THE CERAMICS READER

CW01024652

THE CERAMICS READER

Edited by
Andrew Livingstone and Kevin Petrie

BLOOMSBURY VISUAL ARTS
LONDON • NEW YORK • OXFORD • NEW DELHI • SYDNEY

BLOOMSBURY VISUAL ARTS
Bloomsbury Publishing Plc
50 Bedford Square, London, WC1B 3DP, UK
1385 Broadway, New York, NY 10018, USA

BLOOMSBURY, BLOOMSBURY VISUAL ARTS and the Diana logo are trademarks of Bloomsbury Publishing Plc

First published in Great Britain by Bloomsbury Academic 2017
This edition published by Bloomsbury Visual Arts 2020

Copyright © Introduction and editorial material, Andrew Livingstone and Kevin Petrie, 2017
Copyright © Individual chapters, their authors, 2017

Andrew Livingstone and Kevin Petrie have asserted their right under the Copyright, Designs and Patents Act, 1988, to be identified as Authors of this work.

For legal purposes the Acknowledgements on p. xii constitute an extension of this copyright page.

Artist: Alexandra Engelfriet
Photographer: Danièle Gardyn

All rights reserved. No part of this publication may be reproduced or transmitted in any form or by any means, electronic or mechanical, including photocopying, recording, or any information storage or retrieval system, without prior permission in writing from the publishers.

Bloomsbury Publishing Plc does not have any control over, or responsibility for, any third-party websites referred to or in this book. All internet addresses given in this book were correct at the time of going to press. The author and publisher regret any inconvenience caused if addresses have changed or sites have ceased to exist, but can accept no responsibility for any such changes.

A catalogue record for this book is available from the British Library.

Library of Congress Cataloging-in-Publication Data
Names: Petrie, Kevin, 1970- editor. | Livingstone, Andrew (Artist), editor.
Title: The ceramics reader/edited by Andrew Livingstone and Kevin Petrie.
Description: New York: Bloomsbury Academic, 2017. | Includes bibliographical references.
Identifiers: LCCN 2016043563| ISBN 9781472584434 (paperback) | ISBN 9781472584427 (hardback) | ISBN 9781350025776 (Epub) | ISBN 9781350025783 (Epdf)
Subjects: LCSH: Pottery. | BISAC: ANTIQUES & COLLECTIBLES/Pottery & Ceramics. | ART/Ceramics. | CRAFTS & HOBBIES/Pottery & Ceramics. | ART/Criticism & Theory.
Classification: LCC NK4240 .C47 2017 | DDC 738–dc23
LC record available at https://lccn.loc.gov/2016043563

ISBN: HB: 978-1-4725-8442-7
PB: 978-1-3501-9894-4
ePDF: 978-1-3500-2578-3
eBook: 978-1-3500-2577-6

Typeset by Deanta Global Publishing Services, Chennai, India
Printed and bound in Great Britain

To find out more about our authors and books visit www.bloomsbury.com and sign up for our newsletters.

To our husbands:

Pat Tierney (AL)

Allen Doherty (KP)

Thank you for all your support!

CONTENTS

LIST OF ILLUSTRATIONS

ACKNOWLEDGEMENTS

We would like to thank all of those people who have made this Reader possible. Firstly, we would like to thank Alison Stace for developing the idea and working with us on the early stages. Thanks also to Abbie Sharman, Rebecca Barden, Claire Constable and the additional team at Bloomsbury for supporting the creation and realization of this book. We would especially like to thank our researchers Dr Chris McHugh and Dr Laura Gray on the project for their crucial work in gathering and consolidating the texts and images. We acknowledge support from our academic institution, the University of Sunderland, for providing the space and assistance to make this book happen. We would like to thank the individual authors and the estates of those who are no longer with us for providing your critical voice to this first Ceramics Reader. This is extended to the publishers of books and journals who have also kindly granted permissions, including *Ceramics: Art and Perception/ Technical* from which we drew a number of texts.

Finally a special mention is given to Garth Clark in terms of his scholarly voice and the unconditional sharing of his personal files and thoughts with regard to *The Ceramics Reader*.

NOTES ON THE CONTRIBUTORS

Glenn Adamson led the Victoria and Albert Museum's Research Department before becoming the Nanette L. Laitman Director of the Museum of Arts and Design in 2013. He has written extensively on art, design and craft and his previous publications include *The Craft Reader* (2009) and *Thinking Through Craft* (2007).

Sarah Archer is freelance writer and independent curator. Prior to moving to Philadelphia, she was the director of Greenwich House Pottery and a curatorial assistant at the Museum of Arts and Design, New York.

James Beighton was senior curator at Middlesborough Institute of Modern Art until 2014; he is currently a doctoral researcher.

Kenneth R. Beittel was potter and professor of art education at Pennsylvania State University. He studied pottery in Arita under Manji Inoue, a renowned Japanese ceramicist.

Laura Breen has worked in institutions including the Potteries Museum and Art Gallery, Bolton Museum and Archive and Tameside Museums and Galleries, UK. Her PhD research at the University of Westminster forms part of the AHRC-funded *Ceramics in the Expanded Field* project. She has an MA in Art Gallery and Museum Studies from Manchester University.

Glenn R. Brown is professor of art history and associate head of the Art Department at Kansas State University, USA. A member of the International Academy of Ceramics, Switzerland, he has written extensively on contemporary and historical ceramics.

Marjan Boot was Curator of Applied Arts and Design at the Stedelijk Museum, Amsterdam between 1996 and 2013.

Louisa Buck is an art critic and Contemporary Art Correspondent for *The Art Newspaper*. The author of several books, she was a jurist for the 2005 Turner Prize.

Marek Cecula is a ceramic artist and designer. He was Head of Ceramic Design at Parsons School of Design, New York, between 1983 and 2004, and was Visiting Professor at the Royal College of Art, London, between 2010 and 2015.

Ruth Chambers is visual artist and professor in the Visual Arts Department at the University of Regina, Canada. Her ceramic sculptures and installations address concepts of temporality, beauty and yearning.

Garth Clark is the editor in chief of CFile, an online ceramics resource. With his partner Mark Del Vecchio, he assembled the Garth Clark and Mark Del Vecchio Collection, one of the most significant collections of modern and contemporary ceramics in the world.

Emmanuel Cooper OBE was a distinguished studio potter, editor and writer. His numerous publications include *Ten Thousand Years of Pottery* (2000) and *Bernard Leach: Life and Work* (2003).

Jo Dahn is an independent writer, researcher and curator with a specialism in contemporary ceramics. Her latest book *New Directions in Ceramics: From Spectacle to Trace* was published by Bloomsbury in October 2015.

Edmund de Waal is a writer and artist, best known for his large-scale porcelain installations which have been exhibited in many museums around the world. His bestselling memoir, *The Hare with Amber Eyes,* has won several literary awards. Another book, *The White Road,* was published in September 2015. He lives in London with his family.

Neil Ewins is senior lecturer in design history at the University of Sunderland, UK. His doctoral research was concerned with the impact of globalization on the UK ceramics industry.

Patricia Failing is emeritus professor of art history at the School of Art, Art History and Design, University of Washington, and has written widely on visual art and ceramics.

Silvia Forni is curator of anthropology in the Department of World Cultures at the Royal Ontario Museum. She is also assistant professor of anthropology at the University of Toronto where she teaches anthropology of material culture, ethnography of Africa and anthropology of art.

Christopher Garcia is a ceramic artist and educator based in New York.

Wendy Gers is research associate at the Visual Identities in Art and Design Research Centre (VIAD), University of Johannesburg, South Africa, and was the Curator of the Taiwan Ceramics Biennale 2014.

Andrea Gill is a professor of ceramic art at the New York State College of Ceramics at Alfred University, New York. Her work is featured in several notable collections, including the Smithsonian Institution, Washington, the Los Angeles County Museum of Art, and the Victoria and Albert Museum, London.

Amy Gogarty is an educator, artist and writer who has contributed over 100 critical essays and papers relating to contemporary visual art and craft practice to journals and symposia in Canada and abroad. She taught visual arts history, ceramics history and contemporary theory for sixteen years at the Alberta College of Art and Design in Calgary, Canada, prior to relocating to Vancouver in 2006.

Anthony Gormley is a leading British sculptor who has exhibited widely both in the UK and internationally. He has used clay and ceramic extensively, and his work formed part of *A Secret History of Clay: From Gauguin to Gormley* at Tate Liverpool in 2004.

Laura Gray is an independent writer, researcher and curator based in Yorkshire, UK.

Paul Greenhalgh is director of the Sainsbury Centre for Visual Arts at the University of East Anglia, UK. His previous positions include director of the Corcoran Gallery of Art, Washington, and head of research at the Victoria and Albert Museum, UK.

Holly Hanessian is professor of art and Area Head of Ceramics at Florida State University, USA. She is interested in 3D ceramic printing and recently created a Digital Ceramics Programme.

Tanya Harrod is an independent design historian and writer based in London. She is co-editor of the *The Journal of Modern Craft*, and her biography of the potter Michael Cardew *The Last Sane Man* (2012) won the James Tait Black Prize for biography.

Emily Hesse is artist and curator based in the northeast of England, UK.

Veronika Horlik is an artist based in Montreal, Canada. She teaches art education courses at McGill University, and ceramics at the *Studio de Céramique Alexandra*, Canada.

Lesley Jackson is a writer, curator, design historian and journalist specializing in twentieth century and contemporary design. She is a leading authority on the post-war period and her specialist fields include textiles, furniture, glass, ceramics, metalwork, lighting and wallpaper.

Brent Johnson is a studio potter living in California, USA. He is the author of *Storied Pots: The Life and Art of Dean Schwarz* (2014) and contributed to *Marguerite Wildenhain and the Bauhaus: An Eyewitness Anthology* (2007), edited by Dean and Geraldine Schwarz.

Jeffrey Jones is emeritus professor of ceramics at Cardiff School of Art and Design, UK. He was founding editor of the electronic journal *Interpreting Ceramics* and his book *Studio Pottery in Britain 1900–2005*, a major survey of the field, was published by A&C Black in 2007.

Bonnie Kemske is a ceramicist and writer based in London and Cambridge. She was awarded a PhD in ceramics from the Royal College of Art in 2008 and was editor of *Ceramics Review* between 2010 and 2013.

Laurel Birch Kilgore holds a PhD from the School of Oriental and African Studies, University of London, and has undertaken extensive fieldwork in Malawi. She is author of *Inscribing the Mask: Interpretation of Nyau Masks and Ritual Performance among the Chewa of Central Malawi* (1996).

Janet Koplos is a critic, writer and curator based in Minnesota, USA. She is a contributing editor to *Art in America* magazine, and has taught at both the Pratt Institute and Rhode Island School of Design.

Bernard Leach was a pioneer of British studio pottery and with Shoji Hamada established the Leach Pottery in St Ives, Cornwall, in 1920. His seminal work, *A Potter's Book*, was first published in 1940.

Andrew Livingstone PhD is professor of Ceramics and leader of the Ceramic Arts Research Centre (*CARCuos*) at the University of Sunderland, UK.

Martina Margetts is senior tutor in critical and historical studies at the Royal College of Art, London. She was editor of *Crafts* magazine for nine years and with Alison Britton curated *The Raw and the Cooked: New Work in Clay in Britain*, at the Museum of Modern Art, Oxford and the Barbican, London, in 1993.

Paul Mathieu is a ceramicist and associate professor in the Faculty of Visual Art and Material Practice at Emily Carr University of Art and Design, Canada. His most recent book, *The Art of the Future: 14 essays on Ceramics*, is available on his website at www.paulmathieu.ca.

Natasha Mayo is an artist and senior lecturer at Cardiff School of Art and Design, UK, where she is subject leader for Ceramics.

Christopher McHugh is an artist and researcher based in the northeast of England. Between 2010 and 2013, he was the recipient of an AHRC collaborative doctoral award at the Department of Glass and Ceramics, University of Sunderland and Sunderland Museum and Winter Gardens.

Graham McLaren is head of the Department of Design and Critical Studies at Bath Spa University, UK. Prior to this he taught the history of ceramics at Staffordshire University, UK, and his book, *Ceramics of the 1950s*, was published in 2003.

Mitchell B. Merback is history of art professor at John Hopkins University, UK. He specializes in German, Netherlandish and Central European art of the later middle ages, the renaissance and the reformation.

Bruce Metcalf is a jeweller and occasional writer from Philadelphia, USA. He is co-author with Janet Koplos of *Makers: A History of American Studio Craft*.

Ingrid Murphy is Academic lead for Transition and Boundaries at Cardiff School of Art and Design, UK. Her research focuses on how new and emerging technologies can be used within ceramics practice.

Ruth Park is a ceramicist based in New South Wales, Australia. She was awarded a PhD from Southern Cross University, Lismore, in 2007.

Elizabeth Perrill is associate professor of art history at the University of North Carolina, and consulting curator for African Art at the North Carolina Museum of Art, USA. Her research areas include Southern African contemporary art, the history of ceramics and gender theory.

Kevin Petrie PhD is professor of Glass and Ceramics and Head of Arts at the University of Sunderland, UK. He is author of several books and articles, including *Glass and Print* (2005) and *Ceramic Transfer Printing* (2011), both published by A&C Black.

James Putnam is an independent curator and writer with an interest in the relationship between artists and museums. He is author of *Art and Artefact – the Museum as Medium* (2001).

Imogen Racz is senior lecturer in art history and contextual studies coordinator at Coventry University, UK. Her research concentrates on post-war sculptural and object-based practices, and as well as many articles she has published two books, *Contemporary Crafts* (2009) and *Art and the Home: Comfort, Alienation and the Everyday* (2015).

Philip Rawson was curator of the Gulbenkian Museum of Oriental Art and Archaeology (now the Oriental Museum) at Durham University between 1960 and 1979, and Dean of the School of Art and Design at

Goldsmiths' College, London between 1981 and 1984. He is the author of several books, including *Ceramics* and *Drawing*, both titles published by the University of Pennsylvania Press in 1984 and 1987 respectively.

Sir Herbert Read DSO MC was a literary critic best known for his numerous books on art, including influential volumes on the role of art in education. He was a curator at the Victoria and Albert Museum from 1922 to 1939, and co-founded of the Institute of Contemporary Arts, UK, with Roland Penrose in 1947.

Lizzie Zucker Saltz founded the Athens Institute for Contemporary Art (ATHICA), which she directed for twelve years. A non-profit art space in Athens, Georgia, USA, during her tenure it embraced socially engaged arts practice and curatorial nurturance.

Ingrid Schaffner is curator of the 57th Carnegie International, which will take place at the Carnegie Museum of Art, Pittsburgh, USA, in 2018.

Peter Selz is emeritus professor of modern art in the History of Art Department at the University of California, Berkeley, USA. He was the founding director of the Berkeley Art Museum.

Ezra Shales is an art historian, curator and artist. He is professor at Massachusetts College of Art, USA, and the author of *Made in Newark: Cultivating Industrial Arts and Civic Identity in the Progressive Era* (2010).

Emma Shaw is an artist, writer and researcher based in London.

Scott A. Shields is the associate director and chief curator at the Crocker Art Museum, California, USA.

Rose Slivka was editor in chief of the Craft Horizons magazine from 1959 to 1979. She played a significant role in the advancement of crafts in the United States, and her book *Peter Voulkos: A Dialogue With Clay* was published in 1978.

Matt Smith is an artist whose practice often engages with institutional critique and museum interventions. He founded the UK-based Unravelled Arts project, which commissions artistic installations within historic houses.

Julian Stair is a potter and writer with work in over twenty public collections, including the Victoria and Albert Museum, UK. His doctoral research at the Royal College of Art investigated the origins of English studio pottery between 1910 and 1940.

Brad Evan Taylor is associate professor at the University of Hawaii, USA, where he teaches ceramics. His work explores site specificity expressed through the materiality of clay.

Haruna Tomaru studied at Antioch College, Ohio, and teaches in the Department of Correspondence Education, Kyoto University of Art and Design, Japan.

Mike Tooby is an independent curator based in Cardiff; he also teaches at Bath Spa University, UK. He was the founding curator of Tate St Ives.

Clare Twomey is an artist and research fellow at the Ceramics Research Centre, University of Westminster, UK. She is best known for making large-scale, site-specific installations which employ clay and ceramics.

Jorunn Veiteberg is an art historian and author. She is guest professor at the School of Design and Craft at the University of Gothenburg, Sweden, and she has written extensively on contemporary craft.

Moira Vincentelli is emeritus professor of Art History and Ceramics Curator at Aberystwyth University, UK. She is the author of *Gendered Vessels: Women and Ceramics* (2000) and *Women Potters Transforming Traditions* (2003).

Inga Walton is an independent writer and arts consultant based in Melbourne, Australia. She contributes to numerous Australian and international arts and culture titles, and her work has appeared in several books.

Melania Warwick is an artist, inclusive participatory arts practitioner, researcher, and trainer on behalf of PRIA Arts and Artworks Cymru, UK.

Ian Wilson is a fine and applied arts writer. He is especially interested in ceramics.

GENERAL INTRODUCTION

Livingstone and Petrie

This book is largely focused on what might be described as 'art ceramics' as opposed to industrial design or high performance industrial ceramics. The editors are both academics, and teach ceramics to art students at various levels including BA, Masters and PhD. This book has been developed with our students in mind and several of the texts and themes relate to what we teach and what issues concern our students.

From this starting point, we have attempted to show a range of themes and thinking around the subject of ceramics that will have relevance for other students around the world as well as makers, curators, critics, collectors and those with a general interest. We have deliberately selected different types of text and writing styles. Our selections reflect a range of perspectives including historical, personal, viewpoints from makers, journal papers, lectures and conference papers. Some texts are informal and personal, some polemic, some objective. We have tried not to offer value judgements on the texts and would encourage readers to take a critical view of both the texts themselves and our selection – as we hope this book might help readers establish their own position on the place of ceramics in the world.

Although this is a thick book, there have been limitations to what could be included. Ceramic history goes back millennia and there are already excellent and comprehensive histories available from Emmanuel Cooper's *Ten Thousand Years of Pottery* to Garth Clark's *The Potter's Art: A complete history of pottery in Britain* and similarly his hefty tome, *'American Ceramics 1876 to the present'*. Therefore, this book largely focuses on the twentieth and early twenty-first century. There are areas that are not covered, or at least not in detail, such as industrial ceramics, technical subjects like glazing and wider cultural perspectives. The prime focus is creative practice in Europe, United States and Australia.

We hope that this book will also offer a 'hub' to further reading and have included pointers to this effect. Garth Clark's essay, 'Pen and Kiln: A brief overview of modern ceramics and critical writing' which follows this introduction, provides an excellent starting place for readers to get their bearings on modern ceramics and writing. In this new text, specifically written for *The Ceramics Reader*, Clark presents an overview of the development of modern ceramics and insight into the associated writers who have developed critical ceramics writing. Clark's text provides a knowledgeable contextual timeline, which draws out key players in the near history of ceramics both in the United States and United Kingdom. He elucidates upon the troubled and changing relationship of ceramics to fine art at the same time bringing us up to date with observations on his scholarly position on ceramic art today.

As we gathered the texts, some key players and themes emerged. Some are considered from differing viewpoints, Bernard Leach being a prime example. Perhaps the overriding preoccupation in writing about ceramics is its status in relation to the art world – sometimes referred to as 'the art/craft debate'. Although some readers will want to move on from this, there is still this tension within ceramics which we feel needs to be acknowledged. Other key themes emerge: ready-made versus handmade, status of decoration, relationship to industry and the status of function.

Our selection was also in part based on what texts were available from publishers and writers within budget and time constraints. Images had to be used selectively and we have been unable to include as many as we might have liked. We would recommend that readers have the internet close when using this book, perhaps on a hand held-device, as this will be invaluable in sourcing images of artists work to support your reading.

The book is divided into three sections: 'Ceramics – materiality and metaphor', 'Ceramics in Context' and 'Key themes' – each with a 'Section Introduction'. These three broad sections are divided into subsections that group texts together in themes. The subsections start with an 'Introductory Summary' that gives an overview of the texts in that section. At times we also refer the reader to other relevant texts.

Section One, 'Ceramics – materiality and metaphor', considers the importance of clay/ceramic as a material and the metaphoric meanings it might hold for us. Section Two, 'Ceramics in Context', draws together texts that provide some context for ceramics today. This includes a subsection on historical precedents, which although far from exhaustive offers examples of texts covering some key historical developments in ceramics since the eighteenth century: Wedgwood, the Arts and Crafts Movement, and two texts on mid-twentieth-century developments in Studio Ceramics. The importance of Studio Ceramics is developed further in a designated subsection on this subject. The prominent use of ceramics as a sculptural medium and more recently in installation art has led us to include two subsections on these subjects. Further subsections on 'Theoretical Perspectives' and 'Conceptual and post studio practice' complete the section. The final section, 'Key Themes', allows us to bring together texts on themes that to us seem important and relevant today in ceramics. Of course, readers might disagree with our choice of themes and we welcome this and hope our selection offers at least a platform for discussion. This section in part emerges from our teaching and a 'Key Themes in Glass and Ceramics' module we deliver to second year BA (Hons) Glass and Ceramics students. In these sessions, we use texts to stimulate debate between our students around key issues in Glass and Ceramics. We hope that this section, as well as this book as whole, will provide a similar starting point for others further afield.

PEN AND KILN
A BRIEF OVERVIEW OF MODERN CERAMICS AND CRITICAL WRITING

Garth Clark

This anthology comprises some of the finest critical writing on modern and contemporary ceramics and the editors, Andrew Livingstone and Kevin Petrie, have done a commendable job both in their individual selections and in providing clear and useful organization. Scale is one of this volumes strengths, it's large and expansive. And its timing is pivotal.

The entire paradigm of what ceramics in our culture is today is shifting at unprecedented speed. Ceramics in art is almost unrecognizable from two years ago. Overall contemporary ceramics is going through a change of guard, more radically than anything the field has experienced in 150 years.

It has moved from marginalization to mainstream. It is not a move in progress that might happen as so many articles argue. It is done. Over. Complete. The art vs craft debate is officially dead. Just about every major international art dealer has embraced ceramics. And the design field has absorbed it with gusto, producing hand made as well as industrial. Ceramics populates every art fair and does well on auction. True, its heightened presence during this honeymoon period may calm down in a while, but it is not going away.

Ceramics is not just welcome but is the flavour of the decade. *New York Times* art critic, Roberta Smith, calls it 'the new video', (1) an apt analogy seeing the camera also had to overcome the craft stain to gain entry.

Not all things ceramic are now art. Much of what is discussed in this anthology is still craft, design or whatever its primary practice was when it was made. The makers desire for it be art does not make it so. What has changed is that a small portion of ceramists who actually make contemporary art will be considered for entry and from that group an even smaller selection will pass through the hallowed marble portals into high art.

Today an art student will not be penalized for graduating from the ceramics department. However, they will suffer the same brutal rigor and subjective selectivity as, say painters, thousands graduate each year, a few make the cut. That fate, whatever the outcome, is suddenly personal. Before ceramists could argue that rejection was the medium's fault, no more. Now they fully own their rejection or acceptance.

Inclusion after a long period of rejection results in mixed feelings and often an identity crisis. Ceramics is facing a similar dilemma to that of American gays who are coping with the seemingly sudden shock of the Supreme Court ratification same-sex marriage this year.

Once the sound of corks popping faded away, opinion columns began to express concern that marriage equality heralded the end of gay culture. I hear ceramists saying the same thing about their induction into art. There has been a long build of ceramics as a discrete community with its own discipline, history and aesthetic practice. Does acceptance mean that this micro identity will be overwhelmed and ceramics will be demoted from a great discipline to a mere material?

Source: © Garth Clark/*Ceramic Arts Foundation*.

At first this seems naive. Isn't equality what was sought? Wasn't integration the inevitable result? Parts of the gay movement clearly expected to be equal *but* on their own terms and still separate, keeping everything they had before; a segregated watertight community, their own institutions, art galleries, gathering places, history and philosophy, getting new freedom but giving up nothing in return. In ceramics some believe that when the art rapture came they would make all of the art world's ceramic art.

This perverse reaction is understandable. Both gay and ceramic activists have defined their identity during a state of war, a fierce battle for rights. However, let me be clear, I am not equating a fight for human rights with a turf war in art over aesthetics, but the comparison is nonetheless instructive.

While not all the battles are won, the court victory regarding marriage has sucked some fierceness out of the gay community. Similarly the laying out of the welcome mat from fine art may do the same to ceramics. Winning can dull the knife's edge.

There has long been a warrior culture in ceramic literature. Overnight that role is gone, ceramics can be art. This is good for the greater part allowing the field to be drained of its excess self-pity, whining and victimhood.

The flip side is that fighters might decide to disband. There is no need for this. An enormous amount of work still awaits. And if its skirmishes they want, combatting clumsy early attempts at writing about ceramics by the fine arts, and some inept work by artists who have no chemistry with the medium, it could keep anger at boiling level.

Ceramic scholarship could lose some of its finesse but it will also encounter a smart new audience far less conservative than their current one. It is likely that those coming to ceramics for the first time, from all disciplines in art and design, whether maker or scholar, will be a large proportion of this anthology's readers, possibly even the largest group in time.

They will find our style and tenor a tad unfamiliar. Most of it does not read like traditional art criticism and theory. It is less conceptually biased. Canon barely exists and has never been examined in any depth. And because much has been written by the makers it has a pragmatic flair, nuanced intimacy and personal faith not common in art writing. The language is more poetic and sensual, with blushes of unapologetic romance and even sugary sentiment, elements that the more acerbic art world would brusquely edit out.

It is for these newcomers that I write this introduction. Those who have spent most of their career in ceramics do not need any more explanation of how critical writing on ceramics developed its character. They have lived it.

The Ceramics Reader is a key document for kiln virgins. They cannot turn to their usual source. Academia is still remarkably ignorant of, and prejudiced against, mankind's oldest art discipline. And even when they acknowledge its new presence, they will face a daunting task, catching up with a complex history that is 15,000 years old. The turnaround may well take a generation.

How did writing on ceramics get to where it is today? What route did it take? Why is it such a later bloomer? To begin with the ceramics movement did not really try and grapple with modernism until the 1950s and began as a highly tribal activity, divided by everything from their belief in art to their choice of kiln fuel. The internationalism that other arts take for granted did not arrive until recently and even now, is still underdeveloped. An inherent caution, traditional bias and residence to the new kept brakes on its growth.

There is no one ceramic aesthetic although attempts were made to impose one but the dominant one was thrown vessels in stoneware and porcelain. The only unity aside from clay and kiln came from the shared mission to gain respect for ceramics, outlawed, as it was from the mainstream in contemporary culture. Getting contemporary respect was difficult because from 1950 to 1970 the greater part of ceramic output was imitative or historicist in character.

Before we proceed, why the apartheid? It's a long story. But the short version is Modernism had cast handmade ceramics aside by 1920. It feared that handicraft (as opposed to industrially made wares) would be costly, not serve the proletariat and encourage bourgeois taste. And to be fair the socialist founder of the crafts movement William Morris did complain in his latter years to having been reduced to, 'Ministering to the swinish luxury of the rich'. Modernism, certainly in art, ironically did the same. The Bauhaus worker chairs are now costly trophies in corporate boardrooms.

Refused and alienated, Fortress Ceramica was built, from which we grew our field, defended ourselves against the evils of industrial design, and sent out sorties on attempts to invade fine art. It was a place of safety but not one that gave succor to intellectual or aesthetic challenge. Ceramists were extremely smart, brilliant glaze chemists, well read in their own history but highly suspicious of anything that smacked of academia.

The Fortress created its own, material-specific, cultural infrastructure. This included education, literature, publications, conferences, historians, exhibiting societies, and (albeit very vanilla) critical and theoretical voices. It was a mini-art world that was, paradoxically, anti-art.

Ceramics in 1950s and 1960s ceramics was pot-centric, anti-industry (and therefore anti-design) and while dismissive of art as decadent and egotistic, ceramics lusted after art's stature, power and their marble temples. Asian ceramics was held as the model of purity (forgiving and forgetting slave and child labour) and the Western history of ceramics was dismissed as degenerate. Like most fundamentalism it was defined more by what it hated than what it loved.

Its high priests, those who wrote the dogma, were initially all ceramists. We had no Sir Kenneth Clark or Clement Greenberg. In 1940 Bernard Leach's *A Potter's Book*, was published, republished in 1952 and has never since been out of print. In studios it became known, without a trace of irony, as 'the bible'. It was a dated muddled mix of Edwardian art aesthetics and Zen concepts of beauty buttressed with how-to craft instruction and written in a mild pompous voice.

Leach defined beauty as coming from two sources, dead Sung potters and living Japanese ones from the Mingei movement. In Leach's favor if one was a budding romantic potter at the time with little interest in the contemporary, his book had strong moments, bursts of stirring inspirational prose, in short it was a quasi-religious text.

Only in the mid-1970s did it lose dominance but still has not gone away, an anti-modernist specter still hovering in the smoke of time. One could not write about ceramics until a decade or two ago without acknowledging its presence, if only to repudiate its tenacious creed.

There were other influential maker-writers. In America the more secular and eclectic Glenn C. Nelson published *Ceramics: A Potter's Handbook* in 1966, the best selling ceramics book in the world, and it made him a fortune. Daniel Rhodes wrote a series of four books – from *Clay and Glazes for the Potter* (1957) to *Pottery Form* (1976) – that were also top sellers.

Michael Cardew's *Pioneer Pottery* appeared in 1969. He was Leach's first apprentice so a central tenet was the potter-pilgrim claim of moral superiority based on the presumed 'honesty' of making functional pottery in an era that did not need them.

Pioneer Pottery remains a classic because it is superbly written by a heroic figure, who, unlike Leach practiced everything he preached, almost to a fault. Every page was enlivened by Cardew's sharp intellectual steel and biting wit. But it gave little sustenance to anyone wanting to use clay beyond the functional pot. Turned off by Roger Fry's lecture on modern art while Cardew was a student at Oxford, he was Course Director for MA Curatorial Practice and as much a philistine on the subject as Leach.

In America some writings in the 1960s and 1970s presented clay in hippie garb, a plastic guru that led by touch towards inner-sensitivity. This too was Zen based but coming from a different and arguably more authentic core.

M.C. Richard's *Centering in Pottery, Poetry, and the Person* in 1964 (and now back in print) became a cult classic, earning this wonderfully oblique review from John Cage (she was a member of his group): 'What shall we do with our emotions? Suffer them, I hear her saying. The subject she teaches isn't listed in the catalogues. Sooner or later we know we're studying with her. How is she and where? I am okay and growing, and trying to concentrate on really carrying this through. It ain't easy, or comfortable, but here we are, right? Not only the Devil, but the Lord, too, is on earth and doing His work beautifully'.

Paulus Berenson, a modern dancer in New York in the 1950s who later moved near the Penland School of Crafts in North Carolina was another spiritual clay leader (he and Richards were close). He eschewed the wheel as too mechanical and took to pinching and folding clay as a pathway. His 1974 book *Finding One's Way with Clay*, was similarly a popular magnet for those approaching ceramics within an alternate life-style.

There was life beyond brown stoneware pots. It was just largely invisible and only given attention in print when needed to rile the pottery community, like feeding red meat to carnivores, filling their letter columns with rebuke and derision.

In particular two American movements roiled the ceramics world in the 1950s. The first came from Southern California in 1955, the misnomered Abstract Expressionist Ceramics Movement (also known as Otis Clay). Peter Voulkos was its informal charismatic leader with John Mason, Ken Price, Ron Nagle (albeit from San Francisco) and others in this all-male group. They unshackled the vessel from, tradition and pioneered large-scale abstract ceramic sculpture.

The second was Funk in Northern California beginning around 1959 with Robert Arneson at the helm. This movement was figurative providing a 'dirty' aesthetic of scatology, body fluids and solids, and puerile sexual confrontation, the counter to the 'clean' of Pop, though they travelled parallel roads. Out of this grew the Super-Object a high craft troupe losel style that was closer to the precision of Pop.

Important as these two breakouts were, in 1978, when I compiled the first modern ceramics anthology *Ceramic Art: Comment and Review 1882–1977*, there was almost no writing of consequence about the movements even though nearly two decades had passed. I found only two essays of stature about Voulkos and Co.; Rose Slivka's 'The New Ceramic Presence' (1961) and John Coplans' 'Abstract Expressionist Ceramics' (1964). And none for Funk.

Slivka's essay appeared in *Craft Horizons*, a widely regarded journal published by the American Craft Council. The reaction to her article, hardly incendiary, was apoplectic and hundreds of ACC members resigned over the article.

Welcome or not, Voulkos and Arneson had to live and work uneasily in the Fortress; teaching ceramics, showing in all-ceramic shows, applying to crafts organization for grants, and giving workshops (a peculiar extremely popular and remunerative ceramic obsession as though watching clay being moved around for two days would result in an epiphany). By the mid-1970s the two had become accepted as a heroes, at least within the younger community.

Ken Price was part of the Fetish Finish California art movement that included Ed Ruscha, and Billy Al Bengston. He was scrupulous in avoiding the clay club and that ensured (it took a long time) that he was the first of the revolutionaries to rise into the blue-chip stable of the fine arts.

Back in England, *Art of the Modern Potter* (1969) by Tony Birks, also potter and artist, was the 1970s breakthrough. I was among many who can cite this book as a turning point in my life. It was lightweight in literary terms but eminently readable. The volume was handsome, large format with excellent photogprahy by Jane Coper (Hans Coper's wife). Its effect on the Fortress was electric.

The covers opened like windows onto a new art-based landscape that many had not seen before. Hans Coper and Lucie Rie, its two stars, had been working in Britain for 20 years by the time it appeared, at first to a hostile reception but by now appreciated. It also presented an Organic Abstraction movement that was emerged from the Central School of Art, London. It was already more than a decade old, with Ruth Duckworth, Dan Arbeid, Gordon Baldwin and others.

Finally the focus shifted from the suffocatingly dull rustic nostalgia of the stone cottage to a modernist chic that fitted contemporary urban architecture. It also allowed a more cosmopolitan array of influences.

Lucie Rie channeled the refined sensibility of Viennese Secession Movement. Her first show was at architect Josef Hoffman's modern masterpiece, the Palais Stoclet in Brussels. Hans Coper, previously a sculptor, took the vessel into sensual minimalism and subtle anthropomorphism via his adoration of Brancusi and Giacometti. Ruth Duckworth's work grew out of pre-War European abstract sculpture by Arp and others.

The book was the lead in for Postmodern ceramics, from the Royal College of Art. Unlike previous movements that had to wait sometimes decades for recognition, this was seized upon by the Crafts Council while its artists (Jacqui Poncelet, Elizabeth Fritsch and others) were still at school and given full court treatment with solo exhibitions, catalogues and lively coverage in their *Crafts* magazine, which became an excellent source of critical writing on the field.

America's tipping point for ceramics scholarship was the result of an exhibition, *A Century of Ceramics in the United States 1878–1978,* organized by the Everson Museum of Art in Syracuse, NY. I was lucky to be invited to co-curate the show with artist Margie Hughto, who originated the idea.

All major cultural shifts depend on only three things, timing, timing and timing. So I take limited credit. American ceramics was on the brink of realizing its zeitgeist, pent and ready to explode. The *Century* show just lit the fuse.

Tensions between the pro-art side and the functionalists were at boiling point, a marketplace was finally opening up and museums began to take notice. A huge amount of art in ceramic studios that had barely seen the light of day yet alone a gallery spotlight began to trickle out into the world.

The exhibition, a blockbuster comprising 450 objects, was lavishly funded by the Phillip Morris Company. It received half a million dollars funding from the tobacco company and at least as much was poured into advertising, sending the show on a four year tour of the United Sates.

A documentary with Orson Welles as narrator played on PBS for a decade, and at every stop Phillip Morris would produce double-page colour advertisements in *Newsweek, Time* and announcing its arrival. As a result it racked up attendance records at every museum.

When it reached New York and the Cooper-Hewitt Museum the city's critics came out in full support, Greenberg gave it his blessing, it got raves in Art in America from Donald Kuspit and from John Ashberry in the Village Voice. All declared that the moment for ceramics to bask in fine art sun had arrived. The predictions were premature but it did set the ball rolling.

Ceramics galleries began to open and the medium's rush for fine art status went into high gear. The craft world attracted a huge influx of collectors. And, importantly, better and more serious writing was published. The flagship arrived in 1981, a quarterly, the handsomely designed by Vignelli and Associates, *American Ceramics,* published erratically by Harry Dennis and skillfully edited by Michael McTwigan.

Any discussion of technique between its covers was outlawed (as were advertisements from those selling ceramic equipment or materials), more non-artists were invited to write, a deliberate effort was made to invite known critics with little knowledge of ceramics to contribute in order to lure them into the camp (with mixed success, sometimes ignorance even from a genius, is still just ignorance).

By now the university-based art and craft education juggernaut in the US and somewhat in the UK was in full swing. In the US it was sparked, after World War II, by the GI Bill, and ceramic courses were offered by over 300 institutions.

They were mostly consigned to the basement (symbolic as well as practical) but ceramic courses were popular as an easy and enjoyable elective. So the ceramics community grew fast and big. Even today the National Council on Education for the Ceramics Arts (NCECA) is the largest artist group in the world with its annual conference drawing up to 6,000 delegates.

Book publishers sensed a dedicated niche market and new titles began appearing every month. How-to titles dominated by a twenty to one ratio but monographs and surveys of various kinds hit the shelves as well. Ever since the depth of the writing has increased. *The Journal of Modern Craft* has offered an outlet for peer reviewed academic writing, so does the intrepid *Interpreting Ceramics*.

But this is still scattershot. There is nothing truly programmatic? to build a history of modern ceramic art and no college that teaches this as a subject or a full textbook? But if one looks at the glass half full, the last two decades have been a remarkable period for ceramic scholarship.

The literary canon has grown since 2000 with titles like Louise Cort's *Isamu Noguchi and Modern Japanese Ceramics: A Close Embrace of the Earth* (2003) and *The Temple Potters of Puri* (2013, with Purna Chandra Mishra), Tanya Harrod's magisterial biography *The Last Sane Man: Michael Cardew – Modern Pots, Colonialism and the Counterculture (2012)* and now Edmund de Waal's *White Road: A Pilgrimage of Sorts* telling of the story of porcelain. This was enriched by books of fiction – *The Collector: A Novel* by Tibor Fischer and *Utz* by Bruce Chatwin – and biographies such as *Red Brick, Black Mountain, White Clay: Reflections on Art, Family, and Survival* by Christopher Benfey and T*he Porcelain Thief* by Huan Hsu.

Exhibition reviews gradually emerged in art media with Janet Koplos, a former associate editor of *Art in America* and Roberta Smith at the *Times* taking the lead. Albeit in a scrappy disorderly manner our written record has matured and become palpably richer and more sophisticated.

Huge gaps remain. The library on contemporary ceramics can best be symbolized by the colander. Peter Voulkos is identified as the giant of our field the radical who broke open the vessel in art terms, yet to date there is not a book worthy of his contribution.

The fine arts will bring more scholarship to the table their pockets are deeper. Underfunding has long held back ceramics. And as the marketplace today calls all the shots, museums and the art media will be required to support and document the ceramics now being exhibited and sold.

This is already happening and predictably the results are uneven, the average art writers lack of knowledge, even to the point of not knowing the difference between clay and ceramic, has been an irritation and will be for some time. So will the fact be that every other article on ceramics today will be entitled 'Feats of Clay'. But some writers, unencumbered by the field's traditional baggage, while they may well get a definition or two wrong can also produce fresher, surprising insights that are more entangled with culture at large.

To its credit, art is proving to be a quick learner. In 2007 Barbara Gladstone one of the field's uber-dealers put together what is perhaps the worst show in ceramics I have ever seen *Makers and Modelers: Works in Ceramic*. Today she is deeply involved with the medium, producing one exceptional ceramics show after the other, represents Andrew Lord, and actively encourages her artists to work in the medium.

Matthew Marks also in New York, was so kiln phobic that he forbid the word ceramics from being used in his gallery in relation to the art of Ken Price when he took him on (it had to be called 'fired clay', which of course is ceramics).

Now he has added Ron Nagle to his stable, gave his four-inch high objects a beautiful solo installation and proudly touts the work as ceramic. Also he hosted a major scholarly traveling show in New York *What Nerve! Alternative Figures in American Art, 1960 to the Present* that wove Voulkos, Price and Robert Arneson into the history of avant-garde American art, accompanied by a 368 page book with contributions by the shows curator Dan Nadel and an array of scholars.

From Yale University comes a major exhibition of over 200 works, *The Ceramic Presence in Modern Art: Selections from the Linda Leonard Schlenger Collection*, with a 176 page book, scholarly examination of ceramics and art written by curator Sequoia Miller and Jock Reynolds, the director of the Yale University Art Gallery. The major focus is on the Abstract Expressionist School and Funk but other aspects of ceramics are examined as well.

The Bonnefanten Museum for contemporary art in Maastricht (appropriately located at Avenue Ceramique 250) in cooperation with the Cite de la Ceramique, Sevres, has just opened Ceramix: Art and Ceramics from Rodin to Schütte. It is a giant exhibition of over 250 works that celebrates major artists relationships with ceramics, including 'monograph rooms' for some, where their involvement can explored in detail.

Ceramics exhibitions by major galleries are frequently accompanied by lush large format publications, something the ceramics field could rarely afford. And the exhibitions are achieving huge media coverage reaching audiences twenty times larger than ever visited the Fortress.

It's clear that ceramics in the art world has grown up. Where does this leave the Fortress? Will the new migration away from specialization and towards fine art and design lead to it becoming a deserted ruin? That would be a tragedy but is unlikely. I have spent my entire adult life in this place, more often as a visitor than a resident, and one cannot find a warmer group of artists; sensual, earthy, supportive, generous passionate largely free of pretension and seemingly all culinary masters.

Fears of its demise are premature. Just as gay marriage adds a new profound layer to queer culture so will tearing down the Fortress walls. For too long the field has been hermetic and resistant to anything in the field not of their making.

It needs to be placed with easy access that welcomes the stranger, trains artists who are unschooled in ceramics and informs the writers who have little knowledge or insight. It needs to embrace the multidisciplinary and multimedia incorporation of ceramics into a broader field. It needs to marry with design and that is already happening. In short, it is time for gentrification.

Think of it as a trading station at which roads from all ceramic cultures meet, feverish with activity, exchanges of ideas, a creative free-for-all that is akin to a Burning Man gathering for the newly global kiln clan.

It still has material specific roles to play in encouraging traditional pottery enclaves, in using ceramics in the third world to improve health and generate income, and it needs to keep education alive at a time when it is shrinking. And partnering actively with art and design will transform its role in the twenty-first century.

While this takes place, a time of turmoil and opportunity, this book offers contemporary understanding of the field at its pivot point, a foundation document that everyone will reach for, to be guided and informed, challenged and critiqued, excited and inspired. Perhaps we have a new bible.

References

http://www.nytimes.com/2011/07/01/arts/design/paul-clay.html?_r=0

Printed with permission of the author.

SECTION ONE
CERAMICS – MATERIALITY AND METAPHOR

Section introduction

Ceramics are central to our lives. We live in brick buildings with ceramic tiles. We eat and drink from ceramics. As a material it functions closely to the body in cleansing rituals and as a recipient of our bodily waste. We decorate our homes with ceramics and use them to commemorate personal and national events. Ceramics are also used in industry, from engineered parts for car engines, the tiled surface of the Space Shuttle to internal medical components for the human body. Ceramics and pottery are also a major strand of artistic practice which can be used in very diverse ways from vessels, to sculpture, to surface decoration and in a raw state as seen on the cover of this book.

Clay is perhaps a unique material for the creation of both functional and symbolic objects. It starts as a natural primordial base material that has the potential to be manipulated by human hands into diverse, beautiful and enduring objects. This quality as a material has led to the metaphoric uses of clay and ceramics that permeate culture. The creation of clay into functional and symbolic objects is used in The Bible as a metaphor for the creation of human life. For example, 'But now, O Lord, thou art our father; we are the clay, and thou art out potter; and we are the work of thy hand' (Isa. 64.8). Similarly the Qur'an uses clay as a metaphor in relation to Allah creating the first man from clay, 'Your Lord said to the angels, "I am going to create a human being out of clay. When I have formed him and breathed My Spirit into him, fall down in prostration to him!"' (Qur'an 38.71-72). In 'The Rubáiyát of Omar Khayyám', the Persian Poet, Omar Khayyám (1048–1131) wrote a series of verses in which pots become human like and talk with each other in the pottery reflecting on the potter who made them and their 'life' and uses. The permanence of ceramics is used by poet John Keats (1795–1821) in 'Ode on a Grecian Urn' in which he reflects on the surface painting of a romantic couple on an urn who will never fade or grow old. This powerful ability of clay and ceramics to act as symbol and metaphor in our lives is central to this book and is introduced in the following texts.

Livingstone and Petrie

SECTION 1.1
WHY ARE CERAMICS IMPORTANT?

Introductory summary

In the first chapter of his book, *Zen and the Art of Pottery*, Kenneth R. Beittel describes pottery as the humblest of man's arts. However, he goes on to argue that pottery has a universal and fundamental place in society. He discusses 'roundness', 'centering' and 'wholeness' on micro and macro levels. For example, he links the roundness of pottery to the womb, the family, the horizon and the curve of space, therefore placing pottery and its possible meanings at the centre of everyday life and the universe.

Philip Rawson also argues for pottery's 'intimate connection' with daily life. Because ceramic objects are rooted in function, and the 'ground of daily experience', Rawson believes that ceramics fills a gap between art and life. Ian Wilson's text takes this a step further and reminds us that ceramics are intimate parts of our everyday lives on the dining table and that we enjoy ceramic objects (or not) from childhood to old age. Wilson encourages 'appreciation' of ceramic, whether mass-produced or handmade, in terms of 'recognition of qualities', 'interpreting' and 'gratitude'. This wide ranging text also touches on notions of imperfection and practicality, Scandinavian design and postmodernism – all discussed in relation to ceramics found on the breakfast table!

Although focused on pottery production in the Cameroon, Silvia Forni's text provides a range of examples to indicate the value of ceramics more generally. The Babessi pots that Forni describes are used for cooking, liquids and washing but also have symbolic uses such as washing newborn babies, rites of passage for young men and funerals. The making of these pots is considered to be like giving birth and the pots themselves are thought to be 'actual persons'.

The importance of ceramics in relation to art is one the central themes of many of the texts in this book and Janet Koplos argues two main points on this subject. The first being that ceramics criticism is weak in comparison to arts discourse and second, that ceramics is not the same as painting and sculpture and it will never attain this status. In her observations, she acknowledges an interpretation of ceramics in the twentieth century with regard to an analysis and understanding adopted from fine art discourse. Koplos gives an overview of ceramics writing in terms of international journals and books and acknowledges the strengths and weaknesses with regard to literary critique in the ceramics and crafts field. She goes on to layout her four main considerations for ceramics criticism, stating that a major issue is to intelligently support pluralism.

So ceramics play an important part in our lives – but also have a long tradition of use in rituals around death. Christopher Garcia and Tomaru Haruna give a range of examples including the uses of ceramics in death rites in Maya and Japanese cultures. This article also includes examples of a range of artists who have made works on the theme of death using ceramics including Jorge Llaca, Alison Stace, Forrest Snyder, Keisuke Mizuno and Charles Krafft. The latter is known for his use of human ash in his 'Spone' bone china.

Livingstone and Petrie

1

CLAY AS ELEMENTAL WHOLENESS

Kenneth R. Beittel

What is pottery?

Pottery is the humblest of man's arts. Even before it became metaphor, pottery brought Earth to shine forth in man's world. It is best when it is most earth-honest; that includes process-honest, fire-honest, honesty of being itself. Often a beginning potter will hone a simple bowl down to where it breaks through and will learn that a pot is made of nothing – and earth. A potter's labor is consumed within the work, the craft within the art. Mere expressiveness has no depth compared with rocks and mountains, sand and sea, which speak of being and presence. Forms innovate through subtle differences of individuality within the world's infinite and pervasive roundness. The shape of nothing and of space is curved. The movement of hand and arm, head and trunk, body and mind is curved.

A cup is the sacrament of drink, a bowl the benevolent nurturance of sustenance. We have commerce with 'cupping' and 'bowling', not with objects at rest. But this is all too poetic unless we see the sacred as the everyday. For then again, the potter thinks not, but celebrates at every wedging; meditates on the nothingness of all forms at each centering; dies and is born again at each trial by flame. Young potters are like determined oaks; old ones like flowing willows: their works are at rest in fields and woods and beaches, and contain themselves patiently in museums. Pots play the range of the everyday-sacred, reflecting the vitality of children at play as well as the silence of a holy day. They are all. But actually, a pot's a pot: Earth come to stand as world to man.

A first view of tradition

Through life, we are the same self. We are vaguely conscious that the time zones of childhood, middle age, and old age mesh, and that the meaning of the part is not separate from the whole of life. Similarly, our life and our meaning are not separate from the tradition in which we stand. Our common language is the readiest access to this fact. Tradition, as inherited meaning, shapes the present and portends the future, even as it accords or clashes with these. When we rebel against tradition, knowingly or not, we also fight against our own meaning – when, for example, we feel more restraint than support from our inheritance. Nevertheless, whether we affirm or deny what has shaped us, we still help to create and continue the collective dream that is tradition.

Anthropologists have said that settlements of potters within old cultures are greatly resistant to the influx of foreign influences. Literally and figuratively rooted in the earth, potters partake in a tradition as primordial

Source: © *Zen and the Art of Pottery*. Protected by copyright under terms of the International Copyright Union. Reprinted by arrangement with The Permissions Company inc, on behalf of Shambhala Publications inc, Boston MA, www.shambhala.com.

as the opposition of thumb to fingers is to human evolution. It is not hard to demonstrate the evident anthropomorphism, animism, and mysticism that have persisted within the pottery tradition wherever and whenever it has existed as part of human culture. The hand itself is the earliest container. When something passes from hand to hand, we have the birth of ritual and sacrament. When a bowl or cup is freed from the human hand as a cupped hand of clay, we can take in hand or pass to another hand what the hand has freed from the hand.

Tradition, likewise, can be thought of as what is passed from hand to hand. In pottery, this is literally by 'word' of hand. Moreover, history of meaning and method becomes a master, to whom we are disciples. Discipline then means to be a disciple of someone who hands down meaningful tradition. It is also in this sense that an anonymous cup made five thousand years ago can be my teacher, for the wrought clay can speak across the ages, opening up for me from the bowels of the earth the infinite forms potentially containing meaning, and the very meaning of containing itself.

One does not imitate these forms; one participates with them in the attitude and ritual inseparable from them. We imitate our masters only because we are not yet masters ourselves, and only because in doing so we learn the truth about what cannot be imitated.

Roundness

Modern potters often complain of roundness and symmetry, yet one might as well complain of nature or of the human form. True, roundness and symmetry are not identical, but all roundness touches somewhere on the ideal symmetry of circle and sphere, or gains its meaning in a departure from the circle.

Recently I was led to meditate on roundness from a potter's perspective. I was in my studio, where the roundness of the wheel head seemed to float above the large kicking block beneath. On the wheel head sat a new, full sphere. I thought of the sphere as an infinity of circles, or as moving circles defining a real, ideal, and virtual volume. I also saw how day grows into these forms and how forms cannot be imposed willfully on the clay.

I also thought of the Japanese word *hara* as bodily roundness – the centering of gravity in the sphere of the belly – and of the mind as a sphere with its yin and yang. Generation itself is rounded, in that breasts and testicles and wombs swell with the spherical pressure of growth and the giving of life: out from a center. We round out our days and step within the circle of friendship. Lovers complete endless circlings of embrace. The year goes round. The womb becomes a greater sphere. One generation rounds out and a new one has found its center. We sing a round, dance a round, and drink a round.

The first form drawn by a child is often a rounded enclosure; the roundness of the eye takes in all of this. We have a home when we have drawn our loved ones and our loved things around us. If we must leave home, we make a round trip to return. In our life history, we circle the self we are, will become, and have been, in search of a center.

If value or force pulls a circling up or down, a spiral is created. If it pulls up or down toward a center, we have a vortex. A tendril is a spiral of growth. There is a family circle, and a circle of discussion. Draw a magic circle. A circle can close one out. The horizon encircles us. The infinity of the sky is a dome, the upper part of a sphere with us in the center. Science says space is curved.

A plane circles for a landing, a hawk for its prey. The wild animal goes round and round to make its bed in the tall grass. Kittens, puppies, and babies, before and after birth, curl into a ball. The porpoise takes circling leaps in and out of the ocean. Flowers, fruits, and nuts tell the secret of center, circle, and sphere. So do droplets and snowflakes. As we age, our edges get worn off; we become round like stones rolled by the ocean or a glacier.

Presence and absence alike define roundness: the pocket in the catcher's mitt; the begging bowl; the cupped hand; the nest; the impression of the head in the pillow; the beautiful hollow between a woman's breasts, waiting for the rounded head of the beloved.

Organic thought and creation are round: We begin with the end foreshadowed and we end with the beginning. The last act of a play curves back upon the first curtain. The last brush stroke falls within the sphere set in motion by the first. Our old age rounds out our infancy, and from our infancy we can project the curve of our old age.

The theme and counter theme of music form a circle in repetition, development, and recapitulation. Despair is a whirlpool dragging us down; elation is the spiralling flight of the eagle toward the sun.

In meditating on roundness, I cannot hope to 'round out' the topic here, no matter how long I engage in circumlocution. 'Of all this and more', I say with a wave of my hand, 'the potter's curving nothingness is full.'

Centering

Centering is a quieting of motion without loss of vitality. It is a vibrant containment. Dynamic centering is never accomplished through sheer will and force. If we are off center, we virtually feel lopsided and eccentric; we cannot work unless the clay, in finding its center, centers us. In the East, a potter may meditate before throwing on the wheel. Meditation is a means of finding the mind's still center: the full nothingness through which all forms must flow toward becoming and being.

The potter carries center within, but has achieved this state only through the internalization and idealization of what he has learned through imagery and practice. The beginning potter working with a master has imagery before practice, so that it might be argued that the Ideal comes first. I prefer to think that ideal and practice, like essence and existence, are both primordial and equal.

Centering is more than the quieting of a mass of spinning clay on the wheel. Properly understood, centering reveals the deeper meaning of tradition and ritual. The traditional acts of the East convey wisdom through agreed-upon conventions and rituals. The rituals are not meaningless, as mechanistic and scientific Western minds might believe them to be; rather they constitute sacraments that consecrate the mundane and the everyday. The disciple of a traditional Eastern art is working not on techniques nor even pure mastery, but on the self. It is in making oneself nothing that one is filled with the power within the tradition. The bamboo branch sings through the brush, and the spherical jar through the clay on the wheel, naturally and effortlessly.

Meditation is thus not removed from tradition as understood in the East. Even as hatha-yoga postures can be acts of meditation, the same is true of shooting an arrow from a bow or wedging and centering clay. In subtle ways, the mind negates the mind, requiring one to be a disciple of a deep tradition – to partake, in other words, of the true meaning of discipline. The true self is not the clamoring, willful ego; it is more like the Zen ideal of being totally absorbed in whatever one does, whether chopping wood or forming clay.

After thirty years of pottery, I find that I can center more and more clay on a kick wheel and use less and less speed and energy – as though a tacit knowing between my body and the clay brings us together on center. If I hurry or think ahead of myself, this dialogue falls apart.

In the West, there is the expression, 'he has it all together'. The East is humbler and wiser. If one knows how to center, bodily and mentally, then wherever one is there is a stillness, even if it is in the eye of the hurricane.

Wholeness

Quality and wholeness are the same because it is through the qualitative that we are aware of wholes. Parts do not *describe* the whole; rather they are instances of the pervasive quality of the whole. Thus in art there are no rules or techniques that transfer, without art, from one whole or context to another. Again, a rich and vital tradition teaches us how there can be a rule and no rule simultaneously. It leaves us with a 'rule' of best practice, or an expectancy that is closest to the unexpected. This is not contradictory language. Experience itself is this kind of whole. Never what we expect, it always has its own peculiar pervasive quality. Experience and art, therefore, participate in negativity: they arise from the nothingness between one state of being and one coming into being. Becoming, for anything that will be alive and whole, engages in a freedom not foreseen or foreseeable. One philosopher has referred to art as the free becoming of being.

Artists live in a kind of participatory and anticipatory wholeness. They are committed to the form of things unknown. Tradition shows them that these forms are natural, selfless, and timeless at the same time that they are unique, present, and part of their own destiny. Artists in the East realize that what others may consider useless and neglected are in fact essential to life. The still hub of the wheel is essential to motion, and without emptiness, the bowl cannot overflow with contents. Sculptors who are also materialists do not understand that the dark 'nothingness' within a potter's forms is, in fact, the form. It has separated out a meaningful space from all possible space, and given it wholeness and quality.

Within a tradition one has the patience to be a disciple. The pervasive whole, tradition, is like the whole of one's life magnified. Standing within our life, we are also within the quality of its whole, even though it is unfinished. So it is with tradition: standing within it as a whole transcending many lives, we also stand within its unfinished wholeness. We help to determine its quality even as its quality helps to determine us. We take a share in the quality of our human condition, which is to be both contingent and free.

Extracted from Kenneth R. Beittel, 1989, *Zen and the Art of Pottery*, New York; Tokyo: Weatherhill, pp. 3–8.

2
THE EXISTENTIAL BASE

Philip Rawson

This intimate connection with a potent aspect of daily life and experience is what gives ceramics its particular aesthetic interest. Even though pottery must be based on a technology of some kind, if it is good pottery it always eludes the tyranny of its technology. Even when it employs a technology so elaborate that its processes can only be called industrial, as when ceramic chemists like Höroldt at Meissen were employed on refining glaze colours, good pottery can never use technology in a scientific way, for the sake of calculation, of questioning the material world within a framework of abstract concepts, of seeking causes and logical explanations for results. Instead the resources are deployed and improvements sought ultimately for the sake of living needs; the manufacturing processes and investigations serve a purpose which lies not within their own terms of reference, but within the life of the human beings who use the pots.

The great French poet Paul Valéry has made an apt observation.

> Works of the mind exist only in action. Beyond this action what remains is only an object that has no particular relation to the mind. Transport the statue you admire among people sufficiently different from your own, and it becomes an insignificant stone. The Parthenon is only a small quarry of marble. And when the text of a poet is used as a collection of grammatical difficulties or examples, it ceases at once to be a work of the mind, since the use to which it is put is entirely foreign to the conditions of its creation.

It is easy for us in our day to believe that once we physically possess an object, and can visit it maybe repeatedly in a museum, it is ours in every sense. We believe that we can understand the uprooted works of art we may have wrenched out of their bed in the culture of other peoples. We have even developed a special theory to persuade ourselves that we are missing nothing in works drawn from what was once grotesquely called '40,000 years of Modern Art'. The theory rests upon one misunderstanding or another of that familiar notion of 'pure form' or 'abstract structure'. It is, of course, ridiculous to believe that only the method of arrangement used in an art was of any significance even to the original makers – though they may not have known it! This conception of form will, I hope, be very clearly distinguished from the conception which will be proposed here. Ceramics are, in Valéry's sense, works of the mind; and since this book is devoted to the appreciation of the arts it is their modes of action in the mind we have to explore. If possible we must try and discover, through active use of imagination, how the live meanings of works of ceramic art which played some role in the life of every patron can be revived in our own minds.

There are, of course, many ceramic traditions which have produced works so sophisticated that it is hard to see how they can possibly be called useful. Some of the most elaborate eighteenth-century Meissen fantasies

---

Source: © Philip Rawson/University of Pennsylvania Press.

or sixteenth-century Bernard Palissy wares may seem to be impossibly remote from any conceivable life functions. It would however, be a mistake to interpret such sophistication as 'art for art's sake', as one may be tempted to do. For it is always possible to trace back even the most elaborate of ceramic extravaganzas, perhaps through its historical development, to a point where its feet stand as it were, on the ground of daily experience.

Thus one of the prime reasons why ceramics is such an interesting art is that it fills the gap which now yawns between art and life as most people understand their relationship. To explain the meaning of ceramics can be, in a sense, to explore the historical roots of art as such. For whereas other arts, painting and sculpture in particular, have come for centuries now to resemble cut flowers, separated from the living plant which produced them, in the case of ceramics we are everywhere brought face to face with the root. This appears in the primal interweaving of matter, human action, and symbol that each pot represents. Inert clay, from the earth, is made into something which is directly and intimately related to active craft, to the processes of human survival, and to social and spiritual factors in the life of man, all at once. None of the elements is lost; all are reflected in some sort of balance in each successful work. This then becomes what one may call a 'transformation image', something undeniably material, wearing the evidence of its material nature in its visible and tangible forms and attributes, which at the same time contains so much projected into it from man's daily life and experience at all levels that it can seem to him almost like a projection of his own bodily identity. It thus becomes an external testimony to his existence. By taking an existential back-step, so to speak, we are enabled to witness in humanity's pots a virtually unlimited variety of concrete realizations which un cover and authenticate his life and action in his world of meaning.

The earliest and most important evidence we have about the history of Neolithic man, after his tools, is usually the remains of his pots. Archaeology may even call whole cultures by the name given to the pottery the peoples made and used – e.g. the 'Beaker people', 'the N.B.P. culture'. This, of course, is because pottery is very permanent, even when broken, resisting corrosion. But archaeology – and even art history – look only at the external characteristics of pottery, to classify them according to modern categories of significance, and locate them in a historical system of thinking, which is a special mental phenomenon of our time. This seeks to give to the past a kind of uniform conceptual continuity with our conceptual world of the present, an activity which has its own reason for existing but which can have no bearing in itself on the actual meaning of a pot to its maker or its users. Ortega y Gasset (among others) has pointed out that to create a concept you must leave the sensuous multiplicity of reality behind. A concept is in the mind, one element in the mental order among all the other ordered elements of the world. Pots, however, have always been bedded firmly into the world of their makers' reality, at all sorts of different levels. They are far more than they can ever appear to be as concepts in our academic analyses of 'ceramic history'.

How to make pots by firing clay shapes was one of Neolithic man's discoveries; and pots fall into the category of primary discoveries involving the use of transformed elements of the world. Such discovery and such use are both ingredients in a fundamental act of selfprojection, which enables men to look at and manipulate 'things' they have made. It may well be that the very notion of the 'thing', as a unit which exists and is independent of other 'things', is based in some way upon that fundamental experience of transforming elemental material out of the unbroken tissue of outer and inner reality. What he creates as a self-contained usable object, upon which a man projects his experience of himself, may show itself to him as a separate vehicle of individual being. Whatever the actual case may be, it is certainly clear that pots, even the simplest, can only be 'mere facts' to those of us who classify them academically. To their makers and users they have always been a kind of two-way revelation, first of man to himself as a creative and independently working agent, and second of the world to man as a medium, imbued with 'reality', which he is able to transform. A pot thus 'contains' both the reality of materials and process, and the inner realities of man's sense of identity in relation to his own world of meaning. Ceramics may thus be an important element in the 'world order' created by a culture. In manipulating 'forms' a potter is manipulating and correlating complex meaning-entities.

Since at bottom every pot thus presents what I have called a 'transformation image' of some kind, which lies at a focal point where strands of meaning related to life, use, and symbolic thought are knotted together, it reflects back into the mind of each owner or user an image of himself as existing in his world. A work of high ceramic art may even connect to itself whole chains or circuits of thought, feeling, and value, particularly those related to social status and identity (also valid ecological concepts), by means of the formal symbolism in its elaborated shapes and carefully treated surfaces. All these may be added, perhaps unconsciously on the potter's part, into the transformation image represented by the pot, and may raise it far above the category of primary utensil into a region of sophisticated expression. It may thus reflect into the mind of its owner an extremely complex image of his own identity, status, and personal value.

But here delicate issues of truth and falsehood may be raised. For whenever it has become possible merely to purchase brilliant images of other people's cultural identity without any knowledge of their meanings, first a loss of authenticity, later perhaps corruption and pretence, have inevitably followed; and it has become possible to treat what was originally a live existential discourse with a condensed meaning, as pure convention at the level of mere chatter. This has happened especially, of course, when one culture has adopted the forms and symbolisms of an alien culture (e.g. when eighteenth-century Europe adopted Far Eastern patterns). But it is also possible for people to cease to be aware of the full meanings of the forms used by their own tradition. Potters may then begin to follow mere convention or fashion. Such a failure shows itself in their work, which may slide in the direction of mere dead 'ornament'; this has certainly happened at various times. Even the Meissen decorators often failed to make their Japanese imitations more than 'curious'. But it has happened far less often than we, in our sceptical age, and with our slackened imaginations, may tend to believe. The general plan of this book will be to follow the potter's thought step by step, to trace out the levels and degrees of symbolism involved in the transformation of clay into art, of inert objective matter into a symbolism of being, passing from the simpler levels of fact and use towards the sophisticated expression of clear non-verbal meanings which may rightly be called aesthetic.

'The Existential Base', in Philip Rawson (1984), *Ceramics*, Philadelphia: University of Pennsylvania Press, pp. 3–9.

Reprinted with permission of the University of Pennsylvania Press.

3
APPRECIATING CERAMICS OR SO MUCH MORE THAN JUST AN EGG CUP OR A MILK JUG

Ian Wilson

The manner in which I will be using the word 'appreciation' in this essay takes full advantage of several of the meanings encapsulated in this term, including 'recognition of qualities', 'interpreting' and 'gratitude'. Various pairs of tableware - one member of each pair industrially produced, the other handcrafted – will be looked at, contextualised and extrapolated upon to show how an appreciation of quite ordinary artefacts can involve the user in all manner of socio-cultural and artistic questions.

Aspects to be looked at include the significance of the image, the factory-made versus the handmade object which has no sign of the potter's hand, the beauty of glazes, artefacts which some might consider to be "imperfect", the matter of practicality and impracticality in tableware, and brief glances at Scandinavian design and postmodernism as manifested on the breakfast table.

I do hope that the charge of self-indulgence will not be levelled against me, for the examples to be discussed all come from the shelves of my own dining room. Perhaps I have been a teacher for too long a time, but also inherent in this article is the sub-text of underlining the importance of awakening in the young an appreciation for the plates and bowls which they use daily, and showing them that these are artefacts loaded with both connotative freight and factual fascination.

My plate as a child – I do not believe I am a victim of the phenomenon of 'false memory', but I do recall – with what seems like absolute clarity and surety – demanding to be told why the picture which decorated the 'child-sized' plate set in front of me each morning, was so hideously drawn.

This is an example of the ceramic surface as the canvas for image-making, for this unfortunate scene was presumably intended as the selling point, the commercial 'come on'. Perhaps most perturbing were the legs of the two animals perched on either end of the see-saw – the strange, crude, pedestal-arrangement on which a small, cosily-sized bird, presumably intended to represent a chicken or perhaps a duckling, is balanced, and the distressingly grotesque, misshapen, pointed, hoof-like appendages which serve as the rabbit's paws. These anatomical oddities meant that the plate emanated a sinister, somewhat threatening quality, which completely thwarted any of the appeal that the animals might have hoped to embody.

This is truly decoration of a remarkably crass nature. It could be berated, not because I was the possessor of a precocious artistic awareness, but because imaginative illustrations in children's books had set a standard for what rabbits and chickens – even when wearing clothes – should look like. One wonders whether a plain white plate have been better than this little monstrosity.

Examples of the wholly successful exploitation of the ceramic surface are legion throughout the world, throughout the ages – twentieth century examples range from the wonderfully exuberant jugs and platters decorated by Picasso with such understanding of the relationship between the image and the physical form

Source: © Ian Wilson/*Ceramics: Art and Perception.*

of the artefact, to that "superlatively Surrealist object",[1] Meret Oppenheim's cup, saucer and spoon perversely covered in rabbit fur. My son's appreciation of ceramics started off in a very different way; his cereal was served in a drape-moulded bowl by the South African potter Hylton Nel, decorated with a pale blue-grey snake - so much more potentially menacing and distinctly less 'loveable' a beast to discover beneath your muesli, than unthreatening chickens or cuddly rabbits. With a crafty, scheming look in the eye and scales, which are indicated by boldly incised X marks, the reptile crawls across a bare landscape, which bakes beneath an egg-like sun.

Although Nel was not intending to cater to a child's taste, which, presumably, was the failed intention of the plate which it was my penance to use, it was with real pleasure that my son ran his fingers over the tiny corrugations caused by wrapping the exterior surface in coarse fabric before firing; with what curiosity he asked about the trio of spur marks left by the supports during firing, with what excitement he related the painted snake to those so frequently encountered in the garden, for we were living in tropical Africa at the time. Nel himself has said of his wares 'I do not make flawless things, and if I try, it's a torture. Nor do I deliberately try to create 'imperfect' objects – they come out like that.'[2]

Appreciation of a piece such as this can so easily open out into thoughts about the whole concept of the beauty of things which are 'imperfect' as encompassed in the Japanese term of 'wabi-sabi'.

My son understood and appreciated the decoration on his bowl so much better than I had the picture on my plate, for although he was looking at an image equally 'unrealistic', it was artistically infinitely superior. In terms of current Cultural Studies this opinion might well be seen as sailing close to Matthew Arnold's nineteenth century view regarding the moral improvement which is wrought by 'good' Art, though personally I do wonder what Arnold would have made of this particular serpent.

My egg cup as a child was an object of much four-year old admiration. Somehow I felt that more care and artistry had gone into its making than was the case with the 'See-saw plate', beside which it stood on that kitchen table in Africa, so many years ago. For neither of them is there any indication as to their manufacture, no information is printed on the base – they are thoroughly anonymous factory products.

I suspected that it was not hand-formed, notwithstanding the fact that I was wholly unaware of the existence of industrial moulds. But nevertheless I was a stern little critic even at that young age and can recall the bitter disappointment when, one morning, closer inspection revealed how 'untidily' it had been painted. (Clearly, I had yet to appreciate the the beauty of 'wabi-sabi'.) The question of why a chicken should be chosen to be the container for an egg often struck me as both odd and disconcerting, why a ceramic fowl should be deemed as an appropriate holder for offering the products of its body for human consumption.

Only later did I realise that in a humble, modest manner, it belonged in the tradition of ceramic tableware, which produces platters in the form of fish, or asparagus or maize cobs for the dedicated presentation of these foodstuffs on the table. There are unbelievably extravagant manifestations of this genre, many of which, like my egg cup, have been imitated in a considerably more downmarket manner, rendering them more compatible with the reduced milieu of the suburban family dining room rather than the banqueting tables of Baroque nobles.

The point I am trying to get across is why a child who was not an unusually perceptive little boy and who was growing up in a household where there was no particular 'aesthetic' appreciation of ceramics or the applied arts should have had this early response triggered by the most banal of factory-produced ceramics. I rather hope that I still retain something of the child's ability to discover the extraordinary within the ordinary. We should not neglect to encourage enthusiasm in the young user, and it is in this sense that I feel deep gratitude to functional ceramics for stimulating an awareness that has enlivened so many of the often unstimulating meals I have eaten in homes, hotels, restaurants, cafes, canteens, bars and eating houses from Guadalajara to Siberia.

Next up for discussion is an egg cup in use on my table today and which was made by a final year ceramics student at the university where I taught. How very different it is from the open-mouthed chicken, and what very dissimilar aspirations it embodies from the 'homemadeness' of the Hylton Nel snake bowl, for here there is no perceptible flaw, no mark of the potter's hand comes between oneself and the conceptual message with which the object is associated. It is the handmade imitating the factory product.

Its maker was surely enjoying a dalliance with postmodernist aesthetics, for one needs to keep in mind ceramics created in the 1980's by people such as Matteo Thun and Ettore Sottsass for the Italian-based Memphis design group. This is the overthrowing of the modernist slogan 'Less is more' in favour of the post-modernist proclamation 'Less is a bore'. Here, the 'moreness' is reflected in the wholly unnecessary size, the pomposity with which this egg cup consumes so much of a small kitchen's cupboard-space and implicitly implies that unlimited space is available for the storing of such objects. It is a deliberate flouting of minimalist conventions; the egg is elevated as if upon some inflated cushion-throne, but ironically, humorously, almost self-mockingly the cup overwhelms the object, which it supports.

Turning the focus onto jugs, the sturdy brown example is part of the 'Ruska' series of tableware produced by the Finnish firm Arabia. There is an interesting story behind this famous company which started life in 1874 as a subsidiary of Rörstrand, a Swedish producer of porcelain, and was located in Finland with the intention of making commercial headway in the Russian market. Arabia became not only an important maker of all manner of ceramic goods – ranging from sanitary ware to soup bowls – but also exemplifies how 'industries ... became devoted to current design trends' in a somewhat different manner, one aspect of which relationship is summed up in the words of the glass and industrial designer Kaj Frank: 'unique objets d'art are signed, mass-produced articles are not.'[3]

The mass-produced work of artists and designers who worked for Arabia, such as Ulla Procopé – whose ovenproof 'Ruska' service appeared in the 1960s – was to be found on the dining-tables in many design-conscious homes – young architects were particular devotees – and was contributing to the influence which Scandinavia was exerting in many areas of the applied arts.

There is a robustness about this jug, how very solidly and reliably it stands on the table, how substantial its cylindrical shape is, like the trunk of a young tree and how varied are the colours to be found within the range of 'browns' with which it is glazed.(Incidentally, the name 'Ruska' refers to the changing colours of the leaves for which the autumn landscape of Lapland, in northern Finland is famous.) Yet there is a sophistication to its straightforward functionality when compared to so very many lumpish 'brown jugs' emerging from potter's workrooms, jugs which are neither naïve, nor genuinely artless, merely clumsy.

The other jug could hardly be more different – it is part of the series created in porcelain by Takeshi Yasuda and called 'Creamware'. Its silhouette has a lyrical rhythm, almost balletic when compared with its Finnish counterpart. (If I were to try to find a sculptural comparison for the outline of this jug, it might well be with certain garments created by Japanese fashion designers such as Issey Miyake and Yohji Yamamoto.) The shape is complex, but the overall effect is unified. The handle – which Yasuda terms a 'squirrel tail' – encourages different people to hold it in different ways, and the fluted elegance of the spout allows liquid to be poured with delicate precision. The glaze has a luscious, sensual quality – how right its maker was in naming this series 'Creamware' – which is a truly subtle achievement for one has seen all too many failed attempts at creating a glaze of this shade and density.

Finally, two plates – the one with grey speckles is from the Italian firm Andrea Fontebasso 1760 and it encapsulates an interesting variation on the idea of 'appreciation'. Because of a fault possibly caused in applying the design and exacerbated by the firing, there is an irregularity in the colour which meant that it was not up to the standard for the firm's usual outlets and would thus not be 'appreciated' by the type of customer for whom its wares were intended.

The plate was bought in one of Bulgaria's foreign currency shops, which, at the time (pre-1990) were places where those who had hard currency in their purses could indulge their tastes, but which served also, as in this case, as a dumping ground for goods deemed 'inferior' for the markets for which they were originally destined, but not so defective as to be condemned to the reject bin. I must confess that the flaw no longer distresses me, that it is outweighed by the generous expanse of surface area and the gently sloping gradation from plate to capacious rim. But the plate's special virtue is its ability to enhance almost any food which is served on it – aubergine, squid pasta, a tomato salad, all seem to look their best against this mosaic-like background.

The second plate is hand-made, but its form does not allow it to fulfil its function very adequately – it was purchased with insufficient consideration, allowing myself to be unthinkingly beguiled, I paid and grabbed. A passion, in my particular case, for ceramic tableware, can lead to impulse buying an activity which, more often than not, brings immense pleasure to one's life, the occasional mistake can be trashed, given away (moral qualms might be involved in this option) or kept as a reminder that judgement and discrimination ought never to be wholly cast aside. What one has, in actuality, is a rather substantial plate with only an extremely small flat area, and an impractically wide sloping surround down which food tends to slide and which visually creates a worrying sense of imbalance.

The bold shape, which decorates it is quite pleasing, is interestingly positioned on the 'canvas' of the surface area and there is a rather pleasant washy quality to the green glaze. The cream colour of the background is however considerably less successful, exemplifying what I was saying about a loss of subtlety resulting from the stridency of a yellow note. Possibly intended as a dinner plate, the kindest comment is that it works well enough as a sort of fruit bowl. People who like music talk about it, people who like football will let the food on their plates get cold while they argue about penalties and the decisions taken by referees; we who enjoy ceramics should express our enthusiasm not only in galleries, exhibitions, museums and conferences but also at the at the dining-table and there is nothing wrong in starting to do so when still of so-called "tender years". One should learn from those cultures in which the choice and placement of the ceramic wares turns the dining table into an art gallery.

Responding to the functional and the aesthetic characteristics, the glazes and the dimensional forms, considering the historical aspects, recognizing the wider cultural contexts, relishing the tableware with the same interest and excitement that one enjoys the food – appreciation of this nature enriches our lives from childhood to old age.

Notes

1. William Gaunt, *The Surrealists* (London: Thames & Hudson, 1972) p. 34.
2. In conversation with the artist.
3. Ulf Hård af Segerstad, *Modern Finnish Design* (London: Weidenfield and Nicolson, 1969) p. 40.

This essay was presented as a paper at the 2nd ICMEA (International Ceramic Magazine Editors Association) Conference entitled "Appreciating Ceramics" which was held at Fuping Pottery Art Village, Shaanxi, China, 6th–9th November 2007.

It is reproduced here by the kind permission of the journal *Ceramics: Art and Perception*.

4

CONTAINERS OF LIFE: POTTERY AND SOCIAL RELATIONS IN THE GRASSFIELDS (CAMEROON)

Silvia Forni

Pottery production has been a central activity in the kingdom of Babessi since precolonial times. Used extensively as daily cookware, ritual containers, and prestige items throughout the western Grassfields region of Cameroon, Babessi pots have been part of a network of exchange of objects that has played a crucial role in defining regional cultural identity at least since the eighteenth century.[1] As noted by many scholars, material culture is an essential element in the understanding of the commercial and competitive relationships among independent Grassfields kingdoms. This is particularly true of those items associated at various levels with hierarchical political power through which prestige and identity are defined. Consistencies among regional cultures, then, should not be attributed to a common origin, but considered the result of an elaborate system of commercial and symbolic exchanges through which food, utensils, prestige objects and, in certain cases, institutions and meanings have circulated for centuries among independent polities (Fowler 1997:67).

Even though pottery is an art that is mostly associated with the sphere of domesticity and the realm of women, and thus not immediately associated with political power, Babessi is one of a number of pottery centers that acquired a special regional reputation between the eighteenth and nineteenth centuries thanks to their production of ornate clay pipe heads and elaborate pots.[2] Known for their particular strength and beauty, Babessi pots were sought after as ritual containers, medicine pots, or plates for notables and titleholders, even where locally produced pottery was normally employed in daily use. These pots have acquired functions and meanings specific to each locality.[3] In Babessi they continue to be considered crucial as markers of local identity.

In this article I analyze Babessi pots in light of recent scholarship concerning the inherently social nature of material culture (Appadurai 1986; Hardin 1995; Arnoldi, Geary, and Hardin 1996; Gell 1998). This perspective emphasizes the relevance that objects might acquire in their contexts of production and use, regardless of the labels attached to them once appropriated by others. In particular, art objects, Gell states (1998:17ff.), are 'secondary agents', which do not have the capacity to initiate causal events through their will but that can amplify the effect of human intentionality, thus affecting their social and material milieus. Gell's view then shifts the locus of definition of art objects from their aesthetic or institutional dimension to their indexical quality, thus stressing their ability to affect the con text in which they operate as agents.[4] This particular perspective sheds light on the relevance of the relational dimension in understanding the form, the use, and ultimately the power of Babessi pots, which in virtue of their mode of production and of their function may become agents in particular circumstances.

Babessi pots, as with pots in other African settings (Barley 1994; Berns 1990, 1993; Berzock 2005; Gosselain 2002), are treated as people from the very onset of their making. In the Grassfields, this association persists

Source: © Silvia Forni/MIT Press Journals - first published in *African Arts*, 40.1, (Spring 2007).

throughout their social life, in which, as people, they continue to play a role as containers of substances that insure the prosperity of the society and the respect of its laws. From birth to death and beyond, pots are important agents in social life and are used in the majority of events that mark individual and community life passages. Pots also mediate physically and conceptually between genders, bringing together contrasting discourses of power – particularly the tension between male control over the reproduction of hierarchy and female generative powers – that otherwise are rarely expressed in the official narratives and accounts of local society.

Although these aspects may emerge in a variety of contexts, here I focus primarily on the production process and on selected instances that clearly show the role of pots as actual persons embedded in complex networks of social relations. The examples I have chosen show how Babessi pots are invested with variable functions and meanings, which are informed by the intention of their makers or, more frequently, by their social interactions. In these varied roles as 'social agents', pots embody a broad set of shared meanings and practices, which reveal important facets of Babessi culture.

Making pots, making babies

When talking with my informants in the field about the ideal image of Babessi culture, pots are often described as the 'work of women'. This expression implies that they can be identified as women's distinctive contribution to the family's economy and the community's social life. As in many other kingdoms of the western Grassfields, women contribute to the household's economy primarily through farming, which provides the basis of livelihood and, in many cases, an important cash contribution to the family's finances. Pottery, however, defines the role of women in a way that is perceived to be intrinsically Babessi. Until the 1940s–50s, all Babessi women were taught to mold clay pots. Even though many opted for other kinds of income-generating activities in their adult lives, each woman I interviewed recounted memories of the times spent working at her mother's side, helping with the collection of clay or with the firing of the pots. Young boys and men, on the other hand, would participate in the production of clay pots only as occasional helpers, and even then only in activities that are not directly connected to the shaping of the pot or its decoration.

Making clay pots, which is the most visible form of artistic production in Babessi, is considered the most appropriate 'handwork' for women, and the reason for this is often expressed in metaphysical terms. As many of my older female informants stated, pottery is a 'gift of God to women' which underlines their importance in community life. Although women are for the most part excluded from the local power hierarchy and take no part in official decision-making processes, their fundamental social role as farmers, mothers, and potters is often stressed in conversations with men and women alike. Indeed, each of these three roles underlines the generative and nurturing role of women, whose ability to give and maintain life lies at the core of the wealth and power controlled by the male political hierarchy and of the community itself.

In Babessi, working with clay functions as a very strong metaphor for human reproduction. As noted by Nicolas Argenti, 'It is not the forms of pots, but the technique of potting which is inherently procreational in the Grassfields' (1999:9). In Babessi this is true from the very onset of the process. The site where the clay is collected, called the *mvoh*, is equated to the king's inner room, the most private and sacred core of the palace. This is the place where the king (*fwa*) conceives the offspring who will insure the continuation and the vitality of the kingdom, carefully controlling the vital substance that warrants the existence and prosperity of the village.[5] In a similar way, the *mvoh* is a place of great potential where the material necessary for the production of pots – and, metaphorically, of people – is found.

The association between pots and people is expressed in many ways during the process of pottery making. The bottom of the pot (*nyikuh*) is in itself considered a potential person. Magdalene V., an elderly Babessi potter, once explained to me

> You were very lucky to be able to see how they make pots in this village. In the old times this would have not been easy, as strangers could not witness this process … When god is molding man you cannot know the center of a human being. As god makes it you will not see, you just see the man when it is complete. That is why Babessi people did not want strangers to see how Babessi women were closing the bottoms of the pots.[6]

The bottom of the pot, with its symmetry, balance, and regularity, is like the 'center of a human being', as Magdalene V. put it, that needs to be regarded with care because it contains the potential for human life. Once the process is initiated, in fact, the potter cannot decide to suspend it at her will, but must carry on the building and the modeling to its final form. Should a significant disruptive event occur to interrupt the process, such as an accident or the announcement of a relative's death, the potter may be forced to abandon the bottom before pulling up the walls. In this case the nascent pot cannot simply be thrown back with the rest of the clay and recycled: Either the potter calls on one of her friends or relatives to continue the work for her or, if that is not possible, the bottom is left in a corner until chance intervenes to damage it. Only cracked and broken pots can be recycled and remodeled.

Me boh, the verb used to refer to the molding of clay, is also used to describe the process going on in the womb during the first months of pregnancy. Like pots, children are 'molded' in the womb thanks to the productive and reproductive abilities of women, who are perceived as transforming a soft malleable material into structured beings. The firing process, like labor and delivery, is a critical phase in the making of pots. Although the vocabulary used to describe the two activities differs, many potters told me that having unfired pots is like being pregnant.[7] One should never sell a pot before it is fired, as 'one cannot show a baby before she has delivered'. Indeed many factors could still jeopardize the outcome of the firing. During this period, one should be very careful to avoid quarrels and fights, or even engage in any sort of conversation while placing the pots on the fire. Jealousy, witchcraft, and evil forces may be particularly dangerous during this liminal phase and contribute to the destruction of long hours of productive work. It is only after the pot has been removed from the embers and sprinkled with *ntse* (the red, bloodlike liquid that gives to the pot its final 'skin')[8] that the work of the potter can be assessed and her 'delivery' considered successful. According to Lydia T., 'It is just like when you deliver and you hear the baby crying. Then you can be happy that you have given birth.'[9]

Power and forms

Once fired, pots start their lives as social objects and acquire a multiplicity of meanings and roles. While many are used for cooking and serving food, as storage containers or to cook traditional medicines, certain pots acquire a more distinctive social agency. By virtue of their primary function, Babessi pots undergo a number of semantic transformations over the course of their lives depending on the occasion. In certain ways, then, the plasticity of clay and its potential to adapt to different needs continues even after the vessels are fired.

As in many parts of Africa, Babessi sacred and ceremonial pots are often identical in form to their domestic counterparts (cf. Barley 1994, Berns 2000, Spindel 1989) and it is only through their use that one is able to determine the functions and meanings of the vessels. Cooking pots, which are generally decorated with a simple pattern made by a roulette,[10] may become containers used in a variety of ways both domestic and ritual.

More elaborate anthropomorphic and zoomorphic relief decorations embellish the surfaces of water pots, wash basins, and palm wine pots, whether destined for private use or for public display.

The application of the decoration generally follows a strict sequence that can take from one to four hours, depending on the commission and the inventiveness and skill of the potter. First, she delineates the space for the decoration through the application of two fine parallel coils (*koke*, meaning 'belt' or 'necklace') just below the neck of the pot. Within that space, the potter then composes the decorative program, choosing a subject and the patterns she prefers. Once the space between the *koke* is smoothed with the aid of a leaf, each decorative element is shaped individually and applied directly onto the pot freehand. Together they form one or more continuous rows that wrap all the way around the pot, creating a rich and attractive motif. After she applies the different elements the potter may smooth the decorative surface with her wet fingers or a small leaf, or create a texture with a plastic comb (*satu*).

All the potters I interviewed stated that there is no preferred or 'appropriate' decoration for a water pot and that any image or symbol can be placed on it. For the most part, potters agreed that the decoration of a water pot should not contain images that are 'frightful' (*mebime*, 'inspiring feelings of awe and respect and revealing connection with supernatural forces'), as it is a pot that is placed inside the kitchen from which anyone can drink.[11] As stated by Lydia T., 'one should never be frightened by a water pot, as it is something for all the people.'[12] However, this does not mean that water pots cannot contain images that in Grassfields iconography are related to the power of the palace authorities and of the ancestors. Water pots are often decorated with spiders, snakes, frogs, cowrie shells,[13] and a variety of geometrical patterns, which potters use to reference the spiritual world or even events and spaces connected to the palace. For example, ostensibly abstract designs in fact constitute references to the entrance to the *ngwo* compound (*lo mwaneke*), bracelets given to a princess in the ceremony preceding her marriage (*bulubu* and *mbamba*), or the bamboo windows in the house of a male association (*manjong*). In choosing to apply images that refer to male hierarchy and political power onto a water pot destined for a woman's kitchen, the potters suggest the profound connection between the domestic and official spheres. Even though men control political power and retain exclusive access to the secret knowledge and objects from which that power originates, women are aware that the images associated with its public display represent a wider notion of power that connects human and spiritual worlds in which they also take part. In the interpretations of the potters, cowrie shells, snakes, frogs, and other zoomorphic and geometrical patterns placed on pots give form to different elements of the social space inhabited by men, women, ancestors, gods, and animals. Many of these images, such as lizards or snakes, reflect local belief in the transformative power of kings, twins, and ancestors. Others, like the scorpion, refer to the punitive power of the king. Spiders, chameleons, and frogs may be a reference to the ability to communicate with the otherworld, whereas cowrie shells, bracelets, human heads, or skulls are mainly associated with the life of the palace. However, these images' reference to spiritual, supernatural, and political power is not so strictly or exclusively defined as to prevent potters from applying these decorations to different kinds of containers. Many of the elements placed on water pots can also be found on the more elaborate and 'frightful' palm wine pots (*kuh mendu*), with the possible exception of the snake-spider (or earth spider) combination that is very common on water pots and basins but never found on palm wine pots. On the other hand, images of human heads and human beings, which recall more explicitly the idea of political control and hierarchical power, are found mostly on palm wine pots and wash basins usually associated with men, and never on water jars.[14]

While in other kingdoms of the Grassfields certain motifs (especially those of animals) refer to specific titles and privileges and cannot be used by commoners or women, Babessi potters have the freedom to combine anthropomorphic and zoomorphic images to create their personal decorations. With the exception of anthropomorphic motifs that are generally considered *per se* 'frightful' images, to be placed on special pots, other patterns are loosely characterized in relation to their symbolic and emotional impact. Though never explicitly defined by the potters, it became clear that vessels are *mebime* ('frightful') not because of any single decorative element. Instead, it is their combination and the elaboration of the design pattern that communicates the 'frightfulness' of a pot. A pot identified as *mebime* generally displays an almost mesmerizing decoration, whose design and texture are likely to inspire in the viewer awe and an immediate sense of respect.

Without denying the relevance of the symbolic significance of certain motifs, the attitude of the potters and of many of their customers suggests that the importance and affecting power of pottery motifs does not reside in the univocal and regionally shared association of form and meaning,[15] but in their ability to refer in different ways to hierarchical and spiritual powers. As shown by Argenti, meanings and interpretations of individual icons are subject to a wide range of variability depending on the social and political contexts of use:

> ... [I]n the different polities of the Grassfields, icons are named according to a set of referents which are used dynamically to negotiate one's position in the hierarchy. While iconic representations circulate largely unchanged, whether in clay, wood, mud or stone, the referents of those representations vary as much as hierarchies do between polities.... The motif, in other words, does [not] represent an object but rather the property of transformation; the key to power in Grassfields cosmology (1999:19–20).

This use of images as icons that represent local ideas and aesthetics of power is a common feature throughout the region. However, rather unusually, in Babessi the molding of all anthropomorphic, zoomorphic, and geometrical motifs is always the creative work of women, thus giving a particular meaning to the idea of the property of transformation as the key to Grassfields power noted by Argenti. Whereas in legends, tales, and rituals this property is often represented as the ability to cross the boundaries among human, natural, and spiritual realms and is usually associated with twins, kings, and particularly powerful male figures, according to the potters the idea of transformation refers mainly to generative powers and the ability to mold soft matter into structured beings, containers, and images. Through their generative and creative abilities, Babessi women give shape to essential elements of the kingdom's daily and ritual life, molding both the people and the pots that take part in it.

The visual features of the pots further emphasize this social and relational quality. Babessi style has remained fairly consistent over the last century.[16] However, that is not to say that potters endlessly reproduce a static tradition. On the contrary, they engage in a continuous dialogue with the reality in which they live. Unrestricted by any traditional law in the modeling of their designs, Babessi potters can draw freely from the regional iconographic repertoire or even invent their own personal motifs and derive inspiration from different sources. Potters take great pride in their ability to create new designs and combinations.[17] It is not unusual, for example, to find from time to time modern icons of power such as Nike logos or Coca Cola lettering alongside traditional motifs, applied on pots destined for successful, middle-class, urban households. The freedom of Babessi potters to choose motifs based on their significance, form, or aesthetic appeal allows for an ongoing, though subtle, transformation of the visual power and agency of the pots they produce. In most cases Babessi potters seem more concerned with a pot's final effect than with each motif's semantic reference. The completed pot itself constitutes an index that refers in a multilayered and open way to the role and importance of its owner, whether the owner is the traditional head of a compound or a middle class urban professional, a long-standing male palace association or a newly formed rotating credit group.

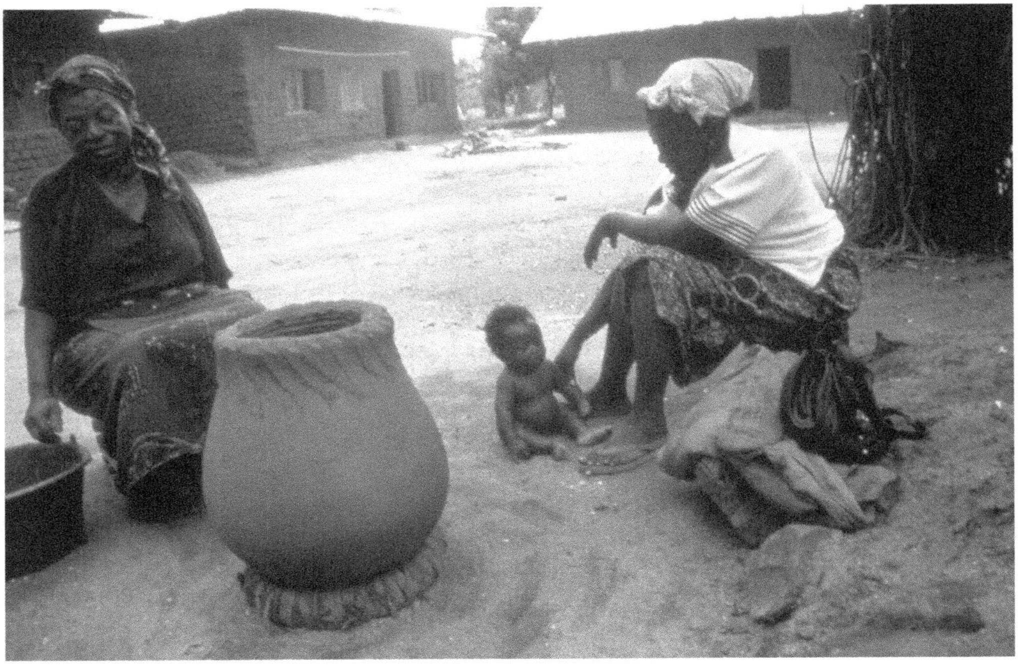

Figure 4.1 Potter Margaret B completing a large water container/photo by Silvia Forni.

Function and social relations

The artistry and skill of a potter as manifested in the regularity of shape and intricacy of decoration are important elements in understanding the ability of an object to affect its recipients. However, formal qualities by themselves are not what render a pot powerful or ritually significant. Indeed, it is necessary to distinguish different levels of visibility and different levels of the understanding of power. On the one hand, the visual power of a pot may be connected to the reiteration and combination of forms – such as lizards, human heads, double bells, spiders, or snakes – associated with metaphysical forces and hierarchical privileges that reinforce the exceptional status of a ritual container. On the other hand, the affecting power of a vessel may originate simply from its use: When employed in a ritual, medical, or social interaction, even ordinary, unembellished cooking pots can become captivating and awesome objects. In this case, the transformation of the pot into a powerful social agent is not attributed to the potter, but to those who acquire and use the pot, those who alter its appearance by drawing on its surface and wrapping leaves around its neck, whether for medicinal purposes or for decorative effect. While visual appearance and the use of medicine might enhance the vessel's power in various ways, a pot's function as container remains central to its agency and determines its role in both private and public domains. Ritual pots and the pots placed on medicine shrines, for example, contain the supernatural powers invested in them by the ritual specialist: Once consecrated through the use of medicine, these ordinary pots become receptacles of benevolent and evil forces that manifest themselves in the actions and public displays of the various groups that compose the articulate hierarchical structure of Grassfields societies. Clay pots are, in fact, kept in the secret houses of the kingdom's regulatory societies and other groups, all generally defined as *juju*,[18] whose masquerades embody the subversive and fierce components of political power, which can be controlled and handled only by male initiates.[19] Whether made 'frightful' through the skill of their makers or through the use of magic, these pots cease to be ordinary objects but become the embodiment of an essentially indecipherable force, which is able to strongly affect peoples' lives.[20] *Juju* pots, in particular, whether they actually contain medicine or rest upon medicinal leaves, are used to share wine among members of the society and are the core of the masquerade's power. As containers of the spiritual and ancestral forces that govern the *juju* society, they are objects that must be treated with great respect and circumspection.

In other instances, the agency of a pot is enhanced by its ability to contain and transform, through the cooking process, culturally significant ingredients. The range of substances that might be contained and cooked physically and metaphorically is broader than that generally defined as 'food'. Indeed, the act of cooking and the subsequent sharing of the cooked food are central to many events that mark domestic and public social life. As suggested by Brad Weiss (1996:27), food is an integral part of the making of a 'lived world of meaning and experience'. Choices and preferences conditioning the selection and preparation of items to cook and the pots to cook them in cannot be assessed exclusively in terms of the functional necessity of nourishment nor even as the enhancement of flavor for the enjoyment of eating.

Cooking in Babessi must be understood in relation to a wider set of sociocultural practices and meanings. 'To cook' (*mena*) is a verb used in Babessi to refer to a number of literal and figurative transformations that occur daily and on ritual occasions. Cooking transforms ingredients from their 'natural' and raw state into a cultural product. This fundamental change is sometimes achieved metaphorically simply by placing crucial ingredients in a clay pot, which even in the absence of fire 'cooks' ingredients into a culturally significant product. Pots can thus be seen as instruments of cultural transformation that are likely to be found in all those instances in which critical passages in an individual's life or in the life of the community need to be culturally sanctioned. Indeed, Babessi clay pots have increasingly become very special cooking containers whose artistic agency has been enhanced by the gradual shift of their use from daily routine to particular events.

In day-to-day use, locally made pots have been largely supplanted by those of cast aluminum and the most common serving dishes are Chinese or Nigerian made enamel pans. The practical advantages of using such durable containers rather than the local clay 'country' pots are obvious.[21] In addition to greater durability, the possession of a good range of 'whitemen pans' is a visible statement of status.[22] Clay pots have not been entirely replaced, however, and they continue to be the preferred choice for occasions in which 'traditional' acts are performed. Because they are molded of clay – the soil of the ancestors – and are produced through processes and skills that have been passed on from one generation to the next, 'country' pots are the proper containers to be used whenever the 'cooking' directly involves social and spiritual forces. Clay pots are themselves the result of 'cooking': They are 'roasted' (*twaghoke*) in the fire, and thus they are the result of a fundamental material and cultural transformation, which in turn confers to them the ability to cook and transform.

Pots and life passages

The powerful and transformative agency of pots is evident in a number of private and public events that mark the life of individuals and of the community. For example, the wide, shallow pots called *ntieke* are commonly referred to as men's wash basins even though they are used for various purposes: to wash hands before a meal, to cover a water pot, or to serve a large quantity of food. They take on other, more spiritually significant roles in life's passages. In Babessi, the *ntieke* is made or purchased to bathe a newborn baby twice a day during the first months of life. The *ntieke* is then kept by the mother in a special place and preserved until the child has grown into an independent adult. Only then is its function fulfilled, allowing the mother to start using the pot as a normal household container. However, if the baby dies soon after delivery, the pot is used to wash the corpse and is broken over the grave immediately after burial. To keep the pot would be a dangerous thing, as the 'cooking' process that transforms babies into fully socialized human beings was not successfully accomplished. This is the only circumstance in Babessi in which pots are broken over the grave. The basin used to wash the corpse of an adult is not broken after burial. In this case, death is not framed as an unsuccessful transformation, but as an appropriate and natural passage to a different stage of life in the ancestral world.

Pots also play a role in other important life passages. For example, in the celebration that marks the official 'graduation' of a young man from the *ngwo* regulatory society in Babessi, clay pots are given away to sanction the passage from neophyte to full member of the society. After several years of initiation[23] during which the boys are expected to serve in the *ngwo* compound taking care of menial tasks and gradually learning the laws of the society, the boys are dismissed from service and given the title of *nchinda*. For the ceremony accompanying the graduation, which is held in the compound of the family of the young graduate, the mother of the young man will make, or commission a potter to make, a certain number of *ntieke*.

When used for the *ngwo* graduation, the *ntieke* is rubbed in camwood just like the body of the young graduate. The young *nchinda* displays his pots as a bride would, all but one of which will be taken away by visiting senior members. The last *ntieke*, which is preserved with great care and used by the young man, is a visible sign of the achievement of a further step towards social adulthood. The pots are used here as an index of the agency of the young graduate, who performs a metaphorical wedding with the older members of the society. They may also be seen as indexes in and of themselves that stand for the life-changing passage that has transformed the boy into a young man.

By contrast, the use of other pots refers more to the social importance of the group than to identification with individual members. This is especially true for pots used by palace societies, quarter assemblies, and for other social gatherings. On most public occasions, pots are displayed as signs of unity and community. In Babessi, a palm wine pot is among the first things that the members of a newly formed male association (*samba house*)[24] or rotating credit group (*njangi*) needs to acquire, as it is considered highly inappropriate for a society to meet and share raffia wine out of plastic containers. However, the use of the clay pot (*kuh chuo* or *kuh meh*, 'group pot') is not just a choice dictated by proper etiquette. Sharing from the pot is an important sign of group unity: Within both age-mate groups and rotating credit associations, each week a different member is responsible for celebrating (or cooking) the meeting (*mena chuo*). The raffia wine brought by the celebrant is placed in the pot and shared among all the members. The pot filled with raffia wine becomes an index of the group's common mind and purpose. For this reason, even though not consecrated with any particular medicine, the pot acquires a very strong power and can be taken as a 'testimony' in case of internal conflicts. According to Michael T., a wine tapper and diviner:

> If one is accused of a crime and he claims to be innocent he might be asked to take an oath over the common pot. A pot from which many people drink has a power, it can affect anyone who is not sincere. If the person is sure that he is innocent, then he goes to the pot when mimbo has been placed inside. He will talk, talk, talk saying that he did not do what he is accused of and he calls on the pot to be his testimony. Then he will drink some of the wine that is inside the pot and everybody else will also drink. If it is true he will live, if he is lying he will die.[25]

Pots' social relevance is strongly connected to their function as cooking containers and to their ability to contain and transform physical and spiritual substances indispensable in individual and community life. Jean-Pierre Warnier (1993, 1999:59ff.) has pointed out the importance of the container metaphor in understanding the conception of social and political power in the Grassfields. According to Warnier, the king, the notables, the compound heads are 'containers' who preserve and administer the 'vital substances' that ensure the continuation and prosperity of the kingdom. As political and family leaders, men control and ensure the potential reproduction of the society through a careful management of the vital substances – i.e., blood, semen, and saliva – that they contain in their bodies. These substances and powers are also embodied in the containers used in private and public rituals that mark many fundamental passages. The emphasis on procreation and transformation, which recurs in many of the critical events of individual and social life, also underlines this extreme degree of male control that characterizes Grassfields hierarchical power structure.

However, the Babessi concept of a potter-God, who molds pots and people out of the clay soil, also suggests a further implication of this metaphor: If bodies are containers, it can also be argued that containers – whether decorated with anthropomorphic and zoomorphic motifs or not – are bodies. The connection between pots and bodies is emphasized in the terms used to describe different parts of the pots, which have bellies (*bvo*), mouths (*chiu*), and necklaces (*koka*). Eating dishes also have a navel (*tuo*). This anthropomorphization of containers states once more the strong connection between the creative and reproductive powers of Babessi women.

However, women's ability to make children, cook, and mold the pots used for social and ritual occasions does not warrant any particular social recognition in the public arena. While women are intrinsically associated with the production and reproduction of the life cycles of individuals, men appropriate these abilities through the ritual use of pots that become containers of the powerful and secret substances preserved in the centers of political power, thus claiming for themselves the life-giving properties that are posited as the root of societal reproduction and hierarchical organization.

Rather than presenting and representing unequivocally symbols of fertility, power, and prestige, Babessi pots display these references in social interactions, thus disclosing different layers of meaning. As shown by the examples above, the understanding of the agency of pots in their context of production requires an investigation of multiple aspects of local society. Pots are the result of the creative agency of their makers who, through a deeply cultural re/productive process, impress in their shape and in their decoration shifting ideas of aesthetics and visual power. By choosing heterogeneous images that refer to traditional and imported iconographies, potters combine apparently inconsistent elements, thus giving life to objects that reflect the plasticity of local culture.

Once made, purchased, and used, Babessi pots may acquire roles and meanings that go beyond the intentions of their makers. Throughout their social life they become agents able to affect their environment. Used in life passages, rituals, and social gatherings, pots acquire a presence that is strongly connected to their ability to contain natural, supernatural, and social forces that inform the lives of groups and individuals. In many instances of their social life, pots embody crucial values at the core of local society and take part in the process of continuous production of culture. Obviously this is not a neutral role. Indeed, the analysis of their context of use and of the social relations they mediate reveals that the secondary agency displayed by these objects is embedded in a network of social relationships that are ultimately – and fundamentally – political. It might be worth noting, as a final remark, that even though the traditional power structure of the kingdom still has a strong influence on the daily life of people, many changes are occurring in response to different challenges. In particular, gender relationships are undergoing significant transformations and there are an increasing number of young women who refuse to submit their productive and reproductive power to male control (Goheen 1996). It might not be so surprising that, along with their role as wives, these young women refuse also to become potters, thus failing to provide a significant material agent for the reproduction of traditional society.

Notes

Research for this article was carried out during three field trips over a period of ten months between November 1998 and February 2001. Funding was provided by the Missione Etnologica Italiana in Africa Equatoriale. A shorter version of this paper was presented in the Art and Agency panel during the African Studies Association meeting in November 2005. I wish to thank Nicolas Argenti, Ivan Bargna, Kathleen Bickford Berzock, Barbara Frank, Wyatt MacGaffey, and Costa Petridis for commenting on earlier drafts of this paper. I am especially grateful to Kinsey Katchka for her thoughtful remarks and patient editing.

1. The Western Grassfields is a region that corresponds to the anglophone North West Province of the Republic of Cameroon. The territory is characterized by high plateaus densely inhabited by a population divided in numerous independent kingdoms, each with its own language and government. Babessi (which the inhabitants call Wushincho) is a medium-sized kingdom located at the eastern end of the Ndop Plain, at the foot of steep hills which delimit the village's territory to the north and east and mark the border with the Bui Division. The village has a population of approximately 12,700 inhabitants, according to the official estimate in 2000, itself based on figures from the 1987 census. In 1992 Babessi was chosen as the subdivisional head-quarters for the area including Bangolan, Baba I, and Babungo; however, this administrative role does not reflect a leadership of Babessi in relation to its neighboring kingdoms.
2. Also the kingdom of Nsei, which is today the most active pottery center of the region (see Forni 2001), was known in the eighteenth and nineteenth centuries for its ornate pots and clay pipe-heads. Regardless of their proximity and the fact that they produce similar types of items, the styles of pots and decorations are rather different.
3. Both Argenti (1999) and Koloss (2000) mention the importance of Babessi pots in the kingdom of Oku. Moreover, Babessi pots are also illustrated in Tardit's volume on the kingdom of Bamum (1980) and they were present in the display of the 'traditional Bamum kitchen' in the arts and craft museum in Fumban when I visited in June 2000.
4. According to Gell (1998:13ff.), art objects are indexes that permit a particular cognitive operation, identified as the abduction of agency, a sign of human agency whose meaning is not fixed, as proposed by a strictly symbolic approach, but inferred from its context of use.
5. Grassfields kingdoms are polities governed by a king and by a hierarchy of notables who control all public political and ritual functions. Although the organization of the hierarchy, the allocation of roles, and rights might vary from kingdom to kingdom, the political structure is fairly consistent. Besides ensuring the government of the village, this hierarchical organization also has strong symbolic significance. As suggested by Warnier (1993), the king himself is considered a 'container of vital substances' indispensable for the well-being of the village. The king, his family, his personal success, and his possessions are important symbols of the kingdom's health, fertility, and prosperity (see also Feldman-Savelsberg 1999). In the palace, the *fwa's* inner room is the most sacred place of all, where only certain categories of notables and the *fwa's* wives can enter.
6. Interview with author, Babessi, December 2000.
7. The reverse association is also true. De Heusch (quoted in Herbert 1993:213) describes in detail Thonga rituals of birth that see the child 'as the product of successful firing', a piece of ceramic ware that has been fired and not cracked. For other associations between cooking and giving birth see Feldman-Savelsberg 1999.
8. Also the final searing of carvings performed by Oku carvers (Argenti 2002) is referred to as 'putting the skin on'. This practice further emphasizes the strong parallel between artistic creativity and human reproductivity that in Grassfields conceptions seems to emerge throughout expressive media.
9. Interview with author, Babessi, May 2000.
10. Roulette patterns on cooking pots are obtained either with a wooden, carved roulette or simply with the dried stem of the plantain flower (*tuo kungo*). Applied decoration is generally reserved for pots that are not handled very often, since the decorative elements may detach themselves with use.
11. In reality, though, men rarely drink directly out of water pots. When reaching the kitchen, a man would generally ask the woman or a child to draw some water for him. This is common behavior throughout the Grassfields and has been noted also by Argenti (1999) in the kingdom of Oku.
12. Interview with author, Babessi, May 2000.

13. Frogs, spiders, and snakes have different meanings in different parts of the Grassfields region. In Babessi, where these images are often found on water pots, the emphasis is placed on the connection of these animals to the realm of water and to the power of fertility.
14. While Babessi potters produce a range of anthropomorphic decorations, generally applied on palm wine prestige pots, they do not create clay figurines such as those created for ritual use by the Mfunte-Wuli who reside north of the Grassfields (Baeke 1995) or the decorative sculptures made by the male potters in the nearby kingdom of Nsei (Forni 2001).
15. Different authors, such as Gebauer (1979), Northern (1984), and Knöpfli (1998), have investigated the meaning of Grassfields symbols. Virtually all the anthropomorphic and zoomorphic motifs may be associated with some form of political and/or spiritual power; however, meanings seem to shift significantly depending on their context of use even within the Grassfields. Thus, defining univocal associations between forms and meanings is almost impossible, even though it is clear that the decorations on the pots make explicit reference to the visual idiom of power shared among Grassfields kingdoms.
16. The consistency of Babessi pottery style is clearly demonstrated by the pot collection of the Bamenda Provincial Museum and the Prespot Museum in Nsei. The Bamenda Museum contains, among other things, a collection of pots from different villages in the North West Province initiated in the late 1950s by American collectors living in the area. The Prespot Museum houses a collection of old and new Nsei and Babessi pots and pipes. It was set up in the 1980s in one of the guest houses attached to the Presbyterian pottery project (Prespot) in the village of Nsei as a sort of reference collection that could inspire the project's creations. Recently, thanks to UNESCO funding, the Prespot collection moved to a separate museum building inaugurated in 2005.
17. All of the potters in the village and also a few of their customers were in fact able to recognize without hesitation a pot made by any of them. 'It is like my handwriting', potter Margaret B. told me once. 'I make my *nyanga* [pidgin term to define any sort of decorations and especially body decorations, which translates the local term *nyaka*] different from the others. People like to buy my pots because I take my time, I do not rush. The others just try to copy what I do, but my own decorations are good (*mejuh*)'.
18. The term *juju* is a pidgin term used throughout the Grassfields region to refer to the masquerades, dance group, and sacred objects connected to palace regulatory societies and male associations. *Jujus* embody sacred powers that are highly respected and feared by men and women alike. The most powerful *jujus*, who appear during annual celebrations and palace-related ceremonies, may not be seen by women or uninitiated men.
19. Ritual uses of pots are not just those connected to the male societies. Pots are also central in funerals and certain healing rituals. However, medicine pots and palm wine pots used in male societies and *juju* houses are considered the most powerful and affecting containers, which can cause real harm to those who are not entitled to see them or those who act against the laws of the society (see also Koloss 2000).
20. The language used to describe the powerful presence of *juju* pots bears strong similarities with the description of Kongo *minkisi*, and ceramic *minkisi* in particular (MacGaffey 1993, Thompson 1995). However, even though they are containers of spiritual forces, Babessi ritual pots do not acquire individuality and personality comparable to that of *minkisi*.
21. When talking in pidgin, Babessi people and traders usually refer to clay pots as 'country' pots, to distinguish them from imported china and metalware, which are always identified as 'whitemen pans' regardless of the fact that most of these containers come from Nigeria. Also, potters commonly make a distinction between *kuh* (generic term for pot) and *kuh mekalema* (whitemen pots).
22. The possession of metal pots and pans is valued also among potters, who never use the pots they make to cook daily meals. In many potters' compounds one is likely to find an even larger selection of metalware than in ordinary farmers' compounds. This is because women potters have more access to cash that they can use to equip their kitchens. See also Barley 1994:72 for a similar situation among the Dowayos in the 1970s. However, it is not only metalware that is sought after and valued; European-style china (porcelain) plates are considered even more prestigious in the Grassfields (at least in Oku) and referred to admiringly in pidgin as 'breakable plates' (Nicolas Argenti, personal communication).
23. Nowadays, boys serve the *ngwo* for a period of about five years, during which time they continue to go to school. In the past the initiation period was between seven and nine years. The boys lived in the *ngwo* compound. Today it

is possible to acquire the title of *nchinda* even without serving in the compound, by simply paying all the necessary fees and taking a short instruction course.

24. Besides constructing their own meeting house in the compound assigned to them by the *fon*, upon their formation *samba* groups need to acquire different objects that will constitute the common property of the group. These include one big and two small drums, a *denge* (thumb piano in pidgin), *shueme* (a fiber and bamboo emblem carried along when samba members are attending a celebration), a *samba* (fiber bag used to collect gifts after performing at death celebrations), *ngio'* (a calabash with long neck), and *kuh meh* (a large clay palm wine pot).
25. Interview with author, Babessi, January 2001.

References

Appadurai, Arjun, ed. 1986. *The Social Life of Things: Commodities in Cultural Perspective*. Cambridge: Cambridge University Press.

Arnoldi, Mary Jo, Christraud M. Geary, and Kris L. Hardin, eds. 1996. *African Material Culture*. Bloomington: Indiana University Press.

Argenti, Nicolas. 1999. *Is This How I Looked When I First Got Here? Pottery and Practice in the Cameroon Grassfields*. British Museum Occasional Paper no. 132. London: Trustees of the British Museum.

Argenti, Nicolas. 2002. 'People of the Chisel: Youths, and Elites in Oku (Cameroon).' *American Ethnologist*. 29 (3):497–533.

Barley, Nigel. 1994. *Smashing Pots: Feats of Clay from Africa*. London: British Museum Press.

Baeke, Viviane. 1995. 'Le système de pensée wùli: les morts, les esprits de l'eau, et la sorcellerie.' In *Objets-signes d'Afrique*, ed. Luc de Heusch, pp. 58–91. Annales Sciences Humaines vol 145. Tervuren : Musèe Royal de l'Afrique Centrale.

Berns, Marla. 1990. 'Pots and People.' *African Arts* 23 (3):50–60, 102.

Berns, Marla. 1993. 'Art, History, and Gender: Women and Clay in West Africa.' *African Archaeological Review* 11:129–148.

Berns, Marla. 2000. 'Containing Power: Ceramic and Ritual Practices in Northeastern Nigeria.' In *Clay and Fire: Pottery in Africa*, ed. Christopher Roy, pp. 53–76. Iowa Studies in African Art, vol 4. Iowa City: School of Art and Art History of the University of Iowa.

Feldman-Savelsberg, Pamela. 1999. *Plundered Kitchens, Empty Wombs: Threatened Reproduction and Identity in the Cameroon Grassfields*. Ann Arbor: University of Michigan Press.

Forni, Silvia. 2001. *Molding Culture: Pottery and Traditions in the Ndop Plain* (North West Province–Camer- oon). PhD diss. Università degli Studi di Torino.

Fowler, Ian. 1997. 'Tribal and Palatine Arts of the Cameroon Grassfields: Elements for a Traditional Regional Identity.' In *Contesting Art: Art, Politics and Identity in the Modern World*, ed. John MacClancy, pp. 63–84. New York: Berg.

Gebauer, Paul. 1979. *Art of Cameroon*. Portland: Portland Art Museum and New York: Metropolitan Museum of Art.

Gell, Alfred. 1998. *Art and Agency. An Anthropological Theory*. Oxford: Claredon Press.

Goheen, Miriam. 1996. *Men Own the Fields, Women Own the Crops: Gender and Power in the Cameroon Grassfields*. Madison: University of Wisconsin Press.

Gosselain, Olivier P. 2002. *Poteries du Cameroun méridional: Styles, techniques, et rapports a l'identité*. CRA Monographies 26. Paris: CNRS Editions.

Hardin, Kris L. 1995. *The Aesthetics of Action: Continuity and Change in a West African Town*. Washington, DC: Smithsonian Institution Press.

Herbert, Eugenia. 1993. *Iron, Gender, and Power: Rituals of Transformation in African Societies*. Bloomington: Indiana University Press.

Knöpfli, Hans. 1998. *Sculpture and Symbolism. Crafts and Technologies: Some Traditional Craftsmen of the Western Grassland of Cameroon. Part 2: Woodcarvers and Blacksmiths*. Basel: Basel Mission.

Koloss, Hans-Joachin. 2000. *Worldview and Society in Oku (Cameroon)*. Baessler Archiv Beitrage zur Ethnolo- gie 10. Berlin: Verlag von Dietrich Reimer.

MacGaffey, Wyatt. 1993. 'The Eyes of Understanding.' In *Astonishment and Power*, by Wyatt MacGaffey and Michael Harris, pp. 21–103. Washington, DC: National Museum of African Art.

Northern, Tamara. 1984. *The Art of Cameroon*. Washington, DC: Smithsonian Institution Press.

Spindel, Carol. 1989. 'Kpeenbele Senufo Potters.' *African Arts*, 22 (2):66–73, 103.
Thompson, Barbara. 1995. *Earthen Spirits: Ceramic Power Vessels of Lower Zaire*. Master's thesis, University of Florida.
Warnier, Jean-Pierre. 1993. 'The King as a Container in the Cameroon Grassfields.' Paideuma 39:303–19.
Warnier, Jean-Pierre. 1999. *Construire la culture materielle: L'homme qui pensait avec ses doigts*. Paris: PUF.
Weiss, Brad. 1996. *The Making and Unmaking of the Haya Lived Word: Consumption, Commoditization, and Everyday Practice*. Durham: Duke University Press.

Silvia Forni (2007), 'Containers of Life: Pottery and Social Relations in the Grassfields (Cameroon)', in African Arts, Spring 2007, Vol. 40, No. 1, pp. 42–53.

Reprinted with permission from MIT Press. ©2007 by Regents of the University of California.

5
CERAMICS AND ART CRITICISM

Janet Koplos

Ceramics is a visual art, although it's not painting, and it's not sculpture. It has its own identity. The position of ceramics today is not a problem. If there's a dilemma, it's that ceramists, having learned their trade at art school, lust after the perceived status of painting and sculpture, whether or not they want to follow the practices of those arts.

Presented at The Ceramic Millennium, 1999, Amsterdam

My subject is criticism, and although I will mention a few artists, my focus is on words more than work. I must warn you that I'm going to be saying some things that some of you won't want to hear. I have two main points to make. One will probably find no disagreement: ceramics criticism is weak if you compare it with art criticism. But my second assertion is that ceramics is not the same as painting and sculpture, and never will be. The situation is complex, and that's what makes it fascinating. But I hope to speak simply about it.

Garth has given me three charges. I'll give my perspective on the present state of ceramic art and its relationship to the art world. This is a basic consideration on which all criticism relies. I'm also going to evaluate the quality of ceramic criticism. And I'm going look at some options for the future.

I will be talking about examples and issues in American ceramics. But the similarity of the issues in other places I know a little about, such as Holland, Japan, and Britain, lead me to believe that the discussion will be relevant to other places as well.

On the one hand, clay is just a material. It can be used to make beautiful things, useful things, thought-provoking things. There is no barrier that keeps clay out of the art galleries. In fact, one sees a considerable amount of work in clay in the museums and galleries of New York and elsewhere. Anthony Caro, Lynda Benglis, Thomas Schütte, Beverly Semmes, Antony Gormley, Charles LeDray, and lots of other contemporary artists work with clay. The Kruithuis Museum here in Holland did a show of great modern and contemporary artists who've worked extensively in clay, from Picasso to Fontana to A.R. Penck. Clay is among the materials that an artist may use to make a form or express a notion in a finished work, not to mention its traditional role in modelling for bronze casting. So there is no stigma to using clay. It's a non-issue.

But ceramics is something else. In the sociological sense, ceramics is a community based on a material and shared attitudes toward working with it. Ceramics has its own teaching programs, its own residency sites, its own publications, its own technical jargon, its own politics, its own galleries and museums, its own history of makers and styles, its own international symposia. This world is, to a degree, independent of the art world, but it brushes up against it all the time, which produces some friction.

Just as the ceramic world is distinguishable from the art world, ceramic art is distinguishable from painting and sculpture – and I'm using that cumbersome phrase 'painting and sculpture' as a broad heading, because I

Source: © Garth Clark/Ceramic Arts Foundation.

dislike the term 'fine art;' which seems to me to imply that everything else is not fine. The aesthetic of ceramics is far from being a single thing, yet there are typical and atypical types, and there are qualities that identify it as a particular and interesting field in itself. So let me venture a few generalities.

Nearly always, a work of ceramic art is an object. Usually it's of throwing size, related to human body scale, even if it's made by some other technique. Most often it is a hollow volume – that is, a vessel. Although it is usually three dimensional, ceramics tends to concentrate on the embellishment of surface more than on the invention of form, and on detail more than on large gesture. Surface and form are often separate considerations in ceramics, which is seldom the case in mainstream sculpture. In general, surface is more important in ceramics than in sculpture.

And ceramics has the additional dimension of an inside contributing to its character, so that it involves a topological transformation of a bulge on the outside being a recess on the inside – a quality that open vessels particularly exploit. Vessels pull vision and imagination into themselves. They focus inward, centered on that interior void, rather than reaching outward to command the surrounding space.

Ceramics is often purely formalist, developing relationships of part or colour for their own inherent satisfaction, rather than for the expression of an external meaning. These relationships of parts typically play on a spectrum of unity or disunity, probably because of that capacity of form and surface to operate independently. It also often incorporates, as a sort of subtext, the history of decorative or utilitarian form, conveying multicultural references. Ceramics has always been richly multicultural encompassing rather than exclusionary. Ceramics may be representational as well. Although political subjects are possible, they have never been so important as in painting. Humour is found more frequently in ceramics than in painting or sculpture. This, I think, shows a wish to follow the practice of painting and sculpture to violate expectations, but without provoking hostility – or taking itself too seriously. Ceramics tends to be easy going as a statement – almost embarrassed to be excessive – yet intense as a demonstration of skill.

Looking at the field as a whole, it's possible to recognize a certain manner. One can also recognize that different character when gallery hopping. If you've been looking at paintings or installations, and you walk into a ceramics show, you have to narrow your focus to smaller scale, attend more to detail and subtler interests. Ceramics seems to ask for intimate address more than painting and sculpture do. Nevertheless, the whole twentieth century drift in ceramics is for the work to be analyzed and understood in terms of expectations adopted from painting and sculpture. Both inside and outside the field, it's the deviations from this typical character that get attention.

While there is no hostility toward clay in the art world, there are negative stereotypes about ceramics in general and assumptions that it is not as interesting, not as adventurous, not as important as painting and sculpture. Often the ceramics field itself seems to share this skepticism! In fact, ceramics, for the most part, operates under a sensitive aesthetic that has more in common with prints and drawings than painting and sculpture. The labour of processes, the vulnerability of the material, do not seem to encourage the grand gestures or flamboyant outrages that our celebrity-obsessed and media-driven contemporary culture responds to. Leading-edge art today tends to challenge traditions and to respond to the world-with social engagement or with irony.

Art has been defined by materials and format. That is, a painting is art whether it is good or bad; it's art by definition, and quality is a separate question. More recently, art is defined by manner and mindset or by context: that is, anything shown in an art gallery is art, even cooking a big pot of food to share and not cleaning up afterwards, or setting out a giant ashtray full of cigarette butts. Skill may be demonstrated, and some recent art even takes virtuosity and obsessive labour as its subjects, but it's the treatment of a subject, not the skill or the labour per se, that makes it art today.

Clay, of course, may match these art characteristics and fit the definition of art without strain. Even works in clay that take the vessel form may do so. Even vessels produced by people who come from a ceramics background by training and socializing may do so. It becomes art by accolade, because it's so good. Thus Betty Woodman, who started out as a production potter, is discussed in art magazines in terms of her innovative and challenging painting, which moves through three-dimensional space discontinuously around the surface of an object or several objects in combination. Thus Robert Arneson is praised by art critics for his irreverent wit, for his skill at mimicry, and for grasping archetypal forces that animate the collective American psyche, as one of them put it. Thus art critics looking at Ken Price's recent vessels respond to their sensuousness, their anthropomorphic mystery, and their striking concordance with the formal insouciance and eye-grabbing colour of a much younger generation of Los Angeles artists, as another critic said. Thus Daisy Youngblood has impressed a succession of art critics with her eerie fragmented animal and human figures with empty eye sockets that seem to give a view into their bleak souls. Clay is not an impediment to art status in any of these examples. Woodman, Arneson, and Youngblood in New York and Price in Los Angeles show at important mainstream art galleries, not in specialized craft or ceramic galleries.

Considering how different the work of these four artists is, it seems clear that ceramics criticism cannot be reduced to a simple formula or set of expectations. Once there was talk about truth to materials, but we've come to realize that one of the truths of ceramics is that it's a chameleon. It can be pretty much whatever the maker wants it to be. Figural, decorative, tactile, architectural, painterly, gestural, pictorial, usable, symbolic of the long continuity of time, symbolic of the fleet passage of time, and so on and so on. It can be formalist, it can be metaphoric. Archaic or space age, sensuous or cold.

Ceramics is a visual art, although it's not painting, and it's not sculpture. It has its own identity. The position of ceramics today is not a problem. If there's a dilemma, it's that ceramists, having learned their trade at art school, lust after the perceived status of painting and sculpture, whether or not they want to follow the practices of those arts. Young art students today, as a legacy of conceptualism, learn that the idea is the important thing, and they should use whatever medium works for it. But ceramics artists don't want to use whatever medium. The clay comes first, as a precondition. Many of them isolate themselves in the ceramic world and don't know what's going on in painting and sculpture. Yet their complaints reveal that they think that the art world is better than their own, and they want access. Actually, they hope that the art world will discover them, come around to their thinking, buy their work for the high prices paintings sell for. They want to be appreciated not by the public but by these elites. If I were being unkind, I'd say that they don't want to play the game, yet they want to win the prize. This is ambition in word but not in deed.

I must emphasize and re-emphasize that the 'otherness' of ceramics, this non-paintingness, non-sculptureness, is a good thing. Ceramics should be accepted and celebrated for its own attributes. What would be gained by every medium trying to adopt the expectations of painting? Art, you know, goes through fads and aberrations, follows social change more often than it foreshadows it, and has lately become so dependent on language and video that one wonders if it's simply going to turn into literature and movies and nothing else! Art does not have a stranglehold on wisdom, and a lot of artists come up empty. So why is there this endless whining about the art status of ceramics as a field? Ceramics is a second-tier aesthetic activity or marginalized *only* if you believe that painting and sculpture define the terms of worthiness; and if you believe that the goals and means of painting and sculpture are the proper ones, then why are you in ceramics? The question is less one of aesthetic hierarchies or exclusion of a material than of identification and self-confidence.

Exactly the same paradox applies in the case of ceramics criticism. If you're comparing it to art criticism, ceramic criticism often isn't very good. It sometimes sounds as unnatural as a speech delivered in a foreign language, and sometime it's just clichéd, because it borrows an established art vocabulary without sufficient regard for appropriateness. This problem has been recognized, so now we have conferences about the need for a language of criticism for clay. But that's still using art criticism as the model and assuming that if we select some nouns and adjectives, by gosh, we'll have our own critical language! But in fact, art words fit styles and visual dynamics just fine, and ordinary language does a good job too. Only art and literary theory and social and political terms seem misapplied. What's needed is not new words, but a framework that adjusts to the specifics of the situation and responds to the particularities of ceramics.

Unfortunately, it's easy to mimic the form of art criticism without the substance. If you act like a critic, you are a critic. All you have to do is use a few popular words, such as 'narrative' or 'hegemony' or 'discourse;' or others borrowed from writing in other fields. You can get away with almost anything, because there's no certification process. Who can measure a critic's performance? Peers could, but professional courtesy tends to keep the lid on that. One might think that editors would put a stop to bad criticism, but for reasons I'll get to in a moment, that doesn't seem to happen. So a lot of nonsense gets written about ceramics. But do remember that a lot of nonsense gets written about all art, and there's a lot of excruciatingly boring writing and a lot of impenetrable stuff. That got really bad in the eighties with theoretical writing based on literary criticism and employing dense, scholarly jargon. The difficulty is compounded in ceramics because of the multiple purposes and goals of clay, and also because of a lack of support structure, such as programs of study that would give a critic a historical and philosophical background and bases for comparison. (Britain, maybe because of its literary orientation, has a stronger recent history of serious, provocative, substantial, and continuous consideration of craft issues and history by scholar/critics such Tanya Harrod, the late Peter Dormer, and others. This exemplary activity has no equal in the USA.)

Ceramics looks to art for the style of criticism, and sometimes for the practitioners as well. Just as there are visitors to ceramics, there are visitors to ceramics criticism. Craft periodicals and catalogues solicit art writers. That has the appeal of broadening the field and getting fresh perspectives. It's sometimes really just a means of seeking legitimation, but if it introduces art critics to ceramics, that can be useful. When writing by outsiders is bad, that may be because they don't know enough, and the writing is superficial – sometimes overly impressed with the fact that clay is a craft material, while not sufficiently examining what's being done with it. Other bad ceramics writing by art critics is that shaped entirely by the idiosyncrasies and established agenda of the critic, whether it's politics, theory, or psychology.

When it's good, writing by outsiders opens new doors. Arthur Danto has applied philosophical questions to the nitty-gritty of clay, using comprehensible language. Other good writing by outsiders genuinely cross-fertilizes, which is the case in recent analysis of Betty Woodman's work by the painter and critic Robert Berlind, writing a catalogue essay for an exhibition in Iowa.[1] He takes a theme of 'between' in addressing Woodman's work. He describes geometric against organic, fact against metaphor, invention against reinterpretation, as well as figure-ground reversals and the relation of the work to both sculpture and painting. He compares her spontaneity to action painting (Abstract Expressionism), and he discusses thinking through the act. Berlind brings a particular painter's sensibility to his essay, producing a rich, rewarding piece of critical writing.

Another institutional or structural problem with ceramics criticism is that the field is narrow, and therefore the pay is too little for anyone to make a living as a ceramics critic. Financial hardship can deter capable writers from pursuing the subject, unless they're really driven to do it, regardless of the lack of reward. Too often criticism is expected to be a charitable donation of time and effort! Another problem is that publications don't develop critical thinking by pushing writers, by sending manuscripts back with challenging questions that require critics to reach more deeply into their resources, both factual and imaginative.

I'd like to look briefly at the magazines, American, plus a few others. *Studio Potter* has always presented serious, insider consideration of a certain range of ceramic work, but it depends upon makers to do the writing, and does not pay for writing. Thus, although it supports thinking, it does not foster the development of criticism from objective writers. *Ceramics Monthly* is both a technical publication and, in a way, an academic one – it's a place where teachers can get visibility to please their university's administration. *American Ceramics* is a sad case, because it once seemed so promising. Under the considered editorship of Michael McTwigan it once presented the most consistent critical exchange the postwar American ceramics field has known. Since McTwigan's departure – for work that would pay well enough to support a family – this magazine has come to owe so much money to so many writers and to have alienated so many gallery advertisers by its undependable publication schedule that it's amazing that it persists in its decrepit state. It's still beautiful and usually worth reading when it does come out. Also on this playing field is *Ceramic Review*, the British technical magazine. The strength of the Australian magazine *Ceramics Art and Perception* is beautiful pictures and international focus. The texts are often light and more character oriented than critical. There seem to be problems with finding writers who are not in some way involved with the people or places they're writing about. Perhaps that's because the pay is so modest that critics can't afford to do it, so friends and associates do. One can't be sure of the critical independence and objectivity of what one reads.

There are also general crafts magazines that include ceramics, such as *American Craft* magazine. Years ago, when it was called *Craft Horizons* and was edited by Rose Slivka, it presented an important bridge to the art world through Slivka's personal acquaintance with such artists as David Smith, Elaine and Willem de Kooning, and the poet and translator Richard Howard. Slivka's own writing emphasized the capacity of craft objects to carry poetic feeling; she took it for granted that ceramic objects can be metaphoric, which is a short-form explanation of what makes something art. Since her time, *American Craft* has been more of a coffee-table magazine than a critical one. The review section was discontinued. The articles are intelligent, but they rarely challenge. The only critical content is one or two single-page reviews. The British magazine *Crafts* also has drifted in a more populist, less critical direction since the days when Martina Margetts was editor, though it still has lots of reviews. It has an inventive visual style and a concise, breezy, and informational verbal style, but the articles are fairly short, and there's less sense nowadays of urgently arguing important issues. The editorial staff of most of these magazines consists of professional editors who are not active as critics, which is different than the pattern of many art magazines and may, in part, explain the different tone of craft publications.

One can look elsewhere for coverage. During the years that Derek Guthrie was publisher of the *New Art Examiner*, that magazine consistently paid attention to ceramics. And the major American art magazines – *Art in America, ArtNews* and *Artforum – have* all given feature treatment to significant ceramic artists, as well as publishing many reviews of clay shows. Ken Price's work has been on the cover of *Art in America*. There are also design magazines, such as *Metropolis* in New York, that include contemporary crafts and take an intelligent, critical approach. Ironically, though, these sources of critical writing don't particularly serve the makers of ceramic art as a group, because not so many ceramists read them regularly thus supporting my point about ceramics being a separate community.

Now, all my comments on these publications have been based on the assumption that an art-type criticism is a need or a desire for ceramics. If that's the case, this publication situation is lamentable. But maybe not. Maybe, like water seeking its own level or a time getting the style it deserves, maybe this writing is what ceramics needs – even if not what it says it wants. Before I go on to consider what criticism might be, let's pause to enumerate the forms of writing about ceramics. I can name the types in just a few words: technical, lifestyle, work documentation, experiential, historical, and theoretical, probably in descending order of frequency. I think that tells us something, and I'll come back to this idea at the end.

Do consider the value of various kinds of writing, now and in the recent past. There are books, whether about ceramics specifically or not, that can be profitably applied to thinking about ceramics. Bernard Leach, despite the fact that he's getting kicked around nowadays, is still useful. He attempted to identify values for ceramics, and that's still stimulating. Books like David Pye's *The Nature and Art of Workmanship* enrich the discussion of labour, which is significant in ceramics. Philip Rawson's historical treatment in his book *Ceramics* tells us how the work can be analyzed and understood, and what ceramics has meant and therefore what it has the potential to mean. M.C. Richards made ceramics a metaphor for living.[2] Henry Petroski's *The Evolution of Useful Things* makes us think about the forms and purpose of objects and tools around us. Garth Clark mapped out contemporary American ceramics history and fearlessly evaluated work, something that's very difficult to do in such a small world. This variety points to the possibilities and maybe identifies the needs. Stop to think: if there consistently is so much writing about technique and lifestyle, maybe that's in fact what's important. Maybe that's the meaning of this activity.

Well, I'm not really a believer in forecasts of anything having to do with humans. You can predict the weather, maybe, but people, and especially artists, tend to come up with options more fascinating than any I could imagine, which is why I hang around them. But I think I can confidently predict that ceramics as a field is not going to be taken up wholesale by the art world. If that's your hope, I'd recommend that you get over it. I don't think it's something to wish for. It would just mean that things would be regarded as poor sculptures rather than good pots, faulted for not being spatially interactive, or on the edge, or whatever.

The situation of photography is a relevant comparison. Photography, like clay, is a medium used by artists to suit their purposes. Yet there continue to be photography galleries and photography departments in museums; 'pure photography' by people who devote their lives to traditional-format documentations of existence in this medium tend to be concentrated in these specialty galleries, rather than being taken up by mainstream painting-and-sculpture galleries. So it is with ceramics, and will continue to be.

The most traditional forms, those that make reference primarily to the ceramic tradition itself, remain in the specialty galleries, outside the usual routes of art critics. This work is covered by specialty criticism, which follows the model of art criticism-but is not the same. It is softer and more sympathetic. (One might note, however, that photography has been more successful than ceramics in establishing itself as an academic field of historic and aesthetic study.)

What should ceramics criticism be? What makes good criticism? My feeling is that learned and intellectual criticism certainly has a place, and that place is academia. Such writing is too specialized and too difficult to be useful in the ordinary consideration of ceramic art in magazines and newspapers. I prefer to think of criticism as a translation service for what is otherwise a nonverbal form of expression. The critic mediates between the work and the viewer, and helps the viewer to see. The critic may have special knowledge, or the critic may simply be a person who looks carefully at art and thinks seriously about it – an ideal viewer who also has writing skills. It has been said that the essential critical activity is not having an opinion, because everybody has opinions; the essential critical activity is giving reasons for those opinions.

If criticism is regarded that way, it surely is an important part of the ceramics world, even if ceramics is not painting and not sculpture. Criticism should be just good, clear thinking, communicated to others. Every field needs that. The problems come when critics think that ceramics should be something other than what it is and turn the heads of the makers. Critics should not write rules, and makers should remember that no one ever did a great or original thing by following what other people claim is important.

I can see four things that ceramics criticism can be. One is analysis of the big picture, ceramics in its context. Another is, contrarily, the intimate consideration of the work as a reflection of the maker and the making. Another is simply the verbal expression of the visual – this is the poetic sort of writing. And another is comparison, the grappling with standards, based on whatever seems important in our time or the past, or commercial considerations or personal goals. All these are forms of criticism. The only things ceramics criticism must adopt from art criticism are seriousness, care, and good writing, not pedantry or pompousness, and not the foolish assumption that what's difficult to understand must be important!

It's essential to think about what the specific nature of ceramic works require as a response. I would argue that in contrast to painting and sculpture, greatness and originality are not essential to the vast majority of the uses and pleasures that derive from ceramic work. Maybe function is important. Maybe virtuosity is important. Maybe perpetuating traditions is important. We all know that there is a place for clay that carries metaphor and meaning. That place is the art gallery. And clay in the art gallery will find consideration in the same vocabulary and against the same standards as any other contemporary art.

But I worry, in any discussion of criticism, that we will forget that there have always been other places for clay, too, where criticism is irrelevant – the dining table, the kitchen and the garden, among others. Clay has always occupied the space between art and life, although that's a space that the art world only discovered a few decades ago. It seems to me that the major issue for ceramic artists to face is resolving their identity and maintaining *plural* choices. The major issue for ceramic criticism is to intelligently support that pluralism.

Notes

1. Robert Berlind, *Betty Woodman* (Fort Dodge, IA: Blanden Memorial Art Museum, 1999).
2. Mary Caroline Richards, *Centering in Pottery, Poetry, and the Person* (Middletown, CT: Wesleyan University Press, 1964).

This essay is reproduced by kind permission of Garth Clark/Ceramic Arts Foundation.

6

DEATH AND CLAY: CULTURAL AND PERSONAL INTERPRETATIONS IN CERAMICS

Christopher Garcia and Tomaru Haruna

Death and clay have gone hand in hand throughout the history of Human-kind. Six of the seven continents have a ceramic lineage and I recently learned that now there's a contemporary ceramic studio in Antarctica.

For centuries, burial practices across the world have involved ceramic urns, ritual figure sculpture, and bowls filled with offerings for the next incarnation. Many of these traditions are startlingly similar from one culture to the next. For example, the Indigenous people of Nicaragua, the Nahuatl, and the Japanese people from the Jomon period both shared a common practice. Both civilizations would bury their dead for a number of years, then excavate the bones and deposit them into a clay vessel that represented a womb. The concept of "rebirth" through a clay uterus holds a strong symbolic message of passage that transcends physical borders.

In the 21st century, death ritual worldwide has slowly phased out the ancient role of ceramics. The use of urns for cremains (mortuary ash) is still prevalent, but western culture has often opted for brass over clay. Ceramics have also lessened in their daily utilitarian use over the centuries. In this steady progress away from our discovery of fired clay, are we also losing a tie to our ancestral origins?

Several cultures throughout time have had a strong artistic and cultural presence in our books and museums. The majority of the ceramic ware that represent the culture's sophistication was often recovered from excavated tombs. It is fascinating to imagine that how a civilization treated death has often been the gauge for a society's progress.

One of the cultures that used some of the most beautiful and mysterious ceramics in death ritual was the Maya culture. The Maya focused mainly on the role that religion played in their lives and were strongly linked to their gods and nature. The Maya religion was based on the "Popol Vuh", which was the collected cosmic myth and story of the Quiche.

There are many symbols of death in Maya codex-style vases and sculpture. Maya religion was dualistic, as expressed by the constant conflicts between good and evil, life and death. Among the deities, there was the Long-nosed God and the Roman-nosed God. These gods of death also had control over the healthy birth of children or an abundant crop. Death not only controlled the end of life, but everything leading up to it.

Among the ceramics made for ceremonial use, there were censers, vessels, and figurines for funeral purposes. Small vases in human or monster form were found in many burial mounds. Codex-style painted pottery is renowned for its representation of Maya religion and myth. They are illustrated with portraits of Maya kings, nobles, and mythical deities. A link between myth and art is shown in funeral pots where the recently dead interact in the Maya Underworld.

The Jomon period in Japan also offers a rich relationship of ritual and clay. The word "Jomon" means a cord-mark decoration or motif. Archaeologists have classified Jomon pottery into many styles and cultural regions. This pottery was mainly made for practical purposes, such as storing and cooking.

Source: © Chris Garcia/*Ceramics Technical.*

Pottery seemed to be the main focus of Jomon artistic expression, but they also made clay figures and ornaments in abundance. Jomon pottery went through a number of notable changes over the 10,000 years of the period, but all the pottery types were unglazed, low-fired wares.

People in the Jomon period buried their dead in pits in the ground or in jars. The basic burial pattern started in the Middle Jomon period and extended to the Final Jomon (specially) in eastern Japan. Before the Middle Jomon, people were buried in a stretched position, later; they were in a fetal position. They sometimes used caves for burials as well. There were many ways of positioning the faces or bodies, by areas or periods, when burying. For instance, stones or vessels were put on the head or chest, or vessels covered the head entirely.

As I mentioned before, there were cases where, after the dead were buried for a while, people dug the bones out and buried them again (secondary-burial "sai-so"), or washed the bones and put them in a jar and buried them (secondary-burial of cleaned bone "senkotsu- so"). Senkotsu-so occurred in Okinawa, and there were also records of it in Kyushu and Honshu.

Sannai Maruyama, an archeological excavation in Aomori prefecture revealed that about five hundred people were living in about one hundred pit-dwellings in a Jomon village structure. There were separate graveyards for children and adults. Children's graves were in the northern part of the community space. They were buried in jars that stood upright in the ground.

Small children and infants were put in jars and buried in or near houses under the entrance. Some jars were buried upside down. Some have been also found with a hole bored in their bases. These holes were ritually cut into the jars, it has been suggested that the hole is probably a passage for the deceased's spirit to be released, or to discourage re-use by a scavenger.

The Maya and Jomon period are just a couple of examples of the value ceramics had in burial rites. Whether it is a universal symbolism of being born of the earth and returning to it, or if it is just the practicality or Symbolism of clay as a vessel, ceramics have had an immense impact on the way we bury our dead. The question now is, does humanity still hold clay as an important symbol in burials? While many contemporary cultures dig graves into clay, is the clay simply a way to fill the hole and cover the dead, or is there more to this ancient medium in our present day?

In my own life and work, I have found a deep interest in the rituals Surrounding death in many cultures. Growing up in Puerto Rico, a Predominantly Catholic island, I had the chance to explore colonial Graveyards and view the relic skeleton of San Pio in Old San Juan's Cathedral. When I travel, I always visit graveyards and catacombs to better understand the culture's view of life and death.

I have addressed the subject of burial in individual works and continuing series over my career. One series that I have been doing over the past six years has involved placing small figures on neglected tombstones across the world. When I travel, I either make new pieces or bring along three or four 3" stoneware figures that I can leave as offerings on graves. This series began after I visited the old Jewish cemetery in Krakow, Poland and was very interested in the simple, direct tradition in Hebrew culture of leaving a small stone as a token to a visited grave. Though there is no definite origin to this tradition, some think it can be traced to the biblical story involving the sons of Jacob piling small stones one by one to build Rachel's grave. The rite now acts as a marker, letting the deceased know you visited and paid your respects. After time, a large accumulation of stones would represent the honor and love the person still receives in death.

Another ongoing series of my work involving death relates to obituaries. I have read obituaries over the years and was often surprised by how a person's life could be summed up in a few paragraphs. In many cases, this written documentation may be the most complete and important archival evidence that they ever lived. Mostly, the information is mundane, telling of 40 years of working for a company, a record of military service, a list of grandchildren left behind, etc. In other cases, fantastic coincidences, moments of triumph or discovery add something a little more special to these departed people. I wanted to find a way to use this interest and turn it Into a commemoration as well as an artistic interpretation.

This series entails an act that I am still not comfortable with. When I find a recent obituary that interests me, I visit the freshly dug grave, pay my respects, and leave with a handful of grave clay. The clay is cleaned and then worked into a figure sculpture relating to the person's condensed existence as told through their obit. The figures are often hard to interpret. I focus on aspects of their lives that interest me and sometimes these different parts cross into strange contrasting symbols. The figures are fired to cone one to five, depending on the clay sample, and then combined media elements, including a bone china skull, are added at the end.

The aesthetic style of the figures are based on the Mexican Calaveras that represent small clay and/or wood skeletons involved in the same everyday activities their living counterparts would be doing.

Mexico has one of the richest and healthiest relationships with death in the world. The well-known Dia de los Muertos celebrates the lives of those who have passed on and the important role death has in our daily lives. The art that has evolved from this culture demonstrates death as not a fearsome thing, but a steady companion throughout life.

The work of Mexican ceramist Jorge Llaca reflects this co-existence and also offers a unique and personal interpretation. Llaca's artistic career has included a diverse palette of mediums and he continues to work in a variety of different materials to bring across his ideas. His ceramic work allows a more visceral approach to his philosophies of life's cycles. The pure physicality of clay gives him the raw material to express the organic, tangible quality he searches for in his art:

> "Our existence is embedded in an endless circle of life and death. We are forced into the conflict, surrounded by metaphors of beginnings and endings. Today, we find the real truth of our existence in recycling and composting: giving to the universe that which has been given to us in life, with the payment of our own death, so life can emerge again."

Llaca's hand-built sculpture, *Toro*, offers the viewer a mythical, nightmarish beast that dwells somewhere in the mind's shadows. The figure of an emaciated cow with a skull for a head is reminiscent of some biblical, apocalyptic message of famine. The terra cotta surface with hints of white softens the piece visually. The remaining flesh has a slight warmth, a tenuous grasp on life, pulsing under the thin skin of clay.

In a more straightforward work, *Like Father, Like Son*, Llaca presents a coffin motif featuring a figure that is solely composed of a head and hands. The wood sculpture representing a coffin is the predominant medium, but not the most powerful. Even with the body being mostly consumed by the tube-like form, the expression on the face and the attitude of the hands speak of the humanity of the metaphorically buried figure. Llaca, in choosing a rough, unglazed surface for the face and hands, has given the features a vulnerability that relate to every mortal being. The title, *Like Father Like Son*, passes on to the viewer the message that death is our parent's legacy; Where they went, we will one day follow.

British ceramic sculptor, Alison Stace, has created work that also deals with the physicality of death, but she is equally concerned with its spiritual significance. The undiscovered qualities of what lies beyond are perhaps unknown to the artist, but her figures have the presence of wise, far-seeing beings that walk between two worlds:

> "My figures are concerned with some of the issues surrounding death, such as the marking of death, connections with ancestors, ritual and memory...They relate to a collective memory and communicate silently with the living. They are guardians of the spirit, mediators between the dead and the living, the past and the present."

Stace has created her own race of beings and imbued them with a mystic quality that is reminiscent of the statues on Easter Island. Both sets of figures have a noble, brooding air about them that exudes a definite knowledge of what is beyond, but they are also stoic, silent. These beings do not offer the message, just the promise of it.

The physical qualities of these tall forms are very hard to pin down. In *Group of Three White Creatures*, the beings stand vigil, their hawk-life faces lifted and alert. Stace explains their strange bodies and faces as a further embodiment of their separate reality:

> "My creatures are related to human figures, but have developed from research into shamans, who take on an animal form as they travel into the spirit world. They are therefore neither human nor animal, and neither real nor imaginary, but instead exist somewhere between the two realms of the flesh and the ether."

Forrest Snyder is an American ceramist living in North Bennington, Vermont, where old New England cemeteries pepper the countryside. Snyder has viewed the tomb stones in these grave yards for years and has grown to accept them as not only historically relevant, but conceptually appealing:

> "Psychologically, these stones aren't morbid or morose, quite the opposite. I view real tombstones as little bits of recorded history, hints at past lives. It's this aspect that really gets me – I like creating images for characters giving the minimal (and sometimes not so minimal) information on a tombstone."

In the towns throughout Vermont, there are cemeteries with gravestones dating back over 250 years. Snyder was documenting the more interesting markers with a pinhole camera and then decided to create his own fictional tombstones out of clay. He took the style of writing, both in font styles and grammar from existing stones to create his own fictional ones. Snyder found a broad, unending source of inspiration in his walks through cemeteries and has documented quite a few brief, but intriguing stories from the graves:

(These epitaphs have retained their line breaks and miss-spellings, and random capitalization from the stones):

> "A thousand Groans his dear remains convey.
> To his Cold lodging in a Bed of clay."
>
> "IN MEMORY
> of Daniel, Son of Mr. Thomas
> Matteson, and Mrs. Sarah his
> Wife; who received a bruise
> between the Stump of a Tree
> and a Rail crouded by a Cart
> Wheel: After continuing
> about Eight hours, Expired
> on the 28th Day of July
> 1787 In the Ten Year
> of his Age.

With this abundant source as a catalyst and high regard for his source of inspiration, Snyder went on to compose his own epitaphs for imaginary characters, Snyder is not only a visual artist, but the care holder of an ancient medium of historic prose and poetry that has found new development in his creations. He presents the works not only on the visual strengths of ceramics and architecture, but as testament to a strong, but mostly forgotten literary style.

Japanese born Keisuke Mizuno addresses the subject of death a little differently than the other artists I've discussed in this article. Mizuno uses the metaphor of attractive, colorful blossoms and fruit to bring about a message of impermanence and decay. The works are beautiful, but deadly, bold, yet ephemeral. These porcelain pieces have the intimacy and lushness of Georgia O'Keefe's flower paintings, but there is the underlying element of death in all the work in this series.

Mizuno's use of clay skulls, bones, ears, shells, keys and other objects as centerpieces to these sensual plant forms have the feeling of foreign objects lured and then conquered by the blossom. Like a Jack in the Pulpit or a Venus Fly-Trap, these fleshy plant/animals consume life and are made beautiful in return.

In *Buddha with the Balance*, the viewer is offered a very clear set of symbols to interpret: A leaf-like base containing discarded flower buds and petals, a part of a clock dial, and a seated Buddha with an obliterated face, balancing a bone on his head. The objects are straightforward, but still mysterious. We are given clues, and a definite story, but we are allowed to use the statements of life and death in the balance, the swiftness of time, and the uncertainty of wisdom or religion easing our inevitable passage from the world in any way we want. *Buddha with the Balance* offers a lyrical emblem of humanity's most private questions for the universe.

If Mizuno's work had an odor, it would be sickly sweet. Somewhat like the smell of rotting fruit, or the smell of an ocean's surf. There is a terrible beauty in these pieces. Like the carnivorous plants I mentioned before, Mizuno uses similar methods to lure and then trap the viewer. The promise of something pleasant becomes an unexpected glimpse at our own mortality.

Of the ceramic artists who speak of death, nobody I know has taken it further than Charlie Krafft. This Seattle based artist has several ongoing ceramic series that have gotten a lot of positive feedback and some unapproving words as well. His Disaterware series, for example, uses the Dutch Delft style of painting to record murders, natural disasters, genocides and whatever other subject you wouldn't expect to see finely rendered on a plate. Krafft has also created molds of guns and other weapons and used the same Delft style blue on white painting on clay reproductions for the "Porcelain War Museum" in Slovenia. This avant-garde approach and irreverent, autonomous motivations have also lead Krafft into funerary works that he has entitled Spone. Spone is, in fact, human bone china.

Krafft has followed in the footsteps of Josiah Spode II who introduced powdered cow bones into his clay in the late 1700's. The addition of this bone ash made the clay more vitreous and translucent. The ceramic industry took note, and Bone China has become a common ingredient in porcelains worldwide. Krafft studied this history and tied in the idea of using cremains for human bone china. The concept was to introduce a very new and different alternative to common burial/cremation practices.

While usually cremated remains are stored or buried in urns made of clay or metal, Krafft's idea was to not just store the ashes in an urn, but to make the deceased into the urn. And, even beyond the traditional urn form, the Spone piece could be in any shape imagined. Krafft has had requests for commemorative portrait plates, a WWII helmet, a bulldog, an image of Ganesh, a vodka bottle, and other commissioned forms. He has also made other sculptural and conceptual pieces, allowing his creative ideas to take shape as well.

The concept of a deceased relative in a jar on the mantle has become more accepted in western society over the years, but Krafft's Spone lingers oddly on the American palette. Some people find the idea of handling an object that was once human flesh disturbing. New takes on death and dying and the disposal of human remains are still strangely taboo in our culture. Krafft has, and continues to push the envelope, offering something tangible, unique and most importantly, a work of art that could eventually persuade society into a new funerary philosophy:

> "What is gained by studying the relationship of art to death is familiarity with the rich traditions of commemoration practiced by different societies at different times. In our society it's an often overlooked utilitarian application of art that deserves more attention than it gets because of our fear of death."

Krafft's recent work in Spone includes a series of ceramic shovels.

He obtained the cremains from unclaimed boxes at a funeral home, so the work could be done without the consultation/permission of the family. The shovels have an acurate utilitarian shape, but like most of Krafft's work, there is the element of finely polished elegance. These shovels beg to be used, but they are too beautiful, too fragile to break ground.

In reviewing historical burial rituals and the diverse work of Contemporary artists, I have found one unifying theme that crosses cultures, times, religions and traditions: Curiosity.

Behind any death ritual, offerings to the deceased, prayer, or individual artistic expression, there is the question "why?" Those of us who are left to wait with the rest of the living want to know what happens and we take on this mystery one way or the other.

For some, religion, tradition and legend ease that need to know and fill in the gap by offering further existence. Others seek a continuation of life through children, deeds, monuments. And then, there are those who see a cycle of birth/life/death and see the soil as our creator and re-creator.

There is a need to know, and one way or another, we're all trying to figure this big question out. I'm intrigued that the humble craft of clay has served humankind so well throughout our history. Perhaps ceramic art will continue aiding us in our questions and philosophies and transcend the advents of a modern age for a clear tie with those who went before us.

This essay is reproduced by kind permission of the journal *Ceramics Technical.*

SECTION 1.2
CERAMICS AND METAPHOR

Introductory summary

Perhaps one of the most famous uses of clay as metaphor in popular culture is the wheel-throwing scene in the 1990 film *Ghost* in which Patrick Swayze and Demi Moore sensually make a pot together. This scene uses clay as metaphor for sensuality and sex. Sarah Archer's essay discusses this scene and also gives examples of how potters are often portrayed rather negatively in TV and films. She concludes with some good tips to prospective TV and movie-makers for 'ceramic' stories.

In 'Analogy and Metaphor in Ceramic art', Philip Rawson argues that our common human experience can allow us to make connections with pots even though we may never 'pick up on' all the references. Rawson introduces a number of metaphoric aspects that might define pots such as the body, containment, inner volume and the 'creative female'. Rawson refers to a broad range of pots from around the world but emphasizes Chinese pieces and how they blend form, decoration and purpose to create meanings.

Laurel Birch Kilgore's text, 'Metaphors, myths and making pots', describes pottery made by the Chewa women in central Malawi. The pots are considered by this community as the signs of a good home and marriage. However, a broken pot is a metaphor for a broken or bad marriage. Pottery also relates to wider myths for the Chewa such as creation myths. The making of pots is associated with fertility, birth and the creation of new life.

Sculptor, Tony Cragg's 'Laibe' (German for loaves) series consist of solid thrown 'vessels' which have been sliced like bread while the clay is still malleable. The pieces might be seen to reference the essential functions of clay as a carrier for food and liquid amalgamated into one sculptural form. The pieces also reflect on making and contradict the norms of throwing and finishing. Imogen Racz's wide-ranging text reflects on how an artist like Cragg uses clay as a sculptural medium for metaphorical rather than functional purposes. Linked to this, she describes some of the divides between art and craft – the craft versus art debate. References to other artists also show how clay is a strong medium for pieces that 'are about but separate from the everyday world, and are non-functional, propositional and symbolic'.

Livingstone and Petrie

7
HEART LIKE A WHEEL: WHAT IS HOLLYWOOD TELLING US ABOUT WORKING WITH CLAY?

Sarah Archer

A special combination of luscious imagery, romance, and personal turmoil makes artists and designers juicy subjects for movies. Such recent examples as *Pollock* and *Frida* aim for seriousness and verisimilitude, but without having known these artists, we can only guess how much these portrayals ring true. My personal favorite movie-subject artist will always be a fictional one: Catherine O'Hara's Postmodern harridan, Delia Dietz, in Tim Burton's 1988 masterpiece *Beetlejuice*. This may seem a surprising confession coming from a decorative-arts nerd, but instead of seeking artful portrayals of historical ceramists, à la the Delftware painter (Griet's father) in *Girl With a Pearl Earring*, I'm much more interested in how craft practice is staged in mainstream popular culture.

Craft and design had me at hello, and I spend so much of my time interacting with people who are on the same wavelength that I often wonder how the rest of the world sees us. Hollywood is probably not the best gauge of this, but Hollywood's widespread influence can't be denied. Most people have had the experience of seeing some aspect of their identity portrayed on screen, whether it be their region, culture, profession, school, or personal style, and thought, 'not even close'. Professional artists and designers who work in clay are not likely to feel much resonance with the ways that movies and sitcoms portray the world of ceramics. This is because most of the time, ceramic practice is deployed as a plot device that signifies personal flakiness, economic irrelevance, a creative 'phase' that puzzles onlookers, or straight-up hippie-dom. I have never seen a ceramic artist or designer portrayed on screen frantically assembling a tenure packet, or preparing work to ship to a gallery, or spending hours updating her CV, or traveling to a residency program in China. Potters, according to Hollywood, are actually just regular people taking a break from reality while their families try hard not to show their growing concern.

Anyone who has spent time in a ceramics studio since 1990 has witnessed a performance of 'Unchained Melody' accompanied by a re-creation of Patrick Swayze and Demi Moore's romantic wheel-throwing scene in the movie *Ghost*. This movie has launched thousands of couples into pottery classes that probably turned out to be both much less sensual and much more challenging than they had expected. Like movies that prominently feature exquisitely appetizing food, *Ghost* used clay (with way too much water, it must be said) to underscore the physicality, earthiness, and messiness of love. *Ghost* probably comes closest of any film or television series to portraying a 'professional' potter on screen, yet the implication is that Demi Moore's character, Molly, 'can' make pots full time only because her husband works on Wall Street. That slip-covered love scene tends to get all the attention, but what I find much more interesting is how ceramics is portrayed as a career in *Ghost*, or more specifically, as the lack of one, and how this point of view has developed a currency all its own in recent decades.

Source: © Sarah Archer/*The Studio Potter* - 501 (C) (3).

Ghost has spawned countless parodies, including portrayals of ceramists by cartoon characters (*Family Guy*) and puppies (*Hollywood Tails*), but the best by far is a 2010 episode of the NBC comedy *Community*. Called 'Beginner Pottery', this episode captures the exquisite torture of a continuing education class gone awry. 'Beginner Pottery' features a priceless scene in which the quietly angry, batik-clad instructor of the ceramics class lectures his students that his only rule is 'no Ghosting', which means that any hint of the Righteous Brothers or of a student coming up behind another while they're sitting at the wheel is strictly forbidden. The drama of the episode revolves around the main character, a disgraced lawyer named Jeff who needs an academic credential to get his career back on track, coming to terms with the fact that he's not especially gifted at most things he tries (including ceramics).

During the course of the class, Jeff finds himself taunted by a local doctor who takes the class simply to unwind from his stressful medical practice. In one scene, the doctor throws large vases effortlessly as beautiful women look on adoringly. Here, ceramics represents irrelevance played for laughs. Like ballroom dancing, beauty pageants, dog shows, and golf, ceramics is presented as an endeavor that elicits intense, cringe-worthy emotion from its irony-free participants. As Jeff pulls an all-nighter researching ceramics (but not practicing it), the humor lies in the life-and-death focus of these overly invested players on a mere hobby.

'Pottery Will Get You Nowhere', an evocatively titled episode of *The Wonder Years* from 1993, focuses on tension between Jack and Norma, the parents of the adolescent protagonist Kevin. The show is set in the late 1960s. Norma, from roughly the same generation as Betty Friedan, experiences a modest creative awakening when she signs up for a pottery class at her local community college. She is proud of her creations, and her counter-culture teenage daughter, Karen, thinks they're creative and bold. Norma's husband, Jack, is irked by her new focus on ceramics and by her sly introduction of her pottery into circulation among the family's regular tableware repertoire. She even replaces his favorite coffee mug with an unwieldy green and yellow creation that he clearly dislikes. Norma's dalliance with ceramics is meant to demonstrate that her character needs a creative outlet and that her husband resents her restlessness.

As in *Community*, ceramics is a lighthearted activity that allows the personal drama (whether funny or serious) to take center stage. So deeply ingrained is the use of clay as a therapeutic tool that it appears to be alive and well in the twenty-fourth century. Two episodes of Star Trek series feature characters using clay as a tool to express humanist values to an artificial (or partially artificial) life form. 'Masks', a 1994 episode of *Star Trek: The Next Generation*, opens in a children's classroom, where Data, the thoughtful and deadpan android, is carefully detailing a clay sculpture of an Enterprise view screen, complete with text that he fashions with a pin tool. Set designer Michael Okuda's classic rounded rectangles are instantly recognizable in the android's creation. Counselor Troi wants Data to explore his imagination and challenges him to sculpt 'music' by trying to think of the images that music elicits in people's minds, then giving those images a form. Data responds by rapidly sculpting a treble clef in bas relief.

A similarly deadpan exchange unfolds between Captain Janeway and Seven of Nine in 'Raven', an episode of *Star Trek: Voyager* from 1997. The captain has invited Seven to visit her Holodeck program, set in Leonardo da Vinci's studio, where she is at work on an earthenware bust of a man. A former Borg drone with a limited capacity for metaphor and irony, Seven half-heartedly attempts to sculpt the clay while complaining that no 'useful task' is being accomplished. Janeway counters that sculpting helps fire the imagination, driving human progress and helping us to think up novel solutions and ideas. In both cases, we find not-quite-human characters, puzzled by the uselessness of working in clay, being encouraged to think creatively about what it can really accomplish. Clearly this is not the task at hand but rather some larger task of sparking creativity so that the amateur ceramists can better perform their real jobs.

The belief that craft practice belongs to the world of hobbies and recreation has clear roots in the second half of the nineteenth century, when the United States was rapidly industrializing and when newly rationed 'leisure time' presented an unprecedented social challenge. What were people to do with all this free time? The original do-it-yourself movement promoted such wholesome activities as carpentry, needlepoint, model-making, paint-by-numbers, and for the really industrious, pottery, with a potters' wheel installed in the basement. All of these activities create a kind of gestural representation of real work and have the patina of practicality: often the end result is some useful or attractive object. Handicrafts were also praised as palatable alternatives to vice and sloth, especially for young people living in large cities. John Dewey's groundbreaking educational philosophies, particularly experiential education, emphasized the benefits of process over the quality of the finished product in craft instruction, and thus Dewey's ideas contributed to the popularity of crafts in schools, community centers, and summer camps. All of this conspired to cast craft practice in a curious light: what was once existentially defined by skill was now pleasurable and worth doing for its own sake, and the quality of the result, once the sine qua non of making an object, was now relatively unimportant. The widespread love of the fun, no-consequences side of craft has both supported and plagued it ever since. Ceramics has gained financially from its popularity as a hobby, but it has lost credibility among those who find the taint of amateurism too indelible to ignore.

There's only one country on earth that would, or could, produce a feature film whose protagonist is a professional potter. Popular culture and craft guru Garth Johnson introduced me to the Japanese movie Ugetsu, a ghost story from 1953 that centers on the supernatural exploits of a rural potter living in sixteenth century Japan. Ceramics occupies a role in this film that another sort of old-fashioned profession like farming could credibly occupy in an American movie. Ceramics is not played for laughs or meant to indicate that the character is artsy or flaky or experiencing a midlife crisis; he's just a rural, pre-industrial man who makes and sells pots. I would love to see a new crop of movie or television characters who, in the spirit of Ugetsu, work in clay for real: designers, professors, entrepreneurs, style icons. Creative fields make for great TV – food, art, fashion, and interior design are all fair game – and ceramics really deserves better than to always be a supporting character. In fact, small craft businesses are full of ingenuity, success stories in a troubled economy, stranger-than-fiction characters, and irresistible eye candy. Imagine a bio-pic about Gertrud and Otto Natzler, full of romance, espadrilles, volcanic glazes, and Neutra houses. Or an addictive HBO series based on the life of Beatrice Wood. Or the story of Heath ceramics, founded by a visionary woman potter and designer, and revived by two inspired entrepreneurs with great taste and great personal style. Put on a clean apron: we're ready for our close-up.

Originally published in *The Studio Potter*; Summer/Fall 2012, Vol. 40 Issue 2, pp. 15–17. Reproduced with permission from *The Studio Potter* and the author.

8
ANALOGY AND METAPHOR IN CERAMIC ART
Philip Rawson

> *There may be many areas of reference, which we shall never pick up in other people's pots. But that is not a reason for restraining ourselves from picking up any at all. We are duty bound to feel for those levels of symbolic coding which can come across on the basis of our common human experiences. For visual art seems still to rest on a kind of onomatopoeia, the performance of acts that come close to imitation.*
>
> Presented at *Ceramics and Modernism,* 1981, New York City

My particular experience with ceramics has induced in me a long view over human history. I shamelessly adopt a perspective, which recognizes the likenesses between men and races rather than their differences. Modernism, seen in this perspective, becomes a problem of another kind than when it is seen from much closer to.

In his early work, that great, much misunderstood, and wrongly denigrated philosopher, Friedrich Nietzsche, developed a thought, which I believe is very important for us as artists and historians. You will find that it goes much farther than that catchword usage, which Garth Clark criticized yesterday. In *The Birth of Tragedy,* particularly, Nietzsche shed light on the ways in which all kinds of human ideas (he was especially concerned with religious and philosophical ideas) repose at bottom, on complexes of metaphor. This implies that each particular experience gains its meaning by reference to others, like a cross-indexing system. We can only explain one phenomenon in terms of others. But habitually recognized similarities take deep root in our minds; and they become so matted together by our regular thinking and speaking that, gradually, they fossilize. You realize I have just been using them: "matted," "take root," "fossilize"! And because such a procedure is so integral to all our dealings with our life and world, they become invisible to us.

Not only that. When they become invisible, the everyday languages based on them cease to question the roots from which they spring. Only the poets and artists awaken the analogies that lie sleeping in their languages by metaphor. For to bring out the true nature of these metaphors can cast suspicion on the whole upper crust of thought, raising radical doubts as to truth and validity. Certain major, central analogies themselves, when they are dragged out into the light of day, can often seem crudely physical—repugnant even—to the refined intellectual mind, ridiculous to the less refined. And what we now like to call "structures" may actually be abstract reflections of the analogical bonds we take for granted between the highly immediate and physical terms of those mutual metaphors by means of which we establish our reality. Nietzsche, indeed, argued that space, as a concept, embodies a metaphor for metaphor itself. I suggest that what we call aesthetic meaning (as well as intellectual meaning) seems to be a function of that metaphorical complex, and that what constitutes the virtue of good art relates to its success here.

I am afraid I cannot agree with that vein of art criticism, which looks on the work of art as simply a new, unclassifiable object, without roots in a language of form. I sympathize with the feeling of disgust with over

Source: © Garth Clark/Ceramic Arts Foundation.

intellectualizing, which that attitude implies. But I do not accept that the major art of the past or of the present actually works at any pure-object level. I think it is probable that the meaning of any artwork we make or perceive rests on its own linked series of analogical references. I was delighted to see so many magnificent metaphors shining out in the Bauhaus, Futurist and American modernist ceramics we saw yesterday morning, even though some of the industrial optimism now seems a little misplaced.

The really vital point is that, in a good work, these analogical references will ultimately reach down to rest on and connect up with certain fundamental and immediate experiences. But it is a horrible error to suppose that any one of them alone can ever be a work's whole content. No single metaphor can ever contain the whole meaning of a work or part of a work. Here, I think, Jungians (not Jung himself) may sometimes be at fault. No true symbol ever refers simply to an object—say to a house or to a nude or to an idea, say, energy. This is where Garth's cartoonist showed his own failings. But insofar as it is a symbol, each work of art constellates its own particular field of analogical reference, which nothing else at all can constellate.

Its metaphors are mutual, two-way, between what is referred to and the pot. One cannot translate the meaning of a picture, a sculpture, a pot, into simple terms by any obvious device. That would short-circuit and destroy its purpose. At the same time, it may help to bring out into the light of day some of the more deeply hidden metaphorical references into our art. To do this may, I think, broaden the analogical bases onto which modern—not modernist—artists may rest their work.

Of course, no one can deny that in every culture there are layers and levels of symbolic coding which will always be opaque to those who were not brought up on that culture. The words of spoken languages may have to be learned as pure conventions. There may be areas of reference, which we shall never pick up in other people's pots. But that is not a reason for restraining ourselves from picking up any at all. We are duty bound to feel for those, which can come across on the basis of our common human experiences. For visual art seems still to rest on a kind of onomatopoeia, the performance of acts which lie close to imitation.

I am afraid I don't personally believe in all this talk of new formal orders, new this, that. The general look of things is not the substance of art. I am afraid I am (maybe) going to tax your patience a little by asking you, for a while, to suspend disbelief. To begin with, the slides may seem to hurry, but I want the formal suggestions of each to lie in your minds as its successors pass before your eyes. I hope you will join me in allowing the forms and colours of works of ceramic art to speak to your sympathies on their own account. The works will be familiar. That is part of my point. I intend to speculate freely.

Our first approach to any ceramic work is made, I think, through its body image. We all refer to the "clay body" it is made of. We talk of it having "foot," "belly," "shoulder," "lip." We rarely talk about its "head," though plenty of pots do have heads and faces added, as does this medieval English jug. There are also beautiful Nabatean storage jars, excavated in the Negev, which wear obvious necklaces. We tend to judge the expression of a pot by the way it addresses us, body to body, and by the way we apprehend the posture it takes, as if it were another body. We read a humanoid high-shouldered posture in these two Finnish pots of the fifties. They withdraw from any intimacy with us, but we feel ourselves into the posture they show. A pot, however, is a body we also feel from within.

We still need, I feel, to adhere to the traditional character of ceramics as implying the image of the containing. So our pots lose if they do not have this double aspect: first, of containing and isolating a realm of space, maybe even sanctifying it; and second, of exhibiting outward forms, which define the container as a special kind of presence in the world, no mere inert object. The ceramic image cannot crystallize if the work has only an exterior, as Bill Daley's fine works show. This T'ang dynasty funeral pot exhibits itself almost like a peacock. But most important, it offers that vital sense of vertical axis, which throwing always gives naturally, but which even very early handmade pots virtually always strive towards. That ceramic axis is no mere expedient. It represents the anthropic vertical: the central column both of man and of his sanctified world, the axis mundi, the lighthouse at the centre of reality, the source and focus of creation.

It is this strong axis for the potter's inner space, which seems to me to differentiate ceramics from all that straight clay sculpture. We are profoundly aware of inner volume which we understand by an inner sympathy as being centred, as we are centred; we know it to have an affinity with our own sense of being but to be, at the same time, set "over there," over against us, so that we can address it as if it were another. A work like this seventeenth-century tea bowl by Kenzan was deliberately made to provide an outer focus for meditation upon the mutuality of being and not being, of interior and exterior, inner and outer—speaking to us, as body speaks, through our hands as much as though our eyes.

The truth is that pottery, as I am describing it, has actually got an iconography implicit in its very existence. It is no game of open experiment. For one of the great fundamental metaphors in ceramics is the creative female. This little Greek goddess from Tanagra is a piece of potter's work. Her shape tells us so. From the symbols of our artistic language, we recognize the source from which men and animals emerge as a mysterious breeding container, generically female. And pots are one of its type of images. Our own bodies are in some sense our feminine component; our clothing of flesh that continually reweaves itself is a function of the creative principle that presents us as beings to others and to ourselves.

The interesting issue, of course, is what it contains. Greek tradition offers us this figurine of about 6,000 B.C. Later, a thought was expressed by the writer Porphyry that the breeding container of the soul was actually a mixing bowl, a krater. This has an unequivocal formal affinity to the figurine: the kind of large vessel in which the Greeks used to mix wine with many other ingredients to produce their invigorating drink. But then, we can only ask ourselves what on earth this cachepot from the second millennium BC Anatolia was meant to be. We do not know, but with its little opening door in its notional pelvis, it can certainly mean something to us. Maybe it received relics; maybe it was a soul house of some sort. It can clearly "give." Early Western men—and most likely early Oriental men—saw the female's productivity as spontaneous; and they seem to have understood the fertility of the earth, metaphorically, as a colossal transcription of this female productivity.

The famous little Paleolithic relief called the Venus of Laussel, and the great breast-and vulva-filled grotto of Pech-Merle, imply as much. They seem to have passed their heritage down to the famous Eastern Mediterranean mother-goddess known to us from Roman times as Diana of the Ephesians. She was the continually pregnant and propagating mother of all creatures, feeding and nourishing them all with her many breasts. This nourishing function of the pot as mother we find alluded to in many pots when they are shaped as breasts. Here is a very early one, from Iran, of the third millennium BC. It may have had some ceremonial function, as suggested by the great multiplicity of breasts. Here is another from the European Iron Age. You can still buy ordinary coffee mugs molded with pairs of breasts.

The ancient European mother goddess is known to us in many guises. Here is one little-known terra cotta from the Balkans—Romania in fact—dating to about 4,000 BC. The painted striations on its body are thought to be images of some kind of active functioning, maybe connected with water. But it is very interesting to find the motif of striations carried through still, not only in traditional Africa, as on this pot with its deep, wavy ridges, but even on this late nineteenth-century art-nouveau vase. I am not, of course, talking of direct cultural transmission but rather of the continuing underground life of metaphors in human culture, perhaps even via human physiology.

For those countries of Western Asia and the Balkans where the ceramic art first flourished were also the home of those mother-goddesses who are still alive as metaphor in modern cultures. This is the course of the river Adonis (or Tammuz, Venus's boyfriend) in modern Syria. The water pours in a torrent from its cave. Once a great temple to the goddess Astarte stood beside it until it was destroyed by the first Roman Christian emperor, Constantine. And also from a site in Syria, of about 1,800 BC, is this goddess holding her vase which overflows with water and fish. We can still find her descendants on the fountains in Western cities, and enlisted to serve as pretty little teapots.

This goddess of ours had another incarnation in one of those cultures that produced one of the greatest ceramic arts of which we know: Crete. Here she is, wearing her flounced skirt, presented in the famous compressed frit sculpture from Knossos, second millennium BC. We can certainly read her as goddess of the waters in this drawing of a Cretan intaglio seal from the same period. In her monster-headed boat she has with her a flowering tree. In personifying her as thoroughly as this, the Cretans did not make the mistake of losing their grasp on her identity as generative principle. The waters were one of her realms—the sea, of course, in Crete. And here we may find her metaphorically incarnated in this gesturing pot with its high, wavy handle, emblazoned with the creatures of her domain.

The pot witnesses her sanctity. It is one of her descriptions, by analogy. No less than the animals, we—her humans—are functionally part of her. She was also goddess of the flowering land and of the mountains. She appears on these other seals in various other guises, as Gertrude Rachel Levy has demonstrated. But as mistress and mother of vegetation, she is embodied in dozens of other Cretan pots now in the Herakleion museum. The way these pots use garlands of the goddess's own flowers to illuminate the sanctity of pot bodies prefigures the floral ornament on tens of thousands of later painted pots; their makers have long since forgotten whose image they were making. The superb floral ornament on this pot shows that the Iznik Turks may have accepted, perhaps, a little more of her than one might imagine, in spite of being Muslims. But the old life-and-death seriousness built into the true mother goddess image is nowadays missing. Of course we make millions of pieces of floral ware without any real concern at all.

Many of us may even feel some slight disgust at the feebleness of our floral imagery. In fact, the boot painters used to keep the goddess very much alive, even in the nineteenth century. The Chiswick press in London was still using this beautiful tailpiece block in the 1860s. I don't think many people would disagree with the proposition that the Chinese were probably the world's greatest masters of the ceramic art as this Ming Cheng-te plate demonstrates. So you will not be surprised if I develop certain notions about the semantics of pottery using chiefly—but not only—their works.

The first point is the basic mode by which ceramics, as I have defined it, spins out from itself an imagery of space. I want to go here beyond the pious generalities of art criticism, e.g. "surface tensions" and "dynamic form relationships" and so on. The great French art historian Henri Focillon developed the idea that space could be incorporated in art according to two chief conceptual poles. They have a variety of possible grades between them. The first implies that the artwork contains within itself all the space to which it refers. In fact, when I was looking for a ceramic piece to illustrate this pole alone, I found it extraordinarily difficult. There are a few African examples and Western Asiatic storage jars, but this fine Chaco canyon mug also shows the idea on its surface. Its ornament consists of concentric enclosures, which address you frontally when you grasp its handle. You seem to be supposed to focus within them, as symbols of order. They may be meant to represent concentric regions of space.

The other pole is represented by artworks, which generate an undefined and unlimited arena of space around themselves. They do this by reaching around themselves, out into the openness that lies about them. They state it without limiting it. This beautiful Chinese Lung-ch'uan Southern Sung spittoon does exactly that. Its body is, of course, an enclosure; but its flat, conical lip embodies a gesture of reaching. It becomes particularly important in connection with something I mention later that you are able to read this shape and its meaning without being able to see the whole contour at all.

Hear are two of the epitomes of the second of Focillon's poles: two ink paintings by major Chinese masters who were working in the thirteenth century when the Sung potters were potting. They illustrate perfectly the way in which the present objects, which are stated by the ink strokes, send our awareness out into the vast-ness of that arena of what they do not state, and which they imply they never could. Instead they point towards it.

I am sure you all know that all the arts of China were fundamentally linear. Calligraphy was the mother of the other arts, the highest and most expressive of them all. This is an essay by aT'ang dynasty monk called Huai-su—a very fine work. It embodies beautifully what the Chinese called "the meaning beyond the text." This meaning is conveyed through the formal and kinetic references of the brushwork, its endless inventiveness, its refusal and ever-changing waves of the Tao—or Dharma as Buddhists would call it. The brushstrokes say what the words cannot. In this very famous portrait of the poet Li Po by the thirteenth-century Ch'an monk, Liang K'ai, the strokes do exactly that. Look especially at the rhythms and at the curves. They took time to make. We must take time to re-enact and read them. Hence they embody time. There is no reason why this whole dimension should be omitted, as it is, from much modernist work.

When we come to Far Eastern three-dimensional art, we find that its surfaces are developed out of very skillful lines. In all three-dimensional art, except that made of transparent materials, it is the visible and tangible that conveys rhythms and reveals volume. Well-developed lines like these not only run to and fro across the flat field but also go over and around, into and out of, the depth of the image. Pick any spot to start on, say a fold of the robe under the hands, and then track it as it runs up, across, around, behind, then forward over again. This is a sculpture, which most emphatically takes time to follow, like music; and hence it must incorporate reading of the time into its image. It was made in Japan in the epoch of the Chinese T'ang dynasty by an artist who was probably a Korean or Chinese working in high T'ang style. Now it is in the Yakushiji Buddhist Temple, Nara.

I have put in this fifteenth-century Chinese painting of the deity of the sun, simply to make the transition from figurative art to ceramics. The whole expression of this image lies in its graduated, curving lines. I hope the formal point of this comparison will be obvious. The curving contour of the T'ang tombware jar is what generates its form. The vigour of the line which is led in space is what makes it so superb. But of course, that line cannot have been made by an actual gesture as painted lines can be. It can only be a thorough going invention, shaped by the imagination and led with the utmost care through a graded series of inflections. It is not casual in the name of inspiration: the resulting form is the full, inflected image of a mobile body, offered to us as a surface illuminating the receptive and the creative at once.

Exactly the same is true of this beautiful Kuan vase, of the Sung dynasty. This shape, like all thrown and turned pottery shapes, is a function of revolution of its contour line about the fixed axis. And the mobile relationship between that line and the axis of rotation is what gives the pot its specific expression. One can also feel the interaction with the opposite contour. The pacing of the lengths of the inflections of the curves is what gives it the rhythmic quality that enlists our sympathetic responses and exhibits the inner functioning of the fluid creative body. It, too, has its own "meaning beyond the text," beyond the objective facts. In practice, all creation of sculptural form depends upon the generation of a continuous, articulate surface, which reveals a variety of implicit structures. Even this modest apple-green eighteenth-century vase has a similar, subtle grading and varying of lengths and qualities of curve. Imagine how banal it could easily become if that little angular inflection at the shoulder were missing. The implications of this for the shaping and our reading of the volumes are enormous. They make it possible for us to read the body as a group of fully intelligible, interpenetrating volumes.

And what about surface decoration? Here a superbly painted overglaze enamel peony swoops around the relatively undeveloped curvature of this bowl. It is undeveloped because, during the Yung-cheng period (1723-1733), such bowls were made as white blanks; we now make our porcelain in the same way. But Chinese artists then used such blanks virtually as canvases on which they painted designs as free and inspired as possible. And since they were true ceramic painters, the better ones laid out their designs in order to express the curvature of the bowl as if it corresponded with the curvature of the painted motif. Here we are again in the presence of a special version of that female ceramic image. And here we need maybe to pick up some of those cultural responses, by using our knowledge. For the early summer peony is a standard emblem in Chinese culture for feminine beauty; it refers directly to the sexual organs, establishing a beautiful visual as well as a notional analogy. And the pot thus conveys a complex and mutual act of metaphorical praise between an image of the female and the rolling year. So the metaphor reaches us in the first place through knowledge as well as through the eye.

In this great Mei-Ping dragon vase, however, we find the interaction of the pot body as spatial presence and surface design carried to an extreme degree. Let us follow through the notional evolution of this pot. First there is the contour, which establishes the surface by its revolving around the axis. This surface moves fully in three dimensions. On it appears a dragon, which represents for the Chinese the celestial and material force permeating the cosmos and its creatures. If an "actual" dragon is coiling among clouds, the shape it naturally takes in space may very well correspond with the three-dimensional curl given to it here by the surface of the pot on which it is depicted. And then we find the image is presented to us by applying the red underglaze to those places where the dragon is not: i.e., it is executed in reverse, and the waves of cloud and water among which this great cosmic energy moves appear to rise in response to the beast's frenetic plunging. Here is a perfect example of the way an image can be extended into several different notional regions by ceramic art alone.

On this Ming plate we have another dragon. He embodies, through a complex of form and cultural knowledge, really very deep feelings. By his greenness, he represents the rising force of the new spring season, circling in and rising from the arena of the dish. He means, in principle, the same as this album painting attributed to Kung Hsien (seventeenth century); but his force is active. The plate was meant, according to Chinese ideas, to be used at that season of the year. It would transmit the appropriate seasonal energies to the person eating from it, for the Chinese and the Japanese recognize that things brought together influence each other.

All things inhabit the stranded weaving of current in the great boiling river of time, the Tao; and the currents that animate one cannot fail to have a powerful effect on another. Good, and hence appropriate, ceramics are therefore good for us in every sense: not because we witness them as external, but because they key in with and co-ordinate the dynamics of our bodily existence.

Here, as a little light relief, is a *famille rose* dish with delicate—no, far from delicate—symbolic allusions. To illustrate how ceramics were woven into life in China, we can read it. To the left is a blue rock, crystallized emblem of that coiling, boiling Tao. Such rocks always have this meaning in China. The two waiting ladies are, of course, imbued with Yin, the dark female essence which forms one polarity of the cosmic movement. They are surrounded by other natural objects, which also burst with Yin essence: the peony, the coiling cloud, the *ling-chi* fungus. And there above them, flying down, is the Phoenix, the sun-bird of noon and high summer, supreme embodiment of brilliant, masculine Yang. They will do each other a lot of good, because the egrets (or cranes) symbolize immortality, or at least the long life which happy and beautifully executed sexual relations naturally produce. How far into semiology and the life order ceramics can reach! This plate if very good for us.

Here I should like to introduce a short digression, just to ride one of my hobby horses, which is relevant to the question of modern ceramics. I have felt, for a long time now, that Western ceramics has been bedevilled by the pseudo-Japanese tea ware, which dear Bernard Leach brought over to Britain, and Hamada's example reinforced. Here is a piece of real Chosen Karatsu. But there are thousands of potters who believe that it is possible, by some kind of direct inspiration, to produce superficially similar pots, either "reticent" (that is to say, undeveloped), or wobbly and kinked ones that will somehow express deep insight by those very properties alone. In the absence of the Japanese tradition, complete with its kinetic roots, I do not personally see how this can be so.

This is where the question of art language as convention emerges. For we must remember that the Japanese inherited and developed precisely that Far Eastern linear tradition (here Korean) with which the peach on this Japanese door is incised. Lucy Rie's teapot that Garth showed was a straight Japanese influence—very common then in Vienna. A similar sense of rhythm and variation embodied in this tradition is actually embodied in even the most eccentric raku tea ware. It appears as a refinement upon that superb Chinese linearism I have been discussing—radical certainty. Here is, first, a Chinese prototype: a rhythmic *i-pin* (untrammeled) painting of Zen monks by Shih-ko. And next, its descendant, a Japanese painting by Korin, following its own careful formulae for radical spontaneity.

One must not miss the consciously radicalist revamping of an old tradition of rhythmic expression which actually contributes to the symbol system of this piece of Japanese tea ware. Nor can we forget that a close and intensely cultivated set of qualities codes the piece into its total Japanese environment: an environment, in fact, from which its whole meaning springs, and in which it is consummated—in this case, a work of garden art shows the links. I do not think it is enough simply to claim, as the artists of Beat Zen used to claim, that we should be satisfied with immediate response to the naked object, pointing nowhere beyond itself. Privately, I think this theory sprang from a misreading of D.T. Suzuki, the pioneer of Zen writing in English. It misunderstands the radical sense of "fullness" implicit in Buddhist intuition. This piece of tea ware relies on what one could call "two-stage" metaphor. It refers to experiences of appearance which are themselves interpreted as indices to the whole of which they are an appearance. The experiences are seasonal and emotional, connected with beloved sanctity and ultimate security, with warmth in the face of change and decline, with the power of modesty in the face of the power of dominion and destruction. For all of these, the pot embodies metaphors, not least by means of the way it was meant to be used, held in the hands at the tea ceremony and gazed deep into.

This question of the more specific fields of metaphoric reference, which pots may embody, I have discussed before in the book. Here, in this tea ware by Koetsu (seventeenth century), we find perhaps an ultimate in subtle statements: Yang white is banded above Yin dark, heaven over earth; they band and part from each other like this in deepest autumn. Yang withdraws upward and Yin fills the abyss; everything is coming to a standstill. Humility, retirement, and autumnal rest are indicated. The striping of the bands is not strict; but it is felt as a shifting adjustment, like the seasonal movement itself. It is the vital key to the meaning. The hands also play a major part in the perception- a tactile image as much as a visual.

This kind of "feeling for" rather than "statement of" is precisely what I mean by complexity of metaphor. The pot is dignified by the cosmic metaphor, just as the seasonal phase is by the pot. The clarity and precision of art is a clarity of pointing, not of bald statement. This Tung-yao celadon goes maybe too far in the direction of statement. It verges on conceit. It tells us a little too exactly that the pot is equivalent to leaves and sprigs; though personally, I can forgive its fancifulness for the sake of its elusive presence and proportions. In a way, I would find it more difficult to accept a Dresden cabbage tureen for its extravagant harshness, or the more extravagant conceits of modernist mannerism, which mimic other objects, like a stand-up comic imitating the president of the United States.

I find the formal allusiveness of this fluted, red Colima (Mexico) tripod vessel infinitely subtle; it does not fall over into conceit, despite its bird-head feet. It claims to turn itself into no actual gourd. Yet the definition of its essence as a pot is pinpointed by strong metaphorical suggestions into our fund of experience; from there, a variety of analogous experiences are awakened to resonate together as we witness it. It and its parts subtend in us a variety of rhythmic acts as we perceive it, appropriate to its status as a pot, body, and container. Its generating contour is superb, counterpointed by the rhythmic flutings; and it has, to the highest degree, that quality of presence I shall be discussing in a moment.

Similarly multi-referential is the glaze on this Sung dynasty Chun-ware dish. This kind of reduced copper flambe seems to have been discovered by the conservative Chun potters by accident. And it was read by the Chinese as a kind of natural cryptography, revealing how the purple energies of heaven—passing through our world from the constellations—penetrate the object and give it quite individual characteristics. My point, in all these last few works, is that the metaphorical image originates in the pot, generating its resonance in us; there was, indeed, a public ready to read the semiotic clues; and we may join that public even before we know we are totally right. There is leeway in the reading for each of us to come up with his or her own valid answers to the question of the object's ultimate meaning. Knowledge can only add to our responses.

How, then, can we look upon this fine piece of eighteenth-century Wedgwood jasperware? It is rigid with signs and symbols, all specified down to the minutest detail. Spontaneity was an irrelevant cultural criterion. The ware relates it to—no, equates it with—the Portland Vase, that great piece of late-classical cameo glass. The design by Flaxman is based on Roman cameos. The lid is crowned by a post-Renaissance, pseudo-Roman, triumphal equestrian monument. One feels that such a meticulous assembling of symbols for the Roman Virtue (supposed to be induced by a classical education) may suggest many things. Among them would be that the people for whom it was made felt happiest living by accepted prescription and learning, rather than by what we would call individual response. There is only one way to read it.

The shape is trimmed and disciplined; one might say lacking in energy. But indeed it satisfies. As the tombstone put it, it is "Pious without enthusiasm." Also, the object seems very self-contained, without interest in its ambience. Probably it would have been virtually an architectural component of the decor of the house in which it sat as an emblem of acquired good manners.

This brings us to a more positive, indeed metaphysical, transcription of the idea of the pot as matrix or material: that is, the notion of presence and presentation. It seems to me to be almost a criterion for judging good ceramics; it goes like this. When one looks at a fine pottery piece, like this Nazca vessel from Peru, from the normal angle of approach—usually from a little above and to one side—it is the surface that invites one to approach it, not the contours. The part that faces us nearest is what we grasp it by, not the remote edges; this in spite of the fact that the surface is a function of its contours. The point is that there is always that about well-conceived ceramic contours, which leads you to the middle of the pot, to apprehend its presence. We perceive a pot not as line but as surface, which moves through well-varied and interesting curvatures. Furthermore, any design added to the body will add to the web of its own curvatures—as it does on this Zuni Indian pot—so that the apparently two-dimensional curvatures of the design, which are actually three-dimensional, supplement, in their own way, the complex curves of the actual surface.

Here is where I have some doubts about the Malevich ceramics. I admire his work greatly for the way it generates that extraordinary sci-fi field in two dimensions. This seems to me not to work on the curvatures of rather feeble blanks. For a pot is, above all, a surface offering a variety of rhythmic inflections; and well-painted ornament participates fully in that curvature. This is why merely globular pots, or pots with over-simple or merely busy contours and ornament appear boring. When the metaphors of the shape are carried through by the coded references of the design, which also help to assert the middle of the visual field, we reach a new level of meaning: here blue yin on white yang body. The drawing, as we read it, runs off along different curvatures into the spaces generated by the pot surface.

In this piece of Northern Chinese Sung dynasty celadon—a bowl just the right size to be held in the paired hands. There can be no mistaking the way the design focuses our attention on the body, itself floral. That shape is certainly the consequence of subtle, linear drawing in space. But try, in your mind's eye, to cut diagonal sections through the volume of the pot and see how interesting the curves that process generates are. The volume is by no means a simple one. It is clear, yet it eludes all the obvious categories of analysis.

To illustrate how a ceramic shape can develop its "presence" through our apprehension of surface as an index of subtle volume, take this piece of Southern Chinese Lung-ch'uan celadon. The fluting and facets make us apprehend it—from the middle—as a complex body; but it can be read as a combination of forms. The floral base is crowned by a kind of inverted pericarp. The neck, which is by no means a hard contour, can be inverted as "impaling" the flower calyx. The rings on the neck have a rhythmic, proportional relationship with the optical spacing, horizontally, of the petals. When you look carefully, the contour is by no means simple. But it is not stressed.

I am putting on this more recent ceramic now, not, I am afraid, to praise it. The glaze is splendidly colourful; but this piece, made in Paris in 1896, is a rather good example of a pot that has almost no middle. It lives, it seems to me, by the kinked lift and tuck-over of its outlines—kinked, if feeling, about halfway up. Its interest is accordingly diminished. Its surface curvatures strike me as fairly feebly developed.

Finally, I would like to show you one or two of my favourite pots, because all of them do something extremely interesting. Here, on this hand-formed pot from Mexico, we see the representation of a centipede. Rather as in the Chinese dragon vase, we see that the three-dimensional surface of the pot gives the centipede's body an "actual" curvature, corresponding to that curvature which a centipede's body in our space would have. But he is, emphatically, not in relief. That would spoil it. He is also shown as "climbing up," "reaching for" the lip of the bowl. His movement is thus an active transcription of the shaped surface of the bowl and a presentation of its nature as centred holder and container. There is a similar concordance of design and shape in this Cretan vase, belonging to the Museum of Herakleion.There can be no mistaking the mutuality of the pot form and the upward-growing plant in white. The loops of the petals rehearse and multiply the loops of the lugs. The form itself is by no means as simple as it may look. Do that imaginary cutting of diagonal sections again, and you get some very interesting results. It is more than likely that this vase was meant to support an actual spray of flowers, which would complete its upper form.

The form of this one, the great Cretan octopus jar, is a direct extension of the last. Here we are back again in the realm of the sea goddess, Our Lady of the Sea. The body of the octopus and the movement of its limbs are firmly related to the curvatures of the mobile surface, so we never have the feeling that we are looking into the space of the jar as if we were looking into an aquarium. The body of the octopus remains on the surface and "realizes" the multi-dimensional curvature of the pot itself. So the curvatures of the tentacles can play games with our perception of that surface, which then becomes a subtle image of space; and the apparent "downward" movement of the animal takes place within a definite "upward current" suggested by the shape of the pot. This is, indeed, a valid presentation of that great lady whose creatures are woven of her own substance; they realize it by their presences, embodiments illustrating her creative activity. The pot also refers us back to that dual function of containing and giving, molding and uttering, which I personally feel we need once again to reach for.

This essay is reproduced by kind permission of Garth Clark/Ceramic Arts Foundation.

9

METAPHORS, MYTHS AND MAKING POTS: CHEWA CLAY ARTS

Laurel Birch Kilgore

In this essay I argue that pottery and other clay forms made by Chewa women in central Malawi collectively reflect recurring themes that resonate throughout Chewa society. My approach is to seek relatedness, searching for the likeness of patterns and motifs from one social space (domestic) to another (ritual). This approach is derived from the idea of 'connectedness' suggested to me by Philip Ravenhill, that the tiniest detail could be connected to a much wider range of semantics, objects, social realms, and ideas.[1] The seeking of relatedness is more than seeing similarities in objects across media, though this is also evident; it is the metaphorical collapsing of ideas (Ricouer 1978, Sacks 1979, Tilley 1999) as they are presented widely throughout social life.

Ravenhill (2000:60) wrote, 'sometimes that which is at first seen as unusual comes to be accepted as a given. The initial why? is not met with a response, and so the question recedes from consciousness and lies dormant, seeming to disappear'. A turning point in Ravenhill's field research was a serendipitous moment when he was told 'sheep have lineage'; and leading from this, 'all things have lineage'. During my field research with Chewa potters, I was told 'it is our custom', 'that is what we do', 'it is tradition', and the initial 'why' necessarily became dormant until a serendipitous moment when a deeper understanding was revealed. As Ravenhill found connectedness through the serendipity of a man talking about a sheep, so too I found that pottery provided an entree into myth, kinship, marriage, and cosmology.

The ethnography of Chewa pottery described herein is the result of extended periods of field research, revisiting the same potter many times from 1988 to 2005. I was apprenticed to Mai Mpokosa, the Namkungwi, an important teacher and keeper of knowledge. The title of Namkungwi is given to a senior woman in the village, respected by all members of the community and chosen by other senior woman to guide the Chief, arrange initiations for girls, and present issues on behalf of the women to the Chief. She is present at both male and female initiation instruction, being initiated in both. This Namkungwi had the patience to teach me to make a rather unshapely pot,[2] but more importantly allowed me to be initiated in the knowledge of women and the specialized knowledge of potters. My most intensive period of research was in 1992, during field research for my PhD. The focus of my research had been the men's secretive society of masking, *Nyau*.[3] However, the study of pottery became increasingly important to my work on masks and masked performances as the cosmologies expressed through these arts were complementary: One enhances understanding of the other. My work among the potters revealed as much about Chewa society, religion, cosmology, and art as the more visible and vibrant masked performance (Lawal 1997).

One recurring image or motif related to pottery was a simple mark called *mpini* that, once recognized, I realized recurred in multiple media, even on masks made by men (Aguilar 1996). *Mpini* are marks such as slash marks, crescents, or circles, and could be combined together in different ways to create larger images or

Source: © Laurel Birch Kilgore.

figures. Markings such as the repetitive indentation marks around the rim of a pot are connected by the word '*mpini*' and by a range of cosmological associations that are found across otherwise seemingly disparate arts. I became aware that *mpini* was more than a mere marking: It was a theme found in art, in language, and in cosmology. In short, it became a metaphor for the connectedness of the Chewa social world.

In the space of this article, I can only discuss a limited range of material, such as tools to make pottery, markings on pots, and myths that are reenacted in the making of pots. However, the connectedness of clay extends beyond pottery to initiation rituals and objects, house paintings, scarification, and rock paintings. Clay is a substance that is present in all of these arts, and pottery-making is a long, technological proces of transformation (through fire) of that substance (Barley 1995; Fagg and Picton 1970; Frank 1998; Roy 1993, 2001). Alfred Gell (1998) describes this process as a magical one, as simple substances are recreated into works of art. For Gell, process is more important than the finished object, as it is the mystery of the technology, the intention of practice, and the metaphorical significance of the actions of the potter that produce the art object and also recreate society. In my field research, the process of pottery-making was the focus of intensive discussion, while the completed object passed from the potter's hands to be sold, burned black in cooking, and eventually broken. In another way of understanding this technological process, the clay undergoes a kind of transubstantiation, a process described by Victor Turner and others (Turner 1967, 1974; Herbert 1993) to explain the role of change through a ritual process. In the making of pottery, the simple, worked clay and water are transformed into a new, hardened substance, imbued with significance from having undergone the ritual process and associated with the divine world or cosmology (Eliade 1958, Fardon 1990; Hinfelaar 1989; Richards 1972).[4]

The pottery process

Pottery begins life deep in the ground as raw clay. As has been done in these hills for many decades, young women dig the clay, forming small mines in the earth in order to procure the clay needed. The clay is then set in shallow pools of water beside the potter's house, where it is cured and prepared for pottery-making. When the potter is ready to work, she takes a bundle of clay to a dry, exposed stone ledge on the edge of village. There she kneads the clay and removes impurities such as stones and clumps of soil. It is then brought back to the house, where the potter prepares to work. She sets a pot of water beside her and brings out a large pot shard that holds various tools. She adds collected bits of old pottery pieces and finely ground bits of old broken pots to the wet clay in order to give it strength.

While the potter works, the prepared clay is covered to keep it moist. The potter begins the pot by taking a lump of clay, tossing it in the air, twisting and shaping and molding it with her hands. She punches the clay lump, pushing her fist into the center to create the shape called *mimba*, 'the womb', and continues to form the pot in her hands. This process takes only a few minutes. She places the emerging pottery form on a large shard of old pottery, which she turns round and round, continuing to shape the pot with her hands. Then she adds bits of moist clay, covering the remaining unused clay each time. She begins building the shape, working up the sides and defining it as she increases the size of the pot. She frequently moistens her hands from the pot of water and works the moisture from her hands into the clay.

As she works with the clay, building the sides, she creates the shape and size desired for a specified purpose. Small, wide pots are made for cooking relish and deeper, rounded pots are used for cooking maize meal – *nsima* – in larger quantities. To shape the pot, she uses various tools whose qualities have associations in Chewa cosmology: Whiteness, shininess, freshness, food, agriculture, and water are all associated with health, well-being, and closeness to God and the ancestors. A cob of maize from the garden lengthens, thins, and smooths the sides. A smooth, white river pebble helps maintain the rounded belly of the pot, and a curved shell rounds the thinner sides. A strip of white sisal, used in making mats and baskets, is now a tool to trim the top before adding the lip of the pot, and a fresh green leaf smooths the rounded rim. Finally, the shiny knife marks the unfired pottery.

The pots are left to dry and harden to the consistency of leather. Often a small fire of twigs and grasses is set in the belly of the pot to ensure the inside is sufficiently dried. Once partially dried, the pots are ready to be trimmed and smoothed with simple metal blades. The potter scrapes the surface of the nearly finished pot, thinning the rounded bottom and cutting away any imperfections in the smooth surface. A knife is used to incise markings (*mpini*) around the rim of the pot. These markings are unique to a particular potter. One woman marks her pottery with simple slash marks around the rim, and another is known for a simple indent made with the handle of a knife, symmetrically repeated around the neck of the pot. One woman is known for the distinctive shape of her work: dramatically horizontal pots with a sharp edge delineating the belly of the pot from the neck. Some place a mark on the rounded underside of the pot, sometimes rendered invisible in the pottery-making process. Because the pots are sold by traders, few outside the pottery area may be aware of these differences, but for the potter community, these patterns and shapes identify the individual potter.

When thoroughly dried, the pots of a week's work are gathered together in a central spot within the village to be fired. The pots are carefully placed in a pile on cleared ground and wooden branches are arranged around them, followed by dry grasses. The dry grasses are set alight and blaze for an hour. During this time, preparations are made to mark the pots once they have been fired.

The women have dug up a special root known as *nkunga*, with red sap that is described by the women as blood. When I twisted the root, it 'bled' and the red sap on my hand indeed looked like a gush of real blood. I was told the sap is acidic, and so it was immediately removed from my hand. The roots are considered sources of fertility and the blood of life, and each living person is associated with a *nkunga* root. The root is used in medicines used for cleansing a woman after birth by helping to purge any remaining blood from her womb. Roots for pottery marking are carefully selected by an older woman, who chooses only old plants. These can safely be harvested, since presumably they are associated with a deceased person; digging a young root associated with a living person is believed to literally cut short that person's life. The root is beaten against a hard rock, just as the clay was beaten against a hard rock, and the root and its sap are placed in a pot of water and worked through. As the red sap is kneaded from the root in the water, it turns milky white and is then left to rest in the water.

As the fire burns down to glowing red embers, the pots are buried in the ashes. The women use long poles to bring the red hot pots out of the fire for the final process. The fired pots are painted with the *nkunga* root solution. The water and sap form a stain running down the interior and exterior of the pots as the whitish liquid sizzles to a dark brown. Once the pots have been stained in this way, they are left to dry and cool.

The incisions and painted patterns of the pots are admired for their beauty: the incisions with the knife admired for symmetry and evenness and the stained patterns from the root drippings for their randomness, chance patterns that seem particularly attractive. The women offer practical reasons for why these markings are made: They are said to demonstrate that the pots are strong, since they do not break when brushed with the liquid while still hot. However, the women also talk about how pleasing the pottery is to look at and admire. There are certain characteristics of well made pottery that a group of potters all agreed were pleasing and beautiful. The color of the fired clay is important; a clear color is preferred to a muddied one. The pottery is better if it has a sheen and the clay is not dull. The brown stains are also transparent, and this transparency is perceived as a kind of brightness valued by the women . During firing a variety of colors appear on the surface of the pot, such as dark blue, orange, and earth tones, and sometimes a grey green shade. The way these colors play on the surface with the applied stain can be very beautiful and renders each pot unique.

Once made, the pottery is taken away to be sold. The beautiful patterns, clear, bright clay, and translucent stains will soon fade in the sunlight and pots used for cooking will become blackened with fires and ash. In time the pots will crack and break. Eventually, some of the old broken pots will become shards for the potter's wheel, and the dust of old pots will be used again in making new ones.

Pots and relationships: Whole or broken

Pots are useful objects. They are used for cooking, for storage, and for collecting water. Porous pots are used as 'refrigerators' for condensing and cooling water. But for the Chewa, these practical uses are only part of a larger, more complex, and cosmological interpretation.

I suggest that, through transubstantiation, Chewa potters create new forms that are life-enhancing. A finished pot enhances the well-being, health, and hygiene of a woman's home. It is a sign of a good life and good food. A good cooking pot is taken as a sign of a good marriage, and in contrast, a broken pot is taken as a sign of a marriage in trouble, demonstrated by a quarrelling couple throwing out a pot and breaking it. A husband should eat from his wife's pot and never from the pot of another woman. A good husband must provide his wife with her cooking pots. If there are marital problems, the wife may show anger by refusing to cook, forcing her husband to find his meal elsewhere. And ultimately, a broken marriage pot is a sign of a broken marriage.

Children, who belong to the mother in Chewa society, are taught when they are very young to eat only from their own mother's pot. Boys initiated into adulthood[5] are told they may no longer eat directly from their mother's relish pot, a smaller pot used to cook precious meat, vegetables, and savories. He can be given his relish on a plate or with his maize meal, but he cannot take it directly from the cooking pot: There is a suggestion of incest when an older son eats from his mother's marriage pot. Young, unmarried men eat from the larger family pot of maize meal, and eventually will need to find their own wives and share food from their own marriage pot.[6]

Other life passages and relationships are signified by pottery. When a woman dies, one of her pots is often broken and buried with her. Broken pots are sometimes scattered over the graves of the deceased.[7] *Mbiyazodooka* ('broken pot') is the name of a particular masked dancer, depicting an outcast from society, one who has no kinship ties to the village and is often associated with the loss of a mother.[8]

Whole pots, ones that are life-enhancing, are contrasted with broken pots as signs of the fragility of human relationships. Smashed pots reflect broken marriages, broken kinship ties, and other broken relationships, and they also signify separation from society, being orphaned or outcast. Whole pots signify marriage, kinship, family, children, sharing food, life, birth. Broken pots are metaphors for death and breaks in social relationships as whole pots are for life and unity in society.

Pots as wombs, birth, and life

The Chewa women with whom I apprenticed spoke of pots as being like a womb (*mimba*), shaped like a pregnant woman. I was told that, just as sexual relations during pregnancy is prohibited, potters in the past could not have sexual relations during the critical stages of pottery-making, such as when pots are being fired, because the technological process of making pots is associated with female fertility, birth, and the creation of new life. The process of shaping the pot, molding it into a womb-like shape, is a mysterious process. Fresh from the potter's hands it is still soft, but over time it matures into a hardened shape that is crafted, marked, and fired into life as a fully formed object.

Among the Chewa, only women make pots, and potters live together in communities of sisters, mothers, and aunts. Most potters learn from their mothers (or 'many mothers', referring to all adult women in the village), as the young girls sit and observe the women making pots, sometimes making small pots of their own with the clay. Older girls collect the clay and help with the firing and retrieving of the hot pottery. A woman may become a potter at any age; one elderly woman, who had been married to a Chief, returned to the village where she was born, and her nieces taught her how to make pottery for sale.

Living in the Chewa community, all the women are initiated in female knowledge. In Chewa cosmology, God is in the soil as well as the sky, and the presence of God in the soil is female. There, deep in the soil, the earth is like a womb giving birth to germinating seeds. I suggest that the pots the women make are metaphors of this knowledge of creation and birth.

Mythological themes

As with pottery forms, pottery-making has myriad associations with Chewa myths, relationships, and beliefs about the creation of life, a fact that became evident to me as I learned the process and its significance from the woman potters alongside whom I worked. Following are two myths, a creation myth and the myth of a legendary rain-maker turned snake (Schoffeleers 1992, Schoffeleers and Roscoe 1985; de Heusch 1982 describe similar myths). Both of these are then interpreted in relation to pottery and Chewa cosmology.

So we begin in the beginning, when man and woman first came to earth, falling from the sky to the barren earth [ground/land] in a cataclysmic torrent of rain with thunder and lightning that made the earth like clay. Rains covered the earth and in low areas rivers and pools of water formed. The rains brought all life with them and imprinted new life in the wet clay on a high plateau that was once hard as rock. Here these first Impressions of life remained as the rains dried and the rock hardened again. As if in proof of these origins, the Kaphirintiwa Plateau in the Dzalanyama Mountains still carries the ancient footprints of men, women, and animals and the imprints of various objects including a cooking pot, a mortar and pestle, and a threshing basket.

The living gathered in the savannah grasses, grown tall and green in the rains. All dwelled in the same space together, including God. Humans, though, were not content, and learned to make fire. They were warned about its danger, but one day, the fires ignited the grasses, which then burned out of control. God escaped high into a tree and then into the sky. Some animals, in rage and anger, ran away from man. Others were frightened and ran toward him and became tamed. As the grasses burned, the air became dry. The season of dryness parched the earth, dried up the pools of water, made the clay hard, and the winds became stronger; but then the rains came again after the winds. Finally the fires died into ashes. Life did begin again, as the seed germinated under the ashes. However, as punishment, man and all creatures now had to die to rejoin God.

This creation myth explains the dry and wet seasons, the mountains of the Rift Valley, and the deep pools of water and lakes. The myth explains the objects of everyday life – pottery, baskets, mortar, and pestle – as gifts that came with the rains, leaving imprints with the footsteps of woman and man and animals. It explains the presence of fire, earth, and water. It explains why God is so distant, why there must be death, and why there is renewed life. It is seen in the grasses that grow green and high, then become parched and dry. It is present morning and evening, in the smell of smoke rising through the thatched roof from cooking fires in every village household. It explains why the Chewa burn the grasses every year toward the end of the dry season, leaving glowing red gashes on the sides of hills that are seen for miles at night time. After the burning, the ash is laid over the barren earth where, with the coming of the rains, the green stalks of maize will come to life again. This myth is not articulated very often, and it took a senior Chief renowned for his love and knowledge of Nyau to tell it to me. Yet people are made aware of all that the myth explains about their lives as part of initiation into adulthood in the village.

There is another important myth that helps to provide insight into the deeper significance of pottery and the pottery making process. In this myth a young man named Mbona had the gift of rain-making. One year when the rains were very late and famine threatened, his Chief called upon him to help make the rains come. Mbona agreed to perform the rain ritual, but warned the Chief that all the people must remain inside their houses for their safety. Mbona flashed his dagger and called upon the lightning and the thunder, and by the end of the dance, the rains were falling. However, a little boy who ran out of his house was struck by lightning and died. The boy's mother, a sister of the Chief, was so distressed she inflamed the Chief with fears that Mbona would take the Chief's power. Eventually the Chief agreed to kill Mbona. Mbona heard of this plot to kill him and escaped. The legend includes different variations describing how Mbona repeatedly escaped the Chief's warriors, even allowing them to try and cut him with daggers, and they failed. Finally, Mbona told the warriors how he could be killed: with a simple sharp blade of grass.

The warriors cut him with the grass and killed him. Mbona's blood flowed, forming first a river, and then a flood that filled a deep pool of water. When the men realized they had killed a spirit and not a man, they built a shrine near the pool. Mbona called to women from the depths of the water, demanding a good woman to be his wife. He selected a mature, older woman, who took a vow of celibacy to become the wife of the spirit. At night, Mbona came to her in the form of a python snake and whispered to her. The woman, then, had authority from the words of the python spirit Mbona to relate his words, warnings, and demands to others. She became a priestess who interpreted the messages from Mbona to the whole society.

These myths of creation are reinterpreted in the materials, actions, and processes of pottery making. Relationships with the earth, soil, and clay, pools of water, fire, and heat cooled again by water, are metaphors that recreate the world in the making of pots: rain and pools of water used in the curing of the clay, hard stone and dryness in the purifying of the clay. Clay Is the substance created in the first rains that brought life to the Dzalanyama Mountains, and the red blood of Mbona Is present in the red clay mined from the deep pools of water. Some of the tools used in pottery-making are from streams or farming (associated with the earth), and the knives are the blades of Mbona's dagger, flashing in the light. Pots are made from the clay that created the world, shaping raw earth into wombs that are metaphors of bearing life, the birth of all that lives. The red of the *nkunga* root sap and the red of iron ore in the deep pools and streams of water are Mbona's blood. The reddish brown stain on the pottery is also Mbona's blood.

The firing of pottery is interpreted as a recreation of the fires that caught the dry grasses in the mythology of creation. In that dangerous moment, pottery wombs may pop, crack, and break. The outcome of weeks of work is decided by the firing, but it is also the moment of mystery, of transformation and transubstantiation from one substance to another, from soft clay to a shaped and hardened vessel. The dry season of fires cools, just as the pottery cools in the embers and ashes. From the cooled ashes, the pots are removed with long sticks and dripped with the blood red sap, reminiscent of Mbona's fresh blood, turned milky white, which then becomes deep brown red like earth on the surface of the still hot clay.

Mythologies relate cosmology of day and night, sun and moon. As the myths explain the cosmology of the Chewa, the women explain how the sun sets into an enormous pot and emerges in the morning as renewed life, giving birth to each new day. The sun returns to the clay womb every evening to be reborn again the next day. Pottery is also likened to the moon, and the various phases of the moon are likened to the various shapes of pottery, from round orb to crescent. The wide, shallow pot made for cooking relish is as beautiful as the crescent moon, similar in shape and with a bright, white-like surface that reflects in the calm way the moon shines.

The connectedness of Chewa Pottery

From the morning cooking fires that heat pots filled with maize meal to the evening ashes, myths are constantly re enacted. From the dusty red pathways leading to villages to the fields of maize and the seedlings covered in ash from the burned dry grasses, images of creation recur. The smell of the first rains falling with thunder and lightning, the sun in the day and moon at night, ground nut tendrils and the deep rich shades of soil, to the evening fires, crescent pots of relish and rounded bellies storing grain or cooling water, everyday life is filled with metaphors. Moments of great upheaval and change, funeral bonfires, initiations of the young into maturity, harvests and plantings, aging and illness, marriage and births, divorces and separations, the teachers and students, and the Namkungwi guiding a new Chief, these themes recur over and again.

The connectivity of color and form recur over and again, as the world is constantly renewed, pottery is constantly being made, and life is constantly changing and repeating in cycles of life and death. Metaphors repeat, interplay, and layer one upon the other. Recurring images and metaphors connect disparate aspects of society, creating and re-creating understanding of a world. The art of pottery-making becomes the art of creation and the completed pot a way of connecting worlds.

Notes

The most important resources in this research are my informers: Isaac Chisati, Bobo Yosiya (deceased), Rosemary N'gonzo (deceased). Chief N'gonzo, Mai Mpokosa, Juliet Ngwira, Nicolas Nigwira (deceased), and Davie Guzani among many. Bobo Yosiya ofiered me the first glimpses into local village life and the Nyau, secretive society of the Chewa people. Bobo died in 1991. After this time, Isaac introduced me to a group of women porters, including Mai Mpokosa, her sister, and her aunt (now deceased); they in particular are responsible for much of the ethnographic data herein. In this journey of connectedness between Chewa potters and the pottery they make, I refer to other works and authors, but I remember the first insights from my academic teachers, scholars in the discipline, and most particularly my teachers in the field: the women who make the pottery and tried their best to teach me. I walked miles to see one such woman, a potter who had declared celibacy and held authority to collect certain substances from pools of water used in her pottery-making and midwifery. Another Malawian woman has allowed me to stay in her home over various field trips in the last fifteen years, and l am honoured to call Juliet Ngwira my dear friend. As pottery is more than an object in relation to other things, the teaching of Christopher Roy instilled the sense of the aesthetic of the object itself. While I believed there was a natural beauty in this particular style of pot, I also learned from Roy a deeper aesthetic appreciation of pottery and African art. Other teachers, John Picton, Allen Roberts, and Mary Jo Arnoldi among them, furthered my learning and I owe them all a debt of gratitude.

1. As supervisor for my MA degree in African Art and Anthropology. Philip Ravenhill explained his theoretical construction to me as part of my tutorials (individual lectures). l will necessarily draw on the research of others in the field, Matthew Schoffeleers (1992, 1979, 1985) in particular, who published the myths l retell.
2. This same first pot and others are now in the British Museum collection. Examples of Chewa clay pots collected in periods of field research are presently on exhibition in the British Museum Africa exhibition and the Smithsonian lnstitution's National Museum of African Art.
3. *Nyau* is a secretive society that is associated with men, but includes all people within the cosmological and religious context. Nyau members perform the Gule Wamkulu (Great Dance) masked dances with women singing and clapping and men wearing masks and dancing. The Gule Wamkulu is performed for funerals, initiations, ancestor remembrance, and rituals for new Chiefs. Nyau is dominant in rural areas of the central region in Malawi, and border areas of Zambia.
4. Reference to the divine, to religion, cosmology and ritual are all present in the work of Victor Turner (1967). Transubstantiation is presented by others, notably Eugenia Herbert (1993) in relation to African iron-making.

Iron-making was historically the male counterpart to female pottery-making in the central region of Malawi, both involving transformation of the earth to hardened usable forms through firing, and both are associated in historical literature as rituals.

5. Initiation of boys is generally from about age nine to mid teens, though some are initiated as early as seven and others are full adults before undergoing initiation. Initiation among the Chewa does not include circumcision.
6. This is also explained in Makumbi (1955), who wrote about Chewa customs in a Chichewa publication stressing that boys should not eat from their mother's relish pot after initiation into the men's society of Nyau.
7. I have visited various graveyards, new and old, and have seen shards and occasionally whole pots on some of the graves. A woman was buried with her pot in one funeral I witnessed, and shards littered the ground around chasms in Nkhuma mountain around the burial sites during the times of wars, most significantly the Nhoni wars (mid eighteenth century) still in the social memories of people.
8. In other research by Philip Ravenhill (personal communication, 1990), if an elderly person can recall a relationship that is still distant enough to be acceptable as kinship, the couple undergoes a ceremony where the families break a pot to indicate that the kinship tie is broken, and the couple is allowed to marry.

References cited

Barley, Nigel. 1995. *Smashing Pots: Works of Clay in Africa*. Washington DC: Smithsonian Books.

Eliade, Mircea. 1958. *Birth and Rebirth: The Religious Meanings of Initiation in Human Culture*. New Yorlk: Harper.

Pagg, William, and John Picton. 1970. *The Potter's Art in Africa*. London: The British Museum.

Fardon, Richard, 1990. *Between God, the Dead, and the Wild: Chewa Interpretations of Religion and Ritual*. Washington DC: Smithsonian Institution Press.

Frank, Barbara. 1998. *Mande Potters and Leatherworkers: Art and Heritage in West Africa*. Washington DC: Smithsonian Institution Press.

Gell, Alfred. 1998. *Art and Agency: An Anthropological Theory*. Oxford: Oxford University Press.

Herbert, Eugenia. 1993. *Iron, Gender, and Power: Rituals of Transformation in African Societies*. Bloomington: Indiana University Press.

Hinfelaar, Hugo F. 1989. *Religious Change among the Bemba-Speaking Women of Zambia*. PhD diss. University of London.

de Heusch, Luc .1981. *The Drunken King, or, the Origin of the Stole*. Bloomington: Indiana University Press.

Kilgore, Laurel Birch, 1995. *Inscribing the Mask: Interpretation of Nyau Masks and Ritual Performance among the Chewa of Central Malawi*. Freiburg: University of Freiburg Press, Switzerland.

Lawal, Babarunde. 1997. *The Gelede Spectacle: Art, Gender, and Social Harmony in an African Culture*. Seattle: University of Washington Press.

Makumbi, Archibald. 1955. *Maliro ndi Miyambo ya Acewa*. Nairobi: Longman and Green.

Ravenhill, Philip. 2000. 'Likeness and Nearness: The Intentionality of the Head in Baule Art.' *African Arts* 33 (2): pp. 60–71, 91.

Richards, Audrey. 1971. *Chisungu: A Girls' Initiation Ceremony among the Bembe of Northern Rhodesia*. 2nd. ed. London: Tavistock.

Ricouer, Paul. 1979. 'Meaningful Action Considered as Text.' In *Interpretive Social Science: A Reader*. ed. Paul Rabinow and William Sullivan. Berkeley: University of California Press, pp. 73–102.

Roy, Christopher. 1993. *Art and Life in Africa: Selections from the Stanley Collection Exhibitions of 1985 and 1992*. Seattle: University of Washington Press.

Roy, Christopher. et al. 2001. *Clay and Fire: Pottery in Africa*. Iowa Studies in African Art Vol. 4. Iowa: University of Iowa Press.

Sacks, Sheldon. 1979. *On Metaphor*. Chicago: University of Chicago Press.

Schoffeleers, J.M. 1992. *River of Blood: The Genesis of a Martyr Cult in Southern Malawi c. AD 1600*. Madison: University of Wisconsin Press.

Schoffeleers, J.M. ed. 1979. *Guardians of the Land: Essays on Central African Territorial Cults*. Gwelo: Mambo Press.

Schoffeleers, J.M. and A.A. Roscoe. 1935. *Land of Fire: Oral Literature from Malawi*. Lilongwe: Popular Publications.

Tilley, Christopher. 1999. *Metaphor and Material Culture*. Oxford: Blackwell.
Turner, Victor. 1974. *Dramas, Fields, and Metaphors: Symbolic Action in Human Society*. Ithaca: Cornell University Press.
Turner, Victor. 1967. *The Forest of Symbols: Aspects of Ndembu Ritual*. Ithaca: Cornell University Press.
Originally published as Laurel Birch Kilgore (2007) 'Metaphor, Myths and Making Pots: Chewa Clay Arts', in *African Arts*, Vol. 40, No. 1, Ceramic Arts in Africa (Spring, 2007), pp. 64–70.

Reprinted with permission from the author.

10
SCULPTURAL VESSELS ACROSS THE GREAT DIVIDE: TONY CRAGG'S *LAIBE* AND THE METAPHORS OF CLAY

Imogen Racz

Abstract

This article discusses Tony Cragg's *Laibe* (1991) in the context of fine and applied arts practice of the time. Just as many British crafts practitioners were concerned with using the vessel as an iconic starting point to explore sculptural ideas, Cragg's *Laibe,* which conflates the vessel form with the suggestion of loaves of cut bread, brings together the necessities for sustaining life in a metaphoric use of form and material. The obvious hand marks while using industrial clay, at once suggests the long history of thrown pots as well as contemporary practices. Like many artists who have used clay as part of a broader range of materials, Cragg collaborated with a ceramicist, in his case during a residency at the European Ceramic Work Centre in the Netherlands. *Laibe* was shown in *A Secret History of Clay: From Gauguin to Gormley* (2004), and the article discusses the critical and exhibiting distancing of art from craft, in spite of the overlaps of concerns.

Introduction

In 2004 Tony Cragg exhibited an example from his series of related sculptures called *Laibe* in *A Secret History of Clay: From Gauguin to Gormley* at Tate Liverpool. This work, which dates from 1991, represents both an early interest in the ceramic medium and an example of how he used the vessel form as a metaphorical starting point to engage the viewer in ideas about the ways in which humans relate to their environment. However, the coming together of clay and vessel creates tensions, not only within art dialogues, but also between art and craft. Unlike other contemporary works included in the exhibition, such as those by Cindy Sherman or Richard Slee, the surfaces of *Laibe* are not used for imagery, are not clothed in a skin of glaze, and do not incorporate wit or irony. The four related vessels that make up the sculpture have obviously been raised on a wheel and the material qualities are intrinsic to their meaning. However, this work, as with the aims of the exhibition, is not about potting or studio vessels, but uses the vessel form within an artistic framework.

Tony Cragg's *Laibe* was only one of many vessels in the exhibition. From Gauguin's *Hina and Tefatou* (1893), which falls within the continuum of his overall oeuvre that depicts mythic scenes related to the folk culture of Tahiti, to Jeff Koon's *Puppy Vase* (1998), which is an ironical sideways glance at decorative and

Source: © Imogen Racz/*Journal of Visual Art Practice*, 2009, 8 (3), pp. 215–228.

sentimental pottery objects, vessels were shown to have played an important part in artistic production over the twentieth century (Groom 2004). This idea had also been explored in an earlier exhibition held in Holland – *The Unexpected. Artists' Ceramics of the 20th Century* (Koplos 1998). This international exhibition, which highlighted the ceramic collection of the Kruithuis at 's-Hertogenbosch, was narrower in its remit. Unlike *A Secret History of Clay* (2004), which included performances and works that were destroyed during and after the exhibition, the objects exhibited at the Kruithuis were self contained and many were vessels that linked to other facets in the artists' oeuvre. Like *A Secret History of Clay* studio makers were hardly mentioned, although the vessel was a key theme. What is interesting in the titles of both of these exhibitions is the degree to which both highlighted the importance of clay in twentieth century art, while acknowledging its historical ambivalence within critical dialogues. What is also worth noting is the fact that many of the artists were reliant on the skills of craftsmen in order to advise on technical and material possibilities and to help make the works.

Contemporary with *Laibe* were a number of English exhibitions that highlighted craft practitioners who were moving beyond the idea of the vessel as something comforting or utilitarian. *The Abstract Vessel: Ceramics in Studio* (1991) exclusively featured studio ceramicists who were making sculptural vessels (Houston 1991). Like the essays included in the catalogue for *Beyond the Dovetail: Craft, Skill and Imagination* of the same year, the role of the vessel in the post-industrial age – when 'honest potting' can be seen as nostalgic, when skills that had traditionally conferred status can be easily produced mechanically, and when most craft practitioners have been through higher education and therefore engage with broad artistic debates – was discussed (Frayling 1991). Unlike the catalogues related to *A Secret History of Clay* and *The Unexpected. Artists' Ceramics of the 20th Century*, the texts for these craft exhibitions and others like *The Raw and Cooked. New Work in Clay in Britain* (1993), engaged with the genre history and moved beyond that to make links with art and its related philosophies (Elliott 1993). As Martina Margetts wrote in her essay for the latter exhibition, the developments in art during the late 1980s and 1990s had led to the role of ceramics being more open to interpretation and connection. She argued that process as product, which was important within both craft ceramics and the sculptural production of artists like Tony Cragg, Richard Deacon and Anish Kapoor, meant that there were close affinities, especially in relation to vessel forms, across the genres (Margetts 1993: 13–15).

However, these links were not discussed within the art journals. There were reviews and articles about *A Secret History of Clay* in the magazines *Crafts, World of Interiors, Ceramics* (Australia) and *Ceramic Review*, but none in art journals. The exhibitions related to craft ceramics were not reviewed outside craft journals. In the article for *Crafts* about *A Secret History of Clay*, Tanya Harrod makes the point that if one looks back over the last half century, it is possible to trace a more inclusive history of art than is normally considered (Harrod 2004: 29). Although there is a rich history of artists making works that could be considered 'craft', including ceramic works, by the 1940s Alfred Barr, Clement Greenberg and Hilton Kramer had chosen to ignore this. This exclusion from and exclusiveness of the allowed history of art is a recent phenomena, but what the works in the exhibition revealed was the diversity of reasons for using the material (Harrod 2004: 32). As the preview in *Ceramic Review* articulated, the aim of the exhibition was to prove that 'clay is a central art' (O. R. 2004: 17). However, the ambiguity of the status of clay has meant that many artists have found it necessary to distance this work from the craft genre. Edward Lucie-Smith's (2004) article about *A Secret History of Clay* in *Ceramic Review* starts with the pronouncements made by Antony Gormley in the catalogue about the differences between art and craft. Whereas art, Gormley states, questions the world and complicates things, craft objects reconcile the needs of human life and the environment. Gormley was unhappy about the state of craft at the time, considering that it had both lost its function and, that in aspiring to be sculpture, vessels were being made that were unsuitable for holding flowers (Gormley 2004: 84). As

Lucie-Smith dryly commented, this ambiguous position also held true for many similar works by artists (Lucie-Smith 2004: 32). What Gormley, as well as many other artists have tended to forget is the long history that craft has of being linked to social and political events and of being for display. Clearly, as Grayson Perry has articulated, the proximity of ceramics to art makes it a threat, in the way that even distant areas of art do not represent. As he said, 'if you call your pot art you're being pretentious. If you call a shark art you're being bold and philosophical' (Groom 2004: 14).

What *A Secret History of Clay,* along with other exhibitions of the 1990s and 2000s revealed was the importance of clay and the vessel as a means of exploring ideas right through the twentieth century. This became even more obvious during the 1980s and 1990s, when both cutting edge craft practitioners and those affiliated with New British Sculpture made vessels in many different materials and forms. Some, like *Laibe* are solid and just suggest a vessel. Some use the containing space to suggest ideas. Some suggest links to architectural ideas or reference iconic works like Duchamp's *Fountain* (1917).

The generation of artists and ceramicists that emerged from the RCA (Royal College of Art) and other London art schools during the 1970s, of which Cragg was one, had been educated in similar ways, knew each other and have remained loosely connected. Their work does reveal affinities. It is not my intention to investigate the relative statuses of art and craft. That has been considered repeatedly over the last few decades. However, through discussing just one of Cragg's sculptures – *Laibe* – and placing it within a broader framework of vessel forms of the time, I intend to cast some light on the shifting relationships between different practices.

Laibe

Laibe is, on the face of it, atypical of Cragg's work. It is not made up of a collection of found or transformed vessels. There is no containing inside. There are no contrasting elements and the surface maps the maker's process. However, I have chosen it because in spite of these apparent differences, it also represents a coming together of many of Cragg's ideas, and the fact that it was exhibited at *A Secret History of Clay* placed it alongside the work of other contemporary artists and, by comparison, reveals much about its artistic context.

Laibe, like others in the series, consists of four solid, unglazed ceramic vessel shapes, arranged into a still life. The original vessels were thrown, with the traces of the potter's fingers remaining mapped into the surface. Each of the components had been sliced, and through the visible pull of the knife through clay together with the outward sag of the slices, the consistency and malleability of the material is evident. The manganese oxide that was added to the fine grained sculpture clay resulted in this work being brown – others in the series are pale. The vessels were fired at a low temperature, meaning that the earth qualities – in spite of being industrially treated – remain (Reijnders 2005: 152).

Cragg has written that his works are intended as propositions rather than dogmatic statements. He wants to create objects that 'don't exist in the natural or functional world', but that can reflect and transmit information and feelings about the world (Cragg 1985: 60). The fact that his sculptures are not meant to be functional is key, especially when considering his works that incorporate references to function, like his vessels or arrangements of furniture. He argues that art is unique in that it does not belong to a particular utilitarian power system that deadens people's responses to everyday life through promoting the consumption of banal, mediocre objects (Cragg 1992: 72–73). For him, in order to express the environment there needs to be a different level of responsibility to making things (Cragg 1988: 63). Art, he feels, occupies a special category of objects that offers itself as 'complex symbols for new experiences' (Cragg 1985: 59).

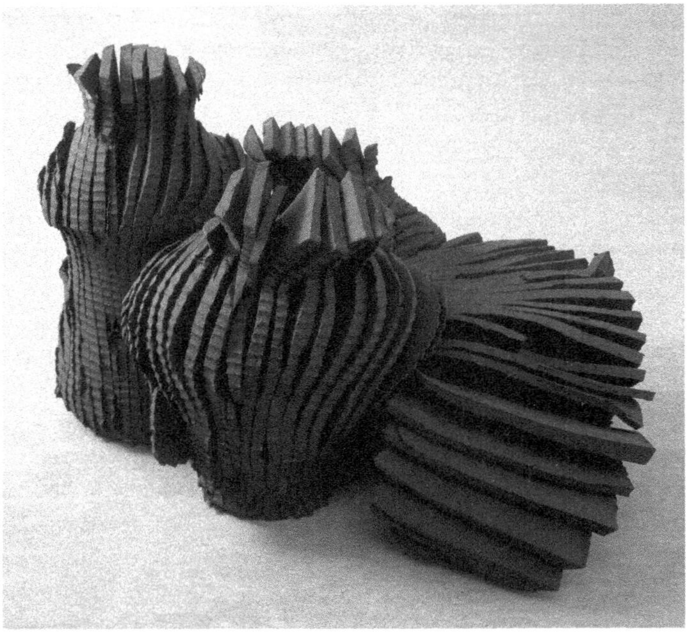

Figure 10.1 Tony Cragg's Laibe (Image of sliced vessel), 2009 – Imogen Racz/Anthony Cragg.

The concept that the objects are about, but separate from the everyday world, and are non-functional, propositional and symbolic, are relevant when considering all of Cragg's work, but especially so when considering *Laibe*. Like so many of his sculptures, it is complexly layered, so that the initial suggestion of four vessels is complicated by their being solid and sliced. '*Laibe*' is German for loaves. The quality and variety of German bread is legendary, but beyond that bread, like vessels and clay, has metaphoric, cultural and ritual resonances, as well as being vital for sustaining life. The very fact of the vessels being so obviously raised on a wheel references the millions of pots that have been made in this way over the thousands of years since the wheel was first invented. The forms of *Laibe*, are what Perry would call 'classical invisible', in being not related to any particular time or culture, but they provide a base that people can understand (Boot 2002: 14). Through this non-determinacy, possible interpretations are left open. While the hand marks and clay surface suggest artisan skills, this is not intended to be a nostalgic reference, nor is it meant to promote a direct link between maker and user in the manner of, for instance, vessels from the Muchelney Pottery or those espoused by Octavio Paz (Paz 1974: 21). Although the elements suggest a link back through time, the slicing (sliced bread) and the industrially produced clay suggest an engagement with contemporary life and commercial production.

In *A Secret History of Clay*, the last room included postmodern ceramics, like *Madame de Pompadour (Née Poisson) Soup Tureen and Saucer* (Cindy Sherman, 1989–91), *Brooms* (Richard Slee, 1999) and *Puppy Vase* (Jeff Koons, 1998). In a manner that would have horrified Clement Greenberg, all were related to the domestic, and verged on kitsch in order to critique popular culture. All were highly finished with a skin of glaze, aping industrially produced ceramics and mocking consumer values. Ironically, the soup tureen and saucer, which was a pastiche of Sèvres wares, and was therefore about 'high' taste, was next to Slee's brooms, which were almost Disney-like in their conception and vocabularies. These were contrasted with Jeff Koons' shiny, oversized sentimental object that links back to industrially produced ornaments. It is the dominance of the image as opposed to the object in these works that connects them both with postmodernity and consumer culture, and which separates them from Cragg's contemporaneous work, which was shown in the preceding room along with sculptures by Richard Deacon and Richard Long. The work in both rooms was about contemporary culture, but was revealed in different ways.

Frederick Jameson's hostility to the cultural emphasis on visual imagery is owing to what he considers its end as being 'rapt mindless fascination' (Jameson 1990: 1–2). This also echoes Cragg's stand against the banal and mediocre. *Laibe* represents the opposite of consuming passions. As a still life, it would come under the category that Norman Bryson would term 'rhopography': 'the unassuming material base of life', the overlooked in a world seduced by plenty (Bryson 1990: 61). It is a humble image that overturns perceived importance. Everyone needs to eat, and the vessel and bread are the basic requirements that are needed to satisfy hunger.

The use of gravity in deciding the final form, rather than the artist 'completing' the work, echoes the ideas of Robert Morris and the soft sculptures of Claes Oldenberg. Allowing the material to move and determine the final shape has become a feature of many contemporary artists' work, including that of David Nash and the wood turner Christian Burchard, but is also something that frequently occurs in Cragg's sculptures. *Wall Peg* (1985), for instance, links to the upright forms of *Minster* (1987), where contrasting circles of materials including rubber, stone, wood and metal, are piled into a spire shape, making a tension between the traditional craft involved in building cathedrals and the industrial, found, and manipulated layers. However, unlike *Minster*, *Wall Peg* is upended and flops out into the space of the gallery suggesting links with minimalism. Each element leans against its neighbour, waiting for gravity to finally pull it to the horizontal. However, *Laibe* is not made up of contrasting layers, but is a whole that has been cut. Photographs of it drying show how the slices are moving outwards at the top, while they are held together at the bottom (Cragg 1993: 10). Unlike the rips and repairs in the work of Peter Voulkos – who was also exhibited at *A Secret History of Clay* – these cuts are not intended to critique the material. The material is just part of the vocabulary of meaning.

Skill

The use of the readymade in Cragg's work prior to the late 1980s meant that there was a distancing of the artist from the means of production. Joseph Kosuth's *Art after Philosophy* (1969) argued that the introduction of the readymade was the point at which traditional skills were finally stripped of past meaning, and where the chosen objects were no more than carriers of propositional content (Roberts 2007: 24). David Pye, writing at much the same time, articulated his anxiety about the loss of interest in workmanship. Without this knowledge of materials and their relevant techniques, the fullest expression and range of qualities cannot be exploited (Pye 1968: 1–3). This lack of tacit knowledge, he felt, represented a narrowing of possibilities. Certainly, clay is a complex medium that requires intimate knowledge about both the forming and the glazing and firing processes, which has meant that most artists who have used clay have relied on the skills of crafts practitioners to advise them. Gauguin, for instance, collaborated with Ernst Chaplet, Miró with Artigas and Caro, Tàpies and Chillida all worked with Hans Spinner (de Waal 2004: 51).

Materials have always been of central significance for Cragg. He uses a broad range, but rather than unmediated natural materials, they have all been modified or are man made, which, he feels, makes them integral with the physical, intellectual and emotional lives of men (Cragg 1985: 60). Until *Mittelschicht* (1984), his works were frequently found plastic fragments related to a specific area, which were arranged into a temporary composition. This sculpture was the turning point at which Cragg began to move back to studio production, where he could explore materials and their roles in making meaning (McEvilley 2003: 168). He felt that the Duchampian strategy of found objects was running out of steam, and that by the middle of the 1980s artists like Gilbert & George, Richard Long, and Joseph Beuys had reduced the difference between art and the everyday world to a critical extent. He wanted to return to the studio and try another strategy. Although this return to making could be seen as a retrograde gesture, Cragg decided to become engaged with it and break the rules on his own terms (Cragg 2003: 201).

With a return to studio practice, Cragg needed to develop his own skills and also draw on those of others. This delegation of manual processes, as well as receiving the advice of material experts, means that he gained the ability to take risks and exploit the potential of each material. In order to develop skills and understanding in ceramic production, Cragg obtained a residency in 1990 and another in 1992 at the European Ceramic Work Centre, the EKWC, in the Netherlands. The stay in 1990 was a trial run in the earlier location in Heusden, when the centre was finding an identity for itself. The 1992 residency was at the new centre at 's-Hertogenbosch, where many artists have stayed to explore the artistic and technical possibilities of the material while assisted by expert technicians (Reijnders 2005: 10). Other artists who have used their facilities have included Anish Kapoor and Antony Gormley, but the centre has also given residencies to well known ceramicists like Ewen Henderson and Philip Eglin (Reijnders 2005: 10). *Laibe* was one of many works produced during Cragg's residencies, where one of the technicians threw particular shapes according to his instructions and then Cragg manipulated the resulting forms in different ways (Geitner 2002: 23).

Photographs of him working at the EKWC depict him actively manipulating materials as well as directing and discussing the possibilities of technique and material with others. This use of people with an intimate hands-on knowledge of a material by a crafts practitioner, designer or artist is a continental way of realizing projects. Scandinavia, Germany and the Netherlands have developed this manner of working in industry since the 1920s, and indeed one of the aims of the EKWC is to strengthen the bonds between ceramics, industry, science and education (Geitner 2002: 12).

In England though, this is less common. Craft practitioners typically work with a narrow range of materials and know them well, but artists have moved away from this deep knowledge and frequently use whatever materials seem relevant to their intentions, without necessarily worrying about artisan skills. Cragg's sculptures incorporate glass, ceramics, metals, plastics, wood and many other materials, so that it would not be possible to become a master of all. Like other artists of the 1990s, like Tracy Emin or Sarah Lucas, he incorporated traditional craft materials according to the intended message. However, unlike them, he was not trying to blur the distinctions between art and life. His themes might be about particular everyday elements, but they were not subjective, intended to shock or just suggest the contemporary. Indeed, the application for his residency at the EKWC stated that he wanted to give the materials 'more meaning, mythology and poetry' (Geitner 2002: 46). The skills used were there to create ambiguities and tensions, to suggest past and present, to complicate rather than to describe.

Skill is a factor that has caused rifts in both craft and fine art over the last few decades. Sculpture has always had less status than painting because of the physical labour involved as well as the fact that so many sculptors traditionally trained with artisans. Even between the 1950s and 1970s, when new materials were being incorporated, many sculptors, like Kenneth Armitage, Reg Butler and Lynn Chadwick, expanded their education beyond art schools by learning welding at classes run by British Oxygen for workers in the building trade (Garlake 2008: 51–62). However, skill in itself has ideologies within different artistic genres and different eras. The obvious hand-made qualities of products designed by William Morris were a subversive stance against capitalism, where the deskilling of workers in factories through mechanization was a key factor in production. Skill was used in modernist art not for displays of virtuosity, but as a means of linking maker to object and for critiquing material. However, more recently these skills have been subdued by a desire to move beyond the studio to situations and discourses not traditionally associated with art. Much contemporary art is suspicious of objects and self expression, with the practice of art operating across formal, cultural and spatial boundaries. With the artist frequently acting as entrepreneur, artistic skill is demonstrated through conceptual acuity (Roberts 2007: 3 and 11).

With the return of Cragg and other British sculptors to a real engagement with material in order to create objects – even if this does call on the skills of others – craft, with a small c, becomes implicated in the making of meaning. As Grayson Perry has stated, the ceramic pots that he makes represent a stand against so much contemporary art, which is not sensuous. Rather than the object being a prop for an idea; 'the hand made object speaks the language of the body, and if we only engage with our heads then we are denying a huge part of the vocabulary' (Buck 2002: 100).

During the 1970s and 1980s there was also a rift in craft between those with traditional artisan skills and those who have been through higher education. This came to a head in 1982, when Michael Brennand-Wood both exhibited in and curated a Crafts Council touring exhibition entitled *Fabric and Form: New Textile Art from Britain*. In the November/December issue of *Crafts* this exhibition was reviewed, with Peter Fuller arguing that the exhibition was an example of 'the decadence of Council subsidized fashions' (Fuller 1982: 43–44), which he felt had already played havoc with the nation's painting and sculpture. He felt that this sort of work represented the breakdown of textile practice and of the special skills and knowledge associated with it. Michael Brennand-Wood's reply was that skill and tradition had not been forgotten, but now textiles no longer needed to be linked to function, to be tasteful, soft or flexible (Brennand-Wood 1982: 44–45).

A similar argument was considered in 1991 by the ceramicist Alison Britton, who in answer to a call by Peter Dormer and David Pye for recognition of the value of traditional skills and forms, also said that crafts could not be nostalgic. She argued that while technical skills formed a basis, the most important thing was going beyond those and making something appropriate for the contemporary world. 'What I would define as our main responsibility is the skilful achievement of relevance' (Britton 1991). Her sculptural vessels of the time were hand built, which allowed her to combine asymmetrical elements and create unusual surfaces and through those means, to reference and articulate particular ideas.

Vessel

In a recent discussion with Edward Allington (June 2009), who is a sculptor of the same generation as Cragg and the New British Sculptors, and who has also made many metaphorical vessels, he claimed that the rich use of the vessel form from the 1980s onwards in sculpture owes much to ceramics and dates back to the artists' student days. Allington started his career as a ceramicist. Deacon is married to Jacqueline Poncelet, who was a ceramicist. Cragg has known a number of ceramicists since being a student. Gormley, Cragg and Kapoor have all spent time at the EKWC, and since 1999 Deacon has spent much time working with the ceramicist Niels Dietrich in Cologne (Kolberg 2003: 14).

Although Cragg, like the sculptors Alison Wilding and Richard Deacon and the ceramicists Alison Britton and Elizabeth Fritsch, studied at the RCA during the 1970s, where the separate courses were taught within small independent departmental units, the students from across the disciplines did meet (Frayling 1987: 144). The Royal College of Art opened its doors to 'aspiring artists, designers, studio potters and sculptors using ceramic materials' in the 1960s, and when there was increased disenchantment with design during the 1970s, many of these ceramic students opted for what has been called a 'para-art activity' (Harrod 1999: 371). Although the structures of galleries, journals and museums have tended to keep the consumption of craft and sculpture separate, certain ideas are relevant at particular times. One of these is the vessel and its metaphorical richness. The ceramicist Edmund de Waal has written that:

> Clay vessels are among the earliest known objects made by humans. Actual containers of food, water, wood or ashes, the mundane and the precious, they have also always been on the threshold of symbolic activities and rituals. They have been used to tell stories and express poetry [...]. Historically and culturally resonant, they are as full of possibilities as ever. (de Waal 1999: 74)

Beyond these metaphors, vessels are also rich in the ability to suggest the experience of the world. The metalworker Michael Rowe, for instance, has discussed vessels as fundamental to human existence and, reflecting his interest in architecture, his vessels respond to some of these concerns. 'We live and move in a world of containers, we put things into containers, we contain things and we ourselves are contained [...] forms within forms' (Bond 1973: 22). In addition they are containers that have an inside and outside, that both occupies and contains space, and through this defines emptiness as presence (Daintry 2007: 9). It is all of these aspects that give the form such enduring resonance. Through considering any of these aspects both sculptors and crafts practitioners are linking their practice to the roots of humanity. It is here that sculptural practice and that of crafts come very close.

This interest in using the vessel form as a means of expression, to create something to look at and that was relevant to the contemporary world as well as reaching back through time, was a common thread in all of the work shown at the 1991 exhibition of ceramicists *The Sculptural Vessel* (Houston: 1991). In this they were similar to the intentions of Cragg at the time. In his essay for the exhibition catalogue, John Houston argued that the role of the vessel in crafts in the post-industrial era is complex as it is a fundamental, timeless and archetypal prop of civilization, and yet its preciousness has been debased through mechanization. In order to give it new meaning, contemporary ceramicists had looked beyond craft traditions to ideas related to architecture, sculpture and painting (Houston 1991: 12). Like the metal vessels of Michael Rowe, for instance, many ceramicists at that time were considering ideas related to deconstructivism, with fractured elements and complex relationships of interior space to exterior form. These aspects were conscious disruptions of the single gesture, raised pot, and their built forms not only created those that were unfamiliar, but also removed the possibility of function and the associated sense of everyday touch.

Cragg has stated that he does not like people to touch his work as he thinks that the eye can take in information at a distance, whereas touch obscures meaning (Schulz-Hoffmann 2003: 296). Clearly touch and sight are very different senses, with touch, both for the maker and user, being related to particular objects, and sight having the ability to give an overview and context. However, bread and vessels, which are implicated in *Laibe,* are the most tactile of human objects. While objects are in themselves instrumental in the formation of consciousness, having the ability to give a sense of separation from the world, they also stimulate remembering (Kwint et al. 1999: 2). The deep knowledge of the feel of ceramics that all humans have; the ability to empathetically trace the makers' finger marks on the surface, together with the long history of cultural resonances, give the material a special place in understanding. Bread, which everyone has eaten, is handled and crumbled in the hands, accompanies meals, and gives sustenance. As Cragg has stated, each material has specific qualities which provides a rich vocabulary in the language of objects

(Cragg 1985: 60). The simultaneous incorporation of subject and metaphor with material increases the suggestive possibilities. These are the means that Cragg uses to re-engage the audience with their man-made environment, a relationship that he believes has been lost in the post industrial world with the emphasis on image and desire.

Other artists working in ceramics, like Grayson Perry, use the proliferation of imagery as a source, and subvert the decadence portrayed through using the vessel form. The very unassuming nature of the vessel, with pretty shiny glazes and colours attracts the viewer into looking, while the imagery repels. Unlike Cragg, it is not the timelessness of the vessel or the material itself that attracts, but the surface available on the apparently docile domestic object that provides a vehicle for illustrating the underside of contemporary life. However, for Cragg, as well as Wilding, Kapoor and Deacon, it is the material, process, and form that help to suggest metaphor.

Cragg frequently creates a tension between the past and present within his work. For many craft makers, this is frequently revealed through the vessel form, and through surface and material, but for sculptors this can cover many areas of practice. Richard Long, for instance, has used the artistic walk as a means of exploring apparently unmediated terrain, in a way that suggests both early man and contemporary mapping. He is only one of many who have explored this type of practice. (Tony Cragg went on an artistic walk along Hadrian's Wall with Hamish Fulton, Richard Long and the ceramicist Jenny Beavan in the 1970s (Beavan interview, April 2006). However, the use of the vessel form gives this suggestion of past and present particular resonances. Much of what we understand about previous cultures comes from shards of vessels that offer glimpses into preparing foods and performing rituals. Clearly archaeology, craft, and art are not the same things. An exhibition in 1991 entitled *From Art to Archaeology*, which featured the work of Richard Long amongst others, discussed those differences. Archaeology is the study of past human experience that is understood through digging up cultural artefacts that have been accreted through layers of the earth. Art does not search for that scientific understanding – although Cragg does frequently include references to scientific study – but where the two disciplines meet is where a pattern has been spotted and corresponds to what touched the creator (Chippendale 1991: 40 and 43). These aspects have been fundamental both within craft and art ceramics.

With the return of Cragg to studio based work in the early 1990s, when he was experimenting with clay; ideas around humanness, archaeology, and ritual were being explored within different areas of the fine arts. In addition, studio ceramics were frequently using the vessel as an initiating point to develop new forms and sculptural ideas. *Laibe*, with its rich possibilities of interpretation that incorporates the past in the present and the universal aspects of human survival within the ceramic vessel form, lies at the heart of these complex and overlapping areas of practice.

References

Bond, D'E. (1973), 'Michael Rowe', *Crafts*, March, pp. 22–25.

Boot, M. (ed.) (2002), *Grayson Perry, Guerrilla Tactics,* Amsterdam: NAi Uitgevers.

Brennand-Wood, M. (1982), 'Reply to Peter Fuller', *Crafts*, November/December, pp. 44–45.

Britton, A. (1991), 'The manipulation of skill on the outer limits of function', in C. Frayling (ed.), *Beyond the Dovetail. Craft, Skill and Imagination,* London: Crafts Council.

Bryson, N. (1990), *Looking at the Overlooked. Four Essays on Still Life Painting,* London: Reaction Books.

Buck, L. (2002), 'The Personal Pots of Grayson Perry', in M. Boot (ed.), *Grayson Perry. Guerrilla Tactics*, Rotterdam: NAi Uitgevers, pp. 92–101.

Chippendale, C. (1991), 'From Art to Archaeology: From Archaeology to Art', in *From Art to Archaeology*, London: The South Bank Centre.

Cragg, T. (1993), *Tony Cragg. In Camera*, 's-Hertogenbosch: European Ceramic Work Centre.

Cragg, T. ([1985] 1998), 'Preconditions' , in H. Freidel (ed.), Anthony Cragg. Material_Object_Form, Munich: Cantz Verlag, pp. 58–61.

Cragg, T. ([1988] 1998), 'Vantage Point', in H. Freidel (ed.), *Anthony Cragg. Material_Object_Form*, Munich: Cantz Verlag, pp. 62–64.

Cragg, T. ([1992] 1998), 'Talking to Andrew Naime', in H. Freidel (ed.), *Anthony Cragg. Material_Object_Form*, Munich: Cantz Verlag, pp. 72–73.

Cragg, T. (2003), 'Tony Cragg talks to Barry Schwabsky', *Artforum*, April, pp. 200–1, 253.

Daintry, N. (2007), 'The Essential Vessel', in *Breaking the Mould. New Approaches to Ceramics*, London: Black Dog Publishing, pp. 6–15.

de Waal, E. (1999), *Design Sourcebook. Ceramics*, London: New Holland.

Daintry, N. (2004), 'High Unseriousness. Artists and Clay', in S. Groom (ed.) *A Secret History of Clay. From Gauguin to Gormley*, London: Tate Publishing, pp. 37–54.

Deacon, R. (2003), *AC: Richard Deacon. Made in Cologne*, Cologne: Walter Konig.

Elliott, D. (ed.) (1993), *The Raw and Cooked. New Work in Clay in Britain*, London: Crafts Council and Oxford: MOMA.

Frayling, C. (1987), *The Royal College of Art. 150 Years of Art and Design*, London: Barrie and Jenkins.

Frayling, C. (ed.) (1991), *Beyond the Dovetail. Craft, Skill and Imagination*, London: Crafts Council.

Fuller, P. (1982), 'Review of Fabric and Form', *Crafts*, November/December, pp. 43–44.

Garlake, M. (2008), 'Materials, Methods and Modernism: British Sculpture c. 1950', *Sculpture Journal*, 17:2, pp. 51–62.

Geitner, A. (2002), *Slip. Artists in the Netherlands and Britain working with Ceramic*, Haarlem and Norwich: Sainsbury Centre for Visual Arts.

Gormley, A. (2004), 'Antony Gormley. In conversation with James Putnam', in S. Groom (ed.), *A Secret History of Clay. From Gauguin to Gormley*, London: Tate Publishing, pp. 82–85.

Groom, S. (2004), 'Terra Incognita', in S. Groom (ed.), *A Secret History of Clay. From Gauguin to Gormley*, London: Tate Publishing, pp. 13–23.

Groom, S. (ed.) (2004), *A Secret History of Clay: From Gauguin to Gormley*, London: Tate Publishing.

Harrod, T. (1999), *The Crafts in Britain in the 20th Century*, New Haven and London: Yale University Press.

Harrod, T. (2004), '"Hidden Depths", A Secret History of Clay', *Crafts*, May/June, pp. 28–33.

Houston, J. (1991), *The Abstract Vessel. Ceramics in Studio*, London: Bellew Publishing.

Jameson, F. (1990), *Signatures of the Visible*, New York: Routledge.

Kolberg, G. (2003), 'Like You Know. Richard Deacon's Ceramic Sculpture', in R. Deacon (ed.), *A C: Richard Deacon. Made in Cologne*, Cologne: Walter König.

Koplos, J. (1998), *The Unexpected. Artists' Ceramics of the 20th Century*, 's-Hertogenbosch: Kruithuis Museum of Contemporary Art.

Kwint, M., Breward, C. and Aynsley, J. (eds.) (1999), *Material Memories*, Oxford and New York: Berg.

Lucie-Smith, E. (2004), 'From Gauguin to Gormley', *Ceramic Review*, September/October, pp. 32–35.

Margetts, M. (1993), 'Metamorphosis: The Culture of Ceramics', in D. Elliott (ed.), *The Raw and Cooked. New Work in Clay in Britain*, London: Crafts Council and Oxford: MOMA, pp. 13–15.

McEvilley, T. (2003), 'Tony Cragg: Landscape Artist', in T. Cragg, *Tony Cragg. Signs of Life*, Düsseldorf: Richter Verlag, pp. 166–173.

O.R. (2004), 'A Secret History of Clay – Preview', *Ceramic Review*, May/June, p. 17.

Paz, O. (1974), *In Praise of Hands. Contemporary Crafts of the World*, Greenwich Connecticut: New York Graphic Society.

Pye, D. (1968), *The Nature and Art of Workmanship*, Cambridge: Cambridge University Press.

Reijnders, A. (2005), *The Ceramic Process. A Manual and Source Book of Inspiration of Ceramic Art and Design*, London: A&C Black, and Philadelphia: University of Pennsylvania Press.

Roberts, J. (2007), *The Intangibilities of Form. Skill and Deskilling in Art after the Readymade*, London and New York: Verso.

Schulz-Hoffmann, C. (2003), 'I don't particularly like it when someone touches my works. Reflections on Tony Cragg's philosophy of sculpture', in T. Cragg, *Tony Cragg. Signs of Life*, Düsseldorf: Richter Verlag, pp. 296–300.

Discussion with Edward Allington, June 2009.

Interview with Jenny Beavan, April 2006.

Published originally in the *Journal of Visual Art Practice*, 2009, 8 (3), pp. 215–228.

SECTION TWO
CERAMICS IN CONTEXT

Section introduction

This section covers much ground with regard to presenting a context for ceramics. While the main focus of the book is based upon studio ceramics and consequential developments, some key historical markers have been included as useful guidance to develop a narrative in relation to the context. There are of course many texts that we were unable to include here that align to those in this section and we hope they will help expand reading with regard to developing a contextual history of ceramics. We begin with Herbert Read's views on decoration with regard to Wedgwood and industrial ceramics. It seems appropriate to include Wedgwood within this contextual framework as studio ceramics fundamentally developed as an antithesis to industrial production, an area explored in greater depth by Glenn Adamson in *The Invention of Craft*. Moving forward, Emmanuel Cooper's text expounds on the move to the hand made within a wider global context and offers the reader a viewpoint of ceramics from various countries.

When surveying studio ceramics Bernard Leach features prominently. He is included in several texts within this book and these intentionally offer varied perspectives with regard to his philosophies and position within the canon.

Sculptural ceramics could be considered as a development in opposition to Leach and a closer alignment with fine art, this is explored through a number of texts that draw on both historical viewpoints and observations constructed at the time of these new developments in ceramics. Seminal texts by Rose Slivka and Martina Margetts offer reflections on the shift in ceramics towards more sculptural applications. The move away from the plinth that accompanied the sculptural arena within ceramics, consequentially encouraged installation-based practice within the field, one that is often evidenced through the presentation of multiple object, alternative spaces for exhibition and site-specific interpretation. Three texts are included here as a means to explore this area within ceramics. Readers might find it useful to explore Claire Bishop's writing on installation within art practice to offer further contextualization.

Theoretical writing with regard to ceramics has developed exponentially within the last thirty years and a deeper critical voice has emerged as can be evidenced in the selected essays in this section, this is supported by Garth Clark in his new text for this reader, which provides a historical narrative with regard to writing in the field. The development of theory and critique has afforded a wider contextualization of ceramic practice, which in turn has offered a much-needed critical position for work that resides within the 'expanded field'.

As lines between fine art and craft became blurred and discussion as to whether the field has become 'expanded' or even 'collapsed', the final heading within this section explores conceptual approaches to ceramics and the more recent phenomena of 'post studio' practice.

Livingstone and Petrie

SECTION 2.1
HISTORICAL PRECEDENTS

Introductory summary

The first text in this section considers the function of decoration and one of the key historical figures in ceramics, Josiah Wedgwood – the eighteenth-century industrialist. Herbert Read begins with an observation to the effect that mankind holds an aversion and is intolerant to empty spaces. This is most notable with reference to 'savage' races and within decadent periods within history. He goes on to discuss Wedgwood and the development of ceramics from the start of the industrial age where the manufactured ceramic ware is presented as an exemplar of the successful use of decoration with regard to function.

Emmanuel Cooper offers a history of the Arts and Crafts Movement and while this text is long, it does cover a lot of international ground and is clear and precise. Its focus on the Arts and Crafts movement is important in terms of helping the understanding of the development of ceramics, not least in respect of the employment of handicraft tradition at the time of increasing mechanization and mass production. This text serves as a grounding and introduction to the development of studio practice covered later in this section.

Brent Johnson gives an intriguing insight to the dialogues about standards in the mid-twentieth century with his description of a debate between Bernard Leach (1887–1979), known as the 'father of British studio pottery' and Marguerite Wildenhain (1896–1985), a Bauhaus-trained potter born in France who emigrated to the United States in 1940. Leach visited the United States in 1950 and criticized American pottery for its poor quality. His position was that pottery should integrate western and eastern craft traditions and that America lacked a central tradition or 'taproot' to build upon. Wildenhain objected to this in an open letter and argued that America could draw on many influences, which was a strength and not a disadvantage. This text also offers a glimpse into the professional lives of these keys players in ceramic history as their fame was developing and demonstrates the growing level of debate which was emerging around 'humble' pottery at the time. Lucy Rie and Hans Coper were also key figures in twentieth-century ceramics and in the following text, Lesley Jackson sets their work in context alongside European design and fine art; in particular the 'contemporary' style of the 1950s.

Livingstone and Petrie

11
THE FUNCTION OF DECORATION: WEDGWOOD

Herbert Read

Before passing on to the possibilities of compensatory qualities in machine art I would like to refer to the function of decoration.

Again there is some confusion of terminology. A form in itself may be 'decorative', but that usually implies the relation of an object to its setting. We decorate a room when we paint the woodwork and paper the walls, but that sense merely implies that we give it color. When we decorate a work of art, an *objet d'art,* as it is then usually called, we add to its form an extra thing which is known as ornament. Ornament can be added to almost any work of art – we add carved capitals and friezes to architecture, color and pictures to pottery; even the cabinet picture is not complete without its ornamental frame. All such ornament is *applied* to the work of art, and this is where the word *applied* has its original and proper sense. But by one of those monstrous misapplications of words which can confuse thought for centuries, the epithet was taken from ornament and given to art. Applied ornament became applied art, and all the commissions of inquiry, all the museums and schools of art in the country, have labored under this confusion for a century or more. The necessity of ornament is psychological. There exists in man a certain feeling which has been called *horror vacui,* an incapacity to tolerate an empty space. This feeling is strongest in certain savage races, and in decadent periods of civilization. It may be an ineradicable feeling; it is probably the same instinct that causes certain people to scribble on lavatory walls, others to scribble on their blotting pads. A plain empty surface seems an irresistible attraction to the most controlled of men; it is the delight of all uncontrolled children. While I think that a little discipline would be a very good thing, I by no means wish to urge the total suppression of the instinct to fill blank spaces. I deal with the question more fully in Part 3. At present, all I wish to insist on is that the instinct is not essentially aesthetic. All ornament should be treated as suspect. I feel that a really civilized person would as soon tattoo his body as cover the form of a good work of art with meaningless ornament. The only real justification for ornament is that it should in some way emphasize form. I avoid the customary word 'enhance', because if form is adequate, it cannot be enhanced. Legitimate ornament I conceive as something like mascara and lipstick – something applied with discretion to make more precise the outlines of an already existing beauty.

Since both our educationists and manufacturers have for so long been blind to the formal elements in art, they have tended to regard ornament as the only essential element, and their failure has been largely due to this misguided attempt to contort and twist and otherwise deform the naturally austere and precise forms of manufactured articles into the types of ornament they mistake for art.

Source: © Herbert Read/Faber and Faber. An extract from *Art and Industry.*

Wedgwood

It would help us at this point to consider two historical attempts to solve our problem. One comes right at the beginning of the industrial age, and is so interesting and instructive that it would merit a separate and exhaustive examination. All the problems that confront us now were obvious to Josiah Wedgwood, one of the greatest of industrial geniuses, a man who in his own lifetime converted a peasant craft into an industrial manufacture, a man who, in whatever sphere he had applied his gifts for organization and rationalization, would have effected a revolution. When the German poet and philosopher Novalis wanted an apt comparison to bring out the essential character of Goethe he thought of Wedgwood. Goethe, he said, is the completely practical poet. 'His works are like the Englishman's wares – extremely simple, neat, convenient, and durable. He has done for German literature what Wedgwood did for English art. He has, like the Englishman, by virtue of his intelligence, acquired a fine taste, which taste is economic in nature. Both men go together very well, and have a near affinity in the chemical sense.'

How illuminating this comparison is for our understanding of Goethe is beside the point, but it gives the real clue to an appreciation of Wedgwood's genius. His name has a quite peculiar significance, not only as a great potter, but also as a leading figure in the development of taste. It was largely due to Wedgwood's activities that the cult of a few dilettanti was taken up and propagated until it became the commercial aspect of that phase in the history of art known variously as the Classical Revival, Neoclassicism, the Empire Style.

Josiah Wedgwood was born at Burslem, in Staffordshire, about July 1, 1730. He belonged to a family which had followed the craft of pottery for many generations, but so far pottery had been little more than a peasant industry. The productions of the primitive kilns of Staffordshire, though possessing simplicity and vigor and a kind of native raciness – qualities which we have learned to respect – had no pretensions to dignity and conferred no prestige on their makers. But toward the end of the seventeenth century two Dutchmen, the brothers Elers, had introduced improved methods into Staffordshire, and their ideas had been taken up by a local potter, Thomas Whieldon. It was with Whieldon that Wedgwood eventually became associated. From Whieldon, whom he joined at Little Fenton in 1754, Wedgwood no doubt learned all that the local tradition of pottery could teach him, but at the end of his five years' agreement he returned to Burslem, determined to strike out on his own.

A potter, no less than a poet, is born, not made; but though Wedgwood could doubtless practice all the processes of his craft with ability and ease, it would be a mistake to consider him as anything in the nature of an inspired artist. Novalis's distinction implies that whereas taste can be formed by application and understanding, art is the product of inspiration or intuition. Wedgwood was primarily what we should now call a great rationalizer of industry; he was bent on eliminating waste, on improving processes, on creating a demand where it had not previously existed. Fine porcelain in his day was a rarity imported from China or the Continent, a luxury for the rich. Factories had sprung up in England (at Chelsea, Bow, etc.) to compete with these imported luxuries, but their existence was precarious and their products were regarded as inferior. Wedgwood's aim was not to compete with the foreign factories on their own ground, but to provide an alternative. In this he succeeded beyond his wildest dreams.

Merely as a technician Wedgwood deserves his fame. He built bigger and better kilns; he improved the wheel and introduced the turning lathe which enabled the potter to give finish and precision to his wares; he investigated and vastly improved the chemical constituents of clays and glazes; he discovered new types of wares, such as 'black basaltes' and 'jasper'; he invented the pyrometer for measuring the heat of the furnaces, thereby first making possible a perfect control of the firing. For this he was made a Fellow of the Royal Society. His practical activities extended beyond his own industry. He led his fellow industrialists in their demand for turnpike roads and canals. As his export trade grew he had to solve difficult problems of packing and transport. He had to arrange an elaborate system of travelers and agencies. At every turn his practical genius triumphed. When he died he was worth half a million pounds – the equivalent, in modern currency, of the fortunes of our great industrial magnates.

All that material grandeur would have passed away and left a name in nothing but the economic history of our country, had not Wedgwood had the wit to discover that 'art pays'. His intelligence was wide enough to admit a considerable respect for the humanities. While cultivating these interests during a convalescence, he fell in with the intellectual society led by Dr. Priestley. He formed a friendship with Thomas Bentley, a Liverpool merchant, described by Priestley as 'a man of excellent taste, improved understanding, and good disposition'. In Bentley, Wedgwood saw his ideal partner – the man who would bring culture into association with his industry and direct his energy into the channels of correct taste. The partnership, formally entered into in 1768, prospered exceedingly, and lasted until Bentley's death in 1780. The letters they exchanged during the period have been published, and are a complete revelation of Wedgwood's mentality, and of the spirit that was to carry through the Industrial Revolution.

Under Bentley's guidance Wedgwood was drawn into the circle of Sir William Hamilton, who was then publishing his illustrated portfolios of Greek and Etruscan antiquities. By his activities the British Minister at Naples had set a mode, and Wedgwood was quick to seize on its significance for him. Once before in the history of art, pottery had been the medium of a nation's highest artistic genius. A Grecian urn was a symbol for all the grace and serenity of the ancient world. Wedgwood determined that pottery should again rise to those heights. The best artists in the land, John Flaxman at their head, were commissioned to copy ancient prototypes or adapt them to modern uses. In a sense they succeeded all too well. A classical mode was imposed upon the whole of decorative art: it might be said that a style of architecture and furniture had to be invented to accommodate the imperious products of Wedgwood's activity. The movement conquered Europe, and dominated a generation. Today we can see that it was only a surface movement, like all culture determined by intelligence rather than sensibility. Wedgwood's ornamental wares have in their turn become antiquities, objects for the curious and the contented. His useful wares, in which his true genius was expressed, are still with us, for we can hardly eat from a plate or drink from a cup that does not bear the impress of his practical genius.

The fate of Wedgwood's pottery is thus very significant for our inquiry. The useful wares which have survived – not as 'works of art', but as the prototypes of the best useful wares still being made by Wedgwood's firm, and by countless imitators all over the world – these wares were the product of the local pottery tradition, selected and refined by the practical genius of Wedgwood, himself a trained potter. In *English Pottery,* a book by Mr. Bernard Rackham and myself, published in 1924, we observed of these useful wares that

> Wedgwood was the first potter to think out forms which should be thoroughly well suited to their purpose, and at the same time capable of duplication with precision in unlimited quantities for distribution on the vast scale now imposed by the great extension of trade which he helped so much to foster. … The shapes are, as a rule, thoroughly practical, and many, such as the round-bellied jug with short wide neck and curved lip, good for pouring and easy to keep clean, have remained standard shapes to the present day. Lids fit well, spouts do their work without spilling, bases give safety from over-turning; everywhere there is efficiency and economy of means.

In these words we defined a machine *art* in its first phase, and with all its essential features. We then went on to contrast the 'ornamental' wares designed for Wedgwood, not by practicing potters, but by independent artists (painters and sculptors) like Flaxman and Pacetti. After noting that such wares mark the beginning of a dualism in English pottery which until then had never existed, we observed:

> From the point of view of the potter it was a misfortune for Wedgwood that the pottery from which he chiefly drew his inspiration for his innovations – whatever virtues it may possess in exquisite beauty of draughtsmanship and gracefulness of shape – was not good pottery. In ceramic qualities, Greek vases of the 'best' period stand far behind the ancient wares of Egypt, Persia, and the Far East, and are inferior even to the unpretentious pottery made far and wide by aborigines in the provinces of the Roman Empire. Their shapes are copied from, or intended to emulate metal-work; nor do they depend for decoration on the plastic qualities of clay. All is left to the brush – never, it is true, more skilfully wielded by ceramic painters than by the best artists of Athens, to the enormous advantage of our studies of ancient Greek life and literature, but with great loss to the value of Greek vases as pottery. Nor was it by vases alone that the eager mind of Wedgwood was stimulated; he was no less interested in the statues, altars, sarcophagi, and reliefs in sculptured stone that the spade of the excavator and the burin of the engraver were bringing for the first time to the knowledge of the world at large.

The source of the dualism of the 'fine' and the utilitarian arts is therefore easy to trace in the limited sphere of pottery. For on the one hand we have the potter relying on his own knowledge of the craft and designing for use; on the other hand we have the potter relying for his design on the outside artist, who is not concerned to design for use so much as for ornament – as an exhibition, that is to say, of his artistic skill and 'taste'.

Extracted from Herbert Read (1961), *Art and Industry: The Principles of Industrial Design*, Horizon Press, New York, pp. 23–29.

Reproduced by permission of Faber and Faber.

12
THE ARTS AND CRAFTS MOVEMENT: GREAT BRITAIN, THE UNITED STATES, GERMANY AND AUSTRIA, SCANDINAVIA, THE NETHERLANDS, HUNGARY AND ITALY

Emmanuel Cooper

> Art made by the people, and for the people, as happiness to the maker and the user
>
> William Morris

As Britain entered the Victorian era the impact of the 'industrial revolution' was beginning to be felt throughout the land and concern was growing as to its social implications. Meanwhile a contest was brewing in the art world between the classicists and those in favour of a revival of Gothic styles in architecture and the decorative arts. Fervent advocacy of the Gothic on the part of such luminaries as Pugin, Ruskin and Morris, informed to a great extent by religious and moral considerations, was to give rise to a wider public debate on the perceived decline in overall aesthetic standards brought about by the mass-production of manufactured goods.

It was within this complex scenario that the Arts and Crafts movement emerged in England during the second half of the nineteenth century. Like so many others, this 'movement' gained its title in retrospect. At the time it centred largely around the far-reaching influence of William Morris's teachings and their manifestation in the form of attempts to revive or retain handicraft traditions in the face of increasing mechanization. The arts and crafts philosophy quickly found favour in Europe and by the turn of the century was being taken up with enthusiasm in the United States. In combination with rapid technological progress, it was to have a profound effect on the pottery industry worldwide.

As the efficiency of manufacturing processes increased, so too did the speed and technical reliability with which ever larger batches of wares could be produced, while economies of scale helped keep costs low and prices competitive. At the same time continual refinements were being made to decorating techniques, greatly expanding the scope for innovation and providing every opportunity for manufacturers to design ceramic products for the mass market that were both visually appealing and functional. Instead, some of the larger factories became preoccupied with creating excessively intricate pieces to show off their new capabilities. Reaction to such work was to contribute to an increasing focus on the concept of 'applied art' and the establishment of specialized art and craft schools intended to ensure that high artistic standards were applied to the design of manufactured goods.

In England one of the first men in public life to express concern over the perceived ill effects of industrialization on artistic and social values was the influential art critic and social reformer John Ruskin (1819-1900), who declared that mechanization was dehumanizing, debasing both the quality of life of the workman and craftsmanship itself. His championship of a craft rather than a machine aesthetic was eloquently

Source: British Museum Press/Reproduced with permission of Curtis Brown Group Ltd, London on behalf of The Beneficiaries of the Estate of Emmanuel Cooper. Copyright © Emmanuel Cooper 2010.

expressed in the second volume of *The Stones of Venice*, published in 1853, in which he argued that the Gothic style was superior to all others since it was the least mechanistic. A great many leading artists, architects, designers and writers of the Victorian era came to espouse Ruskin's views, notably William Morris. While still an undergraduate at Oxford, Morris was deeply affected by Ruskin's chapter 'On the Nature of the Gothic' and his commitment to the ideal of a just society in which hand-crafted work was valued for the creative effort invested in its making and the craftsman spiritually uplifted by his labours. Building on Ruskin's theories, he formulated strong views of his own which soon attracted a substantial following.

It was Morris's writings and example that formed the cornerstone of the Arts and Crafts movement, motivating a number of those working in architecture, handicrafts and both the fine and applied arts to join forces in order to promote simplified functional design, the natural use of local materials and the reinstatement of individual craftsmanship. The Arts and Crafts movement held much in common with the closely related Aesthetic movement, both faction being equally antagonistic towards the mechanical and unfeeling aspects of art in the industrial age. It did not, however, subscribe to the elitist and much-parodied doctrine of aestheticism that enshrined artists in an 'ivory tower' and advocated 'art for art's sake', a phrase coined to sum up the contention that art should be purely aesthetic and need serve no moral, religious or political purpose. One important belief that lay at the heart of both schools of thought was that art should encompass not only painting and sculpture but also everyday objects such as factory-produced flower vases, umbrella stands and tableware. This contributed to the development of a large market for 'aesthetic' objects, which prompted a number of ceramic manufacturers to set up special departments to design and produce art pottery.

As the Arts and Crafts movement spread further afield, a new mode of design and decoration began to emerge. Impressed by the detailed flora in paintings by the Pre-Raphaelites and their followers, and even more so by the distinctive plant and flower motifs that became the hallmark of William Morris's work, European artists and designers turned to nature for their own inspiration. In France this led to the appearance towards the end of the nineteenth century of art nouveau, an extravagantly flowing asymmetrical art style typically featuring sinuous trailing and climbing plants portrayed in an exotic manner. The style was also characterized by the use of coiled or meandering curvilinear ornament, either in abstract arrangements or in more representational plant form, as well as details such as billowing hair, rippling water and draped fabric. In pottery, as in other fields, the art nouveau style was eagerly adopted as a means of breaking away from the relentlessness of historical revivals and moving towards an entirely fresh outlook on product design. Shapes from nature became incorporated into stylized decorative patterns and a new feeling for colour arose – features that would continue to be evident in the designs of pottery manufactured during the twentieth century.

Quickly taken up on an international scale, art nouveau retained its French title in Britain and America while other countries adopted alternative terms in their own language. The London store of Liberty and Co. (originally an Anglo-Japanese warehouse, founded in 1875 as A&C) embraced the new style wholeheartedly. It was soon commissioning ranges of specially designed products and became so closely associated with art nouveau that in Italy the style came to be referred to as the *stile Liberty*. The term 'art nouveau' is taken from the Maison de l'Art Nouveau opened in Paris in 1395 by the collector, publisher, designer and art dealer Siegfried Bing. French art porters whose work was displayed and sold in Bing's showroom include Alexandre Bigot, Pierre-Adrien Dalpayrat, Edouard-Alexandre Dammouse, Auguste Delaherche, Clément Massier and Emile Müller.

Perhaps the major single influence on the European ceramics produced over the last few decades of the nineteenth century was that of Japanese stonewares and porcelains, particularly those associated with the tea ceremony. Following the re-establishment of trade with Japan in 1859 large quantities of Japanese artefacts were imported into Europe and many European artists and designers made visits to the East. The appearance of Japanese arts and crafts at the second of London's great international exhibitions in 1862 created an instant stir, and it was not long before fashionable ceramic pieces designed in the studios of British pottery factories began to follow a vogue for modified oriental styles. The equal impact made in France when Japanese wares were shown at the Paris exhibition of 1878 is reflected in certain aspects of the art nouveau style.

Artistic responses to the social and economic changes of the nineteenth and early twentieth centuries took many forms and varied from country to country. The following section looks at the work of notable ceramic designers, such as William de Morgan and the Martin brothers in Great Britain, George E. Ohr in the United States and the artist-potters in France. It also discusses the work of the art studios that were established by manufacturers to meet growing demand for affordable but well designed and made decorative pottery, and also the art potteries set up specifically to produce art wares.

Great Britain

In the nineteenth century rapid urban expansion, a substantial rise in population and the development of huge overseas markets greatly aided the growth of the British pottery industry, by then firmly centred around Stoke-on-Trent in Staffordshire. Not only did this area lead the world in both the quality and quantity of its ceramic products, but a series of significant technical improvements were made there. Keen to demonstrate the capabilities of its new techniques, the pottery industry deployed considerable ingenuity in creating complex and ostentatiously ornate objects that were frequently more spectacular than tasteful. Companies such as Minton and Worcester took great pride in displaying specially designed pieces at the 1851 Great Exhibition in London, but both the materialistic tone of this event and the poor design of many of the British exhibits drew severe criticism. The overall outcome was the dawning of an era in which good design began to be seen as essential to the success of mass-production.

William Morris (1834-96)

In addition to being a prolific poet and writer and an articulate social idealist, William Morris was a gifted designer and a versatile craftsman. He lectured and wrote extensively on art and craft, arguing that the two should not be separated, and both his writings and his output as a designer and artist-craftsman had far-reaching influence. In the ceramics field they provided the impetus for considerable innovation, by pottery manufacturers such as Doulton and Co. and the Martin brothers as well as by individuals such as Morris's good friend William de Morgan.

As the leading light of the Arts and Crafts movement, Morris was a strong supporter of manual as opposed to machine manufacture and frequently expressed concern over the division between maker and designer. Believing that hand-crafted items enriched the life of both those who created them and those who used them, he was in favour of a craft-based system akin to that of the medieval guilds and argued for the artisan again to be involved in all aspects of production. Morris was also a committed socialist whose ideals centred around an egalitarian desire for art for the common man, although this, like so many of his views, was perhaps informed as much by a deep personal abhorrence of the soul-destroying effects of industrialization and what he perceived as the ugliness of the modern world as by socialism as such.

He did, however, practise what he preached by personally mastering a range of different crafts (even turning his hand to clay modelling) and creating a craft co-operative to build and decorate his new home, the Red House. In 1861 this developed into the manufacturing and interior decorating business of Morris, Marshall, Faulkner & Co. (later Morris & Co.). Founding the enterprise as a company of 'fine art workmen',

Morris enlisted the collaboration of several members of his immediate circle, notably the architect Philip Webb as well as the painters Edward Burne-Jones, Dante Gabriel Rossetti and Ford Madox Brown. The Firm, as everyone involved referred to it, was to exert a fundamental and lasting influence on English interior design. It produced all manner of skilfully crafted hand-built furniture and furnishings for grand houses and churches, including metalwork, stained glass, tiles, fabrics, tapestries and wallpaper. Inevitably, hand-made work of such high quality proved expensive to produce and the enterprise did little to realize Morris's dream of art for the masses.

Inspired by Morris's theories on the vital link between art and craft, in 1884 a group of architects joined forces with decorators and craftsmen to form the Art Workers' Guild, making Morris an honorary member. This led, a few years later, to the formation of the Arts and Crafts Exhibition Society, the aim of which was to increase public awareness and appreciation of hand-making skills. Whilst initially sceptical about the scheme, over time Morris became so enthusiastic that he participated actively in the first exhibition in 1888 (by giving a demonstration of weaving) and took on the presidency of the society in 1891. The following year he was elected Master of the Art Workers' Guild, by then the nucleus of the Arts and Crafts movement.

William de Morgan (1839-1917)

Although William Morris's own work in the ceramics field was largely restricted to creating painted designs for earthenware tiles, his opinions on arts and crafts stimulated numerous potters to experiment and to hone their skills by making objects using traditional hand-making techniques. The potter most closely associated with the Arts and Crafts movement is William de Morgan, a friend of Burne-Jones and Rossetti and a practising devotee of the Pre-Raphaelite style. De Morgan met Morris in 1863 and was persuaded to give up his fine art training to design stained glass for 'the Firm'. He also designed tiles and painted furniture panels, but his personal interest drifted increasingly towards the finishing aspects of ceramics. In 1872, wishing to develop his own work and in particular to try out new glazes, he set up a kiln at his parents' house in Fitzroy Square, London. It was not long, however, before his experiments caused a fire that destroyed the roof of the property.

From then on de Morgan concentrated all his efforts on ceramics, making painted wares based on Turkish and Persian forms and working on ways of accurately reproducing traditional lustre decoration effects. Now living in Chelsea, he set up a showroom nearby and employed several decorators to carry out his designs. His early tile patterns include flowers, birds and animals, often painted in Persian colours on a cream or white ground.

The reputation of William de Morgan grew, and in the late 1870s the distinguished artist Frederic Leighton commissioned him to produce, and advise on the installation of, special patterned wall tiles for a grand Arab Hall he was adding to the Kensington house he had designed and built in 1866. De Morgan's task was to produce tiles that would match as closely as possible genuine Islamic ones that Leighton and his friends had found in Cairo, Damascus and Rhodes. The installation at Leighton House, now an art gallery and museum, reveals no obvious difference between the authentic tiles and those made by de Morgan.

In 1882 de Morgan transferred his business to Merton Abbey in Surrey, close to the new riverside works of Morris and Co., where he established a pottery and employed a thrower to make vase forms. In 1888 (now married to the artist Evelyn Pickering) de Morgan formed a partnership with the architect Halsey Ricardo (1854-1928) with a view to building a factory near his house in The Vale, Chelsea. In due course the business moved into the new Sands End Pottery in Fulham and together the two men began undertaking ambitious projects such as the innovative tiling that characterized Ricardo's buildings. In view of the complexity involved in translating de Morgan's often ornate designs from paper to ceramic, the pottery workshop had to be highly organized, with members of the skilled workforce allocated specific tasks and expected to carry out precise instructions.

Inspired to rediscover 'the lost Art of Moorish or Gubbio lustres' of the fourteenth and fifteenth centuries, de Morgan developed a range of rich lustre colours by employing traditional techniques, for example the use of thick clay pigment and a reduction, or smoky, firing. Much of his work was based on the use of copper and silver, the colours so produced including pink, yellow and grey. The lustre decoration was used to great effect on a limited range of shapes such as tile blanks and vessels, supplied by Wedgwood and other firms but mostly by Davis of Hanley in Staffordshire. Some of the larger shapes were specially thrown to de Morgan's design. His complex lustre effects were often achieved by the use of two or more lustres and the designs, mostly of excellent quality, include animals, fantastic beasts, ornate swirling foliage and ships. So successful were the lustre pieces that in the mid-1890s de Morgan was commissioned by the P&O shipping line to make tile panels for its luxury liners. He also created relief designs for moulded tiles and plates by Ricardo. On the socalled Persian wares he attained a palette of brilliant blues, turquoise, green and clear red, which he used to create flowing designs painted on to a white slip underneath a clear glaze. Much of his colourful decoration has a strong affinity with William Morris's wallpaper and fabric designs.

De Morgan's work was costly to produce, however, and despite its wide artistic acclaim his business was never profitable. Production at the Sands End Pottery continued under his direction until 1907, the pottery itself remaining in operation for four more years, but thereafter de Morgan abandoned ceramics altogether, devoting the last years of his life to the writing of novels.

The Martin brothers

The brothers Robert Wallace, Charles, Walter and Edwin Martin were the first group of English potters to develop a method of working similar to that used by most twentieth-century studio potters, encompassing all aspects of small-scale production. Their business was founded by Robert Wallace Martin (1843-1923), the eldest of the four brothers, who trained initially as a sculptor, principally under one of Pugin's chief assistants, and at that stage would have been influenced by the Gothic revival. In 1860, the year in which his brother Edwin was born, Wallace Martin became a student at the Lambeth School of Art. For a while, attending classes in the evening, by day he assisted the sculptor Alexander Munro, at whose studio he made his first terracottas. One of Wallace's fellow students at Lambeth was George Tinworth, who was later to be recruited into Henry Doulton's pioneering art pottery venture. From 1864 Wallace studied at the Royal Academy Schools and by the late 1860s he had set up his own terracotta workshop, the firing of his modelled sculptures being carried out at Doulton's salt-glaze factory. His production experience was gained by working at potteries in Devon and, for a brief period around 1871, Staffordshire; he also decorated pots fired at the famous Fulham Pottery originally established by John Dwight.

Together with three of his five brothers, Wallace Martin opened a studio at Pomona House, Fulham in 1873, the work they produced there being fired at local potteries. On the strength of the success of this enterprise, in 1877 the Martin brothers moved into a fully equipped workshop (which until then had been a derelict soap factory) at Southall in Middlesex, where they both made and fired saltglazed stoneware. Wallace was responsible for modelling the Martin brothers' strange and innovative 'Wally' birds, grotesque-featured face jugs and other sculpted items. The pottery produced owl-like vessels throughout the many years it was in production. The Martins' eccentric, medieval-style creatures conjure up a mysterious world combining aspects of both the real and the imaginary. The heads are removable from the body, and although not airtight the pieces may have been used as tobacco jars. Many of the face jugs are modelled in much the same spirit, with faces leering out of the side of the jugs.

The pots made at Southall were salt-glazed in subdued colours and the use of painted oxides gave dark blues and purplish and dark browns. As well as decorative vases and jugs with relief, incised or painted decoration, the objects produced include larger architectural pieces such as fireplace surrounds and fountains, as well as chess sets and some tableware. Firings took place twice a year until 1899, when this was reduced to a single annual firing. Within the enterprise Charles Martin (1846-1910) served as business manager and also handled sales at the pottery's showroom in Brownlow Street, Holborn. On the recommendation of George Tinworth, the two youngest brothers, Walter (1857-1912) and Edwin (1860-1915), had both studied at the Lambeth School of Art as well as working for a while at Doulton and Co. before they joined the family business, where both of them contributed to the throwing and decorating of the pots. Walter tended to look after technical aspects of the work such as the coloured glazes, also becoming the most expert at the wheel, while Edwin was responsible for many of the pottery's fish and flower designs.

Thrown ware, especially vases and jugs, made up the majority of the workshop's output, although also made were punch bowls, lamp bases, puzzle jugs, double-walled vases, and miniature tea and coffee services. Stylistically the wares fall into three more or less chronological phases. The first is characterized by classical influences, with decoration carved in deep relief together with incised patterns; this style continued until the early 1880s. In the middle period the predominance of Renaissance and Japanese styles is evident in the softer, more subtly conceived shapes. Although colours and decoration remained subdued, cobalt blue was painted on the grey stoneware body and a rich deep-brown glaze was often applied. The shapes subsequently became simpler and more rounded. Incised patterns were used sparingly and Renaissance designs featuring formally arranged foliage appeared. In the final period, from around 1895, flowing art nouveau lines are introduced, this later work demonstrating an effective integration of form and decoration. A wider range of colours and textured surfaces derived from plant forms and fish were used with considerable success.

When the youngest Martin brother, Edwin, died at the beginning of the First World War, only Robert Wallace Martin, now over seventy, remained. Production at Southall dwindled and finally ceased altogether after Wallace's death in 1923. Over the years a number of assistants had been employed at the Martin brothers' pottery works, but none became well known in their own right. Wallace's son Clement Wallace Martin, who had worked in the studio, continued to make similar wares until the 1930s. The workshop building was struck by lightning and destroyed in 1943.

Christopher Dresser

Although not himself a potter, Christopher Dresser (1834-1904) exerted a powerful influence on ceramics. Widely regarded as the father of industrial design, he worked in a vast range of materials and mediums, among them glass and metal as well as ceramics. He also wrote extensively and influentially on decorative design, notably in his books published in 1862 and 1873. In the 1860s and '70s Dresser worked as a freelance designer, undertaking varied work for a number of different manufacturers, including Minton and Wedgwood. His use of stylized plant motifs reflected his early study of botany, and a government-sponsored visit to Japan in 1876/7 led him to incorporate elements of Japanese design into his work.

In 1879 he set up the Linthorpe Art Pottery near Middlesbrough in association with the businessman John Harrison, and on Dresser's recommendation Henry Tooth, an artist with little knowledge of pottery, was appointed manager. During his three years as art director at Linthorpe, Dresser produced distinctive shapes that combined simplicity with grace. His work there can be divided roughly into two groups. The first consists of vessels carrying stylized animal and plant motifs while the second is made up of often extraordinary shapes derived from a variety of exotic sources, some contemporary, some ancient. A good example of the latter is his 'Peruvian pottery', based on the Pre-Columbian Peruvian bridge-spouted vessel. Most of Dresser's pots were highly glazed, the 'Linthorpe glaze' being characterized by speckled, richly flowing colours.

In 1882 Tooth left Linthorpe to establish the Bretby Art Pottery at Woodville in Derbyshire, in partnership with William Ault. Here umbrella stands, jardinières, vases and hanging pots were produced, as well as pieces resembling hammered copper, bronze and steel and carved bamboo. In 1887 Ault in turn moved on to set up his own enterprise in competition with Linthorpe, the Ault Pottery at Swadlincote, Derbyshire. On the closure of the Linthorpe Art Pottery in 1889, Ault acquired its moulds and continued to produce Dresser's designs – which has caused problems with the attribution of this work ever since.

Henry Doulton

Prominent among the ceramic manufacturers who put art and craft theories into practice is Henry Doulton, who pioneered art pottery by setting up a studio at his factory specifically for ceramic design and decoration. When he first joined the firm built up by his father, John Doulton, it was producing a range of stoneware vessels for domestic and industrial use, but by the mid-nineteenth century, largely as a result of Henry Doulton's own foresight and entrepreneurial flair, the business had greatly extended its product range and had become a major manufacturer of drainpipes and sanitarywares.

The Lambeth-based pottery of Doulton and Co. was thus already on a sound commercial footing when in 1854 the Lambeth School of Art opened nearby. Over the next few years Henry Doulton forged close links with the school, becoming increasingly enthusiastic about the new concept of applying art to industry. This encouraged the school's enterprising art master, John Sparkes, to propose the setting up of a scheme whereby his students could make use of Doulton's factory facilities and decorate pots made in its workshop. The plan proved so successful that in due course Doulton recruited many of the students who had taken part in the scheme and in 1866 his factory began producing art pottery on a commercial basis.

The young decorators employed in Doulton's art pottery studio in Lambeth worked on shapes specially made in the factory and their pots would be dotted among the sewage pipes to be fired in the large salt-glaze kilns. One of his most successful appointments was that of George Tinworth, who specialized in figural and sculptural pieces. Notable among the many women who were employed for their 'finger dexterity and deftness' was Hannah B. Barlow, who became known for her sensitive incised animal designs; her sister Florence and brother Arthur also worked as Doulton decorators. Towards the end of the century over 300 people were employed in Doulton's art studio. Some of the signed work by his protégés was shown in 1871 and 1872 at exhibitions in South Kensington, where it was greatly admired by Queen Victoria, among others. A Professor Archer of Edinburgh, in a review in the Art journal, was generous in his praise and pointed out that Doulton 'played no tricks with the clay by trying to make it do more than it was capable of doing well'.

In 1872 earthenware was introduced into the studio and experiments led to the making of 'faience' (this term covering any earthenware with relief modelling decorated with coloured glazes). Other products that began to be made include white Doulton stoneware resembling marble in appearance, sold around 1887-96 as Carrara. This was usually covered with a transparent matt glaze then painted with coloured enamels or given lustre decoration and gilded. The material could also be modelled in relief or pierced and was often decor ated with foliage designs or strapwork in dull red or sage green.

Production of art wares continued in a separate studio until the First World War. The experimentation with high-temperature glazes begun by Charles Noke and John Slater in the late 1890s was stepped up on the arrival of the ceramic chemist Cuthbert Bailey, who collaborated with Bernard Moore, an expert in the production of Chinese red glazes such as flambé and sang-de-bœuf.

Other British factories Producing Art Pottery

Doulton's example soon prompted other manufacturers to open art studios. In 1872/3 Minton Ltd established its Art Pottery Studio in London at Kensington Gore, fitting it with an unusual kiln claimed to have been designed to consume its own smoke. Pots made at Minton's factory in Staffordshire were brought to London to be decorated so that the artists, in their search for design inspiration, could make use of the South Kensington Museum and the horticultural gardens. Among a number of other experiments that also sought to relate the industrial production of pottery to the work of the artist, both Wedgwood and Worcester set up small art departments for the design and decoration of 'art pottery' that could be produced in their factories.

In 1891 the four Pilkington brothers set up a factory for the production of tiles at Clifton Junction, near Manchester, after suitable clay had been discovered there in the course of a search for coal seams. William Burton, formerly a chemist at Wedgwood, took technical and artistic control; later joined by his brother Joseph, he remained with the enterprise until his retirement in 1915. In addition to wall, floor and fireplace tiles, the factory manufactured a variety of small ceramic items and some decorated pieces; rich, ornate glazes played an important part in their production. In 1900 the Pilkington display at the Exposition Universelle in Paris included architectural earthenware tiles, pots, and a pair of lion figures, made from moulds by the sculptor and painter Alfred Stevens, that were covered with a brown crystalline glaze called Sunstone. Influenced considerably by oriental wares, other dramatic glazes were later developed: one had an opalescent effect, another resembled the skin of fruit, a number of pink and red flambé glazes produced a lustrous sheen, and the development of an iridescent lustre resulted in the production of lustre-painted ware. The company's art pottery studio, set up in 1903, employed the services of many gifted artists and designers of the time, including Gordon M. Forsyth, Walter Crane (the first president of the Arts and Crafts Exhibition Society), Lewis F. Day and Charles F. A. Voysey. The production of ornamental wares ceased in 1937, although tile manufacture continued until after the Second World War.

The Della Robbia Pottery in Birkenhead – which took its name from the Florentine family of sculptors famous for their terracottas of the Renaissance period – produced painted lead-glazed wares from 1894 to 1906. Much of the ware consisted of tiles for architectural use, but in addition relief-moulded hollowwares with bright green glazes were made, and the work was signed by the individual makers. The robustness of Della Robbia earthenware is in great contrast to the delicacy of the vessels produced by the Ruskin Pottery established by William Howson Taylor (1876-1935) at Smethwick, near Birmingham, where commercial production began in 1901. Specializing in decorative wares inspired by Chinese ceramics of the Song and Ming dynasties, Taylor developed a range of original coloured glazes with mottled, flambé, sang de-bœuf and lustre effects, mainly on a porcelain body. His special interest in glazes led to the creation of often spectacular tones. He created multi-layered surfaces of great depth and richness, also devising a range of lustre colours including yellow, orange and pearl. He tended to use simple shapes that reflected those of wares from the Far East. Like many of his contemporaries, Taylor jealously guarded his production methods and glaze ingredients. Shortly before his death he destroyed all his notebooks, with the result that his secrets were lost forever.

Also worthy of mention in connection with rich oriental glazes is the work of Bernard and Samuel Moore. Located at Longton, Stoke-on-Trent, the Moore brothers made a range of high-quality tablewares and ornamental pieces, as well as imitations of heavily gilded Chinese cloisonné enamel and reproductions of Japanese pottery. Burmantoft's, established in 1858 in Leeds and a branch of the Leeds Fireclay Company from

1889, produced wares ranging from umbrella holders and pedestals for plant pots to decorative panels for architectural purposes. The company's faience was made from a hard, buff-coloured earthenware body that took colour well. Production of Burmantoft's art pottery ceased in 1904 but the firm continued to manufacture glazed bricks and terracotta.

The West Country was home to a number of very different workshops. Watcombe TerraCotta Co., established in 1869 near Torquay, made use of a local deposit of red clay to produce fine art pottery characterized by decoration with enamel or turquoise glazes and intricate modelling. Much of the ware was produced by slip-casting into moulds and the range included tea services, plaques, figures and architectural ornament. In 1901 the pottery became part of the combined Royal Aller Vale and Watcombe Potteries and produced a variety of functional as well as ornamental wares. Production finally ceased in 1962. The Aller Vale Pottery, near Newton Abbot, had been set up in 1865 to manufacture a range of domestic earthenware products but later introduced architectural pieces, terracotta and slip-painted ware. After receiving the patronage of Queen Victoria's daughter Princess Louise, the firm traded as the Royal Aller Vale Pottery, selling its products through Liberty and Co. Thrown, moulded and slip-cast wares were made, some heavily decorated (by students from the local art school) with such motifs as seaweed, shells and flowers under glossy glazes. The Liberty catalogue for 1892 lists an extensive range of domestic and ornamental ware with decoration derived from lznik pottery.

At Barnstaple in north Devon, an area renowned for high-quality traditional pottery, Charles H. Brannam introduced Barum wares in his father's old country pottery workshop. Combining fashionable design elements with the characteristics of traditional Devon slipware, the thrown shapes were decorated with sgraffito or painted slips. However, the onset of the First World War forced the firm to abandon many of its earlier styles in favour of simpler wares with monochrome glazes.

In Somerset Sir Edmund Elton opened the Sunflower Pottery at his home at Clevedon in 1881, at first employing a flowerpot-maker to throw pots under his supervision before learning to carry out the work himself. Elton aimed for highly decorative effects. On forms that were modelled and irregular in form he created asymmetrical relief patterns of flowers and foliage, built up of coloured slips with sgraffito outline, which stood on a background of mottled shades of blue and green. In addition he produced pots with raised floral motifs in coloured slip set against streaky grounds, usually in blue, and most notable of all was his development of a range of metallic, crackled glaze effects. The Sunflower Pottery continued in operation until 1930.

United States of America

In the United States the term 'art pottery' is generally used to describe ceramics that were made with a consciously artistic intent during the period roughly from the time of the Philadelphia Centennial Exposition of 1876 until the beginning of the First World War. The making of pottery of this kind was one aspect of a more generalized artistic movement that arose around that time, partially in an attempt to establish a genuinely indigenous American style over a wide range of artistic mediums. Art pottery in the United States encompasses both ceramics made by artist-potters operating independently – for example, George E. Ohr and Adelaide Alsop Robineau – and the work of potters and decorators employed in highly organized factories, who typically worked on shapes specified by the factory and manufactured ranges of art wares for distinct markets.

An extraordinary variety of objects came to be produced in art potteries, some with meticulously painted decoration that was often naturalistic in style, others in which the effect relied largely on form and the quality of the glaze. Pots were made by throwing, by hand-building and by slip-casting and moulding. Although some enterprises such as the Grueby Pottery, were male-dominated, it was by no means unusual in American art potteries for the decorators to be mostly female, and several women founded successful businesses of their own – notably Maria Longworth Nichols and Mary Chase Perry Stratton.

The American Art Workers' Guild, established around 1885 in Providence, Rhode Island, influenced work in the United States for some thirty years. Also important was the establishment of arts and crafts exhibition societies and the publication of design periodicals such as *The House Beautiful*, *International Studio* and *Keramic Studio*.

The creation of art pottery in America started out principally as a leisure pursuit for upper-class ladies, among whom the activity soon became immensely popular – so much so that in many states the lady potters set up societies through which to exhibit and sell their work. When a china-painting class was begun by the Cincinnati School of Design, one of the first students, Mary Louise McLaughlin, grandly proclaimed that 'tidings of the veritable renaissance in England under the leadership of William Morris and his associates' had reached America. Another of the early students at the school was Maria Longworth Nichols, whose father was a patron of the Cincinnati Art Museum. Both women were later to be recognized as pioneers of American art pottery.

Maria Longworth Nichols and the Rookwood Pottery

Maria Longworth Nichols (1849-1932), the granddaughter of a real-estate millionaire, rented a small studio space at the Hamilton Road Pottery owned by Frederick Dallas, where, inspired by books of Japanese prints and by the French and Japanese pots she had seen at the 1876 exhibition in Philadelphia, she began researching into clay, bodies and glazes. Her early work included the development of high-fired 'granite ware' and the making of relief-decorated vases, often with designs featuring aquatic motifs.

Her fellow-potter McLaughlin, meanwhile, had formed an eleven-strong Pottery Club, which she had not actively encouraged Nichols to join. Feeling snubbed by this omission, Nichols decided to set up her own rival establishment where she and her circle could pursue their fashionable hobby of pottery decoration. For this purpose her father bought her a disused schoolhouse, which she named 'Rookwood' after the family estate.

Nichols soon became more ambitious, however, and in 1880 she put the Rookwood Pottery on to a commercial footing, expanding her repertoire of grotesque animals in the Japanese style and continuing to develop her own art pottery alongside the commercial production of items such as tableware, cooking pots and vases. She immediately took on Henry Farny, a well-known artist specializing in American-Indian themes, as a fulltime decorator. For a brief period she also employed Karl Langenbeck (1861-1938), a neighbour with whom she had collaborated early on when he received a set of china-painting colours from Germany and who was now a fully trained ceramic chemist. Another short-lived venture in the 1880s was the Rookwood School for Pottery Decoration, which had Clara C. Newton (1848-1936), a studio potter in her own right, as its secretary and instructor.

The workshop's products quickly won huge popularity and became widely imitated, and it was not long before the Rookwood Pottery was acknowledged as the leader of America's craft industry. As the Rookwood style gradually developed, the colours used in the work became more refined and the forms simpler, decorated with naturalistically rendered plants and animals. In 1883 the innovative use of an atomizer allowed the fine spraying of colours to be introduced, resulting in the development of Rookwood Standard ware whose subtle gradations of colour from dark brown to orange to yellow and green prompt the description 'Rembrandtesque' tones. Crystalline glazes were later used: Tiger Eye was noted for its 'strange luminosity' and its 'striations and sparkling particles of gold', while Goldstone gave the effect of 'glistening particles in adventurine, but rather more limpid'. (William Burton at Pilkington's Tile and Pottery Co. in England achieved similar effects.) Rookwood's matt glazes also became very popular, setting a trend that was followed by many other potteries.

Espousing a philosophy closely akin to that of William Morris in England, Nichols attempted initially to divorce herself from the 'factory system' by holding artistic integrity paramount and running her workshop along philanthropic lines. However, after the appointment in 1883 of a shrewd businessman, William Watts Taylor, as manager, the factory became highly organized, and despite its image as a paragon of arts and crafts ideals, the large demand for Rookwood wares led to the adoption of numerous labour-saving technical processes in the interest of low-cost mass-production. Nichols' aims had been to provide secure employment for talented artists and decorators while fostering originality, shunning duplication and encouraging individuality. In practice, the degree of artistic licence afforded to Rookwood decorators was considerably less than the pottery's prolific publicity would suggest; they are even said to have been fined for misnumbering vases, which were produced according to strict 'division of labour' principles.

After the death of her husband in 1885 and her subsequent marriage to lawyer and diplomat Bellamy Storer, Nichols became less and less involved with the pottery on a day-to-day basis. After travelling in Europe, in 1889 she settled in Washington, leaving the pottery under the total control of Taylor. In due course she transferred her interest in the business to him, but she retained a studio at Rookwood for her own use and there achieved lustrous copper-red glazes. Eventually she moved with her husband to Europe, where she lived for the remainder of her life.

Taylor ran the firm until his death in 1913. Under his management the company flourished and received many prestigious prizes, the first being the gold medal at the Exhibition of American Art Industry in Philadelphia in 1899. The following year its commercial future was assured when the Standard and Tiger Eye wares, displayed by an agent, were awarded the gold medal at the Exposition Universelle in Paris. So impressed were the judges by the artistic quality of the pieces that doubt was expressed as to whether they could in fact be reproduced; when further samples had to be brought over from America as proof, the favourable publicity that ensued was enough to seal Rookwood's high reputation. The Rookwood Pottery continued in production until 1967 and its ware are now much sought-after.

Mary Louise McLaughlin

Mary Louise McLaughlin (1847-1939) was strongly influenced by the display of Charles Haviland's work at the 1876 exposition in Philadelphia. She experimented with painting in slip onto the unfired clay, describing her work as Limoges faience. In 1879 she organized the Cincinnati Pottery Club 'to uphold the standard of good craftsmanship of the best workers in the different branches of pottery'. Ever inventive, McLaughlin not only devised a method of inlay decoration but also discovered the secrets of making high-fired porcelain. This was eventually used for pots, on which she carried out highly skilled decoration very much in the art nouveau style, successfully exhibiting her work at the World's Columbian Exposition in Chicago in 1893.

The Newcomb Pottery

The revolutionary notion that women could be trained in a skill that would enable them to make an honourable living was one of the essential tenets of the Arts and Crafts movement. It was also a primary motivation for the establishment in 1894 of the Newcomb Pottery in the American South, where men made the forms using local clay, while women carried out the decoration using mostly naturalistic designs based on local plants and vegetation.

The pottery was set up at the Sophie Newcomb Memorial College, the women's division of Tulane University, Louisiana, at the instigation of Ellsworth Woodward, a teacher of the decorative arts who was dedicated to the cause of vocational training for women, and his brother William. After a year of experimentation a formal programme of practical training was implemented, leading to an advanced qualification in art and design. One of the main aims of the pottery venture was to provide an outlet for work created by the college's art graduates.

The Newcomb Pottery adhered strictly to the principle of allowing total creative freedom in every aspect of production, even specifically forbidding duplication to ensure that each piece made was a unique and original hand-crafted item. Professional potters were brought in to work on hand-throwing, glazing and firing, as these were considered unsuitable tasks for the female students. Mary G. Sheerer taught underglaze slip decoration and china-painting as well as contributing to the development of a range of products including bowls, coffee sets, vases and table-lamp bases.

Gradually an identifiable Newcomb style developed that made sensitive use of painted decoration and matt glazes. In 1901 a new building – its architecture again true to the ideals of the Arts and Crafts movement – was constructed to house the college pottery and production was increased. Despite substantial demand for its output, the Newcomb Pottery, unlike Rookwood, never wavered in its pursuit of the arts and crafts ideal. It continued to receive financial support from the university and at no time operated on a commercial basis.

Zanesville, Ohio: 'Clay City'

Samuel A. Weller

Samuel A. Weller (1851-1925) established his first pottery in Fultonham, Ohio, producing red earthenware umbrella stands, jardinieres and flowerpots there, before moving to Zanesville. His factory achieved success by manufacturing wares based on Rookwood's while also developing highly individual pieces of its own, often in collaboration with well-known designers. In 1894 Weller acquired the Lonhuda Pottery, where he collaborated with W. A. Long to create the 'Louwelsa' range of slip-decorated vases; these featured patterns of fruit and flowers as well as portraits, often of American-Indians. This production continued until1948.

John B. Owen

The potter and tile manufacturer John B. Owen (1859-1934) moved to Zanesville in 1892, having formerly run his business from Roseville, Ohio since 1885. Employing Maria Longworth Nichols' former colleague Karl Langenbeck as chief chemist, Owen produced wares including teapots and jardinieres. W. A. Long became associated with Owen's pottery from 1896, developing the 'Utopian' range, which was painted with flower and animal designs as well as American-Indian portraits in slip against a dark background.

Roseville Pottery Co.

When Owen moved out of Roseville his premises were taken over by a new enterprise calling itself the Roseville Pottery Co. and making stoneware items for the home under the management of George F. Young; over time the business would be run by four generations of his family. The company later bought out another local pottery and a further two in Zanesville, which became its principal base in 1901 and its exclusive one from 1910. It was at this stage that Roseville began producing a range of art pottery known as Rozane, moulded from local clays, in an attempt to compete with Rookwood's Standard ware. Gradually the firm developed a more original style of its own that featured crystalline glazes. In 1904 Frederick Hurten Rhead (1880-1942) became art director, introducing the Della Robbia range. Under the direction of F. H. Rhead and later his brother H. G. Rhead, further Roseville lines were added, each being given a name indicating its artistic influence: Aztec, Donatello, Mostique, Pauleo. The Roseville Pottery was closed in 1954.

The English-born potter F. H. Rhead had moved to America in 1902, bringing with him a strong feel for modern design, and art nouveau in particular, that was to inspire designers in several factories. He worked for Samuel Weller before joining Roseville. Rhead wrote articles for *Keramic Studio* and in 1910 became an instructor at the University City School of Ceramics in Missouri, later setting up his own pottery in Santa Barbara. Much of his work was based on oriental wares and incorporated conventional modelled or applied decoration.

Other American Potteries

Almost as important as the work of the Rookwood Pottery was that of the brothers Alexander, Hugh Cornwall and George W. Robertson and their father, James. Based in Chelsea, outside Boston, the Robertsons produced undistinguished brown wares until1872 but from then on began to focus on making art pottery, calling their new enterprise the Chelsea Keramic Art Works. Much of their early work, made in fine red earthenware with minutely detailed decoration, was inspired by ancient Greek terracottas. Later, impressed like so many others by the French and oriental pots shown at the 1876 exhibition in Philadelphia, they went on to devise a range of slip-decorated wares and carried out experiments that led to the development of rich red glazes. However, the business was beset by failures and the family came near to bankruptcy.

In 1891 a new business was established on a more commercial basis under the control of Hugh Robertson. Known as the Chelsea Pottery US, its main product became an attractive 'Cracqule' ware, which was characterized by a grey crackle finish used to great effect on both ornamental and functional pieces. In 1895 the pottery moved to Dedham, where the Robertsons traded under the name of the Dedham Pottery; the workshops were closed down in 1943.

Closely associated with the Robertsons' work is that of John Low and the J. & J. G. Low Art Tile Works. The Lows, father and son, worked at the Chelsea Keramic Art Works before setting up their own tile factory in 1878, with George W. Robertson acting as their glaze technician. By 1882 the firm was also producing art pottery jugs and vases with modelled decoration. The potter William H. Grueby (1867-1925) was employed by the Lows for a time prior to setting up his own pottery; where he produced tiles and other architectural earthenware, basing some of his work on historical styles. On visiting the Chicago World's Fair in 1893, Grueby was greatly taken by the work of the French potters Auguste Delaherche and Ernest Chaplet. Their combination of strong form, innovative plant-like decoration and matt glazes prompted him to experiment with developing similar glazes himself. In addition to its existing wares, the Grueby Faience Company began producing ornamental vases, many decorated with vegetal forms in low relief; these were thrown by hand and the designs executed by women decorators following exact patterns. Conceived as a 'happy merger of mercantile principles and the high ideals of art', Grueby Faience came close to realizing many of the ideals of the Arts and Crafts movement.

The influence of art nouveau is much in evidence in the work of Artus Van Briggle (1869-1904) and Louis Comfort Tiffany (1848-1933). Briggle trained as a painter before acquiring pottery skills at Rookwood. His two years' study in Paris had introduced him not only to the latest styles of decoration but also to the oriental wares on display in the city's museums. Back in America he worked on developing matt glazes (attempting in particular to re-create those of the Chinese Ming dynasty) and modelled pots in which design and decoration merged, borrowing heavily from the fluidity of art nouveau. In 1899, suffering from tuberculosis, Briggle left Rookwood and moved to the healthier climate of Colorado Springs. Soon afterwards he set up his own art pottery there, where he designed and modelled vases and plates with relief decoration of plant forms and occasionally animals, achieving a close relationship between decoration and form that was enhanced by the use of monochrome matt glaze. Van Briggle's ceramics were made to a high technical standard and soon became highly acclaimed, but sadly he did not live to enjoy his success. His wife Anne carried on the business, however, and in 1908 she opened a new factory, which she named the Van Briggle Memorial Pottery.

Louis Comfort Tiffany (the son of Charles Lewis Tiffany, founder of the famous Tiffany & Co. jewellery concern) was a distinguished artist and designer in a number of different mediums. A committed devotee of the Arts and Crafts movement, he put the ideas of William Morris into practice in much of his work, as well as in the cooperative ethos of the interior decoration business he set up before developing a greater interest in art glassware. Unlike Morris, however, Tiffany did succeed in producing hand-crafted objects at a low enough price for them to become widely accessible. In Paris Tiffany had particularly admired the lustre pottery of Clément Massier as well as the more avant-garde work of Dalpayrat, Delaherche and Bigot. After buying lamp-bases from Grueby Faience, he began making his own ceramics and showed his first pieces in 1904. Using the same trade name as his glass, he marked his wares Favrille Pottery and offered them for sale in limited quantities at the new Tiffany & Co. building in New York. Some pieces were made on the wheel but most were slip-cast; the decoration consisted of abstracted designs of plants and flowers. To achieve a more natural appearance, for some items he cast moulds from natural plant specimens and hardened them with lacquer. Tiffany's rich and ornate glazes included matt, crystalline and iridescent types; the colours included a splodged green created to resemble moss and others ranging from light yellow to black, suggesting old ivory.

Art nouveau designs continued to influence numerous potters, although some workshops – for example the Clifton Art Pottery, established at Newark, New Jersey in 1905 – tried to evolve a style based on traditional American-Indian pots. Clifton Indian Ware included vases, jugs, mugs and ornamental and souvenir items. The Fuller Pottery, which operated from 1814 at Flemington, New Jersey, produced a range of art stoneware made from the local clay. The art products, including flower-holders in the form of animals, candleholders and clock cases, were fired alongside more commercial domestic wares.

One of the few individual potters to emerge at this time was George E. Ohr (1857-1918). Ohr first learned the craft from Joseph F. Meyer, a friend who later worked at the Newcomb Pottery. After a two-year tour of potteries all around America, Ohr settled in Biloxi, Mississippi, where he opened his own studio. He had an ability to throw extraordinarily thin forms, which he then glazed with unusual mottled, tortoiseshell and metallic glazes. In stark contrast to that of his contemporaries, Ohr's handling of clay was expressionist and gestural (his twisted shapes have often been described as 'tortured'), and as a result his work was little understood or appreciated at the time. He made thousands of pieces, of which no two were precisely the same, ranging from very small items to huge pots as tall as a man. Both Ohr's appearance and his almost surreal art could be said to have anticipated the later Salvador Dali. His unconventional hairstyle, outrageous whiskers and eccentric behaviour – including a tendency to proclaim himself 'the greatest art potter on Earth' – may have been calculated to draw attention to his work; not surprisingly, they earned him the tide 'The Mad Potter of Biloxi'. In 1909 Ohr closed his pottery down after hiding away his stock of pieces, aware, perhaps, that they were ahead of their time. For this reason his work remained largely unknown until 1972, when the cache was sold by his family through a dealer, so bringing a new audience to these exceptional and original ceramics.

Adelaide Alsop Robineau

The painter, potter and porcelain-maker Adelaide Alsop Robineau (1865-1929), a major pioneer of the American ceramic movement, began her career in china-painting before tackling the more exacting medium of porcelain. Although she operated on only a small scale, from a studio at her home in Syracuse, New York, Robineau became an influential potter, producing often highly ornate and superbly executed work. She was also instrumental in disseminating information on ceramic developments and techniques to the growing ranks of American art or studio potters. In 1899 Robineau ventured into publishing with *Keramic Studio*, a magazine aimed primarily at the amateur potter and china-painter, which she continued to edit until her death.

One of many articles Robineau published by the French potter Taxile Doat (who, like her, taught pottery at University City, Missouri) dealt with the making of porcelain and acted as a stimulus for her to extend her own skills. She began learning porcelain-making with Charles Binns, one of the leading teachers of the time, at Alfred University, where classes had been held since 1901. Robineau's pots were mostly decorated with incised and carved decoration enhanced by the jewel-like quality of the matt and crystalline glazes. Her greatest success was the award of the Grand Prize for fifty-five pieces shown at the International Exposition of Decorative Art in Turin, Italy in 1911.

Mary Chase Perry Stratton

Mary Chase Perry Stratton (1867-1961) was the founder of, and motivating force behind, the Pewabic Pottery in Detroit. Like so many of America's female art potters, Stratton first became involved in ceramics through the women's chinapainting movement. Keen to work with clay, she established a studio and workshop in which to experiment with clay bodies and glazes, and in due course this evolved into a full-scale pottery works. The early production of her Pewabic Pottery included vases, teapots, mugs, candlesticks, tiles and lamp bases. Many of the shapes were based on oriental forms and all were hand-thrown then covered with a gloss, matt, lustre, iridescent or flow glaze. Pewabic tiles became the pottery's main product line and numerous commissions for these were received from architects, principally for use in churches and public buildings. In 1966 the pottery was gifted to Michigan State University and in 1981 its long-term preservation was assured when it was taken over by the Pewabic Society.

France

Forming part of wider revival in the visual arts, the studio pottery movement that arose in France in the second half of the nineteenth century was inspired to a large extent by oriental high-fired wares and Middle Eastern earthenwares. Many ceramic artists worked in or in conjunction with factories, while others set up their own individual studios.

Joseph-Théodore Deck (1823-91) was one of the first French potters to create objects in clay that were intended as individual works of art in their own right. Trained as a chemist and sculptor, Deck worked initially in pottery stove factories before settling in Paris and opening his own atelier there in 1856. His early products include Renaissancestyle historicist wares. In common with de Morgan in Britain, Deck was inspired by lznik and Persian pots and lustrewares and based much of his work on them, producing ceramics with floral decoration in turquoise and blue with touches of red and green. Not only is his work of a high technical standard, it is also artistically inventive, the pigments smooth and rich.

Deck's later output was influenced by the imported Japanese stonewares shown at the Paris exhibition of 1878, which stimulated him to make pots fired in the reduction kiln. He achieved some of the first flambé glazes of the period, as well as celadons, which he used over incised decoration; these pieces were first exhibited in 1884. Chinese bronzes constituted a further source of inspiration. In 1887 Deck's book *La Faience* was published and in 1888 he was appointed art director of the Sèvres factory, where he made improvements to the softpaste porcelain and developed a stoneware body for the manufacture of vases, sculpture and garden ornaments.

Originally a lithographer and etcher and sub-sequently a painter (but outshone in this medium by his wife Marie), Félix Bracquemond (1833-1914) not only became involved in ceramic decoration himself (designing large plates that were produced in earthenware by Joseph-Théodore Deck), but actively encouraged other artists to work in the medium. In 1871 he accepted the position of art director at Sèvres, but he stayed there for only a short time before leaving to take up a similar post with the Haviland company. Here he employed the services of such artists as E.-A. and A.-L. Dammouse and Ernest Chaplet. Bracquemond's own designs in earthenware and porcelain were influenced by both Japanese and French Impressionist works.

The New York-born porcelain manufacturer Charles Haviland (1839-1921) established the family business of Haviland & Cie in Limoges in 1864 in collaboration with his father, David, and his brother Théodore. The company produced wares decorated with lines and dabs and featuring small bouquets of lilies-of-the-valley and moss roses. Haviland subsequently settled in Paris, in 1873 opening an experimental studio in Auteuil which Bracquemond directed. In 1881 Haviland himself took over as director, at the same time setting up a further studio in Paris; here Ernest Chaplet worked on developing brown stoneware and later porcelain, too, was produced. The company was dissolved in 1891 and Charles Haviland and his eldest son, Georges, set up a new firm called Haviland and Co.

Some potters responded more freely than others to oriental influences and to the artistic revival of the 1870s by indulging in experimentation and improvisation. Ernest Chaplet (1835-1909) was one of the important early pioneers. For a time he worked at factories such as Sèvres (his home town) and the Laurin firm, making painted earthenwares. In 1875 Chaplet joined the Haviland studio at Auteuil, benefiting from Bracquemond's policy of engaging designers who were already working in impressionist and Japanese-inspired styles. In 1881, influenced in equal measure by the traditional brown stoneware of Normandy and by oriental wares, Chaplet began to produce stoneware in simple forms ornamented with Japanese-derived designs in low relief and coated with rich deep glazes. He later reproduced the classic Chinese sang-de-bœuf glaze. In 1887 he set up his own workshop at Choisy-le-Roi, where he produced more austere forms and developed further decorative glazes. Chaplet was a major influence on numerous contemporary potters, including Albert Dammouse, Adrien Dalpayat and his son-in-law Emile Lenoble, all of whom contributed to the remarkable blossoming of studio ceramics in France.

The French artist-potter Taxile Doat (1851-1939) specialized in the pâte-sur-pâte technique, which consists of building up a raised surface by successive applications of liquid slip, and also produced gourd-shaped vessels, often covered with a crystalline glaze. In 1877 he joined the Sèvres factory, remaining there until 1909, when he travelled to America and helped to establish the University City Pottery at St Louis, Missouri. During the 1890s Doat had installed a kiln at his own home, where he developed flambé, crystalline and metallic glazes. His study *Grand Feu Ceramics: A Practical Treatise on the Making of Fine Porcelain and Grès* was published in the United States by Samuel Robineau. Doat's ceramics exerted a great influence on American ceramists such as Adelaide Alsop Robineau, who published fourteen of his articles in *Keramic Studio*; his articles were also published in other art and craft magazines, including *Art et Decoration*. Doat returned to Sèvres in 1915.

Over the period from 1891 to 1916 radical changes were made to production at Sèvres under the direction of Emile Baumgart and Alexandre Sandler. Experiments with crystalline glazes had been made from as early as 1885, but they did not go into regular production until the mid-1890s, at which time they became greatly admired. Crystalline glazes, with their reflective surface and hint of the exotic, were used by a number of European factories at this time, including the porcelain works in Copenhagen and Berlin, as well being used by many smaller art potteries.

In addition to being a painter, an engraver and a skilled and inventive ceramist, Jean-Charles Cazin (1841-1901) was also an influential teacher, serving as director of the Ecole des Beaux-Arts and curator of the museum at Tours, where he carried out experiments on earthenware. Cazin's work in France was brought to an end when he fled from the troubles of 1871 to settle in London, working there as a teacher both in Kensington and at the Lambeth School of Art; among his pupils were R. W. and W. F. Martin. At the Fulham Pottery he made stoneware jugs and mugs, often with Japanese-style decoration.

Artists such as Auguste Delaherche (1857-1940) productively absorbed the influence of art nouveau. Delaherche's early career was in architectural ceramics, but in 1887 he took over from Chaplet at the Haviland studio and there produced stoneware goblets, tobacco jars and pitchers with the aim of making work that was inexpensive and thus available to all. In 1894 Delaherche left Paris and built a workshop and kiln at Armentières near Beauvais; here he concentrated increasingly on high-temperature glaze effects, later producing porcelain. French artist-potters were among the first to experiment with copper-red glazes inspired by Chinese ceramics and Delaherche's copper-red glazed stonewares were shown to great acclaim at the Exposition Universelle in Paris.

The ceramist Pierre Adrien Dalpayrat (1844-1910) was equally concerned with oriental glazes and achieved spectacular sang-de-bœuf effects in a deep red speckled with green. The sculptor and potter Jean Carriès (1855-94) used wood ashes and feldspar in the production of his glazes, which featured a trickled effect. The influence of art nouveau was particularly evident in vases made in the form of gourds and other natural forms, such as those of Georges Hoentschel (1855-1915), who collaborated with Carriès. Hoentschel was strongly affected by Japanese ceramics and much of his work derived from floral forms. The art nouveau style is also reflected in the thrown forms with matt glazes in yellow, green and buff produced by Alexandre Bigot (1862-1927). Bigot opened a workshop in Paris for the production of vases, figures, tiles and other decorative stoneware with flambé glazes.

Emile Decreur (1876-1953) studied with the sculptor and ceramist Edmond Lachenal (1855- c.1930), from whom he learnt faience techniques, glazing and firing; the two subsequently collaborated. Among Lachenal's work was furniture made in stoneware, which was displayed at the 1900 Exposition Universelle. Decreur also developed an interest in stoneware, experimenting with flambé glazes and ornamental techniques; some of his finest pieces were vases in vegetable forms, with minimal decoration. In 1907 Decreur established his own studio at Fontenay-aux-Roses, where he made both porcelain and stoneware, abandoning ornament altogether in favour of refined shapes and sophisticated glazes. From 1939 to 1942 he served as artistic consultant at Sèvres.

Several showrooms in Paris specialized in promoting innovative decorative art, among them Meier-Graefe's La Maison Moderne and the Maison de l'Art Nouveau opened in 1895 by Siegfried Bing (1838-1905). It was Bing's policy of handling new and experimental work that contributed most to the initial spread of art nouveau in France.

In contrast to their counterparts in Britain, French artist-potters regarded their ceramics as fine art and showed them in art galleries alongside works by painters and sculptors. This fluidity between art and craft allowed fruitful links to be forged between potters, painters and sculptors and industry. The painter Paul Gauguin (1848-1903) worked successfully with clay, collaborating with Chaplet to produce cylindrical vases and mugs in reduction-fired stoneware decorated with Breton scenes featuring figures, sheep or geese, and trees. Gauguin also made vessels and portrait vases, dishes with modelled figure decoration, and later figures such as Eve and Black Venus. His connection with potters prefigured later partnerships entered into by artists such as Joan Miró and Georges Braque, both of whom collaborated with the Spanish-born potter and ceramic chemist Llorens Artigas, and Picasso, who made ceramics at Vallauris in the 1940s and '50s in association with Georges and Suzanne Ramié. Unlike Gauguin, Picasso drew on the traditional brightly coloured tin-glazed earthenware of Spain and southern France and on terracotta wares.

In southern France the Massier family pottery at Vallauris produced a range of lead-glazed decorative ware. In the 1880s Clément Massier (1845-1917) set up his own pottery at Golfe-Juan, where he devised a method of reproducing the traditional lustre technique. His workshop manufactured pots and plaques with richly iridescent nacreous glazes in peacock blue or emerald green, decorated with stylized plant designs including rose, cactus and foliage, which again reflected the art nouveau style. Jacques Sicard, who worked closely with Massier, later introduced the technique at Samuel Weller's pottery in the United States.

Germany and Austria

It was not until the beginning of the twentieth century that the influence of the Arts and Crafts movement and art nouveau – in German *Jugendstil* ('youth style') – gained any great hold in Germany and Austria. The origins of art pottery in Germany owe much to the example set by the Belgian architect and interior designer Henry Clemens van de Velde (1863:-1957). Drawing his inspiration in large part from the arts and crafts ideals of William Morris, van de Velde became a pioneering practitioner of the art nouveau style. He designed interiors for Bing's new gallery in Paris; and when these were shown in Dresden in 1897 they received a much warmer reception in Germany than they had in France. This prompted van de Velde to settle in Berlin in 1900 and later that year the Westerwald district council obtained permission from the Ministry of Trade in Berlin to invite him to contribute to an initiative to reverse the moribund trend of the local salt-glaze pottery industry. Despite his lack of experience in the medium of ceramics, van de Velde succeeded in making full use of the potential of glaze effects. Breaking with tradition in terms of both shape and decoration, in his first designs he introduced fluid art nouveau forms on which he used sang-de-bœuf glazes fired in salt-glaze kilns.

In 1901 Henry van de Velde was called to Weimar, where he conducted seminars at the art school; one of his students was Otto Lindig (1895-1966), later to become associated with the Bauhaus. Another influential teacher was Max Laeuger (1864-1952), potter, painter, sculptor, architect and designer, who contributed to the spread of new ideas by encouraging innovation and employing art nouveau shapes and decoration in his own experimental work in lead-glazed earthenware and majolica. Van de Velde also carried out architectural and design work in Weimar, including the rebuilding of the art school in 1904 and the creation in 1906 of a new school of arts and crafts (*Kunstgewerbeschule*), of which he was appointed director.

In 1903 the Meissen factory commissioned van de Velde to design a tea and dinner service that would be 'modern' in feel but nevertheless appeal to the popular market. After some manufacturing difficulties, the service was finally produced two years later, its elegant forms carrying a linear whiplash decoration in blue or matt burnished gold. Innovative designs were also used for the salt-glazed stonewares produced at Höhr-Grenzhausen, one notable contributor there being the modeller Peter Dümler (1860-1907), who later set up in business on his own.

Peter Behrens (1868-1940) shared much in common with van de Velde. Both had trained as artists before turning to architecture and interior decoration. In 1895 van de Velde had designed and furnished his own house at Ukkel, near Brussels, which became something of an art nouveau landmark and brought him commissions for other houses, mainly in Germany. Five years later Behrens followed suit by designing his own house in Darmstadt together with all the fixtures and fittings, including ceramics; his pottery designs were later used by the company Porzellanfabrik Gebrüder Bauscher, established in 1881 by August Bauscher to specialize in hotel porcelain. One of Germany's more forward-looking ceramic manufacturers, Bauscher was keen to apply the *Jugendstil* to his company's ranges and commissioned artists to design forms as well as decoration. Among others to espouse the new style was the Nymphenberg porcelain manufactory, which in 1906 set up a studio specially for the designer Adelbert Niemeyer (1867-1932) to create decorative pieces.

Work influenced by art nouveau and oriental styles was also produced at the pottery in Altona founded by the German ceramist Hermann Mutz (1845-1913) to manufacture tiled stoves. Mutz and his son Richard (1872-1931) developed a distinctive range of pieces including stoneware vases and bowls based on Japanese pots, on which richly coloured glazes were used. Richard Mutz later produced wall fountains in collaboration with the sculptor Ernst Barloch (1870-1938). After moving to Berlin in 1904 he again collaborated with Barloch to make pots with brightly coloured 'runny' glazes. In 1906 he formed the Keramische Werkstätten Mutz und Rother in Liegnitz for the production of architectural ware.

After working for the large firm of Villeroy & Boch in Mettlach, Jacob Julius Scharvogel (1854-1938) set up a workshop in Munich in which to produce art nouveau-style stoneware. He was later appointed director of the Grand Ducal Ceramic Factory in Darmstadt, where he focused on producing stoneware with rich glaze effects. In 1897 Scharvogel became co-founder of the Vereinigte Werkstätten für Kunst und Handwerk in Munich. Here, in collaboration with Theodor SchmuzBaudiss (1859-1942) and other designers, he made more complex forms with relief decoration. Wilhelm Kagel (1867-1935) studied at the Kunstgewerbeschule at Munich and worked at Garmisch-Partenkirchen before building his own kiln in 1905. He established a workshop for the large-scale but low-cost production by hand of wares that would combine artistic and technical excellence. Working initially in high-fired earthenware and later in stoneware, he often used patterns of garlands and stylized blooms inspired by southern German folk art.

The Rosenthal porcelain concern, founded in 1879 as a decorating workshop by Philip Rosenthal (1855-1937), soon began producing whitewares and opened a branch in Asch, Bohemia. In 1891 production was started at the newly built Porzellanfabrik Philip Rosenthal & Co. in Selb, Bavaria, with a workforce of 225; by 1905 the enterprise employed a total of 1,200 workers. Some of the Rosenthal tablewares were left plain to emphasize the elegance and modernity of the shapes, while others had painted decoration. The Botticelli and Darmstadt services were decorated with slender stems and heart-shaped leaves, the Donatello range with a cherry design. As well as tableware the company manufactured industrial porcelain, along with stoneware and other ceramic bodies. In addition it continued to produce tableware and ornamental pieces in the traditional Westerwald style, using designs that featured relief decoration in blue and grey.

Scandinavia

In Denmark some of the first studio pottery was that made in the 1880s by the designer and ceramist Thorvald Bindesbøll (1846-1908), who worked in earthenware creating vases and other decorative forms that he enamelled in blues, greens, browns, yellows, black and cream, often working from his own watercolour sketches. Between 1883 and 1890 Bindesbøll designs were produced by the factory of J. Wallman (established in 1867 at Utterslev) and other manufacturers in the Copenhagen area.

Another pioneering Danish factory was Kæhler Ceramics, established in 1839 at Næstved, Seeland by Joachim Christian Herman Kæhler for the production of earthenware, initially in the form of stoves (which were manufactured until 1888). In 1872 Herman August Kæhler (1846-1917), who had worked in Berlin, inherited the business from his father and introduced a number of changes, including the introduction of red metallic glazes on well-designed vases bearing motifs of flowers, stylized leaves and other natural forms painted in lustre. When his son Herman J. Kæhler (b.1904) in turn took over the company, he initiated the manufacture of glazed stoneware. Decorated with similar design motifs, the range of items produced included bowls and jars with brushed decoration designed by Herman's brother Nils A. Kæhler (b. 1906). The pottery later began production of architectural stoneware.

In addition to manufacturing its high-quality tableware ranges, the Royal Copenhagen Porcelain Factory also commissioned artists working in various mediums to design individual pieces, for example the Danish sculptor Bertel Thorvaldsen. Also based in Copenhagen, Kongelig Hof Terracotta, the factory of P. Ipsens Enke, established in 1843, became widely known for its Greek-style vases and other classically inspired ceramics. Finely made and often highly detailed, these were exhibited throughout Europe during the 1870s. On some pieces both the shape and the decoration were taken directly from ancient vases, although more freely interpreted styles were also used. Some scenes were copied, with extreme precision, from Thorvaldsen's marble reliefs of mythical and allegorical subjects.

It is the founding of the Central School of Arts and Crafts in Helsinki in 1871 that marks the introduction of the Arts and Crafts movement into Finland, where the influence of the potter Alfred William Finch (1854-1930) and his work at the Iris workshop is significant. Finch, born of British parents, studied in Belgium at the Brussels academy and there learned to make earthenware pottery. On a visit to England in the 1880s he became aquainted with the theories and work of the Arts and Crafts movement. Later, he accepted an invitation from the potter and painter Anna Boch to work at Boch Frères at La Louvière (SaintVaast) in Belgium, where he made vases, goblets, jugs, dishes and plates in red earthenware with simple, almost rustic, slip decoration featuring elements of the art nouveau style. His ceramics were later sold at van de Velde's gallery in Paris.

In the late 1890s the designer Louis Sparre invited Finch to Finland to help set up a pottery at the Iris workshop in Borgå, Porvoo, east of Helsinki that he had established for the production of furniture and glass as well as other art works. Here Finch made a range of mainly functional wares featuring swirling slip decoration in floral patterns, with linear designs often cut through the slip. When the Iris workshop closed down in 1902, Finch was appointed Head of Ceramics at the Faculty of lndustrial Arts in Helsinki, where he experimented with complex high-temperature glaze effects on stoneware.

Important among Finch's pupils at the Helsinki art school are E. Elenius and Toini Muona, who later joined Arabia, Finland's major ceramic manufacturer. For this company they designed stoneware dishes and vases in strong angular forms with monochrome glazes. Around 1900, seeking to put into practice the philosophy of the English Arts and Crafts movement, under the artistic direction of Thure Öberg Arabia commissioned designs from the Finnish industrial artist Axel Gallen-Kallela (1863-1931).

In the early years of the twentieth century many Scandinavian ceramic manufacturers, in common with those in Germany, adopted the technique of high-temperature firing and set up small design studios specifically for the use of artist-potters. Pottery designers thus benefited from having factory facilities and technical expertise close at hand, while in exchange the manufacturer gained an on-the-spot source of original design ideas. In Sweden this arrangement allowed Josef Ekberg, chief designer at the Gustavsberg factory, to produce some notable work, while in Norway it helped the Porsgrund porcelain factory in particular to develop distinctive lines. In Denmark Bing & Grøndahl of Copenhagen, under the art direction of J. F. Willumsen, encouraged individual artists to give free rein to their imagination in the creation of unique pieces.

The Netherlands

A particularly rich flowering of ceramics took place in Holland in the last decades of the nineteenth century. The contemporary emphasis on arts and crafts had prompted the opening of a number of new pottery factories, and four designers – Theodorus Colenbrander, C. J. van der Hoef, Bert Nienhuis and W C. Brower – came to dominate the industry.

The Rozenburg Plateelfabriek was founded in 1883 in The Hague by the German ceramist Wilhelm Von Gudenberg and soon became noted for its creative earthenwares. Experimentation was carried out with the production of high-quality wafer-thin porcelain in eccentric shapes and a new range of colours was used in the decoration, characterized by stylized motifs of flowers and insects. These bone china pieces made a considerable impact when exhibited in 1899 and 1900 and many other factories began to imitate the work. The designs featured elements of European stylistic trends such as naturalism and symbolism as well as being influenced by art nouveau.

The textile and ceramic designer Theodorus Colenbrander (1841-1930) worked as art director at Rozenburg between 1884 and 1889, creating vases, plates and display pieces decorated with painted floral motifs in bright shades of blue, green, red, brown, yellow, purple and white. In addition to being informed by the current European styles, his work showed the influence of batik patterns from the Dutch colony of Java. In 1912 Colenbrander was appointed a decorator at the Zuid-Holland factory, which had been established in 1898 in Gouda. Here he decorated large plates and other ceramic pieces both with patterns based on lznik wares and with hand-painted floral designs, making ample use of brown and matt blue.

In common with many other designers, Christian Johannes van der Hoef (1875-1933) had trained as a sculptor. He designed ceramics for various factories and served for some years as director of the Amstelhoek factory, near Amsterdam. The ideas of the English Arts and Crafts movement were influential in the small workshops at Amstelhoek, which had been set up by W. Hoeker for the production of ceramics, metalwork and furniture. The pottery workshop made functional earthenware in red clay, with red or green glazes. Van der Hoef's distinctive designs for Amstelhoek featured two colour inlaid decoration derived from traditional peasant pottery and incorporated the flowing lines of art nouveau. From about 1908 to 1910 van der Hoef worked for the newly founded firm of Amphora, where he designed both shapes and decoration. In 1910 the Amstelhoek business merged with De Distel, a factory that had been operating since 1895 in the production of painted earthenware and tile panels.

The potter Willem Coenraad Brouwer (1877-1933) worked for a time at the Goedewaagen factory in Gouda, where he had his own kiln. He showed his first individual ceramics in 1899 and six years later moved to Leiderdorp. Using coarse clay, glazed either green or yellow, Brouwer produced chunky vases in simple, rounded shapes with incised decoration, and among his decorative designs were regular, abstract or floral patterns as well as others based on animal forms. His later work includes heavy pots covered in white or grey crackle glazes, his use of slip decoration and contrasting glazes emphasizing the patterns and suggesting the influence of both Dutch peasant pottery and the work of A. W. Finch. Brouwer's powerful designs were also strongly influenced by the play of lines and forms in Maori decoration, which he had studied at the Ethnographical Museum in Leiden.

Bert Nienhuis (1873-1960), who had trained originally as a painter, worked for De Distel from its foundation in 1895 until 1911, becoming head of the decorating department in 1901. Nienhuis developed a distinctive linear style of decoration in light colours on a matt-glazed ground. An influential figure in Dutch applied arts, Nienhuis taught at several art schools, in 1917 taking charge of a pottery department set up at the Quellinus school in Amsterdam. Some of his designs were produced at Goedewaagen in 1935.

Long-established Dutch firms also responded to the growing interest in new trends in ceramic design. From 1877 to 1919 the Delft factory of De Porceleyne Fles, which had been in operation since about 1650, was under the art direction of Adolf Le Comte (1850-1921). Inspired by Japanese styles and techniques, Le Comte inaugurated production of a range of wares with abstract decoration and metallic glazes, later introducing decorative tiles, matt-glazed or painted with enamels and shaped to follow the design.

The sculptor and ceramist Joseph Mendes da Costa (1863-1939) trained in his father's stone-masonry workshop in Amsterdam and studied at the Rijksschool voor Kunstnijverheid before designing production earthenware. Together with the sculptor L. Zijl he became a member of the Labor et Ars group, formed in 1885 as a reaction against sterile academic attitudes to the applied arts. In 1898 Mendes da Costa set up his own pottery, where he made coarsely textured domestic brown earthenware, making use of medieval design elements that endow his work with a curiously mystical quality. In addition he modelled stoneware animals, figures and groups, on which he employed a grey glaze flecked with blue and brown. From the turn of the century Mendes da Costa worked with the architect H. P. Berlage and other members of 't Binnenhuis, an influential association of architects, artists and designers; he also taught at the Industriesschool in Amsterdam.

Other notable European Ceramics

In Hungary the Zsolnay factory, established in 1862 to produce earthenwares, extended its output to include decorative pieces patterned with Turkish and Persian motifs, often using shapes derived from pre-Columbian American and Chinese ceramics. Developed in an experimental workshop under the direction of Vinsce Wartha (1844-1914), the factory's best-known products have a rich red iridescent glaze on which the etched decoration is highlighted with gold lustre.

In Italy the old-established Cantagalli factory was transformed in the late nineteenth century by the two brothers Ulisse (1839-1902) and Romeo Cantagalli. The company is best known for its production of Renaissance-style ceramics, which include direct copies of celebrated Renaissance maiolica pieces. From about 1880 Cantagalli revived lznik pottery techniques and wares of this type continued to be made well into the twentieth century.

Emmanuel Cooper (2000), 'The Arts and Crafts Movement: Great Britain, The United States, Germany and Austria, Scandinavia, The Netherlands, Hungary, Italy', in Emmanuel Cooper, *Ten Thousand Years of Pottery*, London: British Museum Press, pp. 250–279.

Reprinted with permission from Curtis Brown Group.

13

A MATTER OF TRADITION: A DEBATE BETWEEN MARGUERITE WILDENHAIN AND BERNARD LEACH

Brent Johnson

In 1950, the English potter, Bernard Leach, after traveling around the United States, criticized American potters for their poor quality of work. He attributed the problem to a lack of standards, which, in turn, he believed was the result of having no long-standing pottery tradition compared to that of Britain, China and Japan. This touched off a debate on the nature and importance of tradition in the context of the growing studio potter movement that had gained momentum after the Second World War. Marguerite Wildenhain challenged Bernard Leach's ideas concerning the roots of tradition and what she had come to believe was his misguided effort to encourage American potters to imitate styles from the Sung Dynasty and Japanese folk pottery movement. This article explores this debate on tradition in the words of two of the most important potters of the twentieth century.

It was during this same period (1950's) that the center of the modern art movement had shifted to America. New conventions were being established in such areas as painting, sculpture and performance art. New York City and institutions like Black Mountain College were at the forefront of the movement. American potters, too were questioning their own traditions and debating the future of their craft. The commonly accepted view that pottery should be classified a minor or decorative art form was just one of a number of issues up for debate within the context of the newly energized studio pottery movement. To address these and other issues, craftsmen from around the world convened at Dartington Hall, England in July of 1952 for the first (and only) International Conference of Potters and Weavers.

The idea for an international conference of potters grew out of an initial desire by Bernard Leach to organize a major exhibition of British pottery produced since the 1920's. Having turned the business of running the pottery at Saint Ives over to his son, David, Leach had been living and working at Dartington Hall since 1932, where his friends Leonard and Dorothy Elmhirst provided him with a workshop and financial support in exchange for teaching classes. The Elmhirsts founded Dartington Hall in 1925 as a "salon in the countryside" for creative individuals such as artists, architects, performers and writers who lacked sufficient resources and an environment in which to work.

The purpose of the conference was to bring the world's leading potters and weavers together to discuss the status of their crafts and the challenges facing them in a post-war modern industrial world. The conference agenda included lectures, demonstrations, and discussions spread out over a ten-day period. The delegates stayed in dormitories on the premises and took their meals together in the dining hall. In the evenings there were concerts, films and parties, all of which were intended to create a sense of community that would last beyond Dartington Hall.

It was at Dartington Hall that Marguerite Wildenhain first met Bernard Leach. Both were already well known to the world community of craftsmen, Wildenhain for her accomplishments at the Bauhaus and Berg

Source: © Brent Johnson/*The Studio Potter* 501 (C) (3).

Giebichenstein where she created her classic *Hallesche Forms* for KPM (also known as Royal Berlin Porcelain), and Bernard Leach as the author of the very successful *A Potter's Book*.

A key issue taken up at the conference was the growing studio potter movement. Leach summed up the current state of things: "With the extraordinarily large number of people taking up one craft or another after the war, the general standard is not high [in America], nor for that matter is it in any other country. One must concede that at no period in history has so low a standard existed. Too much has happened in too short a time and we are suffering from aesthetic indigestion."[1] In his address to the conferees titled, "The Contemporary Potter," Leach outlined what he considered to be the greatest challenges facing present-day potters. Before discussing the key points of his address, it may be helpful to go back to Leach's first impressions of America.

During that first visit to the United States and Canada in 1950, Leach undertook a ten-week multi-city lecture tour, in which he made stops in Boston, Toronto, Saint Paul, Wichita, San Francisco and the New York State College of Ceramics at Alfred University, traveling some 12,000 miles in all. For his return trip to England, Leach chose to travel by boat to give himself time to reflect on what he had seen in America. He went on to write, "The first new perception which came was a sense of thankfulness that I had been born in an old culture. For the first time I realized how much unconscious support it still gives to the modern craftsmen."[2] As an Englishman who lived a significant portion of his life in the Far East, Leach often expressed his opinions in terms of comparison between the culture and values of *East* and *West*. As an artist, he believed that assimilating the best of both western and eastern craft traditions was not only possible, but necessary in order for the modern potter to be successful, or as he referred to it, "fully integrated." This notion of a potter becoming fully integrated was a core belief and cornerstone of his philosophy. It was also a key area of focus in his address at Dartington Hall.

On the dilemma of the American potter, Leach wrote, "Americans have the disadvantage of having many roots, but no taproot, which is almost the equivalent of having no root at all. American pots follow many undigested fashions and, in my opinion, no American potter has yet emerged really integrated and standing on his own feet; not as much as [Shoji] Hamada in Japan or Michael Cardew in England,…"[3] Leach believed that the craft pottery traditions Europeans brought with them to America died out before they could take root. As a result, the American craftsman didn't inherit a birthright of tradition that produced multiple generations of craftsmen within a family in the same way that Europeans had. "The background of crafts in the United States and Canada differs from that in either Europe or Japan in two ways. In the first place, America as a new amalgam of races does not provide a craftsman with traditions of right making born on its own soil, secondly, its contemporary movement is, by and large, a post-war growth in a setting of high industry."[4]

Regarding Native American craft traditions, Leach saw their pottery and textile traditions as evolved but not integrated into the mainstream of American arts and crafts. "The American Indians of course, together with the folk anywhere, do not proceed on individual choice and the root in their case is the race root. It is a humbling fact that so very few of our evolved, educated, self-conscious, world-conscious potters can stand the test of comparison. And yet a real judgment in pottery must be based upon the highest standards of the past constantly checked by the present, as in all art."[5]

While it was clear to Leach that American potters had been influenced by the great Chinese, Korean and Japanese pottery traditions, he felt they had been unsuccessful at integrating the true expression of those Eastern traditions into their own pots. He refers to such pots as haphazard mixtures of *Bauhaus over Sung* or *Sung over Bauhaus*. "Every modern artist, the potter included, has to find his own world-synthesis of thought and action. He has to choose between East and West or to discover out of his own deep perceptions how they can dovetail. It is a question of marriage, not prostitution. I have seen many stoneware, or pseudo-stoneware pots from coast to coast which are mixtures, 'Sung over Bauhaus,' free form – unintegrated. Can they integrate? Can the free form geometry of the post-industrial era assimilate with organic humanism of the pre-industrial?"[6]

In his address at Dartington Hall, Leach stayed with what were by now familiar themes that centered around the American potter as representative of the struggle to "fully integrate." "I have felt in the months that I spent there that if the American craftsman and artist can find his purpose—find his true role through not having a single pattern of tradition, but all traditions, … then the other problems in the other countries are comparatively easier."[7] Delving further into the topic of tradition, Leach went on to suggest that Sung Dynasty pots made between the seventh and eight centuries represent the highest achievement in pottery—a fact that was not realized in the West until the early twentieth century when large numbers of Sung pots were unearthed in Korea and China during the construction of railroads. "Since that time discerning minds, including those of potters working independently in different countries all the way from Japan to Finland and America, have recognized the highest achievement of men in ceramics is China of the Sung Dynasty; and therein they have found spontaneously a criterion of values or a standard or a measuring rod. Not that such a thing is static either; it is always a moving point. But in looking back at the past we do look for the groundwork of tradition, the groundwork of achievement—that by which we can judge the present."[8]

Having identified the lack of tradition as being the root cause for declining standards among contemporary potters in America, and having explained the concept of "integration" and East-West awareness, Leach left it to Shoji Hamada and Soetsu Yanagi to demonstrate a Japanese model for "integration" and East-West awareness.

At Dartington Hall, Soetsu Yanagi and Shoji Hamada worked as a team in their support of Bernard Leach. Hamada declined to give a lecture; instead he let Yanagi speak on his behalf and that of the *Mingei* movement, while he gave demonstrations. This arrangement worked well and was one they would repeat in subsequent public appearances, according to Bernard Leach who wrote about it years later. "The Buddhist aesthetics expounded by Yanagi held audiences of craftsmen and craft lovers; this philosophy was demonstrated by Shoji Hamada without many words. The double presentation of thinker and maker lit the imagination of art lovers wherever we went. Here was the silent voice of an Oriental telling the West with fresh clarity the virtue of man doing work in harmony with nature as it should be done—with heart, head and hands; here was the example of a potter, far from being dominated by intellect, showing us how it could support intuition in work from day to day—a man balancing in right tension between the two extremes of individualism and non-individualism."[9]

Yanagi suggested that the best way of demonstrating a commitment to society and the establishment of a new tradition is to abandon one's personal identity with one's work. "Almost all craftsmen believe that they are deserving of the honor of signing their names on their wares. Because they call themselves individual artists, their customers and critics, too, appreciate goods with signatures on them. … Signing one's name on one's work is not wrong but from the view point of Oriental religion, it reveals his relative deed of attachment. He signs because he advertises himself through his goods. … Modern fine art may be established in the individuality of a person; nevertheless, craftsmen in the present times should live in society and think of the essential character of craftsmanship. Let us give cheers for that age when again many beautiful unsigned goods are produced. I want to admire the times when such beautiful goods are produced. I want to admire the times when such beautiful goods are used as a matter of course in daily life. It will be the golden age of craft when those many beautiful goods are sold cheaply. … In the Orient where tradition is still retained, such a utopia is still partly to be found. … Mr. Hamada and Mr. Kawai, who are two of Japan's best pottery artists, do not put their signatures on their goods."[10]

The notion that any modern craftsmen, whether living in Japan, Europe or America could live up to Yanagi's standards, to Wildenhain at least, seemed misguided and overly sentimentalized in the American context. While it is true that Hamada and Kawai did not sign their pots, they often sold their best pots in wooden boxes that bore their signatures and a brief description of the pot. Then as now, the boxes serve as a means of authenticating the pots for collectors, thereby boosting their value in the process—a consequence that many have noted hatever runs contrary to Mingei philosophy. As Hamada grew more famous, the demand for his work increased, which in turn drove up the prices of his pots. As a result, the very pots that had once been made to serve the everyday needs of a rural population had become largely unaffordable except to the wealthy and the collectors, thus decreasing the likelihood that they would ever be used at all. Despite these contradictions, Hamada and Yanagi were a hit at the conference. It marked the beginning of their newfound fame in the West and increased their popularity back in Japan.

Having listened to Leach and Yanagi speak and seeing Hamada demonstrate, Marguerite Wildenhain took her turn to give a lecture and demonstration. The title of her talk was "The Potter in the New World." She began by agreeing with the premise that the quality of present day pottery was poor. But rather than blame it on a lack of tradition or intellectualism, she framed her argument around what she saw as a general level of disaffection that had become pervasive throughout modern society. "[A]s I see it, we have lost that intimate correlation of the mind and the hands as a philosophy of life, as it was in the centuries when crafts were all important. ... So if we look at the pots of the last century as a whole, we cannot help but find them wanting, because they do not convey what makes a pot really good—some technique, an imaginative and functional form and a personal idea. ... How do we come to that state of affairs? Don't we have all the technical knowledge, all the machinery and expensive external equipment, all the materials, costly or common, finely ground or coarse as we choose? ... as we are today, we have no real faith in ourselves, nor our work, nor our values. ... We have lost a deep relation with nature, and with that it seems our natural instinct."[11]

She went on to say, "Our difficulties thus lie apparently in the field of ethics and human expression and not in technique. To make hand pottery valid again so that it becomes a virile and creative activity again, it is urgent to raise anew the standards of the crafts, both away from a sentimentality towards their traditional standards in former centuries, but also out of untraditional intellectualism and tightrope walking, fearlessly giving the craftsman a new, more complete, and deeper relation of his work to his life. ... it is not possible for us to go back to the forms and techniques of times that have passed, be they ever so excellent, nor to the standards of beauty in other countries such as Greece or China. ... Creative man has always made things according to his idea without looking too much to the predecessors. ... We are living in the most arid and desolate time for art. To survive, we will have to rediscover those basic cells that are alone the essential cells of creative work and life."[12]

When it was over, the conference was considered a success by its organizers, the Dartington Hall Trust and the attendees. One of the most important outcomes of the conference was that it helped define the modern studio pottery movement by giving it a voice. In this regard, it brought [three of] the world's leading potters: Leach, Hamada, and Wildenhain, together for the first time. But the conference was especially successful for Leach, Hamada, and Yanagi as it gave them celebrity status, which they seized upon by adding several cities to their planned workshop and lecture tour of the United States that followed the conference.

Their first stop was Black Mountain College in North Carolina. A year earlier Bernard Leach had made arrangements with the college for the workshop, but because the school had no resident potter at the time, Wildenhain was asked to stand in as host and teach her own workshop during the week preceding the visitors' workshop. In the period of months between the initial planning and the workshop itself, Karen Karnes and David Weinrib were hired as resident potters at the college. However, it was decided to leave the job of hosting to Marguerite Wildenhain as planned.

The debate over the future of the modern craftsman that had begun at Dartington Hall resumed at Black Mountain College. Once again, Leach characterized the American artist potter as over-intellectualized and a failure in his efforts to integrate elements of the world's best traditions into an evolved American tradition. "The native [homegrown] potter of the United States has not yet arrived at his ultimate goal—a truly American tradition upon which to base his efforts. His greatest present need is the 'digestion' of many diverse influences besetting him both from the Orient and Europe; ultimately this digestion process will lead to the development of a tradition of his own building."[13]

Marguerite Wildenhain responded, "...no culture has a single "taproot" of tradition and that an authentic American tradition would be forged in time through a synthesis of many cultural influences."[14] She believed that America was a melting pot where many traditions had come together, and the notion of there being a single taproot of tradition in any country simply didn't exist. Having heard the same pronouncements by Leach and Yanagi no more than two months earlier at Dartington Hall, she may have taken a more critical view of Leach's ideas. His advocacy for the adoption of standards based on the modern Japanese folk pottery movement was at odds with what she believed, which was that such standards should reflect American styles and values. Leach's repeated praise of Shoji Hamada and the teaching of Yanagi must have caused her to feel outnumbered in her opposition.

Warren MacKenzie was present at both the Dartington Hall Conference and the Black Mountain College seminar. He offers his recollection of the interaction between Wildenhain and Leach. "Two weeks of serving as host [at Black Mountain College] had worn Marguerite's patience...but she never said a word about the potters or demonstrations until Leach, Hamada and Yanagi left to resume their tour. Once they had gone, and while the students were still assembled, Marguerite said, "I want to see you all in the pottery shop at 9:00 a.m. tomorrow." I stayed and went to the pottery shop the next day. At 9:00 a.m. Marguerite walked in and said, "Forget everything you just heard. Now I am going to show you how to make pots properly."[15]

After the Black Mountain College seminar, Marguerite Wildenhain returned to Pond Farm. Leach, Hamada and Yanagi continued their lecture tour with stops at Alfred University, the University of Minnesota, Saint Paul Campus, the Archie Bray Institute in Helena, Montana, Santa Fe, Los Angeles, and eventually San Francisco. While in San Francisco they visited Wildenhain at Pond Farm (her home and studio located in a remote Redwood grove near Guerneville). There they left Marguerite with a memento of their visit by leaving their hand prints and signing their names in slip on the white-washed barn wall. It would be easy to think that the gesture of visiting Wildenhain at Pond Farm could have soothed any bad feelings stemming from their spirited debate over tradition. But that was not the end of it. It was Marguerite Wildenhain who would have the last word in the form of an open letter to Bernard Leach. Below is that letter as it appeared in *Craft Horizons* in the June 1953 issue.

Dear Bernard Leach:

Ever since your first long visit to the United States and your article in Craft Horizons (Winter 1950), so many voices have risen in opposition and in doubt as to the value of what you are trying to convey to us, that I feel the problem needs to be discussed frankly and in public. No one could possibly doubt your sincerity or deny that you wish to foster high standards of craftsmanship. Still, if to arrive at that, you start at a wrong premise, it is obvious that your conclusions must necessarily be erroneous.

It is understandable that you should stress the importance of roots in tradition, so do we all. But tradition is only good when it is alive, when no one is even conscious of it and it needs no praise. The minute, however, that tradition needs artificial bolstering because its design elements no longer have any relation to the present generation, then let us have the courage to throw it overboard. It is time then to search honestly for those forms that are related to us, that express what we feel, think, and believe. It is equally evident that we cannot take over the techniques and forms, the way of life of another culture no matter how excellent.

No, we have no choice but to find our own way to what may become a new tradition for generations to come; no one but ourselves can do that for us, and this is a fact that we must face clearly and unemotionally.

Roots are, of course, wonderful to have, but who has that one single "taproot" you talked of? That single taproot no longer exists in our day. It is probable that it has never existed. No country, no single individual has only one root from which he draws strength. Roots grow when one lives according to what is right for him, when one's life and work are deeply related and when both are closely connected with the country, the society, the ideas of the people around one.

America has roots too, but they are many and come from all over the world, from all races. In this lies its uniqueness, its grandeur—this cementing together of a thousand parts. A country like America cannot have just one expression, one way of doing things. It must perforce have as many forms of expression as the sources of its life as a whole. That is America's beauty and greatness, and nobody would want to see just one single form, one single way of thinking grow on this continent. For our tradition is just the opposite: it stands for the free choice of each individual.

It ought to be clear that American potters cannot possibly grow roots by imitating Sung pottery or by copying the way of life of the rural population of Japan. Conscious copying of the works of a culture unrelated to the mind and soul of our own generation would only produce dubious makeshifts and turn our struggling potters into either dilettantes or pure fakes. As creative craftsmen, we reject the tendency to force our generation into a mould that does not belong to it.

No, if we want the crafts to remain alive and even perhaps grow roots again, we must give young craftsmen all the freedom and education, all the honest experimentation, using every technique and material in any way he chooses. Man needs to find room in the world for growth; he cannot have his mind, his work, his taste and his ideas restricted at the start by taboos and preconceived formulas and rules. We are eager and willing to learn and to try, but no spirit can brook restriction. On the contrary, open up the whole world to us, show us the beauty of all races so that we may learn to see the different elements that have gone into the making of our own background: we have excellent traditions closer to us than the Chinese or Japanese, of equal merit and just as inventive. For these are the qualities we aspire to. In art as in life, the main thing is the divine spark. We cannot quench it in the student without killing it in the man.

(Signed) Marguerite Wildenhain, March 23, 1953.

Notes

1. Bernard Leach, *A Potter In Japan*, London: Faber and Faber, 1960. p. 36.
2. Bernard Leach, *Craft Horizons*, Winter 1950. pp. 18–20.
3. Ibid.
4. Bernard Leach, *A Potter In Japan*, London: Faber and Faber, 1960. p. 34.
5. Bernard Leach, *Craft Horizons*, Winter 1950. pp. 18–20.
6. Bernard Leach, *Beyond East & West, Memoirs, Portraits and Essays*, London: Faber and Faber, 1978. p. 241.
7. Bernard Leach lecture, "The Contemporary Potter," Conference Proceedings, Dartington Hall, 1952.
8. Ibid.
9. Bernard Leach, *Beyond East & West, Memoirs, Portraits and Essays*, London: Faber and Faber, 1978. p. 244.
10. Soetsu Yanagi lecture, "The Japanese Approach to the Crafts," Conference Proceedings, Dartington Hall, 1952.
11. Marguerite Wildenhain lecture, "The Potter in the New World," Conference Proceedings, Dartington Hall, 1952.

12. Ibid.
13. Robert L. Diffendal, "Black Mountain College Holds Pottery Seminar," *Ceramic Age*, Dec. 1952. pp. 54–56.
14. Mary Emma Harris, *The Arts at Black Mountain College*, Cambridge, MA: MIT Press, 1987. p. 232.
15. From an Interview with Warren MacKenzie at his workshop in Stillwater, MN, Sept. 30, 2005.

The preceding article is based on a chapter of the same title that originally appeared in the aforementioned book: *Marguerite Wildenhain and the Bauhaus*. In 2007, it appeared in *The Studio Potter*, Volume 36, Number 1, Winter 2007-8. Copyright © by Brent Johnson 2006.

14

'CONTEMPORARY' DESIGN OF THE 1950s: RIE AND COPER IN CONTEXT

Lesley Jackson

Although the pots of Lucie Rie and Hans Coper stand out as being radically new and distinctive when contrasted with the mainstream British studio pottery movement of the early post-war period, their work takes on an entirely different perspective when considered in a wider international context. Even before Rie arrived in England she was already a veteran of the European exhibition scene, having shown her pots and won Gold Medals at a series of international exhibitions, including Paris in 1925 and 1937, Brussels in 1935, and the Milan Triennale of 1936. After the Second World War there were fewer exhibitions of this type, although significantly both Rie and Coper had work selected for the Festival of Britain Exhibition in 1951, and the same year they were also invited to participate in the Milan Triennale. When they exhibited together again at the next Triennale in 1954, this time it was Coper who won a Gold Medal.

From 1947, when the Triennales resumed, these exhibitions were considered the most prestigious international venue for manufacturers and makers to present their latest work. 1951 and 1954 are acknowledged as being golden years, providing an unparalleled showcase for the flood of new talent which had emerged since the war in Scandinavia, Italy and the USA – the new design superpowers of the 1950s. What suddenly came to fruition at this time was a 'New Look' in design as revolutionary as that introduced in the fashion world by Christian Dior in 1947. This fresh, dynamic and confidently modern style, widely referred to at the time as 'Contemporary', drew on many of the functionalist ideas of the inter-war Modern Movement, but re-interpreted them in a more accessible and visually stimulating form.[1] This was Modernism with a human face, and it reflected the new spirit of optimism at the end of the war, which in turn spawned a renaissance of creativity in the applied arts. Greater familiarization with the output of the leading international 'Contemporary' designers of the post-war period – those who, like Rie and Coper, were working at the cutting edge of the applied arts – throws new light on the work of these potters and the flourishing international design climate in which they were working.

The country which stole the show at the two Milan Triennales of the early 1950s was Finland. Building on the breakthroughs in organic design made by Alvar Aalto during the 1930s, particularly his work in the fields of furniture and glass, Finland rapidly emerged during the late 1940s as a major force in the applied arts. The two leading Finnish designers of the 1950s, Tapio Wirkkala and Timo Sarpaneva, were both glass designers, but the Finns also excelled in ceramics, textiles, furniture and lighting. Although it is unlikely that Rie and Coper would have been exposed to much Finnish design directly during the 1950s (because, critically acclaimed though it was on the Continent, there remained relatively few retail outlets for Finnish goods in Britain), it is nevertheless true that their work and that of the Finns share a complementary aesthetic.

Glass and ceramics provide the most fruitful areas of comparison. Tapio Wirkkala's 'Kantarelli' vases of 1946, for example, inspired by the form of chanterelle mushrooms, are cut with a pattern of fine vertical

Source: © Barbican Centre, Corporation of London/Lesley Jackson lines comparable to the linear sgraffito patterning which was to become Rie's hallmark form of decoration. Although the original source of inspiration was different in each case (Rie was inspired by incised Bronze Age pots which she saw at Avebury during the late 1940s), there are obvious aesthetic similarities between the two end products. Timo Sarpaneva's glass designs were even more sculptural than those of Wirkkala. In his 'Kayak', 'Pot Hole' and 'Lancet' sculptures, the suggestion of the vessel has almost disappeared, and the forms themselves are totally abstract. Sarpaneva was a great admirer of the sculptures of Barbara Hepworth, but the influence of Constantin Brancusi, the father of modern sculpture, is also very much apparent in his work. Coper too was working in the shadow of Brancusi, and his work has a similarly elemental quality.

In the field of ceramics Finland's prowess was entirely due to the achievements of one firm, Arabia. Arabia was unique in the way it broke down the barriers between the studio and factory system: the top floor of the factory was occupied by studio potters who were under no obligation to design for production, but whose work was nurtured by the firm and showcased at international exhibitions, bringing further prestige to the factory. Birger Kaipiainen, who specialized in leggy bird figures, and Rut Bryk, who created large-scale textured tile panels, were two of Arabia's best known artists. Working in porcelain like Lucie Rie, Toini Muona and Friedl Kjellberg created innovative organic vessels, sometimes gourd-shaped, sometimes attenuated, such as Muona's tall wavering 'Grass' sculptures. Although there are no specific areas of aesthetic crossover between these artists and Rie, had she emigrated to Finland rather than to Britain, she would certainly have found a home alongside these artists on the top floor of the factory at Arabia.

The work of another of Arabia's studio potters, Kyllikki Salmenhaara, bears direct comparison with that of Hans Coper. Like Coper she was inspired by ancient ritual vessels, and this led her to develop some potent and highly unusual forms. Working in a coarse stoneware body called 'chamotte' decorated with a rich earthy red glaze, Salmenhaara created a range of exaggerated thrown vessel forms, some tall and attenuated, some squat with tight necks and narrow feet. Like Coper's mature works, these are vessels of extremes, sometimes composite in form, whose visual impact arises partly from their shape, partly from their rich surface patina, and partly from their 'presence'.

In Sweden the major figure in the ceramics world during the 1950s was Stig Lindberg at the Gustavsberg factory. In 1938 William Kåge had radically modernized the firm's tableware production with the introduction of his influential 'Soft Forms' service. After the war the organic trend was vigorously championed by Lindberg, and the elegant attenuated and hourglass forms that characterized Rie and Coper's exquisite wheel-thrown tableware designs are reflected in production form in Lindberg's stylish production tableware designs of the mid 1940s. Meanwhile, in the USA, the Hungarian born Eva Zeisel was working on similar lines with her strongly organic 'Town and Country' tableware for Red Wing Pottery and her sophisticated 'Tomorrow's Classic' range for Hall China. However, whereas Zeisel confined herself to shape design, Lindberg was equally skilled in pattern-making, including both printed and handpainted designs, amongst the former a pattern of fine radiating lines, similar to Rie's sgraffito decoration. Lindberg also had the opportunity to produce one-off studio pieces at Gustavsberg where, as at Arabia in Finland, creativity flourished because of the crossover between studio and production design.

One of the reasons why Swedish design was in such good shape after the war was that, as a result of Sweden's neutrality, there had been continuity of production during the 1940s. The situation was very different in central Europe. During the late 1930s, many artists, designers and architects, particularly those of Jewish origin, were forced to flee Nazi Germany and neighbouring Austria to make a new life elsewhere. In 1938, the same year that Rie arrived in London, the potters Gertrud and Otto Natzler left Vienna to start their career anew in California. The Natzlers worked very much as a team, with Gertrud throwing the pots and Otto creating the glazes. Six years younger than Rie, it would be interesting to discover whether they knew each other in Vienna, as there are some striking similarities of aesthetic and technique between their work after the war. Otto Natzler experimented with thick bubbled glazes called 'Pompeian', 'Lava' and 'Crater', which evoke comparison with Rie's 'volcanic' glazes. Like Rie, the Natzlers chose to work on a modest scale because they preferred the intimacy of smaller pots.

Of their work Otto wrote, 'We feel that pottery is to the visual arts what chamber music is to the art of music.'[2] This comment is interesting because it suggests a way of understanding the closely allied but divergent path pursued by Rie and Coper during the course of their careers. To co-opt Natzler's metaphor, it could be argued that the precise, small scale approach of Rie is analogous to chamber music, while Coper's work opened out formally onto a broader plain, assuming a scale analogous to the symphony.

During the 1930s British studio pottery had been dominated by the rival 'schools' of Bernard Leach and William Staite Murray. By the 1940s, with the withdrawal of Staite Murray from active involvement and the publication of Leach's *A Potter's Book*, the Leach tradition was accepted as the establishment voice and looked set to dominate the 1950s. The famous Dartington International Conference on Pottery and Textiles of 1952, which both Rie and Coper attended, could be seen as Leach's attempt to establish the agenda for the post-war period. However, all that was soon to change as Rie and Coper, championed by Muriel Rose in her book *Artist Potters in England*, began to gain acceptance for their work. By the end of the 1950s it could be argued that Rie and Coper were responsible for a new school of studio pottery in Britain, centred around the progressive retail outlet, Primavera, opened in 1945, and run by another enlightened European, the German-born Henry Rothschild. This school included potters such as Waistel Cooper, Barbara Cass, Ruth Duckworth, Gordon Baldwin and Robin Welch, who exhibited at Primavera from the early 1950s onwards. Although it is true that Rothschild also stocked the work of Leach and his followers, his shop initially provided one of the few outlets for progressive 'Contemporary' craft during the post-war period, and gave the public a rare opportunity to see studio pottery sympathetically displayed alongside 'Contemporary' glass, textiles and furniture.

The potter whose work stands out most obviously as being in a similar vein to Rie and Coper during the early 1950s is Waistel Cooper. Cooper established a studio at Porlock in Somerset in 1950, where he adopted a rough stoneware body and ash glazes. By 1953, when exhibiting at Primavera, his style bore distinct similarities to that of Rie and Coper, both in terms of shapes and surface decoration, although the proportions of his vessels were different. The main areas of similarity were in the use of incised linear patterning inlaid with manganese oxide, and the creation of a surface patina through the abrasion of slips and oxides. Although Cooper denies being consciously influenced by Rie and Coper at the time, and it is true that he came into contact with few other potters during his career, his work must have sat comfortably alongside theirs on the shelves at Primavera, Heal's, and Malcolm Bishop's shop in Manchester (the Primavera of the North), where it was also sold during the 1950s and '60s.[3]

Also working in a similar idiom at this date, and selling work through some of the same outlets, were Brigitta Appleby who ran the Briglin Pottery, Irwin Hoyland, whose work was regularly featured on the pages of the *Studio Yearbook*, and William Newland. Newland, however, was more closely associated with another group of British potters who shared an enthusiasm for Picasso's ceramics, and who were consequently dubbed by the disapproving Bernard Leach the 'Picassettes'.[4] Picasso had first begun experimenting with ceramics in 1947, and was to continue his involvement via the agency of the Madoura Pottery at Vallauris in the South of France right through until the end of the 1960s. Combining his powers as a painter and sculptor, Picasso introduced a new vigour and freedom of expression into ceramics. Amongst his English followers were Margaret Hine, Nicholas Vergette and James Tower. Of their work Dora Billington wrote in 1955, 'To all who saw the work of these three potters [Newland, Hine and Vergette] ... it must have been apparent that English studio pottery is at last acquiring a 'New Look', more in tune with current ideas in house decoration and design generally.'[5] To judge from this, the 'New Look' adopted by the 'Picassettes' was perceived as another equally valid alternative for British potters to follow, along with what might loosely be described as the 'Primavera school'. The aesthetics of the two were not mutually exclusive, however: some of the early vessels of Hans Coper, with bold creamy white designs scratched through dark manganese slip, have a strong graphic quality that clearly relates to Picasso, as well as to Abstract Expressionist painters such as Hans Hartung. As Billington pointed out, the key to the new aesthetic of the period, by this date known in Britain as the 'Contemporary' style, was 'the exciting mixture of sculpture, painting and potting.' A fundamental difference between Rie, Coper and the 'Picassettes', however, was that, whereas the latter endeavoured somewhat self-consciously to produce painting and sculpture in clay, Rie and Coper absorbed the influence of contemporary art on a more subliminal level so that its aesthetics were more deeply and effortlessly integrated into their final expression.

In industrial ceramics three British firms stood out as being at the cutting edge of 'Contemporary' design: Midwinter, Poole and Hornsea. Midwinter introduced American-inspired organic shapes into their 'Stylecraft' tableware of 1952 and the 'Fashion' range of 1955, while Jessie Tait produced simple abstract and stylized patterns, strongly influenced by 'Contemporary' textiles, to complement the newly modernized tableware shapes, including one pattern, significantly, called 'Primavera'. She also designed a range of vases decorated with abstract tube-lined patterns, which appear to show the influence of Rie's work. Interestingly, from the mid 1960s Roy Midwinter took the adventurous step of involving studio potters in the design of new tableware shapes, culminating in the studio-inspired 'Stonehenge' range of 1972 and the 'Stoneware' range designed by Robin Welch in 1979. Given Roy Midwinter's receptiveness to new ideas from other branches of craft and design, it is tantalizing to speculate what might have emerged out of a partnership between Midwinter and Lucie Rie, had Rie been commissioned to design tableware by Midwinter instead of by the more reactionary Wedgwood. Hornsea Pottery, founded in 1949, did not fully mature until the end of the 1950s following the appointment of the designer John Clappison. In his 'Home Decor' and 'Studiocraft' ranges of decorative vases and bowls, Clappison introduced a new range of slip-cast forms combined with innovative relief-moulded textures, both apparently influenced by studio pottery. At Poole the full impact of studio pottery did not manifest itself until the early 1960s with the development of the 'Studio' range. However, during the 1930s the artist Truda Carter (of the original firm of Carter, Stabler and Adams) had introduced a new style of hand-painted decoration at Poole, a technique retained during the 1950s through an updated range of 'Contemporary' patterns. Some of these resemble the organic patterns of Stig Lindberg for his 'Faience' range of tin-glazed earthenware, while others have a linear 'spirograph'-like quality which relates to Rie's sgraffito patterns. The freeform vessels designed by Alfred Burgess Read at Poole during the 1950s (some thrown, some slip-cast) have a plastic quality associated with Rie's tablewares of this date, particularly those, such as her salad bowls, with squeezed oval forms created by manipulating the thrown vessel before the clay had hardened.

Plasticity was a characteristic exploited even more fully through the medium of glass during the 1950s, particularly in Sweden and Denmark. The leading manufacturers were Holmegaard in Denmark, where Per Lütken was the chief designer, and Orrefors and Kosta in Sweden. The type of glass most commonly associated with the period is the thick-walled, organic, free-blown vessel made in smoky colours or in clear glass with deep coloured underlay. In Britain, Whitefriars Glass produced their own version of the Scandinavian Modern style (sold alongside the pots of Rie and Coper at Primavera), while later in the 1960s the firm followed the lead of the Finns in producing mould-blown glass with relief-textured bark and ice patterns. At the other extreme, another type of glass produced in Sweden during the 1950s, which characterizes the period equally well, was the thin-walled, hourglass-shaped 'Tulip' vase designed by Nils Landberg for Orrefors. The key to both styles – the organic and the attenuated – was in exploiting the plasticity of glass to the full, in the first case to highlight the optical effects of glass as a solid but transparent material, in the second by pushing it to the limits of physical distortion.

The approach of the Czechs to glass design was totally different from the Scandinavians. Here the main emphasis was on surface decoration using cold techniques such as engraving and enamelling. These were exploited to stunning effect by artists such as Stanislav Libenský, Valdimír Kopecký, Jiří Harcuba and Karel Vaňura, who had been co-opted to work in the nationalized glass industry after the war. The patterns which these designers created drew on the vocabulary of contemporary abstract painting, but transformed it through the medium of glass into something quite extraordinary and unique. As in the ceramics and textiles of the period, there was a scratchy linear quality to their graphic style which allies it to the work of Lucie Rie.

In terms of vessel shapes, the medium in which some of the closest parallels can be drawn to the early work of Rie and Coper is metalwork. Rie's restrained organic tableware forms are mirrored in the shapes created by British silversmiths such as Gerald Benney and Robert Welch. (They, in turn, were strongly influenced by contemporary Scandinavian metalwork, particularly the designs of Henning Koppel in Denmark, and Sigurd Persson and Sven Arne Gillgren in Sweden.) Similarities extend beyond shape and proportion to surface treatment, such as the use of hammered and tooled relief-textured patterning, trends which would be further developed during the 1960s. The contrast between smooth and textured surfaces was an interest pursued by Benney both in his one-off pieces of silver and his production designs for Viners.

While ceramics, glass and metalwork, being largely vessel-based, are all media in which one might expect to find similarities of form, pattern and surface texture, other aesthetic trends affected a wider range of applied arts during the 1950s. In several branches of design – furniture and lighting in particular – there was a move towards lighter structures and pared down forms: legs made of tapering wood or fine steel rod, as in Gio Ponti's 'Superleggera' chair and Ernest Race's 'Antelope' chair, for example. Seats were made of thin moulded shell plastic, or an open wire grid, as in the furniture of Charles Eames and George Nelson for Herman Miller, and Eero Saarinen and Harry Bertoia for Knoll; and lampshades made of paper, plastic or finely spun aluminium or steel, as in the designs of Isamu Noguchi for Knoll, George Nelson for Howard Miller, Gino Sarfatti for Arteluce, and John and Sylvia Reid for Rotaflex. Lucie Rie, too, moved from the heavier forms of the inter-war period to thinner, pared down vessel shapes from the late 1940s onwards, and one of the reasons why her work looked so distinctive when compared to her contemporaries in England was because it was so much lighter. Interestingly, by the late 1950s, around the time of his move to Digswell, Hans Coper's pots were becoming increasingly weighty and monumental. His monumentalism looked forward to the 1960s, however, rather than back to the 1930s. The forms he had begun to create by the end of the 1950s – less fluid and organic, more regular and symmetrical, often based on discs, cylinders and chalice forms – reveal a potter working ahead of his time.[6] These forms continued to develop during the 1960s, reaching full maturity by 1969 at the time of his exhibition at the Victoria and Albert Museum.

It is also illuminating to consider 'Contemporary' textiles of the 1950s in relation to studio pottery. After the war there were two new trends in pattern design, both influenced by recent developments in contemporary art and both involving abstraction. First there were the energetic, colourful, linear patterns influenced by artists such as Miró, Klee and Calder. In Britain the leading exponent of this style was Lucienne Day, whose 'Calyx' fabric for Heal's, based on stylized abstracted plant forms, set the tone for the decade when it was first shown at the Festival of Britain in 1951. Other British textile designers producing patterns in a similar idiom, many for the progressive firm of David Whitehead, included Terence Conran, Jacqueline Groag and Marian Mahler. Pattern design was, in fact, one of the few areas of the applied arts where Britain led the field internationally during the 1950s, although there were comparable developments in Europe, Scandinavia and the USA. Elsbeth Kupferoth and Cuno Fischer produced jazzy Miró-esque patterns in Germany, for example; in Finland Dora Jung employed abstract linear patterns in her woven table linen designs for Tampella; while in the USA Angelo Testa, Ben Rose, Paul McCobb and Ruth Adler all produced quirky, playful, off-beat, abstract designs. What united many of these 'Contemporary' patterns was a distinctive wiry quality, as though the outlines were etched or drawn freehand with a fine-nibbed pen. Here again the aesthetic quality of this graphic style has parallels in the sgraffito technique used so extensively by Lucie Rie.

The second phase of 'Contemporary' pattern design during the 1950s was influenced by Abstract Expressionism, and these patterns were denser and more textural. Sometimes artists were commissioned to produce designs, as in the scheme launched by David Whitehead in 1953 called 'Painting into Textiles', which involved Eduardo Paolozzi, William Gear and Louis Le Brocquy. The Italians, too, were enthusiastic about inviting artists to design fabrics, and contributors included leading avant-garde artists, such as Gio Pomodoro and Lucio Fontana. This form of abstraction, and in particular the emphasis on grainy, abraded and striated surface textures, clearly relates to the aspirations of Hans Coper during the second half of the 1950s. Earlier he had experimented with bold painterly sgraffito patterns but, dissatisfied with the results, he later turned to purely textural effects created through patina rather than patterns. Although this probably had as much to do with Coper's interest in ancient ceramics and bronzes and the evocation of artificial ageing, clearly there were parallels with 'Contemporary' textiles, such as the remarkable furnishing fabrics known as 'Texturprints' created by Tibor Reich.

Although it would be misleading to suggest that the 'New Look' in studio pottery pioneered by Rie and Coper during the 1950s was simply the result of an amalgam of influences from other branches of the applied arts, there was a well-defined aesthetic context for their work at the time, best illustrated in Britain by the displays of 'Contemporary' design at the Primavera Gallery in London, and internationally at the Milan Triennales. While Rie and Coper deserve to be singled out for the quality and originality of their work, it would be wrong to isolate them completely from the environment in which they lived and worked. A measure of their originality, however, is the fact that whereas the 'Contemporary' style itself had gone out of fashion by the mid 1960s, by this date the pots made by Rie and Coper had become increasingly elemental and timeless, so that they themselves could no longer be judged by the fickle laws of fashion.

Notes

1. For a fuller discussion of 'The New Look' and 'Contemporary' design, including bibliographies, see L. Jackson, *The New Look-Design in the Fifties*, Thames and Hudson, 1991, which contains a detailed Directory of1950s Design; and L. Jackson, *'Contemporary' Architecture and Interiors of the 1950s*, Phaidon, 1994.
2. Los Angeles County Museum of Art, The Ceramic Work of Gertrud and Otto Natz!er, Los Angeles, 1966, preface by Otto Natzler.
3. For further information, see L. Jackson, *Waistel Cooper – Forty Years of Individual Pottery*, Manchester City Art Galleries, 1993.
4. See T. Harrod, 'The Forgotten Fifties', *Crafts*, May/June 1989, pp. 30–3.
5. D. Billington, 'The New Look in British Pottery', *The Studio*, January 1955, pp. 18–21.
6. For a group of documented early examples of these forms dating from 1955 and 1958 from the collection of W. A. Ismay, see Jackson, 1991, op. cit., p. 82.

Lesley Jackson (1997) "Contemporary' Design of the 1950s: Rie and Coper in context', in Margot Coatts (ed), *Lucie Rie and Hans Coper – Potters in Parallel*, London: Herbert Press in association with Barbican Art Gallery, pp. 22–29.

Reprinted with permission from the Barbican Centre, Corporation of London, and the author.

SECTION 2.2
STUDIO CERAMICS

Introductory summary

Studio Pottery is the term used to describe single or small groups of potters working in studios, as opposed to factories, to make individual or small runs of pottery. Tanya Harrod makes a distinction between the 'art pottery' of the late nineteenth century, which usually evolved from experiments in industry and often focused on decoration rather than form. Studio Pottery tends to be characterized by the potter undertaking all aspects of the making themselves from digging and preparing the clay, throwing and decorating to building and firing the kilns. Harrod's text details the developments in this major strand of ceramics in the first half of the twentieth century, with a particular focus on the friendship/rivalry between two of its central figures, William Staite Murray and Bernard Leach. Staite Murray (1881–1962) is known for his stoneware pots through which he attempted to raise the profile of pottery to an equivalence with painting and sculpture.

In his 1940, *A Potter's Book*, Leach brought together his position on standards, materials and methods for pottery. The extracts printed from the opening chapter of 'Towards a Standard', are chosen to give a flavour of Leach's philosophy. Here, he offers a rather polemic view of the differences between industrial and handmade ceramics. He goes on to give a definition of beauty based on the writing of Soetsu Yanagi, the Japanese philosopher and founder of folk craft movement. Leach also gives his views on how to recognize a 'good' or 'bad' pot and some 'constructional ideas' to consider when making.

Edmund De Waal's 'Towards a Double Standard' was chosen as a useful counterpoint and critique of the excerpts above from Leach's 'Towards a Standard'. De Waal sets Leach in context and makes a case for his strengths as a 'mark maker' and creator of subtle ceramic surfaces. He also unpicks Leach's relationship to the East and proposes that the 'standards' Leach set in his public statements are not always reflected in his work. Importantly, De Waal also challenges the narrow ideas of the 'Leach style' – often associated with 'boring brown' pots.

Julian Stair offers a useful history of the origins of studio pottery and references key thinkers of time including Herbert Read, Bernard Rackham and Roger Fry. Stair traces the rise and fall of studio pottery from the re-evaluation of traditional functional ware to pottery as an art form and back again to function.

The Archie Bray Foundation for Ceramics Arts was founded in 1951 by brick maker Archie Bray in the foothills of the Rocky Mountains, Montana, United States. The Foundation supports exhibitions, residencies, workshops and classes and has a mission to 'provide an environment that stimulates creative work in ceramics'. Patricia Failing provides a history of the foundation and importantly the key ceramic artists connected with it such as Peter Voulkos and Rudy Autio. This text also provides a useful overview of the debates and changing nature of American ceramics including function, sculpture, funk and Trompe-l'œil.

To conclude this subsection, Jeffrey Jones' text, 'Studio Ceramics: The end of Story?' offers a strong case for the success of studio ceramics as an art form, which might be heartening for young makers. However, this article was published in 2001 and since then a new strand of 'ceramics in the expanded field' has emerged. So perhaps studio ceramics is not quite the end of the story?

Livingstone and Petrie

15
STUDIO POTTERY
Tanya Harrod

Between the wars ceramics emerged as a new art form, recognised as the quintessence of formal abstraction, compared by critics to advanced sculpture and modern music.[1] The complexity and variety of the so-called 'art pottery' fashionable during the last quarter of the nineteenth century held few charms for the men and women who came to be described as 'studio', 'modern' or 'artist' potters. In the eyes of studio potters 'art pottery' was found lacking on two counts, techniques and sources. Most art pottery came out of experimental studios within the industry where there was division of labour.[2] There was no question of a single potter following through every ceramic process, digging the clay, creating the clay body, building a kiln, throwing, decorating, glazing and firing. Even the most admired figure working within the Arts and Crafts Movement, William De Morgan, was not concerned with the business of forming shapes and some of his most beautiful work was painted onto industrially made tiles. Similarly the artists employed at Doulton's Lambeth Pottery were chiefly concerned with surface decoration. In addition the sources for art pottery were diverse, and closely followed fashions in art, design and collecting. Thus William Burton and the team at the Royal Lancastrian pottery specialised in high-temperature single colour and flambé glazes of the Chinese Ch'ing period. William De Morgan's rich lustre wares were inspired by Hispano-Moresque pottery and his brilliantly coloured green and blue enamels drew on Persian Iznik. By the 1920s all this kind of work seemed to lack what Bernard Leach called 'sincerity'.

The ceramics produced from 1873 by the Martin Brothers might be thought an exception because the four co-operated as a close team, throwing, modelling and experimenting with glazes to make vases with incised and modelled decoration, and their famous grotesque bird and face vessels. But by 1923, when the young would-be studio potter Michael Cardew was taken to the Art Workers' Guild for an evening discussion of Martin ware, their work seemed merely quaint, an array of over-elaborate objects which Cardew felt 'obliged to be polite about'.[3] The early studio potters rejected the decorative eclecticism of art pottery. Instead they substituted what became a modernist orthodoxy which favoured the relatively rough facture and austere shapes of early English pottery and early Chinese wares.

The first real opportunity to see early Chinese ceramics came in 1910 when the collector members of the Burlington Fine Arts Club put on the exhibition *Early Chinese Pottery and Porcelain*. It was rich in pots owned by George Eumorfopoulos, one of a handful of collectors buying early wares, which were being excavated in quantity in the wake of Chinese railway construction at the turn of the century. They quickly became part of a modernist canon of greatness in art. Sung ceramics, as Roger Fry pointed out in a seminal article of 1914, were marked by a strong sense of form,[4] a quality he sought in contemporary painting and sculpture. And the founding of Omega in 1913 by Fry initiated a challenge to the traditional hierarchies which separated the applied and fine arts, non-Western and 'primitive' art and Western art, and the trained artist from the naive or vernacular artist. For Fry's acolyte Clive Bell, 'Significant Form' could be found in a swathe of different

Source: © Tanya Harrod/Yale University Press.

media: 'Sta Sophia and the windows at Chartres, Mexican sculpture, a Persian bowl, Chinese carpets, Giotto's frescoes at Padua, and the masterpieces of Poussin, Piero della Francesca, and Cézanne.'[5] As Bell asserted in 1914: 'No one ever doubted that a Sung pot or a Romanesque church was as much an expression of emotion as any picture that ever was painted.[6] This recognition of the formal beauties of these austere early examples of ceramics meant that potters inspired by early Chinese wares or by what Fry had called 'the noble and serious'[7] early English wares were assured of an informed, if small, audience often with avant-garde tastes. Omega pottery, perhaps surprisingly, drew on rather different sources – principally French country pottery and Mediterranean tin-glaze wares.

The most important potter in terms of the future direction of the studio pottery movement was the sculptor Reginald Wells. He had been making slipware inspired by seventeenth-century English examples from about 1900. But in 1910, the year of the Burlington Fine Arts Club exhibition, he turned to early Chinese ceramics for inspiration. His simple, rather lifeless shapes were clothed in mottled running glazes which recalled Chün and Yüan wares. Already famous for his small boldly modelled bronzes of labourers and countrymen inspired by the painting of Jean-François Millet, Wells's pots seem like a move towards abstraction, a response to the crisis of sculpture before the First World War.[8]

Many of the first efforts inspired by English slipware and Chinese Sung had an undeniably archaeological air. W.B. Dalton, headmaster of Camberwell School of Art from 1899 until 1919, was an early experimenter but his quiet pots were less important than his decision to set up a pottery class at Camberwell in 1909, initially taught by Richard Lunn and from 1915 by Alfred Hopkins. Roger Fry, Reginald Wells and a key figure in the future studio pottery movement, William Staite Murray, all learnt the rudiments of pottery there. From 1919 Charles and Nell Vyse were making thrown stoneware and porcelain directly inspired by early Chinese wares. Nell Vyse was a knowledgeable glaze chemist and they recreated tenmoku, celadons and Chün glazes, carving and incising in the spirit of Tz'ŭ-chou pottery.[9] The Vyses lived near George Eumorfopoulos, studied his collection and were encouraged by him. But to some members of the new studio pottery movement their pots looked like reproductions and were dismissed as too 'competently commercial'. This harsh verdict, delivered by the potter Katharine Pleydell-Bouverie, suggests the hierarchies and groupings that swiftly developed within this new movement.

That there was a more populist sympathy for entirely handmade pottery is suggested by the career of Dora Lunn, the daughter of Richard Lunn, who set up her Ravenscourt Pottery in 1916.[10] It received publicity as an all-woman enterprise and as a fresh-air workplace – 'Pottery in the Garden'. Clear simple shapes and deliberately crude decorations characterised her early work but by the twenties she was following a developing trend and making pots inspired by early oriental wares. Denise Wren, another figure on the margins of this new aesthetic, learnt to throw from a local flowerpot maker in Surrey and set up her pottery at Oxshott in 1919, making pots incised with Celtic designs inspired by Archibald Knox, her tutor at Kingston School of Art.[11] She and her husband Henry Wren were what would now be called 'enablers', producing useful how-to-do-it books, selling kiln designs and holding two-week crash courses in pottery technique.

These early experiments began to seem like a movement after the First World War. A government report on the 1925 Paris exhibition made a sharp distinction between the art pottery produced by firms like Doulton, Pilkington, Moorcroft and Bernard Moore and the 'British Studio Potters' – men and women working alone or in small workshops designing and making pots and figurines.[12] By then there were two further key figures working in clay, William Staite Murray and Bernard Leach, each of whom inspired a band of gifted pupils and who shaped the movement through their personal charisma and a body of proselytising writing.

The special status of studio pottery in the 1920s and 1930s owes most to William Staite Murray.[13] Destined for a career in his father's seed and bulb firm, Murray escaped into the world of 'abstract painting and abstract sculpture' just before the First World War.[14] It was a serendipitous moment and by 1915 he was on the fringes of the London art world, studying Buddhism, painting, experimenting with bronze casting and making earthenware plates at the Yeoman Pottery, Kensington with the Vorticist painter Cuthbert Hamilton. Making pots in a small workshop in the first two decades of the twentieth century (like direct carving in stone, printing expressively with wood blocks or designing for the ballet) was one way of avoiding the potential academicism of easel painting. Murray might have seen the ceramics at Fry's 1910 Post-Impressionist show or known of the pottery experiments made by the German Expressionist group *Die Brücke* around 1912.[15] At the Yeoman Pottery Murray painted abstract designs on plates which suggest that he had studied work by Vassily Kandinsky, who had been a regular exhibitor at the Allied Artists Association exhibitions since 1909.[16] But in 1919, like other early studio potters, Murray began to explore the techniques of early Chinese stoneware.

Within a couple of years Murray had gone beyond the faithful emulation of Chinese wares which characterised the work of Charles and Nell Vyse. His finest pieces from the mid 1920s onwards were monumental forms, occasionally powerfully incised and often painted with abstract marks or stylised birds or fishes. From the late 1920s major pots were given poetic titles – *Cadence* (1928), *Vortex* (1929), *Mare and Persian Garden* (1931). Functional wares were of no interest to Murray who took his cue from the budding art critic Herbert Read, who had declared that pottery was 'plastic art in its most abstract form'.[17] In the same year Murray was arguing that 'A finely proportioned Pot ... is an abstraction, and once we experience pleasure in contemplating it as such, we shall discover the underlying principles of beauty in more evolved forms, in Sculpture and Painting. The forms are abstractions and as such readily contemplated as pure form'[18] From 1924 onwards ideas about thrown pots being 'abstract' or representing a branch of abstract sculpture became commonplace in discussions of studio pottery partly because Murray himself remained close to debates on abstraction in the fine art world. In 1927 he became the sole potter member of the Seven & Five Society, elected at the suggestion of the painter Ben Nicholson. That year he also shared an exhibition with Ben and Winifred Nicholson and Christopher Wood and the following year showed with the Nicholsons alone.[19] He exhibited in the final Seven & Five show in 1935 from which all figurative work was excluded. By 1930 Herbert Read took Murray's pots as a demonstration that 'all art is primarily abstract'.[20] Other critics, in the extensive coverage of Murray's exhibitions, also identified him as an abstract artist or saw his work as a synthesis of abstraction in painting and sculpture.[21]

In 1925 Murray was appointed pottery instructor at the Royal College of Art and was swiftly elevated to Head of Department. Though a practical man, he kept technical instruction to the minimum. Instead his students became aware of his interest in the vitalist ideas of Henri Bergson, the writings of Lao-Tzu and the koans of Zen Buddhism. Murray's group of students rapidly made an impact on the London art world, exhibiting frequently and forming a recognisable grouping, hailed in 1930 as 'canvas-free artists' by Herbert Read.[22] His most adventurous pupil, Thomas Samuel Haile, carried forward Murray's ambitiousness for ceramics.[23] Haile was also a painter, allying himself with the English Surrealists in 1936 and joining the Artists International Association in 1937. The decoration of Haile's pots made plain his interest in School of Paris painters like Pablo Picasso, Paul Klee and Joan Miró – they were the inspiration behind his powerful slipware of the late 1940s. Murray's other favoured pupils – Henry Hammond,[24] Margaret Rey,[25] Heber Mathews, R. J. Washington and Philip Wadsworth – all made pots which remained close to his vision of ceramics as a fine art.

Like many inter-war craftsmen and women, Murray's career faltered in the mid-1930s.[26] His elevated perception of pottery as an art form equal to painting and sculpture found less favour in a period of economic crisis. Many fine artists felt morally obliged to think in terms of design for industry. Murray never entertained such ideas, pointing out that 'You can't make love by proxy'.[27] In 1939 he travelled to Rhodesia, was caught there by the Second World War and decided to make East Africa his home. An attempt to make a pot using local native techniques – handbuilding and firing without a kiln – failed and, remarkably, although he lived until 1962, his career as a potter ended at that point. Haile was killed in a car crash in 1948 while Margaret Rey turned to sculpture. R.J. Washington became a chicken farmer and art inspector, only returning to ceramics in the 1980s. Henry Hammond devoted himself religiously to teaching at Farnham School of Art. Murray's precipitate disappearance from the world of ceramics in 1939 meant that his reputation was largely eclipsed by Bernard Leach who carried on working, lecturing and publishing into the 1970s.

It is hard not to think of Murray and Bernard Leach as rivals. A coldness sprang up between the two men over Murray's Royal College of Art job and it has been argued that they represented different groupings, with Murray charging high prices for ceramics as art and Leach creating 'a living tradition of studio pottery'.[28] The truth was more complicated. They both wrote romantically about the making of pots, both seeing it as semi-mystical activity. Bernard Leach's background was grander than Murray's but he too had been discouraged from becoming an artist.[29] In 1903-5 he studied at the Slade where he learnt to draw with fluent grace. After an unhappy spell with the Hong Kong and Shanghai Bank he attended the London School of Art, met a young Japanese artist named Kotaro Takamura and fell to thinking about his early childhood, spent with his grandparents in Japan. In 1909 he set sail for Japan, planning to teach etching.

Leach's absence from England for the next eleven years meant that, unlike Murray, he missed the crucial years just before the Great War when exhibitions mounted by Fry, Frank Rutter and the Allied Artists Association and other groupings and galleries introduced virtually the entire canon of modern European art to London.[30] Leach's contact with European modernism was more tenuous, taking place at long range, among the wealthy Europhile group of artists, writers and thinkers who formed the avant-garde Shirakaba group in Tokyo. In 1911 he attended a *raku* party where traditionally pots decorated by guests were fired immediately. Leach was fascinated by his own efforts and immediately set about learning the craft. He saw Sung pots in China on visits between 1914 and 1916. For Leach pottery became a metaphor for dreams of an East/West synthesis which he shared with the young Japanese philosopher Soetsu Yanagi. Pots also became a practical demonstration of how the East could, as Leach wrote, 'exercise a wonderful influence upon the soulless mechanical output of Europe'[31]

In 1920 Leach returned to England. In Japan he had read Bell's ideas on significant form with excitement and he must have arrived home with some optimism. With the help of Shoji Hamada whom he met at the end of his time in Japan and who accompanied him to England, he established his pottery by a stream just outside St Ives.[32] Hamada returned to Japan in 1923 but continued to exhibit in England throughout the 1920s and 1930s, offering an 'authentic' neo-Orientalism which helped give weight to Leach's own work. The link with Japan was kept up by the arrival of Tsuneyoshi Matsubayashi who helped Leach rebuild his traditional Japanese three-chambered climbing kiln and generally gave technical advice. In those early years Leach was friendly with Murray and he, Hamada and Murray exchanged technical information, with Murray eager to learn Oriental brushwork from Hamada and the St Ives team interested in Murray's oil-fired kiln.

Leach's early output in England was notable for its range. Almost from the start he worked with stoneware, porcelain, *raku* (this chiefly to entertain tourists who paid to decorate a swiftly fired pot) and slipware, decorated with a range of techniques. The contrast with Murray, who restricted himself to stoneware, was striking (although the price paid was a high proportion of kiln failures and a swift slide into financial difficulty). Nothing can detract from the beauty of the best of Leach's early work. Pieces could be monumental or delicate, and painted, carved or incised with a repertoire of stylised graphic motifs that Leach had built up in Japan – the Tree of Life, the Wellhead, fishes, horses eating seaweed on the seashore and images of 'the peaks of the High Japan Alps'.[33] But in the grand amateur circles in which he had moved in Japan most technical problems were solved either by his teacher Ogata Kenzan VI or at his Abiko pottery by 'the trustworthy and experienced potter who managed my workshop and kiln so admirably, demonstrating by his behaviour the right relationship between artist and artisan.[34] In England, however, the 'right relationship' with artisans proved harder to establish and as a result many uncertain pots were produced.

From the start Leach made functional wares, pleasing cups and saucers and improbably lumpy looking teapots. Part of the reason was economic. For instance he saw tile-making, to which he turned in 1927 and which allowed his genius as a draughtsman full rein, as a 'bread and butter' solution.[35] In *A Potter's Outlook*, an angry pamphlet of 1918 written for the New Handworkers' Gallery, he argued that the lack of 'any acknowledged classic standard of pottery' in England was forcing him in the direction of utility. But he retained vestigial Arts and Crafts ideals in which handwork could save men's souls and halt the progress of industrialisation and in which a country pottery, making a broad range of wares, had a place. At times he also thought in terms of a small factory with some division of labour – Morris's 'Factory as It Might Have Been'. The ideas were reinforced by the visit of Hamada and Yanagi to England in late 1929, bringing with them ideas about the unselfconscious beauties of functional work made by teamwork, a philosophy of art which they called *mingei* or 'art of the people'.[36]

From 1923 Leach had taken on a succession of eager upper-middle-class pupils including Michael Cardew, just down from Oxford, Katharine Pleydell-Bouverie, a boyish, intelligent aristocrat who had taken a few pottery lessons at the Central School, and Norah Braden who had spent six years at the Central School and the Royal College of Art. They in turn set up their own potteries, Cardew at Winchcombe in 1926, Pleydell-Bouverie at her family home at Coleshill in 1925, to be joined there in 1928 by Braden. Other pupils before the Second World War included Charlotte Epton, who married the painter Edward Bawden in 1932, and Sylvia Fox-Strangways who went on to teach at Dartington School in 1926. Harry Davis, a fiercely idealistic autodidact, came to St Ives in 1933 as an employee and married another pupil, May Scott, the granddaughter of the founder of the Manchester Guardian, who arrived in 1936.[37] They set up the Crowan Pottery in Cornwall in 1946. Leach's son David joined the pottery in 1930, a decision which was to have important implications. David Leach trained at the North Staffordshire Technical College in Stoke-on-Trent from 1934 to 1936, acquiring the technical know-how that enabled the pottery to flourish after the Second World War. In 1938, at his suggestion, a local boy, William Marshall, was taken on as an apprentice. He proved an ideal 'artisan' and after the Second World War threw handsome large pots for Leach to decorate.

Leach therefore established a small 'school' of followers which included three potters of great talent. Norah Braden and Katharine Pleydell-Bouverie were seen by the critics as abstract artists celebrated for the pure forms of their stoneware and the subtle effects of their wood ash glazes.[38] Michael Cardew, on the other hand, was hailed both as the guardian of the English slipware tradition and as a Gauguin manqué living in poverty in Gloucestershire. He was certainly difficult, an abrupt handsome figure, brimming with disdain for a London art world which intermittently courted him.[39] Leach himself was less famous than we might suppose during the 1920s and 1930s. He was admired by the same collectors and curators who bought Murray's pots. He had fewer connections in the fine art world than Murray. But he presented himself first and foremost as an Occidental who understood the Orient, constantly setting the aesthetics of the Far East against the materialism and superficiality of the West. His thinking appealed to his key patrons between the wars, the wealthy idealistic Elmhirsts of Dartington, and they funded Leach while he wrote *A Potter's Book* during 1938-9. Its publication in 1940 was timely. His sweeping rejection of industrialisation, his promise of spiritual enlightenment and his confidence about aesthetic standards went far beyond the step-by-step didacticism of a how-to-do-it book. Instead Leach offered the promise of a spiritually fulfilling way of life. For those in search of certainties, *A Potter's Book* became a bible for a war-torn generation and after the Second World War Leach began to seem like the founder of the studio pottery movement. Murray's work and ideas slipped from view.

The men and women in Leach and Staite Murray's circles had a sharply defined vision of what constituted studio pottery. Their elevated discourse was dominated by the act of throwing on the wheel which was granted semi-mystical status. Both Leach and Murray liked to assert that 'a pot is born rather than made'.[40] The critics as we have seen, drew frequent attention to the abstraction of thrown pots and it was this branch of studio pottery which dominated the famous collections made by Eric Milner-White,[41] Henry Bergen[42] and George Eumorfopoulos and the purchases made by the Victoria and Albert Museum.[43] The two canonical surveys of the studio pottery movement, George Wingfield Digby's *The Work of The Modern Potter in England* (1952) and Muriel Rose's *Artist Potters in England* (1955) also remained loyal to what Leach came to call in *A Potter's Book* 'the Sung standard'.

George Wingfield Digby (curator and subsequently keeper in the Textile Department of the Victoria & Albert Museum) and Muriel Rose (founder of the inter-war Little Gallery) helped give studio pottery an identity which also excluded any kind of collaboration with industry. Neither discussed the work of Alfred and Louise Powell who worked and exhibited throughout the interwar years. The Powells are interesting because they combined aspects of the Arts and Crafts project, particularly a concern for the creative satisfaction of a less privileged work force, into the 1930s. Their decorative language owed something to the art potter William De Morgan but it was more reticent, a precise and lyrical version of pastoral, based on the study of wild flowers and plants. Both possessed many craft skills. Alfred Powell, like Henry Wilson, had been trained as an architect in the office of John Dando Sedding, an architect with a supreme sensitivity to workmanship and materials. From 1903 Powell specialised in creating designs for Wedgwood to be painted under-glaze on the firm's pottery blanks. In 1906 he married Louise Lessore and from then on they worked as a team, training women to paint their designs freehand in factory conditions at Wedgwood, thus 'uncovering the love of beauty in work'.[44] The mystical musings of Leach or Murray would have irritated the Powells. Their avowed aim was 'freshly inventive and delightful crockery, as full of fancy as a wood of leaves.'[45] Both in the Cotswolds and at Stoke-on-Trent they sought to encourage creativity among all classes of men and women.

The Powells were greatly admired by another important potter with industrial links. Dora Billington had grown up in Stoke-on-Trent, her grandfather and father had been associated with the Potteries and she had trained at Hanley School of Art, and then at the Royal College of Art where she took over as instructor on the death of Richard Lunn in 1915. In 1919 she started teaching at the Central School of Arts and Crafts in the School of Painted and Sculptured Decoration and by 1936 was giving lectures on pottery materials and chemistry that were so precise and helpful that Murray's students from the Royal College flocked to hear them.[46] In 1937 she published *The Art of the Potter* which argued for a homegrown or European tradition. She had little time for Orientally inspired stoneware, preferring the Powell's decorated wares and enjoying Vanessa Bell and Duncan Grant's 'spirited experiments' in maiolica.[47] She designed for industry as well as working in her own studio, arguing for unity of ceramic practice. Her real influence was felt as a teacher at the Central School. After the Second World War her anti-Orientalism bore fruit, taking the form of a maiolica revival among her more gifted students. They celebrated the ceramic arts of Southern Europe and Picasso's wartime experiments with clay and combined throwing and hand-building to create light-hearted figurines more suitable for the coffee bar than the museum or collector's cabinet.

Between the wars some studio potters had made figurines. The Vyses made a series of urban Madonnas with high cheekbones selling balloons and lavender. Reginald Wells made ceramic variants of his small bronzes. Many of these inter-war figurine makers were women and because figurines were excluded from Wingfield Digby and Rose's accounts of the history of studio pottery these women were retrospectively marginalised.[48] A period eye is needed here. Reginald Blunt's *Cheyne Book of Chelsea China and Pottery* of 1924 makes it plain that figurines had their own band of admiring collectors in the inter-war years. Some collectors bought both figurines and studio pots. The ceramics purchased by the architect Sydney Greenslade for the immensely wealthy Davies sisters of Gregynog included 'art' and 'studio' pottery and figurines.[49] Gwendolen Parnell's characters from Sheridan's *School for Scandal*, Stella Crofts's animals, Madeline Raper's minaturised tudor cottages and Harold and Phoebe Stabler's garlanded putti riding bulls modelled for Carter, Stabler & Adams at Poole were often exhibited alongside pots by Leach, Murray and their pupils.

In 1925; the art critic Frank Rutter reviewed the British ceramics shown at the Paris Exposition of that year. He had been founder of the Allied Artists Association, the radical director of the Leeds City Art Gallery from 1912 until 1917 and had organised the 1913 Post-Impressionist and Futurist exhibition at the Doré Galleries which had included the most wide-ranging group of European modernist art yet seen in London.[50] Rutter praised pots by Reginald Wells and Leach but he reserved his greatest admiration for the 'daintiness of invention and execution' of figurine makers like Gwendolen Parnell, Harry Parr and the Vyses.[51] This seems surprising. Both his response and inter-war buying and exhibiting patterns suggest that studio ceramics encompassed a more varied practice than the later histories of the movement allow – even if ultimately the thrown abstract vessel came to represent modernism in ceramics. *The Times* art critic Charles Marriott was voicing a consensus in 1943 when he argued that there were no British sculptors to compare with Brancusi but that 'pottery is, precisely, abstract sculpture' and that here British artists were proving themselves 'second to none'. In 1945 W.B. Honey, the then Keeper of Ceramics at the V&A, explained of a series of early pots ranging from pre-dynastic Egyptian to nineteenth-century English country pottery: 'They are compositions in line and mass and as such are examples of what is usually called abstract art.'[52] Finally, after the war, T.S. Eliot, a director of Faber & Faber, which published the writings of Honey, Leach and Read, put a discussion of the pure form of pottery and its superiority to painting and sculpture at the heart of his play *The Confidential Clerk*.

Notes

1. For a good account of the early development of studio pottery, see Oliver Watson, *British Studio Pottery: the Victoria and Albert Museum Collection*, Phaidon/ Christies/ Victoria & Albert Museum 1990, pp. 16–24. Hereafter Watson (1990).
2. See Malcolm Haslam, *English Art Pottery 1865-1915*, Antique Collectors' Club, Woodbridge 1975; Geoffrey Godden, *British Pottery: An Illustrated Guide*, Barrie and Jenkins 1974; Peter C. D. Brears, *The English Country Pottery. Its History and Techniques*, David and Charles, Newton Abbot 1971. See Rachel Gotlieb, 'The Critical Language and Aesthetic Criteria of Art-Pottery Manufacturers and Studio-Potters 1914-1934', RCA/V&A MA thesis 1987, for confusions of identity between art and studio pottery.
3. Michael Cardew, *A Pioneer Potter: An Autobiography*, Collins 1988, p. 27; hereafter Cardew, *Autobiography*.
4. Roger Fry, 'The Art of Pottery in England', *Burlington Magazine*, March 1914, pp. 330–5.
5. Clive Bell, *Art*, Chatto and Windus 1914, p. 8.
6. Ibid., p. 58.
7. Roger Fry, 'The Art of Pottery in England', *Burlington Magazine*, March 1914, p. 335.
8. Wells attracted some interesting contemporary comment. See Frederick Lessore, 'The Art of Reginald F. Wells', *Artwork*, no. 8, vol. 2, Dec-Feb 1926-7, p. 234; Ernest Marsh, 'R.F. Wells Sculptor Potter', *Apollo*, vol. 1, 1925, pp. 283–9; Bernard Rackham, 'The Pottery of Reginald F. Wells', *The Studio*, vol. xc, December 1925, pp. 359–63.
9. Richard Dennis, *Charles Vyse 1882-1971*, Richard Dennis/Fine Art Society 1974. Celadon and tenmoku are both stoneware iron glazes. Celadon is a greyish-green or blue and tenmoku a lustrous black/brown breaking to rust on

rims and edges. Chün is an ash glaze which fires to an opalescent blue to purple. Tz'ŭ-chou describes stoneware produced in north China from the seventh to the fourteenth century, characterised by bold decoration which is incised, sgraffitoed, brushed or moulded or employs a combination of these techniques. Bernard Leach, *A Potter's Book*, Faber & Faber 1940, contains good vivid descriptions of most of the glazes and decorative techniques that I mention.

10. Graham M. McLaren, '"A Complete Potteress" - The Life and Work of Dora Lunn', *Journal of the Decorative Arts Society*, 13 (1989), pp. 33–8.
11. Margot Coatts, *The Oxshott Pottery: Denise and Henry Wren*, Crafts Study Centre, Holburne Museum, Bath 1984.
12. Gordon Forsyth, 'Pottery', in *Reports on the Present Position and Tendencies of the Industrial Arts as Indicated at the Exhibition of Modern Decorative and Industrial Arts, Paris 1925*, Department of Overseas Trade 1927, p. 134.
13. This section is indebted to Malcolm Haslam's excellent study *William Staite Murray*, Crafts Council/Cleveland County Museum Service 1984; hereafter Haslam (1984). There is also much of value in Sarah Riddick, *Pioneer Studio Pottery: The Milner White Collection*, Lund Humphries/York City Art Gallery 1990.
14. Haslam (1984), p. 10.
15. On fine art and ceramics see Tamara Preaud and Serge Gauthier, *Ceramics of the Twentieth Century*, Phaidon/Christies, Oxford 1982, p. 82.
16. Anna Gruetzner Robins, *Modern Art in Britain 1910-1914*, Barbican Art Gallery/Merrell Holberton 1997, p. 130.
17. Bernard Rackham, Herbert Read, *English Pottery. Its development from early times to the end of the eighteenth century*, Ernest Benn Ltd., 1924, p. 4.
18. Haslam (1984), p. 71.
19. H.S. Ede, 'Ben Nicholson. Winifred Nicholson and William Staite Murray', *Artwork*, no. 16, vol. 4, Winter 1928, no. 16, pp. 262–9.
20. *Catalogue of Pottery, Paintings and Furniture by Staite Murray*, Alex. Reid & Lefevre Ltd., November 1930.
21. See especially Ede, *op.cit.*, p. 267. Haslam (1984) quotes the important reviews of Murray's work. Murray and studio pottery in general were discussed in *The Times* by Charles Marriott from 1924-40, in *The Studio*, in *Apollo* (founded 1925), in *Artwork* (1924-31) and in the short-lived *Arts and Crafts* (1925-9) as well as in less specialist magazines like *The New English Weekly* (founded 1933) and *G.K.'s Weekly* (founded 1925).There was also interesting coverage in the *Pottery Gazette and Glass Trade Review.*
22. Herbert Read, 'Art and Decoration', *The Listener*, 7 May 1930, p. 805.
23. Barry Hepton (ed.), *Sam Haile Potter and Painter 1909-1948*, Bellew Publishing/Cleveland County Council 1993.
24. Crafts Study Centre, Holburne Museum, Bath, *A Fine Line. Henry Hammond 1914-89 Potter and Educationalist*, 1992.
25. Paul Rice, Christopher Gowing, *British Studio Ceramics in the 20th Century*, Barrie & Jenkins 1989, pp. 78–83.
26. For a more detailed discussion of the 1930s 'problem' see below pp. 118–20.
27. Cardew, *Autobiography*, p. 98.
28. Peter Fuller, 'The Proper Work of the Potter', in Peter Dormer (ed.), *Fifty Five Pots and Three Opinions*, The Orchard Gallery, Londonderry 1983, p. 21.
29. On Leach see Watson (1990); Leach, *Memoirs*; Bernard Leach, *Hamada Potter*, Kodansha International, Tokyo 1975; Edmund de Waal, *Bernard Leach*, Tate Gallery 1998.
30. For an overview see Anna Gruetzner Robins, *Modern Art in Britain 1910-1914*, Barbican Art Gallery/Merrell Holberton 1997. For Murray's involvement in the London avant-garde see Haslam (1984).
31. Bernard Leach, 'The Meeeting of East and West in Pottery', *The Far East*, 12 June 1915, p. 314.
32. *Pottery Gazette and Glass Trade Review*, 1 December 1920 - 'The progress of this Cornish innovation will be watched with more than ordinary interest.'

33. Leach, *Memoirs*, p.73. Also see Sarah Riddick, *Pioneer Studio Pottery: The Milner White Collection*, Lund Humphries/York City Art Gallery 1990, p. 63.
34. Leach, *Memoirs*, p. 119.
35. A phrase used by Katharine Pleydell-Bouverie in a letter of 5 October 1927, Leach Papers 2497, CSC.
36. Oliver Watson, *Bernard Leach - Potter and Artist*, Artis Inc., Japan 1997, p. 19. See also Bernard Leach, *Hamada Potter*, Kodansha, Japan 1990, pp. 162–5, 170–1.
37. For an acerbic account of the Leach pottery see May Davis, *May*, privately printed, Nelson, New Zealand 1990.
38. For an overview see Crafts Council/Crafts Study Centre, Holburne Museum, Bath, *Katharine Pleydell-Bouverie: A Potter's Life 1895-1985*, 1986. For contemporary criticism in which sculptural, architectural and even musical connections are made see W.A. Thorpe, 'English Stoneware Pottery by Miss K. Pleydell-Bouverie and Miss D.K.N. Braden', *Artwork*, no. 24, vol. 6, Winter 1930, pp. 257–65. Paul Rice, Christopher Gowing, *British Studio Ceramics in the 20th Century*, Barrie & Jenkins 1986, pp. 56–64 gives a lively, affectionate account of Braden and Pleydell-Bouverie's work.
39. The best introduction is Cardew, *Autobiography*.
40. Staite Murray quoted in Haslam (1984) p. 70 and Leach, *Memoirs*, p. 146.
41. The key book is Sarah Riddick, *Pioneer Studio Pottery: The Milner White Collection*, Lund Humphries/York City Art Gallery 1990.
42. Eileen M. Hampson, 'Henry Bergen: Friend of Studio Potters', *Journal of the Northern Ceramics Society*, vol. 8, 1991, pp. 74–89.
43. Watson (1990), p. 38.
44. Maureen Batkin, 'Alfred and Louise Powell', in May Greensted, *The Arts and Crafts in the Cotswolds*, Alan Sutton 1993, p. 100. For the social context see Jacqueline Sarsby, 'Alfred Powell: Idealism and Realism in the Cotswolds', Journal of Design History, vol. 10, no. 4, 1997, pp. 375–97.
45. Alfred H. Powell, 'Arts & Crafts: Pottery', *The Highway*, vol. ix, no. 101, February 1917, pp. 79–81.
46. Watson (1990), p. 153.
47. Dora Billington, *The Art of the Potter*, Oxford University Press 1937, p. 110.
48. This point is well made in Moira Vincentelli, 'Potters of the 1920s: Contemporary Criticism', in G. Elinor, S. Richardson, S. Scott, A. Thomas, K. Walker (eds), *Women and Craft*, Virago 1987.
49. Moira Vincentelli, Anna Hale, *Catalogue of Early Studio Pottery in the Collections of University College of Wales, Aberystwyth* 1986.
50. Anna Gruetzner Robins, *Modern Art in Britain 1910-1914*, Barbican Art Gallery/Merrell Holberton 1997, pp. 116–37.
51. Frank Rutter, 'Modern English Pottery and Porcelain', *Apollo*, vol. 11, December 1925, p. 133.
52. Charles Marriott, *British Handicrafts*, British Council 1943, pp.33-4; W.B. Honey, *The Art of the Potter*, Faber & Faber 1946, p. 15.

This was first published as 'Studio Pottery' in Tanya Harrod, 1999, *The Crafts in Britain in the 20th Century*, Yale University Press, pp. 30–42.

Reproduced by permission of Yale University Press
© Yale University Press 1999

16
TOWARDS A STANDARD
Bernard Leach

P 1-4

Very few people in this country think of the making of pottery as an art, and amongst those few the great majority have no criterion of aesthetic values which would enable them to distinguish between the genuinely good and the meretricious. Even more unfortunate is the position of the average potter, who without some standard of fitness and beauty derived from tradition cannot be expected to produce, not necessarily master pieces, but even intrinsically sound work.

The potter is no longer a peasant or journeyman as in the past, nor can he be any longer described as an industrial worker: he is by force of circumstances an artist-craftsman, working for the most part alone or with a few assistants. Factories have practically driven folk-art out of England; it survives only in out of the way comers even in Europe, and the artist-craftsman, since the day of William Morris, has been the chief means of defence against the materialism of industry and its insensibility to beauty.

Here at the very beginning it should be made clear that the work of the individual potter or potter-artist, who performs all or nearly all the processes of production with his own hands, belongs to one aesthetic category, and the finished result of the operations of industrialized manufacture, or mass-production, to another and quite different category. In the work of the potter-artist, who throws his own pots, there is a unity of design and execution, a co-operation of hand and undivided personality, for designer and craftsman are one, that has no counterpart in the work of the designer for mass-production, whose office is to make drawings or models of utensils, often to be cast moulded in parts and subsequently assembled, The art of craftsman, to use Herbert Read's terminology, is intuitive and humanistic (one hand one brain); that of the designer for reduplication, rational, abstract and tectonic, the work of engineer or constructor rather than that of the 'artist'. Each method has its own aesthetic significance. Examples of both can be good or bad. The distinction between them lies in the relegation of the actual making not merely to other hands than those of the designer but to power driven machines. The products of the latter can never possess the same intimate qualities as the former, but to deny them the possibility of excellence of design in terms of what mechanical reproduction can do is blind and obstinate. A motor car such as a Rolls Royce Phantom achieves a kind of perfection although its appeal is mainly intellectual and material. There I think we come to the crux of the matter: good hand craftsmanship is directly subject to the prime source of human activity, whereas machine crafts, even at their best, are activated at one remove – by the intellect. No doubt the work of the intuitive craftsman would be considered by most people to be of a higher, more personal, order of beauty; nevertheless, industrial pottery at its best, done from the drawings of a constructor who is an artist, can certainly have an intuitive element.[1] The trouble, however, is that at a conservative estimate about

Source: © Bernard Leach/Unicorn Publishing Group.

nine-tenths of the industrial pottery produced in England no less than in other countries is hopelessly bad in both form and decoration. With the exception of a few traditional shapes and patterns for table-ware, and others designed by the best designers available to-day and painted by the best available artists (none of whom is a potter), turned out notably by the Wedgwood and Royal Worcester and Minton factories and by the Makin and Gray firms in Hanley, and excluding also a few purely functional and utilitarian designs, some of which are also traditional, such as Doulton's acid-jars, we meet everywhere with bad forms and banal, debased, pretentious decoration – qualities that are perhaps most conspicuous in 'fancy vases', flower-pots and other ornamental pieces, in we find a crudity of colour combined with cheapness and inappropriateness of decoration and tawdriness of form that must be seen to be believed. And although the mechanical processes are indeed marvellous, as for example the automatic glazing, cleaning, measuring and stamping of many millions per month of bathroom tiles, fired in a single non-stop tunnel kiln, the mere fact of their being mass-produced is no reason why these tiles should be as cheaply designed and as dull and miserable in colour as it is possible for tiles to be; nor in the case of hollow-ware is the casting of shapes so exactly and so quickly and with such perfect pastes an adequate excuse for dead shapes, dead clay, dead lithographed printing or the laboured painting of dead patterns. Indeed the more elaborate and expensive the decoration the more niggling and lifeless it is, and the nearer it approaches the long deceased fashion of naturalism of the nineteenth century, when close attention to detail and the careful painting of pictures upon porcelain in enamel colours was considered the summit of ceramic art – 'applied' art with a vengeance! On the other hand, if the bulk of the pottery turned out in England to-day is mass-produced and of inferior form and decoration, its inferiority is not so much due to the manner of its production – for mass-produced wares can not only be of fine quality of body[2] and beautiful in form, if designed by the right men – but for various extrinsic reasons, chief of which is the failure of the manufacturer to interest himself in good design. The want of artistic initiative on the part of the manufacturers must be ascribed to the general lowering of taste under conditions of competitive industrialism. The public is ever increasingly out of touch with the making of articles of everyday use, and although its entrepreneurs, the buyers and salesmen trade, are continually caught out in their under-estimation what people like they cannot be entirely blamed for catering to safe markets. Even if, as Pevsner says, 'one cannot condemn industrialist too severely because he does not jump at suggested artistic improvement', and it 'would be absurd suggest to the producer that he ought to ruin himself for community', there is nevertheless no reason why he should work as far as possible towards replacing bad forms and decorations with good, and realize, in spite of the cheerful assurances of buyers and travellers, that he must cater to bad taste, that of the chief reasons why 'the public (apart from a few hopelessly insensitive individuals) likes' tawdry utensils, is because as a rule it can get no others. Apart from the initial expense of new moulds, and provided a competent designer is available, there is no apparent ground for believing that good commercial pottery should be any more expensive to make than bad.

P7-10

… That the criterion of beauty is a living thing and constantly in flux, is true, but here at least there is a continuous if ever changing consensus of opinion as to what may be called great achievement. In regard to pottery such a criterion can hardly be said ever to have entered the consciousness of Western man. In the East it has long been in existence, especially in Japan, where the aesthetic sensibility of educated people has been stimulated by the ablest of critics for some three hundred or more years. As space will only allow me to speak briefly of this great aesthetic cult and its unrivalled standard of artistic appreciation, I cannot do better than give a more or less condensed and paraphrased extract from an essay on popular, or folk, arts and crafts by Sōetsu Yanagi, the intellectual leader of the Japanese craft movement of to-day:

'I have many occasions to call at the residences of wellknown art collectors, but I find too often that the articles of everyday use in their homes are far from being artistic, to say the least. They often leave me with a sad suspicion as to how much these collectors really appreciate beauty.

'To me the greatest thing is to live beauty in our daily life and to crowd every moment with things of beauty. It is then, and then only, that the art of the people as a whole is endowed with its richest significance. For its products are those made by a great many craftsmen for the mass of the people, and the moment this art declines the life of the nation is removed far away from beauty. So long as beauty abides in only a few articles created by a few geniuses, the Kingdom of Beauty is nowhere near realization.

'Fortunately, in Japan, handicraft objects have been treasured through the channel of ceremonial tea. *Cha-no-yu* in last analysis is a means of harmonizing life and beauty. … It may be thought of as an aesthetics of the practical arts. In all its appurtenances, whether it be in the architecture, the garden, or the utensils, the first principle is utility and the adornment of life with refinement. Not beauty for beauty's own sake, but beauty answering all immediate needs of life – that is the essence of ceremonial tea….

'One may ask, what then is the nature of the beauty which has been discovered by these tea-masters? … In the first place it is non-individualistic. … As in medieval Europe art meant adherence to tradition, so in the East all works of arts or crafts were governed equally by common principles. … Some of the most famous tea-bowls were originally the simplest of utensil in popular use in Korea or China; many of them were the rice bowls of Korean peasants. But the amazingly keen eye of the *Cha-no-yu* master has discovered in these odd, neglected pieces a unique beauty; for what most appeals to him are the things originally made for everyday use. In brief, *Cha-no-yu* may be defined as an aesthetics of actual living, in which utility is the first principle of beauty. And that is why such great significance has been given to certain articles necessary for everyday life….

'The next important aspect of the works of people's art is that they are simple and unassuming. Here the quality of extravagance that is always associated with expensive art objects is wholly absent, and any surplus of decorativeness is objectionable. ... Simplicity may be thought of as characteristic of cheap things, but it must be remembered that it is a quality that harmonizes well with beauty. That which is truly beautiful is often simple and restrained. … I am told that St. Francis of Assisi advocated what he called 'Holy Poverty'. A thing possessed in some manner of the virtue of poverty has an indescribable beauty. Indeed, Beauty and Humility border upon each other. What is so appealing in the art of the people is this very quality … beauty accompanied by the nobleness of poverty. The Japanese people have a special word *shibui* to express this ideal beauty. … It is impossible to translate it satisfactorily into one term, "austere", "subdued", "restrained", these words come nearest. Etymologically, *shibui* means "astringent", and is used to describe profound, unassuming and quiet feeling. The mere fact that we have such an adjective would not call for second thought, but what does call for special note is the fact that this adjective is the final criterion for the highest form of beauty. It is, moreover, an ordinary word, and is repeated continually in our casual conversation. It is in itself unusual that a nation should share a standard word for aesthetic appraisal. Here in this criterion of ours for the best and most beautiful may be observed the fundamental principle of the aesthetic tastes of the Japanese people. … If you have travelled much in rural Japan you must have come across one of these stone monuments, with the

> inscription *Sangai Banrei Tō*, at a crossroad or in a deserted corner. The inscription means "a monument to the unknown, departed souls of the million people of the world". This monument is an expression of the Buddhist's compassion for the countless number of forgotten and uncared-for souls. I am one of those whose prayer it is to erect such monuments in the Kingdom of Beauty.'

Thus from a Buddhist background, ethically much akin to the medieval Christianity on which the neo-Thomists have based their attitude towards art, Mr. Yanagi seems to me in these arresting and moving sentences to have thrown down a challenge not only to his Japanese contemporaries but to us as well – a challenge to our over-accentuated individualism. For one may indeed look back with an acute sense of loss to those periods when the communal element, with its native religious, psychological and aesthetic basis, was all-powerful as an ennobling and transmuting influence and source of life.

A potter's traditions are part of a nation's cultural inheritance and in our time we are faced with the breakdown of the Christian inspiration in art. We live in dire need of a unifying culture out of which fresh traditions can grow. The potter's problem is at root the universal problem and it is difficult to see how any solution aiming at less than the full interplay of East and West can provide either humanity, or the individual potter, with a sound foundation for a world-wide culture. Liberal democracy, which served as a basis for the development of industrialism, provides us to-day with a vague humanism as insufficient to inspire art as either the economics of Karl Marx or the totalitarian conception of national life, but at least it continues to supply an environment in which the individual is left comparatively free.

P17-23

I have often sought for some method of suggesting to people who have not had the experience of making pottery a means of approach to the recognition of what is good, based upon common human experience rather than upon aesthetic hairsplitting. A distinguished Japanese potter, Mr. Kawai of Kyoto, when asked how people are to recognize good work, answered simply, 'With their bodies'; by which he meant, with the mind acting directly through the senses, taking in form, texture, pattern and colour, and referring the sharp immediate impressions to personal experience of use and beauty combined. But as pottery is made for uses with which we are all familiar, the difficulty probably lies less in one's ability to recognize proper adaptation of form to function than in other directions, primarily perhaps in unfamiliarity with the nature of the raw material, clay, and its natural possibilities and limitations, and also in uncertainty as to the more imponderable qualities of vitality and relative excellence of form, both of which are indispensable constituents of beauty. It must always be remembered that the dissociation of use and beauty is a purely arbitrary thing. It is true that pots exist which are useful and not beautiful, and others that are beautiful and impractical; but neither of these extremes can be considered normal: the normal is a balanced combination of two. Thus in looking for the best approach to pottery it seems reasonable to expect that beauty will emerge from a fusion of the individual character and culture of the potter with the nature of his materials – clay, pigment, glaze – and his management of the fire, and that consequently we may hope to find in good pots those innate qualities which we most admire in people. It is for this reason that I consider the mood, or nature, of a pot to be of first importance. It represents our instinctive total reaction to either man or pot, and although there is no guarantee that our judgment is true for others, it is at least essentially honest and as likely to be true as any judgment we are capable of making at that particular phase of our development. It is far better to run the risk of making an occasional blunder than to attempt cold-blooded analyses based upon other people's theories. Judgment in art cannot be other than intuitive and founded upon sense experience, on what Kawai calls 'the body'. No process of reasoning can be a substitute for or widen the range of our intuitive knowledge.

This does not mean that we cannot use our common sense in examining the qualities in a pot which give us its character, such as form, texture, decoration and glaze, for analytic reasoning is important enough as a support to intuition. Beginning with the colour and texture of the clay, one must ask, apart from its technical suitability, whether it is well related to the thrown or moulded shape created by the potter and to the purpose for which the pot is intended – what, for example, is appropriate for a porous unglazed water jug is utterly unsuitable for an acid jar. Does its fired character give pleasure to the eye as well as to the touch; its texture contrast pleasingly with the glaze? Has it where exposed to the flame turned to a dull brick red which contrasts happily with the heavy jade green of a celadon? Does it show an interesting granular surface under an otherwise lifeless porcelain glaze? Has its plasticity been such as to encourage the thrower to his best efforts, for the form cannot be dissociated from its material. The shape of a pot cannot be dissociated from the way it has been made, one may throw fifty pots in an hour, on the same model, which only vary in fractions of an inch, and yet only half a dozen of them may possess that right relationship of parts which gives vitality – life flowing for a few moments perfectly through the hands of potter.

Apart from the basic clay, the form of the pot is of the first importance, and the first thing we must look for is, as already indicated, proper adaptation to use and suitability to material. Without these we cannot expect to find beauty in any of its modes, nobility, austerity, strength, breadth, subtlety, warmth – qualities which apply equally to our judgments of human and ceramic values. Nor do these qualities arise from human characteristics alone, but from a common recognition of forms whether man-made or natural, which we associate with them. Of all forms we know best our own and attach to it the greatest degree of evocative emotion; next come animal, plant and mineral forms; lastly, and mainly in our own time, geometric abstracts, largely the inventions of man's brain. It is not without reason that important parts of pots should be known as foot, belly, shoulder, neck and lip, or that curve and angle should often be thought of as male or female. Beauty of ceramic form, which is at once subjective and objective, is obtained in much the same manner as in abstract (rather than representational) sculpture. It is subjective in that the innate character of the potter, his stock and his tradition live afresh in his work; objective in so far as his selection is drawn from the background of universal human experience.

Subordinate to form but intimately connected with it is the problem of decoration, and the question arises whether the increased orchestration adds to the total effect or not. Decoration will be treated more fully later on, here it is enough to say that, although some of the very finest pots are quite plain, it is nevertheless of the greatest significance. Many a good piece has been spoiled by a weak or tasteless design, printed or applied in one way or another: not only must the pattern be good in itself and freely executed, but it must combine with and improve the form and harmonize with the natural variations of both colour and texture of body and glaze.

The upshot of the argument is that a pot in order to be good should be a genuine expression of life. It implies sincerity on the part of the potter and truth in the conception and execution of the work. By this reasoning we are thrown back upon the oldest of questions, but there is no escaping fundamental issues in discussing problems of art at a period of break-up and change. Art is an epitome of life experience and in searching for a standard in pottery elastic enough to cover both past and present we are compelled to look far afield and to examine the principles upon which the best pots of East and West have been based. In a broad way the difference between the old potters and the new is between unconsciousness within a single culture and individual consciousness of all cultures. And to this one can only add that until a life synthesis is reached by humanity the individual potter can only hope to deepen and widen his consciousness in anticipation and contribution towards that end.

The method by which a pot is formed determines its general character, whether hand modelled or built up out of coils or slices, or freely thrown on the wheel, or thrown in a mould, or cast entirely in a mould – each process conditions the interpretation of the original idea, and each has a limited range of right usage, from the easy flowing application of which follows the sense of satisfaction and adequacy of technique. It is for this reason that the industrial practice of rigidly separating designer on paper from maker in clay is responsible for much of the deadness of commercial pottery, for it is a waste of opportunity as well as a straining of technique to make moulded pots as like thrown pots as possible. The beauty of each method lies in using that method honestly, for what it is worth, not in imitating quite different processes.[3]

The range of plastic beauty achieved in primitive pottery made chiefly by the hands of women without a wheel and with tools only of wood or stone, basketry, textiles, leaves of trees or stitched animal hides, is immense. The whole world seems to have contributed to it during thousands of prehistoric years: Minoan, archaic Greek, African, North and South American, pots of the Black Earth Region and neolithic China, pigmented but unglazed, often so fine that one might be tempted to surrender all claim for the supremacy of eleventh and twelfth century China, were it not for the fact that the general cultural and technical achievements of the Sung Chinese were so much greater. For this reason I shall deal in this book for the most part with wheel-thrown forms, which reached their greatest perfection round about that period.

A pot thrown on a good wheel with responsive clay, but not too soapy in texture, is impressed and expressed, urged and pulled and coaxed through a series of rhythmic movements which like those of a dance are all related and interdependent. The spinning wet clay must be kept dead true to the centre the wheel while it is being hollowed and drawn up, expanded and contracted into a living embodiment of the potter's intention. The preconceived shape will include the mark of each part of the process of throwing, the ribs left by the fingers, the upward thrust of the cylinder from the wheel-head to the major curve of the belly, the fulness or leanness of that curve, the pause and turn on the shoulder, often accentuated with ridge or collar, where convex movement changes to concave, the neck tapering to the lip with a concluding accent and conciseness of finish. Many of the noblest and most spontaneous pots are complete at this point, but others, especially such as are to have a foot-ring or bevelled lip, need to be pared on the wheel when half dry. This cutting off of shavings gives a different and sharper quality of finish: the difference between modelling and carving; and the two surfaces must be brought into harmony with one another.

The foot, upon which the pot stands, should be reasonably wide for stability, but over and beyond that its angles and proportion should relate to the lip, to which the eye instinctively leaps. The cutting of the foot does not end with the profile; the inside of the ring is nearly always hollowed out in the East. Stoneware pots are seldom glazed over the bottom, and the exposed clay tells how thoroughly the potter felt the contrast between the profile with its necessary concluding foot and the perfect curve of the pot through it.

There are many types of foot-cutting well understood by Oriental potters and often associated with certain kinds of vessel or with certain localities, in which refinement has been worked out by a long process of trial and error into a fixed tradition.

1. It is interesting to see an Oriental pick up a pot for examination, and presently carefully turn it over to look at the clay and the form and cutting of the foot. He inspects it as carefully as a banker a doubtful signature – in fact, he is looking for the bona fides of the author. There in the most naked but hidden part of the work he expects to come into closest touch with the character and perception of its maker. He looks to see how far and how well the pot has been dipped, in what relation the texture and colour of the clay stand to the glaze, whether the foot has the right width, depth, angle, undercut, bevels and general feeling to carry and complete the form above it. Nothing can be concealed there, and much of his final pleasure lies in the satisfaction of knowing that this last examination and scrutiny has been passed with honour.

P23-24

Here, for example, are a few of the constructional ideas that I have found useful:

1. The ends of lines are important; the middles take care of themselves.
2. Lines are forces, and the points at which they change or cross are significant and call for emphasis.
3. Vertical lines are of growth, horizontal lines are of rest, diagonal lines are of change.
4. Straight line and curve, square and circle, cube and sphere are the potter's polarities, which he works into a rhythm of form under one clear concept.
5. Curves for beauty, angles for strength.
6. A small foot for grace, a broad one for stability.
7. Enduring forms are full of quiet assurance. Overstatement is worse than understatement.
8. Technique is a means to an end. It is no end in itself. If the end is achieved, and a fine pot comes out of the kiln, let us not be hypercritical about fortuitous blemishes. Some of the most beautiful pots in the world are full of technical imperfections. On the other hand, the Japanese have often gone too far and made pots with deliberate imperfections and overstatements of technical characteristics. This is nothing more than a kind of intellectual snobbery, rather to be expected from groups of second-rate tea-masters, and a very different thing from sanded foot of Ming porcelains or the Korean foot-ring, spur-marked with quartz, whose virtue was the virtue of necessity. There was no question of pose about it. But there comes a time when the accidentals of potting have to be considered consciously as such, and that is the position to-day.

Notes

1. 'Whenever the final product of the machine is designed or determined by anyone sensitive to formal values, that product can and does become an abstract work of art in the subtler sense of the term.' Read, *Art and Industry*, p. 37.
2. '... pottery manufacturers know that mass production can in ceramics, at least as regards the quality of the body, help greatly towards improvements. The reason is that more efficient kilns can be used and better conditions of firing attained.' – Comp. Nikolaus Pevsner, *An Enquiry into Industrial Art in England*, 1937, p. 191 and p. 83.
3. Every designer either on paper or of model parts should have first-hand experience not only of the processes of manufacture, but also of the limitations no less than the potentialities of his materials. What is obviously needed is a new type of designer who knows both approaches to pottery and can therefore keep industry in touch with fresh artistic expression in the studio. Without such an alliance in the near future between artist-craftsman and factory, it is difficult conceive how pots could be made in Staffordshire which would be even respectable in the scale of beauty the world has known. The tendency to employ sculptors and painters of reputation to make designs for the industry is useful up to a point, but it gives no guarantee that these artists know and feel their medium, nor that the factories and their reduplicating processes will do justice to the designs. The link is not close enough.

Extracted from Bernard Leach, 1940 (2011), *A Potter's Book*, London: Faber and Faber, pp. 1–4, 7–10, 17–23, 23–24.

Reproduced by permission of Lord Strathcarron/Unicorn Publishing Group.

17
TOWARDS A DOUBLE STANDARD?
Edmund de Waal

A child may ask when our strange epoch passes,
During a history lesson. 'Please, Sir, what's
An intellectual of the middle classes?
Is he a maker of ceramic pots...'

W.H. Auden, Letter to Lord Byron, 1937[1]

Bernard Leach bridges 'two strange epochs'. The first is the epoch of Auden's poem, when making pots was precious and rarefied, the occupation of a middle-class Bohemian vanguard. Being a potter was a testament of faith. It necessitated having both an apologia and an intellectual argument to justify the strangeness and contrariness of this activity. Leach's life up until the publication of A Potter's Book was a struggle to find ways of justifying and articulating what he did. Making pots and making definitions about making pots were intricately linked. His advocacy for being a potter was all the more powerful and heartfelt because of his early life in Japan, of living and working amongst a supportive and interested small group of patrons. In leaving Japan, he also left a way of living as an artist that seemed purposeful. In arriving in a country that was unaware of his talent, Leach's later years at St Ives and Dartington were an attempt to recreate a space in which to live creatively. What in Japan had been private art, making pots for exhibiting to a tightly knit group of friends, eventually became a public art through his career in England. Leach's studio was open to visitors, for the seasonal tourist trade he demonstrated Raku; he demonstrated throwing to the curious at exhibitions and trade fairs. He wrote passionate letters to newspapers and journals, articles for magazines, and published his pamphlet, A Potter's Outlook.

Other potters of the time did not see themselves as advocates to a greater public in quite this passionate and engaged way. For William Staite Murray, exhibiting his pots in the late 1920s with artists like Christopher Wood and Ben Nicholson, the idea of demonstrating, making the process of art visible, would have been unthinkable and somewhat degrading. Staite Murray's studio was hermetic. As an artist who used clay his conversations were with fellow artists, rather than with an unconnected public. But for Leach, who could not live as an artist as he had done in Japan, making pots and the public role of being a potter began to overlap. And being a potter began to have not only personal vocational significance (following an inner spiritual journey through the respect of materials) but also a public and didactic converting role. Leach becomes the first modern potter, middle class, a maker of ceramic pots, necessarily an intellectual of sorts. Hence the air of moral regeneration noted at his retrospective.

Pottery between the wars is a rootless art. For some critics pottery could be related to the interest in organic form of key sculptors of the day. That Henry Moore collected medieval jugs, noted the critic Geoffrey Grigson, was indicative of this 'romantic' abstraction: 'what is typically English in pottery seems to me never out of touch with the roundness and solidity of natural forms, the human breast or thigh, the tree trunk, the boulder,

Source: © Crafts/Edmund de Waal.

the flint block, if you like, the turnip'.[2] Clay was being used in ways that seemed contemporary: the articulation of forms seemed in Patrick Heron's vivid words to be 'submerged rhythms': 'we feel a powerful pulse in their pots: a rhythm that seems at its most emphatic just below the glazed surface. This is also a characteristic of natural formslogs; boulders that have been washed by the sea; or even in the human figure, where the structural form is below the surface of the flesh – the bone is under the muscle'.[3]

Critics seemed to be interrogating this new phenomenon of studio pottery as to its ambitions. Was it a genuine alternative to industrial ceramic manufacture ('necessary pots')? If so its expense and technical imperfections were manifest problems. Was it a decorative art, a useful resource for 'interior decorators and architects' to employ (nursery fireplaces, earthenware chargers for country-house walls)? Was it an art that was the peer of contemporary painting or sculpture, to be shown in very particular places and ways? Leach is at the heart of this 'strange epoch', attempting new definitions, new ways of selling work, juggling new unequivocal convictions with new equivocations.

Leach was instrumental in defining the canon of pots that potters can draw upon as genuine precursors to this new and hybrid art. His writing established the canon by which his own work was judged. His exclusions (almost all industrially manufactured ceramics, the work of the French pioneer studio potters, any of the highly decorated vernacular English pottery traditions, figurative ceramics in their entirety) remained as startling lacunae in the world of handmade pottery until the late 1950s. But in this epoch, with the canon as yet unossified, Leach's idea of appropriate pots was challenged vigorously. An article by Geoffrey Grigson in The Studio of 1935 shows the combative nature of the debate: 'The best modern analogues for the medieval earthenware or the Siamese stoneware bowl of the 10th century, the T'ang earthenware jar, the Chinese stoneware bowls of the 12th and 13th centuries or the Japanese firepot which were included for comparative purposes in the exhibition were not pots by Mr Staite Murray, Mr Bernard Leach, Miss Pleydell-Bouverie or Mr Michael Cardew … but the Doulton fire-clay crucibles, the stoneware ginger-beer bottles, the mercury-bottle and bungjar shown by Messrs Joseph Bourne.'[4]

Grigson found a 'quality of seemliness and vitality and solid grace' in the work of uninterrupted factory craftsmanship; in porcelain beakers, crucibles, evaporating and crystallising dishes and so on. His ceramic canon, like that of Herbert Read at the same time, is more profoundly demotic than Leach's. As Henry Bergen had said when editing A Potter's Book, coming across Leach's romantic apprehensions as to the reach of English country pottery, there was 'nothing more fatuous than to idealise the past except to idealise the present … even what we call country ware was used only by the better-to-do farmers …'[5] Leach is confronted and argued with: his ideas are taken seriously enough to be given the credit of public disagreement.

The second 'strange epoch' is the epoch of Leach's later life, the 1960s and 1970s. By now pottery was a common recreational pursuit, the stuff of ubiquitous evening classes and craft fairs. The studio pottery movement had burgeoned; potters filled every margin of the countryside. And there were magazines, associations, galleries devoted entirely to the dissemination of handmade pottery. It had become a 'rooted' art and a profession. As had been foreseen at the Dartington Conference of 1952 'to Leach or not to Leach' had become the driving question within this pottery world. Pottery was a new kind of enclosed group – one to which potters became attached through some sort of empathetic election. It was possible to consider 'orthodoxies' within the movement: covert degrees of adherence to Leach's ideas and precepts, overt rejections of his standpoint. But this was less a debate about the relationship between handmade pots and industry, or indeed pottery and contemporary art and architecture, more an increasingly marginalised conversation between insiders. Leach, a man with students but no peers in the West, received less and less of the robust, unsettling debate that had kept his certainties in check.

In the West, Leach has been seen as 'a natural child of the East',[6] someone who 'understood' Japan by birthright and in an almost mystical way. In the East, he has been credited with seeing deeper into the culture of Japan than any Westerner since Lascadio Hearn, of being attuned to the country and the people. Yanagi's description is almost religious: 'We were drawn to each other silently and irresistibly; I think we realised instinctively that our characters were necessary to each other. From that time on he lived among us as one of us. Our spiritual appetites were the same, we moved about in an unknown world, looking for our real world. Our hope was his hope, and our agony was his agony. He probably got nearer to the heart of modern Japan than the ordinary Japanese did. It is doubtful whether any other visitor from the West ever shared our spiritual life so completely.'[7]

Leach is anointed by Yanagi: Yanagi is anointed by Leach. The rhetoric is hyperbolic and overheated and both these friends see each other as the conduit of spiritual truths, as seers. What is curious is that this friendship has been taken so uncritically, that their mutual gratitude and the ways in which they ascribe authority to each other has not been examined. At the start of their friendship, Leach was a trophy for Yanagi, a young artistic Westerner with a bent for talk of aesthetics and spirituality. For Leach, Yanagi was a way into a salon life to which he aspired but had no access. A close and genuine friendship grew out of their interlocking needs but there was always a pragmatic heart as well. For just as Leach's authority in the West was constructed around the mythic story of his knowledge and insight into Japan, of his apprenticeship into the Kenzan school, of his 'natural' absorption into Japanese life, so Yanagi's authority in the West was constructed through Leach's placing of him as not only famous in Japan but amongst the most profound thinkers on Japan.

Stories build up and anecdotes accrete significance over time. Western critics repeated the 'Japanese Potter of St Ives' stories ad infinitum, but the limits of his Japanese world, to his ability to speak, read, or travel independently, to his knowledge of Japanese pottery traditions, have been overlooked. Yanagi's words – 'He lived among us as one of us' – should be read with a clear knowledge of the 'us': a small, attenuated group of elite, mostly English-speaking, aesthetes. In later travels around Japan, Leach is chaperoned by the leaders of the Mingei movement. Leach's Japan is a closely mediated one.

What may seem curious is why Leach's view of Japan should be attractive to Yanagi and other Japanese friends. Why should this characteristic example of Leach's views, when he is writing of the feeling of glazes to the touch, be even acceptable? 'We feel more than a satisfaction through the eyes. Unconsciously our fingers are invited to play over the contours, thereby experiencing pleasure through the most primitive and objective means. Children play with pebbles with a similar awakening of perception, and Orientals have lost touch with the fresh wonder of childhood less than we have.'[8] Leach's constant perception of Orientals as childlike, or mystical, or more attuned to the spiritual – 'Like unspoilt children no ego intrudes' – was a concomitant part of his reading of Oriental pottery as ego-less, mystically alive or, in some nebulous way, spiritual. His discovery of the tactile values of such pottery led him to consider that sense responses were the defining principle, that pots were congeries of feelings. His difficulties with the Kenzan forgeries where he was involved with urbane, complex, 'ego-full' traditions have been explored earlier, but what emerges clearly is that Japan becomes a symbol for Leach of the mysterious rather than the understood. It is this that appeals so strongly to Yanagi.

In this, of course, Leach partly reflects his age. Leach's Orientalism remains that of an Edwardian art-student brought up on the seductive exoticism and melacholy of Lascadio Hearn's prose and the unfocused whimsy of Whistler's vision of the East. This kind of Orientalism was a powerful force amongst Leach's Japanese friends. For Yanagi, as an urbane young aristocratic intellectual, his own relationship with rural Japan was similar to that of an ethnographer. Rural potters or weavers, any Korean makers at all, were almost as exotic to him as to Leach.

For many commentators on studio pottery, as well as potters themselves, Leach and Yanagi's vocabulary has been adopted wholesale: 'As is well known, in general terms the East stands for the importance of the inner life over the external, psychological insight over material forms, the inspiration and generative forces of the artist over the technical triumphs of execution,' wrote Wingfield Digby in 1952.[9] East and West are mediated as soul and mind, inner life and external life, instinctive and critical impulse. These great and pleasingly simple polarities, much discussed when Leach and Yanagi were earnest young men, stayed with them throughout their lives. Indeed so much energy was invested in exploring the polarity, that the suspicion arises that East and West could only be bridged by them. For potters, Leach becomes the interlocutor with the East, the key to unlock the arcane world of Oriental pottery. How this pottery became invested with the arcane has been overlooked.

Leach's reputation as a maker of pots has become entwined with that of his followers. 'Leach style' has become a common, and mostly pejorative, referent. It has come to be code for muddy colours, unarticulated forms, indeterminate Oriental-ish brushwork and a certain modesty of ambition. The idea of a possible function for the pot is seen as the overriding determinant. This is a curious anomaly. Leach's 'individual' pots were many and various in their styles: they cannot be stylised in such obvious ways. It is only a reading of Leach's pots that centres on the most standard of his standard wares that leads to this belief. His early Raku pots, his earthenware chargers, his tiles and fireplaces, his enamel-decorated porcelain, his large tenmoku jars, and his late fluted porcelain bowls are all in flight from any idea of a 'standard range' of pots. The endless repetition proscribed by Leach in a revealing image ('Think of the hours women have spent with knitting needles and in cooking good home-made food. In such they found pleasure and satisfaction as well as work. Repetition for a hand potter is of a like nature'[10]) was never his life. He never gained great technical facility in throwing, and never pretended that he had gained it. He never needed to make such a sacrifice of his time. Throughout his life at Abiko, and in Tokyo, in St Ives and in the Japanese pottery villages, pots were thrown under his direction for him to decorate.

In many ceramic traditions, of course, the roles of making and decorating have been distinct. The paradoxes come in Leach's writing. In Leach's rhetoric of the alienated worker, the factory-hand waiting to be liberated after the war into 'real work', the stress was on that of integration: that at this particular moment in history the potter could and indeed should have control over all the processes of creation. This has been the great and powerful seduction of A Potter's Book: its sense of self-sufficiency. Leach's relationship with those who worked for him in his studios, those whose 'orchestral playing' he 'conducted', seems to stand in direct opposition to such a rhetoric. The workshop 'craft' ethos that he promulgated was based on the centrality of an artist as a catalyst for those whose creativity was of a lesser kind. His views on the craftsman were never complex, his views on the artist, the decorator of the craftsman's work, the conductor of the studio were considerably more flattering. Decorating, like conducting, are more visible roles to adopt.

This is not to suggest that Leach did not repeat patterns. In the standard ware he decorated the majority of the 'marmalade jars' and many of the simple 'zed' bowls, too. In his 'individual' pots he employed the same patterns on pieces widely separated in time: his 'Tree of Life' motif, first used in the 1920s, was still a part of his repertoire in the 1960s. But by both initial training as an art student and by inclination too, Leach was more engaged with the dynamics of mark-making in its widest sense (drawing, engraving, etching, painting, slip-decorating, combed decoration into clay, sgraffito, fluting and so on) than with the dynamics of making forms. His graphic work, etchings in earlier life and pen and wash sketches in later years, fed constantly into his decorations for pots. He initiated ideas in two dimensions, rather than through experimenting on the wheel with alternate forms. Indeed his diagram of how to analyse the form of a pot seems to be not only didactic but of a demonstrably prescriptive bent. The characteristic process for Leach was to sketch pots before they were made: making as exploration of form, as a three-dimensional kind of sketching was not part of his life. This may explain why many of Leach's most resolved works are those where he has strongly delineated the forms to frame the decoration. His dishes made when he was driven by enthusiasm for early slipware, his tall 'medieval' jugs or his slab bottle vases all reveal this clearly. These are pots that have 'sides' to them in the most basic of ways: they are by no means complex forms. Less resolved are those pieces where there is a strong sense of a bravura 'exhibition' at work: the famous Leaping Salmon vase, for instance, only has one satisfactory viewpoint but many 'sides'. It is as close to a picture on a pot as is possible. It ought to represent the nadir of the studio pot within Leach's own philosophy. Yet it remained one of his favourite pots.

Leach's greatest strengths as a potter lie elsewhere. His sophistication in 'mark-making' is matched by his sensitivity to the surface qualities of clay. In his very earliest experiments with sgrafitto there is a caution and inhibitedness to the movements that may reflect his sense of the connections between print-making and decoration. Hamada's sgrafitto bowls of the same period are magisterial in their ease by comparison: there is a real sense of incision through the slip into the clay. But with great rapidity Leach builds up a vocabulary of techniques that allow him a more robust interaction with surfaces of pots: his judgement about when to leave parts of pots unglazed to reveal the colour and texture of the fired clay becomes increasingly fine. His use of applied sprigs of clay in the medieval manner, or of combing directly into the clay itself, shows Leach enjoying this stronger connection. His employment of a considerably wider range of glazes than was generally acknowledged is interesting in that, though the tonal range of the glazes is slight, their texture is often a matter of subtle variation. It is as if Leach's actual interest in pots, though iterated as being in the somatic experience of looking at, touching, handling and using the pot, actually stopped at the surface. This would go some way to explain that whilst the greater part of his rhetorical life was spent in trying to make a space for 'necessary pots' to be appreciated, his pots rarely seem to be an excited or engaged response to the idea or practice of function.

Notes

1. W.H. Auden and Louis Macniece, Letters from Iceland, 1937, page 201.
2. Geoffrey Grigson, 'In search of English Pottery', The Studio, November 1935, pages 256–263. See also Bernard Leach, 'A Potter's Reply', The Studio, February 1936, page 119.
3. Patrick Heron, 'Submerged Rhythms', The Changing Forms of Art, 1952, page 64.
4. Grigson op cit.
5. Henry Bergen to Bernard Leach, ms letter, 7 July 1937, BL archive 3181.
6. Edwin Mullins, 'Leach as Author', The Art of Bernard Leach (ed. Carol Hogben), London 1978.
7. Yanagi, A Potter's Book, page xiv.
8. Bernard Leach, A Potter's Book, page 37.
9. George Wingfield Digby, The Work of the Modern Potter in England, 1952, pages 25–26.
10. Bernard Leach, The Potter's Challenge, 1975, page 19.

Source: Crafts (London, England) no149 30-5 N/D 1997
The magazine publisher is the copyright holder of this article and it is reproduced with permission. Further reproduction of this article in violation of the copyright is prohibited.

Reproduced with permission of Crafts and the author.

18
RE-INVENTING THE WHEEL: THE ORIGINS OF STUDIO POTTERY

Julian Stair

> 'Among professional artists there is... a vague idea that a man can still remain a gentleman if he paints bad pictures, but must forfeit the conventional right to his Esquire if he makes good pots or serviceable furniture.'[1]
>
> A Modern Jeweller, Roger Fry, 1910

> 'The shifting of interest away from the "fine" arts towards the so-called "applied" arts is one of the significant features of the post-war period in England, and nowhere are its effects more readily seen than in pottery.'[2]
>
> Bernard Rackham, 1925

In 1910, the critic and painter Roger Fry attended a meeting of the Society of Arts where a 'vigorous' discussion took place on the relationship between the fine and applied arts, a subject still debated in contemporary craft today. Fry wrote soon afterwards of the 'implied contempt' for the Applied Arts and the association of utilitarian work with 'a lower kind of faculty'. Fifteen years later, a major change had taken place in the crafts; Bernard Rackham's words reflect a movement full of self-belief, confident enough to be dismissive of the 'fine' arts. As Keeper of Ceramics at the Victoria & Albert Museum, his comments were part of a chorus of voices which heralded pottery in particular as a new and radical art form. From the first appearance of the term 'studio pottery' in a trade journal in 1923,[3] up to the beginning of the Second World War, hand made pottery, and the wider studio crafts, were re-invented in a period of remarkable optimism. With this, the era of the *amateur* or *gentleman* ended along with Fry's worries about forfeiting one's right to the 'Esquire'.

The complex threads which account for this transformation of the crafts can be traced through the early critical writing of what is now called 'studio ceramics'. The factors that shaped the inter-war years owed much to the urban environment of London's avant garde and two of this century's most important art critics, Roger Fry and Herbert Read, who were instrumental in shaping this emergent discipline. In just a few decades, studio pottery moved from a crusade of moralism (with its maxim of 'truth to materials') to Modernism. A new critical agenda emerged in which Formalism evolved into ideas of abstraction through the discovery of English vernacular earthenware and an unlikely marriage with early Chinese stoneware.

Source: © Julian Stair.

The context in which these changes took place was less than auspicious. By 1910, the 'utopian' work of the Arts and Crafts Exhibition Society was being widely questioned as one of its most prominent figures, W.R. Lethaby, declared in a lecture to the Royal Institute of British Architects

> 'However desirable it may be to continue in the old ways or to revert to past issues, it is, I feel … impossible. We have passed into a scientific age, and the old practical arts, produced instinctively, belong to an entirely different era.'[4]

If this was a period of uncertainty for the crafts in general it was a time of crisis for pottery, which was unable to achieve the success of other Arts and Crafts media such as woodwork, textiles, metalwork and bookbinding. Pottery had been dependent upon William De Morgan for its identity, and was in a vacuum after the closure of his factory in 1908. Although De Morgan achieved success with his various tile products, by his own admission, pottery came low on his list of priorities

In the order of their importance:

1. Decorative painted panels …
2. Stove tiles and other patterned tiles for various purposes …
3. Plain coloured tiles …
4. Miscellaneous decorated pots-good for wedding presents and the like, but of no use except to put flowers in when they do not run- as indeed now and then they do not. It is very possible that a little further evolution of this work might have really satisfactory results.[5]

Art Pottery, the industrial equivalent of Arts & Crafts pottery, also came in for criticism in the 1910s for its reliance on obsolete Victorian glaze effects and superfluous decorative treatments. In a review of the British entry at an international exhibition in Turin, the pottery (in this case Bernard Moore's) was criticised for allowing technical virtuosity to take precedence over artistic skill

> 'it is deplorable to see prints of village churches and the Grand Canal underlying splendid sang de boeuf glaze.'[6]

The creation of the Design Industries Association in 1915 led to key figures in the Arts and Crafts movement realigning themselves to industry, and small scale pottery production was marginalised further. Even the ceramic work produced by the short lived Omega Studios (1913-1919) did not produce a lasting influence and references to contemporary pottery in the press and major art journals were scarce.

In 1924, however, the studio pottery movement was propelled into the critical limelight through the first references to pottery and abstraction, and within the span of a few years, studio pottery came to epitomise avant garde concepts of abstract art. Although these ideas were seen to be embodied in contemporary work, they arose from a re-evaluation of historical ceramics in the key ceramic text of the inter-war period, *English Pottery*, which was published in 1924 by Herbert Read and Bernard Rackham. Read had joined Rackham in the Ceramics department of the Victoria & Albert Museum in 1922, and their collaboration on *English Pottery* proved to be a successful union of skills and ideas. Rackham's scholarly knowledge of ceramics complemented Read's interest in Modernist poetry and art. But it was Read's Modernist disposition which introduced a new and radical set of criteria and elevated ceramics into the centre of innovative debate. Read claimed that as pottery forms were free from figurative associations they were 'plastic art in its most abstract form'.[7] In re-appraising historical pottery and creating a critical agenda that could evaluate it, but could also apply to modern pottery, Read and Rackham equipped critics and potters with the means to frame contemporary developments. Reviews of *English Pottery* were quick to point this out:

> 'English pottery has emerged from this cloud of classicism, and a much more healthy outlook as to what constitutes fine pottery quality is now prevalent.'[8]

R. L. Hobsan, curator of ceramics at the British Museum concurred.

> 'The true canons of the potters' art, as conceived by our authors, are clearly explained in the introduction, and they are kept constantly in view in the admirable criticisms which run through the book.'[9]

Within months of publishing *English Pottery* Rackham used abstraction as a theme to discuss William Staite Murray's first solo exhibition at Paterson's Gallery in Old Bond Street, claiming that 'Pottery can indeed be plastic sculpture in a purely abstract form.'[10] Five months later Staite Murray reinforced this in *Pottery from the Artist's Point of View*. 'The forms are abstractions and as such readily contemplated as pure form.'[11] In the same year, Rackham widened his artistic net to include the pottery of Reginald Wells 'in its truest forms - [they] may rightly be classed as abstract sculpture.'[12]

This proto-movement grew quickly, attracting other critics who came to regard pottery as the link between painting and sculpture. The Observer art critic, P.G. Konody, stressed the unity of these three disciplines in a catalogue essay for an exhibition which included Staite Murray and Reginald Wells, Paul Nash and Jacob Epstein - 'the modern movement in art is based on a broad foundation.'[13] - while the owner of Beaux Arts Gallery, Frank Lessore, described pottery 'as high as any other branch of sculpture, of which it may justly be considered the most abstract form.'[14]

In the 1920s and 30s studio pottery received remarkable coverage by today's standards, in *The Observer*, *The Sunday Times*, the *Manchester Guardian*, and *The Morning Post*, and in leading journals of the day, *The Spectator, Apollo, Artwork, Burlington Magazine, Sphere, The Studio, The Listener*, among many. Charles Marriott, the art critic of *The Times*, joined this consensus in 1926, and promoted studio pottery over the next decade, spreading the mantra of 'pottery as abstract art' in over 40 reviews and championing Staite Murray above all others. A review of 1927 opened

> 'The difficulty in discussing the stoneware pottery by Mr W. Staite Murray ... is to avoid superlatives ... the works of Mr Murray represent a fusion of painting and sculpture, and the technical beauty of the results goes a long way to show in what direction abstract aims are legitimate.'[15]

Between 1924 and 1930, studio pottery consolidated this position at the core of Modernist critical developments in the Fine Arts, breaking most of its associations with Arts and Crafts ideology . While Reginald Wells disappeared from view, Staite Murray went on to show with leading artists of the era, notably Christopher Wood, and Winifred and Ben Nicholson, whom H.S. Ede (the founder of Kettle's Yard) described as 'a most interesting trinity'.[16] Through Nicholson's introduction, Staite Murray became a member of the notorious Seven & Five Society of Artists and the only potter to exhibit in their annual shows. During this period Herbert Read developed his ideas on pottery and abstraction further and in 1931 published *The Meaning of Art*, which included his famous maxim that 'Pottery is pure art; it is art freed from any imitative intention....'[17] Significantly, the entire section was first published anonymously in the catalogue introduction to Staite Murray's first solo exhibition at the Lefevre Galleries in 1930.

The compelling marriage of Read, the young critic and Rackham, an established curator, which had produced *English Pottery* established new canons of ceramic appreciation and revealed many previously unappreciated qualities of English ceramics. However, close reading of Rackham and Read's ideas and language reveals that a precedent in Roger Fry's Formalism and the renaissance of interest in early English and Chinese pottery of the preceding decade.

At the end of the 19th century ceramics collectors had become interested in vernacular English pottery, in particular early slipware. This spawned a few publications such as Charles Lomax's *Quaint Old English Pottery* of 1909, which Leach copied pots from while in Japan. Reginald Wells, the pioneer of the modern revival, started making slipware around 1900 in the old pottery town of Wrotham, Kent, but abandoned it in 1910 in favour of higher temperature stoneware. The vernacular revival was established in 1914 with the seminal exhibition *Early English Earthenware* at the Burlington Fine Arts Club. However, this interest in slipware did not extend to appreciating the aesthetic value of medieval pottery which was perceived as 'crockery of simple form ... [and] crude designs'. Lomax saw such pottery as simply a precursor to the more decorative slipware

> '.. at length we find the potters assuming more elegant shapes, and attempts being made to relieve plainness by applying ornaments of various kinds and the more frequent use of coloured slips.'[18]

Similarly, the catalogue for the Burlington Fine Arts Club exhibition, *Early English Earthenware* quickly passed over the medieval and slipware pottery in favour of later cosmopolitan pottery, categorising it as unsophisticated and rural 'a purely native product, a rustic craft, home grown and racy of the soil.'[19]

Critical interest in the vernacular amongst museum curators was slow to develop. A younger Rackham, without the counter- balance of Herbert Read, compared medieval pottery unfavourably with the universally admired medieval encaustic floor tiles and relegated it to fulfilling 'the everyday needs of humble folk.'[20] He was also dismissive of Leach's later attempts at a revival

> 'Any attempt to revive ... the use of the actual materials of the 18th century is likely to end in failure ... study of bygone wares will certainly be helpful, but only if the aim of such study is to stimulate the student to fresh ideas of his own, not to save him the trouble of thinking for himself.'[21]

The first critic to appreciate medieval earthenware pottery was Roger Fry. Fry judged medieval pottery on the grounds of form, texture and expressiveness, using new analytical terms such as 'austere rhythm ... structural design .. relation of planes .. inherent unity'.[22] He argued for the work's great refinement of taste and, in the ultimate accolade, compared it to Tang dynasty pottery, 'the greatest ceramics in existence'. Crucially, Fry appreciated medieval pottery for its purity of form and understated decoration and valued it above the decorative slipware of Ralph Wood and Thomas Toft which he saw as degenerate,

> 'a really crude, barbaric and brutally clownish idea of deformation, devoid of a structural sense and vital rhythm, expressive only of a beery jocularity.'[23]

This was a distinction that Herbert Read would reinforce a decade later in *English Pottery: An Aesthetic Survey*[24] where he also classified medieval earthenware with Tang and Sung Dynasty pottery. Through the validation of medieval earthenware pottery, Roger Fry paved the way for the later revival of English pottery effectively launching 'the English recovery', one of the defining movements within English studio ceramics. He provided the critical references that enabled this previously neglected work to rise above the level of curiosity and become representative of a modern movement. Although these ideas were published well before the studio pottery movement's rapid expansion in the 1920s they provided the critical foundation for much of *English Pottery*. Ironically, the slipware revival popularised by Leach and Cardew in the 1920s was built on the historic English pottery Fry and Read dismissed. The 'beery jocularity' of Staffordshire slipware and the 'clownish fancies' of English slipware were to become embedded in the psyche of British studio pottery despite the low opinion of the two critics who were instrumental in launching the movement.

The other great theme of the inter-war period was 'Orientalism'. Less critically charged than the revival of vernacular pottery or the development of abstraction there was still confusion over the means of its introduction to Britain. Chinese pottery in the first decades of was little known, for 'the number of genuine pieces in English or indeed in Western collections generally might be almost counted on the fingers.'[25] Curatorial discussion had been limited to authenticating the few available examples in the West through obscure Chinese literary references. The opening up of China to the West after the Boxer Rebellion in 1900 and the cutting of embankments during the building of railways disturbed grave sites and new archaeological finds provided keen scholars with access to this rare pottery for the first time. In response to this enthusiasm the Burlington Fine Arts Club organised an exhibition *Early Chinese Pottery and Porcelain* in 1910 and the Burlington Magazine published a comprehensive series of articles on Tang and Sung dynasty pottery by the British Museum curator R. L. Hobson. The exhibition was highly influential in showing this very rare work for the first time and in helping curators and collectors to establish its chronology and provenance. 'It may be safely said that until the last two or three years it would have been absolutely impossible to bring together a collection of this character.'[26]

Within the next decade the pottery of China became the subject of intense interest with exhibitions, articles and reviews. There was a wide interest in Chinese philosophy and The *T'ao Shuo* - an anthology of ceramic literature first published in China in 1774 - was translated while Bernard Rackham published '*The Literature of Chinese Pottery: A Brief Survey and Review*'.[27] This scholarly interest was soon translated into contemporary debate, as the new type of pottery exhibited at the Burlington Fine Arts club was seen to reflect a change in aesthetic and critical values, 'taste that tends more and more to favour the simpler and ruder early wares'. The Chinoiserie of the 18th century and Japonism of the 19th century was superseded by a new wave of 'Orientalism' more appropriate to the emerging Modernism. An editorial of 1910 in the Burlington summed up this mood

> 'There are signs that the present rapidly increasing preoccupation with Oriental art will be more intense, and produce a profounder impression on our views, than any previous phase of Orientalism ... To us the art of the East presents the hope of discovering a more spiritual, more expressive idea of design.'[28]

The critical agenda of this early phase of Orientalism in studio pottery was shaped by the debates that framed abstraction and the vernacular revival, ideas that were a product of a wider agenda, before a 'craft' ethic had permeated studio pottery. Again Fry's role in establishing a link between Orientalism and avant garde concepts was pivotal. In an article on the art collector Mr R. Kelelian, Fry revealed how Kelelian's sensibility to modern developments was fashioned by ancient art

> 'His long familiarity with early Oriental art has trained his taste in the search for what is really significant . . . in his choice of modern work ... a man who has handled so many Fayum portraits was not likely to miss the qualities in a head by Matisse'[29]

Oriental art was felt to embody the aspirations of the modern movement and pottery was seen as an integral element. Wyndham Lewis's inclusion of work by the great Japanese potter Koetsu in *Blast*, the publication which launched the Vorticist manifesto, was evidence of the avant garde movement's interest. Hamada, as the first potter to exhibit in Bond Street, represented the living embodiment of this new phase of Orientalism and his exhibitions were soon followed by Staite Murray's Orientally inspired abstract pottery and Reginald Wells's 'Soon Pottery'. The new material of stoneware clay, reductive forms, monochrome glazes, sober colours and controlled decoration were discussed in terms of expressiveness and artistic integrity. Hamada's first exhibition was praised for allowing 'the 'individuality of the potter to assert itself'.[30] From Fry's comparison of English medieval pottery with Tang and Sung pottery - 'some of the greatest ceramics in existence'[31] - early Chinese pottery became the universal benchmark of ceramic excellence. By the end of the decade the critic W.A. Thorpe wrote 'It is said that a man cannot paint who has not studied the Italians; no more can a potter pot who is unversed in Sung.'[32]

The 1920s saw widely differing interpretations of Orientalism by individual potters. The adoption of the 'Sung Standard', the ultimate canon of ceramic integrity, is widely credited to Bernard Leach but, as with the rising interest in slipware, his arrival in Britain in 1920 was fortuitous. The prevailing climate of interest was already established, as he acknowledged. 'Upon my return to England I found the basis of criticism of pottery had shifted. America and Europe had become familiar with earlier work'.[33] Leach's return to Britain from Japan in 1920 may have been timely given the rising tide of interest in Orientalism, but he suffered from a lack of critical recognition, for his interpretation of Orientalism was at odds with the wider consensus. Although Leach's Japanese credentials automatically prefaced every public mention of him, his self-portrayal as a conduit between East and West, and emphasis on tradition seemed parochial in contrast to the more radical ideas which presented Sung and Tang dynasty pottery as icons of modernity. From the very first reference to him in the press which expressed his desire to promote 'hand work rather than machine craft[34]' Leach effectively allied himself to a Morrisonian concept of craft as opposed to that of the Modernist potter, creating individual artworks. Leach's choice to locate his pottery in Cornwall under the patronage the St Ives Handicraft Guild and his ambition to '"turn out more than a couple of thousand pieces per annum for the first year or two."' reinforced this image.

While the critical landscape was developing rapidly, in the early days of studio pottery Leach became marginalised. Abstraction was never linked to his pots although it was a key factor in the appreciation of Staite Murray, Wells and even his pupils Nora Braden and Katherine Pleydell-Bouverie; Leach only made one passing reference to abstraction in an article on Tomimoto in 1931. While Wells, Staite Murray and his 'assistant' Hamada were exhibiting in Bond Street, Leach was struggling commercially with exhibitions at less prestigious galleries. Prompted by worsening financial problems Leach attempted to balance his artistic aspirations with commercial practice but this fraught strategy collapsed in 1927. The Studio announced the 'very interesting experiment[35]' of two simultaneous exhibitions of 'collector's' pottery' in Leach's first Bond Street exhibition at Paterson's Gallery and 'English Slipware … ordinary household utensils' at the Three Shields in the less fashionable Holland Park. Leach's attempts to straddle artistic and commercial markets was unsuccessful, the slipware sold badly and whether his artistic credibility was damaged is difficult to gauge, but he never exhibited at Paterson's Gallery again. After this failure Leach adopted a different tactic and started to show in the emerging specialist craft venues such as The New Handworker's and The Little Gallery. He also began to publish polemical articles which were instrumental in altering the direction of studio pottery. In the same year that Staite Murray was being heralded by Marriott as one of Europe's leading artists, Leach issued a statement

> 'There is a need to escape from the atmosphere of the over-precious; and not only have the new craftsmen to prove that they can be creative, but as "artist craftsmen' they must, if only for the sake of

their art, contribute to national life. A growing public wants to enjoy the use of its crockery, and that can only be if it is inseparably practical and beautiful. …

There is a profound and urgent need for attempting to bridge that gulf soon.'[36]

It is difficult to separate the aggrieved tone of Leach's view of 'over precious' studio pottery from his own commercial problems. Up to this stage in the development of studio pottery, the critical agenda had been firmly placed in the domain of radical Modernist ideas with little attention devoted to vestigial Arts and Crafts ideals. The new radical movement of studio pottery was seen as an adjunct of the fine arts, with an economic identity based on the patronage of Bond Street - one that Leach had previously accepted and aspired to. Until this point, the 'gulf' that Leach identified had not existed, as the making of studio pottery and 'crockery' were accepted as separate activities. Leach was disingenuous in advocating utility as a prime motive, for he survived the early years through a mixed practice of exhibiting stoneware 'museum pieces', producing slipware pottery and making raku for the tourist trade. He also struggled with practical matters as Frank Rutter, a leading critic and member of the Design Industries Association revealed in a thinly veiled criticism

> 'We have been suffering from a teapot with a defective spout. It is most versatile and will shed its contents anywhere besides into a cup. It was bought at a small pottery in the west country. We were attracted by a pleasantly mottled colour and the fact that the maker incises his name on every piece with the place of origin. This, we thought, should be a guarantee of general excellence, and we still think it should.'[37]

The following year Leach published A Potter's Outlook, a diatribe on the condition of contemporary pottery - the same year that Staite Murray exhibited with Winifred and Ben Nicolson at the prestigious Leferve Gallery

> 'What have the artist potters being doing all this while? Working by hand to please ourselves as artists first and therefore producing only limited and expensive pieces, we have been supported by collectors, purists, cranks, or "arty" people, rather than by the normal man or woman … and consequently most of our pots have been still-born : they have not had the breath of reality in them : it has been a game.'[38]

Critical response to Leach's pottery and studio pottery in general started to change after these public expressions of his disillusionment. A year later the Studio Year Book coined the new term 'domestic wares' to describe Leach's pottery and approved of the change in direction of his work which was formerly only 'within reach of the collector' but became pottery 'within reasonable reach of the person of taste.'[39] Leach's critical isolation of the early and mid 20s was boosted by the visit of Soetsu Yanagi in 1929, the leader of the Mingei movement and exhibitions from three of its prominent potters Hamada, Kawai and Tomimoto over the next few years. The momentum Leach gained from Hamada's two exhibitions at Paterson's Gallery in 1929 and 1931 and his joint exhibition with Tomimoto was invaluable as they generated publicity he had been starved of and confirming his oriental 'authenticity'. But the main benefit to Leach was the critical support he received from Yanagi with his unbending moral advocacy of utility, and desire to move pottery 'from the parlour to the living-room and the kitchen.'[40]

By the early 30s the tone of critical writing in the media had changed and the new and fragile edifice of studio pottery started to develop cracks. The response of Charles Marriott, a very public, but less than independently minded critic, reveals this transformation. Having assiduously championed the autonomy of studio potters during the 1920s, believing they should work independently of industry in 'cloistered virtues', Marriott reported in 1930 that Leach's essay *A Potter's Outlook* 'inspires confidence by facing facts and conditions [in] linking up studio and factory pottery.'[41] Reviewing Leach's exhibition at the Little Gallery in the following year Marriott wrote approvingly

> 'The special point of this exhibition is that the articles in it -pots for flowers, jugs, vases, grapefruit and other bowls, ash trays, covered pots for preserves, and pots planted with Japanese dwarf trees - are mostly small, and all of them intended for everyday use and are inexpensive. As a rule, and for good reasons, questions of price do not come into notices of art exhibitions, but in this case price is a definite factor'[42]

Marriott saw Leach's work as pushing individual pottery towards commercial production, approving this on the grounds of its advantages to 'lean purses' and a departure from 'the individual potter stood aloof with museum pieces.'[43]

By the mid 30s studio pottery's high critical standing went into decline. An industrial or 'Machine' aesthetic, the antitheses of a craft sensibility, emerged out of reconstructed industrial production. The Wall Street crash and Depression had profound economic and social consequences and new movements in art developed with radically different conceptual rationales, notably Dada and Surrealism, which undermined studio pottery's reliance on formal appreciation. As Clive Bell wrote

> 'The first movement of the twentieth century, the movement sometimes called "Abstract", at one moment "Cubist", and best fitted, I think, with that … purely chronological label, "post-Impressionist," has, unless I mistake, run its course. It is complete.'[44]

But these factors do not account wholly for the demise of studio pottery as a viable movement within British art. By the mid 30s it was receiving minimal critical coverage from either the broadsheets or the major journals. It is difficult to separate the introduction of Leach's petulant and prosaic agenda with its resultant emphasis on pragmatic factors such as costs and commercial production from the freefall that took place in critical writing about in the early 1930s. In the space of a few short years studio pottery moved from being discussed as a radical new art form and the interface between painting and sculpture to an adjunct of industry where quality was governed by price. The dynamism of Fry's Formalism or Read's ideas of pottery and abstraction which were able to re-contextualise historic precedents within a contemporary Modernist agenda were replaced by Leach's hectoring and moralising tone, originally derived from the writing of Ruskin but mediated through the Japanese Mingie movement. The consequence of this was the demotion of pottery as a viable avenue for artistic practice to a commercial enterprise with bolt- on aesthetics. Whereas it once had a clearly defined position in the art world it was now compromised, hovering somewhere between the gallery and department store. 'The steady working down to common use is wholly welcome, for potting however you may look at it, is a domestic art.'[45] Pottery now had an ambiguous identity and its audience was unsure of its new position. In one of the last articles of the 1930s Jan Gordon of the Observer concluded with an opinion which is still applicable today

> 'Thus potting has contrived to straddle branches, appertaining to Fine Art on the one side and to Craft-Art on the other. … though potters always lay claim to be craftsmen, the high art of potting, that is, the production of rare pieces with unique glazes, belongs to the most high-brow of Fine Arts … Much pottery is abstract Fine Art camaflouged in the sheep's clothing of a humble craft.'[46]

As a result of this repositioning, critical coverage of studio pottery in the national press and art journals fell dramatically away and where it did continue it was less enthusiastic. While Leach's career befitted from this revision of criteria that now defined pottery as a practical craft, and by the emergence of a group of gifted pupils -Michael Cardew, Nora Braden and Katherine Pleydell-Bouverie, who were producing technically competent work at significantly lower prices, the general esteem of pottery fell. Marriott complained of the 'smug bucolic roughness which is the mark of so much modern pottery.'[47] After his vociferous championing of studio pottery during the late 1920s he even lost interest in Staite Murray, writing in 1932 'In his enthusiasm for form and colour in the abstract, he has lately been in danger of forgetting that a pot is after all a pot.'[48] Apollo magazine echoed these criticisms 'his hands are in the clay but his head is surely in the clouds'[49] and condemned his last show 'And can he really reconcile the labelling of his pottery, ... with the abstract significance of form on which he once so much insisted. A pot's a pot for a' that'.[50]

The fall of studio pottery's critical approval was sudden and dramatic but the movement did not disappear, it simply relocated to a new position within the arts, one which is familiar today and loosely titled the 'crafts'. Although outlets such as Muriel Rose's Little Gallery emerged selling studio pottery and imported ethnic folk crafts, this was little compensation for the loss of such galleries as Leferve or Patterson's. The closing remarks of a review of a contemporary Japanese crafts show organised by Leach at the Little Gallery reveal the retail arena into which studio pottery had settled, 'Practising artists will find the exhibition exciting, and the brushes and papers on sale irresistible.'[51] In the course of a decade, studio pottery which had been seen to fulfil the progressive criteria of early British Modernism and burst into the closed sanctity of the fine arts with a momentum that defined itself as a valid new movement was now concerned with the prosaic, of 'representing shillings instead of pounds'.[52] From occupying a central position in national newspapers and the major art journals studio pottery coverage moved from the review sections to the Home pages. The last article to feature ceramics in the Times (Leach, Cardew and Pleydell-Bouverie) before the outbreak of war was a homily on the virtues of slow cooking, *Attractive Fireproof Ware*.

> 'The modern housewife who can usually cook as well as order an attractive meal to-day knows that casseroles in fireproof ware are a necessity for the making of certain dishes.'[53]

After a decade of lively debate, with nothing new to offer, studio pottery fell from critical grace and in the process moved from Bond Street to the High Street.

Notes

1. A Modern Jeweller, Roger Fry, The Burlington Magazine no LXXXVII, Vol XVII, June 1910.
2. The Pottery of Mr Reginald F. Wells, Bernard Rackham, The Studio, Vol 90, Dec. 1925.
3. The Late Robert Wallace Martin, anon, The Pottery Gazette and Glass Trade Review, Sept 1 1923.
4. W.R. Lethaby, Royal Institute of British Architects, 1910.
5. William De Morgan, May Morris, The Burlington Magazine, no CLXXIII, Vol XXXI, Aug 1917.
6. Applied Art At Turin, Burlington No CV, Vol XX, Dec 1911.
7. English Pottery: It's Development From Early Times To The End of the Eighteenth Century, Bernard Rackham and Herbert Reed, London, Ernest Benn Ltd, 1924.

8. Book Review, Gordon Forsyth, Artwork, No 5, Oct-Dec 1925, p. 68.
9. Book Review, R. L. Hobsan, Burlington, Vol XLV No CCLVII, Aug 1924.
10. Mr W. F. Murray's Flambé Stoneware, Bernard Rackham, The Studio, Vol 88, Dec. 1924.
11. Pottery from the Artist's Point of View, W. Staite Murray, Artwork, Vol 1 No 4, May-Aug 1925.
12. The Pottery of Mr Reginald F. Wells, Bernard Rackham, The Studio, Vol 90, Dec. 1925.
13. Catalogue of Pictures, Sculptures & Pottery by some British Artists of To-Day, P.G. Konody, Leferve Galleries, London, Feb. 1926.
14. The Art of Reginald f. Wells Sculptor and Potter, F. Lessore, Artwork, Vol 2, No 8, Cec 1926.
15. Mr W. Staite Murray, Charles Marriott, The Times, 11 Nov, 1927.
16. Foreward to Paintings by Ben & Winifred Nicholson and Pottery by Staite Murray, H.S. Ede, The Lefervre Galleries, London, July 1928.
17. The Meaning of Art, Herbert Read, Faber & Faber, London, 1931, p. 23.
18. Quaint Old English Pottery p. 4, Charles J. Lomax, Sherratt and Hughes, Manchester, 1909.
19. Catalogue of Early English Earthenware p. xvii, Burlington Fine Arts Club, London, 1914.
20. English Earthenware and Stoneware at the Burlington Fine Arts Club p. 265, Bernard Rackham, The Burlington, No CXXXI Vol XXIV, Feb 1914.
21. Domestic Pottery of the Past p. 10, Bernard Rackham, "The Studio" Year-Book of Decorative Art, London, 1922.
22. The Art of Pottery in England p. 335, Roger Fry, The Burlington, No CXXXII Vol XXIV, Mar 1914.
23. ibid.
24. English Pottery: An Aesthetic Survey, Herbert Read, Apollo, Vol II No 12, Dec 1925.
25. Chinese Pottery and Porcelain at the Burlington Fines Arts Club p. 210, Edward Dillon, the Burlington, No LXXXVIII Vol XVII, July 1910.
26. Ibid p. 211.
27. The Literature of Chinese Pottery : A Brief Survey and Review, Bernard Rackham, the Burlington, Vol XXX No CLXVII, 1917.
28. Oriental Art, The Burlington Magazine, no LXXXV, Vol XVII, April 1910.
29. Modern Paintings in a Collection of Ancient Art p. 304, Roger Fry, the Burlington Vol XXXVII No CCXIII, Dec 1920.
30. The Pottery of Mr Shoji Hamada, W . McCance, The Spectator, May 26, 1923.
31. The Art of Pottery in England p. 330, Roger Fry, The Burlington, No CXXXII Vol XXIV, Mar 1914.
32. Thorpe 1930.
33. From the Hand of the Potter p. 225, Bernard Leach, Homes & Gardens, Nov 1929.
34. An Art Pottery in Cornwall p. 1661, specially contributed, The Pottery Gazette and Glass Trade Review, Dec 1 1920.
35. The Studio p. 200, Vol 93, March 1927.
36. Bernard Leach on Crockery p. 14, The Arts & Crafts, Vol 2 No 2, June 1927.
37. In Quest of a Teapot, The Work of the Sudio Potter, Frank Rutter, Birmingham Post, Dec 9 1925.
38. A Potter's Outlook, Bernard Leach, Handowrker's Pamphlets No 3, New Handworkers Gallery, 1928.
39. Pottery and Glassware, The Studio Year Book p. 151, 1929.
40. The Pottery of Shoji Hamada, M. Yanagi, catalogue of Shoji Hamada, Paterson's Gallery, 1931.
41. Stoneware Pottery, Charles Marriott, The Times, March 31 1930.
42. Stoneware Pottery, Charles Marriott, The Times, Oct 29, 1931.
43. Mr Bernard Leach, Charles Marriott, The Times, Dec 5, 1933.
44. What Next in Art?, Clive Bell, The Studio, Vol CIX, No 505, April 1935.

45. Stoneware pottery. Charles Marriott, The Times, May 23 1932.
46. The Rise of Potting, Bernard Leech, Jan Gordon, The Observer May 3 1936.
47. Mr Staite Murray, Charles Marriott, The Tmes, April 26 1934.
48. Lefevre Galleries, Charles Marriott, The Times, 7 Nov 1932.
49. Art News and Notes, Apollo, Dec 1935.
50. Art News and Notes, Apollo, Dec 1936.
51. Conemtemporary Japanese Crafts, Hugh Gordon Porteus, The New English Weekly, May 21 1936.
52. Leach Pottery, Charles Marriott, The Times Mar 23 1927.
53. Attractive Fireproof Ware, Anon, The Times, Oct 19 1938.

© Julian Stair. From Julian Stair, 2002, 'Re-Inventing the Wheel', in P. Greenhalgh (ed.), *The Persistence of Craft*. London: Bloomsbury. Reproduced with permission.

19
THE ARCHIE BRAY FOUNDATION: A LEGACY REFRAMED

Patricia Failing

Reflecting on her long experience as a historian and curator of ceramic art, LaMar Harrington says of the Archie Bray Foundation, 'My strongest impression is that it's always THERE. It's like a source of energy, intense and exuberant in the early days, more subtle in later decades, but always leaving its mark on so many artists' work'.[1]

Accounts of the Bray's impact on its numerous residents, local students, visiting artists, directors and supporters during the past half century are as varied as the tellers of the tale. The energy Harrington perceives is the afterglow of this collective experience, but the Bray's historical 'thereness' was also configured by particular individuals and events. This essay, which is more about how the Bray came to leave its mark than an attempt to quantify its impact, will address some of those particulars.

We can begin with the Archie Bray Foundation's best-known icon, the photograph of a humble brown jug on a makeshift table, surrounded by five men (opposite). The three gray-haired men wear thick suits and ties; the two younger ones are dressed in Levis and chambray shirts unbuttoned to expose their underwear. The youngest has a pen handy in his pocket and only two buttons unbuttoned at the neck. His colleague is unbuttoned to below the middle of the chest and the jaunty posture of his arms (akimbo, hands on hips) replicates the open V-shape of his shirt. The other men hold their arms close to their bodies, and the tallest grips the edge of his jacket, pulling the garment across his chest like a blanket or mantle.

This image documents the 1952 meeting at the Bray of Rudy Autio, Peter Voulkos, and Soetsu Yanagi, the founder of the Mingei craft movement in Japan, ceramist Shoji Hamada, soon to be declared an official Japanese National Treasure, and the Englishman Bernard Leach, arguably the most influential figure in the field of handmade pottery in the early 1950s. The semiology of costumes and poses immediately divides the group: proletarian-cultural worker-ex-G.I.-Montana ranch hand versus tweedy elegance, neat mustaches, and well-knotted ties. Literally forming the sign of a question, the jug handle in front of them inquires, 'Why are you all here? Why is this pot in your picture?'

A plausible reading of this document would be: older, cosmopolitan men have come from afar to speak with promising younger fellows about Japan, tradition, and the modest brown jug. Indeed, during a week-long workshop at the Bray in December of 1952, the distinguished visitors lectured about anonymous craftsmanship and Zen concepts of beauty. They also demonstrated techniques for decorating greenware with Japanese brushes dipped in slip and posed the unfamiliar challenge of working from the hump.[2] Ceramists from all over Montana attended, including Bray employees Autio and Voulkos.

The photograph of a remarkable constellation of characters gathered in a small pottery studio in the dead of winter has come to serve as the first major document of the Bray's historical 'thereness'. Responding to

Source: © Patricia Failling, University of Washington, Seattle.

questionnaires about the legacy of the Bray, residents and visitors from the past two decades often comment upon the awesome prospect of sharing the same workspace once occupied by Leach, Hamada, Voulkos, and Autio. The visit by the avatars of Japanist aesthetics has also nurtured a perception of the Bray in its early days as one of the main conduits of Asian aesthetics in the United States. Leach apparently shared a similar vision: his itinerary for his two U.S. visits in 1950 and 1952 included Alfred University, Black Mountain College, the Pueblo San Ildefenso in Santa Fe, the Chouinard Institute in Los Angeles, and Frans and Marguerite Wildenhain's Pond Farm pottery in northern California. Reviewing his tours in 1953, Leach declared, 'we felt that a start had been made [at the Bray] under Peter Voulkos that held greater promise than any other place which we visited in America'.[3]

The famous photograph now becomes not just a document of the past but a prescient image of the future—the future of the Bray, the younger artists, and the brown jug. Well, maybe not the brown jug. Voulkos and Autio are known for not having followed Leach's prescriptions for a humble pottery 'flowing from a taproot deep in the soil of the past'. Voulkos's aesthetic, in fact, is routinely regarded as having undermined Leach's in the Realpolitik of the U.S. pottery world. In what might be a classic case of Freudian disavowal, Leach seems to acknowledge this shift in the format of his last major book, Beyond East and West, published a year before his death in 1979. In this memoir, Leach reviews his 1952 U.S. tour with Hamada and Yanagi, beginning with the trio's legendary October workshop at Black Mountain College in North Carolina.[4] Their journey also included stopovers in Santa Fe, the Grand Canyon, Seattle, Los Angeles, and San Francisco, Leach reports. He also warmly recalls a visit with his student Warren MacKenzie, near Minneapolis. But not once in Beyond East and West does Leach mention Montana, the Bray, Voulkos, or 'the greatest promise of any place we visited in America'.[5]

So the question posed by the brown jug may be as much about what distanced the younger and older men as what brought them together. In retrospect, their contrasting self-images seem both transparent and complex: on the level of visual cliché, the group divides easily into two camps, the cowboys and the aesthetes. But these aesthetes idealized anonymous, unpretentious peasant potters who lived among the people, worked instinctively, and were not overburdened by theory. The cowboys had M.F.A. degrees. As undergraduates, they had studied with one of the most respected modernist painters in Montana, Bob DeWeese, who remained a lifelong friend and mentor. When the photo was taken, Autio's ambition was to become a sculptor; his heroes were Marino Marini and Henry Moore. Voulkos considered painting to be his primary art form in 1952, although he had decided to make a living as a production potter.[6] In a 1978 interview, Voulkos's main recollection of the Leach-Hamada workshop was Hamada's 'small Buddha sort of hands, sort of fat fingers, you know? The image I got was of this slip coming through his fingers and the facility he had'—a facility he compares to the dexterity of his father, a short-order cook.[7] In another interview he admitted, however, that 'I suppose it was then that I got turned on to what Oriental pottery really was'. Autio remembers the workshop as 'lifting our thinking from one level to another. Hamada decorated so freely. But remember we only had [brief] contact. I think their significance may have been overstated'.[8]

Perhaps the famous photograph should not be seen as a document of transmission (old to young, Japan to Bray, gospel to converts). Another reading might be: the man who takes up the most body space with his open, expansive posture is in charge. The younger fellow is his ally, and the older gentlemen are not where they belong. This interpretation would recenter the Bray's early historical 'thereness' on Peter Voulkos. Considerable evidence suggests that in 1952 and for several years thereafter, if a small, remote, fledgling Montana pottery called 'the Bray' was known to the larger world of American ceramics at all, it was primarily through its association with the name of Mr. Voulkos, who began winning top prizes in national ceramics competitions while still a student at Montana State in 1949. His streak continued in 1950, when he was awarded the purchase prize at the Fifteenth Ceramic National Exhibition, one of the most important national competitions at the time. In 1952, the first prize at the National Decorative Arts and Ceramics Exhibition went to Voulkos; he won the top award at the Designer Craftsman U.S.A. show at the Brooklyn Museum in 1953. In 1954 his first one-person New York show was mounted by the American Craft Council at the America House gallery. He won the gold medal at the International Academy of Ceramics exposition in Cannes in 1955.[9] This unusual series of prizes provoked curiosity and some chagrin, as Voulkos was not associated with Alfred University, Cranbrook, Ohio State, or any of the better-known incubators for successful young ceramists. Judges were most impressed by his wax-resist surfaces and confident wheel work. The narrow-necked bottle and lidded-casserole forms Voulkos preferred during his tenure at the Bray, however, are generic 'good design' of the period and, like the vessels' surfaces, are not especially notable for their fidelity to the prescriptions laid out in Leach's bible of Asian aesthetics, *A Potter's Book*.

In the early and mid-1950s, Voulkos's colleague at the Bray, Rudy Autio, occupied himself with a series of carved brick and tile compositions for several buildings in western Montana. The semi-abstract figures that populate these compositions can be visually related to art-deco cubism, Diego Rivera's murals, medieval manuscripts, or Picasso, but not to Leach, Hamada, or Zen ceramics. By 1955, Autio was also making stacked abstract sculptures that may have encouraged the pot-form assemblages Voulkos began to produce the same year. Although both artists admired Asian ceramics,[10] Autio's sculpture remained firmly grounded in Western formalism. Voulkos was studying classical Western pottery. ('When I came [in 1958] there were books on Greek pottery all over the place, really dirty and muddy from Voulkos sitting there looking at them,' Ken Ferguson reported.)[11] If the Bray's early influence is traced through Autio's and Voulkos's on-site production, there is little to associate the Bray with Japanese aesthetics in particular—were it not for the meeting recorded in the photo of five men with a jug.

Surveying published overviews of Voulkos's artistic development, it seems as if the photograph itself called certain lines of inquiry into being. Whatever the influence of Leach and Hamada on Voulkos might have been, it was not obvious and straightforward. Yet because these artists have been represented historically in a manner consistent with the Bray photograph (cosmopolitan evangelists/precocious Montana frontiersman), the temptation to find a substantial relationship among them has been compelling. Historian Garth Clark, for example, sees the Leach-Hamada Bray workshop as 'particularly far-reaching'. He locates Leach's influence in Voulkos's stack pots of the 1970s, which were divided like Leach's, but with an opposite effect.[12] Elaine Levin notices that Voulkos's slip and glaze palette becomes more similar to Hamada's after 1952. 'Less obvious—and more startling—was Leach's effect on Voulkos,' she decides. 'In a way Leach himself could not have predicted, his philosophy helped guide Voulkos into uncharted territory. The result was not less than an entirely new strain of American ceramics'.[13]

Levin credits Voulkos's encounter with Leach and Hamada for his receptivity to the abstract expressionist painting he first encountered in New York in 1953. Voulkos has repeatedly emphasized the epiphany he experienced during this visit, and there seems little doubt that abstract expressionist painting techniques informed the profound changes in his work from 1955 to 1959. Whether these innovations should be credited more to the influence of Japan or more to the impact of abstract expressionist painting is a by-now-familiar debate. Clark, for example, maintains that the critics who attribute Voulkos's breakthrough to the influence of painting do not understand that 'the primary experience for the potter of the 1950s had been the recognition of the complexity of Japanese ceramic aesthetic'.[14] The debate is still unsettled: can one draw a straight line from the Bray, Leach, and Hamada to Voulkos's revolutionary work of the later 1950s, or was there a crucial detour through abstract expressionism?

Reviewing the range of Voulkos's experiences at the Bray complicates these questions. Voulkos was in residence at the Foundation in the summer of 1951; he left to complete his M.F.A. degree at the California College of Arts and Crafts during the 1951–1952 academic year. He came back to the Bray after graduation.

In the summer of 1953 he taught at Black Mountain College and traveled to New York, returning to the Bray in the fall. In the fall of 1954 he moved to Los Angeles to begin teaching at the Otis Art Institute, but he visited the Bray again the following summer.[15] After that he rarely had contact with the Foundation, although he did conduct occasional workshops with Autio at the University of Montana in the 1960s and 1970s. His tenure in Helena, in summary, was intermittent and relatively short. While in residence he was primarily occupied with production pottery—the cups, plates, bottles, and casseroles that were marketed to a national clientele. Autio emphasizes that he and Voulkos 'never talked about art' at the Bray. 'We talked about how to make things work. If there was any aesthetic discussion, it was only in a joking way'.[16]

'How to make things work' was a huge topic in the West Coast ceramics world of the 1950s. There were few books to consult, and ceramists relied heavily on direct, person-to-person transmission of clay-handling techniques, glaze formulas, and models for kiln construction. Early Bray visitors and workshops provided a kind of foundational resource that college and university programs typically provide today. The relative thinness of technical expertise among West Coast studio potters had an important impact on period practices, according to Voulkos's Los Angeles student and colleague, John Mason:

> The thing that fascinates me about this period is that it had been preceded by a time when there was not enough technical information to continue the craft in a vital way. . . . So there was a period of rediscovery, of learning all this information in order to re-establish the handicraft. And yet at the moment when it was possible to re-establish it, the people who were really involved in it didn't want to re-establish it as a straight craft. They wanted to take it somewhere else outside that straight-line continuity of the craft tradition. And it wasn't just one individual—it was a common feeling.[17]

The 1952 Leach-Hamada Bray workshop was followed by a second celebrity appearance in May 1954, when Marguerite Wildenhain arrived for a five-day session. (These were the only two major workshops held at the Bray before Voulkos moved to Los Angeles.) Renowned for being outspoken, Wildenhain had recently taken on Leach in print. 'It ought to be clear that American potters cannot possibly grow roots by imitating Sung pottery or by copying the way of life of the rural population of Japan,' she wrote in *Craft Horizons* in 1953. 'We have excellent traditions closer to us than the Chinese or Japanese, of equal merit and just as inventive'. Wildenhain's views were consistent with 'the common feeling' Mason described about the desirability of reestablishing ceramics 'somewhere else outside of the straight-line continuity of craft tradition'. 'If a potter's mind, taste, and ideas are restricted from the start by taboos and preconceived formulas and rules,' Wildenhain emphasized in this article, the result will be dilettantes or fakes.[18]

A graduate of the Weimar Bauhaus, Wildenhain was among the wave of well-established émigré artists who fled to the United States in 1939 and 1940. In 1940, she replaced Carlton Ball as head of the California College of Arts and Crafts; in 1942, she started her own school at Pond Farm Pottery, an Arcadian retreat she established near Guerneville, California. Like her Bauhaus mentors, Wildenhain refused to divide art from craft; in her classes she provided a strictly disciplined program of intense training based on Old World master-apprentice models of instruction. Among her pupils was self-proclaimed 'Bauhaus baby' Frances Senska, Voulkos's and Autio's ceramics instructor at Montana State, who also studied with Lázló Maholy Nagy and Grygory Kepes at the Institute of Design in Chicago.[19]

Wildenhain's hand-thrown stoneware pitchers, cups, saucers, and teapots in the late 1940s and early 1950s were an apogee of Bauhaus elegance and craftsmanship. 'The artist-potter is like the priest,' she told her pupils. 'He has dedicated his life to something greater than he—to beauty, expression, art'. For Wildenhain, pottery was a profoundly ethical undertaking, but not one in which a potter necessarily 'loses his soul as an artist if he works in an industrial setup. . . . Let us use the machine when we need it, but let us not adore it'.[20] Ceramist Val Cushing compares her influence to that of Bernard Leach and Charles Harder of Alfred University:

> [They all] changed the course of contemporary American ceramics in the late 1940s and early 1950s. Each in their own way, of course. Leach for bringing Japanese and Chinese pottery techniques to our attention in a profound way—Harder for the educator and philosopher that he was—and Marguerite for her single-minded devotion to standards of quality and hard work [and] for bringing us the Bauhaus and our Western heritage of art theory to weigh against Leach and his Eastern influences.[21]

Wildenhain's reception at the Bray was decidedly mixed. Forty-seven artists attended her workshop, including Senska, Voulkos, Autio, and visitors from British Columbia and Seattle, among them Nan and James McKinnell.[22] The McKinnells were so impressed by Wildenhain that they soon moved to Helena to work at the Bray. Autio, on the other hand, remembers her differently:

> [She was] pretty arrogant. We didn't like that. She couldn't throw as well as Pete and her work seemed hidebound by traditional European techniques. She was intolerant of anyone who made it the easy way, like we had, without apprenticing for five or six years. But she did have her following and she pounded it into them. I didn't think much one way or the other about that workshop.[23]

Voulkos was apparently more impressed. 'Sometimes, when you watch Pete throw, you can see Marguerite Wildenhain,' Senska maintains. 'I learned certain things from her. Pete learned certain things from her'.[24] What Voulkos learned might be indicated in the advice he passed along soon after the workshop to a student considering a graduate degree in ceramics: 'If he wants a Ph.D., let him go to Ohio State; if he wants to teach, let him go to Cranbrook; if he wants to go into industry, let him go to Alfred; if he wants a vacation, tell him to go to the University of Hawaii or Switzerland; if he wants a quickie, he should go to the College of Arts and Crafts in Oakland; if he wants to learn to pot, he should go to Marguerite Wildenhain'. (The advisee was Paul Soldner, who ignored all these recommendations and enrolled in Voulkos's classes at Otis a few months later.)[25]

Voulkos probably shared Autio's allergy to Wildenhain's authoritarianism, and her top-down teaching methods have never been a model for learning at the Bray. But Wildenhain's modernist conviction that imitating ceramic forms from the past was a form of decadence and her encouragement of individual expression provide a more cogent backdrop for Voulkos's professional development than Leach's admonitions about finding a taproot in the soil of the past. As a graduate student, Voulkos's ambition was to study with another ceramist devoted to European modernism, Anthony Prieto.[26] Prieto, head of the ceramics department at Mills College in Oakland, became Voulkos's close friend and mentor. His work and teaching were informed by the examples of Miró and Picasso, and his elegant, narrow-necked pots and abstract surface designs have much in common with Voulkos's vase and bottle forms of the early 1950s. Voulkos and Autio also admired the glazes and virtuoso wheel-throwing performances of Prieto's predecessor at Mills, Carlton Ball, who was gaining a reputation for his large-scale pots. Ball spent several weeks at the Bray as a Fulbright scholar in the summer of 1955. 'I think as far as influences go, Tony Prieto was more important [than Leach],' Autio concluded. 'And Carlton Ball too'.[27]

Had Autio and Voulkos been photographed side-by-side with Wildenhain, Prieto, or Ball, would the historical image of the Bray be different? Were there such a document, it might hedge some of the current assumptions about the weight of the Leach-Hamada aesthetic on the institution's first years of operation. It could also reframe Voulkos's encounter with North Carolina's Black Mountain College in the summer of 1953, which has been represented by several historians as a second chapter in the Leach-Hamada-Bray story.

In 1952, at Leach's request, Black Mountain hosted a two-week seminar with Leach, Hamada, and Yanagi. Marguerite Wildenhain presented the opening lecture. Voulkos was invited to conduct a three-week workshop the following summer by resident ceramists David Weinrib and Karen Karnes, who were carrying on the Alfred/Harder/Bauhaus tradition of superbly crafted production pottery in an academic environment suspicious of such 'bourgeois' production.[28] The functional ware that Voulkos produced at Black Mountain is reminiscent of Prieto's formalism and provides no evident sign of the radical shift his work would undergo three years later. When Voulkos arrived in North Carolina, he was making, in his own words, 'straight pottery,' with everything 'just sort of going through my hands . . . there was nothing of a head trip'. After meeting other members of the teaching staff, including John Cage, David Tudor, Merce Cunningham, and M. C. Richards, he found a new context for his work: he began thinking of pottery as 'inventing with form, not just craftsmanship'.[29]

Daniel Rhodes, with whom Karnes and Weinrib had studied at Alfred, also taught at Black Mountain during the same session. Like Voulkos, Rhodes became 'emotionally involved' with abstract expressionist painting that summer and began painting again himself. Voulkos's involvement came after the workshop when he traveled to New York City, where he stayed with Tudor and Richards and met Franz Kline, Willem de Kooning, Jack Tworkov, and Robert Rauschenberg. Voulkos and his friends agree he was never the same after that trip in 1953, even though he came back to the Bray and its production pottery. The functional ware that won prizes continued to reflect the influences of Picasso, Miró, and Matisse, and there are no overt references to the work of Leach, Hamada, or the abstract expressionists. It seems reasonable to conclude, therefore, that Voulkos's initial receptivity to the new art he encountered on the East Coast probably derived more from his interest in modernist painting, including his own, than from the relatively subtle links we now see between Zen ceramics and abstract expressionist painting techniques. Voulkos's first significant departures from functional pottery began to appear in 1955, after he moved to Los Angeles and immersed himself in contemporary art. 'The biggest thing that ever happened to me was moving to Los Angeles,' Voulkos once said. 'Then I became aware of everything. Everything started falling into place. I began to go to all the openings at the galleries and museums—painting shows and sculpture shows I had never been to before, and I really got turned on to painting like never before—work by New York painters especially'.[30] According to Voulkos's principal biographer, Rose Slivka, some of Voulkos's students in Los Angeles were studying Zen philosophy; at that point he may have began to intuit connections between Zen and the unpremeditated creative processes associated with abstract expressionism.[31]

If contacts with Leach and Hamada did not epitomize Autio's or Voulkos's relationship to the Bray, and if the Bray was probably not a major conduit of Asian aesthetics in the early 1950s, how would the historical impact of the Bray be re-drawn? In both of her monographs on Voulkos, Slivka positions the Bray as a conservative foil for the artist's triumphant breakthrough: by 1956, she says, Voulkos 'had completed the first leg of the journey from Archie Bray classicism to the Los Angeles anything-goes adventurous spirit'.[32] John Mason makes a related point: the revolutionary ceramics produced in Los Angeles in the late 1950s were 'more than just a simple homage to abstract expressionist painting. [The new work] also had a great deal to do with feelings of doubt about pottery. . . . Certainly, Pete really believed that. He had come out of a production situation at Archie Bray to an art school'.[33] In these rhetorical schemes, the Bray is invoked as the contrary of 'adventurous spirit' and 'art'. Was the Bray what Autio and Voulkos had to leave behind to become artists? While working in Helena, neither of them produced the work that secured their current high position in contemporary ceramics.

From one perspective, it could be argued that both Autio and Voulkos as well as Ken Ferguson had to leave the Bray to make the art for which they are best known. The Bray's early artist-directors not only produced inventory for the pottery; they also built and serviced the kilns, kept the books, unloaded clay from rail cars, taught classes, painted woodwork, fixed the plumbing, and swept the floors. Voulkos made production work in the daytime ('a dozen of this, a dozen of that, a dozen of that everyday') and created his own exhibition pieces late at night. Autio followed a similar schedule. According to Ferguson, although they enjoyed and respected each other, the artists and Archie Bray never saw the pottery business from quite the same angle:

> Archie was in a strange position—supporting the pottery but not really understanding what could happen here. I remember one story—Archie talked Pete into making an awful lot of small flowerpots he was going to market through his friend who had a nursery. Voulkos fired all the pots, glazed all of them, and they were sitting on the floor in the front room. Archie came in one evening and there was Voulkos with a large hammer, breaking them all, one by one. Archie stood there and didn't know what to think: he was trying to make a buck, trying to keep the place going, and here's this guy breaking the pots. He said, 'Pete, what are you doing?' Pete didn't answer. He just kept hammering the pots.[34]

During Ferguson's tenure as director (1958–1964), the Western Clay Manufacturing Company, the Bray family business that helped subsidize the pottery, went bankrupt. Ferguson worked evenings and six days a week to make the pottery economically self-sufficient. Given the onerous crunch of day-to-day operational responsibilities, it is not surprising to find that these early directors did not produce their most adventuresome artworks in Helena.

But the Bray energy field that left its mark on ceramics history did not emanate from the early production pottery alone. The Foundation provided unique opportunities in the early 1950s, and not all were associated with celebrity visitors. LaMar Harrington remarked on one of the most significant contributions the Bray made to Voulkos's artistic development:

> [It was] the sheer abundance of material. He could be as prolific as he could be and throw the biggest pots he could throw in part because he had carloads of clay—enough clay to absorb his tremendous energy. I don't think he would have become the artist he did without that opportunity. I also think the look of the brickyard—the slag heaps and misfired bricks—had some effect on the style of his later work. As for Rudy, the slab constructions he made for architectural commissions at the Bray gave him some of the insights that came together in those large figurative pieces of the 1960s.[35]

As do many ceramists, Voulkos perfected his wheel-throwing facility turning out production pottery. He also learned to carry out this performance in public at the Bray. 'A lot of townspeople came out . . . and Archie would take them around and make me throw on the wheel for them,' Voulkos recalls. 'We were a kind of exhibit, which was all right because I was very shy and it forced me to work in front of people'.[36] Today Voulkos has a legendary reputation for these performances as well as the objects he produces: improvising like a jazz musician, he perfected a new method of ceramics instruction, tantalizing his audience with unpredictable orchestrations of chaos and control.

Technical facilities played a significant role in the Bray's development as well. In the early 1950s two of the largest downdraft, gas-fired kilns in the country were built at the Foundation, one for salt glazing and one for high-fire reduction. According to Harrington, these kilns offered the only opportunity in the Northwest to work in the very high stoneware range and with salt glazing.[37] And Ferguson confirms:

> It was one of the best-firing reduction kilns I've ever seen. It had a ton of concrete poured over the arch to hold it into place. It was a big sprung arch held together by large pieces of railroad tie. Wheelbarrows were brought over from the brickyard and the entire door was mudded over with a trowel. It was very

large, with four burners and lots of gas pressure, no forced air, just natural draft. It fired so well because it cooled so slowly and we got very good effects with glazes.[38]

Along with Voulkos's reputation, these facilities drew artists like Manuel Neri to the Bray in the early 1950s. Three artists who would head influential ceramics departments in West Coast universities converged there in 1954 when Robert Sperry arrived to study with Autio and Voulkos. Sperry spent the summer and fall at the Foundation; Voulkos taught him how to throw, and he practiced glazing techniques on pottery Hamada had left behind.[39] Sperry returned to Seattle and taught at the University of Washington, where he encouraged artists such as Fred Bauer and Patti Warashina to visit the Bray in the 1960s and 1970s.

Voulkos was not the only Bray Foundation member to receive national press in the early 1950s. Foundation director Branson Stevenson was featured in *Craft Horizons* in 1953, where he extolled Montana's native clays and glazes. On a trip to New York a year or so earlier, Stevenson met Aileen Webb, founder of American Craft Council and America House Gallery, who arranged for an exhibition of Montana pottery at America House in 1952.[40] "Potters and Glazes of Montana" traveled to several countries in Europe and Asia, showcasing slip glazes from a canyon near Bozeman and local red-iron earthenware clay. By the mid-1950s, the Bray had become known in the Northwest as a center for experimental work with native materials, a reputation that enhanced its regional allure.[41]

But most of all, it could be argued, the Bray Foundation came to be a unique venue for ceramic art because Archie Bray and the other Helena founders of the pottery did not originally envision the Foundation as a platform for major artists like Voulkos and Autio. Like many small-town potteries in the United States, the Bray began as a center for ceramics education where local potters and students could learn new skills, and the teachers could market their work. The Helena model was extravagantly democratic: anyone 'seriously interested' in ceramics who paid a 10-dollar membership fee could have lifetime access to 'a fine place to work'. When it turned out that the first instructors were exceptionally proficient, Bray hoped they might be able to establish a successful business in production pottery. Bray was also the leader of the local Community Concerts program that brought theater and concert performers from all over the world to Helena, and he envisioned the pottery as part of a larger arts complex. His friend Branson Stevenson, an engineer knowledgeable about ceramic materials, applied the Community Concerts model to the Bray Foundation in his own way, contacting the renowned Bernard Leach on his first U.S. tour to arrange for his 1952 workshop in Helena. Archie Bray, meanwhile, helped make Autio and Voulkos local celebrities, inviting friends and Community Concert performers to his brickyard to watch Voulkos perform and pitching Autio's tile and carved brick murals to local builders and architects.

Thus the Foundation began as an unstable conglomerate of educational services, a small business, and a venue for major artists who dumbfounded Mr. Bray by producing the flowerpots he ordered and smashing them before they could be sold. Attracted by Voulkos's reputation and the imprimatur of Leach, Hamada, and Wildenhain, other professional ceramists began to discover the Bray and take advantage of its accessible studio environment. The Bray was never an art school: there were no entrance requirements or required classes. It was not an organization established to nourish and preserve a local craft tradition, as were Penland School in North Carolina or Haystack Mountain in Maine. It was not a potters' guild like those established by Harvey Littleton in Ann Arbor, Michigan, or Toledo, Ohio, which were primarily professional cooperatives. Nor was it a retreat for established artists like New Hampshire's MacDowell Colony or California's Huntington Hartford Foundation.[42] The Bray left its historical mark most of all because it turned out to be an institutional anomaly, a unique space between all the other places for both emerging and well-known artists.

The Bray's evolution from a small-town pottery to a center for ceramic art with an international constituency was erratic and sometimes harrowing. Voulkos moved to Los Angeles in 1954; Autio left the Bray to join the art department at the University of Montana in 1957. Ken Ferguson took over the pottery in 1958. Recruited by Jim McKinnell, Ferguson was a 30-year-old graduate of Alfred University who had never been West until he came to the Bray:

> I figured if the place was good enough for Voulkos, it was good enough for me. If you look at catalogue of ceramics shows in the early 1950s, the pots are pretty bad. You can see just by looking what an explosive effect Voulkos had. His pots were big, strong, superbly crafted, with a good sense of decoration. It was time for him to move on from the Bray when he did. He already had a national following and people were copying his work.[43]

Ferguson was also enticed by the image of the men with the jug: 'I just wish I could have been [at the Bray] when Leach, Hamada, and Yanagi came through . . . that could have been the greatest time ever'.[44]

> The Foundation was in financial jeopardy when Ferguson arrived: [B]ut I didn't know that—in fact I didn't know much at all. . . . I was an Easterner trying to fill Autio's and Voulkos's shoes. Their presence was still felt and I was as much in awe of them as the members. I had to learn how to get along with the people at the Foundation and how to manage the shop. I also became aware of my limitations and soon developed a rhythm of throwing, working, and making functional pots. I had thoughts only of being a potter, not an artist. . . . My most positive achievement during those lean years was keeping the doors open. The pottery was down to $50 in the bank at one point. . . . The brickyard [which had helped support the pottery] stopped work in 1960 and all of a sudden the Foundation was on its own.[45]

In a 1961 full-page feature in the *Helena Independent Record*, Ferguson is photographed next to dozens of lidded jars. The caption reads: 'Only a few of the 500 jam pots produced annually at the Archie Bray Foundation Pottery'. Most of the 2,000 pots produced at the Bray every year are sold locally, Ferguson tells the reporter. Also pictured are Helena hobbyists enrolled in Ferguson's ceramics classes, along with samples of their work. There is little in the report to suggest that the Bray's reputation extends beyond its production pottery, save for a mention of the prize Ferguson had won recently at the Syracuse National Exhibition and a photograph of seven pots created by Bray directors and visiting artists in the early 1950s.[46]

This document is a useful index of the Bray's relative position in the U.S. ceramics world in 1961. As he emphasized later, Ferguson concentrated on building local support and shoring up the pottery business during his tenure at the Foundation. He did invite David Shaner to work at the Bray; Fred Bauer and Angelo Garzio joined him as well. Toshiko Takaezu presented a workshop at the Foundation in 1963. But there were few guest artists and no significant intersections between the Bray and the ceramists who dominate histories of the period today—the group gathered around Voulkos at the Otis Art Institute.

Like Voulkos, Ferguson built up his technical facility making production ware. He was soon creating direct, confident pottery and winning national prizes for his emphatically vertical, modestly decorated, covered jars. Some were topped with oversized knobs, like the jam jars illustrated in the *Independent Record.* He was so affected by the scale of the land and sky in Montana that he continued to turn out casseroles that would not fit in an oven.[47] Leach's visual imprint begins to surface at the Bray at this point: Ferguson's muted, textured glazes and functional stoneware with finger ridges tracking the growth of the pot on the wheel exemplify the U.S. potters' aesthetic inspired by *A Potter's Book.* Like Leach, Ferguson also came to believe that a pot would have integrity only if its maker did, and that whatever was in the potter's soul would show up in his or her production.[48]

Ferguson enlisted Alfred University colleague David Shaner as his successor when he left the Bray in 1964 to teach at the Kansas City Art Institute. Under Shaner's leadership, a new institutional vision was crafted that ultimately configured the Bray as the national resource it is today. The Foundation was in legal trouble when Shaner became director: the Small Business Administration had foreclosed the brickyard, and the pottery was among the assets to be sacrificed to satisfy its debts. 'For five years [1961–1966] the Bray Foundation lay in limbo, putting us in the position of being little more than squatters,' Shaner recounts. 'Just when Senator Mike Mansfield thought a deal to separate the Foundation from the brickyard would be possible, the bottom fell out. The government quickly put us on the public auction block—the physical property, including wheels and kilns, were all tagged to be sold to the highest bidder. We succeeded in purchasing the buildings and contents though competitive bidding.'[49] In the campaign to save the pottery, Shaner proved to be not only a savvy leader but also an effective rhetorician. 'What New York is in communications, Hollywood in the film industry, and New Orleans in jazz, Helena is becoming in the field of creative pottery,' he assured the local press. 'In this field you can't go any higher than the Archie Bray Foundation.'[50]

The aftermath of the successful bid was arduous: another buyer purchased the brickyard, and the pottery's infrastructure had to be cut free from its former parent. A well was dug, water and gas lines laid, and buildings repaired. Shaner supervised this transition while keeping up the Foundation's income flow, selling clay, teaching classes, and producing hundreds of the pots the Bray sold every year. At the same time, he began to think about repositioning the Foundation as a national center for ceramics professionals.

Ferguson was an excellent teacher who developed a loyal following among prominent amateur ceramists in Helena. Shaner observed, when he inherited the clay classes:

> [They were] quite ingrown, and it was like a social club. We sold them clay premixed, and all the firing was done for them. . . . At that time, they had unlimited access to the Bray, and we got in a position where some of them had begun to sell their pots and take orders, almost to the point where when you made pots there was not room . . . in the kiln, and you were making pots to keep the Foundation surviving. . . . Over the years, my thought was to try and get new blood into these pottery classes. . . . I built six kilns for people to help them get set up on their own.

By the time of the auction, Shaner decided that what the Bray needed were opportunities for 'more talented people to come,' so it would 'not be just a Helena pottery situation.'[51]

The National Endowment for the Arts had begun to initiate its grant-making programs in the mid-1960s. 'Since the U.S. government had played Shylock in our procuring the place, it was only natural that we should pursue them for a grant,' Shaner reasoned. In his initial application, Shaner represented the Foundation as 'an experiment of private Ceramic Industry supporting the Creative Ceramic Arts. Its position in the Art World was unique from the beginning,' he writes. 'The Foundation, being self-supporting, provides experience and insight into a successfully operating pottery. This and its opportunity for total involvement set the Foundation apart from all other educational institutions.' He underlined the difficulty 'for a visiting potter to travel to Montana. Ofttimes we cannot serve the most talented or those with the greatest interest.'[52]

Shaner's commitment to national outreach was an essential preface for the Bray's current historical 'thereness.' Endowment funds enabled Shaner and future directors David Cornell and Kurt Weiser to leverage the image of the men with the jug and attract a wide range of the country's most important ceramic artists. Shaner invited Victor Babu, Val Cushing, Wayne Higby, Chuck Hindes, Jun Kaneko, Mick Lamont, and Mark Pharis for residencies. Warren MacKenzie and Daniel Rhodes came to present workshops. 'All [the residents'] expenses were covered by the grant—they just had to concern themselves with getting here and finding a place to live,' Shaner points out.

The march toward artistic professionalism was difficult and controversial. The Foundation's trustees were divided over the wisdom of seeking federal funds for their Montana pottery. Reviewing the new climate at the

Foundation after Endowment funds arrived, Lee Wynn, who contributed the 'Looking in on the Arts' column to the Helena Independent Record, noted with sarcasm:

> You will remember Daniel Rhodes, one of the country's foremost potters and authors on the subject, who was here and conducting a workshop in the early Spring [April, 1969]. Well, he is reported to have said that the Archie Bray Foundation makes more of a contribution to the field of pottery than any other institution he knows of. In order to earn that compliment, the Foundation had to sacrifice something precious to the folks around Helena, though. It used to be a Helena Housewives Haven where many a mother went to make mugs and casseroles and bird feeders. Well, there still are a number of them in the regular classes but the atmosphere is more of a serious instructional one and there isn't room for the mud-dobbers [sic]. Also there are restrictions on the amount of time students may work there. . . . Mud-dobbers, you're going to have to find a new place.[53]

Remarkably, like his predecessors, Shaner kept the Bray on track and advanced his own work at the same time. 'Somehow the workshops and the camaraderie of the art-ists all affected my creativity, augmented my own creative juices. . . . I had to make pots and make them in quantity for the Foundation, but make the public buy what I chose to make'.[54] Shaner had come to the Bray from a teaching job at the University of Illinois, where he was becoming known for pottery that had much in common with Ferguson's. Ferguson taught Shaner to throw, according to LaMar Harrington, 'yet Shaner's work seemed more intuitively formed'. She aptly describes the look of Shaner's pottery as reminiscent of 'the delicate mathematical balance in the profile of classical Greek sculpture and architecture,' but reminds us, too, that his prize-winning entry in the Twenty-fourth Ceramic National in 1966 was a torn, expressionist plate.[55] 'In essence I was trying to save the utilitarian pot,' Shaner admits. 'It was like a mission for me. The university was teaching more avant-garde clay work, and somehow the pots were being made by the granola-type people on the street. . . . I think it was important that I proved that good pots could still be made. . . . It was like putting notes in a bottle and casting them out to sea'.[56]

Shaner's evangelism has been contextualized by Garth Clark. By the mid 1960s, according to Clark, U.S. ceramists 'were beginning to experience a certain anguish. They saw themselves as artists. Many of their peers in painting and sculpture viewed them as equals. . . . But in general the art establishment still viewed them as craftsmen and beneath serious consideration. In this climate, the vessel became a particularly embarrassing reminder of its plebeian roots and was treated with the same disdain and discomfort as the socially ambitious might feel toward their country cousins. The 1960s were therefore characterized by an accent on the sculptural and a denial of pottery'.[57] Clark sees the work of California and Seattle clay artists who made funk sculpture or trompe l'oeil still-life objects as the dominant new production of the 1960s. Like the ceramics created by artists associated with Voulkos in Los Angeles, this new expansion of the field is also largely absent from the Bray's historical anatomy. Former Bray director Kurt Weiser attributes these omissions to a culture clash:

> I think for a long time the Bray was more of an East Coast institution, even though it was in Montana. There wasn't much West Coast influence at all. All the directors, with the exception of Rudy and Pete, were from the East, and Pete completely bailed out after the mid-'50s. Ken and Dave did Alfred stuff. The values that were prior to abstract expressionism lasted a lot longer at the Bray. Ken was into Bernard Leach, and Dave was too. Ceramic comedy never made much of an impact in Montana. But things did change when the Cornells were here—they jumped off in a different direction.[58]

David and Judy Cornell became codirectors of the Bray in 1970. David Cornell was from Kalispell, Montana, and Judy from Rochester, New York: both were graduates of the Alfred University ceramics program. Before Montana, they had been resident artists at the Penland School in North Carolina. In the mid-1960s, Penland became a retreat for university-trained artists working in a variety of craft media, and the Cornells envisioned a rapport between the North Carolina model and Archie Bray's dream of an arts complex serving a wide range of artists. Soon after their arrival, Judy Cornell organized an exhibition of work by noted émigré weaver Ebba Kossick, and David Cornell received grants from the Montana Arts Council and the National Endowment for the Arts to establish a glassblowing facility. Meanwhile, both produced hundreds of pots for the pottery, and David built new kilns, including one for firing with wood. Judy worked primarily with porcelain, and her output changed the complexion of Bray production ware.

The Cornells presided over the Bray's twentieth birthday party. During these two decades, thanks in considerable measure to Shaner's leadership, the Foundation was attracting national as well as local funding. The Cornells not only diversified the program to include glassblowing and weaving, they also invited artists to present workshops whose production clashed with the Alfred aesthetic, among them Patti Warashina, Erik Gronborg, and Betty Woodman. A series of two-year residencies was established; some residents taught classes for the local community in exchange for an opportunity to market their work through the pottery shop.

The Cornells' tenure is often remembered for their tolerance of camping (the Cornells reversed Shaner's adamant opposition to tent-camping by Foundation residents) and for what were known at the time as 'alternative life styles,' but their emphasis as directors was on providing practical, real-world skills and experience. They initiated a crafts apprenticeship program funded in part by the Rocky Mountain Federation of States. David Cornell successfully expanded the Foundation's clay-supply business. Pat Eckman, a resident artist from Indiana in the mid-1970s, spoke for many of his peers in his assessment of the Cornell-era Bray experience: 'I had the choice of going on to college [and] graduate school or coming here. This place is more involved with the real world and its practical aspects than a university. This place provides an artist with the educational aspects of learning about materials and how to work with them, but it also teaches you how to live in the world and sell your work.'[59]

Under Kurt Weiser's directorship (1976–1988), the Bray's profile looks more familiar. Weiser is among the many students of Ken Ferguson and/or the ceramics program at the Kansas City Art Institute to have a sustained relationship with the Bray; this contingent also includes John and Andrea Gill, Richard Notkin, Akio Takamori, Christy Lasater Weiser, Chris Staley, and Josh DeWeese. 'When I got here, the finances were not in good shape,' Weiser recalls:

> I tried to make as many pots as I could and sell as many as I could—anything I thought would make money. I soon realized that making pots and trying to sell them in Helena was not going to sustain the place. I thought the clay business might save us, so I got a friend from Michigan, Chip Clawson, to come out. I thought he could build up the business and he did a tremendous job. As it got progressively easier to run the place financially, the more I was able to do exactly what I wanted in my work. It didn't matter whether it sold here or not—I wasn't making production pots and the artists who came here didn't need to do that, either.[60]

At the Bray, Weiser created elegant slip-cast and porcelain cylindrical abstractions that lean or stretch or bend like a dancer's silhouette. The distance between these compositions and Ferguson's mass-produced jam pots provides a clear visual marker of the Bray's progressive liberation from the demands of a marginal small business to a studio environment that can sustain creative freedom on a regular basis. The new taxonomy of the early 1980s—'vessel-oriented clay object'—seems applicable not only to Weiser's work but to that of Takamori, the Gills, and Notkin: Bray production became more consistent with larger national trends in the late 1970s and 1980s than it had been in the 1960s. Stylistic strategies associated with the West Coast such as funk or the trompe l'oeil 'super object' had largely peaked by the end of Weiser's tenure, and the resilient tradition of the vessel that predominates at the Bray began to exert a new authority in the pluralistic field of postmodern ceramics.

Not all the artists who have flourished at the Bray, to be sure, are vessel makers. In 1984 Weiser was able to negotiate the 'Louisiana Purchase'—the acquisition by the Foundation of the former Bray family brickyard adjoining the pottery. 'People today just can't imagine what it was like before we got the brickyard,' Weiser observes. 'I used to say one of the best things we had going at the Bray was that everyone knew about it but hardly anyone had actually seen it. The place always looked like a junkyard or construction project. With the brickyard property, we could put the clay business in a proper building and build new studios. The residents could stretch out and do things they never did before—like Robert Harrison did'.[61]

Harrison came to the Foundation to do studio work and discovered that 'all of a sudden I had access to acres of land and tons of raw material. Getting that brickyard was like a rebirth for the Bray. I was unexpectedly able to explore some of the larger scale, on-site issues I was infatuated with. That experience really did it for me, in terms of building my confidence and establishing credibility for some of my big outdoor work'.[62] Harrison made three architectural-scale site works at the Bray using material from the brickyard—Tile-X (1985), the Potter's Shrine (1985–87), and Aruina (1988)—which led to a series of outdoor arch and gateway compositions created in the 1990s for other sites all over the world. 'There are many who know you can do experimental work at the Bray, although there is a perception that it's just a place for potters,' Harrison points out. 'There's such a strong desire on the part of many younger artists to explore larger-scale and outdoor pieces, and there aren't many opportunities to do this, especially in terms of residencies. There is potential for stretching out at the Bray that isn't as well-known as it should be'.[63]

Weiser stretched the Bray in other ways as well. 'The National Endowment for the Arts was really important for us,' he emphasizes:

> They would give us funds for visiting artists and workshops; we would find the artists we wanted to have here and entice them with the money. The Asian Cultural Council in New York deserves a lot of credit, too. They helped us reach out internationally and bring Asian artists to Montana; then we would go and visit them. All this was very informal—a person-to-person network—but it helped spread the word about the Bray all over the world. . . . When I met Kichizaemon Raku in Japan, even he knew about the Bray, and we were able to get him out here [in 1987].[64]

The second woman director of the Bray, newly minted Alfred University graduate Carol Roorbach, began her three-year term in 1989. (The first woman, Lillian Boschen, was director for a short time in 1951–52 while Autio and Voulkos were in graduate school; in the 1970s Judy Cornell was associate director.) Roorbach's prominence contrasts with the relative invisibility of most of the directors' female partners, among them Gertrude Ferguson and Ann Shaner, who made crucial contributions to the Bray's forward momentum. Roorbach celebrated the Bray's fortieth anniversary in part by supervising the organization's first long-range plan and accelerating the formation of an endowment. Works of art left behind by residents over the years were collected and organized into the nucleus of an on-site gallery or museum.[65] These activities mark a new level of self-awareness about the Bray's institutional history and its allure for potential residents: the photo of the men with the jug was made into a postcard, which functions as a locally ubiquitous reminder of the Bray's distinguished pedigree. 'When you come to the Bray as a young artist,' Akio Takamori remembers, 'you really realize there's a history here and that it's important for you to be included. The Bray makes you want to be included'.[66]

The Foundation's current director, Josh DeWeese, seems predestined for his job. His B.F.A. degree in ceramics is from the Kansas City Art Institute; his M.F.A. is from Alfred University. He was born in Montana, the son of Autio's and Voulkos's undergraduate painting teacher, Robert DeWeese, and one of Montana's leading landscape and figure painters, Gennie DeWeese. His stylized vessel forms are superbly crafted and expertly glazed with atmospheric surfaces. During his tenure, the pottery shop has revived and now provides a 'respectable' slice of the Foundation's income. ('Josh has done an astounding job selling pots,' Weiser says with admiration. 'When I was at the Bray, Helena was pretty much a *Farmer's Almanac* kind of town; now it's Eddie Bauer. Josh was on to this and has really made the shop attractive to a new crowd of buyers'.)

DeWeese leans on the Bray's artistic legacy in formulating the Foundation's residency program:

> As I think about selecting residents, I always think about working potters. It's a given that there will be good potters working here. What I try to encourage is a diversity of styles and career levels. But the Bray is a place for sculptors, too, and in the 1990s, a lot of the good work is installation-oriented—I'm thinking of artists like Rebecca Hutchinson and Tré Arenz, who really did some interesting pieces here. This is still a clay-based program, and we presume a strong technical background, but the Bray will go where artists want to go. What's so great about this place is that there are no rules here, except that the best artists should have a fine place to work.[67]

From the perspective of Richard Notkin, an artist who has followed the Bray's evolution for a decade and a half, the Foundation's influence can be figured around its directors: 'When Shaner came here, it was really the Shaner Foundation; then it was the Cornell Foundation, the Weiser Foundation, and so on, and now it's the DeWeese Foundation. Even when Ferguson was here, the director was relatively autonomous in terms of determining the program and who would come in. But beyond that, the directors had or have a certain magnetism that draws other artists, particularly young ceramic artists at the early stages of their careers'.

Some residents a few years ago 'proposed a "Ceramic-triangle" T-shirt with three intersections: Alfred, Kansas City, and the Bray'. Notkin goes on to reflect:

> Those links have been central historically, but the Bray network is much wider and deeper. The Bray belongs to a kind of ceramics trade route. The Silk Road didn't just happen; by analogy, neither does the pathway between most artists and the Bray. Young artists who follow the path tend to self-select. They usually have a strong work ethic, a good technical background, and the maturity to work outside an academic structure, where you are not jumping through someone else's hoops. Like me, many of them don't necessarily do their best work at the Bray, but they lay the foundation for inspiration in the future. The collection shows this: most of it is not mature work. It's exciting as a record of transition, a very fertile period in the careers of artists who are now renowned, but who were just artists with a lot of promise when they came to the Bray. Personally, that's what I hope the Bray will always be—a sanctuary for promise.[68]

In the context of historical writing, particular events and people who have consolidated the Bray's institutional impact appear as text or recorded conversations. For Notkin and scores of other artists, by comparison, the Bray's historical 'thereness' is cast in the intangible substance of personal memory. These memories form a matrix of identification, loyalty, and nostalgia that the records show to be tough and resilient, helping pull the

Foundation through its messy divorce and adventurous re-marriage with a nineteenth-century brickyard. The city of Helena has grown up along with the Bray and has provided many forms of critical support. The new frontier for the city, the artists, and the Bray will be to create a sanctuary that works for the next millennium. As Notkin points out, the Bray now has a lot of competition: 'There's a great deal of strength in reputation and history, but cultural memories don't hold up forever. History or facilities are not the main reasons the Bray is unique and important. It's dedicated people doing exciting things that make artists want to be around that energy. That's what has kept the place going and it's the best recipe for the future'.[69]

Notes

Unpublished archival materials, in addition to those cited in the bibliography, include newsletters, artists' questionnaires, and scrapbooks of memorabilia and clippings held in the Archie Bray Foundation Archives, Helena, MT. Bray artists' questionnaires, slides, and resumés, collected in 1977–78 by LaMar Harrington for an unrealized Bray exhibition at the Bellevue Art Museum, Bellevue, WA, are located in the LaMar Harrington Archive, Manuscripts and University Archives Division, University of Washington Libraries.

1. LaMar Harrington, interview with the author, June 1998.
2. 'It was from Hamada that everybody started learning to throw pieces of pottery off one lump of clay. In other words, before that time we'd been making one lump of clay and we'd make a piece out of it, and then we learned from Hamada—you take a great lump of clay and you just keep throwing little bowls off the top of it'. Martin Holt, Interview with Peter Meloy, June 19, 1977. Transcript in Archie Bray Foundation Archives.
3. Letter from Bernard Leach to Peter Meloy, 1953. Copy, ABFA.
4. Leach, Shoji Hamada, and Soetsu Yanagi conducted a two-week seminar at Black Mountain College October 15–29, 1952. Leach met his future wife, Janet Darnell, during this visit. See Mary Emma Harris, *The Arts at Black Mountain College* (Cambridge, MA, and London: The MIT Press, 1987), 231. In several of his publications, Garth Clark incorrectly reports that Leach, Hamada, and Yanagi presented their workshop at Black Mountain in the summer of 1953 and that Voulkos met the trio there a second time. See, for example, Clark's essay "American Ceramics Since 1950," in *American Ceramics*. The Collection of the Everson Museum of Art (New York: Rizzoli, 1989), 200.
5. Bernard Leach, *Beyond East and West. Memoirs, Portraits and Essays* (London and Boston: Faber & Faber, 1978), 244–252.
6. Rose Slivka, *Peter Voulkos. A Dialogue with Clay* (New York: New York Graphic Society, 1978), 14.
7. Martin Holt, Interview with Peter Voulkos, August 7, 1978. Transcript, ABFA.
8. Matthew Kangas, *Rudy Autio Retrospective* (Missoula, MT: School of Fine Arts, University of Montana, 1983), 10. Autio has offered various assessments of the 1952 Leach-Hamada workshop over the years, but consistently acknowledges the impact of Prieto and Ball.
9. Sam Jornlin and Garna Muller, "Chronology," in Rose Slivka and Karen Tsujimoto, *The Art of Peter Voulkos* (Tokyo: Kodansha International, 1995), 161–62.
10. According to Autio, in the early 1950s he and Voulkos were especially interested in the work of Kanjiro Kawai. See Kangas, "Rudy Autio," in *Autio*, 10.
11. Martin Holt, Interview with Ken Ferguson, July 2, 1979. Transcript, ABFA.
12. Garth Clark, *American Ceramics 1876 to the Present* (New York: Abbeville Press, 1987), 101, 167, 170. According to Clark, Leach divided his pots to emphasize the wholeness of the vessel. Voulkos's divisions, in contrast, 'released the parts from the domination of the whole'.
13. Elaine Levin, *The History of American Ceramics 1607 to the Present* (New York: Harry N. Abrams, 1988), 200.
14. Clark, *History of American Ceramics*, 117–118. Writers who 'did not understand' the importance of Japanese pottery included Rose Slivka, author of the major Voulkos monographs, and John Coplans, who organized the highly influential 1966 Abstract Expressionist Ceramics exhibition.

15. Jornlin and Muller, "Chronology," in Slivka and Tsujimoto, *The Art of Peter Volkos*, 161–162.
16. Rick Newby and Chere Jiusto, interview with Rudy Autio, November 3, 1998. Audio tape ABFA.
17. Slivka, *Peter Voulkos*, 28 (as in n. 6).
18. Marguerite Wildenhain, "A Potter's Dissent," *Craft Horizons* (May/June 1953): 43.
19. LaMar Harrington, *Ceramics in the Pacific Northwest* (Seattle and London: University of Washington Press, 1979), 22.
20. Marguerite Wildenhain, *Pottery: Form and Expression* (New York: Reinhold Publishing, 1965), 74–76.
21. Val Cushing, quoted in *Marguerite Wildenhain: A Retrospective Exhibition of the Work of Master Potter Marguerite Wildenhain* (Ithaca, New York: Herbert F. Johnson Museum of Art, 1980), 25.
22. Bernice Boone, "The Archie Bray Foundation and the Pottery," *Quarterly of the Montana Institute of the Arts* (Spring, 1960): 22.
23. Newby and Jiusto, interview with Autio, ABFA.
24. Slivka, *Peter Voulkos*, 12. Slivka incorrectly states that Wildenhain conducted a five-week workshop at the Bray [the correct dates are May 4–9, 1954]. She adds: 'Voulkos worked with her closely, assisting her. She considered him enormously gifted,' 38.
25. Slivka and Tsujimoto, *The Art of Peter Voulkos*, 39 (as in n. 9). The advice was communicated in a letter to Paul Soldner from Nan and James McKinnell.
26. Holt, interview with Voulkos, transcript ABFA, 15. Voulkos reports that he enrolled in the California College of Arts and Crafts because, although he wanted to study with Prieto, he wasn't accepted at Mills College. The College of Arts and Crafts is located in Oakland, not far from Mills.
27. Kangas, *Rudy Autio Retrospective*, 21 (as in n. 8). Prieto conducted a workshop at the Bray in August, 1956. There is considerable confusion in several major publications regarding the chronology of events at the Bray in the early 1950s. The most recent major book on Voulkos, Slivka and Tsujimoto's *The Art of Peter Voulkos*, for example, states that in 1953 Voulkos conducted workshops at the Bray with Carlton Ball, James and Nan McKinnell, Robert Sperry, and Marguerite Wildenhain (62). The Wildenhain workshop was held in May, 1954; the McKinnells first came to Helena for the Wildenhain workshop. Sperry was a Bray resident artist in the summer of 1954; Ball's workshop was in the summer of 1955. There were no ceramics workshops in the summer of 1953, when memorials were held for Archie Bray, who had died on February 17, 1953.
28. Karnes produced Alfred-style pottery, but Weintrab was also beginning to make ceramic sculpture.
29. Harris, *The Arts of Black Mountain College*, 234 (as in n. 4). Also see illustration, 235.
30. Slivka, *Peter Voulkos*, 23.
31. Slivka and Tsujimoto, *The Art of Peter Voulkos*, 111.
32. Slivka, *Peter Voulkos*, 31. She repeats the same sentence in *The Art of Peter Voulkos*, 43.
33. Slivka and Tsujimoto, *The Art of Peter Voulkos*, 42.
34. Ken Ferguson, audio tape, 1974. A copy of this tape was provided to the author by Akio Takamori.
35. Harrington, interview with the author.
36. Holt, interview with Voulkos, 11, transcript, ABFA.
37. Harrington, *Ceramics in the Pacific Northwest*, 24 (as in n. 19).
38. Ferguson audio tape.
39. Kangas, *Rudy Autio Retrospective*, 10, 20 (as in n. 8).
40. Martin Holt, interview with Branson Stevenson, August 2, 1978, transcript, ABFA, 20. See also Branson Stevenson, "Clays and Glazes of Montana," *Craft Horizons* (February, 1953): 42–43.
41. The Bray's reputation is discussed in Margaret Callahan, "The Comeback of the Potter," *The Seattle Times* (April 11, 1954). Clipping, ABFA.
42. Misimpressions persist about the Bray's early institutional identity. Many assume the Bray was originally established to serve the needs of professional artists. For example, Martha Drexler Lynn, a former curator of Decorative Arts

at the Los Angeles County Museum of Art, states in a 1990 essay that the Bray was 'founded in 1951 as a center for advanced study in ceramics'. See "From Vessel to Vehicle'" *Clay Today: Contemporary Ceramists and their Work* (San Francisco: Chronicle Books, 1990), 24

43. Ferguson audio tape.
44. Holt, interview with Ferguson, 22, transcript, ABFA.
45. Ken Ferguson, quoted in "The Archie Bray Foundation," *Studio Potter* 8:1 (1979): 51.
46. Olive Henry, "Bray Foundation Produces Finest Examples of Pottery," *Helena Independent Record* (November 5, 1961). Clipping, ABFA.
47. Harrington, *Ceramics in the Pacific Northwest*, 29. See also Michael Rubin, "Kenneth Ferguson," *American Ceramics* 2:3 (1983), 43–44.
48. Lynn, *Clay Today*, 21.
49. David Shaner, quoted in "The Archie Bray Foundation," *Studio Potter* 8:1 (1979): 51.
50. George Remington, "Sale May Wipe Out Pottery Foundation," *Billings Gazette* (April 14, 1966), clipping, ABFA.
51. David Shaner, "Seven Years as a Director of the Archie Bray Foundation, 1963–1970," transcript of audio tape, ABFA, 7.
52. A copy of Shaner's application to the National Federation of the Arts and Humanities is included in the Shaner scrapbook, ABFA.
53. Lee Wynn, "Looking at the Arts," *Helena Independent Record*, undated clipping, ABFA.
54. Shaner, 'Seven Years as Director,' 19.
55. Harrington, *Ceramics in the Pacific Northwest*, 29. A composition much like Shaner's 1966 prize winner is included in the exhibition.
56. Shaner, "Seven Years as Director," 18.
57. Garth Clark, "Introduction," *American Potters Today* (London: Victoria and Albert Museum, 1986), 13.
58. Kurt Weiser, interview with the author, March 26, 1999.
59. Don Bundy, 'The only art is living,' *Helena Independent Record* (January 30, 1976), 9A.
60. Weiser interview.
61. Ibid.
62. Robert Harrison, interview with the author, October 5, 1998.
63. Ibid.
64. Weiser interview.
65. Diane Douglas, 'The Archie Bray Foundation,' in *The Legacy of the Archie Bray Foundation: Four Decades of Tradition and Innovation in American Ceramic Art* (Bellevue, Washington: Bellevue Art Museum, 1993).
66. Akio Takamori, interview with the author, June 10, 1998.
67. Josh DeWeese, interview with the author, February 19, 1999.
68. Richard Notkin, interview with the author, July 19, 1998.
69. Ibid.

Reproduced by permission of the author.

20
STUDIO CERAMICS: THE END OF THE STORY?

Jeffrey Jones

This article was originally given as a paper at the 'Diversity in the Making: Studio Ceramics Today' conference which was held at Camberwell College of Arts, London, on 15 January 2001. It was published in issue 2 of *Interpreting Ceramics* later that year. Inevitably the text is now dated, not only in the sense that thirteen years have passed since it was written, but also in the sense that the turn of the millennium framed the writing in very self-conscious way. Therefore no attempt has been made to update the text; it is presented here as a period piece with all its outdated references intact.

Introduction

There can surely be no doubt that we have now passed from the twentieth to the twenty-first century and the arguments as to whether the twenty-first century began on 1 January 2000 or 1 January 2001 can be put aside. Whichever date we favour for this significant transition, we might at least all agree that the period of change from one century to another, from one millennium to another, has shown itself (somewhat predictably) to have been a fruitful time for a discussion of the ends of the things. It wasn't until I started to prepare this talk that I discovered that there was a name for this phenomenon: endism,[1] and there is also a name for those of us who dwell deeply on finalities, passings, conclusions and the like. It seems that we are endists and that there are a lot of us about.

You need not look far for evidence of this. Try doing a search for 'endism' on the Internet and see what you get. Or consider the titles of the following books published in recent years: *The End of Science*,[2] *The End of Work*,[3] *The End of Utopia*,[4] and perhaps most notably, Francis Fukuyama's *The End of History and the Last Man*.[5] If all these big things really are over, what then are the prospects for the smaller concerns of life and the chances of survival of more localised forms of human activity such as studio ceramics? Is it time to surrender to this gloomy tendency, accept that what we call studio ceramics has run its course and proclaim the end of that as well? Before becoming too downhearted by what can appear to be the inherent pessimism of endist thought it might be useful to explore the phenomenon in general a little further before coming to any premature conclusions about the end of studio ceramics.

Firstly, let's put aside the more sensationalist manifestations of endism, those concerned with Doomsday scenarios and the hastening on of the end of the world as we know it. There's plenty of that available if you have a mind to look but I should think it is not to the taste of most of us here. However the prevalence of such apocalyptic thought does tell us something about the mood of the times. Paying attention to it can alert us to the heightened feelings which are engendered when there is the slightest suggestion that what we hold to be continuous, solid and reliable is threatened by closure. We should also note that for some people the prospect of the end of everything is exciting; although the end of everything in that instance usually means the end of

Source: © Jeffrey Jones/*Interpreting Ceramics* (issue 2, 2001).

everything that is not to such people's particular liking. That kind of endism can provide an opportunity for some to look forward to the victory of very partial worldviews. This is endism as triumphalism.

In 'The End of History', Francis Fukuyama's much-discussed article published in 1989 and his subsequent book published in 1992,[6] the author talks of the triumph of the West, and the seemingly unstoppable success of the Western idea. He refers to the exhaustion of viable, systematic alternatives to Western, democratic liberalism and says that 'there are powerful reasons for believing that it is the ideal that will govern the material world *in the long run*' (original emphasis).[7] Now, I am here to talk about studio ceramics not political history and theory but Fukuyama's controversial thesis provides an important lesson for us. Fukuyama writes of the triumph of a particular political philosophy but he is hardly a triumphalist, trumpeting the victory of a particular ideology and the end of competing voices. Fukuyama is more concerned to articulate an awkward, dawning truth: that by all accounts, by all reasonable measures of what is going on in the world, Western, democratic liberalism now finds itself with no serious, ideological competitors. To put it simply, Western liberalism has won; it's the end of the story. History, in the sense of events, things happening in the world, will of course continue, but history, in the sense of a struggle for a dominant idea has ended.

In this paper I argue that such an insight can usefully, and I think reasonably be applied to the discourse surrounding studio ceramics and its position within the wider field of ceramics as a whole. I would ask you to consider if we are not justified now in asking the simple question: has studio ceramics won? And, if the answer is yes, is this in any sense good news?

So in framing the title of this paper as 'Studio Ceramics: The End of the Story?' I am therefore not so much concerned with writing the obituary of studio ceramics as with interpreting studio ceramics as an ideological phenomenon, which has at its core an implicit sense of historical destiny and convergence. Studio ceramics is therefore understood here as having taken on a particular responsibility both for articulating the potential of the medium of ceramics, and for nurturing and protecting ceramics as a discrete category of human activity. If, as Don Cupitt suggests, 'what people call history evolves over the weeks and years as the provisional outcome of a contest of stories'[8] then I would argue that we have good reason for recognising that studio ceramics has in the twentieth century been supremely successful not only in achieving a pre-eminent place for its own story, but also in achieving for itself the role of narrator of the ceramics story as a whole. Studio ceramics is the end of the story in the sense that it has come to see itself as the final chapter in the great book of ceramics.[9]

I must emphasise here that I make no claim and offer no evidence that the work produced under the aegis of studio ceramics is any sense better, technically or aesthetically, than any other kind of ceramics. But there is evidence that the ideology embedded in studio ceramics can now be understood as an unrivalled success. Before looking at some of this evidence I should say that my concerns here are with British studio ceramics although my arguments may also have relevance elsewhere. I should also point out that I shall be taking as examples people who make or have made pottery although I readily acknowledge that the term 'pottery' by no means accounts for everything covered by the term 'ceramics'. However I think it is fair to say that British studio *ceramics* has its practical and ideological roots anchored firmly in the twentieth century studio *pottery* movement. There may be some who would fight at all costs to preserve the nice distinctions between these two but I admit I find it difficult to separate them in many, if not most, circumstances. I must risk giving offence by sometimes conflating the two and talking, for instance, of the studio pottery/studio ceramics movement.

Studio Ceramics: Telling the story

In the figure of Bernard Leach, arguably the foremost polemicist of that movement, we can observe someone whose sense of historical destiny was central to his life's work. But as well as making a claim for his own historical importance, Leach was as ready to make a grand claim for his chosen medium, saying that 'the history of man is written in clay'.[10] Leach was not alone in making this assertion, for example Dora Billington stated that 'the story of pottery is the story of civilisation'[11] and W. B. Dalton, who I believe was principal here at Camberwell at the beginning of the twentieth century, described clay as 'man's oldest, if not greatest friend' and went on to say that 'clay lives in and through all the history of mankind'.[12] All three, Leach, Billington and Dalton, wrote pottery handbooks in which varying degrees of technical information are juxtaposed with references to a range of ceramic artefacts from the past. The authors are all humble in the face of the achievements of potters from previous ages but there is also a recognition of the privileged position from which they are writing. For example, towards the end of Billington's book *The Art of the Potter*, published in 1937, in a chapter entitled 'The Pottery of Today', the author writes:

> Although a considerable expansion of studio pottery has taken place only during the last twenty years or so in this country, it has its roots in the last century, when pottery collections were formed and written about, and experiments made, resulting in a gradual readjustment of values. For the first time contemporary pottery could be adequately compared with what had been done before and many attempts were made to recover lost 'secrets' and origins.
>
> Thanks to all this spade work the studio potter can survey the whole field of ceramics and, within the limits of his capabilities, make whatever wares he pleases.[13]

Leaving aside the observation that most studio potters proved to be far more circumscribed in the wares that they made than that which Billington might have hoped for and encouraged, there is a sense here of the studio potter moving towards a privileged vantage point from which the whole field of ceramics can be accessed and interpreted. Billington was neither naive nor unique in her approach; C.F.Binns, Dora Lunn, Bernard Leach, Murray Fieldhouse, all of these writers felt it appropriate to provide some kind of historical survey in their pottery handbooks usually as a preface to the instructions which they provided to their aspiring colleagues, the new breed of individual potter.[14] Leach may have been fussier than most in his choice of exemplary ceramic traditions, limiting himself to Raku, English slipware and Oriental stoneware and porcelain, but the range of ceramic styles and processes covered by the potter-authors referred to above is impressively diverse. The studio potter's inheritance was indeed a significant one, and one that brought with it a good deal of responsibility, as well as a range of possibilities. As the studio potter emerged as a distinct type, so the story of ceramics coalesced as a seemingly coherent field of endeavour with a distinct, historical trajectory.

As the history of twentieth century studio pottery/studio ceramics itself came to be written, its unique, privileged and seemingly conclusive position within the wider ceramics world became ever more apparent. Studio ceramics became, literally, the final chapter in an increasing number of publications which covered the history of ceramics in far more depth than any of the authors of the pottery handbooks had attempted. One of the most ambitious of these publications to have appeared in recent years is *The Potter's Art* by Garth Clark, which is subtitled *A Complete History of Pottery in Britain*. Clark's book, published in 1995, is divided up into four parts: The Peasant Potter, The Industrial Potter, The Artist Potter and then The Studio Potter as the last and longest chapter. In his introduction the author sets out the rationale for this, describing the book as consisting of four overlapping chronologies and he defends this approach by saying:

> This view is perhaps best understood by regarding the narrative as a kind of cultural relay race for leadership in the ceramic arts in which the baton is transferred at certain points from the hands of one potter type to another.[15]

The metaphor of baton passing is a vivid and compelling one, but in its very success as a metaphor there is an uncomfortable reality laid bare at its foundation. This metaphor surely begs some important questions. If we, the studio ceramics community find ourselves carrying the ceramics baton, then where now should we run with it, and perhaps more pertinently, will there ever be any other kind of potter type to whom we can eventually hand it on? It seems as if the race is over but has anyone actually won? Are we really justified in consigning to history those non-studio potters who have played their part, handed on the baton and dutifully stepped aside? There is surely a case for looking more closely at these other ceramics stories and noting, at the very least, that their individual narratives have a life beyond their apportioned stages in the ceramics relay race. I shall briefly look in turn at the stories of these three other potter types as described by Garth Clark, with especial regard to the way that those stories have been positioned within the larger ceramics story. I shall begin by asking, what happened to the peasant potter?

The peasant potter

The extinction of this species has been dated to various points throughout the first half of the twentieth century, their demise hastened by the First World War, or by the Depression, or by the Second World War. Bernard Leach thought he had spotted the last of them in the figure of Edwin Beer Fishley.[16] It is easy to romanticise such a figure; the peasant potter and his story can so easily be assigned to folklore and quaint, British customs rather than to any serious social history. But if we look dispassionately at the fortunes of the places in which these potters worked, what are usually called country potteries, and which I prefer to call small, local potteries, there is a thread of stubborn survival. The stories of two such potteries are extraordinary.

The Curtis family has been associated with Littlethorpe Pottery in North Yorkshire since about 1912 or 1913 when George Curtis started work there as a clayboy. He subsequently became manager and then owner of the pottery through marriage in 1939. George's son Roly Curtis continues to work the pottery although its continued existence as a going concern seems to hinge on plans to reposition it within a heritage context, somewhat in line with other potteries such as Wetheriggs in Cumbria. Littlethorpe has a good claim to be the most intact survivor of this kind of small local pottery, at least in terms of the preservation of the buildings and the continuity of methods of manufacture.[17]

As impressive as Littlethorpe, though in a slightly different sense, is Ewenny Pottery in South Wales. There are records of pottery making in this area since the fifteenth century and there is an oral tradition of a pottery on this site from 1610. For many years the Morgans family worked the pottery and in 1820 Evan Jenkins married into the Morgans and thus was established what surely must be the longest lasting pottery dynasty in Britain. Caitlin Jenkins, who now works at the pottery with her father Alun, is the seventh generation of the Jenkins family to have worked there.[18] Unlike at Littlethorpe, the original pottery buildings at Ewenny, although they survive, are no longer used for pottery making but as a furniture workshop. A newish building provides working accommodation for the potters who continue to produce a range of thrown earthenware for sale through the attached showroom. Both Alun and Caitlin Jenkins have completed BA degrees in ceramics in Cardiff and so can be said to have trained as studio potters. However, Ewenny Pottery itself resists categorisation as a studio pottery and in terms of its market it still operates very much as a small, local pottery. For example, amongst the most striking aspects of Ewenny is that the potters continue to make a living almost entirely through passing trade. The pottery is situated on the road to the coast a few miles away and this must help, but it is not a well-established tourist area. There is some tourist trade but a livelihood is made easier here through what can only be described as local loyalty; people from a certain catchment area in South Wales buying pottery for their own use or as gifts, from a pottery which they more than likely remember from their childhood. This sense of the pottery being able to satisfy a need in the local community is one that many studio potters have aspired to but hardly, if ever, achieved.

Littlethorpe and Ewenny are both alike survivors against the odds, but that is not enough in itself to guarantee the acknowledgement of a studio ceramics community which has often, in real terms, been indifferent to the fate of such indigenous, long standing, local enterprises. Oliver Watson pointed out some years ago that 'it is surprising that Bernard Leach and Cardew did not try to seek out more thoroughly the remnants of the tradition whose passing they so deplored'.[19] There are welcome signs of an awakening interest. Andrew McGarva's well-researched book *Country Pottery* is the first real attempt to cover the field since the Peter Brears book published nearly thirty years ago. But McGarva is selective; unlike Littlethorpe, Ewenny is not listed amongst the surviving potteries worthy of extended comment but then it does not fit his criteria. Ewenny is classed alongside Rye Pottery in Sussex as places which continue to produce (and I quote) ' pots of a decorative nature … developing the 'art ware' style rather than country pots' (original emphasis).[20] In referring to the large amount of this kind of pottery produced over the years by potteries such as Ewenny, Mcgarva makes his position clear:

> It is not by this decorative ware that the country potter's work should be judged. For a historian or anthropologist, they may seem more interesting, and a certain rustic charm in this decorative ware is undeniable. But any potter can see what these old potters made best, with skill and spontaneity, were the 'ordinary' pots for everyday use.[21]

But if ordinariness really is a criterion that should be taken seriously, where should we look for it now? Is the taste of the people who have bought the work of Ewenny Pottery over all these years not ordinary enough to count for anything? Applying a studio ceramics sensibility to small, local potteries inevitably results in an interpretation which gives undue weight to a highly refined taste which hardly connects at all with actual patterns of production and consumption which made and, in the case of Ewenny, continue to make such potteries viable. If the story of these small, local potteries continues to be told through a studio ceramics centred narrative how faithful can that story be to the experiences of the participants within that story?

The industrial potter

It was the relationship between the industrial potter and the studio potter that provided the richest area of debate in the ceramics world during the twentieth century. It is in this area that the idea of a contest between opposing ideological ceramics camps can be most clearly seen. It is also in this area that the 'Britishness' of the debate is most clearly exposed; there are examples readily at hand in other European countries to show that the industrial potter/studio potter contest was not an inevitable historical outcome. Indeed there are examples to be found in Britain which show that at times such a debate was seen as either meaningless or counter-productive. Gordon Forsyth's book *20th Century Ceramics*, published in 1936, gives a good indication of the diversity which can be identified as a prime feature of the inter-war period in Britain. Forsyth saw no need to categorise ceramics and the illustrations in his book reveal an easy acceptance of different ways of making.[22] Similarly, Dora Billington, in an interview published in 1950 was able to say:

> Because I grew up with the industry, I have the feeling that pottery, whether mass-produced or studio pottery, is one thing. I cannot recognise any very clear distinction.[23]

Others, however, did and it was during the middle years of the twentieth century that a contest of a rather undignified kind broke out between those in the ceramics world who on the one hand represented the factory and on the other hand represented the studio. Strong support for industry came from a perhaps unexpected source, namely, W. B. Honey, curator of ceramics at the Victoria and Albert Museum. Honey's predecessor at the museum, Bernard Rackham had been generally supportive of the emerging studio pottery movement in the 1920s through his articles in *The Studio* magazine but W. B. Honey in his book *The Art of the Potter*, published in 1946, showed himself to be far less convinced of their merits. One of the chapters of Honey's book is entitled 'Traditional and Modern Design in English Pottery' and it consists of the text of a paper which was presented to the National Council of the Pottery Industry on 26 March 1945. Honey compares a jug by Bernard Leach to work designed by Keith Murray for Wedgwood. Honey comments:

> I am now offering no opinion on the relative merits of these two widely different sorts of work. But I must point out in passing that the one preserves or revives artificially, for the satisfaction of a cultivated and leisured class of well-to-do patrons, a style belonging to peasant craftsmanship; while the other looks forward to a time when the potential power of a fully mechanized and wisely directed industrial system will provide leisure and amenities for all. The one has no economic reality; the other belongs to the present day. And between them there is really no bridge at all.[24]

Honey's text gave encouragement to a pottery industry which in the early 1950s confidently believed in its power to see off this upstart called studio pottery. The pages of the industry trade magazines of this period provide interesting reading. They are suprisingly generous in their scope, including reviews of studio pottery books and exhibitions, but not so generous in their comments when studio potters or their supporters overstep the mark and make too grand a claim for their approach to pottery making. When they do then the full force of the pottery industry's wrath descends on their heads. A harsh but effective tactic by a reviewer in the November 1952 edition of *Pottery and Glass* was to dismiss studio pottery as a cult and to go on to claim that:

> The originators of this cult must realise that the Second World War destroyed forever the social conditions necessary for its survival. But the legend they created still stalks the land, deluding the minds of innocent art school students and sophisticated housewives, and setting a halo around the head and hands of the thrower in his corduroys.[25]

It is extraordinary that this extract continues to possess such resonance today, nearly half a century on, even though the reviewer was so strikingly wrong when he/she went on to sound the premature death knell of studio pottery by claiming that this 'fashionable artistic cult ... was knocked on the head in 1940, and has been lying on a cold slab in the morgue ever since, awaiting identification'.[26]

Indeed it is studio pottery/studio ceramics that has survived and prospered as the once mighty industry in Stoke-on-Trent has contracted to a fraction of its size half a century ago. But it is not just manufacturing capacity that has been lost; what has also disappeared is the capacity of the ceramics industry to fight an ideological battle. It is to the studio ceramics journals that we must now turn for discussion of ideas and for the airing of opinions rather than to the trade journals. There surely must still be some apologists for the industry who would point out the continuing importance of Stoke-on-Trent to the field of ceramics but we now have to look hard for measures of that importance in terms of a confident voicing of its position. The ceramics industry in Britain may well still have a voice, but if it does then it is one that is increasingly not being heard.

The artist potter

What then of the artist potter? Of all potter types this is the one that appears to be most historically circumscribed. The terms 'art potter' or 'artist potter' are now understood as referring to a type of maker who was active for just a few decades straddling the changeover from the nineteenth to the twentieth century. Such a potter was a product of very specific historical conditions and it may be that the story of the artist potter is best left as a brief but colourful episode in the long history of ceramics. To go back to the relay race metaphor, they did their bit, ran their stage and then handed the baton on to the studio potter who had the privilege of running the final leg. But there are some interesting aspects of the story of the artist potter which are relevant today.

For example, the original representatives of this potter type, in spite of the fact that they were often associated with an Arts and Crafts ideology, were generally unhindered by any qualms about the division of labour. They would frequently employ others to complete parts of the manufacturing process which they were either unable or unwilling to complete themselves. The emphasis was clearly on Art rather than Craft and there was little if any investment in the idea of any particular skill having an intrinsic value within the overall ideology of making. For example the elevation of throwing to mystical heights would have to wait for the emergence of the studio potter a couple of decades later for its realisation.

It is extraordinary to reflect on the way that the completion of every task by the maker themselves has become endemic to the practice of studio ceramics. So much so, that when this code of practice is breached it can seem scandalous to the studio ceramics sensibility. Handing on responsibility for a part of the making is seen as something that artists might do but that studio ceramists should not. There are examples of contemporary fine artists who use clay but are not identified as studio ceramists, at least by themselves, and a strongly defining indicator of this distinction is the willingness of the artist to delegate key tasks. One of the most intriguing examples of this is Cecile Jonhson-Soliz who in strictly descriptive terms is both an artist and a potter.

For Johnson-Soliz craft skills are fundamental to her art; it is important that her work is as well made as it is well thought out. She has, however, no qualms about enlisting help when she needs it and she retains control of all the making processes. It is with considerable skill and sensitivity that she marshals the labour of herself and others as well as the conditions under which her work is shown. She is clear about her intentions and will hand on to others crucial tasks such as firing as long as she is confident that she will get the results she wants. There is no investment on her part in that attenuated self-sufficiency which has become a hallmark of studio ceramics and in abandoning such orthodoxies she creates considerable creative space for herself; space in which the appropriateness of the context in which her work is presented is as crucial as the quality of the artefacts themselves. Johnson-Soliz clearly makes pottery but has succeeded in avoiding classification as a maker of studio ceramics. There are other examples (Andrew Lord is one such) of fine artists who exclusively use clay as their medium, but who have taken great pains to avoid being called studio ceramists. However they have not escaped the often envious gaze of the studio ceramics community and such work is increasingly incorporated into the studio ceramics debate and into the studio ceramics consciousness. However much artists such as Cecile Johnson-Soliz and Andrew Lord would like to distance themselves from the ideology of studio ceramics, it is an ideology that has an increasing capacity for gathering such makers to itself.

Conclusion

To conclude, I would argue that studio ceramics has been the great, ceramics success story of the twentieth century. Studio potters/studio ceramists have established themselves as (to use Garth Clark's phrase) the 'potter type' against which all other potter types are measured. Also, the story of studio pottery/studio ceramics has in the twentieth century been central to the wider story of ceramics, and has offered a paradigm for the telling of stories of other potter types. These other potter types have survived, and cling on to separate identities, but their stories have to a large extent been told through a narrative which has placed studio ceramics as the end point.

To some extent, at least, the stories of the peasant potter, the industrial potter and the artist potter have been told by different kinds of narrators and have been heard by different kinds of audiences. For example, archaeologists and ethnographers are taking an increasing interest in country pottery, the design historian already pays a good deal of attention to industrial pottery, and even the art critic occasionally casts an eye on fine artists who use clay. It is, however, only studio ceramics as a category that enjoys the privilege and responsibility of being able to draw on the diversity of ceramics practice in order to inflect and enlarge not only its own area of practice but also the general discourse around ceramics over which it has a largely unacknowledged measure of control.

I have limited myself in this paper to a discussion of pottery making in Britain, but if there were time to extend my arguments to other branches of ceramics and to other countries then I believe that my argument would be strengthened further. For example, through coming into contact with some of the overseas students in my work at the Centre for Ceramics Studies in Cardiff, I have begun to realise that in very many parts of the world what might be called the studio ceramicisation of ceramic practice is accelerating. In many cultures it seems that the baton is being passed quickly now from peasant potter to studio potter without going through any intervening stages.

To go back to Garth Clark's metaphor of a relay race, I would argue that it is unimaginable, at least in the foreseeable future, that we as a studio ceramics community will have either the inclination or the opportunity to pass the baton on; there is no other kind of potter type on the horizon to whom the baton can conceivably be passed. Perhaps that metaphor itself is now obsolete, that kind of race is over, that kind of history making no longer holds good.

Of course people will continue to use clay to make pots and to make art and the diversity in the making heralded in the title of this conference will, I hope, be a continuing reality. But I also hope that when the story of ceramics is told in future years, the central role of studio ceramics in the narration of the story will be seen to have been discharged with fairness and with due regard for all the actors within that story.

In his article 'The End of History' Francis Fukuyama wrote: 'the victory of liberalism has occurred primarily in the realm of ideas or consciousness and is as yet incomplete in the real or material world'. I suggest that similarly, the victory of studio ceramics can now be observed as having occurred in the realm of ideas or consciousness. I am left wondering whether the completion of that victory in the real or material world would be good news for all makers in clay, both within and beyond the studio.

Acknowledgements

I am grateful to Richard Carlton of the University of Newcastle-Upon-Tyne for material relating to Littlethorpe Pottery and to Caitlin Jenkins of Ewenny Pottery, Bridgend, South Wales for material relating to Ewenny Pottery.

Notes

1. A useful, short introduction to the notion of endism is to be found in Stuart Sim, *Derrida and the End of History*, Cambridge, Icon Books, 1999, pp. 12–16.
2. John Horgan, *The End of Science: Facing the Limits of Knowledge in the Twilight of the Scientific Age*, Reading, Mass., Addison-Wesley, 1996.
3. Jeremy Rifkin, *The End of Work: The Decline of the Global Labor Force and the Dawn of the Post-Market Era*, New York, G. P. Putnam's Sons, 1995.
4. Russell Jacoby, *The End of Utopia: Politics and Culture in an Age of Apathy*, New York, Basic Books, 1999.
5. Francis Fukuyama, *The End of History and the Last Man*, London, H.Hamilton, 1992.
6. Fukuyama's article entitled 'The End of History?' was published in *The National Interest*, Summer 1989, pp. 3–18 and was subsequently expanded into the book entitled *The End of History and the Last Man*.
7. Fukuyama, 'The End of History', p. 4.
8. Don Cupitt, *What is a Story*, London, SCM Press, 1991, p. 20.
9. I am using the phrase 'studio ceramics' here as a kind of short-hand for a body of people and ideas much as 'the West' might be used to stand for both a group of countries and an ideology. Exhibitions, conferences, journals, books, courses in further and higher education all testify to the fact that studio ceramics can be identified as a particular, ideological phenomenon.
10. Annotation by Bernard Leach on the cover of the Summer 1950 edition of a magazine entitled *Far and Wide*. On the front of the magazine Leach has written: 'Write article for this Quarterly this winter: 1000-1500 words. The modern potter - what makes a pot good - The first international conference of artist potters. The history of man is written in clay'. Bernard Leach archive, Crafts Study Centre, catalogue no. 538. (At the time of writing the Craft Study Centre is in transit from The Holburne Museum, Bath, to Farnham Campus, Surrey Institute of Art and Design.) Leach's article was published in 1952 as 'The Modern Craftsman Potter', *Far and Wide*, the magazine of the Guest Keen and Nettlefolds group of companies, no. 20, Spring 1952, pp. 17–21.
11. Dora Billington, *The Art of the Potter*, London, Oxford University Press, 1937, p. 6.
12. W. B. Dalton, 'Just Clay', printed for private circulation, 1962, p. 87
13. Billington, *The Art of the Potter*, p. 108.
14. See C.F. Binns, *The Potter's Craft*, (2nd edition), New York, D. Van Nostrand Company, 1922, (first published 1910); Dora Lunn, *Pottery in the Making*, Leicester and London, Dryad Press, 1931; Bernard Leach, *A Potter's Book*, London, Faber and Faber, 1940; Murray Fieldhouse, *Pottery*, London, W. & G. Foyle Ltd, 1952.
15. Garth Clark, *The Potter's Art: A Complete History of Pottery in Britain*, London, Phaidon Press, 1995, p. 7.
16. See Bernard Leach, *Beyond East and West: Memoirs, Portraits and Essays*, London, Faber & Faber, 1978, p. 148.
17. See 'Littlethorpe Potteries, Ripon, North Yorkshire', R.J. Carlton, a report prepared for Harrogate Borough Council and North Yorkshire County Council by the Littlethorpe Potteries Project.
18. Information provided by Caitlin Jenkins, Ewenny Pottery.
19. Oliver Watson, *Studio Pottery: Twentieth Century British Ceramics in the Victoria and Albert Museum Collection*, London, Phaidon Press, 1993, p. 41, n. 11.
20. Andrew McGarva, *Country Pottery: Traditional Earthenware of Britain*, London, A.& C. Black, 2000, p. 112.
21. McGarva, *Country Pottery*, p. 12.
22. Gordon Forsyth, *20th Century Ceramics*, London, The Studio, 1936.
23. Dora Billington in John Farleigh, *The Creative Craftsman*, London, John Bell and Sons, 1950, p. 189.

24. William Bowyer Honey, *The Art of The Potter*, London, Faber & Faber, 1946, p. 96.
25. 'The Not-So-Modern Potter', (book review), *Pottery and Glass*, vol. xxx, no. 11, November 1952, p. 72. The book under review was by George Wingfield Digby, *The Work of the Modern Potter in England*, London, John Murray, 1952.
26. 'The Not-So-Modern Potter', p. 72.

This essay is reproduced by kind permission of the author and the on-line journal *Interpreting Ceramics*.

SECTION 2.3
SCULPTURAL CERAMICS

Introductory summary

As we saw in the previous section, the term 'Studio Ceramics' tends to relate to vessels made on the wheel, which are functional or at least reference function such as vases, bowls or plates. But of course, ceramic is also a very flexible medium for the creation of other more sculptural forms. By no means exhaustive, this section offers just a few perspectives on the use of clay for sculptural objects from different periods. Those with a particular interest in sculpture and ceramics might like to read the texts in the following section on installation as these texts also deal with this broad area.

'A rough equivalent' by Jeffrey Jones relates to the exhibition of the same name that he curated, in which examples of sculpture and ceramics from the 1950s to 1970s were brought together. The exhibition highlighted similarities in aesthetic between the sculpture and ceramics of the time – especially the 'rough' surface treatments. This text places this work in the context of Leach, critical opinion of the time and also the pessimistic post-war years.

During the period that Jeffrey Jones discussed, the 'Funk' movement was emerging in Northern California in the 1960s, which embraced representation and themes from modern life and popular culture – often with irreverent humour. Scott A. Shields maps this development centring on ceramic sculpture, artist Robert Arneson and the University of California at Davies. He also links the work of ceramic practitioners to painting and sculpture of the time.

By the 1970 the possibilities of what sculpture could be had developed away from the plinth-based object to encompass environments, interventions in the landscape and even physical activities such as walking. Rosalind Krauss neatly summed this development up as 'Sculpture in the Expanded Field' in her seminal 1979 essay of the same name. Ceramic artists adopted this term to describe methods of working with clay that moved away from the traditional studio pottery approach. For example, in installations, performances and more ephemeral presentations using unfired clay. Mitchell Merback's piece 'Cooled Matter: Ceramic Sculpture in the Expanded Field' written for the exhibition 'Cooled Matter: New Sculpture' in 1999 gives an overview of various approaches to ceramics sculpture by Charles M. Brown; Sadashi Inuzuka; Jennifer A. Lapham; Walter McConnell; Katerine L. Ross and Garry Williams.

In her 1961 groundbreaking and much referenced text, Rose Slivka draws links between painting and sculpture and ceramics through a discussion of similarities in technical and aesthetic application. She acknowledges extensions of clay as paint and physicality of shape and scale as abstracted sculpture. The articulation of a new ceramic presence is aligned to the United States and in particular a reinterpretation of the ceramic surface and a representation of classical formal rendering. Although, now somewhat dated, in terms of the development of the ceramics field, this text adds context to a historical narrative demonstrating major turning points within the development of ceramics discourse.

Writing in 1993 for the catalogue of the exhibition, 'The Raw and the Cooked' Martina Margetts comments on the relationships between ceramics and sculpture through the twentieth century as well as making a case for ceramics as a sculptural medium. This exhibition has been included in much discussion and literary comment since its premier, one could draw comparison to the 1988 fine art exhibition 'Freeze' curated by Damien Hirst, in terms of its impact upon the canon. It has been heralded as a turning point in ceramics, particularly in the UK, and should be considered in this context, when constructing a narrative timeline of contemporary ceramic development.

Merback's piece makes reference to British sculptor Antony Gormley, who famously used clay in his various 'Field' pieces between 1989 and 2003. In these works, Gormley worked with communities to make thousands of small basically formed unfired clay figures, which were presented en masse in galleries. The conversation with James Putnam provides thoughts and observations in reference to clay and ceramics by Gormley. He makes a clear distinction between the material and its difference when presented as both art and craft, where he states that art questions the world and craft makes life easier. The format of this text is refreshing and honest in its consideration and application.

Livingstone and Petrie

21
A ROUGH EQUIVALENT: SCULPTURE AND POTTERY IN THE POST-WAR PERIOD
Jeffrey Jones

In his essay entitled 'End of the Streamlined Era in Painting and Sculpture', first published in *The Times* in August 1955, the art critic David Sylvester announced that 'the most obvious difference between the art of today and the art of the inter-war period is that rough surfaces have taken the place of smooth ones'.[1] Sylvester argues that this change reflects the move on the part of post-war British artists away from an impersonal art based on collectivist ideals to a more individualistic art where 'roughness of surface is the symptom and symbol of a revolt against the anti-humanism of the streamlined surface, an assertion of the artist's humanity and of the value of the creative act, considered as an act'.[2]

Sylvester refers to the importance of 'the so-called machine aesthetic' to the Constructivist sculptors of the 1920s and 1930s, whose use of modern materials such as metals and plastics typically resulted in a smooth finish that gave little opportunity for the kinds of gestures that revealed the idiosyncratic touch of the artist's hand. Sylvester extends his argument to sculptors such as Henry Moore and Brancusi, who used more traditional materials and methods of making. He claims that these artists 'have chosen to identify themselves, not with the robot, but with the great impersonal, elemental forces of nature'.[3] The end result, according to Sylvester, was much the same.

Sculptural surfaces that alluded to the kind of purifying, 'blind' effects that the wind, the rain and the sea inevitably have on stone and wood could be equated with streamlined forms and surfaces that were shaped, either literally or metaphorically, by the impersonal power of the machine. In both cases the resulting smoothness spoke of a willing retreat on the part of the individual artist in the face of much greater, universalising forces. In contrast to this, Sylvester states that 'the present age delights in texture and irregularity, exploits the accidental, courts imperfection'.[4]

Sylvester is of course being selective in his arguments and his examples in more ways than one. To begin with, he was talking about painting and sculpture and had nothing to say about ceramics. This is hardly surprising: during the post-war period in British art there were few opportunities for potters to exhibit alongside painters and sculptors, and it is likely that work in ceramics would simply not have been noticed by him.[5] However, in an immediate, visual and tactile sense, Sylvester's conclusions could be applied just as much to ceramics as to painting and sculpture. As this current exhibition 'A Rough Equivalent' demonstrates, there is a roughness of surface on the glazed and unglazed pots and ceramic work of the period that corresponds with the sculpture of the time.

This correspondence opens questions about why such a juxtaposition of ceramics and sculpture might be so long overdue.

Source: © Jeffrey Jones/The Henry Moore Foundation.

One reason - perhaps the key reason - is that during the twentieth century the respective discourses of ceramics and sculpture developed mostly independently of one another. Had Sylvester been aware, for example, of the body of critical writing on studio pottery that preceded the publication of his essay (and indeed been aware of the pots themselves) then he might have found it more difficult to construct and sustain his basic premise. Indeed 'roughness' understood as the celebration of textured and irregular surfaces, the deliberate courting of accidental effects and the aesthetic elevation of the idea of imperfection had been commonplace within ceramics for half a century or more.

In 1940, in what is still regarded by many as the key text of the twentieth century studio pottery movement in Britain, Bernard Leach referred approvingly to the 'accidentals' and 'incidentals' that characterise pottery at its best. The first chapter of Leach's *A Potter's Book* is a sustained and passionate polemic in support of an Oriental aesthetic which, according to Leach, reached its apogee in the potters of the Chinese T'ang and Sung dynasties and continued to hold sway in South-East Asia into modern times. Leach writes: 'in China the clays are often coarse and usually exposed, the glazes are thick, and crackled, and run, and occasionally skip, the brushwork is vigorous and calligraphic, not realistic and "finished", the throwing and moulding are frank, and accidental kiln effects are frequent'.[6]

Like Sylvester, Leach writes as if this was a newly resurrected idea, or at least new for Western artists and their audience.[7] With his early life experiences, philosophy and studio practice rooted so firmly within China and Japan Leach was never able to acknowledge that the acceptance, and even the encouragement, of imperfection as an aesthetic choice had a considerable and continuing history much nearer home. In particular, the use of the kiln as an active, creative and often unpredictable element within the artistic practice of early British studio potters was already well established by 1917, when a reviewer in *The Pottery Gazette* wrote admiringly of the accidental effects achieved by Edward Baker at the Upchurch Pottery in Kent, commenting appreciatively that such effects were due to 'the caprice of the fire'.[8]

This phrase leads neatly to a consideration of a central controversy in sculpture between the first and second World Wars around the role that materials or processes might legitimately play in the creation of art. On one side was the critic Stanley Casson, who, writing in 1930, was appalled by sculptors who 'revel in submitting their wills to the caprice of the media'.[9] Barbara Hepworth and John Skeaping, amongst others, were identified as being responsible for this 'retrograde tendency'. They were guilty of abnegating their responsibilities as artists – 'their chisels are never their own, their hands are never free. The shapes of their otherwise admirable creations conform to the demands of their material in a way which suggests a step backwards in the course of evolution'.[10] Casson's position was clear: 'throughout the sculptor must have absolute control, he must not let his chisel be guided by the accidents of nature, by the cleavages and stratifications that he finds in the stone'.

An alternative view was put forward by R. H. Wilenski, who was more relaxed about the idea of 'collaboration between the sculptor and the essential character of the block of resistant substance beneath his hand'.[11] Indeed, Wilenski's book *The Meaning of Modern Sculpture*, published in 1932, put forward this point as number eight in 'the modern sculptor's creed'. Ideologically this accorded in many respects with the modern potter's creed, which was never itemised as such in the manner of Wilenski's model but was nevertheless eloquently expressed both by the potters themselves through their work and words, and through their staunch apologists writing in the mainstream art journals of the day. In *The Studio* in 1925, Bernard Rackham from the Victoria and Albert Museum said of the potter Reginald Wells that he was one of several artists who had begun 'to find in clay as a material and the kiln an auxiliary agent a sympathetic means of self-expression'.[12] Since the beginning of the twentieth century studio potters had been all too aware that granting a degree of agency not only to their materials, but also to the sometimes intractable potter's wheels and kilns on which the success of their work so much depended, was a combined practical as well as an aesthetic imperative.

That this would lead to a degree of 'roughness' was a justifiable and welcome development within the philosophical positioning of the studio potter as a legitimate modern artist.[13]

It could be argued that in his endorsement of rough surfaces in 1955 Sylvester was (somewhat surprisingly) ignoring the debate about the role of materials in the creation of sculpture that was so important to his inter-war predecessors and (quite unsurprisingly) failing to acknowledge the rich contribution that a consideration of pottery might have made to such a debate. In hindsight Sylvester's essay can be seen more as an attempt at shifting the theoretical and philosophical ground on which British painting and sculpture could be understood and appreciated rather than as a discovery of some major change or innovation within the practice or intentions of the artists themselves.

For both sculptors and potters roughness, imperfection, and a celebration of the active participation of materials and processes had been aesthetically important for some time, but there was something about the post-war context that required such things to be emphasised as part of the contemporary, psychological struggle of human beings to make art – or at least to make painting and sculpture.

This 'something' was famously articulated by Herbert Read in his essay 'New Aspects of British Sculpture' in the catalogue to the exhibition at the British Pavilion at the 1952 Venice Biennale. Read wrote: 'These new images belong to the iconography of despair or of defiance; and the more innocent the artist, the more effectively he transmits the collective guilt. Here are images of flight, of ragged claws "scuttling across the floors of silent seas" of excoriated flesh, frustrated sex, the geometry of fear.'[14]

This passage locates the sculpture of the period within a post-war climate of nervous pessimism, engendered on the one hand by the devastating effects of a second world war and on the other by the very real fear of impending nuclear annihilation. As thousands of people from all over the country made their way hopefully to the South Bank in London to celebrate the Festival of Britain and to dream of a brighter future, a small group of metropolitan artists were beginning to be assailed by existentialist doubts. They were encouraged in their thoughts by the circulation of key texts such as Jean-Paul Sartre's essay on Alberto Giacometti, first published in France in 1948, and soon afterwards by a series of writings by David Sylvester who, according to David Mellor, 'articulated a discourse of existential pathos'.[15]

Central to this discourse was the idea of contingency – the unavoidable riskiness of being in the world, a fundamental human predicament which artists had so long ignored.

In 'The Search for the Absolute' (1948) Sartre points to the numerous public statues based on classical ideals, noting 'we have become so accustomed to the sleek mute creatures, made to cure us of the illness of having bodies: these domestic powers kept an eye on us when we were children; they bore witness in the parks to the conviction that the world is not dangerous.'[16] By contrast, Sartre says that a Giacometti figure 'tells us of the astonishing adventure of the flesh'.[17] This fascination with flesh and skin, not as beautiful, smooth, trustworthy delineators of the human form, but as vulnerable, perishable organs, prone to damage, open to adventure and offering an all too imperfect boundary with the rest of the gross, physical world, came to be a signifier of a post-war art that David Mellor characterises as 'a curious romance of abject material'.[18]

As the 1950s turned into the 1960s the existentialist underpinning of British sculpture became less marked. In the catalogue to the 1967 exhibition *British Sculpture 1952-1962* David Thompson noted an important change in tone and emphasis during that decade, saying of Eduardo Paolozzi and Hubert

Dalwood that the 'feeling of edginess and nerviness, and even violence, is as remote from them as it is from Armitage'. It has to be acknowledged that such a feeling had always been remote from the immediate post-war ceramics world. We look in vain at this time for the kind of anxious texts that would have stirred the ceramics community in the same way that Sartre and Sylvester stirred the sculptors. The general response of potters was to move towards a communal, rather than an individualistic idea of their craft. Working together became the progressive ideal and the reparative and therapeutic value of pottery making was emphasised as part of the practical rebuilding of society. Tanya Harrod notes that 'the craft world became less intellectual just at the moment that large numbers of men and women – in reaction against the harsh disciplines of war – wanted to join in'.[19]

Yet, as work in 'A Rough Equivalent' shows, during the late 1950s increasing numbers of potters were trying to articulate something more individual and expressive in their work. They were perhaps taking a lead from the sculptors, and it should be noted that the dates of most of the ceramics in this exhibition are generally later than comparative work in sculpture, although this could be a function of the particular collections from which this work has been selected. However, it is certainly the case that ceramicists were not without histories of their own where risk taking was encouraged and contingency was there to be embraced.

The majority of work in 'A Rough Equivalent', both sculpture and ceramics, displays formal characteristics that reflect powerful echoes of earlier, essentially discrete discourses. Indeed, sculpture and ceramics have mostly remained as discrete practices until the present day - written about in separate publications, shown in different venues, appreciated by different audiences and assembled within private and public collections that rarely include both kinds of work. The public collections in Leeds and York, from which the works in the exhibition are selected, offer a case in point. The Leeds sculpture collection has only a handful of 'finished' works in the medium of ceramics, i.e. works in clay that are not maquettes or models for pieces later to be cast in other materials. This reflects the widespread neglect of clay as a respectable art material.

Interestingly, as can be seen, the substantial ceramics collections of York Art Gallery include many pieces that have a sculptural intent, although they have remained categorised as 'ceramics' or even as 'pottery' although they have no utilitarian function.

What then, justifies the bringing together in 2010 of the kinds of mid twentieth British sculpture and ceramics that have never substantially been shown together before? Firstly, this is happening in a context where discipline boundaries within visual art are becoming increasingly fluid. In recent years the Henry Moore Institute has facilitated exhibitions that have explored relationships between sculpture and other forms, such as architecture and furniture, making an opportunity to explore relationships between sculpture and ceramics a welcome continuation of that process. Secondly, there is something aesthetically contiguous in the works displayed here - the vigorous surface treatments, roughness of texture and imperfect finish were qualities that were employed by both sculptors and ceramicists of the period and, by the end of the period under review in 'A Rough Equivalent', they were bringing their own histories to bear on work which, half a century later, can be seen to be much more alike than was appreciated at the time.

The phrase 'the patina of pathos' comes close to describing what is going on in all these works. James Hyman uses these words to describe the sculpture of the early 1950s, noting 'the foregrounding of the work's surface' and identifying the 'skin' of the sculpture as a site where harsh treatment was meted out. Significantly he says that these features 'would become even more important in the years that followed' and he additionally mentions the 'frontality of many British sculptures in the late 1950s.[20] This can also clearly be seen in the ceramics and it is particularly obvious in certain pots, where the viewer is put in no doubt that there is a front and a back to the pieces. Appreciating the work in-the-round is not an option and in a few examples this is emphasised by the physical squaring of the pot. The anthropomorphic interpretation of pottery – the idea that the pot stands for its maker, both physically and metaphorically – has a long history and here we see that idea emphasised with appendages on the sides of the pots, like wings or limbs, echoing similar stylistic features in some of the sculptures. We can also note various kinds of oily, waxy, dripping, melting surfaces on both the ceramics and sculpture, as well as evidence of scratching, sanding and piercing.

In calling this exhibition 'A Rough Equivalent', the intention is to draw attention to the surface treatment of certain three-dimensional artworks which use a range of materials such as metal, plaster and clay, which were made in Britain at a particular period and which are drawn from two major public collections situated in close geographical proximity. These artworks forcefully articulate something about the riskiness of making art as well as the riskiness of being in the world – neither ever runs smooth. 'A Rough Equivalent' makes the argument that there is a shared aesthetic between the two disciplines of ceramics and sculpture, despite the fact that there is little in the way of a shared history. An equivalency of sorts is established, although this itself remains contingent on the degree to which the two disciplines continue to make connections with one another beyond the two collections represented in this exhibition. However, this much remains certain: whether looking at the sculpture or the ceramics in 'A Rough Equivalent', you will see no 'sleek mute creatures' here.

Notes

1. David Sylvester, 'End of the Streamlined Era', in *About Modern Art: Critical Essays 1948 – 96*, London, Chatto and Windus, 1996, pp. 49–52, p. 49.
2. Ibid, p. 51.
3. Ibid, p. 50.
4. Ibid, p. 49.
5. The use of the terms 'pottery' and 'potter', and 'ceramics' and 'ceramicist' are often contentious. For much of the twentieth century, and certainly in the post-war period in Britain, the term 'pottery' or 'studio pottery' would have included non-vessel forms such as figurative and sculptural work in clay.
6. Bernard Leach, *A Potter's Book*, London, Faber and Faber, 1940, p. 24.
7. Sylvester acknowledges that the kind of art that he is arguing for is 'a resuscitation of the great *malerisch* tradition but it is much more than a mere revival'. See Sylvester, 'End of the Streamlined Era', p. 51.
8. *Pottery Gazette*, April 1917, quoted in Victoria Bergesen, *Encyclopaedia of British Art Pottery,* London, Barrie and Jenkins, 1991, p. 273. For further discussion of this issue see Jeffrey Jones, 'Potters of Independent Means', chapter 1 of *Studio Pottery in Britain 1900-2005,* London, A&C Black, 2007.
9. Stanley Casson, *XXth Century Sculptors*, Oxford University Press/London, Humphrey Milford, 1930, p. 19.
10. Ibid, p. 20.
11. R. H. Wilenski, extract from *The Meaning of Modern Sculpture* (1932), in Jon Wood, David Hulks, Alex Potts (editors), *Modern Sculpture Reader*, Leeds, Henry Moore Institute, 2007, pp. 106–108, p. 108.
12. Bernard Rackham, 'The Pottery of Mr. Reginald F. Wells', *The Studio*, vol.xc, no.393, December 1925, pp. 359–363, p. 359.
13. For potters, rough surfaces were usually associated with matt surfaces and these were preferred to smooth, glossy ones. See Jones, *Studio Pottery in Britain*, p. 180.
14. Herbert Read, 'New Aspects of British Sculpture', in the catalogue to the exhibition of work at the British Pavilion at the 1952 Venice Biennale, unpaginated. [Henry Moore Institute, Leeds, Special Collections].

15. David Mellor, 'Existentialism and Post-War British Art', in Frances Morris (editor), *Paris Post War Art and Existentialism 1945-55*, London, Tate Gallery, 1993, pp. 53–62, p. 54.
16. Jean-Paul Sartre, 'The Search for the Absolute', (1948), in Jon Wood, *David* Hulks, Alex Potts (editors), *Modern Sculpture Reader*, Leeds, Henry Moore Institute, 2007, pp. 180–188, p. 187.
17. Ibid.
18. Mellor in Morris, 'Existentialism', p. 60.
19. Tanya Harrod, *The Crafts in Britain in the 20th Century*, Yale University Press, 1999, p. 208.
20. James Hyman, 'Henry Moore and the Geometry of Fear', in *Henry Moore and the Geometry of Fear*, London, James Hyman Fine Art, 2002, pp. 6–11, p. 10.

First published as issue 62 in the Henry Moore Institute *Essays on Sculpture* series, edited by Lisa Le Feuvre and Sophie Raikes, to accompany the exhibition *A Rough Equivalent: Sculpture and Pottery in the Post-war Period*, Upper Sculpture Study Gallery, Leeds Art Gallery, 30th Sep 2010–2nd Jan 2011.

22
CALIFORNIA FUNK
Scott A. Shields

Blatant, humorous, sometimes gross, Funk ceramics delight with content, narrative and often a good dirty joke. Although these ceramics can present underlying concepts of seriousness, on the surface they communicate we perhaps needn't take art—and by extension ourselves—quite so seriously.

That the Funk movement in clay began in Northern California in the early 1960s makes perfect sense. During this period, and really for the first time, California artists began producing works of art that were nationally significant, but also specifically local in feeling and inspiration. California itself had come into its own, assuming a central place on the national stage in terms of economics, politics, and entertainment. Art, by extension, assumed a leadership role in what has since become the art-historical canon. Through a new style uniquely Californian, artists produced work that manifested a profound sense of self-confidence coupled with a daring willingness to take on themes that had here-to-fore been inappropriate for art.

California's artists had never been entirely comfortable giving up subject matter, and Abstract Expressionism's obliteration of the representational left artists inquiring 'Where do we go from here?' Californians were among the first artists in the nation to provide the answer by reclaiming the subject. David Park put forth *Kids on Bikes* (1950), a radical reversal from his Abstract Expressionist paintings toward representation—a move that initially confused his colleagues. Soon, however, Elmer Bischoff, Richard Diebenkorn and others returned to recognizable motifs, adapting the gestural brushwork of Abstract Expressionism to the human figure, landscapes and still life. Their efforts earned them the appellation, Bay Area Figurative. That the movement made and indelible and lasting impact on ceramic art is made clear through the figurative ceramics of Viola Frey, who earned her bachelor's degree from the California College of the Arts, where Diebenkorn was one of her teachers. Although Frey made her reputation with large-scale, totemic human forms, these evolved from figurative and animal pieces very much in the Funk mode.

Concurrent with Bay Area Figuration, Northern California in the 1950s became the loci of other movements with equally far-reaching implications, and the Figuratives' interest in representation came to characterize Northern California art in its various forms, such as Beat, Pop and Funk. Beat began with the art, poetry, music and performance that comprised the counterculture taking root in San Francisco's North Beach area. There, artists lived and worked in close cooperation with writers and philosophers, rejected convention and flaunted bourgeoisie norms. Making assemblage from refuse, artists such as Bruce Conner and George Herms recycled the discarded materials of consumer culture, snubbing California's materialism and, at the same time, creating art within their own, meager budgets.

These artists frequently imbued their art with humor, spawning progenitors, most notably Funk. The first manifestation of Funk was not about clay, but about art offering a shared subversive and irreverent spirit. Artists fitting the bill held a 1951 exhibition at San Francisco's Place Bar. Called 'Common Art Accumulations', much of the art was made from found materials.

Source: © Scott A. Shields

A decade later, Pop Art became an international phenomenon. Appropriating the mundane as subject matter, Pop artists serially repeated and heroicized products and celebrities. Whereas in New York, Andy Warhol's images plumbed America's image-clogged culture and pointed out its consumptive nature, California's Pop was more playful and accepting. It too drew upon the products of consumer culture – food, roadside architecture, cartoons and pornography – but its impression of these products was more positive, even celebratory. Brash and rich in excess, California Pop seemed to match the state's newfound sense of self.

Concurrently, Funk once again became the label for the style of art that developed in the 1960s around Robert Arneson, William Wiley, Roy De Forest and initially Manuel Neri at the University of California at Davis, just west of Sacramento. Representational, witty, irreverent and even kitsch, its playfulness masked an underlying concern for more serious issues. An antithesis to New York minimalism, it was perfectly suited to, and representative of, California. Like Pop, Funk utilized banal, everyday objects – but was less detached. Wiley, originally an Abstract Expressionist, began producing work that shared Funk's wit, impertinence and penchant for found objects. Primarily a two-dimensional artist, his works on canvas made him a pivotal figure in the transition of California Funk into an art of self-conscious humor and social critique. His paintings were visionary, critical and highly autobiographical – a tendency he shared with others, including UC Davis colleague Roy De Forest.

Today, however, Funk is most often equated with Arneson and the school of ceramics that developed at UC Davis, which in turn attracted other artists and ceramists to Northern California. Some of Arneson's early pieces were overtly influenced by Pop, which, considering the fact that painters Wayne Thiebaud and Mel Ramos were both prominent Sacramento personalities and teachers should come as no surprise. But Arneson also felt a kinship with New York artist Claes Oldenburg. Arneson laid claim to the Funk label when he submitted Funk John to a 1963 exhibition of California sculptors held on the rooftop of the Kaiser Center in Oakland. A toilet complete with fecal matter, Arneson's submission paid homage to Marcel Duchamp's famous Fountain, a urinal that Duchamp signed 'R. Mutt' and submitted to the first exhibition of the New York Society of Independent Artists in 1917.

Like Duchamp's piece, Arneson's sculpture was considered offensive and was withdrawn and so the artist of course wasted no time in producing subsequent versions of the scandalous piece. Arneson's work, along with that of other artists, became known for its ribald humor, scatological and sexual references, and blatant, in-your-face amateurishness. Even the term 'funk' came fully loaded, stemming from dictionary definitions meaning body odor, the smell of sexual intercourse, and something commonly regarded as coarse or indecent. Yet, three years later, what had begun as anti-establishment art was given institutional credibility when it became the subject of an exhibition curated by Peter Selz at the University of California at Berkeley.

As a teacher at Davis for thirty years, Arneson worked closely with his colleagues, especially De Forest, with whom he produced a series of 37 collaborative pieces called 'Bob and Roy Ware'. Brightly colored and whimsical, the deliberately child-like sculptures were shown and sold at the Candy Store Gallery, a two-room space located in a quaint, shingled cottage in Folsom, near Sacramento. Artist Clayton Bailey designed the poster for the show, calling the results of the collaboration 'pretty nifty pots'.

Arneson was also in a strategic position to disseminate ideas to his many students – both Funk and not-so-Funk – at the University's TB-9 studio. During this energetic period, students, having heard of the surge of activity in the art department, transferred from other departments and other schools to join the confluence. With Arneson's encouragement, they rejected modernist traditions, finding clay to be an adaptable material free of pretensions and thus a perfect medium for their experiments. Many went on to become important artists in their own right. Some pursued a more serious side of art in other media, such as Deborah Butterfield and Bruce Nauman. Others, like Richard Shaw and Richard Notkin, continued to work in clay, but instead of the blatant, unrefined treatment, and fresh-out-of-the jar glazes that Arneson championed, brought trompe-l'oeil precision to their technique. Arthur González continued Arneson's dedication to the figure, but added into the mix specific cultural concerns. Gonzalez reached farther back into Funk's Beat-culture roots by incorporating all manner of found objects—such as fabric, wood, plastic and even American currency.

Others embraced Arneson's – and by extension Funk's – wit and color more wholeheartedly. Of these, David Gilhooly, Maija Zack (now Peeples-Bright), Margaret Dodd, Chris Unterseher and Peter VandenBerge counted among the earliest of Arneson's students, showing alongside him at the Candy Store. Gilhooly, formerly an anthropology major, was one of the ceramists most closely associated with Funk. Best known for his "frog cosmology," he also crafted other animals and, with deference to Pop, depictions of food. Dodd set out to capture California's love affair with the automobile, having a particular penchant for Volkswagen Beetles, and Unterseher made narrative vignettes of daily life. Zack first became known for her paintings of 'beasties' rendered in a joyful, irreverent cacophony of color, image and form and then translated these to clay when she became involved with the Regina Clay movement of the 1960s and 1970s in Saskatchewan. There she worked closely with Victor Cicansky, who had received his M.F.A. from UC Davis, but ultimately returned home to teach at the University of Regina.

Like Cicansky, who created life-like, clay canning jars filled with fruit and vegetables, and also Jeff Nebeker, who used real pastry tools to create his culinary clay delights, Peter VandenBerge began sculpting food, vegetables mostly. His, however, possessed anthropomorphic features. Eventually VandenBerge left vegetables behind in favor of the human figure, specializing in life-sized standing personages, often sporting hats. Ultimately, like Arneson, he encapsulated his personalities into larger-than-life busts and heads. Although Arneson arrived at an endless array of self portraits, VandenBerge produced a wide range of characters, many with elongated heads à la Modigliani and Easter Island.

Although he studied in Wisconsin, Clayton Bailey made his way to California to teach at UC Davis in 1967 and quickly became a leader in the Funk scene. He too used the human form for his ceramics, creating deliberately grotesque figures running the gamut from gargoyles to science experiments gone awry. He also made atomic-age jugs filled with 'Claytonium', which exploded in carefully premeditated fractures or melted in horrific nuclear reactions. Tony Natsoulas, who has been strongly influenced both by Bailey and Arneson, takes his mentors' inspired lunacy a step further – into the realm of high camp. Natsoulas's figures are affected, outrageous in their artificiality, and frequently informed by society's fascination with celebrity and nostalgia.

Other Arneson progeny took cues from Funk but quickly abandoned its earthy subjects to create higher-fire – and higher brow – statements in porcelain. Lucian Pompili became one of the first artists on the West Coast to use porcelain as a sculptural medium. He is best known today for his surrealist-influenced assemblages that juxtapose disjunctive word-play and imagery to create enigmatic statements often deliberately tongue-in-cheek. Tom Rippon, nephew of Sacramento ceramic artist Ruth Rippon, worked for Arneson for three years beginning in 1971, but ultimately earned his M.F.A. from the School of the Art Institute of Chicago. Known for his porcelain figurative assemblages with luscious, satiny finishes, Rippon offers a surrealist take less inspired by Arneson than by the paintings of de Chirico, Miró and Tanguy, and the marionettes of Bauhaus master Oskar Schlemmer.

Elements of Funk have now spread well beyond the Northern California region to achieve international acclaim. The acceptance of silliness, of commercially available glazes and of functionless sculpture for sculpture's sake is now part of the ceramic canon. Artists like Patti Warashina, Esther Shimazu and Charles

Krafft, along with numerous other artists just coming out of art school, continue to keep Funk traditions of humor, whimsy and in-your-face social confrontation very much alive.

Originally published in *Ceramics Monthly* (http://www.ceramicsmonthly.org), November, 2008, pp. 38–41.

Reproduced with permission. Copyright, the American Ceramic Society and the author.

23 COOLED MATTER: CERAMIC SCULPTURE IN THE EXPANDED FIELD

Mitchell Merback

In 1958, the artist Allan Kaprow announced what he saw as the necessary retooling of art in the wake of Jackson Pollock's destruction of traditional painting practices: Pollock, as I see him, left us at the point where we must become preoccupied with and even dazzled by the space and objects of our everyday life, either our bodies, clothes, rooms, or, if need be, the vastness of 42nd Street. Not satisfied with the suggestion through paint of our other senses, we shall utilise the specific substances of sight, sound, movements, people, odours, touch. Objects of every sort are materials for the new art: paint, chairs, food, electric and neon lights, smoke, water, old socks, a dog, movies, a thousand other things. …[1]

Kaprow's clarion call might be read as a reawakening of the modern dream of a far-reaching collaboration between the individual arts, a Gesamtkunstwerk with utopian possibilities. His program, however, signalled nothing so magisterial as a Wagnerian opera. What he was calling for was exactly what he describes: a concrete, non-illusionistic, 'live' art made up of everyday objects, collected in one location or several, and perceived for a period of time no more and no less than the duration of the actions carried out on them, or with them, or around them.

Can art be as simple as this? Can one effectively transform an environment merely by placing or doing things in it? These questions point to an irreducible feature of the gamut of artistic practices we designate with the umbrella term installation: place can become significant, it can become a 'site', through an accumulation of things or activities. In this purely formal sense, vanguard paradigms like Kurt Schwitters's Merzbau constructions, Marcel Duchamp's 'mile of string' installation, Happenings, Robert Rauschenberg's 'combine' paintings, Claes Oldenburg's The Store, Bay Area events like Common Art Accumulations, Robert Morris and Robert Smithson's gallery pieces, Arte Povera, Ben Vautier's Living Sculpture, and Robert Arneson's scatter-pieces are all closely related. Each recognises the art gallery, the high-cultural counterpart to the display spaces of commodity capitalism, as a site where any kind of matter can come to rest and mingle with any other. In the hands of radical American and European artists working after Abstract Expressionism, similar strategies were used to expose the cultural and social specificities of the modernist spaces of viewing. As effective weapons against the false aura of the gallery or museum, they pointed the way towards a 'theatricalisation' of the spaces of art and opened up a new awarenesses of the relationships between objects, bodies, beholders and the sites of their encounter. They criticised the commodification of the portable art object, the 'bourgeois fetish' assailed by the interwar avant-gardes. They worked to negate the modernist separation of the artistic disciplines, establish fruitful areas of practice between media, and defeat the presumed self-sufficiency, or autonomy, of art posited by modernist aesthetics – all of which marks installation and proto-installation as moments of the postmodern as convincing as any other.

Source: © Ceramics: Art and Perception.

That this period of intensive experimentalism – roughly 1958 to 1978 – was also the time ceramic artists were becoming aware of the value of transgression within their own discipline, meant a growing receptiveness to the ideas articulated by the old and new avant-gardes. By all accounts ceramic artists realised the subversive potential of installation strategies only after an appreciable lag-time (though well before conceptual art had run its course in the mainstream). The process of adapting to new aesthetic values and positions produced, as it did in every other tendency in postwar Anglo-American ceramics, internecine tensions, strong and weak work, lasting achievements and dead-ends. Unfortunately, we still have no history of ceramic art which adequately maps and explores this shifting terrain. Conventional wisdom about non-vessel sculpture in the 1970s, as found for example in Garth Clark's American Ceramics, holds that this was a time of 'soft-core Conceptualism,' which 'had the effect of liberalising the ceramist's conceptual bound-aries and conservative tendencies'.[2] In this view, avant-garde experimentation could be reduced to relaxation-therapy for artists and their audiences. Ceramic consciousness need not worry about adjusting its self-image on account of these challenges.

Each of the six sculptors featured in the landmark exhibition Cooled Matter – Charles Brown, Sadashi Inuzuka, Jennifer Lapham, Walter McConnell, Katherine Ross and Garry Williams – demonstrates in his or her work a refusal to remain inside the boundaries which have served, historically, to mark ceramic sculpture as a distinct and separate form of three-dimensional expression and inquiry. Seen against the backdrop of the American ceramics community's yearly ritual of institutionalised conformity – the NCECA conference – it was clear to most viewers that a paradigm of sorts had been breached. This is not to say that any of these artists have made the critique of ceramic norms, institutions and discourses the conscious aim of their work; none are interested in posing, as avant-gardists once did, as the gravediggers of tradition. Nevertheless, their common project of pursuing clay into what critic Rosalind Krauss has called sculpture's 'expanded field' contains within it an implicit critique of every modernist orthodoxy, every norm, that has obtained in ceramic sculpture ever since it first had a vanguard to speak of. Out of an ongoing dialectic of affirmative and critical goals, their work, seen together, poses a credible challenge not only to the long-acknowledged insularity of ceramics consciousness, but to the routines of perception and thought that make such a consciousness possible in the first place.

One of the problems that remained fairly constant for painters and sculptors throughout the 1960s and 1970s was how to theatricalise the spaces of viewing. In the teeth of institutionalised modernist art and critical discourse, this goal was radical for many reasons; but prominent in the minds of many experimental artists was the desire to smuggle 'time', and temporal awareness, into the experience of art. Installation, almost by definition, opens up for its audience some kind of experience of temporality (whether or not time-based media are employed). At a basic level, viewers are made aware that an installation is not a permanent feature of the architecture or landscape, but an ephemeral transposition within or upon it. John Mason's widely misunderstood firebrick sculptures of the 1970s, for example, though made of durable individual modules, confronted the viewer with an explicit sense of the arrangement's impermanence: nothing holds them together except gravity; they are assembled, not constructed; when the exhibition ends they are disassembled and the life-span of the piece terminated. The phenomenological inquiries that animated much Minimalist sculpture began from the premise that the viewer of sculpture would be made concretely aware not only of his or her physical situation, but also of the duration of the encounter, the real-time of the task of beholding. Since then, ambitious installation artists like Daniel Buren, Ann Hamilton, Alice Aycock, Bill Viola, Francesc Torres, Wolfgang Laib, Damien Hirst and many others, have demonstrated a sharpened awareness of how the beholder's experience of space and time are interwoven and mutually inflected.

Initially, in the 1980s, sculptor Charles Brown (who is also the show's curator) approached installation as a staged encounter between the beholder and the specific spatial and material conditions in which experience unfolds. Determined to find an aesthetic language adequate to exploring the vicissitudes of 'memory' (a continuing concern for him), he first worked simply, relying often on the iconic form of the chair to function as a surrogate, or sign, for the body, and therefore as the physical site of memory-work (it is noteworthy that several other artists featured in the show used chairs in earlier works). In tableaux like Chair ... Cello ... Rocks (1988), the chair's presence – isolated on a pile of stones and spotlit – conjured the body's absence; bodily experience had to be supplied imaginatively by the viewer, whose displacement to the margins of the work revealed the spatial determinants of viewing. For Brown to 'stage' memory – its potency and fragility, its recovery and loss – at a particular site meant exploring that same uneasy relationship between memory and materiality that so fascinated Marcel Proust:

> But, when from a long-distant past nothing subsists, after the people are dead, after the things are broken and scattered, still, alone, more fragile, but with more vitality, more unsubstantial, more persistent, more faithful, the smell and taste of things remain poised for a long time, like souls, ready to remind us, waiting and hoping for their moment, amid the ruins of all the rest; and bear unfaltering, in the tiny and almost impalpable drop of their essence, the vast structure of recollection.[3]

In another work from this period, Not Forgetting (1989), Brown arranged two chairs in a line, a few paces apart, so that both faced a shallow beeswax box, which was divided into three compartments and mounted on the wall. The compartments contained identical glasses, one half-filled with honey, the second containing a stone, and the third filled with milk. Here the metaphorical meanings evoked by the substances – nourishment and waste, energy and decay – worked behind the scenes of experience, so to speak, as subsensual triggers of response, conditioning the viewer's perception of the physical space as the site of embodiment, and its transcendence via memory.

Throughout the 1990s Brown's work came to depend less on the imagined physical involvement of the viewer and more on the evocative power of raw, unadorned substances. Organic and inorganic materials were set side by side in simple arrangements of primary shapes, their display almost completely free of manipulation. These interests, and the artist's strategies generally, connected him to a key development in Postmodernism. Ten years ago, when the artist and critic Buzz Spector looked out upon the landscape of contemporary art, he discovered a veritable banquet of sprouting, wilting, hardening and decaying substances – organic matter standing in for the traditional armoury of sculpture's permanent materials.[4] Tracing the appetite for the organic in modern art back to Duchamp's biomechanical images and installations, Spector also found 'new methodologies of incorporation, exhibition and performance' in the art of the late 1950s, which he read as a 'calculated critique of the symbolic detachment of Abstract Expressionist painting and sculpture'.

Instrumental in this critique were the Italians Giovanni Anselmo and Mario Merz, and the Greek-born Jannis Kounnelis, who began in the mid-1960s to introduce inert and active organic materials into sculpture (Kounnelis even used live animals). These investigations into nature's vitality produced what Arte Povera artist-theorist Germano Celant called 'concrete knowledge', and this eventually merged with the growing American involvement with earthen materials both inside the gallery and out. Spector concluded: 'To submit to the powers of the 'given' ... rather than any attempt to master it: this is the meaning that has underwritten the work of many contemporary artists who use the organic.'[5]

For Brown and several of his fellows in Cooled Matter, the powers of the 'given' in any material are best realised when the artist restricts his or her activity to accumulation and simple forms of compositional arrangement. This does not mean, as it may have for Kaprow and his generation, a negation of the artist's creative prerogative. Rather, these artists contrive to frame and format organic processes, to better report on their workings. Implicit Model, Brown's installation in Columbus, consisted on the one hand of a grid-like arrangement of small slate shelves, each one supporting a single loaf of bread, press-moulded in white clay and fired. Adjacent to this wall display, six sheets of Japanese nori seaweed were arranged in a row, like pictures in a gallery; upon their fragile, shimmering green surfaces Brown rendered a sequence of astronomical and geophysical diagrams in gold and copper leaf. Further along the wall another set of slate shelves held carefully moulded funnels made of rice and unfired clay mixed with yellow ochre. On the ground, isolated from the wall displays, Brown placed 'domes' of rock-salt on sheets of black glass; (by the time we reached the gallery the domes were fuzzy with growing crystals). Tempted as one might have been by this pseudo-scientific bric-a-brac to cast Brown in the role of alchemist (rather than, say, physicist), there is nothing esoteric in the transmutations presented in Implicit Model. The fact of their visibility, indeed their 'staging' as phenomena, reveals that the 'model' Brown has in mind is not that of physical but of experiential processes. What the diagrams implied about any theoretical model's incapacity to represent the workings of our physical universe, found a kind of macabre confirmation in their total estrangement from lived experience. Likewise the rows of delicate 'petites madeleine' pastries (the kind that so excited Proust in Remembrance of Things Past), displayed on spartan tables, pressed against the floodgates of memory – only to show their water-tightness (the cookies, too, were made of salt).

Real-time glimpsed in the hot mutability of nature, the (liberating or terrifying) prospect of time's end emblemised by the permanence of matter cooled and lifted above this process, the power of materials to contain 'the vast structure of recollection' – these themes ran through the Columbus show like a red thread. And yet, if the appearance of organic matter in the gallery appeared less than radical to a ceramics audience, it is surely because clay artists have never had need to rediscover materials that change with time or conform to the shape of their container, or that respond synergistically to human action, or that encourage metaphorical associations with earth and landscape. In the studio, clay has always been all of these things. But only when the ceramist defies the eternalising command to fire clay and make its forms permanent can the material most readily simulate the processes of organic change. Two other artists in the show, Sadashi Inuzuka and Walter McConnell, have recognised in clay a material uniquely emblematic of such natural processes. Both have exploited the possibilities of unfired clay, and found it capable of behaving as both inorganic and organic matter. They also share a concern with establishing the space of the gallery as a site whose character can be altered by the deposit of clay in unworked states.

Born in Kyoto in 1951, Sadashi Inuzuka emigrated to Canada in 1981 and has since established an international reputation for his sprawling installations of hand-modelled biomorphs arranged in rows on gallery walls. Influenced in some telling ways by the Japanese Mono-ha (School of Things) movement, which emerged in the 1970s and, like Minimalism, explored the literal qualities of materials to posit 'an alternative structure for the interdependent relationships between consciousness and existence, things and site,'[6] Inuzuka's installations are at once clear-sighted reflections on the constraints imposed on aesthetic experience by the gallery, and romantic paeans to dying ecosystems. In 1995 the Richmond Art Gallery (Canada) became temporary home to Nature of Things, which consisted of 600 of the artist's distinctive, reduction-fired sea hybrids. In an adjacent room the artist poured 6.6 m (22 ft) diameter 'pool' of unfired white slip directly under the gallery's skylight, and ringed it with 400 fired terra-cotta cones (the primary geometry of the floor-piece recalled the mud and stone installations of British sculptor Richard Long). By incorporating these elements into the gallery space, Inuzuka returned to one of the goals of avantgarde practice in the heyday of geometric abstraction: the implied or actual extension of individual works of art into the surrounding architecture. The grid-like arrangement of the multiple units amplified every line and intersection of the gallery's walls, making the perception of scale a function of the relationship between viewer, object and architecture. Thus did Inuzuka place his work in a venerable modernist lineage that Clement Greenberg once termed 'the architectural destination of abstract art'. Nowhere in the Cooled Matter exhibition were the architectural ambitions of contemporary installation practice more fully realised than in Inuzuka's work entitled Same Family. But Inuzuka's aesthetic goals for installation extend beyond the masterful manipulation of space; time is an element as well. For despite the frozen, museological quality of the wall displays, on the floor, in the actual space of the spectator, organic nature ticks along in its shifting appearances. For Same Family, Inuzuka poured a long gangway of white slip to create a dramatic processional path from the gallery's centre to the wall display. Although the physical change is imperceptible, the viewer cannot help but become conscious of the clay's drying process: linear fissures open, interconnect and form that distinctive crackle-pattern familiar to potters (and geologists). One can easily find avant-gardist precedents for this kind of actualisation of clay's self-mutating properties: for example, the site-specific and performative works undertaken by ceramists like Doug Humble, Joe Soldate, or Jim Melchert, whose 1972 performance, Changes, leavened the seriousness of real-time investigations with the masculine chaff of potters-in-arms. Inuzuka's work is, of course, more austere, and the artist's body remains forever outside the work, but it stems from a similar impulse. When he installed Dear Lake in the Burnaby Art Gallery in British Columbia (1996), Inuzuka transformed every square inch of the floor into the dried-up lakebed (in nearby Deer Lake Park) to which the work was devoted 'in memorium'.

As the crackle-pattern emerged, it subtly altered the viewer's sense of the gallery's scale, much as British sculptor Antony Gormley's densely packed floor-piece of modelled figurines, Field (1991), transfigured the gallery's modest structural members into the intimidating stadium architecture of the mass rally. With this potential in mind, however, it was hard to see how Same Family, despite its breathtaking scale, could match up to these earlier efforts, wherein Inuzuka alone commanded the gallery space.

Walter McConnell's work in the 1990s has, in some respects, edged even closer to the literalism and actualism that characterised much of the stronger site-specific projects of the two decades following Minimalism. In other respects it has backed away from this legacy. Early in the decade the artist (now on the ceramics faculty at Alfred University) began a series of terrarium-like plastic enclosures, scaled to the dimensions of the rooms in which they were installed. For 10,000 Lakes (1993) McConnell constructed a semi-transparent cruciform box in the centre of the room, lit it from above, and covered its floor with a slippery bog of moist terracotta, from which protruded press-moulded canoe paddles; opposite the display, behind a patio screen, the artist positioned four mocked-up Adirondack deck chairs. Two years later, in Fecundity in Absence (1995), the simulated lake-bottom sludge was delicately modelled into a seething baroque fantasy of grotesque efflorescences, forms that evoked the exotic beauty of marine life and the fetid horror of sewer waste.

McConnell's new work, Flora and Fauna, installed in Columbus with the help of students, advanced yet further towards this ornamentalising approach to the contents of the plastic enclosure. Like the 'odour of sanctity' that miraculously rose from the decaying remains of medieval saints' tombs, the attractiveness of the organic growth encourages us to overlook its excremental substratum. Meanwhile, the 'fauna' alluded to in the title appear in the form of pastel-coloured, slipcast garden bunnies displayed on little iron stands arranged outside the terrarium; from their bodies protruded a variety of pipe-fittings and connectors, suggesting the obsolescence of their function for an environment that has already evolved alternative means of life-support. These vernacular whimsies aside, it's important to see what makes Flora and Fauna such a conceptually precise work. First we must see in the refusal to make clay permanent through firing more than an avant-garde gesture or provocation; rather, it is an integral part of the artist's strategy for submitting – and submitting us – to the 'powers of the given'. Although the expressive modelling of the 'flora' may, with its strange excremental beauty, distract us from the inherent properties of the material, McConnell makes us aware in other ways that the moist clay is no inert agglomeration, no 'finished' work of art. Rather, it is the vital nucleus of a physical system involving light, heat, vapour and condensed water. In this sense, as real-time systems, McConnell's enclosures harken back to Hans Haacke's Condensation Cubes of 1963-5, clear acrylic boxes containing just enough water to respond to the changing thermal conditions of their particular location at a given time.

And like Haacke's attempt to harness natural forces in closed systems, McConnell's work has grown out of an abiding ecological consciousness (however differently politicised it may be).

Is there a conflict between the two kinds of meaning – one stemming from the artist's sociopolitical concerns, the other stemming from the opportunities for concrete experience that the work affords? McConnell's art, it seems to me, mediates the two. On the one hand we have real-time systems that exist in a space that is frankly architectural. When activated by light and heat, the changing biosphere also references the duration of our encounter with it. At this factual level, such phenomena do not admit transcendence – they are concrete and real, and their spatial and temporal conditions inflect one another to produce an effect of spatialised time. On the other hand, we have an artist determined to expose what is perhaps the key cultural precondition of today's ecological depredations: not merely the alienation of culture from nature, but the displacement of nature by its cultural representation. McConnell's moldering lake-bottoms, by virtue of their presentation and display, can be experienced only as spectacles of organic change. We can certainly choose to read them symbolically, in terms of decay and ruin, and thus as a kind of contemporary memento mori, but this does not fundamentally alter the way these dioramas spectacularise, rather than aestheticise, nature's processes. It is no longer the old lamentable case of our being estranged from what is real in nature, but that the real has been driven to extinction by its ever-widening simulation.

Let us look at this another way. One of the prevalent themes of postmodern writing on our changed relationship with the natural world has been the displacement of nature's reality with its image. Prompted by this radical notion, numerous artists have set about investigating the visual codes by which nature is constructed as form of spectacle, fetishised into a kind of commodity, or evacuated into a simulation. In his commentary on the allegorical character of Sherry Levine's photographs, the critic Craig Owens writes: 'When Levine wants an image of nature, she does not produce one herself but appropriates another image, and this she does in order to expose the degree to which nature is always implicated in a system of cultural values which assigns it a specific culturally determined position.'[7] Chicago-artist Jennifer Lapham's exposure of the way nature is implicated in culture, however, proceeds somewhat differently. In a work called Nest (1996), Lapham took a chair, and buried its functional elements under a cluster of bisque-ware tubes. Visitors to the gallery were able to see the human activity that produced the tubes referenced by a group of Mud-dauber nests which the artist had collected, fired to hardness, and displayed on a glass shelf nearby. So displayed, these specimens could be read as an inspiration and model for the sculpture, especially once their status as labor-products of the Mud-dauber had been transformed by the ceramist's technical intervention. Also, by firing the real nests, Lapham reinvested the objects with the purely cultural significance of fossilised specimens in a natural history museum. Torn from their matrix in nature and its processes, their meaning was now to be derived entirely from the context of their display. In short, they became allegories for the transformation of nature into art through human activity.

More recently, Lapham has parlayed these insights into an investigation of the cultural conventions of nature's aestheticisation – and its transformation into kitsch. Sightings (1997), an installation consisting of small dioramas mounted high on the wall, evoked the numerous ways nature's essence has been penetrated by the representational practices designed to reveal it. From one shelf a gilded crab peered down at us (nature enshrined); behind a miniature white picket fence a bird was laid for electrocution (nature violated); a toy automobile passed beneath a bathroom sink to reach a designated view (nature framed); and upon a boulder a tiny figure planted a flag (nature conquered). At one end of the gallery binoculars were provided to give better access to the inaccessible tableaux, suggesting that our effort at bringing nature's spectacle nearer presupposes a real physical distance.

This same strategy was employed for Lapham's installation in Columbus, entitled Indigenous Interior. In the most discreet corner of the gallery the artist hung vertical strips of bamboo-stalk wallpaper side by side, their repetitiveness pointing to a virtually limitless deployment. Slipcast birds were mounted on the wall so they could perch in the leafy tangle of her virtual jungle. Seen at close range, one could plainly see that Lapham had camoflauged their little bodies with bamboo leaves;[8] only from the remote viewing station of the gallery's centre, where binoculars were dangled for us, could the observer derive a convincing optical unity from the artificial scene – that is, only from a real physical distance, where nature becomes spectacle, could the vision be accepted as 'real'. Lapham wants us to grasp for ourselves how 'sight', and the technological reproduction and packaging of sights for human consumption, construe our experience of site, our sense of being there. In her art, site becomes an allegory for sight because the signs that conjure it (site) refer only to other signs, images of nature rather than nature itself.

Garry Williams, a native of Calgary, is another artist whose environmental consciousness has prompted him to use unfired clay and organic matter in the art gallery, though he has done this, in contrast to McConnell, with the intention of working through the traditional language of nature's aestheticisation. Williams knows that the locus classicus for this language is the garden, the perennial refuge from urban-industrial society. In most of his installations from the early 1990s, he therefore transfigured the gallery into a kind of garden, and this brought into play two rival constructs: the garden as an interior space ornamentalised by natural elements, and the garden as an exterior space, a landscape, restructured and 'tamed' by architecture. As a potter, Williams also knows that the ornamental clay vessel can become a powerful synechdoche for the garden as an aesthetic field stretched between the natural and the architectural. Thus when the artist covered two adjacent mounds of moist clay with live moss for In the Same Breath (1991), he not only evoked the feeling of a calm, meandering path through live nature but played off the processional character of the long gallery space to set up a 'vista' whose picturesque destination was a set of terracotta amphorae suspended from cables. For Cathedrals, installed at the Southern Alberta Art Gallery in 1995, Williams used the principle of the grid to evoke the planned regularity of the industrialised timber forest. At regular intervals on the grid he placed spruce seedlings nestled in hand-thrown vessels; interspersed with these were tall lumber poles, their height adjusted to the slopes of the ceiling.

Thus the title pointed both to the actual interior space of the gallery, whose layout and fenestration recalled basilican architecture, and to the romantic idea of the forest as a quasi-architectural setting for religious experience. What made the overlay of architectural and natural environments compelling, however, was the use of the grid to map every element in a spatial system in a such a way that it could, logically, extend to infinity. 'By virtue of the grid,' writes Krauss, 'the given work of art is presented as a mere fragment, a tiny piece arbitrarily cropped from an infinitely larger fabric. Thus the grid operates from the work of art outward, compelling our acknowledgement of a world beyond the frame.'[9]

All but one participant in the Cooled Matter show employed the grid as an organising principle, and this fact made it possible to judge the merits of each application in relation to the others in the gallery. Perhaps more so than any other, Williams's installation, Genesis, had to contend not only with its neighbours, but with the gallery architecture. A black slate floor, itself a grid of light-hued grout, wreaked havoc with the scale of Genesis, which came to bear an unfortunate resemblance to a miniature golf course. One could, of course, promenade happily enough between the carefully shaped mounds covered with lush green grass, each bordered with neatly groomed pebbles; one might encounter others along the paths, and even make a casual dalliance around the ornamental terracotta basins; one could gaze into these basins, and perhaps reflect on the spiraling imagery of animal and human evolution contained in them. But if I'm not wrong, what struck most visitors to Williams's environment was the un-transcendant drama of the newborn grass which the artist had planted one week before and grown with lamps. Every blade swept upward from its unique location toward the source of light and heat, obeying an inbuilt genetic command. That 'real-time' process, however imperceptible, far over-shadowed the intellectually over-processed evocation of an 'evolutionary time,' which the artist had intended as the symbolic centre of the work.

The recent work of Katherine Ross, who teaches at the School of the Art Institute of Chicago, encompasses many of the strategies and themes I've been tracing in this essay: the use of organic materials in tandem with clay, theatricality, an interrogation of bodily experience, an expanded approach to the gallery space and an ecological consciousness. Since the late 1980s, water has been a recurrent theme in her work. To be sure, not a single drop of the real thing is to be found there, but it does appear in a variety of semiotic capacities: as image, as structural model, and as a kind of ur-symbol for the elemental processes of nature, including those of the body. Water, the same substance Ross locates at the center of age-old human preoccupations with purity and transcendence, is also revealed in her work as the carrier of pollution, disease and death. In two related works from 1989, Joy and Vessels in the Landscape, the artist took piles of slip-cast replicas of plastic detergent bottles and imprisoned them in sturdy cages of chainlink fencing. There the identical vessels came to rest, the undegradable detritus of industrial capitalism, patinated and disgorged by an angry mythical ocean. In this approach to site-specific art, nature appears to have become the artist's active collaborator (rather than merely her subject), and the gallery their common work site.

Water Cure, an ambitious, room-sized installation from 1995, heralded a group of interrelated motifs that have carried through Ross's art to the present. Comprising the work were steel tubs on tables and floor filled with cattle hair, soap, lye and fat; a display table with sand-blasted glass cups inscribed with the names of the most polluted bodies of water; another table with copper-glazed ceramic cups bearing the names of mythical gods associated with water; a series of porcelain tiles with digitally-imaged vignettes of bodies of water; and a video monitor alternating short clips of hand-washing and waves crashing to shore. With repeated viewings, the silent, grainy, slow-motion image of hand-washing becomes disturbing; the performance of the task is lifted above its real duration and made into an emblem of a cultural obsession with hygiene, a 'second nature' as imperturbable as the rhythym of the waves. The cure, which Ross posits as a transcendence of the body's impurities, is no more possible through a cleansing intake of fluids than external scrubbing. From an ecological point of view, we are told – and made eerily aware – that the contamination of the earth's water-bodies filters down to our own.

Ross installed three works in Columbus; together they represented something like a grand synthesis of her ideas and practices. Comfort and Transcendence consisted of a grid-like display of slipcast porcelain water-bottles set against a painted field of 'old hospital green'. On the adjacent wall was Prophylaxis/Hygiene, a long horizontal field, also green, studded by a long row of old porcelain faucet handles, each one inscribed with a single word. Two types of passages – one literary, one spatial – were hereby conjoined in the 'performance' Ross imposed on the spectator. Moving through space to read the handles, we are offered an ominous reminder – by the redoubtable French sociologist Jean Baudrillard – of the frightening depletion of our immune systems, not only by new diseases, but by modern medicine's feverish efforts to eradicate viruses by prophylaxis. Contamination dangers surround the human body in every sphere it inhabits. So it is on the floor, practically under our feet, in the large porcelain tiles of a work called Primordial Waters, that Ross delivers her most explicit imagery: invisible bacteria enlarged to threatening proportions and juxtaposed with arms and legs being scrubbed; cellular bodies colliding with human ones, unbearably confined to the sites of their disinfection.

It is not only the complicated structural and psychological analogies Ross conjures between water, bodies, and vessels, or the semiotics of contamination and cleansing, purity and transcendence, that make her pieces both serious and difficult; rather, it is also the way the artist registers these sources of meaning in a broader field of perceptual possibilities. Like the best installation art, Ross's opens up a temporalised experience of space, and a spatialised experience of time. In 1997 she reincarnated the video sequence from Water Cure, projected it on the rear wall of a long, narrow exhibition space, and laid out a pavement of porcelain tiles to denote the patterns of waves. With its undulating tiles creating a processional path to the virtual space of human action (and reflecting from its glazed surface a distorted image of the hand-washing), the work, titled Effluence, was perhaps meant to thematize a kind of Heraclitan fascination with flowing water as an emblem for time's passage and its stasis. But at the same time the tile-groupings operated as a kind of vitalized grid, capable of extending the aesthetic field spatially, beyond the perceptual limits of the gallery.

Richard Serra once remarked in an interview: 'At least with most sculpture, the experience of the work is inseparable from the place in which the work resides. Apart from that condition, any experience of the work is a deception.'[10] My own reflections would seem to proceed from a similar deception, given that I've spent a good many words describing works that no longer exist and can no longer be experienced. Nevertheless, I have persisted in trying to show how the aesthetic strategies underlying the works assembled for Cooled Matter entail a drastically expanded role for the beholder. As a critic, I believe that a willingness and desire to adapt to this role, despite its unfamiliarity, can help steer us clear of the 'deceptions' that beckon wherever we encounter new works purposefully connected to the concrete fields of their deployment.

What makes site-specific and installation practices valuable above all, are the radical ways they decentre our expectations of where we are to find meaning in our encounter with the individual work. Under the rule of modernist aesthetics, beholders were encouraged to seek meaning in the inner structure, the illusory centre, of the art object – a logical place to look if we believe that meaning has been transplanted there from the psyche of the artist who has expressed what dwelt 'inside' prior to the creative act. Sculpture in the expanded field, by contrast, redirects perception to the 'world' around, the totality in which we encounter objects of every kind, not only art. This has been an invaluable direction for sculpture to take, because it has introduced into our experience of art a testing of our spatial intelligence, an intensified awareness of the radical interdependence of objects with the world. But this brings with it its own problems. In terms of artistic practice, Minimalism represents the paradigm for combating the elusiveness and indeterminacy of what critic Terry Eagleton describes as a 'set of interlaced functions and locations'.[11] Rather than using sculptural materials to ornament and thus transfigure the gallery, Minimalism set itself the task of exposing the conditions that pertained in the supposedly neutral spaces of modernist architecture.

One way it accomplished this was by combining repetition and seriality, by simply placing one thing after another. Without a relational harmony of parts (which Donald Judd once described as 'one of the salient and most objectionable relics of European art')[12] to absorb the viewer in a contemplation of the work, attention could be dispersed back into the physical surroundings and the concrete location of the viewer's body in space – and time. 'One thing after another' offered a means of disrupting those routines of thought that lead many viewers to focus their search for meaning on the unique object, especially objects that wore the traces of the artist's touch like so many certificates of authenticity. Within the history of ceramic sculpture, there are few works that consciously participate in this decentring of meaning. Now, in the era of installation and unabashed intermedia, we have more artists willing to defeat the illusory centre, to re-evaluate 'the logic of a particular source of meaning',[13] and to assert the aesthetic and social value in locating meaning in public, rather than private terms.

The art gallery is the supreme example of a kind of place where the myriad possible functions and meanings of its role as a public space are overcome by a routine accommodation to the hegemony of the private and of the personal. What better place, then, to expose the ideological character of these patterns of thought and experience? The best installation projects, whatever their particular meanings, remind us that there could never be any ground for consciousness other than the real-world conditions we inhabit. Such projects shatter the idealist proposition that, as Eagleton puts it, 'there could ever be a world in the first place without the human bodies which organise and sustain it'. Installation furnishes for its audiences an art that can serve as a model of consciousness in which meanings are shared in the here and now – that is, a public art worthy of the name.

Notes

1. Allan Kaprow, 'The Legacy of Jackson Pollock', (1958), in Essays on the Blurring of Art and Life, ed. J. Kelley (Berkeley, 1993), pp. 7–8.
2. Garth Clark, American Ceramics: 1876 to the Present, rev. ed. (New York, 1987), p. 143.
3. From Remembrance of Things Past, vol. 1, trans. C. K. S. Moncrieff (New York, 1934), p. 36.
4. Buzz Spector, 'A Profusion of Substance,' in Theories of Contemporary Art, 2nd edn., ed. R. Hertz (Englewood Cliffs, NJ.: 1993), pp. 231–43.
5. Ibid., p. 238.
6. For a brief overview, Grace Eiko Thomson's catalogue essay in Sadashi Inuzaka, Dear Lake (Burnaby Art Gallery, Burnaby, British Columbia, 1996), pp. 5–6.
7. See Craig Owens, 'The Allegorical Impulse: Toward a Theory of Postmodernism,' in Art After Modernism: Rethinking Representation, ed. B. Wallis (New York, 1984), p. 223.
8. Not content with this, the artist positioned a few ceramic bunnies, likewise camoflauged, in front of the installation. What attracts this new breed of installation artists to the iconic form of the garden bunny is a question that admittedly baffles me.
9. Rosalind Krauss, 'Grids,' in The Originality of the Avant-Garde and Other Modernist Myths (Cambridge, Mass., 1985), p. 18.
10. Quoted in Douglas Crimp, 'Redefining Site-Specificity,' in On the Museum's Ruins (Cambridge, Mass., 1993), p. 167.
11. Terry Eagleton, The Ideology of the Aesthetic (Oxford, 1990), pp. 288–9.
12. Quoted in Michael Fried, 'Art and Objecthood,' in Aesthetics: A Critical Anthology, eds. G. Dickie and R. J. Sclafani (New York, 1977), p. 439.
13. See Rosalind Krauss, Passages in Modern Sculpture (Cambridge, Mass., 1977), p. 262.

First published in *Ceramics: Art and Perception*, no 39, 2000, pp. 6–15.

Reprinted with permission from *Ceramics: Art and Perception* and the author.

24
THE NEW CERAMIC PRESENCE
Rose Slivka

American ceramics – exuberant, bold, irreverent – has excited admiration and controversy among craftsmen in every field both here and abroad. The most populated, aggressively experimental, and mutable area of craft expression, it is symptomatic of the vitality of United States crafts with its serious, personal, evocative purposes.

As in the other arts, ceramics, also, has broken new ground and challenged past traditions, suggested new meanings and possibilities to old functions and habits of seeing, and has won the startled attention of a world unprepared for the unexpected. (At the second International Ceramic Exhibitions at Ostend, Belgium, in 1959, the United States exhibit, circulated abroad for the last two years, became the focus of the show.) To attempt some insight into what is happening – for it is a happening, peculiar to our time and to American art as a whole – to probe the complex sources of our ceramics and its vigorous new forms is the aim of this investigation.

What is there in the historical and philosophic fabric of America that engendered the unique mood of our expression?

America, the only nation in the history of the modern world to be formed out of an idea rather than geographic circumstance or racial motivations – the country compelled by the electrifying and still new idea of personal freedom that cut through geographic, racial, and economic lines to impel people everywhere in unparalleled scope, rate, and number – was a philosophic product of the Age of Reason and the economic spawn of the Industrial Revolution. In the two hundred years of our short history our expanding frontier kept us absorbed in the problems of practical function and pressured us to solve them in a hurry. We have, as a result, become the most developed national intelligence in satisfying functional needs for the mass (in a massive country), with availability an ideal. The rapidity, the scale, and the intense involvement in mechanization have been unprecedented. If there is, in fact, any one pervasive element in the American climate, it is that of the machine – its power, its speed, its strength, its force, its energy, its productivity, its violence.

Not unified by blood or national origin (everyone is from someplace else), or a sense of place (with many generations of a family history identified with one place, as in Europe), we are a restless people. A nation of immigrants with a continuing history of migration, we are obsessed by the need for arrival – a pursuit that eludes us. And so, we are always on the go. (Our writers – Walt Whitman, Herman Melville, Thomas Wolfe, and, most recently, Jack Kerouac – have struggled for a literary art form to express this.) Having solved our need for mobility by mechanical means, we love engineering and performance and the materials and tools by which we have achieved them.

In our involvement with practical matters, we were too busy really to cultivate the idea of beauty. Beauty as such – the classical precepts of harmonious completion, of perfection, of balance – is still a Western European

Source: © American Craft Council/Originally published in *Craft Horizons*.

idea, and it is entirely possible that it is not the aesthetic urgency of an artist functioning in an American climate – a climate that not only has been infused with the dynamics of machine technology, but with the action of men – ruggedly individual and vernacular men (the pioneer, the cowboy) with a genius for improvisation. Our environment, our temperament, our creative tensions do not seem to encourage the making of beauty as such, but rather the act of beauty as creative adventure – energy at work – tools and materials finding each other – machines in movement – power and speed – always incomplete, always in process.

As far back as 1870, a Shaker spokesman declared that Shaker architecture ignored 'architectural effect and beauty of design' because what people called 'beautiful' was 'absurd and abnormal'.[1] It had been stated by others before and was restated many times since, including the declaration in the 1920s by famous architect Raymond M. Hood: 'This beauty stuff is all the bunk'.[2] A typical American attitude, it may well have expressed the beginning of a new American aesthetic rather than gross lack of appreciation for the old one.

This is the ebullient, unprecedented environment of the art that, particularly in the fifteen years since World War II, has asserted itself on every level.

First manifested in painting – the freest of the arts from the disciplines of material or function – it projected such a presence of energy, new ideas, and methods that it released a chain reaction all over the world, and for the first time we saw the influence of American painting abroad. But nowhere has the impact of contemporary American painting been greater than here at home. Feeding on itself, it has multiplied and grown in vitality and daring to penetrate every field of creative activity.

Pottery, of course, has always served as a vehicle for painting, so this in itself is nothing new. The painted pottery of Greece strictly followed the precepts of the painting of the time in style and quality, while that of Japan was often freer and in advance of its other media of painting, even anticipating abstract modern approaches. Contemporary painting, however, has expanded the vocabulary of abstract decoration and given fresh meaning to the accidental effects of dipped, dripped, poured, and brushed glazes and slips on the pot in the round.

But its greatest and most far-reaching effect in ceramics has been the new emphasis it gave to the excitement of surface qualities – texture, color, form – and to the artistic validity of spontaneous creative events during the actual working process – to everything that happens to the clay while the pot is being made.[3] Clay, perhaps more than any other material, undergoes a fabulous creative transformation – from a palpable substance to a stonelike, self-supporting structure – the self-recorded history of which is burned and frozen into itself by fire.

More than in any other form of art, there is a tradition of the 'accident' in ceramics – the unpremeditated, fortuitous event that may take place out of the potter's control, in the interaction between the living forces of clay and fire that may exercise mysterious wills of their own. The fact that the validity of the 'accident' is a conscious precept in modern painting and sculpture is a vital link between the practice of pottery and the fine arts today. By giving the inherent nature of the material greater freedom to assert its possibilities – possibilities generated by the individual, personal quality of the artist's specific handling – the artist underscores the multiplicity of life (the life of materials and his own), the events and changes that take place during his creative act.

Painting shares with ceramics the joys and the need for spontaneity in which the will to create and the idea culminate and find simultaneous expression in the physical process of the act. Working with a sense of immediacy is natural and necessary to the process of working with clay. It is plastic only when it is wet and it must be worked quickly or it dries, hardens, and changes into a rigid material.

The painter, moreover, having expanded the vistas of his material, physically treats paint as if it were clay – a soft, wet, viscous substance responsive to the direction and force of the hand and to the touch, directly or with tool; it can be dripped, poured, brushed, squeezed, thrown, pinched, scratched, scraped, modeled – treated as both fluid and solid. Like the potter, he even incorporates foreign materials – such as sand, glass, coffee grounds, crushed stone, etc. – with paint as the binder, to emphasize texture and surface quality beyond color. (We are aware that the application of paint as color, with its inherent qualities and dependency for a supporting structure by adhesion to a plane in another material, makes a fundamental difference between the two arts – between it and all other practices of the plastic arts. We are not trying to simplify or equate. We are pointing to those common denominators that have profoundly affected and influenced the new movement in pottery.) It is corollary that the potter today treats clay as if it were paint. A fusion of the act and attitudes of contemporary painting with the material of clay and the techniques of pottery (the potter's hand if not always his wheel is there), it has resulted in a new formal gesture that imposes on sculpture.

In the past, pottery form, limited and predetermined by function, with a few outstanding exceptions, has served the freer expressive interests of surface. Today, the classical form has been subjected and even discarded in the interests of surface – an energetic, baroque clay surface with itself the formal 'canvas'. The paint, the 'canvas', and the structure of the 'canvas' are a unity of clay.

There are three extensions of clay as paint in contemporary pottery:

1. the pot form is used as a 'canvas';
2. the clay itself is used as paint threedimensionally – with tactility, color, and actual form;
3. form and surface are used to oppose each other rather than complement each other in their traditional harmonious relationship – with color breaking into and defining, creating, destroying form.

This has led the potter into pushing the limits of paintings on the pot into new areas of plastic expression: sculptured painting, with the painted surface in control of the form. The potter manipulates the clay itself as if it were paint – he slashes, drips, scrubs down, or builds up for expressive forms and textures. Or around the basic hollow core he creates a continuum of surface planes on which to paint. In so doing, he creates a sculptural entity whose form he then obliterates with the painting. This, in turn, sets up new tensions between forms and paint. It is a reversal of the three-dimensional form painted in two. Now the two-dimensional is expressed in three – on a multiplaned, sculptured 'canvas'. As a result, modern ceramic expression ranges in variety from painted pottery to potted painting to sculptured painting to painted sculpture to potted sculpture to sculptured pottery. And often the distinctions are very thin or nonexistent.

The current pull of potters into sculpture – in every material and method, including welded metals, cast bronze, plaster, wood, plastics, etc. – is a phenomenon of the last five years. So great a catalyst has been American painting that the odyssey from surface to form has been made through its power. Manipulating form as far as it could go to project the excitement of surface values, the potters found even the slightest concession to function too limiting. From painter-potters, they were impelled to become painter-sculptors. Instead of form serving function, it now serves to develop the possibilities of the new painting. However, while this painting generates the creation of forms for itself – often massive in scale – it tolerates the dominance of no presence other than – itself. In his new idea of a formal synthesis, the potter is inevitably pushing into space – into the direction of sculpture.

As a fusion between the two dimensional and the three dimensional, American pottery is realizing itself as a distinct art form. In developing its own hybrid expression, it is like a barometer of our aesthetic situation.

Involvement in the new handling of surface with form, however, cannot rest on traditional categorizing. The lines cross back and forth continuously. While the painter, in building and modeling his surface has reached toward the direction of sculpture, so, too, the sculptor has been independently reaching away from the conventional bounds of sculptural form toward an energy of space and the formal possibilities of an activated surface (with or without color). The hybrid nature of this expression, however, has always been within the realm of sculpture, only to be released as an entity in our time.

Sculpture, as every area of the plastic arts, is reevaluating the very idea that gave it birth – monumentality. A traditional sculptural aspiration, its values, too, have changed. The sculptor today places greater emphasis on event rather than occasion, in the force of movement and the stance of dance rather than in the power of permanence and the weight of immobility, in the metamorphosis of meanings rather than in the eternity of symbols.

Specific to the kinship between potter and sculptor is the fact that clay is a primary material for both (for the potter, the sole material; for the sculptor, one of several). Its tools and methods impose many of the same technical skills and attitudes on both. In general, potter and sculptor share a creative involvement in the actuality of material as such – its body and dimension – an experience of the physicality of an object that in scale and shape relates to the physicality of the artist's own body in a particular space.

The developments in abstract sculpture have decidedly affected the formal environment of ceramists everywhere. The decision of the sculptor to reinterpret the figure as well as all organic form through abstraction and even to project intellectually devised forms with no objective reference inevitably enlarged the formal vistas of every craftsman and designer working in three dimensions.

To pottery, sculpture has communicated its own sense of release from the tyranny of traditional tools and materials, a search for new ways of treating materials and for new forms to express new images and new ideas.

In addition to painting and sculpture, other influences that contributed decisively to the new expression in American pottery were: The bold ceramic thrust of Picasso, and Miró with Artigas, gave encouragement and stimulation to the movement that had already begun here. The Zen pottery of Japan, furthermore, with its precepts of asymmetry, imperfection (crude material simplicity), incompleteness (process), found profound sympathy in the sensibilities of American potters.

The freedom of the American potter to experiment, to risk, to make mistakes freely on a creative and quantitative level that is proportionally unequaled anywhere else has been facilitated, to a large extent, by this country's wealth and availability of tools and materials. It gave further impetus to the potter's involvement in total process – in the mastery of technology and the actual making of the object from beginning to end – in marked contrast to the artist-potters of European countries who leave the technology and execution to the peasant potter and do only the designing and finishing. Aside from the fact that we have no anonymous peasant potters in this country to do only the technical or preparatory work, the American loves his tools too much to leave that part of the fun to someone else. For him, the entire process contains creative possibilities. Intimacy with the tools and materials of his craft is a source of the artist's power.

Spontaneity, as the creative manifestation of this intimate knowledge of tools and their use on materials in pursuit of an art, has been dramatically articulated as an American identity in the art of jazz – the one medium that was born here. Always seeking to break through expected patterns, the jazzman makes it while he is playing it. With superb mastery of his instrument and intimate identification with it, the instrumentalist creates at the same time he performs; the entire process is there for the listener to hear – he witnesses the acts of creation at the time they are happening and shares with the performer the elation of a creative act.

Crafts that functioned in the communal or regional culture of an agrarian society do not have the same meaning in the internationalized culture of an industrial society. Thus, all over the modern world, the creative potter has been reevaluating his relation to function. Certainly, the potter in the United States is no longer obliged to produce for conventional function, since the machine has given us so many containers for every conceivable variety of purposes and in every possible material – plastic, paper, glass, ceramic, fiber, metal – with such quick obsolescence and replacement rates that they make almost no demands on our sensibilities, leaving us free – easy come, easy go – from being possessed by the profusion and procession of objects that fill our lives today. We are accustomed to our functional problems being solved efficiently and economically by mechanical means; yet we are acutely aware of our particular need for the handcrafts today to satisfy aesthetic and psychological urgencies. The painter-potter, therefore, engages in a challenge of function as a formal and objective determinant; he subjects design to the plastic dynamics of interacting form and color and even avoids immediate functional association – the value by which machine-made products are defined – a value that can impede free sensory discovery of the object just as its limitations can impede his creative act. And so, the value of use becomes a secondary or even arbitrary attribute.

Then comes the inevitable question: Is it craft? In the view of this writer, as long as it is the intent of the craftsman to produce an object of craft (the execution of which he performs with the recognized tools, materials, and methods of craftsmanship), and he incorporates acknowledgment, however implied, of functional possibilities or commitments (including the function of decoration) – as long as he maintains personal control over the execution of the final product, and he assumes personal responsibility for its aesthetic and material quality – it is craft. At the point that all links with the idea of function have been severed, it leaves the field of the crafts.

Ceramics, perhaps more than any other craft, throughout its long history has produced useful objects that are considered fine art. Time has a way of overwhelming the functional values of an object that outlives the men who made and used it, with the power of its own objective presence – that life invested quality of being that transcends and energizes. When this happens, such objects are forever honored for their own sakes.

We are now groping for a new aesthetic to meet the needs of our time, or perhaps it is a new anti-aesthetic to break visual patterns that no longer suffice. The most powerful forces of our environment – electronic and atomic, inner and outer space, speed – are invisible to the naked eye. Our aesthetic tradition, involved as it has been with visual experience, does not satisfy the extension and growth of reality in our time. Our greatest sensory barrier to a new aesthetic is visual enslavement in a subvisual world. The aspect of man is no longer the center of things, and his eyes are only accessories of his own growing sense of displacement.

Throughout the arts in America we are in the presence of a quest for a deeper feeling of presence.

The American potter, isolated from the mass market, which makes no demands on his product as a material necessity, is motivated by a personal aesthetic and a personal philosophy. Lacking an American pottery tradition, he has looked to the world heritage and made it his own. For this, he has had to study and travel. Today, with his knowledge about himself, his craft, and his art – historically, contemporaneously, and geographically – cumulatively greater than ever before, the United States craftsman, a lonely, ambitious eclectic, is the most eager in search of his own identity.

All this, then, has made him most susceptible and responsive to the startling achievements of contemporary American painting and sculpture. For better or worse, he has allied himself with a plastic expression that comes from his own culture and his own time, and from an attitude toward work and its processes with which he can identify. The American potter gets inspiration from the top – from the most developed artistic, intuitive consciousness in his society. As always, the artist is led – not by the patron, not by populace, certainly not by the critic – artist is led by artist. The artist is his own culture.

Briefly, the characteristic directions of the new American pottery are: the search for a new ceramic presence, the concern with the energy and excitement of surface, and the attack on the classical, formal rendering.

Pottery, with a continuity that reaches back to the very beginnings of man, has always had a tradition for variety. If there is any one traditional characteristic of American pottery, it is this enormous variety. And if there is anything that distinguishes American plastic expression, it is the forthrightness, the fearlessness, the individuality, the aloneness of each man's search.

Notes

1. John Kouwenhoven's documented study of American aesthetics, *Made in America* (Newton Centre, Mass.: Charles T. Branford Co., 1948).
2. Ibid.
3. The writer does not wish this article to be interpreted as a statement of special partisanship for those potters working with the new forms and motivations. It is an attempt to treat a direction of work which, with its provocative attitudes, has evoked strong response – for it as well as against it. Our partisanship is for creative work in all its variety. We recognize that pottery has as many faces as the people who make it.

Rose Slivka, 'The New Ceramic Presence', *Craft Horizons* 21/4 (July/August 1961).

Originally published in *Craft Horizons* magazine. Reprinted with permission from the American Craft Council.

25

METAMORPHOSIS: THE CULTURE OF CERAMICS

Martina Margetts

All kinds of battles, not just military ones, are fought in the name of civilization. A few have affected the course of culture in contemporary Britain, and with this the current position of ceramics. The battle of the sexes, waged by women to achieve equality with men, has enfranchised the creative achievements of women and the hand processes associated with the crafts and domestic contexts. The current exploration of gender (transexuality and androgyny) in terms of personal and cultural identity, has further liberated conventions of thought. The battle of high versus low (popular) culture has reached a stand-off between the Madonna/Mozart, Dylan/Keats camps, since never again can culture be, narrowly defined within Matthew Arnold's nineteenth-century, socially-improving model. Cultural relativism (the postmodern absence of hierarchy and absolute standards) and multiracialism now rule.

Ceramic art is thriving in this homogenous, relativist climate, aided especially by developments in sculpture and design. Both are engaged in a more variegated, tactile, metaphorical approach. Sculptors aim not to represent the world, but to explore its meaning through materials, processes and the nature and function of objects in a metaphysical way. Designers recognise the significance of emotion in the buying of consumer goods: the need for a light, a kettle, a chair to offer, both functionally and stylistically, a more specialised relationship with its owner' For example, products by the Memphis Group, Alessi, Ron Arad, Philippe Starck, Stefan Lindfors and the lighting designer, Ingo Maurer, all typify this experience.

Ironically, it is the postwar history of ceramics itself, as much as the absence of a sympathetic cultural context, which has delayed the present coming of age of British ceramic art. Despite some experimental post-war ceramics, the twin peaks of Bernard Leach (1889-1979) and Hans Coper (1920-1981) have loomed so large that it seems only now, at the end of the century, that ceramics here can be freely made and assessed across the whole spectrum of structures and purposes. Elsewhere, this tunnel vision has been less evident, especially in the United States and Japan. For example, Peter Voulkos, instigator in the 1950s of Abstract Expressionism in American ceramics, and the revolutionary ceramic artists of the Sodeisha Group (founded in Japan in 1948 by Kazuo Yagi and Osamu Suzuki) created in their work an exciting relationship between form and surface skin. Their works, apparently chaotic in structure, offered, on the contrary, a new sense of order in ceramics, akin to that achieved by Picasso in the fine arts. Newness of feeling led to newness of form.

By contrast, in Britain in the 1950s and 1960s, pots remained within conventional parameters, from William Staite Murray to Sam Haile, while non-vessel ceramics seemed cut off from the artery of mainstream sculpture. Ideas, scale, form and especially the clay material (a provisional basis for, say, bronze sculpture, rather than significant in its own right) were delimiting factors.

Leach's holistic vision, too, of life and work together producing beauty, harmony and a sense of useful purpose, was so compelling that the aesthetic he evolved in ceramics prevailed as a badge of allegiance, a

Source: © Martina Margetts/Museum of Modern Art, Oxford.

symbol of belief. The whole realm of the brown and green betokened these values, becoming a political and social as much as a cultural statement.

The aesthetic charge derived from 'conviction ceramics' manifested itself also, but differently, in the work of Hans Coper, the German engineer-turned-potter who lived and worked in England from 1938 until his death in 1981. The creative strictures he imposed upon himself, his refinement of form which forced him to work, as he wrote, 'like a demented piano-tuner trying to approximate a phantom pitch', led to a goal of continuous production and to the evolution of a family of vessel shapes through a meditative, reductive process rather than one which relied on catalytic radicalism, as in the US and Japan. Eloquence triumphed over eclecticism.

It is not surprising that the 1970s generation of British ceramic vessel makers exploded that territory with a more experimental approach to form and narrative, which Alison Britton explained in her much quoted essay in 1982 (The Maker's Eye catalogue). Most importantly, she connected her concerns in ceramics to Modernism and to other art forms, especially literature and painting, analysing them within and on those terms. During the 1980s ceramics has, like architecture, moved between Modernism and Postmodernism, between an abstract narrative about form (essence) to a literal narrative about content (synthesis). But the explorations mainly evolved round the form of the vessel, with non-vessel ceramic sculpture confined to its black hole. Although cultural support and stimulus existed, in terms of ceramic development in other countries and a large range of ceramic works made by fine artists throughout the century, the critical and institutional biases seemed to work against this area of ceramics flourishing in Britain.

The separate existence of the Crafts Council from the Arts Council, of separate crafts organisations, galleries and departments in museums and art schools, conferred separate intentions on the works, emphasising difference rather than common ground. Added to this was the constricting view of some influential critics and of the public, who conceded that art may present the shock of the new, but who viewed ceramics as an area of conservatism. They preferred to define ceramics in terms of Leachian studio pottery and to link it to the sentiments expressed in, say, Keats' *Ode to a Grecian Urn* (the pot as 'the still unravished bride of quietness … she cannot fade … beauty is truth, truth beauty') rather than to the ravished, faded image of the Bride Stripped Bare in Duchamp's *The Large Glass*.

The writings on ceramics by the late Peter Fuller, and those of Peter Dormer, a critic of wider sympathies but who nonetheless is in favour of 'familiar forms' offering 'solace', relate back to the social context and yardsticks of use and beauty promoted by Morris, Lethaby, and Japanese culture. This is acceptable, of course, as one view of current ceramic practice, but only when it is tempered by a knowledge and tolerance of the alternatives. The danger lies in the public's delight in selectively seeing its own traditionalist biases condoned: consequently, the broader reaches of the ceramic avant-garde are ignored.

The role of ceramics in the 1990s is open to much wider interpretation and connection, especially because the climate of painting and sculpture has been propitious and complementary to it, Since the 1960s, sculpture has broken boundaries of material, and form, as evidenced in the exhibition *Gravity and Grace* of sculpture from 1965-1975, shown recently at the Hayward Gallery: 'The fervent search for other ways of seeing', writes the curator Jon Thompson, 'involved different procedures and methods for making, finding, reflecting, matching, pairing, completing, growing, placing, spacing, and associating. Boundaries grew blurred in a world that seemed to promise a permanent state of change and flux'.

The moral hegemony of Modernism's purist and idealistic fitness-for-purpose ethic, implying an attainable truthfulness, was also outfaced by Pop, performance art, advertising and a manipulative technological revolution. Objects lost their apparent definitiveness (certainly no sculptural figures on plinths) and creative works became touchstones of experience, rather than finite representations and explanations. From the 1980s, process as product in new British sculpture gave it a hauntingly ambiguous aesthetic and an exciting atmosphere of philosophical enquiry. The sculptures of Richard Deacon, Bill Woodrow, Alison Wilding, Tony

Cragg, Antony Gormley, Shirazeh Houshiary and Anish Kapoor have a close affinity with figurative and vessel forms, presenting objects as metaphors, marked and metamorphosed by process.

The choices of materials and techniques, fusing exposed elements with covert messages, has poetically reconnected art to nature, inviting a metaphysical rather than a literal response. In this exhibition, this approach is evident in work by, for example, Antony Gormley, Ewen Henderson, Trupti Patel and Sara Radstone. Their humanistic preoccupation with origins is underscored by their concepts of the natural world. In nature, forms and processes suggest a diagram of forces at work (the four elements, the four seasons, night and day), which need to be harmonised to offer some sense of order and continuity. The psychoanalyst, Carl Jung, recognised that human experience and its conditional process of birth, life and death also demands the reconciliation of opposites. Human aspirations and nature can be related to alchemy, to the notion of transforming nature's prosaic elements and our prosaic selves into a condition of harmony and fulfilment: in this respect, the choice by these artists to use clay is especially appropriate, since it, too, involves the transformation of raw earth through fire into special things of permanence.

The strength of ceramics has always lain in its universality – in terms of geography, form, content and language – a non-verbal, worldwide evocation of spiritual, ceremonial, sculptural and utilitarian functions. The unique versatility of the material, which is able to interpret a great range of styles and ideas whilst retaining its own intimate identity, imbues ceramic works with a particular resonance through time. The sculptor, Eduardo Paolozzi, has emphasised the mix of meaning and memory within the clay material (nature's collective subconscious): 'Shaping a piece of clay is like reading William Butler Yeats poems to the Michelangelo painting of Leda and the Swan – rich in metaphors, intoxicating in its associations and yet mysterious' (*The State of Clay* catalogue 1978).

The coming of age of ceramic art in Britain, when now the conceptual range of ceramics can be more sympathetically viewed and when the works themselves have become more richly inventive, is the subject of this exhibition. Here clay is not a craft material but an authentic medium for sculpture. The works take myriad forms, in concept, scale and meaning: the continuing exploration of the vessel form, fusing the languages of painting, sculpture and architecture in a physical language of its own, is balanced by works concerned with the ironical re-presentation of ceramic traditions; with figuration; with landscape (physical, mythological, metaphorical); and with identity. This latter realm perhaps most potently evokes current concerns in the context of an increasingly synthetic world, a determination to explain to ourselves what we are about as well as how to survive with some sense of values and civilization intact.

Originally published as Martina Margetts, 1993, 'Metamorphosis: the culture of ceramics', in Alison Britton and Martina Margetts, *The raw and the cooked : new work in clay in Britain*, Museum of Modern Art, Oxford, pp. 13–15.

Reprinted with the permission of the Museum of Modern Art, Oxford and the author.

26
ANTONY GORMLEY IN CONVERSATION WITH JAMES PUTNAM

James Putnam

James Putnam I suppose a good way to start would be to ask you what is your first response to clay as a working medium?

Antony Gormley It is the most immediate material that sculpture can use. It is also one of the oldest. Just think of those caves in the Dordogne or in the Haute-Garonne such as at Montespan where there is this loosely modelled bear sculpture formed from the wet clay – still wet! – and completely covered in holes where the Cro-Magnon speared it ritually.

JP There are also many caves that have these wonderful marks left from fingers pressed in the soft layer of clay that covered the rock.

AG Yes, on the roof at Rouffignac, the 'spaghetti' traces of fingers on the roof of the cave that go on for three kilometres. Those ochre hand silhouettes in Peche Merle seem to celebrate the fact that clay is so formable. When I first began using clay I just wanted something that actually carried the sign of touching, of an event between a receptive material and the hand. But I was suspicious of the 'Rodinesque' and the virtuosity of modelling. I want things to be directly made, and in as raw a material as possible, I have always used clay straight out of the ground. I get fantastic clay from a brickworks in Essex, just outside Southend. It's a lovely colour. When the loam comes off the surface you come across this sedimentary layer composed of the oldest igneous rocks that have been broken down to this very, very fine particulate and have sat there, amalgamating over millions of years. I like that, it's as if you're touching the flesh of the earth just like those paleolithic hand impressions.

JP Do you think you will come to use clay more in your work?

AG When I first started using clay I was experimenting with it and I really liked the way it behaves in its different forms, dry and liquid. But since making *Field* I haven't been able to think of any better way of using it. *Field* seems to combine this direct touch, bodies formed not as representation but as event – this act of squeezing in the space between the hands. It is the impression of this moment that gives the form, not an idea about the articulation of an anatomy. Then it is a register of a whole range of touch because *Field* is made through many hands. It's also important to me that the clay we use is liberated from its destiny of becoming a brick. I still want to do a big work in clay: a building in human form.

JP You're referring to your Brick Man, whose maquette is in the collection of Leeds City Art Gallery?

AG It was originally proposed for Leeds but they didn't want it, so now I want to make it in China, quite differently, in a more personal way with each brick made by hand so that everybody has a chance to make a part of it. People would write a message or just sign their names on individual bricks and

Source: © Tate/Reproduced by permission of Tate Trustees.

build up this hundred-metre high building in human form of several million bricks. I quite like the idea that this thing is made from uniform, absolute clone-like units but somehow each one carries an identity and that those identities together make this collective body, in one place, one object.

JP To come back to this current exhibition I suppose what may be an underlying issue is clay's place in the hierarchy of art materials. Probably before the twentieth century it tends to be viewed more as a process material.

AG But that is not true, is it? When you look at Renaissance art and the work of Della Robbia and Donatello, they did some amazing things in terracotta like that fantastic portrait in the V&A.

JP But it's more about how clay is less appreciated, due to its fragility and sense of impermanence, so that the preliminary clay model is often less valuable than the finished bronze cast — it's like how a drawing usually commands less market value than a painting.

AG I am not sure that I accept that, but I suppose in the conventional hierarchy of materials bronze and marble are at the top, lead and wood are in the middle and plaster and clay are at the very bottom. But I think that has all been turned on its head in the last hundred years. When Richard Long poured liquid china clay on the floor of the Tate's Duveen galleries in 1990, there is a work that is absolutely recognisable as a great work of art, and yet it is swept up afterwards and there is nothing left. I think our attitude to time in objects has changed radically so that we can now appreciate things in terms of fragility and temporality and their relationship to an event as much as to their sense of permanence and monumentality.

JP Surely this runs contrary to the notion of monumentality that seems to characterise some of your works, like the colossal *Angel of the North* or your proposed *Brick Man*, or even with *Field* its sheer mass evokes an effect of the monumental?

AG It is funny but I think of *Field* as an anti-monumental monument. It has no inscription, it is not memorialising anything in particular and the reading of it is open – it is a space where what you think and feel is the real subject of the work. I think it asks more questions than it presents certainties. Traditionally the monument has been a bulwark against amnesia to resist the effect that time has on dissolving certainties. *Field* has in-built entropy, it is a fluid, provisional and uncertain thing, and is formed by the space it is in.

JP Going back to the immediate appeal of clay, we could say it has an 'honest', down-to-earth quality to it. Yet its abundance and availability count against it in this hierarchy of fine art materials, also the fact that throughout history it was most frequently used in the manufacture of utilitarian artefacts.

AG But that is why it's so wonderful, because it is inherently democratic.

JP Clay obviously has more appeal to you in its natural state than in its more finished, glazed ceramic form.

AG Yes. I want it to be earth. I am very keen on the colour – the redness of the clay being something to do with the iron in the earth, which is also the iron in our blood, which somehow makes a connection between flesh and planet. That connection is very important. *Field* suggests that the earth holds the memory of our ancestors and also the promise of the unborn. It has a life, a memory and a conscience.

JP This exhibition would seem to provoke the ongoing debate about the differences between art and craft – do you think we are experiencing an increasing blurring of these boundaries?

AG It is very simple to me what the difference between art and craft is. Art questions the world and therefore makes life more complicated; craft is there to make life easier, more liveable. Craft is a reconciliation between the needs of human life and the environment around it. This is a supporting role. It has to do with comfort, shelter, and the support of the body. Art is about complicating things and about providing the mind with alternative avenues of thought and feeling, and can often be contradictory. The two cannot be confused.

JP So when you look at exceptionally fine ceramic objects, in the Oriental porcelain tradition, of superlative form and glaze, do you think they could ever transcend their original utilitarian function and be regarded as sculpture?

AG I think your question relates to the idea of looking for art in everyday objects. That was the Bauhaus ideal, that virtually everything we touch and use every day should be the subject of the same amount of thought and creativity as art – a great idea, good for design but a disaster for art (look what happened to Kandinsky!). Maybe the distinction I've just made between art and craft is truer for the twenty-first century than in any previous era and I think in our time it is as well for the health of both pursuits to keep them very separate. I am often horrified by the things that are supported by bodies like the Crafts Council, there is a sense in which these are objects that have lost their determination to be useful. Aspiring to the condition of the beautiful, they end up in some limbo – vases that refuse to hold flowers, that aspire to the condition of sculpture but don't actually achieve it—burdened by their over-considered surfaces and a design philosophy that has abandoned utility.

JP There is this distinction between the form of the vessel and its surface decoration. As you mentioned, you would like to see some of the magnificent, animated drawings on Greek black-figure ware liberated from their grounds. If we take Picasso's ceramics, perhaps many people rate his paintings on their surfaces as being more successful than the forms.

AG Except when he does those brilliant things when he gets his thrower to throw him a vase and he sort of squeezes it and turns it into a dove. I quite like those pieces where he is morphing the utilitarian object into something else. It's an extension of his bicycle seat becoming a bull's head.

JP Let's return to the fundamental appeal of using clay through the ages. I recall when we were handling and discussing those ancient Mesopotamian fertility figurines in the British Museum you were talking very passionately about clay's direct and symbolic link to mother earth and creation myths.

AG It is extraordinary how universal and similar these ideas about creation are—from the book of Genesis, to the Akkadian and Mesopotamian myths, the Nag Hammadi Gnostic gospel and the Chinese creation legends. This idea of some primeval matter from which man is created by the spit or breath of God. It's rooted very deep in our psyche that a god-like figure creates us from the earth and that we return to the earth.

JP An ancient Egyptian creation myth describes the ram-headed god Khnum as a potter who models on his wheel the egg from which all life was to emerge. There is also the idea of him modelling in clay all the forms in creation – living creatures, plant life, as well as the purely geographic features of the world.

AG One of the things that intrigued me most when I was doing *Field* at the British Museum was this infiltration of individual *Field* figures in some of the museum's exhibition cases, finding a relationship between these lumpish, not-modelled things and the ancient clay figures. Recently when I was in China working on *Field* I was taken to a holy site near Baya'tun in Gansu province, caves that had been visited by pilgrims from the earliest times to the present. At the deepest part of the cave, I was invited to put my hand into a hole where I felt this muddy clay. Then I was told to squeeze and remove the lump I had formed and place it up on a natural rock shelf where there were millions of these impressions that other visitors had made over the years. I hadn't seen that anywhere before and it was absolutely like *Field* – uncanny.

JP As a sculptor, your work involves moulding and casting rather than carving, so I suppose you can relate very closely to that expressive quality of clay.

AG If you are interested in traces, you are interested in the shortest possible bridge between life and the record of life, and so as a medium clay is one of the best things that you can find. There is a feeling when you use it that you are repeating some primal transformation of the unformed to the formed. When you return it to the fire it becomes like stone. That is a very primal alchemy, like commending experience to memory, a fossilisation or fixing of a moment and unlike any of the other techniques – such as 'lost wax' – it is totally direct. I would like to reverse the old hierarchies in that sense too, because clay is a medium that can become an extension of the flesh in a way that no other material can.

JP So, do you think we are going to see an increased use of clay in contemporary art?

AG I don't make predictions but when people have an idea that needs this medium, it will be used and I can't see clay as ever being irrelevant.

JP Do you think clay will become more appreciated as a medium in an era where we have so many synthetic materials? Is it more comforting to get back to such a basic material because it is so natural?

AG I don't think it is an issue of it being natural. Clay has always been the most commonly, universally used material to make the vessels that carry food (nourishment) to bodies, so it assists in sustaining us on the inside while it is also used to make the constructed world and shelter our bodies on the outside. All those visions of the future where we are seen living in plastic houses and surviving on pills have been proved to be complete rubbish. Bricks have great insulation properties, they breathe and are effective in such a range of climates. The brick is the unit, the weave of settled life and it is very much the scale of the brick that is a universal measure of settled human life on this planet. The brick and the pot have been the two things that determine the immediate environment which contains our memory outside our neural structure. This is the most receptive, most telling place of inscription of human experience, and this actually overrides anything I might have said about the distinctions between craft and art. And I don't believe that is ever going to change. I think every, every architect and every sculptor will have to deal with clay, one way or another, for as long as human beings walk the earth.

25 February 2004

This was first published as 'Anthony Gormley in conversation with James Putnam' in Simon Groom (ed), 2004, *A Secret History of Clay*, Tate Publishing, pp. 82–85.

Reproduced by permission of Tate Trustees © Tate 2004.

SECTION 2.4
CERAMICS AND INSTALLATION

Introductory summary

Installation art usually refers to three-dimensional artworks in particular 'site-specific' contexts, which are designed to change the viewer's perceptions of that space. There are crossovers between studio ceramics, which might be used in installations perhaps through the use of multiple units to occupy space, and sculptural ceramics.

This section starts with a clear introduction to ceramics and installation by artist Emma Shaw, who begins with definitions of installation linked to site-specificity. She goes on to provide an introduction to this subject with reference to key artists using the themes of context, multiples, new media, new roles/new voices and spaces.

Ruth Chambers' essay gives another practitioner's viewpoint, but starting from a position of scepticism about the need or relevance of the term 'ceramic installation'. Like Shaw, she offers a range of examples of pieces that 'incorporate, identify with, or are informed by practices within ceramics'. From these examples a range of themes are identified which might suggest that 'ceramic installation' could be positioned as a 'differentiated practice' to installation art as a more general term. The themes identified are process and material, self and body, cultural and historical meaning of the ceramics object, display and presentation and ceramics' relationship to architecture.

Installations using multiples of similar objects have become a feature of some ceramic practices. Glen R. Brown argues that works of this nature demonstrate an ambivalence and tension, in ceramics, based on the position that such works occupy between the ceramic and contemporary art fields. This is especially the case when ceramic vessels or utilitarian objects are presented on mass as one artwork.

Livingstone and Petrie

27
CERAMICS AND INSTALLATION
Emma Shaw

Over the last decade, installation has established itself as a major feature of contemporary ceramic art practice. The term 'installation', more familiar within fine art than in crafts, is now well established within ceramics where it is used to identify and define what is seen as a distinct area of practice. Despite the growing number of ceramic artists who have embraced the strategies and mechanisms of installation art, the literature surrounding the subject is slight, with just a few articles and sub-sections in larger texts.[1]

Many of the themes of ceramic installation discussed – such as memory, nature, bodily experience, archaeology, museology, seriality, repetition, narrative and minimalism – can be seen throughout ceramic practice and therefore are not specific to installation. Janet Mansfield's *Ceramics in the Environment*[2] focuses on large-scale, monumental, environmental and architectural works, many of which may be classed as installation. By any standard, installation is a vast, complex and expanding area of art practice which includes multiple methods and approaches, and is therefore difficult to pin down.

Definitions

Within ceramics, the description 'installation' is often employed as a blanket term to indicate either that the work is large in scale, that it does not fit on a plinth, that it makes use of multiples or that it is site-specific. Although these elements can and do constitute installation, there is a tendency to use the expression as a badge of contemporaneity or to demonstrate a knowingness of art world issues. Installation is rising in dominance to the point where anything can become an installation and where no one seems to make just sculpture anymore. This prompts the question – when does sculpture become installation, and how do we define installation?

The concept of site-specificity underpins most installation work. Issues of space and site are central, where the work inhabits a particular physical space (although is not necessarily bound by the architecture). Installation artists respond directly to space and place, engaging with physical and conceptual contexts, which may include the social, cultural and institutional. Scale is significant; installations are usually large in size, encompassing the whole environment. They are often temporal events, performances or interventions where there is a necessity to record and document. Another key feature is the use of multiples, readymades and of mixed and time-based media.

One of the key classifiers of installation can be directly linked to the experience of the audience. Installation work often embraces the senses, providing an experience or involving the participation of the spectator. One of the defining characteristics of installation lies in the difference between looking and spectating, the latter requiring the active involvement from the audience.[3] This difference is a key distinction between

Source: © Emma Shaw

the classification of sculpture and installation. This aspect or approach to installation is currently under-represented within ceramic installation, which often lacks such a direct engagement with the audience.

Context

In her book *Installation Art: A Critical History*,[4] Claire Bishop makes the useful separation between installation art and the installation of art. However, this distinction is often not acknowledged in the ceramics context where much installation work often involves relocating the same work to a different space rather than, for example, making a site-specific work. The (re)installation of art necessarily involves adapting and possibly rethinking a piece and, although its components may remain the same, the result is arguably a different work, not only because of any reconfiguring which has taken place but also because of the different contexts in which it operates.

Within ceramics, installation has developed within the context of craft so it is not, therefore, surprising that it differs from installation within the art world. The main and obvious distinction is that ceramic installation is made up predominantly of clay/ceramics (although other materials and media may be included). There are, of course, examples of artists working outside of ceramics that have successfully employed clay and/or ceramics in their installation work, however this work is generally classified as installation (rather than ceramic installation) because these artists place themselves within an art context. Their work is not generally medium-specific and, although materials may be an integral part of the work, meaning and content are paramount. Although ceramic art practice has expanded to include a range of methods and approaches, ceramic installation, unlike installation in general, is generally approached from a materials-based, materials-specific perspective, i.e. it is primarily about clay/ceramics and the relationship with clay/ceramics.

Multiples

Most of the strategies identified in installation art are in evidence in contemporary ceramic art practice. The use of the multiple, well established in fine art practice, has found particular resonance with artists using fired clay. Multiples are intrinsically suited to ceramic methods of production (moulding, casting, throwing) and display. This interplay between the original and the copy has proved to be fertile ground for ceramic artists making installation. There are numerous examples including thrown forms (Edmund de Waal, who makes what he calls installation groups or cargoes), casts (such as Clare Twomey's work), the handbuilt (such as Phoebe Cummings, who uses multiple elements to create sculptural installations) and the readymade.

Kerry Harker uses multiple readymade ceramic objects in her installation work. Harker decorates found ceramic forms which provide a 'ceramic canvas' for her painting such as in *Bud* (2007). Mass-produced ceramic figurines dominate Ruth Claxton's installations, which explore ideas about domestic display and ornament. Claxton adds to the ceramic figures using various objects and materials, adjusting, distorting and obscuring the original forms such as in *Land's End* (2007). The use of the multiple in ceramics is often accompanied by significant changes or additions to the space, such as the introduction of furniture or by wallpapering the gallery walls as in Carol McNicoll's installation carried out in Bergen Kunsthall in 2001.

New media

The use of digital media and video are also in evidence. Sadashi Inuzuka (born in Japan, now based in Canada) creates large-scale ceramic installations which include a variety of media (porcelain, video projection, stainless steel and sound) as in *Water trade* (2003). Iranian artist Bita Fayyazi uses ceramic multiples in her installation work which explores unconventional subject matter. In *Road Kill* (1997), Fayyazi combines ceramics, installation, performance and film. This work consists of two hundred crushed terracotta dogs, which were then buried in a grave (a high rise was later built on the site). The whole process of the burial was filmed and the event later screened. More recently, Claudia Clare's exhibition of ceramics and mixed media *Shattered* [5] included a short film that was integral to the exhibition as a whole. Clare is an example of a ceramic artist who has extended her role to include that of writer, researcher, film-maker, ethnographer and political activist.

New roles, new voices

The expansion of installation within ceramic practice is in part a response to recent developments within the wider visual arts and the new opportunities and contexts being made available to artists. The museum has played a significant role in this shift in practice. Changes to the public funding of art put institutions such as the museum under pressure to reform, experiment and to widen and attract new audiences. This allowed new roles for art and the artist to emerge, particularly the role of the artist curator. Museums are now a major site for artists' interventions and they are enjoying a renewed interest from contemporary artists seeking new and alternative contexts for their work.

This way of working is relatively new in ceramics. Ceramics are particularly suited to the museum context; many of our ideas about ceramics and their display are rooted in the museum, linking ceramics with museology and archaeology, and with ideas about collecting and collections. In the past, ceramics have been displayed either as historical objects placed in the vitrine or as commodities found for sale in the museum shop rather than being presented as an expressive medium on its own terms. Ceramic installations challenge these positions and offer an alternative ceramic presence which is not commercially driven or product-focused, but which is instead context and/or content-led.

Ceramic artists have begun to exploit the potential of this relationship. De Waal has fully embraced the museum and the role of the artist curator for example in his site-specific work at the Geffryre Museum in 2001 and also *A Sounding Line* at Chatsworth House in Derbyshire (2007), in which de Waal created new works to be displayed alongside historical pieces.

Working in the context of installation and the site-specific can open up new sites and audiences for ceramics and introduce alternative ways of thinking about this common material. Ceramic artists are now working across conventional art-craft boundaries and across contexts, widening their agendas and audiences.

Recent events such as *Clay Rocks* at the Victoria and Albert Museum in September 2006 reflect these new concerns. The event included Twomey's installation *Trophy*, which provided opportunities for direct audience participation (the audience were invited to take the work away) and Keith Harrison's spectacular installation/ performance, both discussed elsewhere in this issue [6]. Andrew Livingstone's *Tacit* (2006) is another example. Participants were invited to construct a basic clay pot following a set of instructions whilst being monitored by closed circuit television. In a more public space, Canadian artist Rory MacDonald's installations explore the built environment. In *Mur Vernisseé* (2003) he placed cast fragments of ceramic ornamental forms in the recesses of a wall that runs alongside a busy street in Vallauris, France.

These works signify a new level of engagement with context and site for both the artist and the audience. Such direct interactions with the public and with the public space also indicate a more socially engaged practice and propose a new public role for craft, a 'public craft'.[6]

Spaces

Some observers have suggested that there is limited demand for critical writing in ceramics but the fact that there is a growing number of ceramic artists working in this way suggests there is a need to develop a body of critical writing to accompany these new areas of practice. We also need to open up new spaces and audiences for ceramic art. For artists who make non-functional, non-commercial work, or work that is difficult to sell or exhibit, or for artists who want to work site-specifically, there are limited opportunities within the ceramic gallery system. This has forced ceramic artists to find new sites outside of the commercial craft gallery. The recent closure of the Crafts Council's flagship gallery in London provides further evidence of a shift away from the gallery.

Although artists have a significant role to play in identifying new sites and contexts for their work outside of the commercial gallery system, they also require institutional support in the form of financial backing and the creation of new opportunities. Despite the closure of its gallery space, the Crafts Council claims that it is committed to making contemporary craft exciting and relevant to the widest possible audience and that it wants to present craft in new contexts,[7] which suggests the possibility of a wider approach in the future. The introduction by the Crafts Council[8] of the new Spark Plug craft curator award is a promising start which could provide future opportunities.

The emergence of installation in ceramics has opened up new ways of working and resulted in a different awareness of the relationships between site, objects and audience. This shift in practice has liberated ceramics from a commodity-driven gallery system and introduced new possibilities for both the creation and exhibition of works. Crucially, it has enabled a new level of engagement with the audience and allowed access to a wider public. This signals a new era for ceramics and craft in which ideas about the social role of craft and about a public craft can be explored.

Notes

1. Such as Edmund de Waal's *20th Century Ceramics*. London: Thames & Hudson; 2003. p. 183–193 and Claire Twomey's Contemporary Clay in C. Hanaor's (Ed.) *Breaking the Mould: New Approaches to Ceramics*. London: Black Dog Publishing; 2007. p. 36–37.
2. Mansfield, Janet. *Ceramics in the Environment: An International Review*. London: A&C Black; 2005.
3. De Oliveira, Nicolas, Nicola Oxley and Michael Petry. On Installation. *Art and Design*. 1993; 30: 6–23.
4. Bishop, Claire. *Installation Art: A Critical History*. London: Tate Publishing; 2005.
5. Clare, Claudia. *Shattered: An Exhibition of Ceramics and Mixed Media*. London: Gallery West, University of Westminster, 23 May – 2 June 2007.
6. Harrison, Keith. High Tension, *Ceramic* Review Jan/Feb 2008, pp. 42–45
7. Chambers, Ruth. Ceramic Installation: Towards a Self-definition. *Ceramics: Art and Perception*. 2006; No. 65: 81–87.
8. Crafts Council, *Corporate Plan brochure – Putting craft into new contexts*. Available from: www.craftscouncil.org.uk/craftscouncil_corp_brochure.pdf (Accessed on 19 July 2007)

Source: *Ceramic Review* no 229 Jan/Feb 2008, pp. 34–39

28
CERAMIC INSTALLATION: TOWARDS A SELF-DEFINITION

Ruth Chambers

Installation practices have widely influenced contemporary visual arts since the 70s, radically altering the look and meaning of artworks and in particular, the relationship between audience and artwork. Yet, installation is a relatively new and undefined approach for traditional craft media, including ceramics. Predominantly the categories of ceramics discourse tend not to include it. Rather they address the primarily traditional concerns of function, the vessel form, figurative sculpture, architectural decoration and occasionally formalism. When the subject is considered, many ceramists and influential critics suggest that discussions of ceramic installation should be located outside of ceramics, believing the practice has moved too far away from traditional ceramics, in fact, to be considered ceramics.

The term ceramic installation does seem fraught with self-contradiction, theoretical ambiguity and confused lineage. Ceramics is a medium traditionally associated with craft production and defined by its material qualities rather than its expressed content. Installation on the other hand, usually takes the form of a temporary environment specific in both look and meaning to its location, it employs a range of media, and the materials are often non-traditional and secondary in importance to the idea expressed. At the same time there are many emerging and established artists and students who work primarily in installation, define themselves as ceramists, and express strong ties to the craft tradition. They make installations in which the material, history and/or processes of ceramics play a central role. Perhaps as a result of the ambiguities and confusions implied by the term ceramic installation, and as a result of the limited discourse through which to address ceramics in the form of installation, many artists who produce ceramic-based installation self-define their individual practices rigorously. They usually do so in relatively autonomous ways and not often within a category of ceramics installation. As an artist who makes installations, which, consistently employ ceramics, I am not myself completely convinced that a differentiated category called ceramic installation makes sense. Yet the combined richness of this related range of works, the lack of a unifying discourse, and the controversy regarding its lineage, have provoked an exploration of what a collective self-definition might offer.[1]

The pieces discussed here represent various approaches to installation yet all incorporate, identify with, or are informed by practices within ceramics. The meanings of the works relate in greater or lesser degrees to a use of clay, and process and subject and material are intertwined in forms that specifically engage ceramics practice. Moreover, within these works are several interwoven realms or themes, which recur in contemporary ceramic-based installations, supporting a position that such work can be viewed as a differentiated practice. These pieces, some more that others, all investigate relationships between process and material, specifically with regards to the material and processes of clay. As well, the relationship between the self and the body is investigated in particular ways – ways that employ phenomenological strategies and experiential aspects

Source: © Professor Ruth Chambers, University of Regina/*Ceramics: Art and Perception*.

of craft practice and ritual. Thirdly, cultural and historical meanings of the ceramic object, especially with regards to display and presentation, inform much of the work. And finally ceramics' traditional relationship to architecture often contributes conceptual and/or formal content.

As well as viewing the works from the position of a visual artist and from the perspective of my own studio practice I am viewing them through the lens of current understandings of interdisciplinarity, particularly as related to studio-based, rather than academic practices. Canadians Marie-Josee Lafortune and Lynn Hughes in *Creative Confusion: Interdisciplinary Practices in Contemporary Art*, make a distinction between interdisciplinary activities in the arts (in which they include theory writing that deals with culture and cultural production,) and interdisciplinary practices from the social sciences and humanities. For Hughes and Lafortune, art practices use interdisciplinary references in open, metaphoric ways and are not particularly attached to the idea of theoretical progress and currency. They explain, 'In art 'out-dated' theories may very well be resurrected, re-embodied for their metaphoric thrust, aesthetic qualities or for their implicit value systems.' In other words, interdisciplinarity in visual art is characterized by historical, material and theoretical fluidity and improvisation. Many ceramic installations possess those qualities. In Lafortune and Hughes' terms, they 'resurrect and re-embody' theory and practice, specifically from within art and craft, as well as from within related fields. And, they do this in highly metaphoric and open ways (2001: 18).

Mitchell Merback and Glen R. Brown, through their writings about exhibitions of ceramic-based installation provide a starting point for this discussion. In *Cooled Matter: Ceramic Sculpture in the Expanded Field* Merback discusses the exhibition *Cooled Matter: New Sculpture* which coincided with the 1999 National Conference on Education for the Ceramic Arts (2000: 6-15). One of the roles of this exhibition was to propose that installation be given a place in the dominant ceramic canon. Although Merback contextualizes the work in relation to American modernist sculpture, and this paper on the other hand explores how ceramic installation to some extent side steps around modernism and integrates a non-Western and pre-modern craft inheritance with postmodern cultural critiques, his discussion of how meaning and medium are thematically bound together in *Cooled Matter* introduces a point of self-definition and differentiation. Similarly, Glen R. Brown in his discussion of *Beyond the Physical: Substance, Space and Light*, an exhibition which coincided with the American National Conference on Education for the Ceramic Arts (NCECA 2001) and which was intended to further explore what installation practices are contributing to the field of ceramics, theorizes a predominant relationship between medium and content. For example, he identifies the subject of memory as a recurring theme in this exhibition and suggests that the craft tradition, in which meaning is contingent on associations with tradition and the object's place and relationships in space and time, embeds the act of remembering into contemporary ceramics (2002).

In Merback's analysis of the work in *Cooled Matter*, the use of clay is also linked to an exploration of temporality. This has been one of the central investigations and strategies of installation art works for several decades. Many installations have used natural processes and organic materials to draw attention to the passage of time. The subject has gone hand in hand with the artist's abandonment of control through a submission to natural and organic processes. Merback suggests ceramic artists have a significant affiliation for and understanding of temporality as it is related to art process. In his opinion, ceramic artists have always been highly conscious of materials 'that change with time, conform to the shape of their container, respond synergistically to human action, or that encourage metaphorical associations with earth and landscape' (2000: 9). Merback discusses how Walter McConnell and Sadashi Inuzuka make use of clay 'as a material uniquely emblematic of natural processes' both for its associative meanings, and because the material will independently change over time (2000: 9).

McConnell's work *Flora and Fauna* (1999,) includes a plastic enclosure in which wet ornamental floral clay forms initiate cycles of evaporation and condensation that are indexed on the surface of the plastic. In this work and in related works such as *Fecundity in Absence* (1995) and *10,000 Lakes* (1993), McConnell uses the physical and aesthetic properties of clay to comment on contemporary relationships between the imaginary, culture and the 'natural world'.

In contrast, Inuzuka, while similarly revealing though the action of time the physical properties of clay, employs the aesthetic properties of the material to speak about an absence rather than an over-determination of human presence. The avant-garde Japanese movement Mona-ha of the late 60's and 70's is often identified as an influence on his work. The artists of Mona-ha, loosely translated as 'school of things,' used ordinary, unprocessed materials such as stone, earth and wood. The impermanent arrangement and revelation of the qualities of a material in relationship to a site is central to the meaning of Mona-ha work and the artists' role is to simply present the material as it exists in the world with minimal interference of human ego. Material and process as independent agents are integral to Inuzuka's works: *River* and *Same Family* (1999), *Exotic Species* (1998), *Deer Lake* (1996) and *The Nature of Things* (1995), which employ poured clay slip that dries and cracks over time in combination with more intentionally formed and arranged objects.

Other artists working in ceramic installation who integrate the material and processes of clay into the content of their work in combination with the use of additional associative meanings of the material include Japanese artist Satoru Hoshino and American Bill Gilbert. In works such as *Reincarnate/PreCopernican Mud II* (1998) and *Ancient Woodland and Fish of Galaxy* (1994) Hoshino states he uses clay as 'basic matter, or nature, rather than just an art or craft material' (Hoshino and Tani, 2000: 63). He describes his process, through which he piles and squeezes the wet material into geomorphic abstractions that heavily index the hand and body in both surface and form, as that of a joint production between the body of the clay and his own body. Gilbert on the other hand constructs adobe forms with material brought to the gallery from his own land in New Mexico as a way of referencing both ancient cultures and geography, and reflecting on human presence in space and time. Brown discusses how unfired clay in Gilbert's *The Kiss* (2001) is employed to represent a different process of indexing and memorialisation – that of time and the past traced on the earth over eons (2002: 3).

Merback proposes that bodily experience is another common denominator in the installations in *Cooled Matter* - bodily experience both as subject in many of the works and as a phenomenological effect of the installations. He notes that repetition and seriality, in works such as Inuzuka's, functions to engage the viewer's body in the space and shift the locus of meaning away from a precious and unique object. Similarly, Montreal artist and writer Steven Horne outlines a relationship between phenomenology and the repetition of minimalism in contemporary installations that are informed by craft practices but he emphasizes the importance of traditional processes as a third key element in such work. In his essay 'Embodying Subjectivity' from the anthology *Material Matters: The Art and Culture of Contemporary Textiles* he discusses work that 'brings the self back to the body' through the use of minimalist repetition, which he proposes directly inherited from craft traditions (1998: 3). He uses the example of Vancouver based Baco Ohama, who's works such as *In A Valley of Three Poems* (1993) and *More or Less a 1000 Cranes* (1993) inscribe personal memories in hand rolled ceramic coils through a highly labour intensive and ritualized activity. Hoshino's process can similarly be seen to be an embodying activity which ritually re-integrates the self, the body and the matter of the world.

Denise Pelletier's installation, coincidentally titled *One Thousand Cranes,* (2001) is a delicate wall mounted arrangement of tiny glossy white forms, the design of which is based on vessels used to feed invalids in the 19th century. Brown views this work as a memorial and discusses it in relation to his proposition that memory is an encompassing theme in ceramic installations (2002: 2). At the same time, the work possesses many qualities that Horne associates with the process of embodiment. Horne links 'labour-intensive, repetitive, materials based work processes' to a ritualized process of embodiment or, in other words, 'to the integration of self and body, which is achieved through the repetitive, reflective production of material objects' (1998: 36). Without contradicting Brown's analysis, Pelletier's undertaking can be seen to exemplify a process of integration of self and body, in this case, the ritual becoming a reparative memorialisation.

The works discussed above illustrate how repetition and seriality are employed in ceramic installations to reference and enact craft and ritual practices and implement phenomenological strategies. Additionally, for purposes related to narration and symbol, the traditional ceramic object, often a container in multiple, is frequently the subject of ceramic installation. While the material objects of a culture, particularly the ceramic vessel, are dense with associative and metaphorical meaning on their own, when presented in an installation the historical, social and political meanings of the presentation and display of such objects are revealed or amplified.

In Garry William's 1993 installation, *Gold Standard*, six replicas of gilded Wedgwood vases on pedestals stand behind Venetian blinds. On the floor are sixty Mexican olla vases holding grain plants. Play with conventions of the presentation and display of cultural objects is central to his comments on economy, class, craft and colonization. Similarly in *"Ouvre les guillemets..."* (1997), Jeannie Mah plays with the history and associative meanings of a specific ceramic container and its display or presentation. Her starting point is a Kamares cup form, and culture is an underlying subject throughout the piece. Ideas of travel, economy and identity are woven into the representation and display of various specific cups, imagined or real, in a structure informed by cinema and French grammar. My work also incorporates cultural associations of the vessel form. In *Giardino Segreto* (2002), porcelain wall mounted reproductions of Renaissance ornamental garden containers are used in combination with a slide projection of a brain scan over a reproduction of a map, (identified as an Early Cartographic Attempt to Locate Paradise) to explore the relationship of imagination and desire to ideas of utopia and dystopia.

Ann Ramsden's piece *Anastylosis: Inventory* (2002), consists of rows of metal storage shelves on which sit broken and reconstructed commercial tableware, and a 15 m (45 ft) mural documenting the shards as they are ordered before reconstruction. Ramsden purchased the ready-mades, broke them, carefully and aesthetically laid them out according to form and colour, documented the arrangement and then reconstructed the pieces. Addressing the conventions of pottery display, and ceramic archiving, and restoration, Ramdsen's breaking and fixing is a performative and ritualized process, and consequently can be seen to fit within Horne's analysis of reparative works that inherit or reference craft practices.

Many ceramic installations, while addressing the subjects discussed above (material and process, embodiment and ritual, and/or the ceramic object in multiple as subject), concurrently reference ceramic's relationship to interior and/or outdoor architecture. Some in particular bring to the foreground the material's historic relationship with architecture in order to address contemporary critical engagements with the space of the artwork and the viewer in the space. As ceramics has traditionally been used in architecture as decoration - tiles, fixtures, and ornamental vessels for example - and as the two fields resonate with utilitarian and formal parallels, (both play a functional role in everyday life and both integrate two and three dimensional form) it is not unexpected that this complex relationship is an element interlaced in a range of ways with other themes in ceramic-based installations.

For example, in *Somewhere between Denver and Naples*, (1988 and 1992) Betty Woodman uses an installation format to expand her exploration of the expressive play between ceramic surface and form to incorporate shapes and decorations inspired by both architecture and pottery. Ann Agee employs decorated ceramic architectural components in a different way. In *Lake Michigan Bathroom*, (1992) she creates an exquisite blue and white ceramic bathroom, with bidet, toilet, sink, and wall and floor tiles on which are painted images of sewage and water treatment, and establishes a dialogue about modern Western hygiene habits and our use of water resources. And from again another angle, Inuzuka and Gilbert use ceramic references to architecture in conjunction with the material and processes of clay to meditate on place, time and the meaning of human presence and human endeavour.

Alternately, Canadian Rory Macdonald's installations explore material and conceptual relationships between ceramics, the built environment and public space. *Ground Floors* (2001) probes the formal and material qualities of ceramic tile. In this site-specific work, installed in an institutional lobby, an elaborate curvilinear floor-based wooden construction supports tiles, which flow over and around parts of it. In *Mur Vernisse* and *French Faience* (2003), Macdonald inserted compositions made of fragments of cast ornamental forms into spaces in a deteriorating retaining wall running along a busy street in Vallauris France. In *Curb Works* (2003 – 2004), Macdonald casts cracks and holes in city curbs then 'patches' the fissures with ceramic forms hand painted in a traditional blue and white glaze. These projects, through material and gesture, propose a role for 'public craft' that offers both critique and reparation in response to otherwise abject civic space.

Works such as MacDonald's and Agee's collapse together often disparate practices such as design, public art, craft, and installation in ways that are dynamic and critically engaging. Similarly, works such as those by Williams and Ramsden, weave the historical and material postmodern and premodern associations of clay into the contemporary critical context of installation, making sophisticated conceptual contributions to both ceramics and contemporary installation art. Unravelling the theoretical ambiguities of the combination of ceramics - as rooted in medium-specific, preindustrial and craft traditions, and installation - as inherently postmodern and content based rather than material based, remains a challenge. Similarly, viewing ceramic installation as a differentiated practice with delineated parameters has limitations because it potentially diminishes the opportunities an ambiguous position presents for further expanded practices. Yet it is important to note that works such as those identified above, rather than simply and belatedly embracing a trend in contemporary art towards installation, employ the ceramic material - its utilitarian, industrial and architectural heritage - to bring specific and rich meanings to contemporary practices, invigorating and extending current ceramics discourse.

Note

1. British potters Julian Stair and Edmund de Waal note that although artists have traditionally contributed critical writings to the fine art canon, writing from the traditional craft areas by makers has been minimal and often dominated by a very small group of professional writers. They suggest craft theory is at a threshold of development but that ceramics, as a very complex practice, risks being addressed only by criticism that has yet to develop a significant breadth of understanding and propose we circumvent potential 'inaccuracies' (Stair) and 'second rate projection' (de Waal) by rigorously self-defining (1999: 14–18).

References

Brown, Glen R. (2002), 'Memory Serves: Time, Space and The Ceramic Installation', in *Critical Ceramics* June 25 2002.

de Waal, Edmund and Stair, Julian (1999), 'Rob Barnard interviews Julian Starr and Edmund de Waal' in *Ceramics: Art and Perception*, No. 38: 14–18.

Horne, Stephen (1998), 'Embodying Subjectivity', in Ingrid Bachmann and Ruth Scheuing (eds), *Material Matters: The Art and Culture of Contemporary Textiles*, Toronto: YYZ Books.

Hoshino, Satoru and Tani, Aratu (2000), 'PreCopernican Mud Reincarnate' in *Ceramics: Art and Perception*, No. 39: 62–66.

Hughes, Lynn and Lafortune, Marie-Josee (2001), in L. Hughes and M-J. Lafortune (eds), *Creative Con/fusions: Interdisciplinary Practices in Contemporary Art,* Montreal: Optica.

Merback, Mitchell (2000), 'Cooled Matter: Ceramic Sculpture in the Expanded Field' in *Ceramics: Art and Perception,* No. 39: 6–15.

Originally published in *Ceramics: Art and Perception* issue 65 2006.

Reproduced with the permission of *Ceramics: Art and Perception* and the author.

29
'MULTIPLICITY, AMBIVALENCE AND CERAMIC INSTALLATION ART'

Glen R. Brown

Plates extend across the floor in a lustrous, frangible carpet; cinerary urns line the wall in a solemn funereal frieze; empty bowls fall in melancholic disarray; austere bottles silently mill like throngs of somnambulists: in certain contemporary ceramics practice the familiar quality of multiplicity has assumed a disposition that is both novel enough and prevalent enough to warrant inquiry into its origins. No longer to be regarded as simply a consequence of efficiency in the production of utilitarian wares, ceramics multiplicity has served in an increasing number of instances to introduce a new kind of conceptual potential to the ceramic object. Multiplicity might even be said to have acquired an ostensibly symptomatic status in ceramics signification, seeming to indicate a particular ambivalence, an indeterminacy of which most recent work in ceramics is implicitly aware. In certain contexts multiplicity has functioned, whether inadvertently or through a more deliberate strategy, to heighten an unrest that has been brewing in western ceramics at least since the beginning of the last century. Although this agitation ripples through the heart of ceramics as a field its origins are in fact on the periphery, along a kind of seismic fault where two closely related yet manifestly distinct tectonic plates abrade their edges relentlessly against one another. Ceramics multiplicity—in its current, equivocal status as signifier—is born of this abrasion. Multiplicity has acquired its potentially ambiguous meaning within contemporary ceramics precisely because it has attained a privileged position within theories of contemporary art.

The friction between ceramics and art—the endless debate over the precise nature of the relationship between them—seems largely a consequence of perceived continuity in material terms but disjunction on the level of theory. The ceramics/art controversy is perpetual because the two fields that these terms designate appear obviously coterminous on one level—a primary, commonsensical level—but hopelessly estranged on the level on which they attempt self-definition, on which, in other words, they seek to theorize their particular being. The tendency to argue for the conflation of ceramics and art as categories is prompted by the rational observation that little formal distinction exists between a sculpture made of fired clay and one of stone, bronze, plastic, steel or any other substance in which an art object can be realized. Nor is a vessel manifestly different in its physical constitution from many objects that enjoy an unquestioned status as sculpture. Empiricism seems to supports the assertion that ceramics and art are in fact one and the same. On the other hand, few would suggest that theories of contemporary art and what little exists in the way of a codified theory of contemporary ceramics are particularly compatible. Although I will forgo for the present a discussion of what I take to be the key distinctions between these, I do want to forward the argument that contemporary art exists as a field because to some degree its self-definition—its particular mode of representing itself to itself—involves the deliberate externalization of the kind of theory that has provided ceramics with its particular sense of being.

Source: © Glen R. Brown/*Ceramics: Art and Perception.*

Contemporary art defines itself partly against ceramics, and ceramics, in turn, has sustained its sense of self partly by externalizing the central tenets of contemporary art.

On the surface of things, ceramics has much to gain—both in the hard terms of economics and in the more nebulous regions of self-esteem—by performing whatever actions are necessary to dismantle the complementary, mutually definitive relationship that exists between itself and contemporary art. Since the late 1950s there has been no shortage of optimism in some circles that if ceramists could only shake their perceived provincialism by apprising themselves of the latest developments in the art world and revising their practices to produce works of a conceptual nature comparable to that of contemporary painting, mixed-media sculpture, installations, performance or video then they too might earn more than a tenuous place in the art gallery and more than a tiny sliver of the lucrative art market. Were this revolution in theory and practice to occur on a sufficient scale, the debate over the relationship between ceramics and art would no longer seem relevant, and ceramists would enjoy a prestige and prosperity equivalent to that of their peers working in other art media. Finally, achieving the distinction that Marcel Duchamp glibly identified as the ultimate confirmation of an object as art, even contemporary ceramic vessels might be copiously reproduced in the textbooks of art history.

One cannot deny the seductiveness of the dream, although this very observation should give reason to reflect on why such an assimilation has yet to occur. It is widely assumed, and rightly so, that the art world has resisted ceramics' overtures for merger, although the motives frequently attributed to this resistance (such as jealous guarding against the financial perils of an art-market glut or anxieties about heightened competition for limited exhibition space or grant monies) are trivial in contrast with the central problem that contemporary art risks its very identity by too openly internalizing that which it has theoretically externalized—that which provides it negatively with a sense of identity, unity, even fundamental presence. It is, to be sure, a critical issue for the contemporary art world to maintain its sense of difference from the field of ceramics. Ironically, however, there is no question that resistance to the assimilation of ceramics to art has evolved equally as a phenomenon within the field of ceramics itself. Denigrated by some as a debilitating conservatism, a stubborn adherence to the archaic values of the 'anonymous craftsman,' the pronounced skepticism that ceramics as a field has demonstrated toward the idea of assimilation to art seems to me rather a measure of the degree to which ceramics recognizes the source of its very being in difference—the degree to which ceramics exists through a distancing from the theories and practices of contemporary art. The result of a pure assimilation would not, after all, be the ultimate legitimacy of the term 'ceramic art', but on the contrary the expunging of the term 'ceramic.'

As a field, ceramics is understandably conflicted, on the one hand acknowledging that its identity is contingent upon the refusal to become art, while on the other succumbing to pangs of inadequacy, the self-deprecatory effects of its art envy. Alternately construed, ceramics as a field wishes to become art but at the same time recognizes the self-destructive impulse within that wish and resists any specific measures that might go too far toward actualizing it. The most overt consequence of this clashing of drives has been an eruption of ambivalent gestures within ceramics, a profusion of signs that ceramics is struggling in fits and starts both toward and against the object of its desire. Perhaps nowhere are the symptoms of this internal conflict in greater evidence than in the strategic use of multiplicity to position the ceramic work in an ambiguous space between ceramics and art as fields. In certain contexts, ceramics multiplicity has become the signifier of the contradictory impulses that ceramics rarely acknowledges openly yet consistently allows to dominate its covert ruminations on the problematic nature of its being. In its role as a trace of this latent self-reflection, multiplicity has become arguably the most significant trait in contemporary ceramics. Through no other characteristic does ceramics yield as lucid a picture of the inner turmoil of its desires.

The ambivalence of multiplicity in contemporary ceramics is clearly contextual—which is to say that the quality of ambivalence is perceived under certain conditions of ceramics multiplicity and not others. In a utilitarian context, for example, multiplicity generally presents itself as a straightforward consequence of pragmatism. Ceramic multiples are more rapidly produced, more efficiently stacked and fired in kilns, and more easily transported than objects of varying dimensions, materials, and methods of construction. The most common techniques for producing ceramic multiples—throwing and molding—have been in consistent use since ancient times. The persistence of these modes of production, perpetuated by practical and utilitarian objectives, is in fact a principal reason that one acquiesces in the idea of a world ceramics tradition. To a certain degree ceramics as a field has employed its methods of multiple production as European painting once utilized classical form to imply the essential and inalterable nature of its being as a discipline. Within ceramics, the quality of multiplicity has served as a perpetual point of contact between past and present, an ostensible confirmation of the temporal unity of ceramics as a field. Multiplicity is a mainstay of the being of contemporary ceramics, an indispensable signifier of consistency that sustains the impression of a unified practice. Within ceramics, it is on the order of the absolute.

Within the contemporary art world, on the other hand, the quality of multiplicity has since the late 1960s been tendentiously employed in the deconstruction of absolutes, the systematic dismantling of conceptions of unity that previously dominated both classical and late-Modern discourse on art. Multiplicity within contemporary art is linked to a repudiation of the absolute nature of representation and to the displacement of the concept of unified systems of thought with a model based on the endless and indeterminate play of signifiers—a perpetual deferral of meaning. Multiplicity within contemporary art confirms the eclipse of the absolute by an infinite indeterminacy. This indeterminacy evades the paradoxical situation of becoming itself an absolute, an essential characteristic of contemporary art, by recognizing that indeterminacy is not an autonomous state but rather is always contingent upon its difference from the absolute. The absolute is not denied as a concept by contemporary art so much as it is banished, externalized to a position beyond the pale. To the degree that ceramics internalizes the absolute, it confirms its distinction from contemporary art—recognizes a boundary across which the semiotic potential of qualities such as multiplicity cannot be transferred intact. By employing multiplicity to sustain the sense of its own unity as a field, ceramics implicity concedes its separateness from any context in which multiplicity signifies only indeterminacy.

Given the current state of ceramics' contradictory desires towards contemporary art—the conflicting impulses to surrender unconditionally to it and to preserve at all costs an identity separate from it—qualities such as multiplicity have acquired apparent symptomatic status within ceramics as a field. Such qualities can suggest, under certain conditions, the incognizant symbolism of a profound but latent turmoil (although to attribute this symbolism to something on the order of a ceramics unconscious would probably be going too far). There is, in fact, reason enough to assume that in most instances the use of ceramics multiplicity to reflect upon conflicted desire in the field is a calculated gesture that only plays on the sense of an unconscious symbolism. The conditions under which the ambivalence of multiplicity emerges in ceramics are too specific. Exploiting them requires not only a knowledge of the forms and theories central to contemporary art but also of their distinctions from those of contemporary ceramics. The ambivalence of ceramics multiplicity is achieved when one is to some degree conscious of these distinctions yet—whether with naive optimism or with a cooler calculation—seeks to unite forms that carry a certain definitive status within their respective fields of ceramics and art. Ambivalence is the invariable result when the central, even archetypal, ceramic form of the vessel is integrated into the space of the emblematic vehicle of contemporary art, the installation. The result is a hyper-hybrid form that has been rightly called 'ceramic installation art,' a term that acknowledges the uneasy, contrived connection between ceramics and art through the intermediary of a controlled space.

The use of the vessel is key to 'ceramic installation art,' since without it—or an analogous signifier of the essentialism and traditionalism dominating ceramics theory—the word 'ceramic' is expendable to the term, the word art becomes superfluous, and the word 'installation' alone suffices. Contemporary art does not concern itself with the physical nature of media but rather with how those media are dispersed. Clay may be utilized as readily as any other material without compromising the installation's semiotic potential, and hence its identity as a mode of art. The qualifier 'ceramic' only becomes necessary as an appendage to the term 'installation' when clay is confined to an iconic state, when it is made to carry the ideology of the field of ceramics into the realm of contemporary art. Such compromise occurs when vessels, quintessential utilitarian ceramic multiples, are dispersed in space not as a consequence of their use—not, for example, as when bowls, pitchers, or mugs are set on a table during a meal—but rather for the express purpose of employing multiplicity itself as a signifier. Multiplicity remains a trait of ceramics when it is linked to the traditional concern for utility embodied in production vessels. However, when these same vessels are implicity removed from the context of utility—when the potential for their use is suspended—their multiplicity may become significant not as a material but rather as a conceptual trait, a particular kind of conceptual trait that is central to contemporary art. Hence, the ambivalence of ceramic installation art.

While examples of ceramic installation art are now abundant and variable, it may be observed that in all cases a particular condition of their being—of their being qua ceramic installation art—is their ambiguous situation along the boundary between the fields of ceramics and contemporary art. The multiplicity of utilitarian vessels is conventional within ceramics; and the use of clay but avoidance of forms exclusive to the ceramics tradition—as in Antony Gormley's Field for the British Isles, Sadashi Inuzuka's poured-slip installations, or Walter McConnell's raw clay terrariums—poses no unique problems within art discourse. However, introduction of the self-consciously utilitarian multiple vessel to the context of the installation implies a tentative effort to bridge the boundary between ceramics and contemporary art, an effort that cannot be fully acceptable to either—that must, in fact, engender a certain skepticism precisely because it implies that such bridging is possible. The first imperative of systems—whether biological, political, economic, or aesthetic—is self-preservation, and any action that threatens the terms of self-definition is a potential source of crisis. As separate domains, both art and ceramics have a vested interest in quelling the suggestion that their respective signifiers can travel from one field to another without significant reconstitution.

From the perspective of contemporary art there is little question that ceramic installation art—as a marriage of the quintessential vessel and the installation format—runs the risk of appearing naive or opportunistic. It seems to mimic art practices without acknowledging the conceptual basis of those practices. It does not sufficiently challenge objectivity, despite its dispersal of objects in space. It does not openly reject conceptual unities such as historical continuity or the universality of utility. It is not a passage in deconstruction, a disorienting mode of emphasizing the contextuality of meanings, but rather appears to emphasize those meanings engrained by tradition. In short, it seems an ingenuous distortion of the installation as a contemporary art form. Within the field of ceramics, on the other hand, ceramic installation art has a very different significance and is anything but naive. It recognizes the impossibility of opening a true bridge between ceramics and art, and at the same time acknowledges the deep desire for such a bridge. What appears from the perspective of contemporary art to be naivete is within the field of contemporary ceramics an expression of the kind of conflict between desire for inclusion and fear of identity loss that plagues the members of any group that perceives itself as marginalized by a more powerful, prestigious and prosperous other. The ambivalence of ceramic installation art makes it the premiere emblem of the troubled conscience of contemporary ceramics, torn between the impulse to surrender itself unconditionally to the practices of contemporary art and the recognition that doing so would be equivalent to expressing disdain for its own tradition, the beliefs and practices that have given ceramics its sense of identity in the first place.

Originally published in *Ceramics: Art and Perception* 54 (Dec. 2003): pp. 3–8.

Reproduced with permission from *Ceramics: Art and Perception* and the author.

SECTION 2.5
THEORETICAL PERSPECTIVES

Introductory summary

Art theory tends to focus on what art might be and how we perceive it, as opposed to issues such as the biography of the artist or the technical processes used to create the work. Art theory is often developed by art critics as opposed to the artists themselves to form 'art criticism'. This forms what might be thought of as an organized system for understanding art and making judgements about an artworks success. This section on theoretical perspectives gives examples of how both writers and makers have attempted to create theories for ceramics or link ceramics to broader art theories. This is perhaps one of the key areas of tension in ceramics as it is the debate around 'art theory', often known as the 'art craft debate' that has dominated much writing around ceramics in recent years. The key issues here are if ceramics can be seen as art (or is it craft) and how can ceramics be written about in similar ways to Fine Art to develop the medium as an art form in the future?

To open this section, Bruce Metcalf's text focuses on perhaps the most famous artwork (and piece of ceramic) of the twentieth century, Marcel Duchamp's 'Fountain'. This 'readymade' consists of a factory made ceramic urinal, which Duchamp signed, thus designating the piece 'an artwork'. Metcalf argues that this highly influential work presents a 'problem' for the crafts as it led to conceptual art and the idea that art can be anything. Metcalf goes on to propose that the same is not true of craft – and in the light of this he offers a set of lucid definitions for craft. This text introduces the 'art/craft debate' in which mainly the craft, as opposed to art world, has argued for equality between craft and Fine Art. This sets a useful context for other texts in this Reader, which consider this issue. In reference to this text, Metcalf has added an updated addendum specifically for this Reader that further elucidates upon some of the points put forward in the original and updates his thinking on these issues.

Glenn Adamson asks what the modern pot looks like. In order to unpick this question, he goes on to consider the writing of two key thinkers on ceramics, Garth Clark and Philip Rawson (both featured in this book – Clark later in this section). This text centres on Clark and Rawson's formalist considerations of ceramics. Formalism in art theory argues that the formal aspects of an artwork, such as form, shape, silhouette, colour, line and rhythm, take precedence over content when judging the artwork. This text also references the influential American art critic Clement Greenberg who in the 1950s and 1960s was a strong advocate for the formal qualities of abstract expressionist painting. The connections made by Rawson to drawing and ceramics are also considered. In summary, this text offers an introduction to the thinking of two writers who have helped form a foundation for critical thinking about ceramics that is still reaching maturity.

In the Fourth Annual Dorothy Wilson Perkins Lecture at the Schein-Joseph International Museum of Ceramic Art at Alfred University, Paul Greenhalgh begins with some polemic statements from Oscar Wilde on modern life and decorative art. Greenhalgh then proposes his own similar statements on ceramics and their history and goes on to offer sixteen factors 'which contribute to the visual condition of any ceramic object'. These could form a useful set of questions that might be applied to creative objects in order to understand them more fully. He goes on to argue for the need to more rigorously analyse ceramic in order to construct a historiography, that is, the history of the history of ceramics.

The two following texts give perspectives from makers. Edmund de Waal argues that there is a tendency for ceramic makers to remain silent on the meanings of their work and that this is linked to an idea that certain kinds of ceramics, especially Studio pottery, represents an 'authenticity'. De Waal believes that this 'reverential silence' is likely to limit the understanding of objects and he concludes by urging makers to write more about their work.

Paul Mathieu's text 'Object theory' argues for greater consideration of 'objects' alongside 'images' in the art world. This text gives a useful perspective on the art/craft debate and readers might want to consider this in relation to Metcalf's 'The Pissoir Problem'. Mathieu's ideas on objects, containers, and decoration are also interesting to consider in relation to a period in ceramics when the 'Leach style' of thrown brown pottery was overtaken by what Peter Dormer termed 'The New Ceramics'. Here more diverse forms and exuberant decoration came to the fore while still maintaining the vessel as a framework.

In the final text in this section, Garth Clark considers the lowly position of ceramics in the mainstream Fine Art world in the twentieth century. To do this, he creates a list of what he considers to be the top five avant-garde works in ceramics in the first half of the century. He rules out some strong contenders: Tullio d'Albisola, Lucio Fontana, William Staite Murray and Sam Haile. His top five are Kazimir Malevich, Meret Oppenheim, George E. Ohr, Antonio Gaudí, and of course Marcel Duchamp. Only one of these is a ceramist – Ohr. From this list, Clark gives five lessons that the world of ceramics might consider and gives a call to arms for ceramics to better argue its case to be part of the canon of mainstream art. This text offers a position that students, makers, curators and critics could use to locate themselves with or against.

Livingstone and Petrie

30
RECONSIDERING "THE PISSOIR PROBLEM"

Bruce Metcalf

It has been sixteen years since I wrote "The Pissoir Problem." I would not write it today. Why? Because conceptual craft has emerged as a persuasive practice, fulfilling the twin demands of skilled work and interesting concepts. In 1999, I was not sure such a thing was possible. Now I am.

If the essay has any relevance, it outlines the difficult question of which comes first: craft or concept? Young makers avoid this question by giving both an equal status. Or, perhaps more accurately, they regard craft as a convenience, something that can, in fact, be disposed of – or added to – at will. Thus, for instance, we find an ongoing interest in video installations that include crafted objects as a necessary part of the concept.

Young makers are familiar with the conceptual turn, and they can deploy ideas with great ease. They have shown that craft and idea can coexist quite comfortably. My warnings about the difficulty of combining craft with the rigors of concept were misplaced. I was wrong.

I would also change my definition of craft. In 1999, I thought that a piece of craft must necessarily be made largely by hand. This is no longer true. Many craftspeople now produce objects designed on computers and produced by one of the many varieties of 3-D printers. Such objects are craft because they work within the confines of tradition craft genres like jewelry, or they are made in traditional craft materials like clay or glass. The hand is no longer necessary to craft.

That said, I remain committed to the idea that craft and art are not the same thing. This condition has not changed at all. I now talk about the center of craft, and its periphery. There are certain kinds of objects that trade in all or most of the characteristics of craft that I outlined in this article. Many of them do not engage in the discourse of art in any meaningful way. Lacking this discursive nature, I would say definitively that such objects are not art. They are craft. In saying this, I must emphasize that I do not establish a hierarchy. I see no reason to think that art is better than craft. A really good clay pot is still a wonder to me, and I think it is a very high accomplishment. The fact that it might not be art does not diminish its greatness.

So I invite the reader to examine "The Pissoir Problem" at a certain critical distance. Be sceptical. I am.

July 20, 2015

The pissoir problem

Here's my nominee for the most influential piece of art of the twentieth century: a urinal. Not just any urinal, of course, but the one Marcel Duchamp signed "R. Mutt" and called "Fountain". It's an artworld icon: it anticipated the genre now called Conceptual Art by about fifty years. And it poses a nasty problem for craft.

Source: © Bruce Metcalf.

Its history is well known: the story began when Duchamp bought a bicycle wheel and stuck it on a stool in 1913. At the time he made no special claim; he simply spun the wheel occasionally as the thing sat in his Paris studio. Next year, he bought a bottle rack. In 1916, after Duchamp moved to New York City, he wrote to his sister Suzanne to ask her to sign his name on the bottle rack, assigning it the status of "readymade" sculpture. All the while, this activity remained private, unannounced and unpublicized.

Meanwhile, in New York Duchamp and a number of other artists and aficionados founded the Society of Independent Artists, which was intended to be an exhibition society similar to the Parisian *Salon des Indépendants*. The first exhibit was scheduled to open April 10, 1917. Anyone who paid $6 could exhibit two works. Even though Duchamp was a Director of the Society, he apparently didn't like the organization, and decided to arrange a provocation. So he went to the J.L. Mott Ironworks in Brooklyn, bought an ordinary urinal, and submitted it for exhibition. (The urinal was a "flat-backed Bedfordshire", reputed to be smelly and hard to clean.) Predictably, other members of the Society found "Fountain" to be "immoral, vulgar, and simply a piece of plumbing", and refused to exhibit it. Duchamp and his friend Walter Arensberg promptly resigned from the Society. Beatrice Wood was apparently part of the enterprise, for she publicized the controversy in the second issue of Duchamp's journal, The *Blind Man*. Meanwhile, the urinal was misplaced, found behind a partition, moved to Alfred Stieglitz's 291 gallery, photographed, purchased by Arensberg, and eventually lost.[1]

And so a revolution began as a prank. It's not clear that Duchamp was entirely serious when he decided that he could assign the status of completed artwork to an ordinary object. And yet, in retrospect, this humble pissoir embodies several ideas that constitute a paradigm for contemporary art. Most notably, it inverted all the received rules of art making. Where high art was supposed to be ennobling, "Fountain" was strictly low-brow and crudely scatological; where art was supposed to be the result of much training and work, "Fountain" required no expertise; where the experience of art was supposed to be uplifting and pleasurable, "Fountain" presented a conundrum: how the hell could this thing be art? None of the conventional standards of artistic quality applied to Duchamp's urinal: it's one of the first and still probably the best example of anti-art. The idea that advanced art must be disruptive has stayed with us ever since.

Furthermore, "Fountain" didn't require fabrication, it required thought. Whatever makes the urinal into art resides not in the object itself, but in what Duchamp is presumed to have thought about it. (And, of course, what has been written about it ever since.) There's no painting here, no casting, no finishing, no messy and laborious craft. As Beatrice Wood wrote, "Whether Mr. Mutt with his own hands made the *Fountain* or not has no importance. He CHOSE it. He took an ordinary article of life, placed it so that its useful significance disappeared under the new title and point of view -created a new thought for that object."[2] In a single stroke, Duchamp elevated thinking to the essential ingredient of art, and simultaneously delegated the whole business of making to relative insignificance.

In fact, the object itself isn't really necessary. "Fountain" is long lost; a grainy photograph taken by Stieglitz has been quite sufficient to change the course of art history. Surely, every art student in the nation knows about the urinal. Duchamp himself authorized a series of signed reproductions in 1964, which have migrated to museums worldwide. In 1973, Elaine Sturtevant created a substitute original. Since then, Sherrie Levine, Mike Bidlo, Richard Prince, Jeff Koons, Tom Sachs, and many other artists have made similar homages. In one of those great ironies of history, Duchamp's throw-away gesture now stands at the center of modern art: analyzed, institutionalized, and glorified. For better or worse, the pissoir is legendary. "Fountain" became an icon because it summarizes the disruptive tendency of 20th century art, and because it so neatly foreshadows what is now known as Conceptual Art.

Marcel's pissoir casts a long shadow. To any informed observer of the art world, it's clear that Conceptual Art influences all aspects of current art practice, from performance art to contemporary craft. Through the

1980's and 1990's, Neo-Expressionism, Neo-Geo, Primary Image, Chaos theory and Abject Art all came and went. It seems the only authoritative approach left standing is Conceptual Art, an impression strongly reinforced by magazines like *Contemporary Visual Arts* and by the curatorial vision of every Whitney Biennial in the past decade. Of course, the art schools have played along. Students across the country are now expected to explain and justify their ideas, and the graduate art programs most closely associated with rigorous theory are generally the most prestigious.[3] And yet, for all its influence, it's not terribly clear what conceptual art actually is.

The artist-philosopher Adrian Piper has offered a comprehensive and persuasive definition. Writing about artist Ian Burn, Piper suggests that Conceptual art need not have a particular style, and stresses that it doesn't always replace the art object with written or spoken language. Instead, she examines Sol Lewitt's proposition that "... the idea or concept is more important than the object in which it's realized." Piper says that Lewitt was taking

> "... a Platonic view, that the concept of a particular work - any work, be it sculpture, drawing, text, videotape, whatever you like - is a kind of perfect form to which the realization, the actual work itself, is just an imperfect approximation. Just as Plato distinguished between sensory reality and the world of pure forms, similarly Sol, I think, meant to distinguish an actual art object as a sort of crude sensory approximation of an idea, a concept, that can exist only in the intellect; and then to say that it's the idea, the pure concept of the object, that's important.[4]"

Piper notes how liberating this notion of Conceptual art was because it opened all types of intellectual inquiry to artists: social sciences, natural sciences, humanities, whatever. Furthermore, any medium was permissible, for ideas can be made manifest in any material imaginable. But Piper is adamant that Conceptual art still demands a hierarchy. As she puts it, " I propose we think of Conceptual art ... as being art that subordinates its medium, whatever its medium, to intellectually interesting ideas."[5]

The implications of Piper's formulation are profound. Obviously, she does not exclude the possibility of Conceptual craft. But, at the same time, she says that the idea must be more important than any other aspect of the artwork. Material, technique, formal qualities, function, or any other aspect of artwork that cannot be construed as an idea must be less important. According to Piper, if the idea is primary, the medium is subordinated. And the secondary status of medium is important, because the idea must necessarily dictate the medium: the artist should choose whatever material or form that best expresses or communicates the idea. Thus, mediums should change to accommodate different ideas. If the idea takes primary importance, *the medium must be disposable*. Piper's Conceptual artist can not be loyal to her medium: she will unhesitatingly sacrifice the medium if her idea demands it. In effect, Piper has proposed a doctrine of disposable medium, which I will return to later.

Piper's definition reinforces Arthur Danto's thesis, which he first advanced in "The Transfiguration of the Commonplace" (1981) and has refined ever since. According to Danto, art is embodied meaning.[6] Danto arrived at his formulation after seeing Andy Warhol's "Brillo Box" in 1964. ("Fountain" would have sufficed, but it's possible that in 1964 Danto had never heard of it.) He was fascinated by the apparent lack of distinction between a real Brillo box and Warhol's sculpture. Presumably, this lack of visible difference threw all previous art theories out of whack, because all those theories relied upon the visual phenomena particular to painting and sculpture, to draw the line between art and the rest of reality. So, what made "Brillo Box" into art? According to Danto, it was because Warhol's box embodied a specific set of meanings, while the supermarket box did not. These meanings would be legible inside a community of like-minded individuals, which Danto called the "art world".

If Danto's thesis is accepted, the exact form of art can no longer be qualified in advance. As Danto says, "Art can be anything at all."[7] In any realistic assessment of art of the last forty years, it's pretty clear that the art world acts as if Danto's thesis is true. Art can be a urinal; art can look like a Brillo box; art can consist of walking around a gallery with your face painted gold, explaining paintings to a dead rabbit. This is the reality of the art world, and it's tough to argue against reality. The medium, the form, the duration of art: all is now mutable and open for exploration. The only remaining qualification is that art should embody meaning.

Danto's thesis dovetails nicely with Piper's definition: art is embodied meaning; conceptual art subordinates its medium to ideas. One could even stretch Danto's thesis a little, and suggest that all interesting art IS conceptual art. (In fact, Danto used to suggest that art should transform itself into pure philosophy, but he has lately disavowed that notion.)

I would argue that Art-with-a-capital-A, art that makes it into art magazines and big art museums, art that smells of the present instead of the past – all this art is synonymous with Conceptual art. Given the infinite mutability of art today, how can it be otherwise? In order to interpret this vast range of enterprises, the only net that can encompass everything is theory, idea, embodied meaning. Otherwise, how do you tell Duchamp's pissoir from those things in the men's room? It's the concept, and the concept alone, that draws the distinction. After all, you wouldn't want to pee into an icon of modern art, would you?

***

For the past 140 years, craftspeople and their supporters have agitated for equality between craft and art. This has been called the "art/craft debate". In the craft world (a term that I use as an exact parallel to Danto's "art world"), most people seem to have assumed that craft can be art, and that no further discussion is needed. Everybody says the art-craft debate is tiresome and meaningless. In Universities and art schools, one can study "fiber arts" and "metal arts". Publishers certify the equivalence of craft and art by titling books about crafts The *Art of Craft* , *Art that Works*, or *American Art Jewelry Today*. I recall an entire conference devoted to the presumption that craft had effectively become art: it was called "Crossover", which called up images of pottery and furniture and jewelry jumping across some line in the sand, finally becoming real art. The battle is won, the fuss is over, and craftspeople can sleep easily at night, knowing they have breached the walls of the golden gated city.

And yet, I'm not so sure. I maintain that craft and art are two different things, and that they are not fully commensurate. By this, I mean that craft and art are two largely different practices, with largely different boundaries, and each with a different "... yardstick of critical assessment in social and artistic spaces".[8] My argument revolves around two questions implicitly posed by Danto and Piper. First, can craft be anything at all? Secondly, can craft truly subordinate its medium to intellectually interesting ideas? In other words, how does craft measure up to Duchamp's urinal?

***

There are several meanings for the word "craft" in the modern era. One sense of the word points to skillful labor of any kind, as in the skill of playing a violin or the craft of welding. Craft also can suggest a class of objects, and is used this way in *American Craft Museum* or *British Craft Council*. I use the word in this second sense. However, it's not a precise category.

Craft is very fuzzy around the edges: there's no clear line between craft and not-craft. I think craft-as-a-class-of-objects must be seem in terms of degree, rather than a matter of black and white. First of all, craft must be an object, a real thing of weight and substance. Secondly, these objects must necessarily be made largely by hand. While observers in the twentieth century accept the use of machines in craft production (such as table saws or power rolling mills), objects made substantially by machines (like computers) or on assembly lines (like athletic shoes) do not usually qualify as craft. Craft can also be identified by an accumulation of four other factors. These are: 1. the use of traditional craft mediums (like clay, glass, or fiber); 2. the use of traditional hand technologies associated with such mediums (like throwing clay, blowing glass, or raising metal); 3. the use of traditional craft functions (like jewelry, pottery, or furniture); and 4. reference to the history of craft objects themselves (like Sung Dynasty ceramic vases, or Coptic textiles). This list of four factors serves as a checklist for degrees of "craftness": the more an object incorporates of the list, the more craft (as-class-of-object) it is.

(An aside: I should point out that function is not on my list. For any number of reasons, observers have seen craft's usefulness as central to its definition.[9] And yet, even a cursory study of historical craft objects shows that function was never a central defining characteristic: think of textiles woven only for display; of massive silver centerpieces made only to be seen; or of whimsies created by craftspeople after the workday was through, like the blown glass bells made in the Ohio valley glass factories. And, of course, uselessness is a signature of most contemporary craft that aspires to the status of art.)

Discerning shades of craftness is accurate and useful. After all, one of the central enterprises in contemporary craft has been expanding the traditional boundaries. Craftspeople have employed new materials like plastics and synthetic fibers, along with non-traditional technologies like electroforming and computer-aided machining. Similarly, many craftspeople make sculptures (although this is not new at all), and many craft objects do not refer to historical material. The resulting objects have been widely understood to be craft, as in Stanley Lechtzin's acrylic and copper electroform torques, or Lenore Tawney's "Cloud Series" of architectural installations. At the same time, some craftspeople have remained committed to very traditional materials, techniques, and usages. Pure pottery remains a vigorous part of modern ceramics, just as Windsor chair-makers and Harris tweed weavers continue to thrive.

However, my formula of two basic criteria + four additional factors suggests an important conclusion: craft has limits. Some things just aren't craft.

For instance, Clark and Hughto show a photograph in their book, *A Century of Ceramics in the United States 1878-1978*.[10] It's Jim Merlchert's claywork, called "Changes", in which the participants dunked their heads in clay slip, and then were videotaped while the slip dried at different rates. The piece typified many of the concerns of avant-garde artists at the time: making artwork that was ephemeral and thus difficult to commodify; using the body of the artist as raw material; or incorporating duration and transience as necessary parts of the work. "Changes" is a performance, with clear aspirations to be understood as high art. The only possible connection to craft is the use of slip, but it's a tenuous connection indeed. Otherwise, hand fabrication is not employed. Nor are any traditional ways of manipulating clay, nor is there any reference to ceramic history. It's not even an object. In the end, I fail to see how this performance is craft in any meaningful way. It might be art, but it's not craft.

A lot of other things aren't craft either, from Nike® athletic shoes to exercising a dog. Or, from painting on canvas to Bill Viola's installations. My point is this: in response to Danto's implicit question "Can craft be anything at all?", the answer is no. Craft cannot fully partake of contemporary art's infinite expansion into all aspects of life. While Duchamp and his followers could point to absolutely anything and declare it to be a Readymade work of art, the same maneuver cannot be accomplished in craft. Craft is a limited field. Crafts have to be *made*, crafts have to be *objects*, and crafts usually must have some connection to traditional materials, techniques, and histories. Being necessarily limited, craft is thus not fully commensurable with art. It is philosophically different. Like it or not, craft and art are somewhat different things.

The question implicitly posed by Piper's definition of conceptual art offers a further illumination. If art (specifically conceptual art) and craft were truly interchangeable, craft could "subordinate its medium, whatever its medium, to intellectually interesting ideas." Craft practitioners would then serve one and only one master: the idea. However, it's my contention that the primary cause in craft practice is the labor, not the idea.

I come to this conclusion from extended observation of craft education and culture. It's no secret that the majority of present-day craft practitioners were first exposed to their craft in an educational institution. As a teacher for the past 22 years, I have watched hundreds of perfectly ordinary students walk into teaching studios. Some students - not all - awaken. They discover something that changes their lives, and a few go on to make a lifelong commitment to their chosen discipline. I am absolutely convinced that this awakening is to the working of a material, and not to "intellectually interesting ideas". Students respond first and foremost to the material in their hands.

Most crafts teachers realize that students intuitively gravitate to particular a studio: there are clay people, fiber people, metals people, glass people. Some students recognize an affinity to a one material, and these are the ones who major in the subject. I suspect that this process of discovery is closely linked to "bodily - kinesthetic intelligence", the aspect of mind that controls both fine and gross motor skills.[11] What we used to call talent may be a genetic predisposition to respond to certain basic materials. This predisposition appears both as a fascination with, and a gift for working in a particular material. I think every jeweler will understand precisely what I mean here, for they have experienced the same thrill of recognition themselves. While my proposition may seem far-fetched at first, consider that everyone assumes that both Einstein and Stravinski were gifted. Only a few individuals will show a talent for mathematics, or for music. Similarly, only a few will show a genuine aptitude for any craft medium, and these talents are most likely genetically endowed, not learned.

An awakening to the possibilities of working a particular material is only the beginning. In a sense, all mature craftspeople have served an apprenticeship: they spent years learning how to control their chosen medium. The learning process is slow, sometimes tedious, and often difficult. The individual who endures the apprenticeship used to be called a master, but I think Peter Dormer's idea of tacit knowledge is more useful.[12] Tacit knowledge comes only from practical, hands-on experience, and cannot be learned simply by reading or recitation. It takes a lot of practice to learn how to solder with confidence, how to blow a thin glass vessel, or how to cut a perfect dovetail. This knowledge resides in the person, and recent research suggests that it consists of permanently altered neural pathways. In effect, it's equivalent to the first definition of craft that I offered: skillful labor.

Tacit knowledge can have an emotional component. Skilled work brings its own pleasures, often experienced as contentment and an altered brain wave pattern.[13] More importantly, I think, is the fact that craftspeople often develop an intense loyalty to their chosen medium. Their identities are completely wrapped up in their work: Kurt Matzdorf is utterly dedicated to silversmithing; Jack Troy lives, eats and breathes pottery. It's difficult to describe the profound commitment that some men and women feel for their craft, but an extended conversation with any one of them will reveal how deeply loyal they are. It's as if the difficulty of mastering the craft is rewarded by internalization: not just the skill, but also a sense of attachment, historical place, and an urge to pass the knowledge along to younger generations. In an era when we expect youths to be alienated and adults to despise their jobs, the voluntary loyalty devoted to craft is quite remarkable.

Most of those men and women who make jewelry or weaving or ceramics into their life's work, never give it up. I take this extraordinary dedication as evidence that the craft - the tacit knowledge and the emotional attachment to it - precedes all other considerations for the craftsperson. To paraphrase Adrian Piper, I propose we think of the craftsperson as being a maker of objects who will not subordinate his or her medium, whatever the medium, to intellectually interesting ideas. I believe that loyalty to medium is a basic characteristic of craft culture. And as such, loyalty to medium defines a fault line between art culture and craft culture. Recall Piper's implicit doctrine that medium must be disposable, and compare it with the loyalty of the craftsperson to medium. As concepts, they are mutually exclusive: one can subordinate medium to idea, or idea to medium, but not both.

I should make one point clear: this definition does not exclude craftspeople from engaging ideas. Far from it. But it does clarify an essential part of craft culture: many people won't give up the craft they have labored so long to acquire. Their emotional commitment wouldn't allow for it.

(As I write this, I can already hear the complaints, so I offer three clarifications. First, by drawing this distinction, I am not making a qualitative judgment: I adamantly do not think that being an artist is better than being a craftsperson. I am proposing a clear difference. Second, this proposal applies to mature practitioners, not to students who have not yet made a commitment to a life in craft. And third, a craftsperson's loyalty can extend beyond a specific medium, to include a sense of craftsmanship that can apply to more than one craft discipline.)

In contemporary crafts, the idea of making Art-with-a-capital-A is tremendously attractive. When I ask my undergraduate students what they are, every single one answers, "Artist." This is not surprising: they attend an art school; their teachers generally call themselves artists; and the idea of being an artist is far more prestigious and respectable than being a craftsperson. There are thousands who think that the only proper ambition for a craftsperson is to become an artist. So, everyone agrees. It's "art jewelry", "fiber art", "art furniture", and "art glass". The problem is, if craft is really art, it must be compared to all the art that's out there. Those people who claim to be making art/craft have a lot of explaining to do. Craft must be held up to twentieth century theory, because art is inescapably bound to its discourses. In the present environment, when art is almost synonymous with conceptual art, craft must stand next to Duchamp's pissoir, and answer for itself.

The answer says more about craft's difference than it's similarity. Craft can't be anything at all, and thus craft is not fully commensurable with the broadest conceptions of art. Furthermore, craft is permeated by the loyalty of its makers to material and process. In my opinion, any attempt to offer a persuasive argument for craft in the new millennium must take these two properties into account.

My argument depends on the assumption that there is no middle ground – that there is no intellectually rigorous artform that can also insist on loyalty to a medium. The case of painting is instructive. For the last 30 years, painting has been subject to intense scrutiny. Painters have been called upon to justify the continued use of a pre-industrial technology and, in some cases, a demanding skill. The question goes something like this: is painting a better medium for the communication of ideas than any other? I can think of no persuasive explanation that was advanced, and nobody has shown that applying paint by hand to a substrate is any more (or any less) suitable as an art medium. Generally, painting is now seen as one option among many. And the idea of loyalty to painting remains unexplained, even when it is raised. The upshot is that painting, in a delicious irony, has been demoted from its former status as "queen of the arts", and the discipline has become rather marginalized. (Almost like a craft!) Painting now seems to be perceived as a way to generate fantastic images, as in the weird women of Lisa Yuskavage, or a vehicle for fey gestures like Damien Hirst's spin paintings. In either case, commentary focuses on the concepts that are embodied in the images, not on the possibility that the paintings have any particular characteristic that could be manifested only by the process of painting. So, for the moment, the literature suggests that the artworld finds any middle ground highly suspect.

***

So, every craft practitioner faces a choice: What comes first? Does one follow the prescription of Adrian Piper, and put intellectually interesting ideas in first place? Or does one remain loyal to their chosen material and techniques? Which one is sacrificed?

I believe the majority of craft/art practitioners want to have it both ways. They want to appeal to the intellectual rigor of art discourse, but without having to submit to it themselves. The quandary posed by Adrian Piper remains unsolved: if you truly practice a Conceptual art - which is to say, any theoretically persuasive art in the present artworld environment - then you must answer the question, "Would you subordinate your medium to interesting ideas?" Avoiding the question makes the practitioner appear wishy-washy, wanting to have her cake and eat it too.

Anne Wilson presents a case study of a craftswoman who confronted Piper's question. Wilson came from a fiber arts background. She learned how to weave and dye and stitch, and she is an authority on ethnic clothing traditions. Her work made it to the cover of *American Craft*,[14] affirming her prominence in the craft world. But her interest in one material, hair, eventually led her to discard the techniques and formats typical of craft. Wilson's recent collaborative installation (with A. B. Forster), called "Told and Retold: an inquiry about hair", is not craft in any meaningful sense. Its form, execution, range of reference, and ambition clearly announce it as art. When presented with the choice between idea or medium, she gave up her loyalty to craft. I imagine that she would have no argument with Piper. She calls herself an artist,[15] and I'm convinced.

However, Piper's question can be answered another way: one can refuse to subordinate medium to idea. I believe this is the craftperson's choice, and it has its own integrity. One can assert one's loyalty to a medium, and proceed to adjust or modify ideas to fit the medium. Furthermore, such loyalty is both intellectually honest and usually visible in the work.

One of the many craftspeople who made this choice was the jeweler Richard Reinhardt. In a retrospective exhibition of his silver work,[16] I could easily detect his respect for his medium. His craftsmanship was superb, and his forms were developed directly from the process of fabricating them. Each piece would move with its wearer, but they were never intrusive on the body. Reinhardt's restless curiosity about form, reflectiveness, linkages, and motion was obvious. It was wonderful jewelry, even though Reinhardt wasn't terribly concerned that his jewelry be seen as Art. In the end, all of Reinhardt's work was emphatically craft, and none the worse for it.

Reinhardt tailored his ambitions to his medium. I don't think it's any insult to his memory to say that his jewelry cannot be compared at every level with art as Piper and Danto conceive it. While the jewelry clearly embodies Reinhardt's attitudes toward his craft, his clients, and his sense of responsibility as a citizen of the modern world, the objects cannot be seen as Conceptual art. They are not as scholarly as Piper might demand, nor do they trade in theory. To me, Reinhardt's jewelry was so much an object, and so clearly evident of his concern for his craft, that Piper's "pure concept of the object" had only a secondary value. Reinhardt illustrates the philosophical difference between craft and art. He was a craftsman, and a good one. Again, I was convinced.

But these days, everybody wants to be an artist. To the degree that craft intends to take a place alongside of art, craftspeople must assemble a cogent explanation of what craft is, and why. If craft and art are not fully commensurate, as I claim, then this explanation must focus on the differences between craft and art, not their similarities. Those similarities (formal qualities, theoretical stances, etc.) cannot explain why a craftsperson should choose to limit her creative project to a particular medium, nor do they explain the profound emotional bond that experienced practitioners feel for their work. Until these differences are explained, the legitimacy of craft will continue to be questioned. And once we understand exactly how craft and art are not fully commensurate, then we can make persuasive claims for the place and purpose of craft as a distinct creative enterprise.

Bruce Metcalf is a jeweler and occasional writer on craft. His next article for *Metalsmith* will propose a theory of craft.

Notes

1. This history was taken from three sources: Varendoe and Gopnik, *High & Low: Modern Art and Popular Culture*, Museum of Modern Art, 1990; Naumann with Venn, *Making Mischief: Dada Invades New York*, Whitney Museum of American Art, 1996; and Mink, *Marcel Duchamp 1887-1968: Art as Anti-Art*, Taschen, 1995.
2. *The Blind Man*, No. 2, May 1917.

3. Among them: UCLA in visual art, The School of the Art Institute of Chicago in fiber arts, and SUNY New Paltz and Cranbrook in jewelry/metals. For a sceptical view, see "How to Succeed in Art" by Deborah Soloman, in *The New York Times Magazine*, June 27, 1999.
4. Piper, Adrian, "Ian Burn's Conceptualism", *Art in America,* December, 1997, p. 74.
5. Ibid. p. 75.
6. For a brief summary of Danto's thesis, see his introduction to *Embodied Meanings: Critical Essays and Aesthetic Meditations*, Farrar Straus Giroux, 1994.
7. Witnessed by the author at a speech by Danto at the University of the Arts.
8. from an essay in which Danto raises the issue of commensurabilitry: "Quality and Inequality", in *Embodied Meanings*, page 340.
9. For a recent example, see Howard Risatti's essay "Metaphysical implications of function, material, and technique in craft" in *Skilled Work: American craft in the Renwick Gallery*, Smithsonian Institution, 1998.
10. Published by E.P. Dutton in 1979. The picture is on page 207, accompanying text on 198.
11. See Gardner, Howard, *Frames of Mind*, Basic Books, 1983. For a more detailed exploration of bodily-kinesthetic intelligence and its implications for craft theory, see the author's chapter "Craft and Art, Culture and Biology" in Dormer, Peter (editor), *The Culture of Craft*, Manchester University Press, 1997.
12. Dormer, "Craft and the Turing Test for practical thinking", Ibid. p. 137
13. See Csikszentmihalyi, Mihael, *Flow: The Psychology of Optimal Experience*, Harper, 1993. Among jewelers, Carrie Adell has been a strong advocate for the transformative power of absorbed work.
14. Spector, Buzz, "Anne Wilson: Urban Furs", *American Craft*, February/March 1988.
15. In conversation with the author, March 27, 1999.
16. "Richard Reinhardt: Full Circle", Rosenwald-Wolf Gallery, The University of the Arts, Philadelphia, March 20 - May 8, 1998.

Reproduced by permission of the author.

31
IMPLICATIONS: THE MODERN POT

Glenn Adamson

Quick: What does a modern pot look like? Perhaps nothing springs immediately to mind. Glass-walled buildings, cantilevered tubular-steel chairs, geometric paintings: these things we all recognize as emanations of the modern movement. But ceramics have never fit into the picture with quite the same ease, despite the fact that the medium is entirely compatible with certain modernist impulses. A potter can be as utopian as any architect – many have set up their kilns in hopes of making a better world, at least for themselves. Pots can be as functional as any Bauhaus furniture design. And they are inherently abstract, like a modern painting. Yet those who have attempted to outline the contours of the modern pot, makers and writers alike, have always faced certain obstacles. Any handmade object presents a degree of resistance to the frictionless mass production that dictates modern life. Antimodernity remains a central appeal of all the crafts, ceramics included. This quality of counterintuitiveness and contradiction is what makes the modern pot worth examining, but also what makes framing a modernist account of ceramics difficult. So it is no surprise that it took awhile.

As late as 1981, half a century after painterly abstraction and the International Style had arrived on the scene, Garth Clark was still trying to establish a critical vocabulary for ceramics. Moreover, he was almost alone in doing so. Clark's book *American Potters* (1981) – the most condensed of his early statements on modern aesthetics in the medium – is deceptively confident in its tone. But close reading suggests that he was playing defense. Like most who have focused on the medium since the collapse of the arts and crafts movement, Clark felt besieged by the art world's disdain for ceramics, as opposed to painting and sculpture. And in outlining his position, he felt obliged to rely on the language and ideas of those more critically established arenas of the visual arts.

After a few pages of historical exposition, Clark began the main substance of his argument with an anecdote. He described how he was won over from thick, mass-produced 'diner' mugs for his morning coffee, and instead learned the satisfactions of drinking from one of Betty Woodman's flaring, slightly wobbly teacups, which 'has too small a base and too wide a mouth, yet it 'functions' so well in an aesthetic sense that one is prepared to make the effort to overcome its shortcomings in terms of efficiency.' Having thus established himself as an imaginative rather than a doctrinaire modernist, he proceeded in the manner of a how-to author, discussing the various aspects of pottery one by one: function, silhouette, spatial composition, decoration. As Clark conceded, such an 'examination of the individual elements of the pottery aesthetic can become somewhat cold-blooded and didactic.'[1] Yet even today, the passion of the text still comes across loud and clear. His essay was a plea to be taken seriously, a manifesto – and it needed critical buttressing.

Clark therefore relied on two supporting characters in his exposition of the modern pot. The first was Clement Greenberg, who in the 1950s and 1960s had been the most powerful critic in the field of American painting and, to a lesser extent, sculpture. For Greenberg, what made an artwork 'successful' was its ability to embody the basic qualities of its own form – in the case of a painting, flatness, boundedness, and color – while

Source: © Glenn Adamson/The Museum of Fine Arts, Houston.

simultaneously transforming those same properties, allowing us to see their possibilities afresh. He and his disciples, such as Rosalind Krauss and Michael Fried, spent years working on the problems that arose from this 'formalist' logic. Their objective was to ground critical discourse in the properties of a given medium. This approach had its problems, however. For example, there seemed to be little besides Greenberg's critical say-so that could explain why an abstract painting by Jackson Pollock, with its assertion of its own flatness, should not be considered simply a pattern, like so much wallpaper. Greenberg tried to repress this conclusion through ingenious analysis, but the effort left its marks. In the case of Pollock, Greenberg argued that webs of interlaced drips created a field of visual instability, a purely 'optical' effect that transcended its physical reality. But as Elissa Auther and Caroline Jones have both argued, the 'decorative' was conversely stigmatized as a fallen state – something that happened to a painting when it 'failed'.[2] This assumption is typical of the unintended consequences of formalist logic; it inevitably led to exclusions and arbitrary value systems. When the artists of the 1970s, especially those associated with feminism, emphatically rejected Greenberg's aesthetic hierarchy, they embraced ornament as the most promising language of insurrection.

With all this in the air, Clark's triumphant introduction of Greenberg as a critical supporter, right at the end of *American Potters,* was something of a deus ex machina. Just two years previously, in 1979, he had had the ingenious notion of inviting the aging critic to the first of a series of symposia on ceramic art, held in the old pottery stronghold of Syracuse, New York. Greenberg's performance there must have astounded knowledgeable attendees. Not only did he decline to characterize ceramics as essentially decorative (as having failed in advance, as it were), he also dismissed any prejudice against clay as small minded. 'Are ceramists to bother about whether they are put down as potters or hailed as sculptors?' he asked. 'Achievement erases the difference between the utilitarian, the vessels, and fine art, sculpture.'[3] The unexpectedly broad-minded intervention from this irascible and intractable modernist allowed Clark to simultaneously exorcise the specter of pottery's inferiority and also authorize his own application of formalist method. Ceramics, he wrote in the final passage of *American Potters,* 'can and must be judged by the rigorous visual and aesthetic criteria relevant to this medium.'[4]

As useful as Greenberg's one-off gesture of support may have been, Clark was no Greenbergian; as would be true for any devotee of ceramics, his aesthetic purview was far wider. His formalism was more akin to that of George Kubler, the Yale professor of preColumbian art whose 1962 book *The Shape of Time* caught the imagination of many in the fine arts and the crafts alike. Kubler offered a complex, open-minded account of historical change that was nonetheless grounded in materiality. He characterized innovation as a matter of 'drift' within otherwise repetitive series, which might come about through the effect of particular tools, attempts to increase or decrease quality, or simply the accident of inexact copying. (This analysis was partly modeled on that of his teacher Henri Focillon.) Kubler made a stirring argument for his readers to attend to form, not just content: 'We are discovering little by little all over again that what a thing means is not more important than what it is.'[5] But how to apply this lesson to ceramics? Kubler himself had little to say on the subject.

That was where a second supporting character came in: Philip Rawson, a writer as ecumenical in his interests as Greenberg was focused. Rawson had a varied career, working in Britain as an artist, curator (at the Gulbenkian in Durham and the Ashmolean in Oxford), and teacher (at Goldsmith's and the Royal College of Art). He published books on subjects as diverse as Indian and Southeast Asian art, the history and practice of drawing, and artistic eroticism. But it was Rawson's 1971 book *Ceramics* that was important in this context. In a 2010 lecture, Clark recalled his discovery of the text as a revelation: 'In the 1970s I was searching for a deeper understanding of a pot's form magic. But I wanted to negotiate this in cleanly analytical terms. I was at gag point with the treacly, sentimental, overly subjective, belly-button gazing, warm and fuzzy, mud-as-spiritualism school of personal poetry that thrived then and to an extent still does today. ... I needed something harder, flintier, like striking bedrock with a pick.'[6]

Rawson provided this solid foundation. His approach was resolutely modernist, all austere line drawings and precise observation, and it traversed ceramic history with seeming ease. Just as Greenberg managed to compress the oeuvres of Édouard Manet, Paul Cézanne, Pablo Picasso, Piet Mondrian, and Jackson Pollock into a single modernist project, Rawson persuaded his reader that courtly Chinese, medieval European, folk American, and experimental modernist vessels were all in conversation with one another through a shared language of shape and volume. One illustration in *Ceramics* positioned seventy-five black silhouettes of pots in a diagram, organized according to 'morphological relationships reflecting patterns of thought.' The image irresistibly recalls the famous 1936 flowchart of modern art used by the Museum of Modern Art's founding director, Alfred Barr, as the frontispiece to his book Cubism and Abstract Art. Like Barr, Rawson was primarily interested in form rather than in the process of making. Though Rawson did give some information about technique in *Ceramics,* he left the fixation on that aspect of ceramics, so customary in texts on the subject, entirely aside. As he put it, 'Good pottery … always eludes the tyranny of technology.'[7] What the book offers, then, is not just a method of description but also an attitude, in which both objective discussion of technique and individual taste (the 'overly subjective' response to pottery popularized by Bernard Leach) are replaced by a more nuanced language of assessment.

Crucially, Rawson's discussion of the pot form was based on another comparison to a fine-art medium: not painting or sculpture, but rather drawing. Clark calls this the 'primacy of line in pottery form.'[8] It is natural that such an argument should have occurred to Rawson, given that draftsmanship was another area of his expertise. For a formalist like him, the two media had many physical features in common. First, both tend to be practiced at a modest scale. One can find huge drawings and huge pots, but most are of a size to hold in the hands. Second, drawing and ceramics both depend for their formal effects on the relation between silhouette and mass. There is an obvious affinity between the profile of a thrown pot, which traces the more or less rapid passage of the maker's fingers or tool, and the outer edge of a figure drawing. In both cases, a great deal of the action happens at the border between positive and negative space. Less obvious, but just as important, is that what is held within this profile is comparable in its material nuance: the substance of the pot (clay body and glaze) and the drawing medium (chalk, pencil, ink). And finally, one can draw *on* a pot. It is hard to find a traditional style of ceramics in which this is not done, with brushed pigment, lines of sgraffito, or edges of dipped glaze. Some of the finest modernist potters of the twentieth century have even de-emphasized the curvilinear aspects of a pot – its silhouette – precisely in order to emphasize its surface. In the work of Bodil Manz, for example (admittedly an extreme case), the vessel is treated as if it were a rolled-up, continuous sheet of paper.

For all these reasons, it was perhaps obvious to Rawson that ceramics could be treated as something like three-dimensional drawings. But treating the medium as such was also an ingenious maneuver, for several reasons. First, it analogized ceramics to another 'minor' art form, but one with considerably more respectability in scholarly circles. The study of Old Master drawings had long been the province of the refined connoisseur, and so Rawson's discussion of ceramics as a kind of drawing in space provided instant pedigree. This makes his approach sound rather conservative, and to some extent it was. But a second big advantage of comparing pots to drawings was that it allowed him to import an existing critical term associated with modern art – rhythm. Prior to Greenberg's development of a more exacting, medium-specific account of modernism, rhythm (that is, the control of interval, as in music) had been forwarded as the key means of understanding form, a common principle that united all the expressive arts. It was a way of relating abstract painting to contemporaneous experiments in dance and composition, or for that matter to traditional art forms revered by modernists, such as Japanese prints and African sculpture.[9]

Pottery and drawing were obviously rhythmic arts par excellence. In an earlier book, in fact, Rawson had written that rhythm was the most important ingredient in draftsmanship, 'unequivocally present in all good drawing and [itself] a category of form.' If the intervals between various graphic forms 'are not controlled by an imagination capable of creating expressive rhythmic figures or patterns, the design will collapse.'[10] Focusing on rhythm allowed Rawson to highlight the temporal quality that linked pots to drawings. In both cases, the character of the maker is transmitted into the object, much as a jazz musician's personality is expressed in improvisation within a completely internalized sense of order. Thus, one test of a good pot is 'variation in its metre – perhaps itself embodying references to past experiences of measure, musical and/*or* architectural.'[11] Clark, too, stressed the musical qualities of pottery, describing a well-thrown pot's relation between interior and exterior as 'finely tempered' and noting that 'pottery seems itself more at ease with the descriptive language of dance and music than it does with that of the visual arts.'[12]

A final, more counterintuitive attraction of the analogy between ceramics and drawing was the very inadequacy of the comparison. On some points, the mediums are not at all the same. Drawings are flat, of course, and although they can be quite complex in their materiality, they can also be very simple – the most accessible of art media, every child's starting place. Pots, by contrast, are volumetric, and they usually present much higher technical challenges to the practitioner, particularly when it comes to glazing and firing. (Even throwing on the wheel, with its ever-present possibility of imminent collapse, has no real parallel in drawing.) For these reasons, sculpture would have been a more obvious point of reference for a formalist account of ceramics. One can even imagine how such a critical vocabulary might have been established. Perhaps Rawson's idea of the 'compound pot' (that is, one with several juxtaposed masses or volumes) could have been linked to the multipart works of David Smith and Anthony Caro. Unified vessel forms like those of Geert Lap or Alev Siesbye might be theorized according to the minimalist theory of the gestalt, as outlined by sculptors Donald Judd and Robert Morris. But Clark was too canny for that. He knew that in any head-to-head comparison, a pot would always seem paltry in comparison to a sculpture. Just as important, he felt that the temptation to treat pots *as if* they were sculptures, and so ignore the all-important principle of medium specificity, could only result in confused objects that Clark described in unusually harsh terms as 'grotesquely androgynous.'[13]

Drawing presented a very different case. There is no chance that even a very flattish pot (by Elizabeth Fritsch, say) could be mistaken for a drawing, and this absolute categorical separation meant that the comparison (unlike the one to sculpture) could not be played to ceramics' disadvantage. Indeed, as Clark made clear, pottery could even be seen as an improvement on drawing, or at least an expansion of its possibilities. He enumerated ways of marking a ceramic surface that are unavailable in other types of drawing: the perforations and deep incisions that one finds in the work of Lucio Fontana and Peter Voulkos; the drawing-within-depth that is possible in a translucent body like porcelain, as explored by Rudy Staffel; the dramatic contrasts of surface quality that can be achieved through lusters and other glazes, as in Betty Woodman's work; and the tidal 'ebb and flow' of the marks left by the potter's fingers, as in Robert Turner's hand-thrown vessels.

And then there were the spatial qualities of ceramics to be considered. Rawson had discussed the 'floor' of drawings, which he memorably described as 'the ground surface which … rises into the format from under the spectator's own feet.'[14] Even if the floor is not literally depicted in the drawing, one feels its presence and can relate it to one's own position in space. Clark adapted this principle to pottery with particular enthusiasm, writing of the 'implied space' created by a pot's profile. The inwardly curving walls of a pot might be imagined to define a conical volume above the rim, for example, whereas 'if we continue the lines of the foot' of a vessel by a master potter like Richard DeVore, 'they converge at an invisible point below the surface on which the pot stands.'[15] This was a formalist observation, but like Greenberg's discussion of flatness and opticality, it was freighted with metaphorical as well as physical implications. A pot's extension into the volume above and below it is imaginary, like that of a drawing, but that extension occurs in concrete, not just representational, space. These spaces are the actual zones in which we interact with the vessel, placing it on a tabletop, pursing our lips at its rim, or placing flowers into its interior. In effect, the 'implied space' of a pot is the functional arena in which it engages with the world of the everyday.

Rawson expanded further on this point by adopting the distinction between *espace-milieu* (space as environment) and *espace-limite* (space as limit), borrowed from the French formalist art historian Henri Focillon.[16] As Rawson explained, 'Art in the mode of "limit" contains in its own forms all the space it creates. Everything outside that included space is of negative value, meaningless.' In a drawing organized according to espace-limite, the marks usually extend to the edges of the sheet, and in the process construct a space, which may be perspectival or abstract but is nonetheless uniform and defined. A good example of espace-milieu, by contrast, is a Chinese ink painting in which 'a few nuclei [are] scattered over the open space of the format.'[17] In this case, the forms inhabit an unspecified negative space, an undefined void that we nonetheless read as a kind of reality. It was Rawson's insight that pots always inhabit espace-milieu, 'for the pot's own space is continuous with the space around it, into which it extends and which makes it perceptible.'[18] The pot, like one of the focal points in an ink painting, does very little to dictate what happens around it. But it nonetheless conditions that reality. In a sense, it brings its own surroundings into existence, just as a few artful swipes of a brush can create the implied image of a whole misty mountain range.

This realization about ceramic space brought Rawson into alignment with many other paradigmatic modernist statements about the medium, including such wide-ranging examples as Wallace Stevens's poem 'Anecdote of the Jar' (1919) – 'The wilderness rose up to it/ And sprawled around, no longer wild' – the still-life paintings of Giorgio Morandi and the pots of Gwyn Hanssen Pigott that they inspired, and Martin Heidegger's 1950 essay 'The Thing'. As a phenomenologist, Heidegger was interested not in pottery but in existence as such. Yet he seized on the clay jug as an emblematic object: 'The potter who forms sides and bottom on his wheel does not, strictly speaking, make the jug. He only shapes the clay. No – he shapes the void. For it, in it, and out of it, he forms the clay into the form. From start to finish the potter takes hold of the impalpable void and brings it forth as the container in the shape of a containing vessel. The vessel's thingness does not lie at all in the material of which it consists, but in the void that holds.'[19]

For Heidegger, the potter's medium is not clay, but space itself. The thrown walls of a jug may address that space, but the content or purpose of the object remains the voids within it and around it, which it brings into a sort of communion with one another. Heidegger dealt with this idea quite abstractly – the 'thing' of his essay is not a particular jug, but the essence of one. Rawson (and Clark following him), however, believed that the analysis of 'potter's space' could be particularized to individual ceramic objects. It could form the basis of a formalist criticism tailored to the ceramic medium.

In theory, this impulse could have achieved escape velocity. A whole school of 'Rawsonian' writers might have emerged, filling the pages of *Studio Potter* and *Ceramic Review* with intensely detailed, formalist readings of specific pots. Of course, nothing of the kind has occurred. Leading writers on ceramics have remained principally concerned with the more 'subjective' matters of biography, ethics, historicism, and signature style, as well as with more contentious issues like gender, ethnicity, and sexuality. Even Clark never adopted anything like an orthodox formalism. In looking at his voluminous critical output since the publication of *American Potters*, it is striking how little he has constrained himself to the method outlined in its pages. On the contrary, he has championed such artists as George Ohr and Grayson Perry, who (working at opposite ends of the twentieth century) embody just the sort of quasi-sculptural, 'grotesquely androgynous' manner that he seemed to reject. He also has been openly supportive of conceptual currents in ceramics, a lineage that originates from Marcel Duchamp's *Fountain* (1917) and continues through the work of Tony Hepburn, Clare Twomey, and Ai Weiwei. Such artists cannot be understood within a purely formal framework, because their works are propositional and discursive in character.

Here we arrive at a big question: what is the historical position of the modernist pot? This quandary is merely a subtheme in an even broader issue, that of the belatedness of modernism in the crafts at large.[20] Rawson's *Ceramics* was published in 1971, and Clark's *American Potters* a decade later – a decade that witnessed the unleashing of the new dispensation of postmodernism in the arts. By the time Greenberg lent ceramics his grudging imprimatur, the critic's entire worldview had already been dismantled. So these formalist statements were all clearly (and consciously) out of step with the times – they were insights that had worked their way through the discussion of painting and sculpture several decades earlier.

There are two ways of reckoning with this matter of delay. The first is simply to dismiss the formalist critical episode in ceramics as derivative – much as one might disregard Peter Voulkos as a Johnny-come-lately to painterly abstract expressionism. There may be a strong temptation to make such a verdict, partly because formalism seems even more remote now than it did thirty years ago, but mostly because ignoring such 'late arrivals' helps to streamline the great machine of art history. And yet, the most important lesson of post-modernism is that such unilateral, progressive narratives are unhelpful at best. The experience of multiplicity that has accompanied globalism in all its manifestations, including in the world of ceramics, has made us rightly suspicious of transcultural notions such as rhythm, and indeed 'form' itself. In this sense, craft's tendency to come late to ideas, and to preserve them long after their moment of inception, might be viewed as a strength. It results in a layering and fragmentation of positions, a world in which the likes of Grayson Perry and Alev Siesbye can coincide in a single gallery (as they did in Clark's own).

How, then, can we return to the idea of the modernist pot, not just as a postponed introduction of Greenbergian theory into ceramics but also as a concept that speaks effectively to our own moment? Rawson once again provides a clue. Toward the end of his life, he contributed a catalogue essay to a small exhibition titled *Recent Fires: Contemporary American Ceramics* held at the Utah Museum of Fine Arts in 1990. In the text, he made it clear that he had not changed his mind about aesthetic value in the medium: 'This show is not about passing fashion, rather about fundamental quality. All [the artists], of course, are Modernist in one special way.'[21] Rawson devoted most of the ensuing pages to a potted history of American ceramics. (The tables had turned, interestingly, for now it was he who was dependent on Clark's scholarly writings.) At the end of the essay, however, he returned to the themes that had preoccupied him two decades earlier. Back in 1971, he had emphasized the importance of tactility in appreciating a pot, which set the medium apart from mediasaturated culture: 'We live out our lives besieged by arts based upon various kinds of photographs, [and] many of the other artefacts by which we are surrounded are made from materials which by their surfaces communicate virtually nothing to the sense of touch. Even our kitchens are lined in that ultimate in touch-repellent surface, formica.'[22] He now returned to this question in the context of a very different craft market, which had brought what he had called 'sensuous castration' to the field of pottery itself: 'It has become very common for ceramic artists to rely on getting pictures of their pieces printed in nationally distributed magazines. Some have therefore begun to think of themselves as making things expressly to be photographed. … We know that our visual culture is overwhelmingly dominated by 2D surfaces – usually shifting, [and] Post-Modernism cured nothing by adding feebly general ornament. Painting loses *relatively* little by being reproduced [in] printed images in comparison with true 3D arts, especially good ceramics. Part of the real value of this show is that it sets out to restore to ceramics their nature as total 3D conceptions. Pots are not paintings!'[23]

Rawson's conservatism is once again evident here, but so too is his perspicacity. While his gibe about potters making photographic props may seem far-fetched, this was precisely the logic underpinning much craft and design in the 1980s. With the growth of an upscale craft marketplace came gloriously illustrated exhibition catalogues, as well as the transformation of the wordy, spiky magazine *Crafty Horizons* into the more visually oriented, glossier *American Craft*. Even the most austere modern ceramics now circulated primarily as images, rather than things. The ceramic artist and sculptor Peter Shire, who as the only American contributor to the Italian radical design group Memphis (which, it is worth mentioning, covered almost all their furniture in Formica-like plastic laminates) occupies a pole position in the postmodernist vanguard, has attested to this: 'There was never any problem with color separations, it always reproduced true, because we were using synthetic colors in the first place. The priority was to go for the image. The difference was between its existing and not existing.'[24]

Rawson bristled at this mentality. For him, it was essential that objects be experienced firsthand. Moreover, they should be created primarily with tactility in mind: 'A good ceramic piece offers its physical presence to yours, its shapes and transitions to the shaped and positioned grips and strokings of your hands.'[25] In effect, Rawson inverted Greenberg's theory of art without subverting its logic. If a modernist painting must be purely optical, lest it collapse into the decorative, then a ceramic vessel must be preeminently sensual, lest it lose its bearings and its integrity. Yet just as Clark's phrase 'implicit space' is best read metaphorically, so too is this preference for a ceramics of immediacy. Although Rawson no doubt believed that pots were best appreciated through the hands, his insistence on direct access was also an expression of open hostility to the market. Not unlike Ad Reinhardt's monochrome grid paintings, which the artist claimed were impervious to the commercial sphere ('free, unmanipulated, unmanipulatable, useless, unmarketable, irreducible, unphotographable, unreproducible'), Rawson's ideal pot would die quietly in a glossy photo but comes alive in the hands.[26] In the *Recent Fires* essay, he employed a commonplace of pottery culture, Zen aesthetics, to signify this animating spirit. Like most discussions of Zen in England and in the United States, Rawson's use of the term had very little to do with historical Buddhism. It was standard stuff – the cult of the tea ceremony, Bernard Leach, and 'cosmic and social energy flowing around and through the potter.' But Rawson also paused to make a cutting remark about Voulkos and other potters who prized individuality above all. Despite the sources of some of this work in Asian calligraphy, Rawson noted acerbically that 'where there is ambition, there is no Zen.'[27] What he wanted out of a pot was modesty, a thing that seemed easy to give but was getting harder and harder to find.

Clark has necessarily occupied a complex position in relation to the ceramics marketplace; after all, he did more than anyone else to shape it.[28] Yet if he has held any modernist ideal as sacrosanct, critically speaking, it is that an object should be comfortable in its own skin. In a recent polemical lecture, titled 'How Envy Killed the Craft Movement,' Clark echoed Rawson's critique of overly 'ambitious' ceramics, applying the same lesson at a grander scale. In the talk, he looked back on the heady boom of the craft market, and the image-oriented tendencies that it brought, as nothing less than a calamity: "The unending desire to escape craft had, by the beginning of the twenty-first century, left the movement in tatters. … Craft today is completely overshadowed by design and is a less influential element of the visual arts than ever before.'[29] While he supported those ceramists such as Robert Arneson and Ken Price, who in his view produced work that could perform in the broader fine-art world, his energies and sympathies were primarily directed toward objects that were recognizable as pots. Despite his increasing influence, Clark never chose to step outside of the ceramic frame of reference. (An abortive foray into another craft-inflected medium, jewelry, was the exception that proved the rule.) Ambitious as he has always been, he has remained 'medium specific.'

In *American Potters*, Clark described ceramics as 'an art of limitations.' At first, this does not sound like a ringing endorsement. It could even be interpreted – like his condemnation of 'art envy' – as condescending, a presumption that potters should stay in their place. But remember that in Clark's text, we are in formalist terrain, where limits and the way they are addressed are the only source of valid artistic meaning. And a pot has so many different kinds of limits – not only its materiality and the processes of its making but its very forms: 'The elements of foot, belly, shoulder, neck, mouth, and lip remain constant.'[30] Compared to a painter, who has nothing to bump up against but four edges, a potter is positively loaded with constraint.

Today, thirty years later, it is easy to see why Clark eventually abandoned the relatively narrow formalist view that he adapted from Rawson. It left out far too much of the huge and varied world of ceramics, and he wanted to think about every part of that world – not just the aspects that could be appreciated through the fingers. But it is also easy to see why he has retained a strong element of formalism in his thinking. For if the modernist project came late to ceramics, it nonetheless was given a useful corrective upon its arrival. Clark's text, like Rawson's before it, reminds us that form is only ever a matter of implication, especially when it is grounded in functionality. A pot's form produces meaning in a way that is not, after all, only internal, only physical. Its resonances extend out into the everyday, the social, the ethical – what Clark (in his encomium of Woodman's coffee cup) called 'the broader sphere of human needs,' and what Rawson had described more pointedly as 'the gap which now yawns between art and life as most people understand their relationship.'[31]

Only the lucky ones among us have had a chance to hold the works of DeVore, Manz, Lap, and Voulkos in our hands. But even on a plinth in a gallery, or in the pages of a book like this one (despite Rawson's reservations about the loss of tactility), such objects invite us to consider the world that is gathered around them and through them: an espace-milieu. In assembling their collection and operating their gallery, Garth Clark and Mark Del Vecchio have sought to construct an ideal gathering of such imagined spaces. In this effort, they have always placed the modern pot front and center. The ceramics they like best are the ones that seem, initially, to give the least to the viewer: 'sturdy, handsome, in many ways without any pretension.'[32] They are certainly able to appreciate postmodernist pots that jump up and down visually, demanding attention, but it is the subtle and the spatial object that they prize most. Their favorite pots must be met at least halfway. The little 'give' in a rim, the tensile snap of a curved wall, the delicate overlay of one glaze on another – these points of appreciation are to some degree a matter of old-fashioned connoisseurship. But in another sense, they are openings into a whole way of seeing. And in that respect, at least, the project of modern ceramics criticism is always just getting under way.

Notes

1. Garth Clark, *American Potters: The Work of Twenty Modern Masters* (New York: Watson-Guptill, 1981), p. 26, p. 28.
2. Elissa Auther, 'The Decorative, Abstraction, and the Hierarchy of Art and Craft in the Art Criticism of Clement Greenberg,' *Oxford Art Journal* 27, no. 3 (2004): pp. 339–64; Caroline A. Jones, *Eyesight Alone: Clement Greenberg's Modernism and the Bureaucratization of the Senses* (Chicago: University of Chicago Press, 2006).
3. Clement Greenberg, quoted in Clark, *American Potters*, p. 32. Greenberg's talk is reprinted in its entirety in Garth Clark, ed., *Ceramic Millennium: Critical Writings on Ceramic History, Theory, and Art* (Halifax: Press of the Nova Scotia College of Art and Design, 2006).
4. Clark, *American Potters*, p. 32.
5. George Kubler, *The Shape of Time* (New Haven: Yale University Press, 1962), p. 126.
6. Garth Clark, 'Ceramics by Philip Rawson,' lecture delivered at NCECA (National Conference for Education in the Ceramic Arts), Philadelphia, April1, 2010. My thanks to Garth Clark for sharing with me the transcript of this lecture.
7. Philip Rawson, *Ceramics* (Oxford: Oxford University Press, 1971), p. 3.
8. Clark, '*Ceramics by Philip Rawson*.'
9. For discussions of rhythm as a modernist principle, see C. Lewis Hind, *The Post Impressionists* (London: Methuen, 1911); Roger Fry, 'Post Impressionism' (1911), reprinted in Christopher Reed, ed., *A Roger Fry Reader* (Chicago: University of Chicago Press , 1996); Elsie Fogerty, *Rhythm* (London: George Allen and Unwin, 1937), excerpted in Glenn Adamson, ed., *The Craft Reader* (Oxford: Berg, 2010); and Alicia Volk, *In Pursuit of Universalism: Yorozu Tetsugoro and Japanese Modern Art* (Berkeley: Univer sity of California Press, 2010).

10. Philip Rawson, Drawing (London: Oxford University Press, 1969), p. 194, p. 195.
11. Rawson, *Ceramics*, p. 116.
12. Clark, *American Potters*, p. 27, p. 28.
13. Ibid., p. 23.
14. Rawson, *Drawing*, p. 204.
15. Clark, *American Potters*, p. 28.
16. Henri Focillon, *The Life of Forms in Art* (Cambridge: Zone Books, 1992), Originally published as *La vie des formes* (1934).
17. Rawson, *Drawing*, pp. 201–2.
18. Philip Rawson, quoted in Clark, *American Potters*, p.31. See also Rawson, *Ceramics*, pp. 183–95.
19. Martin Heidegger, 'The Thing' (1950), translated by Albert Hofstadter in *Poetry Language Thought* (New York: Harper and Row, 1971).
20. On this point, see my own *Thinking through Craft* (Oxford: Berg/V&A, 2007).
21. Philip Rawson, 'Ceramic Overview,' in *Recent Fires: Contemporary American Ceramics* (Salt Lake City: Utah Museum of Fine Arts, 1990), p. 2.
22. Rawson, *Ceramics*, p. 19.
23. Rawson, 'Ceramic Overview,' p.10. The phrase 'sensuous castration' is from Rawson, *Ceramics*, p. 19.
24. Author's interview with Peter Shire, August 23, 2009.
25. Rawson, 'Ceramic Overview,' p. 13.
26. Ad Reinhardt, 'The Black-Square Paintings' (1963), reprinted in Kristine Stiles and Peter Selz, eds., Theories and Documents of Contemporary Art (Berkeley: University of California Press, 1996), p. 91.
27. Rawson, 'Ceramic Overview,' p. 3.
28. Several essays in Clark's collected writings address this point. See John Pagliaro, ed., *Shards: Selected Writings on Ceramics by Garth Clark* (New York: Ceramic Arts Foundation, 2003).
29. Garth Clark, 'How Envy Killed the Craft Movement' (2008), reprinted in Adamson, *The Craft Reader*, p. 449.
30. Clark, *American Potters*, p. 27.
31. Ibid., p. 26; Rawson, *Ceramics*, p. 6.
32. Clark, personal communication with the author, October 11, 2010.

Originally published as Glenn Adamson (2012), 'Implications: The Modern Pot,' in Garth Clark and Cindi Strauss (eds), *Shifting Paradigms in Contemporary Ceramics: The Garth Clark & Mark Del Vecchio Collection*, New Haven and London: Yale University Press in association with The Museum of Fine Arts, Houston, pp. 36–46.
© 2012 The Museum of Fine Arts, Houston.

Reproduced with permission from The Museum of Fine Arts, Houston, and the author.

32
SOCIAL COMPLEXITY AND THE HISTORIOGRAPHY OF CERAMIC

Paul Greenhalgh

Fourth Annual Dorothy Wilson Perkins Lecture Schein-Joseph International Museum of Ceramic Art at Alfred University, October 14, 2001

There are complex and fascinating questions surrounding what I would call the historiography of ceramics. I thought I would start by describing some of these in the style of one of my intellectual heroes, Oscar Wilde. In the Preface of his novel A Picture of Dorian Gray (1890) he produced a list of short statements that instantly became identified as his philosophy of modern life. In his Art and Decoration of 1894 his introductory Phrases and Philosophies for the Use of the Young brought this list of statements to perfection. My favourites fall into two categories. The first constitute an ethical analysis of (late Victorian) society. In many ways they are a recipe for modernity. They are also funny:

- If one tells the truth one is sure, sooner or later, to be found out
- Those who see a difference between the soul and the body have neither
- Wickedness is a myth invented by good people to account for the curious attractiveness of others
- Religions die when they are proven to be true. Science is the record of dead religions.
- The old believe everything; the middle aged suspect everything; the young know everything.
- To love oneself is the beginning of a life long romance

The second category constitutes, for me, a summing up of what a modern decorative art could and should constitute. Wilde was one of the most important writers on the decorative arts of the fin de siècle period. His cryptic messages have underlying theoretical strength that expose the fundamental importance of decoration. In some respects, he pushed it into the social world by humanizing it. He made decoration synonymous with decorum, with the world of social behaviour:

- It is only the superficial qualities that last
- The first duty in life is to be as artificial as possible. What the second duty is no-one yet has discovered
- No artist has ethical sympathies. An ethical sympathy in an artist is an unpardonable mannerism of style
- There is no such thing as a moral or an immoral book
- No artist ever desires to prove anything. Even things that are true can be proved.

Source: © Paul Greenhalgh.

Underneath these acerbic utterings lies an acute understanding of what is at stake in the struggle for the modern. Key concepts like individualism, progress, artifice and amorality constantly recur in Wilde's fiction and non-fictional works. He has much to teach us about tonight's themes and indeed, I was aiming to start by using his methods in the context of ceramic. So here are my 'Phrases and Philosophies for the Use of Modern Ceramists'. My first ones relate to historiography, or perhaps they are more accurately described as being 'On the condition of Ceramic':

- All ceramic is made of clay but not everything made of clay is ceramic.
- Ceramic is not a material. Ceramic is the name of a genre derived from a small manufacturing district just outside ancient Athens that specialized in funerary monuments.
- Ceramic is the only cultural form that traverses race, class and gender in a seamless continuum.
- Ceramic is the only medium that is universal but can be characterized.

Next, my Phrases and Philosophies on Ceramic Historiography. By historiography, by the way, I mean the fabric of history. Historiography implies the pattern or form of history, not its individual facts. It is the structure that the facts fit into. It is the forest, not the individual trees. Often, of course, people cannot see the forest for the trees.

- Ceramic has no historiography because it has too many histories.
- Ceramic has no history because it has too much past.
- Ceramic survives. Eventually it becomes the only thing the means anything in a culture.
- Ceramic is forced to constantly wear the past in the present but has rarely managed to wear the future in the present.
- Ceramic appears nowhere in 'The Story of Art' because it appears everywhere in life.
- Ceramic is not modernist, but has been deeply concerned with modernity.
- Modernity has been a phased development over several centuries. The phase we have just completed was not particularly conducive to ceramic practice. The next one will be.
- Ceramic is a discreet set of stories within the History of Ornamentation.

The key to the future of ceramic practice is bound up in its relationship to the two most important concepts in Western culture: history and modernity.

Modernity is not a simple matter in relation to ceramics. If we sit down and list the total number of things that influence the appearance of a piece of ceramic we realize that we are dealing with a plural discourse. That is to say, the number of sources and influences coming to bear on the perception of ceramic, both from the production and the consumption end, mean that it is a priori open to multifarious interpretation; it will never have singular or pure meanings. It will always have boundaries that leak, it will impinge on other spheres and will be impinged upon as a matter of course. It is part of its condition. Virtually without effort we can list sixteen factors which contribute to the visual condition of any ceramic object:

1. The maker's personal background (her or his personality, family heritage, sexual preferences, physiology)
2. The maker's social background (her or his ethnicity, nation, religion, geographic region)
3. The technical proficiency of the maker (her or his ability to exploit the material)
4. The consumer's personal background (her or his personality, family heritage, sexual preferences, physiology)

5. The consumer's social background (her or his ethnicity, nation, religion, geographic region)
6. The role of the object (it's function)
7. The history of the specific individual objects (where it has been, who bought it, how it was used)
8. The class of the object within the genre of ceramics (it's status in relation to other ceramic idioms and objects)
9. The technical state of the medium (the contemporary condition of the technology and chemistry of ceramic)
10. The condition of the marketplace
11. Current general political and social trends
12. The history of ceramics
13. The material itself
14. The history of other genres that relate to ceramics
15. Current general styles and trends
16. The social hierarchy of the arts

All of these factors impinge on the maker and her or his audience every time they contemplate a ceramic object. While the factors pertain to all genres in the visual arts, in a number of other genres they are less numerous and more restricted in scope. This in itself has much to do with power. Those practices close to the political and economic epi-centres of society have the ability to control - and eliminate if necessary - external factors that come to bear on them. Expensive objects originating in dominant nations produced for those close to the center of socio-political power, feed into predictable worlds. Painting, for example, and especially large-scale oil paintings on canvas, which have been at the core of the Western tradition, have traditionally had fewer external factors mediating their production. The factors are reduced further still if teams of historians and scribes carefully construct protective quasi-histories.

I would argue that the more complex and multi-faceted a genre's historiography, the greater the number of factors impinging on it, the less likely that it could take part in the phase of modernity we have just finished. From this point of view, while clearly the high modernist canon included objects made with clay, the complex totality that has been the genre of ceramics was at best oblique to the canon, and at worst excluded from it.

Historiography and modernity are intrinsically linked. I should define modernity in order to show why this is. Modernity (and the related terms modern, modernism and modernization) is not a method for making cultural artifacts or a style of art. Modernity is a condition of existence. It implies the tacit recognition that the world is not static but moving, that we are shifting through time in distinct ways, and that there is a structure and direction in this movement. Previous key thinkers for modernity connected these shifts with evolutionary ideas (Darwin), with the metaphysical world (Hegel), or psychology (Freud), yet others with social and economic forces (Marx) and all modernists have been bound up with the idea of progress. Modernity implies that there is a structure to history - a historiography, that moves us through time and is not arbitrary. We can see that modernity has been a phased development.

This phased development has been in process for several centuries. The last phase, when engaged in visual culture, took on a number of macro-mannerisms that were largely dictated by the ideological environment. Most noticeable among these was the rejection of decoration, and especially complex decoration, from architecture and a wide range of cultural artifacts. The elimination of decoration during this phase of modernism has been widely discussed (though rarely explained) and is not the subject of my lecture this evening, but suffice it to say that it should be noted that this forced absence was neither inevitable nor total. Modernity is never single-stranded. Surrealism, for example, maintained and developed a particular sense of decoration and decorum; and many of the designers collectivized as "Art Deco" heroically maintained an interest in decorative language. Nevertheless, the dominant ethic was reductivist and determinist, two qualities that a priori eliminated decoration. For various genres the problem was not simply that they were carriers or vehicles of decoration, but that they were decoration in the most profound sense. They were centred on the production of objects that were profound ornament.

An interesting aside. If ceramic was aggressively excluded from the core project of modernity to the point at which we have to doubt that this particular phase of modernity had no "modernist" ceramics in any meaningful sense, then how could we have a "post-modern" ceramics. How can there be an "after" when there was no "during"? Post-modern ceramic must be premised on the notion that there was a substantial, recognizable modern ceramic. But this was not the case. We must quickly re-iterate. The modernisms we have just moved through constituted a mere phase (actually the third phase) in the ongoing process of modernity. Ceramic continued through that period and there are many masterworks in the medium. And ceramic made a central and powerful contribution to previous phases of modernity. But ceramic practice was peripheral to the third phase of modernity.

We are about to start the next phase. Let's call this the phase of complex modernism. I believe it will contain a good deal of ceramic activity, at least partly because it will be premised on complex relationships rather than reductive strategies.

To return to an earlier point. Ceramic presents us with fascinating historiographic problems. Unlike other key arts it has never had a consistent historiography created for it. (We must remember of course that historiography does not equal truth. It is an invented version of the truth. However, it does have the odd ability to become a surrogate truth for the majority of people). As such, many things are yet to be resolved in the history of ceramic. Things that are fundamental problems that have not been resolved in any real way yet are:

Economic value - The Western tradition has not had a consistent sense of the material value of ceramic. The stock exchange has not regulated it, art dealers have no consistent hierarchy for it, the wider public have no clear sense of the cost of it. This is because history has not allocated it a clear economic structure. Social Function - This is a problem of surfeit. Because it has so many social roles in so many societies that we know so little about, through time, the social function of ceramic is utterly confused. It could be said that we routinely commit category errors with ceramic, allocating roles to objects that were unintended and inappropriate. This of course, can have a devastating effect on their economic value. Genre status - the homogenous nature of ceramic has not been well described. A genre is not simply a set of technologies. A genre is also a set of codes and symbols that allow an object to participate in a complex web of discourse. We need to have an acutely clear idea of what ceramic is before we can enjoy its poetry.

Style - Style has been the principle determinant in the construction of the history of art. Style is the visual fabric that coheres a culture. But what is ceramic style, or more concisely, what are ceramic styles? How do we determine its intellectual (as well as its visual) underpinning?

Classification - where does ceramic come in the class-based socio-cultural world of art? We have enjoyed a hierarchy of visual culture for some time now that was invented during the Enlightenment and brought to its specialized perfection in the last (twentieth) century. It is clear now that this hierarchy is falling apart. How will the next one be constructed?

We could say that these problems are not fair ones, in that they were constructed for other arts and then crudely applied to ceramic in order to de-canonise it. This is undoubtedly partly true. But only partly. The failure to rigorously analyse ceramic as part of the continuum of history, and the insistence on either ignoring it or using it as evidence for civilization, rather than part of it, has also created these problems. Ceramic needs a confident historiography in order to achieve a significant position within the next phase of modernity.

It would be quite wrong to suggest that there had not been numerous major scholarly works on the history of ceramics. Many volumes of stunning exactitude and investigative zeal that have exposed individuals, factories and cultures of ceramic have been published over the last several decades. We no longer have to constantly re-invent the wheel with regard to the history of ceramic. But what is only just under way is the production of a body of work that convincingly articulates the nature and role of ceramics in relation to the macrostructure of culture and society, or that provides us with a larger model of ceramic culture that allows us to position oeuvres and objects in meaningful relationship. But even this project is beginning on an international basis. There are historians, writers and makers grasping the issues surrounding the totality of the genre with a confidence that has been absent for virtually a century. It is vital that this work continue on as the next phase of modernist practice unfolds across all of the visual arts. We all know that ceramic has had a past and can rightfully expect a future; but that that is not the same as to assert that it has had a history and will engage achieve a modernism.

Source: Fourth Annual Dorothy Wilson Perkins Lecture Schein-Joseph International Museum of Ceramic Art at Alfred University, October 14, 2001.

Reproduced with permission of the author.

33
SPEAK FOR YOURSELF
Edmund de Waal

Abstract

The author challenges ceramics practitioners to find their own voice and have the confidence to speak about their work. He is concerned about the interpretative vacuum that opens up when they do not do this, leaving open the possibility of disempowerment on their part. Silence is identified as a marker of authenticity for the potter and the failure to speak up can therefore be understood as a reluctance to put that authenticity at risk. Through reference to examples in Western studio pottery and oriental ceramics, the author concludes that much of this reverential silence is misplaced and only serves to close off opportunities for a richer understanding of material objects such as pots. The author ends with an appeal to ceramic artists to break the pact of silence.

Key Words: Silence, authenticity, studio pottery, Yanagi, Bernard Leach

Is it possible to address those silent and, to some, ineffable objects that we call ceramics, pots, ceramic art, art, and not fall into the trap of using those ever-helpful bits of short-hand (appropriateness, tactile values ...) that seem to arise when aficionados are gathered together? Is it possible to believe with passion that there is a great value to theory and still respond in engaging ways to objects? If theory is of value, why is not this more apparent to potters – and why are not more makers of ceramic art writing about their work? Why this great exercise in cultural ventriloquism on our/their parts? Does our critical language disempower the growth of their critical language?

Ceramics is an art whose practitioners have become peculiarly suited to silence. Their silence about their work and that of their peers has become a symbol for their seriousness as artists, in a way that is radically different from other arts. The truly authentic and serious potter is the one who unknowingly makes pots, whose artistic journey is unmapped, whose silence allows a critical space to open up into which the critic, the curator and collector can step, who allows what could be described as an interpretative vacuum.

A silence or a vacuum allows for aestheticising encounters: Rilke writes in a letter of the 'hours I was able to stand in Rome watching a rope-maker repeat in his craft one of the world's oldest gestures, just like that potter in the little village on the Nile – to stand by his wheel was so indescribably and mysteriouslessly fruitful to me'.[1] Mysteriousness, indescribability, ineffability united with ancient craft: the heady mixture of the encounter between the over cerebral writer and the authentically silent. The makers' silence is fruitful, is necessary for the poet's creativity, the reminder of physicality, of repetition and of a gestural language is the spur for the interpreter. Imagine if the ropemaker had talked. If we examine this vocabulary of interpretation

Source: © Edmund de Waal.

we have more than a list of words to investigate, there is also a way of putting these words to use. And we come up with an attitude and a methodology for approaching the writing on ceramics, what might be termed an ethnographic approach to potters and to the making of pottery.

It is ethnography of a very particular kind. It is based on the positioning of the, normally, Western writer-critic-ethnographer as both 'the man apart', the dispassionate onlooker able to observe the goings-on rationally and impartially, and also to be the intuitive, instinctual colleague of the craftsman, to crouch next to wheel or kiln and enact the pantomime of shared skills. This is the taxing position of the colonial encounter with authentic craft, the problem of 'being there'.

Authenticity is a condition seen in groups that have not yet experienced the rift that Ruskin defined between maker and object within industrial society. Authenticity occurs elsewhere, noticed only by the anxiously inauthentic. Thus in the most obvious of ways it is 'a form of cultural discrimination projected onto objects', and, of course, onto people.

The first marker for authenticity is that the maker of the object must not be self-aware. The process of making must be consuming, thereby allowing little of the destructive self- consciousness that has infected the West. Consider this characteristic piece of aesthetic ethnography by Soetsu Yanagi, the theoretician of the Japanese Folkcraft Movement and interlocutor of Bernard Leach, writing about the Kizaemon teabowl, a bowl that a poor man would use everyday:

> … a typical thing for his use; costing next to nothing; made by a poor man; an article without the flavour of personality; used carelessly by its owner; bought without pride; something anyone could have bought anywhere and, everywhere. That is the nature of this bowl … The plain and unagitated, the uncalculated, the harmless, the straightforward, the natural, the innocent, the humble, the modest: where does beauty lie if not in these qualities … Only a commonplace practicality can guarantee health in something made.[2]

Yanagi's Korean potter, healthily illiterate, naturally aesthetic, too busy to be self-conscious is a vivid example of 'homo orientalis … by nature mystical and concerned with great ideas',[3] the peasant craftsman who underpins the creation of Leach's authentic Orient.

That great list of descriptive words 'the harmless, the straightforward, the natural, the innocent, the humble …' is a lexicon of Orientalist language. These words occur throughout ceramics criticism. A recent paean to the wonders of anagama firing in an American magazine was constructed around them. These words tell of the Rilkean moment of the encounter between the silent maker and the incisive critic. To call it patronising is too facile: listen to the language of Leach when writing on the feeling of glazes to the touch:

> Unconsciously our fingers are invited to play over the contours, thereby experiencing pleasure through the most primitive and objective means. Children play with pebbles with a similar awakening of perception, and Orientals have lost touch with the fresh wonder of childhood less than we have.[4]

Authenticity precedes the fall into self-consciousness, the fall into language that comes in childhood, particularly dangerous for the Korean bowl maker, or the young Japanese potters counselled by Leach who wanted to escape their traditional roles:

> A young 'individual' potter protested that our advice to stick to good old traditions was cramping. Yanagi and I, each in our own way, replied: "Be modest, these results of wild experiment shows indigestion, launch out into new only as you can understand it and feel it, in any case only a few have this natural creative capacity in my country".[5]

The quotation marks framing 'individual' say much about where authenticity is sited and where it is held to be absent in this encounter. For the second marker for authenticity is that of tradition. An easily identified and extensive tradition is a safeguard against the novel. Tradition means knowing your place. Experiment is transgressive. For the writer-ethnographer it means knowing their place. The infantalising of the maker, like their silence, is part of the equation.

The third trace for the authentic object is that it should be made in quantity, preferably for everyday local living. As we have seen this was a principal definition for Yanagi, as it was for Cardew in West Africa. Quantity protects the object from becoming a self- conscious art-object. The valuing or endowing of that object with aesthetic meaning is the province of the collector, not the original maker. It is important that the maker cannot talk of aesthetic value or see aesthetic value as clearly as the critic.

Finally the authenticity must be easily communicable. The 'stylised markers' are both easily identifiable as strange, exotic and 'other', but, crucially, their difference from us, however dramatic, does not finally count for much. When we read Cardew or Leach or Susan Peterson, in their limpid and assured prose, the summary, repeated flashing up of a few images of the authentically exotic in their encounters is always without the mediation of any surprise, astonishment, wonder or bewilderment at what they see. It is as if they had already been there. The Korean potter waiting for his Yanagi, the Nile potter waiting for Rilke, Hamada for Peterson. In some ways, they had: what they see fits in with what they want to see and with what they went to see.

This is our inheritance: a collapsing together of words, ethical positions and attitudes to ceramics centring on an idea that some pots are more 'real' than others. When we read the literature of ceramics, that great and unruly mass of tracts, pamphlets, catalogues, monographs, surveys, 'plain speaking' essays on 'How to Reduce', public quarrels about good practice in magazines, the innumerable murmuring of glaze recipes, this is the vocabulary that underpins the edifice. In the language of praxis, the discourse on technique that occupies the huge majority of the writing about ceramics, this is the foundation stone. For if, as I suggest, the language of authentic making necessitates silence on the part of makers, then how do artists who use clay, makers of pots, ceramists converse except through that low level noise that could, and should, be called potchat? What is that bastardised form 'The Artists' Statement' – 150 words to say where you were educated, who did not influence you, what prizes you won, and a gnomic reference to Morandi – but a failure to understand how language works. Statements that fail to add up. Makers mistake their reverential silence when confronted by the essence of their own objects, the involuntary lapsing into wonder about their own ceramics for the authentic ineffability of 'The pot speaks for itself'. Except that it does not, and others do. There is, after all, such a thing as a platitudinous silence. And it means that conversations about interpretation, curation and display go on elsewhere.

What can we do about this situation? Attacks on canonical works continue to give me great pleasure, as my work on the construction of A Potter's Book shows. But the mere additions of 'neo' 'post' 'anti' or 'meta' to an argument does not qualify as intelligent rethinking of agendas. The scattering of a little post-modern bird seed round ceramics is not going to change the status of theory within our discipline, let alone encourage the rara avis of art criticism to take an interest in pots. And the risk is that the gulf between the makers of ceramics and critics will widen. The commonplace that there is already one language for critics and another for makers will become even truer.

My contention is that we have to reground ceramics within the material cultures from which they come, that is in the materiality of their making and in their commoditisation as objects. Both of these aspects are crucial. If we can take the complexity of the making of objects more seriously, rather than regarding their creation as an essentialist outcome of various cultural factors, then we may find that there is more to talk about in these ineffable objects than we thought. For instance when we overhear anthropologists, ethnologists or other writers on material culture talking what do we learn about the ability of objects to change their meanings? Due to the widely appreciated collection of essays edited by Arjun Appadurai we are familiar with the proposition that things have 'social lives': that is, that the same object can be successively recontextualized and that its meanings are radically contingent.

All objects are 'entangled objects'; entangled in the values of the maker and in that maker's appropriation of ideas and images, as well as the values of those through whose lives it is successively animated. If we believe this then we have to find a critical language that is lithe enough to cope with objects that do not stand still, and which play with the metaphorical references to which any object is susceptible. And if we believe this then we have to find a critical language that can map the influences and relationships between objects, that 'map of misreading'[6] that has proved so suggestive and so useful within literary criticism. 'Misreading' is more than the 'passing on of images and ideas': it is the critical act of interpretation that allows one artist to make space for their own work. Makers of objects do 'misread' in this way; do make those critical decisions about where to work amongst the cloud of presences, do decide about difference or similarity with other objects. If we can learn from the new ethnography that any 'biography of an object' will reveal that objects' meanings, we can learn from some aspects of the new literary criticism that it is often the things that remain unsaid that are most revealing. It is those areas left blank, their terra incognito, that are so intriguing.

Within the contemporary sculpture of this century from Duchampian ready mades, through Pop art to the affectionate interventions of Richard Wentworth, there has been a substantial body of art where the imperative has been to explore how the language of objects can be employed. There has been no great anxiety on the part of critics in dealing with this sculpture. Because it has often been an artistic intervention on a ready made object, rather than its creation per se there has been no expectation of an authentic approach to materiality. If you believe, as I do, that in making something it is possible to enrich even further the possibilities for exploring ideas, then the critical lacunae around ceramics seems even more heart-rending. Where in ceramics is that synergy between criticism and making that has become so common in other arts?

I am a potter who writes not a writer who pots. My writing is a response to areas of difficulty or anxiety within my life as a potter; it is a way of making conceptual space for my work and conceptual space for the interpretation of my work. Writing is another way for me to creatively misread work from the past or the work of my contemporaries, and I stress 'creatively'. Here is Eliot quoted by Venturi, himself an 'architect who employs criticism rather than a critic who chooses architecture': criticism is of capital importance in the work of creation itself. Probably, indeed, the larger part of the labour of sifting, combining, constructing, expunging, correcting, and testing: this frightful toil is as much critical as creative. I maintain even that the criticism employed by a trained and skilled writer on his own work is the most vital, the highest kind of criticism ...[7]

If we can believe this – believe that it is worthwhile to encourage ceramic artists to break the pact of silence – we will have strengthened the vigorous critical pluralism that we all espouse. Hence my slightly zealous attitude.

Notes

1. Quoted in 'Rilke and Things' by Idris Parry from Obscure Objects of Desire: Reviewing the Crafts in the Twentieth Century, University of East Anglia conference papers edited by Tanya Harrod, London, Crafts Council, 1997 p. 13.
2. Soetsu Yanagi, 'The Kizaemon Teabowl', from The Unknown Craftsman, Kodansha International, 1972.
3. Brian Spooner, 'Weavers and Dealers: The Authenticity of an Oriental Carpet', from The Social Life of Things, edited by Arjun Appadurai, Cambridge, 1986, p. 211.

4. Bernard Leach, A Potter's Book, London, Faber and Faber, 1940, p. 37.
5. Bernard Leach, A Potter in Japan, London, Faber and Faber, 1960 p. 88.
6. Harold Bloom, A Map of Misreading, 1974.
7. Robert Venturi, 'Complexity and Contradiction in Architecture', Museum of Modern Art Papers on Architecture, 1966, p. 18.

This was originally published in *Ceramic Review*, 182, March/April 2000 and is an edited version of a paper 'No Ideas But In Things' presented at the Ceramic Millennium Conference, Amsterdam, July 1999. It was later published *in Interpreting Ceramics*, issue 5, 2004.

Reproduced with permission from *Ceramic Review*, *Interpreting Ceramics* and the author.

34

OBJECT THEORY

Paul Mathieu

"A novel is, it often seems, nothing but an elusive search for a definition."

Milan Kundera, "The Art of the Novel".

Among all living things, and possibly inert ones as well, humans are the only ones with the capacity to think (we think). This capacity for thinking gives us a consciousness of the world: we know that we exist, that we are born and that we will die, that we are temporal beings, with a past, a present and a future. And this consciousness requires that we make sense of the world. We do this through language, spoken and written words, literature, fiction, theory, science, religion, history, also with music and song. We do this as well by creating images, and we do it by creating objects. Each of these categories of action upon the world is distinct yet connected to the others. Object making is probably the oldest making activity of humankind and we can speculate that it preceded the development of language and the making of images. To survive in the world, humans first needed tools. Formalized language probably came next, followed by images. If there is such a "genealogy", it is actually of little importance and if there is such a precedence, it remains irrelevant here. Yet, language and images as forms of fiction are closely interconnected while objects are at a farther distance, temporally and ontologically, from language. We now live in a world where language, in all its fictionalized forms, rules the world and it does so largely through images. One of the many forms of fiction language takes is theory, as well as history, and in the present instance, art theory and art history.

And the history of art is really the history of images, and art theory likewise.

In the world as it exists and as we experience it, there are two complementary phenomenon, usually perceived and presented as distinct: i.e. nature and culture. Nature encompasses all the things (among other things) that exist outside humankind yet includes humankind itself, something we too often tend to forget, at our own peril. Nature is construed as either that which is created by divine intervention or that which creates itself through the laws of physics. On the other hand, culture is what humans do to nature. The world of culture is vast and complex, as is nature. Culture includes speech and the written word, sounds and music, movement and everything we humans (and probably other life forms too) make, alter, transform and create. Material culture is more specifically concerned with physical things : architecture, engineering, design, crafts and objects of all kinds (fashion, textiles, furniture, jewelry, pottery and all kinds of other containers in all their forms and materials, etc.), but also with all manifestations of image-making (visual culture), that is to say those things that are best experienced with vision alone, primarily through sight: painting, drawing, photography, sculpture, film, television, computer imagery, all print media, graphic design, illustration, etc., etc. All of these aspects of material/visual culture are contributing their own potential to what is generally known as art, the world of creativity and expression, perception and aesthetics. Yet, the history of art is still largely the history of images, of things that are visually experienced, of visual art. Objects are quite simply ignored.

Source: © Paul Mathieu, Emily Carr University of Art and Design, Vancouver, Canada.

Definitions:

By "image", what do I mean exactly? An image, in the narrow yet specific definition I am using here, is a cultural (as opposed to natural) phenomenon experienced through sight alone, visually. A painting is an image, a photograph is an image, a sculpture is also an image, a tridimensional image but an image nonetheless. A building can also be an image if it is simply looked at, and buildings tend more and more, unfortunately, to have a graphic quality for being conceptualized and generated from a flat image, a plan. Just think of the spatial complexity of Gothic cathedrals, in many ways the ultimate handmade objects, which were not generated from plans at all. If we make some exception for blindness, anything, and certainly any perceptual experience, even sound often, can be reduced to a visual experience. Anything is potentially an image, a visual experience and, of course, any experience can also be expressed in some way through language.

In the world of material/visual culture (all those things humans do to nature), there is another category of things that are not experienced solely through sight, visually, and which do not necessarily necessitate language either, but which require other senses, primarily but not exclusively touch, for a complete experience and a full understanding. These things are what I call here "objects". An object theory is what I am attempting here.

"Every history implies another history, one that is not being told", to paraphrase Michel Foucault. The same is true for theories.

Objects are all the things largely ignored by the history of art, as we presently know it. It is possible if not requisite to obtain a terminal degree and become an authority in art history without ever considering the role and importance of objects within culture. If there is a remaining place where ignorance, prejudice, discrimination, segregation and censorship still exist within the experience of art, it is specifically where handmade objects are concerned, and although this is slowly changing but there is still a significant way to go for parity. Whole "History of Art" have been written which do not contain a single object. These books should have been more accurately titled "History of Images" instead. It would have been more honest.

Despite continuous attempts throughout the preceding century and before to reconcile art and life, to open up the definitions and practices of art, to blur differences and remove hierarchies, the world of art (in its theories, discourses, institutions, power structures, etc.) is still largely and often exclusively, the world of visual culture, of visual art and even more so today with mediated technologies than ever before. This leaves behind large sections of material culture whose contribution to culture is immense, essential and continuous, yet still largely dismissed and/or ignored. The silence is quite simply deafening. There are two main exceptions to this state of affairs: architecture and design, either industrial design (industrially produced things of all kinds) and graphic design (the ever changing world of images constantly altering the visual landscape we inhabit, again, outside and beyond the natural landscape). Architecture and Design have been readily embraced by the theories and studies of visual and material culture; they have been somewhat absorbed and included in what we understand as "art", in all its manifestations and institutions, largely because of their inherent economic power and their importance in the world we live in, in a direct relation to consumerism and capitalism. And the analysis of the importance of power structures is essential to any understanding of theories and discourses. Seen in this light, the art world is largely a marketplace, of things as well as of ideas. This embracing of architecture and design practices by the art world was preceded by the likewise acceptance of photography (in its original materialization, a mechanical and chemical process, now mostly virtual) as a legitimate art form (and it could be said that today 95% of art experiences are mediated by photography and related practices), a phenomenon now repeated with other technologies of image-making, because, quite simply, they were instantly acceptable to a world obsessed by visuality to the detriment of all other senses. If I am not directly interested in architecture and design here, nonetheless, the basic principles behind this theory of objects I am exploring still directly applies to these practices as well, if not at the political level, at least conceptually.

What is an Image?:

First, a better understanding of the workings of images is necessary. How do we experience images, what is their phenomenology? Obviously, images are experienced visually, primarily. This visual experience is one of distanciation, of removal, of separation. Sight establishes difference as rupture, as an opposition. This is even more true within representation. A portrait of your mother, be it a painting, a drawing, a bust, a photograph, a film, a video or even more so, a virtual image, such an image is not your actual mother. Experiencing that image distances you, separates you, removes you from the actual physical experience of your real life mother. It exists in a fictive world and thus, in opposition to reality. It creates another experience, a new experience, powerful and real, yet removed from the reality of a live experience. Images are always representation. Images establish a fundamental opposition between two types of experiences. It polarizes them, as opposites really. All forms of binary oppositions are intrinsic to images. These oppositions between two very different forms of experience are also hierarchical in nature (in either directions) since they cannot possibly be equal. Most importantly, images and all representations are directly connected to language through fiction and the operative power of symbols. Images are always literal and they imply and demand the production of a narrative. This narrative around images often takes the form of a theory (or theories) especially with abstract images which are also representations of something else, be it a geometric form or even a drip or a stain (and in many cases, the fiction often takes the form of myth-making around specific practices or, even worse, personalities). This is where the direct link between images and theories resides. Since our world, and certainly the academic world of institutions where art, visual art, operates, is largely constituted around power structures based on language, texts and images have become the predominant forms for the creation of meaning. This is why a theory of objects, an Object Theory is so important and essential in order to clarify and establish the critical role played by objects, and specifically here, handmade objects.

What is an object?:

Objects are of two main types: TOOLS, which are active (the conceptual aspect of tools is function) and CONTAINERS, which are receptive (the conceptual aspect of containers is containment; that is to say, they establish a transition between interior and exterior, but it is important to keep in mind that this transition does not imply an opposition but a continuity). As always with objects, these differences are not absolute, but complementary. Cars, for example, are altogether tools (when they displace their content) and containers. Tools are different within the general category of objects since they are used to make other objects and these objects are usually containers, at the conceptual level anyway. Yet, containers usually if not always imply a tool aspect as well and they can be used to act upon the world. This is yet another example of the reconciliation of differences, the main framework around which this object theory is constructed.[1]

What is the main characteristic shared by all objects (with the exception of those objects which are primarily tools) in whatever form they take, independent of materials, of the processes, tools, equipment and technologies used in their making, or even when and by whom they where made? My answer is that at the CONCEPTUAL level, all objects are CONTAINERS. They are articulated around the transition between exterior and interior. Containment has to do with the relationship between the object and its environment. Containment bridges an object with its environment. Objects are about difference as continuity, not difference as rupture, which is the operative characteristic of images (if an image always represents something else, an object on the other hand only represents itself). A container is a space where opposites are unified, where differences are reconciled (an object is always altogether an image AND an object...). Containers bring together the extremes in reconciliation; they cancel the dialectical impulse of language, which makes objects so difficult to be understood solely through language (by resisting narrative and theory). All the binaries, polarities, opposites and dichotomies present in language (and implicitly in images as well) are reconciled within the container, within the object. Containers and objects combine in symbiosis the top and the bottom, the front and the back, the interior and the exterior, the surface and the form, representation and presentation, image and object, material and concept, nature and culture, art and life, intellectual experience and physical experience, body and mind, and all and any other binary oppositions we can conceptualize. Objects are always inherently material, inherently abstract and inherently conceptual and these three aspects are equally important and thus, they resist hierarchisation conceptually, beyond market value and consumerism. Of all material practices, ceramics is the most intimately informed by this theoretical and conceptual framework, in its conflation of a volumetric form with a distinct surface.

The example of the frame:

In an art context, the ultimate object is the frame. The frame is the ultimate container for paintings, drawings, photographs and other images. In sculpture the equivalent is the plinth, now largely replaced by the floor of the museum or art gallery as institutions, which become by extension a different version of the plinth. And we have seen the progressive removal of plinths and frames in art presentation in the 20th century where their historical role has been replaced by architecture and by the printed or projected image which occupies the full space of the page or the screen … Yet the frame and the plinth (a form of furniture) hardly exist within the art discourse. How often have I seen in exhibitions and in museums worldwide, paintings exhibited in frames carved and painted by the artist where the identification label simply stated "oil on canvas", with no mention whatsoever of the frame! Total invisibility of the object, even when made by the artist! Does the function of frames render them irrelevant conceptually? Isn't function a concept, anyway? Could this be because they are objects first and not solely images? The frame or the plinth is the space, the place, the site where things change, where the transition between art and life takes place. An image is ALWAYS defined by clear borders. It has edges where things stop and end. An object has ambiguous borders where things start and begin and this is still complexified by the presence of images on objects, when characteristics of images and objects are present on the same thing. Images are always signs for something else. They always represent something else, are stand-in for other things and phenomenon, often images themselves. Objects on the other hand do not represent anything else, they are signs for themselves. You know a chair is a chair because it embodies chair as sign for chair while still being chair as thing. A drawing of a chair also embodies chair as sign but it has lost the materiality of the chair. Such a drawing is then weaker as a tool but more powerful as an image, through representation and the imaginative power of language it opens, at the symbolic level.

Images on objects are also very rich in potential since they bring together two aspects of conceptualization: signs and things. Still, images on objects are not operating like independent images do. An image on an object is framed differently since the frame is the object itself, on which the image is localized. The borders of the images are then different, in concept and in experience, from the borders of images which are independent and separate from a real, physical context. Images are always inside something, they are localized. They have borders and they need a context to operate, frame, wall, museum, book, catalogue, theory, etc. Images are in need of institutions while objects can dispense with them (except politically of course, since in our culture it is institutions that validate all human activities and assign meaning, thus value). Objects are on the contrary conceptually mobile, outside of and independent of context, since they carry context intrinsically, within themselves. They can go anywhere without significant (if any) loss of identity and meaning, which tends to be universal. Objects have no real locality. Again, images are unidirectional, in order to be read correctly and to make sense, while objects are multidirectional and retain their identity even when upside down or inside out. They do not have such a specific viewpoint as images do either and demand to be experienced from all directions. Frames and objects create epistemological breaks, where meaning and understanding is altered, they operate paradigm shifts where a real experience suddenly takes a new form, while still remaining real. Is the frame, the object, any less important conceptually than the image? The frame and the object both define a territory and establish a frontier. Images are localized (you know where they go) whereas objects have no real locality and they go everywhere, and also nowhere, not only physically but especially conceptually where they have no place within existing theories, beyond semiotics, which reduces objects to the status of images …, as social and cultural "signs", anyway. The frame and the object fixes the image and the image is by definition and experience always fixed. When the image changes, it is always really just another version of the same image. It is the frame and the object containing the image (at times just a sign for a sign …) that is, on the contrary, mobile. The frame is a prison for the image yet images are also prisoners of their own selves, even when unframed or independent of plinths and seemingly free from physical constraints. Objects are free. You can always change the frame (and change channels). Frames and all objects are interstitial, they operate in the "space between" and as such they connect to reality and connect two realities, art and the real world. In psychology, the term would be "transitional", but this no place to go there now.[2]

The problem of decoration:

Today, images on objects are largely "decorative" and this decoration has retained none or little of the symbolic power of historical signs (often abstract) on objects, which connected humans among themselves and with the larger world of myths and religion. At best, decoration and surface activation on objects today only plays an iconic role as referent for other signs, for history and for culture (a van Gogh on a ceramic coffee cup). As well, signs on objects today are too often simple optical devices for seduction in order to foster consumerism. That is true for design products industrially produced (and Design now is mostly a stylistic practice concerned with presentation, with how things look, and is based largely on the particular personalities and too often the peculiarities of designers), as it is for handmade unique objects, with few exceptions. The decorative now denotes the superfluous, the unessential; yet, the surface itself of objects, at the conceptual level is not decorative since the surface constitutes a system of signs where everything is on the contrary essential.[3] Historically, the surface of objects, their ornamentation, played a powerfully symbolic role. That surface was never purely decorative. Objects made today need to return to that stage where any marking is essentially symbolic and not only ornamental, empty of meaning beyond optical excitation. Signs on the surface of objects are there to inform us about the nature and use of the object (its ontology), how it is perceived and experienced (its phenomenology) and how we come to understand it (its epistemology). Any other sign on an object is unnecessary. Modernism and modern design have largely resolved this problem of decoration and ornamentation by altogether dispensing with them, yet in the process transforming artworks into museum decorations and material for kitch giftware (a Kandinsky on a ceramic coffee cup). I foresee that this situation will very soon change and due to the expanding role of computer technologies in both the design and fabrication of things, the potential for extremely complex and excessive adornment offered by these technologies will permit the creation of personalized, idiosyncratic and highly varied surfaces on all the things in our daily life. This might create a visual revolution the like of which we haven't seen since the reductive, minimalist, "negative" aesthetics of Modernism.

Abstraction and Conceptualism:

Containers and objects are also the ultimate form of abstraction. They never "represent" anything (except themselves). The resistance of institutions toward objects and toward containment as a concept is a resistance to abstraction as concept as well. By their very nature, objects contest the necessity for institutions, they challenge and contest present knowledge structures and existing hierarchies. It is much easier to simply ignore them. If abstraction as style, abstraction in its visual and formal aspects has been embraced by art (image making) in practice and in theory, abstraction as concept hasn't been fully understood yet. To do so would have to imply a complete reexamination of the contribution to art history of certain practices (largely craft practices where abstraction has existed since the beginning of "culture") which would destroy the present power structure of hierarchies (of materials, of practices, of markets, etc.) created by art history and other art institutions. In the 1950's a prominent abstract painter predicted that we would have a period where abstraction in art would predominate for one thousand year. … By art, as is so often the case, he meant images, paintings, etc. Not only was this important artist proven wrong almost instantly but what is essential to remember here is the complete fallacy of the statement since there had already been a period of abstraction reaching back into the past for at least 30,000 years! But since this investigation of abstraction as a concept was not taking place within image making primarily, but within other practices (object making) which were (and still largely are) deemed irrelevant or even worst, impossible to be considered as valid. The fact that most if not all of these explorations of abstraction within objects was the anonymous labor of most probably women makers is probably a significant factor in this erasure of history, since history and specifically here art history is so obsessively preoccupied with original expression of specific individuals, often males. It is important to realize that within object making not only are the notions of abstraction and conceptualization very ancient, but if we truly reflect upon the generative and operative nature of objects, we discover that such categories as modernism, expressionism, minimalism and even postmodernism, all have very long histories within object making and that objects are actually at the source of these developments in art, even if that contribution has been ignored within art discourses and theories (and will as well likely be denied by many).

Objects are inherently abstract (they can only represent themselves even if metaphorically they often are substitutes for the human body and physically they often act as extensions of the human body). Objects are also inherently conceptual, they are the materialization of an idea, even if that idea, that concept is more often than not function and/or decoration. Yet these notions of abstraction and conceptualization have been appropriated and absorbed by visual art practices and they are now generally perceived as intrinsic and largely unique to visual art (and to language). Object makers need to reappropriate their historical ownership of these terms. Abstraction in art is presented as a phenomenon that had no precedent before the beginning of the 20th century. Anyone remotely familiar with the history of objects knows that this is a fallacy. We are also too familiar with the category of "conceptual art". This is a gross misnomer. Conceptual art is not any more or any less conceptual that any other human activity involving thoughts, including all art forms. Art is, as Leonardo said so well, "cosa mentale", a thing of the mind. That is what we humans do, we conceptualize the world, through consciousness. We do it by creating myths, fictions, narratives, theories, histories, symbols, signs and images, that is to say through various forms of fictions through languages, or again by changing the world, by acting upon it and its materiality, by making objects. Conceptual art would be much more appropriately labeled "immaterial art" since the materiality of that type of art is often absent or irrelevant, but I prefer "contextual art", since it is a form of art that acquires meaning only through context, the institutional contexts of art experiences, the physical context of museums, galleries, magazines, catalogues, monographs and photographs and the literary context of art history, criticism and theory. Conceptual art or as we should really say contextual art does not exist or operate outside these specific contexts. It relies entirely on context for meaning. Contextual art is a better term, more precise, more accurate and above all more honest. Since obfuscation and appropriation of precedence have been trademarks of art history, I do not foresee redress in the near future. But if we were to acknowledge the contribution objects have made, through abstraction and conceptualization, to art history , the whole structure of art history would have to be rethought and the whole of art history itself would have to be rewritten. I am not too hopeful that this will ever happen. It is much more easy to pretend to the continual invisibility of certain practices.

The handmade object:

Again, I propose that a reexamination of the role and importance of handmade objects within culture and their theoretical underpinnings could serve as the basis for a new type of art experience where art and life are truly reconciled, beyond the false promises of new technologies (which are fundamentally little other than pressure to ever more consume), which are nonetheless important tools for new forms of creativity, yet cannot in themselves provide satisfactory answers to the present situation of growing alienation. To make an object by hand, material, technique and skill remain central to the task. And both technique and skill, in a world where mechanization, mediation and industrial processes are the norm, have both lost their historical importance. Technique has been replaced by technology and now by the virtual 'reality' of computers. The skill, the actual manual and physical skill necessary to operate a computer is almost nonexistent. It has been replaced by an expanded role for intellectual skill, but for fewer and fewer people. The other users are just indentured slaves to machines and pawns for consumption. Yet, intellectual and conceptual skills are not absent from handwork. On the contrary, in handwork, the manual, physical skills and the intellectual, conceptual skills are in balance. This balance has been broken by new technologies. These technologies are also language based and rely on a system of codes and of signs. They are primarily visual as well, even if recent advances in haptic experience show promise in reestablishing the role of the hand, which will probably find their primary use in virtual gaming and other forms of entertainment …

The maker of objects by hand is like a virtuoso musician or a professional dancer, while being also altogether composer or choreographer. That performance doesn't have the implicit theatricality and the entertainment value of spectacles, though. It remains a performance without witnesses, which can only be experienced through the product of the performance. If images are inherently spectacular and entertaining, objects are ordinary, quotidian, domestic and based in labor. If images are reflections of the world, objects are actors on the world and their transformative power, while being different is as great and certainly as important.

Handmade objects do not only object to theory, by resisting and undermining language,[4] they contest and subvert contemporary visual art by not being mediated, by operating outside institutional contexts, by being permanent physically and/or conceptually instead of temporary, by being timeless instead of grounded in the instant, in the present, in the fashionable now, by resisting change, conceptual change as well as stylistic change. Here again ceramics is particularly sensitive to this relation to time, in its amazing permanency as possibly the best archival material ever devised, as the memory of humankind. Handmade objects contest design products by being unique and again, handmade. The focus that contemporary design presently puts on style instead of substance, on personality instead of vision, is also in need of reexamination and contestation. And above all, the best, most relevant and potent handmade objects contest and subvert craft practices by going beyond material and beyond technique, by denying the importance of the well made, the tasteful and the personal, to become witness and memory of our present (as well as past and future) times. If handmade objects have become largely useless in a practical sense, they nonetheless remain socially essential, as receptacle for the imagination and memory of humankind, memory of knowledge and experiences. This repository for experiences and memories, historically the domain of objects has progressively been usurped by images which now occupy the central stage in fulfilling that archival role, it seems (just think of photography and digital practices). Yet it might be possible that objects are slowly reclaiming that role now given to images, without notice from anyone and without anybody admitting it yet. Quite simply, just to make handmade objects today is a potent form of contestation and an effective exercise of criticality. This might be where objects most important role within culture resides now, and I repeat myself again, as recipient for the memory of humankind, a memory of knowledge as well as a memory of experiences. It could be argued that the only place where contestation, subversion and criticality, where the real possibility for change resides, remains within those practices that have the making of objects as a central activity. At the very least, they offer a potent if marginalized alternative to the current state of general anaesthesia and physical alienation.

Handmade objects in the global world we now live in have the amazing potential to be transnational and operate beyond geographical borders. Their universality attest to that potential. They can also be truly transcultural, combining various cultures in juxtaposition, blurring identities while remaining significant to the local particularities of makers and users. And most importantly they can also be trans-historical, working timelessly, reuniting past, present and future seamlessly. Only objects, and more specially handmade objects have such a complex role to play within culture now.

Handmade objects contest the contemporary and void the apparent cultural consensus. In handmade objects we find the last traces of what we use to call "work" (beyond agriculture, yet for reasons as vital as producing food) and the last place where effort in use still exists, non-mechanical and non-mediated. And the last place where contestation and subversion is still possible in the cultural sphere. To make an object by hand is a profoundly political act.

If objects and particularly handmade objects have not received the attention they deserve, it is not because they have become irrelevant and meaningless in the world we live in. On the contrary, it is because, of all cultural phenomenon, they imply a complexity that exist beyond language and beyond theory, thus beyond the reach of those who are confined by language and by theory. Images are complicated, they need to be explained, to be fictionalized and they are thus the privileged domain of theory. Objects are much less complicated but much more complex. And this complexity resists language and resists theory. Yet a theory of objects, an object theory remains essential if we are to reexamine and reevaluate, reassess and reposition the important role played by objects within culture.

Notes

1. These ideas were first explored in a text "Towards a Unified Theory of Crafts", published in Studio Potter magazine, and then in "Crafts: Theory and Practice, a Canadian Perspective", published by Ronsdale Press and edited by Paul Gustafson.
2. For the development of these ideas see the work of psychologist Donald Winnicott on the infant/mother relationship and the writings of art critic Peter Fuller ("Art and Psycho-analysis" and "The Naked Artist: Art and Biology", Writers and Readers, London, 1980 and 1983) on this subject relation to the art experience.

3. See Jean Baudrillard in "The System of Objects" for more on this.
4. I have developed these ideas elsewhere around a reading of Michel Foucault's "Of Other Spaces" (Diacritics 16, no.1) and "The Order of Things" (New York, Pantheon), in an article "The Space of Pottery", published in Ceramics: Art and Perception, no. 22, 1995 and originally in Studio Potter magazine. It has also appeared in "Making and Metaphor", an anthology of writings on contemporary Canadian crafts, Ronsdale Press.

Reproduced with permission of the author.

35
BETWEEN A TOILET AND A HARD PLACE: IS THE CERAMIC AVANT-GARDE A CONTRADICTION IN TERMS?

Garth Clark

First Annual Dorothy Wilson Perkins Lecture

Schein-Joseph International Museum of Ceramic Art at Alfred University October 27, 1998

It is reasonable to expect that a paper on ceramic history will be a warm and nostalgic trip through glaze discoveries, quaint old pottery studios, accompanied by a picture gallery of charming, non-threatening pots that one can take home to mother. Ceramic history has tended to be a safe subject, without rancor, unpleasant images or disquieting points of view. Alas, this is not that kind of lecture and instead of being taken into the sedate Zen world of Bernard Leach we will spend much of our time in the land of another Englishman, Thomas Crapper. Crapper, the erstwhile 19th century father of the modern toilet, could never have imagined that his development of porcelain bathroom furniture would eventually lead to one of the great controversies in fine art and provide the arts with its most infamous ceramic object.

The subject of this paper has great potential for misunderstanding so let me begin by refining the thesis and by explaining what this will not be about. Firstly, it is not about ceramics made within the disciplines of design, crafts, or the decorative arts. It is about the relationship between ceramics and the fine arts from 1900 to 1950. Secondly, it is not another art vs. craft debate although this is always a subtext. For the purpose of this talk, let's accept as a given that a part of ceramics is fine art. Thirdly, this is not about whether an Avant-Garde movement exists within ceramics. Of course, it does. Every movement has its interior Avant-Garde element. This stature is easy enough to achieve in our field where one has only to be two steps to the left of Warren McKenzie to be considered a radical.

The question posed in this paper is whether or not the ceramics movement made a contribution to the history of Avant-Garde of the fine arts mainstream in the first half of the 20th century. If it did then why has this never been acknowledged and if it did not, what were the reasons for the failure to be a participant. Then we must ask what the findings tell us about the practice of ceramic art history and what this means for our future. The term ceramics here is used in a neutral form meaning fired clay. There are no restrictions on the type of ceramic object that could be selected; traditional, non-traditional, functional, vessel or sculptural.

The next question, and a good one, is why should we even bother to examine this issue? Does it matter to ceramics whether we are part of Modernist art history or not? The answer is, "yes," it does matter. Modernism is the dominant fine arts theology in 20th century art. Even Post-Modernism depends upon its dialogue and opposition with Modernism for its existence. In the next decade our perceived relationship to Modernism

Source: © Garth Clark/Ceramic Arts Foundation.

will decide our status and whether the practice of ceramics is upgraded or downgraded within the visual arts. Moving up or down this cultural food chain will have practical implications. It will decide what (if any) resources we get to educate, research and exhibit, whether we can sell our art at prices that are competitive with other arts and whether we can get the art press to deal seriously with what we make and do. It will decide whether we become more visible or invisible.

It is no secret that the relationship between ceramics and Modernism has, outside of industrial design, been an unhappy one. Modernism rejected the crafts movement as bourgeois and decadent and no ceramists have made it into the inner circle of the fine arts. Ceramists were often sentimental and historical in their approach to art making, an attitude that was antithetical to Modernism orthodoxy. The emphasis on material and process over concept has further alienated us.

We in ceramics are more or less in the position of an adult child who has had a difficult and unresolved relationship with our tough, rejecting father who is now ailing and before he passes on we want him to acknowledge our existence and validity. In art, just as in life, resolving such an issue is a profound moment—touching, painful, exorcizing—and key to a healthy self-image in the future.

This question is particularly important now. Many of our writers are currently grappling with this issue and it will be one of the key subjects at the forthcoming Ceramic Millennium conference in Amsterdam in 1999. The reason for its currency today is that we are about to enter into an orgy of self examination, a modern ritual which happens when we reach a chronological milestone such as a new decade. Two years from now, we will enter not just a new decade but a new century and a new millennium. There is a palpable and urgent desire to resolve our differences with Modernism before we enter the promised land of a new era.

I have chosen to deal with the subject at its most rarified point of entry, the Avant-Garde. Avant-Garde is a military term that refers to the forces that go out beyond the front lines to scout and occupy new ground. The implications of Avant-Garde are risk taking, blazing new trails, exploring new or forbidden territory and often, engaging in a battle with the forces of status quo to gain a foothold for unfamiliar and often unpopular new forms, ideas or beliefs. The artists who have distinguished themselves in this field of battle such as Duchamp, Malevich, Braque, and Picasso in his early years, are the aristocracy of Modernism and exert particular influence.

In the post-1950's period it is worth noting that what is called Avant-Garde has altered. Many theorists argue that the Avant-Garde no longer exists except as a mainstream style of art making, developed and kept alive for some 30-40 years now by a cabal of university trained artists, academics and curators. The style is characterized by its emphasis on conceptual issues, installation and by a profound, even awed, respect for what are often very small ideas. It feels very academic and, given the fact that it represents the status quo rather than the opposition, it seems fair to compare it to the power and predictability of the Beaux-Arts academies that controlled the arts in the late 19th century Europe.

In order to sort through the ceramic art in the first half of the 20th century in search of objects that could possibly have claim to admission into the Avant-Garde canon, I decided to locate the top five Avant-Garde works in ceramics between 1900 to 1950. After much soul searching I ended up with a list of nine objects by nine artists and finally rejected four objects and reduced this to the required five. It is important to understand that by rejecting work I am not saying that the pieces that did not make the cut were not good as art. It just means that they do not satisfy the definition of Avant-Garde art. One can be a great artist and not truly Avant-Garde and vice versa.

The first of the four artists I rejected is Tullio d'Albisola, a gifted ceramist working in Albisola Mare on the Italian Riviera as a Futurist artist in close association with the movement's founder F. Tommasso Marinetti. Between 1928 and 1939, he created a body of magical table-top limited edition ceramic art pieces, together with a group of other artists know as the "Aeroceramisti," precursors of later work in a similar vein and scale by Ken Price, Ron Nagle, Richard Shaw and others. Futurist ceramics was unquestionably a great moment of innovation for ceramic art, imaginative and exciting, but when tested against the broader art mainstream, the "Aeroceramica" ultimately reveals itself as a secondary, decorative response to Cubist and Futurist painting and sculpture that predates the ceramic work by up to 20 years.

Another contender from Italy is Lucio Fontana, architect of *Concetto Spaziale*, one of the century's great painters, a light artist, jeweler and ceramist. Even though Fontana was one of the greatest artists to work in ceramics and his work in clay from 1928 to 1969 can be considered exceptional, progressive art, it is not necessarily Avant-Garde. Fontana's work is magnificent, overwhelming in its conflicting emotions of baroque essence and reductive passion and I fear my decision may be premature but for the time being that is my judgement and I will hold to this.

The final two artists both come from Britain. William Staite Murray, an intimate of painter Ben Nicholson and sculptors Barbara Hepworth and Henry Moore, was a member of the exclusive Seven and Five Society and one of the few ceramists working out of a fine arts milieu. But his work now has a slightly dated quality and even the most Modernist of his pots, while handsome, cannot be considered radical. The same is true of his student Sam Haile, who taught briefly at Alfred University in the late 1930's leaving an indelible imprint on the American vessel sensibility. Initially a painter, he embraced Surrealism and his pots are thrilling adventures in vigorous form and surface drawing. Yet, good as they are, they cannot be considered pivotal to the Surrealist movement and so, do not qualify as being Avant-Garde.

That leaves me with five artists and their objects which I will present in reverse order of importance, a kind of mutant Miss Universe competition. Fifth is Kazimir Malevich and his teapot from c.1920. When the director of the Russian State Porcelain Factory complained that this lyrical collision of volumes and masses would not function well as a teapot Malevich declared this a non-issue as his object was not a teapot but the "idea" of a teapot. This was the first time that I know of when the vessel was so clearly released to become a vehicle for pure art inquiry. The object itself stands out as a perfect melding of sculpture and utility with neither side yielding much to the other.

Number four is *Object* (1936) the fur covered teacup by the Swiss Surrealist loner, Meret Oppenheim, one of the defining icons of this poetic, erotic, mystifying and dream-based movement. It still has the power to shock, creating a queezy feeling somewhere between lip and gut. Indeed the older it becomes and more aged and questionable the fur seems, the greater the unease it inspires. *Object* works because Oppenheim took the cup and turned it into a player in domestic theater. She exploited 2,000 years of oral connection and served up a disturbing conflict with utility. We respond to the cup, even today, because it provokes a perverse, macabre moment of intimacy, imagining our lips against wet, manky fur straining out a serving of Lapsong Suchong.

Number three is a pot by George E. Ohr or rather "pots" by Ohr. Taking just one piece and showing it as the most radical or significant of his works is premature. Scholarship in ceramics has not yet reached the level where a potter's output is so clearly analyzed that we can identify their masterworks and this is an important point that we will return to later. Ohr is the only ceramist that I believe can hold his own as a primary artist of Avant-Garde sensibility on a par with others in the fine arts mainstream. He is also the only ceramist for whom there is a groundswell of support within the fine arts to be taken seriously as an innovator.

He first started potting in 1879, making mostly domestic ware, novelties and ceramic hardware. His significant work as an artist began around 1893 and continued to 1907, the radicalism seeming to have been provoked by a fire in 1894 that wiped out his first studio. It was a short but explosive period of production. Aside from ceramics, he also took on photography creating bizarre personas around his own face which proved to be as plastic as his clay and as hairy as Oppenheim's cup. He was a performance artist before the term had been coined. He used language, irony and street theater in his work. His pots are marvels: sensual, erotic, energetic, abstract and, at times, sublime. They were about big issues to do with creation, deism, birth, nurturing and the individuality of the human soul.

He even took on a different gender in his work, metamorphosing from the muscled macho ex-blacksmith into a nurturing mother who gave birth at the wheel. Most of his remarks and writings on his role as potter are made in the maternal feminine form. For Ohr, the wheel was the locus of unreleased energy (just as it was later for Voulkos and others) and in his own words, when he first stumbled on the wheel he "felt it all over like a wild duck in water."[1] He always knew that he was a great artist even though few shared his confidence pointing to his seemingly lunatic theatrical behavior to argue that he was merely a Southern cracker. Ohr was certainly not the first genius to take refuge in playing the clown. Duchamp and others have traveled this path as well. As Octavio Paz wrote, "truly wise men have no other mission than to make us laugh with their thoughts and make us think with their buffoonery."[2]

In his own time Ohr was reviled by the Arts and Crafts establishment. His glazes were sometimes admired but his tortured forms were dismissed as antics of a crude Southern huckster. The turn of the century potter, educator and designer Frederick Hurten Rhead dismissed him as a hick "entirely without art training and lacking in taste."[3] The fact that he so offended the establishment is a plus in my books. Truly Avant-Garde art is seditious, devious and the new always provokes fear. Its shatters the calm. It puts fur on teacups.

Robert Arneson argued with me that Ohr was not an important artist because he did not produce a school or students. I though this was a curiously reactionary view coming from an anti-establishment, nose-picking, fecally fascinated artist such as Arneson. But I later realized that what he was saying was that to be taken seriously as an Avant-Garde artist, one must have an impact in one's time and sphere of influence. In other words, its not enough for the tree to fall in the woods, it must also be heard to fall.

There is truth to this but Ohr is a unique case and has to be judged by different rules from those proposed by Arneson because his work never went into general circulation so it could not have an impact in his own day. Most of his work was not exhibited publicly until 1969, 51 years after his death, when over 6,000 pots, the bulk of his œuvre was discovered by J.W. Carpenter, an antiques dealer, in the Ohr family barn in Biloxi, Mississippi.

His rehabilitation began through the fine arts world. Andy Warhol, Jasper Johns, Miani Johnson, Irving Blum and Charles Cowles, being among the first to recognize his talent. Only later, and with foot-dragging reluctance, the afficionados and scholars of the Arts and Crafts movement uneasily allowed this eccentric potter from the other side of the tracks, to say nothing of the wrong hemisphere of the United States, into their fin de siècle world of elegant, upper-middle class bohemianism.

Ohr's radicalism has to be measured by events since 1969 when his work first started to become known. This is an odd circumstance but perhaps an even more demanding test than being rated in his own time. After all, if one can appear Avant-Garde over fifty years after one shuts down one's kiln, that is a rare achievement. And this is the test that Ohr passed. The number of artists who admired, collected and were even influenced by his work is varied and impressive. Aside from Andy Warhol and Jasper Johns, it includes Betty Woodman, Ken Price, Ron Nagle, Kathy Butterly, Babs Haenen, Phillip Maberry and Michael Lucero.

Without doubt Ohr's work (or "clay babies" and "mud fixings" as he called his creations) was the most radical pottery of his time. No other ceramist in America, Europe or Asia was pushing the plastic and emotional boundaries of vessel form, material and content so far beyond the limits of acceptable "good" or even "progressive" taste of the day. Nor can he be defused by his critics as a product of the inbred Southern folk art milieu making weird outsider art, as Ohr's nickname of the "the mad potter of Biloxi" would suggest. Ohr clearly knew what he was doing, took pains to educate himself about his art and its history and consciously abandoned a status quo aesthetic of refined, elegant and static beauty (that he could easily have excelled at).

Declaring himself to be the "second Palissy," he set off, knowingly and ambitiously, down a lonely and, at times, humiliating road to find his own truth.

We have not, as he predicted, "built a temple to [his] genius" in the conventional sense but his work is becoming better understood and appreciated. The Whitney is including his work in their upcoming mega-survey of 20th century art. The critic Roberta Smith recently scolded the Whitney in the *New York Times* for leaving out such a significant artist in a previous, smaller survey. The Victoria and Albert Museum is preparing a definitive exhibition on Art Nouveau for the Millennium celebrations in year 2000 and Ohr will have his place there as well. So the support is growing and my choice of Ohr for elevation to the Avant-Garde canon is not made in isolation.

The second place is a controversial one in some ways. After much consideration it goes to "Casa Battló" (1904-1906) by Antonio Gaudí, the second and last of his apartment buildings. In terms of Avant-Garde use of ceramics in a work of art, this is one of the century's enduring masterpieces. Gaudí's approach to a structure as inherently plastic, organic and voluptuously decorative, was without peer in his time. In a curious way, it is as though Gaudí approached creating buildings as though they were plastic malleable pots. As Rainer Zerbst, one of the authorities on Gaudí's work, writes, even the stone facade of this building was carved so that it would create "the impression of a molded clay sculpture."[4]

It seems quite appropriate that Frank Gehry's Guggenheim Museum in Bilbao, his great masterpiece, should be located in the same country as Gaudí's buildings for there is no way that we could have Gehry's architecture today without Gaudí first establishing a vocabulary for this kind of fluid asymmetrical architecture. I hesitated also because the buildings are after all only faced in ceramic but finally, the ceramics is more than skin, more than just clothing. Ceramics was a primary means of articulation for Gaudí and if stripped of the complex tile elements, their color, texture, historical association, textural contrast and other qualities, a Gaudí building would not be a Gaudí building.

Gaudí's love of the ceramic medium and the core belief in its beauty and primacy as a decorative material is intrinsic to the success of the total vision. The reasons for choosing Casa Batlló instead of say Güell Park (my close second choice) are many including the complexity and diversity of ceramics in this building but as Zerbst writes, "There is probably no other building that better illustrates what is modern in Gaudí's work and that does so with such a sensuous, almost symbolic manner."[5] There is also no other architecture from this period of even the later Art Deco period where ceramics is used as a primary material that rivals Gaudí in terms of art and originality and that includes the work Hector Guimard, Jules Lavirotte, Charles Klein and others.

The first choice was preordained. There is only one ceramic object that has an uncontested place in the Avant-Garde Hall of Fame, Marcel Duchamp's *Fountain*. I am sure that you all know this work but for the few who do not, let me briefly restate its history. *Fountain* was a standard Bedfordshire model porcelain urinal that Duchamp had selected randomly (not because its form was so comely and sexual) from J.L. Mott Iron Works, a plumbing store in New York City. He submitted it to be shown upside down at the Independents Salon in 1917 under the nom de plume, R. Mutt. Even though anyone who paid the entrance fee was supposed to have at least one artwork included in the salon, the committee rejected the *Fountain* on the basis that it was not art.

Duchamp, was on the committee, but the rest of the committee (apart from his cohort, the collector Walter Arensberg) had no idea that it was his work. He listened to them rail against his ready-made and then without admitting authorship, he and Arensberg resigned in protest and the *Fountain* became the cause célèbre of the Salon. Beatrice Wood, later to become the internationally known master of luster pottery, weighed into the fracas in 1917 writing in *The Blind Man* magazine that the reason for the *Fountain's* rejection, that it was not art, was absurd because, "the only works of art that America has given us are her plumbing and her bridges."[6]

Fortunately, it ended up in the studio of Alfred Stieglitz two weeks later where Duchamp persuaded the amused photographer to record the piece on film.

There are several interesting facts about the most famous ceramic art object of the 20th century. Firstly, its life was short, maybe a couple of months at most, and during that time only a couple of dozen people saw the piece in the flesh, so to speak. Wood was one of this small cadre and while we often discussed the *Fountain* and its controversy, I learned little about the object itself. After all the point of the piece was its banality. Its power came from dislocation, moving it from the public men's room to a public exhibition hall. It disappeared shortly after this photograph was taken. Stieglitz probably threw it out with his trash when he moved locations. Duchamp was indifferent to its fate. He did nothing to preserve his ready-mades once they were completed and most of the early works, the *Bicycle Wheel* and *Bottle Rack* suffered the same fate. He saw them as ephemeral, not concrete, allowing them their mortality.

Why did this object have the power to so disturb the art establishment of its day and remain as potent and unsettling an icon today? In 1917, part of the outrage was over this porcelain object's indelicate function in our life. It had to be described carefully in the press as a bathroom fixture, calling it a urinal would have offended standards of decency at the time. Then there is the matter of the charged symbolic imagery. As Duchamp's biographer Calvin Tomkins points out, the urinal has "female attributes that serves as a receptacle for male fluid, thus becomes—even more provocatively than Brancusi's Portrait of Princess Bonaparte—a symbol of the sexual comedy that underlies all of Duchamp's mature work."[7]

Bodily functions aside, *Fountain* offended the arts community on just about every level. It was a found object and no conventional authorship was involved. Even the nom de plume "R.Mutt" seemed insulting as a mutt was slang for a mongrel dog. No skill or craftsmanship was attached to its creation. It was anti-art. It was truly subversive. The controversy over Fountain has continued ever since. Part of the debate is over the aesthetics of the form itself. In theory the "beauty" of a ready-made was immaterial as the work was selected for its conceptual relevance with "visual indifference." Yet, in defending the piece, even in its day, Arensberg, in common with other supporters, was drawn to its visual strength referring to its "lovely form and chaste simplicity." Some saw in this white shimmering object a seated porcelain Buddha while Duchamp's biographer, Calvin Tomkins remarks that it takes little imagination to see the curving lines of a classic Madonna or even one of Brancusi's polished erotic forms.[8]

Stieglitz was also taken by the purity of form. In his photograph he deliberately heightened both the object's sexual and aesthetic qualities through emphasizing the urinal's fecund volume and the lyrical silhouette, casting veil like shadow over part of the piece. In 1964, Alfred Barr, director of the Museum of Modern Art, confronted Duchamp and demanded why, if he had selected his ready-mades with such aesthetic indifference, "do they all look so beautiful today?" "Nobody's perfect," Duchamp replied in vintage style.[9]

As the years pass the *Fountain's* celebrity only increases, as enigmatic and ubiquitous an artwork now as the *Mona Lisa*. In recognition of its substantial influence I curated an exhibition in 1997 entitled "Homage to R. Mutt" to celebrate the 80th anniversary of this Fine Art *Pissoir's* rude arrival upon the art scene.[10] I was astounded by the number of artists working on this subject and the many different materials into which it had been interpreted. The exhibition was only a sampling but included the work of Marek Cecula scatology series, Claes Oldenburg's *soft toilet*, Robert Arneson's first *Funk John*, Ron Baron's *American Standard* and Alfred alumni, Kim Dickey's *Lady J's*, elegant erotic objects that gave women standing equality at the urinal. The *Lady J's* raised a multiplicity of questions about ceramics, beauty, gender role playing, taboos and utility in the private realm of the bathroom.

Included in the show was Mike Bidlo's 1995 homage to Duchamp, entitled, *Origins of the World*, a replica of the Fountain against a painting in the style of Georgia O'Keefe. Bidlo, a leading appropriationist artist, spent two years making over 1,000 drawings of the Fountain that recently exhibited at the Shifrazi Gallery in New York, one of the finest drawing exhibitions in years. All of this serves to illustrate the raw power of ideas, not just those temporal moments of protest but the truly innovative statements that shift our conceptual attitudes permanently and establish new ground.

Our exhibition was hugely popular but response on the part of the ceramics community was surprisingly ambivalent. As much as the *Fountain* symbolizes conceptual freedom it also raises cynicism, fears and insecurities because it has none of the individuality of handicraft, no magic touch from the potter's hand and no palette of exotic glazes to give it the values that ceramics traditionally reveres. The additional rub is that the most famous ceramic object of the 20th century is not made by a ceramist. One could go on to examine this amazing object for hours but the time has come to move on and the closing words on this debate belong to Martin Smith, the British ceramist and head of the ceramics department of the Royal College of Art in London. Smith neatly summarized the *Fountain* fracas when he stated at a conference some years ago that what this urinal proves is that"craft is what we piss *in*, art is what we piss *on*."[11]

What does this add up to? Of the five objects only one was by a ceramist. Even that single inclusion is still highly speculative on my part although support in fine art ranks for Ohr's aesthetic deification is rising. There are no other contenders for inclusion out of the ceramics world that I can present with conviction. One choice is a building by an architect and not an object in the more conventional sense although I have always seen Gaudí's buildings first as sculpture and secondly as architecture. Three of the five objects are products of industry and they bear none of William Morris's virtues of social and aesthetic redemption through craftsmanship and the work ethic. Also absent is the reverence for quoting historical ceramics (mainly Asian), that guided the development of most ceramic art prior to 1950. Yet, all three objects evoke deep resonances, responses and arguments based on familiar and traditional utilitarian roles native to ceramic tradition that the ceramic world, transfixed by outdated conventions of beauty, resisted exploring in a more symbolic manner.

None of the three industrially made works express the ideal of "heart, hand and head in balance—the whole man"[12] that the potter Bernard Leach and the most influential single theorist during this era, proposed as the ideal of ceramic art. One of them is covered with fur so one cannot even see the ceramic surface although we know that it lies there below the hirsute coat. One has to agree that all that Duchamp and Oppenheim did with their found ceramics, with the slightest of modifications, was to contextualize them. But one must also acknowledge that this act proved to have greater impact on our culture's understanding of art than material skill or pyrotechnic bombast, an important lesson.

What can we learn from this? And we should gain some practical knowledge from this kind of exercise. After all, if history is not studied in order to better understand today and to evolve strategies for tomorrow, it becomes little more than academic necrophilia. While the lessons are not necessarily new, they are worth repeating:

One. Ceramics, as a movement rather than a material, emerges from this study as an art of evolution and not revolution. Prior to 1950 the ceramic Avant-Garde does seem to be a contradiction in terms. It is not easy to be a revolutionary when one takes a year or more to perfect a new clay body or when one is maintaining a studio with five tons of complex equipment. As my professor at the Royal College of Art, Lord Queensberry once said, "you do not need to buy a 50 cubic foot kiln to make conceptual statement, get yourself a typewriter instead."[13] (This statement was made in 1974 before the advent of the personal computer.) This rootedness to place, materials and equipment creates a cautious, conservative approach to art that does not prevent but certainly discourages the conceptual agility necessary to be a dealer in Avant-Garde currency.

Two. It is clear that ceramics' long held anti-intellectualism and determined empiricism has exacted a heavy price and left us marginalized in a world of art that increasingly is about ideas and less and less about skill and materials. It is obvious now that the prize for creativity does not go to the potter with the best throwing skills, the most unique glazes or the biggest kiln. Nonetheless, the field does remain dominated by a what Donald Kuspit calls, "a nostalgic reprise and metaphor of nature, often in the form of special devotion to clay and glazing, even fetishizing of them, in an effort to make ceramic work a material epiphany."[14]

Three. We find out from this exercise that our practice of art history is primitive and elementary, still rooted in material culture. We are nowhere near being on a par with the rest of the academic inquires into art and that includes photography, as new an entrant to the fine arts stakes as ceramics. This is one of the major stumbling blocks in gaining a place in mainstream art history and theory. What we bring to this table is usually too rudimentary and too poorly digested to be taken seriously. For instance, what are Peter Voulkos's top ten works? He is ceramics' greatest and best known artist but even for Voulkos this step in scholarly sophistication has not taken place. Two books have been written about him. Both are hagiographic rather than analytical. They are love letters not disciplined aesthetic inquiries. This tends to be the rule in what passes for scholarship in our field.

Four. Can we even list the top ten vessels in 20th century ceramics? No we cannot with any degree of scholarly agreement and while such lists are in some ways specious and artificial, the actual process by which they are arrived at—debate, research, scholarship and comparative analysis—is at the very core of a critical discipline. Our inability to deliver this kind of academic rigor combined with an almost pre-natal hostility to art theory, leaves ceramics inarticulate and unconvincing when we try to enter ceramics into the debate of defining the visual art mainstream.

Five. What is clear, is that even though ceramics has suffered discrimination in a bogus hierarchy of materials that the fine arts erected some centuries ago (which I am happy to report is fast eroding), this is of little consequence. Even if this attitude did not exist, our marginalization has to do with the fact that we achieved very little that could have earned us a place in the front lines of Modernist attack. As Clement Greenberg pointed out at the first International Ceramics Symposium in 1979, ceramics as a field is too transfixed with opinion and not concerned enough about achievement.

Six. What is clear is that nearly all ceramic art of the period from 1900 to 1950 belongs unequivocally in the disciplines of the decorative and applied arts. Had I approached this subject from a design point of view, the tenor of this talk would have been upbeat and filled with exceptional objects and primary contributions. Indeed this would make an excellent follow up paper. At least for the first half of this century, the notion of ceramics as a fine art activity is bogus and can be finally laid to rest. We did not participate except in the most superficial way (Ohr excepted) and the few ceramic works we can point to of mainstream significance were made by visitors to ceramics: Noguchi, Nevelson, Fontana and Archipenko – not by our rank and file.

Finally, I wish to close with two questions as to what we can do about this situation, firstly the action that needs to be taken within art history to make sure that we are properly and accurately represented and, secondly, what we can learn from this exercise and apply to plans for our future.

Let us take art history and examine the challenge. Obviously, we cannot claim a special place for ceramics in the Avant-Garde. We should be grateful to Duchamp, Gaudí, Oppenheim, Malevich and possibly Ohr for ensuring that there is at least some ceramic work in the canon. The focus should be moved from the obsessive search for fine arts legitimacy to real achievement, our considerable contribution to design and architecture. This aspect of ceramics is what bonds us to early Modernism and we should celebrate it more aggressively.

From 1950 the game changes. Even though we contributed negligibly to the Avant-Garde of this period as well, we did make a significant and rich contribution to fine art sculpture and object making. Not only do we have great artists to present (Voulkos, Arneson, Coper and others) but we have great artists who have, from time to time, entered into our world and made work in collaboration with ceramists that is significant art (Picasso, Miró, Chagall, Arman, Fontana, Caro, Cragg and others). Collectively we have a lot to offer. The challenge is documenting, arguing and presenting this fact to a skeptical art history world.

This must be communicated in academic parlance not in the touchy-feely patois of the crafts. We also need to convince art history to expand the vocabulary of art to include some language that is unique to ceramic art, particularly in as it relates to vessels. Then we have to make a more difficult argument, in the face of the Avant-Garde's omnipotence, that being an art of evolution is not an automatic disqualifier. An art of interpretation rather than innovation has a vital role in the broad tapestry of the visual arts.

Wayne Higby located the territory that ceramics occupies in a 1979 address at the first International Ceramics Symposium where he quoted from "Halfway Down" a poem by A.A. Milne:

Halfway down the stairs
Is a stair
Where I sit.
There isn't any
Other stair
Quite like
It.
I'm not at the bottom,
I'm not at top;
So this is the stair
Where
I always stop
Halfway up the stairs
Isn't up,
And isn't down.
It isn't in the nursery,
It isn't in the town.
And all sorts of funny thoughts
Run round my head:
"It isn't really
Anywhere!
Its somewhere else
Instead!"[15]

Our task is to get the fine arts to understand that "somewhere else" is a place worth visiting and taken seriously. Some progress is being made and more critics—Peter Schjeldahl, Donald Kuspit, Christopher Knight, Roberta Smith, Arthur Danto and others—are beginning to address the issue and incorporate ceramics into their vision. We have to provide education, encouragement and practical support to continue this trend.

I realize that I am suggesting nothing short of a complete overhaul of the antiquated and antiquarian apparatus of ceramic art history. We were once moving down this path in the early 1980's but by the end of the decade the ceramics world seemed either to lose will, become distracted or else fear the process which is by its nature tough, elitist and excluding. And just who is the magic "we" that will achieve this. It takes fewer people than you might imagine to effect change. Half a dozen impassioned scholars could turn this around. Ideally, new voices should come from the art history field at large and not just ceramics itself. We want the argument broadened not narrowed.

Getting this going has to be a collective effort. It can come from schools like this, from the International Ceramic Museum in Alfred that sponsored this talk, from other museums that support us, journals, schools, groups such as the National Council on Education for the Ceramic Arts (NCECA) and Ceramic Arts Foundation (CAF). Even individual artists, dealers and collectors who feel that time has come for a more ambitious placement of ceramic's role in the journals of 20th century culture. David McFadden, chief curator of the American Craft Museum has already set off down this path, hosting a series of meetings to try and find out what might be a meaningful new definition for craft today that could lead to a more liberal notion of creative making.

Finally, what of the future? If read superficially this paper seems to be saying to young ceramists today, "you are doomed to play a secondary role for all time, sidelined as a bit player in the fine arts because that is the nature and the karma of ceramic art." No, this is not the case at all. If this lecture has made anything clear at all it is that our fault lines are clearly evident and that we can overcome them. We may not even have a choice in the matter because there is a paradigm shift in ceramics of major seismic proportions, the most far reaching in a century, that is changing the character and landscape of ceramics.

There are several aspects to this shift, but I will focus on only two. The first is specialization. The notion of a single medium artist is under threat. Art education in Europe and to some extent in the United States is turning its back on material specialities as a means of training young artists. It is not just a backlash against craft. Leading schools like London's Goldsmiths College are even rejecting the labels of the fine arts—painter, sculptor, photographer—in favor of a free-wheeling pluralism in which any and all media are part of the mix. If this trend continues, and it seems to be building momentum, then ceramists could well be an endangered species unless a new contemporary format can be evolved for those who work in clay.

One practical impact of this shift can already be felt. More and more artists from the fine arts are now choosing to work in ceramics, among other media. The results are mixed but this is less important in the short term than the fact that ceramists are now facing competition from a group that has better access to the marketing systems and media in the arts. I warned the ceramics community years ago that conservatism in the field could well result in us losing our own market to celebrity players and it now seems possible that this could happen.

The second issue is: "The crafts are dead! Long live the crafts." If pressed for a date of demise I would have to place it around the mid-1980's. It is either an amusing or a depressing comment (depending upon your taste for irony) that none of those whose speciality is writing on the crafts have yet noticed this fact and posted obituary notices. This movement has lost its once grand, idealistic, socialist and aesthetic mission and in contemporary times its philosophy has been shriveled to mean "pretty materials and clever hands."

Our intellectual rhetoric has moved from the lofty heights of Ruskin and Morris to the pablum of Martha Stewart's glue-gun TV consumerism. For reasons too complex to discuss here, the nostalgia that was part of the movement's social traction no longer works on a younger generation. The romance of Medieval craft guilds does not inspire a generation whose nostalgia is for the objects and aesthetics of early industrialization. The crafts have lost the high ground and what survives now is predominantly an industry for delivering gimcracks, novelties and bibelots to gift shops, crafts fairs and Renaissance parks.

Whether we like it or not a new intellectual *raison d'être* has to be developed. The death of crafts on the one hand and the impending death of specialization on the other, mean that we are facing a decade of enforced re-invention which we can resist and retreat deeper into our traditional laager or else we leap in enthusiastically and rewrite the rules so that we become more relevant within our culture. This is an opportunity but with painful consequences if we do not act. To make the navigation through the sea of change less perilous we would be wise to learn from art history and avoid the obvious pitfalls of the past. No matter what we do, ceramics itself will survive in one form or another. But ceramics art, as we have defined it, may not. Failure to take the initiative could mean that ceramists will never outgrow its traditional boundaries and we could end up forever trapped between a toilet and hard place.

Notes

1. Quoted in Garth Clark, *The Mad Potter of Biloxi: The Art and Life of George E. Ohr* (New York: Abbeville Press, 1989), 126.
2. Ibid. 136.
3. Ibid. 139.
4. Rainer Zerbst, *Antoni Gaudí* (Cologne: Taschen, 1993), 165.
5. Ibid. 164.
6. Although the piece, "The Richard Mutt Case," is not signed by Wood but she claims to have written and it is generally accepted as being of her authorship. Wood was one of the three editors with Duchamp and Henri Pierre Roche of the issue of *Blindman Magazine* in which it appeared in 1917.
7. Calvin Tomkins, *Duchamp, A Biography* (New York: Henry Holt, 1996), 186.
8. Ibid.
9. Ibid. 427.
10. From author's notes, 1987. Also see Garth Clark, "Homage to R. Mutt," *Keramik Magazin*, (Nov/Dec, 1997), 29–31 for a more detailed explanation both of the *Fountain* and the R. Mutt exhibition.
11. Bernard Leach quote in *Bernard Leach: Fifty Years a Potter* (London: Arts Council of Great Britain, 1961) and reprinted in Garth Clark, ed., *Ceramic Art: Comment and Review* 1882–1977 (New York: E.P. Dutton, 1978), 86.
12. Author's notes, 1975.
13. Donald Kuspit, "Directions and Issues in the Ceramic Sculpture of the Nineties," *Studio Potter*, (June 1998), 20. This article is worth looking into because it deals with Avant-Garde sensibility in contemporary ceramics. However, I should add the caveat that I disagree strongly with Kuspit's narrow view both of the vessel and what he sees as traditional ceramics. The piece reveals a misunderstanding of ceramic history and makes claims for contemporary ceramics without realizing that they are less innovative than he realizes and are based on "traditional" ceramics.
14. A.A. Milne, *Halfway Down*, p. 81.

Source: First Annual Dorothy Wilson Perkins Lecture
Schein-Joseph International Museum of Ceramic Art at Alfred University October 27, 1998.

Reproduced with permission of the author.

SECTIO[illegible] CONCE[illegible]TUDIO PRACTICE

Introductory [illegible]

The texts in t[illegible]enced, show a transition from what might be considered a 'modernist' position to 'postmodern' position. Craft skills and truth to materials became less important as did the industrial object as a focus rather than the studio object.

Lizzie Zucker Saltz's text gives a polemic critique of critics and their responses to artworks in clay and is chosen as another example of an argument in art/craft debate. This essay also usefully sets a number of artists work in a wider US context including Michael Lucero, Ted Saupe, Charles LeDray, Steven Montgomery, Katherine Ross and Marek Cecula.

Writing for the catalogue to accompany the exhibition 'Dirt on Delight: Impulses that form clay', Ingrid Schaffner discusses a range of works that might be described as 'formless' or in a state of flux. The exhibition featured a wide range of artists working through the twentieth century. Schaffner makes the case that clay appeals to base impulses and working with clay is a primordial experience.

Writing in 2007, artist Clare Twomey's essay for the book *Breaking the Mould – New approaches to ceramics* offers an overview of the cutting edge of ceramic practice at the time. In particular, this text shows how contemporary artists working with clay have blurred the boundaries between craft, fine art and design.

After the turn of the twenty-first century a number of ceramic artists emerged who might be said to have expanded the potential of ceramics by using it for installations, performances and time-based works. Often the finished object was less important than the process of making or the 'completion' of a work through interaction with an audience. Jo Dahn's essay gives examples of projects and approaches by a generation of UK artists including Keith Harrison, Clare Twomey, Conor Wilson, Paul Sandammeer, Philip Lee, Bonnie Kemske, Daniel Allen and David Cushway who are making work 'informed by ideas'.

The use of film, animation and video in combination with ceramics has become more prevalent in the last fifteen years and Andrew Livingstone's text considers this development with reference to examples of his own work and other artists. He introduces the notion of the 'performative other' to describe examples of the use of 'non-ceramic' media being used by ceramic artists often through performance.

For much of the twentieth century, there has been a distinction between 'studio ceramics', pieces made by an individual in their studio, and 'industrial ceramics', mass-produced pieces made through a division of labour. Glenn Adamson describes a new phenomenon in the first decade of the twenty-first century in which ceramics artists are producing work outside of the studio. At times this takes place in industry for example in China where artists like Felicity Aylieff can take advantage of the increase in scale that industry can offer. There is also an emerging trend for ceramic artworks to be 'completed' outside of the studio. For example, Keith Harrison fires his piece in the gallery with the public watching to create performance works. Clare Twomey's 2006 work 'Trophy' consisted of small ceramic birds made by Wedgwood that were placed throughout the sculpture courts of the Victoria and Albert Museum. At a given time visitors were invited to view the work and take a bird home with them. So the artwork was completed outside of the studio with this 'performative' act.

Livingstone and Petrie

36

MANUFACTURING VALIDITY: THE CERAMIC WORK OF ART IN THE AGE OF CONCEPTUAL PRODUCTION

Lizzie Zucker Saltz

> Clay is not like any other art material ...(it) may have had a noble past, but in contemporary life it is as debased as it is ubiquitous; hence the references to and quotations of kitsch ... But clay is also china, plates, and pots. Will it ever rise above this domestic shelf? Should it?
>
> —John Perreault., "Fear of Clay," 1982[1]

From Jessica Stockholder's wastebaskets to Damien Hirst's carcasses, medianomadism practically defines the contemporary artist working in three-dimensions. Yet 17 years after John Perreault made this observation, resistance to the ceramic work of art persists. What accounts for its exclusion from the broad material embrace of our critical climate?

I Taxonomic ghetto

Thumbing through a sheaf of reviews covering Michael Lucero's 1996 mid-career retrospective tour reveals how widespread this taxonomic crisis is, affecting hack newspaper reviewers and glossy art-rag critics alike. Witness Carter Ratcliffe's squirming in Art in America:

> The American Craft Museum [as a] venue had a certain rightness because Lucero uses clay and clay is considered a craft material. Yet I have always thought ... Lucero's esthetic ancestors are sculptors of high modernist ambition, not craftspeople who have opted out of the modernist game. ... The retrospective reminded me of this conflict and then left me baffled. I couldn't see precisely where his allegiances are. Though I still felt certain that he works in a fine-art tradition, I wasn't much reassured by my certainty. Lucero's way of being an artist isn't entirely familiar.[2]

or Edward J. Sozanski attempt to explain it away in The Philadelphia Inquirer:

> Lucero is often characterized as a "craft artist" because he works in clay. In fact, Lucero is a sculptor and painter who happens to like clay's physical properties ...[3]

After reading enough of this you start seething: "Get over it!" Though a minority of Lucero critics do gloss over these issues in order to focus on his particular oeuvre, it's easy to imagine the impact of this critical

---

Source: © Lizzie Zucker Saltz.

climate – one would have to be headstrong, pathologically addicted to invalidation, or outright indifferent to artworld recognition to stick it out. That the latter is the most prevalent attitude was lamented by Gabi Dewald, Editor of the German magazine Keramik, who, in a recent lecture titled "Welcome to the Club of the Outcasts," placed the blame squarely on the shoulders of the international community of ceramists and their collectors:

> [T]hat ceramics as a material is excluded from events such as The Venice Biennale is false. … It is however correct that artists who work exclusively with clay hardly ever make an appearance in galleries, museums … outside the applied arts and crafts industry. … [T]here is a whole web of ceramic facilities that cover the ceramic niche with a protective wrapper and protect the plants from the acid rain of open criticism and free competition. … [these] associations do not offer a critical discussion and confrontation, but try to support the situation through self-confirmation and a kind of confederation of the misunderstood … to what extent are we dealing with the solidarity of outcasts?[4]

As anyone who's ever spent time with a couples counselor knows, blame's a two-way game: Dewald zeros in on artists' material exclusivity as the source of the problem; however, this is not only inaccurate when it comes to real-world exhibition practices – as we will see – but relates to problematic critical assumptions with implications far beyond the critical reception of this one sub-genre. How the ceramic material is manipulated turns out to be more germane to a work's reception than that it is used. Its exclusive use is conventionally antithetical to conceptual practice – the latter aligned with the aesthetics of mechanical reproduction as a kind of short-hand for postmodernity.

But Dewald's personification of ceramics as a field is useful in focusing on the sociology of sub-groups, where the heart of the matter lies. After a three-year hiatus from the "clay ghetto," as it is referred to by its self-deprecating denizens, I was as desensitized as any other upwardly-mobile minority member comfortably ensconced in a liberal enclave – that is, until I pitched a review of Ted Saupe's solo sculpture show at LaGrange College Gallery (just south of Atlanta), to the kindly editor of this very magazine. His tactful email reply – "We're not opposed to covering craft-issued art, as long as it's addressed on a conceptual level." – caused me to bonk myself on the forehead for not anticipating his guarded response, and for not consciously qualifying Saupe's ceramic sculptures in my mind as "craft-issued," although in some respects they are more so than Lucero's. The feeling gave me a flashback to a studio visit that art critic Jerry Saltz (no relation) paid me in the winter of '96, at the end of which he asked if I considered myself "a ceramic sculptor or a sculptor." Sensing that this was a loaded question, I spit out the correct answer, "Sculptor," with a traitorous flush. His telling response was "Good, because there have been no great ceramic sculptors." When I stammered out a meek "What about Robert Arneson?," the notion was swatted away like a fly had landed on Saltz's nose. I was suddenly aware of being in very Nochlin-esque territory – not just because of the startlingly coincidental symmetry of Saltz' pronouncement with the title of Nochlin's landmark 1974 essay, "Why Have There Been No Great Women Artists," but because the fickle nature of artworld validation was as apparent from these margins as it had been from the feminist and multicultural margins, and not uncoincidentally.

II The girly-boys club

So, while I shouldn't have been surprised that a Saupe review would be a hard-sell to a contemporary art magazine, it's a pity, since there's a lot about Saupe's ceramic work of interest to the general art-viewing public. He's like a male Mary Kelly – witty, understated, unpretentious and personal without being self-indulgent.

His diaristic tracings of life as a Boomer-Dad to three young 'uns reflects Saupe's role as a primary bread maker rather than bread winner (his wife is a lawyer). Blue-stained diagrams of domesticity tattoo the surfaces of his loosely modeled male figures and animals: bowls with spoons and pots with ladles decorate grumbling stomachs, a cup sticks out of the side of one fellow's head like a reminder to fetch a cup of juice, a butter dish floats above a pregnant woman with an arrow pointed at her brain, lest we forget she has one. The drawing is as casual as face-doodles scrawled by the phone, as tentative as a Susan Rothenberg. Ladders, stick-figures, shovels, staircases and single shoes all attest to the chore-filled, three-ring circus of two-working-parents-family-life in the '90s. Textual snatches of kiddie babble adorn the pieces – a result of Saupe working with children in his studio. Off-kilter poetic snatches like "Thirst-Day" also recall the purposeful misspellings and absurdist free-associations of the Beat-influenced, pun-fond, California Bay Area Funk of the early-'70s, where and when Saupe began his art education.

But as autobiographical testimony to the slow but sure post-feminist shift in masculine roles, Saupe's sculptures fly right under most critics' radar, their aggressive clayworld-ness acting like interfering static. It's not simply that they are ceramic – as Dewald noted, there have been plenty of critically well-received pieces made out of the material; for example, Jeff Koons' celebrity-as-royalty bauble blow-up, Michael Jackson & Bubbles. But 30 years post-ready-made, Saupe's hand-manipulated surfaces read first and foremost as a sign of the non-industrial in the context of the mainstream artworld, thus regressively Modernist. The clayworld's longstanding critical segregation means it plays by a different set of rules, within which Saupe's infantilized and feminized content has a double-meaning in relation to ceramic artworks' pigeonholing by recent western art history. And rather than some arbitrary ceramist's tick, pimpling his pieces with ancient pot forms reads as consistent with his theme of juggling the personal and professional realms – similar to Gregory Gillespie's canvases' integration of painting-studio references.

Saupe has been a Professor of Ceramics for 18 years, as well as a ceramic materials consultant for an excavation in Kavousi, Crete since 1992, where he has sifted through shards, re-discovering the precise nature of ancient working methods for the edification of archeologists. (Before this series, Saupe made almost exclusively historically-referential vessels – with the significant exception of performance, painting and installation work in the mid-'80s.) Taglines like "Another nod to the minow-ins" and "Sojourn of the Urn" allude to the art of Minoan and Etruscan civilizations – the animals visual quotations from them. Sub-structural supports for large vessels are often called ribs, thus the frequent drawings of externalized rib cages on the figures' torsos punnily refer back to the body's vessel-like qualities. Similarly, penises are replaced with downturned Amphorae jars, their neck-handles reading as externalized vas deferens. Amphorae stored libations, so upside-down they refer obviously to urination. But their hollowness emphasizes the penis as something that fills and empties, a remarkably peaceful and modest metaphor in comparison to typically ever-erectile, western phallic symbols like the skyscraper and gun. Consistent with this, the words "Only a Feeling" are penned just above one figure's penis – it's no wonder one male observer mistook an amphora-penis for an emerging baby, despite the figures' unambiguously male facial stubble and flat chests. Within the clayworld, all these nuances add-up to a pointedly postmodern sense of dual-temporality and info-overload. Yet within the artworld, the plethora of pre-industrial pottery references, especially in the absence of any evidence of the world of electronica – which surely must invade Saupe's domestic sphere in the form of VCR's, cellphones, Game-Boys, ATM's etc. – comes off as peculiarly anachronistic, more evidence of ceramic artists' immersion in Dewald's "Club of the Outcasts."

In the artworld, the politicized craft object has been coopted as aesthetic fodder for feminist and multi-cultural cannons since Harmony Hammond et al. fired the opening salvos, and by now it has been mined almost to the point of exhaustion by au courant conceptualists from Jim Hodges to Elaine Reichek. Yet clay-ghetto denizens have historically evaded just such associations through over-compensatory macho gestures (another factor germane to interpreting Saupe's gentle gender subversions); ceramist and clay-mixer salesman Paul Soldner's ads featuring himself with scantily clad young women are an infamous example.

Commenting wryly on these intricacies is Zizi Raymond's photocollage, reproduced in an exhibition catalogue devoted to Robert Arneson's pedagogical legacy at UC-Davis, which was central to the "Clay Revolution" of the mid-'60s. As a grad student Raymond placed the collage in the hallway of the legendary "TB-9" ceramic facility: it featured Arneson's smug-face – well-known from his myriad self-portraits – grafted onto the body of a naked, female torso. In the same catalog, Ann Perrigo characterized TB-9's atmosphere as a "twilight of straight, white-boy bonding; that ineffable mixture of beer ... cheap cigars, pool and poker."[5] Raymond's collage operated as a sardonic "Abandon Hope All Ye Who Enter Here" warning: no matter how infamous Arneson's sexism, even he could not completely overcome the trivializing feminization of the ceramic medium in the masculinist material pecking order. Bay Area ceramist Ron Nagle recalled that given "the attitudes of the '50s ... It took a lot of guts to make those little dinky things with bright colors on them!"[6] Funk Ceramics was obsessed with bringing high art down to the level of hobby-shop-ceramics, thus its frequent association with East Coast Pop Art. Some even argue that Funk Ceramics pre-dates Claes Oldenburg's Store installation. Regardless, the motivations were quite different, as Bruce Nixon articulated in his TB-9 catalogue foreword:

> Funk ... at least as practiced at Davis, had a singularly suburban character: this was not the funk of the Beats who were citizens of an urban world ... it was an inversion of Pop, but it had none of Pop's highly urbanized East Coast ironies[;] there was instead the zany playfulness of Mad Magazine or the Sunday funnies ... this was the work of a suburban artschool lifestyle, work which meant to offend, but offend with a playful innocence that clearly was not of the city in any way.[7]

As an amazing number of well-known artists, from Bruce Nauman to William T. Wiley, took active part in the early days of this scene, it is not hard to trace Funk's influence to Cal-Art "Bad Boys," or the current revival of "Bad Art."[8]

Saupe's relationship to ceramic's Funk roots is as apparent as his borrowing from pre-industrial ceramic history, yet there are vast differences in the reception of his kind of work and that of a California conceptual object maker, like Charles LeDray, who also addressed ceramic history in a piece called Milk and Honey: 2 Thousand Porcelain Objects (1994–96). A slick vitrine, it contains six glass shelves packed with stark white miniaturized pots whose lack of color implies that their museological entombment has drained them of their life blood and robbed them of their individuality. It's a compact visual essay on the industrial displacement of the ceramic arts, underscored by the fact that LeDray reproduced actual historical vessels, recognizable to those in the know through auteur signatures, such as "The Mad Potter of Biloxi" George Ohr's wiggly vase handles. That only the feet and mouths of most of the pots are visible reinforces this narrative of indifference – they are merely ghosts of pots past.

Critics such as Robert Taplin missed out on these aspects of the piece: "LeDray's conjuring of the one and the many is compact and precise, its myriad tiny bodies all forming part of a single larger body, like a marvelous multicellular creature. ... [It] transmits an exalted sense of limitlessness – the microcosm and the macrocosm in confluence."[9] Taplin's bio-evolutionary reading erases the significance of Le Dray's piece as a literal minimization of thousands of years of specific civilizations' sophisticated, pre-industrial art. Had miniatures of western landscape paintings been used instead, one doubts that this historical angle would have been lost on Taplin. It should be noted that Milk and Honey was recently purchased by the Whitney, a fate unlikely to befall Saupe soon.

Considering Saupe's clay-ghetto status raises larger issues about the formation of our critical expectations: If Saupe was an isolated rural folk artist or a Haitian voudou practitioner, rather than an educated WASP, male college professor, would the perception of his work as "craft-issued" and therefore out of sync, be suspended? Has the incorporation of the aesthetic of mechanical reproduction become naturalized in three-dimensional sculptural production to the point that a critic like Taplin doesn't even take note?[10] Even when ceramic works of art confront industrial issues head on they are often misread and subject to sexist-tinged associations, as was the case in Rita Reif's New York Times coverage of Steven Montgomery's exhibit at OK Harris Gallery. Montgomery's cast and oil-painted engine sculptures appear to be in the process of internally-combusting their exposed raw clay innards. Reif quotes dealer Ivan Karp: "'I was drawn to the machines for their sculptural vitality and wasn't aware of the material...that for me and everybody else was a grand surprise.... Mention ceramics, and most people think of vessels or something adorable or lovable or at least tender.'" Reif adds that for Karp, "Montgomery's objects are not adorable or tender; they are aggressive" – the ultimate in cliché masculine validation and the inverse of Karp's feminine associations. She then defensively explains that the "gallery does not specialize in ceramics, but Mr. Karp...found the works provocative."[11] All this negotiating distracts from the clear opposition in Montgomery's work between pre-industrial, primordial clay and clay as literally molded by the machine age.[12] Montgomery even gives his works ambivalent titles like Partial Yield and Divergence, and is quoted as self-consciously "commenting on [his] distrust of technology," and experiencing a near-fatal auto conflagration after which he never renewed his driver's license. Why ignore the impact of the amorphous, fingered-poked, gaping wounds, so obviously integral to what these pieces are about, and so obviously clay?

III Claystory

As Karp's attitude reflects the artworld's ignorance, and thus insensitivity, to the politics of clayworld history, what follows is a brief, terribly over-simplified history. The education of the ceramic artist differs in significant ways from the standard post-Renaissance, western art history canon that still, by and large, informs contemporary art curators, gallery owners and critics. Few institutions offer Decorative Art History, not to mention ceramic history, and rarely is the 20th century covered, not terribly surprising considering that ceramics was taught in Home Economics departments throughout the '60s in many American colleges.[13] Instead, studio artist teachers cram short slide lectures, and more rarely, readings, into their ceramic syllabi in an attempt to fill in the gaps. Despite this informality, the ceramics major becomes aware that ceramics was technologically and artistically advanced by non-western, pre-Renaissance cultures such as Crete, Asia, South America and Africa; thus they have a de-centered and older take on art history than their fellow studio art majors. Students also can't help but become aware of the pathetic nature of European contributions to ceramics prior to its development of industrial applications.[14] There were European studio potters pre-industrialization, but practically no sculptural production in ceramics until well after the 1400s, when Marco Polo imported Eastern porcelain. In their zeal to avoid expensive imports, various European aristocrats offered rewards to anyone who yielded similar results from the markedly different local geology – a feat achieved eventually by an alchemist in Meissen, Germany. By the time that experimental clay body was perfected, the focus had turned towards the mass production of vessels via slip-casting technologies, using an assembly-line-like division of labor to cast and apply decorative motifs, initially entirely derivative of the Asian imports they strove to undercut.

As the development of a clay body suitable for significant scale sculpture was never an objective – as it was in non-western cultures – the European ceramic sculptural production that emerged was in the form of small-scale figurines with no irregular modeling marks incompatible with casting, the forefathers of the Koons send-up.[15] In the '20s there was experimentation with sculptural ceramics in Europe and America, but cracking plagued larger efforts. Not until the '50s did it become technically possible for the ceramic medium to be used as an expressive sculptural medium in the west in a way that could even begin to rival the production of sculptural ceramics in pre-Renaissance, non-western cultures. This was in no small part thanks to the G.I. Bill, which funded students of Peter Voulkos at the Otis Art Institute, where large scale ceramics was pioneered. This work was promoted in 1961 by craft critic Rose Slivka in her wildly controversial article "The New Ceramic Presence."[16] Thus the use of the ceramic medium in America as an acknowledged Fine Art material has a shorter history than photography, a fact obfuscated by ceramic's ancient patina.

Another bizarre and little acknowledged factor is that sculptors and potters are trained in the same classes in American colleges, often up until the graduate levels – an outcome of the field's newness, the economics of shared facilities, and the medium's historical segregation from craft-phobic Sculpture Departments. Thus a large part of the influential Voulkos aesthetic, which Slivka cannily allied primarily with Abstract Expressionism, was inseparable from the history of American pottery. Broadly speaking, Otis was as much a product of the fact that Bernard Leach, the British craft writer, toured Korean folk potter Shoji Hamada around America in the '50s. Hamada's spontaneous throwing style, it should be pointed out, stood in stark contrast to mathematically-based European methodologies. It took American pottery by storm, soon devolving into oppressive gospel, weighing down the field with Eastern village values of humility and respect for elders inimical to the avant-garde rebellions characterizing mainstream American sculpture and painting.[17] Ceramic students, therefore, see Funk ceramics as a reaction to the Leach/Voulkos paternity, rather than as West Coast Pop, as it is explained in Modern Art Surveys who bother with it at all.

If Voulkos was ceramic sculpture's id and Arneson its ego, than Howard Kottler was its restrained super-ego. Kottler's conceptual approach came out of, but transcended, the dime-store surrealism of the post-Funk "Super-Object" stage in ceramics, in which photographic decal techniques pioneered by sculptors Robert Hudson and Richard Shaw were prevalent. As Professor at the University of Washington, Kottler spawned a generation of ceramic sculptors, among them Michael Lucero, who Kottler brought with him when he filled in for Arneson one term. Kottler's influence accounts in part for Lucero's savvy approach and his early decision to aim for integration into the larger artworld. Kottler's work has been resurfacing recently, following the publication of the posthumous coffee-table book, Howard Kottler: Face to Face.[18] It ages well, anticipating the strategies of artists like Cindy Sherman, whose campy 1990 dinnerware service, Madame de Pompadour (nee Poisson) resembles his many tongue-in-cheek appropriations of European painting in the form of the commemorative plate. In Like Father, Like Son, two Gainsborough Blue Boys were scaled big and little but topped with same-sized large heads, needling the big-headed arrogance of painting's colonial heritage. Yet, Kottler's output was limited – until Lucero, no one had confronted the collision of artworld norms and ceramic sculpture's legacy as coherently, persistently or prolifically.

IV Multiculti aggression

For the last decade, in series after series, Lucero has tirelessly butted up against that old devil, taxonomy, which would be painful to witness, were it not for his work's color-crazy, childlike exuberant defiance. As Jason Forrest nicely put it in a recent review of Lucero's work, "As certain schools of contemporary art continue to undermine the art object, I find a perverse pleasure in Lucero's work. ... I am always intellectually amused...[but] always astonished to find his work categorized as 'craft.' This isn't his problem, but ours for letting 'craft' become the expendable option in the schools of the high-minded."[19] From March '96 through May '98, Lucero's mid-career retrospective of works since 1976 toured to five museums accompanied by a full color Phillip Morris-sponsored advertising blitz. Yet to the chagrin of co-curator Mark Leach, most of the tour sites were craft-oriented: "Much to Michael's misfortune...this recent work seems to rest in a kind of netherland. Critics and curators I otherwise respect put the work down as mere decorated ceramics – not capable of holding up to the criteria, whatever they are, they expect in contemporary sculpture."[20]

Lucero's "Pre-Columbus Series" appropriated the forms of handbuilt figure sculptures from the Americas of 1000 B.C. to 300 A.D., and flooded them with a riot of images from 20th century western art, kitsch and symbols of modernity like bar codes used ironically to date his art commodities. A typical piece is Young Lady with Ohr Hair (1991), whose bits from Sonia Delaunay and Joan Miró compete with cartoon-babyfaces screaming on her breasts, wittily conflating the needy with the satisfying object, as can be said of the hand superimposed over her genitals. Landscape quotes echo Hudson River painters. The hair's resemblance to the tops of some of George Ohr's late-1800s pots completes the stew of cultural references and asserts their aesthetic equality. In Lucero's "New World" pieces (1992–94), many of the same tropes are present, but the bodies are composed of archetypal wheel-thrown pots commissioned from potter Chris Daniels; thus they are tighter as a result of their machine-made symmetry. Lucero reinforced their western post-industrial status by incorporating mixed-media elements like a glass top hat, a baby-carriage, a blonde doll's wig done up in flouncy curls.

Lucero's "Reclamation Series" drove the point home even more didactically by grafting his ceramic history quotes onto the remnants of irreparably damaged found sculptures, like Afro-Carolinian Face Jug connected to the African wood carving in Ivory Carolina (1996). As Kevin Melchionne discerned, he "was not only physically reclaiming the damaged object by way of some ceramic prosthesis, he was reclaiming statuary itself as a viable genre for contemporary sculpture."[21] In "Dog Form with House and Zoomorphic Body Form" he also re-creates missing heads, i.e. their brains. In others, like Shepherd, it's the kitsch body that is recovered. The body/head switches question the Cartesian mind-body dualism implicit in exoticizing and minimizing artifacts from southern climes and "low-art." He also produced a number of non-figural pieces, many of which reference southern bottle trees – the most ironic of these is "Hello Duchamp" (1994), in which he took a copy of Duchamp's 1914 winebottle dryer readymade, reclaiming it from the realm of conceptual art, flipping the tables on whose art is considered "merely functional." Cheekily, Lucero has written his name over and over, one initial at a time, on the upturned vases' bottoms, self-consciously forcing himself into the contemporary fine art dialogue, continuing the legacy of Robert Arneson's Funk John series of 1964–65, made in homage to Duchamp's seminal urinal.

Debuting this year was Lucero's latest series, "Excavations," which functions even more aggressively as a protest against eurocentric critical biases. Each piece is a towering stack of forms glazed together in painterly pours of hot color. In keeping with Lucero's Bay Area breeding, there are plenty of visual puns relating to pottery, such as the real feet painted on the bases of pots at the bottom of one tower, referring to the term "foot" used for the bottom of a pot. Lucero has made towers of pots before, but they were never differentiated vertically as these are – towards the bottom are older references to pot forms and other pre-industrial vessels like baskets, and in one an ancient turtle implies the passage of hundreds of years. Scanning upwards, the references get more recent; the effect is of a time-line represented by excavated slices of pot-piles spanning thousands of years. At the tippy-top are objects unmistakably from our milieu – impersonal scientific beakers top Sunburn, a trashy seafood-restaurant-style pelican sits atop High Tide, a fusty brown academic bust forms the pinnacle of Dora. Large digital alarm-clock faces blink out another ironic reminder of the aesthetic depravity of the present. The joke is clear: the "height" of civilization is both cheesier and more depersonalized than what lies below it. Time does not necessarily equal progress, aesthetic or otherwise.

Despite the support implied by the large touring show and the sumptuous catalogue, with its essay by Lucy Lippard, the critical reception of these pieces is often mixed on account of the same confusions around the reception of ceramic sculpture, which, ironically, Lucero is addressing in his work. If I were to critique this last series I would point out that the work seems a bit rushed and transitional. Still, obviously ignorant of the density of Lucero's prolific output, one hotshot young New York sculptor asked Lucero at his show's opening if he considered himself a potter or a sculptor. "Can you believe it?" Lucero exclaimed when relating this to me.[22]

Though far less sterile, Lucero's work is no less a sculpture about vessels than conceptual object maker Charles Ray's Tabletop (1998) is. Like much of Ray's figurative work, this one is comically abject, an ode to the aesthetic poverty of common domestic vessels in suburbanal environments. Each vessel – several happen to be ceramic – spins atop an embedded, motorized turntable which emphasizes their mechanically wrought symmetry. This symmetry reflects the aesthetic compromises of mass-production – the fewer undercuts an object has, the fewer molds are required to produce it, which in turn lowers the cost of production. Yet Tabletop also reads as a bit passé, considering the downward trickle of tastefulness into mass marketing, from Martha Stuart's invasion of Kmart's linen section to Michael Graves' small-appliance line at Target. Increasingly sophisticated technologies of three dimensional making are making the William Morris and Bauhaus dreams of cheap, but beautiful designed objects suddenly much more accessible, though not via the efforts of the individual artisan as romantically envisioned by the '70s utopian crafts revival. Just as cappuccino can now be sipped across America, the yuppification of common objects – from biomorphic razors to ergonomic computer mice – complicates the reception of a work like Ray's Tabletop. Mass produced is less and less synonymous with aesthetically depraved.

In contrast, Lucero's work is resolutely individuated, which, despite its appropriationist sophistications, to some is a de facto a sign of recherché modernism when it comes to three-dimensional production. Yet, there is no doubt that his towers would feel far less passionate and lively had they been constructed, à la Nancy Rubins, literally out of the found things he recreates through molds, wheel-throwing and hand-modeling. Similar meanings might have been generated, but with an entirely less personal shading – his works, and Saupe's, function more like contemporaneous paintings than sculpture. Yet, in Roberta Smith's New York Times review of "Excavations," she saw fit to compare Lucero to the likes of several older generation California vessel makers with very different artistic intents from Lucero and from each other, saying that he "lacks the refinement and distinctness of ceramic artists like ...Ron Nagle...or Adrian Saxe."[23] A more fruitful approach would have been to consider Lucero in terms of any of the postmodern bricolagists that his immersion in the NYC artworld since the late '70s exposed him to, since his surface treatments so clearly relate to pictorialists like Sigmar Polke, David Salle, Squeak Carnwath or Cheryl Laemmle, the latter who, uncoincidentally, Lucero is married to. Smith confuses sculptural renditions of pots with pots, and ends up applying a double standard to Lucero. For when Smith reviewed German mixed-media artist Thomas Schütte's works the next month, some of which happened to be ceramic, she wrote that "Schütte ... is perhaps too skeptical to unleash such lavish painterliness on canvas, and it is much more immediate and distinctive in clay and glaze anyway. Even in the West we should not require proof that ceramics have long been the painting that dare not speak its name."[24] Never mind that Schütte's glazes are obviously "straight from the bottle," or that his egg forms have been done before by myriad ceramic sculptors (like Grace Knowlton or Sandra Shannonhouse) much better; to Smith he obviously ranks as a "real" artist. Notably, she did not reference one other ceramist in her review of Schütte.

V Manufacturing validity

When Gabi Dewald decried the clay-ghetto's insularity, she didn't explicitly link the problem to the brevity of ceramic's use in the western fine arts. Yet in other young arts like video and computer art, an unevenness is to be expected, as well as a self-protective defensiveness that mars artists' works aligned with many subcultural groups who hide behind their identities. When works of mediocre quality are promoted from within ghettos, such "keep hope alive" efforts earn the well-deserved scorn of artworld critics who see right through the pandering. The downside is that quality work is tainted by association, then dismissed out of hand, reinforcing the self-protective defenses and so on. This dynamic is reminiscent of problems with work shown in the early days of feminism at women-only galleries, or at any venue devoted to a special group, be it gays or disabled peoples – in a limited pool, quality becomes suspect. This is to the detriment of any artist associated with a sub-group, which is why many clay artists like Lucero assiduously shunned clay-exclusive galleries for many years. This contorted ghetto psychology gets wrapped up with issues of self-esteem and the ambivalence of group vs. mainstream identification, which crops up in the critical reception of work made by artists perceived to self-identify as "ceramic artists," as opposed to work made out of the material by artists who are respectable media-nomads. But there are actually a fair number of artists who work exclusively with the medium, who can ignore this state of affairs because their work assimilates easily into contemporary art dialogues.

Katherine Ross creates elaborate installations investigating the twinned themes of contamination and cleansing in relation to the threatened environment. In Primordial Waters, recently in the Columbus (Ohio) College of Art and Design show called "Cooled Matter," Ross transformed soft red rubber hot water bottles into hard, sterile cast porcelain ghosts of themselves, mounted like a marching army on a sickly green hospital colored wall. On the floor were circular areas of familiar white-bathroom tiles with digital images of viral life transferred onto them, as if projected by an enormous microscope. On a tandem wall were a row of porcelain faucets, onto which were printed a quote from Baudrillard about immune systems' increasing inability to guard against disease as an ironic outcome of medical prophylaxis.

In comparison, many of Marek Cecula's similarly themed pieces from his "Scatology" and "Hygiene" series are obviously distorted into suggestive new cast forms that conflate the sterility of sanitation with sexuality, suggesting a psychic numbness and denial of the messiness of the body in the culture that produces such objects. In his newest series, "Violations," the artist took a fragment of a Nazi era dinner service, which he found on the Baltic coast during a recent visit back to his homeland of Poland, as a starting point for the series, in which he accurately recreates pieces from the Nazi service. Cecula's motivation for creating "Violations" was the ways that the shard "provid(ed) a viewpoint that Nazism was not merely overt violence, but a voracious totality, which required its conquest of the domestic sphere and the innocent forms of daily life."[25]

What allows Ross and Cecula's works to cross-over without the frictions that Lucero's work is subject to is not just that the overtly social concerns of these artists are related to their own biographies, but that its encoding in the recognizably anonymous post-industrial aesthetic permits them to pass as "real" artists. Michael Brenson recently articulated the reasons behind these unconsciously agreed upon critical parameters for artistic validity:

> Many artists find themselves having to develop in aesthetic and political climates of increasing suspicion and constraint. Throughout the United States the political right is ridiculing artists, and even the idea of the artist; within the art community, there is widespread contempt for any tendency to romanticize the individuality, personality, hand and heroism of the artist. Monograph and biography are now the disparaged forms of art history. Not surprisingly, much of the most respected new art in Europe and the United States is defined by a noticeable degree of self-effacement. It is intended to draw attention to the ideas, processes, and situations – not to itself as an object (if that is what it is) or to its makers....in other words, as the curator becomes a more and more visible player in the world of contemporary art, more artists are concealing their egos to prove to the art community, to the general public, and to themselves that they are worthy of respect.[26]

This generally accurate description is out of sync with the self-identity of ceramists, who are not in recovery from the star status grandiosity of the post-Pop art boom. Instead, one can see Arneson's obsessive self-portraits, or Lucero's large, visible signatures painted on every single piece, or even Saupe's genteel domestic diaries, as attempts to assert themselves as people making the choice to work in this medium, as if to say: "Hey, I exist as an artist making things outside of industrial parameters, in a climate of dismissal, misreadings and invisibility." Their individuality is automatically humbled by association with Perreault's "domestic shelf." Their work does assert the primacy of the touch, and the persistence of the unique object in defiance of dominant theoretical discourses, and in so doing offers an alternative to submission to the invisible hand of the marketplace.

Kim Dickey has found a way to have it both ways without having to go to the self-conscious lengths that Lucero did throughout the '90s. While Dickey is very much of the clayworld, her work is critically received as being on a high conceptual level, a fact confirmed by her frequent curation since 1996 into galleries associated with conceptually-based art. In one series, she lovingly creates unique, hand-formed urination aids for women called Lady J's – after industry's term for devices that allow women to urinate standing, and which are sold mostly to women aviators and avid campers. Dickey's exhibition of these objects is always accompanied by photo-documentation of women using them, emphasizing their status as functional objects, as well as the cooption of this male prerogative.

Dickey's objects possess every theoretically antithetical characteristic of ceramics in the age of conceptual production: they are glazed using non-industrial glazes that emphasize the crystalline qualities of the porcelain; they are functional and decorative; each one is unique and intended for a specific woman, so outside the mass-market structure; they bear the irregular traces of hand-pinched manipulation which mark them as not being the result of a casting process; and their signature style of erotic-organist form lacks socio-historical specificity. Yet the subversive nature of the artist's feminist agenda, and that the presentation strategy stresses art as the event of interacting with artwork, situates Dickey unambiguously as an artist of the moment. But in many ways Dickey is using all of crafts' warm-n-wooly associations to her advantage, the same ones that many, like Cecula, deliberately eschewed in order to declare their postmodernist allegiance. In other installations, Dickey has placed groupings of vessels on tables, emphasizing their natural habitat, and has also captured the groupings in close up Polaroids called Landscapes, which are in turn whole new works. Like Ross and Cecula, Dickey plays in both clay and non-clay venues, but unlike them, she has not succumbed to industrial anonymity. Dickey employs the risky language of hand-pinched vessels to seduce the viewer into reconsidering their criteria for what is art.

VI Conclusion

Sculptural works produced in the ceramic medium, by artists who use clay almost exclusively as their means of expression, can be as complex, layered and sophisticated as other modes of cultural production. We may like to think that the whole notion of material criterion for art fell by the modernist wayside years ago – an assumption that is in no small part due to the causal relation between conceptual art as practiced in the late-'60s and the dematerialization of the art object. But as conceptual object maker Roxy Paine's '90s glob-producing machine-sculptures attest to, Walter Benjamin's seminal analysis of the impact of mechanical reproduction on pictorial art has become gradually more and more germane to the realm of three-dimensional art production, as the impact of mass-production technologies on three-dimensional art are taken into account. Today, most contemporary critics' judgments of three-dimensional artworks are framed by the recognition that all things in the world are loaded with specific socio-historical associations, which in turn imply the narratives that engage the viewer. What a three-dimensional artwork is made out of is tied tightly to the kinds of meanings/narratives a three-dimensional artwork will be capable of generating.

A few familiar examples ground this notion: Janine Antoni's self-portrait busts, Lick and Lather, engage feminist issues such as self-image neurosis and their related eating disorders by being comprised of soap and chocolate; and Kick the Bucket, David Hammons' standing rings of real Night Train wine bottles, are able to contrast the irrelevance of high art minimalism to gritty real-world issues with a force that would be considerably muted had the bottles in question been cast in bronze or hewn from cedar. This conceptual construct is not, in and of itself, terribly prescriptive in terms of what kinds of materials would satisfy its terms. But since conceptually based art and art criticism are historical outgrowths of the age of mechanical reproduction, the judging of a three-dimensional artwork as conceptually viable seems to have devolved over 30 years into a somewhat ritualized stylized practice, whereby the aesthetic of mass-produced goods is shorthand for an artwork's potential validity.

Contemporary artists have learned to exploit this code handily, but not without some problematic side effects. Our visual landscape is dominated by factory produced objects with a fairly high probability of audience recognition – objects that have been assembled via robotic-aided assembly-lines after their components were melted, cast, jigged, soldered and stamped into existence. Thus the majority of hybridized materials and prefabricated objects that artists make use of are products of corporate structures operating in capitalist systems. All the anonymous individuals who participated in bringing the various materials to market to make these components are collaborators in the artwork, underscoring an artist's acknowledgment that their identities and thus their ideas are socially constructed by marketplace structures – the exact inverse of the individually asserted non-industrial manipulation of raw materials. But because this collaboration is often an unacknowledged aspect of a work of art, incidental to its intended meaning, artists acquire a certain corporate cachet by coopting a finished look that is the result of many others' labors and material technologies, and in turn a validity that manufacturing's aesthetic of anonymity confers in a capitalist culture.

The politics of how the objects may have been brought to the marketplace are also elided. The result is that the sculptural and installational fields are tinged with a psychic numbness and affectlessness, communicated via the collaboration of artists with the anonymous forms of corporate driven reproduction. One gets the sense that many de-politicized artists' subconscious attitude is, "if you can't beat 'em join 'em." In today's art climate, there are signs of shifting, but eking out critical space for the reception of three-dimensional art objects that don't explicitly acknowledge the hegemonic structures of 20th century market economies can be dicey. That this is the case with some of the sophisticated sculptural objects coming out of the parallel but segregated traditions of contemporary ceramic production should be a red flag that we need to reexamine our critical paradigms. Only then will the notable sculptural production of artists such as Michael Lucero, Kim Dickey and Ted Saupe be appreciated in full. And only then will the ghetto walls erode.

Thanks to Tori Arpad and David Zucker Saltz for their invaluable feedback, and to Susan Tunick for her alerting me to the Thomas Schütte review.

Notes

1. Perreault, John. "Fear of Clay." Artforum 20. 8 (1982): 70–71.
2. Ratcliff, Carter. "Chimeras of Clay." Art in America 85.6 (1997): 92–97.
3. Sozanski, Edward J. "An Expansive View of Multiculturalism." The Philadelphia Inquirer 23 Nov. 1997, F15.

4. Dewald, Gabi, "Welcome to the Club of the Outcasts: Why Ceramics Are Not Objects of Art." Ceramics Art & Perception 30 (1997): 107.
5. Perrigo, Ann. Artist's Statement. "The Impact of TB-9." 30 years of TB-9: A Tribute to Robert Arneson. Ed. John Natsoulas, and Bruce Nixon. Davis CA: John Natsoulas Gallery Press. 1991. 103.
6. Ballatore, Sandy. "The California Clay Rush." Art In America Jul.-Aug. 1976: 86.
7. Nixon, Bruce. "The Impact of TB-9." 30 years of TB-9: A Tribute to Robert Arneson. Ed. John Natsoulas, and Bruce Nixon. Davis CA: John Natsoulas Gallery Press. 1991. 13.
8. Solomon, Deborah. "In Praise of Bad Art" New York Times Magazine 24 Jan. 1999, 30–35.
9. Taplin, Robert. "LeDray's Microcraft." Art in America 84 (1996): 84-7.
10. That LeDray individually crafted each of these pots has its own relevance to his work, which as a body is related to obsessive labor-intensive process art, but it does not affect their status in this piece as signs of museum minature reproductions, which are, of course, mechanically reproduced in great quantities, an anonymity underscored by their uniform glossy white glaze.
11. Reif, Rita. "Fantasy Machines From Technology's Dark Side." New York Times 6 Dec. 1998, sec. AR41.
12. A significant number of auto-engine parts use ceramic technology, something which the Detroit born Montgomery would be aware of.
13. Robert Arneson was hired initially at UC-Davis as half-time in Home Economics and half-time in Agriculture! (See Nixon.) There were 127 attendees at the 1967 conference of the nascent National Council on the Education for the Ceramic Arts, this year there were over 3,600, according to Harriet Brisson in "The Story of NCECA" Heroes, Icons History, Memory: The 1998 NCECA Journal. The Proceedings of the 32nd Annual Conference of the National Council on the Education for the Ceramic Arts, Vol. 19, 1998.
14. For a clearly written short historical overview, see Susan Peterson's popular textbook The Art & Craft of Clay. Englewood Cliffs: Prentice Hall, 1998.
15. Large scale wheel-thrown pottery has technically different requirements than hand-built sculpture, related to ceramic's physical properties, such as the molecular compression of the clay caused by the gravitational force of the spinning wheel-head. Pre-slipcasting studio clay bodies had been developed for wheel throwing in Europe.
16. Slivka, Rose. "The New Ceramic Presence" Craft Horizons Jul.-Aug. (1961). Her linking Voulkos et al to Abstract Expressionism rather than their ancient Korean sources made raised the hackles of the craft world. The chain of letters to the editors in response in response literally trailed for years afterwards.
17. John Britt's "I too was a Neo-Leachian" at: www.criticalceramics.org is a hilarious send up of these enshrined traditions.
18. Failing, Pat. Howard Kottler: Face to Face. Seattle: University of Washington Press, 1995.
19. Forrest, Jason. "Subverting All Frames of Reference." Atlanta Journal Constitution 21 Nov. 1997, Q7.
20. Mark Leach quoted by Patricia Failing, Feb. 1995, "Michael Lucero: Homage to Ancient Arts" American Craft, 55.1 (1995): 32-37.
21. Melchionne, Kevin. "Major Alterations: Redrawings by Michael Lucero" American Ceramics. 13.1. (1999) 30–33.
22. Phone interview with Michael Lucero, Feb. '99.
23. Smith, Roberta. "Art in Review: Michael Lucero." New York Times, 19 Feb. 1999.
24. Smith, Roberta. "Art in Review: Shortcoming of Art In the Realm of Tragedy." New York Times, 26 Mar. 1999.
25. Cecula, Marek. Violations, unpublished artist's statement.
26. Brenson, Michael. "The Curator's Moment." Art Journal, 57. (1998) 17–18.

Previously published in *Art Papers*, July/August 1999, Vol. 23, Issue 4.

Reproduced with permission of the author.

37
ON DIRT
Ingrid Schaffner

These days the annals on dirt flop right open to writings on the *informe* or 'formless'. That principle, as theorized by the French philosopher Georges Bataille, itself frequently recourses to mentions of mud. Mud oozes up around the big toe in Bataille's rumination on that appendage, which enabled us as humans to stand erect in the first place. Head to sky perhaps, but feet (and mind) forever mired. Mud is viscous and lugubrious. Smacking of excrement – of excess and expenditure – it is a base material, one of life's raw essences. And it is home to those poor little earthworms Bataille calls upon to help his readers conceptualize the power of the *informe* to confer status so low as to be crushable on the spot and made formless as spit. This peculiar power is what makes the *informe* such a critical operative in recent art history: it undoes a narrative that privileges form, while offering nothing as an alternative. Nothing being everything in the universe rendered formless. In other words, the *informe* is a noun that performs as a verb. Bataille called it a *mode d'emploi*. And given what good use he made of mud, the *informe* seems an excellent rhetoric to employ in a discussion of clay as both material and impulse in contemporary art.

There is even a guide for the discussion to follow: Yves-Alain Bois's and Rosalind E. Krauss's *Formless: A User's Guide*. Published in conjunction with their 1996 exhibition at the Centre Georges Pompidou in Paris, this book puts Bataille's thinking to use by identifying those moments of slippage and rupture that signify the *informe* at work. Take, for instance, Jackson Pollock's 'allover painting', a term that comes to sound like a quaint euphemism once you have seen his expulsive squirts and cloudy skeins obliterate the so-called language of abstraction. Likewise desecrating the field of postwar abstraction are Lucio Fontana's ceramic sculptures with their scatological concreteness and fetishistically fingered surfaces. *Dirt on Delight* includes a work by Fontana – albeit a relatively more figurative one than the *Formless* example, which is impressively compared to a 'massive turd'. And though it's not mentioned in the *Guide*, Pollock also worked briefly in clay. There is a photograph of him in the 1967 Museum of Modern Art catalogue standing over a potter's wheel. With an apron over his shirt and tie, he looks like a butcher, his hands covered in muck. The wheel belonged to an East Hampton neighbour, one Mrs. Lawrence Larkin, who evidently helped Pollock during the summer of 1949 make several abstract ceramic sculptures. The picture of one squished and splattered example looks pretty much how one would imagine a rough sketch of the formless in clay should look.

Since clay was only an incidental medium for Pollock, his work is not part of *Dirt on Delight*. However, the exhibition is teaming with objects, images and gestures that resonate with an appreciation of the *informe*. Pats and piles, drips and smears, pinches and slashes, cuts and holes, squeezes and stretches. The notion of leveling also seems relevant to the exhibition's general lack of formal distinctions. Whether a thing is kitsch, craft, amateur, folk or art does not signify. It's all just so much earthworm castings: material to use. In terms of this show, it's as if clay itself were a leveling medium, a disruptive field of operations in which advancing and

Source: Originally published in *Dirt on Delight: Impulses That Form Clay*, Ingrid Schaffner and Jenelle Porter (editors), Philadelphia: Institute of Contemporary Art, University of Pennsylvania, 2009.

regressing are indistinguishable objectives. By the time we have entered the installation and are surrounded, it's time to drop the *Guide*. (That is, if it hasn't already been requisitioned by the authorities.) As useful as it is for making a theoretical approach to this material, it will only carry us so far in actually engaging with the works on view. The *informe* stops at nothing, remember. Yet, there remains so much dirt to dish. Or wedge.

The first step in working with wet clay is to wedge it. This involves kneading, slapping and squeezing out any air bubbles that might lead to explosions in the kiln later down the line. Physical and direct, wedging offers a useful demonstration for getting to the material at hand: let's just pummel the dirt out of clay. Slapped from all sides, as opposed to squeezed through one reading or text, dirt yields up many possible meanings, associations and histories for those who would engage in working with, looking at and thinking about clay. Ever resilient, it punches back with constant hits of delight. Like sex, the physicality and sensuality of which thrum throughout this exhibition, discerning the dirty from the delightful is inextricably intertwined when it comes to a material as elemental as clay.

'First of all,' observed Rudolf Staffel, 'working with clay (as anyone who's ever touched clay knows), is a primordial experience that is very, very comfortable. I think every infant has manipulated something that was soft and gushy and pleasant to touch.' Staffel's medium of choice was porcelain, the whiteness of which does not mask the smell of the substance of his words. The infantile pleasure of playing with poop is one of life's many early delights, and one sure to mature into neurosis and perversions if not checked by, say, a healthy interest in working with clay. Psychoanalysts may find much to read into all of the sculptural pieces of shit and fecal matter that dot this exhibition. Freud himself would have stopped for a beard-stroking pause over Robert Arneson's *John Figure*: a sculptural toilet all embedded with bodily fragments. Made of stoneware and glazed filthy white, the work, in which a coiling turd figures, completely de-sublimates Freud's contention that the wish to be clean is inseparable from the desire to be dirty.

Sex may not be the first thing that comes to mind when one thinks of Marcel Duchamp's *Fountain*, first shown in 1917. A porcelain urinal now enthroned in the permanent collection of the Philadelphia and other museums of art, modernism's most infamous work of clay sculpture seems the very antithesis of the earthy, handmade ethos of *Dirt on Delight*. Except that Duchamp's cool readymade is never the pure conceptual object it's generally portended to be. Just look at the artist's pseudonymous signature 'R. Mutt', scrawled like bathroom graffiti over the face of the shapely vessel, with its feisty little protrusion, to see how dirty-minded a thing it is. To say nothing of the artist's sense of humor; don't be hasty to dismiss Duchamp's role in shaping the work on view. The *Dirt on Delight* checklist is riddled with titles that pay tribute, however inadvertently, to the master of visual puns, whose great legacy includes plenty of yuks for art. The erotic small sculpture of Kathy Butterly and Ron Nagle, respectively titled *Like Butter* and *Hunter's Tab*, for instance. Clay may even be conducive to piling on the laughs (or smirks) that can kill less resilient works but which are one of the vital signs of the grotesque in art.

When it comes to clay, surprisingly dirtier than shit are figurines. This class of small-scale sculpture has suffered insult ever since one of the founding figures of art history, Joachim Winckelmann, wondered why on earth Europeans had gone to such trouble to discover for themselves China's secret for making porcelain when it was for the most part used only to produce 'idiotic puppets'. Writing during the heyday of royal porcelain production, he considered the taste for figurines by Sevres, Meissen, Nymphenberg – the very patronage of which carried the taint of Porzellankrankeit or 'porcelain-disease', a mania that ruined many an aristocrat's coffer – to be plebian nevertheless. Winckelmann's own Neoclassical ideals, popularized by the worthy pottery of Wedgwood, were based on Greek sculpture, which he falsely believed to have been pure white. He thus failed to see the artistry (or delight) in polychrome sculptures of peewee courtiers, miniature monkey musicians and tiny troupes of commedia dell'arte actors. Nor would he probably have been amused by Ann Agee's contemporary twist on this tradition. Elegant figurines, handmade in multiple, are displayed on a table, like the products of some Rococo cottage industry. Forming a random tableau, they present us with an Arcadia in which butchering a pig is as wholesome and essential as burning a bra.

Prejudices that persist against the figurine grant paradoxical power to those who dare its terms. Aspects of which are expressed by virtually every one of the artists in this exhibition. In turn, their works suggest some similarly dirty words for sculpture: curio, souvenir, tchotchkes and 'little Gramma wares'. The last is how Ron Nagle once referred to the work of Ken Price. Said with all due respect and humor, of course, given that Price's sculptures – their fetishistic finishes and forms – have granted generations of artists since permission to develop their own work along such lines. The dazzling colors and illustrative technique of Nagle's sculptures come directly from the hobbyist's kit and craft of china-painting on prefab porcelain dishes and little statues. Is there anything more proverbially grandmotherly than that? To tally up the score: diminutive scale, decorative surface, exquisite detail, unabashed sentiment and artisanal craft, these are the terms of the figurine. And if they sound familiar, it's because feminism has made them a generative means for addressing issues of contemporary life through art for decades. Issues of identity and craft, consumption and class, domesticity and labor, sex and beauty lie at the core of *Dirt on Delight*, an exhibition as feminist in its political tendencies as figurines are feminine in culture – pretty dirty stuff.

Feminism takes dirt in stride. Think of some of the movement's iconic works: Mierle Laderman Ukeles washing the steps of the Wadsworth Atheneum; Mary Kelly pressing her son's soiled diaper into a *Post-Partum Document*; Anna Mendieta laying down naked in the earth to create an ephemeral *Silhueta* in the landscape. Plus what a field day artists had with the cliché of the female body as vessel, pulling things out and sticking things into holes that were theirs only to mess with. That said, Joyce Kozloff is one of the few leading figures to have made clay a primary material for her work: patterned tiles installed as carpets of color map myriad decorative arts traditions. And there are plenty of dishes in *The Dinner Party* that Judy Chicago threw for women throughout history. In both cases, however, clay is more a surface for painting than a material for sculpting.

Perhaps it was the machismo of clay that used to keep women at bay. One artist in the show recalls encouraging words, heard as a student during the 1970s, from a professor teaching her class how to throw: he said it was good for the bustline! As a student during the 1980s, Kathy Butterly did not see herself working with clay until she saw Viola Frey demonstrate that a woman could. And though Frey's fiber figurine sculptures engage with issues of feminism, she did not actively identify herself with the movement. Nor, generally speaking, have more recent generations wanted to ally themselves with a movement that would seem to situate them in the past or a politics that could limit (or put a stain on) a reading of their work.

And yet, feminism is the context that came up again and again in conversation with artists during studio visits for *Dirt on Delight*. Or simply through the objects themselves, for instance, Jessica Jackson Hutchins's kitchen table bedecked and festooned with papier-maché and ceramic dishes puts family life and art playfully out there (it was originally shown alongside a video of her baby daughter, grooving in her car seat on a road trip). Or consider Jeffry Mitchell's ersatz versions of traditional porcelain pieces all pumped up with emblems of gay identity. Chalk it up to a postfeminist era, when male and female artists alike deploy strategies first pioneered by women during the radical 1970s. It's high time feminists called in their debts.

Not all that glitters is gold, as any prospector will tell. You have to sift a lot of mud to hit pay dirt. Even then it might just be fool's gold, or pyrite, as is the case with Sterling Ruby's sinisterly sexual *Pyrite Fourchette*. Similarly, Nicole Cherubini's *G-Pot with Rocks* is a spectacularly raw-looking vessel festooned in fake jewelry and chains. Indeed, there is a lot of mixing of it up between the crudeness of clay and the exquisiteness of jewels in *Dirt on Delight*. Readers of the *informe* might find in this imagery a near literal expression of Bataille's principle of 'sumptuary expenditure'. Mud being excrement, jewels being money, both are pure waste; and depending on what one is into, ecstatic transactions in loss. However if extreme transgression is not your bag, there are other, no less sumptuary takes on sparkles in and on the mud. One that Eartha Kitt, the chanteuse singer of 'Santa Baby' (and who just died last Christmas) took as her creed. 'I'm a dirt person,' she said, 'I trust the dirt. I don't trust diamonds and gold.'

Since medieval times, sumptuary laws have been used to regulate consumption and keep folks in their place. In Renaissance Venice, sporting gold or silver threads was forbidden those outside the aristocracy whose social status was signified as much by their freedom to wear what even those who could afford it could not. In terms of dirt, it's not so much a question of what is forbidden as what is allowed. Working in clay, artists can build for themselves the treasures, relics and triumphs that signify power, privilege and wealth. Look at all the iridescent and golden effects, the dazzling colors and rich tones on display in *Dirt on Delight*. See the royal retinue of chalices, vases and other ornamental plate. And look closely. Jane Irish's vases, for instance, may at first appear to be homespun versions of Sevres porcelain – robber baron booty for the bohemian set. Until the decorative painting discloses a homeless person's cart, a hotel maid scrubbing a toilet, and other less than charming scenes of contemporary life.

Not always so politically overt, dirt is packed with demonstrations of clay's incipient power to usurp, or at least mess with establishments. The exhibition itself might be seen to represent a major triumph for contemporary artists, who work irrespectively of the old ruling classifications between fine and decorative arts, high and low, artist and folk artist. The work of Eugene Von Bruenchenhein seems relatively obscure; yet this visionary artist is one of the great progenerative figures in Paul Swenbeck's personal pantheon. It was with their actual proximity in mind that Swenbeck created a whole new series of his figurative mandrake-root sculptures for this installation. Meanwhile, at the bitter root of Von Bruechenhein's art was the contention that he and his wife were descended from royalty, so he turned their house into a grotto, stuffed with crowns and other trappings of a lost civilization, including the requisite jungle growth, all made of clay.

Dirt is ground and artists have always covered a vast amount of terrain using clay. Indeed, today's challenge to think globally is one that artists working in clay have acquiesced to for centuries. The authority of East Asian ceramics – its techniques, traditions and aesthetics – is practically a subtext of *Dirt on Delight*. This narrative could be dished in detail through individual artists and their learned predilections for Ming, Tang, Momoyama, *mingei*, celadon, blue and white, crazing, *blanc des chines* and countless other wares and desired effects that originate outside of the European tradition. It could also be summed up in the many references made by various artists to Chinese scholars' rocks throughout the exhibition. Adrian Saxe's raku renditions resemble highly aestheticized piles of shit and push the Japanese principles of *wabi-sabi* and *shibui* – of beauty in humble, natural forms and slightly bitter taste – to an extreme. But Asia is just one hemisphere of the clay globe, which lets artists travel virtually every place on earth, and throughout time. Unlike oil paint, for instance, clay's ubiquity seems to make it the stuff of cultural transcendence. So Betty Woodman's *Winged Figure (Kimono)* draws a fluid line from the drapery of Japanese textiles to Brancusi. A line Arlene Shechet makes a thread of in her sculptures, in which many spouted vessels sitting atop Constructivist bases, merge afterimages of the modernist studio with the many-armed gestures of Hindu deities. Why choose one's gods at the exclusion of others when clay admits all?

The question of taste leads to food. Tell someone 'Eat dirt' and best stand back. Unless you are in some 'geophagic' part of the world, like certain regions in China, Zimbabwe, and North Carolina, where there's no insult in eating the local clay, just good nutrition. (A recent dirt-themed dinner held at San Francisco's New Langton Arts featured a *terroir* tasting.) Building strong bodies is one of dirt's mythic properties – Adam and the Golem were both men made of mud. Though the classic metaphor of the 'human vessel', turns stale in contrast to all the 'flesh pots' on view. From Beverly Semmes's lumpen pinch pots, cloaked-to-choked in robes of color, to Arlene Shechet's ashen-toned abstract ceramic lungs, *Dirt on Delight* is teaming with animate form and visceral clay bodies. Like flesh, clay is largely water. Until it's cooked in the kiln, the ceramicist's oven. It's there that the alchemy of turning dirt into such delights as this exhibition holds ultimately transpires.

And so does this essay, which took off from the notion of wedging, draw to its conclusion with firing. Imagine the smoke curling up from the incense burning in Von Bruenchenhein's 'sensors'. The oil in Saxe's Aladdin*esque* lamp is lit. Beatrice Wood's goblets glow with the radiance of their own iridescent magnificence. And the *nostalgie de la boue* hangs heavy in the air: it's a complicated funk, this 'nostalgia for the mud'. And like the *informe*, it's another term from the French useful for thinking about dirt. To speak of nostalgia of any kind invokes a sentimental longing for something that probably never really existed in the first place. Van Gogh went peasant, Gauguin native, in search of romantically simple lives and imagined communion with the earth. To be wistful for mud, however, seems ill advised, even silly. And yet, *nostalgie de la boue* is not so easily dismissed, given all that it connotes. 'That which is crude, unworthy, degrading': the dictionary definition leaves it at that. But let's not leave out the lingering allure of the primitive, the authentic, the native, the natural, the simple, the handmade: the very non-civilized conditions that Freud himself said every civilization longs for in its discontent. (Bohemia was built from this *boue*.) However correctly they have been deconstructed and disabused within postmodern culture, the critical power of these conditions remains intact.

At least where clay is concerned, as the artists in this exhibition show, not through any sentimental longing, but by smartly crafting their work to represent those conditions – both dirty and delightful – that seem increasingly absent or remote from contemporary life. Especially in this moment, as we all face an economy that has been thrown down the crapper by corporate interests that seem to have run the world into a state of ruin. Dirt has long been the bane and boon of a consumer culture built on entire industries devoted to personal hygiene and cleanliness, industries that simultaneously turn a blind eye to the environment, polluting it to the point of climatic meltdown. Dirt is the antithesis of the virtual and synthetic. It takes but a speck to destroy a disk, a chip, a hard drive – to damage beyond repair the highly polished surface of a Jeff Koons bunny or a Donald Judd Stack. And yet, it is in light of the overproduction of things we don't need, coupled with the avoidance and denial of the stuff that's just there, that artists' use of clay comes to seem not only prescient but also instructive. Dirt is always an option.

Source: Ingrid Schaffner, 2009, 'On Dirt', in Ingrid Schaffner and Jenelle Porter (eds) *Dirt on Delight: Impulses That Form Clay*, Philadelphia: Institute of Contemporary Art, University of Philadelphia, pp. 25–31.

Reprinted with permission from the Institute of Contemporary Art, University of Philadelphia, and the author.

38
CONTEMPORARY CLAY
Clare Twomey

Investigative, non-conventional approaches to clay are endemic of our time. Over the past century, the role of the practitioner has experienced radical change, and this shift in the outlooks and the economics surrounding craft practice has profoundly reshaped the role of the crafts-person. It leaves crafts divided in its indulgences and necessity to our society. This ranges from the bespoke potter to the avant-garde makers who are committed to art production with craft-making at its core, all creating the necessary languages and contexts in which to be relevant and active.

This is an emancipated continuance for clay practitioners who are fully engaged and immersed in current debates in the wider visual arts. This intelligent making in clay is part of a much larger dialogue, placing the principles and dialogues of craft into a relevant role in our visual culture.

This relevance can be seen in the diverse trends of clay activities that fall under this handed-down title of craft practice. There are potters, object-makers, hybrid craft makers, sculptural artists, installation clay artists and temporary time based works. These titles and terms have been borrowed and stolen from other art disciplines to give an identity and relevance to the activities undertaken. This embracing of terminology is vital in forming a context for the artists to place themselves within, the identification through terminology forming a knowledge-base of peers. It helps galleries, critics and collectors recognise what they are invited to be taking part in. It bundles relevant histories together, informing the viewer and artist how to behave, and what references to draw upon when assessing these works. How else could the contemporary clay maker identify their work if not by finding relevance in contemporary terminology?

Craft has now past the point where new makers see an amassed division between terminologies from craft or fine art or many other areas of practice; all references to terminology are, when applied intelligently, inclusive and transferable to practice as a whole-the terminology references the maker's intentions, not a discipline. However, it is vital to acknowledge that the recognition of materials is intrinsic to the content and conceptual language of a piece, and by extension to our reading of the piece as an audience.

The ever more complex and sophisticated uses of clay in [illegible] no doubt that as a material, it has transcended its role as a mere mo[illegible]actice and variety of forms that clay has embraced has led us to fundar[illegible]ng of such practices. There are artists expending great craft knowledge [illegible]working in collaboration with others, there are those commissioning th[illegible]d industry, there are those who borrow and construct. All of these dr[illegible]temporary clay practice.

It is vital to acknowlege the recognition of materials intrinsic to the language.

Source: © Black Dog Publishing.

Object-Making

Object development and all its concerns provides an alluring and endless source of established art dialogue as well as a historical model in clay practice. Over the centuries, clay objects have evolved to suit the needs of the culture they serve. Simple vessels were first used to carry water and foodstuffs and to play a role in the ceremonial rituals of ancient cultures. The forms and surfaces of the vessels developed in order to accommodate changes in culture and usage, maintaining through the centuries a fundamental functionality, whose ghost remains ever present. For an object to forge a new trail, it must reflect some truth in its cultural context, and in the instance of clay, this required some kind of break from its functional milieu. In 1900, the Martin Brothers began making vessels influenced by Celtic, medieval and Persian pottery. By the early years of the twentieth century, however, they had branched off into small sculptures of 'Wally Birds' and grotesque face jugs, influenced by the Gothic Revival, reflecting the indulgence of the Victorian decorative object. 80 years later, Modernists Lucie Rie and Hans Coper took the object even further away from functionality, focusing on the spaces inside and outside the vessel.

Object-making and its history provides a diverse commentary that holds relevance to all forms of practice. This is especially true when comparing work, which exclusively uses clays, referencing its specialist history, to work that is more hybridised, using clay in and amongst other materials.

This dialogue can be seen in the works of artists such as Jessie Flood-Paddock and Laura Morrison, from the 2006 Bloomberg New Contemporaries, who both discuss clay-use in their work as a matter-of-fact, and not as a specialised craft tool. In the work of Hans Stofer (United Kingdom) we see clay used as providing a context within which to discuss domestic and personal histories, and Chad Curtis (USA), who uses clay as a context of place in his miniature landscapes. Maxim Velcovsky (Czech Republic) uses clay as a flexible and locally accessible production material, and as a placement tool for his design objects.

A purist clay object-maker such as Michael Geertsen from Denmark can be seen to be in a long investigation with material and a highly specialist dialogue with form. His work draws on the historical discussion in clay practice of spatial containment, but his abstracted, sliced, rotated and skewed forms reach beyond this discussion to the greater concerns of an artist looking at formal relationships in aesthetics and minimalist languages. The scale and placement of the works create interruptions in perceived understanding of ceramics practice. They are often meandering structures stretched across a wall or peeking from some far off corner, observing rather than seeking centre stage.

In contrast to this exclusive relationship, another maker of objects is Nicole Cherubini. As Mark Dean writes in his exhibition catalogue for *One Part Clay: Ceramic Avant-Garde and Mixed Media*, which took place in New York in 2006: 'Nicole Cherubini's over-accessorised and adorned coil sculptures clearly address the current blurred boundaries between social class and status in our society.' In her work, Cherubini accesses a known ceramic metaphor – that of the vase – and embellishes it with lavish additions of chains, beads and found materials, creating a chaotic and indulgent form. These accessories allow the work to transcend notions of use, and other well-trodden discussions of functionality, into discussions of decoration, celebration, and excess. The vases now read as a canvas on which Cherubini has built her dialogue.

From the objects produced in the 2006 Albisola Art Biennale the object authored by the artist Liam Gillick was a truly subversive clay object. Liam Gillick is an artist who is internationally revered for his articulate and geometric understanding of space and composition. He was invited by the Arts Biennial to take advantage of the ceramic craftsmen in Liguria, an area in Italy renowned for its ceramic workshops. The resulting design was a ceramic column of boldly coloured interlocking forms. The scale of this work tantalisingly reaches just beyond domestic understanding and conformity, yet the individual plates are of a generous but standard scale.

Liam Gillick's trademark attention to material and detail was carried out by the local ceramic craftsmen of the 'fabricas' (small factories) in the town of Albisola, who carried out instructions conveyed by Gillick via e-mail. The result is a striking convergence of two histories. The sharp lines and contemporary sculptural forms are complemented by the craftsmanship evident in the quality of the surface and substance of the material. The merged world of concept and craft knowledge can produce exceptional results.

In contrast to this collaboration but still focusing on the forming of a contemporary ceramic object is the work of Richard Slee. With his relentless intelligence and sensitive wit, Slee has dipped in and out of dialogues of craft practice, enriching clay's understanding of itself. His diverse skills as a clay manipulator have allowed him to engage in a broad-ranging discussion on the various aspects of the 'object', and the way we relate to it Rather than relying on a constant theme in order to give coherence to his practice, Slee's work is in a state of perpetual motion, constantly searching for new vehicles with which to engage in conversations about the domestic real. In some of his work, he makes use of materials and technologies outside of clay practice to further blur our understanding of craft and art He extends his syntax of materials beyond the realm of clay, not because of the shortcomings of the material, but because he is on a constant quest for a new language with which to express his intentions.

Clay practitioners that work in object-making often become associated with a language of the domestic.The association of decorative objects in the home, the scale that these objects and environments usually adhere to, and the intimacy and warmth of the domestic environment, all become an intrinsic part of our reading of the object. The sculptures of Anders Ruhwald (Denmark) play on our understanding of the domestic by drawing on an intelligent understanding of scale and the role of domestic objects. From his physical observations of the body's relationship and interactions with its immediate environment, he creates objects that suggest furniture space and imagined domestic activities. Ruhwald questions the role of the object and our presumptions of forms, creating a sense of discomfort by generating an illusion of softness to touch where only hardness prevails. His pieces deliberately encourage a discussion that echoes from the field of fine art to design, forming contact with the broadest possible range of practices.

Hybrid craft-makers

We can explore the trends in current practice further, by looking at the hybrid work of Barnaby Barford, Jaime Hayon and Marek Cecula. In the same way that other material-specific disciplines are breaking from known formats, these artists are borrowing and lending to and from industry, design and craft practice, creating a buoyant and free-flowing environment of hybrid objects in art, design and consumer products in clay.

Artist and designer Barnaby Barford places clay at the centre of his practice, but often makes use of and designs in other materials. The hybridity in his practice stems from the materials he uses, and the way in which he slips effortlessly from the role of artist to designer to crafts-person and back again, challenging preconceptions in each arena. In his sculptures, Barford cuts and re-assembles ready-made ceramic objects into new formations, creating sophisticated and subversive statements on topical social issues. He is a highly skilled crafts-person, but chooses not to highlight this asset when focusing on the ready-made. He appeals to a new audience-base, which is fluent and engaged in many different aspects of visual culture, and which is becoming the target audience for more and more makers. This confidence and unwillingness to adhere to the traditional rules of crafting is a major departure point in current clay practice, linking people like Barford to the works of artists such as Picasso, Antony Gormley and Rebecca Warren in a pact of high material regard and application rather than a limiting, historical approach to clay. By eroding this boundary, a new generation of makers is broadening the dialogues of application, to a vast sphere with the intelligence of the material application at its heart.

The artist designer Jaime Hayon from Spain has collaborated with ceramics manufacturer, Lladro, to broaden the application of material in his work. He has produced design-esque objects that have the finesse of industry yet the dialogue of art, leaving them more in the design camp than Jeff Koons' sculptures, but less in the art camp than Barnaby Barford's collage ornaments. The hybridity of the objects in this case results from the manufacturing process and how it relates to the product. Hayon's enquiries have created a wonderful and strange new place. His well-understood concepts and well-produced clay application have opened up a genre of endless possibilities to new makers.

The work of Marek Cecula also spans art, craft and design. However, his approach to the collaborative process of creation is a much more concerted one. He deliberately assumes an ambiguous role in the work, creating a layered approach to the creative process. In his *In-Dust-Real* exhibition at the Garth Clark Gallery, New York, he re-fired elegant Royal Copenhagen porcelain dinnerware, in a Japanese-style anagama wood-firing. This traditional approach warped the forms and disfigured the fine surfaces. The craft-aspect to the work indubitably stamped its mark on the ubiquitous product, reversing the 'normal' balance of power between craft and industrial manufacture. The exhibition created a commentary on the nature of mass-production and questioned perceptions of beauty in different cultures.

Sculpture

The above works of small-scale sculpture are the tipping point into an area of larger scale sculptural works. Historically this has been dominated by classical sculpting techniques, but there is a group of artists and crafts-people who, through a liberation of thinking and gallery practice, are making large-scale sculptures in clay. Some of these are stable, some temporal, some using a vast array of clay application skills. Artists using clay and other materials to make works are driving forward the possibilities and contextual understanding of how clay is used and by whom. Marian Heyerdahl, for example, has long used clay as an instrumental part of her exploration of sculpture. She has recently completed a project in China, in which she reproduced 60 replica terracotta army figures as females. The sculptures are contemporary in their historical impossibility – identical to the original finds in scale and material but contentious in their brazen femininity and in the violence and anger that they present to the viewer. Heyerdahl has incorporated site-specific elements in the work, creating and exhibiting it in the location that the terracotta army was found, and going so far as to produce the figures in a factory across the road from the archaeological site.

The American artist, Kristin Morgin takes the fragility and temporality of clay to create sculptures that convey a commentary on contemporary concerns in American culture. The frail and fractured surfaces of her work bind together the complexity of other materials, creating a rich material collage. Morgin writes of her sculptures: 'my works are reminders of what it is to be mortal'. The clay is a key material for its easily interpreted condition, and for its reflection of continual change, which mirrors that of the fading and decaying icons that comprise the work.

Looking more broadly at sculptural clay work being produced, Thomas Schütte is an artist with a dedicated understanding of many materials. His use of clay has contributed significantly to the perception of clay as contemporary sculptural material. His pieces could have been produced in any material, and his choice of clay is one that contributes to the conceptual language of the work. He relates to the connotations of classical crafting that the material carries with it, the elemental nature of the material, and the aspect of the hand-made.

When craft-application borrows concerns and approaches from the world of fine art, the result is a conceptual approach to the work, which needs to be examined using the dialogues that have influenced both fields of practice. With this in mind, it is difficult not to mention the works of eminent sculptors such as Andy Goldsworthy, Richard Long and Richard Wentworth. These artists' understanding of material is sensitive and its application is executed with the finesse of a fine crafts practitioner. It is this sensitivity that has enabled the crafts to appreciate the multifaceted dimensions of application of material and concept.

To examine this broadening of dialogues in clay-based work, it is vital to recognise this influence of the wider visual arts on critical thinking within a specific discipline. This is necessary for viewers, makers and curators alike. For all disciplines to remain 'current' they require an immersion within society and an intelligent understanding about their context.

Gallery as context

In clay practice, the developments in the way that clay is used has been influenced by the shift in the role of the gallery from container of objects to context. The all-consuming dialogue of site-specific work has had a highly influential role on the understanding of craft as an immersed destination, placing it firmly in the context of the broader visual arts.

Antony Gormley's iconic work *Field* is an example of how gallery space is being used as part of artwork. Comprising 35,000 clay figures made by an extended family of brickworkers in Mexico, this work is conceptually and physically dependent on the gallery space for the work and its relationship to be validated. In this installation, the viewer is forced outside of the space, and is permitted only to peer into areas occupied by the artwork and now made physically redundant to the viewer. The artwork itself discusses occupation and population as the invasion of figurines sweeps through the space.

To draw a comparative development in craft gallery practice we can look at the work of Piet Stockmans. This artist was exhibited for the first time in the United Kingdom in 1999 in *UN-Limited*, an exhibition curated by Emmanuel Cooper at the Crafts Council in London. Stockmans' work was placed as part of a group show that explored the concept of multiples. His main work was a piece entitled *Floor Installation* ('installation' is a term that will be discussed in depth later on). It consisted of thousands of blue-rimmed white porcelain bowls sitting next to each other, filling the gallery floor. This created a wash of blue lines, and the impression that the rims were floating above the floor. Only one viewing area was created, with no walkways through the work, resulting in a sense of exquisite, but unattainable beauty. In 1999, in the context of craft gallery practice this work was subversive to the core – bowls with no active function, the bare floor as a display area – it broke all the rules of the sacrosanct singular object. Emmanuel Cooper and Piet Stockmans addressed the future with clear intentions, expanding the edges of crafts-thinking by paying their respect to the craft-object whilst simultaneously subverting it with a thoroughly art-driven motive.

What the works of Gormley and Stockmans do is to converge the audience together, at a point in which they are forced to question the use of gallery space. These artists were able to present a sumptuous narrative before us thanks to the preparedness of galleries to move beyond the object. It is a reflection on the current outlook in art-production that such elaborate works can be created, and that such colossal investments are made in the production of art as a social transcript.

The development of the use of intervention, full-scale installation, construction and environmental art has continued to develop and can be seen as progressing gallery interaction from the works of non-clay artist Felix Gonzalez-Torres to that of the clay work of Keith Harrison. Gonzalez-Torres's exhibition, *The Sweetness of Life*, in the Serpentine Gallery in 2000, helped define a moment when the liberation of interaction became part of the common language in art practice, and by extension in other disciplines. In this exhibition, the artist used wrapped sweets as his material of choice, placing them in various colour groups and formations. The visitors to the gallery were invited to participate by helping themselves to sweets, thus depleting the artwork. Gonzalez-Torres's intention was that 'authorship' of this work was a collaboration between the maker, presenter, owner, and viewer.

This combination of the conceptual alongside firm gallery support can be seen in the work of Keith Harrison as well. In many of Harrison's works, he asks the audience to bear witness to a performance of clay transition as the raw clay is fired, using experimental and public methods, and by this act of watching, the audience become participants in the piece. Similar to Gonzalez-Torres, the performative aspects of Harrison's work means that the work's only remaining outcome is in the memory of the audience. The experimental and temporary nature of Harrison's work can be observed in a five hour exhibition at the Victoria and Albert Museum in September 2006. The first of two works was *Last Supper*, a time-based site-specific work located in the Raphael Room and consisting of 13 electric cooker elements and 20 clay blocks arranged by colour and formation in the pattern of Da Vinci's *The Last Supper*. Over the course of three hours, the elements heated the clay blocks, causing chemical changes in the space and the work. Steam gently left the clay and entered into the atmosphere of the room, creating a physical sense of change and evolution within the audience's perception and understanding of what they were witnessing. As Harrison himself states, 'the process of transformation is an intrinsic part of the work'. In the second piece for this exhibition, *M25 London Orbital*, Harrison constructed a replica of the M25 ring-road around London using 167 Scalextric track sections. *Orbital* negotiated the internal and external spaces of the sculpture court and the central courtyard of the museum. This work was also publicly fired over a five hour period, addressing issues of timebased and performative aspects in clay.

The site-specific aspect of interaction is part of the dialogues concerning the clay practices of Christie Brown, Carol McNicoll and Edmund De Waal. All of these artists have explored the narrative of venue in some depth. In *Fragments of Narrative*, Christie Brown's installation in the massive industrial space of a converted power station in Wapping, East London, she explored craft-dialogues in a 'non-craft' space. Writing about her sense of the space, Brown describes it as follows: 'the scale of the space was daunting and challenging. The structure of the main interior echoed a Romanesque church with high windows and columns and the whole site was filled with the traces and memories of its previous existence as a place where steam power was generated to animate bridges and lifts'. Responding to the industrial enormity of the gallery, she filled the space with life-sized clay figures and torsos representing characters such as Pygmalion, Prometheus and Golem, who had some kind of power association at the heart of their story. This complex concept elevated the figures beyond sculpture into the realm of installation, as the work's dialogue was with the very core of the building's identity.

In 2001, Carol McNicoll was invited to exhibit in the rather grand exhibition space of the Bergen Kunstall. In order to challenge the lofty atmosphere, she papered the walls with patterned wallpaper, and exhibited her work on pieces of historical furniture from the museum's collection, rather than plinths. She then scattered store-bought ceramics and domestic objects throughout. 'The domestic setting, which visual art's avant-garde left behind sometime around 1945 is the context I find most interesting', states McNicoll of her work. In this piece, craft acts as a bridge between ornament and art, home and gallery.

Three years later, in 2004, Edmund De Waal made his site-specific museum intervention in the National Museum of Wales. De Waal took on the role of curator of objects from the museum's applied arts collection, as well as that of a site-specific artist working within the gallery space. The catalogue accompanying the exhibition identifies that 'in this exploration of the collection he selects and arranges part of the eighteenth century porcelain collection and places new work of his own in dialogue with it in the frame of a domestic place setting. It is not only the applied arts that have engaged in rearranging collections.... In 1997 at the British Museum, [Richard) Wentworth juxtaposed Egyptian drinking vessels with that of drinks containers from the museums rubbish bins.'[1]

Installation

This brings us to the undefined area of installation, which can of course take on the above concerns of site-specificity, but also could be a work that fully encourages the audience into a space, encompassing them, and starting to blur the boundaries of art and theatre. In some attempt to give a definition of this practice, which is broad ranging and ever applicable to many different art works of many scales, I look to the critical work of Michael Archer and Claire Bishop. Michael Archer on his view of the term installation writes, 'to call some disposition of materials, objects or artifacts an installation with any degree of authority presupposes familiarity with a clutch of related terms: location, site-specificity, gallery, public, environment, space, time, duration. Consequently, a definition of installation must also shed light upon the contemporary significance of this surrounding vocabulary'.[2]

This openness to definition is furthered in Claire Bishop's view of installation art: '"Installation Art" is a term that loosely refers to the type of art into which the viewer enters, and which is often described as "theatrical", "immersive" or "experimental". However, the sheer diversity in terms of appearance, content and scope of the work produced today under this name, and the freedom with which the term is used, almost preclude it from having any meaning. The word "installation" has now expanded to describe any arrangement of objects in any given space, to the point where it can happily be applied even to a conventional display of paintings on a wall'.[3]

With it clearly established that there is an open interpretation to how this term is used in both clay work and other areas of practice, it is vital to look at works that can demonstrate the rigour and awareness that Archer alludes to. In clay practice this is becoming more and more of a demand, as the term must be understood within the context of making from a broader perspective, rather than multiples and decorative concerns alone. It is also important to recognise that many of the previously mentioned artists who are dealing with temporal and site-specific works have made a considerable and intelligent contribution to this area of practice.

The work of Canadian artist Linda Sormin reaches out to this rigour of contextually understood installation work, with a language so fresh and dynamic it is hard to type. Renaissance-punk is somewhere close to where I find the intentions of her crawling, sprawling structures, which seem to consume the very space they occupy. The effortless chaos that searches to identify itself with the domestic but as an action of conflict to this harmony, leaves the viewer in a blissful hunt for clues and anchors in the work. Linda Sormin states, 'the work demands that I negotiate my presence before it, around it, under it, through it. The site looms above and veers past, willing me to compromise, to give ground. Overbearing and precarious, its appetites mirror my own. I roll and pinch the thing into place; I collect and lay offerings at its feet. This architecture melts and leans, it hoards objects in its folds. It lurches and dares you to approach, it tears cloth and flesh, and it collapses with the brush of a hand. What propels the desire to make and compulsively make? Is this how I reassure myself, prove that I am here? If a tonne of clay is in the room, and over time it is transformed – behaving and misbehaving – because of me, is it through making that I perform identity and establish presence?'

Another artist identifying with installation is Phoebe Cummings. Cummings' work responds to environment and space, playing with expectations of materials and scale, and the psychological space of everyday objects. Often working with unfired porcelain, her work envelops the space and lures you into the notions it creates, encouraging you to find out more about the role of the room. Cummings raises questions regarding the function of a space by playing with time, and with the space as a whole. As Cummings states of her work 'the fragile constructions become impossible objects where the viewer is confronted with their physical presence, and made conscious of their behavior within the room.'

Clay artists working within a contemporary cultural context must have a constant awareness of conscious behaviour. By regarding their audience as sensitive and curious, the objectives of the artists, designers and crafts people must deliberately take command of material concerns and concepts. With the future of all artists becoming hybrid, it is vital that craft makers and material specific makers realise their relevance to making environments.

The acknowledgment that investigative, non-conventional clay making has shifted the role of the practitioner, means that the future is unclear. This is a critical time, an enabling time for makers to redefine their roles in a way that will serve future generations of makers in a hybrid, intelligent and sensitive arts culture.

Notes

1. From the exhibition catalogue *Arcanum: Mapping Eighteenth Century European Porcelain*, National Museums and Galleries of Wales, 2004.
2. De Oliveira, Nicolas, Nicola Oxley and Michael Petry, *Installation Art in the New Millennium: The Empire of the Senses*, London: Thames & Hudson, 1994.
3. Bishop, Claire, *Installation Art*, London: Tate Publishing, 2005.

Originally published as Clare Twomey, 'Contemporary Clay', in Ziggy Hanaor (ed), 2007, *Breaking the Mould: New Approaches to Ceramics*, London: Black Dog Publishing, pp. 26–37.

Reproduced with permission of Black Dog Publishing and the author.

39

ELASTIC/EXPANDING: CONTEMPORARY CONCEPTUAL CERAMICS

Jo Dahn

'In conceptual art the idea or concept is the most important aspect of the work... all planning and decisions are made beforehand and the execution is a perfunctory affair. The idea becomes the machine that makes the art.'

-Sol LeWitt[1]

A cursory examination of a range of ceramics-specific publications will quickly establish that the dominant popular discourse of ceramics still centers on traditional craft practices. It revolves around the handling of the clay material and privileges accounts of technique, process, skill and quality in the production of objects, be they functional or otherwise. Could there be an equivalent to what critic Lucy Lippard influentially referred to as LeWitt's 'de-materialization' in contemporary conceptual ceramics?[2] To discuss ceramics in relation to de-materialization begs the questions: What do we mean by 'ceramics?' And what activities can the term encompass? Such a notion seems irreconcilable with the seemingly insistent materialism of ceramics. But the field is steadily expanding; in this essay I consider the emergence of a conceptual ceramics mode that is tantamount to a new genre and prompts a contemporary reconsideration of LeWitt's formula.

In September 2006, for one night only, in the Raphael gallery at the Victoria and Albert Museum, London (V&A), visitors were treated to Keith Harrison's *Last Supper*, a large table made of building blocks and laden with thirteen stripped down elements from defunct domestic cookers. Each element was mounted on a brick core and swathed in Egyptian paste, a primitive clay that fires to a glassy substance at relatively low temperatures. Attached crocodile clips and electrical wiring were reminiscent of car batteries on charge, while the pastel pinks, greens and beiges of the Egyptian paste harmonized with the colors of the paintings (actually cartoons for tapestries) around the room. Cordoned off towards one end of the gallery, with an exquisite altarpiece in the background, the installation evoked church ritual and of course the title invited a biblical reading. It was also possible to consider it in quite a different way: as Harrison remarked wryly, these ovens had long since baked their last supper. Light levels were low, as befits a room full of Raphaels; when the electricity was switched on, and the current run through one cooker element at a time, the results were subtle. A little smoke, some barely audible crackling, some changes in the surfaces as they heated up and the Egyptian paste fired. This did not deter the enthusiastic audience camped in front of the installation; they seemed to welcome the challenge and concentrated hard so as to catch each effect as it happened.

Last Supper was part of Clay Rocks, one of a series of sessions at the V&A that were intended to raise the profile of contemporary craft.[3] The same evening Harrison's *London Orbital*, a 1:5000 scale version of the

Source: Extra/Ordinary, Maria Elena Buszek, Ed., pp. 153–174. Copyright, 2011, Duke University Press. All rights reserved. Republished by permission of the copyright holder.

M25, London's notorious ring road, was installed in the sculpture gallery. An undulating 38 meter ribbon made from 167 sections of ceramic Scalextric track, with parallel electric elements buried in calcium borate frit and cobalt, wended its way along the floor, out through the doors into the courtyard garden and back again. It was intended to fire, producing bright blue stripes when the current was turned on, but like its namesake at rush hour, it didn't work. The system fused each time Harrison threw the switch. That viewers were eager to witness something new and different was made palpably clear when they assembled to watch *London Orbital* in action. Some of them took their places at least half an hour in advance. They remained in position, unwilling to give up even when it was obvious that nothing was going to happen. Meanwhile, in the Casts Court of the museum, Clare Twomey's *Trophy* attracted a long queue. She had scattered a flock of 4000 little birds in Wedgwood blue jasper clay all around the gallery; some perched on the casts, the rest spread across the floor. Each was handmade and stamped underneath with 'W' for Wedgwood, 'V&A' and the artist's initials '*ct*;' they were instant 'collectibles.' Visitors entered a few at a time; when they left, they could take one of the birds with them – hence the title: *Trophy*. People wandered about carefully, picking their way between the birds on the floor and enjoying the installation before choosing which one to take as their own 'trophy.' They became collaborative performers, active participants in the construction of the work's meaning. On leaving, they were asked to send Twomey a photograph of their bird in its new home. She has received many; *Trophy* continues to develop as it spreads out across hundreds and hundreds of private locations.

'Clay Rocks' was a landmark in the development of a new mode of ceramics practice. The siting of *Last Supper*, *London Orbital* and *Trophy* in an international cultural centre like the V&A is tantamount to institutional validation and suggests that conceptual ceramics, once considered an eccentric minority interest, is becoming mainstream and gaining wider notice. *Trophy* was heralded in the British national press, admittedly as an opportunity to steal something from the museum.

Art historian Paul Greenhalgh situates ceramics amongst those genres 'at the core of the Western artistic tradition.' As a craft medium, it has 'moved through history, adapting, twisting, changing and surviving extraordinary upheavals' during the Modern era.[4] He argues that 'the creation of new genres and the collapse of old ones … is a dynamic process [… and] it is important that we acknowledge our genres; that we continually question them; that we occasionally terminate them; and that we consolidate new ones.'[5] Greenhalgh sees the emergence of new genres as serving the continuous, progressive evolution of social and cultural knowledge(s) and believes that notions of interdisciplinarity will govern the 'next phase of intellectual growth' in contemporary culture.[6] His ideas ring true for the conceptual ceramics discussed in this chapter. They were made by individuals who trained in traditional craft techniques and who may well mobilize aspects of ceramics-as-craft. They have, however, dispensed with the production of ceramics-as-objects-of-exchange, and their work challenges conventional notions of what constitutes and is appropriate to ceramics practice. The key ceramics world trope of the solitary, rural craft potter, spiritually nurtured by handwork, despite (or perhaps because of) material impoverishment, is displaced by urban adventures in collaboration. Contemporary conceptual ceramics operates at the permeable boundary between art and craft, partaking of aspects of both, and ultimately demonstrating (or performing) that permeability. A growing faction amongst the craft community in Britain welcomes this sort of radical re-visioning, as 'Clay Rocks' indicated.

Yet there is still no real consensus as to exactly what the phrase 'conceptual ceramics' covers. Arguably, Western culture in the early 21st century is 'post-conceptual' by definition, and certainly the terms 'concept' and 'conceptual' are used loosely today as buzzwords. As a lecturer in contextual studies at a University School of Art and Design, I routinely discuss aspects of ceramics practice with successive year groups of students. Their understanding of the context(s) within which they are working develops alongside their technical skills and imbues their activities with heightened significance. They would be intellectually blinkered if they were not aware of the so-called 'art/craft debate.' Indeed, many of them have tired of it and are ready to embrace change. There is widespread recognition that, as Alex Buck has observed, the crafts are in a 'complementary, symbiotic relationship with painting and sculpture.'[7] Ceramics courses at colleges all over the world use the vocabulary of conceptualism to signal that they offer the opportunity to explore exciting new territory. The Royal College of Art in London (RCA), for example, declares that 'Ceramics and Glass does not so much imply a fixed set of media, but a site for discursive practice where cultural, social, personal, historical and aesthetic concerns intersect.'[8] Nowadays few ceramists achieve recognition without articulating such 'concerns' and what is generally understood by 'conceptual' is that whatever form their work takes, it is *in*formed by ideas. Tableware, vessels, figurative, abstract forms: all are presented as significant objects whose fullest interpretation depends on a conceptual context and a knowing audience, willing to 'unpack' them. When it was first used, however, in relation to developments in art of the 1960s, 'conceptual' referred exclusively to practices where the art object had been 'de-materialized'. In other words, ideas occupied centre stage and its material character, its 'object-hood,' had become little more than a sign of the intellectual process from which it arose.

Contemporary conceptual ceramics often incorporates performative elements and it is worth remembering that ceramics has long been associated with performances of one sort or another. The tea ceremony for instance—whether in its romanticized, meditative, Japanese form, or as class orientated social display—requires a particular behavior from its participants as well as particular types of objects. And ceramic processes, especially firing, have always included spectacle: to take earth and turn it into something that can be used and admired is the most fundamental kind of alchemy. The transformation from the 'raw' to the 'cooked' fascinates, and watching it can be marvellous. The audience for process-based ceramics performance has increased exponentially over the last twenty years or so in Britain. Master classes, technical demonstrations and the like have become staple fare at craft venues up and down the country. Audiences go to see exactly how things are made, and be charmed by a dialogue with the maker at the same time. This is a form of theatre that can serve to promote an individual's work and boost sales. Though rarely acknowledged as such by the ceramics community, it involves a fetishization of technique and process. Written accounts of such events typically foreground the 'how-to' aspects, and do not address any conceptual or performative factors.

Originally conceived as a rural 'potters' camp' in the 1980s, the International Ceramics Festival in Aberystwyth, on the west coast of Wales, regularly presents a host of ceramists from all over the world.[9] Their performances are usually straightforward expositions of studio craft practices, playing to audiences whose principal interest is extending their own technical expertise. Some are less predictable, however. In 1997, Nina Hole constructed a ceramic 'house' from 'Magma Clay.' Three meters high on a square base, it had two stoke holes and was wood fired under a shroud of ceramic fiber. At 1000° centigrade the shroud was snatched away to reveal the glowing structure. Hole and her assistant Debby English flung sawdust over it to spectacular effect; showers of sparks erupted against the night sky. Activities like this may produce objects: the house was eventually dismantled and reassembled elsewhere, but Hole's process was significant for its own sake, as an event. That same year Maxine O'Reilly built a conical kiln that looked like a large anthill crossed with something from a science fiction novel. When it was fired, O'Reilly played it like a musical instrument, manipulating the flames that spurted from many protruding outlets. There was no product other than the photographic record.

Performance art began in the early 20th century as a radical way to sidestep the commodification of culture. Faithful to its avant-garde, Dada roots, performance art by performance artists (those for whom this form of expression is absolutely central) is often intended to unsettle the audience. Ceramics performances in the 1990s were more likely to impress and astound, and their good (as in friendly) intentions set most ceramist-performers at a tangent to performance art proper. For example, with its loud reggae soundtrack, Katsue Ibata and Rjoji Koie's flamboyant presentation at the 1991 Ceramics Festival was described by one critic as 'splendidly anarchic.' Despite this it resulted in well-made objects that he saw as 'readily understandable in the context of the freely sculptural approach to utilitarian wares that has been the hallmark of the best of Japanese ceramics.'[10] Thus it reinforced, rather than challenged, traditional notions of ceramics. Still, the very idea of ceramics-as-performance gives pause for thought, and it is likely that the growth in process-related ceramics performance prepared audiences for something more.

In 1999, surfing the internet, I came across a site called 'Beyond Utility: Psycho-Ceramics.'[11] As I wrote at the time: 'It features a jerky animation of a live head daubed with slip [liquid clay] by a disembodied hand. I would not like to hazard a guess as to the meaning of the piece, but it is fascinating simply because it exists and demands that we consider it as ceramics. How might it develop? A gradual thickening of the clay layer? A ritual shedding of this second skin? A rebirth?'[12] Six years later, in November 2005, FULL, an event that took place in a Bristol shop window, involved exactly that: a rebirth. Over the course of a very long day, ceramists Conor Wilson and Paul Sandammeer coiled a huge lidded pot, Sandammeer working from within, Wilson from without.[13] Eventually Sandammeer was completely enclosed - buried alive in what looked a bit like a canoptic jar, to be (re)born, like a chick from an egg, when it was slashed open by Wilson.[14] It took 17 hours to build the pot and the shop window set included a 'small shelf holding bottles of water, which were gradually replaced with bottles containing urine.'[15] FULL became a trial of endurance that exhausted both men. Why did they do it? According to Wilson, the performance was an opportunity to relinquish the extreme level of control he generally exerts over environment and materials in his studio. It also tied in with his interest in 'the tension between maleness and masculinity' and led him to reflect on the collaborative process in general: 'two men working together, observed and under a certain amount of pressure, with no guarantee of success. [...] The circularity of the work - one man moving around the circumference of the vessel, the other forming a turning hub; both pairs of hands meeting at the growing wall; two very different male bodies creating a barrier between themselves, which happens to be a very strong signifier for the female body, and which eventually imprisons one of them.'[16] Although FULL utilised craft skills, there was no exposition of technique. Wilson and Sandammeer elected to explore this approach in parallel to their more conventional, studio based object production and, for Wilson at least, there was a sense of escape from the craft of making. Their physical exhaustion is reminiscent of the unsettling nature of performance art proper, which frequently entails extreme bodily states.

While still a student, albeit a 'mature' one, training in ceramics craft techniques, Philip Lee began to imprint his naked torso onto an earthenware slab or a piece of paper using slip. Raw, wet clay can be seen as a primal material; smeared on the body it evokes at once a return to childhood innocence and, in a middle-aged man, a transgression of socialized masculinity. Lee saw himself as 'addressing the taboos associated with exposing the male body' and experienced a personal sense of liberation.[17] His efforts recall early feminist performance. When a naked Carolee Schneeman and friends wrestled and writhed with chicken carcasses (and the rest) in *Meat Joy* (1964) their idea was to celebrate the flesh in a kind of proto-feminist erotics. A similar sense of letting go is apparent in the videos that record Lee's ritualised actions. He has exhibited ceramic slabs imprinted with torsos, but these were signs of his performances, rather than resolved objects in their own right; it was the experience that concerned him, not the outcome. Clay became a means of exploring and expressing masculine subjectivity. Paradoxically, the viewer was invited to objectify the male body: to imagine its collision with the material, to witness its exposure.

In an influential essay, jeweller and critic Bruce Metcalf articulated commonly held views about the nature of craft and art. He declared that 'Craft cannot be dematerialized' and asserted that, 'In the craftworld, objecthood and material come prior to any other considerations,' while 'the first priority of art is to address ideas.' Referring to a performance event in early 1970s Germany, organised by US ceramist James Melchert, Metcalf 'failed to see how dumping a bucket of slip over somebody is craft'[18] and would no doubt similarly dismiss Philip Lee's performance. But could it be ceramics? Installation and performance related work has been steadily pushing back the boundaries of ceramics practice and increasingly the terms 'art' and 'craft' seem irrelevant. Ceramics cannot be subsumed to either; it is an exceptionally elastic and fragmented field, comprising myriad activities and bustling with sign systems. Ceramics can be considered in terms of material culture; of consumer culture; in historical context; as a craft activity; as sculpture; as design; as process; as display; rural; urban; first world; third world; production; consumption - the list is endless. The only dependable common factor is the presence of, or association with, clay in some form. Practitioner David Cushway has commented on how this works for him: 'I'm interested in the way the material adds to the concept … the material's intrinsically linked to the concept, […] I'm interested in all these connotations of what clay is, what it does, what it means and what it can do, and what it's done for centuries: the history of it. And I think you can tap into that and you can use it. […] It's not a craft medium at all - it's a material, it's another pencil.'[19]

Cushway typically initiates transitions from the particular to the universal. Beautiful yet uncanny, his *Sublimation* video (2002) alludes to the fragility of individual life and the indestructibility of a greater life cycle ('earth is where we come from and it's where we return to'[20]). Lasting fifteen minutes, it shows an unfired cast of Cushway's own head dissolving in a tank of water. A skilfully made object, the viewer is witness to its gradual unmaking. Nothing is actually lost for, in principle at least, the material could be reclaimed from the water and reused. Cushway notes that on occasion *Sublimation* has moved viewers to tears.

Collaboration with the engineering department at the University of Cardiff enabled David Cushway to produce films that show mundane domestic ceramics—a teapot, a cup, a milk jug—breaking. Shot at thousands of frames a second, they capture every detail in slow motion. Though they make no overt reference to clay-craft, the film-craft on display is impressive: 'high technology' in action. One at a time, the objects float into view, fall gradually through space and smash in a beautiful, measured, hypnotic ballet of shards. Then the process is reversed, the pieces slowly reassemble and the objects are remade. Becoming more and more complete, they float back up the screen. They are second-hand, industrially manufactured ceramics bought in charity shops (thrift stores). Rejects from the domestic interior, their sheer banality enhances their ability to act as vehicles for symbolic meaning. They are readily imbued with human qualities. A milk jug nose-dives to destruction. As it crumples, a fragment escapes and drifts upwards, to become an instant metaphor for hope. Cushway's films operate with psychic intensity. They are remarkably satisfying to watch; perhaps the visible process of reparation fulfils deep psychological needs.

But the time-based (sometimes called 'durational') aspects of contemporary conceptual ceramics are not confined to performance, film and video work. As Cushway's *Sublimation* demonstrates, raw clay is not a stable material, and consequently it lends itself to open-ended investigations. His *Snowdon*, an unfired cast of an iconic mountain peak, harnesses the future. Drops of condensation on the inside of its sealed glass case show that it is in a state of flux. It appears to be breathing and is gradually accruing a variegated organic surface as molds form. He has set a process in motion so that the object is forever 'becoming;' it will never be completely finished. Where and when is the focal point?

For Clare Twomey, a Polaroid photograph signifies a captured memory: 'a sense of a permanent thing we possess of a moment that has gone.'[21] *The Temporary* (Northern Clay Center, Minneapolis 2006) consisted of a thousand Polaroids installed against a 12-meter wall of unfired red earthenware. The moisture in the wall affected the photographic ink, so that, like Cushway's *Snowdon*, the work entered a state of flux, with the Polaroid images dissolving and running into the raw clay background. In 2007 Twomey revisited *The Temporary* and re-installed it at the Amsterdam Art Fair, but this time she cast the Polaroids in clay, fired and glazed them. The resulting ceramic wafers were taken away by visitors; thus, like her *Trophy* at the V&A, the work has simultaneously fragmented and expanded – a slow, controlled cultural explosion.

Both David Cushway and Clare Twomey see their practice as a form of research. They are engaged in a process of inquiry, an exploration of ideas, predicated on and exploiting the characteristics of clay. The transformation of the material is a central concern and (semiotic) significance unfolds with making. Cushway has articulated this sensibility: 'The whole process of making something can inform the conceptual [...]. I am very particular in that I start with an idea and then render that idea in the best way possible. But I do think that there are times when it is a combination of the two things, of the making and the conceptual, and the space between the brain and the hands can lead you in different ways.'[22] For Twomey, an exhibition is an opportunity for personal reflection, to place her work before an audience and for them to 'test the theory of the work.' Of *The Temporary* she has said, 'it really is a large experiment, it's not completed and I am beginning to understand more about this body of work, between the highly temporal and the object [...] it feels like an ongoing conversation that I am learning about all the time. [...] you only truly understand the work when other people engage with it.'[23]

Twomey's *Consciousness/Conscience* at the World Ceramic Exposition in Korea (2002) elicited a performance from its viewers that clarifies the notion of 'conversation' that she seeks in her work. They were invited to walk across a pristine floor of hand-cast porcelain boxes that had been produced in a Korean factory according to her e-mailed and faxed instructions. On the other side of the floor they found photographs of the same boxes being made, but the floor crumbled beneath their feet with every step. For Twomey the work 'alludes to ...the responsibility we must all take for the effects of our actions upon nature.'[24] The precision, both aesthetic and technical, of the installation was crucial to its success, as was an intimate understanding of the material: the porcelain had to break in exactly the right way, without producing hard sharp fragments. Thinking back to Sol LeWitt's definition of conceptual art, in no way was the execution of this work 'a perfunctory affair.' Yet it does fit some of his criteria in that the object was de-materialized in another way: *Consciousness/Conscience* was only completely realized while it was being destroyed.

Keith Harrison's work also has a peak 'moment' of realization: a distinct time period during which it is completely activated. He sheathes the elements of mundane, domestic electrical appliances with Egyptian paste. Electric fires, storage heaters and the like (such as the cookers installed at *Last Supper* at the V&A) are transformed in this way, then 'fired' at the flick of a switch. The period of 'firing' *is* the work; strictly speaking, everything else is before or after.

In the 1960s, Harrison's father was a senior electrical technician in a university laboratory. His son pays him homage with a re-presentation and performance of the technician role. British ceramics has had a vexed relationship with electricity. The products of the electric kiln have been considered inauthentic by craft traditionalists, who see 'combustion and the generation of flames and smoke as the proper way to fire ceramics.'[25] Wood firing, for instance, feels 'organic' and promotes a sense of continuity with the earliest of potters. With this in mind, Keith Harrison's activities are transgressive; indeed, there is something about his demeanor when he constructs his installations that recalls schoolboy experimentation and situates the viewer as co-conspirator or playfellow. (Perhaps that is why the 'Clay Rocks' audience was so reluctant to give up on his *London Orbital*.)

Some of Harrison's early research was carried out in a laboratory at Imperial College, London, the antithesis of a craft studio. His *Bench Block*, cooker rings stacked inside a striped cylinder of Egyptian paste, has a quasi-industrial 'grunge' aesthetic; a distinctive and intriguing style, dictated only in part by the components used. The execution may not have been perfunctory in Sol LeWitt's terms, but neither was it meticulous. Seen on video, *Bench Block* looks dangerous. It exudes molten sugar (used as a binder for the Egyptian paste) and emits plumes of steam. There is a background of laboratory benches and snatches of conversation can be heard: technical terms like 'resistor' and 'wattage.' Often what Harrison does valorizes working-class domesticity. In one untitled piece, a humble bar fire—the most ordinary form of domestic electric heater, with a bar that glows when the current is turned on—comes quietly to life on a patterned carpet in a corner of Eileen Hogg's living room (she is his wife's grandmother). In the background we hear her asking if he wants a sandwich. The effect is utterly banal yet at the same time mesmerising, as exhibition selector, sculptor Andrew Lord commented: 'At once familiar and outside any thought I have had of 'ceramic' sculpture, it is thrilling.'[26]

For the exhibition *Ceramic Contemporaries 4* (2002) Harrison installed a series of wall heaters in the Gulbenkian gallery at the RCA. At the private view, the line on the floor beyond which spectators could not pass generated a *frisson* of anticipation and by the time he switched the piece on viewers were jostling for position. This was a constituency of believers, a collaborative audience whose level of engagement was thoroughly informed by its intimate understanding of ceramics-as-craft, just like the audience for 'Clay Rocks' at the V&A. Conceptual ceramics may well appeal (and be relevant) to a much wider audience, but it speaks most clearly to those who bring their own experience of methods and materials to bear on their process of consumption. To 'understand' Keith Harrison's work, an awareness of ceramics related technology – specifically of glaze chemistry – is a distinct advantage, and something similar is true of Cushway and Twomey.

It takes a person who has handled clay themselves to fully comprehend what was entailed in making David Cushway's *Breath* (2000). It is a thick clay carton inflated by blowing into it, as one would blow up a balloon, no easy thing to do. The piece recalls an occasion when Cushway was called upon to give artificial resuscitation to a child. Almost prosaic looking, its function is to crystallise his past actions; it was not conceived as an autonomous object. Though not described, the body is evoked and the crux of the work is a strong sense of human presence. *Breath* induces an empathic reaction in the viewer: a heightened awareness of one's own breathing.

In Western art the visual dominates, and although the sense of touch, the haptic system, is important in the crafts, it has traditionally been sidelined.[27] Yet physical manipulation of materials is central to the production of studio ceramics, and touch, in the form of handling, is central to our appreciation, or consumption, of ceramic objects. Bonnie Kemske has spent the last four years exploring the haptic system in relation to ceramics. She made a series of forms that were designed to stimulate a tactile response. Their differently textured, highly crafted surfaces and their density are informed by her research into physiology and the operation of touch at cellular level. For her, the challenge has been to produce objects that speak primarily to the haptic system, whose visual character is almost incidental, a consideration *en route* to a perceptual arena beyond the realm of the visual, so that 'The emphasis … lies not in the objects themselves but in a final sensual tactile experience.'[28] Kemske's work is in some sense time based, for it is incomplete until it is brought into contact with a human body. Once engaged physically, interest in its visual character dwindles; she has observed that when holding and touching her work, viewers may look away and/or close their eyes. The objects trigger social interaction, for individuals are keen to discover and discuss their feelings as they literally embrace each form.

As Kemske's experience suggests, it has become possible to exhibit highly wrought objects that are nevertheless understood to direct the viewer's attention elsewhere than their objecthood and/or their craft identity, an approach that is catching on with other makers. Though well established as a figurative ceramist, Daniel Allen has lately departed from representing the figure as such, in favor of exploring relationship(s) between the body and its immediate environment. He made a perfectly rendered, full size ceramic chair - the battered old fashioned wooden sort found in school-rooms and church halls - and asked someone to sit on it before it was fired, while the clay was still soft enough to take an impression.[29] Somehow the person who caused the distorted backrest and buckled legs is almost visible. The work catches a ghost, a peripheral vision; it holds a moment on 'pause.' Allen's installation of eight (undistorted) empty chairs anticipates human occupancy. Yet it already feels inhabited and every reconfiguration of the furniture provokes a different narrative, from a single melancholy soul gazing out the window, to an entire encounter group.[30] That the chairs are made from clay signals a symbolic reading; that they can be read as 'real' chairs is equally important. The high level of technical expertise – the craft – evident in the look of the work is crucial to its success, but not prime in its construction of deeper meaning.

One might have expected to encounter resistance to contemporary conceptual ceramics from within the craft establishment, and there are indeed those who cannot and never will accept some of the work discussed in this chapter as ceramics. This has not proved to be the case in general however, and an important factor in considering audience response involves the notions of community that pervade what has been called 'the craft ideal.' According to academic writer Peter Hobbis, the craft ideal 'sees human life as essentially communal and collaborative' and believes that individual craftspeople are 'acting positively to serve the interests of others,' so that 'the productive activity of each harmonises with the goals of all.'[31] It is, of course, an ideal that owes much to William Morris' utopian socialist view of craft production as un-alienated labour. It leads to an audience for contemporary conceptual ceramics that is warmly optimistic and willing to engage with practices that challenge traditional notions of ceramics, on the premise that such challenges are well meant because they have emerged from and are rooted within the craft community, however tenuous the link may have become. Audiences for conceptual art in a wider sense are 'cool,' conspicuously flexing their cultural competence and alert to the ironies of the postmodern condition as they swiftly 'unpack' the work, assimilate its message and move on.[32] The warm, energetic response of the craft audience is very different. It is, and here I draw on my own observations, largely without irony, though socially and culturally informed, and uninhibited in its display of enthusiasm. Such viewer competency allows contemporary conceptual ceramists considerable freedom in their modes of practice. They can, as Sol LeWitt put it, let the 'idea become the machine that makes the art' with every expectation of a receptive audience.

For LeWitt and the conceptual artists of an earlier era, the physicality of the creative process became invisible and no longer featured in the discourse that accompanied their activities. For the practitioners I have discussed, however, manipulation of their chosen material is a central consideration. The appearance of their work is distinctive, important, and very often beautiful. Every detail is considered; there is nothing perfunctory about its material construction. On the contrary, it figures large in their construction of meaning. Contemporary conceptual ceramists have not rejected the object out of hand and clay remains central to their activities. But they do apply their craft/material-based skills in new and exciting ways. In a quest to unite aesthetic and conceptual integrity, they seek a symbiotic relationship between idea and object. As much as they challenge and extend the boundaries of what ceramics can be, they also challenge and extend the boundaries of conceptual practice by injecting it with craft sensibilities.

Notes

1. Sol LeWitt 'Paragraphs on Conceptual Art' in *Artforum*, Vol. 5 No. 10 (Summer 1967): 79–83.
2. See Lucy Lippard, *Six Years: The Dematerialization of the Art Object from 1966 to 1972* (1973; reprinted Berkeley: University of California Press, 1997).
3. *Clay Rocks* evening event at the V&A 29/9/06.
4. Paul Greenhalgh, 'The Genre' in *The Persistence of Craft*, edited by Greenhalgh (London: A&C Black 2002), 19.
5. Greenhalgh, 27.
6. Greenhalgh, 'Complexity' in *The Persistence of Craft*, 195.
7. Alex Buck 'The Art of Craft' in *Obscure Objects of Desire*, edited by Tanya Harrod (London, Crafts Council 1997), 145.
8. Course description, MA Ceramics and Glass, RCA website: http://www.rca.ac.uk/pages/study/ma_ceramics_and_glass_151.html

9. For more information, see the Festival website: http://www.internationalceramicsfestival.org/
10. Robert Faulkner, 'Challenging Orthodoxy' in *The International* 1991 (the journal of the International Ceramics Festival).
11. See http://bitter.custard.org/beyond/beyond/psycho The performer is Tonia Clarke.
12. Jo Dahn, 'Ceramics as Performance' in *Ceramic Review* No.180 (Nov/Dec 1999).
13. Coiling is a way of building vessels and other forms from sausage like 'coils' of clay.
14. FULL Plan 9, Bristol 22nd October 2005. See also Jo Dahn, 'Sculptor and Figure' (contemporary trends in figurative ceramics) in *Ceramic Review* No.219 (May/June 2006).
15. Conor, Wilson, reflections on FULL, personal communication (April 2007).
16. Wilson, reflections on FULL, personal communication (April 2007).
17. Philip Lee, personal statement (2003).
18. Bruce Metcalf, 'Craft and art, culture and biology' in *The Culture of Craft*, edited by Peter Dormer (Manchester: Manchester University Press 1997), 70–71. Metcalf was referring to James Melchert's *Changes* performance (1972) which took place at Documenta 5 in Germany. See Schwartz, Judith *Confrontational Ceramics* London: A&C Black 2008. P. 122.
19. David Cushway, interviewed by the author (2001).
20. David Cushway, 'Presence and Absence,' conference paper, *The Fragmented Figure*, University of Wales Institute, Cardiff published in *Interpreting Ceramics* edition 8. (See: http://www.uwic.ac.uk/ICRC/issue008/articles/05.htm)
21. Clare Twomey, proposal for *The Temporary*, 2007 (personal communication).
22. Cushway, interviewed by the author (2001).
23. Recorded conversation between David Cushway and Clare Twomey at Bath School of Art and Design, England, May 2007. Subsequently used as the basis for Dahn, Jo 'In Conversation: Clare Twomey and David Cushway' in *Crafts* No. 207, July/August 2007.
24. Clare Twomey, application statement for Korea 2001 (personal communication).
25. Jeffery Jones, conference paper: 'Singing the Body Electric: A Brief History of Electricity and Studio Ceramics' in *Situated Knowledges*, Design History Society annual conference, Aberystwyth, Wales, 2002.
26. Andrew Lord, 'Selectors' Comments' in *Ceramic Contemporaries 4* exhibition catalogue (National Association of Ceramics in Higher Education and Aberystwyth Arts Centre, 2002).
27. See Pamela Johnson, 'Out of Touch: The Meaning of Making in the Digital Age' in *Obscure Objects of Desire*, 292.
28. Bonnie Kemske, 'Touching the Body: A Ceramic Possibility' in *Interpreting Ceramics* edition 8. (See: http://www.uwic.ac.uk/ICRC/issue008/articles/22.htm).
29. Daniel Allen, untitled, 'the absent figure' series I (2005).
30. Allen, untitled, 'the absent figure' series II (2005).
31. Peter Hobbis, 'The Value of Crafts' in *Obscure Objects of Desire*, 37.
32. For further discussion, see Julian Stallabrass, *High Art Lite* (London & New York, Verso 1999).

Source: Jo Dahn, "Elastic/Expanding; Contemporary Conceptual Ceramics," in *Extra/Ordinary*, Maria Elena Buszek, Ed., pp. 153–174. Copyright, 2011, Duke University Press. All rights reserved.

Republished by permission of the copyright holder. www.dukeupress.edu

40
EXTENDING VOCABULARIES: DISTORTING THE CERAMIC FAMILIAR – CLAY AND THE PERFORMATIVE 'OTHER'

Andrew Livingstone

This text aims to explore some key areas that contribute to an extended vocabulary for ceramics with regards to the employment of clay and in particular its juxtaposition with the performative 'other'. The notion of the performative 'other' references the developing spectacle of 'non-ceramic' medium employed by artists working within the ceramics field and one that is often evidenced, although not exclusively, through video, photography, digital-media and performance. These mediums and methods will be discussed through examples and theories aligned to art practice within the ceramics discourse.

The question of authenticity, in this case I refer to the term (ceramic familiarity) becomes perplexed when ceramic is positioned at the digital interface, and most significantly where new media is integral to the artwork. The reading of ceramic both in conjunction with and through another medium, obviously, distorts familiarity where previously interpretation and critique has been applied exclusively to the material first-hand.

The use of video in particular can be evidenced as a growing spectacle within the ceramic domain, where its location moves beyond documental significance to claim an integral position within practice. Contemporary observations can be made towards the ceramic artist that engages video from numerous perspectives, notably when the video image captures either the movement of, or change in, the material clay, (this often visually presents the alteration of clay as a material) and when the development of a narrative references object or location, both address the notion of time-based activity as well as the temporality of material, object and location. These elements can be acknowledged to clay that has the potential to change, a notion that extends beyond the familiar subject of immortalised fired clay. The association, therefore, with the familiarity of the stable ceramic object becomes fluid, where essentially the movement, alteration, or deconstruction of clay, essentially time-based activities work to distort the notion of familiarity that has been constructed within ceramic discourse. This challenge to the materiality of clay through time-based activity suggests, a form of conceptual practice that integrates the artist, medium and idea within the language and arena of ceramic discourse. The absence of the physical ceramic form, presented through representation suggests that clay has become somewhat dematerialised within the familiar taxonomies of ceramic discourse. If the physical form has become dematerialised how then might a medium such as video be interpreted within the discipline of ceramics?

The theory and practice of video art, has developed as a distinct genre, one that is expressed widely within contemporary practice. Several of the critiques and structures applied to video art might possibly be applied to video work emerging from ceramic artists. This might though, become complicated by the location of such

Source: © Andrew Livingstone.

works within artistic arenas that project quite different interpretation. This text will examine the use of video and digital media within ceramic practice and offer a reading from a discipline perspective.

Extended approaches

The ceramic artist's search for the unfamiliar results in both a re-grounding of the characteristics that define craft - applied art, and in the adoption of elements that usually exist outside of applied art discourse. The ceramic artist's approach to unfamiliarity and extended field of ceramic practice, rightly, will include numerous formats where individuals negotiate certain elements of familiarity. The individual may explore several areas of investigation to include material, object, process, function and history. Exploration of these categories will include works that constitute solely the medium clay but this will, however, also extend to works that engage other media and material. With the development of critical language and the progression of ideas-based focused practice, the evaluation of ceramics, in the traditional sense has, overtime, somewhat altered and as a consequence developed extended vocabularies.

Clay in motion - animation as performative 'other'

There will be much work internationally that portrays clay through the process of animation, however, given the limited space of this short text I will focus on a few examples.

The work *The Deconstruction of Trade*, 2004, (http://www.andrewlivingstone.com) consists of thirteen plates. The plates depict the deconstruction of the familiar willow pattern design into a reconstruction of an urban landscape. The final plate is then animated and projected on a larger scale.

The evaluation of process and technique within the work becomes complicated if we follow the definitions of craft as presented by Metcalf.[1] The primary element, put forward in respect of a definition, is that the work should be substantially, made by the hand. This is difficult to administer, as the thirteen plates that constitute the work are ready-made. The manipulation of the images and the application of the transfers, however, was executed by hand. It should be noted that this process is aligned primarily with industrial processes and, therefore, would not demand a high level of process evaluation and skills critique. The animation was also executed by hand and was part of a complicated process but it should be considered that this artform, however, does not originate or reside within craft practice.

These two elements can be observed within the work, however, these familiar elements have been repositioned. They are elements in transition. The connection with craft's past can be familiarised to the use of the blue and white willow pattern design but this becomes disrupted when the image becomes animated and is projected onto tiled surface. This is also the case if we observe the notion of medium specificity as the work moves from ceramic plate to animation through video projection. Whilst the mediums of animation and video reside outside of the canon of ceramics a continued narrative has been constructed that creates a transition from ceramic to digital media. This transition performs in several ways, on a primary level the static fired image is literally animated as birds fly around the familiar willow pattern design and the crane moves along its axis. In terms of a performative reading, the projection re-animates a historical narrative and extends the reading of the work through an alternative platform, and one where the digital medium has the capacity to perform.

Animation has been evidenced within several works and exhibitions aligned to ceramics over the last decade, many of which engage with the 'clay-mation' process, where small changes/movements within the material are meticulously recorded then speeded up to evidence the change over a given time-period. This process forms part of the work *Absentia* (2011) (Figures 40.1, 40.2 and 40.3)

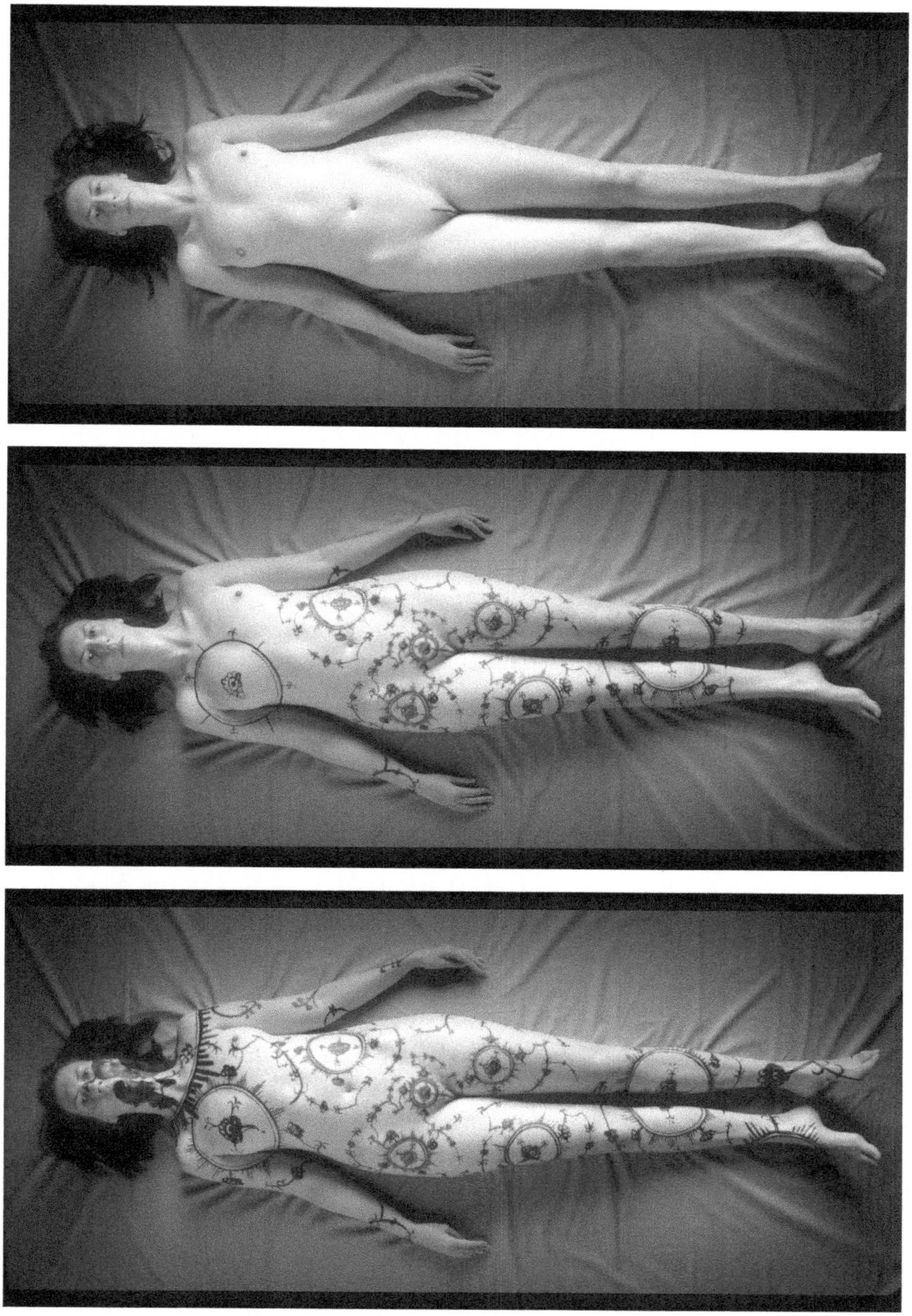

Figures 40.1, 40.2 and 40.3 Absentia, 2010, Susanne Hangaard/Video made in collaboration with: art director: Sofie Fruergaard, cinematographer: Sophie Winquist, editor: Julian Andersen, recordist: Sille Boel, body painter: Patrick Leis and Minerva Fil A/S.

(http://www.susannehangaard.dk/uk/projekter/absentia/index.html) by Susanne Hangaard, where the blue and white Royal Copenhagen fluted motif grows and moves over the artists naked body. Hangaard comments upon the work;

> 'With Absentia I have chosen to let the clay, as a physical material, play a less significant part of the work. Instead, pictures referring to ceramics as well as sound convey the story. My vision is to challenge the way the audience perceive ceramics and the context in which it appears.'[2]

In referencing the work it is clear that clay has a minority part to play, yet a direct connection to ceramics, in this case Danish porcelain, is made through other medium, or what we can term the performative 'other'. You may well be asking, how is this considered ceramic, I would argue that a connection with the pattern in this case the blue and white motif, affords an extended acceptance as the narrative extends from object to video carried by an acknowledgment of the familiar.[3]

Digital media and participant as performative 'other'

The work *Tacit,* (2004), (http://www.andrewlivingstone.com) by myself, investigates both process and technique within the context of installation. The work explores the location of these two elements and how significant they might become in relation to the work when they are repositioned. In the work *Tacit* process and technique are central, whether the spectator activates the work physically or mentally. In the gallery space the spectator encounters wet clay, which sits upon a workstation. A set of instructions on how to construct a pinch pot are located beside the clay and around the room yellow signs are placed informing the spectator that the space is being monitored by CCTV. The location of process and technique within the work is relocated to the spectator (in this case a performative 'other'), as they will become significant dependent upon the spectator's skills when constructing a pinch pot. If the spectator chooses not to construct a pinch pot the elements of process and technique also remain significant as they remain with their conscience. This positioning within the work questions the spectator's own technique and process with regard to making thus fundamentally exposing both elements as concept. That is to say that the idea becomes significant as a result of analysing the skills of the spectator. This work questions the authentic position that process and technique hold within ceramic discourse and aims to relocate them within an extended visual and theoretical vocabulary, this notion is supported by the employment of CCTV within the work, an element that is crucial to the conceptual significance. In examining the digital media contained within this work, simultaneously there appears both a disjuncture and juncture when reading the work. CCTV a surveillance tool, is everywhere in our daily lives, observing our movements, it is also commonplace within galleries, a technical assistant, compliant with the taboo 'do not touch'. Within this work the digital media makes us conscious of the space and the actions performed when making a simple clay vessel. It amplifies the viewer's awareness of their craft/making skills, (an intentional construct of this work), as historically these appear in the upper hierarchy of evaluation within craft/applied art practice. As the arena continues to develop and change, this work both embeds skill centrally, and challenges its reading through conceptual approach.

In contrast to the embedded digital medium within the work *Tacit*, *Teatime at The Museum* (2012) (http://www.davidcushway.co.uk/2012/Teatime_at_the_Museum.html) an artwork by David Cushway, utilises the medium of film as an extension of both object and performer (Figure 40.4). Whilst it might be considered that the film is documentary, Cushway's work and research places the film within the context of

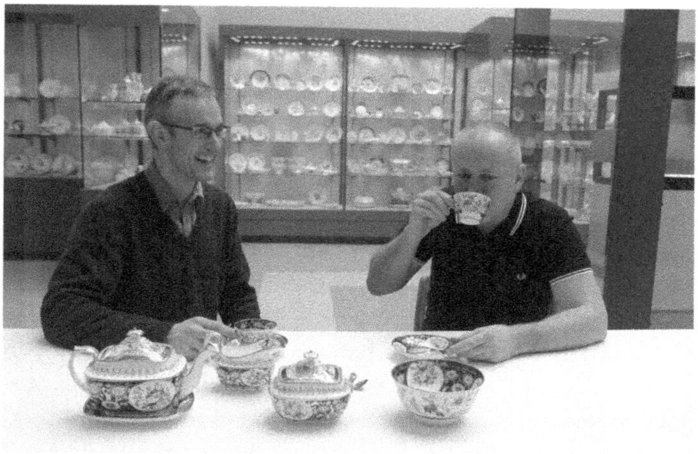

Figure 40.4 Teatime at the Museum, 2012/David Cushway.

ceramics through a post-medium, post-disciplinary construct. That is to say he extends the performance and narrative of 'ceramics' through film, a performative 'other'. The artwork is subversive in approach, as the keeper of collections at The National Museum of Wales, Cardiff, is invited to remove a tea service form the cabinet in the museum and take tea with the artist (both performative actions), a subversive act if you consider both curatorial practice and the removed functionality of objects housed in cases in museums. The re-animation of the objects is central to the work and this is conveyed through the medium of film, this links to the questioning of the museum's role in the collection and communication of objects (in this case ceramics), which is experienced through both visual and dialogic narratives.

Material knowledge

The presentation of clay in unfired form - firstly represented through another medium or secondly when supported by non-ceramic media in either the act of performance or time-based activity - works to dislodge familiarity with clay and question the material itself, more often than not through the object that it assumes. In questioning and exploring the materiality of clay within the constructs of the discipline it perhaps suggests that the notion of *conceptual ceramics* much like *sculptural ceramics* is the product of auto-aggrandisement within its own field.

The symbiosis between object and idea is central to a large proportion of contemporary work, particularly the type of work that is evidenced in this paper. Peter Dormer remarks upon this in his discussion about, medium, object and idea:

> 'Almost any object or part of an object can be put into an assemblage and be described as representing anything that assembler cares to say it represents. What is missing is a congruity between the form and the representation. There is no necessary connection between the medium and the message. It is arguable that much contemporary art, especially installation art, works at this level – the words provide the content and the artefacts are merely pegs. Naturally, in such circumstances, craft knowledge is of secondary or even minimal importance'.[4]

Dormer suggests that there is no necessary connection between the medium and the message and that the object has the capacity to represent a prescribed notion by the artist. This suggestion certainly constructs a valid point that objects exist within complex structures that inform association by familiar recognition.[5] Although Cushway places the familiarity of objects centrally within his works - in contradiction to Dormer's suggestion regarding installation art - he demonstrates a connection between material and ideas, where the tacit knowledge of ceramic is explored and displayed within contemporary practice. In the case of *Teatime at the Museum*, we are able to place a familiarity with the act of taking tea and have an informed knowledge of both the object and materiality of ceramic. Similarly this is a crucial element within Clare Twomey's work, *Is it Madness. Is it Beauty* (2010) (www.claretwomey.com), where the objects, in this case multiple unfired wheel-thrown vessels, rely on inherent physical properties within the clay to both activate and realise the work. *Is it Madness. Is it Beauty* is a performance-based work that consists of a performer (dancer) who repeatedly fills unfired vessels (situated on a large trestle table) with water and proceeds to clean the space with a mop and bucket as the vessels disintegrate over a period of time. The artwork is collaborative in its construction and can be examined from varied perspectives, however, I would like to concentrate on the theme of this paper and the performative 'other'. In this regard, material and process are central as noted above, this references the idea of 'distorting the ceramic familiar' if we consider a vernacular reading of wheel-thrown vessels, that will usually be fired and glazed. It is interesting to note that the skill within the work has shifted from the maker to the performer and our focus concentrated on the materiality of the clay, experienced within a time-based construct.

In an interview with Cushway we discussed the importance of the materiality of clay especially in this context where it emerged that the success of the idea - or its conceptual significance - was heightened if the spectator could identify with the materiality of clay. This would suggest that an informed knowledge of how the material works would in fact enhance the conceptual element of the work.

Materiality and non-ceramic intervention

To explore the use of video within ceramic practice, it seems appropriate to examine the work of David Cushway, and in particular examples of his work that were made over a decade apart. The chosen works explore his approach and use of clay/ceramic through the medium of video and how he has navigated the material from a different perspective within a thirteen-year time frame.

David Cushway positions the materiality of clay centrally within his work whereby the intervention of other media creates a dialogue with ceramic. Although Cushway primarily engages clay within his works, the dialogue created with non-ceramic media introduces the questioning of both materiality and de-materialisation. The work *Sublimation* (2000), consists of a video piece, which depicts the disintegration of an unfired clay head in a tank of water. The video records the clay object over a period of 15 minutes until the head has disintegrated and the clay returns to its non-characteristic form. This work uses video to capture an event, in this case the breakdown of the clay object in water. The reality that this work exists – after the actual event - as solely a video piece, introduces a number of questions that address the portrayal of clay within contemporary practice.

The integration of other media into the remit of the ceramic artist further develops the notion of the de-materialisation of clay. This approach to the juxtaposition of clay with other media is an area of considerable development within contemporary ceramics in that exhibited works are not solely, or even predominantly, constructed from clay but consist of other media and material.

In Cushway's work *Sublimation* (2000) the process of the breakdown of the clay object is an event that ultimately has three elements of representation. The first is the presentation of the actual artwork. This consists of a one off event that is confined to the memory of those who participated in the spectatorship of the event. The second relies upon the documentation of the event through the media of video that is able to record the time-based element of the work through moving images. The third element is the use of still photography, however, whilst such photography enhances the event it gives no indication of the time element involved. The work presented in the exhibition consists of video format and is, most notable in that there is a physical absence of clay itself. Whilst suggesting the de-materialisation of the object in the absence of the material clay, the focus of the work is directed at the object and the process of the change in material. The only possibility for experiencing a simulated representation of the work after the original event is through the medium of video. The presentation of clay through, or juxtaposed with, another medium introduces the question as to how the theories of craft/applied art locate such work when emphasis is constantly afforded to the physical object and the hand of the maker. The observation that can be drawn from Cushway's work is that the emphasis is not placed upon the object directly but upon the process of change within the material. The work *Sublimation* (2000) can, of course, invite multiple readings that can be attached to the significance of the object and, in this particular case, a cast image of the artist's head. Cushway mentions the connection between the making and the conceptual elements contained within his constructed artworks. He states that the process of making can inform the conceptual and this is of central importance within his work. He feels also that this is the same for other artists operating within the same genre where clay acts as the starting point for their explorations. This leads to the question as to whether knowledge of the materiality of clay is required to conceive of the work as conceptual within the context of ceramic practice?

Video and ceramic - conceptual or documental

In offering a reading of video and ceramic initial observation might conclude that the use of video is as a direct result of documental recording of a performance or event.[6] The reading of ceramic through another medium, obviously, distorts familiarity where previously interpretation and critique has been applied exclusively to the material first-hand. How, therefore, can a critique be applied to a medium that is somewhat absent from the language of ceramics? Mona Da Vinci comments upon the medium of video where reference is made to the object in art:

> 'Video successfully bypasses object art, for a new emphasis on connectedness, communication, integers, and vectors, that could potentially lead to a more satisfying and complete synthesis of the artist's full creative powers. Video promises the possibility of providing the intervening conceptual means for the artist to dispense with the artificial or the artifice of art. The medium's capacity for immediacy symbolises "the missing link" that may fill the gap between art and life experience to the contemporary artist. The developmental phase becomes a thing of the past in the video artist's creative output'.[7]

Da Vinci suggests that video contains characteristics that are successful in transcending the object within art. This is to say that video has the capacity to display the conceptual whilst dispensing with the artifice of art. This can certainly be applied to Cushway's work where the video portrays the narrative and informs the conceptual. Particularly, however, with the work *Reconstructing Culture*, (2000) (http://www.davidcushway.

co.uk/2012/Reconstructing_Culture.html) the physical object is presented within the work as a re-constructed physical element, the remains of an event that is translated through the medium of video.

The event captured by Cushway is the destruction of familiar domestic ceramic objects by a hammer. The event in reality would have taken place once, as such a one off performance. The artist would either have had to consign the artwork to a singular presentation, continuously repeat the act of destruction or represent the actions through a suitable medium. Video is perhaps the most suitable medium as it is one that is able to represent the moving image as an event but then repeat the initial event continuously. A direct observation can be made towards the ceramic artist that engages video, most notably when the video image captures either the movement of, or change in, the material clay. The transformation of the material clay is an indication that an external force will be applied to alter either the material, or an object, whether immediately or over a considerable time distance. This notion can be observed in several works by Cushway, where, in the work *Sublimation,* he records the breakdown of unfired clay in water, and in *Reconstructing Culture* where post kiln-fired ceramic is broken by a hammer. Both works engage video to present the alteration of clay as a material and address the notion of time-based activity as well as the temporality of material and object. In an interview with Dr Jo Dahn, she remarked upon the video element contained within the work *Sublimation.* Dahn made reference to an absence of the experience of the quality of material, this she compared to a dissolved clay object in a tank of water in Cushway's studio. She also discussed the nature of video in the work and it emerged that the experience of time that is portrayed through video, evokes a fascination with the process of disintegration. This could be read in terms of documental presentation, which we seemed both to acknowledge, however, the looped video certainly contributes to the idea over making, therefore, it might also be interpreted as conceptual.

Video and the distortion of ceramic – time-based activity and reading

The work of the artists evidenced in this paper, might be acknowledged as being both performance and installation in its construction. Identification of these elements, in conjunction with video within fine art discourse, are offered by Kristine Stiles:

> 'Performance, installation and video often appear together in a single work of art, and all three media share common characteristics that may be summarised as follows. First, the content, form and structure of these, often time-based, media require artists and viewers to engage in and observe temporal changes and duration over time. Second, they include a wide spectrum of aesthetic practices from representation to abstraction, as well as an infinite range of styles. Third, they engage viewers in situations in so far as they often entail a consideration of, or attention to, the experience of a person or place, and they enhance reciprocity between art and viewer as interrelated subjects'.[8]

Temporal change and the observation of duration over time, as indicated by Stiles, forms a significant positioning within the practice of the artists evidenced in this paper. The use of video, as integral to the work, allows for the kinesis of the material clay to be presented. The performance of clay, that is to indicate that an event or alteration of the material occurs over a constructed time element, is presented through video, a significant other within the constructs of familiar ceramic discourse. The absence of the physical ceramic form, presented through representation suggests that clay has become somewhat dematerialised within the familiar taxonomies of ceramic discourse. If the physical form has become dematerialised how then might a medium such as video be interpreted within the discipline of ceramics? In the case of the artists evidenced, video can be acknowledged as a visual representation of the time-based activity that has taken place within the constructed artwork. Whilst this may be considered as fundamentally documental representation, the reinterpretation through the medium of video expands upon the initial event introducing a visual experience that is somewhat unfamiliar within ceramic constructs. Frank Popper offers his views upon the wider significance of video and especially video that expands beyond the notion of documentary:

> 'In video recordings, the search for dematerialised forms of art, the visual and social perception of the environment, the identification of primordial energies, forces and forms in natural space, and the body as the producer and vehicle of language are highlighted. Video recordings have fixed on tape an image of a living situation, one which is not only documentary but a part of the creative moment, implying a visual and temporal extension of the phenomenon observed'.[9]

Popper contends that video has the opportunity to extend the visual and temporal elements of a living situation. This notion has particular significance to ceramics, especially, when the situation occurs over time.

To explore this further, beyond the physical change and recording of the unfired material clay, the following addresses Popper's notion of extending living situations through the medium of video. *Last Supper at the Glynn Vivien* (2011) and *Teatime at the Museum* (2012) are works by Cushway that explore ceramics housed within museums through the medium of video. These works are 'disruptive' in nature, and whilst they could be considered documentary in execution, the content and narratives move beyond documentary. *Teatime at the Museum* has been discussed previously in this paper, similarly *Last Supper at the Glynn Vivien* engages with narrative, where, within this work thirteen members of the general public are invited to choose and talk about an object from the collection at the museum. In observing the content of the work we experience the members of the public discussing their chosen objects. In the context of Popper, the individuals talk about and reference the objects within an extended time-frame experienced through the reminiscence of childhood memories. This connects with Popper's assertion that video extends a living situation and is part of the creative moment, especially if we consider this in relation to the ceramic object, the performer and the medium of film, as a connected construct. In the context of this paper it is appropriate to consider ceramic as it is central to the discipline that we are discussing. We have explored clay and ceramic in several forms within this paper and its connection to digital media. In reference to the objects contained within *Last Supper at the Glynn Vivien* (Figure 40.5), it is worth noting the validity

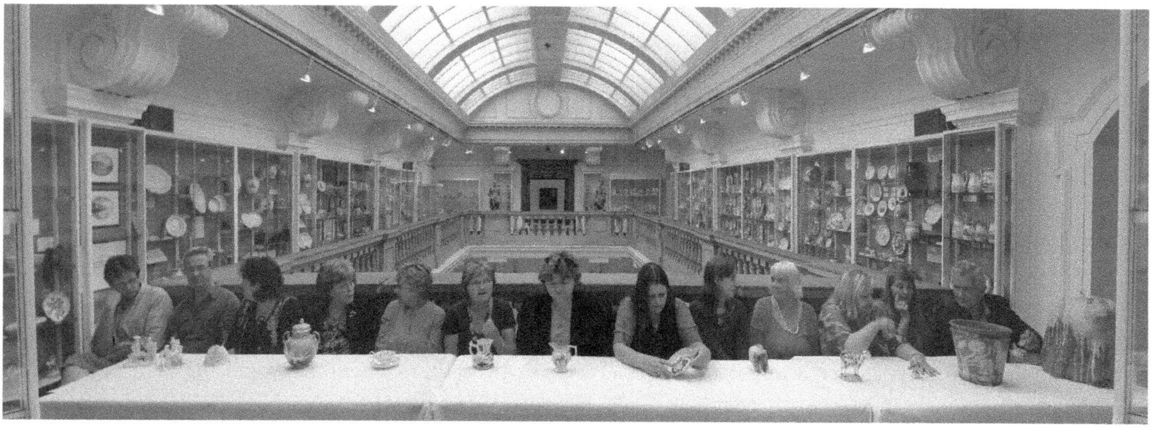

Figure 40.5 Last Supper at the Glynn Vivian, 2011/David Cushway.

of these objects from the collection as 'performative objects' in their own right, a premise articulated by Kristina Neidderer where she argues that;

> 'performative objects". ... would make their users perform in a particularly mindful way. The concept of mindfulness refers here to the attentiveness of the user towards the social consequences of actions performed with the object.'[10]

In the context of this work 'mindfulness' focuses attention on emotional, thoughtful and sensational occurrences based upon the objects presented within the work. This observation in addition references ceramic objects as holders of semiotic significance, as we are able to identify with it as a familiar image. The qualities of the performative nature of ceramics, demonstrates the properties that ceramics possess in creating 'extended vocabularies' for ceramics as a discipline. In this scenario the familiarity of the object has the ability to perform as a conceptual tool.

To explore the notion of time-based activity and the ceramic object further, the artwork *WR14 2AY* (2010) (http://www.andrewlivingstone.com) by myself, draws a two hundred year comparison between the interpretation of landscape, pre and post digital media. This artwork was featured in an exhibition Parallax View (2010), which interpreted a collection of historic 18th and 19th century porcelain housed at the Tullie House Museum, in Carlisle, United Kingdom. Within the collection was a ceramic vase created at the Worcester porcelain factory in 1810 that depicted a hand painted vignette of Malvern Priory. This vase was juxtaposed with a Lilliput video screen that portrayed a recorded six minute film of the same vignette, obviously two hundred years later and through the medium of video. The title WR14 2AY makes direct reference to the postcode and hence the location of Malvern Priory, in the county of Worcestershire in the United Kingdom. These seven characters are a means by which we are now able to locate and position ourselves in the world using digital locational platforms, this is offered in contrast to the painted scene on the vase, when social mobility was very difficult. For those that are familiar with Google Earth, we can even zoom in and get a view of any global location from the comfort of our own home or even on the move via computers and mobile phones.

The footage on the small screen is of Malvern Priory and is shot from a stationary position as close to the viewpoint of the vignette on the vase as possible. This was to prove tricky as two hundred years later the landscape around the priory had been built up and altered. What the viewer gains from this piece of work is the ability to reference a two hundred year time-frame and engage with the dialogue that is constructed between both formats of the presented image. Within this work an extended re-reading of the porcelain vase is offered through the lens of video as a contemporary performative 'other'.

Video and the dematerialisation of clay

The emergence of video within the discipline of ceramics can be actualised as a contemporary phenomenon with a few exceptions. *Changes* (http://jimmelchert.com/portfolio-items/changes/) by Jim Melchert, has been shown retrospectively since its conception in 1972.[11] The initial event was a one off performance, witnessed only by those who were present in the room. All consequential experience and spectatorship has been expressed through the medium of video or written evaluation based upon still photography. The piece was conceived and presented in the early part of the 1970's, when the artist was engaged with the wider research into the ongoing developments of conceptualism and performance art. *Changes*, acknowledged as a one off performance, was recorded onto video, an art-form that whilst relatively new, was being widely used within art practice.[12] The recording of the performance and its retrospective presentation obviously questions the materiality of clay, specifically when reading the work as presented in different formats. Observations will notably be constructed towards the absence of actual physical presence, an element firmly located within the familiar spectatorship of ceramic discourse. This introduces the subject of the transfiguration of the actual three-dimensional form into a reading that invites interpretation through a two-dimensional format. This can be sited as an obvious dematerialisation of the material form, where a two-dimensional presentation can be interpreted as mere representation. The notion of dematerialisation, as mentioned in this text, became an obvious issue, when I discussed the work *Sublimation* (2000) with David Cushway. He said of the work that initially he was working with the idea of just presenting the water tank with the residue of the cast head, however, he felt that the work needed a piece of film, as it brings an immediacy to the work. In our conversation he confirmed that the clay object had become dematerialised as a consequence of the clay constituent being removed, however, he did point out that an informed knowledge of the physicality of clay when placed in water, would contribute to the elevation of the conceptual element within the work.

Conclusion

The use of video and non-ceramic media, whilst acknowledged in both ceramic practice and developing theoretical discussions, occupies a marginalised position in respect of authentic definition. The interrelationship between ceramic and multi-media applications within this paper demonstrates the potential for an extended vocabulary for ceramics, primarily supported by a connection to familiarity (Livingstone: 2008). It is my view that ceramics can be extended through the employment of contemporary 'performative others' which, most notably in this paper, can be associated with digital and new technologies. Although, I have also aimed to demonstrate that there are other strategies that can also be employed and these were evidenced through the performativity of people and objects. In terms of digital media and how we might develop an interpretive language in relation to ceramics - the use of video and digital media within ceramic practice continues to grow and this will no doubt contribute to the development of both the practical and theoretical discourse of ceramics

Notes

1. Bruce, Metcalf. (2000) The Hand at the Heart of Craft, *American Craft, Volume 60, No 4*, August/September (2000), p. 54–61, 66. See article for detailed discussion about the practical use of the hand, including scientific and psychological analysis discussed within the remit of craft practice.
2. Susanne, Hangaard. http://www.suzannehangaard.dk, accessed 21 February 2015.
3. Andrew, Livingstone. (2008) Un-published PhD thesis, University of Ulster, *The Authenticity of Clay and its Redefinition Within Contemporary Practice; Ceramic Familiarity and the Contribution to Expansion.*
4. Peter, Dormer. (1994) *The Art Of The Maker, Skill and its Meaning in Art, Craft and Design.* Thames and Hudson Ltd: London. See chapter *Craft Skills and the Plastic Arts*, p. 35.
5. Lizzie, Zucker, Saltz. (1999) *Manufacturing Validity: The Ceramic Work of Art in the Age of Conceptual Production.* Art Papers vol. 23 no. 4 (July/August 1999) pp. 28–35. 'Today, most contemporary critics' judgements of three-dimensional artworks are framed by the recognition that all things in the world are loaded with specific socio-historical associations, which in turn imply the narratives that engage the viewer.'

6. Michael, Rush. (1999). *New Media in Late 20th-Century Art,* Thames &Hudson Ltd: London, p. 93. Rush discusses the notion of conceptual video ' Some other early explorations in video art came from artists who were already practising their own forms of Conceptual and Minimal art, mingled with the strong influence of Performance art. Much of early video art can in fact be seen, on one level, as the recording of a performance, or what came to be dubbed 'performative' actions.'
7. Gregory, Battcock. (Editor.) (1978). *New Artists Video A Critical Anthology,* E.P. Dutton: New York. See chapter *Video: The Art of Observable Dreams*, Da Vinci, Mona, p. 17.
8. Gill, Perry. And Paul, Wood. (Editors.) (2004). *Themes in Contemporary Art,* Yale University Press in association with The Open University, See chapter *I/Eye/oculus: performance, installation and video,* Stiles, Kristine, pp. 183–230.
9. Frank, Popper. (1999). *Art of the Electronic Age,* Thames and Hudson Ltd: London. See chapter *Video Art,* pp. 54–77, p. 59.
10. Kristina, Niedderer. (2007) Designing Mindful Interaction: The Category of Performative Object, in *Design Issues*: Volume 23, Number 1, Winter 2007.
11. *Changes – Performance with Drying Slip* by Jim Melchert, this film work was shown at Tate Liverpool 2004 as part of the exhibition *The Secret History of Clay – from Gauguin to Gormley*. See exhibition catalogue. Tate publishing: London, pp. 15–17.
12. Edmund, De Waal. (2003). *20th Century Ceramics*, Thames and Hudson Ltd: London, pp. 175–183. See chapter where, De Waal discusses the developments of performance where he states 'Recording the creation or destruction of the object, its reception by the public or its 'life-history' in the gallery through texts, photography or video became commonplace. The art object – and this was increasingly true for ceramics – was becoming 'dematerialised'.

First published Gyeonggi International Ceramic Biennale, ceramics colloquium proceedings, Seoul, Korea 2015.

Reproduced with permission of the author.

41

. . . AND INTO THE FIRE: POST-STUDIO CERAMICS IN BRITAIN

Glenn Adamson

William Staite Murray versus Bernard Leach, Bernard Leach versus the modernists, professionals versus amateurs, modernists versus postmodernists, Grayson Perry versus just about everyone: British ceramics have always been a subject for intense dispute. In some ways the questions have not changed since the days of the Arts and Crafts Movement. Are values such as functionality and simplicity inherently desirable, or are they simply the shackles of conservative thinking? Should pots embody social meanings, and if so, should they be unique and individualist – bearers of the hand's imprint? Or should ceramics be made inexpensively, in great numbers, through the serial production techniques that were perfected in England's pottery capital, Stoke-on-Trent? What is the place of artistic expression in a craft that was, for most of its history, more or less the creation of anonymous workers?

All these questions – which circumscribe the meanings, aesthetics, and social purposes of ceramic art – have been the subject of passionate and articulate disagreement for well over a century, and they are certainly still worth contemplating today. Yet over the past few years there has been an apparent shift in thinking, one which has more to do with the politics of place than the nature of objects. Sites of ceramic production in Britain have remained more or less constant since the nineteenth century, defined by a stable dichotomy in which the studio and the factory are clear opposites. On the one hand we have small, individualized spaces modeled on artists' ateliers. On the other are the large, highlycapitalized manufacturers, mostly located in Stoke. The diversity of making in studios is enormous, ranging from the humble brown pottery of the Leach tradition to the iconic modernist wares of Lucie Rie and Hans Coper to the iconoclastic avant-garde of the 1970s and 1980s, the generation that includes Richard Slee, Alison Britton, and Carol McNicolI. Despite their diversity, however, all of these independent British studio ceramists have thought of their work places as sites of autonomous production, directly in opposition to industry (even in those rare cases, like Slee's, where industrial wares are a stylistic inspiration).

Again, despite this tremendous variation in approach, it is nonetheless striking how stable the spatial organization of studio ceramics has been for the past century. Many theorists argue that craft objects are the authentic trace of the places where they are fashioned. In this case, British ceramics chart a dispersed geography: a vast network of loosely affiliated cells – urban, rural, and suburban alike – which makers have inhabited while pursuing the goal of personal vision. Occasionally these spaces have attained something like mythic status, as is the case with Leach's buildings in St. lves, or Rie's workspace. For the most part though, studios are off-stage. Hidden from view, known only to specialized visitors or perhaps clients at a special holiday sale, they have an air of the sacrosanct, a feeling of autonomy which pervades the products that are made there.

Source: Originally printed in *Contemporary British Studio Ceramics: The Grainer Collection*. All rights reserved © Mint Museum of Art, inc, Charlotte, North Carolina.

Recently though, the medium has taken on a very different set of spatial dynamics, such that it is possible to begin speaking of 'post-studio' ceramics. To say that this is a trend in Britain would be an exaggeration; it is more like a faint stirring, a sign of things to come. And the prefix 'post' (as in post-colonial and postmodern) brings with it a problem: we know what is being rejected, but not necessarily what new, viable options are on the table. Yet it is undeniable that ceramic artists are venturing outside the confines of their protected environments and into the world. The most striking phenomenon is the occupation of a previously ignored middle ground (or more accurately, interface) between the studio and the factory. This strategy abandons the long-established opposition between craft and mass production, hand versus machine, and instead is premised on an industrial craft model (which is to say, highly skilled but serial activities, usually set within structures that inhibit individual workers' creativity).

The irony is that this moment has arrived just as the British ceramic industry has entered what seem to be its death throes. As the Stoke factories close one after another, it has suddenly become clear to some in the field of studio ceramics that industry was not the enemy, but rather a sphere in which craftsmanship was of crucial importance all along. Neil Brownsword has been the leading figure in this regard. A native of Staffordshire, his sculpture is deeply informed by his own apprenticeship in the potteries, and he has conducted extensive filmed interviews with skilled operatives as they ply their trades. In works such as *Salvage Series*, Brownsword has created elegiac portraits of an industry in decline. In his hands fragments, wasters, and cinders become metaphors for the tragic fate of a previously proud community of industrial artisans. Other artists have been drawn to the subject as well – the photographer Dan Dubowitz, for example, has created a powerful body of work entitled *Breaking the Mould*, in which factory spaces are shown eerily empty. In one of his images, shelves full of stacked plaster molds form a monumental framework for a ladder going nowhere. As the potteries of Stoke pass into history, they become available for aesthetic contemplation.

The irony of this discovery is doubled by the fact of geographical displacement. It is the moving of ceramic production to Asia that has created these scenes of melancholic absence; and where skilled jobs have gone, studio potters are following. The trek to Chinese factories, many of which are offering short-term residencies to visiting artists, is becoming almost a cliché of contemporary ceramic practice. British potters hardly have an exclusive claim on this opportunity. The Canadian Paul Mathieu and the American Wayne Higby have been going to China for years, and even contemporary artists like Sam Durant have explored the possibilities that the great ceramic tradition there affords. But the strategy has a special resonance in Britain. As Stoke slides into post-industrial ruin, the rapprochement between mass production and studio craft is being played out not in Britain, but rather halfway around the world. Perhaps it is simply easier to abandon the precepts of your field when you are away from home; but logistically too, the appeal of Chinese manufacturing for British artists is obvious. They can work at unprecedented scale, with a huge range of materials, and the highly skilled (and low-cost) labor available there makes previously inconceivable projects possible.

The recent work of Felicity Aylieff is a particularly direct response to these conditions. Though she is disappointed by much of what is produced in China today ('tired copies of original works made hundreds of years ago;' she notes), Aylieff was nonetheless amazed by the technical facility she encountered on a visit there, and collaborated with artists at a specialist 'Big Ware' pottery to make towering vases considerably larger than herself. The series riffs on the history of Chinese ceramic form and ornament, and perhaps on the trophy-collecting mentality of earlier Europeans who were besotted with Chinese pots (the once common decorative habit of placing a massive vase on either side of a fireplace springs to mind). But mainly they are statements of grand scale, simple and unapologetic, declaring that China is larger than life.

Others who have gone to China take a more playful approach, as is the case with Carol McNicoll. A veteran of the years when British studio ceramics were overtaken by the tactics of radical *bricolage*, McNicoll normally works in a studio that is itself almost a work of art – a potter's nest built of molds, tools, paints, and other detritus. You can take McNicoll out of her home environment, but not vice versa: on a recent trip to Zebu – a city specializing in the industrial production of bone china – she snipped apart the local factory's decals and cut apart their forms, reassembling all this alien material according to her own inimitable sensibility. Like the gesture that Richard Slee made when he went to South Korea recently – a performance piece in which he donned a huge cartoon nose in recognition of a common Asian slang term for Westerners – McNicoll's work seems to self-consciously bear the marks of mistranslation.

Alongside the disappearance of the industrial 'other' against which craft studios were historically defined, a larger framework of art and design practice – postdisciplinary, relational, outsourced, and uncontained – has been emerging recently. This more open attitude to practice offers ceramics a model in which the site of invention is not so much the work as the way of working. As a result, authorship is more widely distributed, in less predictable patterns, than ever before. In this context the craft studio may soon come to seem not so much a bulwark as a burden, both economically and conceptually. For those trying to follow the way to that new, less certain future, Keith Harrison is a good guide – and if his vision is any indication we will be in for some strange and exciting times.

Harrison is the world's first serious practitioner of 'live firing' performances, in which ceramic elements are heated using domestic and hobbyist equipment in front of a watching crowd. Perhaps the most elegant version of this idea was realized in 2003, on a residency in New Delhi, India, where the artist fired colored slip using only the heat of light bulbs, which were in turn decorated by the slip. He has also employed electric heating elements, hob cooker rings, and even the tracks of a toy automobile racing set for the purpose. One of the distinctive features of these actions is that they often fail to work, which Harrison accepts as part of his project. He is not so much a daredevil as a connoisseur of uncertainty, which makes his work particularly resonant for a field in transformation.

But it is another artist, Clare Twomey, who most defines the post-studio moment in British ceramics. Her installation work *Trophy*, shown at the Victoria and Albert Museum on a single evening in 2006, showed that this approach could be as beautiful, poetic, and humane as any handmade studio pot. The idea was simple. Twomey first worked with the British manufacturer Wedgwood to create a flock of bluebirds in jasperware – the colored, matte ceramic body that Josiah Wedgwood himself invented in the late eighteenth century. She then scattered the birds through the plaster cast courts of the V&A. At a prescribed time, visitors were allowed to choose a bird to take home with them. The theme of disappearance is clearly present in this project, as it is in Neil Brownsword's sculptures. But if his work is an elegy delivered at a funeral, hers is the dove released to wing its way skyward.

Twomey recently curated an exhibition at the Middlesbrough Institute of Modern Art (mima), in another former industrial town that has seen its share of hard times. Entitled *Possibilities and Losses*, the show included the work of Brownsword, Harrison, and the North American artist Linda Sormin. Twomey also contributed a piece, entitled *Monument*, in which a gallery is filled with an enormous mass of ceramic shards. Each of these shattered objects has a specific past, more or less unretrievable. And yet there is something optimistic in the work. Here and there, amid the glorious ruin, stands an isolated intact vase or teapot, which has somehow survived its unceremonious dumping into place. And as it turns out, Twomey has sourced all this ceramic from a firm that still survives in Stoke called Johnson's Tiles; they have remained financially viable partly through a strategy of recycling, and these shards will eventually be returned to the factory where they will be ground up into clay dust and reformed into tiles. Like Twomey's birds, albeit less directly, *Monument* will eventually be dispersed into homes across Britain. This is one artwork that stands proudly for the idea of a second chance.

I have two of the little bluebirds from *Trophy* on the windowsill of my London flat today. This is a budding collection, you might say, certainly nothing to rival that of Marc and Diane Grainer's with its scope, scale, and underlying aesthetic convictions. These birds do not define an era, nor do they really map a community (despite the 'relational' gesture of the work). Much of what made studio pottery worth having is absent. There is no expressive gesture, no mark of the hand, no subtle imprint of the workspace. And yet, in these two perky little birds, their tails raised in a permanent gesture of vigilant optimism, I can say that I have an artwork living in my corner. Every day that I keep them, or tell people about them, or write about them in a book, I extend their reach. It's a rather slight vision of the future of ceramics, I know; but at least it's a start.

Originally published as Glenn Adamson (2010), '… And Into the Fire: Post-Studio Ceramics in Britain', in Annie Carlano (ed), *Contemporary British Studio Ceramics: The Grainer Collection*, Yale University Press, Mint Museum of Art, Inc., pp. 199–204.

All rights reserved © Mint Museum of Art, Inc., Charlotte, North Carolina. Reproduced with permission from Mint Museum of Art, Inc., and the author.

SECTION THREE
KEY THEMES

Section introduction

This section brings texts together under a number of themes that we believe to be relevant to ceramics today. The themes are Gender, Sexuality and Ceramics; Identity and Ceramics; Image; Figuration and the Body; Ceramics in Education; Ceramics, Industry and new technologies and Museum, Site and Display. These headings are often interconnected and will have relevance to other sections of this book. We also do not see this as in any way an exhaustive or definitive list but more a series of possible starting points that readers might use to explore themes more deeply.

Gender and sexuality are key issues in art in general and the selections here offer a historical perspective and two more contemporary case studies. The section on identity also connects to gender as well as culture, colonialism and context. The combination of image and ceramic object is a very broad subject and cannot be dealt with in detail here. One text considers the work of Paul Scott known for his printed political ceramics. Readers might also want to read his book on ceramics and image *Painted Clay: Graphic Arts and Ceramic Surface*. Figuration and the body is another substantial area of ceramic practice that we cannot do justice to but the limited selection offers three viewpoints including a substantial overview of practice from Peter Selz. The teaching of ceramics in schools and universities is likely to have an important effect on the future of ceramics as an art form so we have included a short section with two texts that offer some overview and discussion of artist educators as well as an example of recent developments around new technologies. The following section also considers technology and connections between 'art' ceramics and industry. Another major theme for ceramics in recent years have been the context in which objects are made and viewed and this is considered through the texts in Museum, Site and Display.

Livingstone and Petrie

SECTION 3.1
GENDER, SEXUALITY AND CERAMICS

Introductory summary

The important place of women in ceramics is highlighted in Moira Vincentelli's wide-ranging text that encompasses late-nineteenth-century women potters in the United States, the challenges faced by women in the early twentieth century, key figures such as Lucy Rie and Beatrice Wood, figuration, 'feminist ceramics' and the strong influence of women in the late twentieth century.

How museum collections can be accessed and used by diverse sectors of society has been a developing debate in recent years. Artist Matt Smith describes a project that he undertook at Birmingham Museum and Art Gallery in which he produced nineteen art interventions in the galleries which aimed to question and highlight how lesbian, gay, bisexual and transgender experiences might be presented or made more explicit in a museum.

Louisa Buck and Marjan Boot give a useful introduction to the work of perhaps the most famous artist working with ceramics today, Grayson Perry. This text extracted from the 2002 catalogue for the exhibition 'Grayson Perry: Guerilla Tactics' at the Stedelijik Museum in Amsterdam links Perry's work in ceramics to 'psychosexual origins', transvestism and his alter ego Claire.

Livingstone and Petrie

42
GENDER, IDENTITY AND STUDIO CERAMICS

Moira Vincentelli

> Certain versions of femininity and the sexual division of labour have more social and institutional power than others. In order to develop strategies to contest hegemonic assumptions and the social practices which they guarantee, we need to understand the intricate network of discourses, the sites where they are articulated and the institutionally legitimized forms of knowledge to which they look for their justification. (Weedon 1987: 126)

In this chapter I want to examine the way that women in the twentieth century have negotiated a particular field of art practice based on fired clay. Foucault's concept of discourse through which knowledge is classified, articulated and given power can be deployed to assist an analysis based on the idea that words and practices emerge from history to shape the present. Analysis of such classifications can help us to understand more about the construction of the cultural field of studio ceramics and the way women and men participate in it.

The practitioners may be designated potters, studio potters, ce-rami(ci)sts, ceramic artists, clay artists, artists, craftspeople or makers. The names are not innocent. They have a history and carry a trail of associations. 'Potters' have a solid base in tradition and a commitment to function, but the addition of the word 'studio' immediately gentrifies them. Studios are for artists whose work is associated with an identified personal style, thus studio potters produce pottery – usually vessels – in an individual style. Ceramics has a more upmarket ring, but few who work exclusively in fired day actually choose to call themselves just 'artist'. The word has airs – it emphasises intellectual creativity and downplays material manipulation and manual skills. For some 'ceramic artist' may provide a neat compromise. Craftsperson, the politically correct version of the ubiquitous craftsman, is also now sometimes replaced by the more neutral 'maker'. It eliminates that problematic word 'craft' which has proved such a battleground for practitioners. These last words, however, ground the practice again in the work of the hand rather than the head, but align the practitioner to a wider field of cultural production not limited by the medium employed.

Gender and class are part of this equation. Potter has strong male and artisan connotations while studio ceramics gives out a more genteel and female message. Furthermore these designations carry with them overtones of different kinds of practice and technology. In the context of modernism an association with the domestic, the female domain par excellence, is always problematic. As much ceramic art is produced for use or display in the home its relationship to that hegemonic discourse in the visual arts is marginal or possibly subversive.[1]

In the nineteenth century domestic ceramics were produced in factories and catered for a wide market ranging from expensive, refined porcelain to transfer-printed china to inexpensive glazed ware. Country potteries also catered to the need for much functional pottery for the home, the dairy and the garden, but as their market was undercut by factory production they turned increasingly to novelty and decorative wares – even

Source: © Moira Vincentelli/*Women and Ceramics.*

art pottery. The word art attached itself to all kinds of objects in the late nineteenth century setting them apart from the merely utilitarian and lending them superior cultural cachet, in Bourdieu's terms 'cultural capital'. In a period of great social and class mobility material culture was used to signify difference. Art pottery was a signifier of refinement and/or sophisticated avant-garde taste. The pottery itself was usually made by potters – normally working-class men – but the design work and the decoration was assigned to 'the artist' and, as we have seen, ceramic decoration was increasingly associated with women. These divisions were undermined in the development of studio pottery.

It is no coincidence that studio pottery developed in parallel with modernism and its ideology of truth to materials, individual artistic expression, originality, unity of form and decoration, and personal (sexual) freedom. Art pottery was essentially domestic and decorative – sitting tidily and comfortably within the female domain. Early studio pottery was for pioneers whose art practice challenged class and gender stereotypes. Through the mucky work and manual labour of small-scale pottery production pioneer studio potters negotiated for themselves new kinds of identity – different, but equivalent, to the bohemianism of the modern artist. Michael Cardew, an Oxford graduate from the privileged English middle class was making a point as he struggled with the huge bottle kiln at Winchcombe rejecting comfortable urban sophistication in favour of hard physical labour and rural poverty. From an aristocratic background, Katharine Pleydell-Bouverie also renegotiated class and gender identity through ceramic practice when she built the pottery at Coleshill, on the family estate. Learning to throw on a Japanese kick wheel, firing a wood-fired kiln working with Norah Braden in shifts through the night to keep it stoked, experimenting with ash glazes and keeping careful notes – like a scientist – was an unspoken but significant statement of resistance to her assigned place in the social structure.

In the twentieth century, outside industrial production, ceramics found a new role for itself in studio pottery. It was an art practice based on new art ideologies albeit with a direct parent in late nineteenth-century art pottery and many other more distant ancestors in the elite and specialised display ceramics of the past – from Greek black-figure vases, painted maiolica, Palissy dishes to porcelain figurines. Functional wares such as medieval jugs or folk pottery slipware may visually and even ideologically be an inspiration to studio potters, but socially and historically they are a different category of object with more in common with mass produced, everyday china. Even domestic stoneware has always served a specialist market. Its popularity, indeed fashionability, in the 1960s and 1970s can be compared with the democratisation of taste in the period which also saw an expanding audience for modern art. I will argue that the practice of studio pottery has provided an arena for women to act out and renegotiate gender roles and that as a new practice it was more open to innovation and to provide an opportunity for women. However, the practice, like everything else, was also subject to patriarchal ideologies that constrained women's opportunities and confined them to certain kinds of work, or allowed certain work to flourish briefly only to be sidelined quite quickly.

Art pottery to early studio pottery

Art pottery in the late nineteenth century provided new openings for women as decorators and even, to an extent, as designers. The studios at Doulton employed a high proportion of female designer/decorators and gave their employees considerable autonomy, but none went on to work independently. There are no female equivalents of the Martin Brothers.[2] In France, arguably the birthplace of studio pottery, no women seem to have been active, but in the United States a number of the prosperous, privileged, middle-class women who took up china painting very quickly expanded their interests to the whole process of ceramic production. The vogue for china painting acted as a springboard and, although in one sense it was also a trap attracting women into what might be seen as a female ghetto, in another sense it gave some women opportunities. The creative aspects of the art were liberating, but the confidence-building activities of organising societies, exhibitions, teaching, lecturing and writing cannot be overlooked.[3] Women were active as teachers of china painting, but they were also purveyors of the materials and consumers of the products.

China painting has been discussed in chapter 5, but a number of women in the United States extended their practice beyond surface decoration into clay work and technical initiatives. Many of the leading figures were associated with the hugely influential Cincinnati Pottery Club. Its founder, Louise McLaughlin (1847-1939), inspired by the rich effects of barbotine decoration produced in France by Chaplet,[4] experimented with coloured slips and firing to achieve her 'Cincinnati faience'. The technique became widely used in American art pottery. Later she worked in metal but also returned to experiment with earthenware and porcelain.

Maria Longworth Nichols (later Storer) (1849–1932), founder of Rookwood Pottery, used her not inconsiderable financial resources and influence to promote a more complete approach to ceramics. Her own work was inspired by Japanese designs and employed modelled decoration based on fantastic dragons and sea creatures.[5] Another influential figure, Laura Fry (1857–1943), who also studied at Cincinnati and worked at Rookwood Pottery, decorated with incised lines in a style related to the Doulton artist, Hannah Barlow. In line with the technical experimentation characteristic of that circle, she developed a special atomiser spray for applying slips and later became a teacher and professor at Purdue University.

Thus, from beginnings in china painting and art pottery, a number of American women found influential positions as practitioners and teachers in specialised college ceramic departments. Best known of all is Adelaide Alsop Robineau (1865-1929). Originally a painter, like many women artists of the new breed she saw her art as a career activity not merely a hobby. She took up china decoration and became one of the leading figures of the movement as an exponent, as a teacher and, after 1899, as a magazine editor. Her designs were influenced by the trends and publications coming out of Europe which encouraged eclectic borrowings of styles from across the world,[6] but by the end of the century her work was increasingly based on the stylised naturalism of continental Art Nouveau.[7] Soon after her marriage in 1899 she and her husband, Samuel Robineau, took over the magazine *China Decorator* which they renamed *Keramic Studio*. Over the next few years she began to develop her skills as a potter taking lessons from the New York potter, and teacher Charles Volkmar. She produced earthenware and later porcelain and became interested in carving into the surface of the clay. Louise McLaughlin had recently begun to work in this way and her designs had been reproduced in *Keramic Studio* in 1901 (Eidelberg, in Weiss 1981: 76). Robineau was also inspired by Danish porcelain, both Royal Copenhagen and carved pieces by Bing and Grondahl which had had an impact at the Paris World Fair in 1900.[8] Her work at this time was closely aligned with Art Nouveau and she produced high shouldered vases decorated with elegant swirling plant motifs. Ever alert to new ideas and influences, in 1905 she produced a series of vases in what she called 'Indianesque'. These designs were, in part, inspired by the interest in Native American pottery which was promoted through the programmes at Alfred University run by Charles Binns.[9] Later her work is noted for experimental glazes and above all carved porcelain for which she achieved considerable acclaim, both in America and abroad. Her most publicised piece, the Scarab vase, also sometimes known as the '1000 hour vase', marks a departure from Art Nouveau and shows a more directly oriental influence.[10] At a moment when avant-garde artists had rejected the concept of 'finish' in favour of freedom and personal expression, the eclectic and orientalist style and the enormous emphasis put on technique, production time and skill are a far cry from the modernist values with which they are contemporary. These conservative values continue to operate powerfully in the field of ceramics and help to maintain a distance from contemporary ideologies of fine art in the twentieth century.

In his biography of Robineau, Garth Clark has a substantial postscript to Samuel Robineau acknowledging 'the enormous contribution her dedicated husband made to her career'. In this a comparison can be drawn with Denise Wren (1891-1979), an Australian who settled in Britain and was an influential figure in the British studio pottery movement. She too was interested in ceramic technology, throwing and kiln design, and did not allow herself to be constrained by gender conventions. Denise Wren represents an early example in Britain of a woman who was determined to make a career in pottery.

She had been raised in Australia and, by British standards, had a free and unconventional upbringing.[11] As a young woman she developed a feminist awareness and was a supporter of the Suffragettes (Coatts 1984: 10). She studied at Kingston School of Art under the Art Nouveau designer, Archibald Knox, but when his teaching came under criticism and he lost his job she and her sister Winifred and some other students resigned in protest and formed the Knox Guild of Design and Crafts. Denise's powerful personality was one of the mainstays of the group, which exhibited annually at Kingston Public Art Gallery and also at the Whitechapel in London between 1913 and 1939.[12] Her interest in ceramics led her to find a local potter, a flowerpot maker, to teach her to throw and it was from him she bought her first wheel. After she married Henry Wren in 1915 they bought a plot of land and built their own house, 'Potter's Croft', which Denise designed. They ran a pottery and in the inter-war years she produced substantial amounts of vases and decorative pottery. Together Denise and Henry Wren ran short courses, mainly for schoolteachers, and published a number of books, which Denise illustrated with elegant line drawings in the Knox guild style. The books considered especially the way pottery could be used in children's education[13] and laid an emphasis on handbuilding and women's traditional techniques. Denise Wren designed kilns and published the designs so that others would be able to work independently. Her career took a second wind in the 1950s. After her husband died she worked with her daughter Rosemary (b. 1922) running courses, developing saltglazed stoneware, throwing and slabbuilding vases and modelling distinctive elephants for which she received a certain recognition. They were both influential founder members of the Craft Potters Association. Denise Wren was passionately fond of animals, especially birds. She bred budgerigars and parakeets and was an expert bee-keeper. Her finely observed yet stylised bird drawings are a theme that was taken up in the work of her daughter who has specialised in bird and animal forms in stoneware.[14] As a ceramicist Denise Wren's reputation may be modest, yet her life exemplifies the way that pottery offered an unconventional lifestyle free from certain stereotypes of femininity. In another sense her role as teacher and enabler is perhaps not untypical of the way many women have developed their careers.

In 1951 Dora Lunn (1881-c.1955) signed a prepared typescript autobiography, *A Potter's Pot-pourri*, that was never published although it had progressed to the stage of having a preface and excellent photographs with illustrations labelled and numbered for insertion in the text.[15] What happened? Probably by 1951 the life of a woman potter turned teacher, whose work had barely found its way into even the modest canon of studio pottery, was not seen as a very marketable script. However as a record of an individual woman's struggle to become a studio potter at that critical moment when the term was being consolidated, it has no equal. The story is criss-crossed by contemporary discourses around gender, class, money, power and the arts and crafts. It reveals Dora Lunn struggling to build herself into an independent woman potter in a world that constantly poured her back into the mould. The biography throws light on the way models of middle-class femininity inflect the way she thought about herself and effectively constrained her activity.

In examining this material it is useful to deploy poststructuralist theories of the subject which have attacked the notion of rationality and the unified subject and see the individual as taking up different subject positions in different contexts. Sometimes these may be conflicting or contradictory.[16] The autobiography was written in later life with the benefit of hindsight, but not without a vivid sense of the pain and difficulty of the early years. This is despite the high level of press coverage she received for a short number of years between 1917 and 1920 as a media-worthy phenomenon, a woman potter working on her own.

It is a commonplace of a feminist critique of art history to demonstrate the way that women artists are always discussed in terms of their male relations. Nearly every article in the press about Dora Lunn situates her as her father's daughter. She is forever 'Professor' Richard Lunn's daughter.[17] At the beginning of *A Potter's Pot-pourri* – a telling title in itself as a representation of the feminine and the whimsical – she relates that her father taught at both Camberwell and the Royal College of Art. As he was then quite old he was expecting to be dismissed, the plan being that he would run a private teaching studio with the help of his daughter. She had been allowed to work in the RCA studios out of college hours and was learning what she could about pottery. She gives the impression that she felt (as a dutiful daughter) that she needed to do this to help her father. With hindsight she recognised the irony of her situation: 'Anyway I was to be the business manager, secretary and general factotum with my father as the one who really mattered' (AAD 1 66/67: 4). In the event he died in February 1915, just after he had indeed been dismissed but before any such plan could be put into action.

The next stage of her pottery education was at Camberwell. She seemed to have had a few useful privileges because she and her friend, Gwendolen Parnell[18] were allowed to use the studios over the summer vacation. They were deeply disillusioned when the new teacher, Alfred Hopkins, arrived and split the class up, setting the women to paint decorations on pottery he had made while the men were taught to throw. 'All our fond hopes were dashed to the ground! We felt like raging volcanoes! We wondered how the other students could be so docile and contented' (AAD1 66/67: 6). The typescript also contains a wonderful cartoon that Parnell drew to commemorate this insult. She soon left these classes when she realised that she really knew a great deal about pottery and had little respect for the teacher, a relationship that no doubt was not helped by the fact that he was her father's successor.

Strangely, a year later an article in *The Pottery Gazette* 1916 (1 December) entitled 'Pottery training for women' describes the teaching at Camberwell, suggesting that it was precisely designed to offer women the opportunity to set up on their own. It states that 'The first process taught is "throwing" well suited to the delicacy of a woman's hand.' Perhaps their protest had achieved something, although the justification echoes an old stereotype. In the middle years of the war it was probably felt expedient that women should be trained in occupations normally assigned to men.

Despite two offers from fellow women potters to work together, one from Gwendolen Parnell and the other from Frances Richards[19] who had also been a pupil of Richard Lunn, Dora Lunn chose to work on her own. She had recently become engaged and her fiancé had offered some financial backing. In one paragraph she seems to suggest two conflicting positions, the idea of 'a room of one's own' as immortalised by her contemporary Virginia Woolf and, on the other, the idea of a cosy nest for two.

> I began to settle into it, and to feel that it was just the one spot on earth to call one's own. It became such fun to think how equipment could be improvised as the need for it arose, and I looked forward to the day when my fiancé and I could share it together. (AAD 66/67: 10)

It turned out to be a misguided decision because not long after her fiancé became involved with another woman and broke the engagement. Not surprisingly she felt bitter about her plight and very distrustful of men thereafter. She taught two days a week in a school and also wrote occasional articles to supplement her income. She writes, 'I was left alone with a little pottery that I had never wanted for myself alone', and goes on to refer to the pottery as her 'baby pottery' a telling analogy that is made from time to time throughout the text. She determined to overcome her loneliness and 'chose the pottery as a means to this end' (AAD 1: 11).

Pottery involved technologies for which her female education had hardly prepared her. She was impatient with men who treated her with disbelief when buying pipes for the gas kiln, but when the kiln gave off clouds of steam she had to struggle with her fear. But she overcame it – 'I stayed alone till that fear of furnaces was completely conquered' (AAD 66/67: 15).

She set up Ravenscourt Pottery at Hammersmith, originally with the support of a 'patron' who later withdrew, but who encouraged her to exhibit at the British Industries Fair which she did with some success.[20] Single women were fair game especially if they put themselves into the exposed position of publicly selling work at an industrial fair. She describes how a man came up to her and taunted her for being a 'Miss'. The taint of being 'in trade' was still a present reality. She gave employment to a number of other women trainees. Originally she employed a man to throw the shapes but eventually she was able to learn herself. After that she did public demonstrations of the technique for which she had a mystical enthusiasm not untypical of other potters of the 1920s such as Staite Murray.[21] Whether it was carrying heavy loads, getting your hands dirty, dealing with technology, or entering into the world of commerce, she emphasised with some pride that she and her female colleagues were prepared to take on any aspect of the work. All these things undermined the class and femininity of a respectable woman. She makes the point that they were 'women' not 'ladies' with knowing irony.

In 1923 Dora Lunn married Jack Hedges who was an impecunious young engineer. Her family disapproved. The autobiography gives little sense of Jack Hedges as a personality and the couple remained childless. They were never well off, it seems, as she suggested that they could not afford to adopt a child. As the text repeatedly suggests the pottery was her substitute child – 'her baby'. In this respect Jack comes over as a villain.

> Not until after my marriage did I realise how much my husband disliked the pottery. It seemed to him to be a rival in my affection, moreover he was not an artist but a businessman and engineer. (AAD 1 66/67: 81)

When she sold up the pottery she was broken-hearted and felt she had 'to overcome the shock alone'. With startling coolness she says 'I never mentioned the Pottery again' (AAD 1 66/67: 85).

With some educational qualifications she went into schoolteaching, specialising in crafts including spinning, weaving and bookbinding as well as pottery. She had enjoyed school and would have dearly loved to go on to university but 'there were no scholarships in those days' and she had to accept attending occasional classes at schools of art. Like many art teachers she found it an uphill struggle to introduce crafts into the academic environment of the school. Eventually she was able to set up a small studio at her home but was not able to do much work until she retired. She was still nervous about the way it might compete with her domestic life: 'at first I had to walk somewhat delicately and make sure the home did not suffer from any lack of home interest' (AAD 1 66/67: 94).

In the 1930s she began to produce pottery again and make designs for industry. She called the new venture the 'Dora Lunn Pottery'. The name is significant. She chose to identify her work with her own name (before marriage) rather than through the name of the pottery, but in her autobiography she suggests that she chose it, 'wishing to preserve my father's name'.[22] Perhaps she knew only too well that the connection with her father constantly preserved right up to the V&A catalogue was to her advantage (Watson 1990: 215), or perhaps it was a desire to assert her own independence. Her husband appeared to be more supportive of her pottery making in later life.

Dora Lunn's ideals were rooted in arts and crafts philosophies, committed to the value of handcraft and the maker (or worker's) identification with the work Aspects of her decorative style were strongly inflected by continental modernism such as that of the Viennese Secession. Her showroom and her stand at the British Industries Fair were dramatically painted black with black drapes edged with black and silver checkerboard pattern. The pottery was in bright orange, blue, yellow and turquoise, some of it with the same black and white detailing. She also produced figurines and models and her penguins were particularly successful. By contrast, her stoneware vases relied on simple shapes and rich muted glazes in line with the oriental influence in early studio pottery. In her day, Dora Lunn's work was in the forefront of new ideas in contemporary ceramics.

Gendered identities, modernism and studio pottery

As the notion of the independent potter began to spread after the 1920s women become significant, if minority, practitioners in many parts of Europe and America. On the continent the patronage of large ceramic firms who supported and encouraged independent potters/designers to work from studios attached to the factory was important, for example, in Denmark, Finland (Arabia), Sweden (Rörstrand) and Germany. In Denmark Nathalie Krebs (1895-1978) spent ten years working with Bing and Grondahl before she set up the Saxbo Studio where she worked with Eva S. Nielsen (1911-76) until 1968. The works they produced were rooted in a modernist aesthetic and are characterised by a unity of the strong, simple forms designed by Nielsen with glazes by Krebs. The studio became an important training ground for Danish potters. The two most significant British women potters of the inter-war years, Norah Braden and Katharine Pleydell-Bouverie produced work that incorporated ideas of pure form distilled from nature and can be paralleled with work by their contemporaries in fine art such as Barbara Hepworth or Paul Nash. Margaret Rey, a pupil of Staite Murray, is an example of a woman whose work was given recognition in its time, but who ceased to produce ceramics after the war and is now little known.

America greatly benefited from a number of European potters who emigrated in the 1940s. These include Maija Grotell (Finland) (1899-1973) who became an important influence through her work and teaching at Cranbrook Academy in Michigan (see Clark 1987: 270; Schlanger and Takaezu 1996) and the husband and wife, Gertrud and Otto Natzler from Austria and Marguerite Wildenhain (1896-1985). She had trained at the Bauhaus, but moved away from design for industry to make domestic stoneware in a craft tradition after she settled in California in 1942. Karen Kames (1920-) is another ceramicist whose long career is noted for functional thrown ware with forms that suggest a timeless simplicity. The high profile experimental modernism of Peter Voulkos and his students, influenced by Abstract Expressionism was the dominant force in ceramics in the USA after the 1950s. Perhaps it is not surprising that there seems to have been little place for women artists in that circle. Feminist art historians have constantly noted that women artists were particularly excluded from access to the 'avant-garde' and, even when they were there, their work is marginalised in the records of modernism. However, the domestic associations of studio pottery have made it a space where women have found a place in the 'canon' and I want to close this section with a discussion of two of them.

Lucie Rie (1902-1995) and Beatrice Wood (1893-1998) are potters whose long careers gathered momentum in the latter part of their lives. They are considered among the leading potters of their generation in their respective countries. Both were strong-minded personalities who carved out successful careers earning their living by selling work (not really supplemented by teaching). Both had a strong connection with the modernist enterprise. Both sometimes had ways of presenting themselves in relation to men that were surprisingly conventional despite their relatively unconventional lifestyles. Lucie Rie was quiet and measured with everything under control, while Beatrice Wood was altogether more spontaneous and passionate; Lucie Rie was a very private person who rarely spoke about her personal life, while Beatrice Wood's autobiography is frank and revealing. What they have in common is a tendency to downplay their own achievement. Neither had children although both married, in Wood's case twice. Their husbands were not the important influence on their work – but other men were.

Lucie Rie was born into a privileged Viennese family who supported her wish to obtain a good education and art training. Her early training was in the context of the Wiener Werkstätte which in the 1920s was dominated by the decorative and figurative tendency soon to be rejected by the critics of modernism.[23] Lucie Rie was trained in that context but was alert to new possibilities. She was immediately attracted to throwing on the wheel. After her marriage to Hans Rie she had a wheel and kiln installed in their flat, the interior of which was architect designed in a modernist style. The domestic arrangement with the integration of work and domestic life was one that Lucie Rie was to maintain throughout her life. After she came to London she moved into a mews property just behind Marble Arch. The studio was converted from a garage and upstairs was the modest living accommodation where she lived for fifty years.[24] Janet Leach has written a perceptive and interestingly gendered reading of this arrangement.[25]

> The Western world is full of women 'kitchen' potters attempting to work in urban conditions. Lucie's solution to this problem could be held up as an example to other professional female potters, were it not for the fact that she is a very private person and prefers not to have detailed biographical descriptions written of her life-style. Her house and the room where she works are the essence of simplicity. The masculine concept to digging clay, chopping wood, etc. etc. as essential parts of the making process has been answered by her. She proves it is not necessary to dig, chop or use heavy machinery. To me she is important as a feminine 'no-shovel' potter. I have observed many times that the studio workshop requirements of the craftswoman are often different from those of the craftsman. Lucie is the epitome of this observation. The male potter usually likes the feeling of 'going to work', whereas Lucie has integrated her studio and her home in a feminine manner. (Houston 1981: 30)

Lucie Rie is also reported to have said 'I am man-made' (Birks 1987: 7). By this she was referring to the important relationships that she had with male mentors Powlony in Vienna, Plisch, a modernist architect in Vienna, Bernard Leach and eventually Hans Coper.[26]

She sometimes played the 'feminine' role including acknowledging her debt to male colleagues, but she pursued her own work with single-minded integrity. Although never an intellectual, she disliked woolly philosophising and was very focused. Her work was based on wheel and kiln technology, both of which she embraced with enthusiasm. She found equipment that she could cope with in the confined space of an urban studio (even if she did have to load the kiln awkwardly from the top). She was in the first generation of female potters who could use technology for their own purposes, as a tool to achieve an end. She did not fetishise the technology. Her pots are an embodiment of the modernist aesthetic – they are pure form, the surfaces are textured, scored or coloured in ways that are entirely integrated with the form. They make reference to nature – such as rocks, flowers or even fungi – but it is only by the merest allusion. In her later work she moved to an even more poised abstraction using bronze, pink and yellow glazes.

Beatrice Wood's ceramics are much more wild and theatrical. Although she also made figures at certain points in her career, Wood too was immediately attracted to the wheel and to glaze technology and experimentation. Her outrageous autobiography presents a privileged but over protected girlhood. In her own words 'my early life was all mistakes'. She studied in Paris and originally went into the theatre. Her friendships with Marcel Duchamp, Picabia and the important patrons of modern art, the Arensbergs, brought her into close contact with avant-garde art, yet she has suggested that at first she understood very little about it (Wood 1985: 27). She took up pottery in 1933 when she was forty, but her work really developed in the 1940s when she trained with the influential Austrian emigres, Gertrud and Otto Natzler. They taught her throwing

(Gertrude) and how to keep records of experimental glaze work (Otto). Later, Otto and Vivika Heino were important to her development. Although she learned significant lessons from these fine craftworkers, her free spirit always prevailed and the intuitive approach that she had learned from her early circle of friends gave her an alternative source of ideas. In the 1950s she became most noted for dramatic and unconventional lustre glazes. She was also recognised for her figurative ceramics and was amazingly prolific in her eighties and nineties. Her autobiography is largely presented in terms of all the numerous men in her life: husbands, lovers and mentor figures. It belies the basis of her work in a well-organised workshop, carefully maintained notebooks of her experiments and a businesslike approach.

> The fact that I was involved in making pottery, selling it, answering business letters, wrapping packages, changing displays, enriched my activity because it helped form me from a vague person into an articulate one. I was learning that great lesson of discipline. (Wood 1994: 34)

Beatrice Wood made pottery, but here she suggests how it was also pottery that helped to form her identity.

Technical choices

The key signifying technique in studio pottery has been throwing on the wheel. As we have seen, in the first quarter of the twentieth century women often had to go against the grain and claim their right to use the wheel. By the second half of the twentieth century that battle had been won and women as much as men have used throwing as the basis of their work It seems, however, that women have been in the forefront of the reaction against throwing.[27]

As I have shown, throughout history women's ceramic traditions are nearly always associated with handbuilding.[28] It is striking that in the latter part of the twentieth century these techniques have been embraced with enthusiasm by many potters and ceramicists, especially women. It is equally striking that almost none of the women who use these techniques consciously proclaim them as women's techniques, although a number have noted this relationship in writing books which give a context for their practice (see Blandino 1984; Perryman 1995; Rogers 1984).

By the 1950s throwing was the technique that predominated in studio ceramics but a few, such as Ruth Duckworth, chose alternative ways of working. Born in Germany in 1919, Duckworth carne to Britain as a young woman and originally trained in sculpture; however, in the 1950s encouraged by Lucie Rie she returned to college to study ceramics at the Central School of Arts and Crafts in London, where she later joined the staff. Although for a number of years she produced functional wares, in 1960 she followed her personal inclination for sculptural ceramics based on the modernist principles of organic abstraction. She uses handbuilding methods of coiling for her large asymmetrical stoneware vessels and pinching for more delicate porcelain forms. In 1964 she settled in the USA where she taught for many years at the University of Chicago. Unusually she has continued to work on both a large and small scale and has successfully straddled the divide between sculpture and ceramics. Before going to the USA Ruth Duckworth was teaching at the Central School which had always been associated with alternatives to the Leach tradition. Under Dora Billington in the 1950s it had supported the decorative modernism of the group around William Newland and in the next decade it became identified with more sculptural aspects of British ceramics including artists such as Gordon Baldwin and Gillian Lowndes.

Among the most unusual of all the handbuilders, neither figure nor vessel, the work of Gillian Lowndes emerged in the 1960s as an original contribution to British ceramics. As non-vessel form it was hard to classify. When working in stoneware, porcelain and other non-ceramic materials, large and small, she has never been constrained by the conventions associated with the material, yet is ever sensitive to its properties. She is inspired by both manufactured and natural forms and in her work from the 1990s creates wall-hung structures, combinations of clay, metal and found objects (such as chair legs and loofas) juxtaposed in surrealist enigma.

By the 1970s the interest in organic sculptural form manifested itself in the work of a number of artists who used porcelain. Previously a difficult clay to purchase in a prepared state suitable for the studio potter, it became more widely available along with more sophisticated high temperature kilns. There was an explosion of development in handbuilt porcelain. These delicate sculptural forms, the perfect antidote to a surfeit of brown mugs, became one of the hallmarks of the period. Many potters experimented with the medium or worked it occasionally and it became a characteristic British style. Mary Rogers has been the most consistent ceramicist in this genre, creating small-scale sculptural forms inspired by seed heads, petals and shells. She works directly with the clay – pinching, coiling and teasing out the form.[29] The delicate translucency, pale colours and plant and flower references create strong 'feminine' associations which have implications for the reception of such ceramics. They are saleable, but not seen as significant.

I have argued that women's traditions are characterised by simple technology and a way of working the clay that keeps the maximum closeness between the hand and the material. Coiling a pot is a rhythmical activity of short repeated movements which, in the finishing stages, requires smoothing and polishing and a delicate handling of the unfired pot. As we have seen, in many women's traditions this final polishing stage is given a great deal of time. It is valued as a pleasurable activity and the polishing stones are treasured tools passed from mother to daughter. Traditionally the pots are fired in direct contact with the flame in a bonfire. These techniques have been adapted to studio pottery by a number of potters in Britain, most famously by Magdalene Odundo (b. 1950). Originally from Kenya, Odundo became interested in ceramics after she came to Britain. She later went back to Africa for short periods to study ceramics in Kenya, but most significantly she spent three months at the Abuja Pottery in Nigeria while she was a student. Ironically it was at Abuja that she learned to throw properly, but it was the 'African' techniques that were to become so important to her.[30] Her vessels make reference to the natural world – to bodies, nipples, gourds or stamens and they also draw widely on other ceramic forms, especially African shapes, but they are refined down into a distilled essence. They exude a tactile and sensuous experience through beautiful burnished surfaces whose soft sheen speaks the loving attention that has created them. In many ways Odundo's values are strongly identified with modernist ideologies of pure form, truth to materials and 'vitality' – that distillation of life force so sought by early studio potters; but in another sense her ceramics stand in the postmodern world of multi-referencing and shifting identity. Her work appeared in the controversial exhibition *Africa Explores*[31] where it could represent a contemporary African practice, yet it was made in Britain. She is seeking a universal statement, but cannot stand outside the debate around 'black art' or 'women's art'.

Magdalene Odundo loves the construction process of pottery, but she confesses to 'hate firing'. Fire can never be entirely controlled and weeks or months of work can be lost in a moment in a kiln. However, firing is a very visible part of the process on unglazed or burnished pottery characteristic of women's traditions and a number of contemporary women artists have used this. Gabriele Koch (b. 1948) who is of German origin but now lives in Britain, makes coiled, burnished and sawdust fired pots working slowly and rhythmically. Her vessels are serene forms with no sharp angles and no defined base. They seem to communicate the low-tech, but loving, process of their creation. They are 'decorated' by fire: 'I make the form and give that form over to the fire and the smoke'. Her vessels are metaphors of harmony, willing collaborations of potter, clay and fire. From Austria, Gerhild Tschachler-Nagy uses simple salt-fired kilns that she constructs herself to develop her handbuilt pots and sculptures whose finely burnished surfaces are 'painted' and stained by the action of the fire.

Jane Perryman (b. 1947) also expresses a personal identification with her materials and process. Her coiled, smoke-fired vessels are modern original shapes which take inspiration from traditional pottery, the geometric resist decoration (where the colour is applied over paper or leaves, or using wax painting, so the clay shows through in the final effect) reminiscent of such things as African raffia pile textiles. A devotee of Iyengar Yoga she believes that,

> There is a constant mirroring between striving for harmony and balance in making pots. The word Yoga means union of body and soul and a pot is formed by the union of the clay body and the maker. The constant checking, correcting and improving in both disciplines is a life's work (Perryman 1995: 41)

Similar sentiments are expressed by Elspeth Owen (b. 1938) who works in the most simple way of all pinching out the shape while holding the piece in her lap.

> The limited technique and its simplicity leaves a lot of room for an intuitive approach … they hold me and support me as well as me holding and supporting them. (Owen quoted in Perryman 1995: 29)

Many of these potters seem to suggest that they are shaped and constructed by their work just as much as they may construct the piece themselves.

In the last quarter of the twentieth century there has been a great interest in unglazed burnished wares where the surface effects are created by various experimental firing processes, including pit-firing, saggar-firing and sawdust firing. Although such pots are predominantly made by women, men have also used these techniques for their signifying and symbolic message as well as their aesthetic effect. For example, one of the first in Britain to work in relation to an African inheritance was Siddig El Nigoumi (1931-96) (born in the Sudan, but later moved to Britain) **who** used burnishing with sgraffito designs **from** the 1970s. In the United States the African-American ceramicist, David Macdonald has also used smoke firing to create complex sculptural pieces that allude to his African inheritance. However, the unity of handbuilding and smoke firing and the emphasis on the process as a central part of the experience is not so significant among the male artists. They are interested in burnishing for aesthetic effect and are more likely to throw their pots.[32]

Figurative forms

In European ceramics in the eighteenth and nineteenth centuries the figurine flourished in response to an expanding market for all forms of domestic decoration and display. At the upper-class, luxury end were the deftly painted porcelain figure groups of fanciful, even erotic, subjects. At the popular end were Staffordshire figures in brightly painted earthenware of historical and contemporary characters, from highwaymen to politicians and preachers, responding to the popular culture of the day. The market for ornamental animal and figurative ceramics has continued into the twentieth century and in the early part of this century a number of the independent studio potters produced such work.

I want to examine why it was so popular for a brief number of years, why it was seen as appropriate for women and why it was later marginalised in the studio pottery movement. Sometimes the piece was modelled directly as a one-off piece, more commonly the model formed the basis of a mould from which others could be press-moulded. This produced a form of multiple art, relatively inexpensive to produce and a saleable item. By the 1920s more women were seeking an art training with the aim of a career and there is some evidence to suggest that in the immediate aftermath of the First World War there were opportunities, especially in the applied arts. Like china painting, figure models were seen as suitable work for women as they were both domestic and decorative. The subject matter and style of the figure models of the new independent potters were frequently based on themes of women and children. The forms were modelled with a certain breadth of handling and coloured simply, rather than naturalistically, to give a more sculptural effect.

One of the most successful of these practitioners was Phoebe Stabler (d. 1955). She had her own kiln in Hammersmith and produced models that were reproduced by firms including Royal Doulton, Ashstead Pottery and Royal Worcester (Hawkins 1980: 71). Her husband, Harold Stabler, with whom she worked closely, was one of the leading figures in the Design and Industries Association set up in 1915 to improve standards in British industry. From 1921 through to the mid-1930s they worked for Poole Pottery.

Others who had some success in this field include Gwendolen Parnell and Dora Lunn (discussed above), Irene Browne and Stella Crofts, but many others produced examples including Dora Billington who must have encouraged this practice as Head of Ceramics at the Central School of Arts and Crafts in the mid-1920s.[33]

Irene Browne was trained in sculpture and produced plaster and bronze figures and portraits, exhibiting from time to time at the Royal Academy.[34] She took up pottery in 1919 and trained at Putney School of Art. Within the year she was successfully producing stoneware statuettes that were fired at the Fulham Pottery and in 1927 she bought her own electric kiln. Her model of *The Singalese Potter* is an interesting example showing an awareness of women's ceramic traditions. Stella Crofts, on the other hand, was noted for her animal groups with which she had considerable success in the 1920s. Although this field of small-scale ceramic sculpture was not exclusively practised by women, it was one where they achieved a brief recognition only to be forgotten. In a review in *The Studio* of an exhibition of work from the Central School of Arts and Crafts in 1926, it is clear that the new values of studio pottery and design for industry are superseding this kind of sculpture: 'In the pottery section the craze for figure subjects seems to be on the wane. This is a good sign, as the attention given to objects destined to fulfil a practical purpose is more essential'. Slipcasting or press moulding from plaster moulds was not a technique that found favour with the new ideals of 'truth to materials' in pottery. The negative view expressed by Bernard Leach in 1940 was probably already current in the incipient years of the studio pottery movement: 'Plaster has very little life of its own. It possesses no variability which the artist in the craftsman can take advantage of...' (Leach 1976: 95).

In the twentieth century, although many more women entered art schools, relatively few chose to study sculpture. It was the most male-dominated area of fine art training and women had to be very determined to succeed. Ceramics, as an applied art, was much more accessible to women and the small-scale sculpture or figurine offered the opportunity for three-dimensional work without contravening gender norms. But the popularity of this art form was short-lived. The new doctrines of studio pottery gave pride of place to functional vessels while the new doctrines of modernism valued abstract non-naturalistic themes. In Britain in the inter-war years figures were made by women and probably bought by women, but they were quickly marginalised in the art scheme of things. As Charles Marriott, *The Times* critic, wrote of Stella Crofts,

> Miss Crofts is rather too easily successful on the zoological side and would gain from some drilling in what is called 'abstract' composition – designing in shapes that have no illustrative meaning. To go forward she will have to go back a little and study basic rather than incidental forms and characters. (The Times, 1929)

But elsewhere in Europe figurative ceramics were also popular. In Vienna the early severe geometries of the Wiener Werkstätte style were overtaken by more light-hearted decorative designs and a great enthusiasm for figurative forms. Under the leadership of Michael Powlony there was a huge explosion of ceramics produced by students and ex-students of the Kunstgewerbeschule who set up workshops marketing through the Werkstätte. Of the numerous artists who produced for them a large proportion, and some of the best known, were women. Their work was shown at the 1925 *Exposition Internationale des Arts Decoratifs et Industriels Modernes* in Paris to much acclaim and had an immediate impact on American ceramics. This influence was extended later when two of the leading ceramic sculptors, Vally Weiselthier (1895-1945) and Susi Singer (1895-1949) settled in the USA (Clark 1987:69). However, the folksy decorative aspects of the work have not faired well under modernist criticism and have been identified disparagingly with 'feminine' taste.[35]

The Hungarian, Margit Kovacs (b. 1902), who trained in Vienna, maintained her interest in figurative work, drawing also on the decorative folk art of central Europe throughout the 1950s (Pataky-Brestyansky 1961). The Central European tradition has shown more sympathy towards a sculptural approach in ceramics and the field has been less dominated by the ideal of the functional pot.

Under the egalitarian ideologies of Russia after the revolution, there were additional reasons why women were offered opportunities in many different spheres.[36] Natalya Danko (1892-1942) trained as a sculptor and designed architectural sculptures and reliefs throughout her career, but she is most noted for her porcelain figurines (sometimes decorated by her sister Elena). From 1919 to 1941 she directed the sculpture workshop at the state porcelain factory and produced designs for over 300 figures representing contemporary life and events, including poets, peasants and workers in the new classless society. The figures have a lively characterisation in tune with the social realist philosophy of the government. Propaganda porcelain and figures sold well in Russia and abroad where they helped to bring in much needed foreign currency particularly from the international exhibitions in Paris, London and Monza, Italy. In exactly the same period the figures produced by Charles and Nell Vyse of London characters, have much in common with this work They are picturesque images of the working class for sale to the privileged, and they sold well in America.

In Britain the reaction against figurative work in the canon of studio pottery[37] meant that the genre gained limited critical attention and only surfaced through individual practitioners in particular contexts. In the 1930s, in response to the need to teach pottery modelling to large classes of young people, William Ruscoe introduced figure modelling into the training at Burslem School of Art (Stoke-on-Trent). They used rolls of clay to create a characteristic genre of light-hearted/realist subjects.[38] One of his students Annie Potts' self-portrait is a neat expression of gender roles in the pottery industry (illustrated in Audrey Blackman). In the 1950s Audrey Blackman began to work in a similar way. Although not at first aware of the precedents, she based her technique on the metal armatures she knew from her sculpture training. Her rolled pottery figures are witty vignettes of contemporary life and her use of the delicate translucency of porcelain or simple coloured stoneware is notable.[39]

The marginalisation of narrative or realist ceramics has been very strong. Ruth Barrett-Danes remembered vividly the scorn of her ceramics teacher in the 1950s when she suggested she might wish to work figuratively. Only many years later did she gradually begin to incorporate figurative elements into the works she produced jointly with her husband, Alan. However, she has since gone on to work on her own and from the 1980s has been making anthropomorphic animal sculptures stemming from a more literary and imaginative source. Also unusual was the work of Glenys Barton whose figurative work for Wedgwood in the late 1970s led on to her large-scale figurative sculpture exhibited within a fine art rather than a craft ceramic context.

American ceramics have always been less constrained in the kind of approach and imagery used by ceramic artists. There has consistently been more figurative work. The Californian artist Viola Frey (b. 1933) has never been limited by the strictures of craft ceramics and her works draw on kitsch imagery with powerful echoes of folk art. She has taken the ceramic figurine and ironically blown it up life-size (and beyond) to comment, among other things, on the tradition of decorative figures. The brightly coloured, brash figures stand in full frontal pose like Greek *kouros* figures turned strangely banal in their floral frocks or boldly coloured ties. With sympathy, but not without irony, her figures monumentalise the unglamorous everyday fact of contemporary urban existence.

It is not really till the 1990s in Britain that a significant interest in ceramic figurative (and animal) sculpture: has again been given critical attention and encouragement. Characteristic of this recent period many of the artists draw on a much wider range of sources for their inspiration both from ceramic and non-ceramic art. The exhibition *The Raw and the Cooked* (1994), curated by Alison Britton and Martina Margetts, explicitly set out to open up the debate around contemporary ceramics. Over a third of the thirty-two exhibitors were working with human or animal figures: of these the majority were female, most with associations with the Royal College of Art. Sarah Scampton, Trupti Patel and Tracey Heyes examined aspects of the female figure and its relationship to nature and culture. Animal forms, and exotic and mystical beasts were the main theme in work by Susan Halls, Rosa Nguyen and Pamela Leung whose hybrid creatures evoke memories of Chinese popular mythology. Other significant female ceramic artists in this genre include Jill Crowley who creates tender, witty human and animal subjects, Claire Curneen's vulnerable and questioning nudes and Christie Brown's timeless figures – or are they perhaps postmodern ceramic cyborgs escaping any fixed identity? Although women artists are by far the majority, there are some notable male exponents whose work addresses, at times contentiously, issues of gender and identity.[40] For example, Michael Flynn and Philip Eglin do not take the male gaze for granted but rather interrogate notions of masculine identity.

Feminist ceramics

The use of clay and especially the vessel as metaphor for the female body or the womb is a recurring theme in ceramic history. It has been used by artists in this century both to give a timeless significance to the vessel form as in Elizabeth Fritsch's 'Womb Pots', or to make a more overt feminist statement as in the work of Trudy Galley (Canada) or Gudrun Klix (Australia). The Israeli artist Lea Majaro-Mintz has used sheets of clay to invoke primal symbols of creation, birth and death including the sheet of the newly wed.[41]

Inspired by the writings of Gloria Orenstein, the archaeologist Marija Gimbutas and the artist Monica Sjoo, the American ceramic artist Squidge Davis creates sculptural groups, figures and vessels using raku-fired porcelain. They address themes of ancient mysteries: birth, death and regeneration. Her work is inspired by a spiritual quest and a shamanic approach where creativity, healing and therapeutic teaching are united. She sees the work as intimately connected with ancient ceramic traditions but equally aspires to address social issues of today.

Similar sources and motifs have inspired the British ceramic artist, Sandy Brown. She has been open about the way she experiences her own creative processes in a work pattern attuned to her female identity and rhythms.

> I start the making cycle which is usually a menstrually-based month, by drawing. At this time my studio is spotless, tidy and with everything from the last cycle fired and removed. So I have a clean empty space to start anew. I do drawings and paintings first, to exercise the creative muscle, to express feelings which are often directly related to menstruation and sexuality because of the time when I do them … My fingers do it not me, I just follow them about … That process of being lost within myself, exploring darkest inner space, I find tremendously exciting. (Brown 1987)

Her plates and dishes are decorated with free and expressive, usually abstract designs in contrast to the figurative pieces. The 'goddess' images are simple but vibrant forms that correspond to a personal therapeutic activity. Her work blurs the division between artistic creativity and clay work as restorative personal activity, an approach she has developed in her workshops and teaching. Like Julia Kristeva's notion of the semiotic, the figures could be said to represent the often repressed feminine mode of signification which is alternative to the patriarchal symbolic mode as represented in this case by the conventions of studio ceramics. They are out of order. The primeval wildness of the figures decorated in bold stripes and swirling circles defy classification. They are disturbing and provocative.

The power of works that celebrate or explore female sexuality and female symbolism continues to shock The exhibition *Goddesses*[42] that opened in Edmonton in Canada in 1994 attracted a great deal of adverse publicity with accusations of obscenity. The exhibition included the work of Gudrun Klix who uses simple but powerful boat-like forms with evocative titles and metaphorical imagery: *Semele's Pod* or *Boat for the Rainbow Serpent*. Ann Roberts created an installation, *Revival, Regeneration and Rebirth* and Trudy Colley made vessel/women forms. All base their work on metaphor linking back to mythology and the ancient mysteries of procreation.

In considering this continuing distress that is caused by work that addresses issues of female sexuality on women's terms as opposed to through the perspective of the male gaze, we can return to Kristeva's argument that the semiotic mode of signification is destabilising and undermines patriarchal order.[43]

Success stories

In the middle decades of the twentieth century studio pottery offered some opportunities for women who were brave enough to take up the challenge. A few women made it into the highest positions in parallel, one might say, with career women in many other professions such as doctors, lawyers, politicians or academics. It was possible, but women had to be especially able, or dedicated, or lucky. Equally likely was that women had brief moments of recognition only to be forgotten quite quickly as new ideas emerged. Such was the fate of people like Dora Lunn or Margaret Rey or even Dora Billington. In compensation, teaching often offered women a satisfactory career. Dora Lunn's personal history is one that demonstrates the tensions and dilemmas of the choices available to women. In the latter decades of the century women had much greater access to education and training in the arts and by the 1960s art colleges were better equipped and more professional in the range of training that was offered. This was backed by improved facilities in schools for art and craft teaching. The expansion of higher education courses and their liberalisation did not disadvantage women. In Britain the move in the 1960s from Dip. AD to BA and degree status with the requirement of basic educational qualifications made these institutions more acceptable to middle-class women. However, the old disparity between the high numbers of men teaching a predominantly female student body has not disappeared even at the end of the century.

Why was it that women came to the fore in British ceramics in the 1970s? What were the particular circumstances that made it possible? It was a good time for studio ceramics and there were livings to be made selling domestic pots for which there was a growing market. There was an expansion of ceramics courses, both full-time and evening class. The Craft Potters Association set up in 1959 was firmly established and was an important focus. It was dominated by the anglo-oriental Leach philosophies, although Leach himself was only an honorary member and it was riven by division about the amateur and professional. In that familiar model of art historical movements the CPA (and the Leach tradition) represented the old guard to be thrown over. The young men and women who dreamed of being production potters went off to train at Harrow, but the generation of young graduates at the Royal College were seeking new values and a much higher profile for their ceramic work. Garth Clark has suggested that they were promoted like pop stars (Clark 1995: 194). They were urban/e and self-conscious about the potential meanings and aspirations of the ceramic object. Among their teachers was Hans Coper whose sculptural modernism offered an alternative set of values to the Leach tradition. Among their promoters was the newly established Crafts Advisory Committee (later the Crafts Council) headed by Victor Margrie.[44] The macho traditions of the studio pottery movement with its cult of virtuoso throwing and kiln technology was increasingly undermined by the new young ceramicists who valued art ideas rather than craft ideals. Women had less to lose in the overthrow of the old guard and the more liberal attitude to technologies brought opportunities for the liberated women of the early 1970s. As I have shown, handbuilding and figurative form and, as discussed in an early chapter, decoration were all reclaimed for studio ceramics after the 1970s.

But it was not all plain sailing. Carol McNicoll has recalled how the women in her group in the early 1970s had felt marginalised at the Royal College and that sometimes it seemed that all the materials and attention went to the men who were interested in industrial ceramics. The women were left to get on.[45] In that period the feminist movement in Britain was developing at a pace, and although most have not openly identified with that position all have been nurtured by the new self-confidence of women of that generation. As Alison Britton stated about the time of a major exhibition at the Crafts Council in 1980,

> I was conscious of gender at the time of the Crafts Council exhibition. There were quite a few pots depicting men and women in the show, I've often made reference to maleness and femaleness in pots, whether it's in the drawing or the shape. I've not been aware of some of these references until afterwards. I think I drew fish and tulips before I recognised them as male and female symbols. But then I carried on, knowing that. (Britton quoted in Harrod 1990: 28)

Around this point Alison Britton's work migrated from figurative graphic imagery to the more formalist concerns of her large vessels. These are metaphors of traditional ceramic form: slab built, layered with gestural marks and brush strokes that recall abstract expressionist painting or textile pattern. Much more overt in her reference to textile, Carol McNicoll used slipcast ceramic bands to 'weave' her pieces into complex layered forms and bowl-like constructions.

Glenys Barton and Jacqueline Poncelet also used slipcasting which was traditionally associated with industrial production. In 1976 Barton took up a one-year residency at Wedgwood where she first developed her space-age figures cast and then hand-finished. They stood individually or in rows on flat plaques screen printed with photographic images of clouds. The poise and precision of the pieces convey a grandeur belied by their scale. Both artists have since developed in very different ways and identified themselves as sculptors working on a larger scale and exhibiting within the context of fine art galleries. In the early 1980s Poncelet made 'objects', apparently abstract forms that made vestigial references to natural form with brightly painted surfaces, colourful but not decorative, while Barton has continued to work with figures.

Elizabeth Fritsch's work also contravened the rules. Her flattened forms built by coiling and smoothing are vessels of illusion; the syncopated, chequered surfaces and unexpected colours tease the eye. Each ceramic piece is carefully worked out, lavished with attention and then displayed in a group that develops the theme. The groupings evoke distant metaphors of the human, families perhaps, and along with the colours and patterns they demand a contemplative viewer. They are the ultimate pots of the spirit. Of a different generation and a different background, Gwyn Hanssen Pigott has taken this idea and grouped works to great effect. What on its own might be a simple celadon bowl, by arrangement in a group becomes a postmodernist statement.

The bowl has been put in quotation marks, a signifier of containment, nourishment, oriental traditions and orientalist borrowings. These groupings become monuments to the vessel form in history.

In America the position of women in studio ceramics has also been subject to waves and troughs of recognition. Garth Clark ordered his book on American ceramics by decade and it is interesting to note the moments when women appear to be most absent. They have a place in the early years of studio pottery and by the 1940s there is a good proportion of women, a number who have their origins in Europe, but by the 1950s proportionately they are less in evidence dropping to near exclusion from Clark's canon of the 1960s, the high point of influence of the experimental modernism of Peter Voulkos and his followers. Women appear again in the 1970s and by the 1980s are up to one third of the makers represented: still surprisingly low.

Janet Mansfield's book on *Modern Australian Ceramics* (1988) shows a similar proportion with women making up about one third. Peter Dormer's book *The New Ceramics, Trends and Traditions* (1986) also reveals a telling tale with males outnumbering females three to one in his biographies for the USA, while for Britain and Europe numbers are roughly equal.[46] Women, it appears, did relatively better in Britain and Europe than in the USA. One possible explanation is that the whole field of ceramics has less status and therefore women have been allowed in. In the US the higher status of the cultural field of ceramics has been more competitive and hence more male dominated. Certainly the American tradition in ceramics has been much more sculptural and conceptual and closer to fine art than in Britain. The Crafts Council report, *Craft into the Nineties*, shows that ceramics are practised in roughly equal numbers by men and women, but more men work full-time. Women are more likely to work in sculptural and figurative work The survey also showed that women in crafts earned substantially less than men and *Similarity and Difference* (1997), the Australian survey of artists and craftspeople, also found that women commanded lower prices than men in general.[47]

In this consideration of women in studio ceramics I want to stress that there can be no consistent image of progress, but rather moments when what women do is given value and other moments when it is criticised. Whatever the style or the tendency, if it is associated with women it will affect the way it is perceived. However, I hope I have also shown how the practice of ceramics has offered women a space to negotiate new roles and identities in a fast-changing world.

Notes

1. See Reed (1996) for an extended discussion of this, although none of the articles deals directly with ceramics.
2. Overbeck Pottery in America might be said to be a female equivalent of a twentieth-century family workshop. It was set up in Indiana in 1911 by Elizabeth, Hannah and Mary Frances Overbeck who had trained in the art establishments in New York. Elizabeth designed while her sisters decorated (Wissinger 1994). See also Levin, in Kardon (1994: 85).
3. There are large numbers of manuals written by men and women on the subject of china painting. Louise McLaughlin, *China Painting* (1877) and *Suggestions to China Painters* (1884) and Susan Frackleton, *Tried by Fire* (1886) were among the most influential.
4. Ernest Chaplet (1841-1901) worked at Bourg-la-Reine, at first with decorated earthenware, but later experimenting with oriental glaze effects.
5. For further discussion of these figures see chapter 5 and Clark (1987); Callen (1979); Freylinghuysen (1986).
6. These include Owen Jones, *Grammar of Ornament* (1856); Racinet, *Polychromatic Ornamen*t (1873); and Dolmetsch, *Ornamental Treasures* (1896-97) (see Eidelberg, in Weiss 1981: 46).

7. By the 1890s she was studying the new arts and crafts publications from Europe such as *The Studio* and she subscribed to the French publication *Art et Decoration* launched in 1897. Samuel Robineau also translated the treatise by Taxile Doat on the manufacture of porcelain.
8. Eidelberg emphasises that ceramic history has tended to single out Adelaide Robineau because of her later success, yet her move from decoration to studio pottery was taken by a number of other potters, including women in the early years of the century. In 1901 *Keramic Studio* was advertising potter's wheels and Frackleton's Revelation kiln. For example, Clare Pollen set up a pottery in Manhattan and established The New York School of Pottery and Charles Binns established the pottery summer programme at Alfred University from 1901 (see Weiss 1981: 72).
9. Eidelberg argues that she attended a summer course in 1902 (Weiss 1981: 73-6).
10. For a discussion of the production and reception of this piece see Clark (1987: 55).
11. 'My mother was a radical by virtue of her colonial upbringing – her parents saw no virtue in the conventional hieratic behaviour patterns of Edwardian England' (Rosemary Wren in Coatts 1984: 29).
12. For a very positive account of Denise's role in the guild and of her support and friendship with Archibald Knox, see Tilbrook et al. in Martin (1995: 62-3).
13. Henry and Denise Wren, *Handcraft Pottery, for Workshop and School*, Pitman; London (1928); Denise and Henry Wren, *Pottery: The Finger-built Methods*, Pitman, London (1932); Denise and Rosemary Wren, *Pottery Making: Making Pots and Building and firing Small Kilns*, Pitman, London (1952; 1957).
14. For recent tribute to her mother see Wren (1997: 95-8).
15. This is now housed in the Archive of Art and Design (AAD), Victoria and Albert Museum.
16. See, for example, discussions in Moore (1994: 4); McNay (1992: 2).
17. McClaren (1989: 37) suggests that it was Dora Lunn herself who used the title to promote her father's memory. There were no professors at the Royal College till a later period.
18. Gwendolen Parnell had considerable success as a figurative ceramicist between 1916 and 1936, producing historical figures such as Polly Peachum (see Blunt 1973: plates 36-7).
19. Little is known of Frances Richards (c. 1869-1931), but a substantial body of work exists in the Aberystwyth collection and some in the V&A. She is known to have had a kiln in her garden at Highgate and exhibited regularly during the 1920s (see Watson 1990: 233).
20. The files are full of short press reports of her stand at the British Industries Fair. It was especially noted that both Queen Mary and Queen Alexandra were among her clients (AAD 1/68-1983).
21. See the typescript 'A Potter's Potpourri': 36 (AAD1 66/67); also Gotlieb (1988).
22. Graham McLaren suggests that she was prone to overstate her father's role in early pottery education (McLaren 1989: 37 footnote 2).
23. After the First World War women artists predominated in the Werkstätte and in the art college and Birks (1987: 22) suggests that the contemporary critics considered that the domination of female taste encouraged trivial work Similar kinds of criticism occurred in Britain in the same period using gendered language to marginalise women's work.
24. The furniture specially designed by her architect friend, Emste Plischke, was shipped to London and reinstalled in her new flat.
25. Janet Leach (née Darnell) (1918-1997), third wife of Bernard Leach, was American but later trained in Japan. After settling in England in 1956 she became an important figure in the Leach Pottery and a significant artist in her own right.
26. Critics are fairly universal in suggesting that the Leach influence deflected her for some years from her own philosophy of making which owed so much to the modernist aesthetic of continental Europe.
27. It has been suggested that one of the reasons for the enthusiasm for handbuilding in the last two decades of the twentieth century has been that the increased numbers in colleges have made it impossible to provide the equipment and supervision of large numbers of students. Hence the low technology and smaller output of handbuilding has been positively encouraged.
28. I am not discussing slab-building which normally creates angular forms and is a technique mainly used since the beginning of the twentieth century, although at times inspired by oriental shapes.

29. Although by no means an exclusively female form, a number of women have worked in this way making delicate porcelain vessels inspired by organic forms. These include Deirdre Burnett, Anne James, Mary White (Britain/Germany) and Beate Kuhn (Germany). Geoffrey Swindell and Peter Simpson are perhaps the major male exponents. Some of these artists have used thrown forms to construct the basic shape. The American, Rudi Staffels, is another major figure working with the translucency of porcelain but in a more sculptural, expressive way.
30. At Abuja she worked with Ladi Kwali among others and she feels they were among her most influential teachers…' These teachers showed me how to make things work, to be patient, to start something and finish it and never give up. Their lessons taught me humility and respect for the clay' (Berns 1995).
31. *Africa Explores*, an exhibition organised by the Center for African Art in 1991, was seen in Britain at the Tate Liverpool, in 1994. In the catalogue of Odundo's exhibition *Ceramic Gestures* in Santa Barbara, 1995-97, Marla Berns offers a strongly African reading of the work.
32. See for example the work of Duncan Ross (Great Britain) or Pierre Bayle (France) (Perryman 1995).
33. Rothenstein believed it was a form particularly suited to women and encouraged the practice at the Royal College.
34. According to a family manuscript, in 1909 she tried for the Royal Academy Schools but was rejected because she was the only female of a suitable standard. They did not feel they could create a female sculpture class just for her. She was also deemed too old to enter for the competitions. I am grateful to Paul Hyman for bringing this document to my attention.
35. The work is often discussed in the context of Vienna, the training ground of Lucie Rie whose uncompromising modernism rejected such whimsical and decorative tendencies. Although sharing this view, Tony Birks recognises the chauvinism of the critical response to the latter years of the Werkstätte when most of the designers were women (Birks 1987: 22); see also Houston (1981: 13).
36. Even before the Revolution women artists had been particularly prominent in the Russian avant-garde (Parton 1990).
37. For example, the seminal texts on British studio pottery by George Wingfield Digby (1952) and Muriel Rose (1970) make no mention of it. In Birks (1976) the emphasis is on modernist sculptural form and the only figurative work, actually by Ruth Barrett-Danes, is largely subsumed under the chapter on her husband Alan Barrett-Danes. For further discussion, see my catalogue essay on figurative ceramics (1995).
38. The work was publicised by Gordon Forsyth who organised a highly successful exhibition of the work at the Dorland Hall in London and thereafter it had a ready market for a time (see also Forsyth 1934).
39. Rolled pottery figures were used in eighteenth-century Staffordshire to create scenes of contemporary life, notably what are popularly known as Pew Groups: see Blackman (1986).
40. For further discussion of figurative forms see Vincentelli (1995); Fielding (1998); Hamlyn (1994).
41. See the small catalogue, Majaro-Mintz, *Conversations in Clay – She, He, the Sheet and All That* (1988). These works, beyond merely metaphor, also allude to the Jewish practice of displaying the wedding sheet to prove virginity. Her clay sheet with a torn hole in the centre is given the comment 'an embodiment of the devilish need in human society to tread on individual privacy'.
42. For a discussion of the exhibition and the reactionary response that it provoked see Colley (1995). Also included in the exhibition were the figurative sculptures of Michael Flynn.
43. The most recent exhibition of feminist clay art was in Los Angeles 1995/96. *Exploring a Movement: Feminist Visions in Clay*, curated by Jo Lauria, included the work of eighty-three artists (see Kapitanoff 1996: 48-52).
44. Victor Margrie trained at Hornsey in the 1950s in exhibition design and ceramics. Potter and teacher, he was head of 3D design at Harrow and with Michael Casson designed the very successful studio pottery course at Harrow. He was the secretary and later the director of the Crafts Advisory Committee in the 1970s. He was one of the most influential figures in the success of pottery in the early years of the CAC (Harrod 1989a: 36).
45. In a talk at Aberystwyth in 1993 (Ceramic Archive UWA).
46. It should be noted that Garth Clark was an adviser for this book, so undoubtedly had some influence over the people represented.
47. 'If we assume women are just as productive as men in terms of output per hour worked, it is difficult to escape the conclusion that the prices commanded by the work of women craftspeople and visual artists alike are, on average, lower than those commanded by men' (Bardez and Thorsby 1997: 22).

References

Bardez, Claire and David Thorsby (1997), *Craftspeople and Visual Artists in Australia*, Sydney: Australia Council for the Arts.

Berns, Marla (1995) *Ceramic Gestures: New Vessels by Magdalene Odundo*, University Art Museum, University of California, Santa Barbara.

Birks, Tony (1987) *Lucie Rie*, Sherbourne: Alpha Books.

Blackman, Audrey (1986) *Rolled Pottery Figures*, London: A & C Black.

Blandino, Betty (1984) *Coiled Pottery, Traditional and Contemporary Ways*, London: A & C Black.

Blunt, Reginald, with new intro. By J.V.G Mallet (1973) *The Cheyne Book of Chelsea China and Pottery* (first pub. 1924), Wakefield: E. P. Publishing.

Brown, Sandy (1987) *Sandy Brown* (exhibition catalogue), London: Crafts Council.

Callen, Anthea (1979) *Angel in the Studio, Women in the Arts and Crafts Movement*, London: Astragal.

Clark, Garth (1987) *American Ceramics, 1876 to the Present* (first published 1979), London: Booth-Clibborn Editions.

Clark, Garth (1995) *The Potter's Art. A complete History of Pottery in Britain*, London: Phaidon.

Coatts, Margot (1984) 'The Oxshott Pottery: Denise and Henry Wren', in *The Oxshott Pottery*, Craft Study Centre, Bath.

Fielding, Amanda (1998) 'Under the Skin', *Ceramic Review*, 170, pp. 18–21.

Forsyth, Gordon (1934) *The Art and Craft of the Potter*, London: Chapman Hall.

Frackleton, Susan (1886) *Tried by Fire. A Work on China Painting*, New York: Appleton and Co.

Frelinghuysen, Alice (1986) 'Aesthetic Forms in Ceramic and Glass', in *In Pursuit of Beauty, Americans and the Aesthetic Movement*, New York: Metropolitan Museum of Art, pp. 198–251.

Gotlieb, Rachel (1988) 'Vitality in British Art Pottery and Studio Pottery', *Apollo*, 127, pp. 163–7.

Hamlyn, Jane (1994) 'Philip Eglin, Venus Observed', *Ceramics: Art and Perception*, 16, pp. 22–5.

Harrod, Tanya (1989) 'From "A Potter's Book" to "The Maker's Eye": British Studio Ceramics 1940-1982', in M. Casson and V. Magrie (eds), *The Harrow Connection*, Ceolfrith Press, Northern Centre for Contemporary Art.

Harrod, Tanya (1990) *Alison Britton, Ceramics in Studio*, London: Bellew, in collaboration with Aberystwyth Arts Centre, Aberystwyth.

Hawkins, Jennifer (1980) *The Poole Pottery*, London: Barrie and Jenkins.

Houston, John (ed.) (1981) *Lucie Rie*, London: Crafts Council.

Kapitanoff, Nancy (1996) 'Feminist Visions in Clay', *Ceramics: Art and Perception*, 25, pp. 48–52.

Kardon, Janet (ed.) (1994) *The Ideal Home 1990-1920 – History of Twentieth Century American Craft*, New York: American Craft Museum/Abrams.

Leach, Bernard (1976) *A Potter's Book* (first published 1940), London, Faber.

McLaren, Graham (1989) 'A Complete Potteress, the Life and Work of Dora Lunn', *Journal of the Decorative Arts Society*, 13, pp. 33–38.

McLaughlin, Louise (1897) *China Painting. A Practical Manual for the Use of Amateurs in the Decoration of Hard Porcelain*, Cincinnati: Clarke and Co.

McLaughlin, Louise (1883) *Suggestions to China Painters*, Cincinnati: Clarke and Co.

McNay, Lois (1992) *Foucault and Feminism*, Cambridge: Polity Press.

Moore, Henrietta (1994) *A Passion for Difference: Essays in Anthropology and Gender*, Cambridge: Polity Press.

Parton, Anthony (ed.) (1990) *Women Artists of Russia's New Age*, London: Thames and Hudson.

Pataky-Brestansky, Ilona (1961) *Modern Hungarian Ceramics*, Budapest: Corvina.

Perryman, Jane (1995) *Smoke-fired Pottery*, London: A & C Black.

Reed, Christopher (ed.) (1996) *Not at Home, The Suppression of Domesticity in Modern Art and Architecture*, London: Thames and Hudson.

Rodgers, Mary (1984) *On Pottery and Porcelain*, Sherbourne: Alphabooks.

Rose, Muriel (1970) *Artist Potters in England* (first pub. 1955), London: Faber and Faber.

Schlanger, Jeff and Takaezu, Toshiko (1996), *Maija Grotell: Works Which Grow From Belief*, Goffstown: Studio Potter.

Vincentelli, Moira (1995) 'Figurative Ceramics', in *One from the Heart*, Aberystwyth, Aberystwyth Arts Centre.

Watson, Oliver (1990) *British Studio Pottery in the Victoria and Albert Museum Collection*, Oxford, Oxford University Press.

Weedon, Chris (1987) *Feminist Practice and Poststructuralist Theory*, Oxford: Blackwell.

Weiss, Peg (ed.)(1981) *Adelaide Alsop Robineau: Glory in Porcelain*, Syracuse, NY, Syracuse University Press.
Wissinger, Joanna (1994) *Arts and Crafts Pottery and Ceramics*, London: Pavilion.
Wood, Beatrice (1985) *I Shock Myself. The Autobiography of Beatrice Wood*, ed. Lindsay Smith, Ojai: Dillingham Press.
Wood, Beatrice (1994) 'And that is How I became a Potter', *Ceramics: Art and Perception*, 18, pp. 32–35.
Wren, Rosemary (1997) 'Saltglaze at the Oxshott Pottery', *Ceramics: Art and Perception*, 28, pp. 95–98.
Moira Vincentelli, 2000, 'Gender, identity and studio ceramics', in *Women and Ceramics: Gendered Vessels*, Manchester: Manchester University Press, pp. 220–253.

First Published: 2000, 'Gender, identity and studio ceramics', in *Women and Ceramics: Gendered Vessels*, Manchester: Manchester University Press, pp. 220–253.

Reprinted with the permission of the author.

43
QUEERING THE MUSEUM

Matt Smith

As someone who works with clay, I am interested in how archaeologists create narratives of the past from ceramic fragments and vessels. I saw my solo exhibition *Queering the Museum* at Birmingham Museum and Art Gallery (2010–11) as a means of creating a contemporary 'dig' that could allow LGBT narratives to come to light. The exhibition involved placing new works alongside the existing collections and rearranging objects from the permanent collection to recontextualise them. It comprised 19 interventions in the galleries, each of which sought to unpick how lesbian, gay, bisexual and transgender (LGBT) experiences could be interpreted through the collections, and question why LGBT experiences are so seldom included in museum and gallery displays.

Queer has a double meaning: on one hand it is an inclusive term for LGBT and on the other it can mean 'differing from the normal or usual in a way regarded as odd or strange' (Collins, 1982). This opens the term out and enables queer to become a strategy (to queer) which can be used to explore queerness (LGBT identity). *Queering the Museum* therefore worked on two levels. It allowed the inclusion of LGBT narratives into the museum and also repositioned the existing collections into a new framework.

In October 2007 Jack Gilbert (p. 19) argued in the *Museums Journal* that most museums and galleries were failing to 'collect, frame and interpret the lives and experience of LGBT people … not necessarily because individual staff are homophobic but because of institutional failure'. Heimlich and Koke (2008, p. 94) are more forceful, arguing that within museums 'there is still tremendous homophobic prejudice often enacted through the silence, omission and assumptions that are socially dominant'. *Queering the Museum* aimed to negate this 'heterosexual filter' (Petry, 2004, p. 7) that occurs with museum displays, a filter that prioritises the position of the mainstream and negates LGBT experiences unless they are explicitly identified by curators.

By looking at Birmingham Museum and Art Gallery through a queer lens, I aimed to explore what heteronormative[1] assumptions underpinned the working of the organisation and the development and interpretation of their collections, and also investigate why LGBT experiences are so seldom included in museum and gallery displays.

Museums can appear as neutral, democratic spaces. In reality, curators make active decisions about what to collect, thereby shaping what society deems valuable and worth preserving. They also make active decisions about what to keep in store and what to display, and which narratives to tell with those objects being displayed. *Queering the Museum* repeatedly questioned and critiqued these decisions by re-appropriating objects to tell revised stories, removing objects from the stores and placing them centre stage, and placing newly created 'historic' objects within the collection to fill LGBT voids.

Source: © Matt Smith/*Contemporary Clay and Museum Culture*, Routledge Taylor and Francis Group.

There are numerous reasons why museums have struggled with LGBT visibility. Since museums and galleries are usually centred around collections of objects, those groups in society that own, use and consume objects tend to be privileged in museum displays. In addition, since museums and art galleries predominantly use material culture as the basis for exhibitions, they rely on objects to represent identity groups.

It has been assumed that the only difference between gay and straight men and women is that they have sex with people of the same gender. This logic would therefore focus any queer material culture search around objects related to queer sex, which Vanegas explains is:

> an approach that denies other aspects of gay and lesbian culture. Whilst lesbians and gay men have much in common with everyone else – most gay men are more likely to use a steam iron than a cock ring – there are, nevertheless, often distinct dress codes and meeting places, tastes in music and so on. (Vanegas, 2010, p. 164)

Associations between LGBT identities and material culture are therefore much wider and more nuanced than might initially be assumed. As with any minority group, the experience of being in that group is made of many more experiences that those linked directly to differentiating characteristics. However, to be able to draw out LGBT associations with objects in the collections, there either needs to be a high degree of knowledge on the part of the curator, or those links need to be identified within the museum's cataloguing systems and on the exhibition labels, something that is seldom done.

Museums generally label objects with information about their date, material and maker. It is less common for objects to be associated with their owners. As Vanegas has pointed out, the lives of LGBT individuals share much in common with everyone else, so it stands to reason that most objects related to LGBT individuals will be indistinguishable from those owned by other people. Therefore, it is often the personal information about the owners, makers or subjects depicted on an object that will provide a queer association.

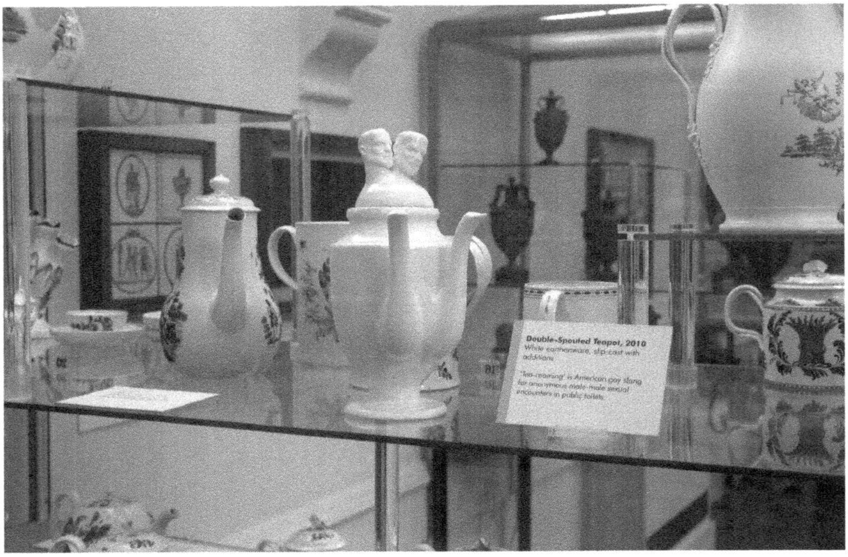

Figure 43.1 Double Spouted Teapot, 2010, photo by David Rowan. Photo is copyright of Birmingham Museum Trust. Work depicted is copyright of the artist Matt Smith.

Birmingham Museum and Art Gallery is one of Britain's largest local authority museums and houses a broad range of objects, from fine and applied art to natural and social history and archaeology. I knew that there were LGBT-related objects in the collection, because I remember visiting the collection in the early 1990s, and reading the label that accompanied the painting *Bacchus* (1867) by Simeon Solomon:

> Solomon's sensual but androgynous images can be linked with his own homosexuality. His career collapsed in 1873 when he was convicted of homosexual offences and spent the last twenty years of his life living mainly in a London workhouse.

I remember my delight at seeing the mention of same-sex relationships being tempered by the link to a criminal conviction. However, while working on the exhibition, the reasoning for this became clearer.

Exhibition labels are usually written with an institutional voice and backed up with documented evidence. Normative thinking assumes people are part of the majority unless there is clear evidence to the contrary. Names and portraits will often indicate gender and race, but less often sexuality. With some notable exceptions, written information about historical queer lives is unusual, and before the decriminalisation homosexuality in 1967 it was often confined to criminal records. The reliance by museums on documented 'fact' means that LGBT histories are often silenced or negative and that heterosexuality is assumed and privileged, encouraging heteronormativity.

An online catalogue search of Birmingham Museum and Art Gallery's collection using the keywords lesbian, gay, bisexual, transgender, LGBT and queer brought up only one result. The keyword 'queer' found a Victorian photogravure of a young girl called Dorothy Drew who was described as having 'a queer kind of elfin charm' (n.d.).

This raises some disturbing questions. If queer associations between objects and their creators, owners and subjects are not identified in the organisation's records, researchers and visitors will need considerable background knowledge to identify any queer relevance in the collection. Rather than being stored in the object records, this knowledge will not be available to other users, who will have to make the discoveries for themselves.

More than seeing this as merely an administrative oversight, Conlan suggested that this lack of identification has the potential to negate identity:

> Omission from the museums does not simply mean marginalisation; it formally classifies certain lives, histories, and practices as insignificant, renders them invisible, marks them as unintelligible, and thereby casts them in the realm of the unreal. (Conlan, 2007, p. 257)

Lucifer and the round room

The first main gallery space within the museum is the Round Room. In the centre of the space, raised on a plinth, is Jacob Epstein's bronze – *Lucifer* (1944–45), inspired by Milton's poem *Paradise Lost*.

Lucifer can be read in a numerous ways, particularly when seen through a queer filter. In *Paradise Lost*, Lucifer is banished to hell following his failed attempt to take control of heaven from God, an attempt borne out of his belief that the angels were equal to God. This struggle for equality is mirrored in feminism and gay rights activism, with Lucifer in the queer role, challenging the received orthodoxy. The desire to challenge an overarching power structure that controls society can be read either as a fight between good and evil or the democratisation of society, depending on one's position. Lucifer's assigned role as the negative counterpoint to good also chimes with queer theory, as Thomas Dowson explains:

> the binary distinction between heterosexuality and homosexuality … resulted from a homophobic desire to devalue one of those oppositions. Consequently, homosexuality is not symmetrically related to heterosexuality – it is subordinate and marginal, but necessary to construct meaning and value in heterosexuality. (Dowson, 2009, pp. 280–281)

The transgressive nature of the sculpture is also seen in its form: Epstein modelled it with a female head on a male body. It is interesting that such a transgressive object can be read as normative by virtue of its status in an authoritative establishment, and this is where the intervention came into play.

Layered on top of the figure was a cape made of two thousand artificial green carnations, sewn together on organza fabric. The *Carnation Cape* (2010) acts as a signifier: letting the visitor know that something is changed.

Interventions remind us that there are many ways of seeing the world: they are perfect agents for queering.

The green carnation, with its 'unnatural' status, was popularised by Oscar Wilde as a means of identifying homosexual desire in Victorian England (Cook, 2003, p. 29). Likewise, the green carnation was taken as a visual key to link the interventions within Birmingham Museum and Art Gallery and placed on all the cases used in the exhibition. Visual signifiers have long been important to gay men as a means of recognising each other. As Matt Cook (p. 132) explains, 'the play of visibility and invisibility, and recognition and misrecognition, were important to the homosexual dynamic in London during the [Victorian] period'.

Within the exhibition, the role of the carnation mirrors the performance of cruising (looking for gay sex): the visitor walks through an ostensibly heterosexual environment searching for queer signifiers that she or he can then choose to ignore or engage with. The carnation visually signified queerness in the way that the use of words such as husband, wife or child on museum labels reinforces heteronormative values.

This play between invisibility and visibility, recognition and misrecognition is key to the strategy for the second set of works – those placed within the museum's ceramic collection.

Upstairs in the industrial gallery

The upstairs floor of the Industrial Gallery was last redisplayed in the 1970s. It employs the traditional museum norms of collecting, cataloguing and displaying to provide curated, 'representative' histories of a subject – in this case, ceramics.

According to collecting theory, this type of collection – and display – would be labelled as male. Baekeland (1981, p. 207) argues that 'women's collections tend to be personal and ahistorical, men's impersonal and historical, just as, traditionally, women have tended to have a relatively greater emotional investment in people than in ideas and men to some extent the reverse'.

By inserting personal, people-centred objects into the cases, the display has been queered, not only through a disruption to the cataloguing systems used by the museum, but also through a 'gendered' assault on the impersonal, male display. Disorder is created within the systematic display, and '[t]he collector's need for order [which is] satisfied by the task of arranging and cataloguing the objects he owns,' is disrupted and contaminated (Baekeland, 1981, p. 209).

The interventions in this gallery are direct responses to the extant collections. The new, queer, objects play with the existing cataloguing rules and infiltrate them with queer narratives to produce new groupings that sit both within and outside the categories. In this way, they echo the ability of many LGBT individuals to 'pass' visually – to go under the radar when necessary and fit in – albeit sometimes only when subjected to a cursory glance.

These new works undermine the museum's position of authority, and place the shared experiences of LGBT individuals in the centre of cultural power. The interventions play with the rules of insider and outsider, adopting queer theory's positions of 'emic and etic' – who is in, who is out (Boellstorff, 2010, p. 208). There is permeability to the distinction as objects alternate between being inside and outside the museum's collections, just as individuals can potentially adopt and discard queer positions.

One of the interventions in the Industrial Gallery is *Double-Spouted Teapot* (2010).

Sited in a collection of earthenware teapots and chocolate pots (for serving hot chocolate), the piece is a play on the American slang term 'tea-rooming', better known as 'cottaging' in the UK, describing anonymous male–male sexual encounters in public toilets.

The piece is cast from a Wedgwood teapot, with a secondary spout added to the front. On the lid, the finial has been replaced by two bearded heads cast from an Action Man figure, the idealised 'boy toy'. Referring to both cottaging and the social niceties of afternoon tea, the piece mashes two very different subjects together, and alludes to the British habit of 'putting the kettle on' when shocking events occur. By taking a norm and subverting it, the piece serves to tell an LGBT narrative while also acting as an agent to queer the exhibition case.

Having two male heads facing forwards with two erect spouts, plays with the viewer's eyes. It is not too large a jump to replace the teapot body with the writhing figures of men. A traditional, functional object has been remade in such a way that it is unable to fulfil its traditional function, thereby achieving a new and different role.

A second intervention in the ceramics gallery was the *Civil Partnership Figure Group* (2010).

In direct response to the eighteenth-century ceramic figurine titled *Figure Group* in the collection, the new piece repurposed the couple's pose and figuration in a same-sex parody of the original piece.

Instead of trying to find or 'out' queer objects in the collection, in these interventions I made pieces that did not exist historically, but could exist now, representing the lives that were lived but not recorded through objects.

Out of the stores

In addition to placing new objects into existing cases, a number of exhibition cases were taken out of storage and placed within the main art gallery spaces. In each of these cases, objects from the museum stores were selected for their ability to act as vehicles to tell LGBT narratives.

Unusually, access was given to all the collections, which allowed for some surprising unions. In the most part these narratives were overlaid on objects which had no intrinsic connection to LGBT lives. In one intervention, *Stereotypes* (2010), three salt-glazed bears were paired with a taxidermy otter. In gay male culture, a bear is a large hairy man and an otter his slimmer counterpart. By placing these four objects together, a visual connection was created that moved the objects from their normal taxonomies.

However the display of a drawing, *Night and Sleep* (1888) by Simeon Solomon, was an exception, and drew on the known queer history of the artist. In response to the 1990s label about Solomon, I had a desire to try to reposition his narrative. While researching his life and relationships – who he had met, where he had met them and what their histories were – it became clear that police records and newspaper reports were the main sources of information about his sex life. It was very difficult to uncover details about the working class men he was arrested with, beyond their names.

I began to sympathise with museum curators – how could stories be told without documented facts? I decided to work with the lack of evidence, rather than against it and Lord Frederic Leighton provided an apt counterpoint to Solomon. Leighton (1830–1896) was working at the same time as Solomon (1840–1905). They were both painters with links to the Pre-Raphaelites and both were seen as great talents at the start of their careers. Solomon's arrests and the subsequent scandals limited his career. Unlike Solomon, Leighton became a pillar of the Victorian art establishment: knighted in 1878, made a baronet in 1886 and raised to the peerage in 1896.

There are numerous indications that, were they alive today, both men would identify themselves as gay. Solomon had many same-sex encounters, two of which lead to his arrest, firstly in London and then in Paris. Leighton was much more discreet about any sexual relations he may have had, whether in England or North Africa.[2] He left no diaries and his correspondence was 'telling' in its 'lack of reference to his personal circumstances' (Leighton House Museum, n.d.). This has led to his possible homosexuality being an ongoing matter of debate.

Within the case, two objects from the collection – the bronze *An Athlete Wrestling with a Python* (1877) by Leighton and the drawing by Solomon – were placed facing away from each other. Accompanying both were contemporaneous quotations about the men at various stages of their careers. A small trophy of a bear, pierced with arrows, imitating Saint Sebastian, was placed by the Solomon drawing, in some small way celebrating his openness and honesty and compensating for the consequences of that honesty.

The comparison of Leighton and Solomon raises issues about how museums can incorporate historic LGBT narratives into exhibitions without resorting to the 'married to his art' (Vanegas, 2002, p. 105) and 'bachelor uncle' (Fellows, 2004, p. 18) euphemisms, when definitive evidence of same-sex intimacy is not extant. Joshua G. Adair (2010, pp. 264–78) argues that we need to rethink the use of the word 'gay'. He agrees with Fellows, who writes:

> One of the most harmful aspects of homophobia is its equating of *gay* with sex alone; that is *gay* tends to be understood quite narrowly as a synonym for *homosexual*. For this reason, it's not an ideal term to use when looking at a person's nature beyond the scope of his sexual orientation per se. But what's the alternative? Resisting the urge to coin a new term for my kind across time and cultures I've decided to make do with the familiar word *gay* and explain what it means to me: a male who is gender atypical (psychologically and perhaps physically androgynous or effeminate) and decidedly homosexual in orientation if not in practice. Thus, my use of the term *gay* encompasses both gender identity and sexual orientation. It is not synonymous with *homosexual*. (Fellows, 2004, p.13; italics in original)

This shift of focus from physical act to gender and sexual difference may be a means of moving the exploration of historic LGBT narratives in museums forwards. Queer becomes a useful tool to start discussing difference that cannot be solely or definitively categorised around sexual orientation.

Conclusions from *Queering the Museum*

Queering the Museum interrogated and drew out LGBT narratives from within the collections at Birmingham Museum and Art Gallery, and laid narratives upon those collections. By developing subjective and tangential links, and developing new artworks to explore narratives, the exhibition highlighted that LGBT stories are all around, but only appear when you look for them. But was it queer?

Queer can be utilised in many ways. As a noun, it encompasses the LGBT 'community' and as such the subject matter explored by the interventions is queer. But this is a limited reading of queer which doesn't address its ability to refer to something 'differing from the normal or usual in a way regarded as odd or strange'.

Queer as a verb brings exciting opportunities for artists: to alter spaces, work in non-normative ways and challenge hierarchies. Unsettling categorisations, disrupting sculptures and displays in the museum and questioning the messages curators tell us, have all in some way resulted in the museum being 'put in a difficult or dangerous position'. Queer – the verb – provides limitless scope for working with museums. Chiming with institutional critique and museum interventions, it can work with or without reference to LGBT narratives. It is concerned with change: re-examining the norm, repositioning the marginalised and subverting the status quo – and thus resonates with outsider status.

Two pieces from the exhibition were acquired by the museum. One of them, *Donkey Man* (2010), explores the sense of finding oneself outside the mainstream, something that most people experience at some time.

Half human, half animal, *Donkey Man* will constantly find himself outside both those categories. The acquisition of the work takes it from the everyday and places it within the museum collection: a place where there is a duty to preserve and care for the object. It sheds its outsider status and is deemed important enough to represent society. In doing so, the museum curators have moved the object 'from the secular, profane, undifferentiated realm of the commodity, and ritually transform[ed] it into a personally and socially significant object' (Belk, 1994, p. 320). It could be argued that having been acquired, the object has lost its queer status.

However, this acceptance is provisional as the label that now accompanies *Donkey Man* makes clear: 'Matt Smith is an activist and campaigner over the issues of lesbian, gay, bi-sexual and transgender identity. His work is highly political and can be challenging, explicit, thought-provoking and funny.'

I question whether terms such as activist and campaigner would be used if I had been working with mainstream identities in the project. I worked on the project as an artist, attempting to explore the museum's systems and taxonomies in order to understand why queer lives were absent from the displays. The labelling goes on to say: 'Smith also engages with society's inability to accept difference' when what I was engaging with was an organisation's inability to portray difference.

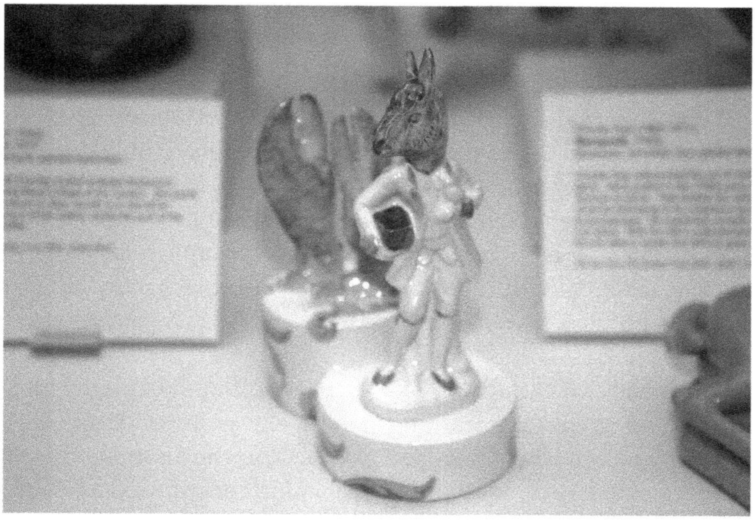

Figure 43.2 Donkey Man, 2010, photo David Rowan. Photo is copyright of Birmingham Museum Trust. Work depicted is copyright of the artist Matt Smith.

However, society's (in)ability to accept difference was engaged with through the evaluation of the exhibition by Maria-Anna Tseliou [2011] from the Museum Studies Department at the University of Leicester. While the sample size was relatively small (31), the evaluation raised some interesting results. Some 45.2 per cent of the interviewees came specifically to the museum to see the exhibition, and of these, 57 per cent identified themselves as LGBT and 43 per cent as heterosexual. When asked, none of the interviewees said that they had found the exhibition provocative, with a sizeable number commenting that they had found it 'thought-provoking, but not at all provocative' (Tseliou, p. 5), with 74.2 per cent of all the interviewees saying that they thought it appropriate to have gay and lesbian culture represented in museums and the other 25.8 per cent agreeing, but with some specifications. This data challenges the museum sector's reluctance to address LGBT lives.

The evaluation also brought the use of the term queer outside the academy into sharp relief. Only 22 per cent of interviewees were aware of the reclamation of the word, with over half of interviewees having negative associations with the word. This raises concerns for its use in projects which are trying to increase and widen social engagement and inclusion.

There are a number of reasons why *Queering the Museum* provoked much positive comment and generated comparatively little protest. Craft, with its association with the homely, the comforting and the feminine, is an ideal Trojan Horse for the politically minded. Working with, bending and distorting museum rules, rather than attempting to overtake or dominate them, allows boundaries to be pushed much further.

Placing a 'homonormative' filter on the work of one museum highlighted a number of issues:

- all objects contain many stories and histories, and curators decide not only which objects are collected and displayed, but also which histories relating to an object are told;
- the freedom that museums allow to artists undertaking institutional critique and artist interventions could be exploited more by curators if museums move away from 'neutral' institutional labelling towards more personal interpretation;
- if museums and galleries are serious about LGBT inclusion, collecting patterns and especially cataloguing terms will need to change;
- possibly most controversially for museums, if objects that are needed to tell a history and to represent society do not exist, museums wanting to be socially inclusive might have to commission an artist to make them.

The LGBT 'community' – if such a thing exists – is fragmented, contradictory and multi-voiced. There are few, if any, unifying activities, events or traditions. It is a group where the shared characteristic is seldom passed down through family lines, so in effect, members of the group have to seek out 'elders' and sources of information in order to discover shared histories. 'Coming out' can be seen as self-orphaning: an admission that you and your parents do not share a common history. I would argue that because of this, the representation of LGBT histories in museums is even more important for this group than for those whose traditions are passed down from parent to child. After all, museums are one of the few organisations placed to preserve and communicate these histories between generations.

If the paucity of LGBT exhibitions is in part due to a lack of historical material culture and written factual evidence, then gay weddings and civil partnerships provide a fascinating opportunity for museums. Although far from adopted by all gay men and women, they are the first positive official recordings of same-sex relationships. As increasing numbers of weddings take place, customs and norms are being created. Clothing, wedding albums, invitations, wedding cards are all celebratory material which can be collected and displayed by museums to tell positive stories.

However, even without uniquely LGBT-related material culture, the interventionist strategies used in *Queering the Museum* enable museums to represent LGBT experiences. As Stuart Frost (2011, p. 19) points out, by taking a tangential approach to museum display, *Queering the Museum* 'underlines the potential that exists for museums to reinterpret their existing collections in thought-provoking ways, and how to integrate LGBT experience and history into permanent galleries'.

Whether mainstream museums will ever seriously preserve LGBT histories, or continue to address them sporadically and temporarily remains to be seen. Many museums present their collections in authoritative ways that do little to make the visitor aware that there are alternative ways of seeing and interpreting them. But simply by having the confidence to explain openly that collections and displays come with 'ideological baggage' (Haacke quoted in Glover, 2011) may be the truly queer way to queer a museum and allow the space for difference to exist.

Notes

1. Calvin Thomas (2009, p. 21) defines heteronormativity as 'the institution, structures of understanding, and practical orientations that make heterosexuality not only coherent – that is, organised as a sexuality – but also privileged'.
2. For more about the perceived links between North Africa and homosexuality in nineteenth-century London, see Cook (2003, pp. 14, 92–3).

References

Adair, J.G., 2010. House Museums or Walk-in Closets? The (non)representation of gay men in the museums they called home. In A.K. Levin, ed. 2010. *Gender, Sexuality and Museums: A Routledge reader*. Abingdon: Routledge. pp. 264–78.

Baekeland, F., 1981. Psychological Aspects of Art Collecting. In: S.M. Pearce, ed. 1994. *Interpreting Objects and Collections*. London: Routledge. p. 205–219.

Belk, R., 1994. Collectors and Collecting. In: S.M. Pearce, ed. 1994. *Interpreting Objects and Collections*. London: Routledge. pp. 317–26.

Birmingham Museums and Art Gallery, n.d. *Photogravure from the Work of Edward Burne-Jones: Dorothy Drew*. [online] Available at: http://www.bmagic.org.uk/objects/1900P102 [Accessed 22 January 2013].

Boellstorff, T., 2010. Queer Techne: Two theses on methodology and queer studies. In: K. Browne and C.J. Nash, eds. 2010. *Queer Methods and Methodologies: Intersecting queer theories and social science research*. Farnham: Ashgate. pp. 215–30.

Collins, 1982. *Collins Dictionary of the English Language*. London: Collins.

Conlan, A., 2007. Representing possibility: Mourning, memorial and queer museology. In: A.K. Levin, 2010. *Gender, Sexuality and Museums*. London: Routledge. pp. 253–63.

Cook, M., 2003. *London and the Culture of Homosexuality, 1885–1914*. Cambridge: Cambridge University Press.

Dowson, T., 2009. Queer Theory Meets Archaeology: Disrupting epistemological privilege and heteronormativity in constructing the past. In: N. Giffney and M. O'Rourke, eds. 2009. *The Ashgate Research Companion to Queer Theory*. Farnham: Ashgate. pp. 277–94.

Fellows, W., 2004. *A Passion to Preserve*. Madison: University of Wisconsin Press.

Frost, S., 2011. Are Museums Doing Enough to Address LGBT History? *Museums Journal*, January, p. 19.

Gilbert, J., 2007. The Proud Nation survey has revealed a shocking reluctance of the museums sector to integrate LGBT material into their exhibitions. *Museums Journal*, 107, October.

Glover, M., 2001. Stop Making Sense. *The Independent*, 20 January. p. 11.

Heimlich, J. and Koke, J., 2008. Gay and Lesbian Visitors and Cultural Institutions: Do they come? Do they care? A pilot study. In: J. Fraser and J.E. Heimlich, eds. *Where is Queer?* Special edition of *Museums & Social Issues: A Journal of Reflective Discourse*, 3(1), p. 94.

Leighton House Museum, n.d. *Who was Frederic Leighton?* [online] Available at: http://www.rbkc.gov.uk/subsites/museums/leightonhousemuseum/aboutthehouse/aboutleightonhouse/whowasleighton.aspx [Accessed 8 April 2015].

Petry, M., 2004. *Hidden Histories: 20th century male same sex lovers in the visual arts.* London: Artmedia Press.

Thomas, C., 2009. On Being Post-Normal: Heterosexuality after queer theory. In: N. Giffney and M. O'Rourke, eds. 2009. *The Ashgate Research Companion to Queer Theory*. Farnham: Ashgate. pp. 17–32.

Tseliou, M.-A., [2011]. *Queering the Museum Evaluation Report*. Commissioned by the author.

Vanegas, A., 2002. Representing Lesbians and Gay Men. In: R. Sandell, ed. 2002. *Museums, Society, Inequality*, London: Routledge. pp. 98–109.

Vanegas, A., 2010. Representing Lesbians and Gay Men in British Social History Museums. In: A.K. Levin, 2010. *Gender, Sexuality, and Museums*. London: Routledge. p. 163–71.

Originally published in *Contemporary Clay and Museum Culture*, Routledge (2016) (eds) Brown, C, Stair. J and Twomey. C, Part V: 19, pp. 196–208

Reproduced with permission of Routledge Taylor and Francis Group and Matt Smith.

44

THE PERSONAL POLITICAL POTS OF GRAYSON PERRY

Louisa Buck and Marjan Boot

Most artists have shied away from making work about the attack on The World Trade Center, but not Grayson Perry. On the large vase *Dolls at Dungeness, September 11th, 2001* (2001), baby-blue infant figures are dotted around a bleak, blighted landscape studded with wooden shacks, electricity pylons and beached boats while overhead war planes, coloured in the same nursery pastel, hover in a gold-lustre sky. As always in Grayson Perry's practice, expectations are confounded and easy interpretations denied. Both attacker and victim appear as malevolent toys, each spewing speech bubbles laden with prejudice and invective: 'macho bull-shitters' explodes from the cockpit of a fighter jet, 'death to all pigeaters' replies a ringleted cutie, while on the ground, a prone baby doll declares 'you can keep your cheap baby milk'. Specific political events are not what Perry chooses to depict here, instead his main concern is with the cultural climate that gives rise to such situations: 'The toys are just as much the bigots and the aggressors as the war planes flying overhead' he comments, 'both are inanimate objects onto which we project our feelings'.[1]

The fact that these comments on world affairs are presented as adornments on a decorative object is both absurd and utterly to the point: Perry is all too aware that you cannot be pompous on a pot. As he has said: '[...] no matter how brash a statement I make, on a pot it will always have a certain humility';[2] and for nearly two decades he has been using this benighted medium as a Trojan Horse to smuggle in serious and sincere comment on the world which he, and we all, inhabit. Grayson Perry has described his early work as 'following the line of most resistance'[3] and although he has refined his approach over the years, this desire to embrace, celebrate and manipulate the improbable, the unfashionable and the unacceptable has never left him.

Perry started making pottery not whilst at art school in Portsmouth, where he made assemblages and bronzes, but at that most underrated and derided seal of learning: the English evening class. It was precisely the low-esteemed status of ceramics, especially within the amateurish context of the evening class, that appealed to him: 'I hated pottery – it was something that hippies did. But I've always been on the lookout for an aesthetic that challenges and doesn't just confirm an idea of the world – I seek out things I really dislike because they have an emotional charge for me.'[4]

Perry's earliest work showed a crude, no-holds-barred subversion of the genteel and humble medium in which he was working. Not only did he revel in his technical ineptitude – dismaying the craft purists with the wonkiness of his early (often glued-together) plates[5] – but he also delighted in combining the most time-honoured traditional English vernacular techniques – painted slip glazes, sprig moulding – with deliberately provocative texts and images that are utterly at odds with the comforting connotations of the medium. On *I am the Centre of the Universe* (1985) a crudely-stencilled flower and phallic rocket are flanked by relief moulds of Masonic symbols and a threatening pair of domestic scissors, while the entire piece is presided over by a swastika-bearing eagle. Another early plate, *Dear Imaginary Mother* (1989), combines the trashiest commercial

Source: © Louisa Buck, 2002. Published by NAi Uitgevers and the Stedelijk Museum Amsterdam.

transfers of flowers, a thatched cottage and poodles with sado-masochistic references that range from an incised text: ('...DREAM THAT YOU WILL ALWAYS TELL ME WHAT TO DO AND THAT YOU WILL PUNISH ME WHEN I AM GOOD'), to a painted image of a spike-heeled female, and mundane objects such as a hair comb, dog collar and dog bowl, which in this context become imbued with specific sexual significance.

In the early 1980s, Perry took part in the activities of the Neo-Naturist Cabaret, and to a great extent the concerns of Neo-Naturism both mirrored and nurtured Perry's own love of the perversely uncool. In a cultural climate dominated by hardnosed, hard-edged Thatcherite consumerism, the Neo-Naturist performances, featuring naked painted bodies and lengthy (and deliberately unrehearsed) rituals and involving New-Age fertility rites combined with folksy domestic science, were outrageously out of kilter with the times. Perry describes Neo-Naturism as 'doing naff things seriously in the nude'[6] and it is Neo-Naturism's paradoxical fusion of serious sincerity with a knowing awareness of the absurdity of their actions which continues to resonate through Perry's pots.

For, however perverse and provocative they may appear, the bleak landscapes, the sexual perversions, the many images of Perry himself, his family and his transvestite alter ego Claire, or the procession of savagely observed cultural stereotypes – housewives, yuppies, car and bike lovers, artworld poseurs – which parade across the surfaces of his ceramics are all rooted in this artist's own reality. Right from the earliest evening class efforts, Perry's pots stand as expressions of his intensely felt personal experience, and this has been explored and refined by his ongoing commitment to psychotherapy, to which he was introduced by his wife Philippa, who is a practising psychotherapist. For many artists – especially in the UK – psychotherapy is viewed at best with suspicion, at worst with derision, but for Perry's work this process of self-discovery has been crucial: 'I've learned a lot about myself and the way people work, it's one of my main subjects. It's a form of interpreting the world in a way that I enjoy – it's as if you have a tool bag but it's too full of crap to be able to find the right tool – and then suddenly someone's shown you a shed and you can find everything: you don't throw the tools away, you just become more aware of where they are and how to use them'.[7] Through his involvement in therapy, Perry has been able to discover and explore aspects of himself and his own identity, and these various roles are constantly played out in his work as well as his life.

Indeed, he attributes psychosexual origins to the very act of making ceramics in the first place: 'I think that the fact that I originally chose ceramics is to do with my particular sexuality: I identify heavily with the feminine and in the young Grayson Perry's mind in his formative years, being female was identified as second class, so with my low self esteem, I identified with the underdog to a certain extent. The low status of ceramics is one of the many layers in the work and the prejudices that everyone has about ceramics – whether they be good or bad is the first filter through which all the work is viewed.'[8]

Intricately entwined with Perry's artistic activities has been the evolution of his transvestism and the development of his feminine other half, Claire. His pottery and his cross-dressing have developed in tandem as psychologically necessary 'underdog' activities. Over the years, Perry-as-Claire has become an integral part of his art as well as his everyday existence. From appearing frequently on pots and in person at the occasional art event, Claire has now emerged as an artwork in her own right, wearing specially made dresses embroidered with talismanic motifs. *The Mother of All Battles* (1996) finds a gun-toting Claire modelling Perry's first textile work, a folk costume in which the vivid applique and embroidered decorations on the skirt and bolero waistcoat reveal what nationalism is capable of unleashing as a bus explodes inside a Star of David, a soldier with an erect penis shoots a baby, and a pregnant cruciform figure is contained within a flaming fighter plane. By branching into textiles Perry again avoids falling into the trap of earnest polemic by using an undervalued craft activity as the unexpected vehicle for serious political comment; and another twist is that, in spite of their handmade, folk art appearance, the designs on this – and all – Perry's textile pieces are computer-generated and mechanically stitched.

In October 2000 Perry staged *Claire's Coming Out*, in which Claire, in a richly-adorned frilly frock, gave a speech and a slide show to an invited audience in which she stated: 'I don't want to be a woman. I am a transvestite. I feel compelled to dress like this by a part of myself that is bursting to find expression: a part of me that is vulnerable, softer, gentler, wondrous and even sweet. A part that as a boy I discarded and buried as a survival strategy in a harsh environment.'[9] Part performance and part significant personal ritual, *Claire's Coming Out* highlighted Perry's increasing ability to move seamlessly between emotionally-charged autobiography and mocking self-parody in a way that makes his work doggedly averse to any neat definitions: dressing up as Claire has undoubtedly imbued Perry with a certain artworld notoriety which he is all too happy to embrace, but his assumption of a female persona remains emphatically part of his own identity. As much as Claire may be integrated within Perry's work, the impact of her presence is all the greater precisely because she is so much more than just an artistic device.

The evolution of Claire as a product of Perry's troubled, violent childhood took place against the backdrop of the blighted terrain of his native Essex, a county that lies to the northeast of London. In this benighted part of the UK – which is the butt of a whole sub-genre of tasteless Essex girl jokes and is much favoured by retired East End gangsters – pockets of rural picturesqueness are surrounded by desolate urban overspill, flat tracts of wasteland and unappealing out-of-town shopping centres. Even though he moved away from Essex in his late teens, this anomalous and contradiction-laden location is regularly evoked as fitting context for Perry's explorations of the paradoxes within his own persona – from the man who is fanatical about physical fitness as well as wearing frocks; the ambitious artist who mocks the artworld, or the accomplished and stylish logo-spotter who also despises the tyranny of fashion. *Driven Man* (2000) finds Perry exploring his love-hate attitude to Essex car culture whilst posing resplendently in his custom-made 'Essex Man' motorbike leathers inspired by the Cerne Abbas Giant; while the seductive appeal of motor machismo and car fetishism also forms the subject of *The Language of Cars* (1999), in which images of the latest top-of-the-range vehicles are finished in mother-of-pearl luster, which, according to Perry, echoes the 'vanities of the boy racer'[10] and float over a series of repeated words – SEX/POWER/MONEY/STATUS/GOD – which read like a capitalist mantra.

However, Perry's preoccupation with his own cultural roots and multifarious individual experiences does not prevent him from citing an ever increasing number of artistic sources. These references can be overt, as in the Kieferesque landscape on *Vase in the Style of Meaning* (1998); or *Punters in the Snow* (1999) whose title and wintry background refer to Pieter Breughel the Elder's painting *Hunters in the Snow*. Then there is a checklist of contemporary art styles and strategies that he satirises in pieces such as *Cliché Artist* (1998), *Gimmicks* (1996) or *Video Installation* (1999), or more discretely with his ever increasing use of carefully researched British, oriental and African ceramic forms and traditions which add more subtle layers of meaning. Although he does not refer to it directly, his use of rumbustious and scatological caricature also places Perry within a tradition of English satirical art as exemplified in the 18th and early 19th centuries by William Hogarth (1697-1764), Thomas Rowlandson (1756-1827) and – especially – James Gillray (1757-1815).

Scratched with graffiti-like directness onto the crowded surfaces of his pots, Perry's grotesquely rendered personages have much in common with Gillray's elaborate and scurrilously bawdy etchings which teem with often hideously distorted figures taken from contemporary life. In the art of both Perry and Gillray, great and grave events of war and politics – along with the foibles and follies of London's society and artworld – are paraded as an uproarious but vituperative masquerade. The enthusiastically kinky mass flagellation of Gillray's *Representation of the horrid Barbarities practised upon the Nuns by the Fish-Women on breaking into the Nunneries in France* (1792) could have come straight off the surface of a Perry ceramic, while Gillray's fashionable women and swells in works such as *High Change in Bond Street – or La Politesse du Grande Monde* (1796) have their 20th-century counterpart in Perry's *Boring Cool People* (1999) or the amoral fashion victims of *Beautiful Murderers dying of Aids* (1997).[11]

Perry's obsessively individual spirit and his commitment to the most directly illustrative forms of communication also point to the profound and enduring influence of Outsider Art, and most particularly the work of Henry Darger (1892-1972). A reclusive Chicago hospital janitor, Darger spent over half a century working secretly on a 19,000-page illustrated fantasy epic revolving around the seven Vivian Girls and their part in a child slave uprising against evil adult armies in the mythical country of *Glandinia*. Perry first encountered Darger's elaborate, meticulously executed scenes of infant rebellion, war and devastation – in which imaginary images were combined with those traced from comics and magazines and painted on sheets of paper glued together to lengths of six to twelve feet – at the Hayward Gallery's 1979 Outsider Art Exhibition, and he felt an instant affinity. 'I felt that they were like one of my pots rolled out. He retreated into his imaginary world full time, but his paintings are visually very sophisticated and not repetitive like a lot of Outsider Art: spatially, compositionally, stylistically and colourwise they change drastically.'[12]

Darger's transgressive images combining (often) hermaphrodite children wreaking havoc and extreme violence have continued both to reflect and to feed into Perry's own iconography. The recent pot *Revenge of the Alison Girls* (2000) directly refers to Darger's mini-army, with Perry's gun-toting hermaphrodite children in charge of a grisly concentration camp devoted to the torture and extermination of adults.

Outsider Art, as the term implies, is made outside any known or understood tradition and without any sense of an audience, whereas Perry's work pointedly acknowledges both, but both artists share a need in their art to sustain and expand the fantasy world of their troubled childhoods, and to depict a parallel universe that fuses internal and external worlds with throat-grabbing directness. Whereas Darger has his Vivian Girls assisted by his heroic alter ego Henry Dargerius and sidekick Jack Evans, Perry's personal pantheon is headed by Claire and Alan Measles, his teddy bear surrogate father, who make repeated appearances, often as heroic figures amidst an array of villainous adults. In the grand lidded pot *Triumph of Innocence* (2000), Alan Measles drives a car while Claire, waving jubilantly, rides on the roof amidst a grisly parade of pre-pubescent children dragging torturously trussed up adults to their imminent execution on a distant hilltop gallows; in *Vase Using My Family* (1998) Measles features prominently as a photographic transfer, and his enduring importance is acknowledged by more appearances as a repeated motif on both the yellow and blue versions of Claire's *Coming Out Dress* (2000).

Over the years Perry's work has evolved from their early defiant roughness to an increasingly ambitious scale and sophistication. As he declares, 'I've come out as a craftsman because, after more than fifteen years, I can't admit that I make them badly anymore; you can't fake roughness.'[13] But as always with Perry, his motives are multilayered. The fact that his ceramics are not just more competently made, but are also more excessively sumptuous in appearance, with an increasingly liberal use of gold lustre and layerings of elaborate decoration, is of course a deliberate strategy. With his abiding desire to be out of kilter with prevailing trends it can be no coincidence that, during the 80s when either high-octane NeoExpressionism or high-gloss production values were all the rage, he was producing wilfully wonky, badly made objects; and now that the British artworld has embraced craft values and a conscious amateurism – whether Paul Noble's intenselydrawn dysfunctional cityscapes, Michael Raedecker's amalgams of oil paint and embroidery, or Martin Maloney's bad paintings and cut-outs – Perry's pots have scaled ever more baroque heights of adornment to become the ultimate in luxury objects.[14]

Although he remains true to his original techniques – all the pots are still laboriously built up from earthenware coils – Perry is now consciously producing work that uses ever more flamboyant means to seduce with their unashamed aesthetic and tactile appeal. 'I'm very reactionary against a lot of modern art in that it doesn't give that sensuous pleasure of the object – often the object is just there to illustrate some point, it's just a prop for an idea. It seems to me that a lot of artists have given up a huge part of their potential vocabulary by abandoning the handmade object: the handmade object speaks the language of the body, and if we only engage with our heads then we are denying a huge part of the vocabulary.'[15]

But revelling in fine forms, rich detail and gold lustre does not mean that Perry has blunted his critical faculties. As he has become increasingly embraced by the art establishment, he has had to develop more subtle strategies to bite the hand that is now saluting him – and beauty is proving to be a powerful weapon. In both their form and the subject matter they depict, his pots continue to play with and off the medium. The ostentatious opulence of *Triumph of Innocence*, with its lushly ornate surface built up of incised drawings, gold lustre, painted glazes and multicoloured sentimental commercial transfers, is deliberately and discordantly at odds with its gruesome subject matter of viciously vengeful infants; just as *I was an Angry Working Class Man* (2001) presents another uncomfortable amalgam in which content is deliberately skewed by style. Nestling within and dangling off the curlicues of this essay in genteel chinoiserie are motorbikes, pub signs and other stereotypical images of manhood, culminating in a lid topped off with the golden figure of a Pit Bull Terrier, the ultimate symbol of English masculinity (much favoured as a status symbol by the Essex male). However, in a characteristic Perry coup de grace, as the manifestations of maleness are reined in by the vase's decorative devices, so this canine killing machine is abjectly defeated, thrown on its back by a kick in the genitals.

Perry's recent and more overt harnessing of his work to specific issues and causes also shows him upping the artistic ante. As well as refining his techniques he has also honed his imagery with what he describes as 'a more organised campaign of images'.[16] Although he always avoids any tight agenda or specific message, in an artworld that tends to dismiss the polemical and view expressions of overt sincerity with suspicion it is nonetheless venturing into risky territory. Specific issues and occasional world events have cropped up in the past – in 1991 his reaction to the Gulf War was to make a Gulf War Dinner Service – but Perry has now become increasingly confident and adept in integrating more widespread concerns within his personal and autobiographical iconography. Here, psychotherapy has again played a significant part. Just as Perry attributes the increasingly childlike image of Claire who, in the past few years has shifted from a middle-aged woman to beribboned pre-pubescence, as being 'about me expressing in a pure form what I've always wanted to express about myself'[17] so the same subtext could be applied to his ceramics, which have gained in coherence without losing any of their psychological complexity. The destruction of The World Trade Center may have been the catalyst for *Dolls at Dungeness, September 11th, 2001* but the vase's infant protagonists can also be seen as Perry's private army of Vivian Girls, waging war on adult violence in a landscape dominated by a nuclear power station that his own father helped to build; just as the bleakly beautiful *We've Found the Body of Your Child* (2000) goes beyond the rabid press coverage of paedophilia to presents an uncompromising indictment of society's ambivalent attitude towards children where they can be simultaneously sentimentalised and brutalised – often by their own parents. In works such as these, Perry can be seen to be continuing to breathe new and incisively relevant life into another unfashionable notion which has always been a hallmark of his work: that of the personal as political.

Notes

1. Grayson Perry in conversation with the author, December 18, 2001.
2. As quoted in: L. Buck, 'Art Rage: Grayson Perry's Unorthodox Approach to Ceramics', Crafts, (1989) no. 97, 38.
3. Grayson Perry in conversation with the author, April 13, 2000.
4. Grayson Perry in conversation with the author, December 18, 2001.

5. *Ceramic Review*, September/October 1988, letter from Molly Williams, Streatham: 'I was horrified when I opened my Ceramic Review to find three whole pages given over to such appallingly badly made work [...] if these horrible dishes and pots are worth showing in colour then you've lost me as a reader.'
6. Grayson Perry in conversation with the author, December 18, 2001.
7. Ibid.
8. L. Buck, 'Grayson Perry: UK Artist Q & A', The Art Newspaper, (2000) no. 103, p. 69.
9. Grayson Perry, 'Claire's Coming Out Speech', Monday October 30, 2000, Laurent Delaye Gallery, london.
10. Grayson Perry website www.graysonperry.uk (notes on *The Language of Cars* [1999]).
11. See ex. cat. J. Gil/ray, The Art of Caricature, london (Tate Britain) 2001, 94, cat. no. 55; and The Annual Report of the Stedelijk Museum 1999, Amsterdam 1999, p. 39.
12. Grayson Perry in conversation with the author, December 18, 2001.
13. See note 8.
14. Grayson Perry was one of eight artists included in 'New Labour', Saatchi Gallery 1 May-19 August 2001, an exhibition devoted to fine artists employing craft techniques.
15. Grayson Perry in conversation with the author, December 18, 2001.
16. Ibid.
17. Ibid.

Louisa Buck, 2002, 'The personal Political Pots of Grayson Perry', extracted from Marjan Boot (in cooperation with Grayson Perry), *Grayson Perry. Guerilla Tactics*, exhibition catalogue, Stedelijk Museum, Amsterdam, Rotterdam: NAI Publishers, pp. 92–101.

Reprinted with the permission of Louisa Buck, Marjan Boot, Stedelijk Museum and NAI Publishers.

SECTION 3.2
IDENTITY AND CERAMICS

Introductory summary

The first text in this section by artist Ruth Park gives an overview of the themes in her figurative ceramic sculptures, which attempt to highlight a 'Eurocentric' or white bias embedded in Australian society. Park discusses a number of her sculptures, which represent the female form to explore her themes.

Aspects of male, as well as cultural identity are brought together in the work of South African artists, Nicholas Hlobo, Clive Sithole and Andile Dyalvane as described by Elizabeth Perrill. These artists reference and subvert cultural rituals and imagery in their works.

Wendy Gers offers a critique of a museum presentation of Kukuli Verlarde's installation of eight sculptures, 'Plunder me Baby', in the Taipei City Yingge Ceramics Museum in Taiwan. This ongoing series of work reflects on colonialism and forms a kind of self-portrait. The pieces also imagine what would happen if pre-Columbian ceramics were to 'wake up' in a museum and what they might feel out of the context in which they were made.

Livingstone and Petrie

45
BODY LANGUAGE: CERAMICS TO CHALLENGE A WHITE WORLD

Ruth Park

Artists who work to a satirical, political or moral theme believe their art can contribute in some way to consciousness raising and change. With an awareness of their intrinsic capacity to touch people, artists can use their exhibited work to challenge, usurp and alter the status quo. My artwork is concerned with highlighting Eurocentric or 'white' bias embedded in Australian society and exposing its impact on others.

Peggy McIntosh argues that being white "... is an invisible knapsack of special provisions, assurances, tools, maps, guides, code books, passports, visas, compass, emergency gear and blank cheques."[1] The term "Whiteness" refers to the historical, social, political and cultural organisation which shapes white people's lives and informs a position of power and dominance.[2] Through my work I hope to contribute to greater community awareness and ultimately positive social change by increasing awareness of the extent these biases encroach on our thinking and our lives.

Lucy Lippard suggests:

> "Artists alone can't change the world. Neither can anybody else, alone. But we can choose to be part of the world that is changing. There is no reason why visual arts should not be able to reflect the social concerns of our day as naturally as novels, plays and music ..."[3]

As my work is intended to critique the power relations within mainstream Australian society, the artworks are directed as much to the general public as they are to an art audience. This factor significantly influenced the style of my work, resulting in a more didactic and unambiguous figurative representation. Stereotypes have also been utilised to aid in communicating this agenda. Stereotypes have routinely functioned within media imagery and language to reinforce and maintain white power.[4] These stereotypes have become an instantly recognisable visual language on which movie characters are based and advertised products promoted. By employing the very language that exploits and reinscribes a dominant white view through my work I am more able to expose and usurp the operation of power. However, this approach is fraught with dangers by increasing the risk of restating and perpetuating typecast images and being misread by some viewers. Whilst mindful of the potential to offend viewers of all races, my approach aimed to use cultural stereotypes to criticise "the very citadels of power."[5] Rather than avoiding such an approach, I chose to directly tackle the inherent difficulties of working with images of race and the prospective audience for which this work was intended.[6]

For example, In My Mind, Under My Skin and the Places In Between, critiques the infiltration and pervasive penetration of white bias into the intimate private spheres of many non-whites' lives, their psyche and the social spaces in which they live. This incursion contributes to undermining a positive self-esteem

Source: © Ruth Park/*The Journal of Australian Ceramics.*

and identity by situating the non-white individual as the 'other' and situating the white person and their experience as the 'norm'.[7]

Many of the art works amplify comments made by women from non-white backgrounds living in Australia who were interviewed as part of a PhD research project at Southern Cross University (2003–2007). This research examined the effects of the over-representation of idealised images of Caucasian women on non-Caucasian women living in Australia. Results revealed the interviewees perceived a negative bias against non-whites through media imagery and visual representations, facilitated through the use of digital manipulation, stereotyping, and physical exclusion and under-representation of non-white women.

They also noted an over-representation of idealised white women in media imagery. This perception was supported by research undertaken by Dianne Sweeney (2001) which documents the over-representation of 'white' women on the front cover of two Australian women's magazines, Marie Claire and Cleo, between September 1995 and October 2000. Sweeney analysed the race of 398 cover-models and found 95.5 percent of Cleo models and 96 percent of Marie Claire models could "be judged to be" white [Caucasian].[8] This was found to be unrepresentative of the multiracial mix within the Australian population which, according to the 1996 Census, found 23.3 percent of the population were overseas-born residents.[9]

In addition to biased media representations, interviewees identified bias in the design, manufacturing and promotion of particular consumer products. These included clothes design, sunglasses and makeup designed for a European body shape and physical structure. These products reinforced many non-whites' sense of having alien status within the Australian community and highlighted a general attitude which failed to consider or appreciate variations in physical features. Interviewees also revealed that various components of women's bodies such as skin colour, hair texture, body size and shape, eye and nose shape were charged with meaning. Some participants first experienced negative stereotyping of body components by certain communities in their country of origin but found this was reinforced upon migrating to Australia where idealised white body images dominate despite multiculturalism.

The topic of a social skin colour hierarchy is explored in works such as Whitewashed and Invisible. Invisible responds to comments by an Aboriginal participant who suggested it was rare to find Aboriginal women in beauty pageants because Aboriginal features diverged 'too far' from the European defined parameters of beauty. This piece comments on their omission from societal images of beauty and through the use of an oppositional image in the form of an Aboriginal beauty pageant winner; I query their absence from this forum. The Makeover and Bad Hair Day deal with body image concerns resulting from the idealisation of the European woman as the universal model of ideal beauty.

The Makeover critiques the brutality involved in many surgical cosmetic procedures. Such surgical intervention is conveyed by the woman from Middle Eastern heritage who is attempting to hammer a nail into her racially specific nose. Rhinoplasty is a popular procedure among Middle Eastern women who desire to change the size and shape of their nose, which they perceive to be too large in comparison to the ideal.[10] Bad Hair Day reveals the preoccupation with straightening frizzy hair, particularly popular among many African women. This frequently involves the application of harsh chemicals to achieve a straighter appearance.

Mirror Mirror comments on the over-representation of idealised images of European women that non-whites are confronted with on a daily basis. Dyer suggests, "White people create the dominant images in the world and don't quite see that they create the world in their image."[11] This piece also responds to comments made by a Chinese participant who, in her mind's eye, perceives herself to be European having blonde hair and blue eyes, often completely forgetting she has an Asian appearance until being abruptly reminded by a reflection in a mirror or shop front window.

The way in which whiteness installs itself as the dominant world view, the standard from which everything else is judged and which has infiltrated every strata of life has been highlighted by the women interviewed.

Listening to and sharing the experiences of those voices marginalised by these biases provided the personal impetus and material to inform this body of work which aspires to social change and believes in the possibility that through the arts we might shake loose entrenched attitudes and forge alternative ways of being.[12] The personal journey accompanying this research has been both challenging and enriching. Throughout this journey I have been forced to confront my own white blindness, and acknowledge that the privileges I enjoy as a white woman result from this cultural domination and they have been achieved at the expense of others. Unearthing the mechanisms for its maintenance will hopefully assist in removing the white blindfold enveloping my own blinkered vision. The process of self-reflexivity attempts to find a space within the gaps; to create room for different ways of thinking, seeing and hoping. As Chambers recounts: "Traversing into the border country, I look into a potentially further space: the possibility of another place, another world, another future,"[13] one which will hopefully embrace diversity and acknowledge the damaging legacy of a Eurocentric heritage.

Notes

1. Peggy McIntosh, White Privilege and Male Privilege, Wesley College Centre on women's working papers series, 1988, p. 189.
2. Ruth Frankenburg, The Social Construction of Whiteness. White Women Race Matters: Routledge, London, 1993, p. 6.
3. Lucy Lippard. Trojan Horses: Activist Power and Power in Art After Modernism: rethinking Representation (New York: The New Museum of Contemporary Art, 1984), p. 344–45.
4. Bell Hooks, Black Looks, Race Representations, Routledge, New York, 1992, p. 2.
5. Art that is not confined to a single context under the control of a market and ruling class taste is much harder to neutralise. And it is often quite effective seen within the very citadels of power it criticizes.
6. Lucy Lippard, "Trojan Horses: activist Power and Power" in Art After Modernism: rethinking Representation (New York: The New Museum of Contemporary Art, 1984), p. 344–45.
7. Cited in Bell Hooks, Black Looks, Race Representations, Routledge, New York, 1992, p. 2.
8. Diana Sweeney, Monochromatism: Representations in Women's Magazines, B. SocSc (Hons) Southern Cross University, Lismore, p. 74–76, 2001.
9. 2.1% of the population were Indigenous although Sweeney's research found only one Indigenous model was depicted on a cover, which represented 0.24% of the total number of cover models. The findings revealed a predisposition towards Caucasians in the selection of models as covers in the women's magazine market which had increased over time and was unrepresentative of Australia's cultural and racial diversity.
10. Iranian woman tend to dislike this racial feature, resulting in an estimated 35,000 rhinoplasty procedures (nose remodelling operations) a year. Scott Peterson, 'In Iran, Search for Beauty Leads to Nose Job', The Christian Science Monitor, 3.9.00. Online: http://www.csmonitor.com/specials/women/mirror/mirror030900.html Accessed 27/11/2001.
11. Richard Dyer, White, Routledge, London, 1997, p. 11.
12. Author: Jennifer Webb, Undoing 'the folded lie': media, art and ethics, New Zealand Journal of Media Studies volume 9, number 1: 'Asian' Media Arts Practice in/and Aotearoa New Zealand. New Zealand Electronic Text Centre, 2005, Wellington.
13. I, Chambers, Migrancy, Culture Identity, Rutledge. 1998.

Reprinted with permission of *The Journal of Australian Ceramics* and the author.

Original Source *The Journal of Australian Ceramics*, Edition 46/1, April 2007, pp. 29–33.

46
RUBBER AND CLAY: SOUTH AFRICAN MATERIAL 'AFTERMODERN'

Elizabeth Perrill

Nicholas Bourriaud described the *altermodern* model as constellations and networks of meaning brought together by the nomad, *homo viator*,[1] a pilgrim in search of truth. In his texts the art world has come to understand there is an international set of 'global nomads,' artists who embody life after the postmodern and create art from networks and shared signs.[2] However, the separation from territory and celebration of displacement, remains a troubling underlying assumption in this self-proclaimed utopian model.[3] By focusing on local meaning and materials, young South African artists offer a subtle challenge to art world jet-setters.

Okwui Enwezor changed Bourriaud's term by one letter and dubbed this new type of artist as a member of the *aftermodern* – those who 'disinherit the violence of colonial modernity.'[4] The growing ability of ceramic artists' to be key players within the global art world side-by-side with peers working in other media can be theorized using Enwezor's *aftermodern*. Utilizing an allusion to Dante's *Inferno*, Enwezor hypothesizes a model in which extant layers of modernity – super-, developing-, specious-, underdeveloped-, or *after-modern* – co-exist simultaneously.[5] Artists flesh-out the possibilities of these *aftermodern* layers with multiplicities of local nuance. Nicholas Hlobo, Clive Sithole, and Andile Dyalvane are members of a South African arts cohort who engage with territories and local meanings, who play with the edges of modernities/post-modernities/the *aftermodern*. Each draws in viewers with aesthetic seduction and then uses linguistic connotations to challenge the viewer and foreground not just African-centered perspectives, but Xhosa, Zulu or local polyglot voices.

Hlobo turns the medium of installation art on its ear and makes it listen to a Xhosa dialect of social development. Sithole creates earthenware works with the materials and symbolism of what African art theorist Sylvester Okwunodu Ogbechie has described as 'indigenous forms of African art whose contemporaneity remains to be theorized.'[6] Dyalvane's stoneware prods at the formation of blended urban/rural identities. Proverbs, metaphors, and material specificity engage close-viewers and plumb these artists' psychological and personal depths.

Rubber and ribbon modernities

Hlobo, a consummate wordsmith, states that linguistic and semiotic interests consistently form the starting point for his creations and traces formative moments in the social-sexual life of Xhosa youth. His solo shows *Izele* (Giving birth), 2006 and *Kwatsiyw'iziko* (Crossing the hearth), 2008 dealt with the acts of intimacy during and prior to birth.[7] 2009's *Umtshotsho* (Gathering) pushed viewers to consider the development of

Source: © Elizabeth Perrill/Correspondence with Richard Dyer at Third Text confirms that copyright is not retained by Third Text because portions of the article have been significantly re-written and re-contextualised.

gender relations and sensuality in young adulthood. Hlobo's works on paper, such as *Umnombo* (Lineage), 2013 connote references to the source of life or the place of one's birth.[8] Each piece takes viewers further into a visual language and metaphor of social and spiritual development.

Hlobo's first two solo exhibitions used relatively obvious physical referents to guide viewers into his iconography. *Dream Catcher* from 2006, constructed from an inner-tube, cut and sewn together with pink ribbon, is at once a phallus, orifice, cliché of an American Indian dream catcher, and/or condom made of rubber and ribbon. It conveys overt references to S&M, the masculine, the feminine, and psychological struggle with the subconscious. Hlobo's sign system was developing; like Joseph Beuys introducing viewers to the significance of animal fat and felt. The predominance of pink and red ribbon, stitching, and embroidery used here are signs for the flesh and blood binding together rubbery skins.

Hlobo's nuance has emerged over several years through materials. Instead of retaining the shape of either an inner-tube or the smooth width of a ribbon, as in *Dream Catcher*, Hlobo's 2009 Standard Bank Young Artist exhibition *Umtshotsho* reflects the artist's growing intimacy with and metaphorical handling of materials. *Umtshotsho's* ornate forms exemplify Hlobo's playful material craftsmanship. All eight individual beings in *Umtshotsho* reach out to the viewer with tentacles; they jiggle and sway when brushed or nudged. Rather than confront a phallus or a condom, viewers explore figures that wiggle and beckon. The rubber that constitutes the figures' flesh is alive; inner-tube rubber and satin ribbons combine with found objects and reproduction colonial furniture in an organic, Baroque manner that encourages exploration.

The word *umtshotsho* refers to a traditional Xhosa youth gathering, a point of departure for the artist to play with adolescence and developing gender identity. At a Xhosa *umtshotsho* youth were historically encouraged to socialize, dance, spar, and practice sexual behaviors such as *ukusoma*, a type of non-penetrative 'thigh-sex'. Hlobo highlights these events as moments loaded with homo- and/or hetero-erotic potential. Yet, as at any party, there are outsiders. The figure and couch component is part of the *Umtshotsho* (Figure 46.1) installation bears the additional title *Izithunzi* (isiXhosa for shadows). The delicate ribbons that stitch together the black, bulging flesh of this 'shadow' spill onto its Victorianate reproduction couch. Ribbon seams and appliqué on the couch blend the sitter and seat, the contemporary youth to post-colonial history. The couch is being consumed by and becoming part of the figure, just as Xhosa culture has taken in and transformed colonial

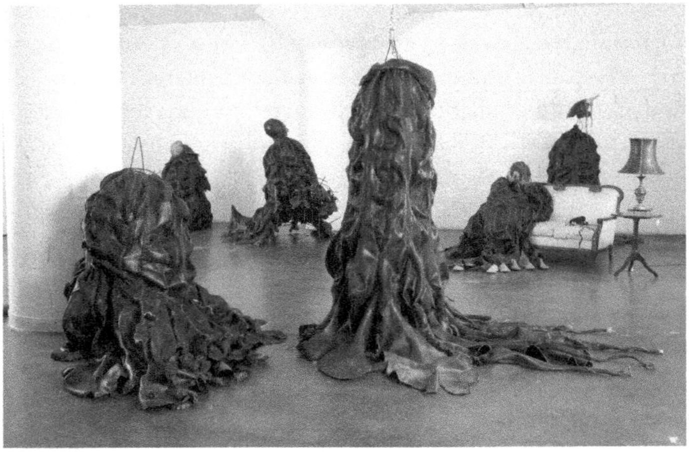

Figure 46.1 Nicholas Hlobo, *Umtshotsho*, 2009, installation with *Izithunzi* and *Kubomvu*, works in progress photographed in the artist's studio. Copyright Nicholas Hlobo, courtesy STEVENSON Cape Town and Johannesburg, photo: John Hodgkiss.

memories and objects as a part of itself. This is a constructed and layered African modernity, the *aftermodern*, as described by Enwezor.

Beyond trans-nationally discernable references to S&M paraphernalia or a cursory understanding of rubber as black flesh, Hlobo also refers to Xhosa rural male nostalgia. For Hlobo and others in his milieu, the patching and reworking of inner-tube rubber by rural men symbolizes the masculine prowess of auto repair. Unexpectedly, the world of car maintenance is woven into the gallery. Indeed, one can see the patches on his purposefully selected recycled rubber, evidence of this history of improvisation during hard times. Hlobo challenges the viewer to delve into ways this material helped construct rural Xhosa masculinity. Speaking of his interest in this material, Hlobo remarked, 'I attribute that to my being a Xhosa man. I think I have great joy of manhood.'[9]

Earthenware masculinities

Ceramic artists are renown for a fetishistic attention to surface and materiality. In the last decade, Clive Sithole, who uses layers of Zulu metaphors and methods in his ceramic creations, has gained some international fame for his coil-built, burnished wares. Though Zulu ceramics have not been well-known for pushing conceptual agendas, the highly imbricated metaphorical relationships that Sithole has developed with this medium bind this art form to the conceptual. In fact, Sithole inhabits a world in which Enwezor's super-, developing-, specious-, underdeveloped-, or *after-modern* abound.

As Sithole's career has developed, he has acquired a grammar of Zulu metaphors related to gender and ancestral respect alongside his mastery of ceramic techniques learned from ceramic doyens such as Nesta Nala, Juliet Armstrong, or Magdelene Odundo. While Hlobo carefully crafts *izinthunzi* spirits and gendered materials into his installation art, Sithole's ceramic medium assumes spiritual and ancestral associations as *a priori*. Zulu beer pots continue to be valued in contemporary Zulu society as highly traditional signifiers used to present sorghum beer to one's ancestors, *amadlozi*. The challenge for Sithole has been to blend these cultural references into his ceramics without allowing them to completely dictate his aesthetic choices.

Zulu beer pots that have historically been made as a women's art form. Sithole's swelling convex vessels often bear the traditional radial symmetries and burnished smooth surfaces that are a part of this gendered tradition. And, as a man working in a historically female-gendered medium, Sithole faces questions from both Zulu-speaking and Anglophone audiences concerning his gender identity. While Hlobo overtly discusses his sexuality as a gay man, Sithole actively obfuscates or elides direct inquires on the topic of his sexuality through avoidance and humor. Simultaneously, he emphasizes his active participation in normative masculine gender roles. As the first-son of a first-son, Sithole bears considerable responsibility in his father's lineage. He has funded costly spiritual events for his family that required the slaughter of both goats and cattle. Sithole maneuvers the historically pastoralist world of Zulu masculinity and the 'great joy of manhood', mentioned by Hlobo. Stating 'My pots are my cattle,'[10] Sithole blends gender metaphors, ceramic femininities and masculine wealth in cattle, just as he blends locally mined Zulu clays with commercially milled stock.

Gendered modernities are layered in Sithole's artistic production alongside his material specificity. For instance, vessels in Sithole's first exhibition in 2001 featured images of cattle and cow horns. He made ties to pastoralism explicit by entitling this exhibition, 'Journey of the Herdboy'. His combination of gendered imagery was obvious to Zulu audiences or those familiar with Zulu cultural values: the cattle that symbolize wealth and masculine success were emblazoned upon his vessels. Yet deeper analysis reveal that this is simply the first layer of connotations worked into these forms. Sithole's imagery depicted cattle in a more representational manner distinct from women's decorative motifs. His works were marked as derived from, but not mimetically traditional. Sithole was aware that scholars had hypothesized that pots decorated with horn motifs and raised bumps on vessels might simultaneously symbolize scarification on women's bodies and the abundance of cattle in a homestead. Sithole was layering his masculine identity on a women's medium with the understanding that he was echoing and amplifying the messages of masculine wealth that were already present in historical ceramic wares.

In a work from 2008, Sithole combines the motif of cattle with rectangular lugs, abbreviated handles, on the sides of vessels that reference men's milk pail carving. Fluent in Zulu, Sotho, and English, Sithole shares Hlobo's love of language and cultural nuance. He is aware of the fact that *amasumpa,* the word for the raised bumps usually used to depict horns on Zulu ceramic vessels, is also the word for the lugs on the side of milk pails carved by men.[11] Thus, Sithole marks his work with iconographic layers of masculine and feminine double entendre through his inclusion of masculine *amasumpa* lug handles. Sithole uses allusion and inference to keep viewers guessing about the gender ambiguity implied by his work.

Sithole's National Arts Council award-winning vessel of 2009 broke with an important formal norm of Zulu ceramics, the feminine convex beer pot shape. Instead, this vessel featured an abruptly concave angle, a technically demanding exploration of form. The abrupt angles of this vessel expose the work to risks of cracking. Though, Sithole is careful to maintain some aspects of his material's strong traditional associations and is playing with these boundaries. The emphatic reference to Zulu culture retained in this work is its burnished surface and flame marks added in a barrel firing after electric kiln firing. The nearly fetishized act of compacting the surface of a clay vessel with a smooth object prior to firing is a hallmark of Zulu ceramics and is obsessed over by artists and collectors alike. The skin of this vessel continues to fetishize surfaces, even as Sithole's work encourages a blurring of binaries in Zulu ceramic production and perception.

Stoneware skins and structures

Another South Africa ceramist whose work challenges pre-conceptions of local meaning versus international appeal is Majolandile (Andile) Dyalvane, of Imiso Ceramics. Dyalvane has been a keen observer of international trends since his first arts workshop abroad at a Danish ceramics center in 2001 and has skyrocketed through national and international design-world ranks with international exhibitions and residencies include the Milan Furniture Fair in Italy (2008), Design Days Dubai in the United Arab Emirates (2013), the Yingge Ceramics Museum in Taiwan (2014), as well as Design Miami and Design Miami/Basel (2104 and 2015).[12] With Dyalvane's inclusion in the Vitra Design Museum exhibition *Making Africa: A Continent of Contemporary Design,* curated by Amelie Klein along with Consulting Curator Okwui Enwezor, one might say he has arrived in the ranks of the global nomad, Bourriaud's *homo viator.*

But this would be selling short the grounded observations that are pivotal in Dyalvane's success and continuing innovations. Ceramic headrests, inspired by Xhosa traditional carvings, were major works in his Nelson Mandela Metropolitan University graduation show in 2003 and later acquired by the South African National Gallery. Soon thereafter, Dyalvane's commercially successful ceramic production focused on the theme of *ukuqatshulwa,* the Xhosa practice of bodily scarification in which the skin is cut and then rubbed with medicinal substances. Dyalvane uses slicing and inserting techniques to connote spiritual healing and enrichment. Unlike Sithole, Dylavane's claybodies, slip-cast, slab formed, and coil-built, do not carry the heady connotations of locally mined materials. Rather, aesthetic choices compliment Dyalvane's Xhosa-based symbolism, "Reds are symbolic of traditional ceremonies and rituals," while "whites are symbolic of new beginnings, spiritual refreshment and purity," Dyalvane explains.[13] Dyalvane even takes his vessels back to his rural home in Qobo-Qobo, Eastern Cape province to serve traditional beer to family and friends.

In a twist on the homogenization that has come of biennale successes for the first wave of Bourriaud's *altermodern* art-nomads, the flurry of international attention inspires an even greater advocacy for local community by Dyalvane and Imiso co-founder Zizipho Poswa. Even the name Imiso is derived from an isiXhosa word meaning "for our tomorrows," implying that the team invests back into their community. Dyalvane and several other South African designers have opened the Imbadu Collective, a name drawing on the term for "a gathering" in isiXhosa. This design collective draws on a "shared experience and background," focused on "being black and coming from this community and the culture."[14] Dyalvane is part of a synergy of creative professionals interested in pulling together in defense of community, building a tighter set of sign systems and experiences than the global nomad.

To this end, Dyalvane has turned his ceramics-based creative energy toward his urban environment, breaking connotations perpetuated during apartheid that black South Africans should only find a sense of belonging in rural spaces. His most recent sculptural works include several sculptures inspired by the view from the Imiso Studio's view of Woodstock, a Cape Town harbor town turned gentrified arts district. In 2006 this view included shipping containers, houses constructed early as the 1880s, and a patchwork of buildings that grew up from the 1950s to 1980s; this neighborhood survived apartheid divisions and miraculously remained a mixed-race "grey" zone while other areas were demolished. Dyalvane's sculptures reflect upon urban gentrification, even as he and his young peers have eased the way for trendy restaurants and "trendy, eclectic 20-somethings armed with lattes."[15] With this recent work Dyalvane questions the changing demographics in what has become one of the world's destination cities.

Conclusion

Nicholas Hlobo, Clive Sithole, and Andile Dyalvane are all deeply informed by cultural nuance and media specificity. Their works reveal ambiguities to the viewer who cares to listen and learn about the local. All imply that the onus is on the viewer to move beyond stereotypes of black masculinity or gender roles, urban or rural identities; the challenge is laid to read the layers of Xhosa or Zulu existences, layers of modernities and contemporary lives. These award-winning, thirty-something artists challenge viewers to see that contemporary artists can retain symbolism that expresses Xhosa or Zulu meanings while appealing to the trans-national viewers at the Tate Modern, a Soho Gallery, or Art Basel Miami Beach. Each demands that the viewer come halfway, with an eye that is knowledgeable and informed, patient and interested in subtle South African materialities.

Notes

1. It seems that Bourriaud undervalues that *homo viator's* search for hope is most often found in *agape,* a thoughtful love of mankind. The key in this new age is not found merely in the act of nomadism or a celebration of the disembodied network. The root and the motivation for artistic pilgrimage lies in the goal of connection. In a humanist understanding of *homo viator,* the development of self involves responsibility, which can remain highly engaged with place and community; one must not 'confuse hope and ambition, for they are not of the same spiritual dimension'. Gabriel Marcel, Homo Viator, Harper & Brothers, New York, 1962, pp. 16–21.

2. This chapter re-engages with the *altermodern* and *aftermodern* concepts originally discussed in Elizabeth Perrill, "South African Rubber and Clay," Third Text vol 26, iss 5, no 118, Sept 2012, pp. 503–514; Nicholas Bourriaud, *AlterModern: Tate Triennial,* Tate Publishing, London, 2009, p. 13
3. Marcus Verhagen, 'The Nomad and the Altermodern: The Tate Triennial', *Third Text,* vol 23 iss 6, Nov 2009, pp. 803–812.
4. Okwui Enwezor, 'Modernity and Postcolonial Ambivalence,' in Nicholas Bourriaud, ed, *AlterModern: Tate Triennial,* Tate Publishing, London, 2009, p. 39.
5. Okwui Enwezor, 'Specious Modernity: Speculations on the End of Postcolonial Utopia', Tate Triennial 2009 Prologue 1, Tate Channel, 24 April 2008, http://channel.tate.org.uk/media/31067749001.
6. S. Owunodu Ogbechie, 'The Curator as Culture Broker: A Critique of the Curatorial Regime of Okwui Enwezor', 16 June 2010, The Zeleza Post: Informed News and Commentary on the Pan African World, Popular Culture (blog) http://www.zeleza.com/blogging/popular-culture/curator-culture-broker-critique-curatorial-regime-okwui-enwezor.
7. Mark Gevisser, 'Under Covers, Out in the Open: Nicholas Hlobo and Utshotsho', in *Nicholas Hlobo,* Sophie Perryer, ed, Cape Town, Michael Stevenson, 2009, p. 11.
8. Nick Shepherd and Steven Robins, *New South African Key Words,* Ohio University Press, 2008, p. 149.
9. Quotation from Mark Gevisser, 'Under Covers, Out in the Open: Nicholas Hlobo and Utshotsho', in *Nicholas Hlobo.* Sophie Perryer, ed, Cape Town, Michael Stevenson, 2009, p. 15.
10. Clive Sithole, Artist Interview, Durban, South Africa, 5 Nov 2006.
11. Juliet Armstrong, Gavin Whitelaw and Dieter Reusch, 'Pots that talk, *izinkamba ezikhulumayo*', *Southern African Humanities,* Dec 2008, vol 20, p. 533.
12. Staff Reporter, "Arts: 'Chameleon artist' takes on the world," *Business Day Live,* 8 Aug. 2012.; Staff Reporter, "Cape Town Ceramist, Andile Dyalvane Wins 2015 Southern Guild Foundation Icon Award," Arts, Culture and Entertainment, *Africa News Wire*, 16 Mar 2015.
13. Megan Diener, "Andile Dyalvane: Artists get all fired up," Design Magazine Blog, 12 Aug 2012, http://designmagazine.co/wordpress/2012/08/12/zizipho-poswaartists-get-all-fired-up/.
14. Khumo Sebambo, "Working hand-in-hand," Design Indaba, 20 Feb 2015, http://www.designindaba.com/articles/creative-work/working-hand-hand-0.
15. Andile Dyalvane, quoted in "Imiso Ceramics: Docks table," Making Africa: A Continent of Contemporary Design, an Exhibition of the Vitra Design Museum and the Guggenheim Bilbao, http://makingafrica.net/2015/04/featured-workimiso-ceramics-docks-table/.

Printed with the permission of the author.

47

PLUNDER ME BABY – KUKULI VELARDE AND THE CERAMICS OF TAIWAN'S FIRST NATIONS: VIRTUAL VENTRILOQUISM AS ARTICULATED IN THE 2014 TAIWAN CERAMICS BIENNALE

Wendy Gers

Abstract

This essay investigates Kukuli Velarde's intervention in the Yingge Ceramics Museum's permanent collection display during the 2014 Taiwan Ceramics Biennale, *Terra Nova: Critical Currents/Contemporary Ceramics*. The ensuing analysis is based on observations of the permanent collection; discussions with the artist and the Yingge Ceramics Museum's exhibition staff; correspondence with Taiwanese academics; and a curatorial project that engaged with post-colonial discourse. The finely calibrated installation of eight sculptures from Velarde's ongoing *Plunder Me Baby* series interrogated the Yingge Museum's problematic construction of Taiwanese ceramics history, and drew attention to the representation of the ceramics traditions of local indigenous peoples. The concept of Virtual Ventriloquism was developed in response to an analysis of the artistic agency associated with Velarde's intervention. Finally, the author advocates for the development of more sophisticated curatorial methodologies that involve the co-production of exhibition scripts for historical and contemporary presentation of Aboriginal material culture, with the representatives of those communities.

Key words

Post colonialism, Virtual Ventriloquism, museum intervention, Yingge Ceramics Museum, Taiwan Ceramics Biennale, first nations, scenography, agency.

Kukuli Velarde's installation of eight sculptures from her ongoing series, *Plunder Me Baby,* in the permanent collection display of the New Taipei City Yingge Ceramics Museum, Taiwan (YCM) was a key work in the 'Post-colonial Identities' sub-group[1] of the 'Glocal Identities' theme[2] in the 2014 Taiwan Ceramics Biennale, *Terra Nova: Critical Currents/Contemporary Ceramics*, (TCB). As the first ever intervention in the permanent collection, it offered visitors an original viewing experience, and facilitated a new way of engaging with the historical narrative presented by the YCM's permanent display.

While in recent years, Kukuli Velarde (b. 1962, Peru) has received considerable acclaim for her ceramic sculptures,[3] it is important to note that her oeuvre is far more expansive[4] and includes written texts about her work. An autoethnographic abrogated[5] 'manifesto' accompanying the *Plunder Me Baby* series contextualizes

Source: © Wendy Anne Gers.

the work, and explains its intentions. After an introductory eulogy to the rich cultural diversity and pioneering achievements[6] of pre-Columbian[7] civilizations, Velarde contrasts her ancestors' cultural universe that was 'made entirely in their image, and after their own likeness' (2014b:1) to that of contemporary subjugated peoples. Velarde suggests that the latter have lost two key resources. Firstly, various forms of artistic expression were modified, diminished or discontinued. The second major depleted resource is personal dignity, an asset that is degraded by endemic local racism.[8] Indigenous and mixed-race people, who constitute the bulk of the Peruvian population, are 'ashamed of their own physical features', and feel 'ugly' next to the Western norms of beauty (2014b:2). Velarde notes 'We became invisible within our own landscape, not anymore the center of our universe, always trying to imitate, recreate, and follow as an attempt to survive …' (ibid). Pratt describes this condition of existential malaise in colonial and many former colonial societies, where 'One is forced to be a second-class member of a club in which membership is not optional …' and where cultural 'unease becomes a source of creativity and experimentalism, as well as exasperation' (2008:226). No doubt motivated by this exasperation, Velarde has developed a sophisticated artistic project grounded in a form of theatrical storytelling.

The *Plunder Me Baby* series offers a polyphonic and palimpsestuous script that responds to some of the negative consequences of colonialism, including plunder of cultural artifacts, violence, racism and the lack of affirmative models for corporal[9] diversity. For example, the plunder of South American artifacts is alluded to in both the nomenclature of the series and formally as each work resembles an iconic pre-Columbian *chef-d'œuvre*. Yet, these historical allusions are immediately subverted as each work features Velarde's 'native-looking' face. These self-portraits express a wide variety of dramatic sentiments ranging from grimaces and pouts, to light-hearted teasing via the blowing of kisses to the viewer. Velarde includes her face in order to 'absorb' and counter the pain of this violent history of plunder. These animated self-portraits also serve as an entrée into the vocabulary of racial slurs used in the bilingual (English/Spanish) titles of each piece, as Velarde 'didn't want it to be perceived as the slurs were being directed to others' (Velarde 2014a, 2015). The theatrical dialogues in Velarde's augmented titles resemble exaggerated melodramatic micro-scenarios for soap-operas. Characters issue demeaning orders and insults (that stress popular racial, gender and class stereotypes), and others respond or evade, in a glib and subversive *tête-à-tête*.

Velarde explained her desire to stage her work within the permanent collection of the YCM when initially contacted about the TCB:

> … I always wonder what would happen if pre-Columbian ceramics in any museum of the world were to wake up from centuries of sleep, what would they think or feel, out of context and stripped of meaning? What would it be for them to be prisoners in a beautiful display? I imagine them in despair, in pain, in fear, and overcoming their defeat; owning themselves, not anymore victims but witnesses of history, transcending their own existence. (2014b:2).

Having previously observed the YCM's problematic display of Aboriginal pottery, the significance of Velarde's request, and the subversive nature of the project, was immediately apparent to me. After lengthy negotiations,[10] the YCM authorized this project.[11]

Before analysing some of the key elements of Velarde's intervention, it is necessary to consider the structure of the YCM's permanent display of the history of Taiwanese ceramics, located in four adjoining halls (numbered 201 to 204) on the second floor. Hall 201 presents an overview of the introduction of glazed ceramics by the Wu family of Chinese immigrants in Yingge from about 1804. It surveys the rise of Yingge as the centre of the Taiwanese ceramics industry, through the nineteenth and twentieth centuries, and includes section that focuses on the Japanese colonial period (1895-1945). Hall 202 considers the production of sanitary and industrial wares in Yingge and concludes with a display of intricate and colourful artistic *chef d'œuvres* by Taiwanese Masters from the 1980s and early 1990s. Hall 203 presents the ceramics of Taiwan's Austronesian-speaking first peoples, in an eerily lit space. The second floor concludes with a dazzling ode to the marvels of industrial ceramics in hall 204.[12]

Poetically entitled 'Shuttle Through Time,' hall 203 primarily presents indigenous ceramics in shard form. The limited English[13] labels fail to elucidate the history of this ancient tradition, which is still practiced.[14] Staff explained to me that the few complete pieces in hall 203 were recent reproductions of ancient Aboriginal forms that the YCM commissioned for educational purposes (Chiang 2015). Despite the recognition of contemporary Aboriginal art and design practices by leading Taiwanese cultural institutions since 1998 (Harrell & Lin 2006:9), there is a no acknowledgement of these practices in the YCM. Visitors to hall 203 have the overwhelming experience of entering a subterranean chamber, as the walls of this supposed 'shuttle' or 'time capsule' are coated with a gritty surface of gravel and sand, indicating different layers of black and grey coloured strata. This tenebrous scenography in conjunction with the lack of contextual information, gives the impression of a mystical or mythical archaeological site, for an anonymous community that has – like Pompeii – experienced a grave catastrophe.

In addition to the evocative room title and sinister scenography, the display of Aboriginal ceramics in hall 203 fails to engage with contemporary initiatives that encourage authorities in 'New World' nations[15] to collaborate respectfully with indigenous communities in heritage projects associated with their past or present. Furthermore, this display ignores national and regional East Asian political endeavors to facilitate 'Island' diplomacy that harnesses indigenous peoples' heritage to foster peaceful alliances among Pacific nations with communities that speak Austronesian languages (Blundell 2011:76). Rather, the permanent collection is a somewhat out-dated incarnation of the YCM as an expression of a specific Taiwanese national ideology that asserts a unique local and national identity, as expressed in a modern ceramic culture based on the the creative reappropriation of Chinese, Japanese and Western traditions and influences. Inaugurated in 1990, the YCM is a county-level museum that was primarily intended to reinforce the commercial activities of Yingge (Chinese) artists and artisans via local exhibitions of their work. It was also intended to facilitate exposure to the international ceramics community, develop tourism and reinforce cultural diplomacy (Muyard 2009:405,407,409,410,412). This role has not evolved significantly since its founding, although the TCB is currently a key event in the 'Cultural New Taipei City' project that presents international cultural events to local residents (Chu 2014).

Velarde's sculptures were displayed within and adjacent to halls 201, 203 and 203. The intervention was accompanied by a bilingual (English and Chinese) explanatory pamphlet. Entitled 'Wanted: Missing and Dangerous,' it invited visitors to embark on a 'treasure hunt' for these mischievous aliens. Commencing in hall 201, the serpentine vessel, *Cholibiris Bicephalus Echidna, The Brown Centipede, Bonita pero peligrosa, como te gustan … Nazca III, Peru AD 400-600*, was installed in a *trompe-l'œil* recessed niche adjacent to a historical Japanese urinal. The title with its sadistic (possibly sadomasochistic) reference to dangerous pleasures clearly set the tone for the ensuing *parcours*. A second work, *Chola de Mierda. Resentida social, socially resentful, she believes she is an equal. Dismissible. Moche, Peru, AD 200*, was perched on an upper shelf of a vitrine displaying eclectic and often poorly-modeled Taiwanese export *bibelots* from the 1950s to the 1970s in hall 201. The title and location of this work communicated powerfully about the international mobility of cultural artifacts, issues of social inclusion and exclusion, and the impossibility of social justice. The two works installed in hall 202[16] engaged in a dialogue around post-colonial racism and gendered sexual voyeurism. This dialogue was augmented by their finely calibrated integration within the meta-text of the permanent collection.

Hall 203, the nexus of Velarde's intervention, contained four works; two within and two were located in the adjacent flanking passages.[17] The initial two sculptures were dramatically lit and placed at eye level, with no protective covers, so as to directly engage with the public. In a corner of hall 203, *Pacharaca Pacharaqueandose Tranquila, tranquila …* was grouped with a series of formally similar, round vessels; yet the head and upper torso of Velarde's sculpture was contemptuously turned to face a side wall. The visitor was forced to walk around the work to discover a pouting, frustrated expression, which was indicative of a greater general malaise within this display. The apogee of Velarde's intervention was the dramatically lit, spectacular, insolent, white ghostly 'monster' with outstretched arms and open paws, *Longa Gatuna, Una Fierecita, Más le Pegas, más te quiere! purrrrrr. … Tamaco/Tolita, Colombia/Ecuador. 300 BC- AD 300.* (Illus. 1), was located in the center of hall 203. It poetically embodied the perturbed, empty-handed, roaming 'spirits' of contemporary first nations artists in this exclusionary narrative. *Longa Gatuna …* is lost in time, a tragic-comic runt, he is 'all bark and no bite.' His story is one of a pithy bravado that fails to hide his vulnerability. There is no supine pity or pious cheerleaders among Velarde's band of eight time fantastic time travelers, who epitomize a diasporic state of 'transcendental homelessness' (Said 1992: xxxiv).[18]

Velarde's intervention ruptures the hegemonic narrative of the permanent collection, but it does not speak for or of the Taiwanese first people, or directly address the problematics of the permanent display. Her sculptures produce agency in terms of affording the post-colonial subject the ability or the means to initiate action in engaging or resisting this exclusionary narrative (Ashcroft 1994), most notably via a strategy that I have called Virtual[19] Ventriloquism.[20] This term embraces both the content and tone of the scripted voice, which is characterized by a drole humour and mimicry[21] and the theatrical context. The latter is over-determined by its *spectacular* scenographic language consisting of a syntax of internal technical structural elements and ordering devices, such as lighting, texts, images, models, sound, colour, architecture etc. Recent advances in Speech Act Theory (Cooren 2010:131,144) suggest (additional) mediating contextual elements including people (visitors), the architecture, administrative and social settings, co-determine or co-define spoken agency by adding, emphasizing, subtracting or invalidating meanings.

In *Plunder Me Baby* this Virtual Ventriloquism is enacted on both a literal and metaphorical manner. On a literal level, the association with the ventriloquist's puppet is reinforced by the human scale of the sculpture's highly animated faces, and the diminutive toy-like appearance of the respective bodies. Like the ventriloquist's puppet, there is an absurd disconnect between the vivacious face, and the detached, static body. The Virtual Ventriloquist metaphor offers more potential than a mere mimic as it speaks 'in the name of' ancient native people of South America, and is *animated* by the various insolent characters that Velarde is invoking. Via its absurd and artificial construction, the ventriloquist effigy acts as a prosthetic device for a *mise-en-scene* of a lively narrative that merges fact and fiction, suspends disbelief and transports viewers into Foucaultian heterotopic spaces of consumption, contemplation and fantasy that have multiple layers of meaning and/or relationships to other spaces and places (Foucault 1984). It is this sense of time travelling that enables spectators to imagine alternative realities and other *modes opératoire* for the representation of the art and culture of indigenous peoples of Taiwan and South America, in the YCM and beyond.

In conclusion, this article has analysed the intervention of eight works from Kukuli Velarde's *Plunder Me Baby* series within the permanent collection display of the YCM during the 2014 TCB. The intervention served as a platform to interrogate different aspects of the YCM's presentation of Taiwanese ceramics history. The author notes that hall 203 fails to engage with contemporary endeavors to valorize Aboriginal culture on a local and regional level. Furthermore, the permanent collection reiterates an ideological bias that blurs specific local Yingge history with national history, to the detriment of Aboriginal ceramics, which are presented in a manner that suggests they are the product an extinct people. A theoretical model of the Virtual Ventriloquist was developed as a means to explore the agency afforded by the theatrical nature of Velarde's work, in association with the museum's dramatic scenographic language, and other mediating contextual elements.

It is hoped that the legacy of Velarde's insolent and jubilatory band of time-travelers is reinforced by this article. However, the aim of this article is not merely to draw attention the YCM's historical narrative of ceramics in Taiwan. Rather, it attempts to facilitate an awareness of the need to develop a set of guidelines or 'best practices' for exhibition scripts for historical presentations of the material culture of indigenous peoples. The author advocates a move away from a 'plunder' display model to a more just, substantive, affirmative and contemporary model that is co-produced with the indigenous peoples in 'New World' nations.

Post-script

I wish to reiterate the significance of this intervention. It was clear from the outset that this intervention was a highly politically charged disruption of the permanent display within the YCM. Museum staff were both gracious and courageous in granting this liberty to a pair of foreign women. The success of this work, in combination with other innovative installations, and the Museum's excellent education and out-reach programs, resulted in over 650 000 visitors to the Biennale which ran from May to October 2014. This is a record in terms of visitors to the YCM, and possibly an international record for ceramics biennales.

In late 2014 and early 2015, exhibition hall 203 was partially renovated. A 'layer' of modern and/or contemporary ceramics made by Han Chinese artists was placed on the upper glass shelf of many display units. These works stand above the Aboriginal shards and works, and supposedly denote a sense of the layering of history. In addition, Aboriginal ceramics are introduced through interactive games and films on large screens (Chiang 2015). But, the wall surface remains unchanged. The problematic reading of Taiwanese ceramics history, to my mind, has simply been compounded. While aiming to express the multiple layers of Taiwan's multicultural and post-colonial history, the layering strategy relegates Aboriginal ceramics visually and symbolically to the lower rung. However, the educational potential of the newly introduced interactive games and videos is significant, as, in the absence of a meaningful historical or contemporary collections, these devices have the capacity to offer a more complete overview of Aboriginal cultures and ceramics histories. However, despite these renovations, the overall structure of the first three halls remains relatively incoherent in terms the development of a sense of chronology or a display that is affirmative and valorizing of Aboriginal traditions.

While this article is critical of an aspect of the YCM's permanent collection, this should in no way be perceived as detracting from the quality of other parts of the permanent display (notably the permanent display on the first floor), or the dynamic reputation of the YCM, with its ambitious international Biennales, extraordinarily successful education and out-reach programs, vibrant exhibition program, and respected local and international artist-in-residence programs.

Finally, I wish to thank Kukuli Velarde, Dr. Frank Muyard (Assistant Professor, National Central University, Taiwan), Dr Elizabeth Perrill (Associate Professor, University of North Carolina at Greensboro, USA) and Chiang Shuling (YCM) for their comments on previous drafts of this essay.

Technical notes

1. The terms Aboriginal, First Nation and indigenous peoples are used interchangeably.
2. Individuals are named in accordance with their respective cultural conventions. Taiwanese individuals presented by family name and then first name.

Notes

1. Other artists included in this thematic grouping in the 2014 TCB were Clementina van der Walt, South Africa; and Lee Yong-ming, Taiwan.
2. Within the Glocal Identities theme, other sub-themes included 'Cultural Identities' and the 'Post-Industrial Landscape'. Other thematic groupings in the 2014 TCB included 'Shattered, Upcycled & Recycled Ceramics'; '3D & CNC Ceramics' and 'Digital Materialities'.
3. Velarde won the prestigious Gold Prize at the 2013 World Ceramic Biennale Korea, Icheon World Ceramic Center, Gyeonggi, South Korea.
4. Velarde's oeuvre includes large oil paintings, drawing installations, video, performances as well as sculpture in other media.
5. The term Abrogation 'refers to the rejection by post-colonial writers of a normative concept of 'correct' or 'standard' English used by certain classes or groups, and of the corresponding concepts of inferior 'dialects' or 'marginal variants' (Ashcroft, Griffiths & Tiffin 2007:3,4).
6. Velarde cites the architectural, engineering, agricultural and the medical arenas as exemplifying this technical prowess.
7. This term refers to the period preceding the American voyages of the European explorer, Christopher Columbus (1451-1506), in 1492. It spans the period from the original settlement in the Upper Paleolithic period to European colonization during the Early Modern period.
8. Velarde explains, 'In a country where most have indigenous roots, discrimination against ourselves is palpable in attitudes and words, often found in assumptions and beliefs that are never questioned' (2014b:2).
9. The term 'corporal' is used as a substitute for 'ethnic' which, to my mind has cultural connotations, and may also have covert racist associations.
10. Staff members of YCM were not familiar with the practice of interventions within the permanent collection and argued that the Biennale should be contained on the third floor and within the entrance foyer. They argued that it should not 'contaminate' the permanent collection as some visitors would be confused or frustrated.
11. This permission was conditional. None of the works in the permanent display were to be moved or removed. This meant that the installation required extensive advance preparation and extremely creative responses as Verlarde's works are relatively large in size. The artist was supplied with ground plans, photos and descriptions of halls 201-204. She designed the installation over a period of 3 months, in close dialogue and with the curatorial team, Yu Gillian Jia-ling (TCB Administrator), Chiang Shuling (TCB Manager), Lin Ching-Mae (Head of Exhibitions) and I.
12. Hall 204 is light and airy, and conveys an overtly futuristic impression with sleek floor-to-ceiling stainless steel display units that contain objects and explanatory films relating to industrial ceramics including dental, electrical, automotive applications. This hall also contains interactive displays that focus on various technical characteristics of ceramics.
13. I note that the bulk of YCM visitors are Chinese-speaking, and that the Chinese labels are most certainly more complete that the English labels.
14. From approximately 6000 BP, Taiwan's Pre-Austronesian Neolithic ancestors transported ceramics from the Southeast of China, and rapidly produced ceramics locally. These first nations peoples are are associated with the Austronesian family of languages that were used as a lingua-franca for trade and expansion in East and South Eastern Asia, from approximately 6000 years ago. The roughly 1200 Austronesian Languages are currently practiced across the Pacific, the islands of South-East Asia (Philippines, Indonesia, Malaysia) and in some Indian Ocean islands including Madagascar (Blundell 2011:76–78).
15. 'New World' nations are countries where the local indigenous people have experienced a history of colonization and subjugation, and was first used in a Taiwanese context by Muyard (2015).
16. In hall 202, *Bien Torreja es esta Chuta, No te vaya a cagar! Don't pay attention to her cojudeces, Nazca phase III Peru AD 500* was installed high up so that it glared down at the spectators. *India Patarrajada. She will do all the*

acrobacies the Master orders, pero no esperes que te quiera mucho ... Tlatilco/Olmec, Mexico. 1200-800 BC, is based on a piece known popularly as the 'Contortionist.' It evokes sexual objectification and erotic voyeurism by placing the work's naked bust and exposed genitals in front of a large mirror, among a row of colourful Modern vases by Taiwanese Masters. The work is conveys a paradoxical confidence and physical ease in what would otherwise seem to see in an uncomfortable acrobatic position.

17. *Desperate House-help, Cha que drama queen la serrana ésta. Cupisnique Peru, 1800-600 BC*, was placed at the entrance to hall 203. The final work in the series, *Care' Huaco 'ta Cariñosa, Fishy, fishy. Do not trust, te va a dar de macanazos. Nazca phase III Peru, AD 500*, depicts a faux mermaid that blows a mischievous kiss at the spectator. It was installed in a niche that offered a spectacular view across the light, airy, entrance foyer of the Museum and the exterior cascades and pond, and hinted at the frustrated situation of a mermaid out of water.
18. Said defines this state of transcendental homelessness as an 'unaccommodated, essentially expatriate or diasporic forms of existence ...' (2002: xxxiv).
19. The term virtual is used to imply a certain essentialism, and not 'digital' or related to information technology.
20. The term ventriloquist is used in a superficial manner within post-colonial studies to refer to the problem of metropolitan researchers 'speaking for' their non-metropolitan subjects. This article proposes another configuration of the term, which effectively refers to the theatrical, performative, and contextual elements of a ventriloquist's show, where the orator is of a non-metropolitan origin, and speaking about non-metropolitan conditions.
21. Mimicry has had lots of mileage in post-colonial studies, and Bhabha notes that it involves speaking with a 'forked tongue' (153) which produces a menacing 'double vision', that discloses 'the ambivalence of colonial discourse [and] also disrupts its authority ... [and] ... alienates the modality and normality of those dominant discourses in which they emerge as "inappropriate" colonial subjects' (155). Bhabha's analysis fails to recognize that mimicry involves a physical and psychological context that can augment or alternatively, can invalidate this discourse.

Bibliography

Ashcroft, Bill. 1994. 'Interpolation and Post-Colonial Agency', *New Literatures Review*. 28–29: 176–189.

Ashcroft, Bill.; Gareth Griffiths & Helen Tiffin. 2007. *Post colonial studies: the key concepts*. 2nd ed. New York: Routledge.

Bhabha, Homi. Of Mimicry and Man: The Ambivalence of Colonial Discourse. In Cooper, Frederick & Ann Laura Stoler (eds). 1997. *Tensions of empire : colonial cultures in a bourgeois world*. Berkeley: University of California Press. pp. 152–162.

Blundell, David. 2011. Taiwan Austronesian Language Heritage: Connecting Pacific Island Peoples: Diplomacy and Values. International Journal of Asia-Pacific Studies, *IJAPS*. Vol. 7, No. 1 (January 2011), pp. 75–91. http://web.usm.my/ijaps/articles/IJAPS-7%281%29-Art4-75-91.pdf Consulted 26/04/2015.

Chiang, Shuling. 2015. Unpublished email correspondence and photos. 27 May, 01, 17, 18 June 2015.

Chu, Eric Liluan. 2014. Mayor's Preface. In: Gers, Wendy (et al.) 2014. *Terra Nova: critical trends / contemporary ceramics. Catalogue of the Taiwan Ceramics Biennale*. New Taipei City: YCM. p.5.

Cooren, François. 2010. Figures of communication and dialogue: Passion, ventriloquism and incarnation. *Intercultural Pragmatics*. 7-1. pp. 131–145.

Foucault, Michel (1984) Of Other Spaces: Utopias and Heterotopias. From: Architecture /Mouvement/ Continuité. In: October, 1984; pp. 1–9. http://web.mit.edu/allanmc/www/foucault1.pdf Consulted 10 April 2015.

Harrell, Stevan & Lin Yu-shih. 2006. Aesthetics and Politics in Taiwan's Aboriginal Contemporary Arts. Paper delivered at the NATSA Annual Conference, University of California, Santa Cruz, 3 July. http://faculty.washington.edu/stevehar/NATSA%20aboriginal%20arts.pdf Consulted 20 May 2015.

Muyard, Frank. 2015. Comparativism and Taiwan studies: analyzing Taiwan in/out of context, or Taiwan as an East Asian New World society. In: Shih Shu-mei and Liao Ping-hui (eds). *Comparatizing Taiwan*. London: Routledge. pp. 13–32.

Muyard, Frank. 2009. Taiwan Ceramics as a Mirror of Taiwan History and its National Culture Shift: The Yingge Ceramics Museum and the Institutionalization of a New Taiwanese Artistic Tradition. In: Frank Muyard, Liang-Kai Chou and Serge Dreyer (eds). *Objects, Heritage and Cultural Identity*. Nantou (Taiwan), Taiwan Historica. pp. 389–419.
Pratt, Mary Louise. 2008. *Imperial eyes: travel writing and transculturation*. 2nd ed. New York: Routledge.
Said, E. 2002. *Reflections on exile*. Cambridge, Mass: Harvard University Press.
Velarde, K. 2014.a. Unpublished interview with the author, Philadelphia, 31 March.
Velarde, K. 2014.b. Plunder Me, Baby. Unublished Text. 05 April.
Velarde, K. 2015. Unpublished email correspondence with the author. 26 May.

Printed with permission of the author.

SECTION 3.3
IMAGE

Introductory summary

The surfaces of ceramics have long been the carriers of painted images, patterns and text that add another layer of meaning to the form. In an article that emerged from her master of fine art (MFA) degree in Ceramics, Veronika Horlik discusses ceramics and painting with the aid of the 'Semiotic Square' as a method to consider binary terms. Horlik uses this method to create categories of ceramics and painting and give examples of practitioners whose work she feels relate to the categories. The artists discussed include Nicole Cherubini, Kurt Weiser, Cindy Kolodziejski, Greg Payce, Kuldeep Malhi, Kim Dickey, Linda Sormin, as well as the author's own work. This essay offers a possible strategy that makers might find useful when considering where their own work 'fits' with in ceramics.

Alongside painting, printing has been a prime method of adding meaning to ceramics since the eighteenth century. The artist, writer and researcher Paul Scott has been one of the prime exponents of promoting the use of ceramics print methods for artists. His seminal 1994 book, 'Ceramics and Print', introduced many artists to the potential of printmaking for ceramics and contributed to a resurgence of these methods in studio practice. Scott is also a thoughtful artist who makes transfer printed ceramics reflecting aspects of politics, the environment and social justice. Amy Gogarty's text traces themes in Scott's work based on what he calls a 'blue and white semiotic'. Readers might also want to consider Kevin Petrie's book *Ceramic Transfer Printing* for a historical overview and methods for printing onto ceramics or Paul Wandless' *Image Transfer on Clay*.

Livingstone and Petrie

48
CERAMICS AND PAINTING: AN EXPANDED FIELD OF INQUIRY

Veronika Horlik

Foreword

2-dimensional and 3-dimensional artworks are read in different ways. In *Sculpture and the Broken Tool* Peter Schwenger writes 'When one views a canvas, the gaze builds up an image *between* the eye and the painting's flat surface ... but the materiality of paint on a canvas is different from the materiality of a boulder on the floor, which is solid, heavy, extended in space' (2005, p. 49). I, like Schwenger, believe that there exist differences in how we relate to and process 2- and 3-dimensional subject matter. Our perceptions may be framed by prejudice, education, and through exposure to popular arts discourses. Today, an increasing number of discipline-based craft practitioners are embracing a multi-disciplinary approach. My own recent ceramic art practice has led me to question whether it is possible to consider contemporary ceramic work through new lenses. Today's ceramic artist can enthusiastically flirt with choices: choosing to work from historical, technical, cultural or conceptual perspectives. Along with artists working conceptually through the vessel form, a strong emergence of large-scale and installation-based ceramic work is hitting the contemporary art scene with fervor, breaking from functional work traditionally associated with fine craft. What roles can ceramics, with its worldly historical roots and tremendous capacity for transference, play in reflecting facets of our current culture and times? Bearing in mind that ceramics is a process that includes imagination, engineering, chemistry, and a technical know-how that can only manifest over an extended exposure to clay and its inherent properties, answers to this question will be found in the field's natural adaptability and innovation.

John Muir once wrote that 'When we try to pick out anything by itself, we find it hitched to everything else in the Universe' (1911, p. 110). When painting and ceramics engage within single artworks, our very understanding of these works broadens. What differences in our reading occur when 2-dimensional representations and ceramics are juxtaposed side by each as in the work of Nicole Cherubini, in contrast to functional ceramic forms that are surface-painted as in the works of Kurt Weiser or Cindy Kolodziejski? In Cherubini's work *Hydras* (2008) the materiality of the clay vessel is amplified by the presence of 2-dimensional imagery. The autonomous 2-dimensional adaptations of her ceramic amphora forms are inextricably linked to the meaning and interpretation of the work. In Cindy Kolodziejski's *Clapping Monkey* (2000) on the other hand, the painting as *skin* to the pot informs our perception of the ceramic vessel by veiling the precise qualities of clay and function it relies on to be recognizable. Both Kolodziejski's painted ceramic surface, and Cherubini's ceramic forms echoed within adjacent images, hold painterly positions within a ceramics practice. Just as fresco painting is inextricably linked to our experience of the architecture it inhabits, so too does painting play an important role in defining these works.

Source: © Veronika Horlik/*Cahiers métiers d'art.*

A few years ago, I was describing to an artist friend that my MFA studies were progressing very well. My friend, seemingly stunned by what I had just said, asked 'I thought you were studying ceramics?' 'Yes' I replied, 'I'm doing a Masters of Fine Arts in Ceramics'. He was dumbstruck to learn of the vast array of contemporary activity taking place in ceramic arts, and ceramics arts education today. Just as the words *fine china* may conjure delicate, white, gracefully decorated tea service wares, the word pottery likely brings to mind a wholesomely handmade vase, teapot, or mug. Pottery, or the vessel tradition, is one of ceramics most common and readily recognizable manifestations among the general public (and sadly also among much of the Art world). When it comes to the discipline of ceramics, pottery is very often the only thing that springs to people's minds. Granted that the ceramics discipline is difficultly pulled apart from its long-standing history in the vessel tradition (and I'll add thankfully so), today's ceramic practices, be they vessel, sculpture, or installation-based, are nothing other than privileged by a rich history and vast scope of activity. The 21st century's continual shifting and expansion of definitions for art have provided fertile ground for discipline-trained ceramic artists to become increasingly interdisciplinary while adhering to a boundary-less conception of expression and innovation within our field. It is indeed possible to proudly retain a die-hard dedication to a medium while at the same time engage in multi-medium approaches that echo within larger discourses of contemporary art. I am very optimistic about ceramics' capacity to enter fully into such a dialog.

The semiotic square

'The square is a map of logical possibilities. … playing with the possibilities of the square is authorized since the theory of the square allows us to see all thinking as a game …' (Katilius-Boydstun 1990, p. 36)

For initiating my exploration into Ceramics and Painting I have chosen to create a semiotic square. The semiotic square, developed by French semioticians Greimas and Rastier in the late 1960's, was designed as a means of both refining and expanding an analysis of oppositions or binary terms. By opposing and triangulating static categories on the square, we open doors to a logic that is dynamical rather than static. This open process parallels efforts within today's craft world to understand contemporary interdisciplinary grey areas of practice.

I have used CERAMIC SCULPTURE and AUTONOMOUS 2-DIMENSIONAL PAINTING as initial binary categories in this heuristic investigation. By considering a variety of contemporary ceramics approaches to form and surface, I make no attempt to validate in a hierarchical sense any one particular method of making over another. Rather, this exploration of cases where ceramics interlaces, overlaps, or interacts with 2-dimensional imagery is intended as a map onto which a variety of artworks may be located for a pragmatic purpose. The square provides a way of visually representing, in one wide-arching single vision, possible relationships generated by expanding on initial categories. It functions as follows: any principal opposition between opposing terms – between (A) and (B) – can be expanded to include a secondary pair of opposing terms between (non-A) or (-A) and (non-B) or (-B). This mirrored second set of oppositions allows us to then open the square more widely through triangulations. Subsequently, each triangulation within the square, thus (A+B), (A+-B), (B + -A), and (-B+-A), holds a natural kinship with each of its initial opposing quadrants. A well-known creative interpretation of the semiotic square is in Rosalind Krauss's 1979 essay *Sculpture in the Expanded Field.*[1] In this seminal text Krauss defines the forms of sculpture emerging in the early 1960's by means of negative ascertainment, defining sculpture by what it is not: not-landscape and not-architecture. In her essay, Krauss describes a 'pulling and stretching' of the term sculpture that had formed in the previous decades (Krauss 1979, p. 30). This pulling and stretching of sculpture's identity resulted in theoretical approaches to sculpture practices of the time to be readdressed. I believe that craft practices and craft discourse find themselves in a similar need for readdressing today.

My primary opposition is (A) CERAMIC SCULPTURE and (B) AUTONOMOUS 2-D PAINTING. The next step is to establish their respective oppositions. Here (A) CERAMIC SCULPTURE refers to ceramic objects set apart from utilitarian or vessel oriented ware. By virtue of conceptual value and function as an aesthetic art object, we can say that ceramic sculpture stands in theoretical opposition to the utilitarian ceramic object. Thus for (-A) we have NON-SCULPTURAL CERAMICS or POTTERY / the vessel tradition. (B) AUTONOMOUS 2-D PAINTING refers to 2-dimensional image-making self-contained within a frame, frame in absentia, contained by the edge of the picture-plane's meeting with the wall (Dewitt 1920, p. 270). Painting here is used as a generalized category of classification, without prejudice towards any one style, type of representation, or technique. Therefore for the opposite of (B) AUTONOMOUS 2-D PAINTING, we have (-B) 3-DIMENSIONAL PAINTING/painting in space (not restricted by the laws of wall-bound 2-dimensionality).

Our initial semiotic square design looks like this:

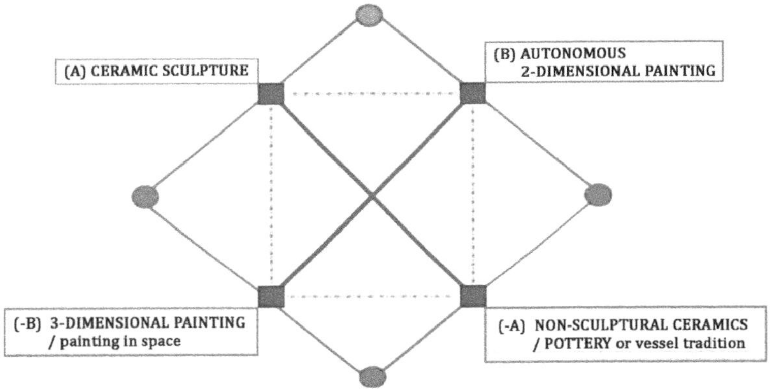

copyright © 2011 Veronika Horlik. All rights reserved.

The next step is to elaborate the square by triangulating off of each initial quadrant.

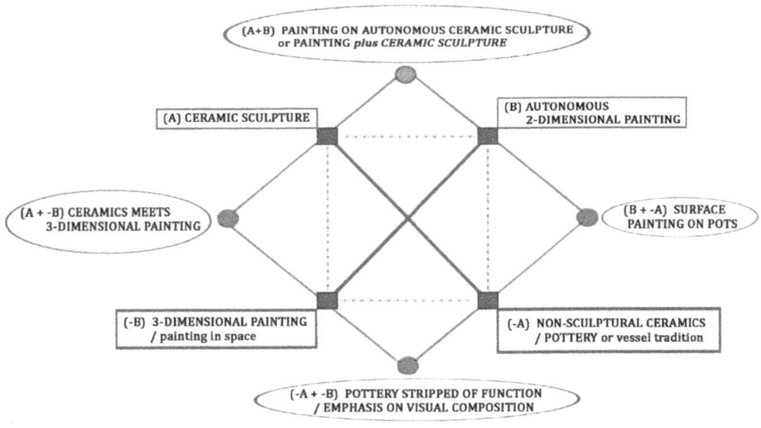

copyright © 2011 Veronika Horlik. All rights reserved.

In what follows, I am will explore each of the four new categories created by triangulating off of the initial square.

(B + -A) Surface painting on pots

A popular misconception distinguishing pottery from other art making is the notion that pots cannot be conceptual, or in a form-follows-function ethic, exist uniquely to fulfill utilitarian functions. Canadian ceramist and educator Paul Mathieu would disagree with the idea that vessel making per se is not a conceptual endeavour. In *The Art of the Future: 14 essays on ceramics* Mathieu eloquently defends that in essence the making of functional and decorative ceramics is a conceptual act:

> ... after all, function and decoration are themselves concepts, something the hegemonic discourses on art history and contemporary art seems to forget [and] ceramics as a distinct art form is predicated on the coming together of pairs of seemingly contradictory conceptual aspects [object and image, form and surface, function and decoration], not to be perceived in opposition or polarity but in continuity, in synthesis and symbiosis (Mathieu 2010).

In her essay *The Essential Vessel* Natasha Daintry states that 'we do not rate vessels like we do conceptual art' (Hanaor ed. 2007, p. 6), 'throwing pots on the wheel or making small pinch-pots in the palm of my hand, I am attending to the simplest things potters do every time they hollow-out a lump of clay. But this simple making of a cup or bowl is also an essay into abstraction, a clothing of emptiness' (p. 8).

When thinking of conceptualism and the nature of the ceramic vessel philosopher Martin Heidegger and his jug come to mind. In *The Thing* Heidegger distinguishes between object and thing, declaring that a thing is an object that sets itself apart from the world it inhabits while simultaneously coming into relation with the existential phenomena surrounding it (Heidegger 1950).[2] Heidegger uses the example of a jug to illustrate his idea which unfolds something like this: The jug is 'ready-to-hand', insofar as it functions effectively without our conscious recognition. The jug is not merely an object at hand however, but rather a thing that stands on its own in the world. Emptiness is what the jug definably holds according to Heidegger, granting it the capacity as *container* to be useful to its user. By holding emptiness, the jug offers a resolute space to be filled, making it a thing with its own capacity to gift. An exchange takes place between the space of 'emptiness' that defines the jug and the outer world surrounding it. The giving jug has its own thing-ness, outside of man's appropriative relationship with it as mere object. 'The vessel's thingness does not lie in the material of which it consists, but in the void that it holds' (p. 169). We become aware of the vessel's gifting nature only when the jug fails to perform its utilitarian function. Heidegger's philosophy locates the function of an object within the interconnectedness of all things, his jug metaphorically stands for all objects that, while serving a function, enter into a form of intricate co-existence with humans. Heidegger's notions on the pottery form bring to mind the paintings of Ben Nicholson of the same era, who strived to embody a similar essence through representations of the pottery form on canvas.[3] Nicholson had an interest in framing an abstracted landscape through exploring the vessel form. This may have been from his acquaintance with his contemporary the ceramist Bernard Leach, both lived and had studios in St. Ives, UK.

The ceramic work of English artist Grayson Perry displays a potent mixture of gender critique, satire, sexuality, violence, autobiographical and cultural references. A dense layering of images causes his dystopic and elaborate representations to hover claustrophobically close to the surface of his simple vase forms. His familiar humble pottery vessel forms (relinquished historically to being a silent, purely functional object) becomes a vehicle, giving all the more potency to his visual subject matter. Instead of sitting on top of the pottery form, imagery is manifest *as* the pot form. If we think here of Heidegger's thingness (which is not found in the object's material, but rather in the void that it holds), Grayson's pictorial subject matter serves what could be seen as both a *giving* and *holding* function. The same imagery on a 2-dimensional surface would be entirely reliant on itself to convey its content. Our perception and reception of Grayson's imagery is made significantly more palpable by the simple pottery form it sheaths. The power of functional pottery as a medium for transmitting, evoking and amplifying our perception of imagery, lies in its humble familiarity and presence in our world as a reliable object.

Another instance where painted pottery plays on our perception has to do with the work's size in relation to our physical bodies, our physical and mental *reach*. When we look at a functional pot, we understand its volume because we hold in our memory the experience of having held similar pots in our hands before. Not only have we held utilitarian pots, but we *engage* with them (be they metal or plastic incarnations of similar forms) as we go about our daily lives.

Cindy Kolodziejski is an American ceramic artist who engages our psychological understanding of functional objects in a most masterful way through the painted image. If we look at her piece *Clapping Monkey* (2000), we see a stretched-out monkey on the surface of a carafe. The pot's elegant form and slim handle is reminiscent of 1950's American metal kitchenware design and this illusionistic metallic quality is emphasized by the image: the monkey painting is warped as our own reflection might appear if we were looking into the surface of a reflective metallic pot. When we look at this piece, we *become* the monkey, looking at a reflection of ourselves. A mental transposition is made possible by three factors: the mirror-effect rendering of the painting; the fact that the reflected face should be our own if we believe in this mirror illusion; and the familiar understanding we experience when we look at a humble and relatable pot form.

(-B + -A) Pottery stripped of function: Emphasis on visual composition

'The body reflects itself in its own seeing, sensing, moving about through he world' (Merleau-Ponty 1964, p. 163).

A vessel provides through its form an accessible enclosure of space, and is defined by the space it makes available to be filled. If a vessel's purpose deviates from the utilitarian, in referential terms it still carries forward qualities of containment and of giving. As Baudrillard points out in *The System of Objects* 'every antique is beautiful, simply because it has survived, and thus becomes the sign of an earlier life' (Baudrillard 1968, p. 88). Similarly, an anti-utilitarian pot holds within itself an earlier incarnation as container and provider. As we will see with the next two examples, the space that *provides* is transposed from the interior to the exterior of a pot.

Greg Payce's clay vessels range from teacup size to human body in scale. In his assemblages of multiple vessels, he uses a sophisticated optical illusion to create figures *between* the objects. Payce says of his work:

> 'The viewer's gaze vacillates back and forth between the positive and negative inviting them to determine possible relationships between the vessel forms and the images formed by the negative space between these forms. This oscillation between image and object creates an illusion of movement which references time-based art forms such as animation and music. I see these works as 3-dimensional manifestations of pottery decoration, not as sculpture.'

These virtual figures (that are created by the silhouettes between the outer forms of the pots) extend into a space beyond that of the actual vessel and are visible only when the pots are lined up at a specific distance from each other. The pot's form itself holds and projects the figures. Payce's vessels function as splendid low-tech analogies for our relationship with contemporary technology. By projecting this ephemeral human form (moving only a few inches causes the figure to disappear from the viewer's gaze), the vessels place us in relation to a projected fantasy, a reminder of our own physical body, its relation to the pot, and its existence in the world.

In *The System of Objects,* Jean Baudrillard explains that in the face of the technological functional object we become dysfunctional, irrational and non-involved, and open to what he calls a 'mythology of the functional' (p. 60). When we become removed from the physical connection to accomplishing daily tasks, our initial enthusiasm for technology gives way to a form of anxiety. In the past century and a half, an upheaval has taken shape in the everyday: many of the objects we use have become more complex than human behaviour relative to them. 'Objects are more and more highly differentiated – our gestures less and less so' (Baudrillard, p. 59). Today technological objects, inferred with abstracted human energy, act in our place, while part of us retreats as mere spectator. According to Baudrillard, faced with ever increasing technological advancements (where machine artificially organizes our reality), man is the one who is turned into an abstraction.

In relation to pottery we have long ago reached a point where technology has achieved levels of production (though not necessarily achievement) that surpass the human hand. Payce's pots, as finely crafted objects, act as extensions of the human gesture, and in turn the human body. They represent effort, creation, and involvement directly. When we look at a handmade pot today, what we see potentially resonates from a place many of us are less and less familiar with – a place of direct connectedness. The figures projected by Payce's vessels make pots themselves appear less abstracted, drawing us nearer into a relationship with the outmoded handmade object.

Combining both the decorative and the anti-utilitarian, Léopold Foulem creates provocative, historically witty, and highly intellectual ceramic vases and other assembled functional ceramic works. In his *Abstraction* series, the holding function of the vessel is rendered impossible by the sealing-off of openings, while another function, that of the pot as unified mass and surface comes into being. The pot as surface not only abstracts the materiality of the object, but equally our relationship to it as a domesticated thing. The outer wall of a pot, traditionally dividing inner and outer spaces becomes a solid pot-plane for projection. Distinct from projecting figures as Payce's vessels do, which draw us nearer to our own body, Foulem's works outwardly project nothing less than the demise of their utilitarian state as simple pots. His *futilitarian*[4] ceramic works are masterful visual essays reflecting his scholarly interest in ceramics as both a distinct art form and vehicle for intellectual change.

(A + -B) Ceramic sculpture meets 3-dimensional painting

When we triangulate CERAMIC SCULPTURE and 3-DIMENSIONAL PAINTING/ painting in space, we arrive at a category that I've called CERAMIC SCULPTURE MEETS 3-DIMENSIONAL PAINTING. In the two previous sections, the utilitarian (and futilitarian) qualities of the vessel informed our interpretation of the broader meaning intrinsic to the handmade ceramic art object. In this section, we rely primarily on our knowledge of image reading as agency of interpretation.

The ceramic works *Braided Blue* (2006) by Kuldeep Malhi, and *Mille-fleur* (2011) by Kim Dickey, use a multitude of clay pieces that act in unison to create a larger image. Unlike mosaic Malhi's mural piece is not flat in physical composition. And although wall-mounted, its pronounced relief places a strong emphasis on sculptural qualities. The visual effect is akin to a woven tapestry in its soft-edged and geometric formation. *Braided Blue*'s minimalist monochromatic gradation has a calming vitality; a ceramic embodiment of the colour field paintings of the 1940's and 50's devoid of the gestural, personal, and painterly approach to colour application. Kim Dickey's *Mille-fleur* on the other hand, is a free-standing 20 foot wide by 7 foot tall wall clad with 15 000 ceramic leaf forms. Dickey used 30 glazes hand-painted onto the pieces to depict an impressionist meadow. The undulated and organic ceramic surface draws our eye into this chiseled block of an imaginary much vaster landscape. The result is an exquisite monolithic cross between Robert Morris' minimalist geometric plywood sculptures of 1964, and the grandeur and lavish colour present in Claude Monet's monumental water lily paintings.

Linda Sormin's work *Mannerplaw* (2003) brings to mind the New York school of Abstract Expressionism. Abstract Expressionist painters exploited spontaneous expression through the happenstance of soiled, spattered, and dripped paint. The painted surface became a space of direct emotional charge, imbued with colour and rawness. Similarly, Sormin's coiled and pinched wildly colourful clay strands manifest as energetic raw gesture. Her improvisational un-orderly ceramic sculptures and large-scale installations are made-up of a repertoire of ceramic techniques including thrown, molded, extruded and hand-pinched clay. Her transparent process amasses her every intimate gesture, while exposing the work to risk through the firing and assemblage processes. Finger pinch marks abound a multitude of chaotic strokes of coloured clay coils, while heavier tool-assisted clay forms act as foundational support. Sormin works the ceramic material into a porous and painterly form that defies any interior or exterior contour.

(A+B) Painting on ceramic sculpture and painting *plus* Ceramic Sculpture

When we triangulate (A) CERAMIC SCULPTURE and (B) AUTONOMOUS 2-DIMENSIONAL PAITING we arrive at (A+B), a category that can be considered in two different ways: PAINTING ON CERAMIC SCULPTURE or PAINTING *plus* CERAMIC SCULPTURE.

(A+B) Painting on ceramic sculpture[5]

If we consider for a moment that postmodern art is an art of impact, surface-oriented intensity, and decentralized sensation (in contrast to a modernist art where meaning, depth, and representation reign), then Ken Price's series of sculpture work exemplifies this category of contemporary ceramics beautifully. Price's amorphous pedestal-bound sculptures (1988 to the present) appear to have simply *dripped* into their voluptuous and slumping positions. However unassuming in their non-representational composure, these fired and painted clay pieces resonate with a seductive intensity. The sculptures' colourful surfaces are the product of numerous layers of acrylic and enamel paints, each sanded laboriously before the next colour is added. The result, a constellation of mottled breaks in colour with visible underlay colours, is a synthesis of surface and form. The visual impact of these pieces far out measures any necessity to derive narrative or interpretive meaning.

(A+B) Painting *plus* ceramic sculpture

The second variation of this last category of our semiotic square, PAINTING *plus* CERAMIC SCULPTURE, describes two distinct media in single artworks. Here I am going to look at the work of Nicole Cherubini, as well as recent work of my own.

Much of Nicole Cherubini's sculpture work is centered on the ceramic vessel. In pieces such as *Hydras* (2008), *Am-4-Ohr-As on Wall* (2008), and *Nestoris II* (2008), her forms reference ancient Greek and Roman ceramic utilitarian ware. In her sculptural assemblages material excess (almost bling) cajoles with the grotesque and the raw, blurring lines between frivolity and tradition. Her large ceramic vessels are exuberantly decorated displaying a wide range of surface treatments: from crude and natural clays, to multi-layered luscious glaze applications at times carefully applied, at times dripping with unruly excess. Unlike the over-the-top surface treatment of the pots however, the pedestals (when used) are pared-down in their construction and materials. And yet, where a more conventional pedestal[6] might assume a non-intrusive role in presenting a work of art, Cherubini's pedestals act as extensions of the vessel forms they support. Everything in the work is in some form of visual conversation with everything else surrounding it. Cherubini often uses 2-dimensional imagery within her sculptural compositions. The 2-dimensional images (c-prints enhanced with drawing and painting) are uncommonly positioned at heights and in arrangements in relation to the sculptures themselves, rather than in relation to the viewer. Again, there is a persistent exchange between all individual elements in the works. In *Hydras* (2008), the framed images are freestanding beside the ceramic work with brightly coloured wood baguettes physically attaching the 2-dimensional to the 3-dimensional.

On the topic of Cézanne's observations on things and vision, Merleau-Ponty writes 'things have an internal equivalent in me; they arouse in me a carnal formula of their presence' (Merleau-Ponty, p. 165). 'The things in the world are not simply *objects* which stand before us for our contemplation' states Merleau-Ponty in describing our relationship with things as interplay between our body, our perception and the things that surround us. In *Primacy of Perception* Merleau-Ponty asserts 'I do not look at an [image] as I do a thing; I do not fix it in its place' (p. 163). In *Painting and the Gaze of the Object*, Peter Schwenger writes 'whatever else painting may be about, it is always about vision' (p. 39).

When a painting is presented in tight juxtaposition to a sculpture, creating an interplay between viewing something that is primarily about vision (2-dimensional image) and something that is primarily about objecthood (sculpture), a widened frame of visual conversation occurs.

In this category, I include my personal ceramic practice. I have been working for several years now on a series of pieces that include large ceramic sculpture and 2-dimensional painting on wood panel. The works in my *BURN* series (2009-2013) possess the potential to break from the fixed conditions which hold them in place: objects and paintings tilt, wheeled structures are ready to change position, and elements are held in place by detachable load-binding straps. I'm interested in an incongruous dichotomy: in how the characters of both the painted image and the object are transformed through their tight and forced juxtaposition. Three areas of interest come together in the BURN series work: 1) The burned landscapes of the Canadian Forestry Industry; 2) A visible play with weight, and the striking of an unlikely balance; and 3) A juxtaposition of two- and three-dimensional media. Through forcing a relationship between object and image, this work examines and emphasizes the very materiality and undeniable physical presence of the ceramic medium.

The impetus for this essay's semiotic square map originated during my MFA studies in Ceramics at NSCAD University when I faced difficulty in positioning my work (theoretically speaking) within a broader discourse of the Ceramics discipline. Discussing the work in terms of simple mixed-media sculpture fell short of acknowledging the craft component to my practice. As a craftperson, my studio practice reflects a distinct commitment to the ceramic process, my practice is thus rooted in ceramics history, tradition, and culture. As with the examples stated in this essay, this cannot be ignored when considering the work.

In this essay, I have reviewed certain artworks where ceramics cross paths with painting, or concepts of painting. The examples that I have used are only a few among an exhaustive list of works that could fit within each quadrant of this semiotic square. The square that I have devised is specific and indeed narrow in scope, though should by no means be considered a firm and conclusive proposition. Kenneth Price once said of his work 'I don't know what to call the new pieces: sculpture, objects, ceramics? I just make them, somebody else can decide what they're called'[7]. This is a sage code of behaviour to follow. It is not up to the artist alone to define where his or her practice resides within an arts discourse; in fact, the artist may not be the works best advocate at all. A problem that occurs within the field of Ceramics however, is that as a discipline it is too often omitted entirely from larger arts discourses. And an ability to be articulate and intelligent about your personal practice therefore is primordial for today's contemporary ceramist. Herein simply lies my grounds for pushing theoretical investigations in this field.

A Word on writing about doing

As a visual artist it is useful to be able to talk about your work, to have the ability to communicate something of the essence of your interest, drive, and direction in the making process. A strong artist statement or theoretical proposition may provide a complementary access point into the work. During a talk on curatorial and exhibition writing that he gave at NSCAD in 2011, Ben Portis stated, 'Good writing [about art] doesn't stand apart from what we are looking at when we look at art. Just as good art should not stand apart from what we are looking at when we look at the world'.[8] Words tend to lock things into place and this can potentially close more doors than it can open. Good writing is a craft in itself – one that makers, having experience in action-based skills and knowledge, may not always master. Describing ideas and processes that take place on physical, non-verbalized levels in an artist's practice can indeed present a challenge. There is the problem of trying to say too much, attempting to create a written equivalent or direct transposition of the artwork in question – 'if it was going to be best to say it in words, I would have been a novelist not a sculptor' a friend of mine once remarked. Then there exists the situation of theorizing art to death by over-conceptualizing, or putting-forth a theoretical groundwork in words that leaves little room for the art to speak for itself – stripping it of innate autonomy in the world. For ceramic artists, ideas are resolved within the act of making, through a rigorous physical engagement with materials and processes. Similarly, writing provides a space for ideas to be manipulated, disassembled, contrasted, re-arranged and worked-out. It is essential for emerging craft practitioners to take interest and delve into an examination of their practice for the full potential of Fine Craft to continue to develop in the 21st century.

Notes

1. Rosalind Krauss opens her article *Sculpture in the Exppanded Field* with a physical description of Mary Miss' Perimeters/Pavillions/Decoys of 1978 and follows with the argument that at that point in the late 70's, sculpture had become a category that was 'almost infinitely malleable'.
2. Heidegger is known for his existential and phenomenological explorations of the question of Being.
3. Benjamin Lauder "Ben" Nicholson was an English abstract painter who lived from 10 April 1894 – 6 February 1982, Martin Heidegger was a German philosopher who lived from September 26, 1889 – May 26, 1976.
4. Futilitarian: A combination of futile: serving no useful purpose, and utilitarian: serving in the interest of utility. My word for vessel-form ceramics that are intentionally deprived of their functional utility in the name of design or creative interpretation.
5. There exists a vast number of contemporary sculptural ceramic works that fit into this category, and the painted or painterly sculptural ceramic surface is not restricted to conventional glaze applications. It is not entirely uncommon for some ceramic artists to use acrylic, enamel, or oil-based paint as a final surface treatment. The American ceramist Peter Voulkos (1924-2002) notoriously and innovatively did not shy away from using industrial paints in adition

to the glazed finishes on his works. Other ceramists known to have used paint as well as glaze surface treatments include Marilyn Levine, Rudy Autio, Pablo Picasso, to name but a few.

6. The pedestal serves the same purpose in sculpture as the frame in the sister art [of painting]; it cuts off the ideal space which the statue [or painting] fills from the real space where it is housed, raising it above the common ground of real life, with its practical and social attitudes, into the realm of contemplation. (Dewitt 1920, p. 288).
7. Price's response when asked in an interview whether 'sculpture' was the correct word to describe his recent work, such as Untitled (1979) from his *Condominium* series. National Gallery of Australia, International Painting and Sculpture, Kenneth Price. [Web published] http://nga.gov.au/international/catalogue/Detail.cfm?IRN=116123 (June 10, 2012).
8. Ben Portis, Currator at MacLaren Arts Center, Barrie, Ontario. *Curatorial and Exhibition Writing*, Lecture at NSCAD University, Halifax, NS. (March 22, 2011)

Bibliography

Dewitt, Parker H. (1920), *The Principles Of Aesthetics* Silver, Boston.
Hanaor, Cigalle (Ziggy), ed. (2007), 'The Essential Vessel' in *Breaking the Mold: New Approaches to Ceramics,* London, Black Dog Publishing.
Heidegger, Martin. (1950), 'The Thing (Das Ding)' in *Poetry, Language, Thought,* Harper Perenial Modern Classics.
Jean Baudrillard. (1968), *The System of Objects*, Verso Publishing, London and New York.
Katilius-Boydstun, Marvin. (1990), *The Semiotics of A.J. Greimas: An Introduction*, Litanus: Lithuanian Quarterly Journal of Arts and Sciences, 36(3).
Krauss, Rosalind. (1979), *Sculpture in the Exppanded Field*, M.I.T. Press.
Merleau-Ponty, Maurice. (1964), 'Eye and Mind' in *The Primacy of Perception*, Memphis State University Press.
Muir, John. 1911. *My First Summer in the Sierra*, Boston, New York, Houghton Mifflin Company, p. 110
Schwenger, Peter. (2005), 'Painting and the Gaze of the Object' in *The Tears of Things: Melancholy and Physical Objects*, University of Minessota Press.
Schwenger, Peter. (2005), 'Sculpture and the Broken Tool' in *The Tears of Things: Melancholy and Physical Objects,* University of Minessota Press.

Web

Mathieu, Paul. (2010), Preface to chapter 4 in *The Narrative Aesthetics. The Art of the Future: 14 essays on ceramics.* [Web published], Available at http://paulmathieu.ca (Oct. 28, 2010).
Payce, Greg. (2003), Artist Statement. [Web published], Available at www.virtualmuseum.ca, http://www.virtualmuseum.ca/sgc-cms/expositions-exhibitions/feu_terre-fire_earth/Artists/Payce/PayceStmtEn.html (Nov. 29, 2010).

First published: *Cahiers métiers d'art: Craft Journal*, volume 6, no 1, Hiver/Winter 2013

Reprinted with permission of *Cahiers métiers d'art: Craft Journal.*

49
PAUL SCOTT'S CONFECTED LANDSCAPES AND CONTEMPORARY VIGNETTES

Amy Gogarty

Paul Scott has achieved international renown in the ceramics world as a teacher, curator and author of two widely-read books, *Ceramics and Print* (A&C Black, 1994/96) and *Painted Clay: Graphic Arts and the Ceramic Surface* (A&C Black and Watson Guptill, 2000). He also makes compelling work. Residing in Cumbria in rural northern England, he recently completed a PhD fellowship from Manchester Institute for Research and Innovation in Art and Design, Manchester Metropolitan University, England. The work discussed in this article relates to research conducted during the course of his PhD,[1] yet it embodies themes that have preoccupied him for some time. These include theories of picturesque landscape painting; the remediation and circulation in print form of such painting; domestic ceramic objects printed with landscape imagery and a host of contemporary issues concerning relationships between human civilization and the natural world.

In 2001, Stephanie Brown reviewed Scott's work with computer-altered, collaged and virtual landscape imagery, wondering if this new direction might ultimately lead him beyond 'ceramic as a physical practice'. She allowed, however, that his life-long engagement with 'the critical potential of banal ceramic idioms' might yet 'feed back into actual ceramics'.[2] Fortunately for ceramics, Scott's new work confirms his commitment to material practice, manifesting the medium's effectiveness both to carry traces of the past and to sustain contemporary inquiry.

Scott constructs highly artificial, theatrical views and artifacts, compounding a miscellany of elements in a process he refers to as 'confecting'.[3] Mixing vintage and modern ceramic dinnerware with printed designs and hand-built sculptural elements, Scott's 'confected' landscapes and contemporary vignettes generate meanings based on what he calls a 'blue and white semiotic'. Originating with Chinese porcelain, 'the most widely produced and distributed object of world commerce before the Industrial Revolution',[4] this semiotic migrated to Europe and became the standard for industrial transfer-printed tableware.

Scott's academic research focuses on historical archives of blue and white ceramic decoration in Britain, Scandinavia, Eastern Europe and elsewhere, with a particular interest in print technology as it relates to picturesque European landscape painting. The concept of the picturesque dominated artistic discourse in the eighteenth century. As defined by one of its chief theorists, Reverend William Gilpin, 'Picturesque Beauty is that peculiar kind of beauty, which is agreeable in a picture'.[5] To clarify exactly what kind of picture he meant, Gilpin proposed rules and schema to organize any landscape into foreground, distance and second distance, such as one might observe in paintings by Claude Lorraine, Gaspard Dughet or Salvatore Rosa.

The transfer process was used to impart detailed imagery onto everyday ceramic objects, contributing to domestic visual environments in which these images circulated as powerful, if subliminal, markers of cultural values and norms. Scott uses the term 'cultural wallpaper' to describe the ubiquitous, if unacknowledged, presence of these objects. Like wallpaper, they contain and define an environment while functioning

Source: © Amy Gogarty/*Ceramics: Art and Perception.*

largely outside the purview of serious art history, which purports to value originality and uniqueness over mechanically reproduced multiples. Museums have not always seen fit to preserve mass-produced objects, a situation Scott criticizes as failing to appreciate the significance these objects hold for ordinary people. He insists that 'industrial ceramics are still used by many people as an art form' having 'relevance to their lives'.[6] Acknowledging its intrinsic and subversive power, Scott adopts the visual style of this outmoded, discredited aesthetic to produce thoughtful and critical works.

Developments in computer graphics software and technology revolutionized the remediation of existing images, altering the process significantly from that used during the heyday of transfer ware. First developed in the eighteenth century and thus contemporary with the rise of the picturesque, transfer ware fueled the expanding middle class' desire for decorative ornaments. Transfer images were created with engraved copper plates similar to those used to make prints on paper. In one process, gelatin bats transferred printers' oil to glazed ceramic objects, which were dusted with overglaze enamels and fired. Later, specialized transfer tissue was used to impart underglaze colour directly to a biscuit surface. This was then glazed and fired, resulting in a permanent decoration that became the industry standard.[7] Scott conducted extensive research in the archives of various manufacturers, interviewing those few engravers who remained working into the early part of this century.[8] In the past, skilled engravers drew upon or 'cannibalized' printed images and copper plates in factory warehouses to create new compositions and genres including generalized views, souvenir plates and commemorative wares. In the often indiscriminate pastiche of unrelated images, Scott recognized parallels to contemporary image-making by digital means. Rather than dismissing these objects as banal, unoriginal or kitsch, he regarded the proliferation of genres as a bonanza, familiar forms to be appropriated, altered and vested with entirely new rhetoric and meaning.

Manipulating images digitally, Scott generates screen-printed decals that incorporate cobalt pigment suspended in a print base. The screened images are subsequently applied to glazed surfaces and fired at temperatures appropriate to the substrate material. The chemical properties of cobalt cause it to bleed slightly into the glaze melt, creating edges that are more subtly blended than those produced using other colours such as red or black. This quality contributed in part to the original popularity of blue and white, as the softened edges related the print more closely to painting.[9] Scott exploits degrees of melt in his work, combining materials such as tin-glazed earthenware, wood-fired, hand-formed and store-bought porcelain into a single work. The substrate modifies the quality of the print – it sits most crisply in the surface of the tin glaze, softens and sinks beneath the glassy surface of the porcelain, and bubbles, melts and moves in atmospheric firings.

These qualities exemplify what media theorists Jay David Bolter and Richard Grusin term the 'twin logics of remediation, immediacy and hypermediacy'.[10] Echoing Marshall McLuhan's claim that the content of any medium is always another medium, Bolter and Grusin define remediation as 'the formal logic by which new media refashion prior media forms'.[11] In this instance, prints on paper remediate oil paintings to be remediated in turn by printed ceramics, and printed ceramics by Scott himself. This chain or affiliation enables the original content of the paintings, landscape, to be continuously repurposed and subjected to on-going historical reflection and analysis. It also reiterates the central role of ceramics in carrying and explicating this content. 'Immediacy' extends the promise of 'access to the real', a condition aimed at through such 'realistic' mechanisms as linear perspective, oil painting, photography, film and virtual environments. Scott identifies aspects of immediacy in the highly detailed representations of landscape created by the copperplate transfer process. Running counter to this, 'hypermediacy' calls attention to the medium itself, substituting for the singular thrust of immediacy, its promised access to the real, heterogeneous spaces and multiple acts of representation.[12] The slight blurring of the cobalt trace beneath the glaze not only heightens the similarity of the printed ceramic to the continuous tone of oil painting, and thus its immediacy, it calls attention to the particular qualities of the printed surface and its constructed or 'confected' nature. This tension between reality and representation heightens the aesthetic response to these works, multiplying potential references and meanings available to what seems on first glance to be everyday functional objects.

This attention to aesthetics and process, seemingly at odds with work that incorporates and/or simulates commercial china, points to an interesting paradox or problematic at the heart of Scott's practice. Conflict between hand and machine processes dominated craft discourse of the Arts and Crafts Movement, as witnessed by declarations such as Oscar Wilde's 'Let us have no machine-made ornament at all; it is all bad and worthless and ugly'.[13] Bernard Leach similarly decried the use of mechanical reproduction on ceramic surfaces, asserting it lacked the 'continuous vital interpretation' necessary for authentic work.[14] Such categorical claims raise red flags for Scott, who believes the material context and use make objects dead or alive, not the specifics of either print or brush.[15] As a young painter, he was drawn to ceramics' capacity to communicate social and political content rather than to technique or self-expression. He clarifies his position, unusual for a studio ceramist, stating 'I operate within, and on the edge of studio ceramics – and completely outside it'. Digital processes allow him to make 'meaningful' forays into the field of studio ceramics, broadening its purview in the process. While appreciating the importance of Leach, he identifies with colleagues working in Eastern Europe and Scandinavia who 'draw on much greater and diverse ceramic practices and traditions … their relationship to industry is much more engaged, thoughtful and productive'.[16] Ultimately, Scott is driven by a desire to develop a working theory of surface, one that exploits the expressive language or semiotic of blue and white ceramics. How he does this is as varied as the project facing him at the time.[17]

For much of his professional life, Scott's work has been recognized as political.[18] Early on, he engaged issues of apartheid, the environment and social justice. Later, he began to address nuclear energy and waste, combining images of the Sellafield nuclear power plant near his home with traditional motifs from the blue willow pattern. Due to the nearly seamless combination of motifs, subversive aspects of these works emerge only with close scrutiny. Other pieces revive an older tradition of featuring industrial landmarks, factories and similar structures set in bucolic surroundings, recalling a time when such structures were objects of picturesque tourism. In some cases, Scott prints the image across the ceramic plate, ignoring conventions of framing; in others, he deliberately encircles views of smokestacks and cooling towers with traditional borders such as the willow or "Marseillaise" pattern to create ironic disjunctions. Some pieces use the process of erasure, mechanically removing areas of pattern from vintage plates and replacing them with collaged commentary. For example, *Scott's Cumbrian Blue(s) After the By-Pass* (2005) overprints an erased segment from a fanciful Spode landscape with a collage of automobiles caught in a traffic jam. Politics and irony are explicit in these works, leading some to wonder if Scott's latest work has traded in politics for politesse. Such a view misses the subtlety and sophistication of this newer work.

One might argue that all landscape, in that it is a representation, is inherently political. As W.J.T. Mitchell asserts in 'Imperial Landscape':

> Landscape is a natural scene mediated by culture. It is both represented and presented space, both a signifier and a signified, both a frame and what a frame contains, both a real place and its simulacrum, both a package and the commodity inside the package.[19]

Scott's confected landscapes embody the disjunctions mentioned by Mitchell, but from the position of one who lives in the country rather than one who looks at it. This is an essential difference in terms of who is speaking and for whom. A series addressing the terrible outbreak of Foot and Mouth disease in Britain in 2001 becomes more affecting when one realizes Scott's home district of North Cumbria was particularly hard-hit: it was his neighbors losing their livestock and his air filled with the acrid fumes of burning corpses.[20] While some examples from this series are so disturbing as to leave little room for nuance, others, such as

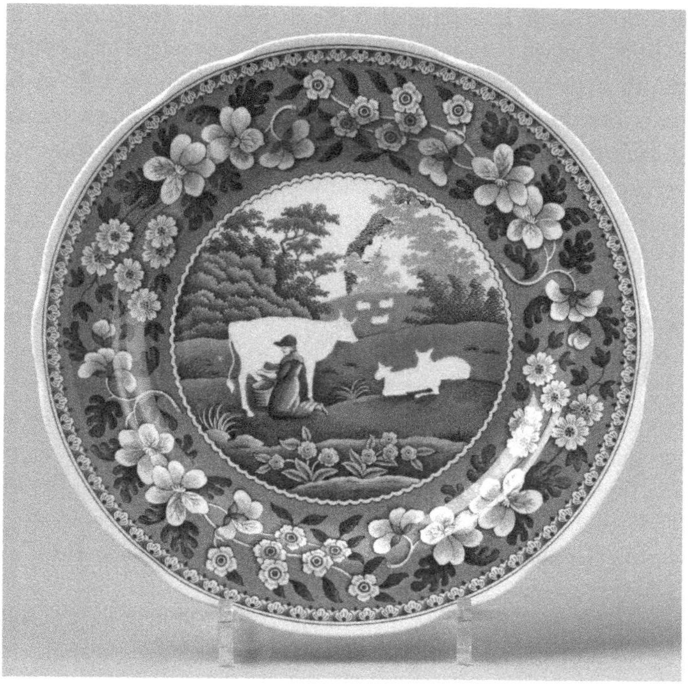

Figure 49.1 Scott's Cumbrian Blue(s) Foot and mouth series, Milk Maid no.3, altered and partially erased Spode blue room, 2003/photo by Paul Scott.

Scott's Cumbrian Blue(s) 2001 Foot and Mouth No:3 (after Thomas Bewick) 3/02 (2001), in which the image based on Thomas Bewick's wood engraving *Tees-water Improved Breed* is rendered with the body of the animal left blank, or *Foot and Mouth* (2003) (Figure 49.1), an altered and partially erased Spode *Blue Room, Milk Maid* plate in which the figures of a cow and two sheep have been mechanically removed, introduce pathos and sense of loss that transcends irony or outrage. The most minimally altered works carry the most punch, as the moment of recognition is suspended until well after the work is first encountered. One contemplates and becomes implicated in his altered Enoch Wedgwood *English Countryside* plates for some time before one notices the wire fence bisecting the rustic image or the cloud-piercing, low-flying military jet.

Insight into the fact that seemingly innocuous images could be perceived as political came to him from an unusual source. Researching transfer ware in Norway and Sweden, he encountered a complex history of foreign designers and decorators brought to the region in the nineteenth century to assist local factory production. Images that appeared generically pastoral to him were perceived by locals as political examples of imported 'English style'. Today they are regarded as embarrassing departures from a larger history of the region's embrace of modernism and modern design. Yet whether acknowledged or not, these works remain as a record of a particular time, influence and political force impacting both nations' history.[21]

This led Scott to re-examine pastoral imagery in Britain with a new understanding of its potential for political content. Living in what appears to many to be an Arcadian village, he is aware of the degree to which his surroundings are industrially formed: farmers compete in industrial economies and use industrial machinery and industrial farming methods to alter the topography of the land. Increasingly, industrial structures such as nuclear power plants and factories encroach on farmland. Scott began to pay attention to the longer history of these encroachments as evidenced in paintings by John Constable, in which the effects of enclosure and the impact of industrial farming after the Napoleonic wars can be witnessed, and in Thomas Bewick's wood-engraved book illustrations and vignettes.[22] Images produced by these artists are more properly termed pastoral or rustic than picturesque, as they depict agrarian landscapes marked by human labour. As Ann Bermingham describes them, rustic landscapes portray 'country lanes, farmlands and river scenes', evoking 'the countryside and rural life' rather than famous views or monuments. What Bermingham calls the 'contradiction between the social reality of the countryside and its idealized aesthetic representation'[23] presents an opportunity to explore similar conflicts today.

Much of this work requires knowledge of country life to grasp its significance. For example, Scott has produced a number of very beautiful prints of hedgerows and fences stretched the length of oval and rectangular platters. To the knowing eye, these hedges are degraded products of industrial methods. Previously, hedges were cut and 'laid', the branches laid flat at the base where they fertilized the plant and formed a barrier to hungry sheep and cattle; new growth sprang from the bottom.[24] Hedgerows can be hundreds of years old, comprise numerous plant species and exhibit regional variation. Tending hedgerows is labour-intensive. Although such hedges present thick, vigorous barriers, pressure from global economies and the general loss of rural labour have led to the introduction of mechanical methods, resulting in the thinning and degrading of hedges over time.[25] The hedgerows depicted on these plates are straggly remnants, elegant in their spiky silhouette yet indicative of neglect and decay. These works offer mute protest as they record changes in our environment and way of life.

Many of Scott's concerns with the environment, sustainability and the impact of industry and progress on rural life come together in his confected landscapes and contemporary vignettes. Vignettes can be understood as the perfect manifestation of the picturesque ideal. Ann Bermingham writes:

> In general, the picturesque landscape aspires to the condition of a vignette – that is, a centralized composition in a shallow space whose boundaries are undefined or shade off … The vignette was well fitted to satisfy the double requirements of nature and imagination: its centralized composition focuses on objects and natural details at the same time that its undefined borders suggest an indefinite extension of the imagination.[26]

Literally deconstructing the picture plane, Scott pares away the distinct divisions of foreground, middle and background proposed by picturesque formulae, rendering them as stand-alone printed forms. Not only does he freely mix found and printed plates with hand-formed components, he mixes realistic and fantasy elements, tin-glaze and porcellanous materials, 'straight' images and 'confected' collage. He draws on strategies used in both commercial kitsch, for example souvenir wares, sophisticated graphic art, for example cubist collage, and digitally rendered images. Processing and reading these works requires an exchange of ordinary logic for a more fluid, heterogeneous approach that engages the imagination.

In the eighteenth century, following the examples of America and France, British gentry feared democratic revolution and the loss of privilege based on conservative values and land ownership. Pastoral images sought to soothe these fears with reassuring images of stable country life. Today, we have different fears: global warming, genetic modification, radiation poisoning and unfettered capital that operates independently of local control. These are fears Scott aims to explore rather than soothe. Standing a romantic graphic tree against a realistically rendered power plant, or posing cows, complete with genetic identification tags and monstrously engorged udders on delicate beds of printed forage, Scott forces us to acknowledge the degree to which we repress, naturalize or simply fail to notice the ubiquitous presence of industry and capital in our midst. Imparting images of machines that empower as well as threaten us on to dinnerware, he admits contagion into the domestic sphere, where ideology has its origin and most potent hold.

That these works are also extremely beautiful heightens the ambivalence and conflict we experience viewing them. Scott makes us recognize the degree to which we are prepared to rationalize and compromise in order to preserve our fantasy intact. Although subtle, Paul Scott's confected landscapes and contemporary vignettes expose contradictions and critique ideological fallacies, making them most political works.

Notes

1. Scott exhibited *Confected Landscapes, Cultural Wallpaper and Contemporary Vignettes* alongside objects from the MMU Special Collections as part of his PhD requirement at the Manchester Metropolitan University Special Collections, Manchester, 19 November 2007 to 1 February 2008.
2. Stephanie Brown, "Pioneer Printer," *Keramik Magazine* 3 (2001), p. 33.
3. Paul Scott, Unpublished notes for PhD.
4. H. A. Crosby Forbes, *Hills and Streams: Landscape Decoration on Chinese Export Blue and White Porcelain* (Milton, MA: International Exhibitions Foundation and China Trade Museum, 1982), p. 1.
5. Ann Bermingham, 'English Landscape Drawing Around 1795', in W. J. T. Mitchell, ed., *Landscape and Power* (Chicago: University of Chicago Press, 1994), p. 86.
6. Quoted in Jo Dahn, *Remember me when this you see* (Aberystwyth: University of Wales and Ceredigion Museum, 2002).
7. Scott discusses these processes in *Ceramics and Print*, second edition, pp. 19–24.
8. Paul Scott, Personal interview 17 July 2007.
9. Paul Holdway and David Drakard, *Spode Transfer Printed Ware 1784-1833* (Old Martlesham, Suffolk: Antique Collectors Club, 2002) p. 77, quoted in Scott, Unpublished notes.
10. Jay David Bolter and Richard Grusin, *Remediation: Understanding New Media* (Cambridge: MIT Press, 1999), p. 21. I have used this text to discuss the concept of remediation and craft more generally in 'Remediating Craft', in *Utopic Impulses: Contemporary Ceramics Practice*, eds Ruth Chambers, Amy Gogarty and Mireille Perron (Vancouver: Ronsdale Press, 2007), pp. 91–110.
11. Bolter and Grusin, *Remediation*, p. 273.
12. Ibid. p. 34.
13. Oscar Wilde, 'Art and the Handcraftsman,' in *Essays and Lectures by Oscar Wilde* (London: Methuen and Co, 1908). Online http://www.burrows.com/founders/art.html. Accessed 07 November 2008.
14. *A Potter's Book* (London: Faber and Faber, 1967), p. 101, quoted in Scott, Unpublished notes.
15. Paul Scott, email to author 7 Oct 2008.
16. Ibid.
17. For example, Scott has used spray paint and stencils to apply willow motifs to buildings, an approach that permitted him to explore issues of scale and architecture not possible within the confines of domestic ceramics.
18. Fiona Venables suggests this in her essay accompanying Scott's exhibition *Paul Scott: Cumbrian Blue(s)* (Carlisle: Tullie House Museum and Art Gallery, 24 May to 13 July 2003): 'The exhibition incorporates Scott's Sellafield pieces, his Foot and Mouth works and a host of objects commemorating political situations and events that have moved the artist over the years, from Apartheid in South Africa to the treatment of Taliban and Al Qaida prisoners at Camp X-Ray in Cuba'.
19. In W. J. T. Mitchell, ed., *Landscape and Power*, p. 5.
20. Dahn, *Remember me*.
21. Paul Scott, Personal interview 17 July 2007. Scott expressed agreement with a proposition put forth by Paul Mathieu that ceramic objects serve as essential archives of historical events and forces. See Paul Mathieu, 'The Brown Pot and the White Cube', in *Utopic Impulses;* eds Chambers, Gogarty and Perron, p. 50.

22. See Ann Bermingham, *Landscape and Ideology: The English Rustic Tradition, 1740-1860* (Berkeley: University of California Press, 1986).
23. Ibid., pp. 10–11.
24. Geoffrey Young, *Country Eye: A Walker's Guide to Britain's Traditional Countryside* (London: George Philip, 1991) pp. 72–73.
25. Paul Scott, Personal interview 17 July 2007.
26. *Landscape and Ideology*, p. 85.

For more information on Paul Scott and images of his work including that discussed in this essay, please see his website www.cumbrianblues.com.

Originally published in *Ceramics: Art and Perception*, no 75, 2009, pp. 51–56.

Reproduced with permission from *Ceramics: Art and Perception* and the author.

SECTION 3.4
FIGURATION AND THE BODY

Introductory summary

The human form has been a key subject matter in ceramic art for thousands of years and this section includes texts that consider figurative works from a number of perspectives. In the first text, Bonnie Kemske describes the background to and development of a series of sculptural ceramic objects 'created by and for the body'. The text gives an overview of the importance of touch as well some examples of exhibitions that have invited visitors to touch objects. Kemske then discusses how she developed her own tactile pieces through 'practice-based' PhD research and how visitors to an exhibition responded to them.

Peter Selz gives an overview of a range of artists, mainly working in the United States, who have made powerful use of clay as a sculptural medium for figurative works. Initially focusing on developments in California and associated artists such as Peter Voulkos, Stephen De Staebler, and Robert Arneson, Selz goes on to discuss 'illusionist' artists including Richard Shaw and Marilyn Levine. Viola Frey's large-scale brightly coloured figures are considered as well as works by Daniel Rhodes, Doug Jeck and Michael Lucero. International artists with connections to the United States are also discussed including German-born Ruth Duckworth who settled in Illinois. Japanese ceramists Takako Araki and Akio Takamori, and Phyllis Green and Marek Cecula are also discussed.

Penny Byrne uses her training as restorer of ceramics to modify vintage ceramic figurines to transform them into satirical sculptures that comment on contemporary issues and politics. The text, by Inga Walton, describes a number of these works and is also relevant for those interested in found objects, political ceramics and humour in art.

Livingstone and Petrie

50
EMBRACING SCULPTURAL CERAMICS: A LIVED EXPERIENCE OF TOUCH IN ART

Bonnie Kemske

I am sitting quietly in the small Japanese tearoom with my legs folded under me. The calm dimness rests my eyes and makes the muted natural amber colors of the room glow. The host sits in front of me. He pours hot water over the bright green tea he has placed in the ceramic teabowl. He rapidly whisks the tea to a froth, picks up the teabowl, turns it, and places it closer to me. I place the teabowl in front of myself, then exchange a bow with the host. I breathe. Then I carefully lift the teabowl into my left hand and feel the warmth of the tea spread through the ceramic bowl to fill my open palm. Molding my other hand around the side of the teabowl, I cradle the bowl that cradles the tea. I raise it slightly, bow almost imperceptibly, turn the teabowl two quarter turns, then raise its smooth rim to my lips.

Cradling the teabowl is not just a function in the Tea Ceremony; it serves as a synecdoche for the Tea Ceremony itself. It is deliberate and considered – imbued with consciousness, self-awareness, and shared action. It is the connection, tactile and spiritual, between you and the host, and the center of your own experience of this sensual art form.

Since this experience as a young Tea student in Japan, through ten years in the ceramics studio producing textured abstracted figurative work, and later as an artist-researcher, I have asked myself how I could capture the evanescent and self-reflective state achieved through the physical experience of Tea in sculptural ceramic objects. This paper tells of the part of this self-reflective journey undertaken as an artist-researcher, and of the experiences arising from it.

My work falls within the area of practice-based or art-based research, which comprises both theoretical and studio investigations, and which results in both critical text and artworks. There is ample support for this experiential model. In 1958 Michael Polanyi articulated the concept of 'tacit knowing' as that which cannot be expressed or taught through language (Polanyi 1958). Since then, tacit knowledge has long been acknowledged and reflected upon within the craft and latterly the art world. Peter Dormer states, 'Craft relies on tacit knowledge. Tacit knowledge is acquired through experience and it is the knowledge that enables you to do things as distinct from talking or writing about them.' (Dormer 1997: 147) He expands this concept by considering the role of the craft practitioner within this 'craft knowledge'. '… [C]raft knowledge … has … a private aspect: craft knowledge resides in individual people. Such knowledge becomes a part of the self. … In most complex crafts there is, for those expert in it, a form of dialogue going on between the practitioner, his expertise, and the goal that the practitioner is trying to make or find.' (Dormer 1994: 18-19) Art-based research had not yet developed during Dormer's time but I believe that we can extend his understanding of the role of the practitioner to include that of the artist-researcher. Anna Fariello continues the discussion on tacit knowledge with this succinct summary, 'While verbal language can provide clues to understanding and can stimulate reflection, it cannot replace knowing the work through experiential methods.' (Fariello 2005: 155)

Source: © Bonnie Kemske/Reproduced with kind permission of Taylor and Francis.

Looking beyond craft theory, a recent book by sociologist Richard Sennett also supports the value of an experiential approach. 'Good work … emphasizes the lessons of experience through a dialogue between tacit knowledge and explicit critique.' (Sennett 2008: 51) In many ways art-based research well represents Sennett's vision of combining 'tacit knowledge' as practice, and 'explicit critique' as theory. The artwork created as part of this research could not have developed without the fundamental interweaving of practice and theory.

Touch and tactility

For many years I had been producing tactile textured ceramic forms as a studio artist. As an artist-researcher I chose to begin the research into tactility, again in a studio setting. I first considered how I might encourage individuals to physically engage with artworks through the qualities of the artwork itself. If I offered them textures that were visually alluring, would they be tempted to touch to verify the quality of the surface? I devised a project to establish which clays and firing temperatures would be most tactilely pleasing. I created almost 100 identically textured tiles in various clays and fired them to different temperatures. However, it became clear very early that there was no universal tactile aesthetic to be found. The tiles were rated differently by myself and others, and rated differently again in a second rating. Research by Charles Spence confirms the changing nature of tactile perception. Spence showed that a texture was commonly rated as rougher if the subject being tested heard the sound of sandpaper being scraped while touching the texture (Spence 2004). Our senses are multi-dimensional and interdependent.

The role of touch

What is touch? I needed to understand the role of touch in our lives theoretically, and to reflect on it personally. This led me to understand touch as our most direct, least intellectualized, sense. It is the grounding sense, the sense of tangibility that places us in the world. As the full proverb states, 'Seeing is believing, but feeling is the truth' (attributed to British clergyman Thomas Fuller, 1608-1661). Yet it seems to me that within our western culture a hegemony of vision erodes our tactile sensitivities.

In Tiffany Field's book, *Touch*, she stated that within our western culture many of us are touch deprived, and she refers to this as 'touch hunger' (Field 2001: 1–17). A quick survey of popular culture illustrates how we search for new ways to incorporate touch in our lives. There are massage chairs, belts, and pillows. Health spas provide access to saunas and jacuzzis. Showers have settings to stimulate the skin. And there are more and more types of massage on offer – shiatsu, Swedish, reiki, and rolfing among others. All these things can be seen as ways of increasing personal touch stimulation in our tactile hungry society.

How much touch we need, how we perceive touch, whether we find it pleasant or distasteful, and how we react to it, vary dramatically from person to person. It is influenced by factors such as our genetic make-up, experiences as a fetus, baby, child, and adult, our gender, the attitudes and mores of our society, our personal circumstances, and our emotional and physical state at any one time. So although touch is a universal experience, it is also an utterly intimate and individual one.

Touch in art

In the world of fine art in the twentieth century, partly as a backlash against movements such as Formalism (from Russian Formalism through to Abstract Expressionism), with its preoccupation with the visual aspects of color, form, line, and composition, artists such as those working within the Arte Povera movement led the way to more fully engaging our senses through their use of non-traditional materials, often mundane materials with which we interact daily (Lumley 2004). This type of work began to challenge the no-touching policies within museums and galleries, and in the past few years curators and gallery owners have been grappling with practical as well as conceptual issues surrounding touching artwork (See Heritage Studies Research Group 2004). Indeed, recently galleries and museums have mounted exhibitions aimed at engaging touch. Three examples in London alone can be given. The Victoria and Albert Museum's exhibition entitled '*Touch Me: Design and Sensation*' (V&A 2005) specifically set out to challenge the anti-touch status quo, and included work by international applied artists. Within this exhibition there were many design items with which visitors could interact, the emphasis seeming to be more on interaction itself than on any tactile experience of the displays. The University for the Creative Arts hosted an exhibition entitled '*HAPTIC: Awakening the Senses*' (UCA 2008), which tried to engage the visitor's sense of touch by providing small touchable samples of the materials used in the artworks. However, this still forced the visitor to rely on touch memory to get a sense of touching the artwork. For '*Jerwood Contemporary Makers*' (Jerwood 2008) seven artists from differing craft disciplines were asked to produce work on the theme of touch on the physical, imagined, and metaphorical levels. Of the work of the seven artists, visitors were allowed to actually touch only one artwork, Clare Twomey's *Witness*, a wall covered with porcelain dust onto which visitors were welcomed to leave their mark. In the remainder of the exhibition we were asked to accept what our eyes told us, to experience the tactile qualities of the works second-hand, through vision and words. Even though the exhibition was themed 'touch', ironically, it left a sense of touch deprivation, the experience remaining anticipative and unconsummated (Kemske 2008: 26). These exhibitions demonstrate that curators did not or chose not to consider the multiple aspects of touch, leaning heavily on single understandings, respectively, interaction, touch as visual verification, and touch as imagined or metaphorical.

The materiality of clay

It was particularly surprising to find such extreme restrictions on actual touching in the Jerwood exhibition because through function and utility crafts or applied arts historically have been the touchable arts. This long history of handling ceramics objects was part of the basis of my decision to situate this research within the field of sculptural ceramics. I feel the familiarity of the material helps us to overcome our reservations about touching artwork. In addition, fired clay has physical properties that are particularly suitable for tactile exploration. It is hard, yet can feel responsive to our touch, partly because it can absorb our body heat. It is a material that enticingly embraces contrast. It can be rough or smooth or both simultaneously. Its heaviness can be perceived as comforting. In addition, it never loses the echo of its making; it is a frozen moment that embodies the act of its creation, a permanent link between maker and the person holding the artwork. I believe that as humans we have an innate and intimate familiarity and sensitivity to fired clay.

Touch and the body

I decided to find out more about the mechanics of touch, or how the body touches, which led to a working understanding of the body's physiology and neuro-physiology. It was the Two-Point Discrimination Threshold Test that led me to fully understand and appreciate that touch is not a single sense and that our experience of touch is very different across different parts of our bodies. This test is used clinically to indicate neurological damage. It also identifies normal differences in sensation. In the test the individual has his or her eyes shut or covered. A two-pointed caliper-like instrument is pressed against the skin at different parts of the body, both points being applied simultaneously. The person indicates whether or not he or she perceives the contact as two distinct points or as a single point. The distance between the two points is made larger and smaller over a series of touchings until a 'threshold' is determined, that is, the widest measurement at which the person still perceives two points to be one.

The differences across the body can be extreme. For instance, the skin of the fingertip and lip is very sensitive, whereas the thigh, forearm, and back is not (Sinclair 1981: 180). Acknowledging the need to evaluate the tactile sensations personally, I had my own two-point discrimination thresholds tested. On my fingertip I perceived any two points closer together than three millimeters to be one point, whereas on my thigh it was 42 millimeters. Indeed, my own two-point discrimination thresholds are in fact rather more acute than average. This may be one of the reasons I am drawn to the field of touch, or perhaps I have become sensitized through the heightened awareness resulting from my work.

Using the results of this test I produced small hand-held textured ceramic forms to be run across the body, creating varying sensations. One particularly successful piece was made to be run down the inside of the arm, evoking a variety of sensations as it travelled across the different sensitivities of the upper and lower arm, wrist, palm, and fingers. If it were not for the continuity of the touch, the same object would feel like many different objects as it travels over the skin.

I found that individuals willingly engaged with these pieces when invited to do so. However, their interactions with them were rapid, both in the speed of their actions and in the length of time they took in exploration. I felt this discouraged a positive reflective experience, such as the one I had had in Japanese Tea Ceremony, and thought larger works might both increase the length of time people took with each piece and slow down their responses.

Looking again at the physiology of touch led to understanding touch not as singular, but as a manifold experience. Distinct receptors have the abilities to perceive and discriminate pressure, texture, vibration, hot, cold, a light touch (Olausson et al, 2002: 900–904), and pain, which includes itch and tickle, and the densities and distribution of these receptors vary across the body. I decided to try to incorporate the multiple senses of touch into the work.

To determine how I might do this, I revisited earlier research I had done into how different cultures interact tactilely with ceramics. I recalled a conversation with Nigel Barley, anthropologist and author at the British Museum (Barley 1994), about women potters in Africa who make pots to fit their bodies to facilitate carrying. I intended my work to be sculptural, not functional, but I thought that creating artworks that fit the body might be one way to try to more fully engage our sense of touch.

Touching beyond the hand

First, I had a plaster cast made of my own body. I built sculptures upon the cast that would then fit against my body. I then textured the surfaces of the forms, using coarse textures where the sculptures rested against the body and fine textures for areas that the hands would have access to. The resultant objects fit snugly against different parts of my body. However, during a three month period of working in Japan, I had no body cast, so I built the objects directly on my own body, that is, I shaped plastic clay against my bare skin, using my body as a mold. This experience was challenging, but also physically engaging, and led me to reflect about my relationship to the pieces I was creating. Here are extracts from journal notes made during the making experience:

- *The clay is cool but warms quickly.*
- *Feels snug, contained, comfortable – caressed?*

- *There's a strong sense of immediacy and intimacy.*
- *A single perspective – an inner perspective of tactile experience.*
- *Until I lift it away from my body it exists solely as part of me.*
- *This piece is an object to me (the subject), but why doesn't it feel like that?*

Being in Japan I looked to Japanese philosophy to understand my experience. It was the work of Japanese philosopher Nishida Kitarō that made me begin to think of the making process as experience, rather than just a way to reach the end-point. Nishida says:

> To experience means to know events precisely as they are. It means to cast away completely one's attitude of discriminative reflection, and to know in accordance with the events. (Nishida cited in Encyclopædia Brittanica 2007)

This is what he calls 'pure experience', a 'direct' experience prior to the separation of subject and object (Nishida 1990: 48), a moment of pre-intellectualization.

> In pure experience, our thinking, feeling, and willing are still undivided; there is a single activity, with no opposition between subject and object. Such opposition arises from the demands of thinking, so it is not a fact of direct experience. In direct experience there is only an independent, self-sufficient event, with neither a subject that sees nor an object that is seen. (Nishida 1990: 48)

The deeper engagement of my body within the experience of making served as a good example to me of this kind of 'direct experience'. I created three pieces in this way and exhibited them in a public art gallery in Kyoto. Finding a way to display the sculptures to encourage touching forced me to consider the role of the gallery and setting.

Touch in the gallery

No matter what has gone into the creation of the specific artwork, the pieces can never be considered outside their context, and one's first encounter with an artwork is most often within a gallery setting. When entering a museum or gallery the sign you are most likely to see reads: Do Not Touch. The sign fortifies the social taboo against touching artwork, but it also serves as a signal to us that there *is* something there to touch, some encounter to be experienced beyond visual engagement. The sign both prohibits us from touching and challenges us to reach out and run a finger over the surface of the art object.

Curators and exhibition designers often reinforce the no-touch policy through the creation of gallery spaces that are dramatic and memorable by using minimal display, specifically designed lighting, and strong focal points. These design qualities, and the reverential hush that accompanies them, often evoke a sense of the church or temple, especially when the artwork is displayed on a plinth, which may evoke images of the altar.

What does this no-touch policy 'do' for the artwork? Where there are large numbers of exhibition visitors there can be protective benefits for delicate or valuable artworks; the social taboo can help prevent breakage, soiling, and can deter theft. The placing of the artwork on a plinth also changes its signification; it informs us that the piece has a considerable monetary and/or cultural value, and it also raises the perceived status of the artist. In addition, not touching precludes individuals from having to know how to physically engage with an artwork, keeping them from the social embarrassment of mishandling the work. It also reinforces elitism within the art world by declaring that 'we' in the art world (makers, curators, collectors) may handle the artwork, whereas 'they' (the public) may not.

In the Kyoto exhibition people did interact with the artworks, but not as I expected. I thought they would fit the works to their bodies in the same positions in which I had made them, but people interacted with them in numerous and creative ways, engaging with them very personally and intimately.

Into the lived experience

Looking to expand my understanding of the intimacy and immediacy of the making, the sense of the work being part of me as I formed it, and the blur I felt between me as subject and the artwork as object, I looked to the French phenomenologist Maurice Merleau-Ponty to try to understand conceptually what was happening in this experience. I carried his concepts of an inseparable mind and body, the 'incarnated mind', and the 'double belongingness' of simultaneously touching and being touched with me into the next stage of making and wrote and reflected on it during that time.

It was clear that I needed to continue to make work using my body but now I wanted to try to create forms that had no conscious design element, forms that were derived solely from my body's own involvement. I was also concerned that in the artworks I had created thus far, the visual aspects were still dominant. In looking for a way to fully engage the body, I came to 'cast hugs', that is, I sat or lay in the studio embracing a large plaster-filled latex balloon until it set.

In this way I overrode my training in the visual aesthetic, using instead only my tactile senses. The works were created through three determinants alone: my body, the state of the plaster, and the sizes of the balloons. After casting a series of 'hugs', when deciding which hugs to further develop into artworks, I first chose those casts that were pleasurable to touch and hold. Secondly, I looked for shapes that might visually entice us to physically engage with the artwork through touching, lifting, handling, and caressing.

I then made molds of the cast hugs and used them to reproduce the shapes in clay, texturing the finished forms, firing, then applying a surface of terra sigillata, which is a fine slip or liquid clay, before a final low firing.

Touch and the embrace

Touch is the first sense to appear in the developing fetus and the last sense to leave (Montagu 1986: 3). As soon as the fetus is large enough, the embrace of the womb is one of the first experiences of touch it has. After birth, infants who are not touched and embraced suffer many disturbing and debilitating conditions, including stunted growth and aggressive behavior (Field 2001: 59–74). Adults as well as children need significant touch experiences in their lives (Field 2001: 91–115) and regular hugging can help people have healthier hearts, especially women (Light, Kathleen C. et al. 2005: 5–21).

We can embrace and be embraced throughout our lives, and the embrace is clearly seen as a positive experience. The Free Hugs Movement video (FREEHUGSCAMPAIGN.org), which shows a man on the street and in shopping malls giving hugs, still circulates on the internet, and is enacted from time to time around the world. Cuddle Parties have been reported in the media (Lusher 2006. See also cuddleparty.com). Having originated in New York these hugging parties are now being enacted in several countries. A cross-over with health, well-being, and religious issues can be seen in the phenomenon that is Mata Amritanandamayi. The laying-on of hands is a common religious activity, especially within some Christian sects; what distinguishes Amma from other spiritual healers is her specific use of the embrace.

> They came by the thousands, from the city and from all over the country, just looking for a hug. But Mata Amritanandamayi – known to her devotees as Amma – is no ordinary hugger. The 50-year-old woman from India, who wears a white sari and a diamond-studded nose ring, is nicknamed the Hugging Saint for the embraces that have earned her a worldwide following. By early yesterday morning, more than 2,000 people had packed the hall at the Manhattan Center on W. 34th St., eager for a moment in the arms of the spiritual guru … (Lebovich cited in Classen 2005: 106).

Extensive field research and the use of methods such as focus groups have given major advertisers an edge on knowing what the public wants. A notable campaign advertising Orange mobile telephones used scenes of young people hugging. An international company as large as Orange using the hug as a marketing image, is a clear indication that hugging is of significant relevance to their young adult target audience.

Age, however, does not seem to deter the need for the embrace. Rose Hacker, a 101-year-old newspaper columnist, wrote, 'Being hugged is the fulfillment of the dream. My parents never touched us – we had a peck on the cheek at most. When my father died, however, he held out his arms from the bed and cried 'Rosie darling.' That was the only time he ever hugged me, and I remember thinking: 'I've been wanting this all my life.' ' (Hacker 2007: 10–11).

The art of the experience

Building on my making experience and understanding the embrace led me to realize that the 'art' of the artwork I was producing was not manifest in the material object itself, but rather in the individual's experience of the object. As Merleau-Ponty said, 'What is given is not the thing on its own, but the experience of the thing.' (Merleau-Ponty 1962: 379) I do not consider the works to be complete until they are held against the body.

At this point it was clear to me that I needed to acknowledge, develop, and chronicle the significance of the making experience. To more fully integrate and reflect on the concepts I was grappling with and the experience of making, I wrote of the experience, intertwining the physicality of the experience with reflections on Merleau-Ponty's writings.

The use of my own body in the making of these artworks had become important, but I did not know how this related to other people's responses to the finished work. My desire was not to have others simply replicate the experience of making. Many of us have felt the thrill of fitting our fingers into the making marks left by the potter of an ancient vessel, but I felt strongly that this 'replication' was not what I sought. Touch is a universal experience, but ultimately, it is also personal and individual, and I wanted each encounter with an artwork to evoke an individual's response drawn from his or her own personal history, not to serve as a personal communication from me as maker to the individual as receiver.

So how did an individual's experience of the work compare and relate to my experience of making? In exhibition I had discovered that, although people did not physically fit the artworks to their own bodies as I had in making, did not in fact 'replicate' the making, I could deduce from the written and verbatim comments I collected from visitors during exhibitions, that we did, in fact, share many of the same emotional and physical experiences. Correlating those comments to the emergent writing style I had developed as a way to bring together my experience of making with my understanding of Merleau-Ponty, I will explore seven themes that arose.

The Thoughtful Body

Sitting on the floor, holding a plaster-filled latex balloon against my bare skin until it sets …
My ankle is pinned beneath the shifting mass that rests on top of it, engulfed by the weight of the soft plaster as it oozes around and over the hardness of bone. I center it to my torso, holding its confined fluidity in place with my legs and arms.

'… it is through my body that I go to the world,' wrote Merleau-Ponty. This could not be more evident than now, as I press my body around this moving, oozing weight. I understand my perception of this mass in terms of Merleau-Ponty's 'lived experience', an experience of and through the body. But Merleau-Ponty's body is not simply a collection of physiological assets; it is inseparable from the mind, just as the mind cannot be considered independently of the body. 'The perceiving mind is an incarnated mind.' (Merleau-Ponty 2004: 34)

Thought and corporeality together are the whole. All I perceive/feel/think is grounded in this, my conscious body, the thoughtful body. It is 'the general instrument of my 'comprehension'.' (Merleau-Ponty 1962: 273)

There were differing ways that Merleau-Ponty's 'lived experience' and 'incarnated mind' were expressed by visitors. Some individuals directly linked body and mind in statements such as 'It's fascinating – and relaxing … It helps you think because it gives you something to touch and handle' or 'The continuous texture is safe and let's you explore it to find new ways – an analogy for new patterns in life.' Also, I believe that statements that indicate a sense of self in relation to the physical experience can express these Merleau-Ponty concepts as well. Visitors used the words 'intimate', 'personal', 'sensual', 'calming', and 'quiet', words that serve as expressions of self-awareness of states of being that transcend the separation of mind and body as they express both simultaneously. Another good example can be seen in this man's comment: 'I feel I should be weeping, having a breakdown, like it's drawing it out of me.'

Overlapping or encroachment

I move my ankle and feel the unstable liquid roll slightly back and forth within its own weight. Squeezing my legs together, my right thigh presses into the heavy liquid, which is surprisingly resistant.

'… there is overlapping or encroachment, so that we must say that the things pass into us as well as we into the things.' (Merleau-Ponty 1968: 123)

I feel the heavy liquid move against my thigh and its resistance to the pressure I impose on it. The liquid mass is distorting, as much as molding to my body, which dents, dimples, and alters under the form's weight. For me, this experience goes beyond Merleau-Ponty's description of an overlapping or encroachment. At this moment I and the embraced form exist only in relation to each other. We connect in an intimate and ever-shifting state of interaction and share influence on each other and presence in the world.

The comment 'You transform something hard and unyielding into something soft, smooth, inviting and irresistible' expresses a state of interaction between body and artwork that is reflective of Merleau-Ponty's 'encroachment', as does 'As soon as I fit it to my body and found a place where it was comfortable, it didn't feel cold or hard anymore.' Transformation expresses the influence that occurs between body and the object being held; each transforms the other. Engagement also signifies a taking in, an encroachment, in comments such as 'It drew me to it', 'It makes you want to lean into it', and 'As sculptural objects these are beautiful, they are also visually very inviting. You want to touch and hold them.' Finally, many people indicated that when embracing the artworks they developed a sense that the objects had become part of themselves. 'Pressing the curvaceous shape into my body felt as if I was hugging an extension of myself' and 'It's so soothing – it sort of melts into your body' are good examples of this.

The shared boundary

The squeeze of my legs moves the skin of my inner thigh across the smooth texture of the mass, an intimate contact that triggers my awareness of its slippery surface. My now-slippery thigh slides over its surface.

Now which is slippery? The form or my inner thigh? And where is the line between me and it? A viscous blur. 'It is as though our vision were formed in the heart of the visible, or as though there were between it and us an intimacy as close as between the sea and the strand. And yet it is not possible that we blend into it, nor that it passes into us …' (Merleau-Ponty 1968: 130–131)

Merleau-Ponty's words refer to vision but I can extrapolate them to include touch. The viscous blur is the connection between me and the mass I perceive, an intimate and integral interface that joins me and it. Yet it is more than merely a shared boundary, a dividing membrane.

A concept closely related to that of encroachment is the blurred or shared boundary between subject (me as maker or an individual as embracer) and object (the sculptural artworks). Some visitor comments addressed this directly, as in 'It's requited – it touches you – you and the work absorb each other' and 'At first it feels cold, but very quickly you can feel it becoming warm. And as you move your hands over it, you can feel where you've been holding it. So you have a sense of how you are changing it as much as it is affecting you. It's responsive.' Others express it in terms of their own bodies: 'I am astonished by the way these rock-like works fit so lovingly around all the curves, the places of my body. They are cool to the touch, and appeal to the sensual, maternal aspects of my being. They are marvelously feminine, voluptuous and strangely comforting.' and 'I like the way the hardness makes me move around and fit my body to it, rather than the other way around. It makes me aware of muscles and my body that I'm not normally aware of.'

The 'and' between subject and object

Shifting forward I press my left forearm into the top of the amorphous mass. It makes only a subtle impression. So I lock my right hand onto my left wrist and bear down again. My arm sinks into the firmness a little more.

My arm presses in, and in doing so,
becomes both sensor and agent, 'the body as sensible and
the body as sentient' (Merleau-Ponty 1968: 136). It both
feels and acts.
'... our body is a being of two leaves, from one side a
thing among things and otherwise what sees them and
touches them; ... it unites these two properties within
itself, and its double belongingness to the
order of the 'object' and to the order of the 'subject' reveals to us quite
unexpected relations between the two orders.' (Merleau-
Ponty 1968: 137)

It is in these dual roles, within this double belongingness,
that Merleau-Ponty explores the 'and' between sensible
and sentient, subject and object, passive and active – two
manifestations of the same body – one experience. As I try
to impress my body into the changing shape, I am aware
of my double belongingness. I feel the mass's physical and
independent presence, but I also feel my influence on its
very existence.

The 'and' between subject and object is manifest in many forms. First, there is the direct influence of the body on the object and the object on the body in comments like 'It's cooling my chest, but warming where my hands are' and 'Because it is ceramic I expected it to be hard and cold. And it was, as long as I was handling it. But as soon as I fit it to my body and found a place where it was comfortable, it didn't feel cold or hard anymore'. Then there are comments that differentiate between self and object at the same time as expressing another kind of inseparable 'double belongingness'. This can be seen in the comment 'It's about me but at the same time it's about this object.' Finally, I believe that some of the more ambiguous comments that express a sense of contradiction may also reflect the 'and'. This can be seen in 'Soft, hard, squashy, resilient – need to touch them!', 'Oddly comfortable – strangely comforting', 'Intuitively you think it won't feel very nice because it's hard and heavy, but it feels good, it's soothing', and 'Isn't it amazing that something so hard can feel so soft?'

Chiasm

Curling over its bulk I add the weight of my upper body to the squeeze. My breasts sink down. I feel the discomfort of their flattened distortion, yet they make only shallow valleys in the shifting mass.

My body is both touching and being touched by the mass I enfold. Awareness shifts from one to the other – toucher to touched, touched to toucher – with little control on my part. This shift is Merleau-Ponty's chiasm, the 'and'. It is 'the motion of perpetual dehiscence, in which perception is understood as a being in momentum.' (Vasseleu 1998: 30) Enclosing this mass within the confines of my arms, legs, and torso leads me to understand that this dehiscence, which is defined as both a gaping and a bursting forth, can be seen as experience itself, a cusp of continuous and never-completed change. '… the idea of *chiasm* [is] that…every relation with being is *simultaneously* a taking and a being taken, the hold is held, it is *inscribed* and inscribed in the same being that it takes hold of.' (Merleau-Ponty 1968: 266)

The chiasm isn't a mechanism, a switch to be thrown that will change one perspective to another. It is the experience of perception, 'the organic relationship between subject and world, the active transcendence of consciousness' (Merleau-Ponty 1962: 176.).

One visitor on leaving the exhibition area remarked, 'I feel like I've still got it against me.' Another said, 'It's almost like your mother. It makes me feel comfortable. I've got, like, a bond with it now. When I'm not hugging it, it feels wrong.' I think these two comments express Merleau-Ponty's concept of simultaneous touching and being touched in that the absence of the object identifies the 'being touched' that had been experienced while caressing the artwork. Then there is the sense of the incomplete or never-ending. This can be seen in comments where the action is seen as indefinite or ongoing, such as 'First you slide your hand all over, then you begin to find the dimples. I just want to explore them. I go back to them again and again.' Another comment also reflects touch as process, rather than as static: 'It's calming and quiet. The texture makes you go into the piece – want to feel the wabi-sabi imperfections. The smoothness feels too hard – you search for the imperfections. The texture makes you explore it.'

Communication/communion/community

I ease back slightly and immediately feel the rounded shape reform. I press again and this time the emerging form nudges downward. The bulge nudges against my pubic bone.

This sensual nudge evokes unstructured yet familiar sensations, not exactly memories, but feelings I associate with warmth, comfort, and an accompanying suggestion of arousal.

'…every perception is a communication or a communion, the taking up or completion by us of some extraneous intention, or on the other hand, the complete expression outside ourselves of our perceptual powers and a coition, so to speak, of our body with things.' (Merleau-Ponty 1962: 373)

I focus on maintaining this hug, my thighs squeezed together, my body curled over, and my arms and breasts forcefully pressing down into the thickening form of the hug.

Is this Merleau-Ponty's communication/communion?
'I am able to touch effectively only if the phenomenon finds an echo within me, if it accords with a certain nature of my consciousness, and if the organ which goes out to meet it is synchronized with it.' (Merleau-Ponty 1962: 369)
There is an unspoken experience of synchronization, of communion, of finding the echo inside of me. I sit with this hug held within the circle of my body and feel the many echoes of experience – echoes of safety, of sexual tension, of great joy, of maternal longing, of motherly love. At this transient, ever-incomplete moment the thickening form and my perception of it coalesce with/within me, my own perception part of the conversation. Yet this is a softly-defined completion, a fullness of uncertainty.

The heavy form my body cradles is quickening and becomes warm against my skin. Ironically, it quickens into solidity. I shift slightly and the stiffening weight no longer follows me. It no longer oozes around me and hugs me; its movement is stilled. I must now press myself around it to maintain the embrace. I become the one who moves.

Another layer of the chiasm, being on the edge of one thing, but continuously being and becoming its opposite, being and becoming neither, the incompleteness. This incompleteness has a depth that avows that there is no purely physical sensation or purely mental reflection.

Each sensation/thought is embedded in a resonance within me that creates the perception, encompassing all that sensation is: spiritual, emotional, mental, physical…

This 'resonance' can be specific in association as in the comments: 'It makes me feel sleepy. Maybe that's because I need something heavy on me to fall asleep. The weight feels safe and reassuring. It feels significant. Also, the texture is important. It feels right. Calming. It wouldn't work if they were soft. The hardness feels strong, safe.', 'It reminds me of large stones in my village in Iran where women in labor press their bodies against the stone to take away the pain. Also, we have stones that we believe take our emotional pain away. We say then that the stone is crying.', and 'The curves of the objects made me think of my family when I touched them, and gave me tears. A very warm feeling.' In these instances the experience of caressing the artwork has evoked particular memories or associations that are separate from the artwork. However, although the resonance within an individual's history is still apparent, some visitor comments also demonstrate that a new association can be created. This can be seen in the following examples: 'It makes me feel slightly more important because now I have a purpose, I am looking after something important.', 'It wants to be held – it doesn't want to be put back in its box.', 'The big smooth one feels like you have to look after it. The others feel like they're looking after you.' and 'I feel that the textured ones reject me.'

These last comments also point to an interesting anthropomorphizing of the artworks that was also evident in other comments from visitors.

Towards an understanding

The gliding of my hand across the surface, the squeeze of my thighs to hold it in place, the press of my breasts and torso against the now well-defined form…

…Perception is not passive; it is the 'lived experience', a direct participation between me and the world.

Completing the circle we arrive back at the 'lived experience'. Comments like 'Without thinking, I stroke it against my cheek. The smooth and meandering surfaces and their weight are just right.', 'It fits. I just want to wrap my arms around it.', and 'When you get it in the right place, it works. It rests on you, feels comfortable.' give a sense of the interaction with the artwork as one that engages mind and body only as an integral experience, where the physical sensations evoke emotional feelings that in turn reinforce the corporal.

The embrace as a shared experience

Visitors' comments also point to aspects of the experience that I did not envision or anticipate. Individuals and family members used the artwork to express and perhaps to strengthen bonds, such as a father who embraced a child who embraced a sculpture, or a mother who embraced her daughter, and an adult daughter who embraced her mother. The embracing of the artwork became a shared experience, as one visitor expressed it: 'The hug is about a closeness, of sharing an emotional charge. I feel like I am getting the charge from all the people who have hugged this before me. It's important that it's been hugged before – that it's a shared hug. The hug gives you emotional energy.' Another visitor put it this way: 'Snuggling up next to an object that 'fits' with your body – quite intimate yet strange, as you are not the only person who 'fits' with that object...it's like sharing the same intimate moment – that is experienced by many others but at different times in different places – people with different associations, experiences and backgrounds.'

Finally, many visitors addressed the hug directly, giving support to the project and the making of sculptural ceramic objects to be embraced. Three examples include 'So comforting! Hugs are the most special thing in my life!', 'I can see that they would fit anyone – after all, hugs fit everyone.', and 'The hardness of the ceramic is interesting – like a hug. A hug is soft but strong and firm too.'

The experience of casting hugs led me to understand the embrace as a positive and transforming 'lived experience'. Visitor comments suggest that they too experienced much the same in their physical interaction with the artworks. I believe that for both maker and embracer the ever-flowing merging and shifting between touching and being touched, and the blurring of the boundary between the body and the object it holds, results in a slide of awareness from the 'object' to the 'experience of the object'. The mind and body, integrally embedded in each other, experience a bodily pleasure that is inseparable from an emotional or intellectual pleasure.

An on-going ending

The sculptural artworks I have created aim to engage the body's sense of touch through corporal interaction. Visitors' comments showed that physical encounters with the sculptures could evoke sensual responses that were both emotional and physical. This was achieved through exploiting a sense of the familiar at the same time as offering tactile and visual enticement with new shapes and textures. The moment of fitting the sculpture to the body within the embrace brought forth a consonance of heightened physical and emotional self-awareness, an engagement of 'the thoughtful body'.

A gallery setting. A woman sits with the sculptural ceramic object on her lap. She settles it comfortably across her thighs, then explores its surface. She lifts the piece and holds it against her torso. Her arms cradle it.

References

Barley, Nigel. 1994. *Smashing Pots: Works of Clay from Africa.* Washington, D.C.: Smithsonian Institution Press.

Classen, Constance (ed.). 2005. *The Book of Touch.* Oxford: Berg.

cuddleparty.com. http://www.cuddleparty.com/.

Dormer, Peter. 1994. *The Art of the Maker.* London: Thames and Hudson.

Dormer, Peter. 1997. 'Craft and the Turing Test for Practical Thinking' in *The Culture of Craft: Status and Future.* Manchester and New York: Manchester University Press, pp. 137–157.

Fariello, M. Anna and Owen, Paula (eds.). 2005. *Objects and Meaning: New Perspectives on Art and Craft.* Maryland: The Scarecrow Press, Inc.

Field, Tiffany. 2001. *Touch.* Cambridge, Mass.: The MIT Press.

FREEHUGSCAMPAIGN.org. http://www.freehugscampaign.org/.

Hacker, Rose. April 1, 2007. 'This Much I Know'. London: *The Observer Magazine.*

Heritage Studies Research Group, Institute of Archaeology, University College London, 20 December 2004. *The Magic Touch: Touching and Handling in a Cultural Heritage Context* (conference).

Jerwood Charitable Foundation. 2008. 'Jerwood Contemporary Makers' (Catalogue). London: Jerwood Space.

Kemske, Bonnie. September/October 2008. 'Jerwood Contemporary Makers'. *Ceramic Review,* Issue 233.

Lebovich, Jennifer. July 19, 2004. 'Thousands Wait Hours for a Hug', New York Daily News, Cited in *The Book of Touch,* C. Classen (ed.) Oxford: Berg, 2005.

Light, Kathleen C. et al. 'More frequent partner hugs and higher oxytocin levels are linked to lower blood pressure and heart rate in premenopausal women', in *Biological Psychology*, Vol. 69, Issue 1, April 2005, pp. 5–21. http://www.sciencedirect.com/science?_ob=ArticleURL&_udi=B6T4T-4F4H9W4-1&_user=10&_coverDate=04%2F01%2F2005&_rdoc=1&_fmt=&_orig=search&_sort=d&view=c&_acct=C000050221&_version=1&_urlVersion=0&_userid=10&md5=cf173da66f7ba15cf6dc6103165f3886. (Accessed: August 14, 2007).

Lumley, Robert. 2004. *Arte Povera*, London: Tate Publishing.

Lusher, Adam. October 14, 2006. 'It's a tight squeeze as British reserve meets the cuddle party'. London: Telegraph.co.uk. http://www.telegraph.co.uk/news/uknews/1531450/Its-a-tight-squeeze-as-British-reserve-meets-the-cuddle-party.html (Accessed: April 12, 2009).

Merleau-Ponty, Maurice. 1962. *The Phenomenology of Perception*, Colin Smith (trans.) London: Routledge.

Merleau-Ponty, Maurice. 1968. *The Visible and the Invisible: Followed by Working Notes*, Alphonso Lingis (trans.) Evanston: Northwestern University Press.

Merleau-Ponty, Maurice. 2004. *Maurice Merleau-Ponty: Basic Writings*, Thomas Baldwin (ed.) Routledge: London.

Montagu, Ashley. 1986. *Touching: The Human Significance of the Skin, 3rd Edition*, New York: Harper & Row Publishers.

Nishida, Kitarō. *Zen no kenkyu*. Cited in 'Nishida Kitarō', Encyclopædia Brittanica 2007, *Encyclopædia Brittanica Online*. http://www.britannica.com/eb/article-5292. (Accessed: 17 August 2007).

Nishida, Kitarō. 1990. *An Inquiry into the Good*, New Haven: Yale University Press.

Olausson, H., Lamarre, Y. et al. September 2002. 'Unmyelinated tactile afferents signal touch and project to insular cortex', in *Nature Neuroscience*, Vol. 5, No. 9, pp. 900–904, published online: 29 July 2002. doi:10.1038/nn896. http://www.nature.com/neuro/journal/v5/n9/full/nn896.html. (Accessed: July 22, 2003).

Polanyi, Michael. 1958. *Personal Knowledge: Towards a Post-Critical Philosophy*. London: Routledge & Kegan Paul.

Sennett, Richard. 2008. *The Craftsman*. St Ives: Allen Lane (Penguin Books).

Sinclair, David. 1981. *Mechanisms of Cutaneous Sensation*. Oxford: Oxford University Press.

Spence, Charles. December 20, 2004. 'A Multisensory Approach to Touch' (conference paper). *The Magic Touch: Touching and Handling in a Cultural Heritage Context*. University College London, Institute of Archaeology, Heritage Studies Research Group.

University for the Creative Arts. 2008. 'Memory and Touch: an exploration of textural communication' (exhibition and conference). http://www.ucreative.ac.uk/index.cfm?articleid=18890. (Accessed: March 18, 2009).

Vasseleu, Cathryn. 1998. *Textures of Light: Vision and Touch in Irigaray, Levinas and Merleau-Ponty*, London: Routledge.

Victoria and Albert Museum. June 16 – August 29, 2005. 'Touch Me: Design and Sensation' (exhibition). London. http://www.vam.ac.uk/vastatic/microsites/1376_touch_me/ (Accessed: June 11, 2007).

Originally published as Bonnie Kemske (2009) 'Embracing sculptural ceramics: a lived experience of touch in art', in *The Senses & Society Journal*, 4.3, 2009, pp. 323–344.

Reprinted by permission of the publisher Taylor & Francis Ltd, www.tandfonline.com

51
VICIOUS FIGURINES: PENNY BYRNE'S CERAMIC ADVOCACY

Inga Walton

They populate antique stores and haunt the cabinets in your Grandmother's parlour: simpering Meissen maidens, archly posed Dresden 'crinoline groups', and swirling pastel-hued gowns on Capodimonte cuties. The quiet aesthetic tyranny of the porcelain figurine is familiar to us all; bucolic milk-maids, prancing horses bearing listless swains, demure courting couples, romping puppies in baskets, tousled-haired shepherds, and nubile nymphs toting garlands of flowers. For centuries these cloying, diabetes-inducing, idealised confections have been avidly collected as a symbol of genteel refinement, and dusted with the most tender care.

Penny Byrne relies on this initial cringe-factor before she assails you with her politically charged and subversive version of this amiable, essentially benign, and much-beloved art form. With a reputation as either decorative or utilitarian, ceramics is not a medium through which audiences generally expect controversial social issues to be explored. Byrne's first major solo exhibition *Blood, Sweat and Fears* in March, 2007 rather pummelled that assumption. "In taking vintage porcelain figures and altering them to change their meaning they are given a jolt into the contemporary world, and updated for the 21st century", Byrne observes, "This antique foundation with my modern layering often makes for a bizarre and confronting mix."[1]

By profession Byrne is a highly-sought conservator and restorer of ceramics and glass, "In that side of my work there's no room to play. It's a very precise, exact, and often very scientific process", she says.[2] Byrne's trajectory as an artist has certainly been an unusual one, "When I finished high school I got into both Law and Fine Arts, and decided to follow the fine arts/ceramics path at the time, which then lead on to ceramic conservation", she recounts. "I decided to study law in the mid '90's as a mature-aged student, fully intending to practice. I have an interest in social justice and human rights issues and, although my degree didn't allow me to specialise, I enjoyed international humanitarian law, feminist legal theory, and family law".

Byrne's first piece, made for a Melbourne Fringe Festival group show in 2005, was assembled from some Dresden ballerina figurines her mother (who owned an antique store in Mildura for thirty years) had given her. "I got a lot of positive feedback about the work, but not many people saw the show, so I decided to exhibit it in the Linden Postcard Show", she recalls, "Unexpectedly, I was one of the winners that year, and the piece sold too which was also unexpected". Byrne delights in the creative and cathartic outlet the works provide for her, a balance to the ethics and restrictions of the conservation process, "I have a great time coming up with the often very political ideas, spend hours sourcing the actual vintage figurines on eBay and in op-shops, and then get a real buzz out of smashing, grinding, gluing, cutting, filling, and painting my little creations", she enthuses.[3]

Byrne's artwork combines the rigour and attention to detail of her exacting 'day job', with the freedom to dismantle and reconfigure objects, just as she does perceptions. "I see my work as political activist art that takes risks, but it also works on several other levels too. In doing so it challenges the notion of the figurine as

Source: © Inga Walton/*Ceramics: Art and Perception.*

sacrosanct object", Byrne observes.[4] "I like to think of my pieces as three-dimensional cartoons", she muses, "This allows me to incorporate my views on global politics, environmental and social justice issues, whilst also subverting the traditional twee nature of the decorative porcelain figurine". Byrne stresses that her works are not provocative merely for the sake of being so, "The aesthetics of my works are very important, and if they don't 'work' aesthetically then they won't have the impact I'm after, and won't provoke and challenge my audience. They draw the viewer in and then surprise them upon close inspection".

No subject seems off-limits to Byrne's pithy perspective, "I am a keen observer of current affairs, news, and pop culture, and get my ideas from what is currently getting my goat. I also like to play with words, and so that comes into it too", she remarks. *The Three Graces-Nip Tuck* (2007) addresses often vexed attitudes towards body image, and the pressure for women to conform to unrealistic beauty standards propagated within the media. Three dolls demonstrate the before-and-after process of a complete surgical transformation, a nod to the popular FX Networks television show. *'I AM a Lady', Insisted Emily Howard* (2006) is a tribute to the flagrantly obvious transvestite-in-denial of the cult BBC series *Little Britain* (2003-06), who prefers outlandish Victorian dresses to modern clothes. With luxuriant chest-hair and a shadow covering most of the clock, Eddie's delicate pose and fine lute playing is still unlikely to convince anyone.

Governmental inaction about environmental issues are of tremendous concern to Byrne. Avian influenza makes an appearance with the "H5N1" (2006-07) works, as the stately upper-classes break out the breathing apparatus while clutching their infected farm-stock. More recently, the equine influenza outbreak which threatened the Spring Racing carnival had its turn with *H1N1* (2007). *She Had Blood On Her Hands* (2007) looks at the cruelties of the fur trade, and the increase in domestic pets being skinned, primarily in China. The pelts are deliberately mislabelled as other species, and bought by a compliant fashion industry, who condone and perpetuate unethical practices in the service of 'glamour'. Byrne's series *Hiroshi and his Friends are Having a Whale of a Time* (2006-07) criticises the Japanese slaughter of whales and dolphins, as cartoon characters perch merrily atop the bloodied mammals. The works are particularly pertinent given the recent clashes in the Southern ocean between marine activists the Sea Shepherd Conservation Society and the Japanese whaling fleet. The new Australian Prime Minister, Kevin Rudd, has been accused of a back-down on previous pledges that a Labor government would tackle Japan directly over the issue, and actively protect the whales.[5]

Similarly, Byrne was moved to document the plight of another much-maligned sea dweller in *Shark Fin Soup, #2* (2006). "I had an idea for [the] work after seeing sharks having their fins cut off...and then being thrown back into the ocean alive. I was so distressed, seeing the finless bleeding sharks...", she remembers. Byrne often finds, or is given, pieces with potential which she will 'rest' until they are right for a concept. Conversely, she will be seized with an idea, as in this instance, and work towards realising her vision. "I got onto eBay and did a search for porcelain sharks, and lo-and-behold there were some available in St. Petersburg, in Russia", she explains, "So I bought them, ground their fins off with my Demel tool, piled them on top of each other, and painted blood running from their missing fins". *How Much Can a Polar Bear?* (2007) ponders the impact melting ice caps will have on the world's largest land carnivores, since bears use the sea ice as a platform for hunting seals, the mainstay of their diet. If the ice melts too early in the year, the bears will be driven to shore, or further out to sea, before they have caught enough food. They will either starve, or drown, and any young are unlikely to survive without adult protection.[6] Clad in flippers and an oxygen tank, the alarming reality of climate change forces Byrne's bear to literally adapt or perish.

Domestic politics are never far from Byrne's mind, particularly the on-going debates surrounding reconciliation, and the 'Sorry' issue. The controversial and divisive question of a formal apology to Aboriginal peoples, and whether compensation should be paid, was recently revived by the Rudd government.[7] *John and Janette Were Ready For the Long Walk* (2006), sees the former Prime Minister John Howard and his wife sweetly clad in the unlikely garb of Aboriginal-inspired dot patterns. Byrne references former Essendon AFL footballer Michael Long's attempt to walk the 658km from Melbourne to Canberra in November, 2004 in a bid to discuss Indigenous policy issues he felt were being sidelined from the national agenda.[8]

In the Land of the Free They Call David a Terrorist, at Home He Was Just a Hick (2006) focuses on the five-year incarceration of (now convicted) Australian terror suspect David Hicks at Guantánamo Bay, Cuba. Known as 'the Australian Taliban', Hicks was captured in Afghanistan by Northern Alliance soldiers and handed over to the US military in December, 2001. Declared an 'unlawful combatant' his trial was delayed on numerous occasions as the legality of the imprisonment of detainees was scrutinised by American courts. Hicks' American military defence counsel, marine Major Michael Mori, became a household name in Australia for his indefatigable work on behalf of his client.[9] This was in contrast to strong criticism of the Howard government (1996-2007) for repudiating its obligation to seek justice for an Australian citizen held without charge by a foreign power, regardless of the allegations against him.[10] Implicit in this work is the hypocrisy of the United States, and the so-called 'Coalition of the Willing', in relation to the Geneva Convention, human rights obligations, and the rule of law.

Byrne reserves her particular ire for the political ineptitude shown by the administration of George W. Bush since the controversial result of the 2000 presidential election. She has devoted several works, some of which she calls "the 'George and Laura' series", to commenting on America's role as instigator of the so-called 'War On Terror' and in the Iraq war (2003-). *George and Laura Were Well Prepared For the 'Long War'* (2006) shows the President and First Lady formally attired and be-wigged, he brandishing a hand-gun as he motions for her hand, she cradling a grenade. *George and Laura Were All Set to Shock and Awe, #2* (2007) is named after the military doctrine based around 'the use of overwhelming and decisive force, dominant battlefield awareness and maneuvers, and spectacular displays of power'. Designed 'to paralyze an adversary's perception of the battlefield and destroy its will to fight', the tactic was implemented by the US military during the Iraq invasion.[11]

Condi Was Blown Away By George's Flashing Repartee (2005) mocks the close relationship Dr. Condoleezza Rice is reported to have with the Bush family. Rice seems to have spent much of her tenure, both as National Security Advisor (2001-05) and Secretary of State (2005-09), in the thankless task of trying to ameliorate some of Bush's more glaring linguistic and policy gaffes (popularly known as "Bush-isms"), and implementing his ill-conceived foreign policy initiatives. "I try very hard to remember that I have to be very disciplined about making sure I'm giving the President the whole story, that I'm making sure he knows everything", Rice has said.[12] Byrne makes her views on the success of this effort abundantly clear; Rice is messily dismembered, as a gun-toting Bush fusses absently with his blood-spattered cravat. Former First Lady, and now a Democratic-party presidential candidate, Senator Hillary Clinton also cops a serve in *Hillary Had Made a Complete Ass of Herself Again* (2004). The price of political expedience is represented as Hillary being forced to assume the part of a brittle and humiliated Titania to the philandering Bill as Bottom.

America The Brave (2006) has a sinister white cherub with a grotesquely leering death-skull face and articulated skeleton swathed in the American flag. He holds aloft a gold fighter-jet with blood spilling onto the decorative tulip base and down his arm. *Mission Accomplished, 1st May, 2003- What a Wank!* (2007) echoes the swaggering bravado of President Bush after he landed in a Lockheed S-3 Viking jet on the deck of the USS Abraham Lincoln, despite the vessel being within range of his helicopter. Against the backdrop of a large banner with its triumphant slogan, Bush announced the end of major combat operations in Iraq. This was widely interpreted as declaration that America had 'won' the war, though the number of American military deaths is climbing towards 4000 (more than the number killed in the World Trade Centre attack), with hundreds of coalition deaths, and reportedly in excess of 151,000 Iraqi civilians.[13] In the face of mounting criticism generated by the banner, a Pentagon spokesman subsequently claimed it referred to the 10-month deployment of the Lincoln, and not to the war.

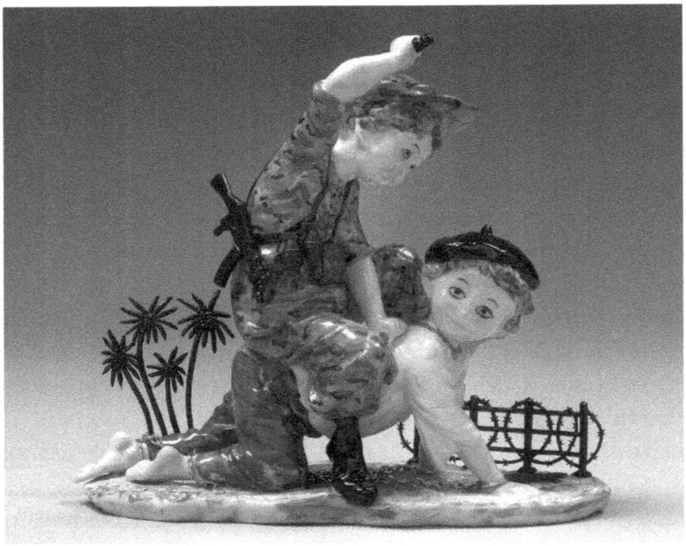

Figure 51.1 Fun and games at Abu Ghraib, 2007, Penny Byrne / courtesy of the artist. Photograph by Jeremy Dillon.

Fun and Games In Abu Ghraib (2004) (Figure 51.1) finds one boy in military fatigues riding on the back of another who is shackled, while cheerfully bludgeoning him amidst palm trees and razor-wire. Of the piece, Byrne recollects, "I found it on eBay...I thought, 'What are these boys doing to each other?', it sat in the studio for a year before it came to me."[14] Abū Ghurayb prison was one of the sites where political dissidents were incarcerated under former Iraqi leader Saddam Hussein. It achieved world-wide notoriety when lurid photographs of the degradation and abuse of Iraqi prisoners by US forces of the 372nd Military Police Company caused a scandal when *60 Minutes II* broke the story in April, 2004. The work looks like the kind of kitsch souvenir service personnel will certainly not be able to purchase at the Army PX supply store in Baghdad![15]

Dying to be with you (IRAN 2005) (2006) is one of Byrne's most confronting works; two blind-folded little boys carrying flower baskets are hanging from individual nooses attached to a central gallows. The artist became aware of the case of two young men, identified as Ayaz Marhoni (sixteen or seventeen) and Mahmoud Asgari (fifteen or sixteen), publicly hanged in Iran's second-largest city of Mashhad on July 19, 2005. Both juveniles at the time of their initial arrest, they were flogged a reported 228 times for drinking alcohol, theft, and "causing public disorder". They were also convicted for the alleged assault and rape of a thirteen year-old boy; gruesome images of their execution were circulated.[16] Controversy still surrounds the charges; most independent accounts contend that no such 'crimes' occurred, and that they were trumped-up by the prosecutors with the connivance of religious authorities. The only 'offence' committed seems to have been consensual sexual activity between the pair.[17] "I saw coverage of it...specifically a photograph of the two boys when they were being hung. It horrified me", Byrne reflects, "I made the work as a direct response to this, and to let people know that there are still places in the word where you can be executed for being gay".

Iran, like several other nations, continues to execute juveniles, and punish rape victims, homosexuals, adulterers, and other 'degenerates' for various 'corruptions' deemed incompatible with 'moral decency'.[18] In a widely-derided appearance in September, 2007 at Columbia University, Iranian President Mahmoud Ahmadinejad said, "In Iran we don't have homosexuals like you have in your country. In Iran we don't have this phenomenon, I don't know who has told you that we have it".[19] With some recourse to ABBA,

Dangerous Liaisons (Going to the Chapel of Love) (2006) reminds us of the continuing struggle faced by the gay, lesbian, and transgender community worldwide to achieve equal rights. With their legal, reproductive, and economic parity still not enshrined in most western nations, Byrne contemplates the fate of those living under more conservative and oppressive regimes where lives are threatened by any exposure to the moral and religious police.[20]

'If Only Gay Sex Caused Global Warming...', Mused Mother Earth (2007), is Byrne's largest work to date, a complicated piece which encompasses many of these disparate themes. Inspired by the article of the same name, it questions the misplaced priorities of certain powerful 'special interest' and lobby groups.[21] They seem overly concerned about so-called 'moral' issues, at the expense of those that will actually decide the future of the planet. "Global warming isn't trying to kill us, and that's a shame. If climate change had been visited on us by a brutal dictator or an evil empire, the war on warming would be this nation's top priority", writes Professor Daniel Gilbert of Harvard University.[22] Beneath a golden halo of knives, a tearful Mother Earth brandishes the twin tablets of 'Stern Report' in one hand and 'Kyoto Protocol' in the other. A grid-locked line of cars wind around the plinth and circumnavigate her like a beauty queen's sash. A pollarded tree sprouts a few feeble leaves in the background, mimicking the forest colours of her dress. The clueless hero, iridescent cape and boots gleaming like an oil slick on a wet road, proffers a dripping petrol-blue rose in supplication. His armoured, oil-drenched steed rears up, mane sodden and eyes bloody. Byrne investigates the politics of 'fear and loathing' in terms of its ability to monopolise debate and derail governmental action; if it's not "indecent, impious, or repulsive", it doesn't register.[23]

Regardless of the subjects Byrne tackles, she is aware of maintaining a balance between raising awareness and appearing to lecture, "Humour, satire, and parody are essential ingredients in my work", she agrees. "Even though a title might sound flippant it is never meant to be, it is meant to make people think...or educate them about a particular issue, as well as to entertain". Byrne seems to have developed a knack for ensnaring viewers, "By doing it in a light-hearted way, it's not forcing it down people's necks, but it's still got a powerful message. People get suckered in by the cuteness, but there [are] other levels"[24] With a keen eye for possibilities and a sharp appraisal of what will prick the conscience, no doubt Penny Byrne will amuse and challenge us with her particular brand of ceramic sedition for many exhibitions yet.

(This article originally appeared in *Ceramics: Art and Perception*, Issue 72, June-August, 2008, p. 15–22).

Notes

1. quoted in Ursula Sullivan & Joanna Strumpf (Eds), *Sullivan + Strumpf 2008*, gallery catalogue, Sydney, 2007, p. 10.
2. quoted in Ursula Sullivan & Joanna Strumpf (Eds), *Sullivan + Strumpf 2007*, gallery catalogue, Sydney, 2006, p. 2.
3. Ibid.
4. Ursula Sullivan & Joanna Strumpf (Eds), op cit, 2007.
5. see, Anthony Albanese & Kevin Rudd, "Action, not words, needed to save whales", Australian Labor Party media statement, 19 June, 2005.

   Malcolm Farr, "Navy to protect whales: Rudd", in *The Adelaide Advertiser*, 19 May, 2007. [on-line]

   "Rudd 'should call Japan PM' over whaling", in *The Age*, 20 December, 2007. [on-line]

   Andrew Darby, "Japan PM defends 'scientific' whaling", in *The Age*, 25 January, 2008, p. 2.

   "Whalers angry at 'eco terror' on the high seas", in *The Herald-Sun*, 22 January, 2008, p. 12.
6. Charles Monnett & Jeffrey S. Gleason, "Observations of mortality associated with extended open-water swimming by polar bears in the Alaskan Beaufort Sea", in *Polar Biology*, Vol. 29/No. 8, July, 2006, p. 681–87.

7. Steve Lewis, "Rudd set to say sorry for openers", in *The Herald-Sun*, 28 January, 2008, p.6.

   Gerard McManus & Carly Crawford, "'Sorry' protest planned", in *The Herald-Sun*, 29 January, 2008, p.7.

   Michelle Grattan, Tony Wright & David Rood, "Nelson seeks to discuss apology wording" & Dewi Cooke, "'Sorry' statement should acknowledge cultural loss, says state leader", in *The Age*, 1 February, 2008, p.4.
8. Stuart Rintoul, "Legend's Long March to PM's door", in *The Australian*, 23 November, 2004. [on-line]
9. Mathew Johnston & Tim Roman, "Fight for fair trial far from over", in *Melbourne University Magazine*, August Edition, 2006, p.15 & cover.
10. see, Lee Sales, Detainee 002: The Case of David Hicks, Melbourne University Publishing (MUP), Melbourne, 2007. www.detainee002.com

    Silvia Dropulich, "Hicks' case leaves no winners- Left or Right" & Tim McCormack, "March 2007: Ideal time to push for lenient deal for Hicks", in *Melbourne University Magazine*, August Edition, 2007, p. 14–17.
11. Harlan K. Ullman & James P. Wade, "Shock and Awe: Achieving Rapid Dominance", National Defence University (NDU), 1996.
12. Julia Reed, "The President's Prodigy", in *Vogue* [US], October, 2001, p.403.
13. Sarah Boseley, "151,000 died in Iraq after US invasion", in *The Age*, 11 January, 2008. [on-line]. Published figures vary, see: The Iraq Coalition Casualty Count: http://icasualties.org/oif & World Health Organisation: www.who.int/countries/irq/en
14. quoted in Joyce Morgan, "Beware, these pretty things bite", in *The Sydney Morning Herald*, 6 March, 2007, p.14.
15. see, Carol Rosenberg, "Guantánamo in pop culture", in *The Miami Herald*, 9 September, 2007 & Ricardo R. Lopez, "Guantánamo- A Cultural Exploration", video presentation, *The Miami Herald* [on-line].
16. see, Report: "Iran: The Last Executioner of Children" (Index: MDE 13/059/2007), Amnesty International Secretariat, London, June, 2007, p.16-17.
17. Doug Ireland, "Iranian Sources Question Rape Charges in Teen Executions", in *Gay City News* [US], Vol. 75/No. 32, 11-17 August, 2005. [on-line]
18. see, Amnesty International Public Statement, "Iran continues to execute minors and juvenile offenders", News Service No: 199, 22 July, 2005. www.amnestyusa.org

    Robert Tait, "Iran hangs man for rapes at 13", in *The Age*, 8 December, 2007, p.20.
19. Ian Munro, "Iran leader met with ridicule", in *The Age*, 26 September, 2007, p.11.
20. Hala Gorani (reporter), "Closet still safer in Middle East", CNN news article, re-broadcast on SBS "World News Australia", 6.30pm bulletin, 28 September, 2007.
21. Daniel Gilbert, "If Only Gay Sex Caused Global Warming- Why we're more scared of gay marriage and terrorism than a much deadlier threat", in *The Los Angeles Times*, 2 July, 2006. [on-line] also at: www.commondreams.org

    Michelle Grattan, "Climate change the biggest challenge, Treasury chief warns Swan", in *The Age*, 1 February, 2008, p.1.
22. Ibid.
23. Ibid.
24. quoted in Joyce Morgan, op cit.

Reproduced with permission of *Ceramics: Art and Perception* and the author.

52
THE FIGURATIVE IMPULSE IN CONTEMPORARY CERAMICS

Peter Selz

Ancient civilizations produced figurative works in clay that tell us about their everyday lives, fears, hopes, and deities. Only in very recent history, during the dominance of the bourgeoisie, has clay been excluded from high art, perhaps because of its humble origins. Its revival as a sculptural medium in the mid-twentieth century was to a great extent due to the innovative ceramics made by Peter Voulkos (b. 1924) in Los Angeles in the 1950s. Before that time, the concept that work in clay must be utilitarian was not questioned, and ceramics was a field marked by distinguished craftsmanship rather than innovation. Ever since, artists have been exploiting the flexible possibilities of clay to create figurative sculpture.

When I first saw Voulkos's gigantic ceramic pieces at his studio on Glendale Boulevard in Los Angeles in 1957, I was stunned. I had never seen clay made into such powerful work as these stoneware pieces with their strong color glazes. They were overwhelming in their sheer physical presence and enigmatic in their technical fabrication. In 1959, as curator of painting and sculpture at the Museum of Modern Art, New York, I was appointed U.S. Commissioner of the *Première Biennale de Paris* and included three large works by Voulkos, who received the Rodin Museum prize for his *Sitting Bull*, c. 1959. A year later I curated a small solo show of six sculptures and six canvases by Voulkos in MoMA's Penthouse Gallery. Here was the work of the man who, by enlarging his vessels and, most importantly, denying any utilitarian function, had changed the craft of pottery into the art of clay sculpture.

Voulkos had been inspired by Franz Kline and the Abstract Expressionist painters, and by Philip Guston, Robert Rauschenberg, and others. Affected also by his study of Zen, he valued process and accident in his work. Although his vertical stoneware stacks have no overt anthropomorphic elements, they are clearly informed by figurative sculpture from Asia and Europe, from the past and present. He was particularly influenced by Japanese Haniwa sculpture, primitive but expressive earthenware figures placed on royal burial tombs from about 300 to 600 A.D.[1] Among modernist works Voulkos admired Picasso's painted bronze and ceramic figures and the inventive, multivalent ceramic sculpture that Miró produced with the fine ceramics craftsman Llorens Artigas. He also expressed great interest in the sculpture of Fritz Wotruba, which he saw in 1955. He has spoken about the Austrian sculptor's method of stacking his bronzes,[2] but he must also have been aware of the universal quality of Wotruba's androgynous figures.

At the Los Angeles County Art Institute (later renamed the Otis Art Institute) during the 1950s, Voulkos taught a group of students who quickly emerged as important artists, including Paul Soldner, John Mason, Kenneth Price, and Michael Frimkess. The youngest of the group, Frimkess (b. 1937), has used figuration in his surface decoration. For example, *CFS004 Plate*, 1982, is incised with primitive human profiles, evocative of children's drawings, and mysterious numbers, and has the rough-looking, asymmetric shape that Frimkess and his Otis colleagues admired in Japanese raku pottery.

Source: © Peter Selz.

In 1959 Voulkos was appointed to the faculty of the Art Department at the University of California, Berkeley. His audacious work there further subverted the prevailing purist taboos that had restricted clay to the making of useful pottery and opened the way for new discoveries by artists such as Harold Paris (1925-1979). When Paris arrived in Berkeley to join the art faculty in 1960, the largely self-taught artist was already well known as a printmaker and had recently begun to make bronze sculpture. During the war he had been assigned by the newspaper *Stars and Stripes* to go to the death camp at Buchenwald. This experience found its reverberations in his *Hosanna Suite*, a graphic cycle of etchings, aquatints, and lithographs, poignant visions of life, tragedy, and death.

At Berkeley Paris saw Voulkos working in the 'Pot Palace', a makeshift basement studio, and was inspired to explore the possibilities of clay. He began creating monumental walls, made of many separate pieces, in which he translated much of the imagery of the *Hosanna Suite* – with its dramatic anxiety and intimate sexuality – into powerful an energetic reliefs. He named these expressive structures *Walls for Mem*, after mem, the thirteenth letter of the Hebrew alphabet; three 'm' places where he had lived (Majorca, Madrid and Munich); and Malach, Hebrew tor the Angel of Death. He completed the first Wall in a twenty-four-hour period of nonstop activity, dramatically grabbing, twisting, cutting, and gouging the clay. *Wall III*, 1962, the last of the group, done with more deliberation, is a great technical accomplishment, almost nine feet tall. (In Los Angeles John Mason had made an even larger ceramic wall in 1960, but without human imagery.) With their bulging humanoid elements, Paris's *Walls* seem to invade the viewer's space. Executed with exuberant passion, they convey what Jackson Pollock may have meant when he spoke of energy made visible in art. The critic Jerome Tarshis concluded, 'More allusive than realistic, [Paris's] walls offer hints of ruined structures and fragmented bodies. Paris managed to bring the Surrealists' interest in psychology and their imaginative treatment of the human body, the concern of postwar European artists to reflect the horrors of war, and the Abstract Expressionists' freedom of design.'[3]

Stephen De Staebler (b. 1933) arrived at Voulkos's program in Berkeley in 1959 after studying theology at Princeton. He was influenced by Voulkos and also by Paris's ceramic walls, with their incipient figuration which he said 'made a strong impression on me, particularly in their tendency to digress to random forms … [TheWalls] were powerful works, and to my eye, the most fully realized imagery. Realized, not in the sense of refinement, but in their fully tactile presence.'[4] Soon, according to Thornas Albright, De Staebler 'became the most original and powerful clay sculptor of the [Berkeley] group.'[5] In 1967 he was commissioned by the Newman Center in Berkeley to design and build a sanctuary, an architectural and sculptural work of liturgical elements. The result, a manifest triumph of clay sculpture in our time, encourages meditation with its judicious placement of objects and austere simplicity. The crucifix is made of high-fired clay and set high on a wall. The sanctuary itself is designed to resemble landscapes in its depressions and rises. contrasting with the crucifix's vertical aspiration.

Both this work and De Staebler's later figurative pieces exploit the essential character of clay: its unpredictable performance in the artist's hands, its wetness when soft and leathery toughness when hardened, its tendency to crack – in short, its truly organic, earthbound quality. His fragmentary figures with their encrusted surfaces recall the static presence of ancient Egyptian sculpture or resemble the eroded survivors of unknown prehistoric civilizations. *Seated Woman with Mimbres Womb*, 1978, suggests the artist's desire to connect a contemporary sensibility to human history. The stacked segments are joined by gravity in the archaic form of the stele; the rounded opening refers to the cavities in the pottery of the Native American Mimbres group.

During the 1980s De Staebler created fragmentary, androgynous winged figures in bronze as well as clay. Incomplete, they convey the precarious quality of life, especially the existential alienation felt by men and women in our time. In a series of human legs made in the 1990s, De Staebler achieved subtle colors by blending pigment with the clay as well as by applying paint to the finished surface. He reduced these fragments to a modest scale in *Three Legs with Sliced Foot*, 1996, disembodied, broken legs that nonetheless convey a poignant sense of human endurance. De Staebler's use of the primal matter of earthenware affirms life's processes of emergence and metamorphosis.

In the San Francisco Bay Area during the early 1960s a new group of ceramists emerged, artists who took it for granted that clay would be used for nonutilitarian purposes. They looked at popular culture for many of their motifs, but in a manner very different from the New York Pop artists, who often created easily recognizable works that would have a ready appeal in the expanding New York art market. The chief artist of this group was the authentic iconoclast Robert Arneson (1930-1992). Arneson first studied at the California College of Arts and Crafts (CCAC) in Oakland, where he was still engaged in producing serviceable pots. Then, as a graduate student at Mills College (1957-58), also in Oakland, he encountered the work of Voulkos, and his work took a more radical direction. While demonstrating throwing pots at the California State Fair in Sacramento in 1961, he sealed a bottle with a clay cap and wrote the slogan *No Deposit* on its body. He called the piece *No Return*. With this symbolic act, he suggested that clay's recent history as a medium merely for mass-produced commercial wares was over. In 1962 he arrived at the University of California, Davis, and before long was the head of the ceramics section there.

The art historian and ceramist Seymour Howard had created a small studio at Davis, which Arneson converted into the now-legendary TB-9 (Temporary Building 9) workshop. As Arneson's former student Richard Notkin recalled, 'TB-9 was a microcosm of these times [the Hippie era]. Anarchy reigned. No overwhelming structure or 'curriculum' to hamper or impede your creative flow. We just worked, and we worked damn hard. We were a ragtag bunch – a group of mud-smeared hairy humans who hung around together – sharing an affinity for making clay into something we hoped would be Art. In short, TB-Niners.'[6] According to Notkin, he and the other students at TB-9 – among them artists as different as Richard Shaw and Peter VandenBerge, as well as Bruce Nauman, Deborah Butterfield, John Buck, and Steven Kaltenbach – learned from Arneson primarily through osmosis.

Work created at Davis, as well as related sculpture and painting done elsewhere in the Bay Area, made without much regard for material or form, was bizarre, often quite ugly and ungainly, yet sensuous. This particular impudent, playful sensibility – which became known as Funk – was unique to the Bay Area. It had its roots in the Beat culture of the previous decade but was also a result of the isolation the artists in this region felt. As Harold Paris explained in an article for Art in America, 'The serious artists, galleries and museums founder in this 'Bay' of lethargy and social inertia. The artist here is aware that no one really sees his work, and no one really supports it. So, in effect, he says 'Funk.' But also he is free. There is less pressure to 'make it'. The casual, irreverent, insincere California atmosphere, with its absurd elements - weather, clothes, 'skinny-dipping,' hobby craft, sun-drenched mentality, Doggie Diner, perfumed toilet tissue, do-it-yourself - all this drives the artist's vision inward. This is the land of Funk.[7]

Aware of this new attitude (it certainly was not a school or movement), I organized an exhibition and published a catalogue called *Funk* at the University Art Museum in Berkeley in 1967.[8] The exhibition included representatives from Davis (Arneson, William T. Wiley, Roy de Forest, and David Gilhooly); Berkeley (Paris, Voulkos, and James Melchert); and San Francisco (Bruce Conner, Robert Hudson, Joan Brown, Manuel Neri, and Peter Saul).Years later Funk was canonized in *The History of American Ceramics*, where Elaine Levin wrote, 'Unlike Dadaism, which aspired to change the world, Funk's intentions were to change the perception of the world by putting familiar objects in an unfamiliar context so that they could be seen afresh.'[9]

Arneson was the exemplary Funk artist, at least as far as his early work is concerned. In 1963 he made a series of clay toilets with turdlike handles and unflushed bowls, johns a great deal more shocking than the ironic soft-vinyl toilets that Claes Oldenburg made two years later. Arneson's *Typewriter*, 1965, with its keys of highly polished red fingernails, signifying the woman as a writing machine, is widely reproduced and has become a sort of standard for Funk. Once clay had been freed from the concepts of honesty and truth (propounded by potters such as Bernard Leach, Shōji Hamada, and Marguerite Wildenhain), the range of its uses became greatly amplified. Arneson continued to explore this new freedom, influenced by a broad range of artists in different media, including Franz Xaver Messerschmidt, Edvard Munch, and Pablo Picasso. In the 1970s he turned to portraiture and self-portraiture. In the large technical feat *Smorgi-Bob the Cook*, 1971, he depicts himself as a chef with a vast display of edibles, all in carefully manipulated perspective. In *Classical Exposure*, 1972, he appears on top of a classical urn with his genitals exposed. In 1982, in response to a disparaging review of an exhibition of California ceramics at the Whitney Museum,[10] Arneson created *California Artist*, a self-portrait in slovenly clothing, standing on a pedestal with a marijuana plant. Later he portrayed himself on the capital of an Ionic column with a pronounced twinkle in his eye and called the piece *Way West of Athens*, 1983.

Known for his work as a portraitist, Arneson was commissioned in 1981 by the San Francisco Art Commission to make a bust of the assassinated mayor George Moscone for the city's new convention center. This splendid bust caused a great deal of public controversy. Below the grinning ceramic likeness, on the pedestal, Arneson inscribed references to the mayor's life and the so-called Twinkie defense used by Moscone's assassin, Dan White. The bust was removed in an unforgivable act of censorship, but it brought Arneson international recognition. Shortly thereafter, feeling an increasing sense of identification with Jackson Pollock, Arneson made a series of sculptures, paintings, and drawings of the iconic American painter. Toward the end of his life he confronted the danger of nuclear war in his work. According to the critic Donald Kuspit, 'his nuclear imagery sharply focuses the fact that there is one serious issue in art today: the re-connection of art and morality – the reconceiving of art as a form of moral politics.'[11]

Moral politics is also a defining issue in the work of Arneson's former student Richard Notkin (b. 1948). From a very early age Notkin was inspired by films on Nazi concentration camps to create work with political meaning. Playful, with an intricacy inspired by Chinese Yixing teapots, his works resemble political cartoons in their use of metaphor and allegory. In his *Endangered Species* series, begun in 1978, Notkin expressed antiwar and other political and social messages, frequently using human skulls of precisely crafted porcelain. In *Vain Imaginings*, c. 1978-79, for example, he placed a ceramic skull on books atop a fastidiously made chess set. The skull looks at its reflection on a television screen, topped by a book, titled *The Shallow Life*, which in turn serves as the base of a coke bottle and a cactus plant. The composition is an evocative version of the traditional memento mori.

Notkin is one of a number of important artists, including Richard Shaw, Marilyn Levine, and Elaine Carhartt, who take advantage of the unlimited pliancy of clay to produce illusionist or trompe-l'oeil sculptures. Richard Shaw (b. 1941), the son of a Walt Disney animator, was trained as a painter and then studied sculpture at the San Francisco Art Institute before he arrived at Davis in 1967. He remembers TB-9 as a 'place of radiating energy.'[12] His work often seems to reflect the cartoon illusionism of Disney movies. To achieve fine detail, he turned to porcelain, which is capable of highly realistic renderings and, fired at high temperatures, yields painterly surfaces. Shaw replicated everyday objects to create startling trompe-l'oeil still lifes. He has also made whimsical, anthropomorphic little statues, such as *Happy Birthday*, 1996. This highly imaginative, striding stick figure – a rather scary birthday guest – has a leg that resembles a tree trunk and a skull wearing a foolscap and offers an apple pierced with sharp pencils, every element precisely rendered in deceptive clay.

Born in Canada in 1935, Marilyn Levine did her graduate work at Berkeley with Voulkos and his group. She specializes in replicating leather goods in stoneware. Her shoes, jackets, suitcases and bags, with all of their scuffs and other marks of human use, are so realistic that the viewer questions his or her perception. Elaine Carhartt (b. 1951) grew up in Colorado and studied in Mexico before settling in Pasadena, where she now produces playful, whimsical creatures of droll humor, such as *Queen*, 1980, a smiling lady riding a fantasy cart, made of bisque clay and then painted brightly with acrylic. This genre in ceramics is comparable to the work of contemporaneous East Coast sculptors Duane Hanson and John de Andrea and related to the work of Super – or Photorealist painters such as Richard Estes, Robert Bechtle, and Ralph Goings. It also comprehends and reaffirms the tradition of the American trompe-l'oeil still-life painters William Harnett and John Peto. Its attitude is very much in keeping with contemporary theory: The French poststructuralist sociologist Jean Baudrillard postulates that in the current era the very excess of images leads the artist to the creation of simulacra and implies that there is no substantial difference between reality and fiction.

Other former students of Arneson, such as Peter VandenBerge and Robert Brady, shared their teacher's preoccupation with the human figure, which they often disfigure or refigure in their sculpture. VandenBerge, born in Holland in 1935, moved with his parents to the Dutch East Indies, then escaped to Australia during World War II before settling in California. Working with Funk artist David Gilhooly at Davis, he made ceramics based on vegetable images, but soon the human figure, and particularly the head, began to dominate his work. A trip to Paris in 1957, including a visit to Giacometti's studio, was of key importance to the young sculptor, and Modigliani, Indonesian aboriginal art, and the great heads from Easter Island also find echoes in his art. His elongated figures combine whimsy and frivolous humor with mock solemnity. *Hood*, 1985, is typical of his mature sculpture. Built up by the coil method, it is larger than life-size, a woman's head mysteriously enclosed in a large cylindrical hood. Eyes peer through slits located far above where the eyes might be expected.

While VandenBerge's busts project a quiet, enigmatic seclusion, the solitary figures of Robert Brady (b. 1946) express vivid torment. Brady suffered a long and agonizing illness when he was sixteen, and there is little doubt that this early trauma affected his work. He studied ceramics at California College of Arts and Crafts and at Mills College before working with Arneson at Davis. His influence by Voulkos is tempered by an affinity for the work of Isamu Noguchi, especially the sculptor's 'sensitivity to material and a sense that he has caressed and loved – made love to – the form, craft and material'.[13] In the late 1970s Brady began a series of distorted masks, informed by the folk sculpture he admired during a stay in Mexico. Later, Sepik River figures from New Guinea and Northwest Coast masks became important sources. *Aground*, 1985, with its large bulbous head, barely supported by its emaciated body and leaning against a grid, wears an expression of alienation and bewilderment, reminding us of Friedrich Nietzsche's phrase 'the eternal wounds of existence' and exemplifying the sculptural eloquence that can be achieved with clay.

Another California artist who makes figurative clay sculpture is Brady's one-time teacher Viola Frey (b. 1933). Frey grew up on a vineyard in California's Central Valley and began working with clay at CCAC. For her graduate studies she enrolled at Tulane University in New Orleans, where Mark Rothko, a visiting artist in the winter of 1957, taught her about the emotional effects of color. Beginning in the 1970s Frey made small, colorful figures that, while uniquely her own, recall eighteenth-century porcelain figurines, Surrealist imagery, and Jean Dubuffet's grotesque *Little Statues of Precarious Life*. She has also produced a series of nonfunctional plates with glazed images that project from the flat surface. In *Crocker Series II*, 1979, her own two large hands, glazed dark blue, are presented prominently on each side of a black-suited man, an image of her friend the ceramist Howard Kottler, who frequently appears in her work. In the 1980s Frey's figures increased markedly in scale, eventually reaching heights far beyond life-size. These figures are carefully constructed of separate ceramic sections, fired individually and then assembled into towering men and women. Strong colors – largely bright yellows and blues – enhance and enliven the surfaces. Typical is *Sky Blue Suit*, 1982, a solitary man with a perplexed expression, dressed in an ill-fitting business suit, standing as an iconic twentieth-century figure.

Although the recent surge in sculptural ceramics began in California, a number of artists working in different parts of the country and the world – Daniel Rhodes, Doug Jeck, Michael Lucero, Ruth Duckworth,

Takako Araki, AkioTakamori, Phyllis Green, and Marek Cecula – have also followed impulses toward the figurative. Often but not always influenced by California ceramics, they address human, animal, or man-made forms, and their approaches are often startlingly different from one another as well as from the traditions from which their work emerged.

Daniel Rhodes (1911-1989) was born in Iowa and turned to figurative sculptural imagery late in his long and distinguished career as a ceramist, teacher, and author of influential technical publications on pottery. Originally trained as a painter at the Art Institute of Chicago and the Art Students League of New York, he began studying at the College of Ceramics at Alfred University in upstate New York and then taught on the Alfred faculty for many years. The ceramics school at Alfred is the oldest and most prestigious institution for the study of clay in this country. Initially set up primarily to train students for the ceramics industry, it was rather traditional until the 1950s, when, partly due to Rhodes's endeavors, it became more adventurous. Rhodes began to make vessels in which he combined clay with metal, wood, fiberglass, and bone. *Untitled (Head)*, 1985, is a late and exceptional work by the artist: a Christian cross embedded in a head of buff clay. As De Staebler did in his crucifix, Rhodes has avoided the trivial aspects of so much ecclesiastical work and rendered the cross as a meditative icon, anchored in earth.

Doug Jeck (b. 1963), working in Seattle, uses clay to form isolated human figures such as the pale ceramic *Projection*, 1977. Like Auguste Rodin's *L'Homme qui marche* (1877/1905), which needs neither head nor arms for its wide, expansive stride, *Projection* is a human torso. But unlike Rodin's sculpture and stemming from a very different time and place, Jeck's nude male is a vulnerable figure with a haunting expression. The head with its inward gaze is superimposed on the beautifully modeled distorted torso, whose pose alludes to classical and Renaissance statues. The work is built of clay slabs that are made up of coils, and it stands without armature on its plinth, which is supported by a wooden base.

Michael Lucero was born in 1953 in California's San Joaquin Valley and educated in Seattle, and he spent a summer at Davis, where West Coast Funk artists such as Arneson, William T. Wiley, and Robert Hudson had an impact on him before he moved to live and work in New York in 1978. *Untitled (Dog)*, 1932, belongs to a series of hanging shard sculptures he made in the late 1970s and early 1980s. To create these works, which defy the expectation that clay pieces should be integral wholes, Lucero strung numerous petals of fired clay, glazed in subtle colors, on multicolored strands of thin telephone wire and then hung them from the ceiling. The shards catch light and under certain conditions shimmer like dry leaves. Unlike Julian Schnabel's broken pottery pictures, which reflect violence, Lucero's fragile dog with its long legs, thin torso, and twisted and looped arms is a delicate spirit image. After this series of weightless sculptures, Lucero made a group of huge, disembodied clay heads with surfaces covered in paintings of idyllic landscapes, which refer to Brancusi's *Sleeping Muse*. In the 1990s he turned to anthropomorphic clay sculptures based on pre-Columbian and Native American sources. More recently he has been working on a series called *Reclamations*, chimerical assemblages of pieces found in antique shops or flea markets and then put back together in what appears to be a topsy-turvy manner and painted or glazed, giving a new and exuberant life to old kitsch.

Ruth Duckworth was born as Ruth Windmüller in Hamburg in 1919. She left Germany to escape Nazi persecution and went to England. Having known since she was a child that she wanted to be an artist, she attended art school in Liverpool. For a time she supported herself by making terra-cotta portraits and carving headstones for graveyards, work indebted to Henry Moore. After an early exhibition in London in 1955, she experimented in a great variety of materials and then decided to concentrate on clay. She went to the Hammersmith School of Art but found the instruction based on the purist potter Bernard Leach's theories too confining and transferred to the more liberal Central School of Art, where she later joined the faculty. Both her ceramic vessels and her reliefs became increasingly abstract, although forms of nature, such as the human body, stones, and seashells, seem to have inspired her.

In 1964 she was invited by the University of Chicago to teach at the Midway studios and she has remained in Illinois since that time. At Chicago she was commissioned to create a monumental wall sculpture, *Earth, Water and Sky*, 1957-68, for the Geophysical Science building. Since that time she has executed many additional mural commissions, exhibited throughout the United States and in England, Germany, the Netherlands, Israel, Canada, and Japan. Her work is distinguished by a sensuous use of materials and simplicity of form. In *Sculpture*, 1988, and *Untitled*, 1997, she develops the structural relationships of geometric forms in Oskar Schlemmer's Bauhaus sculptures – revisiting in her seventies, after many successful transitions, the art done in her native land in the early part of the twentieth century.

The ravaged but numinous Bibles by the Japanese ceramist Takako Araki (b. 1921) present another unique figurative aesthetic. For many years this artist, the atheist daughter of a Zen monk, has turned to the Judeo-Christian book of books as the theme of her work. She produces porcelain Bibles with patient and meticulous attention to detail, making thin sheets that she silkscreens with the sacred text and then tortures into illegibility. Araki has said that her work comments on 'the various cruelties which have been committed for religion's sake throughout history and the false hopes religions have inspired.'[14] Like the British artist John Latham, who destroyed books as his assault on the authority of language and the canon of knowledge, Araki renders scripture into corroded messages, endowing it with transcendent layers of meaning.

The younger Japanese artist Akio Takamori (b. 1950) has been making sensuous vessels marked by erotic narration. He writes, 'I've been in love with the human figure since I was a child in Japan. My father's clinic was located in the red light district of our town; he was a dermatologist and it was always fascinating to watch the bodies of those coming in and out of the place.'[15] He began his study of pottery in Tokyo, but after seeing California Funk sculpture, so totally different from the Japanese traditional discipline, he was eager to study in the United States. He eventually worked with the internationally known American ceramist Ken Ferguson at the Kansas City Art Institute. He later completed his education at the New York State College of Ceramics at Alfred University. Takamori now resides on Puget Sound and is a professor of ceramics at the University of Washington. There he continues to create playful, sensuous, and erotic porcelain and stoneware vessels that relate to Japanese Ukiyo-e woodblocks, especially the work of Utamaro, and Shinto fertility shrines with stone phalluses. They are also related to European traditions: Takamori mentions Brueghel and Picasso as early influences from Western art.[16]

His vessels explore polarities: Eastern/Western traditions, male/female, humanl/animal, birth/death, and interior/exterior. Takamori begins a piece by making drawings on paper, which he uses as patterns to cut slabs of clay, one for the front and one for the back. After detailing and molding the flat slabs into lifelike contours, he fires the piece several times, using polychrome glazes to paint figures and animals, such as chickens or swans, on the smooth surfaces. He may magnify the curves and roundness of the female body to address men's desire for voluptuous women, as in *Thousand Years of Love*, 1988, or address childbirth and its joy and conflicts, as in *Under the Peach Tree*, 1994.

Also discussing sexuality, but from a feminist or postfeminist point of view, is the work of Takamori's U.S. contemporary Phyllis Green (b. 1950). Green produces small mixed-media sculptures, with which she intends to 'challenge the lingering modernist assumption that decoration and ornament, as feminine, are enemies of 'high art.'' [17] In 1994 she exhibited her installation *Turkish Bath*, a collection of abstract, eccentric, playful little sculptures made from a great variety of materials such as clay, velvet, leather, and feathers. As its title indicates, Green's work refers to J. A. D. Ingres's *Le Bain Turc* of 1862. Ingres's salon painting represents nude women, crowded together in their Oriental harem and assuming suggestive poses – a hymn to the glory of the female body as made available to the pleasure of the male voyeur-proprietor. Green's *Odalisque*, 1994, invokes the famous Ingres *Odalisque* of 1814, a painting of a reposing nude, descendent of all the great Venuses in Western art. In Ingres's version the icy colors and sharply delineated lines create a fascinating contrast to the nude's voluptuous pose, again inviting the male gaze. Green's piece is an abstract assemblage that imitates the reclining position of its namesake. On an overstuffed pillow lounges a construction of a large velvet bulb, a stoneware central element with dangerous-looking protuberances, and a long gray velvet tube ending in a yellow aperture – certainly open to many interpretations. It is a most intriguing sculpture, seductive in a very different way from past odalisques.

Marek Cecula (b. 1944) was born in Poland, studied sculpture in Cracow and ceramics in lsrael, went to Brazil in 1962 as a designer of industrial porcelains, then moved to New York in 1977. He set up a studio and gallery, Contemporary Porcelain, in Soho, where he and his wife produced innovative porcelain dinnerware as well as nonfunctional vessels. In 1984 he began teaching ceramics at the Parsons School of Design, and he became head of the department in 1994. His sculpture, made of vitreous china, uses the techniques of industrial design and is associated with an international tendency sometimes referred to as the postcraft movement) that emphasizes a high-tech appearance. During a residence in the ceramics workshop in the town of 's-Hertogenbosch, Holland, he began his *Scatology* series. These sculptures have the stark white finish of commercial bathroom fixtures and are carefully displayed on stainless steel trays. Some of them resemble the lower parts of the human body as well as wash buckets. Cecula followed this group with the *Hygiene* series, of which *Untitled II*, 1996, is a fine example. Here he presents gleaming white basins, of porcelain that simulates vinyl, mounted on high steel stands in a row, like public washbowls, toilets, or urinals. A tubular discharge pipe dangles from each basin, evoking parts of human or animal organisms.

Back in 1919, Marcel Duchamp's urinal *Fountain*, 1913, submitted under the name R. Mutt, was banned from the Independents exhibition because, according to the hanging committee, it was nothing but a 'piece of plain plumbing.' In his historic response Duchamp, writing anonymously, proclaimed, 'Whether Mr. Mutt with his own hands made the fountain or not has no importance. He chose it. He took an ordinary article of life, placed it there so that its useful significance disappeared under the new title and point of view – created a new thought tor that object. As for plumbing, that is absurd. The only works of art America has given are her plumbing and her bridges.'[18] Years later Arneson and Oldenburg made their own derisive sculptural comments on the toilet. Cecula's slick, clean, white bathroom fixtures have a similar satirical realism but a different effect. The emblems of clinical hygiene engender, perhaps inevitably in our era of AIDS, thoughts of disease and death.

The conceivable and actual possibilities of clay as an artistic medium seem to be without limits and are constantly extended. Almost two generations separate Voulkos's wildly Expressionist, roughly textured, gigantic stoneware sculptures from Cecula's basins, with their gleaming white industrial polish. And yet both artists, in their unique ways, crafted vessels made of clay. Their work, like the work of most of the artists in this exhibition, both incorporates and dissents from received tradition, advancing the potential of clay through new and surprising forms.

Notes

1. Karen Tsujimoto, 'Peter Voulkos: The Wood-fired Works', in Rose Slivka and Karen Tsujimoto, *The Art of Peter Voulkos*, exh. cat. (Tokyo: Kodansha International in collaboration with Oakland Museum, 1995), p. 100.
2. Ibid., p. 102.
3. Jerome Tarshis, 'Harold Paris: Emotions in Mixed Media', Christian Science Monitor, 14 December 1992, p. 16.
4. Stephen De Staebler, 'Walls for Mem', in Peter Selz, Harold Persico Paris (San Francisco: Harcourts Modern and Contemporary Art, 1992), unpag.
5. Thomas Albright Art in the San Franclsco Bay Area (Berkeley: University of California Press, 1985), p. 138.

6. Richard Notkin quoted in John Natsoulas Gallery, ed., 30 Years of TB-9: A Tribute to Robert Arneson (Davts, Calif.: John Natsoulas Gallery, 1991), p. 73.
7. Harold Paris, 'Sweet Land of Funk', Art m America 55, no. 5 (March/April 1997), p. 97.
8. Peter Selz, *Funk*, exh. cat. (Berkeley, Calif.: University Art Museum, 1967).
9. Elaine Levin, The History of American Ceramics (New York: Harry N. Abrams, 1988), p. 230.
10. See Hilton Kramer, 'Ceramic Sculpture and the Taste of California', New York Times, 20 December 1981, pp. 31–33.
11. Donald Kuspit, in Robert Arneson, exh. cat. (San Francisco: Fuller Goldeen Gallery; Bentcia, Calif.: Studio AS, 1985), unpag.
12. Richard Shaw quoted in 30 Years of TB-9: A Tribute to Robert Arneson, p. 62.
13. Robert Brady quoted in 'Thomas H. Garver, Sleeping Creatures', in Janice T. Dreisbach, *Robert Brady: A Survey Exhibition*, exh. cat. (Sacramento, Calif.: Crocker Art Museum, 1989), p. 12.
14. Ronald A . Kuchta, *Takako Araki: Recent Work.*, exh. cat. (Syracuse, N.Y.: Everson Museum of Art, 1988), unpag.
15. Akio Takamori with Peter Ferris, 'Vessel Concepts', *Ceramics Monthly* 36, no. 2 (February 1988), p. 27.
16. Ibid.
17. Phyllis Green, artist's statement, November 1994.
18. Anonymous [Marcel Duchamp], 'Comment', *Blind Man 2* (May 1917), unpag.

This was first published as 'The Figurative Impulse in Contemporary Ceramics', in Jo Lauria (ed), 2000, *Colour and Fire: Defining Moments in Studio Ceramics 1950-2000*, Rizzoli International Publications, pp. 159–192.

Reproduced by permission of the author.
© Peter Selz 2000

SECTION 3.5
CERAMICS IN EDUCATION

Introductory summary

In the UK, the teaching of ceramics has reduced in schools in the last twenty years. At the same time university ceramics departments have closed or merged with other subject areas. Andrea Gill reflects on this with an emphasis on the United States and in particular the New York State College of Ceramics at Alfred University. Alongside this she also offers an overview of the development of ceramics in education and some of the key artist educators.

Although many of the core techniques of ceramics have remained the same for thousands of years, new technologies have changed what is possible to create with ceramics. University departments are one context where new experimental approaches have developed. This is especially the case in the last ten years or so when 'digital making' approaches have emerged. This involves the use of computers and equipment such as digital transfer printers, rapid prototyping, water-jet cutting and laser cutting. Holly Hanessian's essay provides a 'snap shot' in time of how a US art department has accommodated this shift in terms of curriculum and studio provision.

Livingstone and Petrie

53
THE INFLUENCE OF EDUCATIONAL INSTITUTIONS ON CONTEMPORARY CERAMICS

Andrea Gill

The future of ceramics as a definable, historically rich, visually potent medium is at a critical point in educational institutions today. After half a century of growth, many schools are eliminated or diluting ceramic programs. A careful look at the history of ceramics in higher education might help generate the energy needed to move forward. There are tangled roots to this history, involving passionate teachers, strong opinions, and diverse traditions. Philip Rawson spoke about this at the 1984 Canadian Clay Conference:

> If one thinks of it solely in terms of a great individual who at a certain time in a city produced something which has got a kind of cachet, one is actually missing part of the point. One of the really important things about ceramics is that there are lines of thought. It is possible to carry through lines of thinking, and intensify them and deepen them and draw in more or make more references to changing conditions. It seems to me that one of the things that (we) might do is to try to disentangle the actual lines of thinking that have gone on from one potter to another.

My teaching position at the New York State College of Ceramics at Alfred University affects my reflections on the relationship between education and ceramic art. Over the years, the faculty at Alfred has addressed many of the questions that have faced the field of ceramics.

Contemporary ceramic art education has its roots in the early twentieth century. Chartered in 1900, the New York State College of Ceramics was primarily an industrial school, but it made connections to art from the beginning. The importance of working directly with materials, with your hands, was an integral part of the progressive theory of education at that time. This created certain opportunities for Alfred. A strange book published in 1906 for parents and teachers, titled *What and How: A Systemized Course of Hand Work*, illustrated projects for young children, including such things as clay modeling and stick arrangement. The book suggested that five pounds of clay is enough for twelve children for an entire year. A quotation introduces each chapter, including this one by the eighteenth- century writer and philosopher Jean-Jacques Rousseau that reinforces the importance of hands-on activities:

> If, instead of chaining a child to his books, I occupy him in a workshop, his hands labor to the profit of his spirit, he becomes a philosopher, though he thinks he is only a workman. Now, of all the occupations which serve to furnish subsistence to man, that which brings him back to Nature again most closely is the work of his hands.

Source: © Andrea Gill/*The Studio Potter* 501 (C) (3).

The connection between this romantic notion of handwork and the development of ceramic programs is easy to see. Clay, an easily manipulated and natural material, is especially suited to these projects. Even in an industrial school like Alfred, clay was also an educational material. Within higher education, demand was growing for teachers trained in "practical arts," so the curriculum evolved to include teacher training. The industrial skills it involved could translate into classroom activities. Many ceramic art programs still in existence today were first located in these early teacher-training models.

That ceramic art has had such a strong connection to primary and secondary education has been a major influence both on programs and on the work produced in them. It helps support artists by providing teaching jobs, but has marginalized ceramics within higher education. In this line of thinking, clay is merely a learning tool for children and college students. It is not part of the serious visual arts curriculum.

Art education has been a good source of income for colleges as well. In 1948 Charles Harder wrote a paper tracing the growth of ceramic art education at Alfred. One of Harder's concerns was the School for American Craftsmen might begin teaching art education in addition to the original mission of training craftsmen as studio artists. At that time, both schools were in Alfred – one supported by Ailene Webb, the founder of the American Craft Council, and the other supported by the State of New York. Harder's paper is an early record of the difference between state and private funding – one driven by budgetary politics, the other by the passions of a wealthy individual. To make his point, Harder gave an overview of how ceramic art education had developed within the college.

Teacher training became important for the College of Ceramics because the original goal of the art program never worked: that the work produced by the artist/craftsmen would affect ceramic industry. Harder identified the original philosophy as the "Handicraft movement," which related to the Arts and Crafts Movement. Harder suggested that this failure was due perhaps to the small number of craftsmen trying to influence a large industry. There was little support for the work from collectors, so few handicrafters could continue making these objects. Ceramics – and the entire handicraft movement – became a hobby for the middle and upper class. This has continued to be a major force in ceramic programs to this day, especially in summer programs and night schools. The huge following of amateurs has greatly affected the field, again providing jobs and studios for ceramic artists. It also colored the entire field as one for dilettantes rather than serious artists.

Charles Binns, brought from England as Alfred's first director, was part of this handicraft movement. He was a ceramic chemist, but his avocation was making copies of Chinese pottery. In his book, *A Potter's Craft*, Binns writes about the beauty of the Song Dynasty porcelains and glazes, but he made stoneware pottery more like the refined Qing Dynasty aesthetic. He spent a tremendous amount of time throwing one pot, making it in sections and trimming the profile to perfection. Although Binns taught industrial ceramics, this object was part of his other persona as a well-educated gentleman. This is the distant beginning of a line of thought that has set one direction of contemporary ceramic work in motion: the interpretation of a historic model, with the intentional or unintentional use of other models, to create a highly individual statement.

In glazing the work, Binns stayed closer to the ideal found on the Song pot: a soft, subtle surface affected by the firing. Binns formulated glazes with 30 ingredients, again separating production from the efficiency of industry. Testing was part science and part art, since the secrets of the Song glaze were difficult to realize with the materials available. This is part of the legacy of the handicrafter's movement. Binns created a serious study of glaze chemistry as an artist's tool.

Experimentation with materials has become a driving force in contemporary ceramics. A copy of Binns' glaze lectures has Maija Grotell's signature on the first page. His legacy is not the beautiful although derivative pottery he made, but the translation of ceramic chemistry into the language of the artist. This is continuing today in the possibilities of new materials and technologies ceramic scientists and engineers are inventing which artists in the future will use.

By the mid- 1930's, two outside forces had dramatic effects on ceramic education: the depression, which almost eliminated the demand for art teachers, and the fact that industry had found what Harder called an "art language," which he does not name in his paper but which I assume was proposed by the Bauhaus. Harder felt so strongly about the new vision for education that, when the dean denied his leave to study the programs in Chicago, he quit, only to be rehired soon after. This new philosophy was supposed to directly affect industry, unlike the Handicrafters who hoped merely to influence it. The craftsman became a craftsman- designer, then an industrial designer, losing the connection to the less practical, amateur Handicrafter's movement. Bauhaus ceramics broke away from traditional forms, but were not that far from Binns' vision of an object with a clear profile and minimal decoration. A new, high quality manufactured ware replaced the slow handmade production of the educated amateur. The ceramic curriculum included only a few courses in liberal arts, painting or sculpture. Instead, there were courses in airbrush rendering, along with industrial mold making and drafting. Any activity that did not have specific industrial applications was suspect.

> The program which we offer is not a sensational one. It offers no guarantee of employment. It demands a lot from the student in the way of application and creative resources. No tricks are used to give the student a false sense of accomplishment by building up his ego beyond justification. Emphasis is placed upon manual training. In short, it is an art program whose whole bias it toward developing personal creative power and judgment on practical lines rather than a short-cut to glamorous or flashy commercialism.

The failure of a creative industrial design program for the ceramic industry is one problem that no one has solved, in spite of Harder's efforts. Ceramic art education in this country has virtually abandoned industrial design. Perhaps Rousseau's romantic workshop – where manual labor leads to enlightenment, not manufacture – has triumphed.

Harder attracted interesting people to this rural college, some to stay, some only to visit. The pre-World War II period was a time of great political uncertainty, but one when ceramics strengthened its position as a creative endeavor within academia. The vision for ceramic art still included traditional references, particularly Chinese pottery, but the freedom to invent form that the Bauhaus movement offered would affect a new generation of artists.

One source of this new vision was Sam Haile, an English artist/potter who had moved to New York City in 1939. According to the story, Harder was on a bus in New York City and saw Haile's work in a shop window. He quickly got off the bus, asked in the shop about the artist and immediately invited Haile to come work at Alfred. A Surrealist painter turned potter, Haile approached the vessel though process, producing work on an impressively large scale. His conversation to pottery has its roots in educational politics: one could not be a Surrealist painter at the Royal College of Art in 1934, but one could take those surrealist images and put them on a vessel. He studied ceramics so he could paint what he wanted, but got hooked on clay in the process. Haile looked at everything in the British Museum, then formed his own eclectic model. The lively Minoan pots were of more interest to him than the perfection of the Song or Qing vase. It was his attitude about the surface that was most remarkable. Haile used pottery as a painterly area. Paul Rice described it in the recent Sam Haile catalog from an exhibition in England:

> The… great difference in Haile's approach was the way in which he used decoration. In almost all forms of pottery the outside line of the pot, the profile, acts as a visual frame to contain the decoration. Decoration is therefor either conceived as a 360-degree abstract pattern which fits this 'frame' from any

> angle, or as separate panels that each fit within a frame. On many of these pots Haile would not allow the decoration to fit within the frame. This had the effect of breaking up the two-dimensional illusion. The sculpted foot and undulating edge were further unsettling elements. The result is that he created an entirely different way of perceiving the space in the pot, and often gave an unsettling feeling that a piece could never be comfortably viewed from any single angle.

In his short time at Alfred and the next year at the University of Michigan, Haile created a body of work that transformed contemporary ceramics. Haile's work and Harder's educational vision defined the new model at Alfred. Haile reaffirmed the idea of the painterly, conceptually layered vessel. This is the line of thought that has produced the "gallery vessel." It has suffered from many poor renditions over the years, to the point that the critic Matthew Kangas can categorically deny its validity. It is the model – particularly as defined by the interest in painterly surface and the redefinition of pottery form – which has inspired many contemporary clay artists. There is no record of Haile being a direct influence on Peter Voulkos, but perhaps photographs of Haile's work in *Crafts Horizon* in the late forties inspired Voulkos to explore the vase and the plate with a new vision. Voulkos is responsible for a techtonic shift in the ceramic world; Haile was the earthquake that started the whole thing moving.

As the gallery vessel became traditional, a new direction and challenge came from "The Beautiful Object for Everyday Use." The genesis of the idea that common objects are artful and how this entered ceramic education can be untangled. There are well-known early champions: the potters Bernard Leach and Michael Cardew; the writer and folk art collector Soetzu Yanagi; and the American response by Warren MacKenzie, his students and other Leach-trained artists such as Clary Illian and Jeff Oestreich. Leach and Cardew recorded their theories in very persuasive texts which have been influencing potters and educators ever since. It is difficult to assess whether it is the work or the words that have set the course. This line of thought not only shaped the work itself, but also validated its position as an intellectual pursuit. This impressed educators, and the doors of academia opened to admit the simple pot.

It was not an accident that Leach's tradition rooted most firmly rooted in Minnesota, of all the United States, although it may have been luck that Warren MacKenzie landed a teaching position in Saint Paul, and not in Santa Cruz, California, where he was living at the time. Scandinavian cultural heritage dominated Minnesota. It recognized the "beauty of everyday things." Ellen Kay, an influential Swedish writer, defined the model in her text, *Beauty for All*, as the simple objects from the 19th- century Scandinavian peasant life. Imbedded in this was a political agenda of nationalistic pride and a belief in social responsibility in all things – including art. The importance of the home, and implicitly of women and children, was central to this theory. David McFadden's book, *Scandinavian Modern Design*, traces this tradition.

The Scandinavian model is a source of another thread in the development of ceramic art and education, which concerns the role of women. The ideal was that beautifully designed and manufactured things remained in the world of daily use. It seemed logical that the Keeper of the Home would make things for the home. Scandinavian designers considered women equal to men when it came to the applied arts. Maija Grotell, an immigrant from Finland, brought this feminine confidence to Cranbrook and infected the American clay scene with it. She was responsible for educating many ceramic artists connected to education. Another model emerges, this time one not for the object, but for the maker. It is true that nineteenth- century women had been influential in the art pottery movement, but these women did not affect contemporary ceramics to the same extent as the Scandinavian design movement did. Ceramic art education has continued to take women seriously. Linda Sikora, an emerging leader in ceramics, continues this tradition at Alfred.

Bernard Leach connected the simple everyday pot to the Japanese Tea Ceremony, specifically in the teabowl. He defined this object for contemporary American and British potters: not merely a simple handmade object of natural materials meant for common use, it embodied spiritual, eternal values with a specific, ceremonial use. In *The Unknown Craftsman*, Soetzu Yanagi argued that the studio potter could achieve this spiritual quality and overcome the banality of industrially produced ware. The style of simple teabowl showed the touch of the maker. It was made coarse, natural materials and did not, in Yanagi's opinion, use vulgar color. The visual qualities imbued the teabowl with a moral position: presenting work that exhibited this aesthetic as *ethical* implied that work which did not look like this was *unethical*. All of this culminated in *STUDIO POTTER*, curiously titled "In Search of the Ethical Pot." It establishes the line of thought: the clay, the glaze, and the firing are defined, then defended by a higher calling for the pot. This work could fit within the hierarchy of academia more easily than the simple pot, due to its moral, philosophical position.

A strong position, especially one that questions the morality of an object, demands questioning. It is logical to find a different line of thinking that would defend another point of view. An explanation can be found in a recent catalog essay by Arthur Danto for the Betty Woodman exhibition in the Stedelijk Museum in Amsterdam. Danto analyses the dichotomy between the teabowl and the vase, in particular the kind of vase Woodman makes, and offers a different reading. Danto uses the vase (as Woodman approaches it) and the teabowl as emblems of the two cultures: The West and The East. Unlike her peers, Woodman rejected the teabowl as a symbolic form, although she allows process and touch to inform the work as much as the Mingei tradition informed the teabowl. She turned to Italian, Etruscan, and Minoan models to explore a European tradition. In Danto's analysis, the teabowl is the Zen Way made real the object that connects the forces in the universe to the soul of the user. The teabowl is a lesson in "applied Buddhism," instructing us as we hold it, moving us to a new state of consciousness. The source of the Western vase is daily life, its history found in the trip to the well or as a container for transporting oil or grains. It embodies the activities and colorful garments of the bearer of the vessel, traditionally a woman. The form refers to the use and the user, the shape of the vase traditionally mimicking that of the female figure. Woodman's vases, although boisterous and colorful, remain within the language of pottery and its function in Western culture. Danto untangled the thinking around the meaning of ceramic vessels for the past quarter of the century.

Ceramic art education began with in the traditional accepted models for the vessel, either for the gallery, the tea ceremony or for daily use. At some point a new era began: it became acceptable to banish potter's wheels from the studio, especially in MFA programs. To understand how ceramic programs removed the wheel, it is necessary to see the connection between the ceramic object, the sculptural object and the artifact. The line of thought becomes clear by examining the sculptural traditions used in ceramic art and education.

Throughout the history of art, the figure was the primary sculptural subject, and ceramics used it either as a sketch for a sculpture or as a figurine. Arthur Sackler, in the introduction to his collection of terra cotta sculptures, writes about the immediacy of clay, how the fingerprint was that of the artist untransformed except by the fire. Other sculptors admired the freshness of the material and often collected the quickly modeled sketches or quite detailed finished works. Classical figurative sculpture has continued to interest ceramic artists.

Sackler's terra cottas are not the same genre as the figurine. Limited in scale and less valuable than small bronze figures, the figurine nonetheless had a robust history into the twentieth century. The figurine implies glaze, usually polychrome, which connects it to the vessel tradition; terra cotta was merely a convenient material for the sculptor. The glazed figurine is now more valuable as an antique than as art. The current industrial version, often poorly made or trite, has destroyed the validity as art for most educators. However, ceramic sculptors and educators in the early twentieth century made figurines. Many had connections to the Wiener Werkstätte in Austria, gaining reputations in this country during and after World War II. Vally Weiselthier, Victor Schreckengosy and Edis Eckhardt, who taught in Cleveland, may have had some influence on figurative ceramic sculpture. Viola Frey's work refers to the figurine, especially in her use of color, but the scale and reference to other sources of figurative language has given her work a power that a small porcelain figurine does not have. Sun Koo Yuh and Michalene Walsh are two younger artists experimenting with this tradition.

Clay has a sculptural history that is as ancient as its use in vessel-making. These objects, collected in ethnographic museums and photographed in beautiful coffee table books, have had a pervasive influence on contemporary ceramic artists. As Garth Clark described it in his short biography of James Melchert, the formal interest was in "the juxtaposition of incongruous shapes without transition." The objects suggested other layers of meaning that attracted ceramic artists. The Leach/Yanagi/Cardew tradition already used artifacts and folk art, but African and Oceanic objects suggested a spiritual power for the maker or user that Western Art objects did not have. The figure, no longer any relation to the trite figurine, was abstracted to a frontal, iconic structure that did not require the difficult modeling skills needed for a more classical rendering.

These artifacts also gave a sculptural language to vessels that did not refer to traditional pottery form. As assignment that was popular a few years ago illustrates this line of thought. The Ritual Object project directed students to make something for a ritual of their invention. Although it relates to the previously mentioned teabowl as a ritual vessel, the assignment was an opportunity to use the artifact as model for sculpture. Arthur Danto, in *ART/Artifact*, warns against using objects with imagined significance or misunderstood meaning as references. The ceramic professor, keen on the idea of the Significant Object and wanting to expand it beyond the Leach teabowl into a more sculptural venue, could easily overlook this detail. To prepare for this assignment, students worked in a dark room and through a series of directives experienced they clay in a private encounter. The intention was to show that clay can have a metaphorical meaning beyond learning a skill, and that they students experienced the material with another level of consciousness. Touching the clay could lead to a significant object that might be poetic, inspirational or transformative. The artifact also gave the ceramic artist a model for color on form that translated easily into glaze.

However, pottery traditions continued as the major influence in clay programs, since many teachers were also potters. Restless with the limited formal language of pottery history, ceramic artists experimented by combining their pots with forms that their colleagues in sculpture departments were making. In *World Ceramics*, Robert Charleston tried to define the new vision, as "abstract pottery," not sculpture, "since it has visibly or by implication an interior as well as exterior shape." The most recent object illustrated in that text was James Melchert's "Wall Vessel," which Charleston described as a pop-art object that "uses clay without regard for the properties normally associated with pottery." The decoration included the impressed image of a zipper, and the form was more like a leather pouch than a pot. It challenged the whole notion on vessel-ness, and what clay can do.

Since the new hand-built pot did not require the potter's wheel, this tool either became a sculpture stand or was thrown out. The work suggested visual and conceptual connections to painterly styles and some more outrageous art movements of the time. The vessel was coincidental, referring to its origins only in the first few inches off the table. Once air-bound, the idea could take off on the lid, or the area that used to be the lid, now permanently attached to the object, suggesting points of view from humorous one-liners to serious social commentary to formal explorations of the figure or abstract form.

Other artist/educators exploited the preconceptions of a ceramic object, infuriating the average potter. Howard Kottler exemplifies the challenge to our sensibilities. As an inspirational educator, he gave a generation students permission to appropriate images and materials from the world of kitsch ceramics. Unscrewing a lid was all the glaze technology needed for this approach, although Kottler was completely knowledgeable in all areas of ceramic technology and history. His attitude about materials and process, combined with his poking fun at tradition, gave ceramic art new roots. The model stayed well within the traditional uses of ceramics materials, although some vocal ceramic artist did not find them acceptable. These objects were in our faces visually but remained within the historical context of the figurine or the vessel. Kottler amended tradition; Mark Burns, Michael Lucero and younger artists like Casey O'Connor followed this new direction.

While Kottler was annoying some potters, an entirely new understanding of clay developed. Some artists addressed the problem of the abstract pot from a more conceptual view. James Melchert's *Leg Pot* series is an example of this exploration. He did not eliminate the interior/exterior language of pottery or get rid of the evidence of the wheel. He used these references to describe a sculptural condition, questioning the vertical, bilateral symmetry of pottery and even the material, adding lead and cloth to the surface. The *Objects USA* catalog, a text almost as important the *Potter's Book*, brought *Leg Pot* and Melchert's line of thinking to a wide audience. Melchert questioned the basic assumptions of ceramics. His intentions were not to eliminate the vessel from serious consideration, but to expand the questions artists could address in clay, using traditional materials in innovative way. Melchert, without giving us a singular, specific visual model to emulate, gave examples of how to ask radical, probing questions of ceramic traditions and gave permission for a new vision of ceramics, one that incorporates ideas from other media. Ceramic sculptors could connect to their work to artists working directly with natural materials such as the Art Povera group in Italy. Melchert's open attitude about process is the type of thinking which will lead to the digital world, either carving clay with a laser or inventing form with a computer program.

This line of thought within the ceramic community can be unraveled back to Melchert's explorations. After leaving ceramics for many years to pursue administrative tasks and a period of interest in other media, Melchert has returned to ceramics, this time addressing title with his questions and provocative answers.

Kottler and Melchert never intended to eliminate ceramic tradition from the dialogue. They were pushing the edges, considering new options. Many artists and educators did not see the difference between expanding the envelope and throwing it away. For some professors, clay had become just another sculptural media, its history and traditions now irrelevant. Deans and search committees like this attitude, as it avoided the issue of "Items Fabricated for Sale," as one writer defined work in the ceramic studio. The traditional sculptural model, the figurine, travelled more easily into sculpture departments, but the vessels often became forbidden territory, especially the functional pot. Educators who prided themselves on their open mindedness about ideas were unable to see pottery as anything except a response to market pressures. Sculptural work, especially when the process was part of the content of the work, was the politically correct ceramic object for serious study.

Ceramic educators now face a real dilemma: should ceramic traditions, laden with a confusing array of conflicting meanings, be part of contemporary ceramic art education, or is clay just another material? The question of "what is *ceramic*" about the object may not be applicable to other work, where the material does not have such tangled roots. It is difficult to ask serious questions in a critique where the discussion dismisses a functional pot as just an item for sale. It overlooks the layering of the historical references, its subtle relationships to form and surface, or its intended cultural implications. The maker of that work does not analyze its visual or contextual components with any vigor, and as a result the work will never rise above the banal. Universities must address the functional potter seriously, in both undergraduate and Master's programs. The romantic notion of the guild apprenticeship neglects the reality of a very expensive educational system. Established potters are naïve to think that they can educate an artist without tremendous time and energy. At best, they can help an educated young potter who now needs some practice.

The problem does not only relate to the issue of functional pottery. How does clay influence the meaning of sculpture? Without adequate knowledge of the references, extracted from the traditions of ceramics, the artist cannot see the work completely. Analyzing its meaning within the context of tradition does not limit its use as a tool for expression. The traditions of ceramics, whether the work appears to be traditional or not, are in the work from the moment the artist touches the material. It is current critical thought, as it as filtered into education, which reinforces the need to understand the ceramic references. It is this line of thinking, now part of the tangle of educational ideas, which should allow a more open approach to making pots, tile, figurines, or sculpture. The ideal education must teach the ceramic skills needed to make the work, not just the words to explain it. Without practice, students are left with theories that they cannot prove.

Opening ceramic work to a variety of interpretations requires asking how factors other than its ceramic-ness have influenced its shape. This question is completely appropriate to evaluating its success. The simple, well-made pitcher, and all other ceramic work, will profit from the dialogue. Without moving outside tradition to find those pertinent lines of thought, the object remains distant, removed from the present and less compelling in meaning. Approaching the work from all angles will ensure an objective response.

The future of ceramic art education depends on knowing when tradition is useful and when to challenge it. New ideas and technologies will push clay in ways that are unimaginable today but will become the traditions of another generation.

Originally printed in *Studio Potter* issue 26 no. 2 1998.

Reprinted with permission from *Studio Potter* and the author.

54
THE DIGITAL FUTURE: REIMAGINING CERAMIC EDUCATION IN THE 21ST CENTURY

Holly Hanessian

If a line drawn in clay can mark time, imagine all the different ways that line can be created today. It can be scraped with a fingernail onto the surface of moist clay, leaving a trace of unevenness that signifies the distinct touch of a human. The line can also be incredibly exact when cut by a laser beam or by a 60,000 psi (pounds per square inch) Robotic Waterjet Cutting system. Consider the state of ceramics today as our culture moves into the information era. Those of us who work in clay have more options than ever seemed possible. We can cut, engrave, and 3D print ceramic artworks objects, or enact age-old rites of fire by hand-stoking a kiln for days on end. In 2009, The Museum of Art and Design in New York City mounted a show called "Object Factory: The Art of Industrial Ceramics." The exhibition included many European designers, whose work emphasized "important technological advances in ceramic material." Little evidence of handwork was visible as designers sliced, deconstructed, and cleverly reassembled ceramic elements pre-made by recognized manufacturers. These hybridized and reconfigured ceramic objects signal that digital technologies are making their way onto the list of tools available to artists and designers who work in clay. Museum shows, begin to establish and promote new emerging patterns highlighting these trends. In 2006, I curated an exhibit titled "The New Utilitarian" at the College of Lewis and Clark in Portland, which examined the place of new technology in the ceramic arts. A diverse group of artists were included, such as Bennett Bean, who built his reputation on hand-built vessels in the 1980's and then switched over to using a three-dimensional imaging program to create strong and intensely beautiful ceramic knives. Garth Johnson, Gary Carlos, and other emerging artists were included, as well as mid-career artists such as Steve Thurston who have started to use these digital technologies with intriguing results.

As computer-assisted technologies emerge in our rapidly changing digital landscape, we educators stand at a critical place. Our field of ceramics has always been process-based and equipment-heavy. In many studio art departments, the ceramics area has begun to expand and merge with larger spheres of design and contemporary art. Given this full plate for art educators who work in ceramics, what are our obligations in adding new technologies into our curriculum? Will these tools become another option for creating meaningful art and well-designed objects? Will these technologies prove truly useful and be equitably available to all students? How and where will they fit into the current model of ceramic education? How do we weigh and balance the value of hand skills in this new mix? These issues are significant and need to be discussed for the mix of creating future curriculum in higher education for all of the studio arts, not just the ceramics studio. Digital equipment and applications offer a significant set of tools for creating innovative artworks and examples in the classroom. The following are descriptions of new technologies that could be integrated into a curriculum standing at the axis of ceramics, sculpture, and digital media.

Source: © Professor Holly Hanessian, Florida State University/*The Studio Potter* 501 (C) (3).

Ceramic digital images or photoceramic printing

Paul Scott and Paul Wandless have both helped usher in the renaissance of decals, silk-screening and other printing techniques currently in vogue in contemporary ceramic art. Paul Scott wrote "Ceramics and Print" in 1994 and is the senior Research Fellow, Ceramics, at the Department of Fine Art, University of Newcastle, England. In 2006, Paul Wandless wrote the book "Image Transfer on Clay" published by Lark Press. Since the publications of these books, new technologies are redefining ceramic industry and are making their way into university curricula, especially in the United Kingdom. Industrial processes able to print very high-resolution images onto ceramic surfaces now exist. One system is electrostatic laser printing, which is revolutionizing ceramic decoration with its small environmental footprint, computer-to-print simplicity and 600 dots per inch (dpi) image resolution. Work is ongoing on the development of ink-jet ceramic printing, and a number of companies are trying to solve the technical hurdles of creating ceramic-pigment slurry ink sets and specially-designed drop on demand (DOD) ink jet print heads. Although no widely available low-cost ceramic ink-jet printing device has hit the market yet, several contemporary artists are using these systems. Minneapolis artist Brian Boldon creates highly realistic photo images using a four-color laser printing process that produces full-color high-resolution images at 600 dpi, which is very near photographic quality.

Rapid protyping or dry printing

Rapid prototyping is the automatic construction of physical objects using additive manufacturing technology with ceramic materials as well as digital printing. Rapid prototyping requires 3-D modeling software to design the form, then the file is sent to a printer, which outputs a 3-D object made of powder and resin. Several innovators, such as John Balisteri from Bowling Green University, have started to experiment with ceramic materials and have fired these with varying results (See *Studio Potter*, Vol. 37 No. 1). In addition to these printers, there are also 3-D scanners, which can capture the geometry of an existing form and allow it to be altered and printed. Michael Eden from the United Kingdom has been working with this process and achieving remarkable results. His artwork is an excellent example of using ideas that clearly express how a 3-D printer can shape ceramics as a material that would nearly unattainable otherwise.

Wet ceramic printing

In addition to the dry powder process, there is a wet clay printing process that extrudes a moist bead of clay, layer upon layer until a shape is formed. In either dry or wet printing, the form is designed using software generated using a 3D image. These images are designed using computer aided design programs or can be imported from a scanned 3D image of an existing object. The digital 3D image is then turned into a 3D file, called an STL file (Stereo lithography). There are several software programs that create STL files and each has its own particular outcomes.

Water-jet and laser cutting

A water-jet cutter is a tool capable of slicing into strong resistant materials such as metal or fired ceramic, using a high-pressure, high-velocity jet of water or a mixture of water and an abrasive. Another option is a

3-D laser cutter, which works by directing the output of a high-powered laser beam onto the material to be cut. The material then either melts, burns, vaporizes, or is blown away by a jet of gas, leaving an edge with a high-quality surface finish. I have been using a 3-D laser cutter on the surface of glazed work, porcelain bone dry and bisque pieces, sheets of acrylic, mirrors, and recently on flexible rubber to create my own imprinting tools for working back into the wet clay surface.

Many of these pieces of equipment are costly, especially the water-jet cutter at $200,000 to $400,000 USD. In addition, they require regular service, and in school settings, student use can be problematic. Funding needs to be allocated for a technician to maintain and operate the equipment. Like other electronics, the price will drop and the technology will be refined as time moves forward. The tools mentioned above have already been introduced into many industrial, interior, and product design programs. I believe that these tools are relevant and should be available to our ceramic students on a limited basis, and that within ten years many schools will have either wet or dry 3-D printers and 3-D laser cutters in their art facilities. Now is the time to carefully consider how we can adapt, develop, and distinguish individual studio art programs. If we take time to thoughtfully create exciting new curricula, we will usher in a melding of realms where handwork mixed with digital tools to create innovative ceramic art.

Folding these new technologies into our current curriculum can be problematic and complicated. Having taught at both state universities and liberal-arts colleges, I have observed that the impetus to change curriculum is usually pushed forward by the following factors: a new, energetic faculty member; university administrators with an agenda to change the mission of the art department; or an accreditation review is on the horizon. Usually the writing of new curriculum happens across disciplines. Our current model of studio education separates out according to materials and disciplines. The painting, sculpture, and printmaking areas, as well as ceramics have distinct sets of course maps. In the last ten years many university programs and art schools like the University of Michigan have merged formerly distinct areas and integrated the media into 2-D and 3-D divisions. It is now common to see ceramics and sculpture grouped together, sharing a curriculum and facility, with some benefits to both areas and some loss for the individual media. With the advent of computer-assisted technologies, which serve specific media areas, art studios will require adjacent computer rooms to facilitate the interface between the technical and the application processes. Additionally, there is the possibility of cross-fertilization with other media areas such as printmaking with digital ceramic printing.

At Florida State University where I teach, we have acquired several new pieces of equipment for a joint facility called "formLab," shared by the art and molecular biophysics departments. We are still in the process of determining which students can use these facilities and where they will eventually be housed.[1] The final determination will depend upon the development of a new curriculum to partner areas of study. Our undergraduate students already have proposals to use the equipment in formLab, yet only a handful can be accommodated. My suggestion is to synergistically partner with other faculty and departments, creating overlapping circles of interest and energy. Using the formLab as a model, my colleagues and I have met and connected with others in the university science community in order to collaborate or write grants, which ends up helping all programs. This spring my BFA/MFA ceramics students created installations and wall pieces based on molecular structures, which were installed in April of 2010 on three floors of the molecular biophysics building.

This particular system works well for the studio art program at FSU. We already have a strong interdisciplinary model, which we call an "intramedia" approach, meaning that students use any art medium that serves their ideas. Ceramics has become one of many materials a student may choose to investigate. This encourages those who are painters to work in clay and vice versa. We have very few students who make straight ceramic art; most use other materials alongside their clay work. This has had a few interesting side effects. The hierarchy of materials falls away, and ceramics is considered as viable as any other material. I do make a point of acknowledging the contemporary craft side of ceramics in my BFA/MFA classes, so that students understand that ceramics has a different material history. When visiting artist Anne Drew Potter came to campus this year she pointed out the importance of seeing ceramics in many of the non-ceramicists studios, concluding that to them it was simply another valid material. I agree that this serves our program well[2]. It is easier to make a case to add new technologies if they serve multiple areas of a studio art program.

FSU's studio art approach is one of many existing models in higher education. Currently there are a handful of universities and art schools in the United States that teach a curriculum using a platform of core ceramic classes coupled with thematic programming. The School of the Art Institute of Chicago is an example, offering an "Extreme Craft" and also a "Designed Object" class" that uses rapid prototyping. These thematic classes follow cultural trends and mirror issues in contemporary art. The problem seems to be finding a curriculum that provides a core foundation with an in-depth overview of ceramic techniques, which also explores contemporary issues and leaves some wiggle room for students to independently make inventive work. When advanced information or a highly skilled technique is needed, will these students need to outsource the technical aspects of working in ceramics to others? The thematic trends that come into our studio art programs are cyclical and based on the aesthetic hierarchies that are fashionable. Handwork is either "IN" or "OUT".

Economies of scale will force many schools to adopt interdisciplinary programs, pairing disciplines and specialties together. In the UK, many ceramic programs have been cut, and others with PhD. programs work with industry in order to defray costs. The downside of this is a possible conflict of interest with corporate research, and a lack of investment in undergraduate education. The Royal College of Art in London, which houses the Applied Art Research-Ceramics & Glass School, has an interesting phrase on their website: "*The materiality of everyday life in a digital age*," which succinctly describes the intersections taking place *both within and outside academia* in England today. Will this leap forward into a digital future create a backlash? I know that I am not alone in the satisfaction I derive from touching wet clay versus pushing keys on my laptop. We need only look to the wood-firing explosion that began in the 1990's and continues today, to see the desire for working directly with materials in real time. At the same time, students and young makers are increasingly comfortable using the Internet as a tool for dialogue, and information, sharing, and marketing. Blogs such as crafttastrophe, extremecraft, and craftmafia disseminate information, provoke and connect people/makers around the globe. The blog Crafthaus has ongoing debates on CAD versus handwork, and another on rapid prototyping. I believe this what the future holds for our students. Those of us who teach need to reflect, engage, distill, and take these ideas into the classroom. I am excited to see what our students will create when they take their digital fluency and re-invent ceramics in ways we can't begin to imagine.

Notes

Below are relevant updates from when the article was first published to now:

1. In 2012 FSU Department of Art created a Fablab for our undergraduate and graduate students to have full-time access to two laser cutters, two Makerbots, a CNC milling machine and an Arduino station. The Ceramics Program in the Department of Art at Florida State University began a new focus area called Digital Ceramics with a course

specifically devoted to Digital Ceramics. This focus area is cross-listed with digital media classes providing students a wider language of skills to incorporate into their ceramic material based studio artwork.

2. In 2014, we created 3D Ceramics Digital Lab, which now houses a 3D Delta Wet Ceramic Printer. We print all types of clay and fire the stoneware and porcelain in our traditional soda kiln.

Originally published in *The Studio Potter*, Volume 38, Number 2, Summer/Fall 2010, pp. 65–71.

Reproduced with permission from *The Studio Potter* and the author.

SECTION 3.6
CERAMICS, INDUSTRY AND NEW TECHNOLOGIES

Introductory summary

This subsection begins with a succinct narrative of the development of ceramics from the emergence of self-sufficient studio ceramics to the use of industrial methods, collaborations with industry and new technical approaches. This text was written in 2009 to accompany the exhibition 'object factory ii: the art of industrial ceramics' at the Museum of Arts and Design New York.

Graham McLaren describes the changes in the British ceramics industry brought about the Second World War, which necessitated a more focused industry due to a reduced workforce. The text provides useful insights into how the industry trade journals navigated issues such as traditional versus 'progress' in design. It also references other influences that readers may wish to follow up including the impact on ceramics of 'connoisseurship' (Bernard Rackham and Herbert Read), Fine Art (Picasso) and the European Common Market.

At times the 'industrial' and 'art' camps of the ceramics world can seem to have very separate agendas. In the text of her lecture, 'Continuity or collapse: Ceramics in a post-industrial era', Jorunn Veiteberg gives examples of artists who utilize industrial skills to make work or operate at what artist Christin Johansson calls the 'borderland between industrial design and fine arts'.

Since the 1990s, the UK ceramics industry has increasingly manufactured its products abroad, notably in the Far East, due to costs. In this context, Neil Ewins considers changes in marketing strategies in relation to 'country of origin' debates.

Maker and educator, Ingrid Murphy discusses 'meta-making and me' in the last text in this subsection, which was especially written for this book. The term 'meta-making' is derived from 'meta-modernity', which according to Murphy is very apt for contemporary ceramics as it relates to a 'field hugely influenced by its heritage, but on the verge of significant departure'. Murphy goes on to give a personal account of her experience of working with new technologies such as 3-D printing, Quick Response (QR) Codes and Augmented Reality (AR). She neatly links her reflections with those of other key thinkers and makers including Richard Sennett, Glenn Adamson, Michael Eden and Hans-Ulrich Obrist to provide an overview of the current positive where ceramics, and crafts in general, occupy a potentially exciting mid-ground between tradition and new technologies.

Livingstone and Petrie

55
TRANSITIONS: A BRIEF HISTORY OF MODERN CERAMICS

Marek Cecula

New roles and functions for ceramics have emerged with the start of the 21st century as a result of developments in the previous halfcentury. With the growth of individual studio ceramics and the shift in those same decades toward new relationships between studio practice and industrial production, the lines of distinction among art, design and industry began to dissolve. This essay analyzes and reflects on the ways in which the medium evolved over the past five decades. This history advances creative discourse on ceramics in general, and on the broad spectrum of cultural production that surrounds this ancient medium.

The late 1950s and early '60s witnessed the emergence and growth of the studio craft movement in the United States and Europe. A number of independent pottery studios were founded, most based on post-Bauhaus craft production. Many drew inspiration from renowned potters such as Japan's Shoji Hamada and Britain's Bernard Leach, to mention only two of the most prominent. These developments also reflected the shifting cultural perspectives of the post-war baby-boom generation. Boomers constructed their own independent perspectives on the modern world and its systems, often challenging the proscribed paths planned for them.

Becoming creative and self-sufficient was the central ideology of this generation; they believed sincerely that the world would be a better place without wars, industrialization, and synthetics (specifically, plastic). Searching for a simpler life and a more natural style of living gave rise to a collective determination to use their own hands to support their basic existence. Adapting creative processes under the umbrella term 'craft', they established low-tech studios and distributed their objects through popular craft shows and festivals. Handmade objects, especially ceramics, became a popular product of the counterculture. With their hand-made honesty, the creative freedom they reflected, and their domestic appropriateness, thousands of ceramics were purchased to warm urban living and signal one's balance with nature (remember your hand-made coffee mug?)

Educational institutions established new craft departments with faculty drawn from practitioners that embraced the romantic myth of the noble potter in the Bernard Leach mode. Alternatively, the departments were headed by the new clay 'warriors' like Peter Voulkos and John Mason, who challenged the functional stereotypes of pottery and transformed the material into viable medium for independent sculpture. Suddenly clay was in vogue. A broad range of graduates with mud on their hands drew inspiration from the magic of wood firing and slab-building; they embraced clay as the means to shaping a freer and better world. In the early seventies, studios of independent craftsmen materialized out of nowhere, popping up in small villages safe from corrupting influence of the big cities. This great movement spread across the Western world, motivating many young people to reject the establishment and look for a better alternative. Clay – humble, democratic, accessible, and literally 'of the earth' – was the perfect ally. Ceramic craft was also associated with the mysticism of eastern philosophy and a deep respect for traditional processes. The popularization of ceramics thus began to take shape within the cultural landscape.

Source: © Museum of Arts and Design, New York.

Many excellent works resulted – high-fired stoneware forms with sophisticated glazes, innovative vessels, functional tablewares, sincere pots, and funky sculptures. Newly established craft stores and craft galleries proudly displayed the handmade commodities to awe-struck consumers seeking something real and honest in an accelerating world. However, many mediocre or plainly bad ceramics were also being produced as craft became a 'therapeutic' hobby to an already comfortable middle-class. The popularization of the crafts sparked its own commoditization within alternative culture and was annexed by the hobby industry, laying in wait and, ready to supply small, inexpensive manual equipment to anyone willing to pay the price. Suddenly there was a proliferation of catalogues with pre-prepared products, pre-packaged 'do-it-yourself' craft kits that catered to anyone who yearned to be artistic. As the handicraft market grew, ceramic hobbycraft became confused with studio craft, or, at least, the two became interchangeable in the public's mind.

This development slowly affected the perception of ceramics, lending a negative connotation to the term, 'craft' and to the profession in general. The craft market became synonymous with gift bargains instead of serious art collecting and the word 'craft' started to lose its original meaning under the patina of popularization and commerce – craft became a category of things, rather than an attitude toward making things. In 2002 the American Craft Museum in NY changed its name to the Museum of Arts and Design acknowledging the end of 'craft' as we knew it.

In late 1970s, another trend in ceramics was emerging. The city dropouts, after spending time in the country, realized that there was more to creative life than growing tomatoes and throwing simple pots with Asian-inspired glazes. Life in the city was once again exciting and vibrant, with boundless cultural opportunities, a flourishing contemporary art scene, and a good economic climate. With industrial lofts available as live/work studios, the city became the place to be for young creative individuals.

For some of these artists, however, returning to the city was not that easy. They had to make compromises in their living and working environment, to simplify their equipment and to deal with the higher costs of urban living. This posed direct new challenges to the creative process and led, in short order, to radical shifts in the nature of hand-made production. The traditional handmade processes were insufficient and the promise of leisure blew away with the country wind. New methods of production were needed – it became clear that more economical and standardized production methods must be adapted to meet greater demands. The country potter had to become an urban ceramist; resourceful, inventive and open to change.

While the studio ceramic tradition was evolving, the ceramics manufacturing industries continued to function and flourish. These firms often had updated technologies and sophisticated systems of production and marketing for their functional and decorative wares. Studio ceramists came to appreciate what industry could offer, such as molding techniques that allowed for rapid serial production, and more efficient techniques of decoration such as printed decals that could be fired on the surfaces of plates and vessels. These two techniques were among those adopted by studio potters.

The acceptance of porcelain as a studio medium had the most dramatic impact on the work of independent artists. Porcelain was special – white, translucent, resonant when struck – altogether a more 'noble' material than humble earthenware or sturdy stoneware. Porcelain also looked fresh and contemporary in comparison to the heavy, brown, and roughly textured clays that had been the norm. Seductive and challenging, porcelain offered an entirely new territory for experimentation and innovation.

Previously, porcelain had existed mostly within the industrial domain and was difficult to obtain for individual studios. Furthermore, few ceramists of the time had experience in working with this material.

In Austria, Kurt & Gerda Spurey were pioneers of porcelain in the early '70s; they created clean white abstract forms from the industrial material. In the United States, Rudolf Staffel explored the translucency of porcelain in his one-of-a-kind vessels, which impressed both his peers and a rapt audience of collectors.

These artists paved the way for porcelain to become a new material in ceramic studios and expanded the medium's creative potential as they linked craft, design, and industry in their work. The industrial slip-casting method of mass production also proved to be effective in small operations and was a good solution to many of the new demands from the urban studio. This process offered almost unlimited possibilities in ceramic forms and made serial production possible. It also became relevant for those who made ceramic sculptures; artworks could be produced as editions or multiples by using plaster molds. This ease of production led to the use of multiples for larger scale ceramic installations.

The fact that rather than having been formed from soft, plastic clay, many of the new ceramic objects were molded in hard plaster or re-cast from their original positives did not remove, wholesale, the hand-made process. Neither did it diminish their value or their ultimate individuality, creatively speaking. Rather, these new processes simply changed the appearance and structure of the form while adding an element of design.

Porcelain took the lead position as the material of choice du jour among designers and ceramists. The pure white material, steeped in rich tradition and history, started to affect the minds and hands of creative people not only from the ceramic medium – other artists and architects recognized its value and the potential of the material, and sought out ways to work with this 'noble' medium. The progressive industries welcomed this artistic influx. Already competitive businesses, they wanted more sophisticated products bearing signatures of somebody well known on the bottom.

In 1961 Rosenthal Porcelain in Germany launched its *Studio Line*, featuring limited edition production in collaboration with internationally renowned architects and artists. Villeroy & Boch Porcelain started to work with designers and sponsored creative projects with various ceramic departments in European and American schools.

On the individual studio front, in both production and unique works, changes were also evident. Small groups of ceramists found ways to get their work into art galleries, and sought critical vindication for their work from collectors and the press. They had something new to offer: works that were fresh and slick, with bright colors, and with forms married with concepts. In California, Kenneth Price, Adrian Saxe, and Peter Shire were among the movement's pioneers. Borrowing from the strategies found in fine art and architecture, the Contemporary Porcelain Studio in New York produced ceramic objects that signaled a departure from large-scale clay sculpture and traditional glazes.

Howard Kottler, a Seattle-based artist, worked with ready-made porcelain forms such as industrially-manufactured plates, and found new possibilities with the use of ceramic hobby materials, especially decals. His approach was both humorous and cynical, and his sculptural objects, ornamental but with provocative social commentary are landmark examples of ceramic work with direct conceptual content. Kottler and others like him had a critical impact on ceramic development by expanding the potential of this medium for creative exploration, without regard for techniques, methods or process. The conceptual act of creativity became the central focus; it was to a great extent, a tectonic shift in the cultural position of the medium.

These bold experiments also opened new territory for collaboration with the ceramics industries which provided knowledge, methods, and access to those who saw manufacturers as natural partners in the creative process. To register this significant shift in the evolution of modern ceramics, it is important to acknowledge some of the people and institutions that set the course along which contemporary ceramics is still traveling today.

In the early 1970s, the Belgian artist and designer Piet Stockmans established a studio practice that embraced both one-off art pieces and functional ceramic designs produced in multiples. In Japan, Masahiro Mori, who had trained as a potter, became one of the most important ceramic designers in this field. He established a collaboration with Hakusan Porcelain in 1956. From 1960 on, he began to develop innovative industrial ceramics and porcelain products. He mixed functionality and sensuality in his forms, blending traditional Japanese aesthetics with modern design. His designs are still in production, and have inspired many designers who believe that good design comes from craftsmanship and deep knowledge of the material. Masahiro Mori died in 1999, leaving a legacy of exemplary utilitarian ceramics which, as a comprehensive body of ceramic design, is both excellent and timeless. Matteo Thun, the Italian designer and architect, and member of the Memphis group, created his own unique style, blending humor and unpredictability with form and function. In 1980, he became the head of the ceramic department at the Art Academy in Vienna, where he changed conventional ceramic education by adding design programs. He encouraged collaboration with industry which gave students the opportunity to become professional designers and to work with ceramic manufacturers.

On the other side of the Atlantic, Parsons School of Design in New York City created a new ceramic design curriculum, a product design program in which students learned how to design and fabricate ceramics. Students achieved, in a short time, a final, ready-to-use product. This was one of the places in which product designers began to make ceramic objects that employed design language and industrial methodology.

In Europe, ceramic educators were more open to design and collaboration with industries, many of which were familiar local enterprises. Ceramic departments in some schools and academies were able to draw upon these resources, but also began to diversify the curriculum beyond industrial collaborations by introducing computer-aided design, software for threedimensional visualizations, and advanced rapid prototyping used for the creation of models.

In s'Hertogenbosch, Holland, a group of local ceramists initiated and succeeded in establishing the European Ceramic Work Center in 1992. With support from the Dutch government, the EKWC, as it is known today, opened its doors to artists, designers and ceramists. Participants are invited to come and explore the clay medium for periods of three months. They have access to a diverse range of ceramic materials and the most advanced equipment, with all the technical support to make a successful project. EKWC has become a place where artists and designers with no previous knowledge of ceramic material can discover the medium's potential, experiment freely, and realize their visions. As many of the artists are not ceramists by training, they bring new insights and ideas to the traditional processes.

It is not surprising that this institution opened in Holland where design exploration had an early start. For some time, Dutch designers were already gaining influence with Droog Design, the vanguard movement, serving as a lightning rod in contemporary design. From the beginning, Droog's product line has been amplified with ceramic designs by such designers as Arnout Visser, Peter van der Jagt, Erik Jan Kwakkel, and Paul Hessels. This group has pushed ceramics to a new level, and in doing so, has stimulated many others to engage in the creation of new ceramic art and products.

One might argue that a new type of ceramic object came into being at this juncture, one that acknowledged the historical evolution of the medium while pointing toward a new synthesis of art, craft, and design in our own time. A new cooperative spirit between the individual studio and the manufactory has encouraged an 'inventive dialogue' that has raised the stature of the industrially produced object. New collaborations were the result.

In recent years, the 250-year-old German firm of Nymphenburg has commissioned designers such as the American Ted Muehling (known primarily as a goldsmith and jeweler), British artist Barnaby Barford, and the inventive Dutch designer Hella Jongerius to create new designs. The Manufacture Nationale de Sevres, founded under King Louis XV of France in the 1700s, invited such artists and designers as Arman, Ettore Sottsass, Betty Woodman, and George Jeanclos to use the material and technical expertise of the Sevres staff to create new works in limited production series. The Royal Tichelaar factory in Makkum, Holland, which first produced ceramics for Droog Design, experiments with new designs and designers on an ongoing basis; their designers have included Marcel Wanders, Studio Job, and Jurgen Bey.

The utilitarian character of the industrial product serves as a point of departure in this new creative approach, showing that almost any object, in the hands of a creative maker and thinker, can be more than what it was originally intended to be. The conceptual layer added to the works makes them updated and contemporary, and aligns the objects to fine art strategies more than to common craft or studio ceramics. As this fusion takes place, traditional divisions and hierarchies among the creative arts become vague and even meaningless. This shift has changed the landscape of our global art and design culture.

Today, theory and practice in art and design is evolving dynamically. In this climate of change, the ceramic medium continues to play a critical role. Due to its ancient traditions, ceramics in general, and porcelain in particular, evoke classic, traditional, and nostalgic forms and decorations. At the same time, the medium speaks to a contemporary spirit through unexpected and surprising forms and new functions. Ceramics have the power to dissolve the time line that separates past and present.

Much of the ceramic output is a high-tech related product since many of the contributors are progressive industries and designers who train in product design, and who show strong interest in adapting and using the new technologies, mixing materials and unconventional forming methods. Synthetic substances are now used to coat ceramic forms; shapes are being cut or modified using high pressure water jets. Designs are created almost instantaneously using rapid prototyping technologies to produce complex three-dimensional models; computer software makes entirely new imagery possible as digital decals. The material has unparalleled versatility.

Another development in recent years is the energetic and inventive reuse of ready-made ceramic forms, ranging from dinner plates to teacups. Unique works by artists using existing ceramics to create new works is emblematic of a new form of creative transformation. Banal industrial shapes or tabletop dishes purchased from Salvation Army stores, updated with whimsical twists, are returning to circulation, forming a new ecology within art as commodity.

The Museum of Arts and Design presents this international survey of ceramics to demonstrate how vital and dynamic this medium has become and how the new developments form a creative mutation in a centuries-old medium. This exhibition has a specific goal; it is intended to illuminate some of the newest ceramic output and to communicate the expansive course of this medium in the current moment of interface between art and design. With the knowledge that ceramics has always served history as an indicator of cultural and technological standards, this exhibition provides fired evidence of the radical shift in the ceramic medium and its new role in our life and culture.

Marek Cecula, 2009, 'Transitions: A Brief History of Modern Ceramics', in Marek Cecula, *Object Factory II: The Art of Industrial Ceramics*, New York: Museum of Arts and Design, pp. 6–11.

Reproduced with the permission of the Museum of Arts and Design, New York, and the author.

56 NATIONAL IDENTITY AND THE PROBLEM OF STYLE IN THE POST-WAR BRITISH CERAMIC INDUSTRY

Graham McLaren

Abstract

This paper argues that the search for an identifiably and quantifiably British style in British ceramics formed a key aspect of the post-war reconstruction of its pottery industry. It seeks to demonstrate that this process was as much about sweeping away internal structures and the boundaries that acted as barriers to change as it was about a reaction to the economic necessities of the 1950s and early 1960s. The paper will show that in order to understand this process we must understand the mechanisms by which the pottery industry evaluated the role of design within manufacturing and marketing processes. It argues that changing systems of communication, both within the industry and between industry and those planning its future, were key facilitators of this process.

Key words

Industry, war, utility, New Look, tableware, Scandinavia, Staffordshire

> '... if we can openly say: This idea is **English**, then we shall keep and win many markets by the one quality which precludes competition ... **our** way, our **national** way.' (original emphasis)[1]

The language used to articulate hopes and fears for the future by the British pottery industry from the mid 1940s onwards has to be understood as part of a debate that had already raged for many years. The ten years before the war had been something of a rollercoaster ride for the British pottery industry, not least in economic terms. The 'answers' to the Depression years had brought new pressures to bear on an industry well known for its insularity, its paternalistic management structures and its conservatism. These forces for change were felt particularly sharply in relation to the design process and to arguments surrounding an appropriate aesthetic for the future of British ceramics. Style and design had always been the most visible aspect of the industry and the one upon which it was most keenly judged.

The lines of communication that alerted manufacturers to issues like these were well established by the years immediately before the war. Industrial and trade organisations, most prominently the British Pottery Manufacturers Federation (BPMF) provided forums where manufacturers could discuss issues of concern face-to-face, whilst trade exhibitions such as the annual British Industries Fair (BIF) offered an opportunity

Source: © Graham McLaren.

to gauge trends in design terms. In reality there is an argument for saying that both of these acted more as brakes to change than providing catalysts for it. Industrial organisations seem instead to have been spaces where the supremacy of the 'traditional' was reaffirmed as at the heart not just of the manufacturing process, but of the very identity of the industry itself, as Sir Henry Cunyngham's (1918) advice on issues of style and demand suggests:

> If the London East Enders want roses on their plates, give them roses - only try and make them lovely roses. If pretty children's faces peep out from among the roses so much the better.[2]

More fruitful in terms of establishing dialogue was the role of print media, and in particular the trade press. *The Pottery Gazette and Glass Trade Review* had been the pre-eminent organ of the industry from the early 1870s, but by the 1930s it had competitors such as *Pottery and Glass*. The approach of the *Pottery Gazette*, almost from its inception, had been to funnel news and advice on national and (crucially) international trends in economic, cultural and design terms into the industry through its pages, and to communicate and even initiate debate on key issues within its pages.

The outlook of the trade press had gradually changed and evolved during the first thirty years of the twentieth century though. Most significantly there had been a re-focusing of editorial attention away from the relationship of the manufacturer to his market. This had been a vital task for the *Pottery Gazette* during the early years of its production, with editorial content 'explaining' often distant markets to the pottery manufacturers, and retailers in those markets learning more of the ware that the British industry offered via richly illustrated advertisement sections and editorial reviews. By the last years of the 19th century however, improved travel and increasingly sophisticated market structures meant that the mediation provided by the press was being replaced by face-to-face contact, a phenomenon noted (1893) by the short-lived trade journal *The Potter*:

> The manner pottery manufacturers have to pay court to the 'American' buyers who come over to North Staffordshire to make their own terms with the makers, is very different to what it was in the old days. The gentleman from the States takes rooms at the North Stafford Hotel, Stoke, and he soon lets it be known that he is willing for anxious sellers to lay their treasures at his feet at his own price.[3]

By the 1930s the focus of the trade press was far more on providing a context for design and production. With this shift came a tacit understanding that both the manufacturer and the retailer were elements within a larger production/consumption cycle.

The space created by these changes was one that demanded a greater contextualisation of the pottery industry and its relationship with larger industrial, social and cultural issues. The battle for this space raged before, during and after the Second World War. It not only set the tone and context for the future development of the industry in terms of the style and design of its products, but brought to the fore a new class of critics and commentators whose role extended beyond rhetoric, becoming substantial and significant forces for change.

Significant amongst these were the writers who had their roots in connoisseurship. They comforted manufacturers, and the retailers who depended upon them by illuminating a readily delineable and separate tradition for British ceramics extending back to medieval times. This approach provided manufacturers with a key underpinning to their belief in the 'traditional' as being central to the industry, and also a demonstrable scale of technical and stylistic evolution against which to judge the success or otherwise of their efforts.

By the early 1940s this approach was receiving official sponsorship via war-time publications. These were designed to give the public a clear understanding of the role of manufacturing (in this case of pottery) in British life. Medieval products were highlighted in this context, being shown to possess '... the everyday characteristics of the people themselves, commonsense and humour ...,'[4] fourteenth and fifteenth century pots '... are robust, generous and hearty and seem to be typical of Chaucer's England'[5] and English slipware and saltglaze types of the sixteenth and seventeenth centuries have '... a peculiar wholesomeness, comparable to that of cottage bread ...'[6]

This view of the past was by no means uncontested. An example of attitudes that used the same historical data to arrive at very different conclusions can be seen in the work of Bernard Rackham and Herbert Read. Their *English Pottery* of 1924 extolled the hitherto unrealised virtues of British medieval pottery which '... are almost invariably well balanced and effective'[7] but, crucially, they emphasise that these wares '... show indeed a dignity which is wanting in most of the later wares.'[8]

How do we explain Rackham and Read's view of the ceramic products of the past as a rebuke to the contemporary industry rather than an affirmation of it? Bernard Rackham was a London-based museum keeper and connoisseur whilst Herbert Read was a left-leaning critic who was to become a key interpreter of continental modernist tendencies in art and design for the British public. Their approach can be allied to the writings of the delineators of tradition in the larger design sense. Rackham and Read's assertion for instance that the quality of 14th century slipware, excelling, they believe, even those of the 17th and 18th centuries is due to '... the use of a narrow range of clay pigments, a simple design serving only to emphasise form, and the avoidance of any confusion between the simple and the crude ...'[9] correlates with John Gloag's later (1947) vision of the medieval craftsman who had '... that deep affectionate sympathy for materials, that sense of apt selection and gay orderliness in the forms of embellishment, which are inseparable ingredients of the English tradition of design.'[10]

Rackham and Read are examples of writers who rose above the narrow confines of discourse within the industry, recognising and analysing larger contexts for its production. Key features of this group of critics included their largely London base and the fact that they questioned the whole basis of a coherent stylistic tradition for the pottery industry, seeing instead the rampant eclecticism and historicism of contemporary production as a problem for it rather than a selling point. Their writing on this issue was largely published outside the trade press but was very fully reported within it.

The views of this group had been receiving semi-official sanction through the work of organisations such as the Design in Industries Association (DIA) from the mid 1930s. This organisation highlighted the reliance of the pottery industry on largely nineteenth century decorative traditions through its journal *Art and Industry*. Overt criticism concealed dangers though, not least the creation of a 'very real hostility'[11] felt by the pottery industry towards this largely London based 'design establishment'. Indeed, a key critic within the modernising tendency, Nikolaus Pevsner, had warned in his seminal 1937 *Enquiry into Industrial Art in England* against a ridiculing of nostalgia and decoration, because this '... can only deter people from studying the modern style, and from trying to appreciate it ...'[12]

The industry would have probably been totally hostile to such pressures for change had it not been for the writing of certain individuals who acted as bridges between industry and government. Of these, the roles of Gordon Forsyth and Harry Trethowan stand out as key to understanding communication systems within the pottery industry during the years spanning the Second World War. Forsyth, Superintendent of Art Instruction in Stoke-on-Trent from 1919 to 1945 was a highly respected figure in the industry and well known nationally as someone who wished to raise the standard of ceramic design. Harry Trethowan, managing director of Heal's Wholesale and Export Limited and a former President of the China and Glass Retailers' Association was a very real influence on the industry from that side of the trade. As a Buyer of ceramics of long standing he was regarded as a man well able to gauge the taste of the buying public, and was therefore held in high regard by the industry. Both were known nationally as well as in the pottery industry, frequently writing articles for the trade press and appearing on various design related committees. They also shared some (but by no means all) of the interests of the modernisers. In particular their view that the quality of basic shape and form was the overwhelming ceramic design issue acted as a valuable point of linkage between their beliefs and those of the 'design establishment'.

During the war years their interest and their work was concentrated largely on the effect of the Utility scheme upon the Staffordshire pottery industry. The Utility scheme was a nationwide plan to provide the country with basic, well designed household furnishings during the war years, concentrating on the needs of newly wed couple and those who had been bombed out of their homes. I have shown elsewhere[13] that the writings of Trethowan and Forsyth played a key role in supporting government policy during the early years of the scheme, emphasising the policy back to the industry through the trade press as a 'new start' that would have the effect of 'cleansing' it of its historicist tendencies. Early articles by both men used terms like 'chastity', 'virginity', 'cleanliness', 'morality', and 'new growth' to describe the potential of the scheme:

> This day of austerity, in every phase of its rationed life, proves to us that hitherto we were wasteful and improvident-wasteful in every section of our life-and the things of which we have been deprived create no real hardship, and life is not really inwardly or outwardly defrauded or constrained. We have in all spheres time to estimate life's true values … how are we going to assess the values, and are we going to be *the better* for having passed through a fire that refines.[14]

This approach was significant because the government had to overcome industrial opposition to Utility ceramics that began as soon as the scheme was mooted. The manufacturers, hoping to preserve as much of their industry as possible, proposed an approach that would have kept planned factory amalgamations and closures (a process known as 'concentration') to a minimum, but which was rejected out of hand by the Board of Trade in favour of a drastic reduction of the industry. Trethowan and Forsyth also had to explain the logic behind Utility as the scheme quickly opened divisions between concentrated manufacturers and the 'nucleus' firms that had been allowed to continue production. These were predominantly the fine china firms with established records of export achievement - and exporting to win hard currency (particularly American Dollars) was a central plank of government economic policy during the early years of the war. Some believed that they saw duplicity between government and the nucleus firms; and although the argument in favour of export earnings eventually proved unassailable it did pose an early and severe problem for those advocating modern design. The output of nucleus firms was overwhelmingly traditional in both form and decoration, with a heavy emphasis on crafts skills that had historically found a ready market in North America. By comparison the competitive earthenware and stoneware sectors of the industry, specialising in low to mid-priced ware bore the brunt of concentration. Ironically, this was also the sector of the industry that had been most amenable to change in design terms, particularly in accepting some of the lessons presented by continental modernism.

By 1945 the leading modernist writers in Britain, critics like Misha Black, Nickolaus Pevsner and Herbert Read could find much to praise in the purifying role of the Utility scheme within British manufacturing industry generally, but were particularly positive about its effect upon ceramic design:

> the utility designs for tableware has probably reached the highest standard of any utility products; and these have been produced naturally within the industries themselves without any of the 'sweat and toil' which unavailingly has been expended in many other fields.[15]

Laudatory remarks like these mask the fact that the confidence expressed in the scheme by key interpreters of it like Harry Trethowan and Gordon Forsyth had been lost by this time. The concentration of the industry had quickly imposed a functionalism far more austere than even the modernising tendency could have hoped for, leading many manufacturers to bracket the stylistic elements of modernism with state control during the war and also (their greatest fear) after it. This general antagonism meant that although the Utility scheme continued to have an influence on ceramic design through into the early 1950s, the argument for it as a viable aesthetic for the post-war world was effectively lost by the end of the war. The critical atmosphere in the pottery trade press of the late war years was one that had moved from an emphasis on the necessities of war and of survival to a questioning of what the future would hold for the British industry. Core to the debate was the issue of national identity. The war had shown that the 'traditional' could earn export income, whilst Forsyth's initial enthusiasm for the Utility scheme had by 1944 turned to writing disparagingly of the '… Elephantine cups, with clogs on for handles' that the scheme produced.[16] Initially then, the debate seemed to lean towards the pre-war eclecticism and figurative decoration generally identified by the pottery industry's friends and foes as traditional to it.

The reasons why this approach did not entirely win the day are varied and complex. One of the most powerful was a quick realisation by the industry that things were not going to be the same in the post-war world as they had been in the 1930s. Most noticeable is the changing attitude towards the consumer during the early post-war years. Harry Trethowan's 1951 comments that 'the consumer is inarticulate'[17] and that 'there is no public taste to cater for … it buys what it sees …[18] are among the last of their type in the industry's trade journals.

In its place the lack of concrete knowledge of what the post-war market would require, together with the vague fear, increasingly expressed, that '… the masses in a generation or so are going to be as discriminating as the connoisseur of today …'[19] led designers, manufacturers and government funded organisations like the Council of Industrial Design (COID) into a struggle to develop an aesthetic which could embody essentially 'British' characteristics (seen even then as a key selling point in export markets) alongside a 'modern' feel.

Against this backdrop the focus of critical debate on the nature of 'Britishness' in ceramic design soon shifted towards the design community. During the early years of the war writing on the heritage of the industry had located it not so much in the objects themselves as in the men and women who designed and made them. Much was made of the irretrievable loss of skills within the pottery industry due to conscription. This was despite the fact that designers in general (and particularly those who worked 'in house') had never been accorded high status within it.

Matters came to a head immediately after the war through the agency of the Britain Can Make It exhibition of 1946. The reaction to the exhibition by the trade press was highly equivocal. The feeling that the exhibition selection committee had chosen '… a limited collection of pottery which will appeal to an even more limited section of the public'[20] was shared by many in Stoke-on-Trent who saw the final display as reflecting the broadly pro-modern and anti-tradition views of the London based Establishment.

The early post-war years therefore saw writing emanating from Staffordshire identifying Whitehall in general and the government funded Council of Industrial Design in particular as conduits for dangerous foreign ideas. Writing under the nom de plume of 'Argus' the editor of *Ceramics*, a trade journal with a distinct emphasis on technical issues summed up the views of many in the industry towards the COID:

> This Council of Industrial Design has for quite a period been a neat little nest where the architects and their confreres have been able to browse in safety and security. It has not, and never will, give anything like commensurate value for its cost … the Council of Industrial Design does not want pruning: It wants cutting out by its roots! [21]

The 1952 editorial that contains this attack is helpful in that it serves to demonstrate that the emphasis for the pottery industry of being under attack from 'the foreign' in terms of design aesthetics was becoming much more focused. To Argus the attack was coming from the Scandinavian form of modernism, promoted in Britain via the COID and identifiable in the selection policies for first the Britain Can Make It exhibition and then the Festival of Britain (1951). For Argus the link between the design aesthetic, government control and society was clear. He saw the Scandinavian approach to modernity as a system that '… has converted Sweden into a nation of flat-dwellers, forever craving after some sort of plant life to cultivate and having to be content with some creeper on the wall or a window box looking out into the street.'[22] He links the aesthetic with a sapping of vigour from the population. Through this process Argus sees Swedish women becoming '… dowdy and frumpish' they '… neither wash their hands nor powder their noses from the time they enter the office in the morning till they go home in the evening.'[23] For Swedish men the penalty for the pursuit of modernity was to be branded as effeminate:

> There are no public houses or bars and you cannot even buy a humble glass of beer … One of the most depressing sights is to see a crowd of young men sitting outside a wayside café fresh from a game or a country walk sipping away at small glasses of lemonade or milk.[24]

In summing up the Scandinavian modern aesthetic for his audience, 'we would call Swedish furniture – Utility furniture'[25] Argus makes a telling link between this brand of modernity, the design intervention of the British government during the war, and the potential danger of future moral and social decay as well as foreign competition.

Whilst Scandinavian modernism was seen by trade press articles such as this to hold out the threat of a homogenised, socialist future, challenges to the Englishness of the English aesthetic were perceived as coming from individuals too. Prime amongst these during the early post-war years was the work and influence of Pablo Picasso.

Exhibited in Stoke-on-Trent in 1950 as a government sponsored touring exhibition, Picasso's work in pottery caused a local furore. The industrial potters saw it as the antithesis of their heritage of careful workmanship and slow design development. Their attitude towards the '… chaotic mysticism of the Picasso School'[26] meant that the artist's name joined terms like 'Jazz', 'Cinema', and 'Futurist' as terms of abuse to describe modernist thinking generally. J W Wadsworth, Art Director of Minton's was asked for example by the *The Pottery Gazette* (1951) to suggest what type of design was likely to be required in the next decade. He was firm in the belief that '… the futurist variety - the product of lazy people trying to set lazy fashions ... the Picasso type … will never have a future in pottery …'[27]

This attitude was not limited to the industrial producer. It is one of the ironies of post-war reconstruction in Britain that these 'threats' are mirrored in writing produced by both industrial and studio potters. Industry and the studio pottery movement had for much of the twentieth century seen themselves as at opposite ends of the craft. To the craft potters, the ideals of the Modern Movement saw a future of large, collective organisations in which the machine dominated and there was no room for the individual craftsman, whilst the rampant, fine art basis for the individualism of Picasso's work shocked and unsettled studio potters like Bernard Leach, who saw Picasso's influence as '… too much from above to below, from the easel to the clay. Picasso is a great and inventive artist, but he is not a potter and his effect on potters has been disastrous.'[28]

Against this background writers sought parallels in the history of the industry. Comparisons were made for example between the disruption of the world of the early potter by industrialisation, and Britain's situation. The language used in writing on the subject is that of the good, the pure, and the 'British' being challenged and threatened by outsiders. A war-time example is provided by Gordon Forsyth's daughter Moira, who produced an influential government sponsored report (1943) on reconstruction in the pottery industry that gives a particularly vivid example of this process. Considering the future of the industry in the context of its past, she puts the break leading to the eventual loss of the medieval tradition as the arrival of the Dutch Elers brothers in the Staffordshire area during the 1670s. They were 'foreigners' to the district who '… conducted their work in great secrecy, apart from the general community' and 'thought in terms of metal rather than clay …'[29]

Out of this she developed a framework for understanding the decline of natural 'good taste' in pottery design over the previous two centuries by ascribing it to the pernicious effect of foreign influence. Hence Josiah Wedgwood is accused of introducing Neo-classicism into the pottery industry as '… a conception foreign to the natural development of the craft'[30] and an outside artist, Flaxman, who '… understood nothing of the processes or of the materials in which his work was reproduced …'[31] thinking '… not in terms of pottery, but of sculpture. …'[32] Similarly, the excessively florid style of the nineteenth century was blamed by Forsyth on the influx of decorators and modellers '… from Sevres and elsewhere who sought refuge here in the Franco-Prussian war ... their idea of a design was to apply a spray of highly realistic flowers indiscriminately to any available surface ...[33]

The question of what made British ceramic design peculiarly 'British' echoed through the 1950s, in that the preservation of a national design identity in pottery was regarded as the best hope for the future. This attitude is apparent as late as 1957 in an argument put forward by the (unidentified) author of 'Tradition and the Something Different' in *Pottery and Glass*:

> the industry will receive a challenge when the European Common Market comes into operation ... Ultimately, this should encourage countries to stick to making what they have become famous for- in other words, to make the best possible use of their traditional crafts, skills and processes - rather than to imitate popular lines from other countries. We can hope that this will lead to a happy state of affairs, of economic advantage to all.[34]

An emphasis on a national rather than traditional design style had other advantages. With the possible exception of the Midwinter company after 1950, the most progressive companies for design during the 1950s were 'out-potters'- firms located outside the Stoke-on-Trent area. Whilst the popular perception of traditional design in ceramics focused largely on the products of North Staffordshire, with the post-war expansion of firms such as Poole, Denby, Hornsea and in Scotland Govancroft the focus of interest in terms of contemporary design began to shift away from Stoke-on-Trent.

Perhaps the greatest change however was in the relationship of ceramics to other industries. Producers were having to face an industrial system that was no longer based on a series of essentially 'island' industries producing design in their own idiom:

> It is, nowadays, becoming increasingly apparent that a link up between pottery, glass and textiles can be a valuable sales aid. Whereas before, or just after the war, the whole idea smacked of being chi-chi, it is clear that the public are growing more and more design conscious. Visible proof can be found in the crowds, purely intent on window shopping and comparing displays, who invade the big towns and cities on Saturdays. As a result, whereas before the war a fashion was prevalent mainly among richer people, today it penetrates to a greater extent down from the West End through every strata and is to be found, though sometimes vulgarised, in every suburban store.[35]

The new 'national' idiom would therefore have to be adaptable enough to harmonise with other design conscious industries. In this sense it was crucially different from the idea of the 'Traditional' that emphasised the past of the pottery or the furniture industries in isolation. *Pottery and Glass* ran a series of articles dealing with the possible integration of different materials which pointed out how developments in transfer technology laid open the way for combining and integrating decoration between different media. It also emphasised the extent to which continental firms were already capitalising on these advances, citing examples such as the links between the German firm Rosenthal and the Swedish glass company Orrefors, offering to put companies in touch with suitable 'opposites' in other materials.[36]

In general though the specialised trade journals struggled with the complexities of explaining this new world to their readership. Instead, a helpful starting point for understanding the form that ceramic design took is provided in the introduction to a survey entitled 'The Potteries in Transition' by George Ratcliffe for the government backed *Design* (1963). Taking as a baseline the survey of pottery design provided by events such as Britain Can Make It, the Festival of Britain, and the souvenirs produced by the industry for the Coronation in 1953, Ratcliffe noted how the 'Britishness' of British ceramic design had developed into a series of motifs based on a mixing of foreign influences and what he regarded as traditional design. Among these new motifs were:

- An emphasis on body material, with earthenware losing its connotations of cheapness, and generally whiter wares being produced.
- A contraction in the number of shapes and patterns available, particularly compared to the pre-war period. This lessened the emphasis on the 'give the customer what he wants' attitude which had been dominant in the industry.
- A new concentration on shape that, although moving away from specific examples, continued to use shapes with historical and national meaning. Ratcliffe cited in particular David Queensberry's shapes derived from the old milk churn form for Midwinter.[37]

Ratcliffe's views would be dangerous evidence to take in isolation, but the early 1960s were a period of general reflection on the post-war years, and by this time there was something of a consensus in the trade as well as among outsiders. 'Post-war British designs of new non-traditional character are selling steadily, and in most cases better than traditional designs of prewar or postwar origin'[38] noted the retailer Angus G. Bell in 1962. He suggested that:

> Continental travel and continental salesmanship brought us both the demand for, and the offer of (at first sight), outlandish designs ranging from almost invisible patterns on the severe white shapes of Scandinavia to the carefree riot of coloured vegetables, etc; from Italy. These things gave our minds a much needed jolt- breached, one might say, our smug, safety first, 'reproduction' defences, and let in the post-war British designers, backed by the COID.[39]

Notes

1. J. Gloag, 'Planning for the Future', *Art and Industry*, 1941, p. 132.
2. Sir H. Cunynghame, 'communication, 31 Jan 1918' *Transactions of the Ceramic Society*, vol. 17, 1918, p. 177.
3. *The Potter: A Journal for the Manufacturer and Retailer*, vol. 1, no. 1, Sept 1893 p. 134.
4. M. Forsyth, Design in the Pottery Industry, Nuffield College Social Reconstruction Survey, October 1943, p. 4
5. C. Sempill, *English Pottery and China*, London, Collins, 1946, p. 11.
6. C. Marriott, *British Handicrafts*, London, British Council, 1943, p. 34.
7. B. Rackham, and H. Read, *English Pottery*, London, EP, 1972, (reprint of 1924 edition), p. 11.

8. Ibid.
9. Ibid.
10. J. Gloag, *The English Tradition in Design*, Middlesex, Penguin Books, 1947, p. 8.
11. 'Design Week in the Potteries', *Pottery Gazette and Glass Trade Review*, April 1949, pp. 375–376.
12. N Pevsner, *An Enquiry into Industrial Art in England*, Cambridge University Press, 1937, p. 10.
13. G. McLaren, 'Moving Forwards but Looking Backwards: The Dynamics of Design Change in the Early Post-War Pottery Industry', in P.J. Maguire and J.M. Woodham, *Design and Cultural Politics in Postwar Britain: The Britain Can Make It Exhibition of 1946,* Leicester Uuniversity Press, 1997.
14. H. Trethowan, 'Utility Pottery, *The Studio*, February) 1943, p. 48.
15. 'Tableware in Wartime', *The Architectural Review*, January, 1945, pp. 27–28.
16. G. Forsyth, 'Planning Prosperity', *Pottery Gazette and Glass Trade Review*, May 1944, p. 262.
17. 'Design Quiz No 3', *The Pottery Gazette and Glass Trade Review*, May 1951, pp. 748–753.
18. Ibid.
19. 'A Layman Looks at Design', *The Pottery Gazette and Glass Trade Review*, May 1945, pp. 259–261.
20. 'Exhibition Forum', *Pottery and Glass*, November 1946, p. 19.
21. Argus, 'Comment' *Ceramics,* vol 3, no. 36, February 1952, p. 454.
22. Ibid, p. 455.
23. Ibid.
24. Ibid.
25. Ibid.
26. *The Pottery Gazette and Glass Trade Review*, April 1950, p. 521.
27. 'Design Quiz No 2', *The Pottery Gazette and Glass Trade Review*, April 1951, pp. 571–575.
28. Bernard Leach, 'The Contemporary Studio-Potter', *Pottery Quarterly*, vol. 5, no. 18, Summer 1958, pp. 43–58, p. 47. Quoted in Jeffrey Jones, 'In Search of the Picassoettes', *Interpreting Ceramics,* Issue 1, 2000.
29. Forsyth, M *Design in the Pottery Industry* op.cit p. 4
30. Forsyth, M p. 10
31. Ibid.
32. Ibid.
33. Forsyth, M p. 9
34. 'Tradition and the Something Different', *Pottery and Glass,* August 1957, pp. 253–254.
35. 'The Link Between Pottery and Furnishings', *Pottery and Glass,* May 1957, pp. 155–161.
36. 'Pottery and Glass in Harmony', *Pottery and Glass,* October 1956, pp. 336–340.
37. G. Ratcliffe, 'The Potteries in Transition', *Design,* no. 177, 1963, p. 48.
38. A. G. Bell, 'Good Design or Good Seller - Can You Have Both?' *The Pottery Gazette and Glass Trade Review*, September 1962, pp. 1089–1093.
39. Ibid.

Originally featured in the on-line journal *Interpreting Ceramics* issue 11 2009.

Reproduced with permission from *Interpreting Ceramics* and the author.

57
CONTINUITY OR COLLAPSE: CERAMICS IN A POST-INDUSTRIAL ERA

Jorunn Veiteberg

A dusty cardboard box filled with broken plates covered with congealed food remains and dirt embellished the cover of *Ceramic Review* No. 233 in autumn 2008. The remains of a long-finished party? Or maybe a hastily packed and forgotten removal box, an expression of a life falling apart? The foregoing event or story is a matter for speculation, but the work clearly met every criterion for what most of us find disgusting and repulsive. On closer inspection, however, it all proved to be an optical illusion. It was not a cardboard carton exposed to the ravages of time, but a work of art created in 2007 by Giampaolo Bertozzi and Stefano Dal Monte Casoni from exclusively ceramic material. Working from their base in the ceramics town of Faenza in Italy, these two artists have, over the years, developed superb technical skills in creating *trompe l'oeil* effects in ceramics. In their hands, clay can be transformed to imitate absolutely any material: metal, feathers, eggshell, bone or paper. Using clay in this way is not unknown in the history of ceramics. In the 16th century, the French ceramist Bernard Palissy was already experimenting with glazes that could imitate semiprecious stones, and he decorated his plates with toads and snakes based on casts of real animals to make his illusions as true to nature as possible. Bertozzi & Casoni's piece contained a small tribute to Palissy in the form of a little snake wriggling between the plates.

However, this reference to one of the forerunners of ceramics and the illusion-creating, visual game is but one aspect of this complex work. Another quote is even more obvious – its title *Brillo Box*. In 1964, American pop artist Andy Warhol exhibited a pile of Brillo boxes at the Stable Gallery, New York. They were stacked like goods in a store, emphasising their *thinglyness*. Shocked, the critics could but acknowledge that visiting a supermarket was no longer any different from going to an art gallery. As the text on the packaging stated, Brillo was a type of soap pad. The brand was not made up, it actually existed. The packaging had been designed some years earlier by James Harvey. Ironically, James Harvey was an abstract painter making a living as a commercial artist while Warhol started out as a commercial artist before breaking through as a fine artist by applying the visual language and techniques of product aesthetics. Warhol did not use Brillo boxes as readymades; as with Bertozzi & Casoni, it was matter of *trompe l'oeil*. His *Brillo Boxes* were created in his studio, The Factory, using wood.

One person who was instrumental in canonising Warhol's work, designating it one of the most important works of art of the 20th century, was the philosopher Arthur Danto. He visited Warhol's exhibition in 1964 and, for him, the Brillo boxes raised a philosophical question about the distinction between art and non-art when the difference is no longer visible. For centuries philosophers have been attempting to define the distinguishing features of a work of art, but with Warhol (as well as with his forerunner Marcel Duchamp) it became quite clear that a work of art does not need to have any particular characteristics. Art can be anything the artist and the artworld public wants it to be, was Danto's conclusion: 'It can look like a Brillo box, or it can

Source: © Jorunn Veiteberg/Crafts Council in partnership with MIMA.

look like a soup can.'[1] It was no longer a matter of looking for a quality in the object itself; it was the underlying philosophy (idea) that counted. Danto, always a warm advocate of artistic pluralism, was of the opinion that this opened the door to a far more diverse art world: 'No art is any longer historically mandated as against any other art. Nothing is more true as art than anything else.'[2]

This way of thinking is also important in contemporary ceramics. Many diverse, even conflicting, practices and attitudes to the medium coexist side by side. So, the fact that I want to draw attention to one current trend in particular does not mean that I consider other ways of working with art and ceramics less important. I read Bertozzi & Casoni along the same lines. These two artists mark an ironic distance to Warhol's work by letting it appear as a forgotten and dilapidated relic from the past. Maybe this kind of art cannot be seen as a guiding light for artists today? Perhaps lasting fame is reserved for just a few select works, while most must content themselves with a few minutes on the pedestal before being taken down and ending up on the rubbish dump? The sculptures of Bertozzi & Casoni remind us that making a ceramic object does not imply that the end result has to look like ceramic, whatever that might be. They do not deny the material or the manual work but they stand for a renewal of ceramics through a 'radical and subversive use, or even abuse, of what was inherent in it and in its history'.[3] It was, however, only after 2000 that they began to make use of materials and techniques known from the ceramics industry. They are not alone in this; it is in fact one of the most central and vital trends in contemporary ceramics and has generated changes in production methods as well triggered new content and the testing out of different ways of being an artist.

Community

At an early stage, Bertozzi & Casoni formed a company for their activity, Bertozzi & Casoni s.n.c., 'in order to construct a profession'.[4] This model for collaboration breaks with the romantic notion of the artist as a person who creates in solitude and is extremely individualistic. They are not the only ones to adopt this kind of practice. Many artists outsource parts of their production, or all of it, but since 1990 we have witnessed renewed interest in collective activities between participants on an equal footing. Words such as group, network, constellation, partnership, alliance, coalition, context and team are used. The message from the anthology *Taking the Matter into Common Hands* (2007) is that communal work forms, pivoting more strongly around process and collaboration, have evolved between artists and between artists and other people. Getting together, being together and working together are more important as an artistic goal than the actual physical result.

Many of the activities of the Swedish group WWIAFM (WeWorkInAFragileMaterial) take on deeper meaning when seen from this perspective. The group was formed in 2001 and consists of nine artists, all alumni of the Ceramics and Glass Department at Konstfack (Stockholm University College of Arts, Craft and Design). Their common projects often have a playful and unpretentious stamp, using materials and techniques in which none of them are experts. It is probably the latter aspect that has prompted Glenn Adamson to assert that 'The best way to understand the group, then, might be to think of them as nine very smart people on vacation from their own cleverness.'[5] However, their common projects are more than creative playtime. It is about applying different forms of 'cleverness' according to the situation, and the underlying driving force is always strong professional commitment in combination with an equally strong desire to challenge and examine the conventions of craft and ceramics. WWIAFM has produced results and events that would not have been created or taken place without collective effort, and that is an essential quality of their work. One example is the video they made in 2005. They call it an educational video, but it is not an instructional film about the work process from *a* to *z*. The music and choreography are lifted from Kylie Minogue's music video *Slow*, but the video shows not Kylie and a thousand sexy dancers on a beach, but the ten craft workers at work – in a life-affirming dance in a workshop with squirting clay and dripping glass. The video is an ironic comment on the myth of the ceramic artist's intense and sensual relationship with the material.

Temp is a Norwegian group that has made a strong mark in the last decade, running a gallery, taking on curator assignments and holding their own exhibitions. The group consists of four women: Heidi Bjørgan, Ruth Moen, Anne-Helen Mydland and Anne Thomassen. All of whom studied ceramics in Bergen. Temp is not in constant activity, but works on a temporary basis according to demand. When invited in 2006 to participate in the exhibition *The State of Things* at Oslo's National Museum of Art, Architecture and Design, the group came up with *Temptation Island*. In this work they have collected, smashed and thrown together everything from design classics to pieces of cheap mass-produced dinner services and their own unique art work, making one gigantic mountain of pottery shards. Or is it a rubbish dump? A tribute to the discipline of ceramics and its traditions or a protest? The work has multiple meanings, but it also represents an accumulation of collective and individual history. The title indicates temptation, but can also be related to the material and the desire to make a ceramic object as well as the urge to smash the result. That which tempts is generally both compelling and destructive at the same time.

Trash and pottery shards

What do the works and activities of WWIAFM and Temp tell us about the state of ceramic practice? They certainly point to potential new strategies for studio ceramics. Their practices would seem to have a lot in common with those of Warhol, whose works Benjamin Buchloh suggests, 'celebrated the destruction of the author and the aura, of aesthetic substance and artistic skill, while at the same time they recognized in that destruction an irretrievable loss'.[6] Contemporary ceramic artists are not content to just produce their own artefacts; they help themselves from the stocks of history, or from the heaps of superfluous objects and trash around us. In the context of art, the boundaries between trash, things and readymades are fluid – but the words still represent very diverse and culturally charged connotations.

One striking characteristic of contemporary ceramics is the recycling of the least valuable things: waste, leftovers, superfluous things or discards. The book *When Trash Becomes Art* (2007) examines this interest in employing 'trash', and presents several possible reasons. It is frequently 'a gesture of protest and provocation', but an existential and psychological cause may also be at the bottom of it. The conditions of modern life cause many to feel fragmented and split, and most of us have experienced being rejected and left behind. Speaking figuratively, our attempts to pick up the pieces of ourselves can be seen as a parallel to collecting what others have rejected. In this context, art made from trash can serve as a metaphor for a society in which many – things as well as people – are redundant and superfluous. Along the same lines, Lea Vergine maintains: 'To save and preserve trash, to try to hold onto it, to help it to survive by rescuing it from the void, from nothingness, from the dissolution to which it is destined, the desire to leave a trace, a sign, a hint for posterity, involves a psychological and a sociological phenomenon at the same time.'[7] Like Boris Groys' statement that 'trash is a collection of physical witnesses that protest against being wiped out,'[8] her words are meaningful in relation to the installations of ceramist Neil Brownsword, who uses superfluous pieces, fragments and waste from factory production as his raw materials. The presentation of these industrial leftovers tells a story of what has been; of threatened or lost knowledge and traditions. It is all about the relationship between then and now with regard to work and values. In this respect, the role of the artist approaches that of both the archaeologist and the anthropologist. In the words of Grant Gibson writing in *Crafts*[9], 'his work today memorialises the human dimension to an industry that's vanishing'. But Brownsword is also an alchemist, transforming worthless material into poetic metaphors. He has clearly heard the protest referred to by Groys and given new and lasting value to 'zeroed out' trash by recycling it as ceramic art.

Already made

There may be many reasons why artists choose to use already made things as materials. The world is full of things, so why make anything new? More and more people are asking this question – which is typical of a postmodern approach to the world. Tanya Harrod sees this phenomenon in relation to the place of consumption in our society.[10] There are currently more consumers than producers, and many artists have built consumption into their artistic practice. At flea markets, second-hand shops or in the factory archives they find things that can exemplify the story they want to tell. In the hands of the ceramist, the readymade commodity is a material on a par with others but it is a material that carries with it memories and opinions from its earlier contexts. In this way, the use of readymades builds a bridge to studies of material culture, providing a wider horizon of understanding than that provided by art history or design theory alone.

Some people deem this strategy to have run its course since Marcel Duchamp used readymades in his art in the beginning of the 20th century. However, the type of dialogue engaged in by contemporary ceramists with Duchamp and Warhol and others in the same tradition is not about repeating old truths, but is more a question of renegotiating in order to say something new. In his book *The Return of the Real* (1996), Hal Foster stresses that such renegotiations occur when the artist experiences the work methods used hitherto as inadequate or without purpose. The strategy is to break with these methods and reintroduce a (more or less) forgotten practice, thereby constructing a new platform from which to operate. Many ceramists have experienced a situation like this, and created a new platform for themselves by opening up to the products and production methods of the ceramic industry.

Incorporating real things into art entails making space for the labour, statements, tracks and comments of others, regardless of whether the things have been bought, appropriated, stolen, given or simply found. The range of subjects is thus neither Nature nor metaphysical questions, but rather what is essentially 'real' life, the everyday. If we disregard this common basic approach, however, there are great differences between the many artists whose creations are based on readymades, both with respect to their reasons for choosing the things and to the ways in which they are used. One interesting example is Clare Twomey's installation *Heirloom*, especially since it blends readymades practice with ordinary ceramic methods.

A butter dish and some other heirlooms found by Clare Twomey at a local garage sale in Swansea in Wales were the core objects in *Heirloom*, which she created for the Mission Gallery in the same city. Not satisfied with just using the collected things directly, she took casts and multiplied them. The title of the installation has several layers of meaning according to whether we consider 'loom' as a noun or verb. Associations with 'looming' coincide with what happens in *Heirloom*: things seem to be floating in and out of the gallery wall. They are partly hidden, partly uncovered. The white colour and the dry matt expression provided by high-fired porcelain lie like a membrane over the things and make them resemble ghosts, appearing as reminders of the suppressed and forgotten. The transformation of all the different things into the same material and colour gives them an ornamental character. Transformation is the essence of ornament, and this process of ornamentalitasion symbolises the metamorphosis from things to memory.

Post-industrialism

By employing techniques or obtaining raw materials or readymades from industry, the aforementioned artists' work binds together two fields that have long been opposed to each other: the ceramic industry and studio ceramics. This opposition has its historical reasons, a discussion of which is not within the scope of this text. However, in our western world, where factory closures are everyday news, it has become clearer to us all that the loss of the ceramic industry entails the disappearance of valuable knowledge and history. Under the new conditions of a post-industrial society, it is no longer meaningful to define oneself in opposition to the industry or to reject materials and methods previously associated with industrial production.

The artist Marek Cecula has taken this insight to heart. As an artist he moves freely between different roles. He designs for the industry while also making unique ceramic objects, sculptures and conceptual installations based on readymades. One of his best known installations, *Porcelain Carpet*, is composed of 144 plates, on which a layer of 'art' is added in the form of a full-format image of a Persian carpet. The image has been digitally transferred and acts as a binding motif.[11] The *Porcelain Carpet* is a work about conventions. While the carpet motif can be said to invite close contact, we are physically alarmed by the porcelain plates on the floor; the fear of breaking something is deep-seated in most people. In this case, the size is decisive for the experience. More than any other genre, installations are about making us aware of how the art is placed (installed) in the space, and getting us to react physically to the situation. At the same time the *Porcelain Carpet* can be read as a tribute to two old handicraft traditions with eastern roots – ceramics and carpet-weaving – presented here through the latest digital technology used in industrial production methods.

Transferring images onto ceramic surfaces has been normal practice in the ceramic industry for several centuries, but frowned upon in studio ceramics. As Paul Scott notes in his book *Ceramics and Print* (2003), this attitude did not start to change until the 1980s. Artists often quote well-known motifs from mass-produced crockery, but submit them to various forms of reworking. Robert Dawson calls his manipulation of the famous Willow pattern 'Aesthetic sabotage'. The pattern was introduced in England as early as 1780 and expresses European admiration for Chinese porcelain and fondness of exotic motifs and dramatic love stories. Its popularity has waxed and waned since then, but it still remains the most sold pattern in the world. Artists Rob Kesseler, Andrew Livingstone and Paul Scott have also reworked this popular pattern, with widely divergent results. Their new interpretations serve to de-familiarise the original and the well-known, breathing new visual energy into the visually hackneyed.

It is not only motifs and printing methods that these artists transfer from the industry to their artistic practice. They also retain the plate as the underlying surface for the prints. Memorial plates and other decorative plates to hang on walls are a tradition with which they are in dialogue. In this respect, these objects have a lot in common with photography, which also serves to preserve the memory of important events and people. Kari Skoe Fredriksen is making an obvious connection when she combines photography and plates. She transfers portraits of women from earlier generations onto plates that are arranged or stacked in ways that we associate with washing up. The stacks of plates act as a background for these portraits on both a literal and metaphorical level. Historically, women's lives have been bound to the home and various kinds of housework, and Kari Skoe Fredriksen's tableaus can be interpreted as highlighting the efforts of our foremothers.

Several of the aforementioned artists took part in the international exhibition *Object Factory: The Art of Industrial Ceramics* curated by Marek Cecula at the Museum of Arts & Design in New York in 2009.[12] This exhibition included innovative industrial design alongside objects made by visual artists for whom the starting point was industrially manufactured. Many different strategies were demonstrated. Kjell Rylander had glued together fragments of different flower-patterned plate rims to make a shape for hanging on the wall. The lack of the main body of the plate removes all utility function from the object. The montage principle is a typical modernistic strategy, while the floral decoration invites reflection on the place and function of the ornament in art. Caroline Slotte presented sculptural objects in which she had stacked second-hand plates of various sizes on top of each other. In the middle of these stacks she had carved out the outline of a miniature landscape, thereby transforming them into a three-dimensional peep-show of great beauty.

These types of visual and formal manipulations can, of course, be interpreted as resistance to the loss of individual, creative autonomy in industrial production. It is also about making our association with things more than just a matter of buying and consuming. But the choice of the plate as material elicits associations with the object culture of both the ceramics industry and our everyday life. The result is art that mixes what the cultural elite has striven to keep separate, i.e. high-value forms with lower forms, the unique with the mass-produced, art with trinkets. The inclusion of things marked by time raises questions such as: Why are things that are chipped and broken worth less? Why is new and young more attractive than used and old?

While a growing number of ceramicists have chosen to work with industrial waste or mass-produced objects, a new type of art ceramics has emerged that takes a different approach to the industry. This kind of ceramics imitates industrial design products in colours and finish, and discusses function with humour and irony. Christin Johansson's *Sanitation with Identity* exhibited at the Køppe gallery in Copenhagen in 2008 is such a project. Fascinated by sanitary porcelain and sterile, clinical environments, she launched a series of bathroom furniture in smooth, pastel ceramic. Women were the primary target group. Here, among other things, they were offered a 'feminoir', a urinal adapted to suit women's anatomy that allows women to urinate standing up. 'My works operate in the borderland between industrial design and fine arts, which in my opinion is one of the greatest strengths of crafts: the freedom to not necessarily be functional but to question and discuss function and design. This is an integral part of the ceramic tradition,' she writes in the catalogue for the project.[13] Many artists and designers now meet in this borderland: The ceramic furniture of designer Maarten Baas is just as much at home here as the 'social furniture' of ceramist artist Anders Ruhwald. Like Bertozzi & Casoni and the other artists presented here, their work deals with what ceramics is able to and has been able to do, and how clay carries culture and history. Paraphrasing Arthur Danto, the authors of the book *Manufractured* (2008) state, 'Now not only might anything be art, but anything might be art, craft and design.'[14]

For the type of work I have presented, being or looking handmade is not an issue. When an artist bases her work on mass-produced patterns, includes readymades, or is attempting to achieve a depersonalised design style, it is, as Danto points out, no longer a question of techniques or hands on practice, but rather a discussion about ideas. Or, as Mark Del Vecchio explains in his book *Postmodern Ceramics* (2001), 'The relationship of ceramics to industry is complex. The issue of craft is not dead, but is re-contextualized.'[15] The label that has been attached to this trend in contemporary ceramics is *post-industrialism*.[16] According to Garth Clark, this not only marks one of the few new directions in contemporary ceramic art; it is nothing less than a whole new order in the field.[17] The previously mentioned opposition that existed earlier between ceramics as an old craft discipline and as an industrial technology has been eliminated by artistic practices that allow the two to overlap. The connecting thread consists of engagement in ceramics as a medium, while the diversity of styles within this new order in ceramics offers a promising perspective.

Notes

1. Arthur Danto, *After the End of Art*. New Jersey: Princeton University Press 1997: 35. Arthur Danto first developed these views in his articles 'The Artworld' (*Journal of Philosophy* 61, no. 19 (1964): 571-84) and 'The End of Art' (1984, published in the book *The Philosophical Disenfranchisement of Art*. New York: Columbia University Press, 1986). He subsequently expounded on his theory in the book *After the End of Art: Contemporary Art and the Pale of History*.
2. Arthur Danto, *After the End of Art*, op.cit.: 27.
3. Marco Senaldi, 'Art lies. Bertozzi & Casoni Time'. *Bertozzi & Casoni Le Bugie dell'Arte*. Bologna: Damiani 2007: 11. Bertozzi & Casoni featured in the Italian pavilion at the Venice Biennale in the summer of 2009.
4. Franco Bertoni i *Bertozzi & Casoni Le Bugie dell'Arte*, op.cit.: 49.

5. Published on www.weworkinafragilematerial.com – We Built This City.
6. Benjamin H. D. Buchloh, *Neo-Avantgarde and Culture Industry. Essays on European and American Art from 1955 to 1975,* MIT Press 2000: 513.
7. Lea Vergine, *When Trash Becomes Art: Trash Rubbish Mungo*. Milano: Skira 2007: 8.
8. Quoted in Ilya Kabakov, *The Garbage Man*, Skrifter series No 1. Oslo: The Museum Of Contemporary Art 1996.
9. Grant Gibson, 'The Kilning Fields', *Crafts* No. 211 (March/April 2008): 24.
10. Tanya Harrod, 'Craft Today Contemporary Concerns', in: Sandy Brown and Maya Kumar Mitchell (eds.), *The Beauty of Craft*, 2004: 41.
11. *Porcelain Carpet* was exhibited for the first time at the exhibition *Groundswell: The Post-industrial Wave in Ceramic Sculpture* in Garth Clark Gallery on Long Island, New York in 2002.
12. *Object Factory: The Art of Industrial Ceramics* was originally produced for the Gardiner Museum in Toronto in 2008 and exhibited in a slightly different version with a new catalogue at the MAD in New York.
13. *Christin Johansson*, Copenhagen: Køppe gallery. [2008]
14. Steven Skov Holt and Mara Holt Skov, *Manufractured: The Conspicuous Transformation of Everyday Objects.* San Francisco: Chronicle Books 2008: 16.
15. Mark Del Vecchio, *Postmodern Ceramics*. London: Thames & Hudson 2001: 178.
16. Ibid.: 176-191.
17. Garth Clark, 'Introduction', ibid.: 24.

First published as Jorunn Veiteberg (2010), 'Continuity or collapse: Ceramics in a post-industrial era', in Jorunn Veiteberg (ed), *Possibilities and Losses: Transitions in Clay*, Crafts Council (in partnership with MIMA), pp. 20–36.

Reprinted with permission from the Crafts Council, MIMA and the author. © Crafts Council (publisher), in partnership with MIMA; author.

58

THE UK CERAMIC MARKETING STRATEGY IN RESPONSE TO GLOBALIZATION c1990–2010

Neil Ewins

Since the late 1990s, ceramic exports from the Far East have surged, and UK ceramic brands have increasingly outsourced production in the Far East or Pacific Rim. The purpose of this paper is to outline changes in UK ceramic marketing, in the context of globalization theories and the work of scholars who have explored 'Country of Origin' debates, such as Papadopoulos *et al.*, (2011), and Magnusson and Westjohn (2011). Using evidence drawn from oral interviews with UK ceramic retailers and ceramic manufacturers, this paper considers responses to the issues created by Far Eastern outsourcing apparent in the changing of marketing strategies. Kitchin and Tate discuss appropriate ways to collect oral evidence. Their 'Interview guide approach' was followed since this enables the interviewee to ask additional questions in response to a reply, for greater clarification (Kitchin and Tate, 2000, p. 213–4). In addition, interviews are considered useful if research is aimed at acquiring information that reflects, 'experience, feelings and opinions' (Kitchin and Tate, 2000, p. 213).

As not all ceramic manufacturers have outsourced production to the Far East, and marketing has emerged that emphasizes 'place of origin', the question arises of whether these approaches are influenced by consumer demand. This research aims to show that reactions to outsourcing are more mixed than have been previously reported, and whilst some ceramic marketing might suggest a need to supply a certain niche, a strong attachment to maintaining Staffordshire production occurs for a variety of reasons.

To many writers the impact of globalization creates deterritorialization, and consumers are increasingly presented with homogenized commodities (King (ed), 1991, p. 6; Tomlinson, 1999, p. 106–49). Taking their cue from Baudrillard, Lash and Urry's analysis of 'global sociology' argued that 'Objects are emptied out both of meaning (and are postmodern) and material content (and are thus post-industrial)' (1994, p. 15). In theory, it becomes the role of advertising to attach imagery and meaning to the product (1994, p. 14–5). Whilst Carroll *et al.*'s analysis of the organization of the UK Ceramic Tableware Industry argued that widespread outsourcing was inevitable because of competition (2002, p. 341) this paper parallels a study by Respicio concerning the Nishijin textile tradition of Japan. Respicio explored issues raised by a craft orientated 'industry' undergoing shifts in production to cheaper places of manufacture (2007). The UK ceramic industry also has a distinctive regional identity and heritage particularly in Staffordshire, and significantly, on occasion, collectable dimensions. However, this research differs from Respicio's paper as it records the visual changes that have occurred in UK ceramic marketing.

Craft skills, the family nature of companies, and the place of production have all been central to the marketing strategies of UK ceramics before the rise of outsourcing, even though the styles of ceramic designs are typically cross-cultural. It was reported that in 'the 1980s and 1990s (and perhaps earlier)', 'medium

Source: © Neil Ewins, University of Sunderland.

ranking firms' were importing undecorated ware from Pakistan, Korea, and China (Rowley, 1998, p. 27). In addition, Royal Doulton announced in 1995 the development of a manufacturing venture in Indonesia.

Broadly, six configurations of marketing have been identified as a reflection of outsourcing. One tendency has been to focus on the Staffordshire brand name, avoiding references to 'place of origin' on the backstamp, and to use only the detachable label or the packaging to indicate a Far Eastern or Asian place of manufacture. It is important to note that when Wedgwood first outsourced its porcelain 'Home' collection to Vista Alegre in 1995, the range was clearly backstamped 'Wedgwood … made in Portugal'. Wedgwood used a detachable label approach when sourcing production in Indonesia.

The next outsourcing example exists where the Staffordshire brand name and 'England' are provided within the indelible backstamp, but the detachable label, or the packaging indicates a Far Eastern place of manufacture. In the manner of Lash and Urry's view, the marketing (or backstamp) creates links with the UK. The word 'England' has in these circumstances come to signify the origin of the brand, rather than place of production. A Johnson Brothers' cup and saucer demonstrates this trend. The printed backstamp reads 'Johnson Bros England 1883' (the year the firm was founded), but the detachable label indicates that it was actually manufactured in China.

A third more unusual trend is for Staffordshire brands, such as Churchill China, to declare in the indelible backstamp that the product was 'Made in China'. A fourth trend has been a shift from stating 'Made in England' to 'Designed in England' to reinforce UK links, without any indication of place of manufacture on detachable labels, or packaging. A fifth approach is to declare 'Decorated in England' which is a reflection of UK firms using imported white-ware, normally from the Far East. Finally, the sixth trend can be a more ambiguous approach whereby one Staffordshire company called, 'Rose of England China', stated on their packaging that mugs were 'Made in England', whilst the mugs themselves are individually marked 'Rose of England, Made in China'.

Changes in the organization of the UK industry were not imperceptible when considering actual marketing, and overall they have implications on both consumers and manufacturers. When the actual origins of UK ceramic brands became decidedly unclear, theoretically, this had an impact on manufacturers who were still producing in the UK. Alternatively, when detachable labels or the packaging indicated that the UK ceramic brand was outsourced, it raised the issue of how consumers responded to these changes. When *Tableware International* published an article concerning the 'country of origin' debate, opinions of UK ceramic retailers veered towards the 'place of manufacture' having limited importance to the consumer (*Tableware International*, 2008). Likewise, and corresponding to Churchill China's use of an indelible backstamp reading 'Made in China' on certain ceramic ranges, a representative of this Staffordshire company when interviewed, indicated that the place of manufacture was more of a concern to the older consumer (Interview 1). These views are more in accordance with Gabriel and Lang's definition of postmodern consumers who no longer search for the 'authentic' (2006, p.88).

However, as part of this research, an interview was undertaken with a retailer in a department store in north of England with a retailer selling Wedgwood, and other brands connected to this group. With regard to shifts in production to Asia, the opinion was that, '… I think they [Wedgwood] under-estimated the customer, and I think the customer is bothered where things are made …' (Interview 2). A central problem described by this retailer was the perception of Wedgwood's value. Prestigious UK ceramic products continued to be retailed at high prices, but because they were manufactured outside the UK, the consumer perceived them as essentially the 'same' as the proliferation of cheap Far Eastern ceramic goods found in supermarkets. It appears, then, that consumers were not oblivious to the detachable labels used to indicate actual place of production.

Does this reaction to outsourcing (albeit to a high-status, heritage brand) explain why some other UK ceramic manufacturers have continued production in the UK? Emma Bridgewater is a Staffordshire-based firm that has remained profitable, and reviews have emphasized how 'every piece is hand-made in Stoke-on-Trent, and Bridgewater, herself, has doggedly refused to outsource production overseas' (Qureshi, 2010, p.14). Hervas-Oliver *et al.*'s analysis of 'regional resilience' has even asserted that Emma Bridgewater and Portmeirion (also based in Staffordshire) have 'generally succeeded' because of competitive design and marketing that 'strongly associate' the product to the region (2011, p. 383). This parallels other interpretations of globalization that foresee local, regional cultures, heritage, identity and continuity becoming re-valued (Corner and Harvey (ed), 1991, p. 24–6). Bridgewater markets a diverse range of surface patterns, often using hand techniques of decoration.

In spite of the Bridgewater backstamp reading 'Hand made in Stoke-on-Trent', when husband and Co-Director of Emma Bridgewater was interviewed, the somewhat surprising attitude regarding place of manufacture was that:

> 'It is not the principal thing.' (Interview 3).

In reality, maintaining production in Stoke-on-Trent stemmed from Bridgewater's desire to create jobs in the UK. Similarly, a Staffordshire firm called Royal Stafford Tableware has created backstamps that emphasize The Potteries and even surface pattern designs incorporating the phrase 'Made in Britain'. This is another example of a type of marketing strategy that has emerged reflecting the impact of globalization. However, the Managing Director of Royal Stafford, when interviewed, established that the motivation for continuing production in the UK stemmed from maintaining design and manufacturing agility issues, rather than a perceived consumer demand (Interview 4).

Nevertheless, adding to the complexity of this area of research there are cases where UK manufacturers and ceramic retailers are less contradictory regarding place of production, and this is of significance. If the ceramic manufacturer is involved in producing the collectable and commemorative category of ceramics, place of production can still be considered to be relevant. The production of collectable ceramics does not align with Lash and Urry's broad assumption that meaning can simply be added to the product wherever it was manufactured. Ironically, Baudrillard's observations regarding collecting behaviour suggested that here there was a greater propensity to search for 'authenticity, craftsmanship, hand-made products, native pottery...' and current research indicates that this tendency still persists (1996, p.75). Finally, it was found when interviewing certain manufacturers that the 'Made in England' backstamp was important for attracting consumers from their newer, growing export markets that are, paradoxically, in the Far East.

Adverse reactions to outsourcing were particularly the case with a high-status UK ceramic brand. Some caution is required if ceramic marketing strategies emphasizing 'place of origin' are assumed to be wholly influenced by an attempt to attract, what might be best described as, the 'Ethnocentric' consumer (Evans *et al.*, 2006, p.209-10). A stronger consensus between the views of retailers and manufacturers regarding a UK place of production depends on the type of ceramics produced, and whether it is aimed at certain export markets. Overall, this individual case study highlights the value of recording actual attitudes in a period of rapid change, and demonstrates that even when examining an industry in isolation, generalizations should be avoided since approaches and attitudes can be contradictory.

References

Baudrillard, J. (1968: reprint 1996), *The System of Objects*, Verso.

Carroll, M., Cooke, Fang Lee, Hassard, J., and Marchington, M. (2002), "The Strategic Management of Outsourcing in the UK Ceramic Tableware Industry", *Competition and Change*, Vol. 6, Issue 4, pp. 327–43.

Corner, J. and Harvey, S. (ed), (1991), *Enterprise and Heritage: Crosscurrents of national culture,* Routledge.
Evans, M., Jamal, A., and Foxall, G. (2006), *Consumer Behaviour*, John Wiley & Sons Ltd.
Gabriel, Y. and Lang, T. (2006), *The Unmanageable Consumer*, Sage Publications.
Hervas-Oliver, J-L., Jackson, I., and Tomlinson, P.R. (2011), "'May the ovens never grow cold': regional resilience and industrial policy in the North Staffordshire ceramics industrial district – with lessons from Sassoulo and Castellon", *Policy Studies*, 32: 4, pp. 377–95.
King, A. (ed), (1991), *Culture, Globalization and the World-System: Contemporary Conditions for the Representation of Identity*, MacMillan.
Kitchin, R. and Tate, N.J. (2000), *Conducting research in Human Geography: theory, methodology and practice*, Harlow.
Lash, S. and Urry, J. (1994), *Economies of Signs and Space,* Sage Publications.
Magnusson, P. and Westjohn, S.A. (2011), "Is there a country-of-origin theory?", Jain, S.C. and Griffith, D.A., *Handbook of Research in International Marketing, Second Edition*, Edward Elgar, UK and USA, pp. 292–316.
Papadopoulos, N., el Banna, A., Murphy, S.A., and Rojas-Méndez, J.I. (2011),"Place brands and brand-place associations: the role of 'place' in international marketing", Jain, S.C. and Griffith, D.A., *Handbook of Research in International Marketing, Second Edition*, Edward Elgar, UK and USA, pp. 88–113.
Qureshi, H. (2010), "From Brixton to Bond and Beyond", *Crafts*, May/June, No. 224, p. 14.
Respicio, N.A. (2007), "The Nishijin Tradition: Past and Prospects, Issues and Problems as Viewed by Various People Involved in Production and Dissemination". Paper for Symposium, *International Research Centre for Japanese Studies*, Kyoto, No. 27, pp. 321–35.
Rowley, C. (1998), "Manufacturing Mobility? Internationalization, Change and Continuity", *Journal of General Management*, Vol. 23, No. 3, Spring, pp. 21–34.
Tableware International (2008), "TableTalk – canvassing the views of the industry", May/June, Issue 3, Vol. 130, pp. 24–5.
Tomlinson, J. (1999), *Globalization and Culture*, Polity Press.

Interviews referred to in this Paper

Interview 1: Churchill China, Tuntstall. Interview with Managing Director of Dining.
Interview 2: Wedgwood seller, department store, north of England.
Interview 3: Emma Bridgewater, Hanley. Interview with Co-Director.
Interview 4: Royal Stafford Tableware, Burslem. Interview with Managing Director.

The following paper was presented to the 16th Biennial Conference on Historical Analysis and Research in Marketing (CHARM), *Varieties, Alternatives, and Deviations in Marketing History*, held at the Copenhagen Business School, Copenhagen, Denmark May 30 – June 2, 2013.

A version of it was published in the 2013 *Proceedings of Conference on Historical Analysis and Research in Marketing* (CHARM), pp. 334–8.

Printed with permission of the author.

59
META-MAKING AND ME

Ingrid Murphy

The position of ceramics within contemporary society is an example of meta-modernity at its finest, it is a field in a perpetual state of oscillation and plurality. Depending on your perspective, ceramics as a material practice is simultaneously endangered and yet, routinely declared as never more potent or valuable to society.

The definition of Meta-modernity by cultural theorists, Timothies Vermuleun and Robin van Der Akker can be easily applied to contemporary ceramic practice; it is that of a field hugely influenced by its heritage, but on the verge of significant departure. In their seminal text "Note on Metamodernism" Vermulen and van Der Akker describe their concept of meta:

> "Meta, for us, signifies an oscillation, a swinging or swaying with and between future, present and past, here and there and somewhere; with and between ideals, mindsets, and positions. It is influenced by estimations of the past, imbued by experiences of the present, yet also inspired by expectations of the future."[1]

This essay is an attempt to hold still this oscillating metronome for long enough to see how technological advances might influence the future of ceramic practice.

On a personal level I experienced this point of oscillation, between the past, present and the future, when in 2011, I had the pleasure of facilitating a shared stage at the International Ceramics Festival in Aberystwyth, Wales between British ceramicist Michael Eden and South Korean Onggi potter Oh Hyang Jong.

There is no denying that the gaze of the three hundred strong audience was fixed firmly on the eight foot high pot growing steadily from Mr. Oh's wheel head, while Michael Eden's Mac Book pro and whizzing cursor merely attracted the odd look of disdain. And indeed, in terms of spectacle it is hard for pixels on a screen to compete with the skill required to produce Mr. Oh's seemingly gravity defying vessel, but when Michael offered a small, glazed, 3D printed, ceramic torus form for audience inspection it drew a modicum of attention away from Mr. Oh.

In this small torus we had binary data given physical form, the digital matrix of bytes had become the analogue compound of clay and glaze. 3D printing had enabled a digital file to become a physical ceramic form. There were a few members of the audience, myself included, enthralled by this object, as it offered a glimpse of into future possibilities. Back on stage, the attention was again with Mr. Oh but it was evident that that torus had formed a small bridge between past and future.

The reaction of the audience did not surprise me in the least. The festival draws from a demographic, for whom, traditional craft skills are of great importance, and the presence of a Mac Book Pro as a tool on the

Source: © Ingrid Murphy.

'stage of craft' was incongruous at best. Such a reaction to technology is common and shows how the rules Douglas Adam's set out in his book "The Salmon of Doubt" still prevail today:

"I've come up with a set of rules that describe our reactions to technologies:

1. Anything that is in the world when you're born is normal and ordinary and is just a natural part of the way the world works.
2. Anything that's invented between when you're fifteen and thirty-five is new and exciting and revolutionary and you can probably get a career in it.
3. Anything invented after you're thirty-five is against the natural order of things.'[2]

The Craft versus Technology debate is not new. It has been a long-standing legacy of Morris and Ruskin's teachings that technological progress is perceived at odds with the poetic evocation of the craftsman and his hard worn skills and material understanding. Technology and the speed of its progress, be it mechanical or digital, is an ongoing debate for makers and theorists alike. To illustrate the never ceasing pace of progress, here is a quote from French poet and philosopher Paul Valéry from his foreword to Walter Benjamin's book: 'Art in the Age of Mechanical Reproduction'

"Neither matter, nor space, nor time is, what up until twenty years ago, as it always was"[3]

This sentiment has never been more apposite when we consider the technological advances of the last twenty years. Society has shifted from a world inhabited by digital immigrants, those born into a pre digital world, to a world inhabited by digital natives. We are fast approaching what *future technologists* Parag and Ayesha Khanna describe as the 'Hybrid Age'.

"The Hybrid Age is a new sociotechnical era that is unfolding as technologies merge with each other and humans merge with technology- both at the same time".[4]

As the "Hybrid Age" attests, we live in a world of co-evolution rather then co-existence with technology. Now that we live in the era of 'big data', it is predicted that we will move away from a society based on causation, (the why of a thing) to a society on correlation (the what of a thing). The implications of this on how and why we make 'things' is immense.[5]

In 2013 the amount of stored information in the world was estimated to be around 1,200 exabytes, to clarify an exabyte (EB) is one billion gigabytes (GB), or in old money, it's a quintillion bytes. This proliferation of information means that less then 2% of the world's information is non-digital, and this relational proportion will continue to reduce. As a ceramicist, and someone interested in the stuff of matter, it is important for me to understand what role material art plays in this post-material world equally I am interested in how the massive computational tools, now available to all, can augment ceramic practice, not only in how we choose to produce a 'crafted' object but how we conceive and perceive it. This requires more than the simplistic approach of replacing a traditional physical process with that of a digital process. It requires us to look more at the 'meta' of our making, the structure that exists above and beyond the *making* itself. To do this it is key to know how emerging technologies as well as technological constructs will shape our future relationships with objects. Just as throughout history, we cannot ignore the pace and influence of technological progress, Paul Valéry's comments of 1936 are still relevant today:

"In all arts there is a physical component that cannot continue to be considered and treated in the same way as before, no longer can it escape the effects of modern knowledge and modern practice".[6]

In my own attempt to embrace these changes, in 2011 I began a Creative Wales funded project to see how digital technologies can be used in my own ceramic practice. In essence I got 'tooled up'.

To quote technology theorist, Tom Chatfield, from his book "How to Thrive in the Digital Age":

> "All technologies change us as we use them: 'we shape our tools, and thereafter our tools shape us.'"[7]

So as my project developed I became a digital journeyman of sorts, learning new skills from the master and font of all knowledge - 'YouTube'. As my new skills merged with my old knowledge it became apparent to me that to fully understand the 'meta' of my own making, and therefore technology's ability to influence it: I needed to break my creative process down into 5 key categories. These were as follows

1. Concept forming
2. The forming giving process
3. Material use
4. Production/fabrication/making
5. Perception/Interaction

As I embraced each new technology be it 3D printing, scanning or augmented reality, I quickly discovered analogies between technological constructs and my own creative process. One in particular was Gartner's Hype Cycle of Technology.[8] Gartner Inc. is a information technology research company whose 'hype cycle' is a graphic presentation of the maturity, adoption and social application of specific technologies. The hype cycle depicts the life cycle of any specific technology as it starts with an innovation trigger, reaches the peak of inflated expectations, falls into the trough of disillusionment, climbs the slope of enlightenment until it eventually reaches the plateau of productivity, a similar cycle to every creative work I've undertaken.

Analogies between traditional craft and digital practice are not new, in his book 'The Craftsman', sociologist Richard Sennett cites the development of the open source software Linux as an example of collaborative craft. Sennett has a very encompassing view of the craftsman:

> "… the carpenter, lab technician and conductor are all craftsmen because they are dedicated to good work for its own sake".[9]

In this expansive view of craftsmen, Sennett also rails against the historical divisions inherent in creative practice:

> "History has drawn fault lines dividing practice and theory, technique and expression, craftsman and artist, maker and user, modern society suffers from this inheritance."[10]

The historical fault line that divides the craftsman - man as maker, from a computer programmer - the operative, would appear self-evident. For one, there is the idea of the hard won craft skill, gained through focused labour. It is cited that it takes 10,000 hours of practice to gain mastery of a skill, this seems distinctly at odds with the 'push and play' sensibility of digital usage, and its world of hyper-mediacy and instant gratification, as opposed to the sense of labour intrinsic in a crafted object. However in my capacity of teaching across both traditional skills and digital applications it is naive to think that proficient skills in software and its inherent applications are not hard won. Trine Webster who teaches digital form and fabrication at Oslo National Academy cites her similar experience in teaching digital fabrication tools to craft students.

> "I think of digital fabrication both as a craft field and a set of tools that come with their own rules for use. To master the tools requires skills, which take about the same time to learn as it takes to master any other craft"[11]

Webster concludes:

> "I am quite sure we have seen the beginning of the use of digital craft. We now have access to a whole range of new tools that allow for a new set of expressions. I think one implication of this will be a monumental shift in the way we understand creation. This, in turn, means we must rethink *what it means to make*, and to *be a maker today*"[12]

With this in mind it is too narrow to focus the impact of new technology at the point of production alone. As stated earlier the impact of new and emergent technology does not occur by merely replacing a hand tool with a digital one, technology is all pervasive in our lives and thus pervades our very psyche, whether we recognize this or not.

In a recent article featured in the Financial Times Glenn Adamson, craft theorist and former director of New York Museum of Arts and Design, comments on the relationship between digital experience and making.

> "Digital experience and tangible making have a dramatic and ongoing impact on one another when it comes to aesthetics … the characteristic features of digital form stretched distortion, filtered colour and backlighting- migrate into analogue design as if unconsciously. Digital experience fuels the imaginative storehouse of the maker, encouraging rapid-fire connection, leaping from one data point to another"[13]

Even at a basic level the internet has facilitated a social revolution in making. Sociologist and media theorist, David Gauntlett in his book *Making is Connecting*, writes of the innate desire people have to be more than mere consumers, they want to make and shape their environment. People not only need to create but want to share their endeavor with others. Web 2.0 with its emphasis on user generated content, facilitates this on a global scale for makers of all kinds, and as Gauntlett states, this creating and sharing 'increases your feeling of embeddedness and participation in the world'.[14]

So technology in this sense does not necessarily affect how we make something but has influence on how we share, access, communicate and develop our making as well as enhancing our wellbeing.

On another level we have the emergence of the open source philosophy and the creative commons license. Open source technology allows anyone to access what was previously the domain of the specialist or researcher. Open source philosophy enables multitudes of makers to share their knowledge, it is truly democratic and non- hierarchical, a collaborative process, where the hobbyist and professional can work together. This inclusivity is akin to that found within craft practice. With open source initiatives there is the advantage of the accumulative power of the crowd, amassing many thousands of 'man' hours towards the development of a shared knowledge, advancing a technology, its application and its creative potential.

However, there is a drawback, the egalitarian inclusivity within the world of open source does bring with it issues of quality and veracity, a characteristic also frequently criticized in the world of ceramics. Equally I have found there is a risk in making an open source technology or software the bedrock of your practice for they can be quickly surpassed, subsumed or indeed even disappeared overnight. Working with open source technologies has taught me not to rely on what is currently existent but to look towards the trajectory and the broader applications of any given technology. In much the same way as it would be unwise to focus this essay on examples of current technologies, it would be outdated by the time the ink had dried on this paper. We need to ensure that our adoption of technologies speak to our inherent creative values. We need to subvert them to our ends, shape our tools to our needs before the tools shape us.

It is easy to be seduced by the apparent sophistication of new and emergent technologies and become consumed with the how as opposed to the why? In my own experience I stared at the 3D printer sitting on my desk for a year before I found a purposeful and creative use for it. Critic and digital theorist Peter Lunenfeld gives us a cautionary note about technological enchantment and how we can be seduced by the novelty of digital objects; "They attract less for what they mean than for the fact that they are".[15]

There are however many ceramicists using digital technologies innovatively to meaningful ends. As mentioned earlier Michael Eden has embraced digital 3D forming and fabrication processes, for Eden the attraction is "that these technologies allow previously impossible objects to be made".[16]

It is interesting to note that Eden's work is frequently produced using non-ceramic materials, however his work quotes so intelligently from the lexicon of ceramics, that it contributes significantly to its material culture.

A leading exponent in the field of 3D printing in clay is ceramicist Jonathan Keep. Keep's use of coding as opposed to off the shelf software is highly innovative. Keep creates his own processing code, which in turn creates digital form. These forms can then be printed in clay using his homemade extrusion printer. What is of particular interest here is that the forms are iterative, in that the code, i.e. the algorithms used to determine the printers movements are created by Keep himself, as opposed to a 3D digital file being rendered by the printer. These codes, which are inspired by the mathematical codes found in nature, dictate how the form develops. Keep's processing code sets both the parameters and potential of the form, this construct would be impossible by any analogue means of making form.

Keep's work does not have the aesthetic sensibilities of what many would see as a digitally produced artifact, but speaks the language of physicality and formal understanding that Keep has honed for years working with clay.

Alongside makers such as Michael Eden and Geoffrey Mann, Keep moves seamlessly between the screen and the workbench, with physicality and materiality at the heart of his making. For these makers, all technologies, be they digital or physical are considered non-hierarchical and subsumed in their practice, there are no historical fault lines here, the wall between the real and the virtual has become permeable.

This new breed of makers, are the subject of Jonathan Openshaw's forthcoming book "The Post-Digital Artisan". Here in a quote form Opensahw's FT article, 'The Craft Makers ahead of the Digital Curve', Hans Ulrich Obrist, co –director of exhibitions and director of international projects at the Serpentine Gallery London, cites the 'porosity of boundaries' brought about by this integration of the physical and the digital:

> "This celebration of the physical is not a rejection of the digital, it's an integral part of the new digital movement.... It's about renegotiating the resources that we have at hand, rather then trying to add new resources to the situation. There's a kind of porosity of boundaries for many of these artists and designer, moving freely between disciplines as they do between media formats".[17]

In my own practice I have focused on the use of technologies in relation to our perception of a ceramic object. Using QR (Quick Response) codes and AR (Augmented Reality) markers to create embedded and interactive content on handmade ceramic objects. Exploring the concept of a 'hacked' object I use 3D digital scans and 3D prints to both physically and digitally hack historical ceramic artifacts.

Recently I have worked collaboratively with artist Jon Pigott to create interactive works. These works, which are kinetic sound sculptures, use the open-source electronic prototyping platform Arduino to create

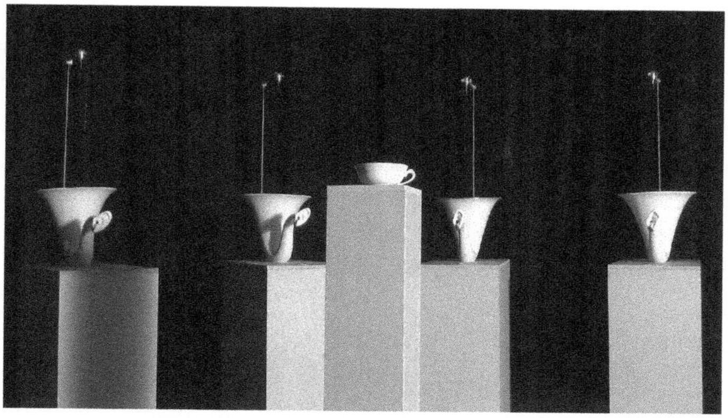

Figure 59.1 The Campanologists Teacup, 2016/Ingrid Murphy and Jon Pigott.

interactive objects. We use sensors and actuators (not to mention a few rubber balls) to explore the aurality of ceramic objects. This combination of clay and electro mechanics makes for interesting bedfellows. In our *bricolage* of hi tech and low craft, we have found a much greater communality in our working methods and processing then we ever envisaged at the outset. For an example of this work view "The Campanologist's Tea Cup" https://vimeo.com/123617368 (Figure 59.1).

Using new technologies has enabled me to animate an inanimate object; when perceiving my work the viewer frequently engages with physical objects and digital content simultaneously. It is the ability to give static objects a voice that is of particular interest, those objects can become palimpsests of their own making. Similarly an object's provenance can be recorded and revealed and in some way may determine its future. This is what I see as one of many trajectories for objects, if we change how we experience them, it will also change how we conceive and produce them.

The science fiction writer Bruce Sterling writes eloquently on the future of objects in his book "Shaping Things", here he discusses the theoretical construct of a Spime. The Spime, as Sterling describes is a futuristic object, which can be tracked throughout its lifetime. It uses six key technologies, including GPS and Radio Frequency ID Tags, these technologies could make it feasible to track the entire existence of an object, from it raw material, through its manufacture, to how it is used/viewed, its ownership, its geographical location, even how it might be recycled into new objects. If the data is recorded, the lifetime of the object can be archived, and searched for, this would not only change how we might approach making an object but how we understand objects in the future. The word spime is a neologism of 'space' and 'time'.

> "Spimes are the intersection of two vectors of technosocial development. They have the capacity to change the human relationship to time and material process, by making those processes blatant and archiveable. Every Spime is a little metahistory generator."[18]

In reality this is not the stuff of fiction, with the advances in I.O.T. (Internet of Things) technology the concept of 'object to object' communication becomes a very real and tangible entity. The Internet of Things proposes that everyday objects have networked connectivity and therefore can send or receive or accumulate data. Interesting to note that in Gartner's Hype Cycle of Technology 2014, Internet of Things technology sat atop the peak of inflated expectations. So in one of my attempts to shape my own tools and use massive computational advances to my own creative ends I designed and made an Internet of Things tea cosy. This tea cosy was made for my elderly technophobe father who lives on his own in Ireland, I was intrigued to see if 'object to object' communication could let me know (un-intrusively) if he was engaged in his daily routine. As a ceramicist the obvious object of choice for routine use was a teapot … so using a IOT device with a heat sensor called a Twine, my twitter account, an IFTT (If This Then That) recipe and a WeMo switch, I 'connected' my father's teapot in Ireland to my own 1950's teasmade in Wales. So when my father uses his tea-cosy to keep his morning brew warm my teas-made lights up and simultaneously pours me a cup of tea … and then safe in the knowledge he's about to sit down with his tea, I can phone him for a quick chat on his landline, which is still his preferred mode of communication.

Writer William Gibson captures the irony of this act in his well known phrase:

> "The future is already here just unevenly distributed".[19]

Which brings me once again to the demonstrator stage at the International Ceramics Festival by now it is 2015 and this time the demonstrators are Jonathan Keep and British potter Lisa Hammond. My view from the stage clearly shows that the audiences attention is now equally divided between Lisa's wheel and Jonathan's 3D printer, they seem to enjoy the fact that Jonathan struggles with the vagaries of clay consistency in the differential atmosphere of the stage, taking comfort in his need for material knowledge with this digital tool. While they are thrilled by the technology they are reassured to see dirty hands!

To end the demonstration Jonathan activates his laptop microphone and captures the ambient sounds of the theatre, this data instantly creates an undulating vessel form on his laptop screen, responding in real time to the noise we generate. Here Jonathan is using the time and space we are in to create the form itself, perhaps a potential forebear of the Spime. On the other side of the stage Lisa is using a freshly sharpened handmade tool to confidently facet her thrown tea bowl, with these sure movements she creates a timeless and beautiful object. As I stand between these two great makers, both making a faceted ceramic vessel, I feel the thrill of oscillating in the present, and it's an exciting place to be.

Notes

1. Vermeulen, Timotheus; Van den Akker, Robin. From webzine "Notes on Metamodernism" October 14 2010. Available online: http://www.metamodernism.com/2010/10/14/what-meta-means-and-does-not-mean/
2. Adams, Douglas. "The Salmon of Doubt'." (Random House 2002) pp. 111.
3. Valery, Paul from foreword to Benjamin Walter, 'The Work of Art in the Age of Mechanical Reproduction' (1936 London) pp. 1.
4. Khanna Ayesha & Parag, 'Hybrid Reality. Thriving in the Emerging Human-Technology Civilization' (2012 TED Books) pp. 2.
5. Cukier Kenneth & Mayer-Schonberger Viktor 'Big Data. A Revolution That Will Transform How We Live, Work and Think.' (John Murray Publishers London, 2013) pp. 13–14.
6. Valéry, Paul., ibid. pp. 2.
7. Chatfield Tom, 'How to Thrive in the Digital Age', The School of Life (2012) pp. 10.
8. From Gartner Inc. http://www.gartner.com/technology/research/methodologies/hype-cycle.jsp
9. Sennett Richard, 'The Craftsman', (London, 2008), pp. 20.
10. Ibid., pp. 10.
11. Webster, Trine. "Digital Craft- How Do We Create With Digital Technology?' from "Materiality Matters" Eds Borda-Pedreira, Joakim & Steinsvåg (Norwegian Crafts 2014) pp. 47
12. Ibid., pp. 50

13. Adamson, Glenn in article by Openshaw, Jonathan, "The Craftmakers Ahead of the Digital Curve". Financial Times. June 16th 2015.

Article available here : http://www.ft.com/intl/cms/s/0/87e1a626-15a5-11e5-be54-00144feabdc0.html#slide10

14. Gauntlett, David. "Making is Connecting" (Polity Press Cambridge, 2011) pp. 56.

15. Lunenfeld, Peter "Snap to Grid. A User's Guide to Digital Arts, Media and Cultures." (M.I.T. 2001). pp. 173.

16. Eden, Michael. "The New Ways- Digital craft Skills and the New Industrial Revolution" from "Materiality Matters" Eds Borda-Pedreira, Joakim & Steinsvåg (Norwegian Crafts 2014) pp. 47.

17. Obrist, Hans-Ulrich in article by Openshaw, Jonathan, "The Craftmakers Ahead of the Digital Curve". Financial Times. June 16th 2015 http://www.ft.com/intl/cms/s/0/87e1a626-15a5-11e5-be54-00144feabdc0.html#slide10

18. Sterling, Bruce "Shaping Things" Editorial Director: Peter Lunenfeld (MIT Press 2005) pp. 43.

19. Gibson, William in an interview for "The Science in Science Fiction" on 'Talk of the Nation', NPR (30 November 1999).

Printed with permission of the author.

SECTION 3.7
MUSEUM, SITE AND DISPLAY

Introductory summary

Ceramics have long had connections with the home and domestic spaces. Therefore, it seems apt that makers have utilized domestic like spaces, in the form of museums that were once homes, for the display of their works. Laura Gray argues that the presentation of ceramic artworks in such museums makes the context a part of the artwork or an additional medium for the artist. In this text, she discusses ceramics installations by Clare Twomey, Edmund de Waal and Anders Ruhwald – artists who work in what Gray calls the 'vessel/installation/sculpture continuum'. Readers might find this idea interesting to consider in relation to Glen R. Brown's, 'Multiplicity, Ambivalence and Ceramic Installation Art', Emma Shaw's 'Ceramics and Installation' and Ruth Chambers' 'Ceramic Installation: Towards a Self-Definition'.

In contrast to Gray's focus on museums that were once homes, Erza Shales poses useful questions about the uses of museums as sites for 'medium-specific' artists who have in recent years been 'mining the museum' for inspiration or as a contextual site to show their work. Artists discussed include Edmund de Waal, Clare Twomey, Neil Brownsword, Charles LeDray and Ai Weiwei.

Artist Brad Evan Taylor's broad ranging text links the transformational aspects of clay to alchemy, science and painting. He goes on to argue for the power of materials, place and time in site-specific immersive artworks.

Mike Tooby gives a commentary on an installation by Simon Fujiwara at Tate St Ives. The installation and wider exhibition offers an example of how an artist has used personal background and biography in combination with aspects of locality and history – including aspects of a museum's history and conceptualization (in this case Tate St Ives).

'Why Clay?' is an interview between artist and curator Emily Hesse and curator and researcher James Beighton. This wide-ranging text covers ceramists working in museums, curatorial approaches, the art/craft debate, ceramics education as well as aspects of Beighton's approach as a curator.

In 'Civic Ceramics: Shifting the centre of meaning' Natasha Mayo and Melania Warwick offer some perspectives on 'participatory art', a term that refers to art works and art projects made through social engagement. This text offers two case studies on the work of Keith Harrison and AJ Stockwell. Following on from this, Chris McHugh, an artist and researcher with a background in archaeology, describes aspects of his project where he researched how an artist might use a museum collection as a basis to engage with communities. In his case, he was 'embedded' in Sunderland Museum and Winter Gardens, UK, and developed a range of projects based on nineteenth-century Sunderland Lustre Ware Pottery. In this text, he focuses on his work with local soldiers who had served in Afghanistan. McHugh reviews two of his artworks and provides a detailed context around the meaning of objects in museums, memorials and other artists' approaches.

In 'Redefining ceramics through exhibitionary practice', Laura Breen traces the developments in ceramic art in the UK over nearly forty years. She does this by reviewing contemporary commentary from the time in exhibition catalogues and reviews. This text very usefully draws together many of the issues and themes (at least in a UK context), which permeate this Reader – in particular the position of ceramics in relation to the wider art world.

Livingstone and Petrie

60
MUSEUMS AND THE 'INTERSTICES OF DOMESTIC LIFE': RE-ARTICULATING DOMESTIC SPACE IN CONTEMPORARY CERAMICS PRACTICE

Laura Gray

Those museums that have formerly been private houses, albeit houses that are somewhat out of the ordinary, and whose interiors have been preserved, are a particularly interesting type of museum. They provide a unique art historical frame for the objects displayed within. The distinctive hybrid domestic-museum environment offered by former homes such as Kettle's Yard in Cambridge, High Cross House in Devon, Blackwell Arts and Craft House in the Lake District, has become of interest to certain artists working in the medium of clay. For some, the museum is also the medium,[1] with the result that the engagement between ceramics and curatorial practice concerned with ideas centring on the domestic has become an important theme in contemporary ceramics. This article investigates how Edmund de Waal, Clare Twomey and Anders Ruhwald have used multiples, installation, and site sensitivity to address the relationship between contemporary ceramics practice and domestic space, or the idea of domestic space, as a frame for, and a participating element in, their work.

Ceramics and domestic space

There are two main strands to the history of displaying ceramics in domestic space prior to the twentieth century: the porcelain rooms of palaces and stately homes; and the more familiar type of domestic space in which most people encounter ceramics – the kitchen dresser, the mantelpiece, ornaments clustered on tables and shelves. Drawing attention to the princely palace or stately home as a site for the display of ceramics serves only to remind us that historically, there have been instances where high status examples of such work, porcelain particularly, have been exhibited in high status domestic space, an environment also considered eminently suitable for the display of paintings and sculpture. Such palaces, of course, served a public, even a state function, as well as containing more private domestic space. In the modern and post-modern periods, the home has been both an important and an undervalued location for encountering art, particularly ceramics. Important because domestic space is the traditional site for encountering ceramics, and undervalued because of an understanding of domestic space as a female sphere, functional associations, the financial value of objects, and the small scale required for display in the home.[2] Nonetheless, certain artists working with clay have chosen to reengage their practice with the domestic – either in terms of the exhibiting site or through engagement with ideas. This article endeavours to understand how and why artists working with clay have sought to return their work to a domestic context or create an association with a type of location that through the modern period was constructed as the antithesis of serious art.

Source: © Laura Gray.

The exhibition *A Secret History of Clay: From Gauguin to Gormley* (Tate Liverpool, 2004) touched on ideas relating to ceramics and the domestic. Amy Dickson, who worked on the exhibition as assistant curator explained in an interview conducted in 2010 how ideas around the domestic were explored in the exhibition:

> traditionally the ceramic vessel is an object that is of the private sphere of everyday domestic life and this show was showing it as a public practice, so I think it was also about this clash between public and private spheres. And the last room was very much about taking it back to a sense of the private and a consideration of how the practice fits with that.[3]

The final room of the exhibition, which showed a Cindy Sherman tea set, ceramics by Jeff Koons, ceramic brooms by Richard Slee, and a version of Edmund de Waal's *Porcelain Wall*, presented ceramic practices that had reengaged with the domestic environment, but prioritized the concept of the domestic over the physical location of the home. The restitution of the domestic as an element in a strand of contemporary ceramics can be seen to indicate a practice that has developed beyond the straightforwardly functional, even when works reference the domestic and take the form of theoretically utilitarian objects such as de Waal's vessels or Sherman's tea set. Though these works might reference domestic objects or the home, they behave squarely as art objects, rather than things to be used.

Tanya Harrod suggests that ceramics have, as participants in the fluctuating relationship between art, craft and the home, 'over the centuries, carried all kinds of high and low art references into the domestic space'.[4] Colin Painter writes in the catalogue for his exhibition *At Home With Art* (Tate Britain, 1999), that 'distinctions between the functional and non-functional are often blurred. It is in this combination of roles and meanings that art can become part of life'.[5] This article sets out to demonstrate that the work of Edmund de Waal, Clare Twomey and Anders Ruhwald takes advantage of this blurring and combining of roles to test and experiment with the expected role of ceramics in relation to the domestic.

The separation of art and the home

From the early twentieth century, in the wake of the Arts and Crafts movement, domestic space was repositioned 'as the antipode to high art'.[6] Christopher Reed quotes Russian artist Alexandr Rodchenko as saying, 'the art of the future will not be the cosy decoration of family homes'.[7] Reed goes on to suggest Dada and Surrealist artists too, with their fascination with the uncanny habitually 'appropriated the accoutrements of domesticity in ways that undermined connotations of homey comfort, while the theoreticians of these movements sustained the anti-domestic rhetoric of earlier modernists'.[8] So where does the powerful modernist rejection of the domestic, and objects with domestic connotations, leave ceramics, particularly vessels, whose suggestion of function makes the home a natural place to encounter them? If serious art has been banished from the home, what does this mean for the status and perception of ceramics that continue to use vessel forms and so persist in their domestic associations? Even the human scale of most vessel-based ceramics is sufficient to align them with the domestic. Mark Rothko, echoing Rodchenko, announced in the *New York Times* that his art 'must insult anyone who is spiritually attuned to interior decoration; pictures for the home; pictures for over the mantel'.[9]

In answer to the call from some artists, including Rodchenko and Rothko, for art not be brought into contact with the everyday (often the scale of works inhibited display in homes), and as part of the desire to find a new kind of space for encountering art, the stark modernism of the 'white cube' gallery emerged in the 1920s and 1930s. In America, 1929 saw the establishment of the Museum of Modern Art in New York. MoMA's founding director, Alfred Barr, did not select the paintings for the museums inaugural exhibition, but he did install them. Barr covered the walls with a natural coloured cloth and eliminated the salon style of hanging paintings. This type of installation looks rather unexceptional now, as this manner of presenting paintings has become so conventional that its significance is completely invisible. But the exhibition contributed to the introduction of a particular type of installation that came to dominate museum practices, whereby the language of display articulates a modernist, seemingly autonomous aestheticism.[10] MoMA's 1934 exhibition *Machine Art* is an example of the simple, spare, pared-down aesthetic which became, and remains, the standard environment in which to view art. This type of presentation of art was a part of the new methodology of display. The development of 'white cube' spaces for the display of art facilitated a severance of art from the domestic elements that had previously been found in exhibition spaces (such as seating, or the 'country house' approach to the display of artworks which incorporated richly coloured walls and dense hangs of paintings). Yet, despite the stark, white spaces of the modern art gallery having become synonymous with the display of art that has 'intellectual significance', artists working with clay have, over the last decade, returned to the domestic environment. Ceramics, after attempts in some quarters to distance the medium from its domestic associations, returned to the home. Artists such as Clare Twomey and Edmund de Waal, with an artistic practice that engages with installation, and the site-sensitive or site-specific, have, on a number of occasions, chosen house museums as a site for their work. In such instances, the house museum not only offers a frame for the work, but becomes part of the work itself. Though in England the concept of the public visiting great houses to see their art collections while the owners were away isn't new, what has changed is the way that artists are actively using the space in which their work is located. The work does not sit passively, but has an active relationship with the environment that it inhabits.

Contemporary ceramics and a reengagement with domestic space

The distinction between the 'thing' and the 'object' is the pivot on which an understanding of the role that contemporary ceramics can play in a domestic setting turns. Louise Mazanti writes of the difference between thing and object, arguing that:

> objects perform a role as aesthetically and formally privileged artefacts independent of time and situation … The thing, on the other hand, belongs to the mundane world of function, actions, drifting meanings, attachments and situations.[11]

She continues, considering object and thing in relation to perception and interpretation,

> in the first case the object controls the situation, in the second, we determine the use and destiny of the thing. The identity of the object is much more insecure than the identity of the thing.[12]

In this instance, Mazanti is shaping her ideas in relation to the work of Anders Ruhwald, for whose exhibition catalogue her essay was written. The key difference that Mazanti identifies between object and thing is the source of meaning and whether that comes from within or without.

> The meaning of the thing is defined by context, situation and subjects. The object rejects this fixation. It allows possible meanings, but keeps an enigmatic layer to itself. In short; the thing is a 'thing'; something we know – the object is a stranger; a piece of art.[13]

The work of both Edmund de Waal and Anders Ruhwald explores the difference between thing and object, and in doing so, disrupts expectation, including the expectation of the conceptual boundaries of artist practice that uses ceramics as a source of meaning and material. The use of domestic imagery, association or location further destabilises the expectations that surround ceramics, particularly vessels. As the work of de Waal demonstrates, the vessel has returned to the domestic environment, but it is a changed vessel, and it is occupying the space on its own terms. There has been a transition from thing to object that allows pots to sit in domestic space but speak the language of sculpture, rather than the language of craft and utility. In the case of de Waal, domestic space has become the site for a more sculptural ceramics practice, a practice that undermines distinctions between sculpture and functional objects.

In the aftermath of the modernist insistence of the separation of the home and the display of art, de Waal has successfully reasserted the domestic environment as a legitimate site of encounter with his artistic practice. This repositioning can be seen as having two stages: firstly, encouraging a rethinking of work in clay as part of the mainstream of visual art, and secondly, returning to the domestic environment with this work, not with, for example, what Reed refers to as the ironic detachment of the Pop artists (Roy Lichenstein's ceramic dinnerware), but with a careful consideration of the space, light and history of the setting, and the movement of the viewer around that space. Edmund de Waal and Clare Twomey have thoughtfully and effectively used the public-private space of house museums for their installations. The installation-like nature of their work uses to advantage what Gill Perry identifies as the fluid nature of the viewer's experience when encountering installation art, in contrast to 'the clearly defined object in the white cube'.[14] In a domestic space, even one that has become a museum, more layers of meaning are possible. Encountering their work in such setting is not simply about attractive placement. For de Waal and Twomey, the museum becomes part of the medium. Largely as a consequence of de Waal's success in working in this way, the engagement between ceramics and curatorial practice that occurs in the practice of those artists that use the house museum has become an important strand of practice in contemporary ceramics, particularly for those artists who work in the vessel/installation/sculpture continuum.

Twomey is less focused on the vessel form than de Waal, though one of her most powerful works to date, *Monument* (mima, Middlesborough Institute of ModernArt, 2009), was made up of a towering heap of domestic ware, which demonstrated not only the powerful effect of massed objects, but the sense of disquiet that seeing broken plates and cups could cause. *Monument* was testament to the continued relevance of the vessel in a greatly expanded ceramics practice. Twomey has also created a number of works specifically for house museums. In 2009 she was commissioned to create a work to form part of an exhibition that celebrated the tercentenary of the birth of English lexicographer Dr Samuel Johnson. Twomey's work *Scribe* was displayed as part of the exhibition *House of Words* at Dr Johnson's House. Beneath a layer of pale blue dust there lies books, paper, quills as if the users of these writing materials have abandoned them at a time of great activity, and have simply never returned. This installation that Twomey created in the garret room of the house pays homage to the six assistants who supported Johnson in his work on his Dictionary of the English Language. The thick layer of blue dust that covers the books, feather quills and stacked papers was created from Wedgwood blue Jasper clay.

Twomey has used blue Jasper clay in her work before, as dust and to make objects. This particular type of clay opens up the work to numerous possible associated meanings. There are shared associations between Wedgwood and Johnson, two great figures of eighteenth century England, who both came from the Midlands. The poignancy of abandoned writing materials left, Miss Havisham-like, to accumulate dust. And the dust itself, creating an association with a struggling ceramics industry, mothballed factories and lost skills. Twomey's dialogue with the house does not acknowledge the space as a domestic environment, though it was, for a period, both home and workplace for Johnson when compiling his Dictionary. Where de Waal would have perhaps pursued an engagement with architecture and space, Twomey engages with the memories contained within the building. A connection with the ephemeral made with an ephemeral material. Though she does not ignore the history of the building, Twomey's work uses the house museum and its history as a starting point for the exploration of more universal strands of thought, such as memory and the passing of time. Her use of dust, butterflies, flowers and birds as motifs in her work evidence these themes, which display a Keatsean preoccupation with transience and permanence. A recent installation by Twomey, *A Dark Day in Paradise*, which is made up of thousands of ceramic butterflies, was created for the Royal Pavilion in Brighton in 2010. Twomey's three thousand black-glazed ceramic butterflies swarmed, hovered and rested in the decadent interior of the dining room of this exotic royal pleasure palace, built in stages for the Prince Regent, later King George IV, between 1787 and 1823.

Not wholly gorgeous to encounter, the glistening black butterflies are transformed into something more unsettling as they crawl over the fruit on the dining table. Twomey has described her concept for this piece as being that a swarm of unsavoury but very beautiful butterflies have landed in the pavilion and they're judging it in some way. Twomey also explained the cloud of butterflies as a romantic image, which have become part of the inescapable, and at time overwhelming, romance of the building.[15] Her idea was to try to embed them, to give the impression that they've always been there and unsettle the visitors who are unsure whether the butterflies are part of the historic interior: an enterprise that could only have taken place in a building with as extravagant an interior as this one. Twomey described the pavilion as a very difficult environment to make for because the interior of the building is so overwhelming; making competing with the decoration for the visitor's attention almost impossible. Nevertheless, the building, with its particular history and associations, allowed her work to have a dialogue in a very particular language that only exists there, in that building. And it is that particular dialogue, the collaborative element, different in every one of the house museums that makes such places rich collaborative partners for contemporary ceramics practice.

Edmund de Waal: Interventions in domestic space

Edmund de Waal's invitation to exhibit his work at High Cross House in 1999, led to an architectural intervention, or installation, of a kind that was new for ceramic practice. High Cross House in Devon, completed in 1932, is a modernist house that was built for William Curry, the first headmaster of Dartington Hall School. At the time of de Waal's project it was open as a visitor attraction, but now is available to rent as a modernist holiday home. The opportunity to engage with the Le Corbusier inspired environment of High Cross House, complete with Bauhaus furniture, allowed de Waal to extend ideas that were already present in his 'cargo' works – groupings, repetition, concealment and revelation.

De Waal began to make work that he called cargoes in order to question the assumption that it was not possible to be a serious contemporary artist and make pots.[16] He called these groups of pots cargoes to emphasize the fact that they were groups, they were multiples - not just the single pot - but also that they were in transit in some kind of way between different cultures – between East and West, but also between art and craft, between sculpture and ceramics. Part of his experimentation with the cargo works was to start putting them in interesting and diverse places, trying to work out why groups of vessels, groups of pots had particular kinds of energy or resonance when they were in particular places. De Waal has said that he was really just trying to experiment with the life of pots, and this idea took hold so that his practice became about making things for places:

> It wasn't just about plonking them on tables, it was more about the discovery of them in those places, so I put them in cupboards or on the ground or high up so you could only just get a sense of them. I was really just trying to experiment with the life of pots, and that's really taken me over. I now feel that that is my practice: I make things for places.[17]

The installation at High Cross House was the beginning of this manner of working, which has become so central to de Waal's artistic practice.

Instead of using High Cross House as an attractive modernist backdrop for his work, De Waal became interested in using the house as a whole, less as an unusual exhibition space, but as a collaborative element with the porcelain. It is this collaboration between domestic space and the vessels that draws out the sculptural qualities, the ability to make references beyond form and material. In the kitchen, an open cupboard reveals a line of porcelain vessels. A single tall, lidded jar sits on the fireplace in the living room.

Pots are where you would expect to find them in a house. But they have the cool stillness of marble sculptures. The possibility of function is simultaneously suggested and denied. With the careful placing of vessels de Waal invites the kitchen cupboard to become a showcase and the fireplace to become a plinth. Michael Tooby writes of these pots in the exhibition catalogue, saying that:

> their 'site specificity' is their domesticity within the furnished modernist house, de Waal exploiting the irony that, in becoming a public gallery, the commission to make site specific pieces enables him to relocate his 'craft' in the realms of both 'art' and 'architecture'.[18]

These are pots, with the suggestions of utility and function that we could expect to find with pots, and though they are being encountered in what was once a home, they assert themselves as works of art through their placement, through their dialogue with the calm modernism of the architecture of the house.

In 1999, around the time of the project at High Cross, de Waal was interviewed for an article in the journal *Ceramics Art and Perception*. He is quoted as saying, 'the whole lazy approach to how ceramics are used, displayed and revealed within our cultural spaces is an important issue that has to be addressed'.[19] With the project at High Cross House, de Waal was taking up this concern directly, and display and revelation still persist as strands of thought in his most recent works that make use of closed doors and opaque glass. At High Cross house, a domestic space transformed into a museum (and back again), ideas of privacy and display, private and public, could be tested through the placement of pots. De Waal, writing about his intervention at the house describes how, 'thinking through where to make pots for in the house made me think about the key places and interstices of domestic life and how these areas change when a house becomes a museum'.[20] De Waal's installation also challenges the modernist separation of home and art, which persists in the idea of the white cube as the ideal space in which to show art, and the modernist desire to see distinction between categories of art.

De Waal continued his concern with the aesthetic of display eight years later with an exhibition held across two galleries. Beginning at Kettle's Yard, the exhibition then moved to mima, where the same works adapted to the very different spaces of the then newly opened gallery. De Waal's relationship with Kettle's Yard was already established and long standing at the time the installation took place, having spent time at the house during his time as a student at Cambridge, 'even when I was reading English I was making pots, and spending time in Kettle's Yard looking at pots and looking at paintings, and the two things really went hand in hand'.[21] The home of Jim and Helen Ede from 1958-1973, Kettle's Yard is another example of a space that has been by turns domestic and public. The house was conceived with the students of Cambridge in mind, and the Ede's open house policy meant that students were able to come to the house and view the collection Jim Ede had created during his time as a curator at Tate during the 1920s and 1930s. In 1966 the house and contents were given to Cambridge University and its role as a gallery was formalised, though the character the Edes brought to the house was retained.[22]

Mima took some of the pieces that were made very specifically for the house at Kettle's Yard such as *A Reading Silence* which was a group of pots placed in a bookcase. What de Waal had done was to remove his favourite books, books that he would read when he was a student at Cambridge and used to visit Kettle's Yard. The books he removed he replaced with his pots. James Beighton discussed the challenges of curating a work made specifically for another space:

> When it came to mima all you had was a gesture of the bookcase, which was just corner shelves, and the vessels that represented the books that were taken out. But there was nothing to represent that books that were left there so in a way it was kind of flipped on its head. The ones that were missing now were the books that were present at Kettle's Yard.[23]

For Beighton, modernism was a central aspect of the relationship between the two spaces. Kettle's Yard:

> manifests modernism, and domesticity in early modernism. And mima perhaps manifests where modernism went, which is the white cube spaces. But it was fundamentally about thinking what are two very different spaces and how can we trace the poetry of that dialogue between the object and space, across those two different spaces.[24]

Anders Ruhwald: Bringing the domestic into the white cube

Ceramics has been moving out of craft galleries into white cube spaces for at least three decades (*Fast Forward* at the ICA in 1985, *The Raw and the Cooked* at Modern Art Oxford in 1993, the inclusion of ceramics at Tate St Ives as reported in 'Ceramics at the Tate', *Ceramic Review* no. 144, 1993). The presence of ceramics in white cube spaces, which are more usually designated for the display of 'fine' art, was part of the repositioning of ceramics as a medium with sculptural potential that *The Raw and the Cooked* aimed for. Anders Ruhwald, while choosing to show his work in conventional contemporary art white cube environments (Lemberg Gallery, Detroit; Gregory Lind Gallery, San Fransisco; Drud & Køppe Gallery, Copenhagen) elects to disrupt the crisp, serious aesthetic by introducing domestic touches such as ribbon curtains, carpets, and visible plug sockets into these spaces. Ruhwald considers that, 'the implication of a domestic setting thus activates a situation that potentially opens up a reading of the work where we engage with the objects at a one-to-one level'.[25] Finding the relationship between audience and sculpture limiting, Ruhwald prefers instead to encourage interaction on a material and practical level, which he does through reference to familiar, functional objects.

Ruhwald writes of his frustration with the earlier conventional display of his work in the exhibition *Keramiske Veje* (Copenhagen, 2004), 'the objects existed in the gallery space as traditional sculptural objects... People could observe them, but there would be no interaction at the material or practical level'.[26] Ruhwald echoes de Waal's frustrations with the limitations of display. Perhaps of particular interest is Ruhwald's belief that the sculptural form and presentation of his work closed down rather than expanded dialogue with the viewer. Raised up on a continuous high plinth, and mounted on the wall, the objects in this exhibition are held apart from the viewer by the manner of their presentation. In contrast, the references to the domestic, both by setting, arrangement and the objects themselves that Ruhwald makes in his later exhibitions such as *You Will See* (Lemberg Gallery, Detroit, USA, 2010-11) and *We float in space and cannot perceive the new order* (Miyako Yoshinaga Art Prospects, New York, USA, 2007) place the viewer and the object in the same space, sharing the same ground.

Ruhwald explains his relationship with the domestic in an article in issue nine of *Interpreting Ceramics*, 'I am interested in working with the 'thingness' of the ceramic object. My sculptures mediate the domestic sphere-not *as* the actual everyday item, but as a commentary *on* that item'.[27] Ruhwald explores the complex relationship between material and form that is at the heart of testing whether vessels can be understood as sculpture, or as having a meaningful relationship with sculpture.

Ruhwald came to the field by making pottery, developing an understanding of 'the potential of using functional forms to mediate concerns that lie outside the confines of pure utility'.[28] For Ruhwald the term *kunsthåndværk* (literally art-craft) is defined by a studio practice that generates carefully laboured objects formally linked to objects of utility but rarely fulfilling that role practically.

In 2008 Ruhwald's solo exhibition *You In Between* opened at Middlesbrough Institute of Modern Art. Ruhwald's approach to mima's white cube spaces was not to revel in the status that such a setting could confer on his work, but instead to undermine this effect. This involved deliberately making gestures of domesticity, with the work itself and in the gallery, to offset the white spaces. *Candle Light* is made up of a simple shelf that has from one end a light bulb hanging down and at the other end a candle sitting on top. The candle is lit and over the course of the exhibition, over the course of each day, it burns down to nothing and another candle is put on and is lit at the beginning of the next day. Over the course of the exhibition wax falls down over the edge of the shelf and a pile of wax builds up on the floor. Curator James Beighton referred to this piece as 'anti-modernist', saying:

> it is very squarely against our gallery spaces but that's something that Anders was interested in, he was interested in the role of decoration, of domesticity in a modernist gallery space. And there were even gestures such as plug sockets … Anders wanted us to fix plug sockets onto the walls, domestic plug sockets, and they weren't to be set into the walls, they were to be on boxes coming out of the walls.[29]

Beighton found the unconcealed plug sockets and cables trailing drawing-like down the wall, as simultaneously 'decorative and uncomfortable' in the gallery space. Decorative because the gallery had hidden plug sockets and cables that could have been used to power *Candle/Light*. The ugly, awkward plug sockets were unnecessary ornamentation, wanted only for the look that they could bring to the space, and the atmosphere they could confer on the pristine gallery.

Beighton considered that, 'the work was trying its hardest to upset the space'. With the use of gold foil Ruhwald 'was interested in referencing the Wiener Werkstätte particularly, so the repetition of that grid structure looks back to Josef Hoffmann's designs. But the use of gold also talks about Klimt and his use of gold leaf on his canvases'.[30] Ruhwald also used ribbon curtains to divide spaces, 'the back gallery was carpeted with ribbon curtains dividing it in two. So Anders is recognising there that they are anything but neutral spaces and I think most of our artists have recognised that they are anything but neutral spaces'.[31]

Conclusion

Christopher Reed has demonstrated that for the European modernists, 'being undomestic came to serve as a guarantee of being art'.[32] As a result the domestic became a site of subversion, 'a staging ground for rebellion'.[33] If modernism suppressed a serious engagement with domesticity, some artists returned with a vengeance to the domestic as a field of enquiry during the shifts in art and design signified by the term 'post-modernism'.[34] This view is supported by the engagement of artists such as Louise Bourgeois and Mona Hatoum with ideas surrounding the home and domesticity, which they have unsettled and destabilised in their work.[35]While Ruhwald, Twomey and de Waal have not been attempting a destabilization of the idea of the home, they have been conducting their own quiet rebellion. The rebellion that they have staged in the house museum and in the exploration of ceramics in relation to the concept of 'the domestic' has been to continue to push the notion of clay as a transgressive material, a valid material for art, as well as craft.

Notes

1. See J. Putnam, *Art and Artifact: The Museum as Medium*, London, Thames and Hudson, 2009 (revised edition) and also E. de Waal, S. Kuhn, J Putnam, *et al*, *Arcanum: Mapping 18th Century European Porcelain*, Cardiff, National Museum Wales, 2005.
2. M. Vincentelli, *Women and Ceramics: Gendered Vessels*, Manchester, Manchester University Press, 2000, p. 128.
3. Author's interview with Amy Dickson, assistant curator, Tate Modern, 2010.
4. T. Harrod, 'House Trained Objects: Notes Toward Writing an Alternative History of Modern Art', in C. Painter, editor, *Contemporary Art and the Home*, Oxford, Berg, 2002, p. 70.
5. Colin Painter, *At Home With Art*, London, Hayward Gallery, 1999, p. 5.
6. Christopher Reed, 'Introduction', in C. Reed, editor, *Not at Home': The Suppression of Domesticity in Modern Art and Architecture*, London, Thames and Hudson, 1996, p. 7.
7. Quote taken from Solomon-Godeau, cited in C. Reed, 'Domestic Disturbances: Challenging the Anti-domestic Modern', in C. Painter, editor, *Contemporary Art and the Home*, Oxford, Berg, 2002, p. 39.
8. Reed, 'Domestic Disturbances', p. 39.
9. Cited in Reed, 'Domestic Disturbances', p. 41.
10. M. Staniszewski, *The Power of Display: A History of Exhibition Installations at the Museum of Modern Art*, Massachusetts, MIT Press, 2001, p. 61.
11. L. Mazanti, 'Life among objects and life among things', in J. Beighton and A. Ruhwald, editors, *Anders Ruhwald - You In Between*, Middlesbrough, Middlesbrough Institute of Modern Art, 2008, p. 57.
12. Mazanti, 'Life among objects and life among things', p. 57.
13. Ibid.
14. Gill Perry, 'Dream Houses: installations and the home', in G. Perry and P. Wood, editors, *Themes in Contemporary Art*, New Haven, Yale, 2004, pp. 231–276.
15. Author's interview with Clare Twomey, 2010.
16. Edmund de Waal, 'Edmund de Waal Part 1: On Location', transcript of an interview conducted for the V&A, available at http://www.vam.ac.uk/channel/people/ceramics/edmund_dewaal_part_1_-_on_location/ (accessed 15.02.2011).
17. de Waal, 'Edmund de Waal Part 1: On Location', accessed 15.02.2011).
18. Michael Tooby, 'Edmund de Waal's Work in Progress', in E. de Waal, E., and M. Tooby, *Modern Home: An intervention by Edmund de Waal at High Cross House*, Totnes, Dartington Hall Trust, 1999, p. 20.
19. As cited in Jeffrey Jones, *Studio Pottery in Britain 1900-2005*, London, A & C Black, 2007, p. 234.
20. Edmund de Waal, 'Making Some Pots for High Cross House' in *Modern Home: An intervention by Edmund de Waal at High Cross House*, Totnes, Dartington Hall Trust, 1999, p. 7.
21. Edmund de Waal interviewed by John Tusa for BBC Radio 3 http://www.bbc.co.uk/radio3/johntusainterview/dewaal_transcript.shtml (accessed 15.02.2011).
22. http://www.kettlesyard.co.uk/house/index.html (accessed 17.06.2011)
23. Author's interview with James Beighton, curator at mima, 2010.
24. Ibid.
25. Anders Ruhwald, 'Functional Languages', *Interpreting Ceramics*, no.9, http://www.uwic.ac.uk/icrc/issue009/articles/04.htm (accessed 14.02.2011), unpaginated.

26. Ibid.
27. Ibid.
28. Ibid.
29. Interview with James Beighton, 2010.
30. Ibid.
31. Ibid.
32. Reed, 'Introduction', in *Not at Home*', p. 16.
33. Ibid.
34. Reed, 'Domestic Disturbances', p. 43.
35. Perry, 'Dream Houses: installations and the home', p. 256.

This article is a revised and extended version of the paper 'No Place Like Home: Curating Ceramics in House Museums', delivered at the 45th Annual NCECA Conference in Florida, April 2011. It was first published in this form in the online journal *Interpreting Ceramics*, issue 13, 2011.

Reproduced with the permission of the author.

61

THE MUSEUM AS MEDIUM-SPECIFIC MUSE

Ezra Shales

Upon hearing of his efforts to found the Museum of Modern Art in New York City in 1929, Gertrude Stein patronizingly informed Alfred Barr that a museum can either be a museum or it can be modern, but it cannot be both.[1] Today, we assume museums and modern art to be compatible. In fact, we even have several such institutions that claim to truck in contemporaneity, that vague term denoting a non-hierarchical and non-deterministic pulse of global visual cultures.[2] And yet concerning the modernity of medium-specific missions, there is rarely consensus. The crux of the debate is whether the medium-specific museum is an isolationist refuge or a place for methodical analysis. To invert Stein's rule of incompatibility, perhaps artists' efforts to confront medium-specificity are a form of nonconformist dissent, a trope to broadcast a condition of self-awareness.

In recent years, the number of artists working in ceramics who are "mining the museum" has grown by leaps and bounds, and these medium-specific projects seem to try to challenge Stein's antinomy. Rarely are ceramic artists' pseudo-archaeological acts as politicized as Fred Wilson's revisionist presentation of the slave economy in the collection of Maryland Historical Society.[3] More common has been a reuse of such modes of display as porcelain chambers, china closets, and *Wunderkammer*; these have entailed both visual emulation and conceptual appropriation. Such medium-specific investigations lie at an enigmatic intersection, the juncture of what was termed information art in the early 1970s (i.e. conceptual art) and what has historically been categorized as the decorative arts. This essay ponders the conceptual weight of the museum upon the artist today, in an effort to inquire if the museum's influence has inspired a genre or constitutes a shared sensibility.

I Tracing lines of retrospection

Artists, like everyone else, often divide in their disregard for museums. Is the cultural apparatus rational and scientific, a crystal goblet holding the finest human achievements, or an authoritarian construct to be mistrusted as propaganda? The museum remains a handy abstract metaphor and a literal technology to visualize the Modernist rupture and its opposite, the grand paternalistic Enlightenment project. This is no great conceptual observation, merely a sociological one. The dusty vitrine remains an art school cliché that signifies the stuffy antique (neither mine nor yours but some superficial and too-conveniently downloadable version). The gilt frame is a shorthand mark to designate rarity and value. It is not only students who use these symbolic trappings (think of Marcel Broodthaers or Ken Lum). "Museum" can be generated with wood molding and a specific patina.

Source: © Ezra Shales.

Self-referential gestures pervade ceramics more intrinsically, in terms of the skin, body, and shape of a pot. Finding a shelf of pots that collated an encyclopedic survey of historic glazes anywhere other than in a ceramic exhibition, one might assume it to be a conceptual installation or narrative structure. But among its brethren it is more often a show of sincere affections and a road map of technique. Such a display prompts questions about the ways that potters and ceramic sculptors access museological contextualization. The unfair generalization holds true that most ceramicists labor with self-blinding devotion to objecthood. Many making a pot in the decades between 1925 and 1975 thought about filling or emptying out that one thing because the idealization of autonomy was a focal point and mission in the twentieth century. Even if pots ceased to be pots, they did not think about orchestrating a room. (A partial exception to this generalization might be Noguchi's assemblages in clay in which sculpture and frame are bound in antithesis, or as a twinned temporal and spatial bind.)

The medium-specific artist can be seen as either committed to the very self-referential rupture that Stein pioneered or as a traditionalist, depending upon the way that he or she perceives time. For the artist trained under the waning sun of Modernism, the issue of disinterest remains an aesthetic but more importantly a social precondition. This makes for a more schizophrenic "shape of time" than George Kubler sketched out in his 1964 polemic.[4] If Postmodernism fractured the notion of artistic autonomy, in educational institutions it only widened the cul-de-sac of individuated practice. Art making is now an eight-lane interstate on which there are mainly lonely solo drivers who lack a clear understanding of their temporal trajectories. The Modernist potter learned to center clay on the wheel and to transcend form through repetition and variation on a theme, but also to work alone, without the past. The Postmodernist might have abandoned the wheel as well as other artistic conventions and has a measuring stick or metronome the self-conscious choreographing of her or his artistic oeuvre. Western art-school graduates are trained to think more easily in terms of their own solo retrospectives than in terms of collaborative work or collective traditions. Their concept of authorship and time is essentially still Modernist, with their own self as the governing principle. This shape of time is a bit lopsided, as the fragmentation of authorship is an accepted theoretical premise but still pursued in practice. (It does seem ironic that Postmodern irony permitted the use of the copy but looked unfavorably upon the re-institutionalization of copying as good pedagogy.) Note, disorder in artistic agency is connected to chronological confusion and cannot be blamed solely on the artist, for museums' categorization of time is at best a sloppy craft, too. Walk through contemporary galleries and you can see that decades and centuries are crutches and constantly leaned upon to designate or even explain changes in style and intellectual attitude; such generalizations are neither nuanced nor genuinely pluralist. Hence my plea for a materialist sense of time.

In her estimation of the constructive confusion surrounding the early *Kunstkammer*, Paula Findlen argues that the "museum [is] foremost a mental category and collecting a cognitive activity that [can] be appropriated for social and cultural ends." Despite such persuasive words, the museum is primarily a material realm where commoditization and capitalist intrigue are maddeningly quantifiable and objects are made to hold time still –behave!– more often than they are permitted to collide and suggest the maddening recursions of visual culture and the unequal speeds at which time's hands spin.

While medium-specificity is often the elephant in the room considered the problem of lesser mortals, in the context of museums this enigma remains something rich and strange. Most museums dock in the treacherous waters of medium-specificity, sorting treasures into fixed moments and material sequences. This used to include a predilection for a focused expertise, but the scholarly orientation in museums is now displaced by an emphasis on collections management.

To return to Stein's antinomy, our working assumption is that a contemporary museum will continually gobble and disgorge youthful endeavors, and yet also that a museum might be purely dedicated to ceramics or glass, as if two such etiquettes were compatible. Are they? One implies taut self-control, the strictest dietary consumption, whilst the other an ominous omnivore. If one's condition is to be so sure of one's chronological location, it would seem to preclude proceeding so boldly as to wall out all other non-like-minded species. However, perhaps the Western museum has a new role as a steward of production in our post-industrial situation. As museums, historic houses, and public cultural centers have multiplied in the last hundred years in Europe and North America at a furious pace, the outsourcing and relocation of actual production has been commensurate. The project of mining the museum might also be explained as a way of coping with deindustrialization. The simulacrum of production has arguably become increasingly emotional and more powerful in an era of out-sourcing.

Today's ceramicists are working with museums in symbiotic relationships as never before, and it is curious to speculate on the pathos with which the contemporary ceramic artist approaches the museological space and collection. Do objects drive production or does their taxonomy or display? How does the individual artist see their situation? Is the museum a place of solace, a locus where medium-specificity seems pregnant with meaning or merely a like-minded pretension?

II Tracing lines of activity

One could argue that the Postmodern era made the museum installation unnecessary and redundant. Decades before the digital database of images erupted and our retinas came to be clouded by the muddy haze of atomized visual culture, there was an abundant interest in recuperating and exercising the codices of historical ornament that Modernism had repressed. For example, each pot by Adrian Saxe is a portable museum. The bricoleur of history creates a condensed "history for dummies" in a highly enriched but ultimately homeless and lonely artifact. While an artist such as Gwyn Hanssen-Pigott might seem relevant, she also falls outside of the medium-specific mining of ceramics because her work is primarily the orchestration of a still-life, not a diachronic and referential passage of time or a gesture that responds to an institutional frame. But a pivotal reference point in the field of contemporary ceramics can be located in its first burst of Postmodernist energy, Ken Price's 1978 installation, *Happy's Curios*.

Price's parody of ethnographic museology and the commercialization of the "tribal" ridiculed the identity politics of ceramic traditions in the same way that Hannah Höch's photomontages dismembered the camera's supposedly empirical eye. Using posters to nominally declare his own work an exhibition of "Mexican Arts," Price undermined the institutionalization of art in witty, acerbic, and critical if opportunistic terms. Naïveté and sophistication were thrown together much the way chronological markers were compressed. The colorful drawings and ethnic appropriation seem to cycle back to the era of the 1930s and the medium to Frederick Hurten Rhead's Fiesta ware. Price's *Death Shrine*, a stacked series of vessels behind a decorative picket fence, seemed to commemorate a mortal collision of art and an innocent visitor that happened in some prior gallery exhibition or a highway fatality. Alongside this gesture of artistic self-effacement Price exhibited an *Inca Self-Portrait* with an outstanding erect phallus protruding from a rather plain bulbous pot. Hubris and humility coexisted and contradicted each other. These works argue both for the necessity of individual genius on the one hand and the total failure of critical categories used to evaluate such a hierarchy. Commemoration and cultural amnesia were endemic in Price's installation. Could "Mexican arts" be made by anyone? Were these "curios" or "art"? While there are still no easy answers to such questions, the framing of artifacts within fences and vitrines clearly established the museum as Price's content.

If Price introduced the genre of mining the ceramic museum, numerous artists continue to probe such questions. By considering a few medium-specific practitioners from the same country, especially the United

Kingdom, one can perceive museology becoming a more ingrained framework in the field and even worthy of designation as a subordinate genre. This selection might appear self-serving, as the British model of the applied arts museum was closely tied to the national system of art education and has exerted enormous influence internationally. However, some qualities peculiar to the museum as a cultural apparatus become tangible threads by collating the work of three distinct artists whose work is radically different in content. If their modes of display are considered in relation to the museum a *Zeitgeist* can be identified. The museum is a modality of display that has a broad bandwidth able to signify or allude to multiple histories, including aristocratic lineage, public culture, participatory spectacles, and regional traditions. These histories are significant forms content among practitioners today.

One of the most self-aware artists to refer to the museum as a paragon is Edmund de Waal. His museological installations call visitors' attention to the subtle nuances of courtly domestic embellishment. De Waal has in fact built a work titled *Wunderkammer* that teases visitors' inability to touch or grasp the totality of the installation. It is a freestanding box the size of Cooper Mini on end, and although the interior is suggestively visible through thin apertures, mere arrowslits, there is no entrance to this room-in-a-room to gain intimacy with the stacks of hand-thrown plates within. De Waal keeps his art out of arm's length in many other installations, and calls attention to this challenge by using titles such as *All You Can See* (2006). The frames and positional dislocation of shelves intentionally limits viewers' satisfaction. The remove also turns a traditionally tactile art form into an optical experience. At his exhibitions in Chatsworth, Kettle's Yard, Cambridge and in the Middlesbrough Institute of Modern Art, de Waal describes his work as "site sensitive." There is a hermetic quality that pervades much of these installations, which is not intentionally frustrating but which is the result of the high degree of refinement with which de Waal is himself comfortable. The artist is able to enter restricted regal homes such as Chatsworth and insert his tableware with aplomb. Although he articulates the hope that his installations at Kettle's Yard are "demotic," the walls and tables and grand piano are peppered with Hepworth and Moore and Nicholson works, no mean litter.[5] The safe havens de Waal selects are modern descendants of the medieval *Wunderkammer* or *Kunstkammer*. He deals in privatized culture, not Richard Slee's domestic jungle of plasticky knick-knackery. His installations coincide with the academic rehabilitation of the princely private space as a place of knowledge building, not simply guarded hoardings of commodities. De Waal is similarly intent on tapping into a sense of awe and wonder –there is nothing populist in that aim. By restricting perceptual access to his work, the art inhabits a rarified place, but to take the artist at his word, these aristocratic spaces become somehow more accessible as aesthetic experiences.

Clare Twomey's installations gently mock the museum even as she uses it as a platform. Twomey's museum is the public, rational space of Victorian order. Her temporary work at the V&A in 2007, *Trophy*, was a one-night stand with the plaster court, the very core collection that was to teach artisans about pattern, ornament, and style. Amid the cacophony of copies of monumental antiquities all made of the same tawny yellowish-white, Twomey scattered four thousand sparrows made by Wedgwood (and herself) in shades of its characteristic blue Jasper body, and permitted museum visitors to pocket them during evening hours. In *Forever*, a work made for the Nelson-Atkins Museum in 2010, replication of a historical object again caused not a lessening of value but precisely the opposite. Twomey's work responds in the affirmative to the eminent Victorians who created the plaster cast court – and their belief that they were facilitating an encapsulated encyclopedic historical and aesthetic experience – while also thumbing her nose at their arrogance. Copying established a *lingua franca* in the nineteenth century, and utilized the recent technical innovations in print to establish an accessible – if imperialistic – grammar of visual culture. Twomey uses replication and large-scale serial production nimbly to access an audience that only such numbers permit. Her work feeds off of this ideal of public culture as a discernable body of images and achievements, and embraces culture as a participatory spectacle. However, she ambiguates by both seeking to deflate the value of the casts and add value to the little blue bird knick-knacks. It is obvious that the birds are kitsch on one level, and yet they also represent an enduring aesthetic achievement, and achieve a value beyond mere kitsch through their association with the value of the plaster casts and museum. Is her work a piece of art because it bears the cipher of Wedgwood as well as the logo of the V&A and the artist's initials? Just as the tradition of a private cultural sanctuary is intrinsic to the meaning of de Waal's work, the concepts of public culture and the universal commodity are essential to Twomey's. Moreover, today's artist labors extremely conscious that production values of documentary photography are of greater importance than actual studio production, and that the museum's efforts at branding and commoditization are a lead to follow, not challenge.

Neil Brownsword exhibits the palimpsests of labor and positions his work in much the same way as a history museum might lay out relics. He investigates the detritus of factory spaces in Stoke-on-Trent, where he grew up, worked, and where he still lives, and presents his excavations of fragments beside his work, as if inefficiency and waste were the central narratives of the industrial revolution. There is a clinical empiricism to Brownsword's flat-footed delivery of these shards as evidence, as they shirk the status of art and more earnestly pursue thingness. Recall seeing objects such as melted glass windows and lead cames preserved from the Great Fire of London of 1666 or the San Francisco earthquake of 1906. Those leftovers are presented as geological strata, existing outside of human intentions. Brownsword exhibits his work in museums alongside such historical shards and has kept the drama of lighting and presentation to a minimum. Paradoxically, his own compelling autobiography is submerged and invisible because of his chosen installation method, unlike Tracy Emin or Damien Hirst, where autobiographical fact trumps material meanings or metaphors. Brownsword's museological contextualization is essential to accessing his work, for it is the history of material culture that he is depositing on a shelf. There is the quotidian, sometimes lovingly scatological and at others a plain unhurried scraping of formlessness and form.

But is the broken cup that is saved for future mending now solely the domain of a museological sensibility? Recently, I looked into a pot that was painstakingly mended with twenty rivets in the eighteenth century, and I began to wonder if such a deed was comprehensible as fact, fancy, or only pure folly in today's world. Is the quiet empiricism that Brownsword accesses one of the last beautiful embers of the nineteenth century to sooth the twentieth century mind, and is it inaccessible to today's emerging artists? Will the antiquarian bent be as obsolete as bowl-mending for future generations? These questions beg a confession. I came of age when museums were backwater harbors, quiet and empty of people, sets of collections still coated with a layer of dust. I encountered artifacts that resembled what George Kubler described as "dead stars," fixtures that were visibly part of the firmament yet illuminating the earth in only a limited way – especially to my ignorant mind. The absence of didactic labels increased these mysteries. The excitement lay in speculating whether I was witnessing the death of a culture or an ember that was about to burn brightly and illuminate my life, my world, and not simply the museum? Kubler notes that "usually our comprehension of a thing is incomplete until its positional value can be reconstructed," and to roam through an encyclopedic museum initially, before the stores and the audio tours and the labels in politically-correct groupspeak, was to continually map out contingent positional values by eye and on foot.[6] What pleasure we might take in a Tracy Emin or what understanding we might have of her blankets is contingent upon knowing her biography, but the resonance through time and space is much the wider in a museum. My hope is that we value medium-specific art which goes beyond self-expression or individual identity so as to value the history of cultural institutions and take pleasure in their lackings and holes as much as their holdings.

These brief interpretations sketch out the ways that the museum is a trope supportive of and relevant to medium-specific production today. The museum is a pivotal metaphor for artistic production, strategy for displaying work, and means of negotiating and/or prompting rupture. A pessimistic reading of this assessment is that the museological frame is a way for medium-specific artists to bypass Postmodernism, plurality, and globalism in order to return to art rooted in and reaffirming a Western hegemony. To gauge the degree to which the museological construct is ubiquitous, it is worth looking at two artists whose work ranges across many media. Charles LeDray, a contemporary United States artist who sews and embroiders, carves bone, also throws pots. LeDray's collections of myriad thimble-sized vessels in a vitrine, such as *2000 Pots* (1993-1996) (or his *Milk and Honey* (1994-1996) and *Thrown Shadows* (2008-2010)), are in the scale of children's dollhouse furniture and they too rely on the museum collection as a tool and mental category. These types of miniature collections were born of the industrial revolution and explosive rise of commodity culture and intended for domestic life but as contemporary methods of display live on only in the public museum. They can signify reliquaries or lost childhoods, among other things. But they are resolutely a museological mode of looking and organizing.

Ai Weiwei is another seminal artist of the moment who also uses the museum as a ploy, albeit to probe national identity. By suggesting that he destroys Han dynasty urns, Ai Weiwei intentionally ruptures value as well as definitions of heritage. Or does he remake these antique commodities when he dips them into viscous paint in saturated colors? The question is whether these altered urns are abused pieces of the public's patrimony or autonomous works of contemporary art. Whereas Price appropriated the artistic voice of the subaltern, Ai Weiwei challenges the technocratic engine of modernization. His repeated gestures that destroy Chinese antiquities –metonyms for the museum– can also be read as attempts to defend the uselessness of the past. His work also becomes auto-ethnography, in terms remarkably more complex than Ken Price's fantastical auto-portrait, when he is considered in terms of the Cultural Revolution of 1965-1968 and the suppression and selective use of national history during that time.

His recent installation of *Sunflower Seeds* (2010) at the Tate Modern can be read as a powerful critique of the cultural institution when it is subject to utilitarian control. By filling up the old power plant as if it were a silo of dead seeds unable to ever germinate, the usefulness of preservation is turned into an absurdity. Many meanings can be extracted from *Sunflower Seeds*. Ai WeiWei turned the museum into a brokerage firm for a dead-end commodity cycle. The seeds were a metaphor for exporting native soil, for the ruin of ecology in the name of progress, and the contradictory ways traditional handicraft is simultaneously fetishized and invalidated, made to speak of the unique human and also the loss of human individuality. But perhaps most rich is the medium-specific meaning of the installation: The seeds mine the nationalist genre of porcelain by mocking its use as a marker of class and civilization – in the West as well as the East. The artist's abuse of ancient urns ultimately seems most comprehensible as an act of empathy with pottery itself and with the museum's right to be a protean graveyard. The ideal that art might be an intangible and uncommodified relationship in lieu of a specific object is now sold in small seed piles in galleries in London, New York, and Paris. These seductive metaphors that momentarily imply that the global networks of power are comprehendible are, of course, precisely the Enlightenment conceit of which the museum was born. In the face of our era of endless waves of commoditization and callousness to acts of savagery justified as so-called cultural regeneration, I can only conclude by acquiescing to Gertrude Stein, and encouraging the artist to mine the museum with Fred Wilson's fire and Neil Brownsword's empathy; forage well and be mindful of the game.

Notes

1. Bruce Altshuler, ed., *Collecting the New: Museums and Contemporary Art* (Princeton: Princeton University Press, 2005), xi.
2. Antonio Negri, "Contemporaneity between Modernity and Postmodernity" in *Antinomies of Art and Culture*, eds. Condee, Smith, and Enwezor (Chapel Hill: Duke University Press, 2008), 23–29.

3. Fred Wilson, *Mining the Museum* (Baltimore and New York: The Contemporary in cooperation with the New Press, 1994).
4. George Kubler, *The Shape of Time* (New York: 1964).
5. Edmund de Waal, *Edmund de Waal at Kettle's Yard, mima and elsewhere* (Cambridge and Middlesbrough: Kettle's Yard and mima, 2007), 127.
6. Kubler, *The Shape of Time*, 97.

Originally published as Ezra Shales (2011), 'The Museum as Medium Specific Muse', In Jorunn Veiteberg (ed) *Ting Tang Trash*, Bergen Academy of the Arts.

Reproduced with permission from Bergen Academy of Art and Design and the author.

62 ENVIRONMENT, ART, CERAMICS, AND SITE SPECIFICITY

Brad Evan Taylor

Metasomatism is the transformation of one rock into another of an entirely different kind.[1] Metamorphosis references the idea of complete and total transformation. The term can refer to matter, or the spirit. Science attempts to explain in quantitative terminology, phenomena and change in our universe. When something is mystical or does not seem to make logical sense, scientists attempt to explain it. The absolute underlying provable truth is the point. Artists are often focused on the emotional result. They generally do not care about the explanation and logical, provable path. The result is what matters. The un-repeatability of the result is what inspires awe in many cases. Alchemy attempts to transmute one substance into another in such a way that the results are repeatable, but not necessarily understandable. Looking at Art, Science, and Alchemy in this way, places Alchemy directly between Art and Science. This creates a path between the two. Bridges connect segmented entities; they allow access of common ground. The connection of seemingly divergent thoughts can sometimes unfold hidden truth.

James Elkins compares painting and alchemy in "*What Painting Is*". He makes the argument that both disciplines utilize a mixture of ground rock and water to elicit a magical transformation. This transformation is hoped to occur in the physical world in the alchemical case. The change is intended for the human psyche in the case of the painter. The first paragraph of the introduction connects the materials and process of painters and ceramists. *"Ceramics begins with the careful mixing of tap water and clay, and the wet clay slip is itself a dense mixture of stone and water. Watery mud is the medium of ceramists, just as oily mud is the medium of painters."*[2] The ceramist is equated to the painter in this statement; the goal being emotional response from the future audience. However, in the ceramist case there are some additional steps; all of that technical transformation which normally accompanies the ceramic process. Ceramists have been known to pray to the kiln gods, and purposefully avoid divulging the "secrets" about the transformation of matter. Ceramists have also been observed pouring over scientific literature in the quest to understand the magical. Perhaps Ceramists bridge Art, Alchemy, and Science.

The divisions between Art, Alchemy and Science were blended in times past. The "Renaissance Man" regularly traversed these boundaries. Leonardo Da Vinci is widely viewed as the all-time heavy-weight-champion of cross disciplinary effectiveness. Scientific discovery, past and present, regularly involves observations and insights which appear to come from the worlds of art and alchemy. Bill Bryson, in "*A Short History of Nearly Everything*", gives several examples of science blending with alchemy during the process of creative discovery, two follow. *"Ernest Rutherford and Frederick Soddy ... discovered that radioactive elements decay into other elements- that one day you had an atom of uranium, say, and the next had an atom of lead. This was truly extraordinary. It was alchemy, pure and simple; no one had ever imagined that such a thing could happen naturally and spontaneously."*[3] This seemed like magic, but it was real. *"Hennig Brand became convinced that gold could somehow be distilled from human urine. (The similarity in color seems to have been a factor in this*

Source: © Brad Evan Taylor.

conclusion.) He assembled fifty buckets of human urine which he kept in his cellar. By various recondite processes, he converted the urine first into a noxious paste and then into a translucent waxy substance. None of it yielded gold of course, but a strange and interesting thing did happen. After a time the substance began to glow. Moreover, when exposed to air, it often burst into flame."[4] This was the discovery of phosphorus. Leonard Shlain, in "*Art and Physics*", makes a case for conceptually linking scientific research and artistic research. His statement directly quantifies this conceptual link, "*Revolutionary art and visionary physics are both investigations into the nature of reality ... While their methods differ radically, artists and physicists share the desire to investigate the ways the interlocking pieces of reality fit together. This is the common ground upon which they meet.*"[5] Note that this statement says "investigations into", and does not simply rely on results. Shlain recognizes that process, the creative process, is paramount. Researchers in all fields become absorbed in the creative process when they are at their best – this is a prerequisite for expansion of the knowledge base.

You might be asking how these observations and stories relate to environment and site specificity in Art. Each of the instances mentioned above involve total immersement by the participants. Complete enthrallment with the materials, ideas, and surrounding environment allow the possibility of discovery; matter, thought, obsession, place, and time coalesce to open windows of discovery. Matter, thought, and obsession are key ingredients in the making of Art Objects. The addition of place and time adds the power of context. Works which include and address place and time acknowledge that living beings are shaped by both "nature and nurture". Advancement, discovery, and adaptation happen constantly within living systems. Evolution is directly linked to place, time, and circumstance. Charles Darwin brilliantly laid out the transformation of living beings in response to the ever changing environment in "*On the Origin of Species*". Clearly context and environment must have enormous power; they have the ability to consistently change the nature of life itself throughout the eons. We are currently recognizing the swiftness of change and the interdependence of all systems with the global climate crisis. Al Gore writes about this emerging truth in the introduction for his book "*An Inconvenient Truth*". "*Our climate crisis may at times appear to be happening slowly, but in fact it is happening very quickly-and has become a true planetary emergency. The Chinese expression for crisis consists of two characters. The first is a symbol for danger; the second is a symbol for opportunity.*"[6]

Perhaps emotion and thought triggered through site specific and environmental art is akin to the Chinese symbology relating to crisis; the danger is in the questions which arise, and the opportunity is in the potential growth from cognizant thought about the questions, and the resulting changes brought about through the inevitable insights. The resulting cultural shift brings winners and losers, much like the evolutionary changes described by Darwin. The scientist Albert-Laszlo Barabasi looks at interconnectedness in his book "*Linked.*"[7] The premise is that computer networks, societies, the spread of disease, and business are all similar in their underlying principles. Change is constant and interconnected. The artist Mark Lombardi explores these concepts in his drawings diagramming the flow of information and money and their relationship to international politics. The FBI actually visited the Whitney Museum in New York City immediately following 9-11 to analyze one of Lombardi's drawings. The work contained information about the interconnectedness of Al-Qaida. Works which incorporate environment and site specificity have additional tools to inspire thought and emotion about connectivity.

Art, at least 'good Art' inspires contemplation, consideration, conversation, and sometimes debate. The intent is often to trigger thought or emotion which is not always explicable in rational, everyday language. Our lifetimes are consumed with the process of making 2+2=4. Making 2+2=5, 6, or 6.66 is another matter entirely. These kinds of rationally inexplicable results are often the goals of Art and Alchemy. The resulting thoughts and emotions exist, but rational, logical, readily explicable explanations for these results are exceedingly fleeting. The human element is magic. The Artist or Alchemist who can evoke the unexplainable is the magician. Again - Transformation is key. I hold the belief that the emotional transformation induced within a viewer, I am speaking about the inexplicable one, is the direct result of the artist's ability to metasomatize matter. The artist might be a painter, sculptor or a ceramist. When an artist has the ability to seemingly transform matter in a magical way, the resulting art inherits some of this ability to communicate on an emotional level.

Artists literally live with their materials. They see, feel, breath, taste, listen and speak, the matter which is metamorphized into the work. This constant communication between artist and matter is what creates the potential for magic. When there is change there is emotion. The artist is coaxing change, using his emotion to communicate with matter and convince it to transmute. The material is in a vulnerable state, it's emotion is changed through this close relationship. When the balance of emotion, communication, and external environmental factors are right, magic happens, matter speaks in an inexplicable way.

This relationship of artist and matter, and scientist and material, is analogous to the psychological theories and arguments about Nature vs. Nurture. How much is hard wired into the material itself? How much is attributable to environment, surroundings, and relationships? How does history affect outcomes? At this point in time there is scientific consensus that environment and surroundings play a significant role in psychological development.

Mark Rothko writes of body-scale to art-scale, environment, and surroundings, and their impact on art experience this way, *"I paint very large pictures. I realize that historically the function of painting large pictures is painting something very grandiose and pompous. The reason I paint them…is precisely because I want to be very intimate and human. To paint a small picture is to place yourself outside your experience, to look upon an experience as a stereopticon view with a reducing glass. However you paint the larger pictures, you are in it. It isn't something you command."*[8] This statement speaks directly about becoming one with your environment. Because he is creating the environment he is also indirectly speaking about becoming one with his materials. This is a statement about immersion in every way possible to the fullest extent. It is about the power of communication when you are part, and aware of your surroundings. This is the power of installation and environment, intimacy through integration. Understanding comes through oneness with place and time.

The physical environment surrounding Jingdezhen, China allowed the development of the world's first porcelain tradition. The chemical composition of the rocks was ideal to create the perfect eutectic to allow melting temperatures low enough to match current firing technology. But someone had to be observant enough of environment to find the right rocks. Looking at scientific phase-equillibria diagrams and comparing chemical analysis of pottery shards from the Song dynasty in the region reveals that the artisans of that time found the mix of raw materials which uncannily matches the perfect eutectic points in the modern diagrams. The only possible explanation is one of an incredibly close relationship of artist, matter, and place. These people had dialog with their surroundings and materials. This invention took place because of the total immersion relationship of artist to material, and artist to environment.

A eutectic is that place where materials, in combination, suddenly become more reactive; the temperature range of the melt suddenly drops and ceramic becomes a possibility. Site specificity could be thought of conceptually as a eutectic. The utilization of the history or physical makeup of a specific locale in combination with a specific mix of concepts, materials, process, and artist interaction can suddenly escalate the potency of a work - cohering that work, in that *specific* place, into a potency not possible in another. The history of Jingdezhen, China, could possibly endow work created using porcelain at that locale with a special significance relating to site specificity; especially if combined with artistic immersion in that intense way which sometimes happens with lifetime obsession. It is not automatic however, all porcelain work which may be created there is not specially infused, only that which finds a way to blend the materials of history, concept, place, action, and 'specificity'. The artist Robert Smithson worked extensively with these ideas of potency and site specificity. He refers to this as "site/non-site". Goals making the "site/non-site" works included first-creating potent work which related directly to a specific location; and second-attempting to transplant portions of the work into foreign locations including galleries and museums. The idea was an attempt to retain the potency of site, by spot-lighting it's singular nature, and then by finding a ways to transfer that captured essence. Psychological linkage to the original "site" was always kept close at hand; however, the works always changed when transplanted, and thus required the designation "non-site" – these were not works simply 'installed' in an indoor or outdoor area for display effect, they were seeking to infuse the non-site with the essence of the original site. This issue is addressed throughout the book *"Robert Smithson: The Collected Writings"*[9]

Ceramic materials have history as old as the earth. The rocks we use to make our work are bound to the history of the planet. The right rocks, the correct proportion, the perfect amount of water to temporarily allow fluidity, the perfect amount of heat, and a dialog with an immersed artisan, allows the metasomatosis of matter and the metamorphosis of emotion to create Art. When you think about it is remarkable that this combination of circumstance and relationship occurs often within our lifetimes. The geologic timescale seems a more likely occurrence of these particular events. The immersion of artist and the intense relationship with matter and environment is the only realistic explanation. Intense interaction speeds transformation.

Clay may very well turn out to be critical matter in the formation of life. It's links to the history of life, and earth, and it's natural ability to focus interaction on an atomic level, make it an idealistic choice for use in environmental works when one wishes to incorporate and utilize the intrinsic history of the material. Because of clay's integral history, it has an ability to speak through eons. Richard Fortey alludes to this probable history in his book "*Life*" *"Clays are entirely inorganic, and have been common since water started eroding rock. The minerals that make them have atoms arranged is sheets, loosely held together: this is why clays are slimy and slippery. Between the sheets other atoms may bind – and in this way chemicals can become concentrated so that they react together. Clays thus provide a natural factory for the doubling the size and complexity of organic molecules. It is curious to recall that in the biblical account God fashioned Adam from inert clay; science may yet prove that clay truly had a role in that most distant genesis of life."*[10] This theory about the possible links between clay and life are explored in detail in "*Clay Minerals and the Origin of Life*"[11] edited by A.G. Cairns-Smith and H. Hartman. Now let me return to another quote from "*What Painting Is*". *"...meaning does not depend on what the paintings are about: it is there at a lower level, in every inch of canvas. Substances occupy the mind by invading it with thoughts of the artist's body at work."*[12] Perhaps work made from clay can permeate the spirit through it's multidimensional history in a way that other materials simply cannot. The magic of emotion transferred through Art relies heavily on the relationship of artist, material, and environment. Clay is an ideal vehicle for the transference of uncognizable thought.

Notes

1. OED.
2. What Painting Is, James Elkins, Routledge, Great Britain, 1999, pg. 1.
3. A Short History of Nearly Everything, Bill Bryson, Broadway Books, New York, New York, 2003, pg. 109.
4. A Short History of Nearly Everything, Bill Bryson, Broadway Books, New York, New York, 2003, pg. 97–98.
5. Shlain, Leonard. Art and Physics: Parallel Visions in Space, Time & Light. (New York, U.S.A.: Morrow, 1991), p. 16.
6. An Inconvenient Truth, Al Gore, Rodale, Emmaus, PA, 2006.
7. Linked, Albert-Laszlo Barabasi, Plume Printing Penguin Group, New York, New York, 2003.
8. Rothko, Mark, *I Paint Very Large Pictures*, (1951), (eds.), Stiles, Kristine. and Selz, Peter. *Theories and Documents of Contemporary Art; A sourcebook of Artists' Writings*. (Berkeley, U.S.A.: University of California Press, 1996), p. 26.

9. Robert Smithson: The Collected Writings, editor- Jack Flam, University of California Press, Berkeley and Los Angeles California, 1996.
10. Life – A Natural History of the First Four Billion Years of Life on Earth, Richard Fortey, Alfred A. Knopf, New York, New York, pg. 39–40.
11. Clay Minerals and the Origin of Life, A. G. Cairns and H. Hartman, Cambridge University Press, 1986
12. What Painting Is, James Elkins, Routledge, Great Britain, 1999, pg. 96.

Printed with the permission of the author.

63 WHEN FORMS BECOME ATTITUDE – A CONSIDERATION OF THE ADOPTION BY AN ARTIST OF CERAMIC DISPLAY AS NARRATIVE DEVICE AND SYMBOLIC LANDSCAPE

Michael Tooby

When artists 'intervene' in museums, the material at their disposal is not merely the collections and the galleries in which they are displayed. At their most ambitious and effective, they take on the entire conceptualization of an institution. This remains the case even when a museum's collections *per se* are not the content explicitly addressed by the artist. Instead, notions of a canon, a shared understood narrative about history, even signifiers of a community's collective identity, may be wrapped in the work's grasp.

Shocked silence
FATHER What?...So we're going to destroy this Leach tea set?
SON Yes
FATHER But isn't it...Valuable [sounds reluctant]
SON I think it's really important to understand that the characters have to destroy this, because as long as this ideal vision exists, it leaves them in the shadows of it.
FATHER I'm not sure what I think about that [shakes head] No, I'm not sure what I think about that. I mean, is that ethical? [concern in his voice]
SON It's ... Necessary

Extract from: Script for "Rehearsal for a Reunion" (with the Father of Pottery) by Simon Fujiwara, 2011–2

This is the moment of truth in Simon Fujiwara's installation, 'A rehearsal for a Reunion (with the Father of Pottery)', shown as part of a large show by the artist presented at Tate St Ives in 2012.

On a video monitor we have seen two figures approach each other and sit at a table, evidently on some sort of stage set. If we have been paying attention to other works in the exhibition, one is evidently the artist, playing the role of 'son'. The other character, 'father', is played by a person who is clearly not the Japanese father described in the script.

The script they have been discussing refers to a tea set by Bernard Leach, and a reproduction Leach/Hamada style tea set apparently made by 'son' and what the script describes as his real father. The characters do indeed proceed to smash up the real Leach tea set. It is a catharsis both for the players and for the audience.

The version of the installation at Tate St Ives used the curved display space originally created for the display of work by Leach, Hamada and their circle (Figure 63.1).[1] The fragments of the broken pots and the

Source: © Michael Tooby.

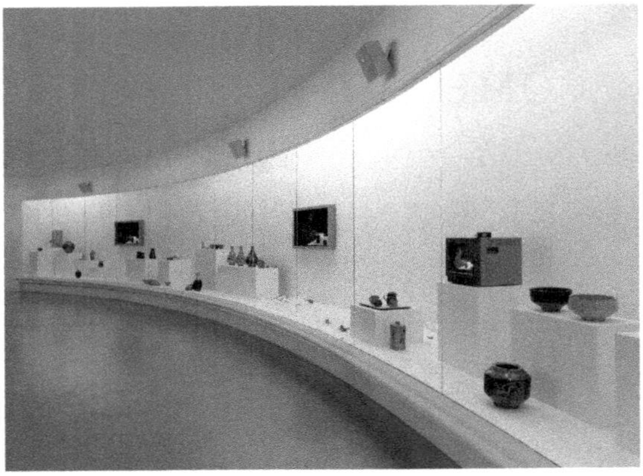

Figure 63.1 Simon Fujiwara exhibition installation, image of upper gallery two, showcase, 2012/Photography © Tate 2012 and Simon Fujiwara.

reproduction pots are shown alongside other Leach and Hamada pots familiar from Tate's past displays, and, less familiar, a kettle, a tea urn and some tea bags, and other bits and pieces, including a book. We presume that the ceramic shards have been carefully kept from the performance shown on screen, and in turn will now be carefully kept for future re-presentation.

In the Tate St Ives version, a variety of details ensure that visitors familiar with the gallery know that the display is a pastiche reproduction of one of the original Tate St Ives historic ceramic displays – a reference made equally explicit in the documentation and visitor interpretation of the exhibition. Plinths are the same plinths used for the collection's Leach and Hamada pots. The wall mounted monitors showing the performance replace paintings such as a William Scott still life.

'A rehearsal for a Reunion (with the Father of Pottery)' was one of a group of installations in which Fujiwara re-presented his own past. The curatorial thesis for the show, entitled 'Since 1982', took at its starting point the fact that he grew up in St Ives, being 11 when Tate St Ives opened in 1993. It was on a scale which might be termed something like a 'survey' if it were by an older artist.

The Leach piece was one of six room-sized installations. Whilst others dealt with Fujiwara's past travels, most turned upon the deployment Fujiwara's autobiographical connections to artists and works of art specifically associated with his own past, and with past St Ives displays: Patrick Heron and the iconicity of abstraction transformed by the metaphor of the teenage bedroom; the fantasised world of Alfred Wallis; and the renegotiation of the symbolization of powerful female artists, with Barbara Hepworth at the centre.

The Leach installation builds on a number of layers of prior knowledge that are articulated in the exhibition wall texts and the standard introductory leaflet. Simon Fujiwara's mother was British and father was Japanese. As a child, he was taken to the Leach pottery (before the renovation which gives it its present character took place). As an adult, he travels to Japan and visits his father, now separated from his mother.

In a generic sense, these interpretative texts embed certain details where jokes and implausibilities prompt doubt. We must assume that he and his father really did meet up at his father's original home town of Mariko (which is easily confused with Mashiko, of course) and had a go at making pots, which then resembled Leach/ Hamada style pottery.

We must further accept that his father really did sketch Leach furniture, and consider making reproduction versions. This historical research is a surrogate research history mapped in the catalogue. It is obvious, meanwhile, that Fujiwara *fils* is posing as a kind of Imperialist traveller connoisseur in the photos of him

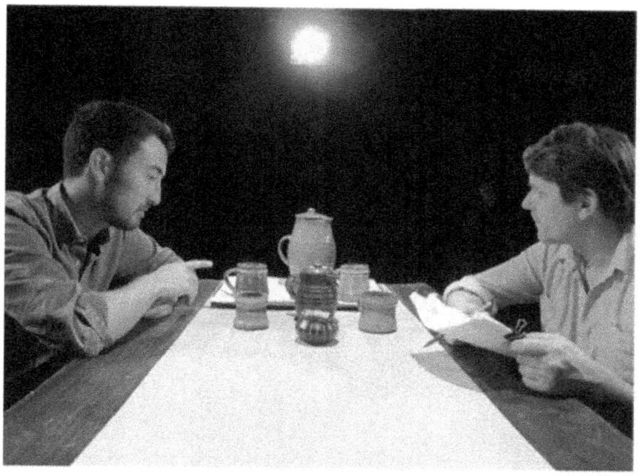

Figure 63.2 Image from 'A rehearsal for a Reunion (with the Father of Pottery) by Simon Fujiwara, 2011–12/Photography © Tate 2012 and Simon Fujiwara.

admiring pots *in situ*. The catalogue images which reproduce past installations referencing Japanese interiors are plainly constructs which play on the real and the distant.

We must therefore test the authenticity of our own reactions when, like 'Father' in the performance (Figure 63.2), the reality dawns on us that it may actually have been a real Leach tea set that was actually smashed up in the performance. We might hope that it may have been reproduction, since it would be such a vandalistic act to attack a real one. Or perhaps we hope it may indeed have been a real one, since that would affirm our own complex of struggles with this father figure.

We also imagine the artist, now in his studio in Berlin, looking back at his younger self, recalling his youth by looking at old photos in books of Tate exhibitions, or finding old posters of Hepworth and Heron in amongst other teenage ephemera. Given the importance of the erotic in his work, was the gallery gendered and eroticized for him? Did it form a nexus of power and authority *vis a vis* his imagined future, or did it offer a model of escape?

Fujiwara's audience - St Ives resident, occasional tourist and penitent acolyte alike – will divide. There will be long time residents who may remember Fujiwara as a boy. There will be those who have moved to live in St Ives in its boom era and know nothing of the pre-Tate town, and of contention around the presence of a figure such as Bernard Leach, and indeed the Gallery itself. There will be others coming as first time visitors anxious to get the basics about this celebrated fragment of art and craft history, wondering where this fits in.

There will be, amongst these different audiences, some who are today part of a nostalgic or historicized vision that Tate, the Hepworth Museum, the renovated Leach Pottery all reconstruct for visitors in search of the 'real' St Ives experience. In contrast, meanwhile, there will be the critically engaged, anxious to know what the dialogue between artist, venue and community is renegotiating on this occasion.

Fujiwara knows that all these potential prior readings on the part of audiences depend on a perception of authority. His own childhood is itself offered as carrying authority – I am actually from this town, and have personal testimony to offer. The show can therefore be read as distinct narratives and symbolisations across these audiences, adopting a certain authority in which ever discourse they require.

In this way it represented a powerful adjunct to the discourse of artists' interventions in and responses to Museums. Most of the projects described in such a category of practice gain their identity from being an interaction with a collection. They may also form a dialogue with architecture and setting. They certainly play with the way Museum buildings become ciphers for authority in the play between those two forms. On some

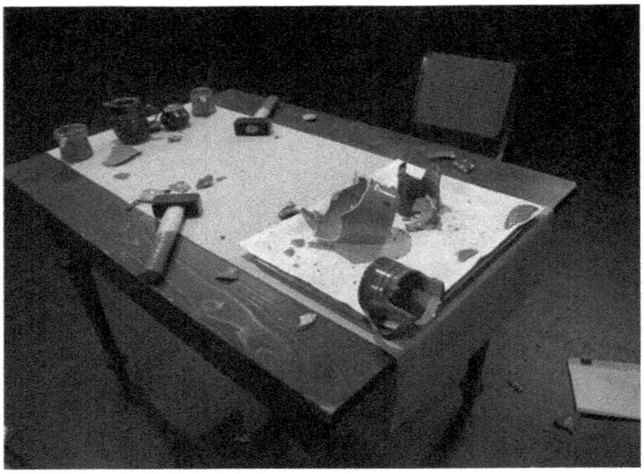

Figure 63.3 Image from 'A rehearsal for a Reunion (with the Father of Pottery)' by Simon Fujiwara, 2011-12/Photography © Tate 2012 and Simon Fujiwara.

occasions, they have invoked the collective memory shared between Museum and audience of the unique identity grounded in the history which both Museum and collection reflect.

Fujiwara's project takes a fresh step in this discourse by embracing the collective memory and the different discourses surrounding the entire programme of the Gallery. He sifts examples of visiting objects from the collection, and plays with the architecture. He references past exhibitions and projects. He makes allusions to marketing imagery used in the early life of the gallery to establish awareness, and to themes current in the debate about what constituted its identity and purpose.

Leach therefore also possesses a multi-faceted identity within Fujiwara's work. He is the father of the craft tradition which, we now take as 'read' in the discourse, he played a large part in creating. The building blocks of Leach's narratice are the imagery of Fujiwara's installation: the marriage of East and West; the renewal of the vernacular craft practice; the enshrining of tradition in the modern. He is the father to the community, a senior figure, of the same generation as Hepworth, the female opposite, who was apparently (in Leach's exegesis at least) pursuing the separate path of high public art.

By reversing the gendering of Fujiwara's parentage – the male father from the east, returning to the east, and leaving the female in Cornwall – Leach the father begets Fujiwara *pere* the son. The father played by the actor in the work, shocked by the vandalism of the pots which "is necessary", neverthless becomes a willing, aware player in the drama (Figure 63.3).

There is also a metaphor of acceptance and rejection going on. What remains of the drama played out on stage and on screen? We are offered the contemporary replication and reproduction as remaining whole, not the original. The new vernacular of the electric kettle and tea bags replace the invented tradition of Leach's adoption of the bowls and vessels of the tea ceremony, as Fujiwara breaks from all three fathers (ur father, real father, role playing father) and they move aside.

Long term local residents visiting his show may recall – and indeed be part of - a social dynamic that might began in the period before and of the first few years of Tate St Ives was the local community's adoption – or not – of the Gallery, and how that operated for different groups within it. One memory will be of a kind of anti-gallery sentiment that mapped class, education, the perception of the visual arts and crafts at a moment just before projects like Tate St Ives itself and the reorganization of the Tate Gallery in London.

The development of Tate St Ives' local education programme at this time, in which the young Fujiwara was indeed a participant, might recall the danger of using historicised or anecdotal recall of the artists and the community. Many artists, then recently deceased or nearing the end of their lives, might either be recalled negatively, or indeed till alive and active in the community – as was the case with artists as different as Patrick Heron or Janet Leach, working as they were in their own studios in the town at the time Tate St Ives opened.

The very immediacy of specific associations living on in the community at that time meant that the allure or negativity of "being an artist" would be loaded with personal associations. Fujiwara, for instance, describes how as a schoolchild he was reminded of Barbara Hepworth's death as an example of the dangers of smoking – and, by implication, not being told about her standing as an artist.

The other contemporary items in the installation offer a different example of the specificity of thinking required about the generic nature of community memory, and its sublimation in reinterpreting that for today's new visitor. We might link the gay politics made vivid and immanent elsewhere in Fujiwara's show to the foregrounding by him of the biography of Leach by the late Emmanuel Cooper: literally an object of display.

This careful placing of Cooper's book, in the perceptions of some visitors, referenced Cooper's own valuable role in the gay community in London and Britain. This was something to which, in his lifetime and at Cooper's death, many in Cornwall showed respect alongside that shown to his work on the documenting of the working ceramics community, and of his study of Leach's life and work.

Such specificities drawn from past shared memory are unavailable to the new audiences for Tate St Ives and the Leach Pottery –as is any anecdotal background for any exhibition.

'A rehearsal for a Reunion (with the Father of Pottery)', meanwhile, has been shown outside the UK in different configurations and contexts, before and after its Tate St Ives showing. We might reconsider the title if seeing the work at, say the Kwangiu Biennale. Who is the reunion with? It is only a rehearsal we are watching – it might never actually happen.

Beyond St Ives, one speculates, the iconography of the 'broken pot' might be foregrounded over the specific location of St Ives.[2] It is important to note, however, that this iconography does not feel immediate for the artist. Whether contemporary makers and ceramic artists who see their careers as positioned within the discourse dominated by and reactive to Leach might feel affronted by Simon Fujiwara's appropriation of it, is beside the point, since his autobiographical claim to his St Ives upbringing allows him to turn the iconography around that very issue. Imagine, he seems to be saying in some moments, growing up in a town dominated by received ideas about art and craft.

To conclude, though Fujiwara rebuilds the museum display, he also rebuilds the ways in which the museum display might prompt associations by its different audiences. And though he addresses a mainstream narrative in ceramic history, he does so from an explicitly autobiographical position which becomes for audiences a point of entry to many shared meanings.

'A rehearsal for a Reunion (with the Father of Pottery)', uses at its core not the idea of a museum display per se, but a notion of value which resides in a canon created by a narrative of 'otherness', dependent on a complex relationship between a community in Britain and a community in Japan. Simon Fuijwara himself is both an individual whose personal circumstance mirrors this communal relationship, and an artist who then transforms his individual circumstance into a rich discourse for a museum project.

In these respects 'A rehearsal for a Reunion (with the Father of Pottery)' is different from many so-called 'interventions' in museums. It takes not a specific fixed display, but a generic curatorial position as its reference point. The order being challenged is not so much the order represented in any fixed way by a museum or a canon, but a set of assumptions about an underlying history and reference set. It shifts the artist's relationship to the audience as a co-curator, taking the audience's part and suggesting that the artist and audience share questions and insights that are dramatized around the body of work, the body of ideas, and the body of apparently external contingent details which turn out to be central – and are having fun with it, too.

All illustrations: courtesy of Tate, for Tate St Ives *Simon Fujiwara: Since 1982* 18 January – 7 May 2012, and © Simon Fujiwara

Notes

1. The author, Michael Tooby, was the first curator of Tate St Ives and, therefore, the author of the displays that Fujiwara was responding to.
2. The iconography of the broken vessel is another line of enquiry that might usefully be developed when considering this work. From Gainsborough's "fancy pictures" to Ai Wei Wei's 'Dropping a Hang Dynasty Urn', physical, moral and ethical integrity has been embodied – or demonstrated as brittle – in the image of the broken or cracked vase. This iconography persists in contemporary practice. The author has, for example, recently described the use of a dropped cup in 'Fragments' and related works by David Cushway, in Tooby, M.: *'Order and disorder: Some relationships between ceramics, sculpture and museum taxonomies' in the online journal 'Interpreting Ceramics', Cardiff Metropolitan University, Issue 14, 2012.*

Printed with permission of the author.

64
WHY CLAY?
James Beighton and Emily Hesse

An interview with James Beighton by Emily Hesse

EH: You are currently a curator, writer and AHRC funded PhD researcher. Is it fair to say that your work in the field of ceramics is the area for which you are most well known?

JB: Yes I think that's probably fair.

EH: So what created your initial interest in ceramics?

JB: In the past I have talked fondly about encountering a Walter Keeler teapot for the first time and the discussions that I would have with the collectors of studio ceramics. This was the moment I became interested in studio ceramics, perhaps, became aware that it was a thing, rather than simply the fact that some people made pots, some people even made money out of making pots. I am becoming more interested in clay on a phenomenological level, a level that takes onboard studio ceramics, but encompasses far more than that. Should we exclude the ceramic model of a witch I made at primary school; the teapot and mugs bought from a local potter by my parents when I was a child and never used; the porcelain dolls that my mother used to make in the 1980s during the hobby craft rage? We use examples such as this to advocate for the value of clay, to justify it as a choice of material for artists, to explain its enduring appeal and current trendiness in the art market. It would seem disingenuous therefore for me not to also acknowledge all those earlier moments when clay made an impression on me. Trivial moments perhaps, moments that we could all drag up from the back of our memories – that's the point.

Keeler's teapot was important in my thinking about clay as a curatorial interest. I became interested in thinking about what clay could say when it was taken out of the realms of the everyday and put within a gallery space – not a shop, not a museum: the purpose of presenting it was not (at least not primarily) about selling it, nor were you presenting a social history of the object – What languages was the object able to speak? Did it bring elements of the everyday along with it? Was it divorced from such discussions as a result? How readily accepted would it be by those people – gallery visitors – who looked at the material and what would they accept it as?

EH: The title of this chapter, 'Museum, site and display', suggests that the role of ceramics is altering in some way. Do you agree that this is so and could you state the reasoning behind your answer?

JB: We have to be cautious of using phrases like paradigm.[1] It's a very popular phrase within the humanities these days and one I think is somewhat overused. The term originates within scientific discourse, where it means a way of working that prohibits any other conceivable way of working, any other truth outside that which the paradigm itself advocates. I can't see that this applies with ceramics. I don't think it is fair to say that the way ceramics are presented in museums presents a truth that denies other possibilities. What we are looking at is something more akin to a trope.

Source: © James Beighton and Emily Hesse / AHRC Heritage Consortium, Teesside University.

That said, I do think there is a shift in the way that ceramicists are working in relation to the museum. This has been the subject of one of the major research projects of the last five years, undertaken by the University of Westminster, *Ceramics in the Expanded Field: Behind the Scenes at the Museum.* The project looked at the idea of museum intervention and a tendency on the part of ceramicists to intervene within museum collections. We are probably quite familiar with the idea of museum intervention by fine artists, a strategy with several decades of history: Miranda Stearn for example provides a helpful analysis of artist's interventions in museums, starting with Hans Haacke in the 1970s.[2]

The fact that there is already such a history of museum intervention in fine art presents some problems as it re-enforces the tendency to look at ceramics as playing catch up with fine art; adopting the tropes of fine art only twenty years or so after fine art has adopted them. I wonder what in particular ceramics has to say as a material that is distinct, that allows it to say something different through museum interpretations than any other material. Now one of those things might be that the material is so ubiquitous, the material surrounds us, it makes up so much of the earth, it is the bricks build the houses we live in, it is the teacups on our tables and the plates we eat our dinner off. But is this enough to suggest that ceramics has a particular characteristic that allows it to engage in museum interventions? Are those artists that are using ceramics in museum interventions really doing something very different to what fine artists were doing when they too were looking at museum interventions? This idea of intervening within the totalizing narrative of the museum collection is interesting in its way, but something else has happened of course with museum collections between the time of artists intervening and the current research around ceramicists intervening and that is that museums themselves are about disrupting these totalizing statements in their collection.

I recently have authored a paper to be delivered at the Gyeonggi International Ceramics Biennial in Korea, which questions this relationship between history and ceramics. It takes as a starting point the museum intervention but then I have wanted to move through to something which I find much more interesting, which is based upon Hal Foster's notion of the archive.[3] What Hal Foster talks about seems to be much more interesting for ceramics because he talks about the way that artists have tended to embrace the overlooked traces of the past and have accumulated them to present a new story, not that is about disrupting a narrative but that rather is about presenting something purely imaginative, a future possibility. That seems to me to be something that ceramics both is engaging with now and is particularly well equipped to engage with. The case in point I used for that work was Neil Brownsword's *Salvage Series* (Figure 64.1), where he takes the industrial residue of the ceramics industry and represents them as an archeological find. But also something that presents a new possibility, a new future. This is something that I see in your own work, where you take, likewise, overlooked material, in particularly locally dug unfired and more recently fired clay and the use of bricks. The bricks found on beaches that were washed up from Victorian towns that were pulled down to be replaced by industry. The way you combine those materials does not present a maudlin reflection of the past, not as a declinist narrative of how our historical past was a halcyon time and everything has gone wrong since then, but rather an imagination of another possibility. It may be a future that doesn't come to pass, but it allows a glimpse of that future.

With artists working in that particular way, as Brownsword, as yourself, as people like Clare Twomey does, you see a case being made for why ceramics might be a particularly relevant material. Precisely because of its ubiquity. So much of the lost and overlooked traces of the past are constructed from ceramics.

EH: You mentioned how ceramicists have interacted with the museum, but what of the actual museum workings itself: mima (Middlesbrough Institute of Modern Art) is primarily a 'modern art' gallery, it has a collection but also during the time you worked there, had a ceramics remit. mima is also part of the Plus Tate network, along with the Baltic, Gateshead, Turner Contemporary, Nottingham Contemporary, Grizedale Arts and so on. As a curator operating

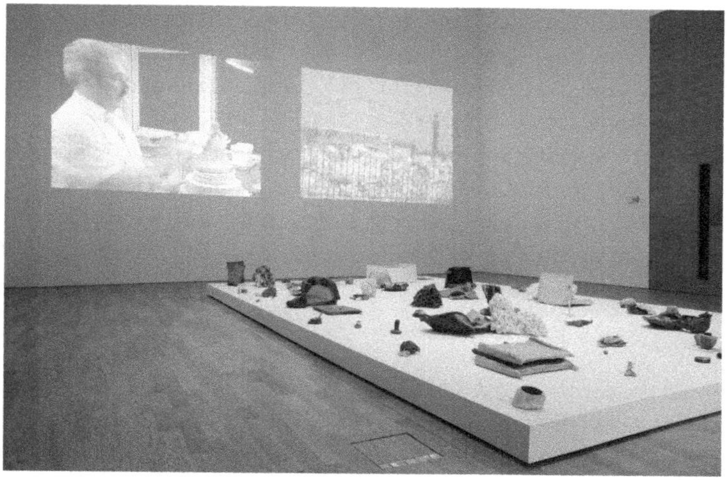

Figure 64.1 Installation image of Neil Brownsword Salvage Series, 2005, in *Possibilities and Losses* MIMA, photo MIMA (Middlesborough Institute of Modern Art).

within this network, was it important to adopt some of Tate's curatorial strategies? For example, their mixing up of 'isms' within shows, their famous juxtapositions, a Monet shown alongside a Pollock. Was this a strategy that you applied when showing ceramics?

JB: It opens up other possibilities for presenting ceramics certainly and it was a strategy that I was aware of. It was also a strategy that Tate had come under particularly harsh criticism for adopting. A critique that still hasn't gone away, especially from the traditionalist reviewer who liked to think that art should be told within the particular linearity of its history. Of course that linearity of history does have a habit of excluding things. It is adept at telling one particular story. One that ignores those works that don't quite fit within the single, comfortable truth: works by women for example, non-western works, works by amateurs, perhaps works in clay.

One of the differences between the opportunities that Tate had and institutions like mima had was the fixity of their collection displays. Collection displays at Tate are major projects, which change slowly and require considerable curatorial resources to achieve. Collection shows at mima were always intended to be much faster paced affairs. They were mingled in with the temporary exhibitions, there was not a permanent collection gallery and so all exhibitions in effect were treated the same. With this came the opportunity and indeed responsibility to find new stories that we could tell with the collection. Some of these stories might be unconventional, ones that perhaps would upset people if shown over a prolonged period of time, but which when presented in a temporary exhibition on for maybe three months, allowed much greater freedom. That would allow us to show for example; Shoji Hamada alongside Alan Green, based upon the particular relationships that both artists had to the material they used; in Green's case the mixing of his own pigment, in Hamada's case the mixing of his own glaze ingredients and digging of his own clay. That would allow us to show Andy Goldsworthy alongside Hamada or Bernard Leach: In particular, one of Goldsworthy's *Torn Pebbles*, a stone that had been fired in a kiln creating cracks and fissures over which the artist had no control. It functioned as an object of sculpture, but also spoke as a piece of ceramics. We were able to present a Julian Stair alongside a drawing by Antony Gormley, where both works showed clear conceptual concerns, both looking at ideas around the containment of the human figure and the oppressive forces that were asserted upon the figure. To do that within a longer standing permanent display would have run the risk of failing to do justice to other, perhaps more important stories. The role that Leach and Hamada had played within the studio ceramics tradition, the role that Goldsworthy and Gormley had played within the post-minimalist sculpture tradition in this country for example.

So awareness of the opportunities that that changing approach that Tate had adopted, as well as the dangers and the risks that you could fall into with that approach were certainly apparent. Underpinning that though, as I have already mentioned, was a questioning of what voices a museum can and should adopt. It's something that has become very important within museum studies during the last 20-30 years or so. That is why I feel that understanding the role of ceramics within the museum now has to be placed alongside shifts in museological thinking.

EH: So you mentioned the showing of Andy Goldsworthy's *Torn Pebble* (1984), alongside a work by Bernard Leach, now not to drag up the old art craft debate, but Andy Goldsworthy is obviously what you would consider a fine artist working in clay. Do you feel the ceramic world feels a hostility to what are defined as, 'fine artists working in clay'?

JB: You could almost go so far as to say that it is the ceramics world's dirty secret. It is something it is obsessed with and yet deeply hostile to. There can be hostility both towards those artists who are working in the fine art field but who happen to use ceramics as well as those artists who have come from ceramics backgrounds but who come to be regarded as fine artists. The level of hostility that you hear in studio ceramics towards some artists who have achieved success in the wider art world, is something that I personally find quite disappointing. Edmund de Waal talked about it in a radio interview that he gave in 2005 on BBC radio 3 with John Tulsa where he described receiving hate mail from other potters.

Notwithstanding this, it seems that whatever new model of research or new way of talking about ceramics arises, at the heart of it, once you strip the layers back, you are left with the debate about the relationship between fine art and craft. It's not that that debate is resurfacing, it's simply to say that that debate never seems to have gone away. In *Material Culture* (2008, Figure 64.2) I presented Hamada and Leach together with Goldsworthy or Stair with Gormley, not because I wanted to introduce a debate necessarily about those two categories but because firstly I wanted to show a similarity between their thinking. I was aware that Goldsworthy and Hamada were adopting similar approaches. I was also aware that the piece by Hamada that I was showing dated from 1921 and the piece by Goldsworthy dated from 1984 and there was something about the turning of its head of the laggardly relationship that I have already mentioned. But over and above that I wanted to show similarity. I wanted to show my perspective, that what we are looking at is quite simply art; this is a perspective informed by how audiences related to what was shown at mima. The idea of craft is very important to me, but I have long since questioned whether it should exist as a category in its own right. Does craft make sense as a term sitting alongside sculpture, installation, video, photography, painting or drawing? I don't think it does. I think it makes sense as a description of an approach to working and that description is as relevant to somebody working in any of those other categories that I have just mentioned. It just so happens that it has become customarily associated with a collection of materials, a collection of media. And that those media are talked about, grouped together, as craft.

Ceramics can be art, but isn't necessarily always art. When we talk about the category of craft and when the institutions are established with a specific remit to look at craft, there is a tendency to merge together anyone with a dedicated practice in a particular discipline. This can elide over the massive differences between two different artists working in the same material. Is it really fair to either, Neil Brownsword or Richard

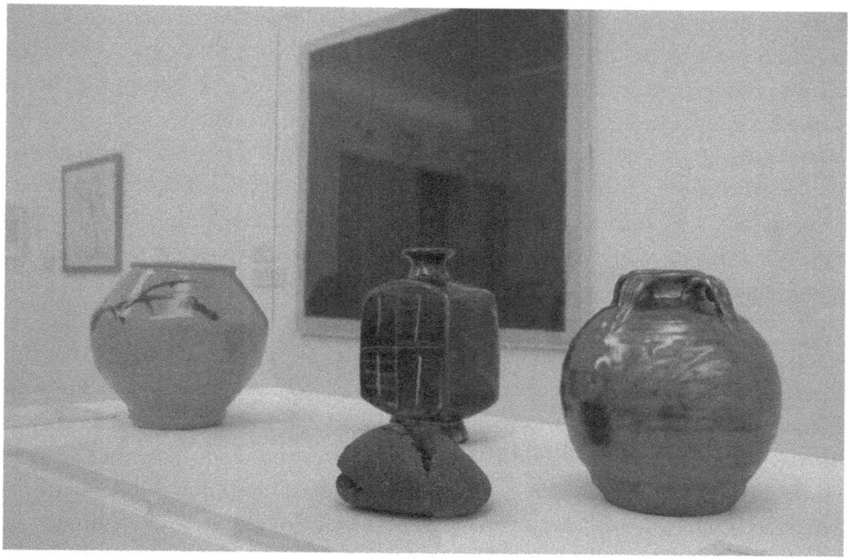

Figure 64.2 Installation image from Material Culture, 2008, (Leach & Hamada), photo MIMA (Middlesbrough Institute of Modern Art)

Batterham for example, to talk about their work in parallel? Is doing so not likely to undermine the sincerity and the conviction with which Batterham has developed his range of forms and run the risk of making his practice (and that of many others) seem anachronistic? I have a deep respect for what potters like Batterham achieve: I don't think I've met anyone yet who doesn't. It can also lead to some very poor work being made under the tag of conceptualism. If you use clay to make work that is about sculpture, performance, video and so on then you should expect it to be judged alongside any other work made in that way, irrespective of material and not retreat back into the discipline of ceramics. Perhaps it is this tendency to focus on the material rather than the message which causes some of the hostility, some of the jealousy you can witness. I feel that this hostility comes from a point of hypocrisy at the end of the day, but hypocrisy is a trait that we all exhibit sometimes, so perhaps we mustn't be too harsh on those who are practicing it.

EH: It's almost as though they have just caught up with Modernism. They need something to rebel against.

JB: I think the studio ceramics tradition has been rebelling against Modernism since it realized that it was a Modernist movement to start with and no longer wanted to be it.

EH: You moved initially to the North East to work as curator of craft at the Cleveland Crafts Centre in 2002. You then moved on to become Curator at Middlesbrough Institute of Modern Art when it opened in 2007, then latterly, Senior Curator. Your first major ceramics show at mima was Edmund de Waal's first UK museum solo exhibition in collaboration with Kettle's Yard in 2007. What was it that you saw in de Waal's work that led to this show?

JB: I think it's worth pointing out that this was also mima's first solo show. First solo show by any artist, so that is quite a strong statement of direction that was being made by mima at the time as an art gallery that was positioning itself within a network of other fine art galleries that had opened up at similar times: Baltic, the New Art Gallery in Walsall, for example. It took some persuasion to get that exhibition on the cards, but once the argument had been won there was nonetheless a willingness to programme a ceramics exhibition as mima's first major solo show. My discussion with de Waal started in relation to a work in the gallery's collection, a small espresso cup. As he talked more fully about his work and about the direction his work was taking him in it became apparent that he was offering something that would suit particularly mima's spaces. It was at the time when he was moving on from making the individual vessels to making the 'cargo series' of vessels and latterly to the larger scale sculptures. He spoke enthusiastically about the way that ceramics could relate to architecture, or comment upon it. I thought as a new gallery that had just been built, where we knew that many visitors were still coming as much to look at the building as they were what was in it, that set up a very interesting dialogue.

There was another factor, which I'm still not sure I can articulate more intelligently than to describe it as a hunch, intuition, if you prefer, which suggested that it might be the right time to do a show like that. De Waal had just been made a professor at Westminster University in 2004, the year I started talking to him. He was also in discussions with Kettle's Yard about a show there, which ultimately became the two venue touring show that I did for MIMA. The Arts Council had been soliciting him to develop a mid career retrospective of his work, and he had been in the Jerwood ceramics prize, so a lot of things were coming together. Other things hadn't happened yet: I remember whilst installing the exhibition itself, having discussions with him and with his studio manager at the time about a little book which he was planning to write which was going to be a fairly straightforward memoir of his family, which turned out to be a best seller.

EH: Your third ceramics show at mima was Possibilities and Losses in 2009, co-curated with ceramicist Clare Twomey and supported by the Crafts Council. What was your vision for this show?

JB: It was based around wanting to extend the dialogue that had been possible with the two previous solo shows (mima had produced a solo show with Anders Ruhwald in 2008). Solo shows present something of a dialogue between the artist and the curator inevitably, but ultimately it is the artist's vision that comes through supported by the curator. It doesn't necessarily give you the scope for the curator to make the assessment of a state of play in a particular field. That was one thing that was motivating me. I wanted to move beyond the solo presentation and look at what could be said about a particular moment in the making of ceramics. It also came about through conversations, as so many of the best ideas do, in this case a conversation with Clare Twomey. She started talking about her area of research, she had been recently appointed research fellow at Westminster University and she was looking at a concept called, 'Installation, Clay and Crafts.' The research was trying to understand how people working with ceramics had started to work on a larger scale, embracing ideas around the installation more fully and moving on from the sculptural ceramics tradition that perhaps typified so much new practice in the 1960s through to the 1980s. It also questioned in what ways, if any, this work could still be considered craft. If ceramicists were adopting the strategies of fine art, if they were presenting it in fine art galleries, was it not simply *de facto* fine art?

So that was one of the questions that I was interested in answering as well. Again, that took a lot of persuasion with the rest of the curatorial team. They felt that if it was artists using fine artists' strategies and simply employing ceramics as a material, then why shouldn't the fine art curator deliver that exhibition? It actually took a long time to get that show on the table. The team had to change before it could be realized.

EH: This is probably your most talked about ceramics show, why do you think this is?

JB: I don't think a show quite like that had been seen on that scale in this country up to that point. It built upon shows like *Spectacular Craft* at the Craft's Council, which certainly showed artists working on a very large scale. But I think there was a clarity to *Possibilities and Losses* that I still hold to be its success. This was built around a very simple principle that we adopted of four galleries and four artists. We had considered doing a survey show, perhaps including twelve artists, really trying to get to grips with what the state of the field was. But felt that with the space we had available, with the budget we had available, it wasn't really going to be possible to do justice to that.

So we moved back to a simple strategy, four rooms four artists that would simply look at four possible ways of working. What grew from that was a real coherence between the four. I won't say that we hadn't foreseen this, because of course we had chosen those four works knowingly but they started to have a different dialogue to just the one we had initially expected them to have. Our initial thinking around the title, *Possibilities and Losses*, was that it was a reflection on the state of a practice in change. A state of change in ceramics. This question of how could you capture something of the excitement that seems to be apparent in contemporary ceramic practice but how also could you capture some of the loss that was inherent in that. The fact that something that many, myself included, hold very dear, the studio ceramics tradition, was being challenged to such an extent to where it perhaps became unlikely that artists would be attracted to working in that particular way anymore. That potential loss was something that I felt.

The show started off as an idea about the position of craft in this moment of change. In the end, the story of change it told was much more clearly about a society than simply a practice: it told stories of towns and industries re-inventing themselves and imagined future possibilities for those societies. There was a narrative running through the show that our audiences really responded to, both locally and nationally. It's a show that gained a huge amount of positive comments from people across the board, both from people that were specialists in ceramics and people that were fine artists. Of course it remains one of the mima shows that is most widely talked about in the ceramics field.

EH: There are few ceramic departments left in universities in the UK. Do you think this is caused by a lack of integration with other disciplines and courses, such as fine art? Do you think ceramics will have to integrate or die?

JB: I haven't worked in education, so may not be best qualified to answer this. I can only speak from the outside looking in. I think it is caused by economic reality, by the fact that ceramics is a very expensive course to run. It's caused by a questioning of how employable or indeed transferable the specific skills that a ceramics undergrad course would teach are valid to other industries. What skills ceramics offer that are better than other courses. It's caused by another economic reality, the decline in the ceramic industry which therefore means there are fewer jobs with those specific ceramic skills than there past were previously.

One thing that we are seeing is at the same time ceramic departments are closing down and selling off their wheels and kilns, certain fine art departments are buying kilns and wheels, to reflect the demand that fine art students are placing on the ability and skills to work with the material. This isn't a new thing by any means. Bernard Leach would often talk of the art students who would come to his pottery seeking further training in ceramics. I'm not entirely sure that the demise of ceramic courses is entirely unhealthy for the future of ceramics. I do believe that the educational segregation that we have seen in this country has contributed to the segregation of the medium as a craft discipline, along with other medium specific courses. We are already at a stage where graduates are coming through who cannot have had access to dedicated ceramics training.

It will be interesting to see what impact that's going to have upon the scope of those artists thinking and the materials they feel able to work in.

EH: Based around that discussion of ceramic education in universities in this country (UK) at the present time, what advice would you give to those students and early career artists or ceramicists trying to fit into the field of ceramics as it currently exists?

JB: Perhaps don't take my advice, look for your own solutions. I hope that these upcoming artists find their own way because I think this is what will set them out as an artist. You are not going to learn how to be an artist by simply going to university. I studied English literature at university, that didn't teach me how to be a writer. It certainly didn't teach me how to be a curator. It's what inquisitiveness artists bring to their time at university that will set them apart. How much they are willing and able to look at what is being made around them, how much they are willing to read what others have said, how much they are willing to look at other disciplines and embrace other ways of thinking. Not just reflect back on the history of ceramics but to think about politics, think about philosophy, think about film and music, think about the sciences and the humanities, think about everyday life. How they reflect the ability to speak in a way that will mean something to a visitor of an exhibition, that will allow that visitor to open up a freedom of thought about a new possibility for their own lives. It's things like that that set a good artist over and above someone who is simply making work because they have been trained in that way. Go out, talk to people, look at what's going on around you and care.

EH: You are currently a student yourself, researching a history PhD on the provision and reception of visual arts in post-industrial towns. Why history?

JB: I wanted to understand a question that I had encountered throughout my career as a curator, the reasons why people have valued the visual arts, especially outside the major metropolises. As a curator it was difficult to step outside the role of advocate and you would tend to select the evidence that supported your viewpoint on the value of art, ignoring others. Using the methods of a historian you are able to adopt a more impartial stance: it doesn't matter to you personally what the results are and if the evidence suggests that on balance people really don't value art at all, then that is also a valid outcome. Increasingly the discipline of history is seeking to uncover previously untold stories. With a turn from the political to the cultural, historians are investigating broader aspects of people's lives. In order to tell these stories, new methods are being employed, including questioning what objects can reveal about the people who used them. Curiously, this has brought me back full circle to ceramics as I investigate the two large potteries in Middlesbrough to understand what they can reveal about the social history of the town. I seem to be spending more time thinking about clay now than ever.

EH: Why clay?

JB: Why not?

Notes

1. An earlier working title for the chapter heading included the term 'a changing paradigm'.
2. Stearne, M. (2013), 'Remaking utopia in the museum: artists as curators', *Museological Review*, (17): pp. 36–47.
3. Foster, H. (2004), 'An Archival Impulse', *October*, (110): pp. 3–22.

Printed with permission of the authors.

65

CIVIC CERAMICS: SHIFTING THE CENTRE OF MEANING

Natasha Mayo and Melania Warwick

The title 'Civic Ceramics' refers to a growing number of practices that concertedly 'shift the center of meaning' from the artwork itself, to the activity of a viewer's interaction, investment and sense of ownership over it. From work that explores the thematic overlaps in ceramics knowledge and studio skill base with its use in society, to practitioners employing ceramic practice as part of direct social engagement, the mapping of coordinates between 'civic' and 'ceramics' enables clear identification of a growing and increasingly innovative movement.

This essay attempts to uncover some of the approaches that are pushing ceramics to the forefront of participatory engagement. It also seeks to explore how we might better account for these emergent and diverse practices that are reawakening the discipline's particular resonance as a politically and culturally responsive material.

Background

At a glance, it can appear that ceramic practice arose fundamentally in response to the need of society and *then* repositioned its profound material sensibility, technical knowledge and ergonomic concerns within more philosophical debate. In following this trajectory, any backward glance can be seen as a threat to what Jorunn Veiteberg describes as the 'visibility' of craft.[1]

The discipline was not however theoretically bereft before this point of departure. Historical reticence or 'silence' within the wider field of craft simply caused many of its concerns to be overlooked.[2] The correlation between ceramics and society provides perhaps one of the field's most integral and authentic debates.

The correlation of 'Civic' and 'Ceramics' equips us with both a framework for interpretation and a mode of practice for examining, at a more nuanced level, the boundaries of the 'intervening space' between the discipline and the community. More than this, it can enable us to identify practices that are creating a virtue of this previously opaque area, by pulling into view the unusual or simply forgotten connections that lie between the community and traditional and contemporary ceramic practices.

In fact, once an investigation of ceramics' connection to a community is undertaken, any previous sense of their separation can become extremely difficult to maintain; from hair dressers' straighteners to spark plug insulators, from catalysts to sensors, ceramics can be found almost everywhere you look and sometimes where you can't. This connectivity persists in all manifestations of studio ceramics to a greater or lesser degree, offering potential dialogue to expand or deepen any imposition we might make upon its form.

It is not surprising therefore, that many high profile, international 'gallery' artist's such as Clare Twomey, Stephen Dixon and David Cushway are developing respected practices engaging with dialogue that

Source: © Natasha Mayo and Melania Warwick

reconnects ceramics with the community that shaped it. Participatory art is no-longer relegated to the margins. As Hal Foster states: 'in the social expanse of everyday life, the possibilities for participatory art are endless'.[3]

Definition of terms

Before continuing, perhaps we need to more clearly define our terms when speaking of 'participation' in art. A common distinction is drawn between 'Participatory Art Projects', and 'Participatory Art' (per se). This distinction usually separates participation in contemporary art practices – such as events-based practice at biennales or contemporary gallery commissions, with social engagement-based projects – such as those working within public, community or socio-urban contexts, often sponsored by local government.[4]

Such distinction fuels the art as 'social therapy' versus 'authentic art' argument, the assumption that Participatory Practice is unable to withstand the critical evaluation of 'art world' critics, specifically because its value is lodged in the interaction between participants (and whatever products or benefits that brings) as opposed to the artwork itself.[5] This is where the relationship between the artwork and its 'point of meaning' has been historically problematic.[6]

Whilst it is well understood that the artistic and cultural life of a society is heralded as a 'barometer of its health' the impact of art that speaks directly to or with society is often met with scepticism. This is in part due to the problem of measuring its transformative capacity; whilst elements of an 'aesthetic encounter' are historically and socially determined, it would be impossible to establish with any certainty the root cause. This in turn, has resulted in methods of critiquing such practice that rarely reflect the complexity of its 'transformative rhetoric' and instead fall back onto more basic arguments.

So what method of analysis should we apply to artists such as Twomey, Dixon and Cushway without omitting or trivializing the strident participatory aspect of their art? The nature of participation, as Kester suggests requires 'new ways of thinking'.[7]

A more progressive approach to understanding the rise in participatory practice in the field of ceramics would be perhaps to question how these practices redefine or transform our understanding of aesthetic experience. And how do they challenge preconceived notions of the object of art?

Case studies

Let us examine dynamic examples provided by Keith Harrison and AJ Stockwell, both of whom engage with dialogue created by the overlap between studio and society. In 'Michael Hamilton', Harrison courts the absurdity that can be found in the life/art juxtaposition, appropriating domestic electrical systems and portable appliances to conduct live firings of Egyptian paste in a living room! This intervening space is also inhabited by Stockwell in 'Bad Teeth' (Figure 65.1) exploring replicated processes in conservation and dentistry. Stockwell creates video of dental paste being used to conserve a porcelain cup and runs it concurrently with the dialogue of a patient undergoing a procedure in a dentist chair.

The significance of these examples for contemporary ceramics debate is two fold: 1) the artists necessarily establish a thorough appreciation of the nature of both contexts in order to succeed in their assimilation of them, 2) the perimeters of ceramics vocabulary was necessarily stretched through its engagement with another field. For example, Stockwell's recognition of the connectivity between use of porcelain paste in conservation and dentistry enabled a far wider exploration, as well as consolidation of her 'expertise' in ceramics process.

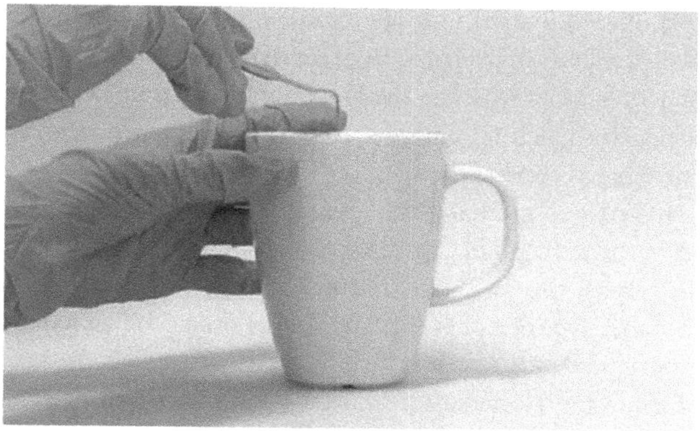

Figure 65.1 Video still Bad Teeth, 2015, © AJ Stockwell.

The same is true of Harrison's exploration of the sensory experience of firing when set in relation to the domestic sphere.

These artists are a new breed of ceramicists, with a plurality of skill base that extends far beyond their own studio in order to facilitate movement between personal and wider social concerns. Such artists are in fact offering living examples of a generative approach to ceramics practice, with projects necessarily responding to context and need as well as retaining concern with contemporary ceramics debate. The benefits for the ceramicist are multifold, extending their engagement with their social and physical environment and mapping previously unchartered areas of knowledge.

Harrison and Stockwell's respective practice undoubtedly widens our appreciation of the remit of ceramics but are we missing something richer contained within these examples by simply accounting for them through conventional methodology? My account tells us very little about the complexities and contradictions of the actual performance of the work. I have simply acknowledged the role of the artist in focusing our attention on certain hidden relationships or correlations in our routine lives so as to challenge our normative assumptions. The actual response of the viewer may in fact bear little or no resemblance to this schema. My conventional critique has of course abstracted the practice from its participatory element.

If participatory and collaborative art practices shift the center of meaning from the artwork, object or event, to public interaction or dialogic engagement, we must do the same in accounting for them. This must be the case particularly when dealing with projects in which the viewer or participant has the potential to reshape and transform the work over time.

A fuller account of Harrison's practice would address the actual rather than the hypothetical experience of participants in the project – the actual experience of entering the living room and the emergent awareness of both the familiarity of the firing methods and difference the work offers in regard its contextual and sensorial impact. To be inclusive of its participatory element would require me to be more attentive to 'agency and affect' – to ways in which the site prompts particular response. I would need to be more attentive to my own and other signals through language and utterance, gesture and movement.

In accounting for participatory arts practice Kester demands that the various contributing factors of a project be gathered together in order to understand how their varying proximities impact upon the meaning of the work and its impact on participants. He terms this engagement 'a field-based approach' whereby analysis arises from inhabiting a space for a substantial amount of time, with attention to the social conditions of space, discursive, haptic, and temporal rhythms of the events that take place there.

The assertion is a simple one, that any thorough analysis of art practice that engages with participatory elements, however marginal, demands in itself a level of participatory engagement to review. Here the theorist or critic becomes, in Kester's terms, 'a genuine interlocutor in the unfolding of a given work, rather than a gray (or perhaps more accurately, white) eminence'.[8] Participatory practice requires a far more nuanced understanding of how an artwork is received.

Traditionally art and art theory is monological; analysis deals with the transformation of materials and intent by an artist, received by the perceptual capability of a viewer – both according to a single consciousness. Once this process becomes social, the 'aesthetic' is considered more as a form of knowledge relevant and communicable amongst a collective, or spheres of understanding. Art practice becomes about the social articulation of aesthetic experience.

If we shift the center of meaning further still toward community based practice, we discover more about how appreciation of craft's social, participatory nature might enable us to better critique ceramics practice in more general terms.

In 'Transnational dialogues in contemporary crafts' ceramist Stephen Dixon, along with other researchers from Manchester, worked with the people of Dhal Ni Pol, Ahmedabad, India, to address the decline of traditional Indian craft skills, in jeopardy through globalization and the speed of market development.[9]

The group sought to raise local awareness of the Pol's unique and endangered architectural and cultural heritage. They first documented their everyday rituals, then began to encourage a new daily ritual around a notional 'doorway', resulting in a series of ceramic installations, temporary site-specific artworks, films and events reflective of the particularity of Pols 'social aesthetic'.

This new ritual was intimately connected to the Pol's everyday and at the same time different, allowing objectivity and enabling the inhabitants to witness their own 'social aesthetic identity' emerging before them.[10]

Conclusion

Whilst the center of meaning radically shifts in each example given in this essay, displaying variable dynamics between craft and its particular social community or constituency, each shift uncovers the discernable connectivity of ceramics to society. The Participatory aesthetic can be seen as returning craft to its origin but not merely by engaging with a community, it recognizes the capacity of craft to motivate exchange and cohesion between those who engage with it, both in regard to making and interacting with it.[11]

Far from posing a threat to the academic vantage point of contemporary ceramics, this 'backward glance' in fact offers a potential means by which to articulate the potential of crafts aesthetic as something more powerful than traditional monological practices. The participatory aesthetic - as plural, fluid and open to risk - can offer us a means by which to better appreciate how craft contains forms of knowledge relevant and communicable amongst a collective, as opposed to remaining discrete and singular.

Notes

1. Jorunn Veiteberg *Objects in Transition The Ceramic Art of Kjell Rylander* Ceramics: Art and Perception No. 61, 2005.
2. See Andrew Jackson, 'Against the Autonomy of the Craft Object', in *Obscure Objects of Desire: Reviewing the Crafts in the Twentieth Century*, ed. Tanya Harrod, London, Crafts Council, 1997, pp. 284–291, p. 285. This notion of crafts 'Silence' is understood as referring to the lack of published account of ceramics historical movements and development. This ties in with Veiteberg's reference to crafts 'visibility' and concerns regarding any loss to its contemporary foothold as a now well theorized and published discipline.

3. Foster, Hal. (1996) 'The Artist as Ethnographer', in *The Return of the Real: The Avant-Garde at the End of the Century*, Cambridge: MIT Press.
4. Belfiore and Bennett (2010) The Social Impact of the Arts: An Intellectual History. Pub Palgrave Macmillan.
5. Kester, G. (2013) *The Device Laid Bare: On Some Limitations in Current Art Criticism, e-Flux.*
6. Clare Twomey (2015) Conference Presentation, Consciousness/Conscience, for Fragile? Conference at the National Museum Wales.
7. Kester, G. (2013) ibid.
8. Kester, G. (2013) ibid.
9. Dixon, S. (2010) Conference Presentation, Transnational dialogues in contemporary crafts, for the Applied Arts/Transnational Collaboration conference, M.M.U.
10. It's interesting to note how an aesthetic experience can become individualized and revealed through participatory practices, to the point where it has the potential to be 'owned and unique' as opposed to generalized and diluted as common perception may have it.
11. Irvine, J. The James Irvine Foundation, explores the various progressive stages of Participatory practice as follows: the official start of participatory arts, is referred to by Irving as 'Crowd sourcing' where the audience is involved in choosing or contributing financially to an artistic product - art exhibitions by community artists or theatre based on community stories come under this rubric. The second stage is co-production, and perhaps this incorporates AJ Stockwell if not in final production then in the pooling of knowledge and conceptual development. This stage often involves an exchange of creative energy between an arts organization and its public. Harrison's involvement of the public as both audience and completion of context also finds a position here.

    The third and most participatory stage occurs when audience members substantially take control of the artistic experience. A professional artist may design the experience, but the outcome depends on the participants. Stephen Dixon and Clare Twomey's practice lies here.

Printed with permission of the authors.

66

CERAMICS AS AN ARCHAEOLOGY OF THE CONTEMPORARY PAST

Christopher McHugh

Introduction

This paper will argue that a socially-engaged ceramic practice may have much in common with the aims of current archaeological approaches to investigating the recent or contemporary past. Both endeavours can be regarded as forms of 'creative materialising intervention' in that they may result in the constitution of an otherwise absent material culture, 'thereby expanding the scope of discursive culture' (Buchli and Lucas 2001a, p. 15–17). This will be illustrated by reference to my own practice-based research undertaken between 2010 and 2014 as part of a collaborative doctoral project at the University of Sunderland and Sunderland Museum & Winter Gardens (SMWG). Responding to the museum's collection of nineteenth century Sunderland lustreware pottery, this project sought to engage and reflect the contemporary community of Sunderland through the creation of a series of ceramic art works and museum displays.

In particular, I will discuss two examples of ceramic artworks I made after holding a focus group and reminiscence activity with a group of eleven Wearside-born soldiers from Third Battalion, The Rifles (3 Rifles). Taking the rich military and naval imagery of Sunderland pottery as a precedent, and concentrating on their embodied experiences and commemorative practices, the project invited the participants to discuss how their tour in Afghanistan, as part of Operation Herrick 11 (2009-10), might be remembered in ceramic.

One of the premises of my approach is that ceramic objects have the potential to remedy the widely observed and problematised 'forgetfulness' (e.g. Nora 1989, Connerton 2009) and dematerialisation (e.g. Renfrew 2003) associated with the current age. As enduring forms of 'external symbolic storage' (Renfrew 2003, p. 188), they may act as material conduits through which ephemeral aspects of human-object relations can be disinterred and manifested. As will be discussed, rather than replicating the problematic of modernity by simply moving the responsibility of remembering to monumental sites of forgetfulness, the challenge of such a project is to explore how these 'micro-local sites of memory' (Kidron 2009, p.5) may then go on to become socially constituted as active loci of creative remembrance.

Archaeologies of the contemporary past

According to archaeologists Rodney Harrison and John Schofield (2010, p.7), the increasing use of archaeological approaches to understand the contemporary past is a reaction to communal forgetting caused

Source: Extracted from 'Community in Clay – Towards a Sunderland Pottery for the Twenty-First Century: Approaching Museum Collections and Communities through Creative Ceramics', PhD Dissertation, University of Sunderland with Sunderland Museum and Winter Gardens, March 2015. This research was funded by an AHRC Collaborative Doctoral Award.

by increasingly rapid technological and social change. This means that the 'recent past seems to recede' and become 'obscured at a rate not known before in human history'. These archaeologies, therefore, are motivated by 'a desire to reconcile ourselves with a recent history that moves at such great speed that we feel both remote from it and disoriented by its passage' (ibid., p.8). Victor Buchli and Gavin Lucas (2001a, p.14), early proponents of a socially-engaged archaeology of the recent and contemporary past, have argued that the abundance of material culture in the present leads to an 'excess of information', which can obscure more marginal histories almost as much as a dearth of evidence.

Although there may be a general feeling that documentary evidence and personal experience render archaeology unnecessary for the examination of our own era (Schofield and Johnson 2006, p. 106), archaeologists of these periods hold that there are always aspects of human behaviour which exist 'outside discourse, unconstituted' and which would remain 'inarticulate' without a materialising archaeological practice (Buchli and Lucas 2001a, p. 12–14). Prehistorian Colin Renfrew (2003, p. 188–189) has warned that the increasing digital expression of symbolic aspects of material culture is resulting in the gradual 'dematerialization of the real world', meaning a future 'archaeology of mind' may be difficult. This 'flood' of electronic information is no longer possible to handle other than through electronic devices (Connerton 2009, p. 124). While digital media have the potential to store memory in a more inclusive and participatory nature (Olsen et al 2012, p. 132), their ability to constitute 'potential memory' for future re-interpretations of the past is contingent upon their durability, which is still open to question (ibid., p. 134). This potential fragility is eloquently illustrated by Ezra Shales' (2013, p. 20–21) observation that, if they were only brought back to life by skilled labour, the one hundred-year old plaster moulds left at the former Spode ceramics factory in Stoke-on-Trent have more potential to be viable carriers of memory than the 'antediluvian computers stacked like logs of wood into closets' at the same site.

Ranging from the traumatic recovery of remains of the 'disappeared' from sites of modern genocide (Crossland 2002) to socially-engaged 'excavations' of 1990s council houses (Buchli and Lucas 2001c), these studies tend to be characterised by a focus on 'the quotidian, the overlooked and 'taken for granted' [through which] the traces of subaltern voices and experience can be constituted' (Buchli and Lucas 2001a, p. 14). These approaches, then, seek to 'presence absence' by 'bringing forward or indeed materialising that which is excessive, forgotten or concealed' (Buchli and Lucas 2001d, p. 171). Through this 'mattering' – making things matter physically and conceptually – these archaeologies, it is argued, may play a role in challenging authoritarian discourses of dominance.

Here, archaeology is construed as an inherently creative enterprise where the past is constituted in the present, both conceptually and materially, rather than being a process where pre-determined givens are simply 'discovered' by excavators (Buchli and Lucas 2001a, p. 16–17). In this way, Greg Stevenson (2001, p. 61), talking about twentieth-century ceramics, likens archaeology to a 'design history of the everyday', where 'social relationships, stories and narratives of how things might have been' are 'designed' by archaeologists in the present. Similarly, Angela Piccini and Cornelius Holtorf (2009, p. 11) argue that, 'like artists, archaeologists actively shape materials in a process of transformation' when they excavate and interpret the past. In this way, both archaeology and art employ a variety of approaches and techniques to make meaning out of material and 'have in common a combination of lab- and field-based practices with material story-telling' (ibid., p. 13).

In, for example, ceramicist Neil Brownsword's re-fired ceramic detritus recovered from pottery sites around Stoke-on-Trent, we can see a similar desire to dramatise, and pay homage to, overlooked and undervalued signs of human labour through creative practice. As he explains,

> The cast clay spares vigorously removed from a mould, or marks remaining on a palette from repetitious lapping motions of mixing enamel, go unnoticed as they possess no inherent value.

> The extraordinary qualities of these material by-products emphasise an individual expression that lies in stark contrast to the effects of standardisation that have rendered evidence of human contact an imperfection. They expose a greater insight into the entirety of each process and the innate knowledge of material, command and timing embedded in each craftsperson. (Brownsword 2006, Chapter 5, p. 3)

While the outcomes and methods may differ in that archaeology recovers otherwise ignored material culture and the creative ceramic practice to be described in this paper makes it through an engagement with a museum collection and associated community, there appears to be much commonality in the aims of the two disciplines. Both attempt to raise awareness of overlooked or hidden narratives of human-object interaction through the constitution of a new material culture – archaeology through its 'critical empiricism' (Buchli and Lucas 2001d, p. 172) and ceramics through its ability to materialise and dramatise – and, consequently, both can perhaps be described in terms of the 'creative materialising intervention' Buchli and Lucas (2001a, p. 17) aspire to. Ultimately, as archaeologist Laurent Olivier (2001, p. 187) highlights, by making new things we are adding to the archaeological record as 'all manifestations that bear witness, physically, to human activity are, by their nature, concerned with archaeology.'

Why ceramics?

As ceramic objects are familiar due to our long association with clay vessels, durable, and capable of carrying a range of meaningful contextual information in form and surface design, ceramic practice provides a particularly suitable means by which ephemeral narratives can be manifested through a process of materialisation. Although it is possible that almost any form of artistic output might enter the archaeological record, it is perhaps ceramics which combine accessibility with the most potential for endurance. Ceramic artist Stephen Dixon argues that ceramic has both charted the development of human civilisation and been central to the development of sculpture due to its material qualities of 'durability, versatility and universality', combined with its ability to carry narrative information:

> Fired clay, although fragile in comparison with some other sculptural materials, is permanent and durable. It will not perish, rot, dissolve or be consumed by animal or insect. Its colours will not fade. Its lack of material value means it will not be melted down for re-use. Ceramic is therefore a uniquely important material for the historian and the archaeologist, for piecing together the narratives of civilisation. (Dixon 2012, p. 3–4)

As Glenn Adamson (2009, p. 36) notes, it is both the fragility of ceramic objects as well as the ultimate durability of their sherds which make them 'our most reliable evidence of human endeavour', arguing that a 'smashed and discarded ceramic pot literally kills time as it waits to be discovered', providing 'a cultural trace that transports a sense of immediacy across the centuries.'

In his discussion of the importance objects play in both 'inscriptive' and 'habitual' memory practices, archaeologist Bjørnar Olsen (2010, p. 160) contends that it is their 'durability' and 'in-place-ness' which situates the past within the present, providing us with a sense of 'ontological security' (ibid., p. 121). Objects often outlast their human makers and users, accumulating over time. These 'intrinsic gathering and enduring capacities of materials' (ibid., p. 110) are particularly true of ceramic objects which may survive as fragments or be treasured as heirlooms or museum objects, both presencing the past in the present and carrying it into the future.

The archival potential of ceramic has led to 'time capsule' initiatives like Memory of Mankind, an online service where participants can upload digital information which is then turned into a decal and preserved by being fired on to stoneware tablets. This ceramic archive will be stored for posterity in a salt mine in Hallstatt, Austria (MOM 2015).

Distributed objects

Although anthropologist Alfred Gell's (1998) work on how objects may extend and distribute the agency of their maker or commissioner has been subject to much debate (see Chua and Elliott 2013), his treatment of artistic oeuvre seems to offer a convincing way of regarding a museum collection, uniting individual agency with wider contexts. Gell (1998, p. 222) contended that there is an 'isomorphy of structure' between the 'internal' cognitive world of the artist and the way it is manifest externally as the artist's oeuvre of 'spatio-temporal structures of distributed objects'. Following from this, he argued that 'what people are externally (and collectively) is a kind of enlarged replication of what they are internally' (ibid.). Here, humans are not confined to the spatial or temporal limits of their body, 'but consist of a spread of biographical events and memories of events, and a dispersed category of material objects, traces and leavings, which can be attributed to a person and which, in aggregate, testify to agency and patienthood during a biographical career which may, indeed, prolong itself long after biological death' (ibid.). As a result, a work of art or craft can be seen to embody something of the mind and will of its maker, which, in turn, may go on to influence others.

As an example, Gell (ibid., p. 221) described a china dinner set, typical of that made by Spode, Wedgewood or, indeed, one of the Sunderland potteries, as a series of objects, each with their own 'micro-histories', which come together to form a 'distributed object' manifesting the 'intentional actions' of the factory's management and design team. If, as Tim Ingold (2000, p. 372) argues, even such mass-produced objects can each be seen as 'originals' rather than 'replicas', often displaying variation due to the 'dynamics of making', it is perhaps possible to discern in the Sunderland pottery collection, for instance, something of the agency of not only the pottery owners who commissioned it, but also of the workers, whose idiosyncratic application of transfers and pink lustre make each piece unique. The challenge of my project in Sunderland was to create a 'distributed object' which referenced the history of the collection, whilst also communicating something of contemporary Sunderland and its inhabitants.

Public and private monuments

Public memorials have often been problematised as forms of forgetting where lived memory is replaced by a constructed nostalgia. Historian Pierre Nora (1989, p. 7) has criticised such sites as materialised forms of forgetting 'where memory crystallizes and secretes itself', rather than existing as a lived, active practice. For Nora, by the time sites of historical significance (lieux de mémoire) are identified as such, they have already ceased to be loci of dynamic memory practice (milieux de mémoire) where mnemonic activities underpin quotidian existence (Cubitt 2007, p. 244). Connerton (2009, p. 29) similarly argues that often the construction of monuments may encourage forgetfulness by conferring the responsibility of remembering to material culture, which may omit as much as it includes:

> The relationship between memorials and forgetting is reciprocal: the threat of forgetting begets memorials and the construction of memorials begets forgetting. If giving monumental shape to what

> we remember is to discard the obligation to remember, that is because memorials permit only some things to be remembered and, by exclusion, cause others to be forgotten. Memorials conceal the past as much as they cause us to remember it. (Connerton 2009, p. 29)

According to Buchli and Lucas (2001b, p.80), in every memorial 'something has been left out or forgotten', while Connerton, makes a congruent point regarding how war memorials often fail to represent the individual experiences of the combatants:

> They conceal the way people lived: where soldiers are directly represented in war memorials, their image is designed specifically to deny acts of violence and aggression. They conceal the way they died: the blood, the bits of body flying through the air, the stinking corpses lying unburied for months, all are omitted. [...] And they conceal the way people survive. (Connerton 2009, p. 29)

This omission may be officially sanctioned or the result of other dynamics, including self-censorship. For example, when asked how they wanted their tour in Afghanistan to be represented, it was notable that the soldiers who took part in my research did not necessarily want the grittier aspects of their experience to be included. According to Cubitt (2007, p. 199), whilst some personal narratives or mnemonic associations may become officially recognised through commemorative objects and practices, thereby gaining 'widespread currency', others may remain 'private or clandestine', or become the 'challenging alternatives' of a specific interest group. Reminiscence expert Bernie Arigho (2008, p. 206) likens people to museums with their own repositories of life experiences, some displayed to the public and others concealed or 'put to one side'.

Of course, inherent in my materialising approach is the danger of replicating this problematic of creating monumental sites of forgetting. My work with the soldiers sought to avoid this by taking marginal aspects of their experience which otherwise might not be represented by official commemorative practices and monumentalising them through materialisation in ceramic. In doing so, it was hoped that these private narratives would become accessible to the public through display, whilst also retaining their links to individual experience. Discussing objects the soldiers had used in Afghanistan during the reminiscence activity concentrated the conversation on external talking points, attempting to avoid potentially traumatic memory triggers and the emulation of the grand narratives of heroism so prevalent in the original Sunderland pottery. As Arigho advises (ibid., p. 209), in memory work, 'It may be easier and more comforting to engage with a concrete external object than to immediately search inwardly for what may ultimately arise as especially cherished or defining life experiences.'

IED Brush

A series of dialogues emerged from the focus group which revealed how the soldiers had negotiated the trauma and rigours of the tour and its aftermath though a variety of person-object interactions. One soldier brought a domestic paint brush to the session which was inscribed with a tally of the number of improvised explosive devices (IEDs) he had found with it while route clearing in Afghanistan (see McHugh 2013). According to sociologist Kevin McSorley (2012, p. 53), the Vallon IED detector used by this solider in conjunction with his brush is 'now the leading edge of the sensorium of contemporary patrol in Afghanistan', its use recorded through the helmet cameras of soldiers, where 'the footage has a singular, unwavering focus: the hands engaged in a deadly archaeology of delicately brushing away dirt and removing stones to reveal the invisible explosive traps'. The archaeological metaphor is apt as the soldier also contributed a knife which he had excavated, describing it as a 'special find' and musing about the narrative that had led to its burial next to a road.

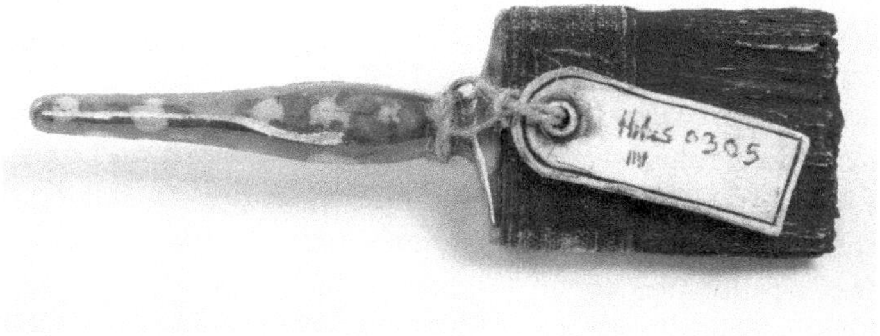

Figure 66.1 Rifleman Hiles' IED Brush, photographed by Jo Howell, Jo Howell Photography (www.maverickart.co.uk).

The familiar appearance of the brush belies an extraordinary history of human-object relations which is only hinted at by the addition of the tally marks. This customization through usage, together with its unusual history, transformed it from a mass-produced object into a decommodified social thing. Similarly to the atom bomb-scarred tricycle on display at the Hiroshima Peace Memorial Museum, 'Taken out of quotidian practice, it invokes and evokes ordinary events and their extraordinary disruption' (Clark 2009, p. 514–515). There can be little doubt that this once ordinary item has potential to offer much as a museum object, providing an unofficial insight into the everyday experiences of a soldier in Afghanistan in the early twenty-first century. However, whether it will be accessioned by a museum or preserved by the soldier as a relic of his time in Afghanistan is unknown. In the domestic setting, it may become an important heirloom, playing a role in framing personal and family cosmologies, or it may simply be returned to its default fate of DIY, perhaps languishing forgotten in a repurposed mug under a kitchen sink or in a garden shed.

Such items may be of 'immense interpretive value' (Schofield et al 2002, p. 4) within museum displays as well as being of significant sociological and historical interest. As archaeologists John Schofield and his co-authors (ibid., p. 7) argue, 'Some material records are central to developing a knowledge of warriors and societies at war that official histories and some archives don't address. What were these combatants like; how did they behave in time of war; how was the world through their eyes?'

Writing about donations to the In Flanders Fields Museum made by the descendants of soldiers who served in the First World War, Dominiek Dendooven also argues that this potentially ephemeral material legacy has evocative and affective potential for museum displays, helping the general public to grasp experiences they can barely imagine:

> Experiences can never be duplicated or revived, and the visceral life-and-death conditions of war are forever beyond reclaim by those who took no part in the struggles. Herein lies the beauty and the power of conflict-related objects, some of which withstand the ravages of time in ways that memories do not. The past may be gone, but sometimes objects retain the power to evoke aspects of that past which gave birth to them, and thereby connect us to our own private and collective histories. Such objects provide us with something to hold on to – they provide emotional and intellectual purchase, turning back the clock of memory. (Dendooven 2009, p. 63)

Dendooven (2009, p. 66) notes that such bequests are often motivated by the fear that with the death of the original owner, the 'meaning of these objects will fade away, and that perhaps one day the object will no longer be recognized as a meaningful war souvenir and will be discarded or sold.' Although donation removes the object from the familial context, it is assumed that 'If the museum accepts the gift, the donor can be sure that the object will be preserved – in theory for eternity and in good condition' (ibid.). In this way, the donation serves to memorialise the relative as well as make their unique human-object experiences accessible to the public.

According to Susan Stewart (1993, p. 135–136), the efficacy of souvenirs comes from their ability to engender a narrative of origin. For Dendooven (2009, p. 66) the recording of such stories must be an integral part of the accessioning process. Such discourses may combine accounts of how the objects were initially acquired and used with reminiscences regarding what role they subsequently played within the family. As Dendooven (ibid.) notes, 'The power of such objects to embody and reconfigure persona and family memories, emotions and crosscutting ideas of identity and genealogy are astonishing as they are currently undocumented.' These items may have 'acquired a patina of emotion' (ibid.), which is obvious to their owners but which might require careful interpretation to maximise their affective potential in the museum setting.

Carol A Kidron's ethnographic studies of the relationships between Holocaust survivors and their descendants suggest that such war trophies or souvenirs taken 'in flight from the deathworld' (Kidron 2012, p. 11) by the survivor generation may 'act as key conduits' (ibid., p. 17) in the mediation of the non-narrative, intergenerational transmission of the traumatic past through a range of embodied object-person interactions within the domestic setting. These 'micro-local sites of memory' help in the 'embedding of the non-pathological presence of the Holocaust past within silent embodied practices' which serve to 'sustain familial 'lived memory' and to transmit tacit knowledge of the past within the everyday private social milieu' (ibid., p. 7). For example, rather than existing as a morbid presence in her home, Michelle's soup spoon, liberated from Auschwitz and used daily to feed her daughter, functioned as a symbol of survival with which her triumph over this near-death experience could be 'routinely re-enacted' (Kidron 2012, p. 11–12).

Although Rifleman Hiles' IED brush was taken with him to Afghanistan rather than acquired there, it nevertheless acts as a reminder of his having survived the detection of at least four significant explosive devices. It is not unreasonable to conjecture that his brush and knife may become significant material referents through which he recounts his experiences in Afghanistan upon return to the domestic setting. Whether it will be possible to 're-enact' the brush through embodied object-person relations in the same way as Michelle did with her spoon is less clear and this question may offer potential for further research.

Kidron (2012, p. 18) has identified a reluctance amongst Holocaust survivors to relinquish their 'deathworld' souvenirs to museums for public display. This tension between private memory practices and public display is further attested to by Chaim Sztajer's ambivalence and possessiveness regarding the display of his model of the Treblinka death camp at the Jewish Holocaust Museum in Melbourne. He is said to have been dismayed at the addition of a glass vitrine, perhaps because he felt unable to access the memories of his exterminated daughter he felt it embodied in the same way as he had when it had been kept at home (Witcomb 2011, p. 47). Kidron (2012, p. 18) also raises concerns regarding the fate of these items as the survivor generation dies. Whilst their children have a tacit understanding of these objects, their grandchildren often have not been privy to these memory practices. It is likely that these once non-verbal relations will have to be explained through a narrative process which fixes them in time and space. To remedy this, it is noted that elderly survivors are increasingly donating 'copies' of these souvenirs to local museums-cum-community centres in Israel so that the domestic contexts of the original items can be maintained while the community can also access this inheritance (ibid., p. 19). Kidron (ibid.) suggests that these centres 'might be explored as niches of intimate materiality in the meso-public domain in which familial interaction can be sustained outside the home without totally sacrificing the mundane living context that has preserved them.'

Rifleman Hiles' IED Brush, the ceramic interpretation of the original object, is a necessarily imperfect attempt to counter this problem of the entropy of private memory, where embodied practices recounted as a narrative by the soldier have been partially reconstructed and translated into a potentially enduring and dramatised ceramic form. Whilst it is impossible to recapture the soldier's person-object experiences with the original item, this work attempts to disinter and monumentalise this story. While the printed tally marks on the ceramic brush hint at its unusual meaning, the work requires an interpretive narrative, and consequently embodies the limitations of my approach. Like Michelle's spoon, the power of the original brush is in its 'material functionality' (ibid., p. 12) which enables us to empathetically imagine what it might have been like to perform route clearing in Afghanistan. Petrified in ceramic, it no longer functions in this manner. Instead, it is an attempt to freeze (Sarmiento 2011, p. 58), or preserve, the story of how an ordinary object came to be used in an extraordinary way. Here, the 'lived memory' (Kidron 2012, p. 18) of Rifleman Hiles is replaced by a monumental, crystallised (Nora 1989, p. 7 cited in ibid., p. 18) form of public memory (see McHugh 2013, p. 80–81). While Michelle's spoon was 'woven into the daily practices of the home', thereby perpetually 'inscribing' the experience of survival (Kidron 2012, p. 12), how the soldier will use his brush away from Afghanistan is unknown. While we cannot predict what will become of this item, an attempt has been made to preserve its extraordinary history through the creation of an artwork and corresponding narrative. Although it is likely that this work will be 'displayed behind glass in frozen sites' (ibid.), this copy means that the original item may potentially go on to perform its silent human-object relations in the domestic setting.

Tattooed pots

A series of jugs made during my research employ a familiar form, which is well-represented in the SMWG's pottery collection, as a medium with which to display a range of narrative and visual information through surface decoration. Some of these jugs present imagery developed from the 3 Rifles focus group, focusing on the soldiers' commemorative tattoos and lucky charms. According to sociologist Les Back (2004, p. 29), tattooing 'involves perforating the boundary between the internal and the external so that the external becomes internal and the internal becomes external.' By committing these tattoos to the surface of pots, the private commemorative practices of the soldiers are made public through a process where ceramic decals are incorporated into the object by being fused into the surface glaze.

The soldiers' tattoos tend to commemorate fallen comrades or deceased family members and, like the 'tattooed' ceramic vessels, these marks introduced into their corporeality act as 'semi-durable' (Pennell 2010, p.40, see also Ingold 2013, p. 94) reminders of the presence of absence. Back's (2004, p. 49) study of the white working-classes of Britain suggests that for this population tattooing provides a hitherto under-appreciated non-verbal means of expressing love and affection, where 'the body becomes a figure through which emotions, affinities, and devotions are inscribed.' The embodied and silent nature of these expressions means that they have often been overlooked, and consequently, the 'complexity' of the 'emotional lives' they represent is 'lost, ignored, or disparaged' (ibid., p. 32). Although these tattoos may last a lifetime, upon death they decay and these records of emotion are lost, possibly to be replaced by similar commemorations in the skin of younger generations. As Back concludes:

> The lines in these tattoos touch permanence but cannot grasp eternity. This has a double consequence for working-class expression because this is often the only medium through which their stories are told. [...] As the cadavers disappear, the traces of their embodied history, of life and love, are lost – they become The Nameless. They pass through hospital wards to the crematoria, to be remembered in the inscriptions made on young flesh that will in turn grow old. (Back 2004, p. 51)

Kevin McSorley and Sarah Maltby (2012, p. 3), argue that the somatic aspects of contemporary warfare, including the inherent harm it causes to bodies, are similarly often denied by dominant discourses. 'The reality of war [they contend] is not just politics by any other means but politics incarnate, politics written on and experienced through the thinking, feeling bodies of men and women' (ibid.). The 'tattooed' jugs attempt to make the embodied shrines of the soldiers into accessible objects which will endure longer than the flesh and around which, it is hoped, a public discourse might emerge.

A consistent theme of *Sensing War*, an interdisciplinary conference organised by the University of Portsmouth in June 2014, was the difficulty of communicating the sensory experiences of war through language (Sensing War 2014). Conference organiser Kevin McSorley (2012, p. 48) has also previously noted that 'the visual grammar that increasingly dominates the contemporary mediascape of the Afghanistan war is lo-fi, intimate, and messy', and inextricably linked to the 'embodied experiences of soldiering'. Whilst acknowledging the difficulty of trying to capture that which is almost impossible to apprehend, the works described above aim to represent the manner in which soldiers coped with the experiences of war and its aftermath through such somatic experiences, presenting this information in a literally 'graspable' form (cf. Connerton 2009, p. 124).

Although these works may require a narrative explanation, they may also be experienced somatically - visually and through touch. As Zachary Beckstead et al (2011, p. 199) note in their discussion of collective remembering and war memorials, it is through the materiality of things and their aesthetic surfaces that 'normally inaccessible feelings' and 'moments of deep affective relevance' are obtained. For Buchli and Lucas (2001b, p. 82), the challenge is to produce a memorial which succeeds in balancing the private need to cope with traumatic experiences with the public requirements of testimony and catharsis. Such a balance might be found in the Massachusetts Vietnam Veterans Memorial, where the incorporation into the architecture of the final letters home of the deceased creates a 'powerful empathic response' (Beckstead et al 2011, p. 202–206), focusing on 'intimate deaths' (ibid., p. 202) and avoiding the jingoism characteristic of many official monuments. Works like *Rifleman Hiles' IED Brush* and the jugs similarly mark an attempt to disseminate individual experiences in the form of publicly accessible artworks, exploring this tension between remembering and forgetting.

Nevertheless, these ceramic works remain static monuments and are once removed from the lived memory of the informants. I have previously discussed how other ceramic items I made as part of my research, notably a pair of jugs made in collaboration with descendants of two nineteenth century Sunderland potters, went on to become activated as loci of remembrance through digital social networking (McHugh 2013; 2016). It is possible that such an approach could also be taken here to animate these pieces. Meanwhile, the question of how non-narrative embodied practice might be addressed by creative ceramics is worthy of further consideration.

Conclusion - ceramics as 'incavation'

The deliberate burial, or incavation, of objects has been practised for millennia in a variety of contexts, including by artists like Claes Oldenburg (Holtorf 2004, p. 48) and Antony Gormley. For archaeologist Cornelius Holtorf (2004), his experiment in incavation is at once archaeological and artistic, leading him to note that, '[whether] one incavates or excavates, archaeologists, and indeed we all, construct the past and its remains like artisans create their craft' (ibid., p. 47). His burial of the remains of 'an extensive breakfast' enjoyed with his friends in Berlin, comprised offerings ranging from 'a cup of coffee with some coffee in it' in Trench 3 to 'an eggcup with some egg shells and a little spoon' in Trench 7 (ibid., p. 45). As such, it is as much a material record of the event as it is an attempt to highlight the 'multitemporality' of the archaeological process, where the artefacts and the site, a town house built in 1899, are 'of the present but also of various pasts and futures' (ibid., p. 47). Holtorf justifies this deposition as providing a 'proactive contribution to the historic process of rendering both the context and the artefact relevant and meaningful in changing and diverse presents' (ibid., p. 48), a rationale which might equally be used to explain the production of new artworks, particularly those based on objects in a museum collection.

Whilst my project certainly tried to communicate something about contemporary Sunderland by producing a material offering to be left behind for the future, it necessarily did not aim to make a comprehensive material archive in ceramic. Rather, by focusing on certain aspects of human-object relationships, it employed the materiality of clay and fired ceramic to raise awareness of some potentially over-looked examples of human experience. As previously discussed, the approach can perhaps be likened more to Buchli and Lucas' proactive materialising project:

> If anything, this is an archaeology of the future, if we take such an oxymoron seriously. Not so much in the sense of 'doing the job' for archaeologists of the future [...], but in the sense of creating the future by being actively engaged in the materialisation of the present – as much as designers, for example. (Buchli and Lucas 2001a, p.9)

Although no objects have been incavated as part of this project, the process where clay is imbued with contextual information through the manipulation of form and surface with a view to preserving something in fired ceramic can perhaps be described as a metaphorical incavation. An attempt has been made to link the past, present and future through reference to the historical collection and the present community. When asked about this tentative definition, Holtorf (2013, pers. comm.) replied that a condition of incavation is the possibility of future rediscovery or disinterment: 'Whether or not a ceramic work is an incavation depends in my view a lot on what you mean by that. For me, an incavation is an act that presupposes the possibility (though not necessarily reality) of subsequent excavation. But I do not own the term...'.

The items made during this project may become accessioned by the museum or collected privately. They may be regularly exhibited or may wait in store rooms to be 'dug up' and re-discovered at times when they offer topical display potential or contextual resonance. Alternatively, they may become broken, discarded or lost, possibly entering the archaeological record as in the case of *Crinson Jug*, one of my other works which went missing at an art fair in Shanghai in 2013 (McHugh 2016).

Indeed, it is necessary to acknowledge Ingold's (2013, p.102) critique of Olsen's (2010, above) assertion of the innate endurance of the material world. For Ingold (ibid., p.94), pots are susceptible to the same kind of 'chronic instability' as the human body, facing the ever present threat of 'dissolution or metamorphosis', and constantly demanding 'vigilance' and care. Glen R Brown (2012) similarly likens pots to living entities, arguing that 'the natural life of a functional ceramic vessel, like that of something literally alive, is fraught with risk'. Much like the transfer-printed items in the Sunderland collection, the interpretation of some of the ceramic objects made during this research may be assisted by information carried in surface decoration. The reading of others, however, notably *Rifleman Hiles' IED Brush*, for example, will require the kind of contextual information provided by museum accession notes. Nevertheless, that they have been brought into being opens up the possibility of their future rediscovery and reactivation through excavation, metaphorical or actual. The challenge is in how the pots might be interpreted subsequently and be sustained as cultural processes, or 'things', rather than merely as material remains.

References

Adamson, G. 2009. 'You Are Here', in deWaal, E. *Signs and Wonders: Edmund deWaal and the V&A Ceramics Galleries*, London: V&A Publishing, pp. 33–47.

Arigho, B. 2008. 'Getting a Handle on the Past: The Use of Objects in Reminiscence Work', in Chatterjee, H. (ed), *Touch in Museums: Policy and Practice in Object Handling*, Oxford; New York: Berg, pp. 205–212.

Back, Les. 2004. 'Inscriptions of Love', in Thomas, H. and Ahmed, J. (eds) *Cultural Bodies: Ethnography and Theory*, Oxford: Blackwell Publishing, pp. 27–54.

Beckstead, Z., Twose, G., Levesque-Gottlieb, E., and Rizzo, J. 2011. 'Collective remembering through the materiality and organization of war memorials', *Journal of Material Culture*, 16, pp. 193–213.

Brown, G. R. 2013. 'Interaction, Intervention and the Will to Preserve', available at <http://www.ceramics-in-the-expanded-field.com/essays/glen-r-brown-phd-usa>, accessed 02.07.2014.

Brownsword, N. 2006. Action/reflection: a creative response to transition and change in British ceramic manufacture. PhD Thesis, University of Brunel.

Buchli, V. and Lucas, G. 2001a. 'The absent present', in Buchli, V. and Lucas, G. (eds) *Archaeologies of the Contemporary Past*, London and New York: Routledge, pp. 3–18.

Buchli, V. and Lucas, G. 2001b. 'Between remembering and forgetting', in Buchli, V. and Lucas, G. (eds) *Archaeologies of the Contemporary Past*, London and New York: Routledge, pp. 79–83.

Buchli, V. and Lucas, G. 2001c. 'The archaeology of alienation: A late twentieth-century British council house', in Buchli, V. and Lucas, G. (eds) *Archaeologies of the Contemporary Past*, London and New York: Routledge, pp. 158–167.

Buchli, V. and Lucas, G. 2001d. 'Presencing absence', in Buchli, V. and Lucas, G. (eds) *Archaeologies of the Contemporary Past*, London and New York: Routledge, pp. 171–174.

Chua, L. and Elliott, M. (eds), 2013. *Distributed Objects: Meaning and Mattering after Alfred Gell*, New York; Oxford: Bergahn.

Clark, L. B. 2009, 'Shin's Tricycle', in Candlin, F. & Guins, R. 2009. *The Object Reader*, London; New York: Routledge, pp. 513–515.

Connerton, P. 2009. *How Modernity Forgets*, Cambridge: Cambridge University Press.

Crossland, Z. 2002. 'Violent spaces: conflict over the reappearance of Argentina's disappeared', in J. Schofield, W. Gray Johnson and C. M. Beck, (eds), *Matériel Culture: The archaeology of twentieth-century conflict*, London and New York: Routledge, pp. 115–131.

Cubitt, G. 2007. *History and Memory*, Manchester; New York: Manchester University Press.

Dendooven, D., 2009. 'The Journey Back: On the nature of donations to the 'In Flanders Museum'', in Saunders, N.J. and Cornish, P. (eds), *Contested Objects: material memories of the Great War*, London: Routledge, pp. 60–72.

Dixon, S. 2012. 'Why Clay?', in *Interpreting Ceramics*, Issue 14, available at <http://www.interpretingceramics.com/issue014/articles/06.htm>, accessed 25.02.14.

Gell, A. 1998. *Art and Agency: An Anthropological Theory*. Oxford: Oxford University Press.

Harrison, R and Schofield, J. 2010. *After Modernity: Archaeological Approaches to the Contemporary Past*, Oxford: Oxford University Press.

Holtorf, C. 2004. 'Incavation – Excavation – Exhibition', in Renfrew, C., Brodie, N. & Hills, C. (eds.), *Material engagements: studies in honour of Colin Renfrew*, Cambridge: McDonald Institute for Archaeological Research, pp. 45–53.

Holtorf, C. 2013. Email correspondence, dated 14.09.2013.

Ingold, T. 2000. *The Perception of the Environment: Essays in Livelihood, Dwelling and Skill*, London: Routledge.

Ingold, T. 2013. *Making: Anthropology, Archaeology, Art and Artchitecture*, London; New York: Routledge.

Kidron, C. A. 2009. 'Toward an Ethnography of Silence: The Lived Presence of the Past in the Everyday Life of Holocaust Trauma Survivors and Their Descendants in Israel', *Current Anthropology*, 50 (1), pp. 5–27.

Kidron, C. A. 2012. 'Breaching the wall of traumatic silence: Holocaust survivor and descendant person-object relations and the material transmission of the genocidal past.', *Journal of Material Culture*, 17 (1), pp. 3–21.

McHugh, C. J. 2013. 'Towards a Sunderland Pottery for the Twenty-First Century: Materializing Multiple Dialogues in Museum Display Through Creative Ceramics', *Journal of Museum Ethnography*, no. 26 (March 2013), pp. 71–88.

McHugh, C. J. 2016. 'The Crinson Jug from clay to the grave (and beyond): exploring the ceramic object as a gathering point', in Christie Brown, Julian Stair and Clare Twomey (eds) *Contemporary Clay and Museum Culture*, London: Routledge, pp. 121–131.

McSorley, K. 2012. 'Helmetcams, militarized sensation and 'Somatic War'', in *Journal of War & Culture Studies* 5 (1), pp. 47–58.

McSorley, K. and Maltby, S. 2012. 'War and the Body: Cultural and military practices', in *Journal of War & Culture Studies* 5 (1), pp. 3–6.

MOM 2015. Memory of Mankind website, available at <http://memory-of-mankind.com/>, accessed 29.09.15.

Nora, P. 1989. 'Between Memory and History: Les Lieux de Mémoire' (transl. Marc Roudebush), *Representations*, no. 26 (Spring; Special Issue: 'Memory and Counter Memory'), pp. 7–24.

Olivier, L. 2001. 'The archaeology of the contemporary past', in Buchli, V. and Lucas, G. (eds.) *Archaeologies of the Contemporary Past*, London and New York: Routledge, pp. 175–188.

Olsen, B. 2010. In Defense of Things: Archaeology and the Ontology of Objects, Lanham and Plymouth, Altamira Press.

Olsen, B., Shanks, M., Webmoor, T. & Witmore, C. 2012. *Archaeology: The Discipline of Things*, Berkley and Los Angeles: University of California Press.

Pennell, S. 2010. "For a crack or flaw despis'd': Thinking about Ceramic Durability and the 'Everyday' in Late Seventeenth- and Early Eighteenth-Century England', in Hamling, T. & Richardson, C., *Everyday Objects*, Farnham, Surrey, England; Burlington, VT: Ashgate, pp. 27–40.

Piccini, A. and Holtorf, C. 2009. 'Introduction: Fragments from a Conversation about Contemporary Archaeologies', in Holtorf, C. and Piccini, A. 2009. (eds), *Contemporary Archaeologies: Excavating Now*, Frankfurt am Main: Peter Lang GmbH, pp. 9–29.

Renfrew, A. C. 2003. *Figuring it out: The parallel visions of artists and archaeologists*, Thames and Hudson.

Sarmiento, J. R. 2011. 'Ode on a Maori Paddle: Ethno/Graphic Glass Art Practice', *Journal of Museum Ethnography*, no. 24, pp. 58–77.

Schofield, J. and Johnson, W. G. 2006. 'Archaeology, heritage and the recent and contemporary past', in Hicks, D. and Beaudry, M. C. (eds), *The Cambridge Companion to Historical Archaeology*, Cambridge: Cambridge University Press, pp. 104–122.

Schofield, J., Johnson, W. G., Beck, C. M. 2002. 'Introduction: matérial culture in the modern world', in Schofield, J., Johnson, W. G., Beck, C. M., (eds.), *Matériel Culture: The archaeology of twentieth-century conflict*, London and New York: Routledge, pp. 1–8.

Sensing War. 2014. A conference held at Friends House, London, 12–13 June 2014. <http://sensingwar.org/>, accessed 29.09.15.

Shales, E. 2013. 'Tools Fit for the External Hard Drive', in Mydland, A. M. & Brownsword, N. (eds) *Topographies of the Obsolete: Critical Texts*, Topographies of the Obsolete Publications, pp. 20–25.

Stevenson, G. 2001. 'Archaeology as the design history of the everyday', in Buchli, V. and Lucas, G. (eds.), *Archaeologies of the Contemporary Past*, London and New York: Routledge, pp. 51–62.

Stewart, S. 1993. *On Longing: Narratives of the Miniature, the Gigantic, the Souvenir, the Collection*, Durham: Duke University Press.

Witcomb, A. 2010. 'Remembering the dead by affecting the living: The case of a miniature model of Treblinka', in Dudley, S. H. (ed), *Museum Materialities: Objects, Engagements, Interpretations*, London; New York: Routledge, pp. 39–52.

Extracted from my PhD thesis, 'Community in Clay – Towards a Sunderland Pottery for the Twenty-First Century: Approaching Museum Collections and Communities through Creative Ceramics', University of Sunderland with Sunderland Museum & Winter Gardens, March 2015. This research was funded by an Arts and Humanities Research Council Collaborative Doctoral Award.

67
RE-DEFINING CERAMICS THROUGH EXHIBITIONARY PRACTICE (1970-2009)[1]

Laura Breen

When the Craftsmen Potters Association launched its magazine *Ceramic Review* in 1970 it selected a title that accommodated forms of practice that stood outside of the studio pottery tradition as well as within it. The magazine's content was focused on hand making, perpetuating craft values, which, as Glenn Adamson has argued, were constructed in tandem with and in opposition to industry.[2] Philip Rawson's book *Ceramics*, published a year later, proffered a different take on the term, addressing the symbolic, tactile and associative values of ceramic objects and the symbiosis of aesthetics and function.[3] However, this paper explores how the designation 'ceramics' has provided a key means of accommodating art-oriented studio practice, delineating a field that has since been reconfigured in relation to changing conceptions of craft and industry as well as work in clay produced by fine artists.[4]

As these additive and unhinging processes encompassed sculpture, ready-mades, concept-led, site-specific and relational works, the trace of the maker's hand and the skilled manipulation of clay became less certain guarantors of a work's status as ceramics. Writing on similar shifts in fine art practice during the 1960s and '70s, Benjamin Buchloh observed that institutional validation and legal position became central to admitting a work into the category of art.[5] Yet, whilst ceramics and craft galleries and publications have largely provided that institutional context for ceramics, public museums and galleries in Britain also began to collect and exhibit contemporary ceramics on a more sustained basis in the 1970s. Faced with practices that straddled existing categorical divisions, they often employed temporary exhibitions as a means of addressing contemporary approaches to medium.[6] Operating at a tangent to its existing discursive formation, these exhibitions provided opportunities to re-negotiate the field's horizons in relation to both new forms of clay practice and those outside its purview. Furthermore, exhibitions had become a central means of separating art from the mass market.[7] As Corinne Kratz has posited:

> Producing and visiting exhibitions [...] can be ways people formulate and sometimes debate notions of quality, worth, and other social values and meanings. These processes entail judgments that help create hierarchies of merit and importance and define such broad fields as aesthetics, history, and morality, as well as particular political economies.[8]

Largely produced by contemporary ceramicists and craft critics, such projects might, therefore, be viewed as attempts to attract new critical audiences and raise the value and status of the art-oriented ceramic practices that were their core focus.[9]

Source: An earlier version of this article was published in the *Journal of Art Historiography*, no. 11, December 2014.

Ambiguities and re-definition

The Anglo-Oriental standard outlined in Bernard Leach's *A Potter's Book* dominated British studio pottery production in the early post-war period, but by the 1960s, inspired by Lucie Rie's functionalist Modernism and Hans Coper's obsessive engagement with form, a new generation of students had begun to explore the aesthetic qualities of the pot.[10] The rejection of function by American makers such as Peter Voulkos and Robert Arneson also had a marked impact, whilst the mobilization of the material and historic associations of clay by artists such as Carl Andre and Judy Chicago would have further repercussions for the field. Pottery was largely regarded as one of the crafts: a set of medium specific disciplines which, as Tanya Harrod has elucidated, occupied an ambiguous position in the post-war period.[11] However, whilst many practitioners had fine art ambitions, efforts to secure the future of the crafts resulted in the foundation of the Crafts Advisory Committee (later the Crafts Council) in 1971. This move demanded a consolidated identity – one that operated in tension with the increasing heterogeneity of clay practice within the arts.

Produced at this pivotal moment, Cartwright Hall's *Modern Ceramics '71* (1971) was one of the earliest attempts to survey the impact that these developments had on ceramic practice. Planned before the Crafts Advisory Committee's inception, the exhibition had no formal affiliation to the crafts. However, the selected practitioners remained united by their commitment to medium-specificity and the use of the term ceramics in the exhibition title was, as with *Ceramic Review*, intended to indicate diversification *within* the field.[12]

In the accompanying catalogue, exhibition organizer John Thompson positioned the artists in *Modern Ceramics '71* within a lineage that included works from the USA, Germany and Japan, which he claimed had exerted a potent influence on British ceramics since the 1950s.[13] The involvement of Tony Hepburn – a vocal advocate of American ceramics whose articles and reviews in UK magazines such as *Ceramic Review* showed a higher level of critical engagement than most other writers in the field at the time – gave further weight to this proposal.[14] Indeed, *The Guardian*'s Northern Arts Correspondent, Merete Bates, used an interview with Hepburn to link the use of clay as a means of expression evidenced in the show to similar developments in the USA.[15]

Discussing the work in the exhibition, Thompson suggested that it had become increasingly difficult to discern between pottery and sculpture in recent years.[16] Despite this, the show was devoid of sculpture from outside the field and addressed the work within the framework of ceramics. This made it difficult to ascertain its merit in relation to the former category. Additionally, although *The Teacher*'s description of the sculptural presentation of Hepburn's *Hanging and Performance* (1971), which required the viewer to stare through a 'building-site peephole', might be seen to support Thompson's standpoint, many of the works were small and fragile. They were, therefore, arranged in vitrines in a more traditional decorative arts approach.[17] In this context, Thompson's rhetoric might be regarded as an attempt to differentiate these works from those with a Leach-inspired focus on the fusion of use and beauty.[18] Whilst the latter risked falling into the category of what Arthur C. Danto called 'mere objects', which were 'logically exempt from interpretation' and, therefore, critical attention, Thompson sought to elevate the status of the works in the exhibition by aligning them with sculpture. Yet, he did not engage with the discourse around it.[19]

Thompson claimed he was keen to show the diversity of the work being produced in clay at the time, selecting over 300 works that ranged from pots by Rie and Joanna Constantinidis to more idiosyncratic press-moulded objects by Paul Astbury and sculptures by Hepburn and Graham Burr. However, the exhibition privileged ceramics that diverged from the Leach standard, rather than exploring the breadth of contemporary practice. It thus reflected current debates about the place of non-functional works within the ceramic field.[20] The fact that the exhibition received the backing of Coper and Geoffrey Doonan – lecturers and artists who engaged with influences outside the Leach tradition – indicated that the exhibition's real achievement was to offer an alternative to the dominant mode of studio pottery practice.[21] It was certainly more successful in this respect than it was in showcasing diversity, with Bates describing the exhibition as 'a shifting initiative' and both she and local collector W.A. Ismay contending that its success derived from its move away from studio pottery in the Leach mould towards art-oriented ceramics.[22]

Although it was independent, the emphasis of *Modern Ceramics '71* was remarkably similar to the rhetoric of the Crafts Advisory Committee, which was founded later that year. Lord Eccles, the government minister with responsibility for the arts, proposed that the Committee would support the 'artist craftsman.'[23] This was a term that Leach had used to describe the role of the contemporary potter in *A Potter's Book* and one that dissociated craft-centred practice from that of the 'designer craftsman', who was the figurehead of post-war initiatives to link design and industry.[24] However, when the Committee's secretary Victor Margrie was asked to elaborate on its meaning in a presentation at the Museums Association annual conference in 1974 he declared:

> We have not attempted to define it, just to use it; to content ourselves with the wide interpretation, which covers those craftsmen who, often rooted in traditional techniques, have an aim, which extends beyond reproduction of past styles and methods.[25]

The Committee's remit was, therefore, defined in the negative, against the emulative approach adopted by many followers of the Leach tradition, rather than by measurable criteria. Nevertheless, it continued to provide support for such work, which still fell under its jurisdiction, and which formed a large percentage of contemporary production. This ambiguity also led to a curious situation where the Crafts Advisory Committee supported exhibitions that included craft media yet aimed to move beyond 'the crafts' and, therefore, its area of responsibility, such as Sunderland Arts Centre's *State of Clay* (1978).

The title *State of Clay* represented a deliberate attempt to move away from the terms pottery and ceramics towards an understanding of clay that showed its wider application.[26] Although the show focused on practitioners with ceramics training, all of the exhibits were explicitly non-utilitarian. Astbury's use of press-moulded porcelain forms, and Glenys Barton's bone china works, which were produced in collaboration with Wedgwood, challenged the ideological opposition to industrial process adopted by many studio ceramicists: a stance that Adamson suggested was central to the 'invention of craft.'[27]

Others such as Gillian Lowndes and Percy Peacock used experimental mixed media techniques. Lowndes was an acknowledged influence on Peacock, having taught on his degree course at Bristol, yet his attitude was equally aligned with critical discussion outside the field.[28] For example, his artist's statement, which listed adjectives for describing clay and his actions upon it, recalled Richard Serra's *Verb List Compilation* (1967-68). Furthermore, in his assertion 'Clay is simply the most versatile material I have found for realizing my ideas,' he prioritised the use clay as a means of expression over that of ceramics as a disciplinary frame.[29] Peacock's work also demanded new approaches to display: modular, floor-based pieces, such as *Impact Imperative* (1978) did not have a permanent formation, nor could they be protected by the glass casing usually reserved for fragile works. These issues made installation difficult for the curators and although Peacock provided details about the scale and format of the work in advance, he was asked to install it himself on several occasions.[30]

In her catalogue introduction, the Crafts Advisory Committee's Marigold Colman stated that the exhibition aimed to create parity between clay sculpture and the Leach tradition.[31] Much like the Crafts Advisory Committee's 'artist craftsman', the term 'clay sculpture' was simply proffered as an alternative to the status quo. In this context, the curators inclusion of a single terracotta maquette by RCA ceramics tutor Eduardo Paolozzi might be viewed as a token attempt to validate the other work as sculpture without forcing the work into direct critical comparison with its contemporaries in that field. However, the same work gains a new resonance when read alongside co-curators David Vaughan and Tony Knipe's catalogue foreword, which discusses experimental approaches to medium and the potential to transcend disciplinary boundaries.[32]

Whilst the exhibition did not represent the state of clay in all its applications, it did include work that challenged existing conceptions of ceramic practice: Peacock's work highlighted the reductive nature of medium-based comparisons and, along with Astbury's and Lowndes's work in particular, foregrounded experimental approaches to media within the ceramic field. The mixed messages conveyed by the *State of Clay* exhibition, its curators and official backers thus exemplified the tension between The Crafts Advisory Committee's support of innovative practice and its need to maintain the distinction of the crafts as a set of medium-based disciplines in order to gain funding.

New standards

Some of the work in *State of Clay*, if not the accompanying rhetoric, indicated that ceramicists were embracing the post-modern collapse of disciplinary boundaries. However, by the 1980s the Crafts Council held increasing sway over the type of ceramic work that was promoted and exhibited in Britain's public galleries. They were particularly supportive of the work and theories of a group of young, critically-engaged, ceramicists who had had graduated from the RCA during the 1970s, which included Alison Britton, Jacqueline Poncelet, Barton and Elizabeth Fritsch. Whilst the Crafts Council continued to support the work of a range of practitioners, discussions about ceramics during this period were dominated by the interrogation of function and containment as subjects and the vessel's ornamental role – all matters that concerned this group. As Harrod has described, earlier examples of expression through craft media were obscured, as if the model of the artist-craftsman, which the Council promoted, was an entirely new phenomenon.[33]

Peter Dormer's *Fast Forward: New Directions in British Ceramics* (1985) brought the perceived dichotomy between Crafts Council-sponsored innovation and Leach inspired traditionalists together with explosive effects. Evincing a strong authorial position, the exhibition was laid out to provide a lineage for contemporary work that stood outside the Leach tradition.[34] It was divided into two main sections – historical and modern – with Dormer suggesting that the historical section should be 'v. critical', showing 'how the modern generation had benefitted from, and why they have reacted against, their recent heritage.'[35] Positioning himself as the arbiter of taste, Dormer then set out to demonstrate this argument through the exhibition's narrative.

The historical section of the exhibition was structured around Clement Greenberg's notion of kitsch something that watered down tradition by adopting its effects without regard for its ideological origins.[36] Dormer illustrated his thesis with objects, using Korean, Japanese and Chinese pots as the unmediated tradition at the pinnacle. He proposed that the work followed a downward trajectory from this point, beginning with Leach, who, he claimed, mistranslated the Japanese tradition and catalyzed the descent into kitsch. His narrative culminated in a phenomenon that he christened 'the ploughman's pot': a label intended to draw an analogy between the Anglo-Oriental pot and the Milk Marketing Board's invention of the ploughman's lunch.[37] This was exemplified by the work of Bernard's son, David Leach.

Dormer's narrative also drew upon the theories of Eric Hobsbawm, who proposed that some traditions were invented in order to create a sense of continuity with the past.[38] Their naturalisation could, Hobsbawm argued, derail the evolution of cultural practices and perpetuate models that are detached from contemporary life. This idea resonated with Dormer, who felt that the dominance of Leach's Anglo-Oriental orthodoxy had led to an elision of the fact that the primary function of pottery in contemporary life was decorative. By exposing the flaw in the standard that Leach laid out in *A Potter's Book*, he cleared a space in which to construct an alternative history, based on decorative traditions. He used the work of two potters to mark the transition between the historical and modern sections of the exhibition: in his notebook he explained 'Very often kitsch has undermined ceramics. However [Michael] Cardew (English trad.) Coper (European) saved the day.'[39]

Dormer's claim that there was a core 'ceramics' to be undermined highlighted the constrictive nature of his outlook. By adopting a linear trajectory he was able to identify Cardew and Coper as the inheritors of those traditions, and the starting point for more recent work, without addressing extra-disciplinary influences. He extended this approach in the modern section of the exhibition, where he juxtaposed contemporary pots with historical objects in order to highlight stylistic affinities. His display strategies included making visual analogies between Janice Tchalenko's brightly coloured work and a 16th century Palissy dish, which inspired her, and the work of Cardew, Glen Lukens and Richard Slee. By doing so he positioned the new works as the logical next steps in the continuous evolution of particular decorative traditions. Dormer also included pieces from Tchalenko's collaboration with Dartington Pottery, indicating that he was keen to explode the opposition of hand-made and industrial, which was at the core of the ideology that surrounded the crafts. Instead, he emphasized the works' shared status as pottery.

Dormer decided to work with the ICA in an attempt to market ceramics to a different audience. Nevertheless, he maintained that the modern pot was a minor art for domestic consumption, which was located between utility and ornament.[40] This created a conflict between the message communicated by the traditional white cube exhibition space, which 'subtracts all cues that interfere with the fact that [an object] is "art"' and Dormer's thesis that the home was the true place for pottery.[41] He was alert to the fact that the small scale of many ceramic forms could leave them stranded in white cube spaces and moved to counteract this by displaying blown up images of details from the smaller works above them. Poncelet's work, in particular, though, highlighted the destabilizing power of context. Dormer stressed that it would be an applied art, rather than sculpture show and Paul Filmer's catalogue essay foregrounded the links between her technique and pottery. However, the work itself demanded open, plinth-based presentation, which emphasized its sculptural presence.[42]

The exhibition closed with works by Rie, Coper, and Bill Newland, which Dormer felt resisted 'the craft fayre content of the post-war pottery revival,' arranged on a series of plinths of different heights.[43] By placing Newland, whose work engaged with design, architecture, figuration and decoration, on a pedestal alongside the celebrated pairing of Rie and Coper, Dormer afforded him a status on a par with these acknowledged greats.[44] Situating the trio's work at the close of the show, he also positioned them as the polar opposite of the kitsch that opened it: an alternative standard, the precepts of which were crystallized in his book *The New Ceramics: Trends and Traditions*, which was published the following year.[45]

Whilst the free use of materials and the appropriation of forms by fine artists had rendered many of Greenberg's arguments about medium specificity and autonomy obsolete by the time of the exhibition, Dormer continued to use them as a reference point. In a draft for a text panel headed 'Familiar Forms' he wrote 'Pottery can offer delight or solace. But it is neither questioning. Nor subversive of the status quo.'[46] This argument turned Greenberg's claim that avant-garde art must challenge cultural norms on its head: whereas the lack of a critical edge had been seen to exclude and marginalize pottery from fine art discourse, Dormer embraced that separation and used it to argue for distinction. The futility of this position was highlighted two years later in the *Vessel* exhibition at the Serpentine Gallery. Curator Anthony Stokes's claim that it would challenge 'the spurious distinctions between the fine arts and the crafts,' may have ignored the continued categorical distinction between the two, but the exhibition demonstrated that ceramic vessels could be used in a variety of ways, challenging any effort impose one definition on them.[47] Viewed with this in mind, *Fast Forward* might be perceived as a bid to argue for ceramics' place as a discrete, modernist discipline at a time when traditional boundaries were being eroded: a situation Dormer later admitted he found problematic.[48]

The use of ceramic forms and materials by artists from outside the field had a more direct impact on *The Raw and the Cooked: New Work in Clay in Britain* (1993). Prominent potter Alison Britton and critic and former *Crafts* magazine editor Martina Margetts curated the exhibition, which brought works by trained ceramicists together with the clay works of established sculptors, at the invitation of David Elliot: Director of The Museum of Modern Art, Oxford.[49] Produced eight years after *Fast Forward*, it focused on the artistic potential of the material.

The initial premise of the venture, provisionally titled: *The Undomesticated Product: New Perimeters in British Ceramic Art* was to demonstrate that:

> Those ceramics, intimate yet referential, which transcend the requirements of utility to deal with views of the world, rather than those of the home, and which unite the concerns of paintings and sculpture in volumetric, decorated forms, can be viewed as a branch of art.[50]

This title and description explicitly declared the preconceptions of ceramic works that the curators hoped to challenge: that they were necessarily domestic and utilitarian. Asserting that, by contrast, the type of ceramic practice the exhibition addressed could be viewed as a *branch* of art, rather than a part of fine art, the proposal might be read in relation to the ideas that Britton set out in her famous 1981 text from *The Maker's Eye* catalogue. Expressing the desire that self-referential works such as her own, which were concerned with the 'outer limits of function', be viewed as a phenomenon that was 'closely in line with 'modernism' in the other arts,' she did not consider the temporal distance between the appearance of 'modernism' in the examples she cited and the ceramic works she described.[51] This might be interpreted as a claim, not for inclusion, which would have demanded a consideration of the contextual specificity of these other iterations of modernism, but for equivalence on the grounds of approach. The *Undomesticated Product…* proposal, albeit twelve years after *The Maker's Eye*, retained a similar concern with elevating the artworld status of a particular area of ceramic practice, without eroding the distinction of medium-specificity. From this perspective, the exhibition might be regarded as a challenge on the epistemological basis of the overarching category of ceramics, which had affinities to similar endeavours to separate artistic and practical photography in the 1970s.[52]

Although the initial sobriquet favoured works such as Britton's, which emanated from the ceramic community and centred on the vessel as concept, the final title, *The Raw and the Cooked: New Work in Clay in Britain*, could encompass a broader spectrum of work. Of those included in the final grouping, Antony Gormley, Tony Cragg, Bruce McLean, Jefford Horrigan and – to a degree – Grayson Perry and Poncelet, all operated outside the crafts. Brian Illsley and Stephenie Bergman were also known for their work in other craft media.[53] However, whilst it is unlikely that any of these artists would align their work with the separate branch of art delineated in the original proposal, they were included in a selection that was heavily weighted towards those with ceramics training who adopted art-oriented approaches. Furthermore, despite Margetts discussing its importance in her catalogue essay, there was no design in this take on 'new work in clay.'[54]

To some extent, the scope of the exhibition was better defined by its exclusions, which Margetts described as anybody 'whose purpose was to make work in clay that was for use, only, primarily for use in a utilitarian way.'[55] Indeed, critic Edward Lucie-Smith viewed the exhibition as a rebellion against the patriarchal figure of Bernard Leach, which maintained many of his values, in particular the rejection of mass-production.[56] This accusation is borne out by the catalogue essays and archival papers, where Leach is repeatedly referenced as both an influence and a force, whose dominance had obscured the diversity of ceramic practice. Indeed, although she discussed how cultural relativism opened the door to new understandings of clay, Margetts's proposal that 'Here clay is not a craft material, but an authentic medium for sculpture,' highlighted her concern with challenging the dominant model of ceramic practice.[57] Her dichotomous stance might, therefore, have been motivated by a desire to counter 'the critical and institutional biases,' which she felt had inhibited the development of non-vessel based ceramic practice in Britain.[58]

The works in *The Raw and the Cooked* were 'chosen out of personal interest,' based on the curators' understandings of ceramic practice at the time.[59] They were then split into loose categories, which changed as the exhibition evolved, and which were not immediately apparent in the final displays. This approach avoided the pitfalls of choosing works to illustrate themes, rather than on their own merit. Nevertheless, by exposing the arbitrary nature of medium-based categorization, it also brought the exhibition's focus into question.

In a revised synopsis of the exhibition's aims Margetts underscored the fluidity of the categories used to plan the show and the potential for cross-referencing works.[60] By contrast, whilst Britton also acknowledged that some works 'cut across categories,' her description of the exhibition as 'a synthesis, as a resolved combination of disparate ingredients, like a meal' suggested an integration that was lacking.[61] Although she claimed that 'the common ground is not just the substance of clay, but the common chemistry and technology that the practitioner has had to grasp with varying degrees of elaboration,' the differing role that medium played within each work, and the varied attitudes to technical prowess, challenged the logic of medium-specific practice.[62]

Whilst this disharmony may have provided opportunities to consider the differences between the exhibits, John Pawson's design, which centred on white plinths and which was used to situate the works in 'as undomestic a setting as possible,' represented a clear attempt to shift them from the category of crafts, into that of sculpture, in line with Margetts's aforementioned catalogue essay.[63] Indeed, Elliott professed that the white cube layout was designed to do exactly that, creating minimum interference with the work and forming a direct contrast with the massed ranks of ceramic vessels found in connoisseurial museum displays.[64] As Brian O' Doherty, in particular, has argued, this approach, often described in terms of transparency or neutrality, can perpetuate the myth of the autonomous artwork.[65] It also encouraged visitors to address the works from an optical standpoint, rather than considering the more nuanced referential qualities of clay, which were signposted by the adoption of anthropologist Lévi Strauss's title *The Raw and the Cooked* for the exhibition.

Elliott hoped the focus on the works engendered by the display would challenge conventional modes of categorization and, in the same vein, The Barbican issued a press release that described the exhibition as 'the first major exhibition to address the issue of how British artists working in clay have broken with the accepted notions and expectations of their place within the arts.'[66] However, the inclusion of work by prominent sculptors such as Gormley and Cragg challenged the idea that there *was* an expected place for artists who worked with clay at that point. These were not works that received marginal billing on their curriculum vitae, but constituent parts of their oeuvres alongside works in other media. Instead, the exhibition might be read as another venture to raise the art world status of works produced within the ceramic field, where medium-specificity still held sway. As reviewer David Whiting suggested:

> ... the show perhaps paints a truer picture of the faltering ceramic push towards fine art – an interesting survey of those makers who, over the last twenty years or so, have tried expand clay's vocabulary. Some have succeeded, many have not.[67]

This tension between disciplinary heritage and ambition was also evident in the curators' catalogue texts: whilst Margetts alluded to the expansion of artistic practice, addressing process and the experiential, she maintained the distinction 'ceramic art.'[68] Similarly, Britton claimed that ceramic objects were universally understandable, yet acknowledged the impossibility of assigning works to a single category. The conflicting emphases of the layout and contents of the exhibition, as well as the literature that surrounded it, thus further highlighted the inadequacies of medium-based definition and the limitations that it imposed on those who confined themselves to the field.

After Modernism

Over the past fifteen years the concept of the expanded field has gained currency in the discourse around ceramics.[69] Taken from Rosalind Krauss's seminal essay *Sculpture in the Expanded Field*, the term was originally coined in response to the emergence of art practices that defied conventional classifications during the 1960s and '70s.[70] However, it was only in the 1990s that the rise of concept and context-oriented practices began to uproot one facet of ceramic practice – the art-oriented strand – from its basis in object making. Whilst *The Raw and the Cooked* included several works in this vein, in 2004 Tate Liverpool mounted an exhibition – *A Secret History of Clay: From Gauguin to Gormley* – that has since come to symbolize this shift.[71]

Co-curated by Tate Liverpool's head of exhibitions Simon Groom and potter and writer Edmund De Waal, the exhibition was an ambitious, if more tightly defined take on medium. Like De Waal's book *20th Century Ceramics*, which provided its starting point, the exhibition had a chronological layout and explored how artists within established art historical movements had used clay.[72] However, whilst De Waal's book also included industrial and studio pottery, most of the precedents in the exhibition – including the artists named in the title – were drawn from the world of fine art.

Groom took the vessel as a key motif in the exhibition, partly, he admitted, because he was frustrated with the hermetic craft discourse that surrounded it.[73] He intended to challenge this insular approach by creating a narrative that exploded outwards from Gauguin's traditional vessel forms, through increasingly larger and more ambiguous works such as those of Cragg and Richard Deacon, before returning the visitor to the domestic-scaled vessel with a renewed perspective.[74] This transition was emphasized by the placement of Clare Twomey's installation *Consciousness/Conscience* (2004) in the doorway to the final section. The work was comprised of 96 ceramic tiles made by Royal Crown Derby to the artist's specification, which the visitor was compelled to step on in order to reach the final section of the exhibition. Crushing them in the process, they engaged with the materiality of clay and broke the taboo of smashing ceramics within a gallery.

Twomey's work led to a room set filled with ceramic objects, which ranged from Slee's brooms, balanced against the wall, to Frances Upritchard's re-purposed stoneware jars, which were displayed in a glass-fronted cabinet. Groom wanted this section to look as domestic and far from a museum environment as possible: an approach that contrasted with that of *The Raw and the Cooked*, where domestic associations were explicitly avoided.[75] It is notable, however, that although James Turrell's *Lapsed Quaker Ware* (1998) and Cindy Sherman's *Madame du Pompadour* tea service (1989-1991) were housed in a glass-fronted case, Andrew Lord asked for his *Profile Vase (Duchamp) 'The Recovery of Meaning'* (2002) to be separated out.[76] This move by Lord – a trained ceramicist who had successfully used sculptural display and the art gallery context as means of communicating the non-functionality of his vessel-based works – highlighted their susceptibility to curatorial re-authoring.[77] Torn from the frame he had inserted it into and attached a biography that reinforced his ceramic training, his vase might be read according to the laws of that field – as a vase. His fierce reaction suggested that the hierarchical distinction between the home as subject of and destination for artistic practice continued to impact on his practice.[78]

Tate Director Christoph Grunenberg described *A Secret History of Clay* as 'The first exhibition to present artists who have worked in clay from the beginning of the twentieth century to the present day.'[79] However, it largely centred on works by artists who had established places in the canonical histories of art. Contemporary practitioners with a ceramics-specific focus were only admitted to the category of 'artists who have worked in clay' to a noticeable degree in the final section. Here, their work was seen to overlap with dominant artworld approaches, rather than vice-versa. Furthermore, whilst staging this exhibition at the Tate – an archetypal modern art gallery – might be seen to signal institutional acknowledgement, it was relegated to a regional outpost and stood apart from permanent collections displays, leaving the galleries' core narratives intact.[80]

Although De Waal asserted that the exhibition offered just one possible history of clay, it constructed a heritage for art-oriented contemporary practice, which collapsed the status-limiting distinction between medium-led and concept-led practices.[81] Krauss observed the emergence of comparable root-seeking strategies, which she regarded as attempts to re-establish boundaries, in response to the expansion of sculptural practice.[82] From the perspective of the ceramic field, the exhibition also, therefore, conformed to Griselda Pollock's description of canon building, forging a 'retrospectively legitimating backbone of a cultural and political identity, a consolidated narrative of origin, conferring authority on the texts selected to naturalize this function.'[83] Situated towards the exit, De Waal's *Porcelain Wall* appeared as the latest manifestation – or even the apotheosis – of this particular history of ceramics.[84]

Composed of multiple ceramic cylinders, which he had hand-thrown, the values embodied in De Waal's work formed an illuminating contrast with the expanded model of authorship evidenced in Gormley's *Field* (1991), which was sited on the second floor. For Gormley, each figure – made by a different individual – was a component of an artwork that he had choreographed, whereas De Waal was attempting to navigate the territory between the hand-making of objects and authorship of an artwork. A mocked-up design for the private view invitation, which incorporated fingerprints, was vetoed on the grounds that it had craft associations, rather than art. However, the text panel that accompanied Gormley's *Field* (1991) stressed that each of the 35,000 figures were handcrafted.[85] These disconsonant examples further underscored the contingency of meaning: De Waal employed an in-built framing device to ensure his work was read sculpturally, privileging the overall concept, whilst the evidence of outsourced hand-making served conceptual ends in Gormley's work. In his catalogue essay, Groom pronounced that shifts in context and display had rendered traditional distinctions between art and craft irrelevant.[86] Drawing on Pollock, it might, instead, be argued that we are 'after' rather than 'post' modernism and that the historic distinctions between art and craft continue to shape the discourse around ceramics.[87]

In a retrospective interview about the exhibition, Groom admitted: 'the more you look, the more artists do work in clay, and so it becomes a bit ridiculous. It's a bit like putting on a show of painting or something.'[88] His words echoed those of Barbara Zucker, co-founder of the USA's first all-female co-operative gallery (AIR). As she posited, although it was obvious with hindsight, it was necessary to declare this work's presence in order to show that it existed.[89] However, whilst De Waal claimed that the collaboration between fine artists and ceramicists had been excluded from history, this accusation might equally be levelled at the institutions and publications that have forged the histories of ceramics.[90] Indeed, in a preview of the exhibition for *Crafts* magazine, Harrod suggested that the exhibition might be a wake-up call for studio ceramicists, as it showed clay work by successful artists whose practice was not ceramic-centric.[91] The subsequent prominence of the exhibition in the critical discourse around ceramics, when compared with its minimal impact on the canonical histories of art, indicates that this was its real achievement.[92]

A Secret History of Clay was produced on the cusp of change: the Crafts Council repositioned itself with regard to both artistic media and exhibitions at the dawn of the twenty-first century. Their own exhibition space was closed in 2006 and they began to work more closely with established museums, including the V&A, to facilitate shows such as *Out of the Ordinary: Spectacular Craft* (2007) and *The Power of Making* (2011). These exhibitions illustrated how craft processes could be employed to a host of ends, which moved beyond traditional craft media and forms. They were part of broader critical efforts to reframe craft as a verb, which pivoted on the idea that 'Craft only exists in motion. It is a way of doing things, not a classification of objects, institutions or people.'[93] Born amidst this climate, *Possibilities and Losses: Transitions in Clay* – an exhibition staged by Middleborough Institute of Modern Art in association with The Crafts Council in 2009 – reflected the contemporary intellectual current and the Crafts Council's new role.

Possibilities and Losses developed from ceramicist Clare Twomey's proposal for a show that would dovetail with her academic research into artists who worked with installation, clay and craft. Twomey and senior curator James Beighton produced the exhibition together, with Beighton selecting Twomey's *Monument* (2009) as a starting point. The work, which Twomey was producing for the Zuiderzee Museum in Holland at the time, was comprised of a pile of ceramic waste from the Johnson Tiles Factory in Stoke-on-Trent. En masse, the fragmentary, broken and rejected objects attained a colossal presence. The work resounded with questions about human mortality and commemoration as well as referencing the decline of the British ceramics industry. However, rather than providing a fixed and insurmountable inheritance, Twomey's take on the past was a temporary agglomeration. A testament to past loss that threatened collapse rather than offering the illusion of permanence, it became material for the present: something highlighted in the titular emphasis on *transition*. Furthermore, taking ceramics as material and subject, and deferring the production of the clay objects to unseen craftspeople in industry, it also raised questions about Twomey's identity as a ceramicist.

Beighton and Twomey were keenly aware that the exhibition had the potential to perpetuate existing medium-based divisions and did not want to produce a survey show. Rather than trying to balance the need for structural organization with the diversity of practices, they reduced its scope to 'four artists, four rooms, four possibilities.'[94] Proceeding from *Monument*, they turned to a pre-existing list of artists with whom they would like to work, selecting works that were united more by conceptual affinity than discipline-specific criteria. However, as the impetus for the exhibition came from Twomey's ceramics-centred research and the other works, necessarily involved clay. It might, therefore, be argued that the academic funding system at that time, which demanded distinction, curtailed the opportunities for intradisciplinary dialogue provided by the work itself.

Fragmentary or process-based, the works in the exhibition confronted the idea of the discrete and innocuous decorative art object. One of the electrical circuits in Keith Harrison's *Brother* (2009) failed during a live firing with a full school group in situ, necessitating an evacuation of the building. Twomey's *Monument* (2009), an 8-metre tall pitcher pile of broken ceramic seconds from factories around Stoke-on-Trent, also required constant invigilation. Neil Brownsword's *Salvage Series* (2005) also focused on industrial detritus: detached from context, the fragments of industrial waste became beautiful artefacts. However, for the final artist Linda Sormin, the confrontation with museum norms was more explicit: curator Beighton was invited to crawl through the paths made available to him on opening night and attack the work with a hammer. Responding to the work, Adamson asked 'Once a museum has staged a ceramic exhibition where most of the clay is either unfired or broken, and which features a curator smashing a sculpture into bits, how in all decency can it go back to placing lovely vessels on plinths?'[95] He also proposed that the four artists in the exhibition had taken on the role of 'self-conscious outsiders,' arguing that this gave them a fresh perspective on medium and describing Brownsword as 'The Historian', Sormin as 'The Immigrant', Harrison as 'The Alien' and Twomey as 'The Curator.'[96] Nevertheless, as artists with ceramic training whose works are mainly discussed within the ceramic field, these roles were only assumed. Equally, the answer to his question about Sormin's work depended on the works being read in relationship to existing perceptions of ceramics, as these norms had already been challenged in other areas of art practice.

Hal Foster argued that artists are often asked to adopt the position of the ethnographer and accorded the right to speak on behalf of a marginalized constituency, to which they are seen to belong.[97] This approach pivots on the idea that those who are culturally or socially 'other' have access to a higher level of access to alterity and, therefore, transformative power. Adamson's description of the artists, as 'other' to the dominant field of ceramics might be seen to fall into this trap. As a model, it reinstituted the dialectic of inside/outside and allowed the institution at the centre – in this case that of ceramics – to appear self-reflexive, whilst leaving its core premise untouched. However, it also reflected the persistence of the category of ceramics and its relationship to academic organization, funding and the market. In this context, Miwon Kwon's argument that

> … the distinguishing characteristic of today's site-oriented art is the way in which both the art work's relationship to the actuality of a location (as site) and the social conditions of the institutional frame (as site) are subordinate to a discursively determined site that is delineated as a field of knowledge, intellectual exchange, or cultural debate

may prove more fruitful.[98] All of the exhibiting artists had established histories of producing site-specific work and had engaged with discursive sites that ranged from climate change to electrical engineering. From this perspective, the museum, as a site that categorizes, could be regarded as another place of friction – one where artists with medium specific training could work through the contradictions of their position. It might further be contended that although they were not comprised of site-specific works, that discursive site – the constitution of the ceramic field – was also the intended and ultimate site of effect for the other exhibitions in this paper.

Adamson proposed that the four artists in *Possibilities and Losses* 'define a moment in ceramic history.'[99] For him, the demise of the ceramics industry and the closure of ceramic-specific courses was leading ceramics to an end of sorts; a scene from which those artists emerged, offering a way forward, which mobilized, but was not constrained by, history. However, the other exhibitions discussed in this paper were, similarly, produced in response to the challenges posed by new forms of administration and practice, from the foundation of the Crafts Council and the growth of fine artists' work in clay to trained ceramicists' engagement with sculpture and installation. As they demonstrated, whilst temporary exhibitions can expand the scope of medium-specific discourse they can also impose alternative, but equally restrictive, frames. Furthermore, the ceramic field has proven adept at reconfiguring itself in the face of change: whilst ceramics courses in Britain have continued to close, 2009 also saw the launch of The British Ceramics Biennial in Stoke-on-Trent, 2011 brought the major AHRC-funded project *Ceramics in the Expanded Field: Behind the Scenes at the Museum*, which this paper forms part of, and in 2012 Cardiff School of Art held a conference with the explicitly separatist title *Ceramics and Sculpture: Different Disciplines and Shared Concerns*. The discourse around ceramics has also been perpetuated through publications including *Ceramic Review*, *Ceramics: Art and Perception* and the online journals *Interpreting Ceramics* and *C-File*, as well as international exhibitions and ceramics biennials. These initiatives have largely remained distinct from, yet functioned in dialogue with, the expansion of non-hierarchical approaches to craft within art and design practice in the same period.[100] Whilst only time will tell if the Adamson's 'moment' will lead to the explosion or reconstitution of the ceramic field, the examples in this paper illustrated that, as De Waal suggested, there is great potential in an approach to categorization that emphasizes the 'perhaps.'[101]

laura.breen@gmail.com

Notes

1. This paper is based upon a chapter of my forthcoming PhD thesis *Re-modelling Clay: Ceramic Practice and the Museum in Britain (1970-2013)*, which is part of the AHRC-funded project *Ceramics in the Expanded Field: Behind the Scenes at the Museum* at the University of Westminster. My research focuses on the dialogue between art-oriented ceramic practice and museum practice since 1970. It concentrates on developments in Britain, as they were embedded in a particular set of socio-economic circumstances, which shaped the evolution of ceramic education and museum practice. Whilst alert to developments in artistic practice outside the field of ceramics, for the sake of clarity, it addresses them only when they impact on that field's constitution.
2. Adamson proposed that craft 'emerged as a coherent idea, a defined terrain, only as industry's opposite number or "other."' Glenn Adamson, *The Invention of Craft*, London & New York: Bloomsbury, 2013, xiii.
3. Philip Rawson, *Ceramics*, London; New York: Oxford University Press, 1971.
4. Edward Lucie-Smith, 'The Biddable Clay', *Ceramic Review*, 44, 1977, 6; Glenn Adamson, *Thinking through Craft*, London: Berg & V&A Museum, 2007.
5. Benjamin Buchloh, 'Conceptual Art 1962-69: From the Aesthetic of Administration to the Critique of Institutions', *October*, 55, 105–43.
6. The predominant means of addressing contemporary practice in the museum since the late 1960s, temporary exhibitions allow museums to explore its rapidly changing terrain without the commitment of permanent acquisition. They also create a time-limited event that demands visitors' presence and can raise attendance levels. See James M Bradburne, 'A New Strategic Approach to the Museum and its Relationship to Society', *Museum Management and Curatorship*, 19:1, 2001, 75–84.
7. Sandy Nairne, 'Exhibitions of Contemporary Art', Emma Barker, ed., *Contemporary Cultures of Display*, New Haven: London: Yale University Press in association with Open University, 1999, 105–126.
8. Corinne A. Kratz, 'Rhetorics of Value: Constituting Worth and Meaning Through Cultural Display', *Visual Anthropology Review*, 27:1, 2011, 21.
9. The notion that the status of ceramics and the crafts might be elevated through the development of a critical framework has been a persistent concern during the period addressed in this paper. As Tanya Harrod has observed, during the 1980s *Crafts* magazine moved to incorporate more critical writing, bringing in writers from outside the crafts world such as Peter Fuller, Peter Dormer, Christopher Reid and Rosemary Hill to engage with these issues. See Tanya Harrod, 'Crafts', *Journal of Design History*. 7: 4, 1994, 299–301 [online]. Available from Jstor: <http://www.jstor.org/stable/1316070> [Accessed 28 January 2013]. This has also led to the growth of critical texts in discipline specific and craft magazines, conference papers and exhibition catalogues. Decades later, in 2004 *Think Tank*; an initiative involving nine key thinkers in the field of craft from across Europe was formed. Its stated aim 'to articulate the significance of the field in the face of rapid change', indicates the continued effort in this area. See Think Tank, *Think Tank. A European Initiative for the Applied Arts*. [online] Austria: City of Gmunden, 2006. Available from: http://www.thinktank04.eu [Accessed 14 February 2013].
10. Bernard Leach, *A Potter's Book*, London; Boston: Faber & Faber, 1986 (Original work published 1940).
11. Tanya Harrod, *The Crafts in Britain in the Twentieth Century*, New Haven: Yale University Press, 1999.
12. Bradford City Art Gallery & Museums, *Modern Ceramics '71* [exhib. cat.], Yorkshire: Bradford City Art Gallery & Museums, 1971.
13. Bradford City Art Gallery & Museums, *Modern Ceramics '71* [exhib. cat.]
14. Hepburn exhibited work in the exhibition and also gave a talk on American Ceramics as part of the events programme: see Merete Bates. 'Breakaway Clay', *The Guardian*, 21 May 1971. Available from: Proquest www.proquest.com [accessed 5 December 2012]
15. Merete Bates, 'Breakaway Clay'.
16. Bradford City Art Gallery & Museums, *Modern Ceramics '71* [exhib. cat.]
17. The Teacher, 'Dig this clay at Bradford', *The Teacher*, 14 May 1971.

18. 'It must always be remembered that the dissociation of use and beauty is a purely arbitrary thing. It is true that pots exist which are useful and not beautiful, and other that are beautiful and impractical; but neither of these extremes can be considered normal: the normal is a balanced combination of the two.' Bernard Leach, *A Potter's Book*, 18.
19. Arthur C Danto, 'The Transfiguration of the Commonplace', *Journal of Aesthetics and Art Criticism*, 33:2, 139.
20. This subject was the focus of Craftsmen Potter's Association secretary David Canter's introduction to the first issue of *Ceramic Review*. See David Canter, 'From the Secretary's Desk', *Ceramic Review*, 1, 1970, 2.
21. Bradford City Art Gallery & Museums. *Modern Ceramics '71* [exhib. cat.].
22. Merete Bates, 'Breakaway Clay' *The Guardian*; William Alfred Ismay, 'Modern Ceramics, 1971', *Ceramic Review*, 9, 1971, 15.
23. Parliamentary Debates, House of Lords, 5th Series, vol 323, 28 July 1971, Lord Eccles announces the formation of the Crafts Advisory Committee.
24. Bernard Leach, *A Potter's Book*, 1. See also Tanya Harrod, *Factfile on the History of the Crafts Council*. Great Britain: The Crafts Council, 1994, 7.
25. Victor Margrie, 'The work of the Crafts Advisory Committee', *Museums Journal*, 74: 3, 1974, 117–118.
26. David Vaughan, interview by Laura Breen, 12 June 2013.
27. Adamson, *The Invention of Craft*, xiii.
28. Percy Peacock, interview by Laura Breen, 19 April 2013.
29. Percy Peacock, 'Artist Statement', *State of Clay: A Sunderland Arts Centre Touring Exhibition* [exhib. cat.], Sunderland: Sunderland Arts Centre, 1978, 39.
30. Percy Peacock, interview by Laura Breen, 19 April 2013.
31. Marigold Colman, 'Introduction', *State of Clay: A Sunderland Arts Centre Touring Exhibition, 5–6.*
32. Tony Knipe and David Vaughan, 'Foreword', *State of Clay: A Sunderland Arts Centre Touring Exhibition,* 3. For further discussion of how meaning is produced through exhibitions in relation to associated texts see Eilean Hooper-Greenhill, *Museums and their Visitors*, London: Routledge, 1994, 115–139.
33. Tanya Harrod, *The Crafts in Britain in the Twentieth Century*, 370.
34. Peter Dormer, *The Crafts in Question: Pot Luck – British Studio Pottery Today, Institute of Contemporary Arts, London, April 30, 1985,* audio, British Library, MP3, 02:04:17, accessed 11 November, 2014 http://sounds.bl.uk/Arts-literature-and-performance/ICA-talks/024M-C0095X0174XX-0100V0. In the discussions at the accompanying seminar 'Pot Luck,' Dormer stressed that he did not wish the exhibition to be didactic, but to provoke debate. However, in order to do so, he took a very clear stance from the outset.
35. Peter Dormer, 'Notebook re: ceramics exhibition ICA Spring '85. Preliminary ideas. Attn: Declan McGonagle', ICA *collection* [manuscript] *955/7/7/29*, London: Tate Archive, 1985.
36. Clement Greenberg, 'Avant-garde and kitsch', *Partisan Review,* 6: 5, 1939, 34–39.
37. Richard Eyre's film, *The Ploughman's Lunch,* which was based on a screenplay by Ian McEwan, brought the Milk Marketing Board's promotion of the ploughman's lunch – and debate about its authenticity – to public attention in 1983.
38. Eric Hobsbawm and Terence Ranger, eds, *The Invention of Tradition,* Cambridge: Cambridge University Press, 1983.
39. Peter Dormer, 'Notebook re: ceramics exhibition ICA Spring '85. Preliminary ideas. Attn: Declan McGonagle.'
40. Peter Dormer, 'Notebook re: ceramics exhibition ICA Spring '85. Preliminary ideas. Attn: Declan McGonagle.'
41. Brian O' Doherty, *Inside the White Cube: The Ideology of the Gallery Space*, California: University of California Press, 1976, 14.
42. Paul Filmer, 'Jacqui Poncelet', *Fast Forward* [exhib. cat.] London: Institute of Contemporary Arts, 1985, 28–32; Peter Dormer, 'Notebook re: ceramics exhibition ICA Spring '85. Preliminary ideas. Attn: Declan McGonagle.'
43. Peter Dormer, 'Notebook re: ceramics exhibition ICA Spring '85. Preliminary ideas. Attn: Declan McGonagle.'

44. Harrod's article *The Forgotten '50s*, which has been credited with raising the profile of the group of artists known as the 'Picassoettes' to which Newland belonged, was not published until 1989. Tanya Harrod, 'The forgotten '50s', *Crafts*. 98:3, 1989, 30–33.
45. Peter Dormer, *The New Ceramics: Trends and Traditions*, London: Thames and Hudson, 1986.
46. Peter Dormer, 'Notebook re: ceramics exhibition ICA Spring '85. Preliminary ideas. Attn: Declan McGonagle.'
47. Andrew Graham-Dixon, 'The Blackboard Jungle', *The Independent, 29* September 1987. [online] http://www.andrewgrahamdixon.com/archive/readArticle/1105> Accessed: 5 June 2013.
48. Peter Dormer, *The New Ceramics: Trends and Traditions*, London: Thames and Hudson, 1994 (revised).
49. Margetts and Britton were not interviewed during the course of this research, which focusses on contemporary archival material, although they provided extensive feedback on the content of this article.
50. Alison Britton and Martina Margetts, 'Draft exhibition proposal', *The Raw and the Cooked collection*. Oxford: Modern Art Oxford archive, about 1991.
51. Alison Britton, 'Alison Britton (artist's statement)', *The Maker's Eye* [exhibition cat.], London: Crafts Council. 1981, 16. This could be regarded as an attempt to argue for the works' status in an avant-garde artworld wherein Clement Greenberg's had once asserted 'In turning his attention away from subject matter of common experience, the poet or artist turns it in upon the medium of his own craft.' Clement Greenberg, 'Avant-garde and kitsch', *Partisan Review*, 6: 5, 1939, 34-39.
52. Douglas Crimp, 'Photographs at the End of Modernism', *On the Museum's Ruins*, 2–42.
53. Whilst Perry positioned himself in the fine art world, he, along with Illsley and Bergman, received attention in ceramics and craft publications and were not, therefore, entirely outside of the field.
54. Martina Margetts, 'Metamorphosis: The Culture of Ceramics', *The Raw and the Cooked* [exhibition cat.] 1993.
55. Martina Margetts, 'Transcript of talk for The Raw and the cooked symposium: Oxford Brookes University', *The Raw and the Cooked collection*, Oxford: Modern Art Oxford archive, 1994.
56. Edward Lucie-Smith, 'The Raw and the Cooked' *Ceramic Review*, 143, 1993, 21.
57. Martina Margetts, 'Metamorphosis: the culture of ceramics', 15.
58. Martina Margetts, 'Metamorphosis: the culture of ceramics', 14.
59. Alison Britton, 'Use, beauty, ugliness and irony' *The Raw and the Cooked* [exhibition cat.], 1993, 10. These loose categories included, at various points, The Person, The Building, The Landscape, The Pot, then Transitional Objects; Abstraction; Landscape; Landscape of the Mind and Appearances; and also Tradition and Irony, Abstraction and the Hollow Form, Nature, Cultural Identity and the Figure. See exhibition notes and press releases in*The Raw and the Cooked collection*, Oxford: Modern Art Oxford archive, 1994.
60. Martina Margetts, 'Revised synopsis', *The Raw and the Cooked collection*, Oxford: Modern Art Oxford archive, 1993.
61. Alison Britton, 'Use, beauty, ugliness and irony' *The Raw and the Cooked* [exhibition cat.], 1993, 10.
62. Alison Britton, 'Use, beauty, ugliness and irony' *The Raw and the Cooked* [exhibition cat.], 1993, 10.
63. Pawson is now famed for his minimalist approach to light and space. Margetts had admired the stark simplicity of his design for an exhibition of tools at the V&A and wanted a similar look. See Alison Britton, 'Transcript of talk for The Raw and the Cooked symposium: Oxford Brookes University', *The Raw and the Cooked collection*, Oxford: Modern Art Oxford archive, 1994.
64. Alison Britton, 'Use, beauty, ugliness and irony' *The Raw and the Cooked* [exhibition cat.], 1993, 9-10.
65. Brian O' Doherty, *Inside the White Cube: The Ideology of the Gallery Space.*
66. David Elliott, 'Letter to John Pawson', [correspondence], *The Raw and the Cooked collection*, Oxford: Modern Art Oxford archive, 10 January 1993; Barbican, 'Press Release', *The Raw and the Cooked collection*, Oxford: Modern Art Oxford archive, 1993.
67. David Whiting, 'Thought provoking, but uneven choices …', *Studio Pottery*, 5, 1993, 10–14.
68. Martina Margetts, 'Metamorphosis: the culture of ceramics', 13.

69. Garth Clark, ed., *Ceramic Millennium. Critical Writings on Ceramic History, Theory and Art,* Halifax, Nova Scotia: Press of the Nova Scotia College of Art and Design, 2006; Cigalle Hanaor, ed., *Breaking the Mould: New Approaches to Ceramics*, London: Black Dog Publishing, 2007; Emmanuel Cooper, *Contemporary Ceramics*, London: Thames & Hudson, 2009.
70. Rosalind Krauss, 'Sculpture in the Expanded Field', *October*, 8, 1979, 30–44.
71. Peter Lewis, 'Fired up: ceramics and meaning', *Fired up: Ceramics and Meaning*, Oldham: Gallery Oldham, 2010, 5–7.
72. Edmund De Waal, *20th Century Ceramics*, London; New York: Thames & Hudson, 2003.
73. Simon Groom, interview by Laura Breen, 12 March 2013.
74. Simon Groom, 'Terra incognita', *A Secret History of Clay from Gauguin to Gormley,* 15–18.
75. Simon Groom, 'Email to Mark Lomas at Doncaster Museum', *Tate archive*, 6 May 2004.
76. Simon Groom, interview by Laura Breen.
77. When Groom and De Waal, replaced the heavy wire armature of his *Profile Vase (Duchamp) 'The recovery of meaning'* (2002) and placed it on a roped-off side table they hoped to create a dialogue with the domestic history of ceramics. For Lord it was a curatorial attempt to return his work to a decorative origin that it never had and, therefore, obliterated the work. See Edmund De Waal and Simon Groom (eds.) *A Secret History of Clay from Gauguin to Gormley*. Liverpool: Tate Publishing (2004): 36; Simon Groom, interview by Laura Breen; Dawn Ades, *Andrew Lord,* Milton Keynes: Milton Keynes Gallery, 2010, 19.
78. See Colin Painter, 'Introduction', Colin Painter, ed. *Contemporary Art and the Home*, Oxford and New York: Berg, 2002, 1–6.
79. Christoph Grunenberg, 'Introduction', *A Secret History of Clay from Gauguin to Gormley*, Liverpool: Tate Publishing, 2004, 9.
80. The reflexive values promoted by Tate Liverpool, which was founded amidst the social and political unrest of the 1980s, operated in opposition to the traditional values that legitimized Tate Britain. See Andrew Dewdney, David Dibosa and Victoria Walsh, eds. *Post-Critical Museology. Theory and Practice in the Art Museum,* Oxon and New York: Routledge, 2013.
81. Edmund De Waal, 'High unseriousness: artists and clay', *A Secret History of Clay from Gauguin to Gormley,* 38–54.
82. Rosalind Krauss, 'Sculpture in the Expanded Field', *October*, 32. 'No sooner had minimal sculpture appeared on the horizon of the aesthetic experience of the 1960s, than criticism began to construct a paternity for this work, a set of constructivist fathers who could legitimize and thereby authenticate the strangeness of these objects.'
83. Griselda Pollock, 'About canons and culture wars', *Differencing the Canon: Feminism and the Writing of Art's Histories,* London: Routledge, 1999, 3.
84. Although De Waal's book does not feature his own work, Groom felt it was essential to include it in the exhibition. Simon Groom, interview by Laura Breen.
85. Tate archive, handwritten note, *Tate archive*, undated.
86. Simon Groom, 'Terra incognita', *A Secret History of Clay from Gauguin to Gormley,* 15–18.
87. Griselda Pollock, 'Un-framing the modern: critical space/public possibility', *Museums after Modernism: Strategies of Engagement*, Malden, MA: Blackwell, 2007, 1–39.
88. Simon Groom, interview by Laura Breen, 12 March 2013.
89. Sandy Nairne, 'The institutionalization of dissent', Bruce W. Ferguson, Reesa Greenberg and Sandy Nairne, eds. *Thinking about Exhibitions*, London; New York: Routledge, 1996, 387–410.
90. Edmund De Waal, 'In conversation with Laura Britton: Rethinking clay symposium, Tate Liverpool, June 5 2004', *Ceramic Review*, 209, 2004, 61. 'Ironically, it is the postwar history of ceramics itself, as much as the absence of a sympathetic cultural context, which has delayed the present coming of age of British ceramic art.' This is something Margetts also suggested in the *Raw and the Cooked* catalogue. Martina Margetts, 'Metamorphosis: the culture of ceramics' *The Raw and the Cooked* [exhibition cat.] 1993, 13.
91. Tanya Harrod, 'Hidden depths: A Secret History of Clay', *Crafts* 189, 2004, 29–32.

92. See, for example, Andrew Livingstone, *Authenticity of Clay and its Re-definition Within Contemporary Practice: Ceramic Familiarity and the Contribution to Expansion*, unpublished PhD thesis, Northern Ireland: University of Ulster, 2008; Wendy Patricia Tuxill, *A Re-Conceptualisation of Contemporary Sculptural Ceramics from a Post-Minimal Perspective*, unpublished PhD thesis, Hertfordshire: University of Hertfordshire, 2010; Laura Gray, On the Transgressive Nature of Ceramics', *Ceramics: Art and Perception*, 89, 2012, 100–103.
93. Glenn Adamson, *Thinking Through Craft*, 4.
94. James Beighton, interview by Laura Breen, 15 April 2013.
95. Glenn Adamson, 'Outsider artists', *Possibilities and Losses: Transitions in Clay.* Middlesbrough: Middlesbrough Institute of Modern Art, 2009, unpag.
96. Glenn Adamson, 'Outsider Artists', *Possibilities and Losses: Transitions in Clay*, unpag.
97. Hal Foster, *The Return of the Real: The Avant-Garde at the End of the Century*, Cambridge, Mass; London: MIT Press, 1996, 302–309.
98. Miwon Kwon, 'One Place After Another: Notes on Site-Specificity', *October*, 80, 1997, 92.
99. Glenn Adamson, 'Outsider Artists', *Possibilities and Losses: Transitions in Clay*, unpag.
100. Glenn Adamson, *The Invention of Craft*, xiv.
101. 'It is a moment caught between pathos (the curator struggling to define an object) and insight (how can we list the objects in our lives?). It seems apposite for those of us who are attempting to find languages in which to talk about objects: how do we move from the unknown into the known. And how do we keep the 'perhaps' alive, how do we find a conceptual and linguistic dexterity in our discourse that prevents a slide into absolutes, certainties, over-robust definitions?' Edmund De Waal, 'Statement', *Think Tank*, 2004 [online] http://www.thinktank04.eu/image/papers/thinktank2004_edmund_dewaal_small.pdf [accessed 18 June 2013].

An earlier version of this article was originally published in the *Journal of Art Historiography*, Number 11, December 2014.

INDEX